SAM JOHNSON'S BOY

BY ALFRED STEINBERG

The First Ten: The Founding Presidents and Their Administrations

The Man from Missouri: The Life and Times of Harry S. Truman

Mrs. R: The Life of Eleanor Roosevelt

My Name Is Tom Connally
(with Senator Tom Connally)

Sam Johnson's Boy: A Close-Up of the President from Texas

"Lives to Remember" Series
Richard Byrd
Dwight Eisenhower
Herbert Hoover
Douglas MacArthur
James Madison
John Marshall
Eleanor Roosevelt
Harry Truman
Daniel Webster
Woodrow Wilson

Sam Johnson's Boy

A CLOSE-UP OF THE
PRESIDENT FROM TEXAS

B Y

Alfred Steinberg

THE MACMILLAN COMPANY, New York

COLLIER-MACMILLAN LTD., London

Library of Congress Catalog Card Number: 68-21306

FIRST PRINTING

The Macmillan Company, New York
Collier-Macmillan Canada Ltd., Toronto, Ontario

Printed in the United States of America

Contents

C . 1

PART ONE

Up From the Hill Country

Chapter 1

CONGRESSMAN WRIGHT PATMAN from Texarkana, Texas, had a unique relationship with certain members of the Johnson family. Not only did he share a seat in the Texas House chamber with Samuel Ealy Johnson, Jr., but he also served with Johnson's son Lyndon in the United States House of Representatives. "I remember Sam Johnson well," Patman once said, recalling their state political service after World War I. "Sam was the cowboy type, a little on the rough side, but he had good principles. He used shortcuts in doing things, and he shouted slogans when he talked. Sam was a very persuasive man; he would get right up to you, nose to nose, and take a firm hold—just like his boy Lyndon."

Sam, Jr., and Lyndon Johnson stemmed from noncowboy dirt farmers, who migrated to Texas from Oglethorpe County, Georgia, in the 1840's. Records are not available, though from their name the first of the American Johnsons probably crossed the Atlantic from England. John Johnson, Lyndon's great-great-grandfather, is the earliest traceable ancestor, and he showed up on the *Survey Book* and *Grant Book* in the Georgia State House as a Revolutionary War veteran, even though he was only eleven when the Minute Men clashed with the British on Concord Bridge that fateful April 19, 1775. After the war, the complexion of Georgia's thirty-six thousand inhabitants was about equally black and white, which meant that even fairly poor whites owned slaves. When John died in 1828, his will ordered that "one Negro girl" be given to each of his two daughters.

His third son, Jesse, who was Lyndon's great-grandfather, was the first Johnson to enter politics. "My grandfather, Jesse Johnson," Lyndon Johnson once cut off an entire generation while seeking votes from a crowd of Georgians, "was elected sheriff of Henry County. Later the people of McDonough in the county elected him sheriff of the inferior court; and thus the Johnson family really got its start in politics."

Jesse was fifty-one in 1846 when he caught the Texas fever. Through the ruse of a joint resolution of Congress, instead of a proper treaty with the

Republic of Texas, John Tyler had slyly annexed Texas a few days before his Presidential term expired in March 1845. This annexation, which had been fought by the North on the grounds that it would produce another slave state, did exactly this. Later that year the largest covered wagon movement in the history of the young United States began rolling. And before it ended, several counties in Georgia and other Southern states were almost depopulated in the hegira toward the promised land.

Despite his age and the coming of the Mexican War, Jesse Johnson organized a swift departure for the great adventure. Included in his covered wagons were his wife Lucy, the youngest of their ten children, the five offspring of their widower son John Leonard, who was a doctor and Baptist preacher, and the family slaves. They crossed the deep-rutted mud of Georgia, Alabama, and Mississippi, ferried over the onrushing Mississippi River, and then bounced over the red hills of Louisiana to the twenty-eighth state. Like the Johnsons, the neighboring Patman clan also made the trek, but their wagons stopped just across the "Loozy-anny" line at a place they named Patman Switch. Here they set up shop as Primitive Baptist preachers. Jesse Johnson wanted a deeper, inland feeling, and he pushed on through Austin, the state capital, in south-central Texas, to a farm at Lockhart in Caldwell County, just south of Travis County, which included Austin.

One of those making the trip to Lockhart was eight-year-old Samuel Ealy Johnson, the baby of the family, who would one day answer Lyndon Johnson's call to "Grandpaw." Sam idolized his brother Tom (Jesse Thomas), who was two years his senior, and when their father died in 1856 and their mother the next year, he followed Tom in his northwest wandering into cowboy country. The two went up to Austin and then turned fifty miles west into what was rather derogatorily referred to as the Hill Country, an area where only Germans and Mormons had set up communities. Besides being afflicted with rampaging Apaches and Comanches, the Hill Country generally had ground that was hard and infertile, a withering sun, a depressing gray-green color, a shortage of rainfall for crops, and an untrustworthy Pedernales River which destroyed hope with its savage springtime floods. At a bleak spot, about thirty miles east of the German town of Fredericksburg, the two Johnson brothers erected a log cabin in 1859, and then, for safety against the Indians, built their barn of rocks with small open portholes through which muskets could be fired.

Sam and Tom saw a fortune to be made in trading with the Germans for their cattle, but this business was hardly started when Texas joined the Confederacy. Sam went back to Lockhart to sign up with Company B of DeBrays Regiment, Confederate Soldiers of America, and the horse soldiers moved out after the Yankees. He saw action at the Battle of Galveston, had his horse killed under him at Pleasant Hill, and gained a reputation for his strength in holding wounded soldiers immobile while they underwent amputations.

During the postwar economic chaos Sam married Eliza Bunton of a founding Texas family and took her home to the Hill Country log cabin. Brother Tom, in the meantime, had joined the Texas State Troops in Blanco County and managed to remain near home during the war. It was in 1864 that he bought a 320-acre spread on the Pedernales, not far from what a century later became known as the L.B.J. Ranch. This property, capable of holding thousands of steers in spacious valley pens, fell into Tom's hands when he paid Old Man Moss's defaulted due taxes on the acreage.

From the ranch the brothers moved swiftly into the cattle business. With German farmers around Fredericksburg willing to sell them cattle on credit, the two organized the largest cattle drives in that part of the country to the railroad towns in Kansas. The size of their enterprise was evidenced by the letter one of their cowhands wrote his father: "The Johnson boys have brought up 25 herds this season, the smallest of which was 1500." Another cowboy described the "johnsons Ranche, Blanco Co. Tex" in this fashion: "This is beautiful country through here: mountains, clear rocky streams, live oak, mesquite . . . stock, abondance of game & Indians once a year."

Yet despite their immense ability at organizing trail drives, their resolute purpose in delivering their cattle after hundreds of dangerous miles, and their strong ambition to be the richest men in Texas, they failed miserably. Part of the trouble was their own lack of adequate business methods; part, the result of operating on credit. John Speer, an early Blanco County settler, wrote: "Tom Johnson, with his brother Sam, had driven about 7000 head of cattle to Kansas in 1870, came home with $100,000 and began at once to pay up for cattle already driven and to buy for this year's drive. There is no doubt in my mind that a good many beeves were paid for twice and some of them three times. When called upon the third time to pay for the same steer, I never heard him [Tom] demanding a receipt."

In 1871 their dream bubble burst. The postwar eastern meat gluttony had attracted ranchers from other areas, and the Kansas cattle market was temporarily overstocked. As a result, they had to winter most of their steers in flat old Kansas, where howling icy winds and a heavy snow season decimated their holdings. When they returned home, finally, they were unable to pay for the cattle they had taken on credit. There were threats in German of lawsuits to come, and Tom unloaded his extensive purchases of Fredericksburg real estate to meet some of the bills. In the end, Sam returned to the family acres at Lockhart, while Tom remained on the scene to suffer insults. Tom died in 1877 when he was only forty-one, and with his passing Sam knew he would spend the rest of his life an economic failure.

It was in Hays County, adjoining Blanco County, near the town of Buda that all nine of Sam and Eliza Bunton Johnson's children were born. Ribald friends teased Sam until 1877, calling him "Gal Johnson" because he had four daughters and no sons. But the name "Gal Johnson" died suddenly in

October 1877 when Eliza gave birth to their first son, Samuel Ealy Johnson, Jr., one day to be the father of Lyndon. Two years later came Tom,
then George, and finally two more girls.

Sam, Jr., grew tall like Sam, Sr., and to differentiate between them in
conversation people took to calling the father "Big Sam" and the son
"Little Sam." Little Sam had enormous ears, skeptical eyes and a habit of
pulling in his chin until it almost disappeared inside his collar. He was his
mother's favorite, not only because he was her first-born male child, but
also for his "magnolia-white" skin, which was a tell-tale Bunton characteristic. He possessed unusual drive and a desire to succeed. Someone close
to him once remarked that everything was "a challenge to Sam; he must
ride faster; plow longer, straighter rows; and pick more cotton than his
companions."

Little Sam spent the first twelve years of his life at Buda. Then Big Sam
developed an emotional yearning for the old trail-driving center where he
and his brother Tom had really tasted life. He had no cash for a return to
the Hill Country on the Pedernales, but Eliza did. For Tom had once given
her a present of "a silver-mounted carriage and a matched span of horses,"
and she had sold them for a good price, enough for a substantial down
payment on a farm about twelve miles west of the old stone barn with the
portholes and the log cabin where they had first lived together.

When their wagons came up toward Austin and then turned west into the
Hill Country, they found that a town was growing up near the stone barn—
a place called Johnson City. Here Little Sam went to school, even though
Johnson City lay in Blanco County and his father's farm in adjoining Gillespie County, to the west. For prestige purposes in political campaigns,
Lyndon Johnson liked to declare later that Johnson City was named after
his grandfather. Actually, when Sam and Tom Johnson fell into financial
difficulties in 1871, James Polk "Jim" Johnson, the son of their older
brother, John Leonard Johnson, took over most of their property in Blanco
County. Jim was a go-getter, and after a few years of owning the unproductive acreage, he conceived the bright idea of manufacturing a town on his
property.

His town, which he named Johnson City in honor of himself, was
to consist of one hundred blocks of houses, a flourishing business district, and a political section centering around a county court house on
the town square. Jim's hope was to have the county seat moved from
Blanco, a town fourteen miles south, to Johnson City, for he believed
this shift would "make" his town and enrich him. By mid-1879 he
had sufficient signatures on a petition to force the issue on the election
ballot. Unfortunately, his scheme went awry by a measly seven-vote
margin.

Yet even though Blanco remained the county seat, Jim Johnson went
ahead and laid out Johnson City on his property. The houses he built

were stone and had an appearance of permanence to them. In time two churches also came into existence, plus a livery stable, general store, a blacksmith shop, a bank, and a schoolhouse. Another disappointment was that the railroad would not install a spur line to Johnson City, but Jim kept his faith that the town would flourish. However, at the time Little Sam Johnson went to school in Johnson City, only a few hundred people lived there, and the chief activity in town seemed to be the domino games that adults played all day long in the town square.

The Johnson family had no savings, except for the paltry butter and egg money Eliza Johnson husbanded deep inside her big zinc trunk and doled out on crucial occasions. As a result, if the children wanted an extra shirt or skirt to wear to school, they had to earn the money themselves. At the beginning of one school term, Big Sam told Little Sam there was not a penny to spare to buy school books and clothes. However, the lad might have some of the family steers to sell if he could find customers. In later years, Little Sam enjoyed telling how he fattened the gift cattle, then slaughtered a steer each weekend and peddled from door to door in nearby towns the steaks, chops, and soupbones he butchered. Another year when the Johnson City barber fell ill, Little Sam bought his chair and tools on credit and cut hair afternoons and Saturdays. Still another year he worked so hard earning a few dollars that his chronic indigestion put him to bed, and his worried mother sent him to West Texas for a rest on the ranch of her younger brother, Lucius Desha Bunton.

In 1896, when he was only eighteen, Little Sam decided to get a teacher's certificate and become self-supporting. This was not a formidable task, for it was general knowledge among would-be teachers that the examiners took all their questions from material in thirteen books. He collected these books, filled a bag with dried fruit and bottles of pepsin pills for his indigestion, and moved in temporarily with Grandma Jane McIntosh Bunton, an arthritic victim, who lived nearby. She had been a schoolmarm in her youth and was pleased to tutor "Sammie," as she called her favorite grandson.

After passing the written tests at Blanco with grades of one hundred in United States and Texas history, Sam plunged into a teaching career. However, he was too ambitious to remain a teacher for long. He spent one year in a single-room country school near Sandy and another closer to home at Hye, a village that early settler Hye Brown had named after himself. Following this second year, he quit teaching because he had barely earned his keep.

Next he became a farmer. At fifty-nine, Big Sam considered himself too old for such labor, and he gladly turned over management of the family farm to his energetic son. Little Sam planted cotton and other money crops and hired farmhands to help him. He also proposed living alone and moved into an unoccupied three-room frame cottage near the Pedernales on the property, about a quarter of a mile east of his parents' larger home.

Big Sam Johnson was a Christadelphian, a minor religious sect which opposed not only the holding of public office, but also taking part in elections. However, Little Sam did not hold to this narrow view, and after a day's work behind the plow he and his friends jawed politics half the night in the little cottage. This politically argumentative group included Dayton Moses, a district attorney for fourteen years; W. C. Linden, a prominent attorney, for whom Lyndon was named; and Clarence Martin, who was married to Little Sam's older sister, Frank. Clarence was Little Sam's closest friend and lived on an adjoining farm. He had served a term in the Texas House and then won election as the district judge of Blanco County in 1902.

It was Clarence Martin who sensed that Sam wanted to get into politics but did not know how to go about it. The unwritten code of the Hill Country Texas House districts gave each of the counties that made up a district a two-year control in rotation of the house seat. For instance, Joseph W. Baines of Blanco County held the three-county eighty-ninth district seat in the 1903-1905 Texas House. Control of the seat during the 1905-1907 session was destined for Gillespie County, where Sam Johnson lived. So Clarence Martin prodded his twenty-six-year-old brother-in-law into declaring his candidacy, served as his campaign manager, and helped him win election.

This was the highest political honor ever achieved by a member of the Johnson clan; and it was, therefore, little wonder that when 1906 rolled around Sam Johnson was unwilling to relinquish his seat. Llano County was next in the eighty-ninth district to claim possession of the state house seat, and as Dave Martin of that county put it to a reporter for the Blanco *News,* he expected justice to be served "under the rotation rule." Martin believed he had a further strong claim because he operated the Martin Telephone Company, which was installing the new-fangled wall receivers and mouthpieces in his area.

But Sam Johnson could not give up the only touch of prestige he had ever known. He exploded his political bombshell long before the July 26 primary and roused Martin to fury by his untraditional behavior. Each raced from church suppers to live-oak grove picnics, shaking hands and expounding his own virtues. Expecting a backlash vote that might defeat Johnson simply because he had dared to run for re-election, the Blanco *News,* which supported him, made a last-minute plea to Johnson's political workers to "get out and shell the woods." Sam Johnson's victory over Martin on primary day buried the rotation rule like a sunken ship.

Membership in the Texas House was hardly a money-making proposition for Sam Johnson and his fellow members. Pay ran five dollars a day during the regular sixty-day session and two dollars a day beyond that for special sessions. However, for those with ambition, the benefits were measured far beyond their meager dollar total. As a rule, the house was a jumping-off place for budding politicians before moving ahead to higher office. It also served as a training ground for young law school graduates before they turned to service as district attorneys or to lucrative private practice. Of course, there were many small-bore local politicos, generally older individuals, who found the state capitol the zenith of their careers.

Sam Johnson seemed to fit into the first category when he rode into Austin for his second term in January 1907, as a member of the Texas Thirtieth Legislature. He had no savings in the bank, but his cheap suit and five-gallon hat were clean, and his big feet were covered with impressive boots that had been hand made in San Antonio. Despite his youth and lack of money, other legislators knew him for his adamant insistence on political independence. One noted publicly that Sam Johnson would "kick like a mule at any attempted domination."

Governor of Texas at the time was Tom Campbell, who ignored the major political issue in the state (which was the liquor question) to promote antitrust and antigambling legislation. Campbell's major achievement was a law supported by Sam Johnson that forbade gambling in futures and outlawed bucket-shop transactions, which were the buying and selling of securities and commodities in the form of bets on future quotations without any actual buying and selling of the property. Unfortunately, Texas speculators ignored the law as much as Campbell ignored the liquor question.

Sam Johnson always remembered this session for another reason. Among the new members was twenty-four-year-old Sam Rayburn, a short, stocky, balding school teacher from Bonham in east Texas, and the two hit it off from the start. Yet there was one major issue separating them, and this was the fate of United States Senator Joseph Weldon Bailey. Bailey's six-year term was to end in March 1907, and because the Seventeenth Amendment with its direct election of senators was still years away, the Texas Legislature would decide Bailey's fate.

Bailey was the prototype of the Texas political scoundrel who enriched himself greedily through use of his political power. Yet because of his handsome appearance, statesmanlike bearing, and Fourth of July eloquence, he set off a huge smokescreen of confusion for those who attempted to judge him. Claude Bower, the historian and diplomat, who knew Bailey in Washington, said he "dominated the Democratic minority like an overseer and considered himself like a conqueror. . . . His speeches were phrased in the best English, though he was prone to draw on his imagination for history when required to make his point. His voice was melodious and when he finished his peroration, his tones lingered in the chamber like the echo of chimes in a cathedral."

Of the two Sams, Johnson saw the real Bailey, the man who was discovered to be on the payroll of Waters-Pierce, a Standard Oil subsidiary.

Sam Rayburn, on the other hand, was completely thrilled by Bailey and told others that "this Adonis of a man with a massive brain captured my imagination and became my model."

When Bailey learned that a revolt against him might be in the making, he quit Washington to rush to Austin "to drive into the Gulf of Mexico the peanut politicians who would replace me with someone who would rattle around in my seat like a mustard seed in a gourd!" Not even his admission to a state legislative committee that he had gained his affluence through the kindness of Standard Oil cost him the support of cheering admirers. In the final vote, Sam Johnson was one of only seven members who opposed him for another term, while Sam Rayburn cast his ballot with the overwhelming majority for Bailey.

This session also had its moments of levity. In one instance, a stern member of the house, who was a minister, introduced a bill making adultery a felony. With lobbyists procuring girls for legislators, the result would have been jail terms for many members. Once the bill was dropped in the hopper, the representative from Travis County, which included Austin, rose, and after praising the bill, he offered an amendment to exempt his county. After loud applause, the entire membership gained the floor one after another to offer similar amendments to exempt their districts as well.

When the session ended, Sam Johnson gave no thought to seeking a third term, for he had picked up large new responsibilities in the interim. Joseph Baines of Blanco, who had held the seat before he did, was a small-town newspaper editor and lawyer, a Civil War veteran, and the appointed secretary of state under Governor "Old Oxcart" John Ireland back in 1882. Baines had three children, the eldest of whom was Rebekah, an energetic and education-loving young lady whom he sent to Baylor College at Belton. Rebekah had not suffered for lack of comforts during her upbringing, but after her third year at college, she said, her father "suffered severe and sudden financial reverses." However, she had remained in school to graduate by becoming the manager of the college bookstore in her final year.

Baines was thoroughly depressed and in financial agony by the time his legislative term expired and Sam Johnson arrived on the scene to succeed him. Rebekah recalled that her father sent her to interview the new legislator, and her memory was that "I asked him lots of questions but he was pretty cagey and I couldn't pin him down. I was awfully provoked with that man!"

However, she also said that she found him "dashing and dynamic." As for Sam Johnson, he quickly decided he wanted to marry the pretty blonde girl, even though her education far exceeded his own. She and her family had moved among the Germans at Fredericksburg, and at every opportunity after the session ended, he rode horseback the fifteen miles from the Pedernales Valley farm to see her. "He was enchanted to find a girl who really liked politics," she said matter-of-factly. He took her to political meetings and oratorical picnics. On one occasion they went to the Confederate reunion, where Governor Tom Campbell and Senators Joe Bailey and Charlie Culberson orated. Insiders liked to pass along the story that after Culberson as governor had made prizefighting a felony in Texas, in order to keep heavyweight champion Bob Fitzsimmons from boxing in the state, the state legislature had "exiled" him to Washington as a United States senator. Another time Sam took Rebekah Baines and his older sister Lucie and younger brother George to hear the "Cross of Gold" spellbinder, William Jennings Bryan, address the state legislature.

The mind and body of Rebekah's father deteriorated steadily, and his efforts to establish a going law practice in Fredericksburg came to naught. When he finally died in November 1906, Rebekah was already supporting herself as an elocution teacher and as a stringer for some neighboring newspapers. Sam Johnson was anxious to get married, but Rebekah had been so attached to her father she delayed a decision. There was also a question of caring for her mother, a matter that resolved itself when Ruth Huffman Baines moved to San Marcos, Texas, and established a boardinghouse for normal-school students attending Southwest Texas State Teachers College.

A still larger problem was not permitted to stand in the way when Rebekah Baines consented to become his bride. At the time Sam Johnson had first gone to the state house, he had no savings. Now he was beset with heavy debts. Quick fortunes were being made and lost in cotton, and Sam had plunged into buying and selling this important Texas crop. Texas cotton was especially in demand abroad, and San Antonio, where much of the trade centered, enjoyed great prosperity between 1905 and 1910. Sam was not one of the fortunates; Rebekah later wrote that he "was dealt a severe blow when the San Francisco earthquake of 1906 wiped out his cotton holdings and saddled him with a debt of several thousand dollars."

But Rebekah saw that somehow Sam retained his optimism and enthusiasm, and she married him in August 1907. The bride was twenty-six and the groom almost thirty. Opinions on the marriage were consistent. Said Oriole Bailey, whose mother was a Bunton and the groom's aunt: "The Baines have the brains and the Johnsons have the guts. The Baines are intelligent but they couldn't put things over. The Johnsons can put things over." Percy Brigham, Blanco banker, who knew both families well, called Rebekah Baines Johnson "one of the smartest women I've ever known. That's where Lyndon got his brains." As for Sam Johnson, Brigham conceded he "was straight as a shingle."

When Sam Johnson took his bride home following the ceremony, it was to the tiny white frame cottage on his father's property, about four hundred yards east of his parents' larger place. The cottage, which fronted about one hundred yards from the Pedernales, was a low structure with a slanting roof over the front porch, three rooms, each about twelve feet square, and a

breezeway, or front to rear open area dogtrot. To the right of the breezeway was the combination living room–bedroom, and to the left was another
bedroom with a kitchen-and-dining-space room attached.

To a town-bred girl with cultural interests, Sam Johnson's spread, which
belonged to his father, could hardly have been a thrilling sight on first or
tenth glance. This was pioneer living, which meant that she "shuddered
over the chickens and wrestled with a mammoth iron stove," made soap
from lye and hog fat, boiled water over the fireplace after hauling it
from the well pump, and read by the light of dim kerosene lamps. A "two-
holer" outhouse in the back yard completed her new way of life. All of the
scene brought to mind the saying of an actual Texas pioneer more than a
half century earlier: "Texas is a heaven for men and dogs but hell for
women and oxen."

Six days past their first wedding anniversary, Rebekah developed labor
pains. Years afterward she wrote that Dr. John Blanton of Buda had come
north to deliver her first baby. But Blanton failed to arrive on time and a
neighboring German midwife, Mrs. Christian Lindig, had to be summoned
late on a Wednesday night. At daybreak the next morning, Thursday,
August 27, 1908, Rebekah Johnson gave birth to her first son in her four-
poster bed. Dr. Blanton came shortly afterward, bounced the baby in his
hands and judged that he weighed ten pounds.

Rebekah's mother, Ruth Baines, was given the honor of being the first
to hold the new baby, who was her first grandchild. Then Sam Johnson's
aunt, Kate Bunton Keele, the younger sister of his mother, expressed her
opinion that she could easily recognize the "Bunton favor" in the brown-
eyed infant with the exceptionally large ears. But Rebekah believed she saw
her father in her son.

By now the sun was out and Sam Johnson wanted the entire area to
know of his good fortune. He raced outdoors, leaped aboard his excellent
gray horse, Fritz, and galloped the quarter of a mile westward to tell his
sleeping parents the news. Then he was off to receive congratulations from
his sister Frank and her husband, Clarence Martin, farther down the road.
In later years the Johnson clan liked to tell the story that Big Sam Johnson,
his white hair and beard flowing, also made the rounds of kin and friends
with word about his fifth grandchild. The Johnsons claimed that Big Sam
sensed a special significance in his new grandson, telling all—"A United
States senator was born today—my grandson." The new mother said that
he even made this forecast in writing to his daughter Lucie. "I expect him
to be United States Senator before he is forty," penned the Christadelphian
who was religiously opposed to politics.

Chapter 2

For three months after the birth of her son, Rebekah Johnson suggested names for the infant only to hear an objection to each from Sam. This continued into November, until one morning when he called to her from the fireplace seat where he laced his boots, "Time to get breakfast, Rebekah."

But she snapped back angrily that she was not making any biscuits until the child in the crib next to the bed had a name besides "Baby." "Now you suggest names and I'll pass judgment," she ordered him.

"Sam was usually the one who issued the ultimatums," she later recalled the incident, but her tone threw him off balance.

He began a recital of his best friends. First, he proposed "Clarence," in honor of his favorite brother-in-law. "Not one bit," she rejected it. Next he suggested "Dayton," after District Attorney Dayton Moses, and again she gave a negative response. He then offered "Linden," after his lawyer friend, W. C. Linden.

This time she approved, but made the condition: "Only if I may spell it as I like." She wanted it spelled "Lyndon," with the middle name Baines, after her family name. "Spell it as you please," Sam Johnson growled. "He will still be named for my friend Linden. Now come cook breakfast; the naming is over."

Lyndon was a pretty baby, as early photographs show. When he was six months old, his parents asked a neighbor who owned a camera to take pictures of him sitting in a wicker-backed chair with a teddy bear in his lap. Although Sam Johnson's term in the Texas House was then about to expire, he was so proud of the pictures that he sent fifty copies of one snapshot to members of the house.

In his effort to support his wife and son, Sam had to spend a great deal of time away from home. Besides grubbing the hard soil on the farm, he traveled widely to buy and sell cattle and cotton and to see prospective customers about real estate. He found the monetary return minute for the time involved. Lyndon's earliest memories include one occasion when his father was gone and only he and his mother were home. He remembers his mother on a dark night, pumping water from the hand pump on the back stairs and crying. Apparently, she was frightened to be left alone and Lyndon sensed it, small as he was. "I'll take care of you, Mama," he reassured her. Another memory is of the time he dipped his toes into the Pedernales River one hundred yards in front of the little house. He remembers the mixed horror and anger in his mother's eyes as she pulled him away and warned him not to go near the "Purd-in-alleys," as the river was called locally. Then there is the third early memory, again involving his mother. This time she pulled her treadle sewing machine into the breezeway on a hot day and worked the foot pedal like a piston.

Lyndon was hardly out of infancy when his mother embarked on a "headstart" program designed to develop him into a genius. She spent many of his waking hours telling him stories from the Bible, history, and mythology. He moved her to delight with his loud demand after each tale: "Is it true, Mama? Did it really happen?" She claimed that before his second birthday she had already taught him the alphabet from blocks. When he was only three, she said, he knew "all the Mother Goose rhymes" as well as a repertoire of Tennyson and Longfellow poems. A year later, he would take his dog "Bigham Young" to Grandpa Sam Johnson's place, read a story to him, and be rewarded with an apple from the old man's desk. At four, his long golden curls bouncing while he concentrated, he could spell "Grandpa," "Dan" (his favorite of the family horses), "cat" and a host of other important words. Rebekah Johnson always had a story or two to relate to relatives about her son's brightness or the remarks he made. On one occasion he bought a little china clown as a Christmas present for his father's older sister, Aunt Lucie. However, he did not want his gift lost in the shuffle of the usual stacking under the Christmas tree, so he gave it to her weeks in advance and informed her loudly, "It cost me a dime and it's worth every penny."

A half mile east of the Johnson house lay the one-room Junction School, where Miss Kate Deadrich taught all the grades from first through seventh. Lyndon was four when he began wandering along the river to the flat near the school at recess time to play with his cousins, Ava and Margaret, daughters of his father's younger brother Tom. Several times the worried teacher delayed classes to walk him home. Then one day his mother, frightened that he might unattended fall into the Pedernales, took him to the side door of the Junction School and induced Miss Deadrich to accept him as a full-day pupil.

The teacher soon discovered that she had a child with a special problem. Called upon to read, little Lyndon insisted that he was unable to do so unless Miss Deadrich held him on her lap, just as his mother did when he read. Miss Deadrich complied, and he worked his way through a primer and a reading book before whooping cough kept him home the rest of the school year.

When Lyndon was five in 1913, the Johnsons moved from the Gillespie County farm near Stonewall the dozen miles east to Johnson City in Blanco County. There were two other children in the family now, Rebekah and

Josefa, and in Johnson City the final members of the family, Sam Houston and Lucia, would be born. In 1913, the town had a population of about three hundred and made a sleepy impression on visitors.

In Johnson City Sam Johnson bought a small house on the north side of a lot a block square. The house had a combination living room–dining room containing a wood-burning fireplace where Rebekah Johnson did much of her cooking, a kitchen with a black, wood-burning stove, two small bedrooms and a screened-in back porch where the children slept a good part of the year. Outdoors, part of the lot held a garden, a barn, water tank, well, and outhouse. Still another large part of the lot was used as a playground by the children. One time Sam Johnson acquired a small cottage, which was to be demolished, and dragged it onto his lot as a playhouse for his children and their friends.

Lyndon Johnson's gnawing desire to become a millionaire was born in Johnson City. For his father's lack of earnings in real estate made it necessary for Lyndon and the other children to wear homemade clothes. A visitor to the Johnsons' white frame, L-shaped little house called the family "terribly poor." The usual diet was bacon fat spread on cornbread, turnip greens, hominy grits, and occasionally boiled beef. Lyndon was indelibly damaged by these early privations, and he reacted to the hardships—some real and some magnified—throughout his adult life.

When Lyndon started the first grade in the fall of 1913, Mrs. Johnson continued her campaign to make him a scholar. In Miss Florence Walker's classroom that year he and Kittie Clyde Ross were acknowledged as the best pupils, and at the end of the year Miss Walker let him read a poem to his classmates and parents. The poem he chose was "I'd Rather Be Mamma's Boy."

But after this initial year, he failed to live up to his promise. His problems were a lack of interest in various subjects, such as arithmetic, a desire to be outdoors instead of in a schoolroom, and a great restlessness that would never leave him. His teachers found him so bursting with energy that, to contain it and prevent pranks, he was loaded with the extra tasks of cleaning blackboards, bringing in firewood, and clapping erasers clean of their chalk dust. Even so, the best grade ever given him for deportment was a "B."

Despite her son's letdown, Mrs. Johnson waged continuous war with him to improve his scholarship. "Many times I would not catch up with the fact that Lyndon was not prepared on a lesson until breakfast time of a school day," she once reminisced. "Then I would get the book and put it on the table in front of his father and devote the whole breakfast period to a discussion with my husband of what my son should have learned the night before." But she pursued him far beyond the table. "By following him to the front gate nearly every morning and telling him tales of history and geography and algebra, I could see that he was prepared for the work of the day."

She also tried to develop cultural interests in Lyndon but failed miserably. This cost money and took part of the few extra dollars she earned giving "expression lessons in a room to the right of the entrance hall of the Johnson home," said one woman. Mrs. Johnson enrolled Lyndon in a dancing class run by Mrs. Stella Glidden, the local postmistress, but he spent the entire time teasing the girls in the class. Mrs. Glidden took as much of this as her patience allowed. Then one day, she said, "He was deviling some little girls. His mother wasn't around, so I just gave him a spanking." That ended the dancing lessons.

Mrs. Johnson next enrolled him for violin lessons with Mr. Brodie in Fredericksburg. This proved her lack of understanding of males, for as a youth of those times put it: "In that area a kid was jeered at and considered a pervert if he played the piano or violin. A kid had to talk big, act big and swagger around. He certainly couldn't swagger with a violin." Lyndon dutifully ran a bow across a violin for six months before he refused to continue.

It was during these early years that Lyndon began paying attention to family stories. As young as he was, he saw that the ancestors who made his chest puff out were not Johnsons, generally, but relatives of the women they married. Two of the women in particular stood out: one was his father's mother, Eliza Bunton Johnson; the other, his mother, of the Baines family.

By the time Lyndon became aware of his grandmother, she was paralyzed, having suffered a stroke in 1912 while sewing a button on her husband's shirt. Thirteen years before she was born, her uncle, John Wheeler Bunton, was one of the magnificent fifty-nine men who signed the Texas Declaration of Independence in the blacksmith's shop at Washington on the Brazos in 1836. Eliza's cousins included Governor Joseph Desha of Kentucky and Mary Desha, cofounder of the Daughters of the American Revolution.

Eliza herself had participated in an adventure whose telling always thrilled Lyndon. Grandpa Johnson told of that day in the summer of 1869 when Comanches caught Tom Felps and his wife while they were fishing in Cypress Creek near what was later Johnson City. A small Negro boy witnessed the scalpings and ran to Judge White, Mrs. Felps's father, with news of the murders. When the grieving judge organized a posse to pursue the Comanches, Lyndon's grandpa, Sam Johnson, Sr., had gone along as a matter of duty, even though his going left his wife and infant daughter Mary unprotected.

They were living at the time in the log cabin by the stone barn with the gun portholes in pre-Johnson City's outskirts. After the posse rode off into the hills, Eliza Johnson was filling a pail with water in the spring near the cabin when she spied Comanches on horseback approaching through the nearby woods. She turned and rushed back to the cabin, swooped up her baby, and despite her tall body crawled into the small cellar beneath the cabin door. From below she closed the trap door and pushed a stick through a crack to maneuver a braided rug over the door. Then she coolly bound the baby's mouth with a diaper rag to prevent her outcries.

Almost immediately afterward, she heard the Indians as they burst into the cabin and ripped the interior furnishings apart. Then she heard them go to the barn to steal fresh horses. When quiet descended, she figured this was merely a ruse, so she stayed in her hiding place. Only when it was long dark outside and she heard her husband's voice calling out, did she push up the floor door. The cabin, so neat before, was a shambles, and the zinc trunk containing their wedding presents now held only broken and smashed items. As for Sam Johnson, he had to admit that the posse had failed to find a single Indian. Not until 1873, after the nearby Battle of Deer Creek, did the Indian troubles finally end. On that occasion, said Sam Johnson, the wounded rangers were brought to the stone barn fortress for care.

Rebekah Baines Johnson was not without her own good family connections to impress her awestruck son. Her grandfather, the Reverend George Washington Baines, had served as minister in the Huntsville, Texas, Baptist Church to which the great Sam Houston had belonged. In addition, for two years at the time of the Civil War, Grandfather Baines had been president of Baylor College at Independence.

One of her prize possessions was a letter Sam Houston wrote her grandfather on November 23, 1857, to extend the time of a loan he had made to Reverend Baines. "My Dear Brother Baines," Houston began, "You will find enclosed your note, and if you will renew it for the same amount of $300 and send it to Mrs. Houston I will be obliged to you. You perceive that I knock off the interest for six years at 8 per cent per annum to one hundred and forty dollars. This I am not loth to do as you have the luck to minister to Congregations who think you can afford to preach to them gratis. If you do not devise some plan to change their practice, they will think that you ought to pay them a good salary for attending church when they could stay at home on Sunday. . . . I am not alluding to charity, tho I think the Scriptures enjoin that as one of the brightest Christian traits of character, but I allude to plain old fashioned honesty of paying what they subscribe. They ought to know that paper currency will not pass in heaven. It must be the coin which is issued from an honest heart. Cotton fields, and cotton bolls will find no market in Paradise. Mrs. Houston joins in affectionate regards to Sister Baines, yourself and family. Truly Thine, Sam Houston."

During those Johnson City years if Lyndon wanted spending money, he had to earn it. He worked occasionally for neighboring farmers and was fairly good at herding goats, though some climbed to the top of poplar trees to eat leaves. He also worked as a "printer's devil" for the local paper and went into the hills with his pals to lay traps. Austin Casparis, who ran the cafe on the town square with his wife Fanny, was a customer for all the fox and raccoon pelts they delivered. On occasion, when one of the boys accidentally killed a skunk, the school was uninhabitable for days afterward should he appear there. With some of his pelt money, Lyndon liked to treat himself to some Casparis Cafe chili. The Casparises said he called chili "Mexican T-bone."

When he was about ten, he also operated a shoeshine stand in the Johnson City barber shop. In those days men would come in for a daily shave and to eye the girls in the *Police Gazette*. These were invariably ladies in embroidered tights who weighed about two hundred pounds. This particular job as shoeshine boy proved embarrassing to Lyndon's father, who was trying to give off an aura of well-being because he was considering a return to politics. He had temporarily taken over the local paper because the owner had been forced to leave for Arizona for reasons of failing health, and Rebekah Johnson was acting as editor of the weekly issues. One day a lecturer came to town and Lyndon went to hear him talk on the value of advertising. "I drank in the words of this stranger," he said later, "and went to my mother and bought space on the front page to advertise my bootblack stand.

"Papa had been on a trip and returned just in time to catch one of the papers off the press. He was so ashamed that for years afterward he told the story of buying a paper so his wife could advertise the fact that his son was a bootblack."

Besides his burning desire for money, Lyndon also possessed at a green age the knack of turning impending disaster to his own advantage. He had a hound dog, named Evelyn, who was his hunting companion. One time when Evelyn gave birth to a large litter, Lyndon's father said he had no alternative but to destroy the puppies. As the tragedy began taking shape, Lyndon ran to the barbershop and talked the barber into letting him put a sign in the window that read: "See me for hound pups." Not only did he save the lives of the puppies, but he also earned money for some Mexican T-bone at Casparis' Cafe.

One year, Lyndon's business energies prompted his Uncle Tom to use him as a decoy to lure other children into child labor. Tom Johnson had a farm south of Johnson City with eighty-five acres planted in cotton. At cotton-picking time, he arranged to have Lyndon round up the youngsters in town for a day filling sacks with cotton. The reward was to be a free ice cream supper.

When the crowd of youngsters arrived in wagons early one Saturday morning, Lyndon bet the girls they could not pick as much cotton as the boys. Aunt Kittie had insisted that the children nap after lunch before returning to work; but when the girls went off to rest, Lyndon quietly rounded up the boys to sneak back to their cotton picking. Unfortunately, when they passed a field where his uncle's steers were grazing, Lyndon made his second bet of the day, that he could ride a steer longer than any of the boys. Not until late in the afternoon did they remember the cotton, and when they limped bruised and skinned to the farmhouse, they not only had to pay the girls but Aunt Kittie also barred them from the ice cream supper.

It was not all school and work for Lyndon in Johnson City. He had such an unerring eye at marbles that he had boxes filled with agates he had won. After a time, marble players refused to let him get into their games. Because he was lanky with an unusually long reach, he played first base in the ball games, which included girls because there were not enough boys available. On a hot summer day, he and his best friends, Tom and Otto Crider and the Redford boys, walked out of town to a road bridge that crossed the Pedernales. Sometimes when they felt lazy they would invite Milton Barnwell, son of old Doc Barnwell, because they could then ride in his donkey-pulled cart to the river. The water under the bridge was known as the "Baptizin' Hole," because the Baptists trudged here to immerse new believers. Lyndon and his pals swam nude in the Baptizin' Hole, and he kept afloat with a primitive sort of dog paddle, never progressing beyond this stroke.

Milton's donkey was so ornery that he tried to throw anyone who climbed his back. This provided another sport and occasional spending money, for the boys took him to the Johnson City baseball field when intertown games were scheduled, and they charged riders ten cents every time they fell off the donkey's back. One of Lyndon's relatives recalled that they never wanted Lyndon to demonstrate because he "had pretty good long legs and he could ride that donkey all evening for nothing."

There were also the Friday and Saturday night movies that Harold Withers ran for Johnson City folks on the second floor of the firehouse. Town wits named the firehouse the "Opera House," because the movies were silent. Lyndon missed few cowboy classics at the Opera House, for Mr. Withers paid him off in passes for distributing handbills of coming attractions.

But the major pastime in which Lyndon and his friends indulged was the contemplation and acting out of the early history of the Lone Star State. The crowded events in late 1835 and early 1836, with special emphasis on the drama of the Alamo, constituted a religious experience for Lyndon.

He pored over the details of the attack by Ol' Ben Milam in December 1835 on the Mexicans holding San Antonio; yelled the patriotic war whoop "Who'll go into Bexar with Ol' Ben Milam?"; and cried because Ben Milam had died leading the successful attack. He felt utter despair in the telling of the massacre of Colonel Jim Fannin and his three hundred and ninety men by the treacherous Santa Anna after Fannin had been assured fair treatment when he surrendered at Goliad on March 25, 1836.

But worst of all and also the most glorious event in Texas history was the tragedy of the Alamo. Just an old Spanish church in San Antonio, it gave focus to a boy's total existence because of what had happened there in March 1836. Outside stood Santa Anna with his army of four thousand; inside were Colonel William Barrett Travis, Jim Bowie, Davy Crockett, Jim Bonham, and the rest of that peerless group of one hundred and eighty-seven. No boy felt prouder than Lyndon when Jim Bonham burst through the Mexican lines and into the Alamo to report calmly to Travis that the aid he had been sent to br   was not available; and the colonel answered just as calmly, "Thank you, Jim. That was a good ride."

Then Travis drew a line in the earth with his sword and said to his men, "I will ask those who wish to stay with me, if any should, to cross this line. Those not wishing to make that commitment are free to leave." What was more Godlike than the reply of sick Jim Bowie when Travis offered the men their last chance to escape? Who could not sob to think of Jim Bowie breaking the silence with "Some of you boys set my bed across that line." And the tears had to flow down Lyndon's cheeks on reading Colonel Travis' letter to his government—the one with the line: "Take care of my son."

No, a boy who cared could never forget the Alamo and the brave men who died there. Not even when the incomparable Sam Houston captured that scoundrel Santa Anna at the Battle of San Jacinto east of Houston on April 21, 1836, and won independence for Texas did the glory of the Alamo fade even the slightest.

In his first year in the Texas House in 1905, Sam Johnson had shown his own high regard for the Alamo by cosponsoring with six other members a bill to purchase the Alamo Mission land for sixty-five thousand dollars. Sixty years later, his son was to say to the National Security Council: "Hell, Vietnam is just like the Alamo. Hell, it's just like if you were down at that gate, and you were surrounded, and you damn well needed somebody. Well, by God, I'm going to go—and I thank the Lord that I've got men who want to go with me, from McNamara right on down to the littlest private who's carrying a gun."

Chapter 3

———————⌣———————

Even as a youngster Lyndon developed still another interest that competed with his dream of becoming a millionaire and a hero. Johnson City oldtimers recalled seeing him hanging around the domino players in the town square and listening to their political discussions. Obviously, this precocious interest in politics was a direct outgrowth of his father's earlier role as a member of the Texas House and his continuing political activities in the district. Despite his father's then lack of a formal title, a stream of visitors came to sit with Sam Johnson on his porch when the family lived in Johnson City. Some wanted his endorsement for office; others came merely to talk politics; while still others asked for his aid in getting pensions. Lyndon often hid in the bedroom behind the porch, his ear against the screen, and listened to the conversation.

When outside politicians came through Johnson City, they paid courtesy calls on Lyndon's father. One Fourth of July, as Mrs. Johnson laughingly recalled the incident, the governor of Texas came to Johnson City for the patriotic ceremonies. Following the spread-eagle speechmaking, Sam Johnson brought the governor back to the house for a big dinner. So many guests found reason to appear that the children were relegated to the kitchen.

During the meal Mrs. Johnson watched, puzzled, when Lucie Price, Sam's older sister, suddenly stiffened, then reached for another piece of fried chicken. Lucie repeated this strange behavior several times before the dinner ended. Later, Rebekah Johnson discovered that Lyndon had hidden under the table to listen to his father and the governor and had prearranged with Aunt Lucie to slip him another piece of chicken every time he pinched her leg.

Among the names he heard his father and visitors mention on the front porch were President Woodrow Wilson, Teddy Roosevelt, Senator Joe Bailey, Governor Oscar Colquitt and Governor Jim "Pa" Ferguson. Some could remember the thrill when Teddy Roosevelt came to San Antonio to organize his Rough Riders for the "War of Eighteen and Ninety-Eight" with Spain. Every afternoon Teddy, astride his horse, would come galloping down the Alamo Plaza near the hallowed shrine, toss his reins to an orderly, and plow into the Menger Hotel for his big daily ration of snorts at the bar.

Oscar Colquitt, a stout little man who was governor from 1911 until 1915, came through Johnson City occasionally, and he always wore a white lawn tie like a city undertaker. Conjecture about Colquitt centered on whether he was a wet or a dry because he had enigmatically come out for local option. There was talk, too, about the big fights he got into over small matters. One squabble that got almost as much attention as the outbreak of war in Europe in 1914 was his battle with the Daughters of the American Confederacy, who believed they were so important to Texas that they merited free and ample office space in the State Capitol. Colquitt also engaged in a cannon exchange with his attorney general, Jewel P. Lightfoot, over the matter of which man should decide constitutional questions.

Political talk on the porch picked up in volume when "Pa" Ferguson jumped into the center ring following Oscar Colquitt. Ferguson, a tall,

plump man, understood the average Texan's delight in political noise, ungrammatical but clever squelches for opponents, the championing of lost
Populist causes, and making a financial haul while holding office. Just as
Sam Rayburn in the Texas House had idolized Joe Bailey, so did Sam
Johnson enthrone Jim Ferguson. Forty-three when he ran for governor in
1914, Ferguson owned the bank at Temple, a title company, a large,
fertile farm, and a breeding ranch. But he astutely affected the manner,
clothes, and talk of a poor and ignorant little farmer. The professional
politicians considered him a minor nuisance candidate when he showed up
on the hustings in his stained clothes as "Farmer Jim, the Farmer's Friend,"
snapping his suspenders, spitting tobacco juice, and getting off earthy remarks about his opponents. So far as the professionals were concerned,
Ferguson "had no more chance than a stump-tailed bull in fly time."

But Lyndon learned through his father that Texans liked a showy candidate who had color. As a poor man, Sam Johnson believed that Ferguson
had even more to offer than a brassy personal show, for Farmer Jim demanded passage of a law to limit landlords to one-fourth of the cotton crop
and one-third of the grain a tenant farmer produced. This issue alone won
him the support of rural Texas. In addition, Ferguson shrewdly won the
support of both the WCTU and the brewers by announcing he would veto
any bill dealing with liquor.

Ferguson won, but after he was inaugurated he proved to be a monster
except on the farm tenancy issue. One year he vetoed the appropriation for
the University of Texas at Austin, a gesture that won him further support
from the predominantly unschooled population. In defense, he called the
professors "liars and crooks." Questioned by reporters about other gubernatorial actions, Pa said, "I am governor of Texas. I don't have to give
reasons."

In 1916 Lyndon watched the excitement of his father and Uncle Clarence Martin as they jumped into Ferguson's re-election campaign. Both
men stumped Gillespie County and Blanco County for him despite the news
that President Wilson and his Cabinet had endorsed Tom Ball, who was
Ferguson's opponent. Clarence Martin went so far as to compose a square
dance in honor of Ferguson's campaign. Some of the lines went: "Swing
your partner and promenade the hall, Vote Jim Ferguson and scratch old
Ball."

Old Ball was scratched, but in 1917 great concern for Ferguson enveloped Sam Johnson. Ferguson, with elastic morals, believed he was entitled to use his political status to enrich himself. Opponents discovered
that he had transferred a $101,607.18 school fund from one bank to his
own bank in Temple, and then lent the money to himself. In addition,
Ferguson had accepted a gift of $165,000 from Texas brewers, a hard,
lobbying group not known for philanthropic enterprises.

The small Johnson home was a scene of dejection when Pa Ferguson
was impeached and remanded for trial on twenty-one charges. Lyndon's

Uncle Clarence was hired as Ferguson's chief defense counsel, and hope rose for his vindication. Sam Johnson listened to the testimony, but he refused to believe that the impeachment resulted from anything except the desire of rich farmers to seek revenge for his farm tenancy proposal. The decision was otherwise. Found guilty, Ferguson was ordered removed from office and Lieutenant Governor William P. Hobby was elevated to succeed him.

Grandpa Sam Johnson had died in 1915, and when his wife Eliza followed him to an adjoining plot in the walled-in Johnson Cemetery on their property in 1917, their son Sam decided to return to the farm from Johnson City. Once more this meant that Rebekah had to give up her town interests for rural privation. She was giving up a great deal, for she had been directing plays in the Opera House, coaching Johnson City High School students in debate and oratory, and earning butter and egg money by her private elocution lessons.

The move back to the farm put Lyndon again into the one-room Junction School where he had once sat on Miss Deadrich's lap. Before graduating from Junction's seventh grade at eleven in 1920, he became well known for his mammoth ego, which sometimes revealed itself in humorous ways. The door of the Junction School stood in the center of the north wall, with a wide blackboard on either side of the door. Whenever a pupil raised a hand and won the teacher's approval to visit the outhouse, he was obliged to sign his name in the corner of the blackboard before going outside, then erase it on his return. Embarrassment forced all pupils except one to sign their names as small as they could write. The exception was Lyndon, who, when he had to go, proudly wrote "Lyndon B." in a large hand on one blackboard and "Johnson" on the other blackboard.

When he completed the one-room Junction School, Lyndon went to the eighth grade in the school at Stonewall, two miles west of the farm. Stonewall was named for Stonewall Jackson, though some transplanted Yankees spread the story that the name came from the many stone walls seen in the neighborhood. Mamma let her older son wear long trousers when he was twelve, but she could not get him to agree to read books. Shortly after he started school in Stonewall, she decided that the walk was too long, and he graduated to a donkey's back for the daily trip. After a time, when she determined that he could get better schooling elsewhere, he transferred to the Albert School, some miles south of the farm. Albert was a stock farming area and was named by Albert Luckenbach for himself. Not far away was the town of Luckenbach that he said was in honor of his parents. Since the town of Albert was even farther away from home than Stonewall, Sam Johnson gave his tall, skinny son a horse for the trip after a while.

Lyndon did not feel the loneliness of the farm as his mother did. To him, the Pedernales was a beautiful river, even though it washed away everything not tied or nailed down in flood time. Nor did he sense the melancholy air that visitors felt among the grayish, low, chalky hills, with their gnarled live-oak trees that were hundreds of years old and the menacing buzzards and chicken hawks that rode the wind streams overhead. To Lyndon the area north of the farm, where he hunted, was the real "Zane Grey Country." There were boulders four stories high, and you had the feeling an Indian war party might be riding over the next rise quick as an arrow. In season the doves were so numerous they sometimes darkened the sky; and deer, too, were plentiful. People claimed that black bear, panthers, buffalo, and Mexican lions once roamed this area as well.

Most of all, when he rode a horse in the Hill Country and wore his high cowboy boots, he felt closer to being a cowboy hero—fast on the draw with a quick trigger finger, utterly fearless, demanding total obedience from others, like "a tall, tough Texan coming down the street." There was only one kind of man to beat this, and that was a Texas Ranger. "When you shoot a Ranger he just keeps coming on," Lyndon once said admiringly.

The air seemed to smell of the frontier, and in truth, from the stories Uncle Clarence Martin told about some of his law cases, it still existed even in Texas cities. Uncle Clarence could get a man acquitted on a murder charge by telling the jury that the victim had been offensive to the killer's female kin. In some cases, he said, he could get a defendant off on the ground he hadn't had time to "cool down" before killing someone who had provoked him.

World War I brought Sam Johnson back to active politics. After he had broken the one-term tradition in his district, William Bierschwale of Fredericksburg, who succeeded him, served four successive two-year terms in the Texas House, beginning in 1909. Sam Johnson had reason to wonder what he might have accomplished had he continued in the house, because in 1911 Sam Rayburn, his acquaintance from Bonham, had been elected speaker.

Bierschwale served until 1917, when Tom Martin of Fredericksburg succeeded him. But when Congress declared war against Germany in April 1917, Martin resigned his house seat after being called to duty in the Texas National Guard. Governor Hobby then ordered a special election in February 1918 to fill his seat, and Sam Johnson, itching to return to Austin, announced his candidacy. When no one else paid the filing fee, he automatically won his old seat back.

A seething disquiet had settled upon Texas with the coming of the war, and Governor Hobby called a special session of the legislature to consider a sedition law. Here and there an accusing voice had been raised about the loyalty of Texas Germans, and hysteria was setting in by 1918. Some demanded prison for the lot, and many spoke of their lack of loyalty to the Confederacy during the War Between the States as proof they could not be trusted.

True, the Germans in Texas had opposed slavery in the middle of the previous century. They had been pioneers in the unwanted Hill Country in the 1840's, at a time when American settlers had avoided that area like the plague. The Americans had gone instead to the rich coastal plain along the Gulf of Mexico, where land was fertile and plentiful, the climate pleasant, and farms not subjected to Apache and Comanche raids. German immigrants had founded Fredericksburg, in honor of Frederick the Great, in a green valley circled by fir trees on the granite and limestone hills eighty miles west of Austin. Other German communities had sprung up at Stonewall, Hye, Albert, and other places in the Hill Country, with a sprinkling of Anglo-American settlers moving in to join them as farmers and ranchers. Relations between the two groups remained friendly until Texas joined the Confederacy. Unwilling to renounce their antislavery beliefs, many of the Texas Germans migrated to Mexico, only to be stopped en route by Confederate forces and slaughtered.

Following the war, relations between Texas Germans and Anglo-Americans gradually improved, though many Anglo-Americans regarded the Germans with continued suspicion because they retained their mother tongue and customs. Rebekah Johnson, who had lived in Fredericksburg, and whose mother, Ruth Huffman, was of German ancestry, once wrote that "Fredericksburg might have been transplanted from the Old World, its customs, ideas and pursuits were unique and forcign."

By the time the special session of the legislature convened in 1918, local Germans were being referred to as Huns and as conveyers of important secrets back to the German High Command in Berlin. The loyalty bill that came before the legislators declared that anyone who was reported to have uttered a disloyal expression was triable for a felony and subject to a prison term ranging from two to twenty-five years. Sam Johnson was responsible for the elimination of one section of the bill that would have permitted any Texan to arrest any person he deemed "disloyal." However, the rest of the bill passed almost intact, with only Sam Johnson and a few others voting against it. In its April 6, 1918, issue the Fredericksburg *Standard* applauded him, pointing out that by his vote he "suffered unfounded and vicious attacks on his character."

When Sam Johnson ran for re-election to the house that summer, he took eleven-year-old Lyndon with him on his campaign. His niece, Ava Johnson, then thirteen, remembered her uncle campaigning in his big Stetson and wearing a shirt collar that "was very stiff." Another who observed him said he was "a good talker and a pretty good entertainer."

Sam had a Model-T Ford he and Lyndon bounced around in while going to political rallies and picnics in the four counties that now made up the district. There were also county fairs and ice cream suppers and an opportunity for Lyndon to listen to his father take thanks from German voters and glibly explain why he had voted against permitting women to have the right to cast the ballot. His wife, who observed him most closely, gave a remarkable picture of her husband that applied equally years later to Lyndon when she said of Sam Johnson: "He was ambitious . . . highly organized, sensitive and nervous; he was impatient of inefficiency and ineptitude and quick to voice displeasure."

He was also shrewd. August Benner, a neighbor who did not like the way the Johnsons used his pasture as a road, ran against him as an "Independent." Benner was not highly regarded in the area, but his German name was expected to be of some help to him. One day, said Lyndon, one of his father's political lieutenants came to the house in great agitation, bringing the report that seventy German families were going to vote for his opponent. When Sam Johnson ascertained that these families lived in a nearby valley, he calmly asked his friend to go there and look up the head of the German clan. "Tell him that the sittin' county judge ain't in good health and that lots of us are thinking that he will be succeedin' the judge before too long."

When the man returned he had much to report. "I went out to the farm," he said, "and found old man ———— sitting on a zinc bucket, and milking his cow into another bucket. His wife was in the loft throwing hay down for the cattle. I told him what you said, Sam, and he came up off that bucket like it was hot. And she nearly fell out of the loft."

Sam Johnson's knowledge of human nature paid off because, according to his son, all the German families in that valley voted for him. If this lesson failed to sink in, Sam Johnson had other sage advice for his son. One of his expressions that Lyndon liked to quote was: "If you can't come into a room full of people and tell right away who is for you and who is against you, you have no business in politics." Actually, said those who knew Sam and Rebekah Johnson, compared to his wife, he was a poor judge of people. "She could read you like a book," said one. His father, who was seldom silent, had another piece of advice for his talkative son. "When you're talkin', you ain't learnin' nothin'!" Lyndon later had this printed and framed, and hung on his office wall.

After the period of bouncing and jouncing over rutted dirt roads for a quick and friendly "Howdy" to voters, firm handshakes, more oratory and anecdotes at live-oak picnics, Sam Johnson was ready for judgment on election day. He won easily over Benner, but his neighbor was so incensed by what he called a crooked election, he asked the Texas House to unseat Johnson. Benner charged that in Kendall County Johnson's friends had managed to keep Benner's name off the ballot, while in Blanco County the Johnson crowd had used "undue influence and intimidation" on voters to discourage Benner supporters. Whatever the truth of his charges, Benner found himself considered a poor sport at home for his cry-babying and a pest by the Texas House, which rejected his plea.

Sam Johnson remained a member of the Texas House until 1925. Although he continued in serious financial straits, he knew better than to let others know his true situation because of its political effect in future elections. Instead he mustered a false front, as revealed by an item in the

Blanco County *Record* of March 26, 1920: "Hon. S. E. Johnson and little son Lyndon were among the prominent visitors in Johnson City this week. Mr. Johnson has one of the largest and best kept farms in this section, and has been quite busy of late supervising its cultivation."

Sam Johnson also knew the importance of getting things for his constituents. Lyndon's memory of that period is of a constant stream of Confederate soldiers, widows, and old Texas Rangers pleading with Sam to help them get pensions and getting the assurance he would assist them. On the other hand, Rebekah Johnson found it difficult to play the political game.

"My mother was sort of aloof," Lyndon once told a reporter. "I remember once on Christmas Eve we were all sitting down for dinner when a road hand came in with his seven children and a cake for my daddy, to express his affection. It was a green cake and terrible tasting. Nobody could eat it. My mother said, 'Oh, my goodness,' and she wasn't pleased at all to have our Christmas Eve dinner broken up that way. But my daddy was very pleased and told them all to come right in."

In the early years of Sam Johnson's second tour of duty, whenever he took the sixty-mile ride to Austin for the legislative meetings, he made Lyndon the family straw boss. This put responsibility on the boy to see that the chores were done. But Lyndon was more interested in managing things than in working directly. So he parceled out duties to his younger brother, Sam Houston, and to his three sisters, Rebekah, Josefa and Lucia. This meant bringing in the eggs, feeding the hogs and chickens, looking after the cows and horses, and filling the wood box next to the stove. When Sam Johnson was at home, it was apparent to him that the work got done despite Lyndon, for his son enjoyed sleeping. He made a morning ritual of stamping toward Lyndon's bed, grabbing him by a leg, shaking it irritatedly and growling, "Get up, Lyndon. Every boy in the county's got a two-hour start on you." He could not bear to hear his son offer as an excuse that a chore should not be done on the grounds that it was too early or too late to do it. "That reminds me of a train in our Hill Country which was brought to the foot of a hill," he told his son. "An old man was sitting there whittlin' and he said, 'You'll never git it started up the hill.' It went up the hill and as it started down the hill, he said, 'You'll never git it stopped.'"

By 1921 members of the Texas House noticed that twelve-year-old Lyndon was his father's shadow in Austin. "He used to bring Lyndon to Austin once or twice a week while we were in session," said Wright Patman, who won a seat in the state house in 1920, following military service in World War I. "Sam Johnson and I shared a desk in the chamber. It was one of those desks that had leg space cut out for two men, and Lyndon liked to stand next to his father or sit with him and listen to the debate. He was around so much that some members thought he was a page and gave him little jobs to do. There was another boy, Homer Thornberry, half of Lyndon's size, who was really a page and the two became close friends. In fact, years later when Lyndon became a United States senator and left the House, Homer got his House seat. Then Lyndon had Kennedy put Homer on the Federal District Court."

Despite the age difference between Patman at twenty-eight and Sam Johnson at forty-three, the two were inseparable. "I was the leader of the anti-Ku Klux Klan forces in the Texas House," said Patman, "and Sam supported my bill to make it a penitentiary offense to wear a disguise to hurt others. Another time, we prevented a known Ku Kluxer from using the house chamber for a meeting. The KKK was at its peak then in Texas, and it took a little guts to oppose it. They didn't bother Sam much, but in Cass County where I lived, they threw rocks through my windows, called me at all hours of the night, and organized the district so that I was lucky to beat the Klan candidate they put up against me."

Since members had no offices but had to do their work either in committee or on the floor, Patman saw a great deal of Lyndon. "He was so much like his father that it was humorous to watch. They sort of looked alike, they walked the same, had the same nervous mannerisms, and Lyndon clutched you just like his daddy did when he talked to you. He was a little on the rough side, too. But there was one real difference between Lyndon and his father. Sam's political ambitions were limited. He didn't have any aspirations to run for Congress. He wanted only local prestige and power, and the Texas House was fine for him as his limit because it was close to home and made him feel important."

Lyndon loved the taste and odor of politics. His mother had repeatedly told him that her father, as secretary of state, had laid the cornerstone of the pink granite Statehouse forty years earlier. Oldtimers remembered that event as well as they did Rebekah Johnson's father, Joseph Baines, who proudly told everyone: "I am a Baptist and a Democrat." Money to build the Statehouse came from the sale by the state of three million acres of Panhandle ranch land for $3,000,000; and there was argument pro and con whether one side or the other was guilty of fraud. The Statehouse stood on top of a river terrace, and at the foot of the capitol hill ran Congress Avenue, the widest street in Texas. Inside, the Statehouse had marble floors, and its walls were crowded with portraits of the famous Texans of the past. A twelve-year-old boy, who thought of all brave men either astride a galloping horse dashing toward the enemy or walking fearlessly in cowboy garb down a dangerous street, could not be expected to have his heart pound at the picture of Sam Houston, the greatest hero of them all. Houston was wrapped in a shabby blanket instead of his fighting clothes and looked more like a poor Roman senator than the Texan he was. But if this was a disappointment, there was a sense of being near the seat of power in knowing that the governor's office was on the second floor of the Statehouse and you could get a good look at Governor Pat Neff almost any day you were there.

Austin had many other attractions, but Lyndon enjoyed one sight every time he saw it. From the vantage of the highest hills, if he looked westward he could spy a low black-green line that actually denoted the beginning of the Hill Country.

His father once explained that back in the days of dinosaurs, volcanic disturbances produced a crack in the earth that extended in a curve northward from Del Rio at the Rio Grande past San Antonio, Austin, Waco, Dallas, and on toward Denison, near the Red River boundary with Oklahoma. The earth crack was called the Balcones Fault, from the Spanish word meaning balcony because of its odd projection. East and south of the Balcones Fault lay the rich coastal plain of Texas, akin to the Mississippi Delta. But to the west of it and extending to the Pecos River stretched the Edwards Plateau, a limestone mesa covering forty counties and equal in size to Tennessee.

The Hill Country, said Daddy, occupied the eastern part of the Edwards Plateau. It began at the Balcones Fault ten miles beyond Austin and ran a hundred miles or so west through ragged, forested low hills, green valleys with only a thin layer of topsoil, and across spring-fed rivers like the Pedernales and the Llano that flowed southeastwardly across the Balcones Fault toward the Gulf. This was home. Beyond the Edwards Plateau, Sam Johnson pointed out, the real Old West still existed in a setting of varmints, cactus, sagebrush, desert and mountains.

Another big thrill for Lyndon came when his father took him occasionally to San Antonio. This was a sixty-mile trip south from the farm and gave him his first direct association with the glory that had been Texas. He was eager to visit Goliad, far to the southwest on the San Antonio River, the "River of Blood," where the scurvy Santa Anna had given his orders to burn the bodies of Fannin's men, who had given their lives for liberty. But the most heart-pounding place of all was the Alamo, which he approached slowly after walking around the square. When he stopped, it was to contemplate that most heroic epic of history as he understood it. "Our flag still waves proudly from the walls—I shall never surrender or retreat" were the magnificent words of Colonel Travis, shortly before the end.

After such contemplation, he was ready for some tamales and chili con carne from the old Mexican street vendors.

Lyndon remembered his father from his Austin days as an agrarian liberal. But other Texas politicians questioned this view. "Sam Johnson ran around with rich lobbyists during the house sessions, even though he was poor," said one. "He was thrilled to be in contact with anyone rich. The lobbyist who excited him most was Roy Miller, who had been mayor of Corpus Christi and was front man in Austin for Texas Gulf Sulphur Company. Roy was the epitome of the lobbyist. He was rich; he dispensed big money and liquor and women to the little people who were in the Texas Legislature. No real liberal would tie in with Roy Miller."

Roy Miller had much to protect, for about 80 per cent of the world's sulphur was mined in three Texas counties. How effectively he operated

became apparent in one instance when a state study valued for tax purposes the Wharton County property of Texas Gulf Sulphur at one hundred
and twenty million dollars. But the final valuation set by the county commissioners was a measly nine million dollars. On the state level, fair-minded
officials believed that the minimum state tax per ton of sulphur production
should be at least one dollar. But the state legislature would not go beyond
thirty-six cents a ton when Sam Johnson was a member.

At the time Lyndon went to Austin with his father, it was commonly
known in the capital that the sulphur, beer, bus, cement, gas, and oil lobbyists were paying the Driskill Hotel bills of many legislators. In some
instances when lobbyists furnished girls to the lawmakers, their upkeep
over the course of the session was handled by putting the girls on the
legislative payrolls. The lobbyists also put out a lavish liquor spread. Men
known to be as "sober as a watched Puritan," at home, turned into
"drinking drys" in Austin. The name "drinking drys" was reserved for
those who ranted against the demon rum in their districts and then poured
gallons of lobbyist firewater down their gullets in their rent-free Driskill
rooms. Even at fourteen, Lyndon must have been aware of some of this.

Yet despite this sordid and disillusioning aspect of politics, Lyndon retained his political ambitions. Anna Itz, who later became a first-grade
teacher, went to the Albert School with him, and she always remembered
one remark he made to her. "It was just after a ball game during recess,"
said Anna, "and we were resting under a tree. He was sitting with his legs
folded. He looked up and said, 'Someday I'm going to be President of
the United States.' "

In 1923, when Sam Johnson was in his fifth and last term in the Texas
House, he decided to move back to Johnson City and concentrate on the
real estate business. Although Rebekah Johnson later wrote that they returned to Johnson City "so that Lyndon might complete his senior year
in school" there, one of her daughters said that the family stayed on the
farm "just long enough for Daddy to go broke." Lyndon tried to place the
blame on the Republican party for his father's troubles, remarking that
Sam Johnson "went broke three times during Republican Administrations."
How partisan this comment actually was, showed from the fact that his
father had named all the good horses on the farm after Democratic Presidents and the worthless critters after Republican Chief Executives.

The senior year at the Johnson City High School was a busy one for
Lyndon. Because the school ended with the eleventh grade and not the
customary twelfth, its seniors would have been juniors elsewhere. There
were five in the graduating class of 1924 besides Lyndon: Louise Casparis,
Kittie Clyde Ross, Margaret Johnson, Georgia Carmack, and John Dolla-
hite. "John was always shy of the girls," said Lyndon, so he had a clear
field with the young ladies, who combined to vote him class president. He

was also first baseman on the school team that played against neighboring town schools, and he threw the discus for a time.

The major event on the school calendar was the annual debating competition for high schools, sponsored by the Texas Interscholastic League. Debaters throughout the state were given the same topic to be argued pro and con; the subject for 1924 was whether the United States should withdraw her troops from Nicaragua, where President Wilson had sent them to prevent a civil war. Despite his mother's coaching, Lyndon could not develop an expressive tone because he mumbled. Nevertheless, he made the team and was determined to win the state meet for Johnson City High.

This involved winning the county title, then the district title, and finally the all-Texas championship. Johnny Casparis, one of the six sons of the cafe owner, was his fellow debater, and the team of Johnson and Casparis mopped up the opposition at the Blanco County meet. When the two went on to the district meet at San Marcos in the southeast corner of Hays County, which lies to the east of Blanco County, Lyndon was so keyed up and self-confident that he had visions of statewide acclaim. But disaster struck, and he and Johnny did not win at San Marcos. Unable to hide his chagrin, the loss immediately brought on nausea. "I was so disappointed," he admitted years later, "I went right into the bathroom and was sick."

Commencement day came on May 4, 1924, on the second floor of the pink-stone high school. Fifteen-year-old Lyndon, standing six feet, three inches, with little flesh on his bones, had the honor of reading the class poem, and the class prophecy of the other five graduates was that he would become governor of Texas one day. School superintendent Edward Bowman passed out diplomas on the stage, and Mr. Glidden, who was the publisher of the Blanco County *Record* and Sam Johnson's faithful political supporter, took note of the graduation. The next edition of the *Record* commended Lyndon and reported that "he is the youngest member of the class and is believed to be the youngest graduate of the school."

But Mrs. Johnson could not get great satisfaction from the graduation. For Lyndon had told all his friends that he was through with school forever.

Chapter 4

⌐⌐⌐⌐⌐⌐⌐⌐⌐

THAT SUMMER OF 1924, after he left Johnson City High School, Lyndon Johnson made one effort to get into the adult work world. This was to take a clerical job his father found for him at faraway Robstown below Houston, but the pay was so slight at a time when the newspapers were bragging about the unparalleled Coolidge prosperity that he quit in discouragement after a few weeks and returned home unemployed.

Even a fifteen-year-old boy could see that prospects for becoming a millionaire in Johnson City were slim. So it was inevitable that the ambitious boy would conspire with his best friends to seek their fortunes elsewhere. Tom and Otto Crider, Otho Summy and his brother, and Payne Roundtree were easy to convince that sunny California was the magic spot waiting for their arrival. "I was very positive and a great persuader," said Lyndon.

All for one and one for all became the motto of the Johnson City musketeers. First off, they pooled their money and bought an old "T-Model Ford" that was on the verge of collapse. "I started with eighteen dollars and few of the boys had more," Lyndon recalled. The car was a canvas-top model without a windshield and required a great deal of cranking before the motor turned over. After the car came the job of collecting food and other supplies.

They quit Johnson City without warning one morning in July. In retrospect, Lyndon liked to call the California trip an adventure—"None of us had been off the farm for a trip longer than the road to town." Some of his companions viewed it as running away from home. Years later, Lyndon told Wright Patman that he went to California because "it meant one less mouth for my poor daddy to feed."

The fifteen-hundred-mile trip to California took almost two weeks. Lyndon had established himself from the outset as the leader, even though he was the youngest. For nourishment, they had bags filled with fatback, cornbread, and molasses. They wanted to keep moving with few stops, so it was only twice a day, said one boy, that they pulled off the road "to gulp down fatback and cornbread garnished with molasses."

"We'd camp out along the railroad tracks at night, and always our first chore would be to dig a hole in which to bury our money," Lyndon said.

"The heaviest member of our party always slept over our cache. We didn't propose to be robbed."

By the time they reached lower California, windburned, sunburned and hungry, they learned firsthand that economic opportunities were only slightly better than they were in the Hill Country. The boys picked fruit under blazing skies in the steaming Imperial Valley and scrubbed dishes in hash houses. Sometimes there were no jobs, and they had to dip into their money bag. "Finally we came to a place where a hole in the ground was no longer necessary," said Lyndon. "The money we had just trickled away. When we were broke and job hunting, we separated." Otho Summy, who would be found playing dominoes under the mulberry tree outside the Casparis Cafe in Johnson City forty years later, could still remember vividly the sad ending of the boyhood trek "to seek fame and fortune in the West."

Lyndon would not give up easily, and for two years he stayed in California. "Nothing to eat was the principal item on my food chart," he said. "That was the first time I went on a diet. Up and down the coast I tramped, washing dishes, waiting on tables, doing farm work when it was available, and always growing thinner." At night he slept outdoors or in cheap rooming houses. His longest stay was in San Bernardino, where he ran an elevator in the four-story Platt Building and also clerked for a law firm. On one occasion, when Charles G. Dawes, the Republican Vice Presidential candidate, came to San Bernardino to yell out one of his gruff and scolding campaign speeches in the fall of 1924, Lyndon agreed to work an extra eight-hour shift in the elevator in order to get two hours off to see his first top-level politician.

By early 1926 he had his fill of California, and now mostly skin and bones, he hitchhiked back to Johnson City. "The trip back home was the longest I've ever made," he said. "And the prettiest sight I ever saw in my life was my grandmother's patchwork quilt at the foot of my bed when I got home."

Even though his mother lost no time, after welcoming him home, in resuming her continual nagging that he go to college, he refused to consider this step. Instead he went to work on a road gang in the county, driving bulldozers and pickup trucks for one dollar a day in pay. Zeke Felps, whose relatives, Tom and Eliza Felps, had been scalped by Comanches back in 1869, said that by 1926 Sam Johnson had been reduced to working as foreman of the road gang and Zeke and Lyndon were in his crew. Zeke recalled it was customary for truck drivers to back up to dirt piles and then join the crew in shoveling the load into the truck. Lyndon was the exception, he said, because he stayed in his truck and catnapped while the others loaded his truck. "Lyndon was no fool," said Zeke. "He was saving his energy to run this country."

Sam Johnson despised the thought that his first-born, the boy of so much early promise, would waste his life on the road gang. He tried sarcasm to jolt a rekindling of ambition in Lyndon, but this had no effect. "It's fine to be satisfied with the simple things," he told him one time. "A man who is satisfied to be a laborer will never have much on his mind. Of course, there won't be much in it, but those who are willing to devote all their lives to a road job really don't need much."

In those days of inflation, a dollar a day was little. Yet is paid for an occasional "Mexican T-bone" at the Casparis Cafe and an occasional date taking local girls to the Opera House silent movies or to one of the Saturday night dances at nearby Hye, Stonewall, Twin Sisters, or the other towns with dance halls. Country bands featuring fiddles and "geetars" scratched and plucked out lively country and western tunes, and sometimes there were square dances. Fredericksburg was the liveliest place with its two thousand citizens and its home-brewed beer, which was in open evidence despite the Eighteenth Amendment. One time when a local rancher was asked by a top federal official what he thought about the effect of a national law, the answer was: "I don't rightly know, Mr. Porter. You see, they ain't put it in down here."

Sometimes Lyndon picked up extra spending money by driving his buddies to and from dances in the county truck. You came into Fredericksburg on a Saturday night down the mile-long Main Street and rode past the old Nimitz Hotel where Robert E. Lee and James Longstreet once stopped. The dance hall would be filled with Germans speaking no English. On occasion, after too much beer, there would be misunderstandings with the Anglo-Americans and free-for-all fistfights would break out.

One time when Lyndon went to a party and returned home with a black eye, his father fumed. "My daddy said, 'Sonny, there are lots of ways of getting yourself noticed. Some of the boys at that party got noticed because they were very handsome; some because they were witty and attractive. But it looks like you chose the worst way—you got mixed up in a rumpus. Next time you want to be noticed, try some other way.'"

In the summer of 1926, when Lyndon was just eighteen, there was a summer revival session in the area, and he joined the Christian Church, even though his mother would have preferred that he follow the Baines' tradition as a Baptist. However, becoming a member of the Disciples of Christ resulted in no discernible change in Lyndon. He was still going out for his beer and occasionally returning home battered. Once when he came in with a cut and bleeding face, his mother sat on his bed and sobbed. "To think that my eldest born should turn out like this," she wailed.

The beginning of a change came on a night in February 1927, when he walked into the house after a rain-swept day on the road gang. "I'm sick of working with just my hands, and I'm ready to try working with my brain," he blurted to his mother. "If you and Daddy can get me into a college, I'll go as soon as I can."

His mother immediately crossed the room to the party-line telephone on the wall and put in a call to Southwest Texas State Teachers College at San Marcos, forty miles south of Johnson City.

Chapter 5

D R. CECIL EVANS, whom Mrs. Johnson called at the small teachers college early in February 1927, was no stranger to the Johnsons. He had become president of Southwest Texas State Teachers College in 1911, when Governor Oscar Colquitt fired his predecessor, and before that he was employed as general agent of the Texas Conference for Education. Sam Johnson met him in the Statehouse, where Evans was a frequent visitor to badger legislators for a higher appropriation for his school and on a variety of other matters, some dealing with education, some not. For years, and unsuccessfully, Evans promoted a bill to provide free textbooks to public-school pupils. Sam Johnson was a member of the minority behind this measure as well as one to continue the teaching of German at state colleges during World War I. During those years when Lyndon's father was in the Texas House, Evans came through Johnson City and other towns to place his school's graduates in local classrooms and he met Mrs. Johnson while paying his political respects.

It was Evans' opinion, when Mrs. Johnson telephoned him, that if Lyndon came right away he could be placed in classes that had begun only a few weeks earlier. To her query about employment for Lyndon while attending school, he assured her that arrangements could be made. Tuition and books would average about ten dollars a month, while board and room would run about one dollar a day at the many boardinghouses in town.

The immediate problem was money. Sam Johnson had none to spare. Unwilling to embarrass his father by asking him to apply for a loan at the Johnson City Bank, Lyndon went there himself only to be coldly rejected. However, his mother had one last hope. Percy Brigham, the banker at Blanco, a town fourteen miles below Johnson City, had once worked as a clerk in her father's law firm and never failed to speak admiringly of her. Lyndon went to Brigham and returned home to report that Brigham had given him a loan for seventy-five dollars—and on his own signature, even though he was only eighteen and a minor.

Sam Johnson had one of his pointed anecdotes to tell his son before he kissed him good-by on the lips and watched him head for the highway with his cardboard suitcase. "This man I knew had a son going to college," he told Lyndon, "and one morning a friend stopped this man and asked him how his son was making out. 'Much better,' he said to him. 'He wrote to me that last term he was at the very top of those who failed.' "

San Marcos was a big place, twice the size of Fredericksburg, with four thousand residents, including the seven hundred students attending Southwest Texas. It lay in a valley surrounded by steep hills, and many of its three-story houses that jutted out of the hills were approachable only by narrow winding roads. Besides being a college town, San Marcos was also a resort town with dozens of cabins alongside the spring-fed San Marcos River. The teachers college covered a twenty-eight-acre hill and had six buildings, including a small library with a mere twenty thousand books, a faculty of fifty-six, a demonstration farm elsewhere that measured forty acres, and three grade schools where local children were subjected to the college's practice teachers.

When Lyndon reached the campus, he checked first with the administrative office to learn about enrollment procedure. The results were like a mule kick in the stomach. He was ineligible to become a student at Southwest Texas because the Johnson City High School went only through the eleventh grade, and was therefore not an accredited school. Dr. David Votaw, who broke the bad news to him, said that there was a way out, however. Subcollege courses were beginning on Monday, February 7, with exams in mid-March. If he got past those, he could begin the next college quarter on March 21. Lyndon said he would take the courses and then proceeded to tell Votaw how he planned to get his college degree in a little over two years of class work.

Grandma Ruth Huffman Baines no longer ran a boardinghouse in San Marcos but had moved in with her daughter Josefa in San Antonio. Lyndon's Aunt Kittie, married to Sam Johnson's brother Tom, did run a boardinghouse for college students in town. However, Aunt Kittie took only girls, and he had to find a room elsewhere while he plunged into six weeks of subcollege-course work. He did this with an intensity he had never before revealed. "I made all A's in the end, except for plane geometry," he said. Math was like a foreign language to him. "My mother came and worked with me all night before the geometry exam, and I got a seventy, just passing."

Mrs. Mattie Allison, who taught the English brush-up courses, said he wrote remarkable themes. One was on politics, she recalled, and she was stunned "that a boy so young could have such a wide grasp of politics." She sent his theme, "Is Thinking Popular?" to the school paper, the *College Star*, where it was printed on March 23, 1927, errors included. In this essay, he bewailed the fact that nonconformists were mistreated by society.

Never did anyone come to town so fast as Lyndon Johnson came to Southwest Texas State Teachers College. This was the case in the jobs he landed, student leadership, and degree earning. His first job was with a cleanup gang that roamed the campus and picked up trash. Dissatisfied with this low-level job, he went directly to President Evans and asked him for a better one. Evans got rid of him by making him an assistant to Leandro Gonzales, the science building janitor.

However, Lyndon returned in a few weeks, barged into Evans' office, and told him he wanted to be of personal help to him. Evans diplomatically pointed out that he already had a full-time secretary, Tom Nichols, to do the office work. But Lyndon was persistent, and in the end Evans wearily agreed that he could become Nichols' assistant, working between classes.

According to Nichols, what next unfolded was flabbergasting. Lyndon jumped up to talk to everyone who came to the office to see Evans, and before days passed, he was asking the purpose of the visit and offering solutions to problems. The notion soon spread that it was necessary to get Lyndon's approval first in order to see Dr. Evans. At the same time, faculty members came to the conclusion that it was essential for them to be friendly to Lyndon, for they believed he could influence the president in their behalf. This erroneous idea developed because the school lacked a telephone system tying Evans' office with those of department heads, and when the president wanted to send a message to a department head or a professor, he asked his part-time aide, rather than Nichols, to run over with the note. Lyndon's tone and attitude somehow gave the impression he was far more than a messenger.

Lyndon fairly overwhelmed Evans by his tactics. In front of faculty members he once slapped Evans on the back in jovial greeting, an act that made eyes roll, since no one else dared do this. When Evans had to attend committee sessions in the Statehouse, Lyndon talked Evans into taking him along to Austin. Evans also turned over to him the job of writing reports to state agencies and replies to letters. "Lyndon," he once told the hurricane from Johnson City, "I declare you hadn't been in my office a month before I could hardly tell who was president of the school— you or me."

Shortly after he went to work for Evans, Lyndon convinced Evans he should rent him the room over his garage. In later years, while on political campaigns, Lyndon got a lot of mileage out of the self-pitying remark: "I lived and slept in the president's garage on a cot." The truth was that he and Alfred "Booty" Johnson, an unrelated Johnson whom he chose to live with above the garage, occupied a room that came well furnished. Their only problem was a lack of bathing facilities, but they dashed across the street and sneaked into the showers in the men's gym when the need arose. One time the athletic coach found them taking showers and after a fit of rage reported "Johnson and Johnson," as they were called on the campus, to the school's administrative office. But this was useless because of the relationship between Lyndon and Dr. Evans. Even though Evans charged the boys a small rental fee, there were times when they could not pay. Dr. Alfred Nolle, the academic dean, said that in such instances President Evans agreed to erase the debt if they painted the garage. In the spring of 1927 the Johnsons painted the garage three times. When Booty needed money but did not want a sweaty job, Lyndon arranged with Evans a featherbedding job for him as an "inspector of buildings."

Lyndon and the other students, as well as the faculty, knew of the dark cloud that hung over Evans' existence. A balding man with large round glasses and a genial expression, Evans lived simply, chided those who put on airs, and spoke in the colloquial vernacular of a rural Southerner. But Evans' democratic ways were suspect in many quarters because his brother, Hiram Wesley Evans, was Imperial Wizard of the Ku Klux Klan, that venomous spewer of bigotry.

Those who knew brother Hiram said that like Cecil Evans he, too, was a cheery affable sort. Hiram Evans had attended Vanderbilt and become a dentist in Dallas, where he was concerned with building a practice until after World War I, when the Ku Klux Klan began in earnest to meet under fiery crosses in open fields and wear white robes and hoods while they planned mayhem and murder for bigotry. Hiram Evans was immediately attracted to the KKK, and because of his professional status, superior ability as a public speaker, and viciousness, he was soon Exalted Cyclops of the Dallas Klavern, the largest KKK phalanx in Texas.

The Texas KKK revealed a spectacular growth under Evans in the early 1920's. There were charges that could not be proved that Governor Pat Neff was friendly to the round-faced, pudgy Evans and to Dr. A. D. Ellis of Beaumont, an Episcopal minister who was then the Texas Grand Dragon. What many noticed was that the Texas Rangers made no effort to arrest Ku Kluxers except when Governor Neff was out of the state. In 1922 Evans acted with impunity in directing the flogging of sixty-two persons at a site alongside the Trinity River. Several of those who were beaten for their anti-KKK activities were also tarred and feathered, and a mulatto physician was castrated. Evans personally branded a Dallas bell-hop with acid.

While Cecil Evans in 1922 was trying to get the state legislature to appropriate more money to expand Southwest Texas State Teachers College, Hiram Evans was elevating one of his KKK boys, Earle Mayfield, into the United States Senate. That same year, Hiram stole control of the national Ku Klux Klan by seizing power from William J. Simmons, the alcoholic Grand Wizard, with the help of the Klan's fifty-man secret police force and the official verdict of the national Klonvocation. Simmons later confessed that "the Klan was one of the World War's most poisonous weeds. It never could have grown up anywhere on earth but in a nation chafing and straining under the emotional stress of war." Simmons also said that his movement had been helped by a movie on the Civil War,

Birth of a Nation, and by the Library of Congress—"which sent me a list of 213 books written on the Civil War Ku Klux Klan."

The respectability of the KKK was astonishing. When Evans visited Washington, D.C., as the Imperial Wizard, one of his chief supporters, Gutzon Borglum, who later was the sculptor of the Rushmore Memorial Presidential Heads in South Dakota, introduced him to President Harding at the White House. Pa Ferguson, a strong opponent of Evans, and eager to promote anti-Klan support behind his wife as a gubernatorial candidate, labeled Hiram Evans the "Grand Gizzard" and the home state KKK the "Longhorn Texas Koo Koos."

Cecil Evans would not enter a conversation that involved his brother. Like most who knew him, Lyndon did not believe he was even in remote sympathy with the Klan. On one occasion, when Lyndon had to characterize him for the school paper, he described the president as "a Democrat, Methodist, member of N.E.A. and Mason." But as long as Hiram Evans remained in the news, Cecil Evans had to carry his heavy burden.

After living in Dr. Evans' garage room, Lyndon did a great deal of boardinghouse and rooming-house hopping. For a time he took his meals at Mrs. Gates's place on Edward Gary Street. The other boys there were glad when he finally moved. In order to maintain a semblance of order at the table, Mrs. Gates insisted that her diners keep their feet on the floor while reaching around the table for food. Several complained that because of his inordinately long reach Lyndon had an unfair advantage. Since pork chops were more expensive than meat loaf, another rule was that on pork chop night each boy would be restricted to one. Lyndon could not get his fill of pork chops, and he took this rule with great displeasure. However, he usually ended up with an extra helping because of his reach. When a diner was absent, Mrs. Gates nevertheless placed a pork chop on his plate. On signal, all were permitted to scramble for the chop, and the loud groans meant that Lyndon had speared it again.

Lyndon gravitated toward boys who were loud, brash, and aggressive like himself. Besides Booty Johnson, who became the college football star, he liked Jesse Kellam, another good athlete, whom he later put in charge of his radio and television enterprise. Still another boy in his gang was Willard Deason, whom he later rewarded with a seat on the Interstate Commerce Commission.

His first meeting with Deason was almost a disaster. The two sat across the aisle from each other in one class, and when Deason replied to a question from their instructor, Lyndon bellowed, "Aw, you're crazy as hell!"

Deason, whose temper was on as short a fuse as Lyndon's, stamped into the hall afterward for a fight. But suddenly an arm enveloped his shoulder, and the owner was Lyndon, who said, smiling, "Well, partner, it's all part of going to college." Deason did not know quite what to make of Lyndon's remark, but he assumed he was apologizing. On that basis they became friends and spent a year as roommates in the widow Pirtle's boardinghouse.

What fascinated Lyndon most about Willard Deason was the latter's phenomenal political memory. When he met someone, he would not only learn the name, but the town where he came from as well. At the next meeting, he would call the boy by name and casually ask how everything was back in ————. Deason was so loyal to Lyndon that when the latter developed a toothache one day, he skipped all his classes to hitchhike with him the fifty miles southwest to San Antonio so that Lyndon's dentist uncle, Dr. William Saunders, could fill his tooth without charge.

Another Lyndon favorite was Horace Richards, who made him green with envy because of his ability to promote harebrained schemes to enrich himself. After one football rally, Horace stood outside the door, and when the fired-up students poured out, he held out his cowboy hat and yelled, "Kick in for the decorations!" He pocketed the money. He had other dubious promotions, with the money to go "to a worthy campus cause." He never mentioned that *he* was the *cause*. For an unknown reason, Richards laughed uncontrollably whenever Lyndon said "Hottentots." Lyndon would suddenly exclaim the word in class, and Richards would be reduced to hysterical laughter, to the puzzlement of their professor. Forty years later Richards told a reporter that he ascribed his low grade in one course to Lyndon's call of "Hottentots."

Vernon Whitesides, who had a thick Texas accent, was important to Lyndon because he was a master storyteller. Whitesides was also the campus agent for Real Silk Hose, and Lyndon was his star salesman. Professor J. B. Buckner, who taught foreign languages, said, "I bought socks from him. Everybody did. Lyndon was such a salesman you couldn't resist him." On one occasion when Lyndon and some of the others in his crowd sat listening to Whitesides' stories, Whitesides punctuated one tale with the comment that he would like to spend the weekend in Mexico. One of the boys said he would supply his rattletrap Ford if the others bought gasoline and food. At this, Lyndon picked up Whitesides' Real Silk sample case and walked out of the room. He returned a few hours later with twenty dollars, saying that he had sold Dr. Evans his umpty-umpth order of socks and had made sales to other customers. So the boys went off in the Ford for a weekend at Nuevo Laredo across the border.

Willard Deason's view of Lyndon Johnson was that "he was always in a hurry on the campus. He never walked with leisure. It was always with long, loping strides, almost like a trot. . . . He was the only fellow I ever knew who could see around the corner."

One of the corners Lyndon saw around was campus politics. When he found out that the school's athletes ran the show as class officers and editors of the publications through their secret organization, the Black Stars, he decided to join their party. Booty Johnson suggested he get on the baseball team and gain eligibility for the Black Stars. However, the coach rejected him as a pitching prospect. Nevertheless, he told Booty to promote him for membership, and Booty put it to the boys that Lyndon might be a dud as an athlete but he was Dr. Evans' right-hand man and "could help us out if we needed it." This proved an enthusiastic rallying point, and Lyndon would have received the necessary unanimous vote had it not been for the single blackball by one member who screamed he was "mad because Lyndon has been courting my girl!"

This rejection provoked Lyndon into attempting his first foray into politics. Not long afterward he sought his revenge through the organization of a new secret society, the White Stars. For class president, he put up Willard Deason against the likeable Black Star candidate, Dick Spinn, who was seeking re-election. "The night before the election the White Stars held a caucus," said Deason, "and we decided we were beaten. I said we might as well go to bed and forget it. But Lyndon wouldn't give up. He spent all night going around to the boardinghouses, calling the girls' dormitory, moving behind the scenes, giving them that old Johnson one-two-three pep talk. The next day I won by twenty votes. When ordinary men were ready to give up, that's when Lyndon Johnson was just beginning."

There was much more than revenge to be gained from the victory. Besides winning a reputation as a politician, Lyndon found that his new White Star power had patronage value. One student noted that shortly after the White Stars gained authority, all inside work jobs on the campus went to members, while Black Stars were relegated to outside construction work and painting.

The rise of the White Stars made Lyndon a controversial figure on the Southwest Texas acres. Those who admired him and those who disliked him tended to be emotional in their views. Some found him "ruthless"; others, "evasive." Some felt he was too obvious in "always wanting to be the head man"; others questioned his motives. "Every action was calculated to advance his career," said one classmate.

As at most teachers colleges, the girls outnumbered the boys. The ratio here was three to one, and with someone as tall and noisy as Lyndon, he had more than his share of girlfriends. This went to his head, said one roommate, who remembered Lyndon's careful preparation when he had a date. He spent a great deal of time examining himself in the mirror. There would be the bow tie to adjust with infinite care, then would come the Stacomb hair grease to smooth down the curls and make his hair shine. Long afterward, he would remain rooted there, "drawing his neck down into his collar so that it would not look so long, and carrying on a lively banter about how irresistible they [he and his roommate] were to girls."

Because students at Southwest Texas came from poor families, social life was modest. The girls in the dormitories held dances, and these drew crowds because they cost almost nothing. When Lyndon had a few extra dollars, he would take his girl to the Palace Theater and then to Williams Drug Store for a soda. Otherwise, he would go to the dormitory dance or for an evening of talking and spooning down at Riverside, the shore area of the San Marcos River owned by the college. Mary Brogdon, the dean of women, was a harsh nightwatchman, and those girls who violated the weeknight ten-thirty curfew could expect a scolding. On occasion, she expelled repeating violators.

As an institution of higher education, Southwest Texas did not rate, compared with Baylor, the University of Texas, Rice, and Southern Methodist. Yet it had a few professors of high caliber who could have fitted in easily with the faculties of these better schools. Two from whom Lyndon took classes were men of such ability. One was M. L. Arnold, the head of the history department; the other was Howard Mell Greene, professor of political science and the debating coach.

Greene was the greater force. A handsome man with a dimpled chin, he wore such disreputable-looking clothes to classes that townspeople thought he was a tramp. Greene considered himself a twentieth-century Thoreau and preached the blessings of the simple life. Such talk stirred other faculty members into classifying him as a leftist. Greene also considered himself a modern Socrates and used his teaching method of throwing questions at his class and leading them on to arrive at the conclusions he had intended they should, before he began. Greene's oft-repeated maxim was that decisions in a democracy must necessarily be compromises of the demands of contending forces.

Greene quickly installed Lyndon as his favorite student. Generally, when he tossed out a question to his class, Lyndon dominated the discussion. Greene thought such forceful talk and energy should be channeled into a political career, and he frequently suggested this to Lyndon. Birdie King, who was in the class and later edited the Texas Federation *News,* heard Professor Greene tell Lyndon to make the United States Senate his political goal.

It was inevitable that when Greene selected his best two-man debating team, Lyndon would be one of the debaters. Elmer Graham, who later became a Baptist minister in San Antonio, was the other debater, and the two boys along with Greene traveled throughout south central Texas to debate other teachers colleges. To while away traveling time, Lyndon and Greene exchanged a host of off-color and smutty stories, all of which appalled the ministerial Graham, who said that Lyndon could spout "a bad word" and Greene could be "quite crude."

Decades later, when Johnson was far into his political career, he wrote Graham that their debating activities had been of enormous importance to him in politics. Johnson went on to say that the need for the two of them to prepare careful arguments on both sides of the debating question, because a flip of the coin would determine their position, made an immense difference to him. But Graham did not react favorably to this letter, for

Lyndon had not only left the preparation of the debate to Elmer Graham, but would not help him organize the material. As a result, it was Elmer's invariable task to open all debates for their side with a presentation of their position. Lyndon's forte, he claimed, was to pounce on a weak point in the opponents' argument and go after it "ruthlessly" with dripping ridicule and jibes, all of which he delivered calmly. Time after time adversaries reacted by falling into hysterical self-defense, which only induced judges to award their decision to Lyndon and Elmer.

Considering his over-full course load, his work for Dr. Evans, door-to-door peddling of Real Silk, White Star politicking, and debating, Lyndon's academic work was necessarily below his true abilities. Years afterward, when his college days took on a magnolia aura, he boasted: "I took forty courses and got thirty-five A's." But though he did well in history and political science and the simple education courses, he fared poorly in science, and his record was blotted with a fail in physical education.

In college Lyndon fancied himself a writer as well as a speaker, and he talked the editor of the weekly paper, the *College Star*, into letting him write a weekly editorial. Then in 1928, after a year of editorial writing, as boss of the White Stars and the patronage the college party controlled, he put himself in as the thirty-dollar-a-month editor of the *College Star*. This job, on top of all his other activities, would have crushed most boys, but Lyndon did not appear to be burdened.

As an editorial writer, he bathed in maudlin sentimentality and super-patriotism. His Thanksgiving editorial in November 1927 said that to him the holiday meant "eating Mother's turkey and basking in her smiles and talking politics with Dad." For Father's Day, he said that in adversity Mamma could rely on "tears," but Daddy "must square his shoulders, resolutely grit his teeth, suppress his emotions and with renewed courage meet the issue." He also lectured students, some of whom were desperately poor, that there was evil in "this swiftly-moving, money-mad age." When Lindbergh flew the Atlantic, Lyndon's advice to his readers was: "Do not sigh for Lindbergh's wonderful luck, but determine to emulate Lindy's glorious pluck."

In other editorials, he presented his already matured views on how to reach the top. One of his editorials noted that "personality is power; the man with a strong personality can accomplish greater deeds in life than a man of equal abilities but less personality." Another time he wrote: "The successful man has a well-trained will. He has under absolute control his passions and desires, his habits and his deeds. This strong will has made of the man a consistent, forceful character." In Lyndon's opinion, "It is ambition that makes of a creature a real man. The great men of the world had inflexible will, resolute determination."

Unlike most students, whose entire existence revolved about Southwest Texas State Teachers College, Lyndon kept an appraising eye on the outside world as well. This was especially true of the political world beyond

the campus. On occasion, when the state legislature was in session, he
hitchhiked to Austin, thirty miles north, to listen to debate in the Statehouse. Sometimes he personally practiced the art of political gladhanding,
which was essential in Texas, where voters were suspicious of standoffish
candidates who spoke too grammatically. Elmer Graham was aware that
whenever he, Lyndon, and Professor Greene went out on debating trips,
in whatever town they landed, Lyndon always established "instant friendships" with complete strangers they met. On the streets of San Marcos,
he hugged and kissed Mrs. Gates, his old boardinghouse matron, on sight,
and he went in for full, hearty handshakes indiscriminately, with his most
fervent clasp reserved for Cayetano Mendez, the Mexican janitor at the
Old Main Building on the campus. One time Lyndon and a friend had
bowls of chili in a restaurant. The food was not high quality, yet on his
way out Lyndon pumped the hand of the proprietress and exclaimed,
"That was the finest bowl of chili I ever ate!"

Nineteen-twenty-eight was a major election year, what with the Presidency, a Texas seat in the United States Senate, all House seats, and
local offices up for grabs. As the year progressed, Lyndon's friends said,
he continually upset their nighttime poker games with his marathon talk
about political personalities and how he would run a campaign if he were
a candidate. What made the 1928 Democratic Presidential nomination
especially exciting to Lyndon was the fact that the national convention
was being held that June in Houston. This was the first major convention
staged in Texas, for the 1920 American Party Convention in Fort Worth
that nominated Pa Ferguson for President was too insignificant to consider.

The school prohibited girls from riding in cars with boys, yet this did
not stop Lyndon from asking a friend with a car to go with him and their
girlfriends to the Democratic show at Houston on June 26. The four
reached Sam Houston Hall in Houston in time for the long speeches and
roll calls. But doorkeepers would not permit the college boys or the young
girls with short, bobbed hair and knee-high skirts to enter without passes.
This infuriated Lyndon, who demanded to see some of the convention
officers. When they came, he immediately waved copies of the *College Star*
in their faces and kept up such a nagging barrage that in self-defense they
wearily accredited him as a working reporter and gave gallery passes to
his friends.

The convention hall spectacle was the biggest political thrill in Lyndon's
young life. Walking about the hall as though he owned it was tall, stoutish
Jesse Jones, the suave Houston real estate operator, whose gift of $200,000
had lured the Democrats to Houston. The Texas delegation, with Congressmen John Garner, Sam Rayburn, James Buchanan, who represented the
Congressional District that included Johnson City, and Tom Connally,
who was running for the Senate against KKK incumbent Earle Mayfield,
could be observed on the floor. There was talk (which turned out to be true)
that many Texas delegates and politicians planned to support Republican

Herbert Hoover if the Democrats nominated Governor Al Smith of New York.

It was Franklin Roosevelt who nominated Al Smith for President and served as his floor manager despite his leg paralysis. The expected fight to keep Smith off the ticket collapsed early, and he easily won more than the necessary two-thirds vote on the first ballot. There was excitement at the end when Roosevelt made a motion for adjournment, and despite the fact that there were few *ayes* and a roar of *nays*, Senator Pat Harrison of Mississippi, the presiding officer, declared the convention adjourned.

When Lyndon and his friends returned to San Marcos, Dean Nolle called him in for special punishment. Nolle admitted, however, that Lyndon gave him such a vivid blow-by-blow account of the convention that he thoroughly enjoyed the recital. At the close, he let him off without taking any disciplinary action.

Lyndon had started at Southwest Texas in March 1927, and he continued classes in each succeeding school quarter, including the summer sessions of 1927 and 1928. During this time he wisely took the five education courses that made him eligible to receive a "Two-Year Certificate," or what was required to become a grade-school teacher in many Texas towns. So in the late summer of 1928, when Dr. Evans learned that Sam Johnson needed financial help, he arranged a teaching job for Lyndon in Cotulla, in southern Texas. The salary was $125 a month for nine months, beginning in September, and Lyndon gave his quick assent to take temporary leave of the San Marcos campus.

In a later letter to his mother he spoke of his "hope that the years to come will place me in a position to relieve you of the hardships that it has fallen your lot to suffer." But in September 1928, as he packed his few belongings, his thoughts were on returning to the campus as quickly as possible to get his degree. If everything went well, the hurricane from Johnson City would be back at college in a year.

Chapter 6

MAURY MAVERICK, that short, thick-chested civil rights champion from San Antonio, once described the one-hundred-and-fifty-mile sweep from his town southward to the Mexican border as a desolate, treeless section where summer temperatures in the cotton fields exceeded one hundred and ten degrees and were slightly lower in the corrugated iron-roofed farm and ranch houses along the way. Once trees had risen here, only to be chopped down to make more room for cotton and cattle.

Cotulla broiled in the sun near the meandering Nueces River in LaSalle County, halfway between San Antonio and Laredo. In bygone days Cotulla proudly upheld its reputation as the wildest spot in the Old West. Old-timers bragged that when the Missouri-Pacific approached the town, conductors called out, "Cotulla! Everybody get your guns ready!" Knocking off sheriffs proved a popular pastime, while all-night brawls were he-man sport for the hordes of cowboys who came in from the range for their fun. Cotulla's most famous citizen was O. Henry (Sydney Porter), who lived outside of town on a ranch and rode in for his mail on his clay-bank pony.

Wild Cotulla no longer existed when twenty-year-old Lyndon Johnson climbed down the Mo-Pac iron stairs at the railroad stop. However, it still functioned as a major cattle center. Close by, the world's largest roundup of wild mustangs had recently occurred and cowboys in dusty clothes were still a common sight. So honored was the cowboy locally that hardly a man in Cotulla, whether bank teller or filling station operator, would be caught outdoors without being clothed in cowboy boots, creaseless cowboy pants, open workshirt, and multigallon hat.

The town was essentially a Mexican center, for of its three thousand residents, about twenty-three hundred spoke Spanish. Everyone lived a segregated existence; the Anglos, west of the Mo-Pac tracks, and the Latinos, east of the tracks in what had once been a separate town called LaSalle. The Mexicans lived in hovels and in depressing poverty.

Lyndon had been hired to teach the fifth, sixth, and seventh grades in the two-year-old Welhausen School in the Mexican part of town. But when he came for his briefing, the school superintendent asked if he would mind serving also as principal, with five teachers and Tomas Coronada, the school janitor, to boss. Lyndon liked the idea, and agreed.

Both teachers and pupils found him a no-nonsense young man. One teacher recalled him as "a firm administrator, a strict disciplinarian." Another description painted him as a person of "great energy, very aggressive, highly creative, and short-tempered." The other teachers agreed that no school where they had taught was run under such stringent rules. One said, "He spanked disorderly boys and tongue-lashed the girls."

One rule he rigidly enforced was that only English be spoken on school property, including the playground. Pupils caught speaking Spanish were liable to be put across his knee and spanked. Many youngsters came to Welhausen knowing only Spanish and therefore had enormous incentive to pick up English. In class, as a teacher, he deluged his pupils almost to exhaustion with arithmetic problems (his own worst subject) and spelling tests. He also spent much time presenting his own highly dramatic version

of Texas' early history, apparently forgetting that his swarthy charges were
related by blood to those on the losing side. Santa Anna may have been
a man of treachery to Lyndon, but he was a patriot to Latinos. Children
whose parents were denied the vote were told that if they "studied hard
they could be President of the United States."

After he rang the school bell in the morning, he would stride into
his three-grade class with his arms swinging. A firmly established routine
called for the thirty-two children to greet him with a song. At that time
the popular vaudeville team of Billy Jones and Ernie Hare made use of a
specialty song as their opening number; and Lyndon taught his pupils a
parody on the same tune, which went this way:

"How do you do, Mr. Johnson,
How do you do?
How do you do, Mr. Johnson,
How are you?
We'll do it if we can,
We'll stand by you to a man.
How do you do, Mr. Johnson,
How are you?"

One morning after he left the room, three children quit their seats
and came to the front of the room, striding along and swinging their arms
in imitation of their teacher. The other children laughed uproariously at
this ridicule of Lyndon. But suddenly they stopped laughing and two of
the arm-swingers raced to their seats. The third one, Danny Garcia, continued his mimicry.

When Danny realized something was amiss, he turned about and there
stood his angry teacher. Years later on television, Danny told what happened. Johnson "took me by the hand and led me into his office. I thought
I was going to get a lecture, but that wasn't it. He turned me over his
knee and whacked me a dozen times on the backside."

As the day wore on, Lyndon combined his teaching with checking on
the other teachers and handling the office work. Dissatisfied with a day in
and day out changeless routine, he expanded activities at a breathless
pace. First he introduced school assemblies where the children performed
before the other children and parents. Then he established competitive
meetings between Welhausen pupils and those in neighboring schools.
These included public speaking contests, spelldowns, baseball games, and
track events. To deliver his pupils to towns miles away, he had to chauffeur
them. This created an initial problem because there were no buses available.
But he questioned the children to learn whose parents owned cars. Then
he talked to car owners to shame, cajole, browbeat, and flatter them into
driving participants to contests. Several parents afterward complained that
he put them on such demanding time schedules and with such frequency
that they considered selling their cars.

Principals before Lyndon had suffered from charges by the school superintendent that they were not holding enough meetings with parents to discuss school problems. Lyndon made friends with an employee in the superintendent's office, and whenever the superintendent was on his way for a surprise visit to Welhausen, Lyndon was notified in ample time by his friend. After each warning phone call, Lyndon rushed outside, rounded up Mexican loiterers, and had them stand in his office facing his desk. When the trouble-seeking superintendent finally poked his head into Lyndon's office, he could only smile disappointedly at what he believed was another of the young principal's frequent meetings with parents.

Cotulla was termite infested. Because of this, almost all houses were built on stilts, some two feet high. When the termites bored through a pole, it could be easily replaced, thus saving the construction of a new house. Lyndon boarded with Sarah Tinsley in the western part of town, and his roommate was the local high school football coach. Both the Anglos and the Latinos made frijole beans, Cotulla's staple dish, and Miss Tinsley was no exception. Anyone who disliked Mexican food would have found Cotulla a nightmare. But Lyndon never tired of returning for dinner at Miss Tinsley's house on poles and finding frijoles on the table.

With all his energy, his duties at the Welhausen School plus the wide extracurricular program he initiated there failed to exhaust or even tax him. When the superintendent held an all-school faculty meeting, and Lyndon learned that Cotulla High School lacked a debating coach, he took on this extra duty at no increase in salary. This required him to go to the high school each day after he closed Welhausen and put in a few hours there. While at the high school, he noticed that it had no literary society. So he organized one even though he found fiction a total bore. Lyndon encroached further into the high school by becoming coach of its basketball team. A girl student said that if the boys were not in the gym when he came, "he would coach the girls' softball team. Even then he couldn't bear to waste time."

Nor were these the limits of his activities in Cotulla. He said he "fell in love with a very pretty girl" who taught in a school thirty-five miles away. One of the problems they had was that she earned twenty-five dollars a month more than he, and he considered this "very humiliating." He took her to movies and local dances and found time to write out her lesson plan for her next week's classes. He never divulged why they finally broke off the relationship.

To top off his hectic activities, he also went to school as a student. That year Southwest Texas at San Marcos had established an extension center at Cotulla, and Lyndon signed up for two courses in each of three quarter terms. It was as though Dr. Evans had established a school outside the school for Lyndon's benefit, because he earned twelve credits, which were added to his scholastic record back on the San Marcos campus. Among his courses were elementary economics, race relations, and the social teachings of Jesus.

In the spring of 1929 the Cotulla School Board recognized a prize work horse and asked Lyndon to return to Welhausen for the next school year. But Lyndon had word from home that his father had hopes of landing a patronage job with the state government and that he should finish his education. He could now put into effect the plan he had brought to Southwest Texas—to combine his junior and senior years into a single year—and finish the four-year course in fewer than three years. So he thanked the school board and left the exhausted educational community in Cotulla behind him.

Chapter 7

In JUNE 1929, when Lyndon returned to San Marcos, the college knew with a jolt that he was back in town. He roused the lagging White Stars and put them back in charge of class offices and petty patronage. In one election for senior class president he bamboozled the opposition. He ran two candidates against the Black Stars' man—one candidate to rage at the Black Stars, the other to claim falsely that he despised the White Stars and was not a White Star himself. The confused electorate gave the second White Star candidate a plurality of votes. In another election he ruined the Black Stars by proposing that the traditional order of voting be turned around so the least important offices be filled first. When the Black Stars fell into his trap, he and his band of schemers quickly nominated and elected the Black Star big wheel as cheerleader, thus eliminating him from probable victory in the contest for class president.

That final year in school he boarded with Mrs. Mattie Hopper, and his roommate was freshman Fenner Roth. Some claimed he chose Fenner as his roommate on purpose because seniors were given freshmen to carry out their chores, and Fenner belonged to Lyndon. This meant a great deal of dashing about for poor Fenner, even though he was a White Star, for Lyndon kept him constantly on the run doing errands.

Student offices poured on Lyndon. He served as president of the Press

Club, with a free trip to the state convention of college journalists at Huntsville. He was also senior legislator of his class, a member of the student council, secretary of the Schoolmakers Club and arranger of its watermelon feast, and a persuasive talker in the Harris Blair Literary Society. In addition he returned as editor and writer for the *College Star*. Despite his reputation as a boisterous teller of obscene stories, when it came to the columns of the *College Star* he decried "the coarse suggestiveness or immoral jokes which some college sheets seem to regard as humorous." He also wrote about the glories of Sam Houston, condemned those who refused to do "good deeds" and reporters who were not "free from any tinge of propaganda," and declared that "the world is looking for men who are not for sale."

Then there was his classroom load. "In order to graduate in 1930," he said, "I took seven courses a quarter." This was in violation of the rules, and Dean Nolle told him so. Yet he permitted him to carry this load, even though he noted that "Lyndon wasn't the scholarly type."

The great prosperity of the twenties had never been noticed in the Hill Country. However, the great depression of the thirties, which was heralded by the October 1929 stock market crash, made poor economic conditions immediately worse. Ironically, Sam Johnson's fortunes improved as mass unemployment and business shutdowns took place. Pat Neff, a former governor, needed voter support to retain his chairmanship of the Texas Railroad Commission in 1930, and he believed that Johnson could still deliver him a pile. So he rid himself of the pressure that Johnson had been putting on him for a job and named him a state bus inspector at one hundred and fifty dollars a month. The inspecting was to be centered at San Marcos, and in the spring of 1930 the Johnsons moved there for a four-year stay. Two of Lyndon's sisters, Rebekah and Josefa, were already enrolled at Southwest Texas, and this move reunited the parents and the two youngest children with the three in college.

In 1920, when Sam Johnson served in the Texas House, he had opposed Pat Neff in his campaign for governor. He also opposed him in his re-election fight in 1922, for he believed Pat was too close with various Ku Kluxers. By then the Nineteenth Amendment, which granted women the right to vote, was in effect, and for the first time Rebekah Johnson went to the polls. Sam had given her to understand that she was to vote for Pat Neff's opponent. But she felt kinship with Neff because they were both strong Baptists, and she confessed to her husband, "When I got to the polls, I just couldn't bring myself to vote against Brother Neff."

Johnson was satisfied in 1925 when Neff was out of office and Miriam A. "Ma" Ferguson, wife of Sam's favorite, Pa Ferguson, took possession of the governor's mansion. Everyone understood that Pa was really governor, and it was commonly known that he had moved a desk into his wife's office to tell her what to do. Unfortunately for Sam Johnson's faith in Ferguson, evidence developed showing that Ma Ferguson handed out two thousand pardons, and in cases checked, Pa Ferguson happened to be the lawyer for some of those involved. Another storm developed over the highway contracts Ma signed, and Dan Moody, the young elected attorney general, ruled them illegal.

Moody defeated Ma Ferguson in 1926, and while he ran the state, Pat Neff went to Washington as a Presidential appointee on the United States Board of Mediation. He made an impressive appearance in Coolidge Era Washington with his long straight back, long silvery hair, black suit, and string tie. But his term ran out in 1928 and he was suddenly on the local scene again, having accepted Governor Moody's offer to serve out the unexpired term of the recently deceased chairman of the Texas Railroad Commission.

When Sam Johnson took the bus inspector's job from the man he had always opposed, he found that his retention of the job depended on that man's success in the 1930 Democratic primary. This put him on the spot, for he knew he had no votes to deliver to Neff. However, he had Lyndon to offer, and he now did so.

In mid-July, in election years, candidates for state, district, and county offices ritualistically appeared at the village of Henle, near San Marcos, for the all-day picnic in the live-oak grove. Each in turn was given an opportunity to "brag on himself" before the crowd of several hundred sunburned spectators, while they ate watermelon and swatted flies.

Sam Johnson thought it was important that he attend and he took Lyndon with him. The crowd was unusually large in 1930, despite the blistering heat. Burly men dragged the speaker's wagon forward and halted it under one of the gnarled live-oaks. Then the master of ceremonies climbed into the wagon and bulled out the name of the first candidate who would start the speechifying. When the man appeared, he stepped into the wagon, and after a short introduction, he screamed out his superior qualifications for the office.

Speaker after speaker tried his spellbinding best, and as time passed Sam Johnson noted that Pat Neff was nowhere in sight. The man who bragged he made eight hundred and fifty speeches when running for governor in 1920 had failed to come to what could be his most important speech in south central Texas. Someone calmed Sam by pointing out that Gregory Hatcher, the former state treasurer who was running against Neff, was also absent.

But when Hatcher's name was called, a man in the crowd said he had come to speak for him. A moment later he stood on the wagon and denounced Pat Neff nonstop in an attack on his personality. Again and again he called Neff a stuffed shirt who never went fishing or hunting, and the crowd enjoyed itself immensely.

After the Hatcher man jumped to the ground over the wagon's lowered tailgate, the master of ceremonies called for Neff. When Neff did not come forward, the Hatcher fans hooted. The announcer was in the midst of declaring Neff the loser by default in the speaking show when Sam Johnson's voice drowned him out. "Get up there, Lyndon, and say something for Pat Neff!" he yelled.

Lyndon came through the crowd almost on the run and leaped onto the wagon. The introduction was simple—"Sam Johnson's boy, Lyndon," and then he began his first political speech. A witness called it "an enthusiastic, arm-swinging defense of Pat as governor and railroad commissioner —a completely extemporaneous and spontaneous speech of approximately ten to fifteen minutes."

It was the hit of the Henle picnic. "Y'uv heard a man say that Pat Neff don't hunt or fish," he said at one point. "I want to remind you of the way those Austin sports come out here into your hills and shoot your cattle when they're s'p'osed to be hunting deer. I ask you if you want a city-slickin' hunter who don't know a cow from a deer to be in charge of your railroad business and your bus line and your oil business, or one whose experience is already tested and proved?"

Following the applause and the whistling, Lyndon walked back to his beaming father, where his second triumph of the day awaited him. Welly Hopkins of Gonzales, a liberal member of the Texas House and a candidate for the Texas Senate, was there to shake his hand and congratulate him. Hopkins was a lawyer of some prominence, his firm serving as counsel to the United Gas Company of Houston and other large concerns. One publication called him a man who "enjoys the confidence of the Gulf Oil Company."

Welly, ten years the college boy's senior, had met him on a recent trip to San Marcos, where he had gone to ask Sam Johnson and others for endorsements. His first question now to Lyndon was "Why did you speak for Pat Neff?"

The reply spoiled the illusion Hopkins had of Sam Johnson's political power. "Because he gave my daddy a job and I wouldn't want to let him down."

"Well, then, how would you like to be my campaign manager?" Hopkins asked.

"Sure I'll do it if I can call all the shots in Blanco, Hays, and Comal Counties," Lyndon shot back at him. These were the largest of the six counties that made up the nineteenth district.

Another experienced politician would have backed away from an inexperienced political would-be who demanded complete control. But Hopkins offered no objection.

School was still on, and Lyndon had to do his classwork on the run during the three weeks remaining in the primary campaign. But the opportunity to try out some campaign techniques he'd been thinking about was too great to resist. Saturation and excitement were the key points. He organized more than a dozen small-town rallies and two big meetings in New Braunfels and San Marcos. He also set up local political machines in all these places, composed and distributed campaign literature, personally collected money from businessmen to pay for the newspaper ads he placed in county weeklies, prodded people relentlessly to attend political rallies, and even organized a traveling claque for Hopkins, which cheered wildly at the mention of his name and treated him to prolonged applause when he spoke.

But while Hopkins believed Lyndon was giving his all for him, Lyndon was busy also in another campaign, said William Kittrell. Bill Kittrell was a lobbyist and a hanger-on in the coterie surrounding Sam Rayburn, the young congressman from Bonham. Wright Patman, who had also gone to the United States House of Representatives, said, "People who wanted to get in good with Sam Rayburn always thought it wise to be nice to Kittrell. Bill was the only man I ever knew who was knowledgeable about every man who walked through the lobby of the Mayflower Hotel in Washington."

In 1930 Kittrell served as campaign manager for Edgar E. Witt, who was running for lieutenant governor. "People in Austin kept telling me about this wonder kid in San Marcos who knew more about politics than anyone else in the area," said Kittrell. "So I looked him up and I got him to make the rounds for Witt, shaking hands with the men on the street, explaining the issues to the farmers, patting babies on the head. We won hands down in a district we had given up as lost."

Welly Hopkins won easily, too, over his opponent Tom Gambrell, and his praise for his young campaign manager was unstinted. Later he rewarded Lyndon by driving him to Monterrey in Mexico for a victory vacation. As for Neff, he failed to win the necessary majority in the primary, and there was a month of concern in the Johnson household that the patronage job would vanish. But the runoff primary came then, and Neff defeated Hatcher, the outdoorsman, by more than one hundred thousand votes. Sam Johnson's job was safe.

Lyndon had every reason to be proud of himself when he got his diploma in August 1930. The only thing he needed now was a job.

Chapter 8

B<small>Y THE SUMMER</small> of 1930, when Lyndon Johnson's mother framed his diploma, the bottom had dropped out of the job market. Banks closed their doors, mass layoffs occurred in factories across the nation, purchasing power plummeted even though prices dropped, and foreclosures on farms and homes grew increasingly common. In education, school construction programs were thrown into trash cans, and teacher loads were increased instead of hiring new teachers. As a result, graduates of the class of 1930 found that opportunities were scarce.

Because of his excellent connections, Lyndon was never scarred by the devastating hand of the depression, though many of his friends went through nightmares to find employment. One of Dr. Evans' apocryphal stories revealed the extremes budding teachers took to get classrooms. As Lyndon retold the tale: "One of the boys in search of a job went before a Hill Country school board. The board was impressed. He was eloquent; generally he was factual; he was impressive. When he finished, the board members asked him, 'Well, we think we would like to have you teach and we would like to retain your services. But tell us, there is some difference of opinion in our community about geography. And we want to know which side you are on. Do you teach that the world is round, or do you teach that the world is flat?'

"The eloquent applicant responded immediately, 'I can teach it either way.' "

Lyndon had more than Dr. Evans working for him. Uncle George Desha Johnson, five years Sam Johnson's junior, headed the history department at Sam Houston High School in Houston, and ever since Lyndon had enrolled at Southwest Texas, Uncle George had mentioned the pleasure he would have if Lyndon taught alongside him in the same school.

Sam Johnson was a nineteenth-century rural type, but his brother George was a twentieth-century city man. Ambition had taken him to Ann Arbor, where he took his degree in history and education at the University of Michigan in 1915 when he was twenty-three. As the sole unmarried child of Sam Ealy Johnson, Sr., and Eliza Bunton Johnson, George was the doting uncle to the thirteen children of his eight brothers and sisters. Among these, his favorites were Lyndon and the three children of his sister Ava. This was fortuitous for Lyndon's Aunt Ava because her husband, John Bright, was a math teacher and Uncle George helped him find teaching jobs. For some years he and Bright taught in the same school at Port Arthur near the Gulf. Then when Uncle George moved to teach in Beaumont, Bright followed and had a classroom down the hall. Uncle George's next move was to Sam Houston High in downtown Houston, and again Bright joined him there. It was only natural that when Aunt Ava's family moved into a house on Hawthorne Street, Uncle George would live with them.

While Lyndon was growing up, Uncle George often visited his family in Johnson City and on the farm near Stonewall. His diction was clearer, but he had the same tell-tale straight-line mouth, elephantine ears, and swinging arm gestures of the male Johnsons, as well as the restlessness and eager desire to talk. He was bald except for fringe hair, and he wore rimless glasses that made him look severely studious. Lyndon remembered that Uncle George had two heroes: Andrew Jackson and Senator Joe Bailey. He never tired of talking about the vigor and brass of old Jackson —the way he could easily frighten his enemies, and the duels he had to protect the honor of his wife Rachel against the many slanderers. As for Senator Joseph Weldon Bailey, Uncle George pooh-poohed the so-called documented stories that had him selling out to Waters-Pierce Oil Company and big business. According to George Johnson, Bailey was the man who gave William Jennings Bryan his ideas in his famous "Cross of Gold" speech. Uncle George was a shouting man when it came to listing the evils of woman suffrage and federal encroachment on the states. But he could be kept off these topics by being asked to recite from the speeches of Joe Bailey, many of which he had memorized.

In the spring of 1930 Lyndon wrote Uncle George that he would graduate in August, and he asked about teaching opportunities in Houston. George immediately spoke to his close friend, Houston School Superintendent E. E. Oberholtzer, and asked for this special favor, despite the retrenchment policy then in effect. More than that, George requested that Lyndon be given a teaching contract at his own school, Sam Houston High.

In June Uncle George sent Lyndon an enthusiastic letter with news that the school board had agreed to hire him as a debating and public speaking teacher at Sam Houston High at sixteen hundred dollars a year. However, there was a slight catch. He would have to wait until a vacancy occurred.

Time was uncomfortably short before the new school year began when Lyndon finally asked Dr. Evans to help him find a temporary teaching job elsewhere. The only opportunity available was a fifty-dollar-a-month post teaching public speaking at Pearsall in Frio County, just north of his old haunt at Cotulla. Lyndon knew he could count on Uncle George's badgering and pushing hard in his behalf, so he took it.

He was careful not to tell the superintendent at Pearsall that he was waiting for a bigger job at Houston, and his hard work during his first six weeks could not have shown more devotion to the high school. But late in October 1930 came the good news he had been waiting for from Uncle George, and he quickly told the superintendent he was leaving. An angry scene developed, and Lyndon was proffered a check for only sixty-seven dollars for his total services. Lyndon not only accepted the check but successfully promoted his younger sister Rebekah as his successor.

Two years earlier, when Lyndon went to Houston for the Democratic National Convention, the big city with its three hundred thousand residents had been a lively, busy place. Sam Houston had named it after himself and it had grown from a few shanties into the biggest money city in the South. Although it lay fifty miles from the Gulf, the kind federal government was in the process of spending five billion dollars to dredge, deepen, widen Buffalo Bayou all the way across the low rolling hills to Galveston and make Houston a leading world port. The city's banks were thick stone structures, and the tasteless rich who filled the vaults with money earned from nearby oil fields and other enterprises developed one of the ugliest residential sections to be found in the entire United States of America. Jesse Jones owned much of the real estate in the downtown area, plus the Houston *Chronicle* and controlling interest in a number of banks and industrial concerns, and he hoped eventually to parlay this money-making mania into his election as President of the country. Local wags said that it was too bad he did not use a little of his money to build a decent restaurant in downtown Houston, for the city was entirely without a good eating place.

In October 1930, when Lyndon returned to Houston, the atmosphere and sights had changed. Thousands of unemployed men stood against walls and sat on ledges in the downtown area. On some streets there were bread lines and soup kitchens for the loitering, unhappy men. Stores had few customers, and people looked seedy.

But Uncle George looked prosperous, with his twenty-eight hundred dollars a year as a teacher, and when Lyndon came from Pearsall to Aunt Ava's house, George immediately insisted that Lyndon live with him. Aunt Ava pointed out that she had no adequate space, for two of her children, Junior and Baby Sue, were still living at home. But her brother proposed that Lyndon share his bedroom with him, and Lyndon unpacked his only suit.

It took him only a few days to discover that Uncle George was the school character at Sam Houston High. Students and teachers called him Senator, and this was readily understandable when you watched his imperious walk and oratorical gestures and listened to his church-organ tone. The school lacked an auditorium, but when the weather was decent, assemblies took place in an open courtyard, with the speakers standing on a second floor balcony. George Johnson frequently forgot he was addressing pupils and gave an eerie imitation of Italian dictator Benito Mussolini, dominating the scene and savoring the inferior position of the crowd, with its upturned heads.

Sam Houston High had begun the school year in its normal, quiet, and orderly way. But all this changed with shocking suddenness when the "Senator's" nephew burst upon the scene. He began by establishing an instant friendship with Principal William Moyes, and when he told Moyes he needed more than the sixteen-hundred-dollar annual salary, Moyes assigned him some extra adult evening classes in public speaking, which paid a dollar and fifty cents an hour.

Moyes also agreed to give him a free hand in developing school debaters into state champions. Sam Houston High School had seventeen hundred pupils, or more than double the enrollment at Southwest Texas State Teachers College. Yet with all this material the high school had never won even the city championship in the annual competition against the four other high schools in town. Lyndon assured Moyes that Sam Houston High would win not only the city championship but the district and state title as well.

The principal took his boast lightly until he found that his newest teacher meant business. Lyndon was listening to every pupil to determine speaking capabilities. Then came reports that dozens of pupils at a time were ordered to remain after school to undergo a hazing and wholesale nagging and scolding because they were not standing or speaking properly as would-be debaters. Day after day Lyndon repeated this process, winnowing out the better prospects and organizing them into teams. The school routine was upset in order to accommodate his program of holding competitions in public speaking between various classes. All the while, he continued keeping pupils after school, working them to the point of exhaustion by requiring repetition after repetition of recitations to the tune of his own "No! No! No!"

His speaking contests continued until Christmas. When one teacher commented that a defeated team took the loss gracefully, Lyndon snapped, enraged, "I'm not interested in how they lose! I'm only interested in how they win!" He ended with Margaret Epley and Evelyn Lee as his girls' debating team, and he was proud when they easily defeated Houston Junior College. His boys' debating team consisted of Luther Jones and Gene Latimer, who were chosen in the school finals by the assistant principal and a local businessman. Luther and Gene, one tall and one short, were much like Lyndon in energy, stamina, and ambition.

Each year the Texas Interscholastic League selected a single debating subject for all Texas schools. The 1931 proposition that came to all debating coaches read: "Resolved, that a substitute for trial by jury should be adopted." The Houston city debating championship was scheduled for April 1, 1931; the district championship for April 18; and the state finals at the beginning of May.

Lyndon allowed for no errors. Classes did library research on the jury question, and he collected arguments pro and con. He went over all possible points and rejoinders with his two teams, made them practice against each other and cut in with his own clobbering suggestions. When he believed his four debaters were growing sharp, he scheduled practice debates on the jury system with other schools. Moderation was not in his character, and he scheduled fifty such sessions! On a twelve-day trip to south and central Texas, he put his group into daily contests, and opposing teams offered no real competition. They had their easiest time with Pearsall, the school he had deserted to come to Sam Houston High.

By now, Houston papers were taking notice of Lyndon and his debaters. One newspaper gave him one hundred dollars, which he was to award to his best debater, but he wisely split it among Margaret, Evelyn, Luther, and Gene. The four were so heavily involved with the jury question that it was drowning out all other thoughts. A teacher charged into Lyndon's class one day to complain that Gene Latimer's work in her class had gone from excellent to poor, and she demanded that Lyndon let up on the boy. She also expressed her entire lack of interest in his program. But by the time she left, he had talked her into staying after school to judge practice contests and chauffeur his debaters to outlying schools for speaking dates.

At the end of March, from Principal Moyes down to the school janitors, Sam Houston High was at fever pitch. Lyndon's debating teams had won every practice session, and now only the official contests stood in the way of glory.

The first test came on April 1 at the Taylor School, where hundreds could not find even standing room at the city meet. Lyndon's foursome breezed through the contests and were given a hero's welcome back at Sam Houston High. The Houston *Chronicle* of April 3 published the remarks of Principal Moyes about "L. B. Johnson, who is making a great record in his first year as a teacher in a Houston school." A victory luncheon by the Kiwanis Club further extolled Lyndon.

But he was taking no chances in preparing for the district meet. He ordered still more library research on the jury system and put his debaters through several additional practice sessions. As a result, the second hurdle, on April 18, was as easy a victory as the city contests. Only the state contest among district champions now remained, and the school's cheerleaders yelled the enthusiastic crowd hoarse as Lyndon and his carefully trained four left for Austin.

In the opening round Lyndon was stunned when Evelyn and Margaret lost to the girls' team from Victoria and were eliminated. But he still had his boys' team, and he was certain Luther and Gene would win. They had come through sixty-five successive victories without a loss, and by now they were talking about juries in their sleep.

The boys did well and came to the final, breathless debate against the team from Sherman, Texas. When the ordeal ended, the judges formed a jury and gave their verdict: Sherman was declared the victor by a vote of three to two. On hearing the news, Lyndon wept as unabashedly as Luther and Gene.

Nevertheless, Houston was proud of its debaters and their teacher, and Lyndon regained sufficient composure to promise victory next year. The Houston *Post-Dispatch* held a banquet in honor of the team, and though he was only an honored guest, Lyndon thought of his father's job and asked that Pat Neff be invited as main speaker. Even though the Houston School Board was ordering salary slashes for the coming year, Lyndon was singled out for a raise of one hundred dollars.

Despite his defeat by a single judge at the state contest, Lyndon planned as strenuous a build-up to win the 1932 title. When school started in September 1931, he had already mapped out an even longer series of practice debates. In addition, he intended to send his best speakers to dozens of assemblies in other high schools where they would talk on "timely civic projects." Luther Jones had graduated and was now going to Rice Institute in town, but he was too valuable to lose. So Lyndon flattered him and called on his loyalty to persuade him to help on the high school program with no pay. Spent at the end of Lyndon's "treatment," Luther agreed, even though it meant cutting dangerously into his time to study his college subjects.

Then, as suddenly as the Johnson hurricane had hit Sam Houston High, it moved eastward to Washington, D. C. The spark was the happenstance of the death of a man whom Lyndon had never met. The man's name was Harry Wurzbach, and he had lately served as Republican congressman from Texas' Fourteenth Congressional District.

Chapter 9

HARRY MCLEARY WURZBACH of Seguin, Texas, was one of those insignificant political figures in history whose passing has a cataclysmic effect on the careers of other individuals. Of German and Irish ancestry, Wurzbach was born in San Antonio in 1874, educated in law at Washington and Lee College in Virginia, and he served in the Spanish-American War of 1898. Afterward, he worked his way up from a small law practice to become prosecuting attorney and judge of Guadalupe County. Wurzbach proved unusual in one respect, and this was his affiliation with the

Republican party, a much despised political organization in the Solid South, where it was equated with Negro interests, high protective tariffs, and Wall Street. When Senator Warren G. Harding ran for President on a platform of normalcy in 1920, Wurzbach joined the ticket as a candidate against Democratic Representative Carlos Bee of San Antonio, and both Harding and Wurzbach had no trouble demolishing their opponents. Wurzbach's achievement was the more remarkable considering that not since Reconstruction days had Texas sent a Republican to Congress.

Sam Johnson, who was then in the Texas House, took Wurzbach's victory like a kick in the stomach, for Blanco County was one of the eleven counties in Wurzbach's Fourteenth Congressional District, a lengthy stretch encompassing Hye near the old Johnson farm and Corpus Christi two hundred miles below, where Sam's friend, lobbyist Roy Miller, had been mayor. It was an unpleasant fact to Sam that the entire Texas Legislature and Congressional delegation were Democrats—except for Wurzbach, who represented Sam Johnson's home county.

Democrats talked away Wurzbach's 1920 victory by calling it an accident. But in 1922, when he won re-election, this argument died, and Sam Johnson joined other Democratic politicians in discussing how to eliminate this uninvited guest who sat at the head of the table. In Guadalupe County, which was Wurzbach's home ground, the leader of the Democrats was J. Alvin Wirtz, a thirty-four-year-old lawyer who served in the state senate. When the Republican regulars in the Congressional District expressed their dislike of Wurzbach because he ignored them, Wirtz combined forces with them behind the scenes to oust Wurzbach. But the congressman had the last laugh: He won re-election in 1924 and again in 1926 despite this combined effort. Aware of what he faced, Wurzbach had appealed directly to President Calvin Coolidge and was granted the only federal-patronage and pork-barrel appropriations in Texas. Since two-thirds of the district's residents lived in Bexar County, which included San Antonio, Wurzbach wisely obtained large appropriations for the military complex surrounding the city.

By 1928, when Wurzbach was firmly entrenched in office, the Democratic machine of Bexar County put up Augustus McCloskey of San Antonio, president of the popular Highway Club of Texas, as his opponent. Wirtz in Guadalupe County, the Democratic machine in Bexar County, and the Anglo dictators who ruled the southern "Mexican" counties combined with such effect that Wurzbach was finally defeated despite the Herbert Hoover victory over Catholic Al Smith in Texas. But Democratic joy was short-lived. Wurzbach complained to his friend, Speaker Nicholas Longworth, that he had proof going to waste of ballot box stuffing by Democrats in his last election. Longworth ordered a Republican-dominated committee to investigate, and on February 10, 1930, almost a year after McCloskey was seated, he was ousted, and Wurzbach reinstated by the Republican House.

Fourteenth District Democrats resigned themselves now to a string of Wurzbach re-elections that would go on until he died or quit office. But there was good news shortly after Wurzbach won his sixth term in November 1930, when he complained of stomach pains. This news proved of even more vital importance in the Capitol in Washington, for the organization of the House might very well depend on Wurzbach's health. The 1930 House elections gave the Republicans 217 members; Democrats, 215; Farmer-Labor, 1; and 2 vacancies. But much could happen before the House convened because, although the Seventy-second Congress had been elected in November 1930, it would not actually meet to select officers until December 1931.

While 1931 passed slowly, there were groans from both parties as ten members died. Five were Democrats and five were Republicans, including Teddy Roosevelt's son-in-law, Nick Longworth. But of those elected to replace them, seven were Democrats and only three were Republican, with the result that the Democrats held a two-seat lead at the end of October.

Republicans had hopes of having the two vacancies filled by the GOP, and with the promise of the single Farmer-Laborite to vote with the Republicans on electing a speaker, they believed they could regain control before the thirteen months of inactivity ended in December. But consternation descended when word came that Wurzbach had entered the hospital in San Antonio for a stomach operation. The first word from the Santa Rosa Infirmary was that his abdominal surgery was successful. However, three days later a blood clot stopped his heart, and he died on November 6, 1931.

Even before the eulogies were spoken, major political warfare erupted. Lyndon Johnson heard about it from Welly Hopkins, who had kept in close touch with his former campaign manager at Sam Houston High. Welly reported that he was going to campaign for Richard Kleberg (pronounced *Clay-burg*) whenever Governor Ross Sterling called the special election, and he suggested that Lyndon take time off from his debate coaching to campaign for Kleberg, too. This might turn out to Lyndon's advantage, because Dick Kleberg was the son of Robert Kleberg, owner of the King ranch, and everyone in Texas knew the King spread was the largest in the world. Lyndon jumped at the chance.

The political warfare was national, state, and local. Representative John Nance Garner of Uvalde, Texas, was after Sterling to set a date without delay for the special election, for if the Fourteenth District sent a Democratic replacement for Wurzbach, Garner, who was minority leader in the House, would be certain of sufficient votes to elect him speaker. Then the publicity he would get as speaker and as the leading opponent of President Hoover would help him corral the Democratic nomination for President in 1932, which was his real goal.

But Sterling was not in a mood to take orders from Garner because Sterling was in the midst of a major fight with Jesse Jones, the leading Garner supporter. Before he became governor, Sterling, whom other Democrats derisively called the Big Fat Boy Babbitt, was known as one of the richest men in the state. He was a principal founder of the Humble Oil Company, and in Houston he competed with Jones by virtue of his ownership of the Houston National Bank and the Houston *Post-Dispatch.*

This had made Jones wild with determination to smash Sterling, because he wanted no competition in Houston as the city's money man. When the depression deepened, Sterling did not retrench as his advisers advocated, but expanded his holdings instead and finally overextended himself. Jones then called a meeting of other "civic-minded" Houston bigwigs to determine how Sterling could meet their notes. First Jones stripped him of his bank, and then he took away his newspaper, for he opposed all thought control except his own. Since Jones already owned the Houston *Chronicle,* he was concerned that local animosity might arise if he ran the *Post* as well. So he tossed the *Post* into the lap of his admirer, former Governor Bill Hobby. In one of the few recorded kind deeds of his existence, Jones told Hobby, who had no money, that he did not have to make any down payment for the paper but could pay off the low purchasing price out of the *Post*'s profits.

Sterling was still far from broke, but Jones had put him into a stupor. This had come on top of another jolt Sterling received. The great east Texas oil field, one of the world's biggest oil strikes, had its first gusher in the little town of Kilgore in November 1930. But the following August, when violators of state production limitations had helped slash prices to ten cents a barrel, Sterling declared martial law in east Texas and sent in the Texas National Guard to enforce oil scarcity. This brought on newspaper attacks and private letter denunciation, which worried Sterling because he wanted a second term as governor. There was also statewide ridicule of Sterling, because his order to the National Guard had been: "Shut them wells."

So the combination of his Jesse Jones troubles and the martial law uproar did not put Sterling in a mood to help Garner. But Garner was relentless, as were his friends, and finally the governor set the election for November 24, with the candidate winning the most votes, even if not a majority, to be the victor.

"Richard Kleberg was a hidebound reactionary, and how anyone who called himself a liberal could work for his election was inconceivable," said a top Texas politician.

But Lyndon Johnson knew why he wanted to work in Kleberg's campaign. So did others in the motley crew who combined in Kleberg's behalf in the two-week campaign that November. Twenty-three-year-old Lyndon hoped for a political job, and Welly Hopkins wanted a strong association with the congressman representing his district. Hopkins had been a member of the Texas delegation at the 1928 national convention, and although he had even stronger state political connections now that he was "the youngest state senator," he had no firm strings out in Washington.

Alvin Wirtz, who would later be known as Lyndon Johnson's political godfather, also knew why he was campaigning for Kleberg. "Wirtz was the logical man to be elected to Congress," said Representative Wright Patman. "He was about forty, then, and he made a fine impression. He stood about five feet ten inches, had a big head, the shoulders and stance of an athlete, and possessed a conspicuous and impressive face. He was a sincere liberal in social causes and was considered an expert in water, oil, and gas law, which brought him a lot of rich, conservative clients."

During the late twenties, while he served as a state senator, Wirtz became the Texas lawyer for the Samuel Insull Industrial Enterprises. Insull, a clever Chicago financial manipulator, was a master holding-company developer. His scheme involved getting control of a small public utility company, then using its total worth to "buy" control of a second utility not quite twice the size of the first. By repeating this process a dozen times, he pyramided a small initial investment into a colossus. However, his entire empire depended on the well-being of the smallest company, for if it should collapse, his entire enterprise would crumble.

As a Texas state senator, Wirtz became interested in developing the Guadalupe River, and with Insull's backing, construction of privately owned dams took place on the river. Then in the late twenties Wirtz extended his interest in dam construction to the Lower Colorado River, a six-hundred-mile-long stream that begins in west Texas, flows through the Hill Country and Austin, and empties into the gulf at Matagorda Bay. The Lower Colorado River is not to be confused with the mighty fourteen-hundred-mile-long Colorado River, which splashes through Colorado, Utah, Arizona, Nevada, and California.

Insull liked the idea of a Texas empire, and construction began on the Hamilton Dam in the Lower Colorado River, eighty miles upstream from Austin. But in the 1929 stock market debacle the Insull empire suffered a crippling blow. When all his holding companies collapsed, President Hoover ordered his arrest. Insull fled the country for Greece.

By now Wirtz had moved from Seguin to Austin, where he established Powell, Wirtz and Rauhut, the leading law firm in the capital. But he could not give up his desire to see the Lower Colorado capped with several dams, and he won court approval as the appointed Texas receiver of the Insull properties, including the unfinished Hamilton Dam. Wirtz's plan— to turn the privately owned defaulted property into a public project— entailed state and federal approval and financing. So when Richard Kleberg said he would support a Lower Colorado River Authority, Wirtz campaigned enthusiastically for him.

Roy Miller, with Texas Gulf Sulphur money behind him, served as

Kleberg's campaign manager, and Roy knew exactly why he backed Kleberg. The King ranch maintained its business office in Corpus Christi, and during the years Miller was mayor there, he and the elder Kleberg had been friends. Roy was counting on Dick Kleberg to help fulfill his long-time dream of federal pork-barrel money to build Corpus Christi's port facilities. He had never been able to talk to Wurzbach about this, because Wurzbach was interested chiefly in getting federal dollars for San Antonio projects.

Still another Kleberg backer, and the most unlikely of all, was Maury Maverick, San Antonio's fighting liberal and scion of one of Texas' first families. When Maverick decided to go into politics in the mid-twenties, he saw he could make no headway in the hierarchical trappings of the San Antonio-Bexar County Democratic machine, so he helped organize the Citizens' League, whose avowed purpose was to oust the existing machine and install its own. Maverick performed the first successful surgery on the existing machine when he won election as Bexar County tax collector in 1928. Two years later Citizens' League members were swept into office as county judge, sheriff, and attorney.

In 1931, when Wurzbach died, Maverick wanted to run for Congress, but the Citizens' League was not yet ready for the eleven-county fight that was involved. Moreover, Roy Miller had already induced seven Democratic county caucuses to come out for Richard Kleberg. As a result, Maverick and the Citizens' League also announced their support of Kleberg, even though Carl Johnson, the San Antonio-Bexar County Democratic machine-backed candidate, was as liberal in his political outlook as Maverick.

The campaign was over almost as soon as it began. Lyndon Johnson went back to Blanco County, where he made some talks and personal appeals for Kleberg votes, even though he had never met the man he praised so vociferously. Bill Kittrell, who had asked Lyndon to campaign for Lieutenant Governor Edgar Witt the previous year, expressed puzzlement over the young teacher's championing of Kleberg. Said Kittrell, "There were a lot of voters who resented Kleberg because he was the owner of the largest cattle ranch in the world and was extremely conservative."

Welly Hopkins carried a larger speaking load than Lyndon. His line was an emotional burst about "the patriotic achievements of the Kleberg family in Texas, from the Battle of San Jacinto to the present day." At the same time, Alvin Wirtz was assuring German leaders in the Hill Country that Kleberg's German ancestry had brought him anguish, too, during the monstrous intolerance during World War I. And Maury Maverick was finding something fishy and smelly about liberal Democratic candidate Carl Johnson because he had been endorsed by San Antonio Mayor Chambers of the Bexar machine. Roy Miller took a racial tack, combining it with romance by telling crowds at political rallies that Kleberg was "a cowboy who understands and sympathizes with the Mexican-American people of southwest Texas." As for Kleberg, he left his magnificent ranch to give short, general speeches in Spanish and German.

Eight candidates plus supporting speakers stumped the district. Seven of the candidates were Democrats, though all except Kleberg and Carl Johnson were without hope. The sole Republican candidate, C. W. Anderson, who had been Wurzbach's attorney, considered his chances to be good if the Democratic vote were badly split. But Anderson's expectation was dashed when Wurzbach's brother, who was a member of the Citizens' League, came out for Kleberg.

No matter how loud the political oratory by Kleberg's champions, Roy Miller did not consider him a shoo-in. Roy was right, for the returns on Tuesday, November 24, revealed that Bexar County, with an expected two-thirds of the total, gave Carl Johnson 12,970 votes and Kleberg only 8,476. Other returns from northern German communities, where votes were small, showed Kleberg far ahead of Carl Johnson.

But Miller had been prepared for Carl Johnson's wide margin over Kleberg in Bexar County. An urgent call had gone out earlier to the southern counties, where Anglo political bosses could deliver a vote for any candidate they favored up to the limit of the poll taxes the bosses had paid. Fraudulent votes could be burned with impunity after the election, but poll tax receipts had to be recorded under state law. Some bosses paid poll taxes for all the local inhabitants of cemeteries and then voted for them; others ordered their frightened Mexican residents to show up and vote as they were told.

Kleberg's margin over Carl Johnson in these counties turned out to be ten to one. And one week later the state canvassing board declared Kleberg the elected representative of the Fourteenth Congressional District with a total of 19,038 votes, compared with 13,945 for Carl Johnson and 5,759 for Anderson, the Republican candidate. Ironically, seventeen years later, when Kleberg accused Lyndon Johnson of engaging in fraudulent vote tactics in his 1948 Senate race, Lyndon retorted over statewide radio, telling about Kleberg's own vote trickery: "You weren't told of the bloc vote in a box behind the locked gates of the King ranch, where not a single vote went to Johnson."

Following Kleberg's victory, Lyndon asked Welly Hopkins to talk to Kleberg about giving him a job on his Washington staff. Hopkins did this; then to pressure Kleberg from another source he also had a long conversation with Roy Miller about Lyndon's free and effective campaigning for Kleberg. Miller agreed to recommend him to Kleberg as a possible secretary, even though he had never met Lyndon. Sam Johnson also got into the pressure act. He had known Alvin Wirtz for years, and he too asked Wirtz to talk up his boy Lyndon to Kleberg.

While all these activities were percolating, Lyndon walked back to Aunt Ava's house one day after school with Michael Spampinato, Sam Houston

High's band director. "Mike," he confided, "I don't know whether I want to stay in teaching or not. I think I would like to get into politics."

His fate was settled only three days after the election. On Friday, November 27, a messenger from the office brought a note to Lyndon's classroom with word that Mr. Kleberg was calling from Corpus Christi. Lyndon ran to the office and picked up the telephone. Kleberg wanted to know if he cared to come to Corpus Christi to discuss his possible employment as a Congressional secretary. This was the dream come true. But instead of babbling with obsequious thanks, Lyndon replied that he would have to discuss this first with his uncle and he would then call Kleberg back with his decision. When he hung up, he turned to Helen Weinberg, a history teacher, who was present in the office, and yelled excitedly, "Mr. Kleberg wants me to be his private secretary!"

Welly Hopkins said that Lyndon and Sam Johnson drove through his home town of Gonzales to tell him they were on their way to Corpus Christi. That night, said Hopkins, Lyndon called him with word that Kleberg had hired him.

On November 29, Kleberg made it official when he notified reporters Lyndon would be his assistant when Congress convened on December 5.

Washington was filled with Congressional secretaries and clerks. Yet when Lyndon left Houston, the *Post-Dispatch* gave him a royal send-off. "Young Johnson, only twenty-three years of age in 1930-1931, his first year as debate coach at Sam Houston, turned out a winning team. . . . Himself an orator of much ability, Johnson coached with a contagious enthusiasm which made him a favorite, not only with his own pupils, but with the entire school."

Chapter 10

A WASHINGTON POLITICAL career that was to span four decades began for twenty-three-year-old Lyndon Johnson that December. "Kleberg and I rode up on the train together to Washington," he recalled the start of the exciting experience, traveling in the company of a man whose front door at home was twenty miles from the entrance gate. He also remembered a slightly lesser thrill—"This was my first train trip outside of Texas."

There was drama on their arrival at the sooty, cavernous Union Station. The Capitol dome rising through the bare-limbed December trees in front of the station looked like the picture in the history books. Then there was the noisy crowd yelling for taxicabs; and when he walked through the mob, politics was the common language, for many of the men addressed each other as "Congressman."

Kleberg had reserved a suite for himself at the plush, carpeted Mayflower Hotel on Connecticut Avenue, and Johnson's first concern was to find a cheap room for himself. He soon discovered that the most popular place for single young men who worked on Capitol Hill, as the legislative area was called, was the Dodge Hotel, a deteriorating old structure that had at one time catered solely to women.

Now the women were confined to the upper floors in the Dodge, and the men had the lower floors below the street level. Although the accommodations were second-quality, the hotel was only a block south of Union Station and a few blocks north of the Senate Office Building, the Capitol, and the House Office Building. For twenty dollars a month, a person shared a room with another occupant. The bathroom at the end of the hall served all tenants on the long floor.

When Johnson carried his cardboard suitcase into the Dodge lobby and registered, the room he shared with another young man was two flights beneath the street. Yet he soon found out that he could not have chosen a better place to live, because the Congressional employees who stayed at the Dodge formed an intelligence force on national politics. Although they continually complained that they were not given credit for being far superior in brain power to the members of Congress who employed them, this did not detract from the fact that they knew what was happening on Capitol Hill and the story behind each move. Simply by living with them at the Dodge and picking their minds wholesale, Lyndon realized he could have a superb, up-to-date picture of events and power struggles on the Hill.

To help Johnson meet his first bills, Kleberg signed a statement making his pay retroactive to November 24, the day of the election. Kleberg also set his salary at thirty-nine hundred dollars, or seventy-five dollars a week, which was a handsome level, considering that it was twice the earnings of Sam Johnson back in San Marcos. However, Kleberg proved whimsical about Johnson's salary, cutting it to three thousand dollars on March 1, 1932, raising it back to the original figure on May 1, then cutting it by eight hundred and fifty dollars eleven months later. This made it difficult for Johnson to plan ahead or to send the same amount of money to his mother to help meet her expenses.

Although Johnson had landed in a new environment, he never knew a lonely moment. An hour after he moved into the Dodge Hotel's sub-sub-basement, his instant friendship technique made him an old pal of everyone on the floor. There were handshakes and jokes, first-name intimacy and arms around shoulders, loud laughter, and Johnson offers to lend anything he owned. Good fellowship talk went on almost the entire night.

By morning, Johnson was considered almost an oldtimer by the others, and he stuck closely to those who, he believed, could teach him the Congressional ropes in a hurry. The boys ate lunch either in the House or Senate cafeteria, and Johnson put this hour to double purpose. One Senate clerk said that when the gang met, Johnson always rushed to the front of the group with his tray, collected his meal on the run through the food maze, dashed to a big empty table and gulped his food before the others arrived. With his lunch already out of the way, he was now free to pump the others about their work and the Congressional routine. If he thought an answer unclear or silly, he cut in to argue. Said one of the lunchers, Johnson was "the greatest argufier any of us had ever seen." Dinner at the Dodge Hotel was too expensive for the boys, though it was a treat to be waited on by wooly-gray-haired shuffling Negro waiters who had the right combination of antebellum subservience and graciousness. So for dinner they walked to the nearby All States Restaurant, where a tasty plate-filler cost fifty cents. Here, while they ate the "Fo'-Bitter," as the southern boys named the meal, Johnson again swallowed his food frenziedly and then threw more questions at the other boys.

This process of picking minds continued at night back at the Dodge. One resident said it was "like living in a permanent debating society, with Lyndon as the focal point." On and on the questions came with an unrelenting intensity. A Congressional press secretary who observed it carefully concluded, "This skinny boy was as green as anybody could be, but within a few months he knew how to operate in Washington better than some who had been here twenty years."

While Johnson was putting the Dodge Hotel gang through his own Congressional educational paces, "Mister Dick," as Kleberg preferred being called, was learning almost nothing about his job. In time this would mean that constituents who wanted help from their congressman would stop at Johnson's desk for business and then visit Kleberg strictly for social amenities. Kleberg occupied suite 258 in the six-hundred-and-ninety-room Old House Office Building, which sat above the partly constructed New House Office Building that would be ready for occupancy in 1933. Kleberg's office was the typical cramped affair, complete with black-leather buttoned sofas and overstuffed chairs, sixteen-foot-high ceilings, plentiful spittoons, and a screen in front of the congressman's private washstand.

Johnson had no intention of observing the caste system of Capitol Hill, where Congressional employees knew their place and abstained from familiar relations with their employers. On one of his first days at work he suggested to Mr. Dick that they call on the Texas senators and cement a warm relationship. Kleberg agreed, and they walked through the Capitol and then crossed the street to the Senate Office Building for a chat with Senators Morris Sheppard and Tom Connally. Both men were considered high quality by their colleagues, as Johnson had learned from secretaries, and what was impressive about their offices was that they were much larger than House offices, had many more employees, and had a more thorough yet leisurely atmosphere. Connally, with a flowing mane, almost Prince Albert–length suit coat, and a notoriously sharp tongue for Republicans, had no memory of this early meeting with Johnson. But Arthur Perry, Connally's press secretary, whom the senator ignored, recalled that Kleberg told him in a needless plea that "he wished I would teach his new secretary everything I knew." Perry's mind was one of the many that Johnson drained at the Dodge Hotel.

After his introduction to the two Texas senators, Johnson attempted to establish instant friendships with other members of the House from Texas. However, this proved impossible, except in two instances, because of the natural arrogance of congressmen toward lowly employees from whom they expected subservience. The two exceptions were Wright Patman and Sam Rayburn, and their friendship hinged initially on the fact that he was Sam Johnson's boy.

"Lyndon dropped in my office almost every day," said Patman. "He was a very good friend of my secretary, Russell Chaney, and I thought he came in only to see Chaney. But after I had to get rid of my secretary and send him back to Texas, Lyndon still came in. Now that he was grown he reminded me more and more of his father, Sam Johnson.

"He wanted to talk politics—who was doing what and what the probable outcome would be. He seemed especially interested in the fight I had started to impeach Hoover's Secretary of the Treasury Andrew Mellon on a serious conflict-of-interest charge. I got this set up for hearings before the Judiciary Committee, but the day Mellon was to testify Hoover lifted him off the hook by letting him resign and flee to London as American ambassador to Great Britain.

"Lyndon also liked to ask questions about the dirty political fighting that was part of Texas electioneering, and he enjoyed hearing whatever you told him about the earlier-day doings in local politics."

Sam Rayburn may or may not have really remembered Sam Johnson, with whom he served a single term in the Texas House from 1907 to 1909, when old Tom Love, the Catholic-hating dry from Dallas, was speaker. But after Lyndon used his father as his calling card, Rayburn found his instant friendship ability a heart-warming pleasure and told him to drop around whenever he wished.

This was an excellent contact because every member of the House knew that Sam Rayburn was a man on the rise. Two years after Sam Johnson had left the Texas House, Rayburn ran for speaker against three opponents. He was a crude, untamed sort then, and when he won over

Governor Colquitt's hand-picked candidate, "Sam jumped up and gave a cotton patch yell and sat down real quick—like he was ashamed of hisself," said his floor manager.

Rayburn came to Congress in 1913, with the Wilson influx, by the narrowest of margins. The opportunity arose when Choice Randell, representative from the Fourth Congressional District, quit to make an unsuccessful race for the Senate. Rayburn had seven opponents in the House contest, and it went down to the final wire in doubt. Of the 21,236 votes, he emerged with less than 25 per cent of the total. Yet his vote of 4,983 gave him the election, for the highest vote of any other candidate was 4,493.

When Rayburn first came to Washington, John Nance Garner let him share his office until one became available for him. And as the bald but fair-haired boy of Garner, Rayburn was given a coveted post on the House Interstate and Foreign Commerce Committee. Here old-timers recalled that he buttered up Committee Chairman William C. Adamson, who also became his sponsor.

But before long Garner realized that Rayburn intended to compete with him eventually for House leadership. In 1924 their relationship grew strained, said Tom Connally, when Garner tried to get House Democrats to elect him minority leader. By chance he discovered that protégé Rayburn was quietly boosting Finis Garrett of Tennessee, the state where Rayburn was born, for the same post. When Garrett won, Garner lost his enthusiasm for the double-dealer, though he let him stay in his private drinking club.

During Rayburn's early House period he was known for his coarse practical jokes. But he subdued himself on purpose, adopted a dour expression, and clothed himself like an undertaker. Despite his early poverty, while in Congress he managed to acquire a comfortable two-story white colonial house on a substantial farm-ranch near Bonham. This was essential for prestige purposes to impress visiting politicians, who noted the permanent roots in the soil of Texas with approbation. Lyndon Johnson caught the significance of this facade on early visits to Bonham. He listened with interest when Rayburn told company he was "busy as a cranberry merchant" on the farm and detailed so many orders to "Old Henry," his colored herdsman, that he gave the impression he was first a farmer and second a member of Congress.

The Lyndon Johnson–Sam Rayburn relationship developed quickly into a son-father kinship. "Sam had married Metze Jones, the sister of Marvin Jones, a member of the House from Amarillo, in 1927," said Tom Connally. "In fact, Sam and Marvin got married at the same time in a double ceremony. But on their joint honeymoon, the bridegrooms did such powerful drinking that the brides fled in the middle of one night and later got divorces." After that Rayburn called himself a bachelor and became a doting uncle to his flock of nephews and nieces. When Johnson came onto the scene, Rayburn added him to the list at first and followed by giving him special attention.

This warm relationship grew obvious when Johnson developed pneumonia and was rushed to a hospital. On regaining consciousness, he found the sad-faced chairman of the House Commerce Committee sitting next to the hospital bed. "Now, Lyndon," said Rayburn, "don't you worry. Take it easy. If you need money or anything, you just call on me." Johnson recalled later, "The most comforting moment in my life was to see that man sitting there dribbling cigaret ashes down his vest."

When Lyndon Johnson had been in Washington only a short time, he made instant friends with William S. White, a young Texan who reported on Capitol Hill for one of the wire services. White said that Johnson was a most unusual Congressional clerk, for he asked "endlessly varied" questions that were focused on a single point: "Who has the power and how is it exercised?"

Johnson's questions were intended to flatter White, his first solid newsman relationship, because he already knew the answers to the questions he asked. The most powerful man in Washington was Cactus Jack Garner, and he exercised his power by bedeviling President Hoover in his efforts to combat the depression. Johnson was also aware that in the House, below Garner, Texans wielded an inordinate amount of power. Sam Rayburn was chairman of the Interstate and Foreign Commerce Committee; Marvin Jones headed the Agriculture Committee; Joe Mansfield, crippled and consigned to his wheelchair, bossed the Rivers and Harbors Committee; Hatton Sumners, the Judiciary Committee; Fritz Lanham, Public Buildings and Grounds; Guinn Williams, the Territorial Committee; and James Buchanan was ranking Democrat on the powerful Appropriations Committee. No other state ran even a poor second to Texas in House power.

That is what made it astounding when Lyndon Johnson, the new secretary to the new congressman, engaged Speaker John Garner in a political battle—and won.

The episode began when Garner was sworn in as speaker on December 7, 1931, and began to cast about for additional powers to add to his already immense authority. By custom, individual House members named local postmasters, and the President honored such patronage by nominating these appointees for Senate confirmation. Garner decided that a new custom was in order and he decreed that in the future the speaker would control all Post Office patronage appointments in his home state.

This nervy move was sullenly accepted by several Texas congressmen who were not anxious for a run-in with Garner. Johnson learned of it through the Dodge Hotel intelligence service, and in great excitement he passed the story on to Bill White. The "Garner steal" made angry reading in Texas papers, and so heavy was the local protest that the speaker hastily withdrew his proposition. However, he was so chagrined by the Texas furore that he checked to find the source of his trouble. Shortly afterward, a group of Texas congressmen heard him complain: "Who in the hell is this boy Lyndon Johnson? Where the hell did Kleberg get a boy with savvy like that?"

So it was that the man who exercised the most power learned that he could be undone politically by a twenty-three-year-old greenhorn Texan who held no power.

Chapter 11

To LYNDON JOHNSON 1932 was an immensely important year in his political development. It would have been enough to learn the extremely complex House procedures. But in addition to his education, Johnson had a ringside view of the power struggle between the Democratic House and the Republican President. Furthermore, the year involved the entirely new experience of helping direct Kleberg's campaign in the midyear Democratic primary.

Kleberg's victory in November 1931 had given the Democrats two hundred and eighteen members to the Republican total of two hundred and fourteen. And by this slim margin Garner gained the right to operate on Hoover. Reporters on the Hill said that Garner was a much tougher man now that he could smell the sweet Democratic Presidential nomination. The death of Nick Longworth, the House Republican leader, was also a factor in Garner's increased toughness. Together, Longworth and Garner had acted as though political parties had not separated them. Longworth called him "Jack" in floor debate, and Garner affectionately referred to him as "that bald-headed coot"; and after the House finished for the day they went arm in arm to Garner's hideaway "Board of Education" room to "strike a blow for liberty," which was the signal to down another glass of bourbon and branch water.

Johnson saw how pleased House Democrats were whenever Garner returned their greetings as he made his way through them in his forceful stroll from the speaker's office across the hall from the chamber to his presiding seat on the dais. At sixty-three he had snow-white hair and eyebrows and went for days without shaving or bathing. He was a superb rough-and-tumble debater and well worth the study time of the former debating coach at Sam Houston High.

Garner operated with the ease of a man who had spent twenty-nine years learning his trade in Congress. He had begun his politics in the Texas House, where he managed to land on the committee to reapportion Congressional Districts. This gave him the opportunity to carve out a new Fifteenth Congressional District to his own measurements in the twenty-three hot and thinly populated counties in the pocket between the Rio Grande and the Gulf of Mexico. His efforts paid off, for he won election to Congress in 1903 representing a Congressional District as large as the state of Virginia.

Texas congressmen chuckled over the cheap suits he bought, the penny cigars he smoked, his efforts to induce suckers to play poker with him, his fervent championing of low tariffs except on mohair, which his District's goats produced in enormous quantities, and his opposition to pork-barrel appropriations for Northern states. As he put it, "Every time one of those Yankees gets a ham, I'm going to do my best to get a whole hog."

By the spring of 1932 Johnson was getting a strange picture of national politics. Democratic irresponsibility was apparently the most effective tool for ruining Hoover's chances to win a second term as President. The depression was renamed the Hoover Depression by the Democrats; and he was called cold and cruel and heartless and a do-nothing President responsible for the "Hoover Breadlines" and the "Hooverville Shacktowns." Some Democratic copywriters went so far as to declare him a murderer that spring when Secretary of War Pat Hurley gave orders to Army Chief of Staff Douglas MacArthur and his aides, Dwight Eisenhower and George Patton, to chase the Bonus Army out of Washington by tanks and guns and fire if necessary.

Garner led the attack on Hoover, and Rayburn was his faithful aide. To gain the publicity he needed to win his party's nomination, Garner later bragged, "I fought President Hoover with everything I had under Marquis of Queensberry rules, London prize ring and catch-as-catch-can rules."

When Hoover proposed a government lending program through a new agency to be called the Reconstruction Finance Corporation (RFC), Garner proceeded to mutilate the bill, even though he agreed with its purpose. His mutilations included knocking out RFC authority to lend money to farmers for crops and livestock, to cities for public works projects, including slum clearance projects, and to industry to modernize plants. Even so, Garner would not permit what remained to clear the House until Hoover let him name two of the five RFC directors. One was Jesse Jones, the Houston tycoon. Garner also continued his hold-up for fourteen months of Hoover's proposal to authorize the Federal Land Banks to buy farm mortgages from private banks in order to end foreclosures on tens of thousands of farmers who could not make mortgage payments.

When President Eisenhower was in the White House during the nineteen-fifties, Rayburn would not permit Democratic attacks on him. "Any jackass can kick down a barn," he warned his party men, "but it takes a good carpenter to build one." In 1932, however, Rayburn showed no such sympathy for a Republican President, and he delighted in mean attacks, which he proudly called "giving it to Hoover with the bark on." One of his repeated charges was that Hoover planned to abolish segregation in the South if he won a second term.

The Democratic National Convention was slated for the Chicago Stadium at the end of June, and the Texas Congressional delegation was already holding noisy spring meetings on the best tactics for storming the convention and installing Cactus Jack Garner in the Presidential slot. Welly Hopkins and Alvin Wirtz, who came to Washington occasionally, had been selected as convention delegates by the state convention, and both believed that Texas was going to have its first man in the White House.

During all this hubbub, "Mister Dick" Kleberg remained fairly oblivious to these goings-on. Garner had put him on the House Agriculture Committee, but he had joined an exclusive golf club and was rarely in committee. What roused him most during that spring was the announcement by Thurmond Barrett back in the Congressional District that he had paid the filing fee as a candidate for Kleberg's seat.

Sam Johnson liked to boast that he could tell the outcome in advance of any local election. If he actually possessed that gift, his boy Lyndon did not inherit it. When Barrett announced his candidacy and Kleberg sent Lyndon Johnson back to Texas to manage his campaign, Johnson was glad that he had talked the Houston School Board into giving him a leave of absence renewable yearly, instead of forcing him to resign. His anxiety was directly related to the lack of interest by the Citizens' League in Kleberg.

The vote of the Citizens' League bloc appeared uncertain, primarily because Kleberg had ignored the League once he went to Washington. Another reason for the cooling-off was that the Texas House was again reapportioning Congressional Districts, this time using the 1930 Census of Population. The League expected the city of San Antonio to be taken out of Kleberg's District and given its own House member in 1934, so there was little urgency in renewing support for Kleberg.

One widely circulated story was that the League had offered to sell its votes to the highest bidder, then "tendered their support [to Kleberg] for four thousand dollars in cash and the promise of the Post Office for one of their group." The story continued with a description of a plane flight to Texas by Lyndon Johnson, serving as Kleberg's bag man, with the money and a promise to name Dan Quill, a League man, as postmaster of San Antonio. What makes the story sound suspicious is that the League could have obtained a much larger grant from Kleberg than these meager terms.

The cactus truth was that Kleberg did win the support of the Citizens' League in Bexar County on primary day and won nine of the other ten counties as well. The only embarrassment in the election was suffered by Lyndon Johnson. For the only county Barrett won was Blanco County, the home base of the young campaign manager.

Chapter 12

LYNDON JOHNSON WAS in the huge mob of cheering Democrats facing the East Portico of the Capitol that cold, damp March 4, 1933, when Governor Franklin Delano Roosevelt of New York and Speaker John Garner were sworn into office as President and Vice President. The Texas members of Congress and their office aides still felt bitter because Garner had not won the Democratic nomination at the 1932 Chicago convention. The double chagrin was that after three ballots, when Roosevelt was past his convention peak, Tom Connally saved him by engineering the Roosevelt-Garner ticket, to the anger of other Texas delegates. Johnson in retrospect some decades later called the inauguration, with Roosevelt's chin-up "The only thing we have to fear is fear itself," the most exciting inauguration he had ever attended.

The economy, which had shown marked improvement from the summer of 1932 through November, dropped to its lowest ebb since 1929 by inauguration day. Concern was widespread that Walter Lippmann, the brilliant columnist, was correct in his earlier judgment of Roosevelt as "a pleasant man . . . without any important qualifications for office." But beginning with his bank holiday to prevent the total ruin of the nation's monetary system; and racing through his slam-bang "First Hundred Days" with their welter of legislation; his "Fireside Chats" over radio like a Dutch uncle to his kin; and his optimistic air; Roosevelt erased all earlier images. Lippmann admitted he had been in error and said that what Roosevelt had accomplished to revive public morale was comparable to what had occurred after "the second battle of the Marne in the summer of 1916."

Roosevelt's efforts to create employment and increase purchasing power had a massive effect on the activities of Congressional offices. Amiable "Mister Dick" Kleberg did not feel this personally, for he was spending much of his time improving his golf game at the Burning Tree Country Club in nearby Maryland. However, Johnson was well aware of the step-up in mail and personal requests from constituents. When the mail ballooned, he brought it down to earth by staying at the office as late as necessary to clear the load each day. He soon learned that Mister Dick's constituents were pleased with such swift responses. Mister Dick was pleased, too, because he did not have to bother to read the letters or dictate answers, but merely signed the most important replies.

Johnson was also the official greeter to the increasing number of persons who dropped in for guidance through the burgeoning Washington maze of alphabetical agencies. No request was too small or too large, and Johnson found that he could perform an inordinate amount of work over the telephone. Besides the legwork it eliminated, the telephone permitted him to sound more authoritative and demanding than he could have been in person with high government officials. As a result, he began spending a larger part of his day as a telephone bloodhound tracking down the civil servant who handled the specific problem he wanted solved. He was relentless in not accepting a *no* answer. Where the Executive Branch could not handle a problem, he dropped private bills for Kleberg's constituents into the House hopper. In 1933 Kleberg's name appeared on thirty-three private bills.

Because of the agricultural-ranching nature of Kleberg's District, much of Johnson's telephoning was to the Department of Agriculture. Here he could expect full cooperation because Kleberg was on the House Agricultural Committee. In 1933 the activity that brought the Department the most business was the Agricultural Adjustment Administration (AAA). This was an effort to administer planned farm production scarcity in order to raise depressed farm prices. Jerome Frank, an able lawyer, was the general counsel of AAA, and Johnson had almost daily telephone dealings for a while with his brilliant young staff, whose roster included Adlai E. Stevenson, Abe Fortas, Thurmond Arnold, and Alger Hiss. On occasion he had to visit the AAA offices, and he dealt with these individuals in person.

In his face-to-face meetings with the New Dealers in the AAA and other new agencies, Johnson was extremely self-conscious at first. Many of the young men were Ivy League in schooling and smug manner. They were also better dressed than he and apparently were not working for the money. Years later in a speech Johnson revealed his dislike for this group by remarking that the New Deal "brought the professors and more crackpots and dreamers to Washington than you ever saw."

Not contented merely to run Kleberg's office, Johnson tried to be legislator as well. For instance, when the AAA bill came to the House for consideration, Kleberg told Johnson he planned to vote against it. In his opinion the bill proposed "socialism," because it planned to pay farmers who agreed to restrict their acreage with money taken in from a tax on grain millers and other food processors.

Johnson, however, decided that Kleberg had to vote for the AAA, and he devised a scheme to force him to do so. First he made a quick sample of the mail from the Fourteenth District and drew up a set of figures that showed sentiment for the AAA running thirty to one back home. Then he telephoned the secretaries of several liberal congressmen and made a tabulation of their support for the bill. Next he confronted Kleberg with his tabulations, and after showing him his findings, he said, "You can't vote against it, Mister Dick."

But Kleberg still insisted that "the bill is socialistic." Finally, Johnson told him he intended to quit if Kleberg voted against the bill. This, rather than the scribbled numbers, gave Kleberg pause, and he consented to vote for the AAA measure.

Besides the AAA bill, Kleberg fell in Johnson's line by voting for the National Recovery Act (NRA) when it came to a House vote on May 26, 1933. However, after this he made use of a handy technique for eluding Johnson's pressure. For example, when the Tennessee Valley Authority bill came to the floor for a vote, he was not to be found.

The free hand Kleberg extended to Johnson on office management also included the hiring of additional help. When Johnson decided he needed reliable assistants, he brought Gene Latimer and Luther Jones, his star Sam Houston High School debaters, to Washington and the Dodge Hotel sub-basement. He put Luther on the payroll at twelve hundred dollars a year, and in July 1934, when Luther told him he wanted to attend Georgetown University Law School, he helped him get an increase of one hundred and fifty dollars a year. Since Kleberg's payroll was limited, Johnson used well-known House subterfuges and had the House Post Office with its ample funds pay Gene Latimer's salary of seventeen hundred and forty dollars.

Both boys discovered that working for Johnson in Washington was no different from being on the high school debating team. They were expected to work late each day, come to the office on weekends if he ordered them, and undergo several beratings and apologies each week.

By 1934 Johnson was aware that most congressmen were lawyers, and that this profession was an excellent open door to a political career. So when his two office slaves told him they were planning to start law school that fall, he decided he would too. Gene enrolled in the Washington School of Law and Luther in Georgetown. Since Georgetown was a prestige school, Johnson joined Luther in the nighttime classes in torts and other subjects.

But he went only a year to Georgetown before law bored him and he dropped it. Russell Morton Brown, who sat next to him in some classes, said that Johnson frequently complained to him that the professor "is not telling me anything I don't know."

Brown, who later became a high-earning Washington attorney, lacked money at that time to purchase law books and pay his tuition. When Johnson got wind of this, he told Brown to report to Kleberg's office and he would put him to work. Unfortunately, when Brown came to the office, Kleberg's staff money was in full use and the House Post Office refused to pay his salary. So Johnson called people at the Department of Agriculture with whom he had been dealing and placed Brown in a clerical job there.

Brown found that even though he was not working for Johnson, he was expected to accept all Johnson recommendations for alterations in his appearance, personality, and habits. On one occasion Johnson told Brown, who lived at the Dodge, that he did not look too respectable and told him to buy a new suit. When Brown complained that he had only enough money to pay his twenty-dollar rent bill, Johnson told him to go to Grossner's on F Street and charge the suit to his account. After a few months passed and Johnson wanted to make certain Brown had not spoiled his credit by failing to meet the monthly payments at Grossner's, he hinted bluntly, "Let me know when your suit is paid for, Russ, because I want to buy one when it is."

Johnson wanted to take part in all the activities of the House, and he did not consider that he was demeaning himself by taking on even menial assignments if they brought him into association with a widening group of congressmen. House Disbursement Office records do not show it, but long-serving members of the House remember Johnson serving as a doorkeeper on the "Democratic Door" for a time. Jennings Randolph, who came to the House from West Virginia in 1932, said, "I recall the tall, gangling fellow on the door. It was Lyndon, and he was there a few months, bringing into the chamber cards from visitors who wanted us to go out to the lobby for a chat. He got to know dozens of us that way."

While Johnson was widening his contacts with legislators, he also took charge of the organization Congressional aides had formed for themselves. "It was fascinating to watch Sam Johnson's boy wind up in the best seat at the head table of Capitol Hill employees only a year after he came to Washington," said Wright Patman.

Congressional secretaries had their own club, the "Little Congress," which they modeled after the House of Representatives. The Little Congress elected a speaker and conducted sessions according to the parliamentary rules of the House. When Johnson first heard of it, he asked one of the boys at the Dodge how its officers were chosen. The answer was that the Little Congress followed the seniority system as did the House, and the speaker was the active member who had joined it earliest.

"Why don't you run for speaker, Lyndon?" another Dodge tenant hooted.

"I might do just that," he replied.

Johnson soon developed his plan. He went first to a few meetings and saw that not only was the meeting room half empty but the same members were at each meeting. When he questioned some who were members but did not attend meetings, he learned that they found the sessions too boring, its leaders too dictatorial.

With the aid of a half-dozen friends at the Dodge who worked for representatives, he put his plan into action. Each man was given a certain number of House offices as his responsibility. In each, he was to talk to the staff to win promises to join the Little Congress and attend meetings. They were promised the bonus of excellent speakers and renowned guests if they voted for Lyndon Johnson for speaker. For those who were half-way softened up but not entirely convinced, Johnson came around in person for the final persuasion.

Membership in the Little Congress expanded rapidly within a few weeks, and then one night came the election of new officers. Quickly one of Johnson's lieutenants placed his name in nomination for speaker, running against a Congressional secretary who had been active for years in the Little Congress. The Old Guard should have been suspicious when there was only standing room in the House committee room where the Little Congress held its meetings. But not until the vote came in showing Johnson an easy victor did the old members catch on to what was happening. "Who is that guy?" his defeated opponent bellowed. "He comes to one meeting and takes over the place!"

Afterward, Johnson raced to tell Rayburn, Patman, and Vice President Garner of his success. The first two congratulated him, but Garner had advice. "Quit gloating and learn to heal the wounds of those you defeated," he told Johnson. "You need to have friends on both sides of the aisle, and you won't be much of a speaker if you don't"—he passed along his own experience.

As matters turned out, besides gaining a wide reputation among Congressional aides as a sly politician and a good engineer of surprise *coups*, Johnson delivered on his promise to make the Little Congress livelier. Several members of Congress came to speak on national and international affairs and to answer questions from the floor. The most explosive meeting was the occasion when Senator Huey Long of Louisiana spoke. "Kingfish" Long, the Senate's loudest-mouthed filibusterer, planned to run against Roosevelt in 1936, and he welcomed any platform where reporters were present. Long was convinced his enemies were out to assassinate him, and he was certain it would be done with bombs. He had hardly begun speaking to the Little Congress when a photographer's flashbulb popped. Long screamed that he had been shot, and the meeting ended in wild confusion.

By mid-1934 most of the crowd at the Dodge recognized Johnson as a "comer," though none knew where he was going. It was commonplace to predict a political career for him, but at what level it would be no one would guess. His conversation seldom strayed from politics, and even when

his friends dragged him to Griffith Stadium to watch the Washington Senators lose another baseball game, he ignored the game completely and
talked politics almost nonstop through the nine innings of play. When they
went fishing in the bay, he would not throw a line over the side but held
forth instead on politics. On some occasions friends induced him to attend
meetings and dances of the Texas State Society, yet even here he remained
the politician at work. One friend said that at the Society's dances Johnson
"usually danced with the wives of Texas congressmen, rather than with
the single girls."

When Johnson returned to Texas during this period, he felt like a politician and a millionaire, for he normally visited the King ranch to discuss
business with Kleberg, if the congressman was there. Johnson once described the King ranch to the United States Senate as being equivalent
in size to a piece of land "one-half mile wide and three thousand miles
long, running from New England to California." The ranch was started
modestly in 1851 by Captain Richard King, a steamboat captain on the
Rio Grande. In time he expanded it to one million and a quarter acres
that overran five counties. A month's difference in seasons existed between
the northern and southern ends of the ranch, and an old Texas couplet
went:

> "The sun's done riz and the sun's done set
> And I ain't offen the King ranch yet."

Captain King's daughter, Alice Gertrudis King, married Robert Kleberg,
and Mister Dick Kleberg was their son. The original ranch had been named
the Santa Gertrudis, and when the family developed its own breed of
cattle by crossing a slate-gray Brahma bull with a shorthorn to produce the
large, cherry-colored bull, it too was called the Santa Gertrudis. Almost
a million head of cattle roamed the ranchland under the watch of seven
hundred Mexican vaqueros, all expert with the lariat and the six-shooter.
Some were the third generation of their family to work on the ranch,
and their pay was one dollar a day plus horses and board.

When Johnson came to the ranch house, he traveled in an old Ford
he had bought. He so identified with the King ranch family that the seat
covers in the car had the Running W brand of the King ranch as part
of their design. He went about the house freely, and the elderly matriarch,
with whom he had made instant friends, shed her normally imperious
manner in his presence because she reacted to his aggressive, energetic
personality.

The Klebergs were willing to let him use any of their facilities because
they believed his aid essential to keep Mister Dick in Congress. The extent
to which he used their property sometimes surprised his friends. "One time
I went to Corpus Christi to attend the state American Legion Convention,"
said Wright Patman. "Lyndon came to see me while I was there. He told

me to collect as many of the Legionnaires as I wanted, and he'd take us out on a wonderful outing on Dick Kleberg's big boat. He was the host when we came on board, and he impressed everyone."

Chapter 13

SAM JOHNSON, THE bus inspector, suffered insecurity again in 1932, for Pat Neff left the chairmanship of the Texas Railroad Commission to become president of Baylor University at Waco. After C. V. Terrell won election as Neff's successor, Sam cultivated Terrell and his secretary in their Statehouse office in Austin to build good will in order to keep his job.

Terrell's secretary was Eugenie "Gene" Boehringer, a good-natured girl who came from east Texas near the Louisiana border. Sam struck up easy talk with Gene, and naturally told her about his wonderful son Lyndon who was helping to run things in Washington. After a few visits he began to think of her as a prospective daughter-in-law, and he promised that the next time Lyndon came to Texas he would arrange for them to meet.

The day came when the two Johnsons walked into Terrell's office. Lyndon made instant friends with Gene, but when he asked her for a date that evening, she turned him down on the ground that her boyfriend from Henderson, a budding lawyer named "Log" Lassater, would not approve. Undeterred, Lyndon said he knew few girls in Austin and wondered if she would line up blind dates for him when he came through town. Feeling sorry for him, Gene agreed "to get dates for him on the weekends when he came in unexpectedly."

Gene had a wide acquaintance with young Austin girls, but there was one friend she did not offer as one of his blind dates. She was black-haired, brown-eyed Claudia Alta Taylor, who had graduated from high school with Gene's kid sister Emma in the Black Belt cotton country back home in Marshall. Claudia, or Lady Bird, as she was known, was shy and dowdy and Gene Boehringer went out of her way to teach her younger sister's friend about style and to make her less reserved and sad.

At Gene's suggestion, Lady Bird had attended the University of Texas at Austin, more than three hundred miles from her home, and here she obtained a second-grade teacher's certificate in 1933 and a B.A. in journalism the following year. As a bonus for her 1934 graduation, her father agreed to send her on a vacation to Washington and New York. Shortly before she and Cecile Harrison, her roommate, left Austin by train, Lady Bird visited Gene in Terrell's office. After listening to her plans, which included only sightseeing ventures and taking in a few plays, Gene wrote Lyndon Johnson's name and phone number on a slip of paper and gave it to Lady Bird. "Call him when you're in Washington and he'll show you a good time," she promised.

However, Lady Bird was too shy to call Johnson during her stop-off in Washington. On her return to Austin, she told Gene there had been no need to call him because Washington was filled with "Texas-exes," or University of Texas alumni, and she knew many of them. "Besides," she added, "I would have felt odd calling up an absolute stranger."

But on a September afternoon a few months later, while Lady Bird was visiting Gene Boehringer, Johnson walked into the office. Gene had arranged a date for him with Dorothy McElroy, who worked in the office, and he had come in to pick her up near the close of the work day. Lyndon took one look at Lady Bird and immediately trained his attention on her. Lady Bird remembered him as "excessively thin and the most outspoken young man" she had ever met. Since he could not change the evening's arrangements, he invited the three girls to join him in drinks after work. Here he managed to talk privately to Lady Bird before leaving with Dorothy, and he asked her to meet him for breakfast the next morning in the Driskill Hotel dining room.

Lady Bird made no definite reply. But the following morning she rose early and paid a call on Hugo Kuehne, an architect whose office happened to adjoin the Driskill Hotel. Her father had asked her to see Kuehne about remodeling their house near Karnack, and this seemed as good a time as any to take care of this chore. It was on her way out of Kuehne's office that she peeked in the window of the Driskill dining room, and her eyes met Lyndon's. He remembered: "I was sitting at the front table waiting for her, when I saw her come out of that office. I've always doubted whether she would ever have found the courage to walk in there otherwise."

This proved to be her last free move. "I had a sort of queer moth-in-the-flame feeling," she said. After eating their steaks, eggs, and hominy grits, he led her outside to his Ford, and in minutes they were speeding down a highway. He talked with hardly a pause for breath for hours.

"He told me all sorts of things that I thought were extraordinarily direct for a first conversation," Lady Bird said. He recited the details of his schooling, his salary as Kleberg's secretary, the amount of insurance he carried, "his ambitions and about all the members of his family." Then his inventory recital over for the moment, he demanded that she marry him. Since they had spent only these few hours together, Lady Bird concluded, "I thought it was some kind of a joke." She gave him an evasive reply.

Johnson had to return to Washington in a few days, and he began monopolizing her time. It soon became apparent to her that if she did not quit their quick friendship and run, she would be completely enveloped by him. But she let matters slide. The day after his proposal he took her to meet his parents, and he spoke as though she were already in the family. Another day they visited the King ranch, where he introduced her to Mister Dick and his wife and mother. When the haughty, condescending Alice Gertrudis King Kleberg, whose ranch was far larger than the entire state of Connecticut, ordered Lady Bird to marry the young office servant of her son, Lady Bird was too awed to take offense.

Day after day he proposed to her, but she gave him no direct answer. Finally, when he said he had to leave for Washington, she asked him to take her to Karnack to meet her father. This was three hundred miles northeast of Austin and on the road to Washington. A problem arose because she also had a car and could not leave it in Austin. He solved this by driving her car while a friend, Malcolm Bardwell, Maury Maverick's secretary, drove behind them in Johnson's car. Before they left, Lady Bird called Dorris Powell, her next door neighbor in Karnack, and asked her to have the house cleaned. "The water pump is broken," Mrs. Powell said sadly.

Gangling Thomas Jefferson Taylor, II, Lady Bird's father, hit it off immediately with Johnson. He was a coarse, direct man who was as talkative as Lady Bird's beau, only he spoke in an Alabama accent. Wright Patman, who knew Sam Johnson, also knew Lady Bird's father. "When I was a boy," said Patman, "my father used to repair and adjust cotton gins in the fall just before the picking season, and he used to take me with him on some trips close to home at Hughes Springs. Every year we'd go the forty-two miles to Karnack, where Ol' Man Taylor had a gin. Taylor never talked about anything except making money. He also owned a lot of land and had a general store, and I remember he would complain that he had some stuff in the store that hadn't moved in fifty years. He married twice more after Lady Bird's mother died."

Taylor was born in Alabama in 1875 to a mother who was married four times and had thirteen children. After country school he moved to Karnack, Texas, near Louisiana, during the late eighteen-nineties. The village of Karnack at that time had a population of one hundred and was a minor center for the surrounding cotton farms. Nearby Caddo Lake, the South's largest natural lake, covered seventy thousand acres in a romantic setting of cypress trees and Spanish moss. Starting as a penniless sharecropper, Taylor kept his mind on money-making, acquired a little land of his own, dabbled in cotton and oil, serviced farmers with his cotton gin, and owned a general store that carried an advertising sign that denoted his philosophy: "T. J. Taylor—Dealer in Everything." In spare time, he bought catfish caught in Caddo Lake and shipped them in ice and salt to New York markets. But even here, before packing the catfish, he removed the fish eggs, which he sold as domestic caviar to eastern dealers.

The first of his three wives was Minnie Lee Patillo, with whom he had gone to country school at Evergreen, Alabama. Minnie was shy, yet she was also headstrong and was used to having her own way. So when Tommy Taylor, who had gone to Texas to earn his fortune, returned to Alabama and asked her to marry him, her father's declaration that he would never consent to Taylor as a son-in-law helped goad her into eloping with him.

Tommy brought Minnie to a large, white-painted structure in Karnack, which was known locally as the "Brick House." Besides being the only brick house in town, its bricks had been made by slaves. Taylor was by then coming up financially, knew how to get along with the "Niggers," who were all over the area like weeds, and was so forceful in his business dealings that he acquired the nicknames "Mr. Boss" and "Cap'n Taylor."

While Mr. Boss was plunging into his money schemes from dawn to late evenings, Minnie Taylor soon grew to detest the dullness of Karnack. Each year she fled the area, and her husband explained that she had gone to Chicago for the "opry" season or to Shreveport for stage plays. At home she tended to seclude herself and spent much of her time reading the set of "classics" that she had brought from Alabama.

Minnie Taylor's problem was not really boredom. Her medical history revealed nervous breakdowns, painfully wracking headaches, and inflammatory rheumatism. She became a food faddist, forbidding any serving of meat in her home. In the house and out, she dressed in gossamer white, swathed her head in veils, and trailed a heavy perfume odor. Unfriendly local gossips claimed she was as bald as an alligator, though a neighbor girl swore that Mrs. Taylor had sent for her many times to brush her long blonde hair.

She was seldom without a complaint of bodily troubles. On one occasion, when she took sick, the attending doctor performed an operation on her on the dining room table. Another time, when she suffered a nervous collapse with great depths of depression, her husband sent her in desperation to the Kellogg Sanitarium in Battle Creek, Michigan. But the mysterious techniques it boasted of to cure mental ailments did not work, and she returned home as miserable as when she left Karnack.

In her few painless moments, she called her big bluff husband "Dearie," and although he took pride in her cultural interests, there was no money in them, so they bored him. A family story about his lack of artistic interests told about his bringing his bride to their home and proudly showing her the red and white oilcloth he had spread over the dining room table.

Despite her attempt to live in a created dream world, Minnie Taylor went through the stark reality of having three children. The first, Thomas Jefferson Taylor, III, was born in 1901; the second, Anthony J., in 1905. Then on December 22, 1912, when the boys were eleven and seven, thirty-nine-year-old Minnie had her final child, a daughter, christened Claudia Alta Taylor in a Methodist ceremony. Minnie had named her daughter after her older brother Claude, a well-to-do bachelor living in Alabama.

The years of the mother-daughter relationship were few. When Claudia was a baby, her mother suffered another nervous breakdown. Nursemaids had to take care of the child, and Alice Tittle, one of the Negro maids, renamed her by accident when she looked into her little face and exclaimed, "Why, she's as purdy as a lady bird." From that time forward, her original name was discarded by relatives and friends.

When Lady Bird was only five, Minnie Taylor tripped over the family's collie on the circular stairway. Her fall brought on a miscarriage and blood poisoning developed. She died at the age of forty-four in September 1918.

Lady Bird once admitted that she had "a childhood dread of loneliness." Unable to tend to his business and raise three children, Cap'n Taylor took the easy way out of his difficulties. He dispatched the boys to boarding school and kept little Lady Bird with him while he pondered a solution. During the day she played in the general store, and at night he bedded her on a cot on the second floor. Once when she lay in bed, she pointed to long boxes that were stacked nearby and she asked her father what they were. They were coffins, and he told her laconically, "Dry goods, honey."

Even in his preoccupation with business deals, Thomas Jefferson Taylor realized that the general store was not a proper home and playground for his daughter. So when she was six, he wrote to Effie Patillo, his old-maid sister-in-law, and told her to meet the Southern Railroad on a certain morning. Cap'n Taylor proved himself a thoughtless man when he would not close down his "Dealer in Everything" general store for a few days in order to deliver his daughter safely to the pine country of Alabama. Instead, he bought a single one-way ticket and lifted Lady Bird to the train's platform, after attaching a tag to her clothing giving the conductor pertinent information about her destination.

Not long afterward, Effie Patillo, or Auntie Weh or Aunt Effie, as the sad little girl called her, returned to Karnack with the child and the two moved into the Brick House with Mr. Boss. Aunt Effie, at thirty-nine, was a thin, sickly woman of a bewildered nature and highly naive. Neighbors said she needed as much care and guidance as the child she was rearing. But the two apparently had a hovering guardian angel, for no serious mishaps occurred.

Aunt Effie could take only so much of Texas at a time. Frequently she and Lady Bird boarded the train for long visits back to relatives in Alabama, and it was as a result of these excursions that Lady Bird's Texas talk acquired a thick Alabama brogue. Aunt Effie was close to her bachelor brother Claude, and he too doted on his shy niece. However, he lacked any understanding of children, for he tried to force his own enormous interest in get-rich-quick-without-working stock market schemes on his only niece. Lady Bird later claimed that "he taught me to study stock market quotations before I was twelve." Uncle Claude also sent her books on accounting principles as birthday presents, as though by some magic she might understand them.

Fortunately for Lady Bird, Mrs. Dorris Powell, a next-door neighbor who was appalled by Aunt Effie's vagueness, willingly served as Lady Bird's substitute mother. As a child, it was Dorris who had combed Minnie Patillo Taylor's long blonde hair, and she told Lady Bird about this and other stories involving her mother. Yes, everyone in town remembered the way Mrs. Taylor came around and called a political candidate a "slacker" because he wasn't in uniform in 1917.

For seven years Lady Bird went to the neighboring one-room-plus-outhouse Fern School. Then in 1924 Aunt Effie took her to the nearby town of Jefferson, where they lived in an apartment Monday through Friday during the school week and then went back to the Brick House four miles outside of Karnack for the weekend. Finally after the two spent two years in this routine, Cap'n Taylor asked them to move back to the Brick House full time. He bought Lady Bird a car, taught her to drive at thirteen, and told her to commute daily to Marshall, a town fourteen miles away, for her last two years in high school. Marshall was a Black Belt town with a total population of about sixteen thousand. Few of the Negroes went to school, and those who did presented no problem to the whites, for total segregation was enforced. The teeming black population in Marshall lived in rickety shanties and was the source of much local laughter because of its superstitions.

Because of her deep-seated shyness, Lady Bird derived immense satisfaction when her grades were low enough in the class of twenty-eight at Marshall High so that she would not have to deliver the valedictorian or salutatorian speech at graduation. Emma Boehringer, Gene Boehringer's sister, was tops in grades instead, with Maurine Cranson nosing out Lady Bird for second honors in the small graduating class of 1928. The school paper noted that Lady Bird's favorite expression was "Why?" and that her ambition was to be an old maid.

Although Aunt Effie insisted that her fifteen-year-old charge was too young to go to college, Dorris Powell's mother managed a talk with busy Cap'n Taylor at the girl's request. The result was that Aunt Effie and Lady Bird rented an apartment in Dallas from which Lady Bird went daily to a junior college. Despite her upbringing as a Methodist, after enrolling in St. Mary's Episcopal School for Girls, the Dallas junior college, Lady Bird became an Episcopalian. For the first time she was also on her own, when Aunt Effie felt so worn out at fifty that she entered a Dallas nursing home.

Upon Lady Bird's graduation from St. Mary's in 1930, Aunt Effie proposed that the two return to Alabama for the girl's next two years in college. However, by this time Lady Bird had met Emma Boehringer's sister Gene, who told her she should go to the University of Texas in Austin.

Aunt Effie pulled one way and Gene the other. Finally Gene wrote a long letter to Mr. Boss about being patriotic to Texas institutions, and Taylor sided with her. The impact of Gene on Lady Bird was tremendous, if for no other reason than the start it gave to the fateful steps leading to her meeting with Lyndon Johnson. But in addition, said Lady Bird, Gene was "a catalytic agent bringing out qualities you might conceivably have. She made me feel important for the first time."

Fellow students at the University of Texas nevertheless remembered Lady Bird for her shyness and her unstylish clothing. She learned to dance, and for a time had a boyfriend named Harrell Lee. She also forced herself to take part in many activities. The 1933 yearbook, *The Cactus,* labeled her as the publicity manager of the University of Texas Sports Association.

After Cap'n Taylor's loud-talk dinner with Lyndon Johnson at their first meeting in September 1934, Taylor was impressed with him. "Daughter, you've been bringing home a lot of boys," he chortled. "But this time you've brought a man!" Taylor was feeling good at the time. He had married and divorced his second wife and was planning a third marriage to a woman decades younger than his own fifty-nine years.

Early the next morning Mrs. Powell walked into the Brick House to meet and observe the suitor of her darling little Lady Bird. She took an immediate jealous dislike to Johnson. When Lady Bird walked Lyndon and Malcolm Bardwell to the highway for their ride back to Washington, Mrs. Powell was horrified that Lady Bird and Lyndon kissed. "Don't do that!" she yelled at Johnson. "Hurry up, go on—or the Ku Klux Klan will get you!"

Once back in Washington, Johnson put in his usual hectic day, managing Kleberg's political business, and gave his evenings to Georgetown Law School. Yet he found time to bombard Lady Bird with daily letters, and he sent her an inscribed photograph of himself in shirtsleeves. He spent hours on the inscription; the final message read: "For Bird—A lovely girl with ideals, principles, intelligence and refinement, from her sincere admirer, Lyndon."

The letters and picture plus some long-distance phone calls were designed to bring him an affirmative answer when he got his next opportunity to return to Texas for Kleberg. "I don't think Bird ever had a chance to say no—if she wanted to," said one of Johnson's Dodge Hotel cellmates.

Seven weeks after their first meeting, he suddenly appeared at the Brick House and accepted Taylor's invitation to stay overnight. He persisted in his demand that they get married "not next year after you've stayed home a year . . . but about two weeks from now, a month from now, or right away." Although she refused to give him a definite answer, he talked her into riding with him to Austin on a three-hundred-mile jaunt to look at rings. Here she let him buy her an engagement ring but not a wedding ring.

Afterward he left her and drove to Corpus Christi to handle some

Kleberg chores, while she returned home. Dorris Powell was upset when
she saw the ring. She argued that Lady Bird was too young at twenty-one
for marriage, that she should see more of life first, and she "begged her to
wait six months." But when Lady Bird asked her to go along on the forty-
mile drive to Shreveport to purchase a trousseau, Mrs. Powell in defeat
accompanied her.

Still, when she got back to the Brick House, Lady Bird made one last
attempt at independence. This was to run to Alabama to discuss Johnson
with Aunt Effie. Their conversation took place in her aunt's hospital, and
her foster mother begged her not to marry "a stranger whom you've known
less than two months. If he loves you as much as he says he does, he will
wait for you," she said. But Lady Bird was talking for the sake of talking
and the attention she got from her aunt and other relatives. One said that
after Lady Bird showed her Lyndon's inscribed picture, she remarked that
she didn't know if she wanted to be called "Johnson for the rest of my life."

Lyndon was at the Brick House when she returned from Alabama. He
and Cap'n Taylor wanted to know what Aunt Effie's advice was. Her father
reacted explosively. "Lady, if you wait until Aunt Effie is ready, you will
never marry anyone," he said. Then when they were alone he urged her to
marry Lyndon, even though they had known each other only a short time.
"Some of the best deals are made in a hurry," he assured her.

The next morning Lady Bird decided to drive to Austin for a talk with
Gene Boehringer. When Johnson insisted he would go along for the ride,
she packed the clothes she had bought in Shreveport and put the suitcase in
his car. Johnson quickly placed a long-distance call to Dan Quill, who was
Kleberg's Citizens' League appointee as postmaster in San Antonio, and he
barked out orders to Quill to arrange for his wedding that evening in the
Alamo town. Then, when he and Lady Bird drove out of Karnack, he told
her about the call and added, "We either get married now, or we never
will." She made no protest when he said he was driving to San Antonio
instead of Austin, though she continued to discuss the pros and cons of
their marriage mile after mile. In addition, at one stop she called Cecile
Harrison, her college roommate, and asked Cecile to stand up for her at
her wedding ceremony that evening in San Antonio.

Dan Quill always took a request from Johnson as an order, and he made
no exception this time. First, he took out a Bexar County marriage license
and dated it that day, November 17, 1934. Then he filled in the names of
the bride and groom, pondering awhile because Lyndon had referred to her
as "Bird." Finally he wrote "Bird Taylor" in the space for the bride.

Quill then rushed on the double to St. Mark's Episcopal Church, to
which he belonged, and burst into the rector's quarters. Reverend Arthur
K. McKinstry, later the bishop of the Episcopal Diocese of Delaware, who
was St. Mark's rector, was outraged by Quill's request. "You're asking me
to perform a justice-of-the-peace ceremony," he snapped at Quill. "I don't

marry people that fast. I want to get to know them, meet with them two or three days to talk with them, and explain the seriousness of marriage."

McKinstry said that his remarks only led to further remonstrance by Quill. "Johnson has only one day in Texas. Then he has to return to Washington." He stretched the truth to convince McKinstry that he should make an exception in this case. Finally, McKinstry agreed to do so.

After completing their four-hundred-mile drive from Karnack to San Antonio, Johnson called Quill to learn where the ceremony would take place. Quill told him and added that Henry Hirshberg would serve as best man. Hirshberg, a Harvard-trained lawyer practicing in San Antonio, had insisted that Quill be best man, but Quill had argued even louder that Hirshberg serve.

Johnson claimed that Lady Bird was still discussing whether to go through with the ceremony as they entered the church. Quill, Henry Hirshberg and his wife, and Cecile Harrison were already present. Years afterward McKinstry recalled, "It was a simple, quiet service with no music and only two or three witnesses. Lady Bird turned to her intended, the man who was to be known as the great master of details, and asked, 'You did bring a wedding ring, didn't you?' 'I forgot,' he said."

Johnson gave Quill an ordering stare, and Quill rushed out of the church and ran to the nearby Sears, Roebuck store. When he was confronted with telling the size of Lady Bird's finger, he solved this problem by galloping back to St. Mark's with an entire tray of cheap wedding rings. Lady Bird chose one that fitted, and Quill dashed back to the store with the tray. The ring cost two dollars and fifty cents, and this became Quill's wedding present to the Johnsons.

Following this, the ceremony proceeded without further mishap. But there was one jarring moment when it was over. As the Johnsons left St. Mark's, Reverend McKinstry called after them, "I hope this marriage lasts."

There was a wedding supper at St. Anthony's Hotel. Quill suggested a toast to Lady Bird, but when he saw the wine prices he blanched. Hirshberg tactfully remembered that he had a bottle of wine at home, and he returned with it a short time later.

After a wedding night at the Plaza Hotel, Lyndon called his parents, and Lady Bird telephoned her father and Dorris Powell. Rebekah Johnson covered her feeling of rejection at not being told about the wedding in advance by promising Lady Bird a special wedding present—a lilac "sweetheart pattern" quilt she had made. Then the newlyweds left on a Mexican honeymoon, before going to Washington for the opening of the next Congressional session.

Chapter 14

L ESS THAN SIX months after Lady Bird's first visit to Washington as a tourist, she returned in December 1934 to set up house as a bride. They spent their first night in the capital in an upstairs room at the Dodge Hotel, and in the morning he introduced her to his dozens of friends as they came up from their underground rooms. From the Dodge they moved into a subleased apartment at the swank Kennedy Warren on Connecticut Avenue. But from here they moved in a few weeks to a small single-bedroom apartment at 1910 Kalorama Road.

Mister Dick Kleberg had a wedding present for them. This was a five-hundred-dollar-a-year increase in pay over the thirty-four hundred dollars Lyndon had been drawing since the previous July. Out of this three hundred and twenty-five dollars a month, he kept one hundred dollars for his personal expenses and insurance. No more money went home to Mamma. With her two hundred and twenty-five dollars, Lady Bird paid the rent, which ran to forty-two dollars and fifty cents each month, bought an eighteen-dollar-and-seventy-five-cent government bond each payday, got a few essential pieces of furniture, paid the once-a-week colored maid three dollars, and spent the rest on food and clothing. She developed into a bargain hunter and asked for seconds and irregulars in the department stores. Food was extremely cheap, considering Johnson's salary during the depression. Stores sold butter at fifteen cents a bulk pound, coffee was twenty cents a pound, and several cuts of meat as low as ten cents a pound. Johnson's cigarettes, which he chain-smoked at the rate of three packages a day, were a luxury even at two packages for a quarter.

All her life Lady Bird had been waited on, and she had never worked for money. "I had never swept a floor and I certainly had never cooked," she admitted. From this extreme, she had to move toward the other, for Johnson was a big eater, and he liked a clean place. On their honeymoon she saw that he relished the hottest and spiciest Mexican foods, and he told her he expected her to learn how to prepare them.

However, the first book she bought was a plain American cook book, and it was with such recipes that she made her stab at stove work. Their first guests were Maury Maverick and his wife, an occasion for which Lady Bird prepared a simple meal of baked ham, rice, and lemon pie. They ate in the living room, and the folding cot she had bought for overnight company was pushed against the wall. "I'll never forget that rice," said Mrs. Maverick. "It tasted like library paste."

The thrill of having Maury Maverick to dinner was many-faceted. Most important was the prestige it gave the young Johnsons, for Maverick was now a member of the House. Redistricting had resulted in the removal of Bexar County from Kleberg's District, and San Antonio-Bexar was now the Twentieth Congressional District. When Maverick decided to run in 1934 as the Citizens' League candidate in the Democratic primary, he knew he could not win without the Mexican vote. The United States Census classified Mexicans as "Negroes," and local Democrats had made use of this to prevent "unbought" Mexicans from voting in the lily-white Democratic primaries. Sherwood Anderson, novelist friend of Maverick, said that the stubby, homely Texas liberal had made it to Congress "by buying the Mexican vote." What Maverick had accomplished was to get President Roosevelt to order the Census classification of Mexicans changed. The grateful Mexicans in Bexar County responded by voting him the Democratic nominee.

Besides having a congressman to dinner, Johnson gained the thrill of entertaining a man whose ancestors were so directly involved in Texas and outside history. The Maverick clan was among the most distinguished families of Texas. Maury's granddaddy had signed the Texas Declaration of Independence in 1836. Captured in battle by Santa Anna, Sam Maverick was marched sixteen hundred miles to military prison at Perote, Mexico. Lyndon Johnson thrilled at the repetition of Sam Maverick's words when the Mexicans offered him his freedom if he would not take up arms again against Mexico. "To say that I would lay down the arms of my country would be a lie," he said. Sam Maverick later became mayor of San Antonio and gave his name to the English language because his cattle were unbranded. A human "maverick" came to mean an independent person on the roam.

The Mavericks were also closely related to other famous Americans. Sam Maverick had been a kinsman to James Madison, and Maverick's son Albert had married into the distinguished Maury family of Virginia. Other Maury Maverick ancestors included Charles Lynch, the famous Judge Lynch whose name also became part of the language, and Meriwether Lewis, of Lewis and Clark Expedition fame during the Jefferson Administration.

If you eliminated Maverick the congressman and Maverick of the famous ancestors, what remained was a fascinating dinner guest. He was a strange sort of Texan because he was an active member of the American Civil Liberties Union, and he could be roused to enormous anger when telling about mean practices against the underprivileged. He spoke enrapturedly on the subject of President Roosevelt, and he expressed low regard for Vice President Garner, who he claimed had worked for his defeat in his Congressional race. Maverick's view of Washington was that it was flooded with "crooked lawyers and people who want favors to which they are not entitled." His ambition, which he freely expressed to Johnson and others, was to run against Senator Tom Connally in 1940.

At dinner, Maverick was also a humorist. He inscribed a picture of himself, "To Lyndon Johnson who got me started." When he said his real name was Fontaine Maury Maverick, and Johnson wanted to know how he got rid of his first name, he said he had been working bees for his cousin on a hot day. "An old man was driving our heavy load and us up a hill, and the horses couldn't make the grade," said Maverick. "So the old man turned to me and asked, 'What's your name?' I told him, 'Fontaine Maury Maverick.' 'You'll have to drop part of that name, or these horses will never make it up the hill,' he said. 'I'll drop the Fontaine,' I told him, and we made the hill."

Practice in entertaining the Mavericks came in handy, for other company descended on the Johnsons. Aunt Effie came up from Alabama, miraculously cured of the ailment that had hospitalized her. And at the same time Uncle George Johnson, the "Senator" from Sam Houston High, came to eat and sleep in their apartment while he took in the sights. Uncle George could not stay more than a few days, but he promised to return soon, while Aunt Effie told the newlyweds she planned to live with them half the year and spend the other time in Alabama.

When the Seventy-fourth Congress convened on January 3, 1935, Lady Bird learned that politics engrossed Lyndon. He introduced her to Sam Rayburn and told her that Rayburn expected to become the next House speaker. Representative Henry T. Rainey of Illinois, who had been elected speaker when Garner shifted to Vice President, had passed away after the last Congress adjourned, and Representative Joe Byrns of Tennessee, who was majority leader, was counting on his seniority to elevate him into the speaker's chair.

Rayburn had put his name on important New Deal legislation, written by the young team of Tommy Corcoran and Ben Cohen, and he believed that this prestige plus the support of true southerners would help him upset Byrns. From his Senate perch, Garner meddled in the speaker fight in behalf of Rayburn, until the Byrns crowd told him they would oppose his renomination for Vice President in 1936 unless he quit lobbying. Although Garner had been wailing that "the Vice Presidency doesn't amount to a hill of beans," he quickly withdrew his support for Rayburn, and Byrns easily won the speaker contest.

Throughout that session the Capitol was in an uproar over legislation, and from his vantage place in Kleberg's office Johnson felt the excitement engendered by the Roosevelt revolution. White House aides swamped House and Senate offices to work up support for such important bills as the Works Progress Administration (WPA), or the program of work for relief checks instead of direct relief checks mailed to the unemployed, the Social Security Act, and the National Labor Relations Act to guarantee the sanctity of employee elections for union representation.

Mister Dick Kleberg was even more disenchanted with this Second New Deal than he had been with the First New Deal in 1933. But Johnson continued to manage his affairs and prevent ruptured relations with the Administration. Some who came into the office gained an impression that Kleberg was working for Johnson instead of the other way around, just as Dr. Evans at Southwest Texas State Teachers College had come to the conclusion he was working for Lyndon.

A Texas politician who had been observing this situation in Kleberg's office said that Kleberg was oblivious of Johnson's management of him. But at the beginning of summer in 1935, Mamie Kleberg, Mister Dick's wife, came through the office and expressed her concern over Johnson's domination.

"Dick," she told her husband in a loud, angry voice, "do you know that that boy Lyndon is fixing to run against you for your seat?"

Kleberg asked what he should do about Johnson.

"Fire him!" she demanded. "Throw him out!"

Kleberg was not a bad sort personally, said the Texas politician, and he hesitated to fire Johnson. But when Mamie Kleberg repeated her demand, he told Johnson he was finished.

Johnson's firing might have been disastrous to him. But instead it proved to be the best thing that could have happened, for it jolted him out of the employee ranks and into the employer caste, from which he could move on to the legislator level.

Of course, at the time he did not know this, and he scurried to Sam Rayburn and then to Maury Maverick with his wretched news. Sam's assurances, while the cigarette ashes dropped on his vest, were not comforting because he could not put Lyndon immediately on his Commerce Committee staff. Nor did Maverick have a staff opening.

"But Maury had something better to offer," said one of his friends. "Maury was one of a half dozen F.D.R. protégés who could barge into the President's office without making an appointment two weeks in advance. He went over to see Roosevelt to ask if there wasn't some sort of a job Lyndon could handle in the White House. And he couldn't have picked a more opportune time. F.D.R. had just approved establishing the NYA (National Youth Administration) under his four-billion-eight-hundred-million-dollar WPA program, and he had the job of naming forty-eight state NYA directors.

"Maury told F.D.R. he had just the man to direct the Texas NYA—Lyndon Johnson. He gave the President a big pep talk about Lyndon, and F.D.R. seemed interested until he found out that Lyndon was only twenty-six years old. Then he scoffed about giving this job to a child. But Maury pumped his engine harder and argued that it was Lyndon's very youth that would give him the advantage of understanding the young people who had to be helped. 'After all,' said Maury, 'you need someone who's honestly interested in helping his own generation work their way through high school and college and improve themselves, rather than sit around unemployed.' By the time Maverick left, Roosevelt hadn't given his okay, but neither had he turned down Lyndon."

After this meeting, Maverick turned the pressure on Roosevelt. Stories leaked to reporters claimed that Johnson was Mrs. Roosevelt's protégé and that she was insisting to her husband that he name him Texas NYA director. "One day Sam Rayburn, who had never been friendly toward me, came to see me," said Senator Tom Connally. "He wanted me to ask President Roosevelt to appoint Lyndon Johnson to run the Texas NYA, and he said he knew this fell in my patronage basket. Sam was agitated and wouldn't leave until I agreed to do this."

While all these activities were proceeding, Kleberg was looking for a new secretary. Lyndon Johnson expressed an interest in helping him find a successor, and when Kleberg said he was willing to take his advice, Johnson relentlessly began promoting his twenty-one-year-old brother, Samuel Houston Johnson, for the job. Sam had graduated in law the previous year from Cumberland University in Tennessee, and though he was actually a mild and sensitive sort, Lyndon assured Kleberg that Sam was energetic and outgoing. Worn down by Lyndon's persuasion, Kleberg agreed to hire his younger brother at Lyndon's top salary of thirty-nine hundred dollars.

And in July 1935 President Roosevelt turned Lyndon's disaster into advancement by naming him director of the Texas NYA.

Chapter 15

J OHNSON MOVED SWIFTLY and without hesitation into his new job. He had called reporters from Washington, and when his plane landed at Austin, he held a press conference. In answering questions, he struck several jaunty poses characteristic of Roosevelt and gave a drawling imitation of his way of speaking. "As ah see it now," he said in summary, "ma job is ta work maself out of a job." He had to leave for a conference with "ma friend" Governor Jimmy Allred at the capitol, and when he walked out of the governor's office, he told the same reporters that Allred had assured him of his cooperation and the use of state facilities.

Immediately afterward he flew to several Texas cities for talks with mayors and to explain the NYA to reporters. As he put it, the NYA was "primarily intended to furnish aid to worthy students and to give an opportunity to young men and women to ground themselves in industry that may pay them dividends in the future."

That he managed to collect as much publicity as he did was surprising because he had so much news competition. Will Rogers and Wiley Post crashed to their death in Alaska; there was a Joe Louis fight; the Texas Centennial celebration for 1936 was winning federal funds; and Congress was appropriating a great deal of money to deepen and widen the ships' channel cut from the Gulf to Houston fifty miles inland.

The San Antonio *Express* of August 6, 1935, carried Johnson's picture plus his statement that he planned to open his central NYA headquarters in Austin on August 15. This left him only a few days to begin operations, and he operated with apparent frenzy.

When it came to picking his staff, Johnson went directly to his old school friends to be his assistants. "I was called one day by Lyndon to meet him in San Marcos the next day at 7 A.M. in the old Post Office cafeteria," said Sherman Birdwell, a classmate at Southwest Texas State Teachers College. Jesse Kellam, a White Star athlete in the Johnson days, received a similar call.

At seven the next morning he told them bluntly that they were going to work for him. Both voiced strong protests, but Johnson ignored them. Birdwell was then setting up a foreign service center in Austin, and the project had not yet jelled. However, Johnson painted such a picture of his and the program's need for Birdwell that he finally agreed to forget about his own project and become a Johnson assistant at the NYA.

As for Jesse Kellam, he had moved ahead swiftly in the teaching field and was now a deputy state supervisor of education. Johnson's tack was to tell Jesse that he did not want him to give up his job, merely to leave it for a short time. Jesse said he might take a two-week leave of absence at most. Lyndon begged him for a month, and Jesse reluctantly agreed, if Johnson would arrange it with his boss. That was all Johnson needed. A quick telephone call to the state director of education, and Kellam's services were his for a month. As things turned out, at the end of the month Johnson put in another call and had Kellam's leave of absence extended a year.

Johnson also went after Willard Deason, whom he had made president of the senior class at Southwest Texas. Deason was working for the Federal Land Bank in Houston, and he did not want to leave. "Help me out for two weeks," Johnson begged him. Deason said he would come for that short time. But once he came, Johnson dangled the post of assistant state director of the NYA before him, and Deason remained.

Birdwell, Kellam, and Deason showed up early on opening day at the decayed Littlefield Building in Austin where Johnson had acquired offices on the sixth floor. When they came upstairs, they found Johnson already on the telephone. "His work day always started early," Birdwell said with some disgust.

When President Roosevelt established the NYA, he allocated twenty-seven million dollars of WPA funds to Aubrey Williams, NYA's administrator, for his first year of operations. In a hasty figuring, Roosevelt computed that one hundred thousand college students working on federal projects and each being paid fifteen dollars a month, and two hundred thousand high school pupils getting six dollars a month, would be covered that first year.

However, the demand for NYA jobs far exceeded the paltry allocation, and Williams found himself besieged by state NYA directors for more than the average handover of only six hundred thousand dollars. Williams was described as a "gaunt, zealous, wavy-haired, hollow-eyed" man, and for good reason. He called his first Washington conference of state NYA directors on August 20, 1935, to settle this question before it got out of hand. Johnson flew in for the meeting and he stole much of the publicity and was in the few newsphotos printed nationally when he told reporters he was the youngest NYA state director. More important to the Texas program, he made an excellent impression on Aubrey Williams, who was also from the South, and he came away with a fuller money pot than Williams had originally planned for Texas. What he gained primarily was a little extra money to teach trades to those not in school.

There was not a moment to spare when he returned to Austin. "It was August, and we were getting young people on the payroll so they could go to school in September," said Sherman Birdwell. " 'Put them to work; get them in school!' Lyndon kept hammering at us."

He beefed up his staff and passed word along that he expected everyone to work overtime and weekends. All his top aides did so without complaint. "For a time after we began to work," said Johnson, "I tried to be the first man on the job every morning, but I found I had just set up a contest."

Johnson suffered a major blow when he discovered that the old Littlefield Building had never been connected to the power lines of the Austin electric company. Instead it had a weak electrical power generator in the basement, and the building superintendent "cut off the juice" promptly at 10 P.M. When the lights on the sixth floor went out at ten o'clock his first overtime night, Johnson groped his way in the dark to the basement. But the superintendent was completely indifferent to his pleas and threats to turn on the power. By the time he crept back in the dark to the sixth floor, he saw flickering light when he opened the door.

One of the men had found nineteenth-century gas jets protruding from the walls. He turned the handle of one and struck a match, and the gas ignited. The gas company for some unknown reason had never disconnected the Littlefield Building's jets. So every night came the ritual of striking matches to ignite the gas; and the staff stayed past midnight before crawling down the stairs to the street. Johnson insisted on being the last one to leave, and when he did he turned off the gas jets.

The paper work was enormous, and the visitors' list was a who's who of Texas education circles. Each morning and afternoon the twice-a-day mailmen brought heavy canvas bags crammed with filled-in application reports from high schools and colleges to make them eligible for NYA funds. And with the mailbags came a steady stream of principals and deans pleading their case for money. On one occasion the dean of the University of Texas came to beg the twenty-seven-year-old director for an addition to the quota of seven hundred and fifty students to receive NYA aid at his school. Johnson and Deason told him bluntly that if he got more, then other Texas colleges would have to be cut. "I felt like I had blood on my hands," said Deason.

All of Johnson's employees found he would not tolerate inefficiency or slow work. Once, when he rushed through the offices to check on activities after midnight, one man was sitting behind a high stack of letters with a look of hysteria on his face. Johnson demanded to know what the trouble was, and the clerk complained that his job was futile. He was answering the letters one at a time from the top of the stack, and he was finding later letters from the same deans and principals lower in the pile, complaining that their earlier letters had not been answered.

Johnson was enraged. Sandwiching the stack of mail between his hands, he turned it upside down. "Start from the top now," he ordered, "and you'll get their latest letters first. That ought to cut your job just about in half."

The Texas NYA provided aid to eighteen thousand students, by giving money to schools and letting the schools decide which needy students to select for part-time work in libraries, labs, and college offices at thirty-five cents an hour. Johnson's program also aided an additional twelve thousand youngsters, who were out of school, in learning trades and doing useful work on local public projects. Early in his program he talked the head of the state highway department into lending tools and trucks so that NYA recipients could build roadside picnic areas, repair school buildings, and construct swimming pools, playground facilities, and tennis courts. Johnson also established training centers for girls who wanted to learn sewing and nursing aid and work shops for boys who wanted to learn to repair appliances and automobiles and become carpenters and electricians.

Because his "beat" was the largest of any of the forty-eight state directors, he had to spend much time traveling, setting up local projects and then returning to check on their progress. His practice was to drop in without notice on inspections, and what he found sometimes made him furious. On one occasion he drove into a San Antonio park where he had allocated funds to train recreation and athletic directors. He found only the project supervisor present, and his replies to questions regarding the where-abouts of the trainees were evasive. Johnson not only fired the supervisor but closed down the project.

With a welcome assist from the Roosevelts, Johnson's NYA program gained national attention in 1936. Mrs. Roosevelt started it by sweeping into Texas with her large entourage of female reporters. On reaching Austin, she told her traveling reporters and local newsmen that she had come to Texas to find out why the Texas NYA director was doing such an effective job. She burst into his sixth floor office in the Littlefield Building; then the two, after her quick handshake, hurried to East Sixth Street to watch NYA girls operating sewing machines in a training program. Next they sped to local colleges to discuss the NYA with officials and recipients. Mrs. Roosevelt was the godmother and guardian of the NYA, for it was she who had convinced her reluctant husband that it would not involve the same regimentation of youth that Hitler and Mussolini were practicing in Germany and Italy. Following her enthusiastic praise for what she found in Texas, she departed, after shaking Johnson's hand again.

As for President Roosevelt, Jesse Jones had induced him to visit the state during the Texas Centennial Exposition in 1936. Johnson learned of the time schedule for his drive between Fort Worth and Dallas, and he lined the highway with hundreds of shovel-wielding NYA boys. When the President's motorcade drove past them, the boys saluted Roosevelt with their shovels. Had the President examined the line closely he would have seen a tall, thin young man with a frozen smile on his face standing in front of the shovel saluters.

Lady Bird waited until Lyndon had passed his first operational crisis in the late summer of 1935 before leaving Washington for Austin. Here she rented a furnished house from one of the professors at the University of Texas and they moved into it.

She saw immediately that the Lyndon Johnson of Austin was far different from the Lyndon Johnson of Washington. Instead of being an employee, he was an assured employer giving orders to a large group of underlings who looked up to him as "the boss." He often did not come home for dinner, and when he showed up at 1 A.M., he expected her to prepare a fresh meal. Or he might suddenly appear with a half-dozen assistants and tell her to feed the entire group. Her specialty was round steak and vegetables, a cheap and easy meal to prepare on short notice. Decades later Sherman Birdwell recalled that she made the only spinach he would eat. Willard Deason liked her cooking so much that he found reasons to drop in at meal time. Lyndon carried on a monologue with his aides when they came to the house on a social visit, his loud voice booming a half block away. Lady Bird was quiet, and one of Lyndon's friends said that her speech at the time contained such Texas gems as "Y'all come back real soon, hear now"; "if God be willin' and the creek don't spill over"; and "noisier than a mule in a tin barn." But she was trying hard to be the boss's dutiful wife, and the staff at the NYA liked her.

Johnson spent part of his time cultivating businessmen so that they would hire the NYA trainees his program had developed. This was a crucial matter, for the upgrading of skills was of no value if the young people could not be placed in private industry. This activity put Johnson on the luncheon circuit as a speaker at Chamber of Commerce and other organizational functions. Here he frequently had to defend the NYA against smug jibes that it was a costly and meaningless boondoggle and a further intrusion of the federal government into local affairs. Johnson's typical answer was an emotional retort instead of a wise diplomatic reply that might have gained him the support of the sneering businessmen.

He cultivated reporters and tried to get them to write favorable stories that would increase public support of his program. His closest newsman friend in Austin was Charles E. Green, who wrote a column, "Town Talk," for the local *American-Statesman*. Although he had no need to do so, Johnson tried flattery and gifts to make his friend friendlier. Green said, for instance, that invariably "Lyndon introduced me as the man who introduced him to Lady Bird. That is not exactly so, but I did know Lady Bird before she knew Lyndon." Green came frequently to the house on San Gabriel Street, which he described as being on a lot that was "wooded, with a creek behind it—a lovely place to sit in the dark and listen to the wild life." Once, said Green, when he visited the Johnsons "Lyndon was wearing a pair of huaraches, or Mexican sandals, some friend had given him. I admired them, and he took them off and made me take them."

Green favored the NYA program and was willing to give both Johnson and the NYA a plug. But Johnson could not tell a simple, straightforward story and Green could not write a believable account. One of Green's columns in the *American-Statesman* contained the following:

"Sure," says Dir. Johnson, propping his feet on the desk and grinning broadly. "I guess I know a little bit about the youth's hard lot in life. You don't mind if I relax, do you."

I didn't. In fact, a man talks much better when he does relax. Then he told me how he started out.

"Received my early education in a country school in the Hill country. After schoolin', I got a job as a day laborer on the highways. I chopped weeds, earned a dollar here and a dollar there, always with an idea in my mind of finishing a college education."

It was this same desire which put Lyndon Johnson into college. He worked and studied at San Marcos. He learned how it felt to come home at night dog tired, turn on the lights, and try to whip a tired body into shape to absorb some mental training.

Later he went to Pearsall, then to Houston.

At Houston, he taught public speaking.

"There was a kid named Gene Latimer. When he wasn't running around with the drug store gang, or delivering parcels, he was practicing debating. He had a knack at debating. I left for Washington. He left for South Texas and started driving a truck. I kept hearing from him. He wanted to go to school. So I brought him to Washington.

"Now young Latimer is standing on his own two legs and is doing a good job for the government. . . .

"It used to be before American civilization became so complex, that a man could bundle up his family in a covered wagon, strike out and hew out his own destiny in some new country. There were numerous things for the young man coming up.

"When the depression hit, the plight of American youth, the great throngs that haunted the drug store corners, the pool halls for lack of something better to do, was brought to the government's attention.

"After all, the boy of today is the citizen of tomorrow. If he grew up without an opportunity, the ability that he had would become warped. He would become disgruntled and a unit to be added to the reds and other malcontents who seized such opportunities to spout their ideas of dissension. . . ."

The messenger boy comes in and Mr. Johnson takes his feet off the desk. The boy hands him a sheaf of telegrams. They are telegrams from schools, stressing new needs. The drouth is hard here, or the cotton crop has been poor there. All funds will be needed. Please don't forget this or that school.

Mr. Johnson is back at work.

Somewhere, somewhere along the line, another boy will be salvaged from the local gang or the local drug store corner loafer's brigade. He'll be placed in a school room and given a chance to become an active, alert, loyal citizen of a country big enough to look after its youth.

One of the characteristics Lady Bird noticed in her husband was that he never opened a book or magazine. She began to mark passages she thought he should see, and she took to walking after him, attempting to read aloud to him, just as his mother had walked to the gate with him while instructing him on school work. But her efforts were insignificant compared with the influence of their landlord on his thinking.

Dr. Robert Hargrove Montgomery, who owned the house they rented, was also professor of economics at the University of Texas. His specialty was cotton marketing, and his book on that subject in 1927 won him critical praise. Montgomery's love was the New Deal, and like a good professor he could raise his voice louder than Johnson's in lecturing his tenant on the meaning of the Roosevelt revolution. Montgomery hated monopolies and cartels, and saw the Roosevelt program, with the exception of the NRA, which abetted industry's self-controlled production and price decisions, as an antitrust effort. The trusts were to blame for the nation's ills, he argued. "Businessmen without competitors will set prices at the most profitable level and produce only what the community will buy at those prices. When the wealth and power of the community is in a few hands," Montgomery told Johnson, "our free business enterprise system will be gone."

Johnson had never before thought of the New Deal as having a cohesive philosophy, and Dr. Montgomery made him see for the first time that all the sprouting alphabetical agencies including his own were tied into a pattern.

Chapter 16

Iₙ AUGUST 1935, when Lyndon Johnson became Texas NYA director, he was too young and inexperienced to trust with state policy decision-making. For this reason, the Washington Administration took painstaking efforts to select one of the state's non-office-holding liberal leaders to watch and guide him. The man chosen was Alvin Wirtz, the former state senate leader and receiver for the defunct Insull Industrial Enterprises, who had recommended his friend Sam Johnson's boy Lyndon to Kleberg in 1931. As chairman of the Texas State Advisory Board of the NYA, Wirtz soon found himself in frequent meetings with young Johnson to discuss plans and projects. Before long he was flattered to discover that Johnson had adopted him as a "political daddy," to promote Johnson's future, just as the young man had adopted Wright Patman, Sam Rayburn, and Maury Maverick as his Washington political daddies.

Wirtz was a good choice as a Texas daddy because he enjoyed wielding political power behind the scenes and had no desire for public recognition. He liked being a maneuverer at state Democratic conventions, serving as a delegate at national conventions, and exerting his influence with the large German bloc vote in Texas. His frustration was that he had never been able to put any of his selected candidates either into the Governor's Mansion or into Congress.

In 1930 he thought he had a governor in Barry Miller. But this was the year that Ross "Big Fat Boy Babbitt" Sterling beat Ma Ferguson in the Democratic run-off primary. Two years later, when Sterling ran for re-election against Ma, Wirtz campaigned against both. Frequently, when Wirtz met with Lyndon Johnson on NYA matters, the conversation veered to Texas politics and Wirtz spoke of the 1932 primary contest as one that left a stench that smelled worse than Fort Worth with its odoriferous packing houses. After the Texas Election Bureau, the state's unofficial vote-counter, showed Sterling as the winner, Pa Ferguson got in touch with his crooked friends in Longview and Nacogdoches in northeast Texas and they rewrote their votes so that Ma Ferguson ended up with a state total higher than Sterling. Normally the sitting governor controlled the September state Democratic convention that affirmed or threw out the primary decisions, and Wirtz attended the state convention that year to watch Sterling reinstate himself. But Pa Ferguson came early, made promises to delegates about what he would do for them when he sat at his desk in Ma's office, and the convention named his wife as the Democratic nominee. Wirtz's abiding axiom was that no Texas election was over until the last crooks finished changing the votes in their counties.

Wirtz detested Pa Ferguson. Yet he considered it his public duty to confer with Ferguson when the run on the banks began early in 1933. Ma finally accepted Wirtz's advice on orders from her husband and declared a bank holiday, closing all Texas banks temporarily until the new Roosevelt regime in Washington could work out a federal program to save the country's jeopardized monetary system. As a lawyer, Wirtz worried that he had told Ma to do something that exceeded her authority. So he had Welly Hopkins, his successor in the state senate, push through a bill to validate her action.

"Alvin Wirtz knew how to carry buckets of bubbling acid on both shoulders without spilling a drop," said Senator Tom Connally. "He had some of the most reactionary and ignorant Texans as his law clients, and he pursued their interests ruthlessly against a lot of helpless people. On the other hand, he loved Roosevelt and the New Deal, and when he acted on his own, he was a champion of public power and federal welfare programs."

His work as an adviser to Johnson at the NYA was an example of his interest in social welfare. So was his relentless effort to establish public power benefits for the people living in the Lower Colorado River area.

Ever since 1930, when he became the receiver for the Insull private power holdings on the Lower Colorado River area centering around Austin, Wirtz had labored to convert and expand those properties through public power projects. This had required the backing of the state, and in February 1935, when Governor James V. Allred was in office, the Texas Legislature finally approved the establishment of the Lower Colorado River Authority. Only with the help of Allred, Texas' most liberal governor since Jim Hogg years back in 1891–1895, did Wirtz cross this first hurdle. The legislative sanction permitted the LCRA to use the flood waters of the Lower Colorado River in ten counties for flood control, power production, water conservation, and irrigation. But until the LCRA obtained federal money, it would remain a paper plan.

Wirtz quickly established an organization to manage the Authority. He became the general counsel and put his young friend, Ralph W. Yarborough, then a lecturer at the University of Texas Law School, on the board of directors. So at the same time that Wirtz was working with Yarborough on public conservation, he was working with Johnson on youth conservation.

Wirtz had supported Kleberg in 1931 because Mister Dick had given his word he would vote for any Congressional appropriations to develop the Lower Colorado River. However, Representative James P. "Buck" Buchanan of Brenham, Texas, was his key man in Washington, for Ol' Buck represented the Tenth Congressional District, which included Austin and surrounding counties. Buchanan's value multiplied severalfold in 1935, when Joe Byrns relinquished his post as chairman of the House Appropriations Committee to become speaker. Through seniority, Ol' Buck was suddenly elevated to the chairman's seat, and he now possessed the most powerful voice in the House in determining the federal budget. He had merely to nod, and Wirtz's dream for the Lower Colorado River would become a reality.

Buchanan had been raised during an era when federal spending except for war was considered almost un-American. Born in 1867, during the rough Reconstruction days, he came to Washington with the Woodrow Wilson regime. His colleagues at the time recalled him in his handsome Prince Albert long-tail, square-cut coat; and despite his shift to the soft collar by 1930, he was generally regarded as an old-fashioned man. He was normally cautious, said Tom Connally, except for one activity, and this was "his foolhardiness in playing poker with John Garner," considered the best poker player on Capitol Hill. He had none of the airs of the typical imperious House committee chairman. In floor debate he spoke so softly he could not be heard six feet away; and in his office, instead of portraying a forceful congressman dealing with constituents, he always sat curled up almost in a ball in his swivel chair, with his cigar shifting nervously from one side of his mouth to the other as he spoke.

When Franklin Roosevelt became President, Ol' Buck heartily approved his moves to carry out his campaign pledge to slash government spending. He applauded Roosevelt's Economy Bill of March 10, 1933, cutting government payrolls and Congressional salaries by one hundred million dollars, veterans' benefits and military pay by three hundred million dollars, and public spending programs by two hundred million dollars.

But Roosevelt changed from a cutter to a spender shortly after Congress approved the Economy Act in mid-March, and his inflationary program jarred Buchanan's long-held philosophy. Ol' Buck was suspicious of the way new alphabetical agencies exploded into being like popcorn. He did not like the roughshod manner in which the downtown crowd tried to take over the Legislative Branch, and on one occasion he added a provision to a deficiency appropriations bill that prohibited independent government agencies from supplying Congressional committees with their own employees on a part-time or leave-time basis. But he was a good soldier in supporting the President's important bills, no matter what he thought of them personally, and it was he who piloted Roosevelt's 4.8-billion-dollar work-relief appropriation through the House.

Wirtz was anxious to get four dams built on the Lower Colorado, and he did not want to wait the usual several years before the first shovelful of dirt was turned. Ordinarily he would have to make his request for money to the House Rivers and Harbors Committee, and he was certain of favorable action here because Joe Mansfield, the wheelchair-ridden congressman from Columbus, Texas, was chairman of the committee. But there was a long rigmarole to follow: surveys by the Army Engineers Corps, local hearings, and then committee hearings. Even once Mansfield's committee acted favorably, this would only authorize the project, and the process would have to be repeated at the House Appropriations Committee, which determined the amount of money to be granted to authorized projects. Nor was this all, for all of the House actions would have to be repeated in the Senate, and by then five to ten years would have disappeared.

There was a quicker way. Congress had established a Public Works Administration with a blank check appropriation of three billion three hundred million dollars in June 1933. This was a program specifically designed to revive heavy industry by spending money to construct new schools, airports, sewage and water supply systems, highways, hospitals, and other large projects which would employ a great many persons and give the steel, cement, coal, machinery, and other major industries the opportunity to sell their products. The PWA program was being run by Secretary of the Interior Harold Ickes, a man who so feared scandal and waste that he moved slower in approving projects and disbursing money than a miser.

Wirtz had determined that he wanted PWA money for the Lower Colorado River Authority, and his easiest way to get some was through Congressman Buchanan. First of all, he pointed out to Ol' Buck, the money was already appropriated, so there was no need to ask Congress for additional money. Second, the Authority had unanimously agreed to change the name of Hamilton Dam to Buchanan Dam. Hamilton Dam, which had been in the midst of construction when the Insull empire collapsed, was not just a little two-bit dam. Wirtz had gone over plans of this structure eighty miles upstream northwest of Austin with "Honest Harold" Ickes, as the President called the tight-fisted PWA administrator, and Ickes knew of its size. In fact Ickes had written that the Hamilton-Buchanan Dam would impound about a million acre-feet of water, placing it among "the biggest twelve or fifteen in the world." Of the other three dams, the largest was the Marshall Ford Dam, to be built twenty-six miles above Austin. If Buchanan could hold a secret, Wirtz told him, the name of this dam was to be changed to Mansfield Dam, in honor of the Rivers and Harbors Committee chairman. The last two dams, smaller in size, were the Austin Dam and the Roy B. Inks Dam, the latter three miles downstream past Austin.

Buchanan was convinced by Wirtz of the necessity of getting PWA money from Ickes, and he took the matter up with Roosevelt. The Presidential decision was to make an initial appropriation of twenty million dollars from PWA money, including a five-million-dollar expenditure by the Bureau of Reclamation for flood-control work.

By the beginning of 1937 about twenty-five hundred workers were employed on the construction of the Buchanan Dam, the L-shaped mammoth structure that would drain an area covering thirty-one thousand square miles. In mid-February Secretary Ickes came to Texas in the midst of a wild dust storm to dedicate the Buchanan Dam and break ground for the Marshall Ford (Mansfield) Dam. He complained about the dust and the Napoleon Suite that he occupied in the ritzy St. Anthony Hotel in San Antonio, and he commented bitterly that "the greatest pressure for public works funds came from Texas." Ol' Buck Buchanan had not made the trip to the Buchanan Dam, and worried friends who noticed he was absent on his day of days learned he was ill back in Washington. He had spent three evenings in a dentist's chair having all his teeth pulled and suffered severe chest pains afterward.

All the pieces of the jigsaw puzzle fell into place on February 23. Johnson had come to Houston on NYA business the day before, and he had stayed overnight with Uncle George at Aunt Ava's place. In the morning Uncle George went into the bathroom to shave before going to Sam Houston High, and Lyndon came in to talk to him before he also left the house. The Houston *Post* lay open on a bench, and while they talked, both suddenly stared at the top front-page headline: CONGRESSMAN J. P. BUCHANAN OF BRENHAM DIES. Old Buck had died in Washington the day before of a heart attack.

Uncle George was first to express an opinion. "You ought to run," he told Lyndon. "And I'll bet you'd win, too." Lyndon had to admit he believed Uncle George was right.

Alvin Wirtz also agreed that Johnson should run, though he was not as sure of victory. The forty-eight-year-old Wirtz had almost suffered apoplexy when he first heard about Buchanan's passing. He had been counting on Ol' Buck to get him the extra millions the Lower Colorado River Authority needed via the Congressional appropriations process. In addition, he had been talking to Buchanan to exert his committee power to push the Justice Department to put a half dozen of its best lawyers on a troublesome matter that had recently arisen. The Lower Colorado projects were being menaced by four private power companies which had brought suit to enjoin the Authority from constructing the Marshall Ford Dam.

Wirtz needed a man in Washington whom he could trust to promote with tireless energy the completion of the dams. Johnson was probably too immature at twenty-eight to be an effective congressman on important national and international issues. But he was on solid terms with key members of Congress, and he knew the ropes for dealing with the Executive agencies.

Johnson put up no argument when Wirtz insisted that he run. Wirtz had no campaign money to offer him, but he said he would guide his campaign, write his speeches, and bring pressure on local political bosses he knew. Johnson would have to put on a strenuous ten-county campaign, work night and day and weekends almost without letup.

Lady Bird was more practical when Johnson told her he planned to run for Buchanan's seat. "I went over for a talk with that wonderful man Alvin Wirtz," she said. She wanted to know what Lyndon's chances were and how much the campaign would cost.

Wirtz pointed out that before Johnson announced, he would have to quit his NYA job. If he lost, he might not get another job as good as this one from the Administration. As for his chances, they would depend primarily on who his opponents were; and there were several, Wirtz believed, who could defeat him. Blanco County, which contained Johnson City, had been removed from Kleberg's Fourteenth Congressional District and was now part of the Tenth District. There might be resentment in the other nine counties of the Tenth against a candidate whose home county was johnny-come-lately Blanco. As for the expense of running a decent campaign, "he said it would cost about ten thousand dollars just to get in the race and make a good try for it," Lady Bird quoted him. But what he had to say did not discourage her.

On February 28 Lady Bird called her father long-distance to ask him to lend her the ten thousand dollars, as an advance on her inheritance. When Minnie Patillo Taylor died in 1918, Texas community property laws awarded her three children half of her husband's estate. At that time, probate records of Marshall, Texas, in Harrison County, where Karnack lay, estimated the total inheritance under this arrangement for Lady Bird and her two older brothers—Thomas Jefferson Taylor, III, and Antonio—at $40,762.50 for 11,966.4 acres of land in Harrison County and $8,627.50 as the value of their father's "Dealer in Everything" general store in Karnack. During the 1920's, her father had paid off her two brothers but delayed doing this for Lady Bird because of her young age. He had not given Lady Bird a dowry when she married Lyndon. Instead, in 1936 he told her the time was not far distant when he would be able to pay her the inheritance coming to her through her mother's share of his holdings. It was in November of that year, their second wedding anniversary, that Lady Bird and Lyndon signed papers from her father that set a future payment of $21,000 as the full settlement of her mother's estate.

When Lady Bird called him three months later for an advance of $10,000 on the total, Taylor said he could let her have money only as a loan and not as part of her inheritance. She said she would be willing to do it on this basis and he replied, "Well, Lady, today's Sunday. I don't think I could do it before morning, about nine o'clock."

That same day Johnson resigned his NYA post and became the first to announce for Buchanan's seat. Hardly had he returned to the office the following day, Monday, March 1, to clear out his belongings when a call came from the White House. "One day Aubrey Williams, who directed the NYA, got hold of me at the White House," Thomas G. Corcoran, a

Roosevelt "Brain Truster," remembered. "Williams said, 'Tommy, you've got to get the President to make this guy Johnson lay off running for the Congressional seat down in Austin. He's my whole youth program in Texas, and if he quits I have no program down there.'" Corcoran went directly to President Roosevelt. "I told the Old Man," he said, "and he gave me orders to get this guy Johnson to lay off that House seat. I tried to find Johnson, but before I could he had quit his NYA job and filed for Congress."

The announcement of his candidacy came from Aunt Ava's living room, and he repeated it from the porch of the Johnson City house where Sam Johnson had spent so many hours discussing politics and political favors with visitors and pleaders. Almost all the four hundred residents of Johnson City came to hear their hometown boy read his short statement, and curious reporters from various newspapers in the Tenth District were on hand to talk to the first candidate for Buchanan's seat. Wirtz had insisted that Johnson publicly announce his candidacy even before Governor Jimmy Allred set the election date, because with no other opponents yet in the field he would get undiluted press coverage. Sam Johnson spoke of his immense pride in his son, though he had to be careful not to grow too excited, for he had suffered a heart attack in 1935 which had forced him to quit his job in San Marcos as a state bus inspector and return home to Johnson City.

After Johnson announced, Wirtz went to the Statehouse to push his good friend Governor Allred into Johnson's corner. However, Allred, a former professional baseball player, was just as adept in fielding political batted balls, and while he gave the impression he might favor Johnson, he said nothing. Wirtz was hardly out of Allred's office when he learned that the governor had promised to support Buchanan's widow if she ran. This almost floored Wirtz because he was aware of the potency of the sympathy vote.

Fortunately for Johnson, Mrs. Buchanan took herself out of possible contention with a public announcement on March 2. But again Wirtz grew jittery when he found out that Allred had offered to support any candidate Mrs. Buchanan named to finish her husband's term. This time she said she would not express a preference, and there was joy in the Johnson camp.

Wirtz's next bit of strategy was again an effort to jump the gun. When Allred let slip to him that he planned to announce on March 6 the date of the April special election, Wirtz pushed Johnson into making his opening campaign speech on March 5. Hurried advance planning compressed into only two days made possible a smooth show when the Johnson entourage came to San Marcos for the kickoff. By choosing his old college town and by calling Dr. Evans, Johnson was assured of a large and friendly audience who would applaud their brother alumnus.

It was obvious to Wirtz that almost all candidates would come out

strongly in support of popular President Roosevelt. So the campaign would
be essentially without issues. But Johnson would get nowhere unless he
could make voters distinguish between him and the other candidates.

The Wirtz strategy revealed itself in the San Marcos opener: Other
candidates might say they backed Roosevelt, but Johnson was the only
true supporter. "If the people of this District are for bettering the lot of
the common man," he declared at San Marcos; "if the people of this
District want to run their government rather than have a dollar man run
it for them; if the people of this District want to support Roosevelt on his
most vital issue, I want to be your congressman. But if the people of this
District don't want to support Roosevelt," he read the words of corporation
attorney and lobbyist Alvin Wirtz's ghostwritten speech, "then I'll be content to let some corporation lawyer or lobbyist represent them."

Shortly after Allred set the election date for Saturday, April 10, the
field grew cluttered with eight other candidates. For a few days Pa Ferguson
threatened to compete with the nine. But he finally decided to stay in
state politics, and the race lost a great deal of potential color.

Wirtz assessed Johnson's chances with pessimism when the final filing
date passed. At least four of the candidates were better known than he,
and anything could happen in a race with so many candidates. Nor did
Wirtz ignore the fact that Austin normally provided 40 per cent of the
ten-county vote and three candidates claimed Austin as their home town.

One candidate worrying Wirtz was C. N. Avery of Austin. Avery, who
was thirty years older than Johnson, had served in several elections as
Buchanan's campaign manager, and for five years was his secretary in
Washington. Avery had begun his campaign with handshaking tours of
Williamson and Washington Counties, and judging by the condition of
his swollen right hand, he had aroused enthusiasm there. Avery also
possessed the advantage of having Tom Nelson, the political boss in the
Round Rock area north of Austin, as his brother-in-law. "When James
Buchanan found out he was going to die," said Avery, claiming heir's
rights, "he called me to Washington and asked me to run." As for Johnson,
the youngest candidate, Avery downgraded him with the comment: "I was
serving on the Texas Highway Commission. Lyndon's father brought him
to me and wanted me to give him a job. I told him I would, but that I
thought he ought to go back to school."

Another front-runner was Merton Harris of Smithville, a former assistant
attorney general and an experienced campaigner. Four years earlier,
Buchanan had defeated him by a margin of only a few thousand votes
out of fifty thousand. Harris seldom failed to tell audiences that his wife
was the sister of the late Captain Randolph, for whom Randolph Field was
named.

Since Avery and Harris were both acknowledged admirers of President
Roosevelt, Wirtz put his strategy to work to create a difference where none

existed. He chose as his key issue the emotion-laden topic of Roosevelt's proposal to "pack" the Supreme Court, a subject getting the hottest play in newspaper headlines and editorials. It mattered not to Wirtz that Avery and Harris and three other Democratic candidates besides Johnson had declared themselves in favor of the scheme to increase the size of the Supreme Court from its current membership of nine to a new maximum of fifteen justices, in order to gain a majority of New Dealers on the Court. For every time that these five candidates said they backed the Roosevelt plan, Johnson denounced them as opponents of the plan and called himself "courageous" for being the only candidate to support it.

Of the three Democrats besides Avery and Harris who came out for the court-packing, Wirtz recognized well-liked Williamson County Judge Sam Stone as the most dangerous. Of lesser concern was Ayres K. Ross, who had run against Buchanan in 1932 and lost by thirty-four thousand to twelve thousand. Ross was running as the Townsend Plan candidate, promoting the old-age pension scheme of Dr. Francis Townsend, the "Haggard Messiah," as part of the press had labeled him. Ross had no chance, because Roosevelt's Social Security Act had taken the starch out of Townsend's high collar. Nor did Ed Waller of San Marcos, a perennial candidate who filed in every election and ran for the publicity he collected.

Only with two of the Democratic candidates did Johnson actually have a legitimate difference on the Supreme Court issue. One was state Senator Houghton Brownlee, who Wirtz believed would collect many conservative votes as well as the Ferguson support, because his campaign manager was the nephew of Pa Ferguson's closest friend. But Brownlee's total could be small because he owned a race horse breeding farm and championed legalized racing at a time when sentiment against betting on horses was running strong in Austin.

By far the stronger of the two Democratic candidates against the Court-packing proposal was Polk Shelton of Austin, an outspoken Democratic liberal who supported the New Deal social legislation and disagreed with the national Administration on the Court issue. Shelton's advantages were that he was an excellent speaker, a World War I veteran, an active leader in the American Legion, and the son of a fabled Travis County district attorney. Shelton's campaign line came out clearly in his opening speech at Taylor on March 12, when he told of his support of Roosevelt in 1932 and 1936 and denounced his Court-packing rivals as "Me too" men who practiced "rubber-stamp statesmanship."

Shelton had another advantage that infuriated Wirtz. Governor Allred had assigned several of his aides to guide him, and it was apparent that Allred had let his own opposition to the Court-packing plan put him in Shelton's corner. When confronted with evidence that his insurance commissioner and others were busy in Shelton's behalf, Allred called this nonsense, though he acknowledged that Polk Shelton had been instrumental in his own victory in the gubernatorial race of 1934. Wirtz had chosen

Claude Wild as the front man for Johnson's campaign, and Allred told reporters that what his aides might be doing for Shelton in their private capacity was more than counterbalanced by the fact that "Claude Wild, who has been very active in both my campaigns for governor, is managing the campaign of Lyndon Johnson."

Wirtz knew that Johnson's youth would play an important role in determining his outcome in the contest, and Wirtz gambled that his youth and enthusiasm were assets. So while the other candidates went about their campaigns in a deliberate fashion, Johnson entered the month-long contest on the run and never stopped for breath. Campaign aides and reporters on his trail called him "the Blanco Blitz," and for good reason. From daybreak to midnight he raced through towns and villages, shaking hands along Main Streets, popping into stores to ask for votes, and passing out handbills which proclaimed him "big enough for the job, young enough to get it done." The handbills also characterized him as possessing "a dynamic personality who knows Washington and can get things done for the District."

There were also the two hundred meetings where he spoke from platforms and atop boxes. Proudest of all was Rebekah Johnson, who sat beaming on the stands while he ripped the squadron of opponents with sneering sarcasm and painted a glowing picture of his own qualifications. Lady Bird was too shy to feel at ease on the stand or to campaign for Lyndon. "I did not have the gumption to share in it," she later recalled that campaign, "although in 1937, a wife didn't campaign," she added in justification of her inactivity.

The speeches pounded away on the agreed-upon theme. "I didn't have to hang back like a steer on the way to the dipping vat," he told an applauding audience. "I'm for the President. When he calls on me for help I'll be where I can give him a quick lift, not out in the woodshed practicing a quick way to duck." When an occasional questioner brought up the fact that Colonel Avery, Judge Stone, Merton Harris, Townsend's man Ross, and Ed Waller also favored the Court-packing bill, Johnson called this untrue and labeled his collective opponents as "eight in the dark."

Wirtz's stroke of genius went far beyond giving Johnson a false issue within the Tenth Congressional District. He extended it all the way to Washington by his effort to seek recognition for Johnson as President Roosevelt's personal and only defender in the election. Broadsides were rushed to the White House to show that Johnson was fighting a lonely battle for the President's "Court-unpacking" bill, as the young candidate was calling it in speeches. This might prove to be the most important election that year, said Johnson-oriented reporters, because it provided the first test of popular sentiment on Roosevelt's Court proposal. Wirtz had first developed this line in preparing Johnson's kick-off speech at San Marcos, and copies were available for Administration officials. "The eyes of the nation are focused upon us," Johnson asserted in that speech. "This national issue, which you will vote on, is commanding the keen attention of the people throughout the country."

Any check by White House aides would have revealed that outside of the Tenth District the rest of the country was oblivious of that campaign. But Roosevelt was feeling the effects of major Democratic Congressional opposition for the first time, and he was eager for friends, no matter how lowly placed. He had good reason for his anger with the Supreme Court, and he had expected no real opposition from Congress, especially after his almost total victory over Alf Landon in November 1936.

The "Horse and Buggy" Court, as he denounced the judiciary, had made mincemeat of his New Deal. The "Nine Old Men" who tottered to the Bench had begun their dirty work by declaring the Connally "hot-oil" act unconstitutional in January 1935. Then the following May, the Court invalidated the NRA and the Frazier-Lemke Farm Mortgage Moratorium Act and barred the President from firing a commissioner on the Federal Trade Commission. Next, in January 1936, the Court knocked out the AAA by deciding it could not restrict farm production and abolished the Bituminous Coal Commission, which Roosevelt had designed to halt overproduction in the mines and regulate labor relations.

A man like Roosevelt could not be expected to accept this wrecking of his New Deal with equanimity. And in February 1937, when he declared war on the Supreme Court in order to change its complexion from reactionary to liberal, he expected to find Congress behind him. Therefore, when Vice President Garner, the two senators from Texas, and liberal senators from other states called Roosevelt's proposed tampering an interference with the independence of the Judiciary, he was stunned. However, his Dutch blood would not let him backtrack, even though there were broad hints from a few members of the Court that Roosevelt should drop his plan because the Court would change its view of the New Deal legislation.

All this was suddenly injected into the Texas Tenth Congressional District race in March 1937 when Postmaster General James A. "Jim" Farley came to Texas supposedly to dedicate some new post offices. After addressing the Texas Legislature and promoting Roosevelt's Court scheme, Farley held a news conference. Asked about the special election in the Tenth District, Farley replied that he expected President Roosevelt's "champion to land on top." The Austin papers the following day carried Farley's quote in a three-column ad that claimed a vote for Lyndon Johnson "was a vote for Roosevelt and his program."

Merton Harris, who was as much behind the Court bill as Johnson, fired off a bitter telegram to Farley and demanded an explanation. Back came the reply: "Am not taking sides in the Congressional race." But this hardly erased the benefit given Johnson by Big Jim's news conference comment.

Other solicited Administration comments also gained newspaper attention. Aubrey Williams, head of the NYA, gave a government-agency type
of praise by declaring Johnson "one of the ablest state directors we have
ever had." A stronger statement came from Elliott Roosevelt, the second
oldest of the President's four sons, who was running a radio network in
Texas with money he had borrowed from the head of the A & P grocery
chain. Elliott publicly wished Johnson "a glorious victory" in his race. An
effort to win Mrs. Roosevelt's endorsement when she went through Texas
in March failed. Instead of commenting on the Congressional contest, she
told stories about her Uncle Teddy Roosevelt's son Quentin, who once
put his pony on a White House elevator and on another occasion climbed
out on a White House flagpole and lowered the flag to half-mast.

When April came, the Blanco Blitz stepped up his dashing pace.
Jesse Kellam, who had succeeded him as Texas NYA director, Willard
Deason, Sherman Birdwell, and other old college and NYA friends
were spending time whipping up support for him among young voters who
had received NYA aid. Rebekah Johnson was calling friends to make
certain they would vote, and Sam Johnson tried hard to remain calm.
Wirtz sought to gain additional support in Austin by asking Mayor Tom
Miller, who favored Roosevelt's Court bill, to speak out for Lyndon. But
Mayor Miller was committed to another candidate, though he said he
would vote for Johnson. Wirtz also introduced Lyndon to Mrs. Charles
Marsh, wife of a successful newspaper publisher, whose chain included
two Austin papers. Mrs. Marsh was so impressed with the young man
that she induced her husband to support him.

The election would come on April 10, and Wirtz planned Johnson's
final rally as the campaign's climax the night before the voting. However,
as that last week began, Johnson developed stomach pains. It became
an effort to denounce the "eight in the dark," and he could barely speak
out his sole foreign affairs plank, that he "would not cast a vote for participation or intervention in a foreign war."

Two days before the election, his pains were so sharp that he had
to be rushed to an Austin hospital. The emergency operation that removed
his appendix also removed him from his campaign, and he lay in a
hospital bed while he listened to a stand-in deliver his final campaign
speech over the radio. "Seems to me Lyndon had been complaining about
that appendix for some time," said a friend. "But this sure was a good
time to have it out—at least as far as the publicity was concerned."

The vote was surprisingly light, less than half the normal fifty thousand
total. But there was never any doubt who would win once the first
returns were announced. Wirtz's strategy had paid off handsomely. Johnson's home county, Blanco, gave him more than twice the total of his
combined opponents. Austin, where the NYA was centered, also gave him
a large vote. And when the District's preliminary total was announced
over radio, Johnson had twice the votes of Judge Stone, his nearest rival.

Yet even though he was elected, he had received only 27 per cent of the total votes cast.

"My darling boy," his mother wrote him when his victory was assured, "Beyond 'Congratulations Congressman,' what can I say to my dear son in this hour of triumphant success? In this as in all the many letters I have written you there is the same theme: I love you; I believe in you; I expect great things of you. Your election compensates for the heartache and disappointment I experienced as a child when my dear father [Joseph Wilson Baines] lost the race you have just won. How happy it would have made my precious noble father to know that the first born of his first born would achieve the position he desired."

PART TWO
FDR's Boy

Chapter 17

IT WAS BENEATH the dignity of the President of the United States to equate the correctness of his course with the election of a twenty-eight-year-old Texan to the House. But Franklin Roosevelt did just this in the spring of 1937.

Roosevelt was not a man who could abruptly end a fight when the other side indicated its willingness to capitulate. After he had scathingly attacked the Supreme Court in February 1937, its nine concerned members agreed privately to end their opposition to the New Deal. As one observer put it: "A switch in time saves nine."

On March 29, in the midst of Johnson's campaign, the Supreme Court began its quaking surrender to the President. That day the Court reversed itself on the constitutionality of state minimum wage laws to protect women, approved a rewritten Frazier-Lemke Farm Mortgage Moratorium Act, and the Railroad Labor Act, which provided for mediation of disputes and collective bargaining on the railroads. Then on April 12 the Court upheld the Wagner Labor Relations Act, permitting free elections on union representation and secret bargaining votes by employees, and barring management from engaging in "unfair labor practices." Chief Justice Charles Evans Hughes also passed word along to the White House that elderly reactionary Justice Willis Van Devanter would retire, giving Roosevelt his first opportunity to put a man on the Court.

Yet despite the Supreme Court's capitulation, Roosevelt would not abandon his plan to pack the Court to assure himself of its continued submissiveness. Many of his New Deal supporters in Congress expected him to go on to other matters now that the New Deal legislation would no longer be declared unconstitutional. But Roosevelt proved adamant about his Court bill, and an enormous battle took shape between him and prominent members of the Senate and House. Roosevelt's ire was now directed toward Congress, and he put in motion a foolish attempt to "purge" his Court-packing opponents in the next year's Democratic primaries.

In the midst of his early fight with Congress, Roosevelt soon felt exhausted, and he went to Texas at the beginning of May for ten days of fishing in the Gulf of Mexico. While he fished for tarpon from the deck of the Presidential yacht, the U.S.S. *Potomac,* temporary White House headquarters were established at the Hotel Galvez, a hundred yards from the Gulf at Galveston. Here came reports that Senator Tom Connally's presentation to the Senate Judiciary Committee of an anti-Court-packing petition signed by twenty-five thousand Texans was a telling blow against the plan. Mayor Tom Miller of Austin, Wirtz's close friend, had been sent to Washington to offset the Connally petition. To his claim before the committee that Lyndon Johnson's victory proved that the people of Texas favored the President's bill, committee opponents sneeringly commented that Johnson's success was based instead on "the large number of federal grants to the Tenth District."

When Roosevelt read Miller's statement, it buttressed his fallacious belief that young Johnson had been the sole pro-Court-bill candidate among the nine who ran. Apparently he missed another story in *The New York Times* which reported the appearance of fifty anti-Court-bill Texans before the committee. They insisted that Johnson's victory had nothing to do with the Court bill, and as proof, several who came from Austin said they had voted for him.

On May 2, when Governor Jimmy Allred flew to Port Aransas to visit Roosevelt aboard the *Potomac,* the President knew full well that Allred's support of the New Deal ended at the entrance door to the Supreme Court Chamber. He permitted Allred to go through the protocol routine of welcoming him to Texas. Then to emphasize how he thought about things, he told Allred he planned to end his vacation on May 11, and he asked him to be sure to bring his true Texas champion—that newly elected Congressman—to meet him when his ship docked.

By the time Johnson and Allred flew to Galveston in the early morning hours of May 11, Johnson had not only recovered from his operation but from the two-week enforced recuperation in a hospital bed. He had lost several pounds from his skinny frame, and the new suit he bought for his Presidential meeting made him look like a beanpole draped in black. Both Sam and Rebekah Johnson were understandably proud that their son was to meet a person whose name was mentioned with awe at home. Lady Bird, who had not been invited, was even more excited than the Johnsons. Just a few years before, when Lyndon worked for Kleberg, there were several occasions when she had hung around outside the black iron fence at the White House with her camera in hopes of catching a glimpse of the President. And now Lyndon was actually to meet him.

Johnson stepped onto the Galveston dock determined to do more than shake hands with Roosevelt, drawl out the Hill Country greeting of "Howdy," and then fade away. When Allred introduced him to the President, he immediately attempted to make instant friends. He used a warm, familiar tone as though the two were jolly equals, referred to top national politicians by their first names or nicknames, asked personal questions about Roosevelt's family, and began drawing Roosevelt out on his fishing luck.

Instead of staring at Johnson as though he were mad, Roosevelt enjoyed talking to this cocky young Texan. Yes, the fishing was pretty good—he had caught two tarpon, one of which weighed ninety pounds and was almost five feet long. How would Lyndon like to join him in the dockside ceremonies and sit next to him in the open car on the way to the railroad station?

A front-page photo in the next day's papers across the nation showed Roosevelt shaking hands with Johnson, with Allred standing between them. Both Allred and Johnson wore garish orchids pinned to their lapels. In the ceremony ashore, Mayor Levi of Galveston formally welcomed the President to his fair city and Governor Allred presented him with a new fishing rod. A photographer snapped a picture of Roosevelt in the car with his gift fishing rod held upright and a grinning Johnson at his side.

Once the car made its triumphant way past cheering crowds to the railroad siding, Roosevelt asked Johnson to come along on the Presidential train as far as Fort Worth. There was a stop at Houston where, Uncle George later told Lyndon, he was ready to burst with pride on learning that his nephew was with the President. There were crowds along the right of way, and their enthusiasm gave Johnson his first insider's view of the great love of the people for their President.

A major stop came at College Station, near Bryan, on the campus of Texas A. & M. Although Elliott Roosevelt had never gone to college, as a personal favor to his father Allred had named Elliott to the board of governors of Texas A. & M. When the Presidential train stopped at the campus, Johnson learned that local rumor had it that the President had come to speak here in order to further his son's political ambitions. One story was that Roosevelt had promised to appoint Allred to the Federal bench, when his term expired, in exchange for his support of Elliott to become lieutenant governor of Texas. Johnson met his first Roosevelt son at this stop, and he discovered that he and Elliott were the same height, six feet, three inches. Elliott's size drew a laugh from the crowd when the President referred to him as "my little boy."

Afterward, when the train pulled out for Fort Worth, Johnson remembered that the President was especially interested in the Navy, having served as Assistant Secretary of the Navy during the Wilson Administration. On the spot, Johnson peppered him with questions about American warships and expressed his own interest in American sea might. This line of talk was rewarding, said Johnson, because Roosevelt told him, "I can always use a good man to help out with naval matters in Congress." Then when Fort Worth hove into view and Roosevelt began his good-by to Johnson, he suddenly reached for a sheet of paper and scribbled a telephone number on it. "Here's a telephone number," he said, handing Johnson the paper. "When you get to Washington, call it and ask for Tom. Tell him what we've talked about."

Lyndon left for Washington from Austin that same day, and Sam Johnson, though pale and weak from his heart ailment, accompanied him to the train station. Sam reminisced about his old friend, Wright Patman, talked about his integrity and his staunch liberal stand, and advised his son: "When you have a doubt about how to vote on a bill, wait for the second roll call and then vote with Wright." Later Lyndon inscribed a photograph of himself to Patman, paraphrasing his father's words, with: "When in doubt vote with Wright—Daddy." Before the train pulled out, Sam Johnson climbed two of the stairs of the railroad car and kissed his son proudly on the lips.

When Johnson walked into the House of Representatives to begin his Congressional service on May 13, 1937, he could measure the distance he had come in a short time by the fact that he was now the "colleague" of Mister Dick Kleberg, Wright Patman, Maury Maverick, and Sam Rayburn. Speaker Joe Byrns had died during Johnson's time in Austin with the NYA, and Bill Bankhead of Alabama was now speaker, with Sam Rayburn as majority leader.

Bankhead swore Johnson into office. Then the national wireservice photographers took their picture. Bankhead placed a hand on Johnson's shoulder and told the reporters they were looking at the "youngest member of Congress." Luther Johnson of Texas, in the House since 1923, expressed his displeasure because he could no longer be designated on roll calls and in debate as "Johnson from Texas."

Not even his publicity as a "Roosevelt boy" helped Johnson when it came to getting a high-priority office. Freshmen members were shunted up to the fifth floor of the Old House Office Building, and Johnson found his new home was Room 504. Another congressman commented on the fifth floor: "In that attic you're about as far removed from what's going on as it's possible to get in Washington."

Almost as soon as Lyndon Johnson walked into Room 504, quarters he was to occupy for twelve years, he put in a telephone call to the White House and asked to speak to "Tom." This turned out to be Thomas G. Corcoran, the short, ebullient Irishman who had called him in Austin just two months earlier to ask him not to run for Congress. "Tommy the Cork," as the President had dubbed the coauthor of the Public Utility Holding Company Act and his favorite accordion player, had been expecting Johnson's call. On the President's return from his Gulf fishing trip, he had spoken erroneously about the young man who was so interested in the Navy and who had defied so many local political leaders by running alone among nine candidates in favor of the Court-packing bill. Corcoran was impressed with the speed with which Johnson had added himself to the list of Roosevelt protégés. "The Boss met Lyndon in

Galveston and invited him to ride across the state in his train. That was all it took—one train ride," Corcoran said in admiration. "Lyndon was an operator."

Corcoran told Johnson that he had an important friend in the White House and to expect a good committee assignment. Part of this comment was clearly illustrated not long afterward when Representative Fred Vinson of Kentucky, a power on the House Ways and Means Committee and later Chief Justice of the Supreme Court, took Johnson aside one afternoon on the House floor. The House Ways and Means Committee wrote tax legislation, but Democratic members of the committee had an extra function of determining the House committees on which freshman Democratic Representatives would be placed.

Vinson, who resembled a sad camel, told Johnson, "Young man, I'm indebted to you for a good dinner and an excellent conversation." Johnson said that Vinson then went on to explain, "I was invited to the White House for dinner, and the President was, as always, a most delightful host. I kept wondering just what it was he wanted from me. I knew it was something. Finally, he said casually—oh, very casually—'Fred, there's a fine young man just come to the House. Fred, you know that young fellow, Lyndon Johnson? I think he would be a great help on Naval Affairs.' He meant the Naval Affairs Committee, you know." Fred Vinson added that the Ways and Means Committee Democrats would put him on the Naval Affairs Committee, chairmaned by Carl Vinson of Georgia, no relation to Fred Vinson. So Johnson became a "junior legislative admiral."

With Lady Bird soon to arrive in Washington, Johnson was suddenly confronted with the problem of renting an apartment for them. The burgeoning of government agencies, a lack of construction during the depression, and the influx of tens of thousands of additional employees into the Washington area had resulted in a serious shortage of apartments. But Johnson was fortunate. The day after he was sworn in, Representative Jennings Randolph of West Virginia, who remembered him as a doorkeeper in the Kleberg years, sat down next to him in the House chamber. Randolph had watched Johnson's swearing-in the previous day, and he asked Johnson if he had found a decent place to live. When Johnson shook his head, Randolph told him, "I know a couple from Charleston who are living here but are being transferred to Pittsburgh by the Social Security Board. They asked me if I knew someone who wanted to rent their furnished apartment."

"Lyndon grew wildly excited," said Randolph. "He demanded that I give him the Ourbachers' address, and he ran out of the chamber immediately to rent it. There was a four-poster canopy bed in the apartment, and when Lyndon became famous the Ourbachers called it 'the Johnson Bed.' "

Johnson's salary as a congressman was ten thousand dollars a year. This came to eight hundred and thirty-three dollars a month, a substantial sum for the depression year 1937. Lady Bird said, however, that she and Lyndon had agreed to repay the ten-thousand-dollar loan from her father at the rate of five hundred dollars a month, and this put them back on the same standard of living they had known when Lyndon worked for Kleberg. But this situation soon eased, for Aunt Effie, who began spending about half of each year with them, paid many of their bills. In addition, one of Lady Bird's friends laughingly recalled, the young congressman's wife augmented their funds by picking up empty Coca-Cola and milk bottles she found in the street and returning them to grocery stores where she collected deposits on them.

In the summer of 1937 Lyndon's joy in being a congressman was severely dampened when his mother sent word that his father had suffered another major heart attack. Instead of putting him into an Austin hospital, Rebekah Johnson said that Daddy had been taken to the hospital at Temple, in Bell County, one hundred and fifty miles north.

Johnson waited until the first session of the Seventy-fifth Congress adjourned on August 21 before going to Texas. By the time he reached Temple, it was evident from the oxygen tent surrounding Sam Johnson's bed and the grimly solicitous faces of the nurses that his condition was precarious. However, spending much time with sick people made Lyndon queasy, and after a short visit with his father he returned to Austin for talks with Alvin Wirtz, Mayor Tom Miller, and E. H. Perry, his latest enthusiastic political "Daddy" on the local front. Then he proceeded with some fence-building among lesser political figures in his District before driving back to the Temple hospital. Here, Sam Johnson was talking as though he knew his end was near.

When he celebrated his sixtieth birthday on October 11, 1937, Sam begged his son to take him out of the hospital and back to the Hill Country. Lyndon argued that he needed an oxygen tent and none was available in Stonewall or Hye. But his father pleaded with him to bring his clothes from the hospital room closet and help him dress. "Lyndon, bring my breeches to me," he demanded weakly. "I'm going back to that little old house in the Hills where the people know when you're sick and care when you die."

Lyndon finally agreed to take him to the Austin house he now rented from his late opponent, state Senator Brownlee. Here Sam seemed to improve. Then only two weeks later, on October 23, he died.

The funeral was held the next day, on Sunday, and Little Sam's remains were laid to rest in the family graveyard near Big Sam and Eliza Johnson. Rebekah recalled that his favorite poem was "The House by the Side of the Road," and that he was a man incapable of bearing a grudge. His friend, Lon Smith, paid him final homage with a graveside talk that included the lines: "He was a man; take him for all and all; I shall not look upon his like again."

Lyndon endured such agonies at his father's passing that Lady Bird made a note to keep him away from burial scenes in the future. "Lyndon suffers so at funerals," she said.

But he was so much the politician as well as the sufferer that he could not refrain from making some small personal use of his father's death. "My daddy's last words were, 'Son, back up the President,' " Sam Johnson's boy told a reporter.

Chapter 18

B EFORE HE LEFT Texas to take his seat in Congress, Lyndon Johnson had issued a manifesto to his constituents, telling them what they should expect from him in Washington. "I'm not going to get up and make a lot of speeches this first term," he said. "I don't believe I can set the world on fire and go up there and reform the United States of America right away."

For a Texan who liked to talk, Johnson was extremely quiet in his early years in the House chamber. On May 26, 1937, he inserted an expected eulogy of Ol' Buck Buchanan, his predecessor, into the Appendix of the *Congressional Record*. This was accomplished without a single word being spoken aloud on the House floor. Then in 1938, he had floor clerks insert in the Appendix a copy of a speech he had given over radio in Austin on housing and a Jefferson-Jackson Day speech by his friend Welly Hopkins, now risen in the world as a special assistant to Attorney General Homer Cummings.

But this reticence to speak on the House floor was of no consequence, for the measurement of his true effectiveness came elsewhere.

His operating motto was: "Nothing is too good for the voters of the Tenth District"—and he put in long days to prove it. Any town wanting a new post office building found a champion in Room 504 of the Old House Office Building. Postmaster General Big Jim Farley was readily available on this score. Or perhaps there were WPA projects or money from other federal programs that Tenth District towns desired. Harry Hopkins, the WPA chief, had been alerted by the White House to consider Johnson among his special friends.

When a constituent wanted to get a private bill through Congress to pay a damage claim against a federal agency, or when Tenth District projects needed new Congressional appropriations, Johnson could be seen rushing about Capitol Hill to lobby with key congressmen who determined the fate of such matters. Senator Richard Russell of Georgia said that the young man from Texas pushed and prodded him personally to have the Senate Appropriations Committee boost the money grant on specific appropriations to a higher level than that approved by the House.

On those occasions when he failed to win satisfaction through direct confrontation with his colleagues, Johnson worked through their staff aides, whom he had known from the good old Dodge Hotel days. Said one of those friends, "Johnson was a real pusher. He was maybe a little cocky and sometimes made people sore, but he got things done. He was a sharp trader, and he knew how to get what he wanted."

The factor giving him immediate prestige on Capitol Hill was the widely spread report that he was a special favorite of the President. His meeting with President Roosevelt at Galveston, the newspaper pictures taken there, and the story of his ride with Roosevelt to Fort Worth (Johnson added to the length of the ride by claiming to have gone all the way to Washington with F.D.R.) were worth at least a dozen years of seniority on the Hill.

"In Washington, the word had gone out: 'Be nice to this boy because he is the President's protégé,'" said Tommy the Cork Corcoran. When Johnson was invited to a White House Sunday breakfast of scrambled eggs with Maury Maverick and the President's young cousin, Joe Alsop, who had come to Washington to write a column for the New York *Herald Tribune,* the Tenth District Texan was the envy of older New Deal Democrats who never got this invitation. Just as at college, where faculty members believed he had influence over Dr. Evans, so congressmen believed he had an inside track with the President of the United States. Because of this, said Corcoran, "he found other congressmen were asking him for favors, and his prestige on Capitol Hill was sky high."

Johnson did not orient himself entirely to the Legislative Branch, Corcoran noted, but also worked hard to spread his prestige and power among Executive agencies. "He deliberately cultivated all the young New Dealers—the young men on the White House staff and the young lawyers around town like myself," said Corcoran. "Gradually these guys found they were working for Lyndon Johnson. They'd carry his requests to the President or to the agency heads. He got more projects and more money for his District than any other man in Congress," added "Baron Munchausen" Corcoran, who was emerging as Johnson's chief propagandist and promoter.

Johnson could handle much more work than most of his House colleagues because he visualized every day as a special crash program. Keeping current was the key to the way he managed his office. On the first day he got off the Old House Office Building elevator and approached 504, he said, he found a staggering pile of thirteen bulging mail sacks outside the door. They only served to reinforce his view that if work were not handled immediately, it would soon swamp him.

As in the NYA, he soon gained a reputation as a slave driver with his help. He kept his crew working evenings and weekends, and he had blistering words for those who failed to measure up to his standards. "The strangest part was that no one quit or told him off, no matter how he overworked or bullyragged them," a Congressional colleague said. On one occasion Johnson told a new employee to call a government agency about a request from a constituent. The man did, and a few hours later Johnson came to his desk and asked for the result. "The thing is settled," said the aide, "because they insisted they couldn't do what you wanted."

Johnson's face turned livid with outrage. "I didn't ask you to get me a negative answer!" he screamed. "Call them back. Say that I want this done for certain and get an affirmative answer."

Worriedly, the man called the agency again. But when the official who had rejected the claim came on, Johnson's man snapped in his boss's peremptory tone, "Congressman Johnson will be satisfied with nothing less than affirmative action on his request."

The official agreed with little argument. "From then on," said Johnson's employee, "I concentrated on getting affirmative results, not negative."

The names of Johnson's office help had a familiar ring, for he needed old and tried employees whom he knew he could drive as hard as he drove himself. He hired Sherman Birdwell, his college friend and NYA aide, as his secretary in June 1937, at twenty-seven hundred dollars a year. Then in August 1938, he replaced Birdwell with Gene Latimer, his Sam Houston High debater, paying him Birdwell's salary. But he paid Luther Jones, his other debater, only eleven hundred a year. When Mister Dick Kleberg dropped Lyndon's brother, Sam Houston Johnson, and cut off his salary of thirty-nine hundred dollars a year, Lyndon put Sam to work as his office greeter at seventeen hundred and forty dollars a year. Sam's salary was paid by the House Administration instead of the office funds allotted his older brother. For a time, Birdwell and brother Sam moved into a three-bedroom apartment with Lyndon and Lady Bird and shared expenses. Luther Jones had to double as Lady Bird's escort to plays at Washington's National Theater, while Carroll Leach, a second-line debater at Sam Houston High, was put on Lyndon's payroll in the second-line role of "valet and driver."

Lyndon also found a job for his sister Rebekah at the Library of Congress, and he made free use of his mother, who wanted to keep occupied now that Sam Johnson was gone. Mrs. Johnson was frequently helpful in doing research on Texas history. Once when he had to speak to Texans of Bohemian extraction, he asked her, "Mama, tell me what I ought to say." She prepared a summary several sheets long dealing with the history of

Bohemian settlements in Texas and short biographies of their outstanding leaders who had come from this western Czechoslovakian province.

Despite his youth and lack of seniority, Johnson's approach to his job made him a far more effective congressman for his constituents than Buchanan. Some of Johnson's friends compared the way he ran his office business to the operation of a retail store. When a constituent-customer entered and wanted something, the staff's job was to satisfy the customer with the least possible delay. Those who wrote in were in the "mail-order" end of the business. One time Johnson received a letter from a man in Bastrop County who complained angrily that he had been trying for years without success to collect on his claim at the Veterans Administration. Johnson replied by return mail that he was looking into the matter.

On each day that followed, he sent the man a franked letter relating the progress he was making with the leviathan agency. The VA chiefs had no rest from his bombardment of demanding phone calls. Finally, five days after the Bastrop County man's letter came in, Johnson reported to him that a check was on its way. All this was not kept quiet, for Johnson leaked it in detail to Texas reporters who wrote stories about the "can-do" congressman.

Johnson worked hard to cultivate Texas editors and reporters, for he knew the good or harm they could do him. One of his press friends was Sam Fore, editor of the paper at Floresville, Texas, south of the Tenth District. Floresville lay in Kleberg's District, and Johnson had originally made instant friends with Sam in order to gain support for Mister Dick when he worked for him. In 1938 Fore asked Johnson for a favor in return. Sam knew a bright boy in Floresville who reminded him of Johnson in his manner, approach and background. The boy's name was John Connally, and he came from a large, poor family. Sam said he would consider it a great favor if Johnson could help Connally find employment so that the twenty-one-year-old lad could complete work on his law degree at the University of Texas.

Johnson wrote to Jesse Kellam, who had replaced him as Texas NYA director, to find a spot for Connally. Kellam did so. Then in November 1939, Johnson brought Connally to Washington to be his secretary at twenty-six hundred dollars a year. Just two months later he raised him to thirty-nine hundred, but dropped him to three thousand and eighty dollars seven months later.

One of his father's remarks that Johnson often quoted was: "Lyndon, you're going to have the friends you are." This was proved several times during Johnson's career, but it was never more obvious than in Connally's case. Like Johnson, John was brash, talkative, homey, scheming, and he could be ruthless. People noticed that he had Johnson's facial expressions, slouched like him, and possessed his dramatics. After a time, they even sounded alike.

The result was that Johnson adopted Connally as his first protégé, after almost putting Gene Latimer and Luther Jones in that category. His sponsorship of Connally would lead in time to his appointment as Secretary of the Navy and to his election as governor of Texas. For the first time Johnson found he had an employee who was not averse to criticizing him when he thought he deserved it. This criticism ranged from the way he handled political issues to the way he shook hands.

"John Connally taught me how to shake hands," Johnson once admitted. He said he had been a finger grabber until Connally told him he would make a better impression if he took full grasp of the other person's hand and pressed it hard. While Johnson was always careful to praise Connally in public, Connally was not as discreet. On one occasion he dissected Johnson in this fashion: "In some ways he is unlettered. . . . Not the most well-read. . . . At times he can be almost brusque and rude, but is always determined, always firm, working for perfection."

Lyndon's team also included Lady Bird. One of his first orders after he won the election was that she memorize the names of every precinct captain in the Tenth District. In Washington it became her duty to chaperone visitors from his District to historic sites. She guided some through the Capitol, took dozens of children on tours of the Smithsonian Institution, where the big attraction was Lindbergh's small one-seater plane, and rode alongside the Potomac to Mount Vernon. Lady Bird said she stopped counting after her visits to Mount Vernon passed the two-hundred mark. Once she took a group to Mount Vernon in a snowstorm, and when she found the gates closed she overcame her shyness and took on her husband's demanding tone. Employees who recognized her from her many previous visits not only opened the gates, but permitted her and the other Texans to roam about the third floor of George and Martha Washington's home, normally off-limits to tourists. "Y'all come back soon, hear now!" she told groups of visitors on parting.

Lyndon also asked her to keep a scrapbook of his newspaper clippings. In time she had more than thirty large, leather-bound volumes. In addition, he gave her a movie camera and requested her to take pictures that would be useful to him in future campaigns. She gained valuable experience as a cameraman when Eleanor Roosevelt came from the White House one noon for a luncheon in her honor at the Congress Club, an organization for wives and daughters of congressmen. Following this thrilling hour photographing the First Lady, Lady Bird went to Texas at Lyndon's suggestion to make a "pictorial story" for Tenth District voters about the problems in the District, such as slums, drought, and floods, and what he was doing in Congress to solve them.

Lyndon once tried to justify his continuous rush and total immersion in his job and his harsh treatment of office employees by telling Lady Bird, "Every job I've had is bigger than I am, and I have to work twice as hard as the next man to do it." But those who knew him said he was entirely devoid of humility. It was simply a case of possessing enormous

energy, open-end ambition, and a general dissatisfaction with the way subordinates worked. Said Lady Bird, "Lyndon was always prodding me to
look better, learn more, work harder. He always expects more of you than
you think you are really mentally or physically capable of putting out. It
is really very stimulating. It is also very tiring."

She called him "an exhausting man to keep up with. . . . Lyndon is a
great hand at saying what he wants and then expecting me to implement
it." He expected her to handle all the small details of his existence. Her
friends said that when they visited her, Lyndon "would rush in from another room and ask, 'Bird, where's this?' or 'Bird, where's that?' and she
knew personally where everything was." It was her job to see that his
shoes were shined, his cigarette lighter filled, and his clothes laid out in
the morning. On the other hand, she said, "Lyndon is a little incensed if I
want help on trivial things."

One of Lyndon's continuing projects was to "redo" her. Some who
knew Lady Bird at this time said that she was a "tacky" dresser. Lyndon
set out to remodel her. He insisted that she wear bright lipstick and avoid
full skirts and low-heeled shoes. He made her cut her long hair and get
rid of thick-weave clothes—"I don't like 'horse-blanket' suits," he told
her. His favorite color of cloth for her was "salmon," and he would not
let her wear what he called "muley colors," the dull grays and browns.
When he found that even when she bought clothes of his favorite color
her style sense displeased him, he began the habit of buying clothes for
her.

Only on a single issue did she best him. Lady Bird desperately wanted to
live in a house of her own. In five years of married life she could count
ten apartments they had rented, and she wanted no more of this type of
existence, despite his insistence that he liked apartment-living.

When she began house-hunting, he told her pointedly that it would
not look good back home if word got out among voters that he owned
property in Washington. However, she ignored him and continued her
search. Finally, she found three houses she could live with, and narrowed
this down to the house she wanted off Connecticut Avenue in northwest
Washington at 4921 Thirtieth Place. Lyndon and John Connally were
discussing political business one day when she burst in with the story of
the eight-room, two-story, brick colonial house she had decided they
should buy.

After she finished her description, he turned back to Connally to continue their talk. This so infuriated her that she cried out, "I've lived out of
a suitcase ever since we've been married. I have no home to look forward
to, I have no children to look forward to and I have nothing to look forward to but another election."

Lyndon looked at Connally and said, "John, what do you think I ought
to do about that house?"

"I would buy it," Connally counseled.

He weakened further when Aunt Effie agreed to make the down-payment. "Then she just wrote in her will that this was an advance on what she planned to leave me," said Lady Bird.

Even so, Lyndon would not give in without a struggle. He refused to accept the owner's "rock-bottom" selling price, and for a time endangered the transaction. But finally the owner agreed to meet Johnson's demand that he go two thousand dollars below his rock-bottom figure, and the Johnsons became the owners of a sixteen-thousand-dollar structure.

Chapter 19

WHILE ALMOST ALL other members of Congress were content to gain power through the usual process of committee seniority, Lyndon Johnson was too impatient to wait the years required. Instead, he based his quicker reach for power on the device of the "political Daddy," that he perfected.

Foremost among his daddies was, of course, President Roosevelt. The basis of the President's fondness for him, the false belief that Johnson had been the only candidate in the special election to support his Court-packing bill, had provided the young Texan with an open door to the White House. "He could always get to the President," said Tommy Corcoran with admiration. And if he could not reach the President on his first call, he could always reach Corcoran, or Jimmy Roosevelt, the President's oldest son, whom reporters had labeled the Crown Prince, or Grace Tully, the Chief Executive's assistant secretary, whom insiders called Duchess.

Because of his reputation as a Roosevelt protégé, Johnson was *ipso facto* regarded as a 100 per cent New Dealer. He was not put to the test of voting on the Roosevelt Court-packing bill, for Senate action had tabled it by the overwhelming vote of 70 to 21. But two months to the day after he took his oath, he had the problem of supporting or opposing the President. The Federal Land Banks, which Hoover had established to lend money to farm owners, had charged 4 per cent interest. In 1935, with Roosevelt's blessing, the interest rate was lowered for two years to 3½ per cent by Congress. This was a lower rate of interest than other federal lending agencies charged, but there was no outcry of favoritism.

At the end of 1936 private industry underwent a revival, and *Time* magazine, analyzing the condition of the economy, described a "depression vanishing into memory." National income was up 50 per cent since 1932, and unemployment was down from fifteen million persons to eight million. Roosevelt believed the time had come to balance the budget by slashing WPA appropriations, ending PWA, and cutting other emergency programs, such as the lower interest charge to farm-owner borrowers.

However, the farm lobby had too many friends in Congress, and a bill went to the White House to extend the low rate. Roosevelt vetoed the bill and a fight took place in the House on the question of overriding his veto. Sam Rayburn was the President's chief defender, arguing that "if we are to do this for the farmer, we will be asked to do this for the urban home-owner." When the *yeas* and *nays* were counted, Johnson did not appear in the President's phalanx but stood with Wright Patman in helping to override the veto by a vote of two hundred and sixty to ninety-eight.

The chances were that Roosevelt never noticed where Johnson's name was entered on the overriding vote, for the President had much more important matters on his mind than the vote of an insignificant freshman congressman. Sitdown strikes were plaguing industry; overseas the Spanish Civil War raged, Nazi threats were bombarding Austria, Mussolini was standing on his balcony and screaming out new plans of conquest beyond Ethiopia, and Japan had begun a major savage attack to conquer all of China. Then as the summer progressed, a national stench developed over the appointment of former KKK member Senator Hugo Black of Alabama to the Supreme Court. Finally, in October, the economy had collapsed anew.

Johnson's memory was that shortly after he came to the House he had to make a decision that could have ended his political career. As he told the story many times afterward, "I was one of the three Texas congressmen who backed the first minimum wage law in 1937. The other two were defeated in the next election." However, his memory was faulty, for the House vote came on June 14, 1938, instead of 1937, and fifteen House Texans out of twenty-one voted for the measure. The bill passed by the overwhelming vote of two hundred and ninety-one to eighty-nine.

Astute Alvin Wirtz remained Johnson's Texas Daddy until his death. The completion of the Lower Colorado River projects remained tenaciously the goal of Wirtz, and became one of Johnson's goals, too, because they were located chiefly in his District. This meant that Johnson had to act as legman, meeting with Secretary of the Interior Harold "Terrible Tempered" Ickes, a man who was convinced that competitors were trying to undermine his status with the President. Ickes not only considered Johnson a "White House boy" who might do him some good with the President, but he also developed a fondness for the talkative, enthusiastic congressman. He liked Johnson's company so much that in the early summer of 1939, for instance, instead of attending a function for the visiting King and Queen of England, Ickes went to Johnson's residence for a stag party Johnson was holding for Maury Maverick. Ickes reported his enjoyment at the shirt-sleeves affair, gossiping about politics with newly appointed Supreme Court Justice William O. Douglas and other Johnson friends.

Wirtz discovered, in going over the complexities of the river projects, that Johnson possessed remarkable ability to memorize figures, dates, and descriptions at first hearing. But unless he had the opportunity to repeat these within the week, his mind erased them entirely. Wirtz also considered him to be a man with a sharp mind. "I've seen engineers and rate experts start explaining a detailed matter to Lyndon," Wirtz once said, "and he'd show complete understanding before they got halfway through the talking, and he'd be asking for the next problem. He had the quickest, most analytical mind I've ever seen."

But if Johnson could make instant friends with Roosevelt, Cabinet members and Hill Country politicians, he was a dismal failure when it came to establishing good relations with private utility officials. With them he revealed a sharp and irascible temper when they refused to surrender to Wirtz's public power authority.

On one occasion patient Wirtz brought impatient Johnson to a meeting with private utility company officers to discuss the sale of the firm to the Lower Colorado River Authority. Johnson was soon embroiled in argument with the company president and in a burst of anger told him to "Go to hell!" This ended the conference, for the utility men immediately stalked out of the room.

Wirtz told Johnson he would like to speak to him privately in his office and left the meeting room. The Lower Colorado River Authority directors who had witnessed the episode congratulated Johnson on his tough approach, and he expected further pats on the back from Wirtz.

Instead Wirtz waited until Johnson had closed the door behind him, then scolded him like an errant child. "Listen, Lyndon," he said, "I've been around this business a long time. I know it must have made you feel good when those other fellows told you what a great man you are for advising the president of a big, powerful utility company to go to hell. But it broke up the meeting, and we still have to settle the issues we called the meeting to discuss.

"I learned one thing a long time ago, Lyndon," he continued. "Sure you can tell a man to go to hell—but he doesn't have to go."

Johnson shook his head with momentary deflation.

By his mature approach Wirtz managed to mollify the insulted utility president, and other meetings took place. Johnson made no further outbursts, and finally in January 1939 Wirtz was able to announce that the LCRA had completed the purchase of that company's properties in sixteen counties.

When Johnson asked Wirtz how to go about bringing electricity to the rural areas of his District, Wirtz explained the complexities of the Rural Electrification Administration's rules to him. The chief stumbling block was the REA provision that in financing farm electrification the agency required a minimum population of three persons per square mile. Obviously, the Hill Country, with only 1.3 persons per square mile, could not qualify.

But there might be one way to get around the rules, said Wirtz, and that was for Johnson to make use of his friendship with the President. Johnson agreed that it was certainly worth a try, so Wirtz put LCRA engineers and draftsmen to work preparing maps, photographs, and tables of figures for Johnson's use.

Tommy Corcoran remembered the day a determined young congressman walked into the west wing of the White House with a pile of photographs and brochures for an appointment with President Roosevelt. "I went in to see the President," Johnson said, "and before I saw him they warned me, 'When you get in there, he'll filibuster you to death. You won't get a word in, and Pa Watson [the appointments secretary] will have you halfway down the hall before you realize it.'

"Well, sir, I went in prepared. I had a picture of the Buchanan Dam and a transmission line—the President loved to look at pictures—and I meant to show him first the Dam and then the line, and tell him how the power from the Dam went right over the heads of the people, and they couldn't get any, though they helped pay for it—water, water everywhere, and not a drop to drink; power, power everywhere, and the people can't get it.

"I showed him the picture of the Buchanan Dam and started to speak," said Johnson, "but I got no further than 'Mr. President' when he broke right in and said, 'That's a multiple-arch dam, Lyndon, and I do believe it's the largest multiple-arch dam I've ever seen.' And he went on and on about the multiple-arch dam, but I knew I was being filibustered all right. But finally I got in my line about water, water everywhere, and power, power everywhere and he told Missy [Marguerite LeHand, his secretary] to get John Carmody on the line—he was power commissioner."

Roosevelt's telephone voice was a shout that required the listener on the other end of the line to hold the receiver about a foot from his ear. As for John Carmody's voice, Harold Ickes once characterized the head of the REA as having a "hog-calling voice."

"John!" Roosevelt bellowed, "there's a young congressman in my office, Lyndon Johnson; he's an old friend of mine." When he explained Johnson's proposal, Carmody shouted back that there were too few farms and ranches and too little demand to justify distributing power in his District. Above all, Carmody added, the District needed three times its population to qualify for financial aid to get electrical power.

"Well, John," Roosevelt shot back, "there's no rule that doesn't have an exception. And besides, John, those people down there breed pretty fast, you know."

With Roosevelt's consent, the REA rule was ignored solely in Johnson's District. However, before the Hill Country farmers could get electricity, they had to establish an electric company to transmit the power to them. It was out of the question that a private utility company would bear the large expense of providing such service, especially since the odds were that it would be a money-losing proposition.

But Wirtz and Johnson already had the answer that had prompted them to go to Roosevelt in the first place. The REA made thirty-five-year loans, preferably to "farmers' cooperatives and other nonprofit organizations" to finance the construction and operation of rural power systems. With the President's approval of the tapping of available power supplies, Wirtz and Johnson contemplated the organization of a cooperative to transmit electricity to members.

There were scoffers who insisted that farmers would not pay for electricity despite its greater convenience over smelly kerosene that had to be poured into lamps and stoves. But Johnson returned to Texas from Washington and held a series of meetings and private talks with farmers and ranchers, and everywhere he met with enthusiasm. He offered a new Stetson hat to anyone who found a farmer who did not want electricity brought to his farm, and as his campaign for a cooperative lengthened, he boasted that he never lost a single hat.

Wirtz handled the legal problems in establishing the cooperative after the farmers voted for its establishment. What resulted from Johnson's campaign was the Pedernales Electric Co-operative of Johnson City, the largest cooperative in the entire nation. When the REA gave its approval in September 1938, Johnson spoke on that occasion and said: "It isn't talk any more for farm women, to whom electricity has always been a faraway thing. Within a few months they can lay aside their corrugated washboards and let their red hot cookstoves cool off while they iron on a hot August afternoon. The farmer who has been dragging water out of a well with a bucket all his life can not only get himself an electric pump to do the work, but he will have power he can afford to buy to run it."

Bringing electricity to the Pedernales Valley was indeed a major achievement for Johnson. In honor of the hard-working founder of the Pedernales Electric Co-operative, when the central headquarters building was completed in Johnson City, a plaque attached to its exterior read: "A Product of the Faith, Ability and Foresight of Lyndon Baines Johnson, while Congressman Tenth District 1938." Local wags marred the dedication of the plaque by spreading word that Johnson had written the message.

Wirtz's social welfare interests also extended to public housing. In 1937, when Congress established the United States Housing Authority for this purpose, Wirtz became a director of the Austin Housing Authority. One of Wirtz's friends, E. H. Perry, who was a lesser "Daddy" to Johnson, became the head of the local Authority, and together with Mayor Tom Miller these three developed a public housing plan for Austin. Their goal was the construction of six hundred public housing units, with money to be obtained by a five-hundred-thousand-dollar appropriation from Congress and the sale of bonds, of which the USHA would purchase 90 per cent of the total.

Johnson took on the job of building public support and promoting approval of the projects with the USHA in Washington and the appropriation through Congress. Wirtz could write touching speeches, and Johnson delivered them with feeling. One he gave over radio station KNOW in Austin on January 23, 1938, said in part: "Last Christmas, when all over the world people were celebrating the birth of the Christ child, I took a walk here in Austin, a short walk, just a few blocks from Congress Avenue, and there I found people living in such squalor that Christmas Day was to them just one more day of filth and misery. I found forty families on one lot, using one water faucet, living in barren, one-room huts. There was no electricity.

"One typical family—living in one room without a single window—slept, cooked, ate there, while the mother bent over a leaky tub, washing clothes for the little money they had; the father lay ill with an infectious disease. There were ten children, all under sixteen."

Johnson got the half-million dollars, and the project was completed.

Sam Rayburn remained Johnson's Daddy throughout his House years. From the first weeks of Johnson's top-speed service in the Lower Chamber, "Mister Sam," as Johnson called him, worried that his running pace would burn him out before his time. Lady Bird agreed with Mister Sam, commenting that "Lyndon behaves as if there were no tomorrow coming and he had to do everything today."

Rayburn was a slow-moving man who managed to do a great deal of work before he sat down to an evening game of dominoes in his hotel lobby, and he talked to Johnson about the folly of operating at top speed without respite. "You remind me of a feller down my way who was gonna get married in the afternoon and he picked cotton till noon," he told Johnson. "Well, he'd made up his mind he was gonna be prettied up for his own wedding, so he went ahead and took himself a long, leisurely bath, and then he was afixin' his sideburns and duding himself up slick.

"Well, another feller come abustin' in and warned him he was gonna be late for his own wedding. So the bridegroom started to fret about it. But suddenly he quit fussin' and burst out laughing and said to his friend, 'Shucks, no use hurrying. They cain't do no business till I gets there.' "

Yet even though he frequently cautioned Johnson to slow down because "they cain't do no business till you get there," he had other rules that seemed on the surface to conflict with this warning. Once when Johnson said he was tired, Rayburn scowled and said, "Never say you're tired, Lyndon. Pretty soon you'll get to feeling sorry for yourself, and then you're through."

"Lyndon grew fast as a member of the House," said Wright Patman, "because he already knew the ropes when he first came. Besides, he was recognized by all members as Sam Rayburn's special boy; and if there were any doubts, Lyndon could always show them a certain key he carried in a pocket. This key gave him status.

"When Jack Garner was speaker, he operated his 'Board of Education' in a room below the House Parliamentarian's office in the Capitol. Top members came around after work to discuss House business and 'strike a blow for liberty' with bourbon and branch water. Then when Garner went over to the Senate as Vice President, and Sam Rayburn became Majority Leader, he copied Garner with his own 'Board of Education.' Every evening House leaders and his special friends came out of the woodwork and went to Sam's place. Sam let it be known that only two House members had keys and didn't have to knock to gain admittance. I had one key; Lyndon had the other."

As a general rule, Johnson kept his Executive Branch Daddy and his Legislative Branch Daddies as separate entities, for he knew that if he asked one to exert influence on his behalf with the other, he would be diluting, rather than strengthening, the Daddy concept. Only on rare occasions did he act on his own to bring the Daddies together, and at such times he made certain he was the maestro.

"I remember once he had an idea that Roosevelt should give a surprise party for Sam Rayburn," said Tommy Corcoran. Roosevelt was then handling vexing international problems relating to the approaching climax between the West and the Berlin-Rome-Tokyo Axis Powers, as well as the legislative struggle to repeal the Neutrality Acts that were hamstringing American foreign policy. Yet he permitted Johnson to talk him into a January 6 birthday party for Mister Sam in his Presidential office. "The President went for it," said Corcoran, "and Lyndon arranged it, brought Rayburn down to the White House on some pretext and all the Texas delegates went with him. He even bought a big Texas hat for the President to give him. I couldn't figure out why he was doing all this. Then the papers came out the next day and there was Lyndon, standing right between the President of the United States and Rayburn. That was the first time I really knew that an operator was loose."

One factor that damaged the father-son image that Mister Sam sought with Lyndon was the young man's unwillingness to play a subservient role. On the contrary, he constantly offered Rayburn advice on House business and looked bored whenever Rayburn started preaching to him. Rayburn went so far on one occasion as to characterize Johnson as "a damn independent boy; independent as a hog on ice."

During Johnson's first few terms in the House, Rayburn was well aware that in a showdown between himself and the White House, Johnson would take the position of the President. This was clearly revealed in mid-1939 when CIO boss John L. Lewis curdled his beetle-brow and denounced Vice

President Garner as "a labor-baiting, whisky-drinking, poker-playing, evil old man."

Cactus Jack Garner grew suddenly alarmed that Lewis' characterization of him might damage his candidacy for the Presidential nomination in 1940. Despite the assurance of Senator Tom Connally that the Lewis comment would only increase his chances because of Lewis' enormous unpopularity, Garner called Rayburn and demanded that he get the Texas Congressional delegation to pass a resolution absolving him from all charges by the labor leader. The short, bald majority leader agreed, without having to be reminded again that Garner's friends in the House were so numerous they could make Rayburn speaker when Speaker Bill Bankhead either retired or passed away.

That same day Rayburn's secretary, who wore cotton housedresses to the office, telephoned Texas congressmen, and a special caucus took place in defense of Garner. After a great deal of cussing of John L. Lewis, one Texan proposed the highly unrealistic resolution declaring Garner a teetotaler and a friend of organized labor. This appeared to be a resolution that would meet with Garner's approval, and Rayburn put it to a vote.

Unfortunately, when the tally was completed among the twenty-three men present, there was one vote in opposition, and this had come from Lyndon Johnson. Called upon to give his reason, Johnson said he "couldn't subscribe to any such language; and besides, the delegation will look foolish because everyone knows that Garner is a heavy drinker and that he is bitterly opposed to labor." Rayburn was astonished to the point of speechlessness by his protégé. But the rest of the delegation was not. Hardly had Johnson offered his opinion, when the room erupted in a shrieking, obscene two-hour argument between him and the others, who insisted that he fall in line and make the resolution unanimous.

Unknown to Rayburn, when his secretary called Johnson about the delegation caucus he immediately telephoned the White House and asked for advice from Daddy Number One. Although Roosevelt had not yet made up his mind whether to run for a third term, he opposed Garner's candidacy and wanted no action from the Texas delegation. The result was that Tommy Corcoran, WPA Administrator Harry Hopkins, the newly appointed Supreme Court Justice William O. Douglas, and Interior Secretary Harold Ickes called Johnson to pass along New Dealer policy regarding Garner.

It was Roosevelt who later filled Ickes in with the events of the Texas caucus by repeating Johnson's first-hand description of the imbroglio. Johnson's picture of the two-hour fight moved him to uproarious laughter. So did Johnson's description of what followed:

Rayburn, in exasperation, took Johnson to his office in an effort to convince him in private to sign the resolution. But after a careful presentation of the reasons why Johnson should sign, he saw he was not making any impression, and he snapped, "Lyndon, I'm looking you right in the eye!"

"And I'm looking you right back in the eye!" Lyndon replied sacrilegiously to Daddy Number Two in Washington.

Finally the two returned to the delegation, and Rayburn announced his failure. This led to renewed bickering, and in the end the weary Texans shoved the job of saving face for Garner onto Johnson by asking him to write a resolution he would sign. He agreed to do so, but never did, and the John L. Lewis charge against Cactus Jack went unrebutted. Not long afterward, when Garner declared his candidacy for the Presidency in 1940, Roosevelt remarked, "I see that the Vice President has thrown his bottle— I mean his hat—into the ring."

Carl Vinson, who was chairman of the House Naval Affairs Committee, was another "Daddy" to Lyndon Johnson. Vinson, twenty-five years Johnson's senior, had come to Congress from the red-clay village of Milledgeville, Georgia, in 1914, and through the process of successive re-elections had risen through seniority to committee chairman. Vinson was a man neither President Roosevelt nor his House colleagues cared to anger. He considered himself the overseer of the naval establishment as well as the leading promoter of an invincible armada, and possessed nicknames that described him well: the Admiral, the Swamp Fox, and the Old Operator.

The Admiral was not taken in by the well-fitting uniforms of top naval officers and their excellent posture. He sat round-shouldered and enjoyed chewing on cheap cigars and spraying the always nearby spittoon while he scolded Annapolis' finest for not doing a better job in behalf of the Navy he loved. With his glasses bridging the tip of his nose, he would lean forward and chide an officer who conjured up possible problems. Vinson's advice, always delivered in a thick drawl, would be, "Now, admiral, don't take off your shoes till you come to the creek." His most frequent remark was, "You don't learn nuthin' by talkin'," an axiom talkative Lyndon Johnson used on many who tried to interrupt him. This was a variation of a quotation Johnson had heard his father use repeatedly.

Some of those associated with Vinson affectionately called the Old Operator Uncle Carl. "Uncle Carl ran his committee like a tight ship," said an aide. "He allowed a freshman member of his committee one question the first year, two questions at hearings the second year, and so forth. He made an exception of Lyndon." His most typical remark to committee members and Navy top dogs when they discussed problems was his assurance of "I'll he'p ya."

"There were certain things Lyndon picked up from his association with Uncle Carl—and some things he didn't. It didn't take Lyndon long before he was as rousing a champion of a tremendous military establishment as Vinson. If both had their way, the country would have been totally mobilized all the time. On the other hand, Lyndon never developed Uncle Carl's hatred of the United States Senate. Vinson called it 'the quote Upper

House unquote.' Obviously, Lyndon couldn't hate the Senate because he
intended to become a senator one day."

Vinson's chief enemy in the Senate was Senator David Ignatius Walsh,
chairman of the Naval Affairs Committee. Walsh was not only Vinson's
competitor, who diluted his own authority in dealing with the Navy, but
Walsh did not accept the twice-over invincible armada stand of his House
counterpart. The Massachusetts senator had come to the Senate upon the
death of Henry Cabot Lodge, who had been Woodrow Wilson's implacable
foe. Walsh was a notorious homosexual who sought companions in the
lower rungs of the Naval Academy staff. He also drank a great deal, hob-
nobbed with isolationists, and saw no pressing need to prepare the nation for war with Hitler. One time he stumbled drunkenly into the Mayflower lobby and urinated in the water fountain, in full view of a large
audience.

Lyndon Johnson's special friend on the Naval Affairs Committee was
Warren "Maggie" Magnuson, a handsome young bachelor from Seattle,
who had come to Congress three months earlier than he. Magnuson had
landed on Vinson's committee without an assist from the White House because the Navy's heavy installations in Washington had produced the
unwritten rule that the Puget Sound Navy Yard member of the state's
delegation be placed automatically on the committee. "Maggie was a gay
blade," said Vinson's aide. "He and Lyndon knew how to play up to
Uncle Carl, and by doing so they could get whatever they wanted from
him. Vinson's wife, whom he referred to as 'the sweetest woman who ever
put on a dress,' was an invalid. He never went to a White House dinner or
on a Navy cruise because he went directly home to her hours before Congress adjourned for the day. Maggie and Lyndon brightened Uncle Carl's
day by dropping in and telling him humorous dirty jokes and the details
of amorous escapades, which he enjoyed with real vicarious pleasure."

"Lyndon and I were very young and very aggressive, and we were
more available than the older members to travel on special chores for
Carl Vinson," said Magnuson. "When a problem arose with the Pacific
Fleet or at a Navy yard, Carl would say, 'You two fellows go and find out
about it for the committee.'

"One time he sent us to Alaska where we investigated what was happening at Dutch Harbor and Kodiak. We found the United States Army and
Navy were almost at war with each other as to which service would have
jurisdiction over various activities. The problem, as we saw it, was that
the Alaskan installation was not big enough for two separately operating
services. We talked informally to the Navy people there, and we brought
back information to Vinson so that he could make a stab at settling the
interservice argument. Then another time Lyndon and I went to Alaska
again, and we worked out a plan for coordinating all services there. When
we reported back to Vinson, he ordered the Department people in charge
to come in, and he had them put our plan into effect.

"Lyndon and I always called Carl Vinson Admiral. We could get around him easily after the first few years—Lyndon more easily than I because he used me as a straightman and he had the southern syrup. But we started out wrong at our first committee hearing under Vinson when Lyndon and I peppered Administration witnesses with questions. Afterward, Admiral Vinson told us bluntly, 'I want to see you two boys in the back room.'

"When we walked in, he let us have it without wasting time. 'You two are nice young fellows, and I'm sure you have the interest of the Navy at heart,' he told us. 'But we have a rule in the committee. We call it seniority. Each of you is entitled to ask only one question this whole year, and two next year.'

"Sam Rayburn had a similar idea about young spouting congressmen. He called Lyndon and me in early and advised us, 'I want you two to keep your mouths shut on the floor. You won't know what the score is for a long time. Also remember, don't get involved with broad issues, because you have to get re-elected; and if you get into the big issues, the voters will think you aren't taking care of your District's problems.' "

If Uncle Carl thought that one of his young committee members was trying to imitate him by writing hard-hitting reports, he enjoyed chastising him in print. Once, when Johnson wrote a strong report condemning Standard Oil contracts with the Navy, the printed document contained a follow-up section by Vinson with the introductory comment, "This statement made by Mr. Johnson contains many errors of fact."

Magnuson said that the way he and Lyndon got to Carl Vinson "was through the fact that he was a recluse. He went home early each afternoon to take care of his wife, and he never invited anyone to visit him. But he was a very curious man, and every morning he wanted to know what had gone on in the House after he left the day before. We started by filling him in; then we told him stories, and before long we were in solidly with the Admiral.

"Vinson was a great admirer of the way Lyndon used anecdotes to prove a point. For instance, when Vinson complained that he couldn't get a sub-committee to do its obvious work, Lyndon told him about 'Hard-Head' Jackson, the great fullback. 'Hard-Head's team was behind six to nothing,' said Lyndon, 'and they were on their opponent's ten-yard line in the last quarter. The coach sent in a signal, ordering the quarterback to give Hard-Head the ball. But the ball was handed off to another man who lost three yards. The coach was frantic and yelled, "Give it to Hard-Head!" But again someone else got it and lost several yards. This happened twice more, and the coach rushed out on the field. "Why didn't you give the ball to Hard-Head?" he demanded of the quarterback. "Him didn't want the ball," was the reply.'

"For years Lyndon warned employees to whom he gave deadlines, 'I don't want you to get stuck in a snowdrift like Magnuson.' Few had any idea what he was talking about, but he was referring to the time I went up to Alaska for the Vinson Committee while the question of fortifying Guam was moving along toward a vital vote. Because of their headcount of members in favor and members opposed, Rayburn and Vinson called me to return to Washington immediately. However, there was so much snow at the airport that the plane couldn't take off. Rayburn and Vinson managed to stall the vote for three days until I got back to the Capitol. 'I got stuck in a snowdrift,' I tried to explain to them. But they didn't believe me, and Lyndon picked up my words as a refrain to his own employees. Just how important was my return came clear when the Guam fortification bill won by a single vote."

Despite the interest Vinson and his two young storytellers had in creating an invincible armada, the mood of Congress and the country ran in the opposite direction. Years later Johnson described the Naval Affairs Committee as among the most powerful in the House. But until World War II approached, it remained as a secondary committee. Even though President Roosevelt's favorite Department was the Navy, he could not get it the appropriations he desired so long as the principal theme in the nation was to remain aloof from the gathering storm being brewed by Nazi Germany and autocratic Japan. By the subterfuge of diverting PWA money to construct two aircraft carriers (the *Yorktown* and *Enterprise*), the heavy cruiser *Vincennes* and hundreds of smaller naval vessels, Roosevelt played an independent hand. But so far as the power of the Vinson Committee was concerned, it was merely gaining practice for the destructive years ahead.

Chapter 20

"LYNDON AND I spent a great deal of time talking about the Senate," said "Maggie" Magnuson, "because we both wanted to be senators." Until the summer of 1938, when Lyndon met the statutory minimum age requirement of thirty years, such talk remained academic. But even after that it sounded unreal.

First of all, Senators Tom Connally and Morris Sheppard of Texas were popular and powerful senators and were generally considered to be lifetime fixtures in the Upper Chamber. In addition, outside of the Tenth Congressional District, Johnson was hardly known in his state. "I never heard of Lyndon until the nineteen-forties," said Ralph Yarborough.

He possessed still another drawback. While he was a favorite of President Roosevelt, Maury Maverick, older than he and with far more experience, was an even closer Presidential protégé. The short, rawboned, loud-voiced Maverick represented far more of a romantic tie with the aggressive early West that Roosevelt admired than did Johnson, whose specialty was relating the sad, primitive living conditions he had known as a child.

Furthermore, as a longer-serving congressman—and with far more prestige—Maverick held a priority over Johnson in Administration backing if a Senate seat should fall vacant. Johnson also realized that Maury Maverick would be the liberal candidate of Roosevelt, above all others. Maury's large-scale activities in civil rights and labor matters tied his umbilical directly to the emotional, philosophic New Dealers, while Johnson's New Deal friends were the hard-headed, practical daily bread-and-butter sort whose liberalism referred to reforming the stock exchange, building public works projects, and fighting Eastern monopolies.

When Maverick first came to Congress, there were those who predicted his early political death because of their belief that he was an alcoholic. Some of his friends worried that he was on a tequila jag, drinking the pure, white juice distilled from the cactus plant that made you feel the next day "like the thorns are all coming out on your body." They could see that instead of walking, he staggered, and once when he lurched into Senator Sheppard's office, a frightened clerk called the police, and he was dragged out despite his resounding assertions of sobriety. This backstage judgment of Maverick proved entirely false, for when Congress adjourned in 1935, Maury went to the hospital where surgeons removed a large tumor from his spinal cord.

Maverick's championing of minority groups earned him the enmity of the Democratic machine back home in Bexar County. When he ran for re-election in 1936, a never-ending campaign barrage subjected him continuously to the charge of being a "dangerous radical." His chief opponent, a gentleman named Seeligson, who had been Maverick's college classmate and was the first cousin of noted author John Dos Passos, grew hoarse calling Maverick a "Red" and "a rich man." There was only one way "to skin Seeligson alive," said Maverick, and this was to reply in kind, labeling his opponent as "a country-club Communist."

Maverick won this distasteful contest, and he returned to Washington even higher in Roosevelt's esteem. Then when the Court fight developed, and Senator Tom Connally was among the leaders of the opposition, Maverick, as a Court-packing-bill backer, felt his White House stock skyrocket.

Always regretting that he had seen no action in World War I, President

Roosevelt was much impressed with Maverick for having been badly wounded in the Argonne Forest, where he collected a Silver Star for gallantry. Roosevelt had been counting on him when he first came to Congress to serve as one of his champions for a strong national defense program. But Maverick was frank to admit to him in 1935 that he was an unequivocal pacifist. Nevertheless, Roosevelt had Democrats on the House Ways and Means Committee assign him to the House Military Affairs Committee, which dealt with Army matters. Here Maverick attracted wide national attention by proposing that Eric Remarque's *All Quiet on the Western Front* and Dos Passos' *Three Soldiers* be made required reading in the Reserve Officers Training Corps. However, by 1938, with the relentless aggressions of the Hitler government in Germany—the Nazi takeover of Austria in March and mounting pressure on Czechoslovakia to permit her dismemberment—Maverick dropped his pacifist stand and became a leading advocate of Roosevelt's fifty thousand military airplane construction program and the training of ten thousand pilots.

Maverick's attitude toward Johnson from the beginning of their acquaintance was that of a benevolent uncle to whom a youngster with problems could turn for aid. He had taken this approach in 1935 when he importuned Roosevelt to make Johnson head of the Texas NYA; and he made himself available when Johnson returned to Washington as a congressman in 1937 and needed a listening post. Thirteen years older than Johnson, Maverick did not consider his Tenth District colleague any challenge to his senatorial ambitions.

It was Maury's liberalism in a land of reaction that abruptly changed this situation. Johnson, who had carefully hewed to a pork-barrel philosophy in his approach to political issues his first term, had no opponent when he ran for re-election in 1938. Maverick, however, had succeeded in uniting the mean, the rich, the ignorant, and the bigoted against him in 1938. Political boss P. L. Anderson, who also tripled as police and fire chief of San Antonio, and Sheriff Owen Kilday put up Bexar County assistant district attorney Paul Kilday, brother of the sheriff, as Maverick's primary opponent.

Big ranchers, who had been saved by New Deal measures, and the local gambling interests opened their purses and poured out money in behalf of Paul Kilday in the large Mexican section of San Antonio. Ironically, these Mexicans, who had gained the vote through Maverick's effort, now sold their votes in order to gain more than their small relief check payments or the going rate of pay of only ten cents a day to pick nuts in the "pecan capital of the world." The result was that Kilday easily defeated Maverick.

But Maverick still harbored senatorial ambitions, and he ran for mayor of San Antonio in 1939 in order to maintain his availability and make a record as a city reformer. This time Maverick avoided the Democratic party label and ran on a Fusion ticket. He also called on his Mexican friends and asked them not to sell out for a few dollars.

When he won and immediately inaugurated a far-reaching program of administrative and social reforms, Boss Anderson almost suffered a heart attack, and some of his friends conjectured as to who would inherit the two-inch-long diamond he wore in his tie. Anderson and Sheriff Kilday decided to deprive Maverick of his victory, and they waited only two weeks to take action. First, they attempted to disgrace him, a tactic designed to force him to spend all his time defending himself. The preceding mayor had issued a permit to a Communist organization to hold a meeting in the city auditorium two weeks after Maverick took office; and when the day approached, Anderson and Kilday spread word that Maverick was responsible for letting the meeting take place. A planned riot occurred at the auditorium, and when Maverick ordered a police guard to the scene to maintain order, several persons were injured by Anderson's club swingers. The more fervent right-wingers burned Maverick in effigy, while the local press denounced him for not revoking the permit.

Later that year Maverick's attackers tried a more extreme approach. This time they arrested him on the charge that he had violated the law by paying the poll tax of another person. The prosecution's argument was that David Dubinsky, head of the International Ladies Garment Workers Union, had contributed one thousand dollars to Maverick's mayoralty campaign and that Maverick had given two hundred and fifty dollars of this sum to a local union. Anderson and Kilday's tortured reasoning was that this union had paid the poll taxes of several Mexicans with the contribution, thus making Maverick guilty of a crime.

Maverick successfully got out of this action and went on his tempestuous way until 1941, when he ran for re-election as mayor. This time his adversaries were busy passing out dollars to Mexicans in the slums, and the vote showed him a loser by a thousand ballots. After this, though he remained a strong Texas voice of liberalism and a force in state elections, the frog-faced battler was no longer a contender for a seat as United States senator.

Despite Maverick's political misfortunes, he continued to be of help to further Johnson's political career. In 1939, for instance, when Alvin Wirtz, Johnson's principal Texas "Daddy," wanted a prestige Administration job in Washington, Maverick held talks with President Roosevelt and Interior Secretary "Honest Harold" Ickes to arrange something for him. During the discussions Maverick discovered that Ickes' Undersecretary was being pushed out, and he besieged Ickes with arguments why Wirtz should replace him.

Ickes, who came from Chicago and had been a long-time Bull Moose Republican opponent of trusts and cartels, could not picture Wirtz in the job because of his earlier association with Samuel Insull. However, Maverick proved a convincing lawyer, and Ickes noted in his diary that he had held "an initial prejudice against him [Wirtz] but later I became persuaded that I had been misinformed." Ickes had Maverick write a letter of recommendation to him for transmission to Roosevelt; and in passing it along to the President, Ickes also praised Wirtz as a "convinced liberal, one of the ablest lawyers and most upstanding men in Texas," whose "handling of the Lower Colorado River project has been masterly, both as a lawyer and as a negotiator."

In giving Wirtz the appointment, Roosevelt's interest in him extended far beyond the Interior Department. Nominally, Wirtz was to supervise the construction of the Shasta and Grand Coulee Dams. However, his chief assignment became that of keeping the various fighting elements of the Texas Democratic party in a New Deal pattern for the 1940 Presidential nominating convention. And in accepting this responsibility, Wirtz had only one young, loping, elephantine-eared Texas congressman in mind as his assistant. So with the Senate's approval of Wirtz as Undersecretary of the Interior, Lyndon Johnson entered into statewide Texas politicking for the first time.

This Texas assignment was of vital importance to Roosevelt, for he believed that the popularity of the Democratic party was on the downcurve, making the twenty-three Texas electoral votes a crucial matter in the 1940 election. In addition, Roosevelt was well aware that the big-money interests in Texas were already conspiring in a "Stop Roosevelt" campaign, their strategy being to send a noisy anti-Roosevelt delegation to the Democratic National Convention.

In mid-1939, those close to the President believed he would not run for an unprecedented third term. But when the European war erupted in September with the savage aggression and dismemberment of Poland by Nazi Germany and Stalin's Soviet Union, White House insiders concluded that Roosevelt now considered himself a necessary President for the wrathful years ahead.

However, Roosevelt refrained from any overt statement in this direction, and his silence encouraged several Democrats to make a bid for the nomination. Slow-moving, slow-thinking Secretary of State Cordell Hull, an old sixty-nine, believed he had the President's nod for 1940. So did gladhander Jim Farley, the ever-smiling but grudge-nursing Postmaster General. And so did Harry Hopkins, formerly WPA chief and now Secretary of Commerce. But Hopkins had hardly set out on the road to meet with local party chiefs when he had to rush to Rochester, Minnesota, to remove a stomach cancer late in 1939, and he dropped his Presidential ambitions for good.

By far the strongest Democratic contender was Vice President Garner, who had developed steadily as the party's anti-New Deal symbol. At the outset Garner had given the impression he was a liberal, said one observer, "because he has the frontier spirit of square-dealing and a native sympathy for the underdog. He takes a frontiersman's pride in being very much on the level and in having a reputation for being self-reliant and having guts." But the man with the "leathery red visage of the plainsman, cold blue eyes, a compact head with curling gray hair, and a tight, down-curving mouth" revealed his conservatism as the scope of the New Deal broadened.

Early in 1940 Roosevelt grew concerned that Garner would win the Presidential nomination unless he were headed off. "He told us that Garner had to be sent home permanently to his six thousand neighbors in Uvalde, Texas, so he could add to his millions as the champion trader of ranches, beehives, banks, goats, sheep, and cattle," said David K. Niles, an assistant to Harry Hopkins and the President. "And this crucial task went to Alvin Wirtz. Besides, F.D.R. was tired of being addressed by his Vice President as 'Cap'n.' "

Wirtz's assignment was formidable. Roy Miller, with Texas Gulf Sulphur money behind him, had already opened a "Garner for President" head-quarters in Washington and was using all his lobbying techniques on under-paid Washington correspondents for newspapers around the country. Back in Texas, E. B. Germany, a party power and outspokenly anti-Roosevelt, was entering Garner in various state Presidential primaries and making quick forays into Wisconsin, Illinois, and other states to fashion an over-whelming delegate count before the Democratic National Convention con-vened in Chicago on July 15. When banking, real estate, ranching, and oil money began pouring into the Garner war chest, local New Dealers con-sidered their cause lost. It was a fight between "the Roy Millers and Amon Carters on one side," the Dallas *Morning News* of April 9, 1940, quoted Roosevelt supporters, "and seven million Texas citizens" on the other side. Reactionary Amon Carter was the immensely wealthy owner of the Fort Worth *Star-Telegram*.

With Congress still in session Johnson remained in Washington to serve as liaison between the White House and Wirtz, who had returned to Texas for direct confrontation with the E. B. Germany–Amon Carter crowd. Armed with a dam to dedicate and dozens of Interior Department installations to inspect, Wirtz had more than two months of official cover for his important political hatchet job.

"Wirtz assails 'Garner for President' forces," *The New York Times* of April 7, 1940, acknowledged his appearance on the local scene. The Garnerites, said Wirtz—in a line of argument he had carefully developed with Harold Ickes, Johnson, and Tommy Corcoran—were "inspired by Wall Street bankers." Their attempt to enter and win state primaries, he went on, revealed they were "trying to defeat President Roosevelt's chances of a third term even at a cost of a do-nothing Republican Administration."

Stung by Wirtz's charges, Germany countered with the argument that Roosevelt was not running for a third term, and what Garner was doing was what any loyal Texan would expect from the second ranking Democrat. Furthermore, he said, the 1938 Texas State Democratic Convention had endorsed Garner for President, as had the Texas Democratic organization in March 1940.

Wirtz's answer to Germany was to pay for a statewide radio broadcast by Pa Ferguson, long a Garner detractor. Farmer Jim put on his usual good show, telling radio listeners that he had "knowed John Garner for thirty years." After a repetitious assessment of the Vice President as a man short of brains and ability, Ferguson declared this was so because "the Lord just dint do enough for John Garner." Harold Ickes also got into the act with an open letter to Amon Carter, whose Fort Worth *Star-Telegram* had jibed at pro-Roosevelt Democrats as "carpetbaggers and outlanders." Said Ickes, "When the President shall have been re-elected in November, you and other such 'leaders' will be the first to hie to the pie counter."

On April 9, 1940, when the Nazis ended the "phony war" of six months of inaction following the plundering of Poland, by invading Norway, Wirtz and Johnson had no doubt that Roosevelt would run again. However, because of the historic opposition to a third term, Roosevelt's strategy remained that of arranging for the weakening of anti-New Deal forces while he maintained a sphinxlike silence about his political future. Nevertheless, Wirtz now began pushing openly for the selection of Texas delegates to the national convention who would be for Roosevelt.

Wirtz knew that his chief effort had to be directed toward the Democratic precinct conventions scheduled for May 4. These fifty-five hundred precinct conventions selected delegates to the two hundred and fifty-four county conventions on May 7 and these in turn chose delegates to the state convention powwow at Waco on May 28. It was at the state convention that delegates to the national convention would be elected, so the major job was to control the precinct conventions, where the road to the national convention began. But the ineptness of the New Deal Democrats in Texas was so marked, Wirtz wailed to his Washington associates, that they were spending all their time talking to each other about their problems instead of making plans to capture the precinct conventions.

As an alternative to this situation Wirtz tried to effect a compromise with Myron Blalock, Texas oilman and state Democratic chairman. Both would work at the state convention to send a delegation to the national convention that would be divided one-third for Roosevelt, another third for Garner, and the last third for Garner only on the first ballot. However, when Blalock refused to accept his proposition, Wirtz concentrated on doing battle at the precinct level.

On April 24, Wirtz made a statewide speech from Dallas, urging Democrats who attended the precinct conventions to "elect only men known to be New Dealers at heart." Then he and Johnson and Mayor Tom Miller of Austin worked up a four-point resolution to be voted upon by the precinct meetings. The resolution declared:

"One. We endorse the humanitarian and forward-looking administration of our National Government under the peerless leadership of President Franklin D. Roosevelt and our distinguished Texan, Vice-President John

N. Garner; Two. We nominate our native son, Vice-President John N. Garner as nominee for President; Three. We condemn the stop-Roosevelt movement and our delegates are instructed and shall pledge themselves that they shall never become a party thereto; Four. We instruct our delegates to the county convention, state convention and national convention, insofar as this resolution is concerned, to vote as a unit."

When Mayor Miller tried to win agreement from E. B. Germany for his support of the "Harmony Resolution," Germany immediately "smelt a rat" and countered with his own proposal. This was a four-line resolution endorsing "the Roosevelt-Garner Administration" and calling for the instruction of delegates to vote for Garner for President.

All the precinct conventions were scenes of antagonism when the two resolutions were introduced, and the results showed both sides about evenly divided. Then three days later at the county conventions the count revealed the Garner Resolution with a plurality of votes but without a majority. A smaller number had approved the Harmony Resolution, and still others came out for delegations favoring a third term for Roosevelt or for uninstructed delegations to be sent to the state convention.

With the state convention only a few weeks away Roosevelt grew concerned that the Garnerites would control the selection there of the Texas delegation to the national convention. He became so convinced that Texas was lost to him under the trend of events that he ordered Ickes, Corcoran, and Johnson to call Wirtz and impress upon him the importance of winning Blalock's approval of the Harmony Resolution.

In the Johnson-Wirtz call, Wirtz pointed out that Blalock might be more amenable if he received a communication directly from the White House. However, Roosevelt could not bring himself to what amounted to a public brawl with Garner. So he accepted Wirtz's alternative, which was to have Sam Rayburn send him and Blalock identical telegrams, declaring that the state convention should emphatically endorse the Roosevelt Administration, select delegates who would support Garner as a "favorite son" candidate, and vow not to join a "stop Roosevelt" faction at the national convention.

Unfortunately, by the time Roosevelt called Majority Leader Rayburn, he had reached the erroneous conclusion that Johnson was a major political power in Texas. Because of this belief, he told Mister Sam that he wanted him and Lyndon to sign the telegrams to Wirtz and Blalock. This brought a quick *no* from Rayburn, for, said Ickes, Sam "did not want it to appear that in a Texas political matter, a kid congressman like Johnson was on apparently the same footing as himself, the majority leader."

But Roosevelt held a trump card, and this was his knowledge that Rayburn wanted very much to win second place on the Democratic ticket. If he failed to sign the telegrams, Garner might win the nomination for President, and this would eliminate Rayburn from consideration for the Vice-Presidential nomination because of the Constitution's restriction against both candidates coming from the same state. In addition, Rayburn realized that if he did not sign the telegrams and Roosevelt won renomination, Roosevelt would not put him on the ticket.

So one Monday afternoon in May a smiling Lyndon and a scowling Sam went to the White House to show copies of the telegrams to Roosevelt and then release them to the press. Roosevelt later confided to Ickes that in effect he had "told them benignly that they had been good little boys and that they had 'papa's blessing.'" Ickes' diary notation was that Roosevelt "treated them as political equals with the malicious intent of disturbing Sam Rayburn's state of mind."

Toward the end of May, when delegates came to Waco for the Democratic state convention, Wirtz expected a cut and dried meeting because Roosevelt had agreed to accept Blalock as the next Texas national committeeman in exchange for his approval of the Harmony Resolution and telegram. But no one had bothered to check with Maury Maverick, who was then mayor of San Antonio. The Nazi panzer divisions had raced into the Low Countries on May 10 and then into France, and Maverick saw no point in playing games with Garner now that the Second World War was broadening.

He entered Waco at the head of a large iron-lunged force, calling wildly for a third term for Roosevelt. In the area around the Raleigh Hotel, he and his followers staged an enthusiastic parade complete with a full-pitched sound truck booming out harsh words against all political wheeler-dealers. He yelled about "a fix at Dallas in advance" and bellowed that he would take over the state convention if it were not run fairly.

When the convention opened on May 28, Maverick proposed that his good friend and Roosevelt supporter, Houston's Mayor Oscar Holcombe, be named temporary chairman. However, Wirtz was ready with his "Harmony" slate, which included Germany as presiding officer, Mayor Tom Miller as keynote speaker, and Maury Hughes as permanent chairman. His invitation to the Maverick-Holcombe group to join the Harmony organization was rejected a moment after the offer was made, and was followed first by leather-throated denunciation and then by fist fights and flying chairs. Only the threat by the Waco police and state highway patrolmen to use their guns on the politicians finally produced a semblance of order.

But it did not last long. With E. B. Germany in the chair, Wirtz motioned that they vote on his Harmony slate. Germany mumbled something, there was some shouting, and Germany announced that the slate had been approved by a voice vote. A three-hour riot followed, with bloodied faces, torn clothes and broken furniture. Said police chief Maxey, who watched the primitive carryings-on, "You'd never know they were supposed to be the smartest men in Texas." Maury Maverick, responsible for the trouble originally, tried to restore order and failed. Mayor Holcombe was also unsuccessful, as was Elliott Roosevelt. Finally Pat Neff with his Baptist preacher's voice quieted the crowd, and the remaining convention work was disposed of before the fighters gained their second wind. Garner was named the "favorite son" candidate of the forty-six delegates to the national convention and a "stop-Roosevelt" strategy was outlawed. Blalock became the Texas national committeeman; Wirtz, the Texas delegation member of the national convention's platform committee; Rayburn, head of the Texas delegation; and Lyndon Johnson, vice chairman of the delegation.

This was Johnson's first participation in a national convention, and the pandemonium in the Chicago Stadium on July 15 was sweet music to him. When he first joined Wirtz in Chicago, Wirtz's concern was that Garner with the help of Farley and Cordell Hull would use their vast political experience to prevent Roosevelt's renomination. It was common knowledge that Farley, who had come to Chicago a week early, was in daily touch with Hull in his Carlton Hotel apartment in the capital and with Garner at the Washington Hotel. Garner had to be called during the day because he was known as a "nine o'clock fellow." Farley, whose chief forte was his ability to remember names and whose charm was his smile that included even his bald head, was as convinced as Garner that the two could prevent a third term. "Jim, the two of us can pull together to stop Roosevelt," was a statement Farley claimed had been made to him by Garner.

Tagging along with Rayburn and Wirtz, Johnson gained valuable insight into convention politics. On one occasion, to test Farley's gullibility, Rayburn lugubriously told the genial Postmaster General that he was "incensed over the way Garner was being handled." Farley expressed heartfelt thanks to Rayburn for his words, but later he said, "I did not take Sam's tears too seriously, as he was a red-hot candidate for Vice President."

Wirtz's ability to reach Roosevelt impressed Johnson. Once when he and Wirtz learned through the gossip ring at the convention that Farley had expressed hope for a long and drawn-out convention as the best way to cool Third Term ardor, Wirtz put in a hurried call to the White House and won Roosevelt's approval of a short and peppy convention. One of Wirtz's many concerns was that delegates might succumb to the anti-third-term propaganda after a few mornings of reading Colonel McCormick's ultra-right-wing Chicago *Tribune*. Johnson and Assistant Secretary of the Interior Oscar L. Chapman were then neighbors and friends at the Kennedy Warren Apartments in Washington, and Wirtz put the two young men to work visiting state delegations to pump for a reversal of convention procedures. Wirtz's proposal was to nail down the Presidential nomination without delay and then take up the party platform, instead of the usually reversed order. However, on this point he ran afoul of Secretary of Commerce Harry Hopkins, who was operating as Roosevelt's convention manager, despite his total lack of infighting experience. Hopkins had his headquarters in a third-floor suite at the Blackstone Hotel, and for privacy he had installed a direct line from the bathroom to the White House. The room was so small that he had to sit on the toilet when talking to the President. "Harry was damned mad with Alvin Wirtz for trying to mastermind things," said David Niles, Hopkins' aide, "so he sat on his 'throne' and got Roosevelt to order Wirtz to stop promoting a different order of convention business."

Farley, thirsting for a top nomination, believed when the convention formally convened that he could defeat the third term. In a telephone call to Hull on the eve of the convention he told the Secretary of State to tell Roosevelt at their usual Monday meeting that "the temper of the delegates was bad; that the real Democrats were annoyed; that the majority did not want to vote for the third term; that if they had their way they would nominate Hull and myself; and that they resented the presence of Hopkins in Chicago."

But this was the bleating cemetery whistling of a beaten man who was trying to reach beyond his depth, for Roosevelt, with the aid of Wirtz and others like him, had painstakingly arranged his own "draft" for a third term. And the pieces were already in place from the moment the organist entertained the stacked galleries with a sprightly rendition of a popular song called "Franklin D. Roosevelt Jones" and was followed by the resounding pro-Roosevelt cheers that came relentlessly from Chicago's superintendent of sewers, who was bellowing through a microphone in his hiding place in a small basement room under the stadium.

There was little drama in the Presidential nomination contest itself, despite the discord Farley was attempting to create on the convention floor. On the first ballot Roosevelt won renomination overwhelmingly with 946½ votes, while the three conspirators showed a total of only 72½ votes for Farley, 61 for Garner, and 6 for Hull.

However, the fight for the Vice-Presidential nomination was another story. Sam Rayburn believed that his moment of glory was at hand, and at 2 A.M. on July 18, only three and a half hours after Roosevelt won renomination, Rayburn called a caucus of the Texas delegation. Wirtz and Mayor Miller, who were committed to Mister Sam for Vice President, conducted swift lobbying among the sleepy delegates to bring unanimity for Rayburn, while Johnson attempted to railroad this through from his vantage point as caucus chairman.

But the Garnerites, still fuming from the small vote their man got in the Presidential nominating contest and belatedly angry with Wirtz for his "Harmony" victory at the state convention, refused to accept Rayburn. Coarse words were exchanged with Wirtz and Johnson, and the Garner group put up Jesse Jones as their Vice-Presidential candidate in opposition to Rayburn. Elliott Roosevelt, who was present, shocked Rayburn when he announced for "Jesus" Jones, as his father so derisively called the conservative RFC chief. But he should not have been surprised, for Elliott had lost five hundred thousand dollars on his Texas radio chain, and Jones had personally bailed him out. This was not an act of charity on the part of Jones, because he knew the chain's potential under proper management, and he proved this by turning the network into a big moneymaker.

Johnson ordered a search for missing Texas delegates to complete the showdown caucus vote. One was found dead in his hotel bed, a few were too drunk to walk, and billionaire Sid Richardson came bursting into the room to announce that he had been held up and robbed in the elevator. The open warfare between the Rayburn and Jones followers continued past dawn, with Rayburn holding on to a majority of the delegation's votes, yet unable to win the near unanimity he needed from his own delegation if he were to impress other delegations.

"While the caucus was still in session," said Senator Tom Connally, "Jones went out to scout among other delegations. In a short while he returned with a deep scowl on his face. 'No use bothering any longer,' he advised us loudly. 'The President wants Henry Wallace for Vice President.' The announcement ended our meeting."

There was another Texas caucus later that day, with Wirtz and the disappointed Rayburn unable to display any enthusiasm for Wallace, whose candidacy they had been asked by Roosevelt to promote inside their delegation. Elliott Roosevelt boasted that he had told Jim Farley, "If you nominate Jesse Jones, I'll second it." Many in the Texas delegation told Wirtz and Johnson that they opposed Wallace because as Secretary of Agriculture he had permitted AAA regulations to ruin the cotton export market, a matter of vital concern to Texas because 90 per cent of her cotton was normally shipped abroad. Rayburn found few members friendly to him because of the general opinion that he had overdone the "good soldier" act by seconding Wallace's nomination on the convention floor. In the end, under the majority rule the Texas delegation decided to cast its entire forty-six votes for House Speaker William Bankhead.

Left to its own devices, the convention would have followed the lead of Texas and chosen Bankhead over Wallace. Much alarmed by the growing revolt against Roosevelt's dictation on the Vice Presidency, convention leaders had pleaded with Mrs. Roosevelt to come to Chicago. The mood in the stadium was ugly long before she arrived. But her effective speech abruptly changed the charged atmosphere. Said Jim Farley, "There is no doubt in my mind that Mrs. Roosevelt's appearance and her speech about the burdens of the Presidency in critical times saved the day for the President." As it was, unpopular Henry Wallace barely squeaked through by a vote of only 627 out of 1,100. But this settled the ticket and permitted the weary delegates to quit broiling Chicago and prepare the fall campaigns.

On September 16, 1940, Sam Rayburn finally achieved a twenty-five-year ambition, when the House elected him speaker to succeed William Bankhead, who had died the previous day. But Sam was a worrywart who foresaw a short tenure for himself because of the political trend. Despite the fall of France and the heroic air battle over Britain that summer—factors that should have united Americans behind Roosevelt—the *Fortune* maga-

zine poll in August showed Roosevelt only three and a half points ahead
of Wendell Willkie, his Republican opponent. Al Smith had come out for
Willkie, the former president of Commonwealth and Southern Utility
Corporation, and there was talk that John L. Lewis and *The New York
Times* were planning to desert the Democrats.

To top off his worries, Lyndon Johnson reported to him that Pat
Drewry, chairman of the Democratic National Congressional Committee,
was not doing his job properly, and the Republicans stood a good chance
of picking up the votes they needed in November to gain control of the
House and name their own speaker. Patrick Henry Drewry came from the
old plantation country in the eastern Tidewater gentility area of Virginia,
and since 1933 was the ranking Democrat behind Carl Vinson on the
House Naval Affairs Committee. Drewry was a philosophic type—quiet,
withdrawn, and unassuming—who was proud of his pork-barrel Appomat-
tox Military Park and his steadfast efforts to win increasing naval appropriations for Hampton Roads. Pat had ingratiated himself with Roosevelt,
even though he was "an old school Virginia conservative," because of his
continued warfare with the Harry Byrd anti-Roosevelt political machine
that held dictatorial power over Virginia Democrats. It was for this reason
most of all that Roosevelt saw to it that Drewry in 1935 became chairman
of the Democratic National Congressional Committee, which raised funds
and parceled out campaign money to Democrats running for Congress.

Agitated by Johnson's comments that Drewry was neither gathering contributions nor being of assistance to campaigning Democratic congressmen,
Rayburn met with House Majority Leader John McCormack of Boston and
passed on some of his mounting hysteria to McCormack. Then the two
rushed to the White House to discuss their problem with the President.
Roosevelt had the latest House count, which tallied 260 Democrats, 168
Republicans, 2 Progressives, 1 Farmer-Labor member, 1 American Labor
member, and 3 vacancies. This meant that the Republicans would have
to unseat fifty Democrats in November to win a majority of the 435
House seats. On the surface such a gain seemed implausible, but Roosevelt's mood was then one of impending doom on his own race against
Willkie.

"What do you suggest?" Roosevelt gulped, in Johnson's version of what
Rayburn told him afterward about the meeting.

"Put Lyndon Johnson in charge and give him a free hand," Rayburn and
McCormack replied.

Roosevelt said, "Sold. Tell Lyndon to see me tomorrow."

Mild Pat Drewry turned livid with outrage when he found he had been
undercut by Johnson. But he swallowed his shame without protesting to
the White House on learning that it was Roosevelt who had given the
young Texan the green light. Let the young whippersnapper run the Congressional campaign show, said Drewry, but the title of chairman of the

Democratic National Congressional Committee would never pass on to him.

The next morning Johnson was ushered into Roosevelt's second floor bedroom, where the crippled President ate breakfast before starting his official day. Johnson went over his plan to save the House for Roosevelt, and after each had smoked several cigarettes in excitement, Johnson left almost on the run to rent a downtown office where he could be on his own and away from Pat Drewry. Within three hours after his meeting with Roosevelt he had his office, several employees, furniture, and a half dozen telephones.

Johnson later claimed that through telephone solicitations he raised sixty thousand dollars in just a few weeks. Drewry disputed this, asserting that only twenty-five thousand, one hundred and eighty-one dollars were collected. Drewry did concede, however, that most of the money raised came from Texas, with E. S. Fentress, the newspaper publisher, topping the list with a five-thousand-dollar contribution for Congressional candidates.

During October 1940 when Johnson was involved with the House campaigns, his telephone pitch for money was that, with the nation's defense program beginning to burgeon, Texas business and industry stood to lose billions in contracts if Republicans won control of the House. And when it came to giving money to candidates, he worked directly with Roosevelt to determine the recipients. Johnson also said he was on the phone hours daily talking to Democratic congressmen back in their districts, offering advice and passing on strategy ideas for their use.

On election night, November 5, 1940, Roosevelt arranged a direct phone tie-in from the dining room of his mother's house in Hyde Park, New York, to Johnson's Washington office. There was excitement and pride when the thirty-two-year-old Texan broke the news to the President that not only had the Republicans failed to gain control of the House, but they had lost five seats to Democrats.

Some political observers gave credit for the Roosevelt victory to the President's humorous and sarcastic refrain of "Martin, Barton, and Fish," to ridicule three House Republican leaders. More said he had won because of the tense international situation, and in winning had carried Democratic candidates for Congress into office on his coattails. But Roosevelt believed that in addition to these major factors, Lyndon Johnson had been of positive help to him; and the 1940 campaign dated Johnson's status as a national politician.

Chapter 21

FOLLOWING THE EXCITING political events of 1940, in which he had played a wide variety of roles, Johnson could not stomach the thought of returning to his usual House routine. One of his dreams was to become a Presidential adviser, and Harold Ickes noted in his diary on January 2, 1941, that Johnson made an indirect stab in this direction. "I told the President," wrote Ickes, "that it was the opinion of Lyndon Johnson that if he should call in Sam Rayburn, John McCormack, and Jere Cooper [the ranking Democrat on the House Ways and Means Committee] for a quiet dinner or lunch to discuss the makeup of the committees for the new session of Congress, he would be able to get pretty much what he wanted. It is terribly important that the new House be organized by the friends of the Administration." Ickes passed along a reminder of Johnson's claim that he had made possible the Democratic House victory, plus the warning that if he did not take Johnson's advice, "there will probably be little chance of carrying a majority of the Lower House in the election of 1942." This advice was superfluous, for Roosevelt was in daily touch with the House leaders on this and other matters.

Earlier, Johnson, with ambitions to land on the control board of the Democratic National Committee, telephoned Ickes with the news that he had induced Rayburn and McCormack to speak to Roosevelt on this score. The two had urged Roosevelt "to have Johnson appointed acting secretary of the National Committee in place of Chip Robert." The reason for the phone call, Ickes related, was that "Johnson wanted me to say to the President that this ought to be done quickly. I passed this on to the President [and] he said he would try to get hold of Flynn [Democratic National Committee chairman and boss of the Bronx] by telephone that afternoon and see what could be done." Johnson was counting on the truth of Washington gossip that Roosevelt had criticized Robert because of the "government contracts Chip's firm had been securing" and had spoken sharply to Jim Farley about Robert's socialite wife, Evie, as a woman who "talks too much." But nothing came of his effort to get Chip Robert's job.

Had he cared to leave Congress, Roosevelt would have given him a major appointment in his Administration. But Johnson had no desire to give up the independence of a congressman for the subservience required of a civil servant. In fact, Roosevelt had earlier offered to name him as boss of the REA, and was somewhat surprised when Johnson rejected the job.

Johnson had still another ambition—to go to the Senate—but in 1941 when the Seventy-seventh Congress convened on January 3, he believed he was as far away from this goal as he had been in 1937 when he first discussed the subject with "Maggie" Magnuson. The same two chief stumbling blocks lay in the path of those dreams; and their names were Tom Connally and Morris Sheppard. Every Texas politician knew both were well liked throughout the state, and neither had to fear strong opposition in his next re-election contest. Shrewd, tart-tongued "Tawm" Connally, tall, curly-locked, and black-suited, had gone to the House in 1917 and then to the Senate in 1928, rising to power on the important Foreign Relations and Finance Committees. He had opposed the NRA codes as a serious violation of the antitrust laws, and the Court-packing bill as an unconstitutional move to abridge the independence of the Judiciary. But on all other matters he had been a consistent New Deal supporter of immense help to Roosevelt in leading the Senate fight to end the Neutrality Acts and promote aid to Britain in her war against Nazi Germany.

As for Morris Sheppard, even his few enemies agreed he could be re-elected to the Senate for life. He had gone to the House in 1902, succeeding his father, who died in office. Then in 1912, when Joe Bailey quit the Upper Chamber, Sheppard defeated Colonel Jake Wolters, the "wet" candidate, for Bailey's seat. The short, good-natured Sheppard was the author of the prohibition amendment and served as Roosevelt's workhorse as chairman of the Senate Military Affairs Committee. Sheppard's ambition, which he freely expressed, was his desire to be the longest-serving member of Congress in American history.

While Johnson chafed over his lack of political opportunity, only three months after the new Congress began, fate stepped in to help him. On Friday, April 4, 1941, one of his friends phoned him with the news that Sheppard had suffered an intracranial hemorrhage. Five days later he died at the age of sixty-five, the victim of overwork on his committee during the period of vast defense expansion, said his doctor.

Johnson knew at the moment when he learned of Sheppard's death that he would run for Sheppard's unexpired Senate term. Sheppard would have been up for re-election in 1942, and Johnson realized that if he did not run for his seat now, it would be virtually impossible to dislodge whoever was the incumbent next year.

Texas law required the governor to call a special election between sixty and ninety days after a Senate vacancy occurred, if Congress were in session when the senator died. The law also required the governor to appoint an interim senator to serve until the newly elected senator could take his seat. This made the key figure in the Sheppard aftermath the youthful, fifty-one-year-old Governor Wilbert Lee O'Daniel, and no one could predict what "Pappy" O'Daniel would do, because he did not take kindly to being told what rules to follow.

Johnson had met O'Daniel only a few times and knew him as a man who could turn a homely phrase to ridicule Roosevelt and the New Deal. But O'Daniel's greater reputation was that of king of the American hillbilly politicians and one of the strange personalities Texas politics washed ashore from time to time.

He hailed from Ohio originally, where his father worked in a plow factory, and after graduating from business college in 1908 at the age of eighteen, he became a stenographer in a flour milling company. He had such a gift of gab that he moved into sales work and was so successful that by 1929 he was sales manager of the Burrus Mill and Elevator Company in Fort Worth. Despite the economic crash he managed to triple sales of the firm's "Light Crust Flour" and became company president in 1930.

O'Daniel owed his start as a public figure to some unemployed musicians who offered to form a hillbilly band and sing twangy and doleful cowboy ballads over radio to help sell his flour. O'Daniel was uncertain what the connection was, but he hired them for a few shows and found his sales were increasing rapidly. This gave him the idea he might expand the flour market in person, so he bought a large, old bus, installed a public address system, and went on long tours of west Texas with his "Light Crust Doughboys." Everywhere the turnout was a sea of sunburned faces, and the crowds showed their appreciation of the hillbilly band and O'Daniel's homespun comments that he delivered in a drawl.

In 1935 he started his own flour company, the W. Lee O'Daniel Flour Company. He had begun life as Wilbert O'Daniel, then had changed it in Texas to Wilbert Lee O'Daniel to show his Confederate sympathies, and finally settled on W. Lee O'Daniel as a less humorous name. The old advertising ideas had proved profitable, and he retained them in the new company. The hillbilly band remained the basic ingredient in the radio and road shows; and in 1936 it became more of a family affair with his son Pat on the banjo, son Mike on the fiddle, and daughter Molly joining in the sad and romantic songs with Texas Rose. O'Daniel's trademarked flour was the "Hill Billy" brand, and beneath the goat on the flour sack was an O'Daniel rhyme with a bold printed line at the bottom of the sack that read: "Please pass the biscuits, Pappy." From the day when the new flour sacks were put on the market, O'Daniel gained a nickname that never left him—"Pass the Biscuits, Pappy."

Pass the Biscuits, Pappy was early aware of his special appeal to old people and to small-town Texans. They liked his handsome face, his clean appearance, his ever-ready stock of quips, and the wide grin he could turn on like a spotlight. It was obvious to onlookers that he could easily transfer this appeal to politics—and he did.

In 1938, after telling Texas over statewide radio that he was thankful for the more than fifty thousand letters and postcards he had received begging him to run for governor, he said he would. Pappy faced twelve opponents in that contest to succeed Governor Allred, and he suffered from a total lack of political experience. But he blithely campaigned like a relaxed winner, with a platform championing the Ten Commandments, the Golden Rule, "more smokestacks and businessmen; less Johnson Grass [a pestiferous weed] and politicians," and a thirty-dollar monthly old-age pension. While the elderly considered him their champion, there was shrewdness in proposing the pension, because those over sixty-five could vote without paying the state poll tax of one dollar and seventy-five cents.

"Play it again, Pappy," came the calls from every audience after the hillbilly band plunked and pleenked through one of Pappy's compositions. He had become a song writer, and in his opinion the numbers that helped his campaign the most were "Your Own Sweet Darling Wife" and "The Boy Who Never Gets Too Big to Comb His Mother's Hair." Pappy's campaign was unusual for other reasons. Besides offering the hillbilly show at every stop, he also had on hand a large supply of Hill Billy Flour, and he peddled sacks of flour to the crowd like a pitchman in a medicine show. Afterward he ridiculed politicians with such humor that some people claimed they heard at his shows the only carefree laughing since the depression came to Texas. Finally, Pappy passed small flour barrels into the crowd with a plea for campaign contributions to be dropped into the slot. Texans whose ancestors came from Tennessee said that from what the old folks had passed along, the nearest comparison to Pappy was "Slim Jimmy" Jones, a clown and mimic, who used those tricks to beat James K. Polk for governor in 1841, despite Polk's prestige as a former speaker of the House of Representatives in Washington and Andrew Jackson's protégé.

Pappy proved immune to all attacks as he went on his merry campaigning. When opponents pointed out that he had failed to pay his poll tax and was unable to vote in the election, Pappy's rejoinder was, "I didn't pay my poll tax because I was fed up with crooked politics in Austin and hadn't intended to vote for anyone this year. I didn't know I was going to be called upon to run." Next his opponents discovered that he had always voted Republican, an odd past for a Democratic candidate. At several of his rallies, ringers in the audience would shout at him for an explanation. Each time he would listen intently to the jiber, pause, then turn to his band and call out, "Shake up another tune, boys." Opponents made as little mileage in discussing O'Daniel's war record during the Great War of 1917 and 1918. It turned out that his sole activity had been to paint his flivver red, white, and blue and drive it in patriotic parades.

"Pappy's gonna win but I ain't for him," was the common comment of city voters who professed embarrassment with the hillbilly candidate. However, they must have voted for him because he swamped his fellow candidates in 1938. Horror at what had occurred was soon felt in some circles when Pappy made his legislative proposals. For instance, he asked for a law to encourage outside industry to move into Texas, and said he would see to it that these new industries could pay as low wages as they desired. If workers objected, he promised, he would throw them into prison, where they would work in gangs picking cotton. He also asked for an increase in old-age assistance programs, and proposed that it be paid for by a trans-actions tax on consumer goods. During his campaign he had opposed a sales tax. When the state legislature would not pass his bills, he denounced it with the nine-cylinder word *recalcitrant*. Despite his failure to come through on his campaign promise of a thirty-dollar-a-month old-age pension, the elderly believed his cry of martyrdom, and he won an even greater victory in his bid for a second term in 1940, when he collected 645,000 votes. The small minority of Texans who were college graduates and listened to Pappy's campaign speeches, and saw the popular reception they com-manded, had good reason to believe Artemus Ward's judgment that "the trouble with Texas is that they know so many things that ain't so."

O'Daniel waited ten days after Sheppard's death before announcing on April 19, 1941, that the special election would be held on Saturday, June 28. The Texas House, long at odds with Pappy, passed a resolution on April 10, proposing that he resign as governor and accept an interim ap-pointment to the United States Senate from Lieutenant Governor Coke Stevenson, who would then automatically be elevated to the Governor's Mansion. Pappy cackled that he understood too well that the house wanted to get him out of Texas, and he denounced the lower house with vehemence.

The truth was that he had discussed just this move with his buddies: Maco Stewart, the moneyman from Galveston; Jim West, the Houston oil, lumber, and cattle tycoon and reactionary publisher; and Carr Collins, wealthy Dallas radio magnate and mineral oil producer. The three agreed that if he held the interim appointment as senator, he could run with the prestige of the officeholder in the special election in June. But what if he lost the special election? He would be out of politics entirely, and this would never do. So the group strategy was that Pappy should appoint the weakest available figure as interim senator, a person who could not com-pete with Pappy in the special election.

Pappy's silence regarding the interim senator produced a flurry of news-paper speculation. First, the papers said that the late senator's widow, Mrs. Lucile Sheppard, would be named; then Jim West's name came up; and finally Austin correspondents decided it would be Hal Collins, the brother of Carr, a rich laxative manufacturer and an exchanger of jokes with Pappy. But Pappy O'Daniel said that his choice would be none of these, and suggested that reporters cover his speech and radio address from the San Jacinto Monument on April 21, the place and the day that General Sam Houston captured Santa Anna in 1836 and won Texas' independence from Mexico.

A large and excited crowd showed up for the one hundred and fifth anniversary of the Battle of San Jacinto to hear what Pappy had to say. He began with a long encomium of Sam Houston, went into various aspects of his career, and devoted paragraph after paragraph to his thirteen years as a senator before the Civil War. Long after puzzled reporters wondered what the point of such details might be, Pappy suddenly announced he was naming Sam Houston's last surviving son, General Andrew Jackson Houston, as interim senator.

Newsmen recalled that on his way east from Houston to San Jacinto, Pappy had stopped at the bayside town of LaPorte, at the shacklike home of Andrew Jackson Houston, for a ten-minute chat. Pappy now told his audience how he had broken the news to Sam Houston's son and of his own comment afterward that went: "General, do you know what caused that sun to suddenly burst through those dark and heavy clouds? It appears to me as if our great and good loving God has just spread the clouds apart so the spirit of your illustrious father could smile down upon his son on this particular scene and see the big smile on your face."

An outcry of indignation swept the state with the news of Pappy's appointment. That legendary Texan, Sam Houston, had been born in 1793 and his son, Andrew, sixty-one years later, while Sam was in Washington serving as a senator. This last link to Texas glory was therefore almost eighty-seven, and reporters who talked to him found him sick and senile. A cheap and shoddy trick by Pappy, said opposition papers, to name a man who could not oppose him in June. Pappy declared this to be nonsense and called Houston a well-qualified Democrat. But quick research produced the fact that the new senator was a lifelong Republican; he had run three times for governor, with his most aggressive contest against Jim Hogg, the illustrious Democrat, in 1892, when he won only 1,300 votes out of 600,000 cast. The last time A. J. Houston had been in the news was several years before when he had tried unsuccessfully to prevent the unveiling of a bronze equestrian statue of his father at Hermann Park in Houston, on the ground that Enrico Filberto Ceracchio's work did not resemble Sam Houston.

The old man's two daughters pleaded with him not to go to Washington for the few months he would serve, but to take his oath at home instead. However, the honor of representing Texas in the United States Senate was too great to pass up, and he boarded a train for the capital, after resting a month following his appointment. He managed to survive the trip to Washington and was sworn in and worn out by the oath-taking ceremony administered by Vice President Henry Wallace on June 2. Capitol historians gaped on discovering he had been sworn in ninety-five years after his father had undergone a similar ceremony in 1846!

After this he came twice to the Senate Chamber, where he introduced a bill to appropriate two hundred and fifty thousand dollars to complete the San Jacinto Memorial. Assigned to several committees, he attended only a single committee meeting. Then on the advice of the Capitol physician to whom he turned for aid to relieve the pains he was suffering in his stomach region, Senator Houston traveled the forty miles to Baltimore to have the experts at Johns Hopkins examine him. Here a checkup revealed a tumor of the pancreas, and instead of letting him live out his life as best he could, surgeons assured him that they could remove the tumor successfully, despite his age. So he underwent the operation, only to die of postoperative shock on June 26, five days after his eighty-seventh birthday and two days before the special election to fill his senate seat. O'Daniel, in a quick eulogy without benefit of research aid, revealed his ignorance of Texas history when he called Houston "the son of the Hero of the Alamo."

All the while Andrew Jackson Houston's tragedy was running its course, the campaign to elect a senator to replace him and serve out the rest of Sheppard's unexpired term continued apace. On April 19, when O'Daniel set the date for the special election as June 28, an immediate convulsion stirred newspaper kingmakers and dozens of Texans who wanted to be senator. The reactionary Dallas *Morning News* promoted Garner until the white-thatched former Vice President said he preferred his retirement in Uvalde, where he was busy with the two banks he owned, the largest herd of goats in the world, and his new activity constructing cheap houses for Mexicans. Some critics said it was wise of him not to run because he would have lost votes with his whining voice, disreputable clothes, and his once-a-week shaving schedule.

Another oldtimer's name came into the Senate picture when Pa Ferguson rumbled about making a try for Sheppard's seat. Pa asked Texans to send him postcards and letters to assure him of needed support. He failed to disclose the result of this appeal, but on May 10 he announced he did not choose to run. "Me and Ma will support Governor O'Daniel," he said, and if O'Daniel did not run they would back the man "who would do the least harm in Washington."

Several unknowns paid the one-hundred-dollar fee and entered the race quickly, though the first major candidate to announce was rugged, handsome, thirty-four-year-old Texas Attorney General Gerald Mann of Sulphur Springs. Mann, who was widely admired throughout the state, had been an exciting forward passer and all-conference quarterback at Southern Methodist before going to the Harvard Law School, where he worked his way to a law degree as a preacher. After only five years of law practice he ran successfully in 1938 against O'Daniel's choice for attorney general, Walter Woodul, who was then lieutenant governor. He amassed such a superb record prosecuting loan sharks and antitrust-law violators that Pappy's friends wanted Mann bought off and asked the governor to do so. Pappy's proposal was to offer him the post of chief justice of the Texas Supreme Court, but Mann rejected this high honor and ran for re-election as attorney general in 1940.

Next to announce was Martin Dies of Orange, the forty-year-old son of a former congressman by the same name. As chairman of the House Un-American Activities Committee, Dies had managed to put his name into the language. To superpatriots his name was synonymous with *hunter of Communists,* while to the Left *Dies* meant *witchhunter.* The husky, fleshy-faced Dies hoped to advance to the Senate as the self-appointed defender of "Americanism." When Secretary of the Interior Ickes heard that Dies planned to run for the Senate, he intended to deflate him by disclosing that Dies "hadn't paid any taxes on his house and lot for eight years." But Dies got wind of his scheme and paid in full the amount he owed.

Another early entrant was Hal Collins, Pappy's pal and producer of Crazy Crystal Water, a laxative that the Federal Pure Food and Drug Administration was trying to put out of business. Hal enjoyed a reputation for the poor taste of his radio commercials. Week after week he told listeners: "When I was a kid I used to have a shotgun, and when that shotgun got clogged up I used to take a ramrod and shove it through. Now Crazy Water does the same for you."

He had created a sensation at the second State Democratic Convention in September 1940 at his home town in Mineral Wells, where as keynote speaker he blasted the New Deal and President Roosevelt. Elliott Roosevelt was in the crowd, and after an emotional defense of the Administration he threatened the frightened Collins with mayhem. Collins' candidacy for the Senate in the spring of 1941 appeared to supporters of Pappy O'Daniel as a double cross of their hero. But insiders wrote him off as a seat-warmer who would campaign praising Pappy until the governor considered it propitious to jump into the race. When he did, Collins was expected to end his candidacy.

A logical candidate for the Senate was Congressman Wright Patman, the promoter of the soldiers' bonus, low interest rates for borrowers, and a plentiful supply of money in circulation. Patman's well-publicized hatred of bankers was bound to attract the large Populist vote in rural counties, though his mild speaking manner was in sharp contrast to the fighting words that came from his mouth. That Patman showed genuine interest in the Senatorial contest became evident when he wired the Secretary of State to tell him the closing date for filing. Patman was also talking to Texas radio officials about acquiring broadcasting time to present his views state-wide.

However, Patman had hardly begun his inquiries when massive White House pressure made clear that Roosevelt opposed his candidacy. The reason for this became apparent within a few days. On San Jacinto Day, Lyndon Johnson was in Austin to address a joint session of the state legislature. Those who heard him found his speech singularly lacking as a commemorative address in honor of Sam Houston. Instead, what he delivered was a smooth speech on the national and international crisis written by White House speech composers. The obvious purpose was to reveal him as a statesman concerned with the basic affairs, rather than a spread-eagle Independence Day orator. The country must mobilize for war. "The truth is we don't have any time," he said. "We don't know, in days, hours, weeks or months, when this hurricane may come to us." Then in words more befitting a President than a four-year representative, he went on: "I come to you as a friend of American labor. But to labor I want to say this: When you vote to strike, you must think not only of your liberties but also of those superior liberties of every citizen of your country. . . . I have been the friend of business and industry. Your government can call on you and you are bound to respond when it must defend you and your precious advantages. . . . I have fought a long battle for the farmers. But to farmers I say: Government can call on you, too, and you must answer. The security of the whole country is above that of any single group—labor, capital, or farmer."

Afterward Johnson held a meeting with Pappy O'Daniel and cautiously sounded out Pappy's intentions on the special election. Pappy, at his disarming best, piously told him he would not run for the Senate. Those who saw Johnson when he left the governor's office said they had never seen him look so happy.

President Roosevelt was to hold his scheduled news conference the next day, April 22, and a half hour before it took place Johnson burst into his Oval Office after an airplane ride from Austin and a taxi trip from the airport. Johnson told him about his successful speech with the standing ovation by the legislators that concluded it, and passed on the news that Pappy was out of the race. Roosevelt also glanced at a statement Johnson showed him that announced his candidacy for Sheppard's seat and suggested that Johnson read it to the newsmen from the vantage point of the White House steps.

A few minutes later, surrounded by reporters, Johnson stood outside the West Wing of the White House, where he prefaced his announcement by emphasizing that he had just come from Roosevelt's office. Later an excited group of reporters crowded around the President's desk and asked him to comment on Johnson's announcement and the special site where he broke the news. Roosevelt, who had failed almost totally to "purge" Democrats in the 1938 primaries for having opposed his Court-packing bill, would not come out flatly behind the young Texan.

"First, it is up to the people of Texas to elect the man they want as their senator," he said. "Second, everybody knows that I cannot enter a primary election." No one corrected him that this was a general election, in which all parties would have candidates, and not a primary election. "And third," Roosevelt said emphatically, "to be truthful all I can say is that Lyndon Johnson is a very old, old friend of mine." When he added that reporters could ignore the rule against verbatim quotation and quote him directly, news stories in Texas the next day said that Johnson had the "blessing" of the President. Some reporters took note of the fact that after publication of the "very old, old friend of mine" remark, Wright Patman did not enter the Senate race.

Longtime political observers later declared they had never seen a motlier crew than those who ran for Sheppard's unexpired term in the spring of 1941. The final printed ballot contained the names of twenty-nine candidates, including twenty-five Democrats, two Republicans (Politte Elvins and Enoch Fletcher), one independent, and a Communist (Homer Brooks). One writer said that the cast in "the election would have shamed Hollywood."

In addition to two congressmen (Johnson and Dies), other politicians in the contest were Attorney General Gerald Mann and Governor O'Daniel, who eventually became a candidate. There was also a Baptist preacher whose heavy-drinking press agent turned out handbills calling for a return to prohibition. Beyond these candidates, other campaigners included a plumber, a laundryman, a bootlegger, a geologist, a chiropractor, an admitted kidnapper, a lawyer, radio commentator, laxative manufacturer, two heavily bearded men who claimed this qualified them, a Naval Academy graduate who wanted an immediate declaration of war against Japan, another candidate who wanted a five-ocean Navy, another who would make the Trinity River navigable, and still another whose vague campaign promise was that he "would fight it out to the end."

Dr. John R. Brinkley of Del Rio was also in the race. Brinkley owned one of the most powerful commercial radio stations in existence, and used it to peddle his goat gland preparation for rejuvenation. He had run three times for governor of Kansas and had almost won once with a write-in campaign. Brinkley promised to cover Texas in his campaign "like the morning dew."

Then there were the men who claimed kinship with famous Texans of the past. One was Joseph C. Bean, who said he was related to Judge Roy Bean—"the law west of Pecos." Another was Edwin Waller, III, who said he was the direct line kin of Edwin Waller, who he said "committed the first overt act of the Mexican War" back in 1846. Still another, Ashley W. Crockett, the Granbury publisher and grandson of Davy Crockett, talked thirstily like a candidate but failed to pay his fee.

First of the army of candidates to show life was Hal Collins, who took his Crazy Crystal band, singers, and sound truck out on the hustings in mid-April. Hal's special gimmick was to give away "a real nice $29.95 mattress" to the largest poll-tax-paying family present. At Austin, he gave away fourteen mattresses to a family with thirteen children.

But Collins proved to be exactly what the experts had predicted, for when Pappy O'Daniel finally announced his candidacy on May 19, the mineral oil millionaire immediately withdrew from the race. Teased by newsmen for a month to declare himself in or out of the Senate contest, Pappy had stoutly maintained he would not run unless the "recalcitrant legislature" passed his five-point program. This consisted, he explained, of a bill to end the poll tax, a constitutional amendment barring deficit spending, a transactions tax to meet his proposed forty-million-dollar-a-year old-age assistance package, a bill to abolish capital punishment, and another to establish an office of auditor–budget director.

However, when May began slipping away, with the legislature passing many measures O'Daniel opposed and ignoring his program, he decided he could wait no longer. He announced his candidacy over statewide radio from the Governor's Mansion, and gave as his reason, "We got the job done in the legislature." Listeners across Texas could hear the roaring laughter from the large crowd in the mansion when O'Daniel mimicked President Roosevelt's news conference blessing of Johnson by referring to Roosevelt as "mah very old, old friend." Afterward Pappy let reporters ask him questions. In 1940, he had criticized state officeholders who retained their jobs while running for offices other than the ones they held, and he later had introduced legislation to force such candidates to quit their jobs. But when reporters now asked Pappy if he planned to resign from the governorship while campaigning for the Senate, he snapped, "I should say not!"

The campaign was off to a slow start, with Johnson ranked as the weakest of the big four candidates despite his public clutching of Roosevelt's coattails. Joe Belden, a student at the University of Texas, who had applied Dr. George Gallup's popularity polling methods with remarkable success in the 1940 contests for President and governor inside Texas, was again at work with his Texas Surveys of Public Opinion. Belden's Polls had achieved such standing that they were syndicated in newspapers throughout the state and were thoroughly studied and analyzed by the candidates. His May 4 published survey on the 1941 race made Johnson's cause appear hopeless; for O'Daniel led with 32.8 per cent of the voters, Mann was second with 28.2, and Dies was close behind with 27.9 per cent, while Johnson was far down the track with only 9.3 per cent.

Other professionals attempted their own forecasts based on the size and nature of the crowds at the campaign kick-offs of these top four adversaries. Mann and Johnson had the largest and most enthusiastic crowds; Dies was dull and O'Daniel suffered a cloudburst.

Attorney General Mann's crowd at Sulphur Springs cheered itself hoarse throughout his recital of his platform, just as crowds had done when he cocked his arm and completed a forward pass back at Southern Methodist. What he promised if elected to the Senate was an "unbeatable" United States Army, all-out aid to Great Britain, a forty-dollar-a-month wage for Army draftees, increased pensions for the elderly, and an FBI investigation of suspected subversives that would dwarf anything Martin Dies' House Un-American Activities Committee could possibly undertake. As for the current raft of strikes in airplane defense plants, Mann promised to work for a law to make them illegal. He also emphasized his support of President

Roosevelt, telling the crowd he had sent him a congratulatory telegram following the national convention at Chicago.

The tall, rippling-muscled Congressman Dies made his opening speech at Greenville, where, in a speaking voice superior to that of most radio announcers, he cried out almost despairingly about a secret army of subversives "much larger than the United States Army," with a Communist party spending ten million dollars a year and foreign agents running organizations holding a "membership exceeding seven million" subversives, dupes, and crackpots. Dies went on to condemn the CIO and praise the AFL, and he proclaimed himself an independent supporter of President Roosevelt. When he explained that he would do more for Roosevelt as a senator because "I am not a yes-man, or a green-man, or a showman," the crowd understood that he was referring to Johnson as the yes-man, Mann as the inexperienced green-man and Pappy, of course, as the showman.

Lyndon Johnson's kick-off came at familiar San Marcos on May 3, before a crowd his friends estimated at seven thousand and his detractors at five thousand. He wore his hat with the brim upturned in the Roosevelt style, and he used many of the President's gestures, though for a former debating coach he was a drawling mumbler. The town was choked with chartered buses and cars from points five hundred miles distant, and on hand to lead the "Hooray for Johnson" parade to the San Marcos Auditorium was the Austin High School band that Johnson's friend, Mayor Tom Miller, had sent for the occasion.

In this prepared speech Johnson referred time and time again to his theme, "Roosevelt and Unity," a tag to be used throughout his campaign to cement his platform together. For those who were deaf or could not read this slogan banner, an immense blown-up picture showed Johnson shaking hands with the President. Johnson's talk left no doubt that he was for Roosevelt on domestic issues, and he was for him on foreign issues. And he wanted it understood that a vote for him was a vote against Hitler. As for talk of war, he pledged, "If the day ever comes when my vote must be cast to send your boy to the trenches, that day will Lyndon Johnson leave his *Senate* seat to go with him." This remark brought the most applause.

Governor O'Daniel was the last of the big four to open his campaign. He left the mansion on June 2 for a day at Waco, which he considered his lucky city because he had made his first speech there when he ran for governor in 1938. The opposition press derided Pappy for his small crowd that day—an estimated three thousand persons, compared with the twenty-five thousand in attendance in 1938. Jim West's Austin *Tribune,* however, viewed his opener as a major success, considering that these few thousand persons braved an afternoon-long cloudburst to watch his show. The governor came as usual with his hillbilly band, his special sound truck with the dome on top like the state capitol, and his usual mouthful of quips. With a straight face Pappy said his platform would again be "one hundred percent approval of the Lord God Jehovah, widows, orphans, low taxes, the Ten Commandments, and the Golden Rule." But this time he was also adding "a common touch with the common man."

He promised he would go "easy" on the others in the race because "there are twenty-eight of them, and when you get to fighting too many snakes at once, one of them will sneak up and bite you." Nevertheless, he pulled the trigger of his double-barreled scattergun on his three chief opponents. "You know that feller Lyndon Johnson is so friendly with the President they tell me he can just walk in the White House and fry his breakfast eggs on the White House stove," Pappy said. "And that Martin Dies feller, he can't get into the White House barn, even with his Trojan Horse." Pappy also insisted he was not against Roosevelt: "I would be some help to that boy, and not just carry water." Then he went into what his opponents called "Pappy's Mother's Day Speech," which made many in his audience cry. Near the close he said he had the peace of mind to campaign for the Senate only because he had achieved such remarkable success in getting the state legislature to pass his twenty-two-million-dollar tax bill to pay for increased pensions. This brought feeble cheers from the old people in his audience, though the legislature had really approved the Morris Omnibus Tax Bill and not the transactions tax Pappy wanted. The omnibus bill contained no sales tax but stressed instead an increase in tax rates on natural resources extraction; nor did it earmark receipts for old-age pensions. Johnson's reported retort to Pappy's claim of legislative success was: "I think he might be feeling the effects of Johnson Grass."

Heavy spring rains and cold weather hampered all candidates as the campaign got under way. Alvin Wirtz had quit his job as Undersecretary of the Interior in order to mastermind Johnson's campaign. When Roosevelt first heard of his intentions, he called Wirtz and suggested he take a leave of absence for the duration or cook up a batch of Interior projects "to inspect" in Texas, and then return to his Washington post afterward. But Wirtz wanted a clean break in order to return later to his lucrative law practice, and he rejected Roosevelt's suggestions, though he agreed to negotiate the purchase of Saudi Arabian oil for the federal government when the election was out of the way.

The neat, long-faced Wirtz had planned a moderately heavy campaign schedule for his protégé, but when Joe Belden's May 4 poll showed him with less than 10 per cent of popular support, he replaced it with a saturation program. Wirtz planned to launch it as soon as the spring rains stopped but an uneasy Johnson refused to delay, and in a beating rainstorm he took off by plane for talks with local political leaders around the state. In west Texas, floodwaters reached the running boards of cars; in east Texas, the wind was like a Longhorn whip.

A week of lunches and dinners in soggy clothes, while Johnson privately qualified his support of Roosevelt by denouncing any federal regulation of the oil industry and weak federal action against defense strikes, brought on a serious throat infection that put him in the hospital for ten days. But Wirtz was ready for this crisis. While Johnson lay ill in bed, one of his friends, Everett Looney, a former assistant attorney general, took over his speaking dates in north Texas; County Judge Roy Hofheinz of Houston, his radio talk; and Wirtz, his speaking engagements in south Texas. Hofheinz scoffed at O'Daniel for concentrating on the social security issue "as the challenge of the hour when England is in trouble," while Wirtz kept repeating, "If someone else is elected and not Johnson, then Senator Burton K. Wheeler [an America First isolationist leader] will say in the Senate that it means the President is all wrong on his foreign policy."

By the time he was able to leave the hospital, Johnson was certain that his illness had doomed him as a candidate. This made the publication of the next Belden Poll a double shock to him. During his enforced idleness, his popularity had increased from 9.3 per cent to 17.6 per cent. All three of his chief opponents had lost ground; Pappy O'Daniel dropping from 32.8 to 22.4 per cent, Gerald Mann from 28.2 to 26.8 per cent, and Martin Dies from 27.9 to 26.2 per cent. What had happened primarily was that the weather had kept the three from making public speeches, while Johnson's friends had kept his name in the limelight. In addition Wirtz had cleverly spread the false rumor that President Roosevelt would soon come to Texas to speak in Johnson's behalf. Uncertain how to take this rumor, the Texas Legislature approved a resolution inviting the President to inspect the busy defense plants sprouting throughout the state.

Besides his news conference remark about his friendship for Johnson, President Roosevelt early put the prestige of his Administration behind the young congressman. When Harold Ickes came to the White House for a meeting on defense oil problems, Roosevelt warned him not to do or say anything that might harm Johnson's campaign. The implication was that Ickes was to lay aside his name-calling and regulatory battle with the Texas oil producers for the duration of the Senate race. Roosevelt also wrote a note to Jesse Jones, now his Secretary of Commerce, to put his home state prestige behind the thirty-two-year-old candidate. However, Jones remembered too well Johnson's efforts against him as chairman of the Texas delegation caucus at the 1940 national convention, and the President's note went into his "file and forget" box. On May 23, 1941, Roosevelt followed up with a second note that read: "I sent you a memorandum on May fifteenth in regard to Texas. I hope you received it. What is the answer?" Jones paid no more attention to this note than he did to the first.

Still other help came from the White House. Harold Young, top aide to Vice President Henry Wallace and a Dallas resident, returned to Texas to assist Wirtz. Bill Hassett, assistant press secretary to the President, got an assignment to write telegrams of support to be sent Johnson at strategic times under the signature of high Administration officials. Roosevelt also arranged to send Johnson telegrams on various public issues to be read by the candidate on big speech nights. In addition the President asked Steve Early, his press secretary, to promote Johnson with Washington correspondents whose work appeared in Texas newspapers. Two who wrote up Johnson as "an unusually able and enterprising congressman" were the boy columnists, Joseph Alsop and his partner, Robert Kintner, with whom Johnson had long before made "instant friends." Alsop, who was known as the "Cassandra of Washington" because of his tediously gloomy column, was the grandson of the sister of President Theodore Roosevelt and Elliott Roosevelt, who was the father of Eleanor Roosevelt. With this special Roosevelt tie, being the grandson of Eleanor Roosevelt's aunt, Alsop was a frequent guest at White House Sunday morning breakfasts, to which Johnson came on occasion as a Roosevelt protégé. In one of their May syndicated columns, Alsop and Kintner poured out the story of a President pleading long and hard with the young Texan to run for the Senate before the reluctant Johnson finally agreed. Their picture of the meeting had Johnson begging off because of the detriment of his youth, his lack of campaign funds, his infected tonsils and his worry that if he should be defeated he would be damaging the President's cause. But, claimed the columnists, the President convinced him when he said that "the times were difficult and that the Administration would need every possible support for its foreign policy."

The cluttered race began thinning out as the weather started clearing. Several candidates dropped out, though their names remained on the ballot. Dr. Brinkley quit on June 6 to concentrate on his goat gland business, and he asked his supporters to vote for Governor O'Daniel. One minor candidate called a meeting of the other inconsequential candidates to decide which one should remain in the race and get the support of the others. Nothing came of this minor league convention.

Handsome Attorney General Mann had set a grueling schedule for himself of three hundred speeches and twenty-five thousand miles of travel. It was apparent to the pros that he was blundering from the start, for he failed to inject the humor into his speeches that Texans expected from their politicians. Instead he emphasized the weighty 3,331 legal opinions he and his staff had written, the 1,806 courtroom cases he had tried, and the million dollars in fines he had won for the state in antitrust actions. At every stop he condemned Congressmen Johnson and Dies for "deserting their posts" during a time of crisis; yet he insisted that the race was solely a contest between him and O'Daniel. As evidence he pointed to the Belden Poll of June 8, which showed him in first place with 27.0 per cent and O'Daniel second with 25.6 per cent.

However, Mann was taking no chances, and he had a collection of condemnatory comments for all three opponents. He labeled Dies' Congressional work as inadequate and called it a tea party compared with the search he would make for un-American Americans. He also had choice denunciations of his governor's tactics, and warned the elderly that Pappy's professed interest in them was based solely on their freedom from paying the poll tax as a requirement for voting. To offset Pappy's success with Bible Belt Texans, Mann carried a Bible to his political rallies and belted it hard at times to emphasize the rectitude of his cause.

For a candidate who insisted that Johnson was not in the running, Mann spent an inordinate amount of time criticizing him. He made a big show denouncing Johnson as the darling of the CIO, arguing that Welly Hopkins, now general counsel of John L. Lewis's United Mine Workers, was active in Johnson's campaign. Wirtz squelched this attack by handing reporters copies of a letter Mann wrote to Hopkins, asking for his support. Mann also hit at Johnson for not reporting all campaign contributions. This brought a quick hackle from Harold Young that Mann was a "cry baby." Young pointed out that he had made a contribution to Mann's campaign for attorney general in 1938, but "my contribution did not appear upon the sworn statement of contributions received by the self-advertised honest attorney general." Mann struck back at Young by charging that federal employees in Texas had been threatened with the loss of their jobs if they failed to vote for Johnson.

By now, with his nerves frayed by his aggressive and driving campaign, Mann reacted emotionally even to pinpricks. Mann had a plaque hanging on the wall behind his desk, and the inscription read: "I sacrificed no principle to gain this office and I shall sacrifice no principle to keep it." When, from one speaker's rostrum, Johnson ridiculed the wall fixture and called it "a bought plaque," instead of ignoring him, Mann told reporters shrilly that his Bible class had given it to him when he first took office. He was so worked up and close to tears as he gave his explanation that several reporters laughed.

When Mann tried to rip away the Roosevelt flag enveloping Johnson, his younger opponent was more than equal to the exchange. While he had been a consistent supporter of the President, said Mann, this did not mean that he had to be a blind follower. Furthermore, he went on, he was certain Texans would not tolerate White House dictation so that "one candidate must be crammed down their throats." Johnson tossed this aside with the comment that "you are not electing a yes-man, but a man to whom Roosevelt will say *yes*." Then to throw another brick through Mann's self-proclaimed glass wall of honesty, Johnson gave out his view that there were some law partners of officeholders who were sneaking off with "huge receivership fees."

One of the unexpected happenings during the campaign was the way Martin Dies faded as a candidate. When he talked to the Mothers of Dallas on communism inside the American Youth Congress, he could evoke hysterical cheers and applause. But he gathered only listless audiences elsewhere. Close observers said that his one scary message was soon a bore, that he lacked an organization, he spoke infrequently, which gave the impression he was not putting out his best, and he was inept in his press relations. Some attributed his decline to his constant sneering at hillbilly music. When Dies mentioned Pappy O'Daniel, it was generally to wail that he should not be sent to the Senate because he "has to have a hillbilly band to play for him while he stops and thinks." One of the charges Dies made against Johnson was that his fellow House member had written friendly letters to a Texas German whom the Dies Committee had on its lists as a Nazi. Reporters called this an unfair attack on the ground that the German had written to Johnson first and a congressman was supposed to answer his mail.

Because Johnson had begun so low on the Joe Belden Poll, Wirtz believed that only an opulent campaign would move him into contention. Federal law limited Senate campaign expenditures to twenty-five thousand dollars, but Wirtz knew that honesty on this score would result only in a disastrous defeat. A single statewide radio talk cost thirteen hundred dollars, some highway billboards two or three hundred dollars, a small newspaper ad fifty dollars. At these rates, twenty-five thousand dollars would not get a candidate out of his own back yard.

There were charges later that the Johnson campaign chest in 1941 exceeded five hundred thousand dollars. The candidate's submitted report claimed receipts of only nine thousand six hundred and forty-five dollars and expenditures of eleven thousand eight hundred and eighteen dollars and fifty-three cents. Of his contributions, Johnson said that twenty-five hundred dollars came from his wife, another such sum from E. S. Fentress, the publisher, five hundred dollars from Clara Driscoll, the Texas national committeewoman, fifty dollars from Miss Lucinda Rayburn, sister and Washington hostess of Mister Sam, and twenty-five dollars from I. Zlotnick, a Washington furrier.

"The half-million-dollar figure was closer to reality," said an associate of Alvin Wirtz. "Lyndon had a personal airplane, hundreds upon hundreds of campaign workers, extensive newspaper ad coverage, a large number of expensive radio broadcasts, cash prizes for those who came to his rallies, a bigger telephone bill than the White House, and the saturation of the entire state with highway billboards showing him and Roosevelt shaking hands. The way one reporter put it was that 'Lyndon either spent a fortune or he has more friends who will work for nothing since slave labor.'

"Wirtz collected a large part of the campaign's finances from Brown and Root, a construction company he had been promoting. George and Herman Brown were two young fellows who had gone into business with George's father-in-law. During the depression, things went so sour for them that creditors took away their equipment, and they were at the point of bankruptcy. At this low ebb Wirtz helped them land a paving contract in Guadalupe County where he had lived, but this didn't help them because they lacked the trucks and equipment to fulfill the contract. So Wirtz stepped in and got the Travis County Commissioners at Austin to lend them, illegally, Travis County equipment to complete a state road contract in another county. Had this ever leaked out, all of them might have been in serious legal troubles, but the equipment was quietly returned after the pavement was down, and Brown and Root was saved from bankruptcy.

"Later, Wirtz awarded them the contract to build one of the dams on the Lower Colorado River, and Lyndon Johnson helped them acquire highly profitable cost-plus federal contracts, such as the construction of the Naval Air Training Base at Corpus Christi, the largest in the world. By 1941 they were fast becoming multimillionaires, with Wirtz representing them as legal counsel, and Lyndon helping them get business as constituents of his.

"So it was natural when Lyndon ran for the Senate and Wirtz managed his campaign that George and Herman Brown would pour money like water into his race. The Bureau of Internal Revenue later uncovered some of the subterfuges they used to get around the financial campaign limitations of the law. One of their widely used schemes was to issue big bonuses to employees during the campaign period, and these individuals gave their 'bonuses' to local Johnson campaign managers. Another trick was to pay high 'fees' to lawyers connected with the Johnson campaign, and these fees passed into the campaign money chest. Since the passing along of the money was done almost entirely through cash, it was difficult to check, but Internal Revenue obtained sworn statements. However, when Internal Revenue was on the verge of taking criminal action against Brown and Root, Wirtz and Johnson paid a call on President Roosevelt, and action was stopped. Some years later when there was talk of reviving the issue, all papers involved were removed from a fire-proof building in Austin, dumped into a quonset hut, and went up in ashes when the quonset hut was leveled by bursting flames."

As June hove into sight, Pappy O'Daniel found himself unable to quit Austin and start his campaign. Pappy was yelling at legislative leaders to adjourn the Texas Legislature so he could fill his special sound truck with gas and get his campaign rolling. But the legislature would not adjourn because members suspected he wanted to veto some of their major bills and have them out of town and unable to override his vetoes. This brought on a blistering tirade against the legislature by Pappy over statewide radio, and charges that members were crooks in league with lobbyists. Pappy's radio programs came weekdays at noon and at 6 A.M. on Sundays. "They are out to get me," he said in a helpless tone during one noontime broadcast. "It seems to me they don't care which one of the other candidates gets elected just so it isn't me." But, he added in a tone filled with resolution, the people would not let "them" get him. Pappy said he could not understand "the stubbornness of the legislature for not adjourning." The only explanation he could find, he insisted, was that they did not know about the state's need for Pappy as a senator; and you could tell this because they sat down "to big plank steaks for lunch every day" and they wore "suede shoes."

After his June 2 kick-off at Waco, Pappy O'Daniel's fury with the Texas Legislature for pinning him to Austin grew. He did not enjoy reading the first Belden Poll in June, which showed Mann ahead of him, and Dies and Johnson not very far behind. As a substitute for his own personal effort, Pappy sent out his three children—Mickey-Wickey, Patty Boy, and Molly—along with the hillbilly band, to campaign for him with songs and stories until he could join them.

It was now or never for Johnson and Alvin Wirtz, and Johnson's June campaign evolved into a mammoth effort, which required an army to prepare and implement. Wirtz saw to it that dozens of cities and towns had active Johnson organizations, which held meetings, passed out handbills and buttons, and utilized local radio time. In Houston, where among several "Johnson for Senator" groups schoolteachers had organized a Johnson Club for their former colleague, Johnson's regret was that his Uncle George, who had predicted he would one day become a senator, had died the previous year. Along the Rio Grande, Wirtz was competing with friends of O'Daniel to buy off county political dictators to "bring in" a big vote for their man through their usual ballot-box-stuffing techniques. To impress Texans, who were universally impressed by bigness, at one stop Wirtz induced fourteen mayors to form a welcoming committee for Johnson. In the ten German counties, where polls showed overwhelming opposition to war between the United States and Hitler's Germany, Wirtz went personally on a speaking tour, though he won few promises of support for Johnson. Wirtz also made extensive use of newspaper publisher friends of the young candidate.

The principal newspaper advocates of Johnson were Charles E. Marsh and E. S. Fentress, who had combined their publishing realm into a fourteen-paper chain. Marsh, a confidant of Vice President Henry Wallace, wrote most of Johnson's campaign speeches and traveled throughout the state with him on campaign swings. Marsh and Fentress's championing of the underprivileged was met with some sarcasm by reporters and copyreaders on their newspapers, who were paid a wage limited to from ten to fifteen dollars a week. Another newspaper-chain publisher printing a running accolade of Johnson was Houston Harte of San Angelo, whose friendship with Johnson went back to the Mister Dick Kleberg days. Said Harte: "I went to Washington seeking a community loan. Dollars were scarce in West Texas in those days. . . . I ended up on a cot in a one-room place. There were three other cots in the room. On one was Arthur Perry, who was Senator Tom Connally's secretary. On another was Congressman Ewing Thomason's secretary, Bob Jackson, who is now editor of the Corpus Christi *Caller-Times*. Congressman Kleberg's secretary, Lyndon Johnson, was on the third."

Wirtz's strategy was to have Johnson begin his campaign as a statesman and then outdo Pappy O'Daniel as an entertainer. At the outset, therefore, Johnson offered a serious seven-point program based on his theme, "Roosevelt and Unity." Among these planks were his call for delivery of a large supply of war matériel to beleaguered England; United States occupation of Greenland, Iceland, Dakar, the Canary Islands, and Cape Verde; the equipping and training of a two-million-man Army; the drafting of business executives for defense plant management; and the drafting of unemployed women for defense work. A vote for Johnson, he maintained to early audiences, was a vote against Hitler.

But as the campaign progressed, Wirtz soft-pedaled issues to stage for Johnson what one observer called "the biggest musical comedy and floor show in the history of politics." It was hokum of proportions not even O'Daniel had been able to attain in his sideshows of previous campaigns. A Johnson rally included a swing band screeching out jazz, a blackface act, dancing girls, an overweight singer of patriotic songs, a large-busted, shapely girl singer, comedy routines, a long patriotic pageant, a lottery—and finally a speech by Johnson.

Someone remarked that if all the persons involved in the Johnson stage show and in his local organizations (including the army of advance drummers who preceded the show from town to town) bothered to vote, he was certain to win the election. Before each rally Wirtz sent trained advance men days ahead to build up excitement and drumbeat local citizens to attend, with their many newspaper ads, radio blurbs, and offers of money awards at the Johnson meeting. Others were busy marring Texas outdoor scenery with billboards showing Johnson and Roosevelt shaking hands; and still others were pasting "Franklin D. and Lyndon B." car stickers by the thousands on windshields. Full-page newspaper ads announced the "patriotic rally" for "Roosevelt and Unity" that was on its way to the lucky town. Johnson was hailed as "the native Texas candidate" (in contrast with Ohio-born O'Daniel); and other references noted him as "the six-foot-three-inch friend of Roosevelt" and "the young man from the Hill Country" who was always "riding high."

On the day of the rally Johnson's plane might land in a cow pasture if the town did not boast an airstrip. Local dignitaries would be rounded up like cattle and brought to the landing strip to extend a warm greeting, and amidst the fanfare of sirens and shiny automobiles plastered with campaign material and bunting he would be transported to the scene of the big meeting. This was usually the town park, complete with a bandstand to which the crowd had been enticed despite the mosquitoes and searing heat by the promise of free defense bonds and stamps to holders of lucky raffle numbers. Behind the bandstand, viewers saw the bigger-than-life picture of Roosevelt and Johnson in their never-ending handshake, with the "Roosevelt and Unity" title below the picture painted in good old patriotic red, white, and blue. Also in full view of the crowd was the squirrel cage that contained the lottery tickets for the money prizes.

The show blasted off with some pieces of ear-jarring jazz by the John-son Swingsters, professional musicians attired in white jackets. Then while the echo was fading into the stifling summer heat, out stepped two-hundred-and-eighty-five-pound Sophia Parker, whom the master of cere-monies introduced as the "Kate Smith of the South." An eyewitness re-corded that Sophia "wore a tarpaulin white evening gown decorated with red, white, and blue"; the perfect costume for belting out "I Am an American."

Then, after she begged the audience to join her in singing a chorus of the song, she blared it out again. This time when the crowd finished ap-plauding itself, she introduced a shapely girl who twanged out "I Want to Be a Cowboy's Sweetheart" in a style reminiscent of Pappy's daughter Molly and Pappy's specialty singer Texas Rose. Now came the hillbilly combo with the guitars and fiddle to plunk out songs of cowboy hangings and general misery. Then the "Kate Smith of the South" again appeared in center spot with her rousing "Dixie" and "The Eyes of Texas Are Upon You," and when she finished the pretty girl returned to crackle through "San Antonio Rose."

But these were only the opening acts. Next came the pageant—"The Spirit of American Unity"—whose tone and approach were an obvious steal from a popular radio show called "The March of Time." The announcer, a trained radio performer with a deep velvet tone, first put in a plug for defense bond purchases by the audience and then solemnly declared that "The Spirit of American Unity" they were about to witness was paid for by "the friends of the President."

The pageant began with a grim recital of the dismal situation in which the country found itself before Roosevelt was elected: the stock market crash; mass unemployment and hunger; and a cruel federal government unwilling to help the people. (All the while the Swingsters played funereal music.)

Now came 1932, and the announcer's voice lost its lugubrious tone as he described Roosevelt's smashing victory over that devil Hoover. (A bugle gave out a military burst.) "When Roosevelt became President the banks were popping like popcorn!" cried the narrator. He told about the bank holiday of March 1933 "to save the American banking system," and he moved on to the relief program, the Civilian Conservation Corps to put young men to work on reforestation, the NYA, NRA, and REA. (The music turned happy and rhythmic, and he boomed ecstatically, "People were eating chicken and ice cream again!")

Then suddenly his happy expression gave way to sadness. "But all this could be swept away!" (Frightening music.) "So the people re-elected our great President!" (Trumpet calls of triumph; then silence, followed by troubled music.) "Hitler came and Germany threatened the world again. What could Americans do about it? They elected Franklin Delano Roosevelt to a third term!" (The band broke into "Happy Days Are Here Again," and the crowd cheered.)

The music stopped. "The war in Europe was getting closer to the United States," shouted the narrator. "Franklin Roosevelt needed a man who loved his country, who loved the people!" (The band blew out the opening of "God Bless America.") "President Roosevelt endorsed this man. This man is *Lyndon Johnson . . .*"

At this, the dignitaries on the stand rose in a body and stood at attention. Then from the rear, Johnson suddenly popped onto the scene with his hands held high while he pleaded helplessly with the crowd to end its hog-calling cheers. Finally, on signal, his bellwether shills in the crowd stopped their cheering, and there was silence.

If he did not want the pageant to be the high point of the rally, the young candidate had to be dramatic in his own right. Off came Johnson's big white hat with the upturned brim, and he tossed it on the floor as though to signify he meant business. Then he began reciting his prepared speech, which contained several references to himself and Roosevelt. A few minutes of this and he stopped to take off his jacket. Then after a few more paragraphs he jerked his tie loose, and a minute or two later he tore his shirt open, as he reviewed "eighty years of the Johnson family's war record" (which had ended with the Civil War). And once he finished the written text, he made a big show of tossing it over his shoulder and telling the crowd, "Now let's get down to my country-boy style of talking." Out would pour his stock of Hill Country homilies—mostly wise things "my Daddy taught me." He would have some humorous stories, the declaration that he was "the best qualified candidate," and sometimes he would ridicule his opponents, making use of his remarkable ability to mimic their way of talking.

After his speechifying ended, the crowd hushed while the squirrel cage was brought forward. This was the main event and the chief crowd attractor. A hand went into the cage, and a lucky number was produced. The announcer read the digits in a shout, and a squeal of joy and a shriek generally greeted the close of the reading. Then the proud winner came forward for his defense bond. At one rally Mayor Tom Miller of Austin handed out one hundred and seventy-five dollars worth of defense bonds and stamps to lucky number holders. One wag commenting on this aspect of the Johnson rally said: "That Lyndon Johnson sure is a handy man to have around between pay days."

Although his three children and Texas Rose were out on the hillbilly hustings, O'Daniel chafed at his own forced inactive campaign from the Governor's Mansion. True, he was broadcasting every weekday noon from his comfortable confines, giving him an opportunity to tell the people around the state that he thought his opponents were "political waterboys" and "coattail candidates." And every Sunday morning at six he was on the air, posing as the religious candidate by urging listeners to go to church. But he missed the sound and feel of the crowd and the personal pleasure of putting on a show.

This was why he could no longer stay in Austin to scold the state legislature for not adjourning when the first week of June disappeared. He told his people over the radio to expect him on his travels across "byoo-ta-ful" Texas. Then he was gone from the capital for his campaign debut at Houston with the nine-piece band, sound truck, Mickey-Wickey, Patty Boy, Molly, and Texas Rose. After his medicine show and after collecting the small flour boxes he passed out to the crowd for contributions, Pappy headed north to Dallas; then he cut out west, where one hundred performances later he closed his campaign routine at a raucous fun rally at Lubbock, south of the Panhandle.

Johnson gave away money and Pappy collected it; otherwise their shows were similar, except for Johnson's professional pageant. Those who watched both men campaigning agreed that Pappy was a natural comedian with a sharp wit which turned out remembered phrases. Pappy's hillbilly band did not meet the level of the Johnson players, but Pappy's boys could wail out some loud, plaintive numbers, and Texas Rose was hard to beat when she sang "A Good Man Is Hard to Beat." Son Mike, the master of ceremonies, had been briefed on the Johnson show, and he had his own copycat Americanism speech to deliver, which he followed by getting the crowd to join him in "God Bless America." Then came Pappy without formality, because he held to a firm rule that no little pipsqueaking local politician could introduce him. He had his homey ramble about his honest platform as a starter, while his crowd slapped mosquitoes on their sun-scorched cheeks. He wrapped himself in the Ten Commandments and the Golden Rule and let everyone know his whispered secret that he was the only one in the race with so lofty a purpose. Frequently he invoked audience participation in his talk. "There's a new moon out tonight," he told one crowd. "Have you all made your wishes yet? All you O'Daniel supporters make that wish right now." Following the homey bits, Pappy tore into the Texas Legislature and lobbyists, and he was assured of prolonged cheers when he told how he was fighting for the people against "influence peddling politicians" who had "mahogany-lined offices." There were no cheers when he passed out little flour boxes and asked for donations afterward.

Johnson could not hope to match Pappy's natural touch, which brought him close rapport with crowds. To the end of his campaign, whatever aphorisms he uttered he continued to attribute to his Daddy. "My Daddy always said to me: 'Lyndon, take care of the people and the election will take care of itself,'" was one he used to show how responsive he was to the needs of Texas. "My Daddy used to say, 'Come now, and let us reason together,'" was another maxim he employed to explain that he was not a stubborn noncompromiser. He had come across this expression in the Book of Isaiah while leafing through the Old Testament at the time he was Mister Dick Kleberg's secretary, and over the years he adopted it as his principal saying.

But his principal campaign weapon to the day of voting remained his constant reminder of his close relationship with Roosevelt. "Yes, I am a yes-man to the Commander-in-Chief, as every good soldier should be in time of war and national emergency," he shouted from the speaker's platform. "I am a yes-man for everything that will aid in the defense of the Republic."

He was always quick to add that there were special advantages in being a yes-man to the President. In a single year, he boasted, he had obtained more Treasury money for his District and for the rest of Texas than the combined total of the other twenty members of the Texas delegation in the United States House of Representatives. "That's because I know the ropes," he confided. Among the projects he had recently landed, Johnson recounted, were the forty-five million dollars as a starting expenditure to build the Naval Air Base at Corpus Christi; the Orange and Houston shipbuilding yards; the Naval ROTC unit at the University of Texas in Austin; and the Naval Reserve Station near Austin.

As his campaign moved toward the homestretch, the special gimmick of the Johnson campaign became his reading of telegrams sent him by President Roosevelt. These messages showed "proof" not only of Johnson's strong voice at the White House, but also Roosevelt's willingness to give Johnson credit for almost all vital actions he was taking.

In one speech, for instance, Johnson said he had told Roosevelt to sign the farm parity bill that Congress had passed. During the next few days, when speaking to farmers, Johnson repeated this statement until that climactic moment at which he said the President had sent him a telegram on this issue. Roosevelt's wire, which Johnson read twice to the crowd, told him that the President thought he would be pleased to learn he had signed the bill calling for parity payments up to 85 per cent of the base year prices of covered commodities. At Fort Worth on May 23, Johnson's speech contained advice to Roosevelt to declare a state of national emergency. When the President did so on May 27, Johnson aides claimed that the Chief Executive had acknowledged the candidate's excellent suggestion.

In a broadcast from Houston Johnson read a telegram from Roosevelt in which the President invited Johnson to "come in and talk to me" about the Texan's old-age pension plan. Roosevelt went on to say he agreed with Johnson on the need to reduce the age of eligibility from sixty-five to sixty and "reminded" Johnson that the two had discussed this before and their views had been incorporated into the Democratic National Platform of 1940.

When Mann kept up his attack on Johnson for deserting his post, Johnson gave reporters a copy of the telegram he had sent Roosevelt, saying he would return immediately to Washington if he were needed "in the national emergency." A few days later he read Roosevelt's reply over radio. The President had ordered him to stay in Texas "to present the issues through personal appearances," and should he be needed in Washington, Roosevelt pledged he would immediately send for him. There was still another reason why it was necessary for him to continue his campaign, said Roosevelt. "The people of Texas by taking part in the election of June 28 of a United States senator thereby present a convincing demonstration of our democratic process at work."

On the days when Johnson had no telegram from Roosevelt, he had wires of support from other Washington officials. From his pockets he would extricate pieces of paper that offered first-person praise from Vice President Wallace; Frank Knox, the Republican Secretary of State; Harold Ickes; and Carl Vinson. He even had the support of Representative Melvin Maas, the ranking Republican on the House Naval Affairs Committee. To foster the idea among out-of-state Texans, Sam Rayburn sent him word for publication that he planned to cast an absentee ballot for Johnson.

From time to time, when Wirtz and Marsh believed he might be overdoing the Roosevelt pitch, Johnson told how he differed from the Administration. For his oil backers he announced his opposition to federal control of oil production, which Ickes favored; and he defended the 27.5 per cent depletion allowance for oil, the tax break that had raised many Texans to millionaire status. He also came out against ending the tax favoritism of community property laws enjoyed by Texans and opposed by Treasury Secretary Henry Morgenthau.

With Johnson eulogizing the President and reading telegrams from him, it was natural that his opponents should declare a close kinship with Roosevelt. Dies called him a "humanitarian," and Mann managed a note of fervor in his voice when mentioning the President. O'Daniel also found it wise in the closing weeks of the campaign to praise the White House occupant. He told his rallies he had written a song for Roosevelt in 1932, voted for him in 1936, and always stood ready to pray for him. "So onward, noble President," he sang his 1932 song, "we pledge our faith in you. 'Cause when we see your smilin' face, we never can feel blue."

When Johnson insisted that O'Daniel and the others were "definitely opposed to the President's policies, either openly or by subterfuge," Pappy said just as loudly that he liked "that boy" Roosevelt. He would go to Washington to rescue Roosevelt from the "professional politicians," said Pappy. Those were the ones who were the radical spenders, and when he got to the Senate, he promised, he would kick them out and retire the entire national debt. And that went for all the others in Roosevelt's crew, those planners and spenders who "couldn't run a peanut stand." This last remark gave Johnson the opportunity to cry out publicly at one of his rallies, "Do you think men like Secretary Hull, Sam Rayburn, Secretary

Knox, Secretary Stimson, Wendell Willkie, Vice President Wallace, Jesse Jones, and Tom Connally are back-slapping, pie-eating, pussyfooting professional politicians who could not manage a peanut stand?"

O'Daniel had interesting thoughts about other people and institutions. When he went to Washington, he said, he would keep a wary eye on the Texas Legislature to see that it continued to do his bidding. "While I'm gone, I'm going to put Texas politicians on probation," he drawled in his acquired Southern dialect, and if they failed to meet his requirements he would be back to punish them. He put this threat to music, and at every rally his hillbilly band played this new hit: "I'll Be with You When I'm Gone."

Once he went to Washington, he promised, he would purge all senators who did not vote for his antistrike bill. Other promises included forcing the federal government to go on a cash budget that included boosting federal old-age pension money for Texans. "I might have to twist their tails in Washington," he said, if United States senators proved as stubborn as Texas senators. "We will get the job done no matter how loud they beller or how many are in the herd. When I worked on a ranch the way to make the old cows move faster was to twist their tails." As for Johnson, Mann, and Dies, he said, these "pretty boys" with their "Clark Gable pictures on all the telephone poles and trees" claimed to know farming; but they really did not and they "wouldn't know which end of the horse to put the bridle on."

By the third week in June the campaign reached the fever stage. Supporters of the different candidates were easily moved to fist fights and foul language. Almost every rally witnessed some spilling of blood when hecklers dared to interrupt proceedings. O'Daniel had liked the Belden Poll at the outset when he was running far ahead of the pack; and so had Mann and Dies because they were only around the next bend. But none of the three could find anything worthwhile about Belden's work when the June 21 poll catapulted Johnson into first place. While the Johnson camp showed elation and declared its man the winner, Mann charged anew that federal employees in Texas had been pressured by Wirtz and Young to support Johnson or face unemployment. Johnson's new standing in the poll served as an impetus to an even greater outpouring of emotions by the camps of his three opponents.

During the final period Pa Ferguson, who had dropped completely from sight, came alive. "It occurred to me one day," he told a reporter, "that if we could get O'Daniel in the U.S. Senate, Coke Stevenson, as lieutenant governor, would automatically become governor. Well, O'Daniel wasn't doing any good. Polls showed it and so did somep'n else. I called up Coke and said, 'How come you ain't out there helpin' O'Daniel get elected to the Senate so you can be governor?' "

Coke opined he "hadn't thought much about it."

"Well, you better get busy," Ferguson said he told Coke Stevenson. "Better take to the stump and let all your friends know that a vote for O'Daniel is a vote for Stevenson."

Ferguson got busy, too. "I rustled around among my hog herd and raised about seven hundred dollars," he said. He claimed he spent this money for an ad that ran in five papers and told people to vote for O'Daniel because Coke Stevenson was also "a pension man" like Pappy. If all of Stevenson's friends voted for O'Daniel, he urged, Pappy's victory would then become a "double-barreled cinch."

Johnson developed a serious skin rash in the final push. Doctors diagnosed it as resulting from nervous tension, but Johnson would not ease his pace. He had more telegrams to pull from his pockets and more rallies to attend. And the Belden Poll at the wire showed his popularity soaring to 31.2 per cent against 26.7 for O'Daniel, 25.2 for Mann, and only 16.2 for Dies. For a few days world events gave evidence of relegating the Senate race to a minor place, for in the last week of the contest Nazi Germany invaded the Soviet Union. But after Roosevelt and Prime Minister Winston Churchill of Great Britain offered aid to Soviet dictator Josef Stalin, Texas interest in the home contest was renewed.

This was shown by the mammoth rally Johnson held at San Antonio on June 25. Rebekah Johnson had left the hospital in Temple to be with her son, and he walked out on the platform with his arm around her. His last major rally came the next night at Houston's Sam Houston Coliseum. O'Daniel had sent Roosevelt a strange proposal to create a separate Texas Army and Navy to help the United States meet its defense needs. There were four thousand at Johnson's meeting at Houston, and he read a Roosevelt telegram that had been sent to him instead of O'Daniel on the O'Daniel proposal. Hysterical laughter greeted Roosevelt's description of O'Daniel's offer as "preposterous."

Johnson made his last speech from the porch of his family's Johnson City house. Then early on election day, Saturday, June 28, he voted in his home town and later went to an Austin hotel a few blocks from the Governor's Mansion. He was so exhausted that he could not sleep and had to take a sleeping pill to knock himself out until the returns began coming in that evening.

O'Daniel had returned to the mansion from Lubbock, and he had arranged a victory party that night. Hundreds were there by 9 P.M., but there was no holiday air. Guests milled about listlessly, and Pappy sat sweating profusely as the early returns put Johnson in a substantial lead.

Five hours after the polls closed, Johnson's lead stood at three thousand. The next morning, with his lead over O'Daniel growing, the front-page headline of the Houston *Post* read: JOHNSON, WITH 5152 VOTE LEAD, APPEARS ELECTED. The unofficial count made by the reporting newspapers for the Texas Election Bureau gave Johnson 167,276 votes; O'Daniel 162,124; Gerald Mann 134,871; and Dies 71,275. Bob Johnson, manager of the Bureau, stated flatly that with 96 per cent of the votes counted and only an estimated twenty-five thousand still out, Johnson would win "barring a miracle." Mayor Tom Miller of Austin was reported preparing a statement that he would run for the vacated House seat of "Senator Lyndon Johnson."

Elated by the election returns, Johnson telephoned Wirtz and began speaking of his Senate plans. But Wirtz was suddenly pessimistic. "Just wait, Lyndon," he said, "by tomorrow you won't have anywhere near a five-thousand-vote lead."

Pappy O'Daniel refused to concede, and Wirtz knew the reasons. Texas liquor lobbyists had met with fifteen Texas senators in secret when the first returns were totaled. Charlie Marsh's Austin papers, the *Statesman* and *American*, and Drew Pearson's syndicated column, "The Washington Merry-Go-Round," told a story of plotting by these two groups of O'Daniel haters to "steal" the election for him. There were votes to be changed to boost O'Daniel's total and cut into the Johnson figures, in order to get Pappy out of Texas, they claimed.

The June 30 headline on the Dallas *News'* election story read: "Only Miracle Can Keep FDR's Anointed Out." But the following day's paper revealed a Johnson lead of only 701 over Pappy. By that day's close, Johnson's lead had dwindled to 77, as "corrected totals" began coming in from rural counties in east Texas and Mexican counties in south Texas. Then on July 2, with "all votes counted," O'Daniel was declared the winner by a margin of 1,311 votes.

O'Daniel said he had won because of the votes at the end "from the forks of the creeks." But the Waco *Herald-Tribune* reported, "The people who counted the election returns of the last 20,000 votes were very puzzled as returns came in from the far places whipping Governor O'Daniel into victory by a few hundred votes. But Ferguson was not puzzled by this, nor were the brewers." Pa Ferguson's explanation to a writer was that "while one dry senator in Washington might do little harm to the beer and whisky business in Texas, one dry wartime governor such as O'Daniel could knock it cold."

Many of Johnson's friends expected him to contest the election, but on Wirtz's advice he did not, even though he had ample evidence of skulduggery. An estimated ten thousand votes had been thrown out in Harris County (including Houston), where Johnson was popular. The reason given was that voters were supposed to cross out the names of twenty-eight candidates and leave only the name of their choice on the ballot paper. In these ten thousand votes, the explanation was given that voters had crossed out the names of all Democrats except Johnson's and then had neglected to cross out the names of the Republicans, the Communist, and Independent candidates in the other columns. For this same reason a pile of Johnson votes in Wichita Falls had been discarded. But this made no difference because Wirtz knew that had they been counted for Johnson, the pro-O'Daniel-for-senator gang would have merely "corrected" more returns for their man elsewhere.

In its last meeting, on July 3, 1941, the Texas Senate voted to permit its investigating committee to examine the peculiar election. In addition, E. B. Germany, chairman of the State Democratic Executive Committee and Garner-for-President leader in 1940, wired the United States Senate's Committee on Elections to probe the vote. But in both instances requests were made to look into the financing of Johnson's campaign, and Wirtz helped quash both inquiries. Martin Dies, who at first blamed his own defeat on "Communists and the Fifth Columnists," said later that Johnson's enormous violation of federal limits on Senate campaign expenditures had also ruined him.

When it was over, Johnson went to the airport at Austin for a flight back to Washington. He suffered from a loss of weight and a severe sore throat, and his rash burned him. Reporters asked him about his intentions regarding the strange last-minute vote, and he told them wanly, "That's the ball game. My vacation is over."

Back in Washington, Roosevelt growled at him, "Next time sit on the ballot boxes." But it would be seven long years before he would try again.

PART THREE

War, Wealth, and Wirtz's Boy

Chapter 22

WHEN LYNDON JOHNSON reclaimed his House seat in July 1941, he had nothing to show for his hard-fought, heavy-spending Senate campaign except a sore throat and skin rash, an echoing horselaugh from Texas politicians who had outwitted him, and a loss of face at the White House.

Sam Rayburn tried to soften the blow by showing him a quotation from a Texas editor who had earlier run for governor against Pappy O'Daniel. The observation noted: "No candidate who talks sense and acts like a human being has a chance to beat this political freak." But the disappointment did not fade easily, especially when Texas papers reported Pappy basking in his "victory," and expressing his intention to delay his swearing-in ceremony as a senator for a month because of more important business, such as marrying off his daughter Molly to a doctor.

Johnson's loss of face at the White House was the most painful aftermath of his defeat by Pappy. The President had injected himself into the campaign as directly as he dared, following his chagrining failure to purge anti-Court-packing Democrats in the 1938 primaries, and Johnson's defeat in 1941 had left an even sourer taste. Nor could Johnson count on indirect White House favors, for Tommy the Cork Corcoran, his chief White House booster, had become a painful bore to Roosevelt and had sunk into the oblivion of a lucrative Washington law practice. So the glory of the young Presidential protégé was tarnished; and the formerly wide-open door at 1600 Pennsylvania Avenue was now only slightly ajar.

It was apparent to Johnson, and to many others, during that summer of 1941 that an air of war pervaded all of Washington except in the Capitol. When Roosevelt had signed the Lend-Lease Act in March, he had declared, "We must now become the arsenal of democracy." In May had come his declaration of a state of national emergency, to be followed the next month by his announcement of large-scale aid to the Soviet Union, which was under direct assault from the Nazi Panzer divisions and the Luftwaffe. Defense industries were springing up in all parts of the country, and young men, whose numbers had come up in the national draft lottery known as the Selective Service System, were filling the hastily erected military camps. Yet while Congress authorized and appropriated money for all these activities, it basked in a business-as-usual mood and a "let's stay out of the war" attitude.

The collision course on which the President and Congress were riding came to a crossing in August 1941, when the House took up the question of dropping or extending the Selective Service Act. Years later in a moment of ego-soothing about his failure to become a senator in 1941, Johnson told an audience that the Almighty had arranged his defeat by Pappy O'Daniel in order that he should personally save the military draft.

Selective Service had gone into effect in October 1940 with authority to draft nine hundred thousand young men for only a one-year service "unless Congress declares that the national security is imperiled." Although President Roosevelt had declared a national emergency the following spring, the Justice Department advised him that this did not bind the Legislative Branch. Therefore, the draftees would be out of the Army in October 1941.

Reports reached Roosevelt that massive indignation had spread among draftees and their parents when they were questioned about staying in the Army after the year expired. Observers expected desertions by the tens of thousands, and soldiers were said to be commonly adopting the slogan "Ohio," or Over the Hill In October. Because of such emotional outpourings Roosevelt's first inclination was to permit the draft to die a natural death and rely on volunteers to fill the Army posts. But Secretary of War Henry L. Stimson and Army Chief of Staff General George C. Marshall raised such a storm that Roosevelt agreed to ask Congress for an extension of the draft, though he insisted that the strategy and infighting be left to Congressional leaders.

Johnson was a member of Speaker Rayburn's inner circle on this issue. The first task was to determine how House Democrats felt about an extension, and Mister Sam put Johnson to work under Pat Boland, the majority whip, to assist him in making a pro and con head count. Rayburn also asked Maggie Magnuson to help, but Magnuson opposed the extension of the draft.

The initial tally showed overwhelming Democratic agreement with Magnuson's position, and to add to Rayburn's consternation, Minority Leader Joe Martin passed along word to his friend Sam that the Republicans had decided to oppose any extension. However, Rayburn would not quit, and he ordered Majority Leader John McCormack, Johnson, and Boland to initiate a broad program of converting Democrats through direct appeals and political promises. Genial Pat Boland, the former Scranton carpenter, possessed a whip organization broken down into geographic regions, and his effort was intensive. So was Mister Sam's work in button-holing members, and Johnson had numerous opportunities to observe Rayburn's technique. As one member described it: "Mister Sam is terribly convincing. There he stands, his left hand on your right shoulder, holding your coat button, looking at you out of honest eyes that reflect the sincerest emotions."

Secretary of War Colonel Henry Stimson, once a Roughrider ally of Teddy Roosevelt and the aggressive Secretary of State under President Herbert Hoover, was a man who believed that the highest glory of other men was to die in battle. A blunt person, he told Rayburn's strategy crew that he wanted "unlimited" service for all draftees; and he had an ally in Johnson. However, Rayburn knew this measure would never pass, and though he mentioned it as his own proposal in his first round of button-holing Democrats, he agreed without argument to a compromise bill, which provided for a maximum thirty-month service, a limit he had favored from the start.

When Rayburn and Joe Martin set the vote on the thirty-month draft for August 12, Sam had expected Roosevelt to go to the phones in the final crucial week. But the President could not be reached. He had slipped out of Washington for his first meeting with British Prime Minister Winston Churchill and had traveled to Argentia Bay, Newfoundland, where the two announced their Atlantic Charter on the day of the draft vote.

Mister Sam was suddenly in a panic without the comfort of having Roosevelt on hand to make the last-minute pleas to House Democrats, and he was open to suggestions, wise or foolish. One time-waster was Johnson's suggestion that he ask Secretary of State Cordell Hull to help. Although Hull had served long as a House member from Tennessee, he was creaking old and Rayburn knew he was held only in bored esteem by the general membership. Nevertheless, he settled for an open letter from Hull to the House, and Hull, who was bitter with Roosevelt for having left him behind on the trip to meet Churchill, hoped to prove from the response of the House that he had a large Congressional following. However, his letter favoring the draft was ignored.

By now the speaker knew he was on his own and would have to call on all his knowledge of parliamentary trickery to save the draft. He kept this to himself as he lined up his debaters and ordered the Democratic whip organization to work over wavering members on both sides of the political aisle.

He chose Johnson as one of his key speakers even though his protégé, already four years in the House, had yet to make a major address. Johnson wanted to impress the House, and he worked hard on his August 8 talk. But he marred its effect because he could not avoid blustering about the special bravery of Texans in their historic past.

"I know how Texas boys feel," he bragged. "I am one of them. Texas boys come from a race of men who fought for their freedom at the Alamo and Goliad and San Jacinto. . . . They had little equipment and what they had was poor. Every time they fought, they were greatly outnumbered. But they fought anyway, because they were battling for their homes, for their religion, their liberty of conscience and action, for a government of, by, and for the people. . . . Texas boys prefer service now to slavery later."

Two days before the vote Mister Sam disappeared from Washington and showed up at his birthplace, near Kingston, Tennessee. He told one old woman whom he visited that he wanted to wash, and asked for "an old wash pan and an old sack towel like I used to use." Country people said he kept looking at the hills where he had played a half century earlier. Then, this brief respite over, he returned to Washington determined to use every trick necessary to gain House approval for the draft extension.

When the roll call came, a reporter noted that the galleries had been filled by the antidraft leaders with soldiers and "pathetic-looking mothers carrying American flags." Johnson, Boland, and the regional whips stood at the Democratic doors for a final urging of members as they trooped to the benches, while a tense Sam Rayburn stationed himself behind the tally clerk to make a running count as the names were called in alphabetical order. From the corner of an eye he could see Republican leaders signaling some members not to vote the first time through the roll but to wait until the second roll call when they could judge how many extra votes they needed to kill the bill.

The moment the clerk finished the call of the four hundred and thirty-five names with that of Orville Zimmerman of Missouri, however, Rayburn glanced at the totals and shouted, "On this vote two hundred and three members have voted *Aye*; two hundred and two members have voted *No*, and the bill is passed!"

Republican leaders angrily demanded that the vote be reopened to changes and additions, as was generally done, but Rayburn, who loomed like a cord-high pile of bricks, summarily rejected this demand. The votes were frozen, he said, and the most he would permit was a recapitulation of the actual voting. Republicans agreed to this because they planned to offer a motion immediately afterward to reopen the entire issue. But when the original tally was repeated and the last House member on the alphabetical roll was answering, Rayburn lost not a moment to declare, "No correction in the vote, the vote stands, and the bill is passed, and without objection a motion to reconsider is laid on the table." When Republican Representative Dewey Short of Missouri started complaining that he had heard no motion to reconsider, Rayburn gaveled him into silence, and the bill was successfully through the House.

The international crisis deepened that fall. The Germans raced on toward Moscow; the Japanese occupied French Indochina. On September 4, a German submarine fired torpedoes at a United States destroyer that had been tailing her; an American steamship was also reported torpedoed and sunk; and on October 30 a United States destroyer was sunk off Iceland while on convoy duty. When Japanese Ambassador Nomura and Special Envoy Saburo Kurusu met in November with Secretary of State Hull, the public knew that fateful negotiations were under way between Japan and the United States. Then came Sunday, December 7, and the carnage at Pearl Harbor.

"A day that will live in infamy," President Roosevelt had denounced the Japanese attack when he asked Congress the next day to declare war on Japan. Johnson voted for war on December 8, and three days later, after Germany and Italy had declared war on the United States, he voted for war against these two nations. Immediately after this second vote, the Navy ordered him to reserve duty.

On January 21, 1940, Johnson had received a commission as a lieutenant commander in the Naval Reserve. At that time several other congressmen had joined, including Maggie Magnuson, who held the same rank as Johnson. Had Johnson been drafted, the chances were he would have failed his physical. Besides suffering from a perennial kidney ailment, sore throat, and painful sinuses, he was so high strung that the slightest tension caused him to break out in an unsightly skin rash. But exams for Naval officers were superficial, and he had easily won his commission.

Along with Johnson, many other members of the House were called to duty. Magnuson left for sea duty in the Pacific, and Johnson's assistant, John Connally, now an ensign, went to work on training and manpower problems in the office of Navy Undersecretary James V. Forrestal. Johnson's orders were to report to the United States–New Zealand Navy Command in San Francisco, and from what he had learned from phone calls to the Navy he would be occupying a safe desk in San Francisco for the duration.

En route west he grew furious with the minute role he would be playing in a worldwide war. At Denver he got off the train to visit his brother Sam, for whom he had landed a job with a defense agency. Sam had married in 1940, and his wife Albertine had presented his mother with her first grandchild, Josefa Roxane Johnson, born in September 1941. Lyndon told Sam he was sorry he had left Congress, and he wailed: "I'm not doing anything. I would be worth more to the country in Congress than I am in this assignment. I'm going to Washington and talk to the Boss. He's got to do something about me."

Having decided he would not like San Francisco duty even before he arrived there, Johnson requested permission to return to Washington to settle a personal problem only a week after reporting to the office of the chief of the United States–New Zealand Navy Command. Permission granted, he flew back to the capital and induced Roosevelt's secretary to give him a few minutes with the President.

This was an extraordinary achievement considering Roosevelt's involvements at that moment. Churchill was then visiting the White House, and the two were heavily engaged in discussions to favor the European Theater and put off major action in the Pacific until after Hitler was subdued. Roosevelt was also giving much of his time to supplying immediate help to beleaguered American islands in the Pacific and to the Philippines. In addition he was examining and approving a plan to move one hundred thousand Japanese-Americans from their West Coast homes into inland concentration camps to appease hysterical Californians. Further activities involved establishing twenty new war agencies, setting production goals for tanks, planes, ships, guns, and other war matériel, and managing the usual Presidential duties, such as dealing with Congress on authorizing legislation and the budget, running the sprawling federal establishment, directing a political party, and shaping public opinion.

Roosevelt had neither the time nor the inclination for the old-style gabfest with Johnson, and he showed it by the brevity of their meeting. What sort of duty did Lyndon want? He was in the Navy but he could not run a ship, fly a seaplane, or command a station according to Navy protocol rules. Maggie was going to special school to equip himself for regular duty aboard a destroyer or cruiser. Did Lyndon want this? Johnson's frown left only one alternative. By the dozens, Roosevelt had begun to send politicians in military uniforms on useless overseas inspection missions to get them out of his hair. What he now proposed was that Johnson make a survey of military supplies in the Australian area. Johnson quickly agreed because it involved a trip to a war zone, and Roosevelt wished him Godspeed.

However, wartime paperwork snafus kept him in San Francisco until May 6, when his orders finally came. By the time Johnson reached Auckland, New Zealand, on May 21, 1942, and shot his first tourist-style film footage with the movie camera he had brought with him, the Japanese military machine had captured the Malayan Peninsula and Singapore, smothered the last American resistance on Bataan Peninsula and the small watchdog island of Corregidor in the Philippines, overrun the Dutch East Indies, Guam, and part of New Guinea, that large strategic island north of Australia, and threatened an invasion of Australia. About the only valuable asset salvaged from this onslaught was General Douglas MacArthur, whom President Roosevelt had ordered to leave the Philippines rather than be captured and proceed to Australia to help plan the eventual defeat of Japan.

Two days after his landing at Auckland, Johnson flew on to Sydney, Australia, where he took more pictures before continuing on to Melbourne, near the southern tip of the Australian continent, where General MacArthur maintained headquarters. Here he and two other "inspectors" visited the Southwest Pacific Command headquarters on May 25 for a staff briefing, and Johnson let words fall to the effect that he had been a congressman and was a close friend of President Roosevelt. This bit of intelligence was reported to General MacArthur, who invited the three inspectors to his private office afterward for a personal meeting.

At this time MacArthur was an angry man on several counts. First, despite the order from President Roosevelt that he leave the Philippines, his many enemies in the Navy were spreading the falsity that he had deserted his military subordinate, General "Skinny" Wainwright, and thousands of his men on Bataan. Second, MacArthur was enraged because Roosevelt had divided the Pacific zone into three military commands, even though MacArthur had warned him that the separate commands could result only in "divided effort, waste, duplication, and undue extension of the war." MacArthur had asked for a unified command with himself in charge, but Roosevelt had named Admiral Chester Nimitz in charge of the Central Pacific command; Admiral Richard Ghormley over the South Pacific; and MacArthur over the Southwest Pacific, extending from Australia through the Philippines in the north and from the Solomon Islands to Sumatra in an east-west boundary. MacArthur's other major cause for funk was his inability to induce General Marshall to allocate a significant share of American military production to the Pacific fighting. Some of MacArthur's friends claimed that Marshall was punishing him because of a personal desire for revenge. During the mid-thirties, Mrs. Marshall had just finished hanging almost forty pairs of curtains at their residence on a newly assigned post when a telegram came from Chief-of-Staff MacArthur ordering Colonel Marshall to report immediately to another post. The decision to give priority to the European theater, however, had nothing to do with curtains: It resulted from an agreement between Roosevelt and Churchill.

For a busy commander MacArthur spent an inordinate amount of time with the three inexperienced military inspectors. One of the three later recalled that he "paced back and forth behind his desk" and "would refer to a map occasionally . . . giving us the big picture. We were all a little awed by the man." Afterward MacArthur told subordinates that Johnson was to get special treatment because he was a protégé of the President and could bring the MacArthur message directly to Roosevelt's attention.

Orders had come for MacArthur to participate in joint offensive action against the Japanese in order to produce a victory that would buoy faltering American morale. Part one would be action at Guadalcanal at the southern end of the Solomons on August 7, under the direction of Admiral William "Bull" Halsey. Part two would be MacArthur's effort to take the Japanese strongholds at Lae and Salamaua on the east coast of New Guinea and clear away the menace that threatened Australia. Action against Lae would come with a penetrating bombing raid on June 9, which would begin the softening-up process.

Johnson and the two inspectors who accompanied him did some rummaging through the various installations in the Melbourne area for a week. Johnson shot more footage, then he and his two buddies, Lieutenant Colonels Samuel Anderson and Francis Stevens, flew back to Sydney on June 3, then to Brisbane the next day and on to Townsville, a rather desolate spot at that time on Australia's northeastern corner. Here the bombing groups were getting ready for the Lae attack on June 9, and the three insisted they be taken along on separate planes as observers.

Anderson's plane went into Lae and returned safely; Stevens' bomber was shot down and he was killed; Johnson's plane never got to Lae. On page seven of *The New York Times* of June 12, 1942, Byron Darnton, the *Times'* war correspondent in that theater, had a description of the June 9 mission that contained the following:

Representative Lyndon Johnson of Texas, who is a lieutenant commander in the Naval Reserve and a close friend of President Roosevelt, paid a visit here yesterday and took off on a bombing mission for Lae, New Guinea. The plane piloted by Lieutenant Walter Greer of Russellville, Ark., developed mechanical trouble and was forced to return without reaching its target. But the Representative got a good first hand idea of the troubles and problems confronting our airmen and declared himself impressed by the skill and courage of the bomber crews and fighter pilots.

Questions arose afterward regarding the completeness of Darnton's dispatch. Lieutenant Greer died a few years later in a stateside crash, so he was not available to confirm Darnton's story or various other versions of the same episode. In another account of this flight Greer's B-26, the *Heckling Hare,* developed engine trouble, fell behind, and was gunned by eight Japanese Zeros before crawling back with a badly damaged fuselage to Port Moresby, MacArthur's forward headquarters in southeastern New Guinea. This was the version that MacArthur's Melbourne headquarters accepted, though Johnson later embellished it by telling a Waco, Texas, reporter that the Zeros knocked out one of the engines and wounded several crewmen.

After Lieutenant Greer's B-26 landed at Port Moresby's Seven Mile Strip Airfield, Johnson decided to leave the battle-readiness zone to do more inspecting in Australia, and he flew back to Darwin on the north-central tip of the "Downunder" continent following a single day at the advanced headquarters. The weather was excellent for taking pictures, and the countryside was so much like the brush-covered, dry, semidesert of west Texas that he grew homesick. Then on June 12, after photographing some kangaroos and koala bears, he decided to return to "MacArthurland" all the way down the continent some twenty-five hundred miles to Melbourne.

This resulted in his other adventure in a short military service. Lieutenant General George Brett, the senior army commander under MacArthur, had been told to be nice to Roosevelt's young friend; and he gave Johnson the use of his personal plane, a Flying Fortress named *The Swoose,* from a combination of swan and goose. *The Swoose* set off on the long flight with Major Frank Kurtz at the controls, and the flight proved uneventful until he lost his way. In late afternoon, with his gas supply running low, Kurtz managed to make a safe landing on an Australian ranch field. William L. White, a roving editor of the *Reader's Digest,* recorded Johnson's remarkable ability at instant friendships in his wartime best-seller, *Queens Die Proudly.*

One of *The Swoose*'s crewmen told White:

We got out. Pretty soon Australian ranchers began crawling out of holes in the ground—I don't know where else they came from—and right away Lieutenant Commander Johnson gets busy. He begins to get acquainted.

They tell him where we are and some of them go off to get a truck to take us into town where we can telephone, and more keep coming, and Johnson is shaking hands all around, and he comes back and tells us these are real folks—the best damn folks in the world, except maybe the folks in his own Texas.

Pretty soon he knows all their first names, and they are telling him why there ought to be a high tariff on wool, and there is no question he swung that country for Johnson before he left. He was in his element. I know he sure swung the Swoose crew. He can carry that precinct any day.

On the ride into the nearby town of Winston, Johnson was sorry he had not loaded his movie camera in time to photograph the kangaroos that kept popping across the road. Then after a good meal and a night's rest at the local hotel he rejoined *The Swoose*'s crew, who had remained with the plane, and the flight continued without further mishap to Melbourne.

By June 18, after less than a month in that area, Johnson had seen enough of Australia in his free-lance inspections, and he passed word to MacArthur's headquarters that he was leaving for the United States. This immediately spurred the general into swift action, and he told Johnson to report to his office that day. MacArthur had learned that the Navy lieutenant commander had become thoroughly indoctrinated with his own belief in the primary importance of the Southwest Pacific Area, and he had a special reward for Johnson as a steadfast reminded for him when he returned to Washington. This was to award him the Silver Star, the country's third highest military decoration, for having participated in Lieutenant Greer's abortive flight to Lae. No one else on the plane, including Greer, was decorated.

With a heavy trowel, MacArthur's citation for the award spoke of Johnson's "gallantry in action" for evidencing "marked coolness in spite of the hazard involved. His gallant action enabled him to obtain and return with valuable information." Years later MacArthur confessed that if he had been able to look into the future he would have given Johnson an even higher award, perhaps the Congressional Medal of Honor for that painless half-hour flight. "If I had known that this young officer was going to be President," he said laughingly, "I might have taken better care of him."

Most members of Congress who had gone off to war had left their offices in the hands of their staffs. But with John Connally, his top aide, also in the service, Johnson had asked Lady Bird to sit at his desk and make a stab at the mail and call government agencies for constituents. Lady Bird, who was too shy for such activities, gained some backbone by asking John Connally's wife Nellie to help her. To save money, because Lyndon had to give up his Congressional salary of ten thousand dollars a year for the three thousand dollars' pay of a lieutenant commander, Lady Bird rented their residence for one hundred dollars a month and shared Nellie Connally's double bed in her fifty-dollar-a-month apartment in nearby Virginia. In recalling the exciting few months when she and Nellie had great fun playing at the politics they had heard Lyndon and John chew over with hardly a pause for breath, Lady Bird said that one morning she might talk to Mayor Tom Miller on the telephone from Austin "about a new abattoir that they just had to build, and materials were scarce, and next talk to somebody on the telephone who wanted a government priority for something else." But without Lyndon's presence, his office had little activity; for businessmen who were seriously seeking contracts switched their appeals to the office of influential Congressman Albert Thomas of Houston, who had a mania for getting federal money for Texas.

Alvin Wirtz and Tom Miller were also available to help Lady Bird. In fact, the two took on a major chore in the spring of 1942 when Johnson was in Australia by managing a drive to have his name put on the Democratic primary ballot. The petitions they submitted to the secretary of state contained twenty-two thousand signatures, and with no other candidates in the race, a victory for Johnson was assured.

To while away part of her spare time in Lyndon's absence, Lady Bird played a starring role in a homemade movie friends were producing in Washington. This was an amateur, silent film called "Heaven Will Protect the Working Girl." Lady Bird took on the role of Petunia, the heroine working girl. The setting was 1910, and Lady Bird's clothes were of that vintage. Mary Rather, who had worked for Alvin Wirtz before coming to Lyndon's office after his 1941 Senate campaign, acted the part of Petunia's mother.

After his Silver Star award on June 18, Johnson decided to go home, and he flew north from Melbourne to Sydney and then back to New Caledonia, in the Loyalty Islands, a thousand miles to the east. There were more movies to shoot and more sights to see, and by the time the Navy PBY plane reached Suva, on Viti-Levu Island in the Fijis, on June 22, his overexertions brought on violent shivering despite the heat. Doctors diagnosed him as suffering from pneumonia and rushed him to a hospital. Lady Bird was shocked to hear Lyndon "was gravely ill in the Far East," a message that did not reach her until he was far along in his recovery.

Not until the Fourth of July did the hospital release him. This was four days after President Roosevelt had issued a directive ordering all members of Congress to leave military service and return to their legislative duties. Several congressmen, including Vincent Harrington of Iowa, who later died in active war service, chose to ignore Roosevelt's order, but Johnson had had enough. Two weeks later he was back in Washington, a civilian again after six months of military duty, thirty pounds lighter as a result of his bout with pneumonia, and the possessor of reels of movie film of Australia, which he would run off for friends hundreds of times in the years ahead—and always to the same refrain: "The Australians are the kind of people you can go to the well with."

Chapter 23

J OHNSON RETURNED FROM his short inspection trip to Australia in a fighting mood, and determined to serve as spokesman for "Americans out there." Before settling into his Congressional routine, he finished writing a report on his Southwest Pacific Area observations. Then, following a bombardment of phone calls to White House aides to arrange an appointment for him with the President, he drove to the White House early one morning on the invitation of Roosevelt to talk during the President's breakfast. By then Roosevelt could have wallpapered the entire White House with reports he had received on the Pacific front.

Roosevelt was not in a happy frame of mind at the time, because of a variety of Allied setbacks. A few weeks earlier an American convoy to Murmansk had suffered a loss of twenty-three of its thirty-four ships; a gigantic German offensive against Stalingrad was approaching its climax, with a Nazi victory threatening to produce a German-Japanese linkup in Asia Minor; and in Africa, General Erwin Rommel's Afrika Korps had chased the British Eighth Army into a tiny pocket near Alexandria following the capture of Tobruk. Roosevelt was also filled with concern because he had agreed to Churchill's demand not to undertake a cross-Channel invasion of the European Continent that year, and this was already bringing recriminations from Stalin. Still another Roosevelt anxiety was his decision ordering untried Major General Dwight D. Eisenhower, his new commanding general in Europe, to throw his green troops into *Torch,* an invasion of Northwest Africa "not later than October 30."

Without any knowledge of these events Johnson proceeded to sour Roosevelt's day further: Many high officers in the Pacific were "incompetent"; a shortage of equipment existed; and "we have no plane which will match the Zero," he charged. Worst of all, he added, soldiers in the Pacific were furious about "politics and business as usual back home."

When he left his report with Roosevelt, he went afterward to the Capitol, where he proceeded to tell Sam Rayburn the same conclusions. Mister Sam tried to calm him with a story he used for just such occasions. "I've just received a cheerful letter from a fellow whose problems remind me of yours," he related. "He said that one of his bald-faced heifers had broken her back and died; some hunters had set fire to his oatfield stubble; a tornado had blown down his windmill; some storms had killed all his chickens; the rain soaked his oats so they couldn't be stored. And he ended his letter with 'Hoping you are the same, I am, truly yours.'"

In the autumn of 1942, when the aged battleship *Oregon* was scrapped, Johnson asked to be the main speaker on the ceremonial program. This provided him with a national audience, and he spent his allotted time pounding nails into the home front. "What about the scrapping that needs to be done elsewhere?" he shouted. "What about dollar-a-year men who make us wonder whether we hadn't better devalue the dollar a little further? What about overstaffed, overstuffed government? While we have fighting to do abroad, we have scrapping to do at home. Scrapping of dead-wood in thinking, of inefficiency in methods—yes, and of ineffectiveness in men; men who have become entrenched in power, men who love their country and would die for it, but not until their own dangerously outdated notions have caused others to die for it first.

"Today," he went on, "there are thirty-three federal agencies working on the postwar situation—exclusive of Adolf Hitler's men, who are working on the same situation in case we don't win." To cover all bases, he also had harsh words for war plant workers who did not show up on the assembly line every day, and for management concerned with profits rather than production.

Over in the Upper Chamber, thick-lensed Senator Harry Truman of Missouri, whom Sam Rayburn had begun to include in his "Board of Education" coterie of late afternoon drinking pals, was running a special Senate watchdog committee which acted like a truant officer over the war production program. Johnson thought there was room for a similar committee in the House, and he talked it over with Rayburn. But Mister Sam said he would not offend the chairmen of the House Military and Naval Affairs Committees by promoting Johnson as the Truman of the House. In fact his good friend Gene "Goober" Cox from Camilla, Georgia, had made a similar proposal for himself months before the Senate set up the Truman Committee and had got nowhere with his bill. Furthermore, said Sam, if a congressman went out to do some firsthand inspecting at a war plant, he would see only machines and ovens and fan belts, and he wouldn't understand any explanation of what was going on there.

Johnson did not quit at this point. Instead, he walked into Carl Vinson's office, told him the latest obscene scuttlebutt, and although he was only the seventh-ranking Democrat on the Naval Affairs Committee, when he left he had Vinson's word that he could be chairman of a five-man subcommittee to investigate the procurement program of the Navy as well as its management of sea warfare. Only days later he was already in business with a subcommittee hearing room, the nucleus of a staff, and an agenda of investigations.

Vinson believed he had forced Johnson into an insignificant operation when he allotted him only a small sum of money to manage his subcommittee. But Johnson outfoxed the "Swamp Fox" himself. Instead of using his funds to hire a few clerks, he employed only Naval Reserve Officers on loan from the Department, and thus he let the Navy pay for his investigation of its activities. Besides opening up the possibility of commanding an enormous staff at no expense to the subcommittee, Johnson had no fear that he might be bossing a disloyal staff, for the Reserve Officers he sought had only recently acquired commissions to avoid being drafted into the Army as privates. Before their hurried change into Navy uniforms, all had worked in other agencies as lawyers, economists, accountants, and investigators. For help in filling the top job of counsel, Johnson called on his friend, Supreme Court Justice William O. Douglas, the former head of the Securities and Exchange Commission. His sole stipulation was that Douglas send him a non-Jew because "those Navy officers are anti-Semitic and I don't want extra trouble." Douglas filled the order with Donald Cook, a newly sworn in junior Naval officer, who had served as assistant director of the SEC's public utilities division.

The man most impressed with Johnson's staffing technique was Uncle Carl Vinson, who believed before this experience that he knew everything there was to know about Congressional committees and their operation. In short order he became an imitator, and his full committee's staff also resembled a Naval station. However, no matter how many junior officers Vinson hired, Johnson always maintained a substantial margin over the full committee in his subcommittee. Other committee members found this peculiar, for the full committee's scope was much broader than that of Johnson's subcommittee.

Yet, even with his large staff of bright young men, Johnson could not hope to gain the prestige of the Senate's Truman Committee, for that committee operated as the arm of the entire Senate and had the blessing of President Roosevelt to roam through defense agencies and war plants to uncover mismanagement and fraud in the entire war production program. The Truman Committee's voice was so powerful that at one point President Roosevelt acceded to its demand and entirely revamped the structure of Washington war agencies.

· Johnson's subcommittee, restricted as it was to the Navy, nevertheless found much to criticize with the way its top men managed their jobs. Many of the subcommittee's reports were highly critical of the Navy's procurement methods, an area directed by Undersecretary James Forrestal, a short, pugnacious, thin-lipped, broken-nosed, trigger-tempered former investment banker. Johnson also had some run-ins with the Secretary, Frank Knox, the Republican Vice-Presidential nominee in 1936 and Chicago publisher, as well as with Knox's special assistant, Adlai Stevenson, whom Johnson had known in the early New Deal days at Agriculture.

Although the subcommittee had five members, it was strictly a Johnson show. As a staff employee saw it, "The other subcommittee members were relatively contented men, unlike Johnson who was a bundle of nerves and was bursting with energy and ambition. They weren't going to kill themselves working—and he knew it. So before long he was totally in charge of what was investigated, the actual investigations and hearings, and the reports. And he had the staff in a bind, too, because they had the impression that if they ever complained about working nights and weekends, he would report them to the Navy, and they would be shipped out to sea."

Among his subcommittee reports was one condemning the Navy for stationing four thousand enlisted men at desk jobs in Washington when they could be serving on warships. The humorous aspect of this report was that it was written by Johnson's Naval Reserve assistants at their civilian desks in his subcommittee office. In another report Johnson lashed the Navy for allowing a private oil company to milk its vast Elk Hills Field in California for outrageous profits. When the Navy rewrote its contract with the company, Johnson said his exposure of the situation had saved the government millions upon millions of dollars. Still other reports hit at absenteeism in Navy war plants and a scandalous draft deferment program for civilians in those factories.

He was particularly incensed with absenteeism. In 1943 he introduced a bill to require Navy contractors to send the names of unjustifiably absent men to their draft boards. He also promoted a "Work or Fight" measure, which would give the federal government authority to freeze war workers on the job, and draft anyone who refused to take a war job. While labor leaders attacked him now for the first time, charging that he had "sold out to the war profiteers," Johnson said his bill would only catch "the loafer, the inexcusable absentee, and the slacker." In one speech to justify his stand he told about his plane ride in the attack on Lae and declared that the B-26 had been hit by Zero fighter guns. "When I watched those boys fighting to keep that plane going, something was burned deep into me," he boomed. "When those boys and others like them come back, I don't want to see the bitterness in their faces, the disillusionment in their eyes, which would come from the knowledge that there was something more I might have tried to help them—and didn't do it."

Too energetic to restrict himself entirely to his subcommittee's work, Johnson involved himself in many of Sam Rayburn's problems. "Here I am, one of the most inexperienced members of the Texas delegation, talking about one of the most experienced," he crooned at a Dallas tribute dinner honoring Rayburn.

But Rayburn was using him more and more as a sounding board and strategist. Late in 1942, despite large-scale lobbying against the bill, Johnson joined Mister Sam in the buttonholing brigade to win House approval of legislation to lower the draft call to eighteen-year-olds. Then in January 1943, when Rayburn barely won re-election as speaker by a vote of 217 to 206, Johnson sat in on the later strategy meetings to keep the Democrats united. Southern Democrats had evolved a technique of defeating Administration bills by deliberately failing to answer roll calls. Rayburn, who had turned quite conservative after the international situation had removed the glow of the New Deal for him, believed that the Southerners required only "time enough to let off steam and patience—plus a little quiet persuasion to convince them to pick up their hats and walk over to the floor." At Johnson's suggestion Rayburn took the newly elected members to the White House, where he hoped the President's charm and Dutch-uncle talk would swing them into line. On one occasion, when he signaled a group to leave, Roosevelt cut in with "Father Sam, you want to send the boys to bed too early."

Uncle Carl Vinson was also permitting Johnson to express his opinions on major actions before the full committee, and sometimes he got rid of staff aides at Johnson's request. One of Vinson's associates said: "During World War II Uncle Carl had an ensign named Dick Wels on the full committee's staff. Wels had come from the SEC where he had run an investigation of Ed Noble, who owned the Lifesaver Company and had served as an FCC commissioner. The SEC investigation dealt with determining whether Noble had put undue pressure on radio station WMCA in New York to sell out to him.

"Warren Magnuson was one of the congressmen on Lyndon's subcommittee, and one day when Maggie was supposed to be out of town, Wels had breakfast at the Shoreham and saw Maggie at another table with Tom Corcoran, Noble's attorney. Wels had a low opinion of Corcoran because they had a run-in during an SEC investigation of the business manipulations of a shady big-time New York operator, whom Corcoran also represented.

"When Wels got to the House Office Building that morning, he called Mary Spargo at the Washington *Evening Star* and asked her to telephone Maggie and needle him with—'I thought you were supposed to be out of town?'

"Maggie got mad as hell when she tracked him down, and he asked Lyndon to help him teach Wels a lesson. Lyndon went to Vinson, told him

Wels was trying to draw a bad conclusion about Maggie's meeting with Corcoran, and asked permission to punish Wels.

" 'I took care of that little sonofabitch for you,' Uncle Carl, laughing almost hysterically, told Maggie afterward. What happened was that Lyndon had called the Navy and had Wels ordered to report immediately to Atka in the Aleutian Islands, even though he had never undergone Navy indoctrination and didn't even know how to salute. Then the next day Lyndon said that maybe he had been too hasty. So he called the Navy again and had the order changed so that Wels had to report to Kiska Island instead, which was even further away from civilization than Atka."

The war put bulging muscles into an economy that had been sickly for more than a decade. Texans flooded Johnson's office with requests for assistance in landing contracts and doing business with the government. The depression psychology was fast disappearing in a wartime boom of Texas millionaires. Texas, bragging about how big the state was and how heroic its people, was adding a new boast: "Hold my baby while I shout how rich I am."

Johnson was especially helpful to George and Herman Brown, whose Brown and Root Company of Houston had been so helpful to him in his 1941 race against Pappy O'Daniel. Johnson's aid in getting them the Corpus Christi Naval Air Training Base construction contract ballooned their fortunes as the initially modest base grew into a one-hundred-million-dollar project covering three counties and twenty thousand acres. But this was only one segment of their business: They developed during the war into one of the world's construction giants through the assistance of loss-proof, cost-plus contracts from government agencies. As a lucrative side-line they also produced hundreds of destroyer escorts and moved into oil and gas production.

In return for his aid in keeping them posted on proposed federal projects and in making timely phone calls to war agencies, the Brown brothers let Johnson use their private plane for flights between Washington and Texas, gave him free space in their Brown Building in Austin, and the assurance of full backing in political campaigns.

While Brown and Root got the bulk of contracting aid in Johnson's office, many other Texans were also assisted. Edgar M. Linkenhoger, a spinach trucker in Robstown, where Johnson had his first job after finishing high school, was only one of several who emerged as big-time war contractors. Back in Karnack, Cap'n Taylor, Lady Bird's father, gained a windfall of seventy thousand dollars when the federal government decided that his lot near his store was the best among the dozens under consideration to hold the enormous Longhorn Ordnance Plant. Neighborhood gossip, of course, was that Taylor's son-in-law had swung the deal in his favor.

The wartime affluence that he was instrumental in creating for numerous Texans was a source of both happiness and dissatisfaction for Johnson.

Outside of his own ten-thousand-dollar-a-year salary as a congressman and Lady Bird's twenty-one-thousand-dollar inheritance from her mother's estate, Johnson considered himself the poorest Texan he knew. He was still as far away as ever from achieving his goal of becoming a millionaire. When he had returned from the Pacific in mid-1942, he and Lady Bird had considered buying a small Texas newspaper. But the negotiations had resulted only in Johnson's embarrassment because he had lacked the necessary cash to complete the deal.

Alvin Wirtz had been scratching his head in search of a legal way to make his young friend rich and at the same time keep him in politics. As a pointed reminder of the degree to which he expected Wirtz to find him an open door to affluence, Johnson sent him a large framed photograph of himself with the following inscription: "To my friend, Alvin J. Wirtz, who can do anything better than anyone else."

Late in the fall of 1942 Wirtz had the answer. A few years earlier a man who owned a small radio station in Austin had offered Wirtz ten thousand dollars to straighten out his miasma of troubles with the Federal Communications Commission. Wirtz had agreed to take on the job, but shortly afterward he had gone to Washington to be Undersecretary of the Interior, and he did not intercede for his client. When Wirtz checked the situation late in 1942, the three new owner-partners of the station, KTBC, had not only inherited the old owner's troubles, but were also losing about seventy-five hundred dollars a year because of these FCC restrictions. For two years the FCC had taken no action to approve their sale of the station to still another would-be owner because of his right-wing conservative beliefs.

Wirtz's thorough inquiry revealed that yet another would-be purchaser had obtained an option to buy the station, pending FCC approval, from the estate of the right-winger, who had died in 1942. But with tourniquet pressure Wirtz believed the new option holder could be persuaded to relinquish his right to purchase KTBC. As for the station as a business prospect, it could become an immense moneymaker with the help of extraordinary favoritism from the FCC.

The background was this: In January 1939, the FCC had issued a license to Dr. James G. Ulmer to operate a new radio station in Austin with the call letters KTBC. Ulmer owned a half dozen other stations in Texas, and his company name was the Texas Broadcasting Company, hence the call letters. That same year Ulmer sold KTBC-Austin to A. W. Walker, professor of law at the University of Texas; State Senator Robert A. Stuart of Fort Worth; and Robert B. Anderson, the twenty-four-year-old Texas state tax commissioner and future general manager of the five-hundred-thousand-acre W. T. Waggoner Ranch and still later the Secretary of the Navy and Treasury under President Eisenhower.

Within a few months these three owners found themselves with too many other commitments to devote the time required to run the small station properly and lobby the FCC to approve an increase in its power.

For these reasons they sold KTBC for eighty-seven thousand five hundred dollars to Jim West, Sr., a self-made multi-multimillionaire, whose holdings included the Austin *Tribune,* which rivaled Colonel Robert McCormick's Chicago *Tribune* at heaping invective on Roosevelt and his social welfare programs.

For a shrewd businessman, Jim West appeared to have paid too much for KTBC. The station at that time had to share its transmitting wavelength with the campus radio station at Texas A. & M. Its assigned transmitting power was extremely weak—only two hundred and fifty watts. And it could broadcast solely during daylight hours, with the Texas A. & M. station holding the right to decide what hours it wanted to be on the air, instead of sharing time equally. But West considered the price fair because existing radio station licenses were a premium buy. With an acute shortage of broadcasting wavelengths, the FCC had almost stopped its allocation of new space on the dialing band. Furthermore, West believed that once the FCC approved the sale of the station to him, he could next prevail on the federal agency to sanction an increase in KTBC's capabilities.

West never had a chance. President Roosevelt had appointed a new FCC chairman, James Fly of Dallas, who was an aggressive New Dealer. Fly held the West purchase-option papers for six months before he made his decision. His ruling was to revoke KTBC's license to operate.

Pending the result of an appeal by the three owners, the FCC permitted the station to continue in operation. Then in the spring of 1940 it rescinded its revocation order. The owners again negotiated a contract with West, but with business poor as a result of the FCC action, West dropped his purchase price option to thirty-two thousand dollars. Once more West filled out the necessary papers for the FCC, and they had hardly arrived in Washington when Fly let fly with a public condemnation of newspapers that were attempting to monopolize communications in their cities by purchasing radio stations. Afterward Fly notified West that he was putting his application in a "pending" file; and despite numerous attempts by West to get a decision that would either approve or deny the sale, the FCC maintained total silence. Two years later, in 1942, Jim West died with his application still "pending."

By the time Wirtz investigated KTBC, Jim West's son Wesley W. West had agreed to assign his late father's option to E. G. Kingsbery, a wealthy Austin businessman. This presented a mammoth stumbling block to Wirtz, for Kingsbery had every intention of submitting his purchase request to the FCC. But having heard the optimistic story of the future possibilities of KTBC, Johnson was insistent that Wirtz devise strategy that would somehow give him the station.

A few days before Christmas Ray Lee, the postmaster of Austin and a friend of Wirtz and Johnson, telephoned Kingsbery and told him that Johnson was in town and wanted to talk to him that afternoon in his Austin Congressional office. Lee did not divulge the subject, and Kingsbery went out of curiosity. When he walked into the office, Johnson greeted him affably and mixed some eggnog for him with "cream one of my constituents gave me." Over their drinks, Johnson reminded Kingsbery that he had given his son an appointment to the Naval Academy the preceding year. Then he told Kingsbery he wanted his help in buying KTBC as a present for his wife.

Before the visit ended, Kingsbery finally said he would drop his option and permit Johnson to deal directly with Wesley W. West as his replacement. This required a Christmas Day 1942 drive by Johnson to the opulent West ranch near Llano for a talk with West and his attorney. Then a few days later, at the request of Wirtz, who was handling the radio station purchase for Johnson, West's lawyer certified to the FCC that the West estate would relinquish its right to purchase KTBC if the three owners would sell the station to Mrs. Lyndon Johnson.

After this, matters moved swiftly. Wirtz met with Anderson, Walker, and Stuart, the three owners, and drove a hard bargain. KTBC's equipment was worth almost thirty thousand dollars, but Wirtz said his client would not pay more than seventeen thousand five hundred dollars, or an amount equal to the station's debts. Before they could protest, Wirtz said he had seen their books, which showed revenues of twenty-seven thousand dollars for the past year and expenses of thirty-four thousand five hundred dollars. They agreed to his offer.

Following this success, Wirtz had to prepare the statement of purchase and would-be ownership for FCC approval. He had told his excited young friend at the beginning of the negotiations that Johnson must not be the recorded purchaser because one FCC requirement was a pledge to devote "full time and energetic effort" to the operation of the station. There was bound to be a negative report from one of the lower echelon FCC investigators if Johnson were listed as the owner. Furthermore, his political career could be damaged by a charge that he was using his political power to enrich himself. By listing Lady Bird as the owner, said Wirtz, Johnson could have his cake à la mode.

The statement to the FCC was filled out with Lady Bird as the prospective proprietor. For a long moment Wirtz was hard put to submit concrete evidence of Lady Bird's past successful business experience, as was required by the FCC. But he got around this by writing a fanciful account of the few months she spent in Johnson's office when he was in the Navy. He also had to submit her personal balance sheet, and he showed her net worth at $64,322.50, part of which was in real estate (her Uncle Claude who died in 1941 left her some Alabama acreage) and part in liquid assets ($21,000) from her mother's estate. She also gave notice to the FCC that she had written a check for $17,500 to be held in escrow until the FCC made its ruling. Asked later where she got the money for the down payment, Lady Bird said one time that it came from a bank loan, and on another occasion she explained: "Daddy had made about three little forays to me about how he'd like to pay me off—that is, pay me my share of my mother's estate. He had remarried and I think he didn't like to have it hanging over his head."

Since 1939 the Wests had failed to make any headway with the FCC. But Lady Bird's application, which was dated January 2, 1943, won FCC approval only twenty-three days later on January 25.

The three former owners were curious to see how Lyndon Johnson would overcome KTBC's deficiencies. "We did not have a network, and we couldn't operate at night," said Professor Walker.

Jesse Kellam, Lyndon's college pal and successor as head of the Texas NYA, became general manager of KTBC at Lyndon's request, and he supplied an answer that became the standard reply whenever reporters asked questions. "Lady Bird took one look at the layout and said, 'I don't know much about radio, but I do know something about cleaning house,' " Kellam explained. "She bought a pair of coveralls, a bunch of brooms and mops, and some soap, and for a solid week she worked on that little walk-up, two-room radio station until it fairly sparkled. It was my job to go around town and pay all the bills that had piled up in the name of KTBC. The bankers were glad to see me coming. She worked eighteen hours a day for five months before we brought the station into the black."

There is no question that Lady Bird made the interior of KTBC shine in those early months she spent at the station. At one point Lyndon, who thought she might be scrubbing too hard, wrote her: "If you don't start writing me more often I am going to have you drafted into the WACs. Then you'll have to write your next of kin at least twice a month." However, what changed the fortunes of KTBC had its basis in other activities than cleaning and mopping.

The primary change came when Alvin Wirtz wrote out a request with Lady Bird's signature, asking the FCC for permission to increase the station's transmitting power from two hundred and fifty watts to one thousand. Lyndon also told Wirtz to request permission to broadcast twenty-four hours a day instead of the few daylight hours then allowed. When the requests came to the FCC, the agency was then reeling under sharp Congressional attacks for its alleged favoritism toward Administration supporters and for hiring leftwing employees. Chief among the attackers were the Dies Committee and the Cox Committee in the House. The Democratic whip organization counted noses and found that an amendment to the FCC appropriations bill to eliminate its entire appropriation had majority support. Only Sam Rayburn's impassioned appeal from the floor saved the FCC. Said an observer, "The majority was against him, but for a brief moment they listened and accepted his appraisal."

As a reward to the speaker's friend and to give the Administration a louder voice in Austin, the FCC was generous with the Johnson station. Not only did it permit the increase in power to one thousand watts and unlimited broadcasting hours, but it gave KTBC its own wavelength.

Then CBS pushed the station into big league advertising revenues by giving it network affiliation. In addition Lyndon Johnson took a direct hand in fashioning an aggressive policy to increase advertising.

In August 1943 KTBC showed its first profit—eighteen dollars. By 1948 Johnson was telling his friends that he was a millionaire; by 1962, KTBC had an estimated market value of seven million dollars.

Chapter 24

WHILE JOHNSON WAS putting in his six months with the Navy in 1942, Alvin Wirtz spread the story that he planned to run once more for the Senate against Pappy O'Daniel. Pappy's immediate term as senator expired in January 1943, and he faced another primary contest in the summer of 1942 for the next six-year term in the Upper House. Wirtz was not serious because he knew that his protégé had as little hope of getting an honest count from the beer lobbyists as he had in 1941. But Wirtz had good reasons for spreading his rumor. First, he considered this necessary in order to keep the absent young man in the news; and second, he wanted to inject some doubts among the complacent anti-Roosevelt Texas Democratic regulars that everything was longhorns and Stetsons for them.

However, few Texas regulars took Wirtz seriously, because Johnson was in uniform and out of the country. Even if he were a civilian and at home, his name did not frighten them because they considered him a dead Senate candidate after his race against O'Daniel the previous year. In fact, the regulars enjoyed a good laugh when they learned that while Wirtz was talking up Johnson for a rerun against Pappy, he was handling a write-in petition to help Johnson hold on to his House seat.

Nevertheless, Texas regulars continued to find Wirtz a thorn under the saddle and a major mystery. One question that bothered them was his untiring effort to promote Johnson. Some said it was the result of having only daughter Ida May at home, and no sons. Another puzzler was how he dared champion Roosevelt when almost all his law clients were rich Texas regulars.

There was one man who took Wirtz seriously when he promoted Johnson for another Senate try, though he would have preferred a candidate without Johnson's reputation as a loser. This was President Roosevelt, who despite his worry over the sorry war situation in early 1942, felt his old, throat-clutching concern over Texas. Once more, Roosevelt had developed his fixation that big Texas would be a pivotal state in the next Presidential election. If this were the case, and a Republican isolationist should become President because of a Democratic loss of Texas, Roosevelt saw his own postwar proposals going down the drain. It was essential, therefore, that O'Daniel be retired from the Senate and be replaced by a popular Democrat who could help swing the state into the Democratic column in 1944.

As a result of his concern Roosevelt called Wirtz to Washington for White House talks. Only one outside lobbyist tried to influence their discussion, and he was Elliott Roosevelt, the President's son, who promoted Gerald Mann for the job. But Roosevelt's frown led Mann to run instead for a third term as attorney general.

By a process of elimination Roosevelt and Wirtz finally agreed that their choice would be former Governor Jimmy Allred, who had introduced Lyndon Johnson to the President back in 1937. After Allred had retired as governor in 1939, Roosevelt had given him a lifetime seat on the federal bench. A White House call now found him not the least enthusiastic about resigning as Federal District Judge to run against Pappy O'Daniel. But the bait was sugar-coated with the promise to appoint him as judge on the higher Circuit Court of Appeals should he lose. On this basis Allred threw his cream-colored Stetson into the ring.

The object of all this scheming and concern was not a happy man at that time. The tall, heavyset, handsome Pappy O'Daniel had brought his ingratiating grin with him to the Senate, yet he was almost friendless among his Democratic colleagues. Tom Connally, his fellow Texas senator, shuffled off purposefully in the opposite direction whenever Pappy approached him. For one thing, Pappy had irked the Upper Chamber by leaping to his feet to deliver his maiden address only two days after his swearing-in, instead of holding to silence his first year as long-standing custom decreed. His speech was a disorganized, jumbling harangue against the Selective Service Act, containing such unrelated thoughts as "I do like hillbilly music." Then after this puzzling debut he rode off in a cloud of such thick anti-labor and anti-New Deal dust that the only senators who would talk to him were right-wing Republicans. He promoted bills to end the TVA, REA, and the minimum wage law, and he attempted to attach riders to legislation that would have abolished overtime pay, picketing, and the closed shop. Within a month, despite his good-natured personal prattle and easy smile, he found himself written up in political columns as a sorehead and crackpot, and he got the blunt word from the White House that he was on the proscribed list for patronage and pork barrel. But despite his total lack of influence in the Senate, Pappy liked Washington and he wanted to stay in the capital and be called Senator.

Allred understood full well the immensity of his task in campaigning against the wooly but wily Pappy O'Daniel. What optimism he possessed came from the fact that former Governor Dan Moody was also running. Moody, the "redheaded boy governor" from 1927 to 1931, belonged to the Texas regulars, and Allred was counting on him to split the conservative vote with Pappy.

Pressed by Roosevelt, Allred went out to "shell the woods" from one corner of Texas to the other, giving oral battle all the way. But no serious speaker could compete with Pappy once he climbed into the $15,000 sound truck that oilman Jesse McKee had given him and went out to war on his opponents. The top of the sound truck was a replica of the capitol dome, and when the hillbilly acts ended, the dome was raised and Pappy sounded off beneath it. "I'll tell you my program," he drawled. "It's this: There ain't gonna be no gas rationing in Texas; we ain't gonna lose the war; and there ain't gonna be no run-off primary." One big applause gatherer was his description of Washington as "the only lunatic asylum in the world run by its own inmates." Another howl of delight amid the mosquito slapping was his characterization of Allred and Moody as "the gold-dust twins." Whenever he thought he was being too funny, he trotted out the campaign-tested tear-producer that his daddy had been so poor that he was buried in overalls. And as in the earlier campaigns, he evoked enormous crowd sympathy when he cried out: "You know what they're sayin' 'bout me now? They're sayin' that my poor ol' mother was a washer-woman."

Walter Winchell, the New York gossip columnist and friend of President Roosevelt, wrote that the President was directing Allred's strategy. As part of it, Lyndon Johnson, fresh from the Navy, and Speaker Sam Rayburn were expected to return to Texas during the last part of the July 1942 primary to speak in Allred's behalf. However, Johnson had no intention of involving himself in anyone else's campaign, and he offered as his reason his own recent return from the war and a bout with pneumonia. As for Sam Rayburn, he was in the midst of laying out a speaking schedule for Allred's campaign when his office was flooded with "vicious" correspondence, foul-word threats against his life if he showed up on the campaign trail that summer. One unobscene letter warned him to stay on his farm "during your vacationing, commune with nature there. . . . You will then be refreshed and strengthened, a wiser one, and will make no mistakes, and you do not want to make any more." Rayburn decided not to campaign for Allred.

Moody's presence in the race prevented Pappy from gaining the necessary majority in the primary and forced a run-off August race between Pappy and Jimmy Allred. Pappy howled that if the cheaters had not stuffed ballot boxes for Allred, a run-off would not have been needed. This was too much even for the Texas regulars' leadership, which had come out for Moody, and their spokesman, E. B. Germany, replied that O'Daniel's total would have been far smaller if the crooked crowd of Texas Republicans hadn't crossed over to vote in the Democratic primary for Pappy.

O'Daniel knew that his strength lay in his unique style of campaigning, which made any serious opponent look ridiculous. Day after day during the run-off, his capitol dome truck carried him along the entertainment and slander trail. At every stop he charged that Allred had pocketed a bribe of $200,000 paid him by "Communist labor leader racketeers," with another $200,000 to be added after the election.

The old folks and the poor ranchers and farmers formed the hard core of Pappy's support, as they had in the past, and when the election day returns started coming in, a facsimile of the 1941 race between O'Daniel and Johnson seemed likely. In the end the election was close, with O'Daniel emerging victor by 451,359 votes to 433,203 for Allred. Tom Connally groaned that because of a measly 2 per cent margin he would have to suffer the presence of O'Daniel for another six years.

Following the election, true to his promise, Roosevelt nominated Allred to the U.S. Circuit Court of Appeals, only to have Pappy block the nomination through the use of Senatorial courtesy. Later, when Johnson became senator, Truman nominated Allred to the Federal District Court and Johnson helped with his confirmation.

After Allred's defeat in 1942, Roosevelt paid no attention to Texas. One casualty was his relationship with Johnson, which dwindled almost to the point of nonexistence. However, a year and a half later, following his return from the Cairo and Teheran Conferences, Roosevelt once more gave thought to Texas politics.

He had returned from his meetings with Churchill, Chiang Kai-shek, and Stalin with a fever and an unabating cough, which worried his wife because he showed none of his previous bounce in throwing off such ailments. Approaching his sixty-second birthday, he looked like a worn-out old man. But at Teheran he had settled the issue of a springtime 1944 Second Front invasion of northern France, the establishment of the United Nations, and the Soviet Union's entrance into the war against Japan once Germany was defeated.

Despite his waning physical condition, Roosevelt was considering a fourth term, and to him Texas loomed once more as the bellwether of Southern Democrats. Alvin Wirtz was again a welcome White House visitor, but Wirtz had a problem that needed settling before he could devote full attention to the job of making certain that Texas send a pro-Roosevelt delegation to the Democratic National Convention in July 1944.

His problem was his law client, the construction firm of Brown and Root, who faced civil and criminal suit by the federal government over tax matters and aid to Lyndon Johnson in his 1941 Senate bid. Brown and Root's troubles began in October 1942 when intelligence agents for the Bureau of Internal Revenue uncovered evidence of the company's secretive techniques to get around the laws regulating the maximum political contributions. According to Internal Revenue agents the company had given bonuses ranging from $2,000 to $54,000 to officials of its subsidiaries to be turned over by them to the Johnson campaign. At the time the agents were finding pay dirt, Wirtz voiced a strong patriotic complaint to Internal Revenue Commissioner Guy Helvering that his men were interfering with the company's heroic war work to build plants, hundreds of ships, and other battle necessities. Because of Wirtz's White House influence Helvering called off further investigation for several months, but permitted a resumption in June 1943. Strong-language phone calls from Johnson failed to halt the work, though the agents were warned by Washington headquarters to be "extra tactful because of complaints which were being registered in Washington relating to investigating political donations." Finally by the end of 1943 the work was completed, and the Bureau of Internal Revenue was prepared to assess Brown and Root a tax charge of $1,062,184.87 plus a fraud penalty of $531,002.45 on its business operations for 1941. In addition, the Bureau's decision was to request that the Justice Department prosecute the company for its political donations to the Johnson campaign.

On January 13, 1944, Johnson and Wirtz had an appointment with Roosevelt, and the President agreed that in many instances "prosecution" was actually "persecution." On this basis he thought something might be worked out for Wirtz's harassed client. He put in a call to Elmer Irey, the Treasury Department's chief legal enforcement officer, and ordered him to get a full teletyped report on Brown and Root from the Dallas Internal Revenue office and bring it in person as fast as he could rush it to the White House.

After Irey delivered the teletyped papers, Roosevelt took swift action. Instead of the $1,593,187.32 tax charge and fraud penalty, the total assessment was lowered to $372,000. As for the proposal to prosecute Brown and Root for their political contributions, Roosevelt ordered this abandoned. Johnson was later asked by Drew Pearson what had taken place in his meeting with the President. His reply was that the Brown and Root tax troubles had not been mentioned. Instead, he said, the discussion had centered on public power issues plus a strong plea from him as well as from Wirtz for Roosevelt to put Sam Rayburn on the 1944 ticket and drop Vice President Henry Wallace.

With the Brown and Root matter settled, Wirtz began his large-scale effort to send a Texas delegation pledged to Roosevelt to the national convention. Johnson agreed to serve as one of his assistants, but because the new Congressional session was just under way and his Naval Affairs subcommittee had several investigations of Navy Department skulduggery in progress, he found excuses for not returning to Texas for the necessary field work.

Still another event held Johnson in Washington. After experiencing three miscarriages, Lady Bird was finally expecting her first child in March 1944. Aunt Effie lived with them the year round now, but she was of no help because her invalidism kept her in her room, and Lady Bird had to care for her.

When March came, Johnson decided to spend the last evenings of vigil with Lady Bird instead of working late in the office. By the middle of the month he was so tense that he asked Willard Deason, his college roommate and NYA deputy, to stay with him and play dominoes each night. For three evenings they played one match after another. They were in the midst of a hard-fought game when Lady Bird asked them to take her to the hospital because her pains were coming regularly. Instead of putting the dominoes in the box, they let the pieces stand and rushed her to the hospital. After Lyndon registered her and learned that the frequency of Lady Bird's pains meant a delay of at least several hours, they drove home and resumed their game of dominoes.

After each game Lyndon dialed the hospital for the latest report. At last came word that he was the father of a baby girl. This time he made race-course time driving back to the hospital. The elevator was painfully slow carrying him and Willard to the delivery floor. When he got out and saw a nurse carrying a baby, the proud new father ran to her and bellowed, "Is that baby mine?"

"Hell, I don't know," the nurse told him, turning away. "It's somebody's . . ."

Almost overcome by his new status, Johnson raced to a telephone and called Sam Rayburn. "It's a red, crying, screaming baby girl!" he shouted. Then he called everyone on his office staff to break the important news. The following day, when he passed out cigars and candy, he announced that the baby had been named Lynda Bird, a combination of his first name and the second part of Lady Bird's nickname.

A week later, Lyndon drove to the hospital to bring Lady Bird and Lynda home. An immediate problem arose because neither parent had the slightest idea how to care for an infant. When Lynda developed colic and the doctor was not available, the distraught father grew hysterical with concern that she was dying. In his anguish, his first thought was to get advice from J. Edgar Hoover, the FBI chief, who lived across the street, but Lady Bird reminded him that Hoover was a bachelor. Finally, Mrs. Ollie Reed, the wife of a doctor and their next door neighbor, heard his shrieks of despair and hurried across the lawn. Once she saw what the problem was, she took charge and calmly soothed the parents and the infant. Lynda's colic disappeared, and Mrs. Reed undertook to teach Lady Bird the fundamentals of good infant care.

In the meantime Wirtz was suffering a major disaster in Texas. Despite his entreaties to local Democratic leaders, an overwhelming number of the springtime Democratic precinct conventions chose anti-Roosevelt delegates to the county conventions and passed resolutions favoring the sending of uninstructed delegates to the national convention. The county conventions, which selected delegates to the state convention at Austin to be held on May 23, proved even more disappointing. Not only did a majority of the county conventions want an anti-Roosevelt delegation sent to the national convention, but they also favored ordering Texas' Presidential Electoral College selectees to vote against Roosevelt, even if he carried Texas in November.

Wirtz attributed his defeat primarily to the Supreme Court decision of April 3, 1944, in the case of *Smith vs. Allwright*. In this eight-to-one opinion, with only Justice Owen Roberts dissenting, the Court ruled that Negroes could not be barred because of their color from voting in Texas Democratic primaries. Texas Democrats, who had play-acted the fiction that their party was a private association in order to bar Negro members, were wrathful at this decision. In the heat of the moment, most succumbed to the charge of Texas regulars that Roosevelt had been responsible for the Supreme Court's action.

Wirtz also attributed his defeat to the absence of big-name Texans in his fleet of persuaders. The biggest was Sam Rayburn, who had considered helping him and then reconsidered because of the pull of his own yearning to be the Vice-Presidential nominee with Roosevelt. So Sam had gone out campaigning for national convention delegates, riding the slow trains to California that spring because of his fear of air travel. Sam had invented the word "grumlins," and in his speeches he applied it to those who complained about the war leadership to the point of disrupting the national effort. He numbered the Texas regulars among the grumlins, defining one of these creatures as "a fellow with a big mouth who at breakfast drinks orange juice and coffee, eats cereal, two eggs, and toast; then feels sorry for himself as he grumbles at his wife because she has used up her red ration stamps for meat and is unable to give him bacon." He said they were people who had "jaundice of the spine in 1940 when confronted with the Hitler menace, and enlargement of the spleen in 1943 when Roosevelt was winning the war."

In mid-May, Johnson went to Texas for the State Democratic Convention, and he met beforehand with Wirtz, Mayor Tom Miller, Jimmy Allred, and other Texas loyalists to discuss ways to steal the convention from the reactionaries who held majority control. Wirtz's plan was to get the jump on the Texas regulars when the state convention convened in the Texas Senate chamber the following Tuesday, May 23. He expected the keynote speech to drive many delegates out for a drink, and as soon as the speech ended, he planned to make the motion to put loyalist Allred in charge as temporary chairman. If he could push the vote through swiftly, Allred could win, and then the regulars would be hog-tied.

However, things continued to go wrong for him. When the state convention opened, State Democratic Chairman George Butler proposed that the keynote speech be eliminated, for reasons of harmony, and placed the name of former Governor Dan Moody, a leader of the Texas regulars, in nomination for temporary chairman. Wirtz argued strenuously that the omission of the keynote speech would be a mistake. When he lost, he nominated Allred to oppose Moody. Again he was defeated, for Moody emerged the winner by a vote of 940$\frac{7}{12}$ to 774$\frac{5}{12}$.

At this point Wirtz decided to "go for broke" by making the motion to require Texas Presidential electors to vote for the Presidential nominee who won the popular vote in the November general election. Hardly had he made this proposal, which would have been a routine motion in most other state conventions, when he was greeted with foul shouts, and fistfights broke out between regulars and loyalists. Reporters noted that in the general melee his motion precipitated, two former state senators were punching each other in front of the rostrum. When the disorder continued without letup, Johnson decided to take a hand in settling the trouble, and he climbed to the platform to discuss a compromise solution with Chairman Butler. But the sight of Johnson on the platform led Texas regulars around the senate chamber to train their cursing on him. Much of what they yelled was profane; among the cleaner calls were: "Throw that Roosevelt pin-up boy out of there!" and "Get that goddam 'Yes-man' off that platform!"

Butler finally restored quiet, and when delegates were back in their seats, he ruled that Wirtz's motion was out of order. This brought on an appeal by Wirtz and further disorder, and when Butler once more restored a semblance of quiet, the convention threw out Wirtz's appeal by a vote of 952 to 695.

This vote had scarcely been announced when Mrs. Alfred Taylor, the affirmative former president of the Austin League of Women Voters, gained the floor and asked "all loyal friends of our dear President" to follow her and Alvin Wirtz to a separate state convention in the Texas House chamber elsewhere in the same building. The organist immediately struck up "Good Night, Ladies" as Texas loyalists began leaving the senate chamber. Wirtz's strategy was to leave Allred behind in the senate to keep an eye on the regulars, and poor Allred felt like a lonely intruder at his own hanging when the doors closed behind the last loyalist.

Once in possession of the house chamber, Wirtz's friends elected him temporary chairman and Mrs. Taylor secretary. Johnson's friends yelled that they wanted a speech from him, and only reluctantly did he walk to the rostrum. Then instead of the rousing condemnation of the Texas regulars in the senate that delegates were expecting, he spoke as though the loyalists had done wrong. They had quit the senate chamber, he said, because they were "prompted by suspicion that the intentions of the winning side were not in line with Texas democracy." But suspicion was not fact, he said to a silent audience. "Before we go off half-cocked, it's extremely important to give every Democrat and every so-called Democrat another opportunity to say whether he expects to vote for the party nominee. When

I bolt a convention," he yelled, "it's going to be a Hoovercrat convention." To his way of thinking, under the American system of majority control, the pro-Roosevelt loyalists had been treated fairly in the other convention.

Despite the crescendo of boos that greeted Johnson, Wirtz stood by his protégé and wearily proposed and won approval of a motion to check on Johnson's proposal. A committee was appointed to ask the leaders of the regulars, whose convention was still in session in the senate chamber, if they would support the national ticket.

The reply came swiftly. The senate convention's answer was the passage of a resolution ordering the twenty-three Presidential electors to vote for any man except Roosevelt. When the news reached the loyalist convention meeting in the Texas House chamber, Tom Miller, who had been elected chairman of the rump group, roared at the regulars as "evil men who would destroy the President, our Commander-in-Chief!" After this, the rumpers voted to send their own delegation to the Chicago national convention, naming Senator Tom Connally and speaker Sam Rayburn as delegates-at-large and making formidable Mrs. Clara Driscoll, a Johnson financial backer in 1941, chairman of the delegation.

Roosevelt's view, without knowing the details, was that Wirtz had made a botch of things. He got in touch with Texas regular E. B. Germany and asked him to meet with Wirtz and Johnson to effect a coalition between both groups. But Germany rejected the proposal and organized Democrats in six Southern states in opposition to a fourth term. In retaliation many Texas loyalists proposed the formation of a third party to support Roosevelt. However, Wirtz talked the hotheads out of this disruptive move.

The Texas Democratic primaries were scheduled for Saturday, July 22, 1944, and the Texas regulars singled out Johnson and Rayburn for a special effort to oust them from Congress. To the regulars, Johnson's crime was that he constantly invoked the name of Roosevelt; Rayburn's, that he was the key figure on Capitol Hill in promoting Roosevelt's legislation through Congress. So to set an example for other Texas congressmen, Texas regulars solicited contributions among their richer brethren and laid plans for the political liquidation of these two.

Because they had well-financed opponents, neither Rayburn nor Johnson went to the Chicago national convention in mid-July. Rayburn found himself faced with two antagonists, state Senator G. S. Morris and George Balch. Balch had run against him in 1942 and picked up 10,000 votes, but Rayburn understood that the Texas regulars had put their money on Morris. That Morris meant business came clear to Rayburn when he returned to his Fourth District and learned that Morris had already shaken hands with 30,000 people, and his literature was spread around the District like raindrops. On almost every telephone pole signs proclaimed: "No Seventeenth Term." Morris' pitch was that Sam believed in "creeping socialism," and he lashed him over radio and from the stump for being a champion of big government. Rayburn was the man who had it in his power to kill a half-million-dollar appropriation for the Fair Employment Practices Committee and failed to do so, Morris charged at every stop. Sam was frightened and his bald head perspired profusely during the rough campaign, but he emerged the winner in a close contest, gathering 22,052 votes to 16,705 for Morris and 816 for Balch. Sam said afterward, "I have it from reliable sources that upwards of $200,000 was spent to beat me."

Johnson took the news that he had an opponent as a personal insult of enormous proportions. The Texas regulars hoped to retire him by sponsoring Buck Taylor, formerly a committee clerk in the state legislature and currently the publisher of *The Middlebuster,* a mimeographed four-page political sheet that came out irregularly. "Lyndon Johnson, tall, gaunt, dynamic young Congressman of the Tenth Central Texas District," the Houston *Post* described the worried House member. The *Post* also called him "a spare, hollow-eyed person, thin, restless, intense in his work, of boundless energy."

It was Wirtz's idea that Johnson refrain from an open campaign, for this would dignify Buck Taylor and show Johnson's concern. Instead, Johnson remained publicly silent, while his friends talked him up throughout the District, and newspaper reporters whom he knew mentioned him favorably. Even the *Post* story, which portrayed him physically as a candidate for a tuberculosis sanitarium, emphasized both his ability to help his District and his importance in Congress. He was a man, said the account, who "works one day on the local business of helping egg and poultry producers stay in business, the next on the gigantic task of shaping future American military policy."

In the early period of the primary campaign Buck "The Middlebuster" Taylor was the epitome of the inconsequential opponent. He traveled about the District to the church socials, picnics, and fairs, and he took a conservative, states' rights line in his radio appearances. Johnson's intelligence sources called him a bust.

But suddenly, as the last ten days of the campaign arrived, the Taylor campaign rushed forward like a cyclone. The District was so saturated by anti-Johnson literature that the mail service had to work overtime. Taylor's *Middlebuster* campaign issue was written by high-priced talent hired by Texas regulars and was an easy-to-read condemnation of Johnson. Then there was *The Dirt Farmer,* whose attacks on Johnson made *The Middlebuster* look tame. A mailed picture showed Johnson shaking hands with a man he had never met and an adjoining picture revealed that man shaking hands with a Negro. The caption under the pictures read: "If you want to avoid this, get rid of this man." Still another piece of campaign dirt was a postcard that went to the entire polling list of the District's ten counties, including Mrs. Rebekah Johnson's house in Austin. The postcard claimed that Johnson intended to destroy Texas' "White primary." Hardly had the mailmen distributed these cards when they had to spread franked copies of a speech by Representative John Gibson of Georgia. Gibson, a correspondence school lawyer, ranted on about the Fair Employment Practices Committee and implied that Johnson had been a principal instigator in the Roosevelt program to help Negroes find jobs on federal war production projects. Johnson's friends nailed this lie immediately, pointing out that he was "on record in public meetings against the FEPC."

Johnson did not know what to expect as the final few days before the election arrived. Radio programs originating in other Texas cities were almost as easy to tune in throughout the Tenth District as Johnson's KTBC. Daily, paid campaign broadcasts emanating from WFAA in Dallas and WOAI in San Antonio vilified Johnson and praised Taylor. Then during the last two days of the campaign a deluge of telegrams came from outside the District carrying the message that Johnson was "hostile" to war veterans. Johnson reacted by spending an entire day on the telephone calling voters in his District.

The effort undertaken by the Texas regulars failed, for Johnson carried nine counties, losing only Washington County. His vote margin over Taylor was a large two and a half to one, but his personal rancor marred the victory. First he raged to reporters that his enemies had spent more than forty thousand dollars in the final ten days on their hatchet job; then he indulged in emotional self-pity, wailing that "it was the slimiest personal attack on an official within my memory."

If Johnson derived any pleasure from that year's Congressional primaries, it came from the ending of the political careers of other members of the Texas delegation. That year Texas loyalists were so strong in the Second District that Martin Dies decided to retire from Congress rather than chance defeat. But even greater joy came from the results in the Fourteenth District. Mister Dick Kleberg appeared to be a fixture there until a small news item ran in papers on D-Day, June 6, 1944. The mother of a thirteen-year-old page working in the Capitol told reporters that her son was forced to give Mister Dick a "kickback" of $39 from each of his monthly $129.50 pay checks.

The reporters questioned Kleberg, and cornered Mister Dick finally admitted he was making "deductions" from the lad's wages. He was not the only congressman doing this, he stressed. In fact, it was a common practice for members to make "deductions" to help them pay office expenses. As the news stories pointed out, Kleberg was part owner of the million-acre-plus King ranch.

Kleberg did his cause further damage when he fired the boy. But his undoing was inevitable because of the meanness of the practice and the appearance of the news story in the June 6 newspapers, at the very time countless American lives were being lost in the landings in Normandy. Kleberg was finished when the wife of Captain John Lyle, on duty in Italy, filed in behalf of her husband. Lyle, who did not return home to campaign,

was an easy winner, and Kleberg responded by coming out for Governor
Thomas E. Dewey of New York, the Republican Presidential nominee.

While Johnson and Rayburn were being plagued by campaign opponents,
Alvin Wirtz was plowing ahead relentlessly on two fronts to fulfill his
pledge to Roosevelt. At the national convention, the job was to put Texas
behind a Roosevelt nomination; back home the task was to bring about a
Democratic victory in November and make certain that the Presidential
electors would cast their ballots for the victor in Texas.

Two Texas delegations swept into sweltering Chicago in mid-July 1944.
Each was a noisy band attired in expensive cowboy hats and boots, and
each was eager for battle. The loyalists cheered themselves hoarse for
Roosevelt. The regulars whooped it up for Virginia's Senator Harry Byrd,
symbol of a weak central government and no civil rights for Negroes.

Before the convention formally convened on July 19, the pushing, shoving, and foul-name calling between the two Texas Democratic delegations
augured chaos for the entire convention. Robert Hannegan, the young St.
Louis boss who was now chairman of the Democratic National Committee,
viewed this warfare as a danger to his scheme of putting over Senator
Harry Truman, his political sponsor, as the Vice-Presidential nominee. So
when Hannegan learned that all loyalist delegates planned to vote for the
renomination of Vice President Henry Wallace, he made a swift decision.
Senator Abe Murdock of Arizona, chairman of the Credentials Committee,
announced it on July 17—only the regulars would be seated, and they
would cast the state's forty-eight convention votes.

Again Hannegan had a change of mind when Dan Moody of the Texas
regulars seconded the Byrd nomination and his delegation of regulars then
remained sullen and glued in their seats during the Roosevelt ovations.
Hannegan's enormous displeasure revealed itself when he named the
absent Lyndon Johnson of the loyalist delegation as an assistant sergeant-
at-arms of the convention. Then came Credentials Committee Chairman
Murdock's decision to seat both delegations and split the vote equally
between them. Texas National Committeeman Myron Blalock, who was a
member of both delegations, immediately wrote a note to Hannegan, telling
him "to please go to hell," and half the regulars quit the convention.

On the Presidential nomination, the remaining chastised regulars gave
twelve votes to Byrd and twelve to Roosevelt. The loyalists, of course, cast
their twenty-four for the President. The issue was now the Vice-Presidential
nomination, and Ed Pauley, treasurer of the National Committee, came
around for a secret talk with Blalock, Wirtz, and Tom Miller. Hannegan's
decision to give seats to the loyalists required a quid pro quo. As matters
then stood, Wallace appeared to have an excellent chance to win renomination on the first ballot. Pauley demanded that the Texas delegations pass
on the first ballot, and Miller agreed for the loyalists. He kept his word,

and Truman won the nomination on the second ballot after Wallace failed on the first ballot by one hundred and sixty votes.

Riding the crest of the Texas loyalists' success at the National Convention, Wirtz vigorously began anew his battle at home with the Texas regulars to gain control of the voting privileges of Democratic Presidential electors. It was the unusual Texas party system that gave him a second chance. Following the spring conventions and the summer primaries during election years, Texas was treated to a second trio of conventions—precinct, county, and state. The state convention came in September and was considered the "Governor's Convention." This was the party get-together where the governor customarily announced his program (and expected quick passage) and named the state Democratic chairman and members of the State Executive Committee. Beyond these activities, the chief work of the Governor's Convention was to certify the winners of the Texas Democratic primaries so that their names would be placed on the general election ballot in November.

Governor Coke Stevenson was looking forward to a pleasant September convention that would operate as smoothly as the meeting in 1942. However, his expectations collided with the determined will of Alvin Wirtz, the stubborn Dutchman, to use the Governor's Convention to undo the work of the May State Convention, which had ordered the Texas Presidential electors to vote for any man except Roosevelt, should he win. In his army Wirtz, who had a great dislike for Stevenson, counted on the help of more than a score of lieutenants, including Johnson, Mayor Tom Miller, and Jimmy Allred. Surprisingly, Wirtz faced the unusual opposition of Sam Rayburn, who believed that the scrapping of the Texas regulars and loyalists at the Chicago Democratic National Convention had cost him the Vice-Presidential nomination. Philosophically also, as Rayburn confided to friends, he had as little use for the liberal Texas loyalists as he had for the encrusted Texas regulars, even though his name was on important pieces of New Deal legislation.

Wirtz decided early to concentrate on controlling the 254 county conventions that met shortly after the primaries to choose delegates to the Governor's Convention in September. Alerted to his strategy, the well-heeled Texas regulars reacted by ordering their bully boys to frighten pro-Roosevelt delegates at the county conventions. But Wirtz had sent out word to his own crews of battlers, and the county conventions turned into roughneck gatherings and delegates by the dozens left for home with black eyes and bloodied noses. In the end, when they adjourned, it was apparent that Wirtz's men had been more convincing, for a majority of the county conventions supported the Roosevelt-Truman ticket.

When Coke Stevenson saw what had happened, he hurried to Washington to confer with Rayburn. At Sam's request, Vice-Presidential nominee

Truman escorted Coke to the White House on September 6 for a conference with Roosevelt. The President was ill from the effects of his rigorous trip to Hawaii at the end of July, where he had discussed strategy to defeat Japan with General Douglas MacArthur and Admiral Chester Nimitz, and he could not abide talk of dissension and trouble in Texas. Roosevelt quickly agreed with Stevenson's proposal that the loyalists should unite with the regulars. However, Wirtz (who was contacted) rejected this proposal. Stevenson then suggested putting two sets of Presidential electors on the ballot so that the voters could decide whether they wanted electors who were bound to the Roosevelt-Truman ticket or electors who would vote against the ticket. Roosevelt thought this novel idea to be fair, but again Wirtz would not agree. As a friend of his expressed his philosophy: When you have the enemy on the run, don't end the chase. Stevenson went home with his mission a failure.

Wirtz showed Johnson how a master politician operated at the state level. Before the Governor's Convention convened on September 12, Wirtz was already on hand holding a series of friendly and earnest discussions with influential delegates. If Texas were lost to Roosevelt, the Republicans would take over the national government, he argued, and what would happen to all the federal money that the Democrats were pouring into Texas?

When the convention began, his swift actions were brutal. Without delay, he promoted Jimmy Allred into office as chairman of the gathering. Then on the following day, he put through a hair-raising purge. George Butler, who was Jesse Jones' nephew and lawyer, was removed from his key office of state Democratic chairman and replaced by Harry Seay of Dallas, a close friend of Wirtz. Next Wirtz had fifty of the sixty-two members of the State Executive Committee expelled and replaced with his own selections, which included Sam Rayburn's friend, Bill Kittrell, as secretary of the committee. Wirtz also tore into the Texas regulars who had caused him to do so much work. These were the fifteen Presidential electors selected among the twenty-three in the May state convention who would not promise to vote for Roosevelt. All fifteen were purged and replaced with loyalists. Afterward, when Secretary of State Sidney Latham, a Stevenson appointee, refused to certify the new slate of electors, Wirtz rushed a case to the Texas Supreme Court and won a quick and favorable decision on September 23. For a man who sought only justice for Roosevelt in Texas, Wirtz had emerged as the political boss of the Democrats.

Now it was the turn of the Texas regulars to say they would not abide by the decisions of the majority at the state convention. In a political broadside, they condemned the Wirtz organization as the tool of "Bronx Negro politicians, the Communists, the CIO Political Action Committee, and other big city machines." Then they entered the Presidential contest as a separate Democratic party, naming Senator Byrd as their candidate. Byrd refused the honor, and they were left in the peculiar position of being on the ticket without a candidate. As a last resort, they asked voters to insert the name of any Democrat other than Roosevelt on the ballot.

Even though Roosevelt should have been pleased with Wirtz's handiwork, he remained fearful that Wirtz might have stirred up a hornets' nest among Democrats which would help the Republican party in Texas. His concern was heightened when the public opinion polls agreed that Texas was the key state in the election. If Roosevelt won Texas, they said, he would win 286 electoral votes, while Dewey would lose the national election with only 245 votes. But if Roosevelt lost Texas' 23 electoral votes, he would have a total of 263 and Dewey would become President with 268 votes.

Because of his poor health, Roosevelt could not undertake a national campaign in 1944, and large Roosevelt rallies were staged by his friends in the various sections of the country. An enormous rally was held at Wichita Falls, with Wirtz in the shadows, while Johnson, Rayburn, Wright Patman, Tom Connally, and Allred were the featured speakers. Little else was done in Roosevelt's behalf in Texas, but he needed no help, for when Texas voted, the Roosevelt total exceeded 800,000 votes. Dewey had only 191,000, while the Texas regulars had only 135,439 supporters. The electoral count revealed how wrong the pollsters were. Roosevelt amassed 432 electoral votes and Dewey only 99.

Chapter 25

D ESPITE THE SWEEPING success of Alvin Wirtz in his hammer blows at the Texas regulars, none of his new power could rub off on his protégé within the Texas political structure. Nor could Johnson move upward in political authority in Washington, even with the support of his Capitol daddies. So when the Seventy-ninth Congress met in January 1945, his ambitions seemed to be stalled permanently at the House level.

The chagrining thing to him was that his friend, Warren Magnuson, without half his push and drive and without political daddies, was now a senator. When they had done their mutual confiding over the years about their ambitions to become senators, even Maggie had assumed that Lyndon would reach that goal long before he would because of the many important people Lyndon bragged were working to promote his career. In fact, from the initial goodwill Maggie had when he first came to the House, he soon appeared on the downgrade, for his political stands were not popular with the leadership. He had voted against Selective Service and later opposed the extension of the draft; in 1943, he led the House fight to repeal the poll tax, which only served to antagonize the Southern bloc that held power in the Lower Chamber; and he brawled publicly with the War Department over the Army's mistreatment of the Abraham Lincoln Brigade members, young left-wing Americans who had fought in the Spanish Civil War in the mid-thirties against the Franco insurgents. But now Magnuson had won election to the Senate and was living evidence to Johnson that politics was not predictable.

Johnson had too much energy to subside in the humdrum political situation in which he currently found himself. He needed an outlet until the opportunity came to move forward again, and he concentrated on what had equal priority to him with his political ambitions. This was his dream of becoming a millionaire and putting on a show like the Klebergs, Richardsons, Carters, and Wests, with all the comforts of Eastern potentates.

The Austin radio station, officially in Lady Bird's name, was his open door to riches, now that the FCC had given KTBC such advantages as vastly increased transmitting power, its own wavelength, and twenty-four-hour-a-day broadcasting rights. Soon after these grants, he began putting in as much time on KTBC business as he did on his Congressional duties. When friends could not reach him in his House Office Building suite, they knew they could find him in Austin.

Lady Bird was needed for the facade of signing all checks and reports for the FCC, but Johnson was the station's boss. Besides Jesse Kellam, his other chief assistant was Walter Jenkins, a young man he put on divided duty between his Congressional office and KTBC business. Johnson saw what all radio station owners know, that the key to the station's success was its ability to attract buyers of radio time. But in addition to enjoying total success in his requests to the FCC, he differed from most radio station proprietors in his relentlessly aggressive campaign to sell time. He personally hired the station's salesmen, and chose those who were talkative, pushy, energetic, and willing to work overtime. Each man operated on a short leash, for Johnson insisted on knowing everything he did for the station. Every salesman had to submit a detailed daily statement, listing separately each company he visited, the sales pitch he used, what the results had been, and what future prospects were. Johnson studied these statements carefully, and the salesmen who failed to meet the quotas he set were sent on their way. He also maintained a chart on which he plotted in each small time segment of each day the money that sponsors were paying the station. If any week failed to show improvement over the preceding period, he made endless soul-searching analyses to determine the reason.

In still another important way Johnson differed from most radio station owners. This was his unwillingness to accept the station's profits as the end-all of his wealth-gathering. He saw the station as a bank teller's cash drawer, the contents of which could become the stake for greater gains. Wirtz told him that bank stock was skyrocketing in value, and he advised him to plow much of his profits into this area. Johnson did this, and he also moved into land ownership. He was clever in the way he picked up valuable Austin real estate without putting up cash. When homebuilders advertised their subdivisions over KTBC, Johnson said he was willing to cut the time price slightly in exchange for "a few of your little old lots." With land values on the increase, these lots he picked up in Austin became an important source of his blooming wealth. Yet as he once admitted, he could have had a good start in real estate a decade earlier if it had not been for his father. Before he went to Congress, he said, he and Lady Bird had an opportunity to buy six hundred acres of good land for only six dollars an acre. When he told his father about it, Sam Johnson, who had worked unproductively many years as a real estate operator, "got up from the front of the fireplace, stalked into the kitchen, and said to his wife, 'I never thought I'd raise a boy that didn't have more sense than to pay six dollars an acre for land!' "

One personal satisfaction Johnson derived as a radio station owner came when he hired Dr. Cecil Evans, who had been president at Southwest Texas State Teachers College, as one of his news commentators. The biggest satisfaction, however, came from the steadily increasing profit showing. Yet this was diluted by a fear that labor unions might destroy what he was so carefully creating.

In the spring of 1945 officers of the Communications Workers of America told him that they intended to unionize the station's employees. This infuriated Johnson because if they succeeded he would no longer be the total master of the staff. Texas was then the scene of much labor violence, with the end of the war removing the restraints against unions organizing workers by threatening strikes. When Johnson heard a rumor that the CWA planned to throw pickets around his station and destroy its transmitter if he refused to unionize KTBC, he called employees and old friends to a meeting and begged them to guard his property against violence. Among those who agreed were Jake Pickle, who would one day occupy Johnson's House seat; Joe Kilgore, also a future congressman; and Merrill Connally, one of John Connally's many brothers. The group came armed with guns and took up strategic positions. But CWA picketing failed to materialize, and KTBC remained a nonunion shop.

In the late period of 1944 and the early months of 1945, while Johnson was a regular commuter between his Austin radio station and his Capitol office, military events piled on top of each other as the final period of the war began. In Europe the Battle of the Bulge had cast a black shadow

over the nation's optimism before German Field Marshal Karl von Rund-
stedt's army suffered 120,000 casualties and disintegrated. Afterward the
grueling Allied push across the Rhine and toward the Elbe River got under
way, as the Germans retaliated with V-2 rocket blockbusters on London.
Simultaneously, General Douglas MacArthur's forces were liberating the
Philippines, while Fleet Admiral Chester Nimitz was producing a frightful
loss of American lives by imbecilic frontal assaults on the islands of Iwo
Jima and Okinawa.

As the war moved into this decisive phase, Johnson thought more than
ever that what would speed final victory was a home-front assault on
absentee war plant workers. Judge Howard W. Smith's House Rules Committee, which believed itself the nation's champion against New Deal
legislation, agreed with him and permitted his revived "Work or Fight" bill
to be reported to the House floor at the beginning of the Seventy-Ninth
Congress. Despite bitter denunciation from both the AFL and CIO that
Johnson's bill was designed to permit management to get rid of union-
active workers, Johnson stuck to his charge that he was solely after the
absentee "vermin"; and the House passed the bill in February 1945, shortly
after Johnson returned from a trip to Austin.

While earth-shaking events were happening with breathtaking speed
abroad, Vice President Harry Truman had become a member in good
standing of Sam Rayburn's "Board of Education." Every day after hours he
enjoyed walking the length of the Capitol from the Senate dais to the
speaker's House-side hideaway to join Sam and his friends in political talk
and "strike a blow for liberty." The blows Truman struck consisted of
bourbon and branchwater snorts, in contrast to Johnson's double scotch
blows. Wright Patman, who still had his private key to the room, found
Truman in agreement with his own populist anti-Wall Street beliefs, while
some of the others invited to attend the board meetings thought the time
best spent in reciting funny stories. Besides the politicians, Lew Deschler,
the knowledgeable House parliamentarian, was a daily guest, and *New
York Times* reporter Bill White, Johnson's special friend, was frequently
asked by Rayburn to join the group.

Sometimes, in the early months of 1945, Truman came to Rayburn's
special room, stood upon the frayed rug before the fireplace or flopped
into a black leather armchair, and talked about his belief that Roosevelt had
not long to live. "Truman once told me about a dream," said Mister Sam.
"He said he awoke in a cold sweat, for he had dreamed that the President
had died and he was called into service." Truman's buddy, Eddie McKim,
who had been a sergeant under Captain Harry in Battery D of the 129th
Field Artillery in World War I and was now the Vice President's special assistant, talked about the day the previous summer when President Roosevelt invited them to a White House showing of the movie *Woodrow
Wilson*. When they left, McKim said he commented on Roosevelt's sickly

appearance and told Truman, "Hey, bud, turn around and take a look. You're going to be living in the house before long." Truman's reply was: "Eddie, I'm afraid I am, and it scares the hell out of me."

When Roosevelt returned from the Yalta Conference in February 1945, his facial skin looked waxy, and he had trouble closing his mouth. But Rayburn and others who talked to him found his mind totally clear and alert. Sam was surprised that in his condition Roosevelt would use up so much of his remaining energy to come to the House on March 1 to give Congress and the nation his report on the Yalta Conference. At a dinner not long afterward Sam could no longer contain his thoughts about Roosevelt, and he spoke indiscreetly to the gathering. "This country is in for a great tragedy," he said. "I don't think the President will be with us much longer."

The end came on April 12, 1945. Shortly after 5 P.M. that day Truman strolled into Rayburn's "Board of Education" room for a bourbon and branchwater and was greeted with a message from Sam to call Steve Early, Roosevelt's press secretary, at the White House. Rayburn remembered later that Lew Deschler and Bill White were there when Truman asked the White House operator to connect him with Early. Early's voice was choked as he told Truman to "come right over." Rayburn had been watching Truman make the call, and he remarked, "Truman is kind of a pale fellow anyhow, and he got a little paler, and he hung up the telephone." When Truman turned to the others, he gasped, "Holy General Jackson!"

Not long after Truman left the room for his ride to the White House and the Presidency, Johnson loped into the board room and heard the news that Roosevelt had died that afternoon in Warm Springs, Georgia. Everyone present was in his own dungeon of grief, and even reserved Sam Rayburn was roughly brushing away the tears.

The man who kept his wits at this hour of national despair was Johnson's friend, *New York Times* reporter Bill White. He knew that his editors would rightly be expecting a story from him on Roosevelt's death, and he saw an opportunity to give his pal, Lyndon Johnson, good publicity at the same time. His story pitch, he told the Washington editor of *The Times,* when he called his office, should be the impact and reactions of a typical pro-Roosevelt congressman to the President's passing. Asked whom he would select as his "typical" congressman, White gave the name of Lyndon Johnson.

In the story that *The Times* printed, White had Johnson describe the impact of Roosevelt's death in this fashion:

"I was in the speaker's office when it came. The phone rang and the speaker answered. He didn't say anything at all that I could hear—just a kind of a gulp. Finally he said the President was dead.

"I was just looking up at a cartoon on the wall—a cartoon showing the

President with that cigarette holder and his jaw stuck out like it always was. He had his head cocked back, you know. And then I thought of all the little folks, and what they had lost.

"He was like a daddy to me always: he always talked to me just that way."

White went on with a Johnson declaration that he had entered politics solely because of Roosevelt's example: "I don't know that I'd ever have come to Congress if it hadn't been for him." Yet another paragraph was carefully designed to portray Johnson as an independent.

"They called the President a dictator and some of us they called 'yes' men. Sure, I yessed him plenty of times—because I thought he was right—and I'm not sorry for a single 'yes' I ever gave. I have seen the President in all kinds of moods—at breakfast, at lunch, at dinner—and never once in my five terms did he ever ask me to vote a certain way, or even suggest it. And when I voted against him—as I have plenty of times—he never said a word.

"When my baby [Lynda] was born, I never dreamed of mentioning it to him, but somehow he found out about it and a White House car turned up at my house and brought a book. It was a book about Fala, the President's dog, as a gift to my daughter. The President had autographed it—they were calling him a 'master' then. He autographed it, 'From the master of the pup.'"

The climactic note in White's creation, depicting the impact of Franklin Roosevelt's passing on a congressman who had been his true follower yet had somehow managed to remain independent, came with the description of Johnson reading Sam Rayburn's pen and ink tribute "in a bold, old-fashioned hand" to the fallen leader. He quoted Johnson as crying out at the close, "God! God! How he could take it for us all!"

Chapter 26

AS PRESIDENT, Franklin Roosevelt considered himself the leader of the Executive Branch, to whom Congress was an alien organization to be bought, coerced, flattered, threatened, or dined to give him the legislation he wanted. When Harry Truman succeeded him, he brought a differing concept of his office, for he did not want to cut the umbilical cord to the Senate nor alter his personal relationship with his friends on the Hill.

Although he undertook to populate the government with Missourians, he established Leslie Biffle, the astute secretary of the Senate who was from Arkansas, and Sam Rayburn as his top legislative advisers. To Biffle and Rayburn he was always "Harry," and never "Mr. President." Biffle had a special office telephone, one with a red, white, and blue cord, that bypassed the White House switchboard and rang directly on Harry's desk. Whenever he had business to transact in a hurry, he never hesitated to call the President. On the other hand, Rayburn did not like the coldness of the telephone and preferred face-to-face meetings instead. This pleased Truman, who thought he might be lonely as President so far from his old comrades in the Capitol. "Just any afternoon after five o'clock," he told Sam, "come in the east entrance of the White House over by the Treasury, and walk through there and come up to my study. I'll be in there."

The stocky, bald man with the dour expression had no intention of wearing out his welcome, so he did not come too often, though Truman never tired of him. In fact, because of Truman's admiration and respect for Rayburn, he proposed and won approval from Congress for a change in the Presidential succession law to make the speaker next in line if the President died (there was no Vice President) and not the Secretary of State.

In the fall of 1945, after V-J Day marked the end of World War II in Asia, as V-E Day had done in Europe the previous May, Rayburn made one of his visits to Truman's study, and when he returned to the Capitol, he thought he had some good news for Lyndon Johnson. Truman had told him that the newly formed United Nations would hold its first General Assembly and Security Council meetings in London in January 1946. Truman's plan was to name Senator Connally, who had participated in the writing of the UN Charter in the April-June 1945 San Francisco sessions, as United States representative, or Ambassador, to the Security Council.

Rayburn's excitement over this news was that if Connally accepted, Johnson could run for his vacated seat. But at Johnson's request that he call Ol' Tawm, he refused. Sam could not ask Connally what he planned to do, nor could he nudge him toward acceptance, for their relationship was properly civil but nothing more. The truth was that Rayburn had put himself into the position of a political debtor by asking Connally a half dozen times, years before, to use his political patronage authority and make his sister Katy's husband, W. A. Thomas, collector of Internal Revenue at Dallas. When Connally came through at last, Sam was bound by his own code not to make any move that Connally might interpret as being unfriendly. Johnson's hopes to run again for the Senate collapsed when Connally finally shrugged off Truman's offer because of his preference to remain as chairman of the Senate Foreign Relations Committee.

After this disappointment for Johnson, another opportunity for advancement suddenly hove into view when Governor Coke Stevenson passed word along that he had no intention of making an unprecedented try for a third term in 1946. Texas politicians agreed that what really motivated "Calculating Coke," as they commonly called the governor, was his determination to run against Pappy O'Daniel for the Senate seat in 1948. Coke's "I do not choose to run" statement reached Alvin Wirtz at a time when he and his loyalist friends were planning a meeting of the Democratic Executive Committee and a party banquet in Dallas in January 1946. Wirtz immediately telephoned Johnson and told him to take time off from his radio and Congressional business and be on hand to promote himself.

Other would-be candidates had the same idea, and the Committee invited four—Johnson, Jimmy Allred, R. W. "Bob" Calvert, and ousted Texas University president, Dr. Homer P. Rainey—to speak at its meeting. Later, the four displayed their affability to the banqueters at the Adolphus Hotel. Here, with an arm around Lyndon, Mister Sam pointedly reiterated a remark he had been using recently, "I don't intend to endorse one of those Democrats who sit on the fence and talk like a Republican." However, Johnson failed to make a positive impression at this Dallas love feast.

Lyndon had a second chance in April when the most popular living American, General Dwight D. Eisenhower, flew to Denison, Texas, with Sam Rayburn to visit his small, woodframe birthplace alongside the Cotton Belt Railway tracks. Eisenhower's relationship with the place of his birth was almost traumatic, for it signified an unhappy period in his mother's life. Failing in business in Hope, Kansas, David Eisenhower had deserted his wife and sons, Arthur and Edgar, and fled to Denison where he took a poorly paid job with the Cotton Belt Railway as a shop foreman. He then suffered remorse and wrote to his wife Ida to join him, and here the general was born in 1890. Until the end of World War II, whenever Dwight Eisenhower had to list his place of birth he invariably wrote "Tyler, Texas."

But every hero is expected to visit his birthplace, so Eisenhower finally had to go to Denison. Because the city was in Rayburn's District, Mister Sam also went through torture, for he was deathly afraid of airplane travel, yet he made the flight with Eisenhower. Festivities called for a visit to the house of origin, a parade, a Texas barbecue, and some oratory at Denison's Forest Park. Rayburn knew that reporters and photographers by the dozens would be in Denison to cover the events, and he arranged a prominent place for Johnson in the roster of speakers. However, instead of a sparkling speech about himself and the general that would give him widespread exposure throughout Texas, Johnson misread the occasion and spoke chiefly about himself and Sam Rayburn. "Speaker Rayburn has been like a daddy to me," he said, "guiding me in my early years in Congress, and now he is guiding the entire House of Representatives in these crucial times."

The immense crowd had not come to hear a tribute to Rayburn, and Johnson's talk fell flat. Other speakers who also praised Rayburn suffered a similar fate. However, in Johnson's case the price was high, for Wirtz advised him not to run for governor but to bide his time some more, with an additional term or two in the House.

If Johnson thought, after his hopes for the Senate and the Governor's Mansion were dashed, that he could coast to an uncontested primary victory in 1946, he was sadly mistaken. Charles King, only a student at the University of Texas, filed for Johnson's House seat, and this was good for a laugh throughout the District. But Johnson did not laugh when he found that the Texas regulars were financing and masterminding the candidacy of a stronger opponent, Hardy Hollers, who was a district judge.

Newspapers called the show Hollers and Johnson put on a "torrid" campaign. It was the first time since 1937 that Johnson conducted an intensive, personal campaign, and it revealed how concerned he was that an upstart might actually push him out of politics. All of his office files underwent examination to cull the favors he had done for individuals and firms in his District; and several typists worked overtime sending these requesters a reminder of what Johnson had done for them in the past and a request that they now reciprocate by voting for him. He also raced about the District for pep talks, speeches, and handshakes, and he passed out truckloads of watermelons, but he found himself on the defensive because of the nature of the Hollers campaign.

Hollers and his backers believed that the sure road to victory was a relentless attack on Johnson for his unusual rise from rags to riches while supposedly being totally involved with his political duties in Washington. What Hollers hollered at every stop was his charge that Johnson should be in prison instead of running for office. "If the U. S. Attorney was on the job," Hollers shouted, "Lyndon Johnson would be in the federal penitentiary instead of in the Congress of the United States. . . . Will Lyndon Johnson explain how the charter for KTBC, owned by Mrs. Johnson, was obtained? Will Lyndon Johnson explain the purchase of his house on Dillman Street [a duplex he had bought in Austin], his acquisition of rental property in Austin, and his mushrooming personal fortune?"

Johnson had no intention of permitting Hollers to draw him into a long explanation of his business affairs. But Hollers' persistence in repeating his charges finally forced Johnson to make what he hoped would be a satisfactory answer. This was his statement that Lady Bird had purchased the Austin radio station with a bank loan of ten thousand dollars and that KTBC's assets at the end of 1945 were only eighty thousand dollars.

Hollers called both statements far from truthful: Lady Bird had frequently claimed she had made a down payment of seventeen thousand, five hundred dollars from the twenty-one thousand dollars her father had given her as part of her mother's estate, and if KTBC's assets were so small, how were the Johnsons able to buy so much Austin property? Hollers scoffed at her claim that her father was well-to-do and able to give her thousands of dollars, for he asserted that an examination of Dun and Bradstreet would show that Mr. Taylor had no credit rating.

Johnson tried to change the tenor of the campaign by pointing to the large amount of federal money he had personally been able to get for the District. But some of Hollers' supporters called him a piker compared with Albert Thomas, who represented the Eighth District. Thomas could claim more than a billion dollars he pushed through the House Appropriations Committee in ten years, which brought two large Navy hospitals, a VA hospital and regional center, the Houston Coliseum, the new Houston City Hall, school buildings, airfields, ordnance works, flood control projects, Navy Yard, and money to dredge the Houston ship channel to the Gulf.

So the campaign went down to the wire, with Hollers certain the voters would consider his charges, and Johnson worried that his political future was dead. But when the votes were counted, Johnson won easily. It was only after he went back to Washington that he grew angry that he had not swamped Hollers. A friend of his said, "He simply could not understand how any of them [the voters] came to oppose him."

It was after the Hollers campaign that Lady Bird was expecting again. However, she suffered her fourth miscarriage and Johnson's hope of having a son vanished. He later detailed how this miscarriage came about, in a long discourse on his wife's bravery. "I remember one time Bird was running a high temperature, but she insisted that it was all right for me to go to the office. The minute that I left the room she called the doctor. She was bleeding and in terrific pain with a tubular pregnancy, but she just wouldn't admit pain, or ask for mercy."

Lady Bird had good reason for not asking Lyndon to stay home. One time when she was away, she said, their daughter Lynda Bird contracted "a very mild childhood disease called impetigo. You would have thought Lynda Bird had cancer the way Lyndon behaved! He called Mrs. Albert Thomas [the wife of the congressman from Houston], who got a doctor, and she came over and helped him out. Lyndon since then considered himself and Lera Thomas veritable lifesavers because that skin eruption didn't finish her."

Not long after Lady Bird's fourth miscarriage, Aunt Effie's liver ailment grew more serious. She no longer enjoyed arguing with Dr. Reed, their next door neighbor, whether violets were weeds or flowers; nor could she serve tea, graham crackers, and sugar cane bits to visitors. At her own request she left the upstairs bedroom in the Johnson house and returned to Montgomery, Alabama, to enter a sanitarium. In the fall, Lady Bird visited the frail woman and stayed a month with her. At the end of that time, when Aunt Effie rallied, her doctor believed Lady Bird could return to Washington without worrying about the sixty-six-year-old woman.

Hardly was she back in the capital, said Lady Bird, when "a doctor confirmed that I was pregnant again." This became the basis for Lyndon's insistence that she refrain from traveling to Alabama in January 1947 when word came that Aunt Effie was dead. To keep her at home, he also had a long conference with her doctor, who then told her she might lose her child if she went. So Lady Bird did not attend the funeral of the devoted woman who had given most of her adult life to her.

However, this caution paid off in July 1947 when Lady Bird gave birth to her second daughter. Lyndon was again disappointed that he did not have a son, but he adjusted to the situation. It was his idea to give the infant the same initials as all other members of the family. As a result, she was named Lucy Baines Johnson.

"It's cheaper that way," he once explained away the oddity of identical L.B.J. initials, "because we can all use the same luggage."

Chapter 27

WHEN JOHNSON TOOK time off from KTBC business to return to Washington for the opening of the Eightieth Congress in January 1947, he was witness to an unusual political situation. For the first time since 1930 the Republicans were in control of the House, having swept the Congressional elections in 1946.

Sam Rayburn pouted at this state of affairs that elevated Republican Joe Martin into the speaker's chair by a majority exceeding sixty votes. Sam said point blank that he would never serve as minority leader, but Johnson led the Texas delegation in buttonholing other House Democrats in working up a draft of Rayburn, and finally Mister Sam consented. When Johnson saw that Rayburn lost the use of the 1944 limousine that came with the speakership, he and others undertook a drive to give him a free car. With Sam setting a limit of twenty-five dollars that a single congressman could contribute, a total of four thousand dollars was collected and Sam became the owner of a 1947 Cadillac. Unfortunately, the money raisers had not considered the expense of employing a chauffeur, and Sam had to pay a driver two hundred dollars a month to transport him around Washington and back and forth to his farm at Bonham, Texas.

The winning of both the House and Senate by the Republicans in 1946 was not a surprise to either party. One Texas Democrat tried to explain the loss by saying, "Harry Truman was hoeing when he should have been plowing." As the European war had drawn to a close in the spring of 1945, economists had pulled their pipes out of their mouths long enough to predict that a postwar economic depression would result in an unemployment toll of eight million. On the basis of this intolerable estimate and to prove that federal idealism was the wave of the future, Truman asked Congress in September 1945 for an "Economic Bill of Rights." His latter-day Bill of Rights would guarantee everyone's right to a job at decent pay, an adequate home, medical care, proper education, free competition, and high price supports if he were a farmer.

The reaction of Republicans and most Southern Democrats was immediate. A dangerous radical was living in the White House. Not long afterward, when Truman replaced Roosevelt high appointments with his own men and then failed to win implementation of his Economic Bill of Rights from Congress, New Dealers also soured on him. Constant newspaper attacks on him for cronyism, for the widespread labor-management troubles that abounded, and a general public desire to get rid of lingering wartime controls over prices and rents also reduced Truman's popularity. The Gallup Poll public esteem thermometer, which showed an initial reading of a feverish 87 per cent, showed a chilly drop to 32 per cent by the fall of 1946.

Johnson's experience in preventing union representation for employees of KTBC destroyed the last vestige of liberalism within him. When the Republican leadership in the Eightieth Congress wrote the Taft-Hartley Bill, Sam Rayburn denounced it as a "punitive labor bill." However, Johnson thought the measure was excellent because it made the closed shop illegal, barred jurisdictional and sympathy strikes and mass picketing, opened unions to lawsuits, forced unions to show their financial records, and gave the President authority to obtain injunctions to prevent strikes involving interstate commerce, public utilities, and communications. While Rayburn led the House fight against the bill, Johnson voted for it. Then, after it passed Congress and Truman vetoed it, Johnson was numbered among the necessary two-thirds House vote that overrode his veto.

Johnson's opposition to the Administration revealed itself also when Truman presented Congress with a strong civil rights program. Among his ten planks were provisions for an antilynching measure, an FEPC, the end of Jim Crowism in seating and in using toilet and restaurant facilities in interstate transportation, and a guarantee of the right to vote. Senator Richard Russell of Georgia, the darling of the Dixiecrats, cursed the Truman proposals as a scheme to establish an "American OGPU," or Communist secret police apparatus. Johnson was among those raising their voices in the House Chamber to denounce these Truman proposals. While Sam Rayburn would not support the Truman civil rights program because to do so would mean his political death back in the Fourth District, privately he called the willful destitution of the Negro race by whites "an excellent breeding ground for the worst things in life."

No matter how frequently Johnson opposed Truman, Rayburn never attempted to scold or punish him. Ever on the alert to promote his protégé, he saw to it that Johnson was made a member of the twenty-three-man Select Committee on Postwar Military Policy. Then in 1947 he found a place for Johnson on the newly created and influential Joint (House and Senate) Committee on Atomic Energy.

On the Joint Committee on Atomic Energy, Johnson repeated the pattern of his operations on the House Naval Affairs Committee. Said one member, "Lyndon saw that most members were either too busy with their other committees or too prone to laziness to do much work, so he filled the gap and gained a voice far out of proportion to his seniority status in Congress." Johnson also added to his power by becoming friendly with David Lilienthal, the first head of the Atomic Energy Commission and the former chairman of TVA. With Lilienthal he liked to reminisce about his New Deal connections, while peppering him with advice. In his diary Lilienthal described the drawling Texan as "an able young man, definitely liberal, shrewd, full of savvy, and a great break, for that Committee can make or break us." On one occasion Lilienthal and Sumner Pike, another AEC commissioner, came to the Capitol to lunch with Johnson and listen to his outflow of suggestions, including repeated advice that they "develop Forrestal [the Secretary of the Navy and later the first Secretary of Defense] and Symington [the Secretary of the Air Force]."

Only days after Truman had taken office, American Ambassador to the Soviet Union Averell Harriman flew back from Moscow and arrived breathlessly at the White House to tell the new President of his "fear that you did not understand, as I have seen Roosevelt understand, that Stalin is breaking his word." The word of the Soviet dictator had been given to hold democratic elections in liberated Poland, but "democratic" to Stalin meant "pro-Soviet Communist." Truman, who was untrained in foreign affairs, was impressed with Harriman's fervor, and he immediately accepted Harriman's view that the Russians planned "a barbaric invasion of Europe."

Truman's first act to implement his new policy was to end Lend-Lease shipments to the Soviet Union and demand that Stalin repay the eleven billion dollars in Lend-Lease aid in the common war against the Nazis. Then, after his unproductive sessions with Stalin at the Potsdam Conference in the summer of 1945, when Stalin asked for a six-billion-dollar rehabilitation loan, Truman told his Secretary of State, James Byrnes, to drop it in the "forget" file.

With his belief that the Soviet Union planned to carry on where Nazi Germany finished, Truman considered it essential that most of the nine million Americans in military uniforms be kept in service. However, the national demand for demobilization following the unconditional surrender of Japan was too great to stem. Johnson found Truman's position one of the few on which he could agree. But though he favored a multimillion-man force, he was also caught in the web of home pressure, to which he yielded. He boasted to a reporter that in a single day he succeeded in winning the release of one hundred and eighteen Texas G.I.'s from military service. When letters from wives and mothers flooded his office, he warned Admiral Louis Denfield, the Chief of Naval Operations, who had been called to a hearing before the House Naval Affairs Committee, that he had to empty more ships of their sailors. "Something has to be done about it, or it's going to get out of hand," Johnson told him.

But Johnson had a change of heart after the military services complied with orders from the White House and slashed their forces to a million men, and sons and brothers from the Tenth District were once more safely home. He now called for a massive military buildup and made friends with Administration officials who believed that a confrontation with the Soviet Union was inevitable.

When Truman proposed his "Truman Doctrine" to Congress on March 12, 1947, Johnson joined Rayburn in pushing the measure through the House. Turkey, with a right-wing dictatorship, was undergoing a severe financial strain in maintaining a six-hundred-thousand-man force in combat readiness against possible Soviet attack. At the same time, with the British Army about to pull out from Greece, the Royalist Greek autocracy did not appear capable of maintaining its control in the face of civil insurrection by Greek Communists aided by Communist governments in Yugoslavia, Bulgaria, and Albania. The Truman Doctrine proposed to provide United States support for "free peoples who are resisting attempted subjugation by armed minorities or by outside pressures," with the words "free peoples" loosely interpreted to mean anti-Soviet. In a House speech for the four-hundred-million-dollar appropriation requested to put the doctrine into effect, Johnson rattled war drums as he shouted, "The only thing a bully understands is force, and the only thing he fears is courage."

Six years earlier he had sought the aid of Vice President Henry Wallace when he ran for the Senate against Pappy O'Daniel. Johnson was always especially pleasant to Wallace's chief aide, Harold Young, who worked hard alongside Alvin Wirtz in his campaigns. One time Johnson put into the *Congressional Record* his warm tribute for Young, remarking: "Just to talk to him, if he isn't too busy with phone calls back to Dallas to Bill Kittrell, George Purl, and Martin Winfrey, is a liberal education. Harold is always selling Dallas, and if you know Harold, you know Dallas."

By 1947 Johnson no longer knew Harold Young, and he had only harsh words for Wallace. A few months earlier Truman had fired Wallace from his post as Secretary of Commerce after Wallace delivered a Madison Square Garden speech that was highly critical of the President's foreign policy toward the Soviet Union. When Wallace came out against the

Truman Doctrine, Johnson labeled him an "appeaser" who wanted to bribe Russia. Johnson also warned Wallace that in his planned speaking tour of Texas in the near future, he would not get anywhere with the "clear-eyed, stout-hearted Texans."

By early 1948, despite a problem of increasingly slurring diction, Johnson was making rousing warlike speeches in Texas. In a radio talk of March 24, 1948, he said, "I came home to talk with the people in my District. I've talked with farmers, merchants, workingmen, businessmen. With mothers and ministers. With young men subject to selective service or universal military training. Knowing that I am the senior Texas member on the House Armed Services Committee and a member of the Congressional Joint Committee on Atomic Energy, people have asked me: 'Are we going to war? If so, when and why?' "

Johnson said there was only one answer. "Let's program now. Let's mobilize our men, our industry and our brains." In his view, the country would be derelict if it did not become a national armed camp, instantly ready for war. Those who opposed his position, he said, should be exposed by having their names inserted on "a tablet of enduring bronze" in "everlasting letters" so the appeasers would always be known.

Although Johnson's field of military attention had been the Navy, he was convinced that the major element in preparing a World War III readiness force was the construction of a super-Air Force. Neither President Truman nor Secretary of Defense Forrestal shared this view, for they favored a balanced military force, with land forces and the Navy given almost equal attention.

This reasoning did not stop Johnson, and he worked behind the President's back with Stuart Symington, the Secretary of the Air Force, who believed in air supremacy just as he did. This was indeed unusual behavior for a Presidential protégé, for Truman had brought Symington to Washington in 1945 from St. Louis as part of the "Missouri Gang," and promoted him rapidly in a variety of assignments. In private life Symington had headed the Emerson Manufacturing Company and had won national recognition for his successful settlements with labor unions, especially with a Communist-dominated union. Truman first placed him in charge of the Surplus Property Board; then named him Assistant Secretary of War for Air in 1946; and when the Department of Defense was established in 1947, Symington wrote the section creating the Department of the Air Force, and Truman chose him as its first Secretary.

At first Symington met privately with Johnson and like-minded congressmen to express his position, but he soon made public his lack of loyalty to the Administration by testifying openly before Johnson's committee that the Air Force should get almost the entire defense appropriations pie instead of the "balanced" piece advocated by both Forrestal and Truman. Symington also compounded his insults to a President who would not fire him by making speeches across the country that were critical of the Administration's position on the Air Force.

Shortly after Johnson met the "Big Bomber Boy," as Symington was known, he proposed that Symington reciprocate for his aid by traveling to Texas in his behalf. "In 1946," said Symington, "Lyndon asked me to go to his District and help him in his Congressional campaign." Johnson later told David Lilienthal that Symington had been of important help to him in his contest against Hardy Hollers; and Lilienthal reported that Johnson "tells a story of how Symington flew down to some Texas shindig and could do anything—making cooing speeches to the farmers; eat barbecue with the ranchmen; make a speech about Czechoslovakia to a Czech group."

"Johnson was as hot as I was for a seventy-group Air Force," said Symington, "and he was the Congressional leader on this issue. We arrived at the seventy-group figure because I asked General Carl Spaatz how many groups we could cut to without hurting our national security. Spaatz said seventy was the bare minimum, a figure that happened to coincide with what was in the Finletter Report to the President. Actually, a 'group' was not an unchangeable number. It meant only that there would be three wings, with a varying number of planes in each wing depending on the type and purpose. Truman was dead-set against the seventy-group program and wanted only fifty-five air groups."

At one point, when he was heckled and harassed by Johnson and Carl Vinson, Forrestal sought to settle the controversy by promising he would permit Symington to demothball eleven groups of stockpiled World War II B-29's. But Johnson remained dissatisfied and continued to push for seventy supermodern groups, despite the Truman complaint of its upsetting effect on the federal finances, should he make it part of his budget. When called before the House committee, Symington said he could not understand why his proposal was causing so much concern because a buildup to seventy groups would cost only an extra eight hundred million dollars. Forrestal disputed this and provided evidence to show the cost would be an additional fifteen billion dollars instead. When Congress passed the money Symington had requested, instead of firing him, Truman announced he would not spend the money.

Despite Johnson's prominent role in the seventy-group Air Force fight and in the appropriations squabble to implement the Truman Doctrine, he was not as well known to the House membership as he had been in the New Deal days. For one thing he no longer possessed the gilded magic of being a Presidential protégé; and for another, he could not work up enthusiasm for spending part of his day in the cloakroom, joking and talking to other members. He felt he had outgrown the House and walked a treadmill. Still another reason for his relative obscurity was his frequent absences in order to pursue his dream of becoming a millionaire.

George Smathers, who came to the House from Florida in 1946 and later became Johnson's closest friend in the Senate, never met him in the House. "In fact," said Smathers, "I wasn't even aware of his existence until one day when I visited the office of Helen Gahagan Douglas [an actress and a Representative from California]. She had a big theatrical picture in her office of a shiny-haired fellow, and I thought the inscription on it was really warm. I asked her who he was, and she said, 'His name's Lyndon Johnson. He's from Texas.' "

Chapter 28

A$_T$ THE BEGINNING of 1948 two facts stood out clearly in the Texas political scene. Senator Pappy O'Daniel had suffered a monumental decline in statewide popularity; and Alvin Wirtz and the loyalists, who had wielded organizational control over Texas Democrats in 1944, were once more on the outside looking in.

As a senator, Pappy had found himself increasingly in opposition to his Democratic colleagues, and in return they avoided him as though he were the bubonic plague. His primitive proposals to reduce wage earners to a feudal existence, his extreme isolationism, and his attacks on Democratic leaders reduced his party status to that of a crackpot. Few Democrats cared that he had gone home to Texas to campaign against a fourth term for President Roosevelt in 1944, but they were aroused after Roosevelt's death when he attacked the late President and his "smear artists of the New Deal" for what he called an effort "to establish their Communistic setup of a bureaucratic dictatorship." As one Texas politician put it: "How can Pappy claim his political platform is the Ten Commandments and the Sermon on the Mount when he keeps calling those who disagree with him 'vipers, snakes, liars, and hypocrites'?"

Pappy's antics stopped amusing most Texans. On the hillbilly hustings, crowds were smaller and sometimes unfriendly. At a rural stop he was pelted unmercifully with rotten eggs and tomatoes, and at a Houston rally audience booing drowned out his entire speech. For a time he threatened to quit the Senate and run in 1946 for another term as governor, but at the last minute he failed to file. His excuse was that he had "to stay in

Washington to fight the British loan." The war-prostrated British Government was asking the United States Government for a loan of four billion dollars.

What really finished off O'Daniel were revelations by the Dallas *News* of his profitable real estate deals in Washington. Among his exposed ventures was a purchase of a building for fifty-four thousand dollars and its resale for one hundred and twenty-seven thousand dollars. Then there was the notoriety his son Mickey-Wickey picked up from newspaper stories when he boosted rents in the Dallas apartment house he owned immediately after federal rent controls ended. It had been Pappy who had shouted insistently in the Senate Chamber that controls were unnecessary to keep rents from skyrocketing.

While Pappy O'Daniel spun into his decline, Alvin Wirtz and the loyalists were being pushed from their control over the state Democratic organization as a result of the governor's election in 1946. When Governor Coke Stevenson had announced his intention to retire from the Governor's Mansion after five-and-a-half years in office, Wirtz had hoped that loyalist control of the party machinery would assist Johnson in a race to succeed Stevenson.

But when Johnson bowed out, the leading candidates were Beaufort Jester, the darling of the "Donkeyphants," or Texas regulars, who was then serving on the Texas Railroad Commission, and Dr. Homer Rainey, whom the board of regents had ousted as president of the University of Texas for seeking greater academic and administrative freedom from the regents.

"Beautiful Jester with the marcelled hair," as his opponents labeled the former attorney for oil interests, was known for his antilabor, anticivil-rights, and anti-Truman stands. One of his chief campaign charges against Rainey was that he permitted copies of *U.S.A.* by John Dos Passos on the university's library shelves. When Rainey countered by denouncing Jester as a former Ku-Kluxer, Jester scoffed that the former university head and professional baseball player "had lost his fast ball and curve ball; and all he's got left is a mud ball."

The two landed in a run-off primary, but in the second go-around on August 2, 1946, "Beautiful Jester with the marcelled hair" swamped Rainey by a 2-to-1 margin. This gave Jester control of the September Governor's Convention, and he replaced Wirtz's friends—Harry Seay, chairman of the State Executive Committee, and Bill Kittrell, the secretary—with R. W. "Bob" Calvert and Vann Kennedy.

After only a year in office Governor Jester appeared to be unbeatable should he try for a second term or contest Pappy O'Daniel for his Senate seat in 1948. Wartime industry had changed Texas from a rural to an urban society, but a rural philosophy against labor unions and Negroes still held sway. When police roughed up pickets and strikers in several cities, no daily paper voiced objection. Jester called for law and order, and he won wide support by pushing bills through the legislature to bar strikes in public utilities and other named industries and to provide workers with a "right to work" without being forced to join a union. The CIO should not be permitted inside Texas, he said, because it was run by "Communist racketeers." Jester was also applauded by business and industry, farmers, and newspapers when he became a prime mover in organizing Southern governors to oppose the Truman civil rights program.

Johnson watched the Jester performance with enormous interest because the governor lay athwart his own plans to contest Pappy O'Daniel in 1948. Should Jester run, Johnson knew he would have no chance against the governor. But if Jester had no interest in the Senate, then Johnson reasoned that his own chances depended on his ability to create a conservative image for himself.

First order of business was to rid himself of the Roosevelt subway strap to which he had clung all these years, and which had now changed to a noose. It mattered little that he had taken antilabor and anticivil-rights stands in House votes, or that he had successfully prevented the unionization of his radio station. What was needed was a public denunciation of the New Deal and a confession of his early sins.

One of Johnson's friends was big Ed Clark, who had been Jimmy Allred's secretary of state and would later be Johnson's ambassador to Australia. Clark, already a wealthy lawyer, lobbyist, and banker, was known as "Mr. Ed, the Talking Horse," due to his reputation as the most garrulous man in Texas. Johnson held no secrets from him, and Clark later told a reporter that his friend deliberately set out to woo "the people of substance" in the big money center of Dallas so that they would establish a "working political relationship to each other."

On this score Johnson's rehabilitation began with his request to the Associated Press to interview him in 1947. In the widely publicized story that followed, he declared the New Deal to be "a misnomer." He went on to say that the only so-called New Deal programs he supported were the "development of water power and other natural resources." To be more explicit, he said, "I believe in the REA and think all-weather roads should be built to every farmhouse." On another occasion, Johnson kicked Roosevelt by telling reporters that in the New Deal period he (Johnson) had been "a young man of adventure with more guts than brains."

In April 1947 Joe Belden made his first forecast of the 1948 Senate contest when he pitted several Texas politicians in a popularity contest with Pappy O'Daniel. The results in the Jester-O'Daniel competition gave the governor 75 per cent. Former Governor Coke Stevenson stood almost as high against Pappy with 74 per cent, while Johnson, Jimmy Allred, and Wright Patman were all at the 64 per cent mark.

The chief result of Belden's first poll was that it ruptured relations between O'Daniel and Coke Stevenson. Pappy told Washington reporters that

Coke would be an "ingrate" if he ran against him the following year. Pappy's version of recent Texas history was that he alone made Stevenson his lieutenant governor in 1938, which made possible Stevenson's rise to governor in 1941, when Pappy resigned to become a senator. O'Daniel also claimed that when Stevenson retired from office at the end of 1946, he had tried hard to get Truman to appoint him to the federal bench as a going away present. To all this Stevenson replied coldly that he was entirely free of debt to Pappy. In fact, he insisted, "if it hadn't been for the support I gave him, O'Daniel might have been defeated by Johnson."

In June, when Jester gave no encouragement to friends who wanted him to run for the Senate, Joe Belden made another public opinion survey that excluded him. This time Belden interviewers premised a primary that included only Stevenson, Johnson, and O'Daniel. His results, printed in the Dallas *News* of June 8, 1947, showed Coke with 55 per cent of the votes, Lyndon with 24, and Pappy with 21 per cent.

A year and a half earlier, when Stevenson tapped his Stetson on his head and walked out of the Governor's Mansion, he told reporters he intended to "return to the hills" and stay there permanently. To a query about his desire to become a senator, he replied, sucking on his ever-present pipe, "I never had any ambition in my life to go to Washington as a senator. I'm just not fitted for the Washington pattern."

But Texas politicians and editors agreed that with the results of the Belden Poll showing him far in the lead, Stevenson would come out slowly and calculatingly from retirement and make the race for the Senate. They were right, for on January 1, 1948, he announced over statewide radio; and he did so at a propitious time—just before the kickoff of the Cotton Bowl football contest at Dallas, when most Texans had their sets turned on to cheer S.M.U. against Penn State.

Coke let it be known he was offering no long string of worthless platform planks. All he would promise, he said, was a hard effort to bring about federal economy, a tax cut, an increase in Social Security payments, states' rights, and "the complete destruction of the Communist movement in this country." He also reminded listeners that when he had succeeded O'Daniel as governor, he inherited a debt of thirty million dollars. When he left, he said, the state treasury reported a surplus of thirty-five million dollars.

Other than for an occasional fracas with the state senate, Coke Stevenson had proved a popular governor with both conservative voters and publishers, and newspapers now praised his hat-in-the-ring opener as a "characteristically homely, simple speech." Short biographies of him noted that he had been born in a log cabin in Kimble County in central-west Texas in 1888. Besides the log cabin, his name was an asset, for he was named after Richard Coke, the Texas governor back in 1873 who chased the Republican carpetbaggers from the state. He was so poor as a child, said friends, that he did not own sufficient clothes "to dust a fiddle." But he was ambitious and energetic, became a cowhand as a youth, then worked in a bank as a janitor and advanced to bookkeeper and cashier while studying law. Once he hung up his shingle, his law practice grew along with his reputation, and after serving as a county judge, he went to the Texas House in 1928, where he was elected speaker in 1933. Voters made him lieutenant governor in 1938, and he moved on to governor in 1941.

Unfriendly reporters called him "Calculating Coke" from the time they first tried to bait him and found they could not arouse him emotionally. Even some of his friends said he possessed an interior stoniness. He seemed to operate from carefully considered plans—like a good chess player—and when he made a move there was nothing spur-of-the-moment about it. His flaw was that once embarked on a poor course it was difficult for him to change. Yet his calculating and planning paid off well financially for him. In his rise from the log cabin, he became president of a hotel, owner of an investment company, a cattle loan firm, a hardware company, and a bank, and these provided him with the extra money to buy a fourteen-thousand-acre spread sixteen miles southwest of Junction near the magnificent falls of the south fork of the Llano River. Few activities afforded him so much pleasure as cutting hay and shearing sheep on his ranch, and then relaxing in his brown canvas pants and matching brush jacket, black leather cowboy boots, open collar shirt, and big hat.

Following Stevenson's announcement for the Senate, a half-dozen other candidates paid the one-hundred-dollar filing fee. Most prominent among these was George Peddy, a Houston lawyer long an active foe of the Ku Klux Klan. Others considered likely candidates were Jimmy Allred, Wright Patman, Lyndon Johnson, and Martin Dies. But Allred declared he would not run if Johnson were a candidate; Patman and Johnson refused to talk; and Dies conjectured whether an honest and legal campaign could win.

What was happening to Johnson was that after waiting seven years for the opportunity, he had developed cold feet. The threat of Beautiful Jester with the marcelled hair was gone, but the early-1948 Belden Polls put Coke Stevenson so far out in front that it was painful for him to read the figures. The February poll, for instance, gave Stevenson a 4-to-1 margin over Johnson, and while the following month's poll cut this to 3 to 1, Stevenson's lead still seemed insurmountable.

Wirtz had given no consideration to the fact that Johnson might not want to run. However, when he, "Mr. Ed, the Talking Horse" Clark, Tom Miller, and Raymond Buck, who had been his official campaign manager in 1941, talked to Johnson, they found him in a depressed mood. Wirtz suggested a test of his popularity—a statewide broadcast over the Texas State Network. It should be on a subject dear to Johnson, one into which he could pour his heart, and afterward they would study the reaction.

Johnson made this radio speech on March 24, 1948, and he delivered a rousing, superpatriotic call for war mobilization. "We went into two world wars unprepared, and let's not do it again!" He hammered away on the urgent need to prepare for war with the Soviet Union. Afterward, he and his friends examined the newspaper reports of the speech, and what Johnson read discouraged him further. Few papers gave it more than a brief mention. One called him weak on foreign affairs; another quoted a Dallas *News* editorial that referred to him as a "bellboy for his District."

Filing deadline for the July 24 primary was June 11, and while more than two months still remained before the deadline, Wirtz started worrying that Johnson would file for the Tenth District's House race and not for the Senate contest. Wirtz learned from talks with the unhappy young man that Johnson, as much a result of the Belden Polls as of the inconsequential reaction to his warlike radio speech, was seriously considering writing off the Senate try. Furthermore, Lyndon had sheet after sheet of names of local precinct captains in many areas who had been put on the state payroll during the long Stevenson tenure as governor and who still held their jobs. All could be expected to work for their old boss.

Urging and nagging did not move Johnson, as he seemed to fall into a state of despondency. "Lyndon was probably putting it on," said one of his friends, "because he was a tough character and he wanted to be senator more than anything else in the world right then. But Alvin Wirtz was having his doubts, and when he told several of us to stage a big show begging and pleading with Lyndon to run and making him jealous that one of us would run if he didn't, we did this."

Most of those whom Wirtz chose for this task were simultaneously Johnson employees at his radio station KTBC and operators of the supposedly rival Austin radio station KVET.

In 1945 Johnson had held talks with John Connally and his brother Merrill, his old college chums Willard Deason and Jesse Kellam, and Jake Pickle, Bob Phinney, and "Mr. Ed, the Talking Horse" Clark to suggest that they organize a new radio station in Austin under his *sub rosa* guidance. Since most were World War II veterans, he told them to use the station letters KVET. Just what share of the proceedings was to accrue to Johnson was never divulged, but Wirtz and Johnson helped the group fill out the FCC forms. When the question of a pre-existing business address arose, Johnson could not lend them his Driskill Hotel address where KTBC was housed because a reporter might chance on the connection and make political hay. The easiest solution would have been to rent a room as a dummy office in an office building, but instead Johnson concocted another falsification for them. Years later the *Wall Street Journal* called it "The Story of the Crowded House at 1901 Dillman Street."

In 1943 Johnson had purchased a duplex at 1901 Dillman Street in Austin's west-side residential area, and he lived in the upstairs apartment when he went home to Texas, with the downstairs rented out year round to pay the mortgage. The KVET license application that was sent to Leonard Marks, Johnson's Washington attorney on FCC business, listed

1901 Dillman Street as the place of business of the Connally brothers, Walter Jenkins, Willard Deason, Ed Clark, Jesse Kellam, Jake Pickle, W. E. Syers and Bob Phinney. What should have aroused FCC suspicions that this was a phony business address was its location in Johnson's residence. But even more damaging was the fact that on the Johnson license renewal submitted afterward for "Lady Bird's station" John Connally, Deason, Kellam, Pickle and Syers were listed as employees of KTBC, supposedly a competitor of KVET.

However, it was the Johnson connection that not only made the FCC ignore such obvious reasons for throwing out the KVET application but grant the station a license and heap special favors on it. For example, a San Antonio station seventy miles away from Austin had been awarded the wave length 1300 kilocycles. KVET told the FCC it wanted wave length 1300, and before it started operations the FCC announced that the San Antonio station had "voluntarily" shifted to a less desirable wave length, giving KVET the 1300 spot. Other government agencies also were affected by the Johnson connection. When KVET's new 211-foot broadcasting tower was set in place early in 1946, the Civil Aeronautics Administration ordered it removed as a serious danger to airplane travel. But a few weeks later the CAA retracted its order and declared that no threat existed. Another Johnson-connected benefit was that outside of his own station KTBC, the only other Austin radio station to gain national network affiliation was KVET.

On the evening of May 11, 1948, several of the KTBC-KVET crowd plus other Johnson hangers-on climbed the stairs to the second floor at 1901 Dillman Street for a final effort to beg and plead with Johnson to run for the Senate and to arouse his jealousy as a last resort should he refuse.

By now it had become a game of repeated meetings with Johnson and loud demands and louder refusals. This was the showdown. "We talked and talked, trying to prove to him that he could beat Stevenson," one present that night later recalled. "We taunted him; we sweet-talked him. We tried every argument any of us could think of."

Stuart Long, an Austin newsman who was there, said Johnson pushed aside all pleas, "said *no* and went to bed. We sat and talked, eight of us, all convinced that former Governor Coke Stevenson could be, and should be, defeated. Finally we agreed that John Connally should run. He was big and handsome with three brothers who were even bigger and more handsome, and their father looked like Old Man Texas himself."

In the morning, said another in the group, "we told Lyndon that since he wouldn't run, we wanted him to help us elect John." Johnson listened in seething rage to the plan to buy "surplus command cars, and put John and his father and brothers in each of them and send them over the state, campaigning by public address system on the cars."

Finally he bellowed the group into silence, said he would hold a news conference that afternoon in the penthouse at the Driskill Hotel, and promised he would have something worthwhile to say.

At his crowded news conference Johnson announced for the Senate and told reporters he would have been a senator seven years earlier if there had been an honest election in 1941. "I was urged to contest that result," he said, "but I tried to be a good sport. Lots of people said they'd support me next time [1942]—but the war intervened." He called himself the most qualified candidate, pointing to his standing as third in seniority on the House Armed Services Committee and membership on the Joint Committee on Atomic Energy, as well as being so influential an individual congressman that he had forced President Truman to halt the sale of war plants and surplus military hardware. He also ridiculed Coke Stevenson as too old for the Senate. Stevenson was fifty-five, while Johnson was thirty-nine, and Lyndon told the reporters: "I believe our senator should be young enough to have energy for the work . . . You've been fed up with has-beens."

On June 7, when filing closed, ten candidates had paid their one hundred dollars. As was expected, Wright Patman and Jimmy Allred backed out, and Pappy O'Daniel announced he was retiring from politics when his term expired. Pappy said he was not quitting because of the polls and insisted that if he ran he would win re-election easily despite his enemies—"the labor leader racketeers, Communists, parlor pinks, etcetera!" One west Texas paper hailed his approaching retirement as the only constructive action in his ten-year political career. Johnson chose Pappy's announcement as a good time to hit him and Stevenson with the words Pappy had used in his 1942 campaign against Allred and Dan Moody: "One of the gold-dust twins is out. Now we stand one down and one to go."

Friends of Martin Dies had paid his filing fee, and the former chairman of the House Un-American Activities Committee quickly took to radio to pound away at Johnson. Dies had no argument that Johnson failed to meet his own standards of patriotism, for Johnson had voted to continue the HUAC and to hold in contempt of Congress Hollywood writers who refused to declare they were not Communists. Instead, Dies used ridicule and a charge of fraud. In his opening speech he said he had heard that another candidate was "our old vaudeville friend of the 1941 Senate campaign, 'Me Too' Johnson." Dies went on to promise he would continue to expose the flagrant violation of campaign spending rules by the Johnson camp in 1941. As for Stevenson, Dies predicted that no one would find out his views because "Coke makes a business of keeping them to himself, like an old woman about her age."

However, Dies was out of the campaign almost as soon as he had entered it. After his radio speech he got in touch with young Attorney General Price Daniel and requested that Daniel either permit him to spend sixty thousand dollars without prosecuting him or promise to prosecute all candidates who spent more than the legal ten thousand dollars. Daniel said he would take the latter course, which Dies interpreted to mean that Daniel would enforce the law vigorously against him while ignoring what his friend Lyndon Johnson spent. For this reason Dies suddenly withdrew from the fight on June 17 and explained to a reporter for the Dallas *News:* "It cost me fifteen hundred dollars to make the single broadcast I made while I was in the race. Multiply that by twenty-five broadcasts and see if the politicians are staying within the ten-thousand-dollar expenditure limit."

Wirtz had planned a lavish campaign for Johnson. When he, John Connally, and Raymond Buck opened campaign headquarters in Austin, George and Herman Brown were called into consultation to help finance the Johnson effort. Postwar government contracts had held up well, and with part of their profits they had paid one hundred and forty-three million dollars to buy the government-built Big Inch Pipeline to supply the East with natural gas. Besides construction projects of all sorts the Brown brothers had also moved into profitable oil production and were a major industrial force in the regional economy.

In addition to Brown and Root support, Johnson found campaign money help from Wesley W. West, the Houston oil tycoon and son of the late New Deal hater, Jim West. Aircraft companies, thankful for his fight for the seventy-group Air Force, also paid some of his bills, as did the major rubber companies, whom he had helped when they wanted to buy surplus government factories producing synthetic rubber. Johnson also had the active editorial backing of Amon Carter's right-wing Fort Worth *Star-Telegram* as well as the Hearst papers in Texas, for his friend Ed Weisl, attorney for William Randolph Hearst's newspaper empire, emphasized his vote for the Taft-Hartley Act in promoting him to the Hearst family.

Johnson's opening speech came at Wooldridge Park in Austin a week after he became a candidate. There was not enough time to create public interest in his campaign, and outside of a few curious on-lookers the crowd consisted of Johnson's core of backers and his family. Not a single time did he mention Truman's name, nor did he evoke any memories of the Roosevelt years. Instead he spoke in explanation of his campaign's theme, "Peace, Preparedness, Progress." *Peace* meant threatening the Soviet Union with war; *Preparedness*, vast rearmament; and *Progress,* "protecting the public from both selfish labor and selfish capital" and "a federal policy leaving to the states those matters which are state functions, such as civil rights."

Of course, Rebekah Johnson clapped until her palms ached. But what perturbed Johnson was that the next day's papers gave his speech less attention than they usually accorded a local wedding. Wirtz, Connally, and Buck agreed with him that something spectacular was needed to get his campaign rolling.

Wirtz was aware that Johnson's body reacted to the state of his mind. When he was depressed, his sinuses bothered him more than usual; when he was nervous, a skin rash appeared. So when Johnson doubled up in pain a few days after his kickoff speech, Wirtz thought at first that the cause was psychological. However, the pain did not vanish and a medical examination revealed the existence of a kidney stone. It was now Wirtz's turn to grow depressed, for the doctor suggested an operation. Chances were that this would put him out of the campaign, or at most permit him a few weeks of tired campaigning before primary day.

But there was an alternative, and Johnson took it. At the Mayo Brothers Clinic in Rochester, Minnesota, doctors were on occasion successfully dissolving kidney stones, making an operation unnecessary. When Johnson called Sam Rayburn and told him of his trouble, Rayburn asked his friend Jacqueline Cochran, the well-known aviatrix, to fly his protégé to Rochester.

A day later she delivered him safely, and he was hardly into a hospital nightgown before he became the despair of the hospital staff. One distraught nurse reported that while he underwent treatment she could not get him off the long-distance phone. He made so many special demands and used his room, waiting rooms, and the central floor nurse call area so intensively as a temporary campaign headquarters that the hospital staff admitted to exhaustion and bewilderment by the time his kidney stone either dissolved or passed out of his body.

In the few quiet minutes he had, Johnson did a great deal of thinking about the way other Texans had campaigned in the past and about what would prove sensational in his own campaign. Tom Connally, who was well-read in American and foreign history, and who well knew the rules of grammar, always campaigned with an outpouring of humorous stories, which were delivered as ungrammatically as if he were an illiterate ranch hand. The Texas trick was to sound spontaneous, and not formal and heavy the way Johnson knew he had in his opening speech. "Someone asked Pat Neff how he prepared his speeches," Johnson later said about his research on the subject. "Neff said he wrote them out and memorized every word and gesture. Governor Hobby said he made an outline and built his speech around it. Ol' Jim Ferguson said, 'I fill myself plumb full of my subject, stand up, and let her fly!' "

At the time Johnson was exhausting the staff at the Mayo Brothers Clinic, Wirtz was busy in Austin dissecting the initial campaign efforts of Coke Stevenson and George Peddy. From what they had already done and from information from his spies in their camps, Wirtz knew that neither intended a full-throttle campaign.

For an experienced politician Stevenson's antics were astonishing. After an early period of rushing about to cut ribbons at opening ceremonies on new bridges, shake hands with every policeman in downtown Dallas, and chance food poisoning at barbecues, picnics, and Rotary luncheons, Coke suddenly disappeared from sight. Reporters were stunned to find him doing heavy ranchwork on his spread near Junction, and from the way he talked, he had a heap of chores to do that had priority over any campaigning for the United States Senate. Then, when he finally returned to the campaign trail, he rode slowly from town to town in an old Plymouth driven by his one-armed nephew Bob Murphy, "who wore a dirty straw hat on his head and a plug of tobacco in his jaw." Newsmen called attention to the fact that Coke had not bothered to glue "Stevenson for Senator" stickers on the Plymouth's bumpers.

While Wirtz found Stevenson's campaigning amateurish, he was professional enough to know that this might have little meaning, for Coke had a solid following. But George Peddy was another story. As a man with a small initial brigade, his strategy should have been to campaign like a bull stung by a bee. Instead Peddy planned to spend little money or energy, hoping to pick up votes through radio calls for a "preventive" war against Russia. His principal campaign program was to come on radio every evening at six-forty-five and threaten to demolish Russia if she did not "take her bloody hands off the throats of the people of Eastern Europe."

After two weeks in Rochester, Johnson came home bursting with nervous energy, and Wirtz filled him in regarding the strange campaigning of Stevenson and Peddy. Back in 1941, Wirtz reminded him, the only way he could compete with Pappy O'Daniel had been to put on a bigger carnival show than the old hillbilly. In this election, with staid Stevenson trailing exhaust from town to town in an old car and Peddy planning few personal appearances, Johnson needed speed, accessibility and novelty.

Because Johnson was not fully recovered, Wirtz started him off by arranging for a cheering crowd and a radio address in Houston on June 7. Here Johnson tested out the strategy of slashing at Stevenson and ignoring Peddy. "Peace, Preparedness, Progress," he shouted before ripping into the former governor as "a calculating, do-nothing, fence-straddling fraud." This taunting speech exhilarated Johnson, for he knew that ridicule was the best weapon against a man with a reputation for respectability . . . who would not answer in kind.

Next, the Johnson campaign surprise was uncovered. Some reporters claimed that it was Wesley West who owned the big helicopter and lent it to Johnson. But the Johnson headquarters in Austin insisted that a group of veterans had purchased the five-seater in Detroit and had it flown to Texas for his use. Whichever was the case, the helicopter was the gimmick Wirtz believed would make deserters of Stevenson's supporters.

On June 13 Johnson, Wirtz, Connally, and a pilot took off in the *Johnson City Windmill,* as the candidate had christened the helicopter, for a campaign swing through northeast Texas. As was expected, few persons in that area had ever seen a helicopter before, or for that matter, a United States Senate candidate, and the tour was a rousing success.

On his first day out Johnson talked to an estimated six thousand people in a dozen towns. After that he set a quota of twenty towns a day for the rest of that trip, because the helicopter proved so maneuverable. It required

neither a concrete landing site nor a runway, but could settle down with
ease inside a baseball park or a pasture, on a road, town street, or building top. Moreover, the powerful public address system the machine carried,
with speakers set between the wheels, enabled Johnson to give a speech
while hovering in the sky. "Hello . . . down there," he enjoyed startling
farmers and townspeople from the air. And when they stared open-mouthed
toward heaven, he continued, "This is your friend, Lyndon Johnson of
Johnson City, your candidate for the Senate, dropping in to say good
morning." Above Forney, he shouted down, "How's the gang in Adams'
drugstore?"

On landing in a town, he raced down the main street, his awkward
loping form and swinging arms coming to jarring momentary stops while
he shook hands and introduced himself as the next senator. If his small
army of advance men rounded up a few hundred persons to greet his helicopter, Johnson would follow his "Howdy and shake" with a short talk on
"Peace, Preparedness, Progress." Then he and his small entourage raced
back to the helicopter and took off, to expressions of amazement on upturned faces. After this first campaign foray Wirtz told reporters that
Johnson and his flying machine "were setting the woods on fire, and people
were talking about Johnson long after the helicopter departed."

When he first learned of the *Johnson City Windmill,* Stevenson sucked on
his pipe thoughtfully and told worried backers who suggested he should
campaign by airplane: "No, thanks. I'll keep my campaign down to earth."
As for Peddy, he scoffingly commented that "the *Johnson City Windmill* is
the name of both the helicopter and its occupant."

Nevertheless, supporters of both men showed open concern when Joe
Belden's poll came out on June 20. The popularity figures gave Stevenson
46.6 per cent, Johnson 36.8, and Peddy 12 per cent. Peddy's name had not
been included in earlier polls, but his friends had expected him to do
better than a measly 12 per cent. The high elation in the Johnson camp
stemmed from Belden's admission that he had conducted his survey before the flight of the *Johnson City Windmill.* "From the time it took me
to make three speeches and spend a week in the hospital," Johnson jeered,
"Coke Stevenson, the do-nothing candidate in the senatorial race, dropped
from 64 per cent to 46 per cent." Johnson asked those persons who had
told pollers they were "undecided" to make up their minds to "vote for the
man who will give Texas a doer and go-getter in the United States Senate."

Wirtz knew that Peddy would study the Belden figures carefully and then
reset his campaign to ignore Stevenson and concentrate on attacking Johnson, for it was fairly obvious that Stevenson would not get the necessary
majority of votes cast in the July primary, and would thus be forced into
a run-off, unless Johnson gained a majority and ended the matter at that
point. Peddy's only hope of getting into that run-off would be to close the
gap between himself and Johnson and emerge as second man.

The Peddy headquarters research crew scoured Johnson's voting record in Congress as well as his past speeches, in order to demolish him. One Peddy revelation was that Johnson had years earlier voted against the appropriation for the House Un-American Activities Committee. There were also broad hints that Johnson had been running a radio station behind the facade of his wife's name on the ownership papers, and that he had neglected his Congressional duties. His absentee record for 1948 revealed that he had failed to vote on a half-dozen vital measures. But Peddy's major charge against Johnson was that he had failed to live up to a promise he had made to Texas voters in 1941. "In the 1941 campaign," said Peddy, "Lyndon Johnson gave his word that if he had to vote to send any mother's son away from her to fight for his country, he would resign from Congress and go along and fight side by side with that boy. Did he keep that promise?" he asked rhetorically. "*No.* The record is clear. He never did resign from Congress."

Johnson wisely refrained from answering Peddy, and for lack of a public brawl Peddy could not make headway for himself.

A far more serious concern for Wirtz was that Stevenson might successfully tie a Truman label on Johnson. This would devastate his campaign, for no name in Texas was so disliked as that of the President. At the springtime precinct conventions, the chief sport had been cursing Truman and calling for his defeat for the Democratic Presidential nomination that summer. The cursing had resumed when the first state convention met in May at Brownwood in Brown County. Adrenalin poured over Truman's veto of the Taft-Hartley Bill, his proposal for a ten-point civil rights program, and his order to Attorney General Tom Clark—"a traitorous Texan"—to bring suit against California in the Supreme Court to assert federal ownership of the offshore tidelands oil. It was Governor Beauford Jester's order to the state convention to send an uninstructed Texas delegation to the Philadelphia Democratic National Convention in July and to take care that the delegation contained no Truman men. Jester's wish was the convention's command, though for prestige purposes two Truman friends were made members of the delegation. These were Senator Tom Connally, who was named vice chairman, and Sam Rayburn, who had already been selected by the National Committee to serve as the permanent chairman of the Philadelphia Convention.

While Johnson waited for Stevenson to handcuff him to Truman, he made his own attacks against the President. He called the civil rights program "a farce and a sham—an effort to set up a police state in the guise of liberty." Repeatedly, he told listeners, "I voted against the so-called poll tax repeal bill" and "I have voted against the Fair Employment Practices Commission. If a man can tell you whom you must hire, he can tell you whom you can't hire." He also harshly condemned the Administration's military program as "too little and almost too late."

Before the Stevenson advisers could solidify a pro-Truman attack on Johnson, an outside event turned their guns around. The Texas Federation of Labor held its annual session at Fort Worth on June 22, and what began as a fairly quiet meeting convulsed into a major attack on Johnson. For fifty years Texas craft unions had held to the firm rule never to endorse a political candidate but to stick to bread and butter issues. However, at Fort Worth, the Taft-Hartley Act and other antilabor bills aroused speakers to intramural bellowing, and eventually the voting record of Johnson on these measures was mentioned. The six hundred delegates let out wave after wave of blasphemous, cheering approval when Brother Wally Reilly of the Dallas AFL charged that "Lyndon Johnson has disqualified himself in the eyes of the working people of Texas by supporting the Taft-Hartley Act and the Case Bill." A motion was made to vote on this, and the convention endorsed Coke Stevenson for the Senate and denounced Johnson, thus ending its political nonpartisanship. When the delegates poured out of Fort Worth for home, reporters said they were vowing "to get Johnson for his remarks and retire him from office."

When word of what the Texas AFL had done reached Johnson and Wirtz, they were almost overcome with elation. Johnson lost no time in going on the offensive and attacking Stevenson as the darling of the unions and liberals. "Labor leaders made a secret agreement with Calculating Coke they couldn't get out of me," he shouted happily in public. "Reports reached me that a few labor leaders, who do not soil their own clothes with the sweat of honest toil, have met in a smoke-filled hotel room in Fort Worth and have attempted to deliver the vote of free Texas workingmen through the endorsement of a candidate without a platform and without the courage to take a stand on the issues now confronting American labor.

"I hope every laboring man will write Calculating Coke and ask how he stands on the Taft-Hartley Law. If my opponent has promised to repeal the law, the people have a right to know. If he has not made such a promise, the people have a right to know. Also, I think the laboring men should ask their leaders to tell them openly why they wanted the unions to break a fifty-year precedent and endorse a faltering candidate who did not have the courage to sign or veto the state's vicious antilabor law when he was governor."

Stevenson found himself in a miserable position. Very conservative and anti-organized labor politically, he nevertheless debated whether the union endorsement meant the additional votes to give him a majority in the primary or whether it would cost him a net loss of votes. Because he could not make up his mind, he remained silent on the issue and lost the opportunity to place a radical horse-collar on Johnson.

With a month left to the campaign, Johnson gloried in the opportunity he had to unplug his political umbilical cord from the Roosevelt-Truman heritage. July came and the *Johnson City Windmill* increased the tempo of its campaign hops, so that Johnson could step up his baiting of Stevenson with appeals to audiences to find out how "the pipe-smoking, do-nothinger stood on the anti-Communist Taft-Hartley Law."

All sections of Texas felt the presence of the helicopter. On many of the campaign flights, said a reporter, Johnson did not overlook the individual voter. After startling a farmer weeding a field by his overhead greeting, Johnson would order his pilot to land. Then he would leap out, ask the farmer if he could help him in the day's work, and before the farmer could say *yes,* Johnson would "wring his hand and ask for his vote; run back and take off." Whenever he spied a train stopped on a siding, he ordered the helicopter docked, and he would handshake the crew into at least temporary support before the *Johnson City Windmill* rose and blew off their work hats. Sometimes, instead of landing in a town, he paused overhead and called out to people on the street.

But he tried to make at least eight big town stops a day, where he could interlard a ten-minute talk on "Peace, Preparedness, Progress" with blasts at Stevenson on Taft-Hartley and Truman on the nation's defenses. To make these stops pay off, Wirtz devised a system to have Johnson broadcast over radio each night and detail where he would be traveling the next day. This involved bragging about the size of that day's crowds and exhorting listeners to have their town's turnout tomorrow dwarf the figures he recited. In these radio talks Johnson told about himself in a folksy way and tied his ancestors into the glories of Texas. He had his nonmilitary great-grandfathers performing heroic deeds in Texas' fight for independence and in the Mexican War, and he said that Johnson City was named for his grandfather (instead of Great-Uncle Jim Johnson). At the time of his radio broadcasts, his advance agents were already in the towns ahead, making all arrangements for a peppy greeting and large turnout. If the weather did not permit the helicopter to land at the scheduled time, the advance men had an emergency band and singers on hand to occupy the crowd until Johnson arrived. On occasion Wirtz worked out a special extra gimmick on the helicopter gimmick. One such stunt occurred at Rosenberg, near Houston, where the *Johnson City Windmill* landed on top of a building, and Johnson spoke to fifteen hundred persons standing in the street below him.

As the last few weeks of the primary began under the broiling Texas sun, Stevenson still refused to tell nagging reporters how he stood on Taft-Hartley. However, he said the time had come to be specific about a number of subjects, and he offered them his "Bill of Particulars." This turned out to be a series of generalities, including a hope that United States military strength might grow mightier, that soaring federal tax rates might end, and the cost of living be reduced. After demanding anew why Stevenson continued silent on Taft-Hartley, Johnson besplattered his "Bill of Particulars" with the ridiculing comment that Calculating Coke was for virtue and against sin. "It reminds me of the Mother Hubbards our grandmothers used to wear," he drawled at one crowd in a loud mumble. "It covers everything and touches nothing."

Down the homestretch Johnson and Peddy invaded the larger cities, while Stevenson continued riding with Nephew Bob in the old Plymouth from small town to small town. En route, Stevenson's strategy was to buy only five gallons of gasoline at one time. This gave him the opportunity to talk to dozens of gas station owners and attendants, but wasted valuable campaign time that could have been spent with larger groups.

The Dallas *News,* which supported him, reported that before he had his morning sausages, pancakes, and coffee, he shook hands with fifty people. On a single day, said Stevenson, he walked ten miles along the main streets of towns he visited. Ten days before the close of the campaign he said he had driven fifty thousand miles, crossed through two hundred and eleven of the state's two hundred and fifty-four counties, and shaken two hundred thousand hands. To counter the magnitude of these figures, the Johnson headquarters declared that Johnson's helicopter had given him audiences of four hundred thousand Texans and carried him to three hundred and seventy speeches. Peddy could not compete in the battle of the numbers, so he continued to attack Johnson for not having resigned from Congress after Pearl Harbor as he had promised. Peddy also accused him of wanting to share atomic secrets with "Godless Russia."

On July 21, three days before the election, the Belden Poll gave Stevenson 43.2 per cent; Johnson, 38.8; Peddy, 14.5; while the combined obscure candidates, including Terrell Sledge of Kyle and Cyclone Davis of Dallas, owned a measly 3.5 per cent. Stevenson doubted Belden's accuracy and predicted he would win 55 per cent and make a run-off unnecessary. Johnson also called the poll incorrect and said he would collect 52 per cent and Stevenson only 38 per cent. Johnson also asked his campaign workers to make that last minute push, in order to make sure that "Texas isn't going to send an old man or an appeaser to the Senate."

On Saturday night, July 24, 1948, when the Texas Election Bureau received its unofficial returns from reporting newspapers across the state, Joe Belden was more pleased than any of the candidates. For his poll had proved quite accurate, with Stevenson collecting 477,077 votes, or 40 per cent of the total; Johnson, 405,617, or 34 per cent; and Peddy, 237,195, or 20 per cent.

The reaction at the headquarters of the candidates was one of sorrow. Stevenson was unhappy that he would have to continue driving through Texas for another month of campaigning in the run-off primary. The Johnson camp's gloom was occasioned by its realization that Johnson had trailed Stevenson by more than 70,000 votes. This appeared to be too great a margin to overcome by August 28, especially since a preponderance of Texas counties, local politicians, and newspapers favored Stevenson. How to overcome the handicap of losing almost all large Texas cities and winning only 72 counties compared with Stevenson's 168?

Chapter 29

THE MONTH OF August 1948 was the most crucial time in Lyndon Johnson's entire political life. If he could not overcome Coke Stevenson's 71,460 lead in the first primary by August 28, he knew he would be politically dead.

This was why several of his friends could not understand his hurried departure by plane the day after the primary. But Johnson had good reason for quitting Texas with suddenness, for he had learned that Stevenson planned a trip to the capital for talks with Congressional and Administration officials on foreign and military affairs. Friendly reporters and photographers were going along, and it was apparent to Johnson that if he were not on hand to talk down Stevenson in Washington, Calculating Coke would impress many Texas voters as a man familiar with the big problems.

Congress had adjourned in June, in order to make way for that year's Presidential nominating conventions and campaign. However, at the Democratic National Convention in steaming Philadelphia, unpopular Truman, in control of the convention's machinery, demolished the supporters of General Eisenhower to win the nomination; and in his 2 A.M. acceptance speech he stuck out his jaw, stared defiantly through his thick eyeglass lenses, and twanged out a call to the "do-nothing" Republican-controlled Eightieth Congress to return for a special session on "Turnip Day," July 26.

This eleven-day "Turnip Day" special session was a scene of wild disorder, with Republican spokesman Senator Robert A. Taft denouncing Truman for calling Congress back to Washington, and Truman, in turn, issuing daily gibes at the Republicans for continuing to "do nothing." While this warfare boomed, Coke Stevenson's slow train pulled into Union Station, and he began a long series of local trips to Capitol Hill and downtown offices for statesmen talks.

Johnson stayed on his trail, and every time Stevenson told reporters he had spoken with a Cabinet officer or a senator, his opponent was "Johnson on the Spot," with his own longer list of conferees. When Stevenson reached a high point in Cabinet talks, enjoying a long session with Secretary of Defense Forrestal, Johnson was angered that Forrestal did not immediately reciprocate by offering him the same privilege. But Forrestal still fumed over the team of Johnson and Air Force Secretary Symington operating behind his back. In fact, Forrestal had only the week before told President Truman he intended to fire Symington for insubordination, for slyly using his original speech at Los Angeles instead of the corrected copy from Forrestal's office. However, Johnson kept calling until Forrestal said he could spare a few minutes from his hectic involvement with Russia over the closing of land approaches to Berlin. Afterward Johnson told reporters he had induced Forrestal to increase his contracts with Consolidated-Vultee at Fort Worth so that three thousand additional aircraft employees would be hired. In addition Johnson said that he was so good a salesman that President Truman had agreed to permit two Missouri-based anhydrous ammonia plants to move to the Houston area. Here they would supply synthetic rubber plants, which, Johnson added, were in operation only because he had single-handedly prevented their closing.

Back in Texas, Wirtz had winced every time he picked up a paper and read about Coke's meetings with Undersecretary of State Robert A. Lovett, Senator Tom Connally, Senator Arthur Vandenberg, Forrestal, and other Washington figures. Hurriedly, he and Johnson headquarters speechwriters wrote an attack on Stevenson's trip to the capital, and Carl Estes, the newspaper publisher in Longview who supported Johnson, recited it over the twenty-station coverage of the Texas State Network. But Wirtz did not let the matter end here, for he took out a full-page ad in the Sunday edition of the Dallas *News* of August 8, and ran the Estes speech in total.

The ad carried the notation that Texas veterans of World War II had paid for it, and the speech carried the title: "Why Silent Coke Fled to Washington to Take the Shortest Short Course in History on International Affairs." Intertwined with its clawing at Stevenson, the speech declared that "if Lyndon Johnson is defeated, every CIO-PAC-AFL labor boss in the country will hail the victory—'Operation Texas'—and the march of decentralized industry to Texas, I warn you, will stop—while Calculating Coke calmly lights his pipe."

On their return to Texas both candidates swapped whip-flicks before officially beginning their campaigns. When Stevenson proclaimed foreign policy out of bounds as a campaign issue, Johnson called this nonsense and said that Stevenson was an isolationist. Stevenson replied by labeling Johnson as the number-one pinup boy of the CIO, and Johnson hit back with a broadside and a story to show that Stevenson was unqualified to be a senator.

"Calculating Coke reminds me that when I was a boy," said Johnson, "my daddy brought home to our rocky little cotton farm one day a brand new hired hand. This fellow admitted he hadn't ever chopped cotton, but he was willing to try. Daddy took him out to the cotton patch, handed him a hoe, and pointed to the cotton and the cockleburs around the cotton plants. When daddy came back in about an hour, that man had the prettiest stand of cocklebur weed you ever saw, and there wasn't a single stalk of cotton in sight."

Wirtz decided that Johnson should kick off the second primary by going after the 237,195 votes that George Peddy collected in the first primary. This strategy became obvious when the Johnson entourage traveled to Center, in Peddy's home county, for his opening speech. Here he appealed to the five hundred who showed up to transfer their Peddy support to him. He declared himself a political soulmate of Peddy and said they were in total agreement on international, national, and state affairs. But there was little applause, and Peddy did not step forward to throw an arm about him.

After this small-town kick-off, Johnson revealed to reporters that he planned to step up his campaigning tempo with emphasis on winning big-city votes. He pointed out that in the first primary he had carried only Austin, and it had been a mistake to go after the rural and small-town votes. This concentration on cities would rule out using the *Johnson City Windmill,* he said. Instead, he would jump between cities by plane and use mammoth motorcades between airports and downtown areas.

His special focus on city campaigning required a much larger campaign staff to make the phone calls, prepare the leaflets, and write the formal speeches. Reporters found Johnson campaign workers in offices at any hour of the day, and the pounding of typewriters went on around the clock. Johnson assembled a staff of speechwriters who could turn out talks on short notice. Horace Busby, a student at the University of Texas, caught the Johnson flair for ridiculing Stevenson and for homespun tales, and Johnson made him his chief writer despite his youth. Another writer whom he used extensively was Phil Fox, a former Ku Klux Klan publicity man, with steady ability to grind out news stories for reporters.

Following the momentum of his mission to Washington and the press interest it generated, Stevenson gave evidence of conducting a spirited campaign by delivering a few hard-hitting speeches. But suddenly he disappeared from sight, and after some days of his silence, reporters recalled that the last time he vanished they found him on his ranch. They found him again at home on the range, and when a newsman asked with disbelief why he was not campaigning, Coke said nonchalantly, "I had to get some hay cut, arrange to have the goats sheared, and round up and spray a bunch of cattle against flies. Did you ever see a stump-tailed bull in fly time?" he added.

In the second week of August he was once more back on the campaign trail with Nephew Bob and the old Plymouth. He had read about Johnson's trip to Center, and he carefully praised George Peddy. The Johnson jibes that he was senile had apparently angered him under his calm exterior, for he took to calling attention to his physical trimness. "Lyndon's been calling me a pipe-sucking, coffee drinker and a calculating old man," he told crowds. Then he flexed an arm muscle and pointed to his lack of a paunch.

"I want you all to see me and judge whether I have one foot in the grave."

Lyndon Johnson was all mouth and no brains and was the leading example of a do-nothing congressman in all of Washington, Stevenson charged. "When my opponent landed his helicopter on this very spot," he told one audience, "did he tell you of any bill he ever introduced in Congress in eleven and a half years? Did he ever write and pass a bill which would aid the average citizen of the United States? I can't find one. If he has passed one, it would be nice for him to point it out. Ask him if he ever even introduced a bill. My opponent has been talking about high prices. Did he ever introduce a bill to lower them? There has been a lot of talk about aiding old folks. Did the other candidate in this race ever introduce a bill which would give the old people more benefits? Why, when I became governor, the average state old-age assistance check was $8.34 a month, and I had it raised to $23 before I left."

Johnson reacted immediately to Stevenson's assertions that he was a zero congressman. Instead of insisting that he certainly had introduced a bill during his six House terms—one to draft war plant absentees—he held up four fingers to crowds and shouted, "I got four large dams to power Texas war factories and light farm homes. After the war I prevented the closing down of the synthetic rubber industry in Texas by the Rubber Act of 1948, which I got through the House. For my nation, I also ran an errand to stop the sale at junkyard prices of our war plants, worth $1,258,000,000, which are so vital to our defense program. For my nation, I also ran an errand which helped us get the seventy-group Air Force to protect Americans against communism." But judging from the greater applause Stevenson kept getting for asking his questions than Johnson got for offering a count of the pork barrel he collected for Texas, this exchange was in Stevenson's favor.

So Johnson stopped making his answer and returned to the chief charge of the first primary. "My opponent says he's against the hoof-and-mouth disease in Mexico," he told audiences, "but he won't say whether he is for or against Taft-Hartley." Even when Stevenson made public a letter in which he declared himself in favor of the Taft-Hartley Act, Johnson pretended he did not know this, and called Stevenson "the silent whip of the labor bosses. Communist labor czars have loosed the biggest slush fund in Texas history to defeat me!" he shouted from speaking platforms. "Those big labor racketeers have voted to destroy me!" In Dallas, when reporters pressed him to name the labor czars, he said he meant "James C. Petrillo, that's who. He will not let our children record their fiddle playing." (Petrillo was head of the American Federation of Musicians and an opponent of "canned" music for radio stations.)

By mid-August, the two candidates were slandering each other at a swift pace. They added a new charge by each accusing the other of operating a huge and illegal political slush fund. When retired General Ira Eaker came home to west Texas on a visit and gave several campaign talks in Johnson's behalf, Stevenson called this open proof that the Hughes Aircraft Company, who employed Eaker, was footing a large share of Johnson's enormous campaign expenditures. Johnson played the part of the injured, innocent party and demanded to know why he should follow the ten-thousand-dollar legal limitation on campaign spending while Stevenson ignored it with impunity. "Who is paying for the eleven-hundred-dollar newspaper ads and the three-hundred-and-thirty-dollar billboard posters for Stevenson on the highways?" he complained in his best outraged voice. "In a twenty-five-mile stretch from Sugarland to Houston, there are seven such Stevenson billboards."

The truth of the matter was that with both headquarters heavily over the ten-thousand-dollar limit, neither dared register a formal complaint, for the party making a complaint would have faced exposure for similar violation.

By the third week of the campaign, observers said, Johnson's voice was a sore-throat croak, his eyes were black-circled and deep inside their sockets, and his face seemed to be skin stretched over long bones. But compared with sweaty Coke Stevenson ambling about in ranch clothes, Johnson was the picture of the millionaire Texas campaigner. Old-time Johnson City residents, who remembered the boy whose mother sewed his pants and shirts, now saw a new Lyndon attired in two-hundred-dollar tailor-made suits and the softest calfskin shoes his Boston cobbler could turn out for his size-fourteen feet. He wore only silk monogrammed shirts and gold cuff-links, and he told time from an expensive Lecoultre alarm wristwatch.

Since his marriage he had given Lady Bird the job of laying out his clothes each morning, shining his shoes, filling his pens and cigarette lighter, and putting the correct pocket items in place. But when faced with his uphill fight against Stevenson, he gave Lady Bird orders to help in the campaigning, and he hired a valet to take over her duties for the duration.

Lady Bird's problem in assisting him was that she had never lost her shyness. The most she had been able to muster for him in the 1941 campaign was a quiet "Ha-dee" when she was introduced to strangers. But Lyndon's order was her command, and she tried to be useful.

Years afterward Johnson magnified her role in 1948 by saying, "Bird set out to organize the women. She hated to fly. It always made her sick, but she got busy and flew all over the state." In truth, outgoing Marietta Brooks of Austin, whose husband Max had gone to college with Lady Bird, headed the Women Volunteers for Johnson. One of Mrs. Brooks' tasks was to complete a list of women's organizations throughout the state and make use of her own extensive membership and leadership in Texas women's clubs to create warmth for Johnson among all such organizations. When Lady Bird told Mrs. Brooks she wanted to help, Marietta, who knew of her shyness, arranged with a clubwoman friend in each of dozens of towns to invite other clubwomen to meet Lady Bird over a cup of tea.

Alvin Wirtz also had a suggestion for Lady Bird. Why not try Coke Stevenson's stunt and pick up the gas station vote for Lyndon? Lady Bird was willing, but she would not go out alone. So Mary Rather, Johnson's secretary who had once been Wirtz's secretary, was detailed to accompany her. Mary recalled later that she and Lady Bird drove out of Houston one morning and Lady Bird "suggested that we buy only five gallons of gasoline at a time so that we could stop at more places and ask people to vote for Mr. Johnson. Just before we got to Madisonville, which was our third stop of the morning, Lady Bird said, 'You ask them this time, Mary, I don't believe I can do it again.' "

With Lady Bird not at his immediate command to soothe him, Johnson's temper frequently went on a rampage in the final period of the campaign. If his hotel breakfast did not reach his room quickly, he could bullyrag an aide and sometimes he created shouting scenes in hotel lobbies in full view of outsiders. When he was told in advance that the organization he would meet at the next stop would not expect a speech, and he found on his arrival that he was scheduled for a talk, he would bellow at campaign aides afterward, "I thought it was just gonna be coffee, doughnuts, and bullshit!" Some reporters who covered his campaign said he reminded them of the bouncing ball on movie screens over the words of songs for audience participation. One newsman called him "a sight to see. While talking, he may, among other things, move from chair to chair around the room, pace the floor, puff cigarettes endlessly, rub salve on his hands, take a digestion tablet, gulp water, and use an inhaler in his nose. He's just too nervous to remain still."

When the last two weeks of the run-off got under way, Lady Bird stepped up her visits to clubwomen's receptions. Called upon to talk at many stops, she knew of the pride Texans had in their history, and she concentrated on giving a quick picture of Lyndon's ancestry. Although her history was at wide odds with the facts, it was warmly received by the ladies, especially her erroneous statement that her husband's great-grandfather, Reverend George W. Baines, "converted Sam Houston."

As the last week of the campaign came on, she dropped most of her remaining receptions to accompany Lyndon in an exciting airplane invasion of Texas cities. Cheering caravans met their plane at airports, and sirens chewed the air as the highly organized Johnsonites escorted their candidate into town for his speech. A flood of campaign postcards and leaflets had preceded the spectacular arrival to let citizens know that their future senator was on his way. "We're comin' round the mountain and don't anyone slow down," Johnson screamed hoarsely at his August 26 rally in Dallas, and his claque went wild.

Stevenson also quickened his pace down to the wire, as he and one-armed Nephew Bob drove faster between towns. He and Johnson continued to indict each other's campaign spending, and the two never let up charging the other with being pro-labor and radical. At Houston, the United Steelworkers of America decided to ask its ten thousand members not to vote for either labor-baiter.

Johnson had set his final rally for San Antonio on Friday, August 27, the day of his fortieth birthday and the day before the election. He had asked Lady Bird to speak from the platform, and though this request frightened her, she reluctantly agreed. Then when she found she did not know how to write a speech, she and her close friend Scooter Miller, the daughter-in-law of Roy Miller the lobbyist, composed one together.

Lady Bird decided to drive with Mrs. Brooks to San Antonio for the rally, because Marietta had arranged a reception for her in a small town en route. They started from Austin on a leisurely ride when the car suddenly left the highway and turned over twice. "All I could think of as we were turning over was I sure wished I'd voted absentee," said Lady Bird.

Luckily, when she and Marietta extricated themselves from the wreckage, neither had suffered broken limbs. Despite her torn clothing and aching body, Lady Bird struggled back to the highway and flagged a passing car. By now Marietta's wounds looked worse, and she was sped to a hospital. But Lady Bird continued on to her reception where she borrowed a dress from her hostess and shook hands with the two hundred women in the receiving line.

Afterward she went on to the big San Antonio rally, where the crowd of fourteen hundred in the Municipal Auditorium Circle sang "Happy Birthday" to Lyndon. In his speech, he told the crowd that he regarded San Antonio as his "home town" because his father and grandfather always had their boots made here. Then when he finished by asking the audience and radio listeners across the state to be sure to give him a birthday present at the polls the next day, Lady Bird was escorted to the microphone to make her first radio speech.

"When we got back to the hotel around midnight," said Lyndon, "I told her we'd better go to bed, but she said she had to go on to Austin that night to do some last-minute campaigning in the morning. As she changed for the trip, I saw those big bruises, and she had to confess about her car accident." However, instead of ordering her to rest or see a doctor, he let her return to Austin where she, Rebekah Johnson, and Lyndon's three sisters, Rebekah, Josefa, and Lucia, spent election day dividing the Austin phone book into five parts and calling telephone numbers one after another to request votes for Lyndon.

At midnight, Saturday, August 28, the wired returns cooperating newspapers had sent to the Texas Election Bureau showed a neck-and-neck race between the two rivals. Stevenson was ahead by 1,894 votes, with a total of 470,681 to Johnson's 468,787. At 3:30 P.M. on Sunday, Stevenson's lead dwindled to 315 votes. Johnson had been up all night listening to returns, chain-smoking and pacing, and he told John Connally, who dropped in, "It's tighter than a tick."

By midnight, with an estimated 10,000 votes still out, Johnson swung in front by 693 votes out of a total of 980,877. Stevenson had remained at his ranch near Junction, where he planned to issue his victory speech, but when the vote shifted to Johnson, he suddenly feared that a swindle was in the making, and he hurried to Austin. Gone now was his characteristic calmness as he made frantic, belated calls to his county managers to "check the results closely." What disturbed him most of all were reports that Johnson and Wirtz had been in touch with the Anglo dictators of the Rio counties and that skulduggery was in the works in that area.

However, by Monday night, two days after the election, Stevenson had re-established at least surface composure when the Election Bureau announced he had regained the lead. This announcement put him ahead by 119 votes with an estimated 400 additional votes to be counted in six counties, including two Stevenson strongholds. Stevenson's smile was back on his face on Thursday, September 2, with the press release of the Texas Election Bureau that the count was now complete and the Junction rancher had won the primary by 362 votes. The Election Bureau also reminded newspaper readers that its own count was unofficial and that the State Executive Committee would meet in Fort Worth on September 13 for the official canvass, with the results to be presented to the state convention the following day for confirmation. Then even though the Bureau had called its September 2 vote final, it made a change in the totals the next day to cut the Stevenson lead to 114.

At this point, the battle appeared won. But suddenly Stevenson's smile vanished, for he heard that Alvin Wirtz had gone out of town and that John Connally, who rented the downstairs of the Johnson duplex, had gone to the Rio counties. The disquiet in the Stevenson camp became an uproar the next morning, Saturday, September 4, a week after the election, for a telephone call from a Stevenson supporter told ominous news. Precinct 13 in the county seat of Alice in Jim Wells County, a bleak mesquite patch holding impoverished Mexicans, had revised its vote. Instead of the originally reported 765 total for Johnson and 60 for Stevenson, its new figures read 967 for Johnson and 61 for Stevenson. By the simple process of adding these extra 203 votes to the finals of the Texas Election Bureau, Lyndon Johnson now led by 87 votes, and there were no more votes to count!

The Johnson headquarters and its candidate naturally showed their elation at this "corrected" figure that gave Johnson the Democratic nomination. Bill White, Johnson's newspaper friend at *The New York Times,* later wrote that "what rescued Johnson in the end was his old friendship for the Mexican ranch hands and a few of their untypical patrons." But Coke Stevenson was described as "fighting mad" as he told reporters, "I was beaten by a stuffed ballot box. And I can prove it!"

From Stevenson's tone, Johnson knew that he meant to use any means available to have the Precinct 13 additions thrown out. But he was ready for battle, with Wirtz heading a crew of about a dozen lawyers, including former Governor Allred, highly respected John Cofer, "Mr. Ed, the Talking Horse" Clark, and young John Connally, whom Wirtz employed in his own firm as a junior lawyer. If the fight should spill over into Washington, Wirtz had already arranged for the free help of three Johnson friends, Thurman Arnold, Abe Fortas, and Paul Porter, who formed the firm Arnold, Fortas and Porter. All this was not lost on Stevenson, who also assembled a top-notch legal staff, with former Governor Dan Moody as his chief adviser.

While both sides measured each other's fighting capacity, the man who had brought on the controversy and thereby controlled the political destiny of Johnson and Stevenson found the excitement he had engendered quite amusing. He was forty-six-year-old George Parr, a resident of the tiny town of San Diego and commonly called the "Duke of Duval" because of the stranglehold he had on the affairs of Duval County. But Parr might just as well have been called the "Duke of Jim Wells" because of his hold on that neighboring county, or the "Duke of Nueces County." In addition to his dictatorial power in these three counties, George Parr had a good working relationship with Anglo bosses of fifteen adjacent counties.

The sun-baked fiefdom in the mesquite had begun with Archie Parr, George Parr's father, who held a state senate seat for twenty years so he would be available in the Statehouse in Austin to effect a profitable trade of Duval County's vote for political and financial favors from power-hungry politicians and the oil interests. He employed George as his page in the senate, and in 1926, when George finished law school at the University of Texas, he gave him his political baptism by running him for Duval County judge. To make certain he won, Archie Parr permitted no other names on the ballot.

In this land of cracked-clay soil and an occasional cactus among the tangles of mesquite shrubs, the Parrs ruled like czars over the hordes of hungry, illiterate, frightened Mexicans. An educated Mexican could cause trouble, so the Parrs saw to it that little of the school funds went into education. The result was that Duval ranked two hundred and fifty-third of the two hundred and fifty-four Texas counties in literacy. Duval County's low position was even more shocking considering that the entire state of Texas stood close to the bottom of all forty-eight states in literacy.

When the old man died, George Parr carried on the family's work. He built a bank in his Duval headquarters town of San Diego and another in Alice, in Jim Wells County, to the east; came into possession of seventy thousand acres on which he constructed a fancy mansion, a swimming pool, and a race track; and entertained worried politicians who wanted to win elections so much that they were willing to add to his vault cash.

The base on which this empire stood was the worried little peon, whose family subsisted in the shacks of the squalid slums that Parr owned. Parr liked to come swaggering into San Diego with his tough, unshaven Mexican bodyguards surrounding him and sit at a table and dispense favors or disfavors to his long line of downcast subjects, who came to beg for food or work. What made the Mexicans so important to George Parr was that he paid the poll tax for each, and his head count became the number of votes he could promise a man running for Congress or statewide office. Sometimes when the total number of votes offered did not arouse sufficient interest, poll taxes were paid for the names on gravestones in Mexican cemeteries.

Despite their shenanigans, the Parrs were seldom in trouble. Once when the state supreme court ruled that Archie Parr had to open the financial records in the Duval County courthouse to a taxpayer, the courthouse was leveled by a devastating fire. Another time, a fearless United States attorney in San Antonio checked George Parr's income tax and found that he had failed to include his entire income. One item was twenty-five thousand dollars in cash that an official of a construction company doing business in Duval County had "placed in a little black bag" and delivered to Parr. The federal indictment against him noted that he was also collecting large sums of money as protection payoffs from houses of prostitution and moonshine and gambling businesses. However, blue-eyed George managed to stay out of prison when the judge put him on probation, after warning him to keep out of trouble. But Parr could not, and in 1936 when he was caught erasing words granting oil and gas rights on property he owned from a notarized document, he was sent to prison for nine and a half months as a probation violator. There were many raised eyebrows throughout Texas when Governor Jimmy Allred and the entire Texas Senate as well as the attorney general sent a plea for freedom in his behalf to the federal court.

After Parr was released from the El Reno prison, he started in where he had left off, though he felt the burden of being deprived of full citizenship rights. An effort to get a Presidential pardon from Franklin Roosevelt failed, but even without this he moved back into close association with top politicians.

Election after election, the Texas Election Bureau received Parr's peculiar vote totals, but since the Bureau was only the unofficial vote tabulator for associated newspapers, its officers merely scratched their heads and shrugged. After all, the governor's September state conventions never challenged the Parr figures in confirming winning primary candidates.

There was no logical explanation for the candidates George Parr favored, because their political views were of no interest to him. Ever since Mister Dick Kleberg ran in his first race in 1931, Parr saw to it that the world's leading rancher had his undivided support. This continued until 1944, when the two quarreled and Parr pushed his Nueces County chips into the corner of John Lyle, who was serving in Italy at the time. This, plus Kleberg's notoriety at the time for demanding kickbacks from his Congressional employees, ended Mister Dick's career.

On the other hand, Pappy O'Daniel, who held the same generally reactionary views as Mister Dick Kleberg, could never gain the use of George Parr's paid-up poll tax voting list. In the 1941 Senate race, the Duke of

Duval gave Lyndon Johnson 704 and Pappy only 50 votes. Nor did he ever find kinship with Beauford Jester or the Neff family. In 1946, in the governor's race, he gave Grover Sellers 1,735 votes and Jester an implausible zero; for attorney general, Parr used the same figures and gave Price Daniel the 1,735 and Pat Neff, Jr., none.

In the past Parr had always bestowed his largesse on Coke Stevenson. This started when Coke first ran for lieutenant governor under Pappy O'Daniel, and it continued throughout his terms as governor. But when Stevenson campaigned for the Senate in 1948, his lieutenants sent him word that the Johnson camp had been talking to Parr and had apparently won his vote for the Johnson cause. This proved to be the case in the first primary, but Stevenson was not disturbed because he figured that in a million-vote run-off fight, blue-eyed George with the false, friendly smile would not be able to dictate the winner with his paltry few thousand votes.

Stevenson's judgment seemed to be severely shaken when the returns came in to the Texas Election Bureau. Suddenly he realized that in a close race Parr could be influential. He knew that Parr would delay sending in his vote totals until he determined how many of his paid-up poll tax votes to use. Parr apparently used his entire list in Duval County when he sent in his late total of 4,622 for Johnson and only 40 for Stevenson; and for Nueces and Jim Wells Counties, where his control was not as strong, he submitted 5,925 votes for Johnson and 328 for Stevenson. These votes came in along with the odd returns from San Antonio and the rest of Bexar County, where rumor had it that for a $35,000 handout from Johnson's headquarters the sweeping 12,000-vote margin for Stevenson in the first primary was changed to a 2,000-vote Johnson victory in the run-off. But as long as Stevenson found himself with a margin of 114 votes at the close of the Texas Election Bureau's count, he saw no reason to protest.

This complacency, of course, vanished when the rumors started that John Connally was on his way to visit Parr. Another rumor had Johnson on the telephone demanding that Parr uncover at least 115 more votes to put Johnson ahead of Stevenson. The story was that George yelled back that he had shot his bolt in Duval County by using up his entire register of paid-up poll-taxers and did not care to get into serious trouble by going beyond his list; but that he knew of some unused paid-up poll-taxed citizens in adjoining Jim Wells County and would see what he could do in Alice, the county seat. Rumor or stories, Stevenson saw facts; and these revealed that a week after the election Precinct 13 ballot box in Alice showed a "corrected" total, which gave Johnson 202 additional votes and Stevenson one vote and put Johnson in front by 87 votes.

Stevenson's first recourse should have been to appeal to Governor Jester, who had never received George Parr's aid. But "Beautiful Jester with the marcelled hair" had gone to New York to preside at the meetings of the

Interstate Oil Compact. Then to add to Stevenson's troubles, when the meetings broke up, Jester remained in the East to search for his missing half-brother.

Without Jester's aid, Stevenson realized he was entirely on his own. Nor could he count on help from the supposedly Jester-controlled State Democratic Executive Committee, for a hurriedly appointed subcommittee composed of Johnson friends met in Austin and after a few minutes announced that nothing illegal had occurred in Alice's Precinct 13 voting.

This small episode, to lend an air of legality to George Parr's handiwork, showed Stevenson he would have to wage a bitter fight on four levels— federal, state, local, and in the newspapers. He recalled that on Thursday, two days before the Precinct 13 "correction" came, Johnson had told reporters, "We've won!" At a news conference Stevenson brought up that remark and explained, "On Thursday, at noon, my opponent issued a victory statement and urged his friends to do their duty. Almost immediately last-minute gains for my opponent began to roll in from those counties of south Texas which are said to be dominated by a single man."

This brought a loud laugh from Parr, who admitted he was the man Stevenson meant. He called Stevenson a poor loser, kicking at him with "In previous elections, the district has gone for Stevenson with as much enthusiasm as it has gone against him in this year's Senate election. I never heard a complaint from him then about the bloc vote in Duval County."

Johnson also jumped into this vocal exchange by going on radio with Lady Bird on September 6. After solemnly declaring, "I didn't buy any votes," he went on to argue that he knew of many other voting places where crooked work favored Stevenson. "You weren't told of the bloc vote in a box behind the locked gates of the King ranch, where not a single vote went to Johnson. Nor of the box that came in Tuesday in another county where the Johnson vote was zero." He tried to even the score for Precinct 13, in Jim Wells County. He also talked about his 1941 campaign and how he had been "counted out" because he had not bothered to have his men watch the vote count. "This time it was different," he said. "Ten young friends of mine who are war veterans volunteered to obtain the official votes from county chairmen." He spoke for eight minutes and when he finished, he pulled Lady Bird to the microphone and she stammered through a short defense of her husband that Alvin Wirtz had written for her.

This vocal sparring continued, with Stevenson demanding that both sides permit the state senate to determine the authenticity of the Precinct 13 vote. To this Johnson hotly replied that he would not agree because Stevenson was on a "crony" basis with the upper house's leadership. But he would have no objection, he added, if the FBI made an investigation that not only covered Jim Wells County but also several other counties that had cheated for his opponent.

Stevenson's lawyers told him not to bother because J. Edgar Hoover lived across the street from Johnson in Washington, and they had far more than a neighborly relationship. Nevertheless, Stevenson insisted that it be done, and a request went to Johnson's good friend Attorney General Tom Clark to investigate the Parr-controlled counties. Clark replied that he was turning the matter over to a Mr. Rosen in his Department, who would look into the charge at some time in the future.

Stevenson next decided to move directly on Parr. First, he sent two former FBI agents to San Diego on September 7, and he joined them the next day when they walked into Parr's office and demanded to see the Duval County voting list and marked ballots. John Connally had preceded the Stevenson trio to San Diego, and Parr was primed for their visit. He laughed them out of his office with a reminder to Stevenson that he could not comply because he (Parr) was not an election judge.

Stevenson and the ex-agents did not put up an argument but sped instead to Alice, the scene of the "crime." Here they were surprised to find that the newly elected chairman and secretary of the Jim Wells County Democratic Executive Committee, Harry Adams and H. L. Poole, were on their side. But the two said they had been unable to take possession of the Precinct 13 voting list, which voters were required to sign, for Tom Donald, the old committee's secretary and an employee of Parr's bank, had locked it in the bank's vault.

When Donald refused to show Stevenson the voting list, Stevenson called Captain Frank Hamer of the Texas Rangers, who came speedily to Alice. The next morning everyone in town turned out to watch Stevenson's foursome approach the bank's entrance, which was guarded by Parr's sullen *pistoleros*. All members of the Stevenson party wore short-sleeved shirts on purpose, to show they carried no guns. There was a moment of heavy confrontation at the bank door, but the *pistoleros* slunk away when Hamer motioned them to step aside.

This time Donald took the voting list from the vault and said they could examine it, providing they did not copy any names on paper. The ex-FBI agents noted that the first several pages contained names written in black ink and in many different handwritings. However, the final 203 names were in blue ink and in the same handwriting. The obvious conclusion was that this final group comprised the "correction" Parr had added a week after the election. Unable to write down the blue-ink names, the two managed to memorize several before Donald snatched away the book and returned it to the vault. An immediate check afterward revealed that three of the "voters" had long been in the cemetery, while two who were alive denied they had voted.

In a further meeting with Adams and Poole, the Stevenson party learned that the new County Executive Committee would meet at 11 A.M. the next day, Friday, September 10. The two assured Stevenson they had sufficient support to throw out all the votes in Precinct 13, which would give him the Senate election.

Apparently the Johnson crew in Parr country believed this too, for frantic telephone calls went to Wirtz's office in Austin. It was now the turn of the Johnson lawyers to save their man, and the small army of learned attorneys met within the hour to plan their move. Unaware of the possibilities of the law, and concerned that he was finished, Johnson disrupted the meeting with his loud nervous talk and pacing. According to an associate of Wirtz, Lady Bird was present at this exhibition of near-hysteria, but later in describing her experience to a woman reporter she said, "The nicest thing about it for me was the fact that I would often see Lyndon being the calmest one of a group of very capable, tough, hard men—all the lawyers who were working with him and advising him. I was just glad to see that he could be—and the times required it—so calm and level-headed."

The battery of Johnson lawyers reached a quick decision. Only a friendly state judge could help them. Judge Roy Archer, who sat in Austin, a long distance from Alice, was a man they knew well, and they presented him with a Johnson petition to bar the Jim Wells County Democratic Executive Committee from examining the Precinct 13 vote. This legal plea claimed that Stevenson and his ex-FBI agents had "entered a conspiracy" to have the Alice box "thrown out on the grounds of fraud and irregularity"; and that Captain Hamer had used "threats and intimidation" on Adams and Poole to throw out the vote and give the state election to Stevenson. The lawyers were in a sweat while Judge Archer slowly read the petition, because the new county committee was scheduled to meet at 11 A.M., only a few hours away, and could complete its action before Archer moved. By then it would be too late to save Johnson. But at 10 A.M. the judge provided a cliff-hanger ruling when he issued a temporary injunction forbidding the county committee to reconsider the vote in Precinct 13. Archer also ruled that the issue should be heard again in the district court in Alice on the following Monday, September 13.

This was the day when the Johnson lawyers faced still another hurdle—the official canvass by the State Democratic Executive Committee meeting in Fort Worth. As a preliminary, a seven-man subcommittee including two representatives from each of the two camps began a count of the ballots at noon in the ballroom of the Blackstone Hotel. Wirtz had planned to remain in the background, but when Jerome Sneed, one of the two Johnson choices, suffered a heart attack in the elevator, Wirtz joined Mrs. Alma Lee Holman in glowering at Albert Sidney Johnson and Mrs. Claude V. Hudspeth, who represented Stevenson.

Even before Jim Wells County was reached in the count, there was trouble for Johnson. Tom Abney, chairman of the Democrats of Harrison County, where Lady Bird was born, declared his county's vote in error because many voted who had not paid their poll tax. If these were removed, the Johnson total would be cut 140 votes, and the controversy over Precinct 13 in Alice would become academic. There were immediate gasps and protests from Johnson partisans, and several of his lawyers held whispered exchanges with Abney. Finally Abney said he would let the original vote stand.

The adding machines worked until four-fifteen in the afternoon, when the total was read with the Precinct 13 "correction" included. Albert Johnson called out his objection, and Alvin Wirtz launched into a legal argument for the inclusion of the final Jim Wells County vote. Tempers were short, and subcommittee chairman W. B. Simmons screamed at Wirtz, "Leave out all those high-sounding words!" In the vote that followed, the subcommittee divided three to three. This gave Simmons a vote, and when he cast it in favor of Stevenson, Mrs. Holman cried out, "You are disenfranchising Jim Wells County!"

That evening the full Executive Committee met to settle the same issue. The ballroom resembled a courtroom, with lawyers for both sides milling about and dozens of thick law books on the center table. Lyndon and Lady Bird, both with forced set smiles on their faces, sat in the front row facing the committee, while Coke Stevenson puffed nervously on his pipe a few feet away.

Chairman Robert W. "Bob" Calvert set the rules, following the reading by Secretary Vann Kennedy of the subcommittee's majority report (to exclude all votes in Precinct 13 and elect Stevenson) and the minority report (to include Precinct 13's votes). Contending counsels would be granted forty-five minutes apiece to present arguments; then the vote would come, with each district casting two votes.

Clint Small, representing Stevenson, chose to make his case by reading affidavits from some of the live ghost votes among the controversial 203. Bluntly he emphasized that "the issue before this committee is whether Precinct 13 in Jim Wells County is to *elect* a United States senator to serve six years." Lawyers John Cofer and Charles Francis jumped up repeatedly for Johnson to jibe at Small's affidavits from nonvoters who charged that their names had been voted.

Cofer spoke for Johnson in his allotted time, and almost his entire forty-five minutes passed in ridiculing Stevenson and praising Johnson, instead of examining the merits of the Precinct 13 votes. "I can wave two affidavits for every one Small can wave," he said in deprecation of his opponent's strong arguments, "but I don't want to waste the committee's time with such nonsense." He also unraveled a long yarn about a man he met in Duval County who "told me that Lyndon Johnson was the best congressman Texas ever had." This brought roaring cheers from the anxious Johnsonites present, and a reporter noticed that Johnson acknowledged this tribute with a smile, then "waved his hand for quiet" when he thought it had gone on long enough.

When Cofer sat down, Calvert called for a vote on the issue to throw out all the votes of Precinct 13. This count had not gone very far when

Wirtz looked stunned. Vote after vote favored Stevenson, or throwing out the controversial Precinct 13. Nor did this trend end, for of the first 31 votes, 21 favored Stevenson. The gloom on the faces of Lyndon and Lady Bird was akin to panic, because fewer than half the total votes remained to be counted.

One observer said he remembered how quiet it was when Tom Moore of Lockhart was called on to vote. Moore shouted his support for Johnson, and after him came a long succession of Johnson votes. Before the end, it turned into a horse race, and finally Calvert read the results: 29 votes for Johnson; 28 for Stevenson.

Pandemonium took over and the air filled with ear-ringing yippees and wahoos. Johnson was still accepting congratulations when Calvert recognized Mrs. Seth Derbandt of Conroe. Then the celebration suddenly ended when she announced she was changing her vote from "Johnson" to "present."

So the vote stood at 28 to 28 unless Calvert cast a tie-breaker. But Calvert would not vote, and he gaveled his announcement that the state convention would have to argue the issue through from the beginning when it met the next day. As an afterthought he asked if any absent members had entered the ballroom since the vote was completed, and he had his gavel raised to adjourn the meeting when someone screamed from the doorway, "Let me in! Let me in!" A man came flying into the room, and he called as he dashed toward Calvert, "I'm Charlie Gibson from Amarillo and I vote for Lyndon Johnson."

With Charlie Gibson's vote the count was again 29 to 28 in favor of Johnson, and the ballroom witnessed a second celebration for him, even noisier than the first. Stevenson's group stamped out midst loud booing.

It was late when the party ended, but Wirtz and Johnson got little sleep that night. On the other side of Fort Worth, the two thousand delegates to the governor's state convention were to meet in the Will Rogers Auditorium the following morning, and there was much work to be done before then. Governor Jester was in town, and Johnson went to see him to ask for his support, only to find that Stevenson had been there before him. In 1946 Jester had controlled the September state convention at San Antonio with ease, and he expected to continue his domination here in Fort Worth.

However, Wirtz had other ideas. He, Maury Maverick, and Byron Skelton of Temple formed a ramrod of "Loyalists for Truman" and talked long and hard to influential delegates to deprive Jester of power over the state organization because of his role earlier that year in helping to organize the Dixiecrats.

By morning the mood of the convention was set. When two Houston delegations showed up, the convention witnessed several fistfights before a roll call vote ousted the anti-Truman delegation. States' rights delegations from Dallas and three counties were also ordered to leave the auditorium, and to show Jester how weak he was, the convention ousted his man, R. W. "Bob" Calvert, from his post as chairman of the State Democratic Executive Committee, and also replaced the national committeeman. But the climax came for Wirtz when the delegates shouted their approval of the 87-vote victory for Johnson and ordered his name put on the ballot for the November election against the Republican candidate. Johnson now made his appearance, and after telling about his ordeal of "a hundred long days of campaigning," he pledged he would "spend the next six years making Texas as good a United States senator as I possibly can."

The action of the state convention, and the decision of the state court at Alice the day before to continue the injunction against a re-examination of the Precinct 13 votes appeared to be an insurmountable wall to many Stevenson supporters. But the former governor would not quit. "Some half million good solid Texans voted for me as their senator, and they have been defrauded and robbed," he told a reporter. He knew he had no friends in the state's court system or in the state Democratic organization. If he wanted to continue the fight, there was only one immediate course still open—to battle Johnson in the federal courts.

At 4 A.M. on September 15, hours after the convention ended, two Stevenson aides knocked on a farm door in east Texas and roused a tiny old man. He was Federal District Court Judge T. Whitfield Davidson of Dallas, who was on vacation from his duties in the North Texas Federal District. The judge made some coffee, then sat on his porch, where he read a petition from Stevenson for a temporary restraining order barring the secretary of state from printing Johnson's name on the November ballot. The two men supplied Davidson with some details of what had occurred at Alice, and when they finished, he signed the order and set a hearing in federal court in Fort Worth on September 21.

When news of Davidson's injunction reached Johnson and his lawyers, they were thunderstruck. The law set September 17 as the official deadline for certifying party nominees on the November ballot, and if they could not act until after Davidson's hearing on September 21, it would be too late even if the old judge ruled in Johnson's favor. Nor was a favorable decision from Davidson likely, for he was known for his highly conservative views.

Wirtz, Allred, and Cofer moved swiftly on September 16 by appearing before the Texas Supreme Court. But although they made an intensive plea for a *mandamus* petition to force Secretary of State Paul C. Brown to certify Johnson on the ballot, the court refused to act. This led George Peddy, the third runner in the first primary, to reappear in the news with a suggestion that his friends should consider a write-in vote for him for the Senate in November.

On September 21, the fight to the political death continued in Judge Davidson's courtroom in Fort Worth. Johnson and Stevenson had arrived in town the day before, each surrounded by his faithful dozen lawyers, and they stayed in hotels a block apart. A newspaper photograph of the court-room scene revealed a tired and worried Johnson dressed in a neat suit and sporting a wide, flower-design tie. Lady Bird sat next to her husband and looked even glummer than he.

In addition to his lawyers, Stevenson had brought several brave Mexicans from Parr's domain and they were prepared to testify that Parr had voted their names without their knowledge. Stevenson also had evidence to show that Parr had voted dead people. Pointing to Stevenson's side of the courtroom, Cofer called the Stevenson petition and evidence nonsense. The simple truth was that Stevenson was a "poor loser" who would not abide by the decision of his party, Cofer told the court.

This brought anger to Davidson's face, and he said bluntly to John-son's lawyers that they had not produced "one word of evidence to dis-prove this plaintiff's claim that he has been robbed of a seat in the United States Senate." When he suggested that both men allow their names to go on the November ballot, Johnson's attorneys said *no*, and gave as their reason that he had been honestly elected. Davidson soon had enough of the swarming lawyers, and on the second day of hearings, he named United States commissioners to investigate the voting in Jim Wells and Duval Counties and report their findings to him on September 27. In the mean-time, the temporary restraining order would continue. Almost apoplectic, Jimmy Allred pleaded with the old judge to hand down a decision on the spot in order that Johnson could appeal it immediately to a higher federal court.

When Davidson refused, Johnson and Allred flew to New Orleans, where they met the next day with Chief Judge J. C. Hutcheson of the United States Fifth Circuit Court of Appeals. Allred begged Hutcheson to dismiss Judge Davidson's restraining order. However, Hutcheson said on September 24 he could not act without the other two judges of his court, and he promised to consider the petition when his court convened in At-lanta on October 14. Allred almost sobbed as he told Hutcheson it would be too late. But Hutcheson was obdurate.

Word from Parr country to the Johnson headquarters was that the United States commissioners were getting nowhere in their search for evidence. In the investigation in Duval County, the Mexican stooge tax collector admitted that "yes, many several thousands" of poll-tax pay-ments had been bought by outside parties, but after a sharp stare from Parr, he said he could not remember who. Oral reports to the commission-ers confided that Parr had voted twice as many names as were in the polling list books. This contradicted the inside informant's story of the Parr-Johnson phone conversation in which the Duke of Duval said he could not give him more Duval votes because he had already voted the limits of his poll taxers. When the commissioners asked for the polling lists, a Parr employee apologized profusely that he had taken the lists home and his wife had burned them by mistake while house-cleaning.

The commissioners experienced similar frustration at Alice, in Jim Wells County, where they investigated the shenanigans in crucial Precinct 13. Subpoenas could not be served on Tom Donald or Louis Salas, the presiding judge in the election, because both had been called suddenly to Mexico "on business." However, the commissioners managed to locate the two ballot boxes for Precinct 13. They were one foot high and resembled metal cookie jars, except for the padlocks on them. But the padlocks on these boxes that spelled the fate of Johnson and Stevenson were open, and their keys hung from the boxes. Johnson's attorneys on the scene put up strenuous argument as to which box should be opened first, and the commissioners finally accepted their priority.

When this first box was opened, it contained only unused ballots. What had happened to the marked ballots that were supposed to be inside the box? A Parr man shrugged and said that the illiterate Mexican janitor must have thought they were trash to be burned. Another argument by the Johnson lawyers brought weary agreement from the commissioners to delay opening the second box until the next day. When it eventually was opened, it was empty.

While the commissioners were searching for evidence, President Truman came through Texas on a whistlestop schedule of nineteen pep talks from the rear of his Presidential train, the *Ferdinand Magellan*. Vic Messall, his former secretary, had called Texas politicians in advance to pave the way for a friendly reception at each of the stops. Messall warned Truman not to go to Texas because of the threats made by responsible Texas Democrats. One had boasted that "they'd shoot Truman if he went down there, that no-good s.o.b. and his civil rights." But Truman had ignored the threats, even though he knew that the Democratic party was in national disarray, and Texas was heavily stocked with hotheads. But so were other Southern states that year, where the Dixiecrat Democrats were running a States' Rights party ticket of Governor J. Strom Thurmond of South Carolina and Governor Fielding Wright of Mississippi. And there was also party trouble in the North for that matter, where the left-wing Democrats under the name of the Progressive party had nominated the ticket of former Vice President Henry Wallace and Senator Glenn H. Taylor of Idaho.

No ugly incidents developed during Truman's campaign run through Texas. In fact, Governor Jester, the Dixiecrat, showed up at trainside on September 26 to welcome him to the land of the Alamo. Sam Rayburn rode through the state with his friend, and for a short time Johnson was aboard for talks with the two. When the train stopped at San Antonio, there were many quizzical exchanges among local politicians who learned that Truman had spent a half-hour with George Parr. Immediate speculation was that Parr would get the Presidential pardon he yearned for (and not long afterward, he did).

Before Johnson left the *Magellan,* he gave Truman and Rayburn a rundown on the current status of his contest with Stevenson. That Truman did not quicken to his recital with maudlin emotion was to be expected because of Johnson's opposition to the Administration's domestic and defense programs. But if Sam Rayburn wanted anything for his protégé, Truman was willing to do what he could. The truth was that he was more concerned about how a Johnson victory might influence his own uphill fight against Governor Tom Dewey of New York, the Republican Presidential nominee.

After Johnson left the train, Truman put in a plug for him at every whistlestop. At Austin, Temple, Waco—it was the same exhortation to the large crowds: "If you Democrats send senators like Bob Kerr and Lyndon Johnson to Washington, we'll certainly make the Republicans dance."

Throughout Monday, September 27, Truman worked his way north toward the Red River. The climax of the day was to come at Bonham, where he would deliver a nationwide radio address from the local football stadium that evening and then spend the night at Sam Rayburn's two-story white colonial house. Shortly before the train reached Bonham, the frightened train crew reported a helicopter descending on them. The train stopped, and the helicopter landed alongside. It was the *Johnson City Windmill,* and out stepped Lyndon Johnson. He rushed aboard the train and was all smiles as he burst into the President's compartment.

Much had happened since he had left Truman. Judge Davidson had reopened the hearings that day and ordered all Jim Wells County ballot boxes impounded. But what Davidson was doing would become entirely academic tomorrow if all went as expected.

The story was this: Three days earlier, when Judge Hutcheson told him and Jimmy Allred that he and his two associated judges on the Federal Circuit Court would hear his appeal from Federal District Court Judge Davidson's actions on October 14, Johnson appeared doomed.

But rumors spread throughout Austin on September 25 that Johnson's high-powered Washington attorneys were attempting to bypass Hutcheson's court by bringing action directly before the Supreme Court. Stevenson was suddenly ill from the thought that Johnson might find a way out of his tight box just when Stevenson's victory seemed assured. That same day Dan Moody, head of his legal help, called the Supreme Court office of Chief Justice Fred Vinson in Washington to learn if the rumor were true. Vinson did not come to the phone, but assurances were made by one of his clerks that the Chief Justice knew nothing of such activity.

However, a major move was already under way. The man who was directing the Washington operation was wispy Abe Fortas from Memphis,

Tennessee, a former SEC attorney, general counsel of the Public Works Administration, and Undersecretary of the Interior, succeeding Congressman John Dempsey of New Mexico, who had succeeded Wirtz.

Johnson had known Fortas since 1933 when he worked for Kleberg, and Fortas, just out of the Yale Law School, came to Washington to work on sugar problems for his professor, Wesley Sturgess, at the Agricultural Adjustment Administration. From the start Johnson had found Fortas quick to do favors, offer advice Johnson wanted to hear, and listen to his rambling thoughts on legislative strategy. Fortas loved political intrigue, and through Johnson he could enjoy an exciting, vicarious existence. Besides his fondness for politics, law, and the violin, Fortas shared an interest in military matters with Johnson. Others acquainted with the facts of their military experiences were amused when the two talked military strategy, for one had spent about half an hour in a danger area flying toward the attack on Lae, and the other had served a month in the Army in 1945 before being discharged with tuberculosis of the eyes.

"I was in Dallas taking depositions on an antitrust case," Fortas once recalled how he became the key man in the settlement of the 1948 Senate contest for Johnson. "Suddenly I got a call from Alvin Wirtz. Wirtz said, 'Lyndon's here in Fort Worth and he's in trouble. Come over right away.' "

It was Fortas who told Johnson, Wirtz, and Allred to appeal to Judge Hutcheson; and when that failed, Fortas took the first plane to Washington. Once his plane landed, the man Fortas hurried to see was Justice Hugo Black. Each Justice was assigned a judicial circuit; and Black handled the Fifth Circuit, which covered six states, including Texas, and was in administrative control of Judge Joseph Hutcheson's Circuit Court of Appeals. As a Supreme Court Justice, Black's credentials were laughable. His only previous experience on the bench was his year and a half of service as a police-court judge in Birmingham, Alabama, and he had gone directly to the Supreme Court from the United States Senate, where he was noted for running ruthless hearings on lobbying. His appointment in 1937 had caused a national furor, for his youthful membership in the Ku Klux Klan was exposed.

Yet Black's chief interest on the bench was civil liberties, and Fortas, who had gone into private practice in 1946, had a similar interest that brought him into warm friendship with the Justice. This was not to his disadvantage now when he took Johnson's election problem to Black and discussed it in detail in the Justice's chamber in the Supreme Court Building a block from the Capitol and the Senate Office Building.

The result of their conversations became public on September 28, 1948, when Black issued an order setting aside Federal Judge Davidson's ruling that barred Johnson's name from appearing on the November ballot. Black's order, dated hastily by hand to make it effective before Davidson could hear another day of testimony, declared that federal courts lacked jurisdiction over state elections. On this basis, the case had to revert to the state court that ruled Johnson must be certified as the winner, and Stevenson's case must be dismissed. By Black's order Johnson would be the next Senator from Texas.

Stevenson's face was the picture of death when Judge Davidson told his counsel that he had to end the case and wire the secretary of state to put Johnson's name on the ballot. "The United States Supreme Court has altered my opinion, but it hasn't changed my mind," Davidson announced sadly. Off the record, he pointed out that four years earlier Black had voted the opposite when the Supreme Court ruled that federal courts could interfere to see to it that Negroes were not barred from voting in Texas primaries. He also noted that Black had ignored the fact that the Stevenson-Johnson controversy had involved a federal office. After adjourning his court, Davidson blasted Black by calling his order "unduly hasty and probably unlawful."

Johnson accepted his victory with an aggressive condemnation of Stevenson and the federal government. In a public statement he said, "After leading by thousands of votes for days in the 1941 election, I was finally counted out [cheated], and took it like a man. This time Coke, the self-proclaimed friend of the county courthouses, ran over the 254 Texas courthouses to reach a federal judge at daybreak near the Louisiana border to put in a civil rights program for himself in Texas." Johnson also thanked Black by calling the order he had issued "reassurance that we will not return to the days of the carpetbaggers and to control of our destiny by the federal government."

In the November election Stevenson asked his supporters to vote for the Republican candidate, Jack Porter, a Houston oil man. But party regularity was still so great in Texas that Truman carried the state by almost a half million majority over Dewey, and Johnson beat Porter by three hundred and fifty thousand. Afterward, the Jim Wells County Grand Jury hit at Johnson by declaring there had been "a complete lack of responsibility in the handling of the ballots in the August primary."

The new senator from Texas did not permit such minor attacks to disturb his exhilaration on reaching this political mountaintop. In fact, as soon as Porter conceded, he had an enormously humorous story to tell friends.

It went as follows: Little Manuel was sitting on the curbstone and crying. Another Mexican came up and asked, "What's the trouble with you, Manuel?"

"My father was here last Saturday and he did not come to see me."

"But your father has been dead ten year, Manuel."

Manuel sobbed louder. "That is true. But he was here last Saturday, and he voted for Lyndon Johnson, and he did not even come to see me."

PART FOUR
Whales and Minnows

Chapter 30

THE SENATE OFFICE Building lay only a few minutes away from the Old House Office Building, across the grassy knoll that stretched before the East Front porticos of the 751-foot-long high-domed Capitol Building. But to reach the SOB from the Old HOB had taken Lyndon Johnson eleven years of dreams and two hard-fought, dirty political campaigns. In terms of personal cost, the 1948 fight against Coke Stevenson had been physically expensive; and old friends who saw him when he returned to Washington for the Eighty-first Congress were shocked at his appearance. The long squabble over the fraudulent George Parr votes had melted twenty-five pounds off his skinny frame, turned his skin scabby from nervous tension, made his hand shake when he drank his double scotches, and increased his cigarette consumption past the daily three-package point.

There were other costs, less easily measurable. His efforts to become rich in a field regulated by a government agency had been given an airing during the campaign; and the rotten innards of Texas politics had been starkly exposed. How would Johnson react? Would he be humble as a senator to the point of humility? Would he be a quiet nonentity, hoping to prove by diligence that he would one day be worthy of his post?

Johnson may have been weary when he showed up at the Capitol in December 1948 with Homer Thornberry in tow, but he acted the role of the big winner who had no regrets or explanations. From his House office phone he ordered Lady Bird to arrange a reception for Mister Sam's sixty-seventh birthday on January 6, and he took Homer on a swift tour of the offices of House friends and to meetings of Rayburn's "Board of Education." At one of the Board's sessions, when everyone present, including outsiders such as Attorney General Tom Clark and Air Force Secretary Stuart Symington, held glasses aloft to "strike a blow for liberty," Johnson voiced a complaint. "How am I supposed to drink with that old buzzard watching me?" he asked, pointing his glass at a portrait of former Senator Morris Sheppard, who had once occupied his Senate seat. Sheppard had been the author of the Eighteenth Amendment, ushering in Prohibition during the Roaring Twenties. Rayburn solemnly promised to remove "the spy" by the next day.

"Lyndon's shift to the Senate completed a circle," said Wright Patman. "A quarter of a century earlier, when I served in the Statehouse with Sam Johnson, Lyndon became good friends with one of the pages, a twelve-year-old boy named Homer Thornberry who was half his size. They used to run in the halls and yell and wrestle. Homer was in the Austin City Council when Lyndon ran for the Senate in 1948, and Lyndon had him run for the House seat he was vacating. After they both won, Lyndon arranged to have Homer take over the same office he had occupied all the years he was in the House."

This was Room 504 of the Old House Office Building, and by the time Capitol laborers had Johnson's possessions on the way to the Senate so that Thornberry could move into 504, Washington correspondents were finding the Texas contest for the Senate an interesting subject. Drew Pearson, who had supported Johnson against Stevenson, dubbed Johnson now in his syndicated column as "87-Vote Johnson" and "Landslide Lyndon." Further newspaper comments on the election came when Coke Stevenson arrived in Washington with Dan Moody to urge Senator Carl Hayden's Committee on Rules and Administration to hold hearings leading to Johnson's expulsion. Hayden, who was a good friend of Sam Rayburn, gravely agreed to examine the charges, and he left Stevenson dangling until July 1949 when he threw his case into the trash can. The committee's reason for upholding Johnson was that it needed the actual ballots to check for fraud, and since they had been destroyed, the committee had nothing to investigate.

If anything, the slurring nicknames and the Stevenson action had the effect of increasing Johnson's normally aggressive nature. From the start he disarmed suspicious senators he did not know by sticking out a hand and saying, "Howdy, I'm Landslide Lyndon." He also worked adroitly to get more than a freshman senator's appurtenances. The Senate rule was that all freshmen be assigned three-room suites, with the few four-room suites assigned strictly according to seniority. But Johnson fast-talked Joe Duke, the new Senate sergeant-at-arms, into awarding him Suite 231— a four-room office, and he soon wedged twenty employees into three of the rooms. Another supposedly firm rule permitted freshmen senators a maximum of three telephone lines. Johnson had four, and he immediately put employees to work calling the offices of the other ninety-five members to ship him autographed, framed photographs of their senators to go on one of his walls.

Then there was the car-parking gambit. The Senate provided an underground garage across the street from the SOB where members parked. In addition, high seniority senators had special places at the curb outside the building. On the first day he drove to work, Johnson blithely parked his car immediately outside the busiest entrance to the Senate Office

Building and down the stairs from his own special office. Every morning after this he parked there, until one day he found another car occupying the space. Outraged, he telephoned Capitol Police Chief Captain Olin Cavness and blistered his ear with profanity. "Get that goddam car out of there right away!" he ordered Cavness.

Leslie Carpenter, who sent news stories from Washington to the Houston *Chronicle* and several small Texas papers, said that the police chief made a check and reported back to Johnson that the space belonged to a senator with top-level seniority standing. "Well," Johnson bellowed at him, "while I'm getting some more seniority, you put a Capitol cop there every morning to guard my space until I get to work!"

For a never-disclosed reason, Cavness stationed a policeman to stand in that space every morning, regardless of the heat, cold, or rain, to keep all other cars out until Johnson's car arrived.

As a senator, Johnson continued to overwork and bullyrag his staff, just as he had his smaller crew in the House. Carpenter quoted him as saying, "There are no favorites in my office. I treat them all with the same general inconsideration." Early each day, after he put on the clothes Lady Bird had laid out for him and finished breakfast, he headed by car through northwest Washington toward the Capitol. "He'd pick me up on Connecticut Avenue," said Mary Rather, his secretary, "and by the time I sat down he was giving me instructions. I learned to keep my notebook outside my purse. By the time we reached the office, he had outlined a whole day's work for me and had given me orders for the others that kept them jumping all day long, too."

Johnson's staff contained many familiar faces. His first administrative assistant was John Connally, who lived close by at 3895 Rodman Street. Connally stayed only a year because he wanted to get back to Texas and start working his way up to millionaire status like Lyndon. To replace him, Johnson elevated Walter Jenkins and named Warren Woodward next in line behind Jenkins.

Johnson always referred to Jenkins by his full name. "Look, 'Walter-Jenkins,' call so-and-so and tell him this," Johnson would say, or " 'Walter-Jenkins,' come in my office." Johnson also liked to tell others that Walter-Jenkins had known no other employer than he. Before World War II, when Jenkins was a senior at the University of Texas, a nervous friend asked him to go with him to Johnson's office in Austin to apply for a job. Johnson frowned and scowled at the jobseeker, but he liked Jenkins and offered him a patronage appointment in Washington. Jenkins hesitated when Johnson said he would have to drop out of college immediately and get on the train for the capital, but Johnson assured him the opportunity was too good to pass up. Besides, he could finish his degree at night at Georgetown or George Washington.

When Jenkins eagerly walked into Johnson's House office, he learned that a patronage job did not necessarily involve working on Johnson's staff.

Instead, members of the majority party in the House were apportioned shares of the large number of menial jobs in the Capitol—messengers, elevator operators, or doorkeepers—and they had exclusive control in filling them. Johnson's patronage job available for Jenkins turned out to be that of a Capitol policeman. Jenkins took it until Johnson finally gave him a clerical job in his office, and he finished college at night. When World War II came, he saw service in Africa and Italy.

One who knew Jenkins well, as a member of Johnson's House staff, said, "Walter did not seem to fit in with the rest of Lyndon's loud and aggressive gang." But Johnson never had reason to doubt Walter-Jenkins' loyalty to him, and when he acquired his Austin radio station, Jenkins worked with him on checking ad salesmen's reports and other station problems. Eventually Johnson rewarded him by naming him corporate treasurer.

Another who did not seem to fit in as a member of Johnson's Senate staff was his brother Sam. Divorced in 1944, Sam found jobs in private industry before coming to work as a sixteen-thousand-dollar-a-year clerk for his brother. Sam's sensitive nature could not bear up in Lyndon's tense atmosphere and full routine, and as time passed it revealed itself in his steadily worsening posture and bad habits. "Sam had a terrible battle with the bottle," said Wright Patman, "but to his credit he overcame this weakness entirely."

Still another employee Johnson brought to the Senate with him was Horace Busby, the short, curly-haired young speechwriter he had used during the campaign. Busby, whose political philosophy at twenty-four was in accord with the Far Right of the Texas regulars, had been a liberal editor of the *Daily Texan*, the student paper at the University of Texas, and Johnson introduced him as "my bomb thrower." Busby later recalled his first day in Johnson's Senate office. He and Warren Woodward reported the same morning, and, said Busby, "we put in a typical day, one which ended after midnight. When we asked our new boss where we could spend the night, he said he had thoughtfully reserved a room for us at the old Dodge Hotel basement, where he had stayed his first night in Washington twenty-five years before."

As Busby said, working past midnight was not an unusual experience. At a staff meeting, Johnson told his employees that he expected them to answer six hundred and fifty letters a day, handle five hundred telephone calls, and charm about seventy visitors. Each employee was ordered to keep daily tabs on letters answered, telephone calls, and conversations with visitors. This was not make-work, with the cards later being dumped into a file cabinet. Instead, Johnson collected them and studied each carefully. Clerks who failed to measure up were called in for a scolding. Late one night when he walked through his rooms and riffled through the in-boxes, he counted forty-five letters that had not been answered that same day. "There are forty-five good Texans who did not get the service they deserve today!" he bellowed.

Besides the normal flow of letters, Johnson added to his staff's workload in order to carry out a scheme to insure his re-election in 1954. First he asked all two hundred and fifty-four Democratic county chairmen to send him the names and addresses of individuals who had supported him vigorously in 1948. Then from the master list of eight thousand names supplied him, his office sent out one hundred sugary letters a day, or about four letters a year to each enthusiastic supporter. Johnson also established a local intelligence system when he induced precinct captains to send him a confidential list of influential persons in their precincts, tell whether each was pro- or anti-Johnson, state the reasons for the position taken, and quote directly what each was saying about him. From these precinct reports, Johnson gained valuable insight into the kinds of letters to send these people and what to say to them in person. Still another effort to spread his name was the use of the common scheme of franking out speeches by the hundreds of thousands and supplying free seeds and the Government Printing Office's popular booklet on *Child Care*. Yet another name-spreading plan was to offer presents to parents who named their newborn babies "Lyndon." After a time his standard present was a free calf. Within a few years, dozens of little Lyndons were growing up in Texas, and in 1951 he showed a reporter a cluster of twelve pictures on his wall of smiling boys all named Lyndon.

For a time Johnson ran his office around the clock on an assembly-line basis. He divided his staff so that at every hour during the twenty-four, typewriters would be pounding and the growing volume of mail answered. At some time during each shift he came dashing through the office rooms and called out like a cheer leader, "C'mon, let's function . . . let's function." Only after the work cards revealed a decline in office efficiency did he discard this administrative nightmare.

A reporter who wrote a friendly article about Johnson called his staff the "youngest, the poorest paid, and the most overworked" on Capitol Hill. Even when they went home after hours of overtime, they could expect a phone call at 2 or 3 A.M. with instructions for extra work to be done early the next morning.

On one occasion, when Johnson faced a revolt by the wives of his employees because of the overtime situation, he took quick action to settle the problem. His solution was not to cut working hours but to hire the wives to work in the office alongside their husbands. "I don't want some wife at home cryin' her big eyes out about the cornbread gittin' cold while her husband's busy doin' somethin' for me," he explained. Soon he had seven married teams on the same oppressive schedule. When any of them had a complaint, it was not wise to confront Johnson, because he was expert at turning the issue around by his own fault-finding and ridicule. Instead, they went to Lady Bird with their problems, and she softly promised to talk to Lyndon. But no improvements were ever noted.

Besides maintaining the daily piecework schedule, Johnson was rough on employees who did not dress according to his taste. His personal preference was for what he considered to be a "masculine" style. He liked full-cut suits with extra-long, roomy jackets that covered his slouch, and he insisted on trousers that reached the floor. One fashion expert attributed his trouser length "to his Texas childhood where it was a sign of affluence to have plenty of fabric in your clothes." He would not abide any suggestions from his San Antonio tailor, whose "fitters quail before the notorious Johnson temper—plus the vocabulary that goes with it." He could never own enough suits. One time he walked into the house with delivery men bringing nine suits that he had bought at a single fitting, and he told friends that they cost him more than two hundred dollars apiece. He also liked the feel of his silk, monogrammed shirts and liked to run a palm over the solid gold cuff-links that were engraved with a map of Texas. To offset his dark suits, he wore the "fat Max" ties with colorful designs, and to offset the ties, his handmade shoes were shined to a mirrorlike gloss. Throughout each day he bent down about a dozen times to buff his shoes and restore the shine. What disturbed him most about his appearance was his thinning hair, but he distributed it carefully in a pompadour and used Stacomb grease to keep it in place and shiny.

Frequently he lined up male employees, criticized their attire, and made suggestions. In his inspections he straightened ties and pointed out an urgent need for a haircut. New employees received personal instructions on how to knot a tie properly, and they were told never to undo the knot but to loosen the noose and slip it over their head. "Tying and untying a necktie ruins it," he said. "Tie it once and slip it off your head without untying it. Pull the knot back where it was when you had the tie on and hang it on a doorknob." Les Carpenter noted that on a visit to Johnson's house, he found "all the second floor doorknobs flooded with expensive neckties." The girls he employed could also expect his criticism when they were overweight or did not apply sufficient makeup. Once when he buzzed a girl to come in for dictation and she entered his office, he told her bluntly, "Why don't you put on some lipstick, and then I'd like you to send a letter to . . ."

All Johnson employees were expected to be totally subservient to him, yet brutally aggressive with outsiders in promoting his interests. These two characteristics became the hallmark of the Johnson man, and to insiders at the Capitol, anyone who worked for him was immediately tagged. His demand for foolproof answers from his staff in turn provoked an inquisition of government agencies by his employees, much of it useless and excessive. On one occasion, said Carpenter, Johnson asked an aide to find out when the Army-Navy football game was scheduled. "The Navy says the game's to be played on December 2," the assistant told him. "That's fine!" Johnson roared, "but what does the Army say?"

As his day moved along, between committee hearings and Senate floor action, Johnson continued his House practice of spending hours making dozens of phone calls. A friend said, "Leave Lyndon Johnson in a room with a telephone, and he will make a long-distance phone call." The walls of his Washington and Austin homes were studded with telephone outlets, in case he felt the urge to make a call. One of the trees in his back yard in Austin was wired for sound with a thirty-foot extension-corded telephone. Horace Busby was to meet him during an afternoon at the Dallas Airport, and when he came he found Johnson pacing back and forth like an expectant father outside a three-phone-booth set. "Watch those phones!" Johnson screamed at him. "I've got a long-distance call working in each."

At lunchtime Johnson generally ate in the Senate restaurant. George Smathers of Florida, who defeated Senator Claude Pepper in 1950, often ate with Johnson after he came to the Senate. "Lyndon was the biggest eater I ever watched," said Smathers. "He would eat two large meals and gulp them down as though he were starving. Nobody could slow him down." Johnson would have liked nothing more than to make a lunch of chili, but this was not a specialty of the Senate kitchen. Friends made it a rule to have a pot of chili on the fire when he was expected. He had an inordinate penchant for Jalapenas, fire-hot peppers, and when Lady Bird scoured Washington for some without success, he called the local head of the Safeway chain, told him he was an important senator, and won his "cross my heart" promise to stock Jalapena Peppers for him in the future.

Johnson habitually took a break during the day's work, and this came late in the afternoon when he walked southward the length of the Capitol to Sam Rayburn's "Board of Education." If he failed to appear at Mister Sam's by 5 P.M., the phone rang in his office. Rayburn would be at the other end of the line, and without identifying himself, he would bark, "Tell Lyndon I'm waiting for him." Then he would hang up just as abruptly.

Because he worked late, Johnson had a ready excuse for avoiding the Washington cocktail circuit. Nor did he consider evening parties more than time wasters. Lady Bird experienced difficulty in getting him to attend those functions she considered necessary, yet when he did go, she was invariably embarrassed. "I noticed that Lyndon was usually the hardest one to persuade to leave, after being the hardest one to get there," she said dryly.

Lyndon expected Lady Bird to pitch in on office chores, and she willingly did. It was still her job to serve as his valet and make certain his first morning coffee was scalding hot. But she had the new task of calling Mary Rather shortly after 9 A.M. to ask, "Who's in town from Texas today?" If the visitors were important politically or financially back in their home towns, she called them and invited them to lunch or to see the sights of the capital.

After Aunt Effie's passing, Lady Bird grew closer to her formidable mother-in-law, Rebekah Johnson. Rebekah was approaching seventy, and she came often to Washington to fulfill her growing interest in her family tree, or "kinship hunting," as she called it. She and Lady Bird spent hours in the genealogy room of the sparkling white Annex of the Library of Congress, where the older woman tried to establish at least a tenuous connection between the Johnson clan and early British royalty. Lyndon was especially interested in determining his first American ancestor, but when his mother told him it was a "John Johnson" of Alabama, he expressed sharp disgust that the name was so common and dull. "Without even a middle initial," Lady Bird said he wailed.

Lady Bird, who was trying to come out of her shell, found Rebekah Johnson's atmosphere far from the exciting one in which Lyndon was enveloped. Once she explained her mother-in-law by saying she "made a ritual of little things." The frequent visits of his mother also served to remind Lyndon of bitter episodes in his past that he had forgotten. Once he recalled a recitation contest in Stonewall that he wanted to win. "My mother had been an elocution teacher, and she felt sorry for Walter Peter because he spoke broken English," he said. "She took him in and coached us both. I was still feeling sorry for Walter when the competition at Stonewall began because he had that broken German accent, and she couldn't get it out of his system. So I'll be damned if they don't bring in first place for Walter. Of course, those judges were German, too."

With the working hours Lyndon kept, there were no evenings at home for relaxation. Only on Sunday did he ease off the pressure on his staff. This was a day for inviting top aides, reporters, and visiting Texas bigwigs to his Thirtieth Place house for barbecue and talk. After the stand-up dinner, Johnson would lead the way to the living room, where he sat on the wall-to-wall carpeting and held court without respite until guests went home. He was especially adept at mimicking the talk and mannerisms of fellow politicians, and his "Harry Truman" was hilarious.

While the profits from KTBC, his Austin radio station, were shooting upward at a swift pace, Lady Bird had remodeled the two-car garage into a family room and the unfinished third floor into a commodious guest room. In addition, Johnson had written to the president of Wiley College, a Negro trade school at Marshall, Texas, in Lady Bird's home country, and asked him to send him his best cook. This was Zephyr Wright, who prepared daily meals, Johnson's beanless chili, and the favorite of the Sunday crowd—her homemade peach ice cream. To help Zephyr get along in high-priced Washington, Johnson found a patronage job for her husband, Samuel Wright, in the Senate. Besides Zephyr, Lady Bird also employed Mrs. Helen Williams to do the housework. Despite having two servants at home, plus a swelling bank account, Lady Bird could not alter her tight budgeting way of life. While Lyndon could come home, as he did one time, with three new cocktail dresses and five hats he had bought for her, Lady Bird still returned bottles to the store for the two-cent deposit and purchased only "seconds" and "irregular" sheets and pillow cases.

As a result of her activities and Lyndon's long working day, the Johnsons saw little of their daughters. Willie Day Taylor, who had done office work in Johnson's 1948 campaign, came to Washington from Texas afterward to be a clerk in his Senate office. She was not long in Washington when he gave her the additional task on her government salary of tending to Lynda and Lucy when he and Lady Bird could not be home. Lady Bird said she "became almost a second mother and my daughters called her Wil-Day." Sometimes when Wil-Day was not available, Mary Rather pitched in as baby sitter. On other occasions Dr. Reed, the next door neighbor, spent the evening with the girls. A neighbor down the street once commented that "the little Johnson girls are being raised by a committee."

Lady Bird insisted that the girls spend summers in Texas. She recalled one nightmare when she, Lyndon, the girls, and a cat drove sixteen hundred miles to Texas. "The terrified cat wanted to get out of the car every inch of the way," she said, "and Lynda cried constantly, 'Are we almost in Texas, Mama?' " Traveling with Lyndon alone was a difficult assignment. When he was only a passenger in the car, he gave driving instructions without let-up to the person behind the wheel; when he drove, he shouted epithets at other drivers he believed were impeding his speeding progress.

When the girls were of school age, Lady Bird's program was to send them to Camp Mystic at Hunt, Texas, during the summer, and then put them into an apartment in Austin under Willie Day Taylor's care throughout the first school semester. The girls spent the second semester at home attending Washington schools.

Of the two children, Lyndon's favorite was his younger daughter, Lucy. Lynda was told she could not go anywhere without taking her little sister along. Lady Bird once admitted that this caused serious problems, for Lynda reacted at first by staying home rather than take her sister, but later she took to eating candy bars at an insatiable rate. When Lyndon remonstrated with her because she was growing grossly overweight, this nagging and concern by her father, whom she seldom saw, only served to increase her appetite and weight. Soon it developed into a major issue in the Johnson household, and when Lyndon shouted that no more candy could come into the house, Lynda secreted it in closets and under mattresses. Not until several years passed did she give up the candy hunger and reduce her weight.

His favoritism for Lucy became obvious one Valentine's Day when he drove to Middleburg, Virginia, in a pounding rainstorm and brought back a six-week-old beagle puppy for her. The pedigree papers revealed its name was "Thomas Jefferson," and this appalled Lady Bird because it was her father's name—Thomas Jefferson Taylor. However, Lyndon had an answer. He renamed the puppy "Little Beagle Johnson," keeping intact the identical initials for all members of the family.

Tragedy almost befell the household one day when Little Beagle was missing. Johnson went across the street to J. Edgar Hoover's house and asked him to put the FBI on the dog's trail. Hoover said he would do what he could for his friend, and a short time later he ordered a stakeout, with his agents alerting veterinarians in the Washington area against a possible dognapping. Three days later a stranger brought Little Beagle to a vet and reported that a car had broken his leg. Despite the absence of any collar on the dog, the vet had been called so many times by FBI men that he guessed correctly that this was the FBI's "Most Wanted" dog. An hour later the newest L.B.J. was at home.

Chapter 31

W HEN THE EIGHTY-FIRST Congress convened on January 3, 1949, eighteen freshmen senators walked down the aisle to be sworn in as members. Of these, fourteen were Democrats, eight of whom had ousted Republicans. The result was that the Democrats had regained control after two years of Republican management.

While the Republican leadership still fumbled in shock over the unexpected Truman victory against Tom Dewey, the Democrats momentarily gave the appearance of a revitalized, energetic force. This party attitude at the beginning of the session revealed itself in the committee assignments parceled out to freshmen. While the crushed Republicans put their new members on such miserable committees as Rules and District of Columbia, Majority Leader Scott Lucas of Illinois treated his new members generously.

Chairman Millard Tydings of Maryland, who bossed the powerful Armed Services Committee, agreed to take on four new senators rather than permit higher seniority senators on poor committees to transfer to his bailiwick. He made only one stipulation, and this was that no Northerners be among the four freshmen. Those Lucas eventually selected for Tydings were Lyndon Johnson, Estes Kefauver of Tennessee, Virgil Chapman of Kentucky, and Lester Hunt of Wyoming. Chairman Elbert Thomas of the Senate Labor and Public Welfare Committee wanted the liberals among the freshmen added to his committee to help promote President Truman's Fair Deal program. The four he got were Hubert Humphrey of Minnesota, who had precipitated the battle of the Democratic National Convention of 1948 with his insistence on a strong civil rights plank; Paul Douglas of Illinois, former economics professor and Marine hero; Matthew Neely of West Virginia, at earlier times a senator for sixteen years and a man noted for having memorized the Bible, Shakespeare's works, and the best of English and American poetry; and Garrett Withers of Kentucky, successor to former Senator Alben Barkley, who resigned to become Vice President.

Clinton Anderson of New Mexico, formerly Truman's Secretary of Agriculture, and Guy Gillette of Iowa, a seventy-year-old politician who had served in the Senate during New Deal years, went on Chairman Elmer Thomas' Agriculture Committee; Frank Graham, former president of the University of North Carolina, who succeeded the late J. Melville Broughton, who died in March 1949, went on the Judiciary Committee bossed by Senator Pat McCarran of Nevada; Robert Kerr, recently governor of Oklahoma, won assignment to the Finance Committee run by Senator Walter George of Georgia; and Russell Long, the thirty-year-old son of the late Huey Long of Louisiana, and Allen Frear of Delaware went on Banking and Currency, chairmanned by Senator Burnet Maybank of South Carolina. For his second committee, Lyndon Johnson landed a spot on the Interstate and Foreign Commerce Committee, which exerted powerful influence on the Federal Communications Commission.

After Johnson succeeded in getting his four-room office suite, four telephone lines, and his special parking space, he had time to study his ninety-five colleagues. While many of his fellow freshmen colleagues were telling reporters the issues they hoped to promote in the Eighty-first Congress, Johnson was diagnosing the power structure of the Senate. His simple analysis contained only two categories: one column titled *Whales* and a second titled *Minnows*. Under Whales, he listed only a handful of names, both Republican and Democratic; the rest were all Minnows. It was his intention to get into the Whale column in the shortest possible time.

The top name on Johnson's list of Whales was Richard Russell, Georgia's junior senator, a bachelor suffering from emphysema. In his twelve-line biography in the *Congressional Directory*, Russell listed himself as having been born in the town of Winder, Georgia, in 1897, and tersely recited a background that included work as a lawyer, speaker of the Georgia House, governor, and membership in the United States Senate since 1933. Had he recorded his legislative "musts," the top three would have been the construction of a massive military machine, the acquisition of an outrageous amount of pork-barrel projects—from military bases to agricultural research stations—for his state, and a frontal attack on the aspirations of the South's Negroes to acquire full civil rights.

Russell's power to influence American military strength stemmed from his position as second Democrat on the Senate Armed Services Committee; and the fruitful realization of his pork-barrel propensities came from his chairmanship of some subcommittees of the Senate Appropriations Committee. His strength in fighting civil rights for Negroes did not derive from committee power but from his assumption of leadership of the Southern bloc, or Senate members from the eleven states that had seceded from the

Union to form the Confederacy in the Civil War. The Southern bloc met informally from time to time to discuss such matters as strategic filibustering against anti-poll-tax bills and what to do to end discriminatory freight rates against their section by railroads. Most members would have preferred that their spokesman be white-haired, calm Walter George, the senior senator from Russell's state, but Russell came early to meetings, sat in the chairman's place, and aggressively dominated proceedings. The general unity of the bloc on the issue of civil rights spread into other areas, with the result that Russell, as self-proclaimed spokesman, possessed enormous power in working closely, now with Senate Republicans to prevent passage of President Truman's liberal Fair Deal program, and now with Northern Democrats on foreign aid and military matters. Russell's power was accentuated by the fact that he had mastered the Senate's complex parliamentary rules and was currently the leading expert on how to disrupt activities at will should the Southern bloc fail to establish a controlling coalition.

Another Whale in the Johnson ledger was Senator Walter George, a member of the Upper Chamber since 1922. George was a short, heavy-set man who wore thick-lensed glasses and old blue suits, and though he was past seventy, his mind was sharp and his walk stately. He had begun life as the son of a poor tenant farmer but rose to become a distinguished lawyer and judge before entering the Senate, where he eventually held the chairman's seat on the powerful Finance Committee and second-ranking Democrat's place on the Foreign Relations Committee. President Roosevelt unsuccessfully tried to purge George in 1938 because of his opposition to the Court-packing plan, yet George always referred to himself as an "80 per cent New Dealer." During World War II he wrote much of the tax laws and was chiefly responsible for the passage of the G.I. Bill of Rights in the Senate. George disliked Senator Russell on two counts: first, because he worked overtime to win recognition as leader of the Southern bloc; and second, because of the rough campaign his father had waged against him for his Senate seat in 1926.

Like Russell's power, Senator George's authority extended far beyond his seniority rank, but for an entirely different reason. When George stood up and expounded on a bill in his organlike basso profundo, he was one of the few senators in history who could sway the votes of his colleagues by a speech. It was early apparent to Johnson that if you had a bill to get through the Senate, it would be worth whatever effort was needed to get George to speak for it. While Senator George liked to tell about his pet parakeet, which perched on the top of his head as he shaved every morning at five o'clock, and about the pleasures of a quiet afternoon nap on the porch of his remodeled sharecropper's cottage back home in Vienna (*Vy-yenna*), Georgia, he carried with him a profound sadness. He could never end grieving for his son Marcus who was killed in action during World War II. In addition he felt eternally in the clutches of the Georgia

Power Company and Coca-Cola, which financed his campaigns and were key political masters in Georgia. "George could have taken the chairmanship of either Foreign Relations or Finance when their chairmen died," said Tom Connally. "He wanted Foreign Relations, but his sponsors told him it had to be Finance, so I got Foreign Relations. Later Senator George rewrote the Roosevelt Administration's Excess Profits Tax so that Coca-Cola benefitted by eleven million dollars a year."

Tom Connally was still another Whale to Johnson, even though he was a nonarguing workhorse for Truman's foreign policy. Connally's special forte was his fund of stories and his ridiculing technique in debate, which shattered opponents. He silenced one talkative and combative Republican senator on an important bill by telling him, "We'd make a lot more progress if you approached this problem with an open mind instead of an open mouth."

Whale Democrats also included Senator Harry Byrd of Virginia, a hidebound reactionary whose power stemmed from his high seniority on the Armed Services and Finance Committees; Colorado's Ed Johnson, Western champion of the South and chairman of the Commerce Committee; Brien McMahon of Connecticut, spokesman for the liberals and antimilitarists on economic and atomic energy subjects; Pat McCarran, Nevada's short, barrel-chested, cold-eyed anti-Semite, champion of higher silver prices and the importation of Basque sheepherders, and the autocrat of the Judiciary Committee, which controlled over 40 per cent of the Senate's legislation.

Two other Democrats completed the roster of the Whales. One was genial Scott Lucas, the majority leader, who determined which bills would be called up from the Calendar for floor action and the committee assignments for freshmen senators. The other Whale was taciturn, slow-moving Carl Hayden of Arizona, second-ranking Democrat on the Appropriations Committee, who took his seat in Congress when Arizona became a state in February 1912.

Although Senator Kenneth McKellar of Tennessee was chairman of the Appropriations Committee and was elected President Pro Tem of the Senate in 1949 to preside in the absence of the Vice President, he was not a Whale. McKellar had dissipated his standing and reputation by carrying on a ceaseless war with David Lilienthal, former chairman of TVA and Atomic Energy Commission. Signs of his senility were already in evidence—pounding his gavel in mid-afternoon to start the Senate's day of debate when the Senate had already been in session for hours; and rushing like a schoolboy every Saturday matinee to the neighborhood movie house for a cowboy show.

The biggest Whale on the Republican side was Senator Robert Taft of Ohio, son of the former President and a hard-running candidate for the Presidential nomination since the 1940 clambake. The humorless Taft was a believer in the "trickle-down" school of economics, which proclaimed that adding to a manufacturer's profits automatically provided more jobs and wage increases. However, he was far to the left of his party in championing federal aid to education and public housing. In foreign affairs Taft held firmly to his isolationist position. As "Mister Republican," now that Tom Dewey had been forcibly retired from politics, Taft served as his party's spokesman in opposing the Administration's program and deriding the President. After Truman won the 1948 election, Taft told reporters, "It defies all common sense to send that roughneck ward politician back to the White House." As for his view of Republican policy under a Democratic President, he said bluntly, "The business of the opposition is to oppose."

After Taft, the principal Republican Whales in the Senate were H. Styles Bridges of New Hampshire, ranking Republican on the Appropriations and Armed Services Committees, and Kenneth Wherry of Nebraska, the minority leader. Both Bridges and Wherry were rabid isolationists and extremely conservative, with a fierce partisan dislike of Democrats. Bridges was a wasp attacking Tom Connally's defense of the Truman foreign policy, and though he was almost always swatted down with insults and ridicule, he was back the next day for further fighting. The Democrats nicknamed Minority Leader Wherry "the Merry Mortician," because he spoke with pleasure about his business back home as an undertaker, with a growing Democratic clientele. They also hooted at him for his frequent twisting of words: When discussing defense matters, Wherry invariably referred to the "Chief Joints of Staff"; native Indian soldiers were "gherkins"; Senator Morse was "the Senator from Junior"; and he agreed with Joe Martin, leader of the House Republicans, that something should be done about "the anti-Sherman Trust Act."

Another Republican Whale was Arthur Vandenberg of Michigan, who had ghost-written most of Warren Harding's speeches in the 1920 "Back-to-Normalcy" campaign. Vandenberg had gained the august aura of an elder statesman in January 1945, more than three years after Pearl Harbor, simply by renouncing his isolationist beliefs in a Senate speech. In the Republican Eightieth Congress he had served as chairman of the Foreign Relations Committee, and as the Senate President *pro tempore*, which put him first in line to succeed Truman, according to the existing Presidential succession law. Because of Vandenberg's prestige among his Republican colleagues in foreign affairs, Truman had sought to buy him with presents, invitations to White House functions, and appointments to membership on American peace treaty and military alliance delegations abroad. Truman also deferred to him by letting him name administrators of several international programs. One Vandenberg choice was Paul Hoffman, the public-minded head of Studebaker cars, as director of the Marshall Plan operation for the economic reconstruction of war-torn Western Europe.

The closest approximation to Walter George on the Republican side of the aisle was Eugene Millikin of Colorado, a bald, heavy man whose humor-filled expression belied the calm conviction and logic he revealed in debate, which brought members flocking to the chamber to hear him.

Beyond Taft, Bridges, Wherry, Vandenberg, and Millikin, Johnson saw only Republican Minnows, though some were larger than others. Together with the Democratic Whales, the Republican Whales formed a rare elite; and he intended to join these big fish.

Chapter 32

DESPITE HIS MASTERY of parliamentary tactics and his ability to cow most Northern Democrats, Senator Richard Russell lacked a secure base of operations in 1949. First, the two other strong men in the Southern bloc, Walter George and Tom Connally, refused to show the slightest subservience to him in carrying out strategy. Then there were Estes Kefauver, the freshman from coonskin Tennessee, who moved swiftly to establish identification with Northern liberals; Claude Pepper of Florida, long a fighting liberal; Frank Graham of North Carolina, who believed the time far overdue for ending the South's mistreatment of her Negro population; and the two Phi Beta Kappa senators from Alabama, Lister Hill and John Sparkman, who felt bound to join the Russell oratorical tirades only for their own re-election purposes.

Russell had no doubts about the loyalty of the freshman senator from Texas, for one of the first decisions Lyndon Johnson made as a senator was to adopt Russell as his "Daddy." The flattery and attention Johnson showered upon the latest in his long line of political Daddies were well-received, and what pleased Russell most was the young Texan's apparent earnestness in declaring that Russell could win the Democratic Presidential nomination in 1952. Johnson was also a good audience for Russell's favorite stories, which concerned his wonderful mother who reared fifteen children on the thousand-acre farm, while her husband spent most of his time away serving as chief justice of the Georgia Supreme Court. Most important, Russell was grateful to have an energetic and bright ally in the fight ahead with the Truman Administration.

President Truman had dropped his first gauntlet in February 1948, when he sent his ten-point civil rights message to Congress. Then in his State of the Union Message in January 1949 he delineated a broad twenty-four-point Fair Deal program, calling for the repeal of the Taft-Hartley Act, compulsory health insurance, low-cost housing, extension of Social Security, an increase in the minimum wage law, and his unpassed civil rights program.

Johnson found himself torn between two Daddies, for Russell immediately blasted the Fair Deal, while Sam Rayburn assured Truman he would do his best to give the proposed legislation a fair hearing in the House. In fact, Mister Sam had acted in advance of the Message to "pull the teeth of the Rules Committee," where "Goober" Cox of Georgia, Judge Howard Smith of Virginia, Bill Colmer of Mississippi, and John Lyle of Texas had combined in the past to keep liberal bills from reaching the House floor. Sam's technique had been to get favorable House action for a new procedure, permitting committee chairmen to bring bills directly to the floor if the so-called traffic-directing Rules Committee failed to clear bills after holding them for twenty-one days.

Although Joe Martin, the House minority leader, glumly commented that "Mr. Truman ought to be able to get anything he wants from Congress," Senator Russell was not that pessimistic. From Daddy Rayburn, Johnson had learned that Truman and Vice President Barkley had been conferring with Charlie Watkins, the Senate's parliamentarian, to find a way to curtail Southern filibusters, and he passed along their plan of strategy to Daddy Russell.

In recent years Russell had been applying the filibustering tactics to motions to take up bills he opposed. As a result, his talking marathons had been directed at preventing passage of the motions to take up the bills and not at the bills themselves, giving him two filibustering opportunities on every civil rights proposal. What Truman and Barkley now decided was to attempt a rerun of the previous year's fight to extend Senate Rule XXII to motions as well as to actual bills. Rule XXII, known as the Cloture Rule, or Anti-Filibuster Rule, permitted an end to debate on a bill when two-thirds of the senators present on the floor voted to do so. The preceding year Senator Vandenberg, then the Senate's president *pro tem*, had ruled against the liberal Democrats and Senator Taft when he found for the Southern bloc that the procedures under Rule XXII were applicable solely to throttling debate on pending legislation but could not be applied to motions to take up bills.

The man who agreed to lead this second Truman fight for the Rule XXII change was "Silent Carl" Hayden, the chairman of the Senate Rules Committee and the Senate's power on pork-barrel public works appropriations. The last known time Hayden had given a Senate speech was back in the twenties, when he led a six-week filibuster against the construction of the Hoover Dam near Las Vegas. So there was enormous press interest on February 28, 1949, when word reached Capitol reporters that he planned to make a speech that afternoon.

Silent Carl made his proposal as scheduled, but Russell had his drawling stalwarts ready; and for ten days they talked day in and out with objections to the use of the Cloture Rule to cut off debate on motions. Johnson was eager to do his part, and despite the fact that he had yet to speak on the Senate floor, Russell gave him the spotlight on March 9. On the morning of that big day, the balding, charm-laden Georgian gathered reporters around himself and urged them to hear Johnson's maiden speech that afternoon if they were after a front-page story.

Newsmen knew this was an exaggeration, but they filled the press gallery to hear what Russell's protégé, Landslide Lyndon, had to say on cloture. What they heard was a Johnson attack on Truman that began by saying he was so lucky to be the White House occupant that he should shut up, and ended by declaring him bent on becoming a dictator.

"Mr. Truman went out to the people. He talked to them, telling them his views again and again," said Johnson. "I rode with him on that train awhile. I saw him before daybreak, waiting to speak to the people who gathered round the rear platform as early as six o'clock in the morning. I saw him still speaking far into the night. Over and over again I heard some of his close associates say, 'If only we had a few more weeks, there would be no doubt about the outcome.' "

Only the Southern senators stood in the way of Presidential dictatorship, he argued. "A man elevated to the office of the Presidency has virtually unlimited power of influence over his countrymen. His own personality is a force of great impact upon all the people of the nation and, in fact, upon the people of the world. Add to those powers directly all those less conspicuous powers of his aides, his administrative agencies, and the multitude of channels which feel his influence, and you have a force no other representative government has ever entrusted for long to one man.

"If on occasion, you grant to this titular head of government the further intoxicant of an overwhelming majority of loyal supporters in the Legislative Branch, then you have a force well-nigh irresistible.

"There is no one to check and no one to balance!"

Vice President Barkley brought matters to a climax the next day with his ruling that cloture could be invoked to choke off further debate on a motion to bring up a bill. Russell was prepared for him, for he had already discussed with Senator Vandenberg the union of their forces in appealing for a Senate vote against such a Barkley ruling. When Vandenberg rose and denounced the Barkley decision as an incorrect interpretation of Rule XXII, reporters conceded another victory for the Southern bloc. But Senator Taft challenged his Republican colleague's stand and began to round up Republicans to support Barkley.

The vote came after ten days of sharp debate. Vandenberg and Taft competed eagerly for Republican votes, and when the countdown came, Vandenberg had twenty-three Republicans to offer Russell, while Taft's army numbered only sixteen. The total vote was 46 for the Vandenberg-

Russell view and 41 for Taft's. Word was sent to President Truman, vacationing at Key West, Florida, and he knew that his Fair Deal was dead.

After its victory over Northern liberal Democrats and Taft Republicans, the Southern bloc met in celebration. Russell angrily argued that the opposition must be taught a lesson by tightening Rule XXII still further. Connally and George took the view that this was being needlessly vindictive, and both were surprised when freshman Johnson jumped into the argument with a strong defense of Russell's position.

A few days later he went further. The existing rule permitted an end to debate by the favorable vote of two-thirds of senators present on the floor. On March 15, 1949, Johnson cosponsored a rule change that would require the affirmative vote of two-thirds of the Senate's entire membership, or a minimum of sixty-six votes, to put cloture into effect. This further extension of power for the Southern bloc was voted by the Senate as its new Rule XXII.

Following the cloture fight, Johnson gave Russell ample proof that he was worthy of being his protégé. Not only did he speak out against Truman's civil rights plans, but he also supported the proposal of little Senator Allen Ellender of Louisiana, the cooking champion of the Senate as well as its leading globe-trotter at public expense, to cut back the existing low minimum wage.

In addition Johnson supported Senator Pat McCarran's anti-Eastern and anti-Southern European peoples Immigration Bill and voted to override the President's veto. Among bills he cosponsored was one to end federal control over natural gas prices; another would undo the Supreme Court's 1947 decision that gave "paramount rights in and power over" offshore oil-bearing tidelands to the federal government. Johnson also saw much merit in Senator Russell's version of civil rights, which was a proposal to move Southern Negroes to Northern states at federal expense. When President Truman expressed mild complaints to Rayburn about his protégé, Mister Sam replied defensively, "I doubt if a man can be a liberal senator from Texas."

Besides his troubles with the Senate over cloture, Truman faced a host of other serious problems in 1949. An economic backslide hit the nation early that year, and though unemployment rose sharply, Congress would not take swift emergency action. Nor would Congress act on his tax reform program. On of Truman's goals in the Eighty-first Congress was the revision of the tax laws in order to eliminate existing special favoritism. By knocking out tax havens and the major loopholes, his economists estimated, tax revenues would increase by four billion dollars.

Unfortunately for Truman, the major tax haven was the 27½ per cent depletion allowance to oil producers, which reduced their tax bills to an insignificant level and made millionaires a common sight in the industry. "The united stand of Texas congressmen put it on the books in the twenties," said Tom Connally. "We could have taken a 5 or 10 per cent figure, but we grabbed 27½ because we were not only hogs but the odd figure made it appear as though it was scientifically arrived at. Then after we forced it onto the Internal Revenue Code, it became political suicide for any congressman from any oil state to oppose the depletion allowance."

Connally, too busy working with Truman and the new Secretary of State Dean Acheson on the provisions of the European mutual-defense alliance, known as the North Atlantic Treaty Organization (NATO), had no time to defend the give-away to Texas oilmen in 1949. The industry did not forget this. But Johnson had time, and he acted as a man possessed in discussing the retention of the depletion allowance with Harry Byrd, who was chairman of the Senate Finance subcommittee on the Truman tax proposal. His talk was unnecessary, for the anti-labor, anti-Negro, anti-foreigner, anti-federal-government spending (except on defense), and anti-Truman Virginian had no intention of permitting the four-billion-dollar Truman tax bill to come to a vote.

In exchange for this promise by the apple-cheeked Old Dominion apple-grower, Johnson agreed to fall into line in attacking Truman on the Armed Services Committee, where he and Byrd served. When Truman's old Senate pal Mon Wallgren lost his re-election contest for governor of the state of Washington in November 1948, Truman appointed him chairman of the National Security Resources Board. Wallgren moved to the capital, took a suite at the Wardman Park Hotel, and proceeded to direct the President's advisory board, which was entrusted with the job of coordinating military, industrial, and civilian mobilization programs in case of war.

Byrd thought it would be uproariously humorous if, after letting Wallgren establish himself at the NSRB, the Senate humiliated him and Truman by not confirming his nomination. Vindictive attacks on Wallgren began flowing from Byrd's Armed Services subcommittee where the Wallgren nomination had gone for examination. Finally Wallgren could not stand the attacks, and he begged Truman to withdraw his nomination. Truman did this in May 1949, making the observation "there are too many birds [Byrds] in Congress." Afterward, Johnson explained to the Senate that he and Byrd had killed the nomination "because of his [Wallgren's] lack of a military background to cope with the many complex security questions." Truman reacted to such excuses by naming Dr. John Steelman, a labor-management conciliator, as acting head of the NSRB.

Lyndon Johnson played an even more central role in 1949 in humiliating Truman on another nomination. In June the President sent the Senate the nomination of Leland Olds to a third term as chairman of the Federal Power Commission. Since FPC matters fell into the bailiwick of the Senate

Interstate and Foreign Commerce Committee, the Olds nomination went
to big, burly Chairman Ed Johnson of that committee, who was no friend
of Truman.

When the Colorado senator permitted the summer to disappear without
holding hearings on the Olds nomination, Truman asked for an explanation, even though he knew full well what the cause was. The Natural Gas
Act of 1938 gave authority to the federal government to regulate the movement of natural gas in interstate commerce. Not much was done in this
area until 1947 when Leland Olds, after prodding by a Supreme Court
decision, decided that the FPC should regulate the sale and prices of natural
gas. This immediately aroused the fury of the big producers, who were
planning major price increases now that kitchen stoves in the East had been
converted to use natural gas. One FPC study revealed that as little an increase as five cents per one thousand cubic feet of natural gas would
boost the value of the Texas Panhandle holdings of Phillips Petroleum by
four hundred million dollars.

Other firms stood to gain corresponding hundreds of millions from price
increases to captive consumers, and an immense behind-the-scenes effort
developed to remove the influence of Olds, who was oriented in his views to
consumers. Back in 1944 Senator Ed Moore of Oklahoma, an oil producer
and know-nothing friend of Pappy O'Daniel, had fought against the Olds
renomination of that year. But Moore's fulminations were child's play compared with what the industry now planned for the short, bespectacled, mild
FPC chairman.

One effort was directed toward removing pricing authority from the
FPC; another, to smearing Olds and bringing about the Senate's rejection
of his nomination. Senator Robert Kerr, freshman from Oklahoma who
was under cursory Senate investigation for having ignored campaign expenditures laws, handled the first approach; Lyndon Johnson, the second.
That Kerr had a personal stake in the outcome did not stop him from
taking the lead, for the millions that his Kerr-McGee Oil Company stood
to gain overrode every other consideration. The Kerr Bill, cosponsored by
Lyndon Johnson, calling for the abolition of federal regulation of natural
gas prices, was soon introduced and sent to committee for hearings.
Eventually it was reported out and won Congressional approval, only to be
vetoed by President Truman.

As owners of the Big Inch and Little Inch natural gas pipelines, Brown
and Root had a big stake in the outcome of the Olds nomination. The industry was aware that Alvin Wirtz was attorney for Brown and Root and
Texas "Daddy" to the junior senator from Texas. With these facts fitting
into place, when Chairman Ed Johnson of the Commerce Committee replied to Truman that hearings on Olds would finally get under way after a
four-month delay, Texas producers smiled smugly on learning that Lyndon
Johnson would serve as chairman of the Olds Subcommittee, and every
member of his subcommittee favored the Kerr Bill.

Johnson started the hearing on September 27, 1949, and within a few days he had the national press in an uproar denouncing him for character assassination of the gentle, little man in the defendant's dock. The Milwaukee *Journal* declared, "Natural gas, and natural gas alone, is the point at issue in [the] outrageous attack on Olds' nomination. Communism and all other charges are pure smear tactics." The Washington *Post, New York Times*, Kansas City *Star*, and a host of other papers took a similar position. To the editor of the Denver *Post,* who wrote he was smearing Olds, Johnson sent a letter charging that the opposite was true, that Olds' friends were smearing him. He added in this letter that the reason President Truman had renominated Olds was that he was trying to curry political help from the "Communist American Labor Party" of New York which had sent Vito Marcantonio to Congress.

One afternoon in Austin, Ralph Yarborough, a leading Austin lawyer and formerly a presiding county judge and University of Texas Law School lecturer, paid a call on Alvin Wirtz at the law firm of Powell, Wirtz, and Rauhut. "I was sitting alongside Wirtz at his desk when the phone rang," said Yarborough. "Wirtz picked up the receiver and talked almost a half-hour; his talk consisting almost entirely of questions of the type a lawyer might ask in court. 'First, ask him this—,' he said into the phone. 'Then ask him if he—.' When he finally hung up, Wirtz told me that he was masterminding by long-distance Lyndon Johnson's hearings on Leland Olds' confirmation. He explained that Lyndon called him every day to report on proceedings and to get more questions to be thrown at Olds and other witnesses."

Johnson's technique was to hurry Olds' friends through their testimony and dismiss them without subcommittee questioning. On the other hand, opponents of Olds were helped with their rehearsed testimony whenever they faltered, and they were later asked one leading question after another, the answers to which were further condemnation of the FPC chairman. As for Olds, he was put through a handwringer to squeeze away his self-respect. Thirty-four witnesses came, most with a view to slandering Olds. Mrs. Roosevelt was one who testified in Olds' behalf, while President Truman blasted the "great corporations" intent on taking over the FPC and said that any Democrat opposing Olds "was a traitor to his party."

The object of this bullying subcommittee attack was a fifty-nine-year-old New Yorker who was educated at Amherst College, where his father had been president. Afterward, Olds became a Congregationalist minister, then labor editor of the *Federated Press* from 1922 to 1929, when Governor Franklin Roosevelt put him in charge of the New York State Power Authority. Following Olds' successful negotiation of the St. Lawrence Seaway Treaty Agreement with Canada, Roosevelt brought him into the FPC in 1939.

In the subcommittee confrontation, the Wirtz-Johnson line of questioning concentrated on Olds' years with the *Federated Press*. Evidence revealed that the *Federated Press* had sold its syndicated columns to any newspaper or magazine wishing to be a subscriber, and one of its one hundred subscribers was the Communist *Daily Worker*. This fact was a gold mine for setting off smearing charges against Olds in the subcommittee hearing. In addition Wirtz had carefully gone over the two thousand columns Olds had written for direct comments and innuendoes to tie him to the Communist party. Olds readily admitted that he had been a radical during the twenties, though never a Communist, and the gleanings Wirtz found in his writings included a concern that American churches suffered from "decay," that big business was growing bigger, and public ownership of railroads and utilities was superior and fairer to consumers than private ownership.

The Johnson-Olds exchanges were sharp and repetitive, as Johnson hammered away at these points. Failing to trap Olds into admitting he had probably been a Red, Johnson attempted to bully him into a statement that he still held his early views. Olds steadfastly denied he did, only to find the same question thrown at him again a few minutes later in a varied form. Finally Johnson ended the hearing and reported to the full committee that his seven-man subcommittee was in unanimous agreement that Olds should not be confirmed.

The fight now moved to the Senate Chamber, where Johnson found himself directing his first floor action. A quick count of members' views on Olds revealed that an overwhelming number opposed his confirmation. But Johnson would not call for an immediate vote because he wanted to savor the situation at least a few days from center stage.

He was not attacking Olds on behalf of Texas producers, he told his disbelieving colleagues. "Through eight elections in twelve years of public life, I have been opposed by the power and gas lobby of my state," he claimed. Anyone who examined Olds would know he was a dangerous radical. "Leland Olds had something in mind when he began to build his political empire across the nation; he had something in mind when he began to smear and besmirch all those who disagreed with him; he had something in mind when he chose to . . . plot a course toward confiscation and public ownership. . . . There were Americans of liberal views who expressed their thoughts and maintained their purpose without choosing—as did Leland Olds—to travel with those who proposed the Marxian [*sic*] answer. . . . He spoke from the same platform with Earl Browder [head of the American Communist party]."

Olds hated private industry, Johnson shouted. "Leland Olds' record is an uninterrupted tale of bias, prejudice, and hostility directed against the industry over which he seeks now to assume the powers of life and death." The pity of the matter, said Johnson, was that he had to do his duty even though it might cost him Administration support. "I do not relish disagreeing with my President and being unable to comply with the requirements of my party. But I can find no comfort in failing to do what I know in my mind is right." If only someone in the White House had done some homework, Johnson maintained, it would easily have been determined that Olds was not a loyal Democrat. "In 1924, Leland Olds left the Democratic party—if he was ever a member," thundered Johnson, "to vote for Senator Bob La Follette. And in 1928 Leland Olds left the Democratic party—if he was ever a member—to vote for Herbert Hoover." Yes, Olds was a living lie, a myth claiming to do "tireless battle with the dragons of 'special privilege,' " when all he was trying to do was to show other bureaucrats that they need merely to "jump on the power lobby to deserve confirmation." In summary, said Johnson, "Olds was . . . not a Communist" but "the line he followed, the phrases he used, the causes he espoused, resembled the party line today."

Senators Wayne Morse of Oregon, Hubert Humphrey of Minnesota, William Langer of North Dakota, Paul Douglas of Illinois, and George Aiken of Vermont defended Olds. But their cause was hopeless, and when the vote came shortly after midnight on October 12, the Senate rejected him by a tally of fifty-three to fifteen.

Sometime afterward Johnson's old college debating coach, Professor H. M. Greene, commented on his student's instinct for the jugular when he discovered he faced a weak opponent. "Well, I would say at times he would grow almost ruthless," Greene remarked. "When he knew he had the advantage, why, he could become ruthless."

A month after the Olds rejection Johnson went to Texas with Sam Rayburn for a "feast of reconciliation" with the various Democratic factions at the new Shamrock Hotel in Houston. Rayburn, who had not been pleased with the excesses of the Johnson attack on Olds, took his protégé along one afternoon on a visit to the campus of the University of Houston.

They stopped for a chat with the president of the university, who turned out to be E. E. Oberholtzer, former superintendent of Houston schools and the man to whom Johnson's Uncle George had appealed to give Lyndon a teaching job at Sam Houston High School.

Oberholtzer recalled the incident, and in feigned official seriousness asked if Johnson had finally returned to end his leave of absence and resume his debate coaching. "Go ahead and take it, Lyndon!" Rayburn urged him.

Chapter 33

Oɴ ᴊᴀɴᴜᴀʀʏ 6, 1950, Lyndon Johnson combined a celebration of his first anniversary as a senator with Sam Rayburn's sixty-eighth birthday when he and Wright Patman cosponsored a bipartisan luncheon in the Capitol for Mister Sam. For the occasion, Johnson invited President Truman, who came in good humor, despite the wreckage of his Fair Deal by a Democratic Congress and the recent loss of mainland China by Chiang Kai-shek's plundering warlords and Nationalist politicians to the vengeance-seeking Communist forces of Mao Tse-tung.

It was a decade earlier that Johnson had slipped President Roosevelt a Stetson to hand Rayburn as a birthday present, and he did the same now with Truman. Roosevelt had made little of that episode, but Truman centered his speech to the roomful of guests on the hat. "Sam is the only man I know who could stay in Washington over forty years and still wear the same size hat he wore when he came here," he twanged out in his hurried Ozark dialect. When Truman shaped the hat and set it on Rayburn's "head of hide," Mister Sam evoked thunderous laughter by pulling the hat down over his ears and eyes.

At that luncheon Truman found time to chide Johnson gingerly about his lack of loyalty to the Administration. Johnson disagreed with him, pointing out that he had been instrumental in getting Truman's friend Mon Wallgren approved as a member of the Federal Power Commission, after the Olds incident. Truman did not argue this point, though the price of Wallgren's confirmation had come high, for Wallgren had promised the Senate committee he would not fight against price increases requested by the industry.

"I'm loyal to you, Mister President," Johnson protested. "I'm just like the farmer back in the Hill Country where I come from who was hauled before the judge because he punched his wife and blacked her eyes. This farmer threw himself on the mercy of the court and said he beat his wife only to protect the reputation of the judge. 'Your honor,' he said, 'yesterday when I came before you, you called me a drunken bum. And when I got home and told my wife what you said, she got so mean and abusive about you for what you called me that I just couldn't set there and let her talk that way about you.'" Truman found the story funny, and the brutal Olds ouster was not mentioned again.

The aggressive recent additions to the United States Senate worked hard to establish reputations for themselves in a variety of specialties. Paul Douglas delved into unethical behavior of public officials and into the details of appropriations bills to fight for the elimination of fat and waste— "Oh, build me more stately dams and rivers and harbor projects, oh, my Congress," he chided the Army Corps of Engineers; Hubert Humphrey in endless talk was wrapping himself in the mantle of the poor and the minority groups; Estes Kefauver was carving out the area of organized crime; Bob Kerr was championing big pork-barrel appropriations and tax breaks for special interests; and old Matt Neely hoped to bring elected officials and self-government to the District of Columbia following an absence of almost eighty years.

After the Olds squabble, Johnson's mail from Texas revealed great emotional interest in witch-hunting among government employees for Communists. He realized this was a fertile field for gaining public attention, despite brickbats from some editors. But the area was soon pre-empted by a young Republican senator.

Forty-year-old Joseph McCarthy of Wisconsin, a restless and ambitious liberal Republican, was in a quandary regarding a means to lift himself out of the obscurity of a Senate nonentity. After Johnson's exhibition on the Senate floor to crush Leland Olds, McCarthy ran into George Dixon, syndicated political humor columnist and son-in-law of Senator Dennis Chavez, once a Senate clerk but now chairman of the Public Works Committee. In his melancholy manner McCarthy asked Dixon's advice on how to gain publicity, and Dixon suggested that he hire George Waters, the assistant city editor of the Washington *Times-Herald*.

McCarthy was scheduled to speak on February 9, 1950, at the Lincoln Day Dinner at Wheeling, West Virginia, under the sponsorship of the Ohio County Republican Women's Club; and Waters, his new publicity man, tied together paragraphs from a twelve-article vaguely written series on "Communists in the Federal Government" by Willard Edwards, a reporter for the Chicago *Tribune*. Three days after the Johnson-Patman luncheon for Rayburn, McCarthy took a leaf from the Olds hearings by astonishing Waters with a falsehood added to his speech that became the ad lib of the decade. "I have here in my hand a list of two hundred and five—a list of names that were made known to the Secretary of State as being members of the Communist party and who, nevertheless, are still working and shaping policy in the State Department," McCarthy charged in his nasal and ponderously weary delivery.

McCarthy had no list, but his fakery gained national headlines when President Truman vehemently denied the charge instead of ignoring his existence. After this McCarthy was off and running as the leader of the lunatic army to disrupt government service and policy during the next five years. When the McCarthy course was run, and the roadside lay strewn with destroyed lives, Johnson eulogized the enterprising Wisconsinite on the Senate floor in this fashion: "Joe McCarthy had strength, he had great courage, he had daring . . . There was a quality about the man which compelled respect."

Faced with the problem of staking out a specialty, Johnson fell back on his old standby—championing massive military mobilization and a sky darkened with military planes. Less than three weeks after McCarthy first opened the sewers of guilt by association, Johnson went to Atlantic City on February 28, 1950, for a speech to the American Association of School Administrators. Their concern at that time was a shortage of teachers and schools operating on double shifts, and though Johnson had been expected to talk about these problems as a former teacher, he chose as his subject, "Our National Security."

In his speech he condemned the nation and the Administration for not being aware that the survival of the country was at stake. "For five years we Americans perhaps have to some extent isolated ourselves behind the security of an atomic monopoly. We were tired from the exertion of war, weary of crisis. We concentrated our national energy and our national talent on our own comfort more than on our security." But the time had come to mobilize, "making full use of this nation's scientific and technological resources. . . . The facts are grim, but we must face them."

Several newspapers publicized his speech. However, his hope for national attention was not met; and, in fact, several Texas opponents sneeringly charged that he wanted everyone else forced into defense work, while he continued to concentrate on his radio station.

Fate gave Johnson another opportunity that summer. Almost five years had passed since the end of World War II, and in that time the Truman foreign policy had held firmly to the George Kennan plan for containment of Soviet communism in Europe. Greek-Turkish military and economic assistance under the Truman Doctrine had kept these countries solvent, and the puzzling closing of the borders by Communist Bulgaria, Albania, and Yugoslavia had dried up supplies for Red guerrillas inside Greece. Then had come the remarkably successful Marshall Plan to rehabilitate the economies of Western Europe at a cost to the American taxpayers of seventeen billion dollars. The Russians, noting a setback, reacted by closing Allied land routes to Berlin, a crisis Truman overcame by airlifting supplies to the beleaguered city until Stalin admitted defeat in the spring of 1949 and reopened the highways and train circuits to Berlin. That same year the North Atlantic Treaty Organization was fashioned as a deterrent to Soviet invasion of Western Europe, and Truman named General Eisenhower as NATO's Supreme Commander of Allied troops on the continent.

Although American foreign policy in Europe proved a brilliant success, there was little to cheer about in Asia since the end of World War II. Here the chief tasks were to tame the warring tendencies of the Japanese people, to push for an end of European colonialism, hand out economic aid to prevent the spread of communism, and end the civil war that was devastating China.

General MacArthur's remarkable skill as a military leader was almost overshadowed by his superb redirection and rehabilitation of postwar Japan. And with little protest from the British and Dutch Governments, American pressure brought about the liquidation of their colonial empires in southeast Asia. However, France would not grant independence to its Indochinese colony, arguing with United States State Department officers that to do so would encourage its African colonies to demand their independence, too. Other deficits were the Communist troubles in the Philippines, where the countryside was no longer safe for travelers, and the Korean Peninsula, where the Soviet forces held the northern half and refused to permit an election to unite the country.

China was the most urgent problem, but there was nothing Truman could do to save it for the West. Once the Japanese invaders surrendered in 1945 after seven years of war, smashing civil war had resumed between the Nationalists under Chiang Kai-shek and the Communists under Mao Tse-tung. In an effort to bring peace to tortured China, Truman had dispatched General George Marshall to the Asiatic mainland to end the military confrontations. Marshall achieved paper success in 1946 by arranging a cease-fire and battlefield truces, plus an agreement by the Reds to recognize Chiang as the head of the Chinese Government. But this was illusory, for full-scale civil war soon broke out again.

American aid continued to pour into China for Chiang Kai-shek, but despite two billion dollars worth of economic and military aid Chiang's faltering regime failed to improve the economy in the areas it controlled. Nor was it able to gain popular support. Wallowing in corruption and brutality, his government offered the people no more hope than the equally barbarous Communist crew. When the Communists took Peking in January 1949, the Chiang regime was riding an irreversible course to total defeat. That December when he fled with a few thousand followers to Formosa, the major postwar victory of the Communists had arrived.

While great anxiety spread over the Truman Administration as to the significance of the Chinese Communist victory, many Republicans and some Democrats attempted to pin the blame personally on Truman. One who did was a high- and thin-shouldered young congressman from Massachusetts named John Kennedy. Although Truman was willing to forgive Johnson for his many attacks on his Administration, this Kennedy attack was never forgiven.

Johnson's opportunity to carve out his own Senate area of action came finally as a result of trouble on a little-known peninsula on the Asiatic mainland. This was the divided country of Korea, a place that the Joint

Chiefs of Staff and General MacArthur had excluded from the vital American defense perimeter. MacArthur's exclusions encompassed far more than Korea, for, as he put it, any American who advocated a land war in Asia should have his head examined.

Korea, which juts south into the Yellow Sea and touches Manchuria in the north at the Yalu River, had led such an unobtrusive existence for centuries that it was known as the Hermit Kingdom. However, trouble arose in 1894 when Japan fought China and won the "complete independence" of Korea from the Manchu Dynasty. Then a decade later, control over Korea became the direct cause of the Russo-Japanese War of 1904-1905. Following this conflict, Japan, the new world power, annexed Korea.

One of President Roosevelt's World War II goals was the formation of an independent Korea, and at Potsdam President Truman believed he had Red Dictator Joseph Stalin's word that this would occur. Since the Soviet Union was not yet a participant in the war against Japan, Stalin had no objection to American occupation of Korea at the close of hostilities in order to accept the surrender of Japanese troops stationed there. However, Truman's military advisers committed a blunder when they insisted there were not sufficient American troops in that general area to handle the surrender. On this basis, Truman agreed to a temporary division of Korea at the Thirty-Eighth Parallel, with American troops handling the surrender below that latitudinal line and the Russians above it. Afterward there would be a joint trusteeship pending a free election and unification.

The maddening problem was that once the Russians accepted the surrender of the Japanese forces, they clamped a blackout curtain at the Thirty-Eighth Parallel and proceeded to establish a Communist dictatorship in the north. When diplomatic efforts by Truman failed to move Stalin, the President induced the UN to hold an election in South Korea in May 1948, and old Syngman Rhee, a militant nationalist and a Princeton graduate, became President of the Republic of South Korea (ROK).

Syngman Rhee ran a quasi-dictatorship, where opponents were imprisoned or vanished completely and where his forty-five-thousand-man police force was under orders to treat crowds at political meetings of other parties like insects. In September 1948 he ordered the slaughter of twelve thousand left-wing Koreans at Yosu, and at Cheju his forces slaughtered an estimated fifteen thousand.

While the Truman Administration was aware of these atrocities, it did not divulge them to Congressional committees or to the public. Nor did it relate the vast corruption of the Rhee regime and its lack of interest in needed social reforms. Complaining one time to Senator Harley Kilgore of West Virginia, a special friend from his Senate days, Truman railed at Rhee but concluded, "We haven't any choice except to support him because he's our S. O. B."

Rhee created a special problem because South Korea had a population of twenty million and North Korea had only ten million; and Rhee believed his destiny called for war to reunite his land by using his larger force. If he should embark on an invasion of the north, Truman's concern was that he might drag the United States along with him. This would be the tail wagging the dog, or a gross interference in American foreign policy, for as General Eisenhower, Admiral William Leahy, Admiral Chester Nimitz, and General Carl Spaatz had written him, "The Joint Chiefs of Staff consider that, from the standpoint of military security, the United States has little strategic interest . . . in Korea." Nevertheless, Truman believed he had no choice other than to strengthen Rhee, so he ordered the American Army to train a sixty-five-thousand-man ROK Army, and he won Congressional appropriations of one billion dollars for economic aid.

By 1950 both Rhee and his northern Communist counterpart were conducting testing raids across the border, and a few pitched battles ensued. The climax came on June 24.

That day Truman dedicated the new Friendship Airport south of Baltimore and then headed for his home in Independence, Missouri, for talks with his brother Vivian relating to the sale of part of their mother's farm to construct a shopping center. It was almost midnight that Saturday evening when Secretary of State Acheson telephoned with news that North Koreans had crossed the Thirty-Eighth Parallel in force. Truman agreed that Acheson should ask the UN Security Council to meet the next day to consider a condemnation of the Reds and order their withdrawal.

There was a point in calling for the meeting because the Soviet delegation had walked out of the Security Council in protest of its failure to oust Nationalist China (Formosa) from the permanent seat for China on the Security Council and replace her with Communist China. With the Soviets absent and unable to cast a paralyzing veto, the Security Council approved what Acheson requested by a vote of nine to zero.

It was Truman's belief from the reports he received that the ROK Army was well motivated and trained. But when it stampeded at the sight of Red tank battalions, Truman ordered General MacArthur to take time away from his occupation duties in Japan to direct American air and naval forces against the invaders. When this failed to slow up the North Koreans, Truman committed American ground forces to the struggle on June 30, under the guise that they were a United Nations army. This was now the war on the Asian mainland his military advisers had so strongly opposed; but Truman believed that an actual invasion of a country under American guidance by an enemy army of several hundred thousand soldiers could not be ignored.

Lyndon Johnson wasted little time after American ground involvement in Korea began before making his move to run the "Truman Committee of the Korean Conflict." From his front-row Senate Chamber desk, he rose one afternoon in July 1950 and proposed the establishment of a

Preparedness Investigating Subcommittee in the Senate Armed Services Committee. He had talked it over beforehand with Senator Russell and asked his help in convincing Chairman Millard Tydings to give him the subcommittee despite his lack of seniority.

When Tydings first heard of Johnson's resolution, he liked the idea so much that he decided to take charge of the subcommittee and run it as chairman. With a war on—or a "police action" as Truman called it—the Preparedness Subcommittee was bound to get front-page attention by holding hearings on the lack of preparedness of the Defense Department for the conflict and by exposing the usual foul-up in defense supply programs and war-plant management. For a week Tydings consulted with Russell on the hearings he would hold and what staff aides to employ. Then one day he saw Johnson in the Marble Room off the Senate floor and he gasped like a man in pain when he told the young Texan he would give the subcommittee to him.

There was ample reason for Tydings' grim appearance and for his decision. He knew by then that he was in the fight of his political life. Two terms a member of the House, then for the next twenty-four years a United States senator, the tall, lean, angular-faced eastern shore Marylander had successfully come through the effort of powerful Franklin Roosevelt to purge him in 1938. Ironically, the menace in 1950 was an upstart member of the Republican Senate minority named Joe McCarthy.

Tydings' troubles had developed a short time before the outbreak of the Korean fighting when President Truman asked Senator Tom Connally's help to save the morale of the State Department. Connally held Secretary of State Acheson in high esteem, even though he knew that Acheson smirked privately at him, and he considered approaches his Foreign Policy Committee might use to protect Acheson and his Department from the daily McCarthy attacks. In Connally's view the best approach was the direct one of having a Foreign Relations Subcommittee investigate McCarthy's charge that two hundred and five Communist party members were State Department employees; and the ablest man to run the investigation was Tydings, then fourth in seniority on the committee.

Connally selected Tydings because the Marylander's right-wing conservatism would seemingly make it impossible for McCarthy to question his motives. In the New Deal era Tydings had voted against unemployment relief, low-cost housing, farm relief, the NYA, and anti-poll-tax bills; during World War II he opposed Lend-Lease aid to the Soviet Union and fought for higher taxes on low incomes; and after the war he sprinkled the pages of the *Congressional Record* with a wild lot of anti-civil rights, anti-labor, anti-farm cooperatives, and anti-federal-spending speeches. Yet none of this past record helped him when he confronted an alley fighter like McCarthy, who had not the slightest intention of letting anyone stunt the great career he saw ahead.

When Tydings requested that McCarthy supply him with the list of two hundred and five names, "the junior senator from Wisconsin," as McCarthy invariably referred to himself, could not do so because he had no list. In a belligerent tone he replied that he could not trust the list to a Red stooge like Tydings. But, said McCarthy to reporters, he might tell the name of the "top Russian espionage agent in the United States." Pressed for the name, he said it was Owen Lattimore, professor at Johns Hopkins; and he added that Lattimore was also a long-time adviser to the State Department.

Lattimore, an authority on the Far East, was then on a UN mission to Afghanistan, but he flew back to Washington to defend himself before the Tydings Subcommittee. Here, with the brilliant help of his attorney, Abe Fortas, Lyndon Johnson's Washington lawyer-adviser, Lattimore battled McCarthy's charge of evidence from his writings and from the testimony of witnesses. Yet McCarthy managed to come out of it an even bigger hero to his growing following by labeling Tydings' clearance of Lattimore and the State Department a Red plot.

Because of the frenzy he was able to whip up every time he made charges, the Senate Republican leadership recognized McCarthyism as a potentially powerful electioneering weapon for the coming 1950 campaigns, and they joined McCarthy in attacking the subcommittee's report. Senator Bourke Hickenlooper of Iowa, who served on the subcommittee, took the lead, and he was seconded by Senate Minority Leader Kenneth Wherry of Nebraska, blubbery Karl Mundt of South Dakota, and Robert Taft.

It was in July 1950 that Tydings learned McCarthy planned to invade Maryland during the fall campaign in a well-financed effort to unseat him. For this reason Tydings turned over the Preparedness Subcommittee to Lyndon Johnson, and made his own plans for survival. But he had no chance, even though the Republicans put up dull John Butler, who worked for the City Service Commission in Baltimore. A massive distribution of faked photographs showing Tydings with known Communists and doctored letters and broadcasting records doomed the four-term senator, and he lost by fifty thousand votes.

When Johnson took over the Preparedness Subcommittee on July 17, 1950, Doris Fleeson, syndicated political columnist, whom he had cultivated, predicted:

Because an obscure Senator named Harry Truman parlayed an innocuous resolution for similar policing of World War II into the Presidency of the United States, unusual interest attaches both to the [Johnson] subcommittee plans and to the personality of its chairman. It is already being said that Lyndon Johnson wants to be President, which is legal. It can be added that ever since he entered the House in 1938 [sic] his bright brown eyes have been fixed on America's defenses from a front-row seat.

To make certain he would run his own show, Johnson won permission from downcast Tydings to name the three Democratic members of the subcommittee. He realized that if he should name Tydings, Russell, or Byrd, he would have to take a back seat even though he was chairman. So the Democratic makeup of the Preparedness Subcommittee came to consist of Johnson and the three freshmen who had arrived with him in the Class of 1948—Estes Kefauver, Virgil Chapman, and Lester Hunt. Then when Styles Bridges, the ranking Republican on the Armed Services Committee, named himself, toothy Leverett Saltonstall, and pugnacious Wayne Morse of Oregon as the Republican complement of the subcommittee, Johnson was ready to begin operations.

From the start Johnson believed he could control all three Democrats, plus Saltonstall. This left two doubtfuls: Bridges, who never forgot he belonged to the opposition, and Morse, whose political purpose seemed to be that of making his fellow senators angry as he rasped them too frequently with the most ungenerous tongue in the Upper Chamber. Fortunately for other senators, Morse telegraphed his intention to let out a withering blast by wearing a flower in his buttonhole. The sight of the flower was a warning that he planned to speak before the Senate adjourned for the day.

That several of Johnson's friends were Morse's enemies did not foretell a warm relationship between the two. For instance, Abe Fortas, who had saved Johnson's political existence by inducing Justice Hugo Black to sign a strange ruling that made possible his victory over Coke Stevenson in 1948, enjoyed a name-calling feud with Morse that went back to World War II. At that time Morse was serving on the War Labor Board, and Fortas, as the Undersecretary of the Interior, had ignored the WLB's wage freeze and increased take-home pay for John L. Lewis' United Mine Workers. For this, Morse had labeled Fortas a "trickster" and a man who engaged in "fixing" tactics; and Fortas returned the language in kind by describing Morse as "unscrupulous, undignified, and irrational." In a letter to Morse, Fortas wrote: "It is useless to argue with a man who conducts himself as if he were bereft of his senses."

Before getting down to the task of finding flaws in the Administration's handling of defense matters, Johnson took his subcommittee to the White House to seek advice from the old master of defense production investigating. (Johnson had already received several tips from Stuart Symington, his friend inside the Administration, as to which activities were most vulnerable.) Truman was pleased with Johnson's thoughtfulness and promised him in a voice choked with emotion the fullest cooperation of the entire Executive Branch. Truman also reminisced to the seven about his old committee and recalled how important it had been for him to read the voluminous reports of the Civil War Congress' Joint Committee on the Conduct of the War, for this Congressional committee had hamstrung Lincoln and prolonged the war by directly interfering with military strategy and operations. "So don't be 'Monday morning quarterbacks' by meddling in strategy and policy," he warned. When the group marched out, Truman called Johnson back. "Make sure you've got the support of the minority members of your committee on everything you do. And make sure all your reports are unanimous—otherwise the Senate isn't going to listen to you."

Afterward, Johnson met with reporters and told them that he was motivated solely by the national interest in undertaking hearings and investigations. Wrote one observer: "Tall, talkative Lyndon B. Johnson uses picturesque profane Texas talk to deny he started the committee for political reasons."

Again he selected Donald Cook, the "tough-talking, fast-moving" counsel of his World War II House Naval Affairs Subcommittee, as his top lawyer. Since World War II Cook had directed the Office of Alien Property, spent two years in private practice, then returned to the SEC as one of its five commissioners. Cook had not wanted to leave the SEC, where he had now risen to vice chairman, but Johnson's request was his command, and the most lenient conditions he could get from Johnson were to continue working days at the SEC and then spend his evenings and weekends as the subcommittee's counsel. Johnson's promise to use his influence later with Truman to boost Cook into the post of chairman of the SEC was enough to induce Cook to take on this rigorous routine.

Besides Cook, Johnson appointed Horace Busby to shift to writing chores and administrative work for the subcommittee. He also named Lyon Tayler as chief investigator and ordered Walter Jenkins to find the time from his duties in Johnson's Senate office and as a checker of time sales activities of the Johnson radio station to help write the subcommittee's monthly report. In time the Johnson subcommittee employed twenty staff members and several unpaid advisers.

"Johnson was rough on all the wheeler-dealers he hired on his subcommittee staff," said one Senate employee. "He screamed at them any time he felt like it and no one ever answered back. They all had the hope that he would help them into top jobs afterward. There was John Connally, who became Secretary of the Navy; and Ken BeLieu, an Undersecretary of the Navy. As for Cook, through his influence with Truman Johnson boosted him into the chairman's seat at the SEC in 1952, later helped him become chairman of American Electric Power Company and offered him the Cabinet post of Secretary of the Treasury."

Even before the Preparedness Subcommittee held its first meeting on July 31, 1950, Johnson was highly critical of the President for not mobilizing the nation and installing World War II controls to fight the North Koreans. Johnson was especially vehement about Truman's failure to call up the National Guard and reserves immediately, because they were trained and ready for action. In a time of war, he chided the Administration, these men had no business being kept on a weekend and summer encampment routine. At the very time he demanded Korean action for the National

Guard, President Truman had already begun to call up National Guard units. In less than a year 110,000 men from 1,457 units were in action.

Johnson also demanded that strict price and wage controls go into effect. Truman had wanted to ask Congress for a price control law, but when Sam Rayburn reminded him how unpopular price limitations by government agencies had been during World War II, he dropped this idea. Instead he asked Congress for priority and allocations control over raw materials, for a boost in taxes, and a restriction of consumer credit.

The first witness called to testify before the Preparedness Subcommittee was Defense Secretary Louis Johnson, who had served as an Assistant Secretary of War during Roosevelt's second term and as Truman's financial angel during the 1948 campaign. Louis Johnson was an easy man to criticize. First of all, it was generally accepted that Truman had ousted Jim Forrestal to repay Louis Johnson for his help in 1948. According to many Washington correspondents, this firing was said to have brought on Forrestal's mental collapse and finally his suicide in May 1949. The truth was that Forrestal's insanity was known to his friends and to Truman long before Louis Johnson appeared on the scene, and this condition had forced his retirement.

Louis Johnson was also an easy mark for other reasons. He despised Secretary of State Acheson and believed that many in his department were not trustworthy. The harm in this was that he turned on his barrage of contempt for Acheson before Congressional hearings and to individual congressmen over the telephone. But Louis Johnson's real Achilles heel was his insistence on a cut in the defense budget in the months before the outbreak of fighting in Korea. In January 1950 he told reporters that a budget of thirteen and a half billion dollars was sufficient for the next fiscal year beginning in July, even though the Joint Chiefs of Staff had set twenty billion as a minimum. The Defense Secretary's smaller budget had produced such sharp wrangles with Congressional committees that in order to win approval he had dispatched General Eisenhower to Capitol Hill to tell the committees that the budget was "fairly well on the line between economy and security."

Once the war began, Louis Johnson became the scapegoat, with the argument that if he had asked for six billions more, the invasion would not have occurred. His loss of face was so complete that, despite his position in the Cabinet, the Preparedness Subcommittee did not treat him with any show of respect. In fact when Truman fired him a month later, Lyndon Johnson told reporters that pressure from his subcommittee had forced Truman's hand.

Actually, when the Korean War was only a few weeks old, Truman made the quick judgment that Louis Johnson would have to be removed from the Pentagon. One afternoon in July he asked his daughter Margaret to drive him to Leesburg, Virginia, about fifty miles from Blair House, the official Presidential residence while the White House was being rebuilt. General George Marshall was living in retirement in Leesburg after serving two years as Truman's third Secretary of State, and Truman had come to discuss national problems and nudge him toward becoming Secretary of Defense. Margaret Truman remembered her father's vexatious back-seat driving on the way to Leesburg and back to Washington. "He lets you pass a corner and then says, 'You should have turned there!' " she complained. But Truman completed his mission, and Marshall replaced Louis Johnson in September 1950.

As watchdog over the Korean War defense program, Johnson's Preparedness Subcommittee turned out forty-six unanimously approved reports which covered a wide range of defense activities from the letting of contracts to the shipment of war products. His first investigation centered on the Munitions Board, a staff agency to the Secretary of Defense, which controlled strategic and critical material stockpiling, coordinated interservice logistics, established procurement and production schedules, handled industrial mobilization, and planned economic warfare against American enemies.

Johnson went after the Munitions Board because of its questionable program of selling government-owned factories and facilities from its national industrial reserve. Only a few years earlier he had pestered government administrators to dispose of surplus rubber plants to concerns that promised him personally they would construct new rubber factories in Texas. Now he wanted to know if the Munitions Board had sanctioned the sale and dismantling of so many rubber plants that the country faced a rubber shortage.

The hardest part of the investigation was getting it started. A letter to Hubert E. Howard, Munitions Board chairman, asking him to cooperate with the subcommittee's investigators, went unanswered. Succeeding letters also were ignored. Finally Johnson's rage, following three weeks of such tactics, produced the first recognition of the subcommittee's existence.

Johnson was determined that Howard must pay for his inaction, and his report of September 19 made clear his wholesale condemnation of the Munitions Board. "If the diligence with which the Munitions Board addressed itself to our inquiry is any measure of the manner in which it attends to its other duties," read one scathing conclusion, "its competence would seem to leave something to be desired." Johnson went on to charge that "the vast organization dealing with surplus disposal, rubber production, and other matters made critical by the Korean War was proceeding at certain points on the continuing basis of the postwar policy of general demobilization."

Arthur Krock, editorial-page columnist with *The New York Times,* played a strange role over the years with Joseph Kennedy to promote the elder Kennedy's political ambitions for his son Jack. Krock was also useful to Johnson. Following the publication of this first subcommittee report,

Krock hailed it as "a model of its kind in that (1) it is unaffected by partisan or political considerations; (2) goes to the heart of the subject of military surplus disposal of rubber stockpiling; (3) gives specific instances of sleeping bureaucracy and the successful methods employed to awaken it."

In establishing his own Truman Committee, Truman had said at the time: "We haven't any axes to grind, nor any sacred cows. This won't be a whitewash or a witch hunt." He had also said that his committee would not operate merely to get some headlines. On reading the Preparedness Subcommittee's first report, while resting in his underwear in his second-floor front bedroom in Blair House, Truman concluded that Johnson had diligently met his own criteria. His first order of business afterward was to give Munitions Board Chairman Hubert Howard his walking papers. Next came a directive to his National Security Resources Board chairman, former Air Force Secretary Stuart Symington, to halt the sale of so-called surplus rubber plants and give priority to the expansion of synthetic rubber facilities. Johnson's subcommittee press agents later claimed that this first report and Truman's order to increase synthetic rubber production saved the federal government a billion dollars because an abundance of synthetic rubber was later produced at low prices.

After this first report was issued, the possibility arose that it might be the last because of the sudden turn in the two months of fighting in Korea. In the first few days of their all-out invasion of South Korea, the North Korean Communists had killed, wounded, or captured half the ROK Army of ninety-six thousand men, and most of the rest had deserted. MacArthur had only four part-strength infantry divisions on occupation duty in Japan, and he threw two into battle with the North Korean invaders, even though the Americans were outnumbered by one hundred to one.

At the beginning of August an American disaster approached, for American troops were clinging precariously to the beachhead of Pusan, at the bottom of the Korean peninsula. It was now that MacArthur proposed one of the most daring maneuvers in military history. Opposed by the Joint Chiefs of Staff, but with the blessing of Truman, MacArthur led an amphibious landing at Inchon, on the west Korean coast near the ROK capital of Seoul, halfway around the peninsula almost back to the Thirty-Eighth Parallel. The Inchon landing came on September 15 and was a remarkable success. Within days an eastward race across the Korean waist choked off all supplies heading south for the invaders below the Thirty-Eighth Parallel; and without food and ammunition one hundred and thirty thousand North Koreans surrendered.

At the outset Truman had accepted the position of Secretary of the Army Frank Pace that the American goal was to expel the aggressor from South Korea. But when South Korea was cleared of the enemy, and Syngman Rhee had returned to Seoul, Truman was no longer satisfied with his original objective.

Had he been willing to settle for the Pace position, the war would have been over at this point. However, his Missouri anger was aroused because the United States had been forced into a conflict only five years after World War II; and as he explained to Senator Connally, he was enlarging his objective so that the United States would "convince the North Koreans they are vanquished and that further aggression doesn't pay." Orders went to MacArthur on October 2 to cross the Thirty-Eighth Parallel and not to halt until he had captured all of North Korea to the Yalu River border with Manchuria. A major blunder had begun.

With an irrepressible drive to the Yalu well under way, Truman flew to Wake Island to meet General MacArthur on October 15. Truman's second thoughts about the drive north were revealed by one question he put worriedly to the general: "What are the chances for Chinese or Soviet interference in the Korean fighting?"

MacArthur replied that he had examined the various intelligence reports from the State Department, the CIA, and his own headquarters staff and found nothing in them to advise of probable direct military action by either Communist nation.

Seated at the meeting table in the Wake Island tent was a Truman adviser who agreed with the general. He was a bald young man named Dean Rusk, whom Truman had elevated to Assistant Secretary of State for Far Eastern Affairs from his post as director of the State Department's Office of United Nations Affairs. The promotion had come to Rusk even though Truman knew of his membership in the Forrestal–Loy Henderson group that had operated to hamstring him on the establishment of a Jewish state in Palestine.

It was Rusk who actually had the correct answer to the question Truman had thrown at MacArthur. Only a few weeks earlier the Indian Ambassador to Red China had informed Rusk that the Chinese Army Chief of Staff had told him on September 25, 1950, that China would not "sit back with folded hands and let the Americans come up to the [Sino-Korean Yalu] border." However, Rusk did not bring up this warning at the Wake Conference. "I was among those who thought they would not come in," he said afterward. "I was wrong."

Unaware of this note to Rusk, MacArthur blandly gave Truman assurances that despite a Red Chinese force of three hundred thousand men just across the Yalu, the Chinese would not enter the fighting. "If they tried to get down to Pyongyang [the capital of North Korea], there would be the greatest slaughter," he said like a Delphian oracle. As for the Russians, MacArthur said that they could not bring in many soldiers in time, nor were their planes and pilots of good quality.

On November 26 Truman's worst fears were realized when two hundred thousand Chinese soldiers crossed into North Korea from Manchuria and quickly enveloped the first American forces that had reached the Yalu. Soon the two American armies—the Eighth Army under General Walton Walker and the X Corps under General Ned Almond—began their headlong flight south toward the Thirty-Eighth Parallel. The fact that Walker and Almond were not on speaking terms did not help the situation. For a time it seemed that the Americans would again be pushed back to the Pusan beachhead, but the line eventually stabilized near the border latitude. Truman's angry comment was: "I traveled fourteen thousand miles to Wake Island to get a lot of misinformation."

Hysteria flamed across the nation when the Chinese hordes began their intervention and American casualty rates skyrocketed. Johnson thought the moment ripe for another of his total mobilization speeches and he spoke on "The War for Survival" on the Senate floor on December 12. "This is not World War II all over again," he said to the packed Senate press gallery, whose members had been alerted to "an important Johnson speech" due that afternoon. "This is a struggle without precedence in human experience," he insisted. "The American people are fed up with double talk in Washington. . . . We have committed ourselves to a policy of not committing ourselves. What is the result? For the common defense we have thrown up a chicken-wire fence, not a wall of armed might. . . .

"Is this the hour of our nation's twilight, the last fading hour of light before an endless night shall envelop us and all the Western world? This is a question which we still have in our power to answer. If we delay longer, we can expect nothing but darkness and defeat and desolation."

In Johnson's view the United States stood at its most dangerous moment. "We are at war not merely with Communist China, but with all the military strength and both the physical and the human resources behind the Iron Curtain. Our primary and immediate goal in this war is survival." The nation must become an armed camp, he repeated his favorite theme. There must be "immediate, full mobilization of our available manpower" and a "prompt mobilization of our economy" with nondefense spending cut to the bone.

This "chicken-wire" national defense speech attracted the attention of several large daily newspapers, but if Johnson thought that Truman would call him over to the White House and tell him he was accepting his armed-camp scheme he waited in vain. First of all, Truman had enormous contempt for "two-bit strategists" in Congress, and his view of the chairmen of the Armed Services Committees was that they were swollen-headed men who "had to have seventeen-gun salutes, parades, etc., as often as they could find excuses to visit Army posts and Navy bases." Second, Truman was too embroiled with the press at the time because of a deliberate editorial misquoting of his remarks at his November 30, 1950, news conference to make it appear that he planned to use nuclear weapons in the Korean War. Third, he was having trouble with MacArthur, who in his anxiety had forgotten his basic principle of avoiding a land war in Asia and demanded that the war be extended to China. Fourth, Republican Congressional leaders were making life uncomfortable for Truman by their increasing personal attacks.

Nor were these all. Truman was still mourning the death of his boyhood friend and press secretary, Charles Ross, who died at his job on December 5. In addition, he was spending late evenings and early mornings writing wrathful longhand letters to those who had attacked him or his family. One went to a music critic at the Washington *Post* who had reviewed the singing concert of Margaret Truman and came to the conclusion that "she communicates almost nothing of the music she presents." This Truman reply, which became a collector's item, was eventually sold for fifteen thousand dollars. As General Marshall assured Truman, "The only thing the *Post* critic didn't criticize was the varnish on the piano." In another letter Truman wrote that he would not appoint John L. Lewis as a "dog catcher."

"My God!" cried his friend Sam Rayburn. "Why doesn't someone down there in the White House hide all the lead pencils from Harry?"

Chapter 34

As the korean War grew in unpopularity, the Democratic party was forced on the defensive; yet the personal stock of Lyndon Johnson rose sharply. It was the war's erosive effect on the Democratic leadership in the Senate that gave him the early opening he sought into the Upper Chamber's power hierarchy. The majority leader, whip, and committee chairmen, who had seemed indestructible, were suddenly outside of politics in 1950, and there were vacancies to be filled.

With a party so obviously divided by sectional stands on economic and civil rights questions, the Democrats for decades had experienced tremors when it came to voting on their Senate leaders. In 1949 the hope of the victorious Senate Democrats had been to elect a majority leader without any show of acrimony. But Northern liberals insisted on a man who favored the Truman Fair Deal and civil rights program, Southern conservatives rebelled and sought one of their own to run for the job. Said "Maggie" Magnuson, "But the Southerners knew they couldn't elect a Southern majority leader because of the civil rights issue, and at the same time the liberals were in a similar power standoff. So both groups went on a hunt for a compromise 'in-between' senator, preferably someone from a border state like Kentucky, where Alben Barkley, the last majority leader, came from, or someone from the West."

Unfortunately, an in-between senator was not easy to find in January 1949, and when liberal Scott Lucas let it be known that he was available, the Democratic caucus elevated him from whip to majority leader. Francis "Frank" Myers, a Pennsylvania Fair Dealer, emerged from the caucus as majority whip, giving the Southern bloc a double defeat. However, the Southern bloc immediately expressed a rationalized but insincere fondness for Lucas, remembering that he had opposed a strong civil rights plank in the 1948 Democratic Convention's party platform and conveniently forgetting that he had voted for a permanent FEPC, an anti-poll-tax bill, and to sustain President Truman's veto of the Taft-Hartley Act. The Southern bloc pointed out that Myers had also favored a weak civil rights plank in 1948.

The Lucas-Myers leadership did not prove to be the catastrophe some Southerners had predicted, because of Southern domination of the major Senate committees, Northern Republican eagerness to combine with the Southerners against the Truman Fair Deal, and Senator Russell's parliamentary schemes to thwart the bringing of civil rights measures to the Senate floor.

During 1949 and 1950 tall, nattily dressed Majority Leader Scott Lucas, whose joys in life were fishing and hunting vacations, keeping abreast of Major League baseball scores, and attending American Legion conventions, dutifully trooped each Monday morning to the White House for sad legislative leaders' meetings with the President. Here the monotony of his recital on his lack of progress in furthering the Administration's domestic program became a painful ordeal for both him and Truman. Twice he had to be hospitalized in exhausted frustration.

Lucas was not a man to call names even in his frustration. But Les Biffle, Truman's spy in the Upper Chamber as secretary of the Senate, fanned the flames of Truman's quick temper with frequent telephone observations of what the Southern bloc and Senator Pat McCarran, who was Truman's pet hate in the Senate, were doing to damage his program. Biffle, who used his sumptuous office dining room located across the hall from the Senate Chamber for lavish luncheons for top-ranking senators and as a late-afternoon and evening saloon, picked up much valuable information while acting as a gracious host. It was Truman's belief that when Lucas and Myers gave him a figure denoting the maximum support he could expect from the Senate, Biffle would be able to round up an additional ten.

By the time a few months passed and the Fair Deal lay in its bed of quicksand, Lucas asked Truman to cut his "must" legislative program in order to make the record look better. In a threatening mood Truman sent word to Congress that he might "even get on the train again and make another tour around the country." Truman did go out West in a political swing in the spring of 1950 in order to arouse citizens to demand action from Congress, but he failed to communicate what the specific bills were that he wanted Congress to pass, though he drew loud cheers in calling his legislative opponents "reactionaries, greedy men and calamity howlers."

The Korean War was President Truman's worst communications failure. Herbert Hoover, brought back to the living world by Truman's generosity in naming him head of a commission to investigate government efficiency, repaid him by calling for a pullout from Korea. Joseph Kennedy, using his status as a former ambassador, spoke out for an American withdrawal from Asia and Europe. On an opposite tack, Lyndon Johnson was hitting at Truman for a "makeshift mobilization" and Senator Wayne Morse, who also favored an enlarged war, declared that Truman had made "a mistake not to permit the Chiang Government to proceed with guerrilla warfare in China and to bottle up his forces on Formosa."

An inability on the part of President Truman to explain satisfactorily why the United States was fighting in wintry Korea and suffering mounting casualties made sizeable Republican gains inevitable in the 1950 Congressional elections. He could point out, as he did in private to British Prime Minister Clement Attlee, that the real aggressor in Korea was the USSR, reacting from its containment in Europe by attempting to spread communism by force in Asia. But the Soviet Union was not directly involved in the war, except to supply matériel and military advisers, and it would be difficult to state this properly to the American people, who saw Chinese and North Koreans shooting and killing their sons. The low national morale that already existed would have dropped even further had publicity been given to the frank observation of General Omar Bradley, chairman of the Joint Chiefs of Staff, that this was "the wrong war, at the wrong place, at the wrong time and with the wrong enemy."

Fearing that a public explanation of the Soviet role would only serve to encourage "preventive war" addicts to shout for World War III with the USSR, Truman attempted a "stand up now and be counted" justification for American participation, which later became known as the "domino theory." As he explained to various congressmen the reason for the large number of American casualties far across the Pacific, South Korea was like a small lead domino in a row of upright dominoes. If this first domino were pushed over, he said, the domino behind it would then topple, and this would continue until all the dominoes fell. So, he asserted, the job was to keep this first small domino from being pushed over if you didn't want all the dominoes to fall. If Korea dropped, he said, the Chinese Communists would then invade French Indochina, then British Hongkong, then Malaya. In this step-by-step aggression, the fight would eventually reach the shores of the United States. Therefore, if Americans wanted to stave off eventual direct confrontation with the enemy on United States soil, they must prevent the smallest domino from falling at the outset, Truman completed his explanation.

"This was a scary thought," said Senator Tom Connally, "but it didn't contain a seed of logic. In the first place, China, the biggest domino, had already fallen, and this had not made us quake. If we subscribed to the domino theory, we should have sent ten million American boys to fight on the side of Chiang Kai-shek's armies in the civil war of 1946–1949, which involved a half billion Chinese. The unvarnished truth was that we were in a war because the North Koreans had invaded our ward in force, and we didn't believe we would have to commit many American troops. And we were still fighting at the end of 1950 only because we had invaded North Korea after we cleared South Korea of Communist soldiers. Truman's real goal there was not to keep the Reds from taking over the Republic of South Korea, but as he said in a March 20, 1951, statement that he never made public, he wanted to establish 'a unified, independent and democratic state' in all of Korea—north as well as south. This was impossible even in South Korea so long as Syngman Rhee was around and as long as the people were so grounded in corruption."

The United States Senate, which had recessed on September 23, 1950, to go out on the campaign trail, returned to Washington on November 27, and the chief order of Democratic business was the selection of a new majority leader and whip.

Qualitatively, the unpopular Korean War and spreading McCarthyism had wiped out the Senate Democratic leadership, plus Armed Services Committee Chairman Tydings and Labor Committee Chairman Elbert Thomas. While the Eighty-First Senate in 1949 had revealed a Democratic majority of twelve, the 1950 elections had reduced the Democrats to a forty-nine to forty-seven lead. Majority Leader Lucas had lost by almost three hundred thousand votes to former House member Everett Dirksen, and Majority Whip Myers went under by more than one hundred thousand votes to James "Big Red" Duff, the liberal Republican governor of Pennsylvania. A newcomer from California who had won because he had out-McCarthied Senator McCarthy in running against Representative Helen Gahagan Douglas was thirty-seven-year-old Representative Richard Nixon. Nixon had made his reputation as a member of the House Un-American Activities Committee, taking the lead in the Alger Hiss affair. Sam Rayburn warned senators who came to convivial meetings of his Board of Education not to trust young Nixon, whom he called "that ugly man with the chinkapin [dwarf chestnut] eyes."

This time the choice of the Southern bloc for majority leader was Ernest McFarland from Arizona, a round-cheeked, heavyset man who came to the Senate in 1941 after serving six years as Pinal County judge in the old Apache country. Although McFarland maintained that he had an 85 per cent party regularity, the Southerners noted that he had opposed the FEPC, the health insurance proposal of Federal Security Administrator Oscar Ewing, and the Brannan Farm Plan of Secretary of Agriculture Charles Brannan, which would pay farmers the difference between the actual market prices they received and parity support prices.

McFarland was known for the flower he wore in his lapel and the friendly smile that sat on his thick features, as well as for his repetitious call for an increase in the price of gold from thirty-five dollars an ounce to fifty-six dollars. Silent Carl Hayden, his fellow Arizonian and long ago editor of the Tombstone *Gazette,* considered it a pleasure to work with Senator Russell to accumulate support in McFarland's behalf, and a few weeks after his effort began, Hayden said that thirty-five senators had agreed to "a spontaneous draft of Ernie." He and Russell wanted Lucas to resign as majority leader before his term expired in order to install McFarland before some of their strength evaporated. But Lucas, who had been pushed about and denied support for almost two years, stubbornly refused to quit.

This extension of time pleased the Senate liberals, who were trying to develop support for another Westerner, Joseph O'Mahoney of Wyoming, a short, slight man with an angry disposition when he suspected favoritism toward big business. O'Mahoney's chief supporters were three: Senators Lester Hunt of Wyoming, Brien McMahon of Connecticut, and Clinton Anderson of New Mexico. Late evening meetings at McMahon's house on Woodland Drive, down the street from Tom Connally's place, witnessed the impassioned talks of Paul Douglas to the sixteen to nineteen senators who came, that O'Mahoney was needed as majority leader in order "to save the soul of the Democratic party."

But the Southern and Western blocs for McFarland were too strong even to consider a last-minute liberal bloc offer of an O'Mahoney withdrawal in exchange for the naming of a few additional liberals to membership on the Senate Democratic Policy Committee. As a result, when the Democratic caucus met on January 2, 1951, a smiling McFarland accepted slaps on the back and handshakes as the new majority leader. At this point the liberals would have settled for John Sparkman of Alabama for majority whip. However, friends of Lyndon Johnson, led by Bob Kerr of Oklahoma, a loud and demanding extrovert, had deluged McFarland in the weeks before the caucus to accept Johnson as whip, until McFarland broke his silence to say magnanimously that he had no objection. But Ernie's smile faded because Lyndon Johnson walked out of the caucus selected by acclamation as the number two man in the Senate's hierarchy, after only two years as a member.

Johnson's immediate rewards as majority whip were the prestige of having his own private office in the Capitol (in addition to his office in the Senate Office Building across the street), a special staff, and the privilege of occupying the front row, center aisle desk on the Senate floor whenever McFarland could not be present. The private office was hardly more than a tiny hideaway; the staff consisted of only the secretary to the majority, Felton "Skeeter" Johnston, and two clerks; and McFarland was seldom absent. Nor was the whip an important functionary, for his chief task was to collect information showing how each Democratic senator planned to vote on the major legislation. Skeeter Johnston, who amassed such data, merely turned it over to Lyndon Johnson, who in turn passed the records along to McFarland. If an effort was undertaken to request or pressure an occasional senator to change his vote, this task belonged to McFarland. Some senators, like gruff, barrel-chested little Pat McCarran of Nevada, gave strict orders to Skeeter Johnston never to ask them for their position on an issue.

But if the immediate rewards were small, the long-term gains were important. Individual senators began seeking him out to gain his aid in convincing McFarland to call their bills off the Senate Calendar and bring them to the Senate floor for consideration. The number of such requests became considerable during the session. In addition McFarland took him on occasion to the legislative leaders' meetings with the President, and he gained a more comprehensive insight into the meaning of legislation from the point of view of the Executive Branch.

At no time, however, did Johnson permit his minor duties as whip to interfere with his work as chairman of the Preparedness Subcommittee. This was where the publicity lay, and as the subcommittee hacked away at the Truman Administration's handling of defense and war matters, his reporter friends on *Time, Newsweek,* and the Sunday *New York Times Magazine* were able to convince their editors that he deserved special attention. *Collier's* and the *Saturday Evening Post* spread his name through profile articles, though his good friend Les Carpenter angered him by writing in *Collier's* that he was a Vice-Presidential possibility for 1952. What should have aroused his displeasure in the Carpenter article was his portrayal as an unpleasant boss, a loud show-off, and a man who was so nervous that when he worried he developed "an irritating rash on his hands and certain internal disorders." The *Saturday Evening Post* article claimed that he would not think about any subject other than politics while in Washington, refusing to be "trapped into thinking about or discussing sports, literature, the stage, the movies or anything else in the world of recreation." The *Post* also called him a vicious automobile driver who screamed, "Get out of the way!" at other drivers; a man whose wife seemingly ran a radio station in far-off Austin "by remote control"; and a politician who Stuart Symington said was "a man of destiny."

Public accounts of his Preparedness Investigating Subcommittee were invariably glowing. He "has already shaken Washington" with his "running investigation of the Defense program," reported *Nation,* which characterized him as "mildmannered but determined." *Newsweek* hailed him as the country's "watchdog-in-chief," and, to the vast amusement of his colleagues, who knew him as a man who scratched himself and belched whenever the impulse overtook him and as a man on the make with loud profanity and impatience, reported that "his manner is quiet and gentle, and everything he does, he does with great deliberation and care." *Business Week* looked into his future and said that "at forty-two, Johnson stands where Truman did at fifty-seven." *Nation's Business* portrayed him as probing the "extravagant use of manpower for noncombat needs, military air junkets, rent gouging, waste in construction and procurement." Although *Nation's Business* lauded him for saving taxpayers a billion dollars, Johnson later asserted that during the Korean War his subcommittee, operating under a total budget of only two hundred and seventy-five thousand dollars, had saved the Treasury five billions.

Among his colleagues there was general scoffing about the subcommittee's value, though there was admiration for Johnson's ability to gain publicity. One such senator was Harley Kilgore of West Virginia, a close Truman friend, who despised Johnson for his attacks on the Fair Deal and the Administration's handling of defense matters. Kilgore, a member of the Appropriations Subcommittee on the Defense Department's budget, once told a reporter: "Lyndon had only about twenty people, including typists and Donald Cook and David Ginsberg, digging up material for the Preparedness Subcommittee. At the same time, the General Accounting Office, which is a part of the Legislative Branch, had more than five thousand accountants, auditors, lawyers, and investigators doing the same work. Here was the GAO supplying the Appropriations Committee with immensely valuable and detailed accounts of illegal and extravagant spending of federal money, which we on the committee used without fanfare, while the piddling work of the Preparedness Subcommittee frequently landed on the front pages. Lyndon got his greatest publicity exposing a Texas farmer who bought a million dollars worth of government surplus airplane parts for six-and-a-half dollars and resold them to the Air Force for sixty-three thousand dollars. This was part of a GAO report."

Besides learning how to get a few headlines and many news stories, Johnson also had the opportunity in April 1951 to learn from Senator Russell how to usurp power from powerful colleagues. The issue was General MacArthur. Once back to the Thirty-Eighth Parallel, MacArthur had chafed about what he called the "Accordion War," with each side in turn advancing until it outran its supply line and then retreating on the defensive. To reporters and congressmen, MacArthur declared, "There is no substitute for victory," and he demanded that Truman turn over the direction of the war to him. What he would do, said MacArthur, would be to establish a blockade of the coast of China, an air bombardment of her factories, the use of Chiang Kai-shek's Formosa-based troops in Korea, and an invasion of South China by Chiang's soldiers. This effort to force Truman's hand by continued insubordination reached a climax on April 11 when the President called a news conference at 1 A.M. to announce he was firing MacArthur as a Constitutional necessity in order to maintain Presidential primacy over the military.

The national uproar against Truman for his action was enormous, and his concern was that MacArthur would prove a major disruptive force on his return home after an absence of fourteen years. This appeared to be borne out by the size of the crowds that cheered him in his coast to coast triumphant tour. It was Tom Connally's delight that MacArthur suffered his only embarrassment in Dallas. While traveling in a motorcade between Love Field and the city's center, the smart-looking motorcycle policemen made a sharp turn at one corner while MacArthur's car continued straight ahead. The general was finally found walking about in downtown Dallas in search of his hotel.

In Washington MacArthur moved a joint session of Congress to eye-wiping and nose-blowing with his emotional address. "As chairman of the Senate Foreign Relations Committee," said Connally, "I planned to hold hearings on the MacArthur dismissal because I figured that day after day hearings would dissipate the high public regard for him and he would become a bore. Dick Russell heard about it, and he argued that since the military aspects of the MacArthur squabble were involved along with foreign policy, Foreign Relations should hold joint hearings with his Armed Services Committee. I agreed, and we worked out an arrangement to alternate daily serving as chairman of the joint hearings of our committees. But no matter how early I came each day to the hearing room, Russell was already occupying the chairman's seat with Lyndon Johnson close to him. It would have taken a public row to budge Russell, and he knew I wouldn't because it would make me look petty when we had a serious matter to consider in the joint hearings. So Russell hogged the MacArthur hearings from beginning to end. The worst part about it was that the Republican senators present—Knowland, Styles Bridges, and Hickenlooper—were vicious in picking on Administration witnesses, especially on General Omar Bradley, and Russell did nothing to keep them in line."

It was also in 1951 that Lyndon Johnson first divulged publicly his desire to become President of the United States. This came about that spring when I interviewed him for an article I was writing on the whips of Congress. Each house of Congress had, of course, two whips—one for each party—and the men involved were Johnson and Saltonstall in the Senate and Democrat Percy Priest and Republican Leslie Arends in the House.

Johnson was outraged when he learned he would be only one of four men featured in the article. "The whip's job is a nothing job," he told me as we walked toward the buttoned, black-leather-upholstered furniture in the President's Room off the Senate floor. From Lincoln until Franklin Roosevelt, Presidents had come to this room during the closing hours of each session to sign last-minute bills.

"Skeeter Johnston can keep track of the way the Democratic senators are going to vote without wasting any of my time," said Johnson. He sat with his knees pressed against mine, a hand clutching my lapel, and his nose only inches away from my nose. When he leaned forward, I leaned backward at an uncomfortable angle. "Hell," Johnson asked loudly, "why don't you write a whole big article on just me alone?"

"What would the pitch of an article on you be?" I countered from my strange sitting position. "That you might be a Vice-Presidential candidate for 1952?"

Johnson sat back and glanced about the empty room. "Vice President, hell!" he whispered. "Who wants that?" He regained his voice. "President! That's the angle you want to write about me."

I smiled at the obvious impossibility of Johnson's ever becoming President.

"You can build up to it by saying how I run both houses of Congress right now," Johnson urged, leaning forward again so that I was bent backward precipitously once more.

From my uncomfortable position, I asked for an explanation of this extraordinary remark.

"Well, right here in the Senate I have to do all of Boob McFarland's work because he can't do any of it," Johnson began. "And then every afternoon I go over to Sam Rayburn's place. He tells me all about the problems he's facing in the House, and I tell him how to handle them. So that's how come I'm running everything here in the Capitol," he finished, gripping me above the knee.

Chapter 35

IT WAS DURING its final few years that the Truman Administration grew chaotic and endangered the continuing rule of the Democratic party. A moment to pull itself together came in July 1951, when Soviet dictator Joseph Stalin agreed to permit the North Koreans to negotiate an armistice at Kaesong, near the Thirty-Eighth Parallel. However, Truman stubbornly refused to budge on one of the proposed Red armistice conditions. This was a term calling for a total exchange of prisoners of war, and to Truman this smacked of forced repatriation. His insistence that not a single prisoner being held in South Korea be sent above the demarcation line against his will meant that the war would continue throughout the rest of his Presidential period. Following Truman's decision that democracy be applied to prisoners of war, eighty thousand American casualties occurred, and domestic displeasure with the war added immensely to the chaos in Washington.

These last few Truman years placed his Administration among the most investigated Administrations in American history. Senator Clyde Hoey of North Carolina, never without his high, stiff-winged collar and early-nineteenth-century clothes, continued to hit at the "Five-Per-Centers," or the peddlers of influence who claimed they knew how to get government contracts or licenses. Republicans began to beat the political drums with charges that Truman cronies were getting "mink coats and deep freezes" for their inside help. Democratic Senators J. William Fulbright and Paul Douglas went after the strange loans and deals made by the Reconstruction Finance Corporation, and Fulbright titled his report "Favoritism and Influence." Truman finally put Stuart Symington in charge of the RFC and ordered him to clean up the place. Then Republican Senator John Williams of Delaware made a one-man show of tax scandals, and his revelations involved a large number of employees of the Bureau of Internal Revenue, including its top administrators. When the House Judiciary Committee began investigating the Justice Department and Attorney General Howard McGrath would not cooperate, Truman fired him. Senator Pat McCarran, silver-haired, silver-tongued, silver-minded Nevadan, punched at Marshall Plan aid from his perch as chairman of the Senate's special "watchdog committee" on foreign aid. McCarran was also hauling Administration officials and others before his Internal Security Subcommittee to undergo grillings regarding possible Communist affiliations. He and McCarthy were now competitors.

Then there was the Senate's Preparedness Subcommittee, with its chairman, Lyndon Johnson, deriding the Administration's air war program as being fraught with "abuse, misuse, and disuse of power," casting aspersions on the three service chiefs, and denouncing the stockpiling of strategic commodities program for not stockpiling enough. Later examination revealed that many stockpiling administrators were overbuying to help their friends in industry get rid of surpluses and create artificial shortages in commercial markets. Sam Rayburn's angry comment about what was happening sounded like a call for sanity: "Everyone down my way says Washington is talking too much. They're tired of this investigation and that investigation. There's a time to fish and a time to mend nets."

While Johnson's national star was rising, his home base security in Texas underwent a jolting decline in 1951. Alvin Wirtz passed his sixty-third birthday in May, and despite his joking comment to associates in his law firm that he could draw Social Security in two years, his existence continued as hectic as it had been during the last three decades. This year's political troubles within the state were more serious than usual for him and for his political protégé, Lyndon Johnson, but he expected to come out on top, as he had with such regularity in the past.

Besides putting pressure on hundreds of local politicians to keep them working in Johnson's behalf, Wirtz was also working late for Brown and Root. George Brown, the ruddy-faced, blue-eyed driving force of the aggressive concern, faced labor problems from more than a score of trouble-making unions in 1951, and Wirtz was given orders to handle this situation. As a lawyer Wirtz took a legal approach and filed suit against twenty-one AFL unions. This case plus others, all piled on top of his political activities, depleted his energy. On October 27, badly in need of recreation, Wirtz went to a football game involving his alma mater, the University of Texas, against Rice. The excitement and the noisy crowd triggered a heart attack and he suffered the indignity of dying in public. Ed "The Talking Horse" Clark offered Wirtz's eulogy: "He could tell Lyndon something was silly. No one could do that now. He molded him."

Without Texas Daddy Wirtz, for the first time in his fourteen years in Congress Johnson was abruptly forced to handle his own state political relations. Wirtz's death came at a most inopportune time, too, because Johnson knew he was no match for the young, power-hungry, money-hungry, handsome man who occupied the State Mansion in Austin.

Two years earlier, when Beauford Jester was found dead on a train on July 11, 1949, his forty-two-year-old lieutenant governor, Allan Shivers of Port Arthur, had moved into the governor's chair. Shivers, whose father had been a moneyless district judge, had a grounding both in politics and in a desire to become wealthy and powerful that was the equal of Lyndon Johnson's. He had toiled in a sawmill after school at thirteen; worked his way through college selling shoes; and Lady Bird's 1933 University of Texas yearbook, *The Cactus,* ran a picture of the tall law student and noted that he was president of the student assembly. When Shivers went to the state senate in 1934 as the youngest member in history, he followed a straight, ultraconservative line on social legislation, while making himself the champion of a proposal to extend the boundary of Texas twenty-seven miles into the Gulf of Mexico. Shivers married well—the daughter of John Shary of Shary Enterprises—and became the general manager of his father-in-law's businesses, which included banking, cattle raising, real estate, citrus orchards, and newspaper publishing. It was after an outstanding two-year record in Africa and Europe as a World War II soldier that Shivers ran in 1946 for lieutenant governor and won a run-off Democratic primary contest against Boyce House, the Fort Worth reporter-humorist. Then three years later, after putting Beauford Jester's reactionary "People's Path" program through the state senate, he became the state's top politician following Jester's fatal heart attack.

Shivers rushed swiftly to consolidate his power before old Texas politicians like Alvin Wirtz and Maury Maverick could cut him down to size. Only months after he became governor, Shivers organized a massive purge of party workers that went deep into the precinct levels. As he expressed his philosophy, "Every active political enemy of mine should expect, and receive, the works."

By September 1950, when the Governor's State Convention convened, said Sam Rayburn, the delegates were so cowed you could almost hear them "moo." Jester and Coke Stevenson before him had followed the practice of permitting the caucus in each state senate district to choose its members—one male and one female—to serve on the State Democratic Executive Committee. Shivers, however, demanded total loyalty on that committee, and he assigned Jake Pickle, who had left the Johnson camp to serve as Shivers' "thinking and planning" aide, to screen each caucus choice like an FBI agent. Anyone not meeting the criteria of 100 per cent loyalty had his name crossed out, and Shivers wrote in a name of his own choosing. Then at the Governor's Convention, which Pickle also organized for Shivers by filling it with Shivercrats from the precincts and counties, the governor's hand-picked State Democratic Executive Committee and his platform won swift approval from the rubber-stamp convention.

Ever-loyal Administration Democrat Sam Rayburn perceived the menace to the national party that Shivers might present in 1952. Shivers had been elected chairman of the Southern Governors' Conference of states'-righters and was also chairman of the Interstate Oil Compact Commission, which wanted Congress to overturn the Supreme Court's decision favoring paramount rights to the federal government over submerged offshore lands. To Mister Sam it was apparent that if a Republican Presidential nominee took Shiver's position on both these issues, Shivers could take Texas into the Republican column.

It was after Wirtz's death that Johnson, too, grew concerned about Shivers, but his worry was that the governor might try to unseat him in the Senate in 1954. This brought him into seeking a private talk with Rayburn away from the Capitol on what to do about the Shivers menace. To entreaties that the speaker come to his house one evening, Rayburn agreed only on the condition that Lyndon promised "not to turn on that blamed television set."

The strategy they developed was to operate at two levels: Rayburn was to find a liberal, energetic man to run for governor against Shivers, who was counting on no opposition; while Johnson would work personally to change Shivers' views and bring him into line with the national party.

"Sam Rayburn and R. T. Craig approached me in February 1952," said Ralph Yarborough. "Right off, they tried to pressure me to run for governor against Allan Shivers, but I didn't want to because I intended to run for attorney general, an office I believed I could win. They persisted and persisted, and finally I agreed when they assured me of all the financial help I might need. I knew they didn't think I could win because I wasn't well known throughout the state. However, I went down and filed after their promise of campaign funds."

It was Shivers' turn now to show his political muscles. "I was coming up for re-election in 1952," said Senator Tom Connally, "and I kept hearing that Shivers was planning to contest me in the primary. This made no sense because he couldn't hold on to his power over the state Democratic machinery if he went to Washington. Then I found out that Shivers was really intending to get me out of the Senate, but he planned to do it by using Price Daniel, who was the state's attorney general.

"When I came home to look into my prospects, friends told me that Price Daniel had got word from Shivers to run against me. Shivers had promised him the support of the state Democratic organization, and for insurance Daniel had gone ahead to organize his forty deputy attorneys around the state as his local campaign managers against me. I also found out that Lyndon Johnson had been over to talk with Shivers and promised to support Price Daniel. It wasn't many years before that Lyndon sent me a copy of a speech he made in which he said, 'Every Texan thrills when from the gallery he watches Tom Connally lead debates on American foreign policy in the Senate.' Now, he was apparently no longer thrilled. Some reporters told me that Lyndon wanted me out of the Senate so that he wouldn't have to be called 'the junior Senator from Texas' in floor debate, but I preferred to believe that Shivers had made him shiver. I finally concluded that renomination would not be worth what a state campaign would cost me and my friends in money, toil, and in the tax it would impose on my strength and health. So after being in Congress since 1917, I announced my retirement from office."

Neither Johnson nor Rayburn showed up when the springtime state convention met at San Antonio on May 27, 1952. It would have embarrassed Mister Sam if he had attended even as an observer, for Shivers was as solidly in command as a dictator in a totalitarian country. Of the 1,152 precinct conventions that had been held at the outset, 1,009 were Shivercrat gatherings; at the next level, 254 county conventions, the Texas loyalist liberals had controlled only 26; and now at the state show 3,500 of the 4,000 delegates were behind Shivers. Asked if he would support Rayburn for the Democratic Presidential nomination, Shivers gave the sarcastic reply: "I would like to know what his views are." To this, Wright Patman said, "Sam Rayburn's views were well known long before the governor was born."

The convention issue between the Shivercrats and the loyalists was an old one—should the Texas delegation to the national convention be forced to agree to support whatever national ticket was nominated? John D. Cofer, one of Johnson's principal attorneys in his 1948 post-election fight with Coke Stevenson, served as loyalist spokesman now that Wirtz was gone.

But his demand that all delegates to the Chicago convention take a loyalty pledge triggered succeeding waves of catcalls from Shivercrats. Fiery Maury Maverick, continuing symbol of liberalism in Texas, made an attempt to repeat Cofer's demand and was drowned out by massive booing. And like the Maverick of old, he reacted by leading his small army from the convention hall with pauses en route for fistfights and head-pounding of Shivercrats with convention banners. "We will throw you out of Chicago!" he warned the laughing Shivercrats as he led his contingent into a driving rain. Shivers considered the loyalist departure an opportunity to declare that he intended to "keep the Democratic party out of the hands of the ultraliberals, left-wing self-seekers."

"After the state convention," said a later associate of Lyndon Johnson, "Shivers got on a plane and flew to Washington, because he was worried about what Maverick might do in Chicago, where Sam Rayburn would be the permanent chairman of the convention and old Maverick friends controlled the machinery. Lyndon wasn't the type who would go to the airport to meet his own mother, but he was there to meet Shivers' plane. And he spent days shepherding Shivers around Washington for talks with people on Capitol Hill and at the Democratic National Committee.

"For someone who was supposed to be a smart politician, Lyndon failed completely to realize that Shivers was scared to death that he and his hand-picked delegation might not be seated at Chicago. If he wasn't, he would be ruined in Texas. Even the oldtimers who sat around the courthouses and whittled all day would have said, 'If he ain't got sense to be seated, he ain't got sense to be governor.' But Lyndon did not see this because he was thinking only about himself in 1954. So he was as charming and as helpful as he could be to Shivers.

"Unfortunately, Rayburn could not be convinced by Shivers' palaver that he intended to support the party's nominees, and the discussion ended without any Rayburn promise to help him be seated in Chicago. Nor was Sam pleased when the pile of Texas Dixiecrats began drifting into the convention hotels when he went out to Chicago. This time, as in Washington, Lyndon heeded Shivers' command and met his plane at the Chicago Midway Airport. Then he rushed him to the Blackstone Hotel for another talk with Rayburn, who had assented only a few hours earlier to the seating of the Maverick-Cofer delegation. Lyndon pleaded with him to change his mind, and finally Sam said he would when Shivers made a solemn oath to be faithful to the party's nominees.

"There was still much work for Lyndon to do in Shivers' behalf, because Maverick intended to fight to the finish. Both the Maverick and Shivers delegations were really armies, for each had forty-two Congressional District delegates, twenty delegates at large, and sixty-two alternates. Every night the rich Shivers gang parked in the best hotels in big private suites, while the Maverick crowd jammed into small rooms at cheaper hotels, but during the day both armies were at the convention hall, where the creden-

tials committee listened to their arguments. Here Shivers promised to abide
by the majority vote at the convention and support the party's candidates,
and the committee chairman, Senator Earle Clements of Kentucky, who was
a pal of Lyndon, pushed through a unanimous committee vote to seat
Shivers.

"This riled Maury Maverick, who know Shivers was lying, and on July 21
when the convention opened and his delegation was ordered upstairs into
the gallery, he denounced Frank McKinney, the national chairman, for
'bootlicking the Dixiecrats.' But McKinney thought he had Shivers covered
on opening day when the convention approved a resolution binding all
delegations to a loyalty pledge. However, Shivers weaseled out of this later
by claiming he could not agree to a pledge that would bind the September
Governor's Convention. So when he returned to Austin, he let out noise
that he had defeated the entire national convention. He said he had gone to
Chicago 'unpledged and unbowed, and I still am.' Sam Rayburn was the
angriest of all because of the personal treachery practiced on him."

There was more important work at the convention than the seating or un-
seating of the Shivercrats. A party ticket had to be selected, and Johnson
was put into the uncomfortable position of being a Senator Russell supporter at the same time that Senator Mike Monroney of Oklahoma was
leading the drive for Sam Rayburn's nomination. On the first ballot fourteen
candidates collected a total of 1,229 votes, with Senator Estes Kefauver
emerging first with 340; Illinois' Governor Adlai Stevenson second with
273; and Russell third with 268. These top three gained on the second
ballot, but the contest was actually over before the third ballot got under
way, when President Truman flew to Chicago and scolded party leaders for
their failure to put over his choice, Governor Stevenson, as the party
standard bearer. Once this conversation ended, Stevenson leaped to a total
617½ votes and the Presidential nomination on the third ballot, while
Kefauver receded to 275½ and Russell to 261. Senator John Sparkman of
Alabama went on the ticket as the Vice-Presidential nominee.

Acting out of concern that Shivers might yet run against him in 1954
unless he continued to appease the governor, Johnson's troubles were only
beginning after Shivers reneged on his pledge of party loyalty to Credentials
Committee Chairman Earle Clements in Chicago. Energetic Ralph Yarborough, in his gubernatorial campaign against Shivers, was telling campaign crowds he was a "Sam Rayburn Democrat." Johnson knew that this
would offend Shivers, and he asked Mister Sam to repudiate the man he
had asked to run. Rayburn would not do this, though he backed off from
Yarborough in a far more telling way. "Rayburn and Craig had solemnly
promised me campaign funds," said Yarborough. "But they failed to raise
a dime for me. I was entirely on my own, without money, and almost unknown."

Proof that Rayburn was not raising money for Yarborough pleased

Shivers, who hoped to cream the Austin lawyer with his own lavish campaign and ring the death knell of Texas liberals. But his pleasure turned to wild anger when the Texas Election Bureau announced the vote late Saturday, July 26, 1952. On learning that Yarborough had won an unbelievable 36 per cent, Shivers bellowed at his campaign aides: "That jerk shouldn't have got more than 20 per cent."

Johnson's appeasement of Shivers extended also into that fall's Presidential campaign between Adlai Stevenson and General Eisenhower. The warm-grinning general, who might have had the Democratic nomination in 1948, removed himself from any political role only to surface in 1952 as a Republican. The only time he had voted was in 1944, when he cast a ballot for Franklin Roosevelt. In 1949 Senator Henry Cabot Lodge, convinced that Senator Taft was a frozen isolationist, had unsuccessfully sought his removal as chairman of the Senate Republican Policy Committee. After that, fearful that Taft might become President in 1952, Lodge began the process of wooing General Eisenhower in order to induce him to seek the Republican nomination. This involved a trip to France where Eisenhower served as Supreme Commander of the Allied Powers in Europe to implement NATO's mutual military defense force. Lodge and other travelers painted a horrifying picture of the future, should isolationist Taft direct American foreign policy, and begged Ike to save the Free World. The general played hard to convince, though he later admitted he decided to run when Sam Rayburn's friend, Jacqueline Cochran, flew to France to show him movies of a fifty-thousand-person crowd cheering "Ike for President" at a midnight rally in New York.

The Taft forces had no intention of fainting at the sight of amateur politician Eisenhower, and by convention time Taft counted almost the necessary six hundred and four votes in his corner. It was at this point that the Eisenhower strategists devised a plan to undo Taft's delegates; and the route chosen was to prevent the seating of enough Taft delegations to swing the nomination for the general. As a test case, Texas became a crucial state. Earlier in the spring, Democrats for Eisenhower invaded the Republican precinct, county, and state conventions, and Donnybrooks were the order of the day as Republican regulars sought to maintain their long-held power. Two delegations roared into Chicago early in July—one for Taft and one for Ike—and each claiming to represent Texas Republicans. The outcome depended on which candidate's backers made the most promises to delegates about future patronage appointments and pork-barrel projects. Which side won this struggle became clear when the convention voted to seat the Eisenhower delegations from Texas and Georgia. At the end of the first ballot on the Presidential nomination, a bitter Taft heard the announcement that he trailed Ike by 595 to 500. Then before a second ballot began, a shift of Minnesota's 19 votes to the general gave him the nomination. Senator Richard Nixon became his running mate after Nixon's backers lied to Eisenhower that he was forty-two years old instead of thirty-nine.

With his own renomination as governor out of the way, Allan Shivers decided to get his pound of flesh from the Democratic party for attempting to control him at Chicago. In a message to Governor Stevenson he demanded to be told how the Democratic nominee stood on the Supreme Court's Tidelands decision of June 5, 1950, which stated that the federal government possessed paramount rights to the submerged lands off Louisiana and Texas. Stevenson suggested that Shivers visit him in Springfield, Illinois, on August 23; and here, without any of his characteristic flashes of wit, he bluntly told the Texan he supported the Court's decision.

This was precisely what Shivers had expected him to say, for he had already determined to support Eisenhower and needed a public excuse. In his keynote speech to the September Governor's Convention at Amarillo on September 9, he denounced the Stevenson-Sparkman ticket and told the head-nodding delegates that they would still be Democrats in good standing if they voted for Eisenhower. This the convention proceeded to make official by approving a resolution urging "all Democrats who have pledged support to Stevenson and Sparkman to reconsider their action and actively support Eisenhower and Nixon." Price Daniel, seeking election to the United States Senate as a Democrat, also endorsed the Republican ticket.

Johnson's dilemma deepened when state headquarters for Stevenson opened in Dallas on September 22. Rayburn was there to declare his intention of campaigning throughout the state for the Democratic ticket, and he denounced "captive Democrats" who wore their big, gilded "Me for Ike" buttons and deserted their party along with the governor, "who could shiver but could not dance to the music of the Democratic hoe-downs." Tom Connally and Cactus Jack Garner, along with six Democratic congressmen —Wright Patman, Albert Thomas, Paul Kilday, Bob Poage, Clark Thompson, and George Mahon—had come out for Stevenson, but Johnson kept his silence. However, this did not deter Mister Sam from claiming that his protégé believed as he did. Reminding those present that three weeks earlier in a statewide radio broadcast he had quoted Johnson as saying, "Bolting the party won't solve anything," he went on to add that Johnson had told him: "Granting that Stevenson is wrong on this question [title to the Tidelands], does that make Eisenhower and the reactionary-isolationist Republicans right on every great issue?"

Johnson's crisis was at hand when Adlai Stevenson took Sam Rayburn seriously that Johnson was his stout defender and promoter. One day Johnson's phone rang and the Democratic nominee was at the other end of the line. He would be coming to Texas late in mid-October, said Stevenson, and he was lining up Texans to introduce him at his planned five stops. He would be flying in from California to Fort Worth on October 17 for a speech, then make another that same day at Dallas, next take a sentimental five-hundred-mile train trip to Uvalde, and finally swing up to San Antonio and Houston. Sam Rayburn had promised to introduce him at

Dallas; Jack Garner, of course, at Uvalde; Paul Kilday and Maury Maverick at San Antonio; and Tom Connally at the Houston rally. Would Johnson introduce him at Fort Worth?

Johnson would not give him a direct reply, and immediately after he hung up he telephoned Shivers to report the Stevenson call. He wanted to know if Shivers would be angry if he occupied the Fort Worth rostrum with Stevenson, and if this were the case, he would give his regrets to Stevenson that he had to be somewhere else that day. Shivers thanked him for calling to relate his problem and magnanimously told him he should not only introduce Stevenson at Fort Worth but he could also ride around the state with him. He assured Johnson there would be no hard feelings if he did.

The Fort Worth rally proved the coldest of the Stevenson stops in Texas. Johnson and Rayburn met the chubby, blue-eyed, bald nominee at Meachem Field, and at the political meeting Johnson's mild introduction characterized Stevenson as "a square shooter" and "more than a fighter, he is a statesman and an administrator of ability." In turn, the Illinois governor graciously misinterpreted Johnson's lack of enthusiasm and told the crowd, "I thought when he got through he was going to introduce Ben Franklin. A little flattery is all right—as long as you don't inhale."

Rayburn said that Johnson would have to be seen with Stevenson at each stop for the sake of the national party. This was an ordeal at Dallas, despite the applause Johnson drew from the party claque in the crowd when he was introduced along with Congressman Kilday, Judge James Sewell of Navarro, who was the state Democratic chairman, and Mister Sam's sister, Mrs. W. A. Thomas. He was seen to frown instead of smile at Stevenson's humor when he quoted Sam Houston's advice: "Never ask a man where he comes from: If he is a Texan, he will tell you; and if he isn't, you should never embarrass him." Nor did he reveal any interest when Stevenson related that one of his forebears, Josiah Hughes Bell, had gone to Texas in 1818 and established the town of Columbia, the first capital of Texas. "President Houston had his office for a time in a house in Bell's yard," said Stevenson. He was sitting on the point of his spine as Stevenson lambasted the Republicans for the economic depression of 1929 and ended with a quote from Sam Rayburn—"In 1932, you couldn't find a jackrabbit on the north plains that didn't have two men chasing it. And when they finally got it into the stewpot, they called it 'Hoover Beef.' "

There was the long trip to Uvalde for breakfast with Cactus Jack Garner and a Stevenson speech in front of the house of Tully Garner, the son of the former Vice President. On the ride to Uvalde, Stevenson talked about his chances of defeating the general. Dick Russell had come out half-heartedly for the ticket, but Governor Jimmy Byrnes of South Carolina and Senator Harry Byrd of Virginia were in opposition along with Shivers, and in Florida there had been trouble a week earlier when Senator George Smathers said he would introduce Stevenson at the Tampa meeting if he could tell the gathering why he disagreed with Stevenson on several issues. Sam Rayburn groused about a meeting he had held with Jimmy Byrnes over a bottle of Jack Daniels Green Label sour mash in a dizzying but fruitless encounter to keep Byrnes within the fold. Mister Sam said he had also talked to other Southerners and warned them that "the South must give the Negroes a better break if they want to prevent passage of federal civil rights legislation. You can't filibuster forever," he claimed he told them.

Jack Garner fed the arriving Democrats a breakfast of smothered fried pheasant, fried ham and eggs, scrambled eggs, hot biscuits, steamed rice, Uvalde honey, orange juice, and coffee. All the guests ate as though it were their last meal, and Stevenson commented, "If I stayed here long I'd be too fat to leave Uvalde." Later, after the old man introduced him on the carpet grass lawn surrounded by century-old oak trees, Stevenson spoke to an enthusiastic crowd. Then his entourage had to rush to make the San Antonio and Houston meetings that same day. At San Antonio, at 11 A.M., Stevenson worked off his breakfast placing a wreath at the statue of Ben Milam in Milam Square and going on a guided tour of the Alamo with Maury Maverick. When he made his speech with its well-chosen words about the bravery of the Alamo men, seated on the platform, besides Kilday, Johnson, Rayburn, Jimmy Allred, Maverick, Homer Thornberry, and former Austin Mayor Tom Miller, were several district judges from George Parr's country.

Stevenson, who was a sensitive and perceptive man, was well aware of Johnson's lack of zeal in his behalf. This view was buttressed later by Johnson's other activities in the campaign. Although the Texas senator had agreed to speak for the ticket over radio, he managed to elude Stevenson's aides who were scheduling him for several radio appearances. In the end he spoke only once over radio, and he avoided any mention of Stevenson's name throughout the talk. Much of his speech centered on his own activities as senator, plus a strong condemnation of politicians who wanted to "rob Texas of her Tidelands" and a weak plug for Senator Sparkman, "the able Southerner on the ticket."

His harrowing experience of walking the spiky Shivers fence finally ended on November 4, when the estimated five million dollars spent in Texas for Eisenhower resulted in his carrying the state with 53 per cent of the 2,075,946 votes cast. Stevenson was convinced that Johnson should be numbered among those who contributed to his defeat in the Lone Star State, but Mister Sam would not permit the harsh judgment of betrayal to besmirch his protégé. In a public statement for the record he declared, "Lyndon did everything—everything—I asked him to do during the campaign."

Chapter 36

I N 1952 JOHNSON'S mind was filled with two other important matters besides the paramount issue of appeasing Allan Shivers. One of these efforts was to establish himself as a comfortable Texas rancher, an appearance that he believed vital to his political future. The other was to boost himself from the millionaire to the multimillionaire class.

One weekend during the preceding autumn, Lyndon, Lady Bird, Stuart Symington, and his wife Evelyn flew to Texas as the weekend guests of wealthy Wesley W. West at his ornate ranch near Llano. That Saturday West suggested they go to Dallas for an SMU football game, and they flew in his private plane to Love Field. The ostentatious display of dozens of other multiengine airplanes by wealthy Texans come to Dallas from all sections of Texas for the game that day reminded some reporters of the death and wounds other Americans were suffering at the same time in Korea. Mrs. Symington's reaction to the rows of private planes was one of awe—that they were "lined up like a fleet of cars."

"After our weekend," said Symington—whose additional purpose in going to Texas was to discuss with West and Johnson campaign funding and tactics should he run for the Senate in Missouri in 1952—"Lyndon and Lady Bird took us on a tour of the ranch area west of Austin, where he was born. When we came to the ranch his grandfather had owned, he said he was thinking of buying it. In contrast to where we had been, it wasn't much of anything. There was an old woman living in the rundown ranch house when we walked in, and Lady Bird took us around to its rooms, saying in each one, 'If we did this or that here, we could make it look real nice.' It had a marvelous fireplace for big logs, and not far from the house was a quaint, walled-in family cemetery. Lyndon also showed us a little cottage close by that was near the Pedernales River. A Mexican family lived in it, and Lyndon said he had been born here."

Gaunt and feeble Aunt Frank, Lyndon's eighty-one-year-old relative, and widow of his father's favorite brother-in-law, Clarence Martin, owned the ranch and the dilapidated ranch house. In order to exist, she had been selling the land piecemeal, and its size was now shrunken to two hundred and forty-five acres. Lady Bird described the seedy ranch house as looking "like a haunted house in a Charles Addams cartoon," when she saw it for the first time in a decade.

But to Lyndon it conjured up visions of a ranch that would be important in his political years that lay ahead. A few hours' ride from Washington sat Monticello, Jefferson's home, and even closer lay George Washington's Mount Vernon, both places undoubtedly vital in impressing colleagues of those early Presidents. A duplex in Austin was hardly the setting for a man who nourished Presidential ambitions. He would have to entertain hordes of visitors, feed them, bed them, and make it appear that he was always accustomed to the best in life. Therefore, he had to have Aunt Frank's place. When the old lady offered little protest to his proposition that she trade the ranch to him for her subsistence and the little house in Johnson City that his father had owned, the deal was completed.

Once he became a rancher, Johnson plunged with zest into the task of turning the old ranch into a showplace. Max Brooks, the architect and husband of Marietta Brooks, who had been with Lady Bird in the campaign auto accident in 1948, drove out to Johnson's piece of the "Purd-in-alleys" River landbed to assess what was required to make the place sparkle. The original house built by Sam Ealy Johnson, Sr., was constructed of thick stone walls, and the decision was to remove all the wooden additions that had been made over the years. This stone nucleus became the living room, with a hooded, four-foot-wide fireplace and beamed ceiling. Around this room a two-story ranch house was constructed with a sitting room, dining room, two bedrooms, and kitchen on the first floor and five bedrooms and baths upstairs. Johnson's first actions in acquiring Aunt Frank's property were to christen it the L.B.J. Ranch and to plot where he would place the radio-telephone central and the innumerable telephone plug-ins. Lady Bird had the more practical job of furnishing the ranch house, and she accomplished this with characteristic frugality. Learning of an old lady in Washington who wanted to sell some furniture, Lady Bird bargained with her for her entire household of furniture, and bought it all for three hundred dollars. Then when Lyndon bought his first cattle, he had the appurtenances he deemed so vital for a national politician from Texas.

When Sam Rayburn first heard that Lyndon had become a rancher, he scratched his bald head with a hairy hand and said jokingly, "Thank God! Now Lyndon will talk about something else besides politics."

However, Johnson already had something besides politics to occupy his time. The radio station was doing well, and his Austin properties and Lady Bird's Alabama pine-tree acreage were advancing swiftly in value. Yet Johnson remained dissatisfied that his total net worth had not climbed into the five- or ten-million-dollar class. He saw his great opportunity in 1948, when the television industry first revealed its possibilities. But that same year the FCC invoked a total freeze on allocating TV channels and said the suspension would last until it devised a national plan of distribution of the limited number of available channels.

Politicians knew that ever since the FCC was established in 1934, it was highly susceptible to political pressure. One story making the rounds related to the occasion when Democratic National Chairman Bob Hannegan asked FCC Chairman Wayne Coy to approve a radio license for a Missouri friend. When Coy said he would give the applicant fair and equal consideration, Hannegan warned him, "That won't be enough!" Regarding KTBC, the Johnson radio station in Austin, there was no argument that the earlier license request for that station by Wesley West's father, Jim West, had been turned down because the elder West was a right-wing extremist.

So, while the FCC worked on its national TV channel distribution plan, it did Johnson no harm to land a seat on the Senate Interstate and Foreign Commerce Committee, which handled FCC matters. Nor were his chances of landing a TV channel lessened when he became majority whip, or when Sam Rayburn's nephew and office assistant, Robert Bartley, was named an FCC Commissioner by President Truman.

The long freeze lasted until early 1952, when the FCC finally made public its national allocation program. The Fort Worth–Dallas area was to get five standard channels (Very High Frequency or VHF stations); Corpus Christi, two VHF channels; yet Austin, in the center of a large and well-to-do consumers market, was to get only one standard channel. Austin was also to get two Ultra High Frequency, or UHF channels, sometimes called "educational TV channels," but since existing television receiver sets were capable of receiving only VHF, for all practical purposes this meant that whoever got the license for the VHF channel would immediately enjoy a lucrative monopoly.

An expected scramble for Austin's only standard TV channel mysteriously failed to materialize. The Johnson application, legally signed by Lady Bird, went to the FCC in Washington, but not a single competitor filed for the VHF channel. An FCC official later admitted "it looked fishy," and Tom Potter, who applied for the UHF channel, which would not have an audience until special TV receivers came on the market, had this to say about his own failure to apply for the VHF channel: "Lyndon was in a favorable position to get this station even if somebody had contested it. *Politics is politics.*"

On July 11, 1952, after processing seven hundred applications, the FCC announced its first-batch license awards for fourteen new TV stations across the country. When Johnson failed to find his approved application among them, he put in an angry call to the agency. Three days later the FCC said that Lady Bird's application for Channel 7 in Austin had been approved on the eleventh but had not been announced by error.

KTBC-TV was now in existence, and after Johnson landed affiliations with all three major networks—CBS, NBC, and ABC—he pushed hard to get the necessary equipment despite a Korean wartime shortage of electronic gear. With breathtaking speed, he had his station operational by October, in time to show viewers Eisenhower's campaign trip in Texas and his greeting by Shivers and Price Daniel. There were also immediate money profits, for KTBC-TV's transmission arc included 203,500 home TV sets, a thriving market for major advertisers.

At the time the FCC allocation suspension was still on, Johnson had already given thought to creating a television empire. About one hundred miles north of Austin lay Waco, and before his Austin channel was approved, Johnson made plans to expand into Waco TV.

In February 1952 he wrote to the FCC, saying he was inquiring for a constituent who wanted to know the status of an application for a VHF standard television station in Waco by the rival KWTX Broadcasting Company. His constituent, he said, was also considering filing an application for Waco's VHF Channel 10. Johnson's letter came when the FCC had already decided to award the VHF station to KWTX under its national unfreezing program. But Johnson's missive caused gasps at the FCC, and when it issued licenses that July it was silent regarding Waco.

A year later, when the FCC was about to license Channel 10 to KWTX, Johnson again wrote to the agency, this time on "Office of the Democratic Leader" stationery. His tone was cold and threatening as he demanded that the FCC give "serious consideration to this problem [the Waco allocation], based on its merits," before deciding whether the Waco KWTX group should be granted a TV license. Once more the FCC officers fell into a state of paralysis. Not until a year and a half later, after it became apparent that Johnson's constituent was himself, did the FCC seem to gather sufficient courage to award Waco's Channel 10 to the rival KWTX Broadcasting Company.

What gave some FCC commissioners backbone to vote as they did was the fact that Johnson, through Lady Bird, had earlier requested the agency to grant him a license to control Waco's other TV station, the year-old UHF "educational" channel station, KANG-TV. The Johnson request was an astonishing puzzler to the FCC, for this weak station was a heavy money-loser because of the old story of television receivers that could not tune it in. The FCC's impression was that Johnson no longer coveted Channel 10, and on the same day that it sanctioned KWTX's control of Channel 10, it told Johnson he could buy KANG by paying $25,000 to its owners and assuming its outstanding debts of $109,000.

Neither the FCC nor the KWTX owners of Channel 10 saw any sense in Johnson's purchase of KANG-TV. First, it was bound to lose a continuously large amount of money because it could not attract listeners. Second, Waco had what already amounted to a two-VHF station system, for the VHF channel at Temple, about twenty-five miles away, beamed programs that came in clearly on Waco home receivers.

However, only days after his purchase of KANG-TV, Johnson revealed his true intentions. KWTX owners had been in the process of completing an affiliation with CBS, while coldly stalling off hard-selling pleas of smaller ABC for affiliation. But less than a week after Johnson acquired KANG-TV, CBS notified KWTX it was dropping all consideration of an affiliation. Instead, said CBS, it was affiliating with Johnson's KANG. With great concern the KWTX owners raced to acquire the second-rate ABC affiliation, and again they were told that the affiliation was going to KANG-TV. Because a firm rule of the networks had been to avoid any association with UHF "educational" stations, this move by the networks to tie in with Johnson's UHF station meant only that the networks were lending themselves to some diabolical scheme that Johnson was hatching. Left now with only local programming, KWTX-TV suffered still another blow when the FCC sanctioned an increase in transmission power at Johnson's Austin TV station from its one hundred kilowatts to two hundred and forty-seven. This meant that Austin's Channel 7, with all three national network programs available to it, could reach into seven hundred and forty square miles of KWTX-TV Waco's broadcasting arc.

KWTX immediately demanded that the Justice Department take antitrust action against the Johnson company's "monopolistic activities," but it knew that the senator's political connections were too strong to move the Department into a legal suit against him. When it registered a similar complaint with the FCC, KWTX-TV realized nothing would result here either.

What lay ahead was attrition and eventual ruin, one of Johnson's many lawyers told Wilfred Naman, a large stockholder in KWTX as well as its attorney. The other major owners of KWTX agreed to this bleak picture of their future, and Naman was authorized to discover what Johnson had in mind. "I visited with him both in his office in the Capitol and then out at his home in Washington," Naman told John Barron, a reporter for the Washington *Star*. "I also recall once during these negotiations I had a conference with him down on his ranch."

Johnson's proposition was simple, and he stated it bluntly. He proposed to transfer his valuable network affiliations to KWTX, but in return he wanted controlling interest in KWTX-TV plus a large stock share of its profitable radio station in Waco. At first the owners screamed that this was not an honest proposition. However, the TV station had begun to lose money operating without network connections, and the owners settled down in earnest to cut Johnson's terms as far as he would permit. The final agreement gave Johnson 29.05 per cent of KWTX stock, and he closed down KANG-TV, which he had used to achieve his goal. With KWTX-TV's "stripped-down" value estimated at three million dollars a few years later, the Johnson share was worth almost nine hundred thousand dollars.

Part of the arrangement was the agreement to let Johnson name three members of the KWTX board of directors, and those he chose were Jesse Kellam, Donald S. Thomas, a Johnson lawyer, and A. W. Moursund of

Johnson City, a local judge who was involved in several business deals with Johnson. The majority board members would do no more than mumble in talking to Johnson's three, yet this did not affect the company's profits. In fact, the board aggressively added to Johnson's wealth by purchasing 75 per cent of the stock of a TV station at Sherman, Texas; 78.9 per cent of a radio station at Victoria; and 50 per cent of a TV station at Bryan. Although the FCC had a rule against permitting an educational station to convert to commercial use, it made an exception in the case of the Bryan station after the Johnson men joined the board of KWTX.

After his Waco triumph, Johnson considered the Rio Grande Valley a fertile area for expanding his TV interests still further. A minor search revealed that O. L. Taylor, who owned KRGV-TV in Weslaco, only a dozen miles from the Rio Grande, had money troubles because the FCC limited his transmitting power to 28.8 kilowatts, and he could not get any network to affiliate with his station. When Johnson learned that another initialed Texan named H. C. Cockburn held an option to buy 25 per cent of the stock for one hundred thousand dollars and was waiting for FCC approval, he offered Taylor a more consolidated deal. In return for 50 per cent of the stock of KRGV-TV, Johnson offered to give him five thousand dollars in cash and lend the television station one hundred and forty thousand dollars repayable at 7 per cent interest. He also agreed to lend one hundred and three thousand dollars to a radio station owned by Taylor.

Taylor was willing to take Johnson's tougher deal because of the proposed loan to his radio station, but he said he had already agreed to H. C. Cockburn's proposal, which was in process of getting FCC clearance. Nevertheless, he also agreed to accept Johnson's proposition if it could be made legal.

This proved a simple matter, for the FCC threw out Cockburn's claim and approved Johnson's proposal. Then several weeks later the FCC authorized an increase in KRGV-TV's transmitting power from its low 28.8 kilowatts to 100 kilowatts. This was followed by network affiliation with NBC and ABC. Next, Taylor merged his radio station with KRGV-TV, and despite the vaulting advertising business he sold his entire operation to Johnson for an additional one hundred thousand dollars. Four years later Johnson in turn sold his Weslaco holdings for one million four hundred thousand dollars.

So the Johnson money-power drive nurtured by his aggressive political power advanced rapidly and easily. And his political power set upon the security of several million dollars moved forward with similar ease.

Chapter 37

D URING THE EARLY evening of Tuesday, November 4, 1952, when
Johnson switched on a television set to Austin's only station, his own
KTBC-TV, election returns from around the nation made it obvious from
the start that Eisenhower was trouncing Stevenson. Network commentators
were assessing the victory as stemming from the general's late October
promise at Detroit "to go to Korea in person if elected and put an end to
the fighting," plus his repetitious proposal "to clean up the mess in Washington." But the truth was that American affection for Eisenhower as a
war hero was an equally significant factor in his election.

Johnson was far more interested in the Senate races, where a total of
thirty-six contests had been fought. His scorecard showed that twenty sitting
senators were winning re-election, while in sixteen other contests nonsen-
ators were ahead. One of the freshman winners was Stuart Symington,
whose candidacy in Missouri had originally been opposed by President
Truman, who had ridiculed him as "Little Lord Fauntleroy." Symington
had campaigned for Johnson in 1946 and 1948, and reciprocally, Johnson
went into Missouri in 1952 to campaign for him. In fact, he spent so much
time on the Symington campaign that Stevenson aides called it his crutch
to avoid campaigning in Texas for their man. Johnson had also put a
substantial amount of Brown and Root money behind Symington to pay
his campaign costs. Said Herman Brown with some bitterness afterward,
according to Selig Harrison, who interviewed him for the *New Republic* in
1960, "I gave him some money and I sent a man down to help at Lyndon's
instigation. But Symington has very little ability, the least of any of them.
I've got a nigger chauffeur [Patrick Milton] who's got more ability than
Symington—though maybe I oughtn't to express myself so frankly."

There was one election result that really caught Johnson's attention.
This was in Arizona where Ernie McFarland had fallen to unknown Barry
Goldwater. As the significance of McFarland's defeat settled upon him, an
enormous thought enveloped Johnson. The Senate Democrats were now
without a leader. A new one would have to be found before the Eighty-
third Congress assembled on January 3, 1953—and why shouldn't it be he?

Johnson put in a call to Richard Russell at his mother's house in
Winder, Georgia. The senator was not there, so Johnson telephoned the

Federal Building in Winder, which served as Russell's office away from Washington. Russell was there. Johnson's first order of business was to overurge the Georgian to run for Democratic leader to insure his refusal. The second order of business was to make Russell suggest that Johnson himself try for it with Russell's backing.

When Johnson begged Russell to seek the Democratic leadership, Russell thanked him and then rejected the plea. First of all, Russell pointed out, he had no desire to give up his current role as Democratic leader in the Senate on defense matters or as boss of the Southern bloc on civil rights prevention. Second, since the Republicans had won control of the Senate, he would only be the minority leader, a minor position without leadership powers, for these were the prerogatives of the Republican majority leader. The minority leader might effectively throw rocks into the wheels of the Senate by opposing the majority leader's efforts to push the Administration's program through the Upper Chamber, but still, he would merely be reacting and not leading. If there were any saving graces to the job they would come in extra patronage and White House meals and conferences in order to neutralize him. Russell's third (but most important) reason for not running for minority leader was that as the head of the Southern bloc (Connally was gone and Walter George had been appeased to the point where he had made the nominating speech for Russell at the 1952 national convention), he carried a stigma that would be impossible to overcome in attempting to create good relations with Northern and border state Democrats.

But why didn't Lyndon run? he asked. He would have the head start of a fairly united Southern bloc behind him without being totally characterized as a member of that bloc. His best friends were the border and Western senators Clint Anderson of New Mexico and Bob Kerr of Oklahoma, and he ought to claim regional kinship even if he were a Southerner. In a reluctant tone, Johnson finally said he would run, though he repeated that he would not if Russell should change his mind.

That same evening Johnson made several phone calls. One connected him with Senator Earle Clements up in Morganfield, Kentucky. Johnson had known the fleshy Clements as a New Deal and Fair Deal congressman during the three years he served in the House before returning to Kentucky as governor in 1948. Then when Clements came to the Senate in November 1950, Johnson frequently took him along to meetings of Sam Rayburn's "Board of Education." Clements would be useful to spread doubts in liberal Democratic circles that Johnson was a typical Southern reactionary; and Johnson's opening gambit was to offer to make him minority whip in exchange for his aid promoting Johnson for minority leader. Clements was highly flattered, considering that he was only a two-year senator, and when he quickly agreed, he was bombarded with orders to secure the votes of almost twenty liberals.

Other telephone calls went out in the days that followed to Bob Kerr, Clint

Anderson, Allen Frear, Mike Monroney, Carl Hayden, Maggie Magnuson, and Dennis Chavez. Chavez was eager to support him if Johnson would in turn help quash his recent Republican opponent, Pat Hurley, who was preparing a case to have the Senate throw Chavez out of office on grounds of voting irregularities and general fraud in the New Mexico Senate election. Johnson promised aid. He also phoned each of the six Democratic freshmen, ostensibly to congratulate them and to let them know that the Democratic whip was thinking of them.

By early December, Johnson knew he had far more than the needed majority of forty-seven Democrats, and at first he found it amusing when he learned that some of the Northern Democrats were promoting seventy-six-year-old Jim Murray of Montana as his opponent. Murray, many times a millionaire, had voted a straight New Deal and Fair Deal course since coming to the Senate in 1934. As chairman of the Labor and Public Welfare Committee, he was known for the strong federal-aid-to-education and housing bills he reported to the Senate floor, as well as for his hard but unsuccessful fight to promote the Full Employment Act in 1945.

But Johnson's amusement turned to rage because even a dozen votes for Murray would undo Clements' campaign promoting the idea that Johnson was essentially a liberal despite his anti-civil-rights stand, his anti-labor votes, and his attack on Leland Olds. When he learned that Hubert Humphrey was leading the small pony pack for Murray, he called him shortly before Christmas in an effort to buy him off.

Winthrop Griffith, one of Hubert Humphrey's assistants, later reported on Johnson's technique. First, he played dumb and asked Humphrey to aid him at the coming caucus by swinging some liberal votes to him. Humphrey replied that he could not do this because he was supporting Murray.

"You can't win!" Johnson snapped.

Then over and over again he asked Humphrey to change his mind; but the skinny Minnesotan, who was known as Gabby and Flannelmouth to his colleagues, talked longer and louder than long, loud-talking Johnson to defend his action. Finally Johnson threw out a big piece of bait. "I might want to make you my whip, Hubert," he said.

However, despite the thrill of being offered the second place among Senate Democrats at a time when he was the most ostracized member, Humphrey said he could not go back on his word to Murray. Nor would he bite when Johnson spoke about filling the two Democratic vacancies on the Foreign Relations Committee with sound liberals.

Shortly before the January 2, 1953, Democratic caucus got under way, Humphrey and Lester Hunt of Wyoming paid a call on Johnson. The two realized that Murray could not win, even though they had a list of twenty Democrats supposedly pledged to him. This time Humphrey was willing to give up on Murray if Johnson would put Paul Douglas and Herbert Lehman of New York on the Senate Democratic Policy Committee.

Johnson hardly let Humphrey and Hunt begin their bargaining attempt when he asked coldly, "How many votes do you think you have for Murray?"

Humphrey pulled out a list and began to read the names, only to be interrupted by Johnson's scoffing voice time after time. "No, you don't have him. I do," Johnson jeered. When the list was depleted, a dejected Humphrey again asked Johnson to put two liberals on the Senate Democratic Policy Committee.

"I don't have to give you anything. I have the vote," Johnson told him.

At the Democratic caucus, Humphrey was stunned when Murray's total included only Murray, Humphrey, Hunt, Douglas, and Lehman. In telling about the caucus embarrassment afterward, Humphrey recollected only three votes for Murray, and that he had quickly moved to make Johnson's election as minority leader a unanimous vote. "I had to protect Jim Murray," he said. "I couldn't let it get back to his home state that he had received only three votes."

When the caucus accepted Johnson's choice of Earle Clements as minority whip, the forty-four-year-old Texan rose and gave his Democratic colleagues a teacher-pupil speech that foretold what lay in store for them during the next eight years. He intended to be the total boss who would represent the Democratic party in its approach to the Republican President and in its own effort to acquire a new personality.

Chapter 38

I N JANUARY 1953 Harry Truman went home to Missouri as a laughed-at figure. A provident history would one day paint over his failure to gain approval for his Fair Deal and his inability to instill ethical behavior throughout the federal officialdom. History would then highlight him as a top-ranking President because of his spirited foreign policy to rebuild Western Europe and contain the Soviet Union, as well as his courageous act in meeting the initial, massive Communist invasion of South Korea.

Dwight Eisenhower was now in power, after decreeing that his Cabinet and other male witnesses on the east Capitol stand wear Homburgs at his prayerful inauguration. Voicing a vague program of generalities, which he called a "crusade," he was ready to embark on eight years in the Presidency.

Senator Robert Taft had determined that the Senate of 1953 was to be the creature of one man—himself. Calming down to a slight degree after the "steal" of the Republican Presidential nomination from him by Eisenhower, he had traveled to New York on September 12, 1952, for a breakfast conference with Eisenhower at his Columbia University residence at 60 Morningside Drive. As president of Columbia, Eisenhower never wandered outdoors for a stroll without his service revolver. But on this occasion, said insiders, it was Taft who disarmed him and won his approval for a Taft statement that they not only had hearts that beat in unison on domestic issues but their differences on foreign policy were only "differences of degree." Adlai Stevenson's wry comment on "Ike's surrender at Morningside Heights" was that "it looks as if Taft lost the nomination but won the nominee."

Taft also attempted to control the selection of several Cabinet members. When Eisenhower ignored his suggestions for Secretary of Labor and named Martin Durkin, a Stevenson supporter and president of the AFL Plumbers' Union, Taft denounced his appointee to the press as an "incredible" choice.

In addition, before the Eighty-third Congress convened, Taft bluntly told Styles Bridges, the preceding Senate's minority leader, that he would have to relinquish his post as Republican leader. Bridges considered this an insult because he predated Taft as a senator by two years and his loss of face among his colleagues would be ruinous. But he read the seriousness of Taft's intent in his face, and he agreed with only a weak complaint to become the honorary Senate president *pro tem,* handing the majority leader's office to the Ohio senator.

Senator Taft evinced little concern that his side of the Senate aisle contained only one more member than minority leader Johnson's side in January 1953. It was a principle to him, he said, that Oregon Senator Wayne Morse, the harsh-tongued former law school dean and government administrator, should be punished for bolting the G.O.P. and declaring himself for Adlai Stevenson in 1952. Despite Morse's assurances that he would vote with the Republicans to organize the Senate, Taft viewed this as a meaningless gesture. For even if Morse voted with the Democrats, this would only produce a forty-eight to forty-eight tie, and Vice President Nixon could then cast a tie-breaking ballot. Taft's decree was that Morse must be removed from his seat on the Armed Services and the Labor Committees, and to dramatize his plight, Morse came to the opening day of the Eighty-third Congress with a metal folding chair that he intended to plant in the aisle between Taft and Johnson. Taft angrily ordered the secretary of the Senate, Mark Trice, to get rid of the chair and sit Morse down on the Republican side as an ostracized object lesson.

"If Taft could punish Wayne Morse," said Senator Kilgore, "some of us liberals reasoned that Lyndon ought to do the same to Price Daniel, Harry Byrd, Olin Johnston, and one or two other Democrats who supported Eisenhower. But Hubert Humphrey, who said during the 1952 campaign that he would swap three Southern senators for Wayne, now argued that we should be nice to these traitors because we needed all the Democratic votes we could tally if we wanted to take over the Senate in 1954. What we should have done was to ask Wayne to become a Democrat. After all, Harry Truman offered to make him his Attorney General in 1951." Senator Paul Douglas was another who wanted Johnson to invite Morse to join the Democratic party. "Should we drive him, at the point of a bayonet, back to the Republican party and say, 'You are an Ishmael, you can find refuge nowhere'?" he asked.

But Johnson wanted no part of Morse, the old enemy of his 1948 Washington attorney, Abe Fortas. Besides, even a Morse vote would not unseat Taft as majority leader. As a result, when the Senate Republican caucus of January 13 removed Morse from his committee assignments, Johnson refused to let him stay on his committees as part of the Democratic party's quota of members. After an unsuccessful effort to win his seats back as an Independent, Morse found himself relegated to the dismal swamp committees dealing with public works and the District of Columbia. By now his anger centered on Johnson instead of Taft, and he told Senator Douglas that he intended to campaign against Johnson in Texas the following year. Johnson's reaction on hearing this was one of pleasure, for Morse's pro-Stevenson and anti-state-tidelands-ownership stands would be valuable assets in Johnson's favor when he ran for re-election in 1954. But for the record he told a *Time* reporter that his retort to Douglas on being warned of Morse's threat had been: "You aren't trying to argue that we should give in to political blackmail, are you?"

Exhilarated as much by name-calling as Johnson was by power, Morse shot back that Johnson was "more Republican than Democrat" and "a follower, not a leader." On a trip to Houston afterward, he told reporters: "Why don't you elect two senators? You have none now. Price Daniel represents the oil and gas industry and Lyndon Johnson represents Lyndon Johnson." Yet this feud was not destined to last beyond the 1954 elections because each became suddenly the most important man in Washington to the other.

As the head Senate Democrat, Minority Leader Johnson lacked Taft's power and skill; but he intended to have both in time. And while he waited, he knew his first order of business was to consolidate his own authority among the Democrats.

One important job was to convince the six new Democratic senators that they were heavily in his debt. When he assigned each to a major committee, he let it be known that this was a revolutionary move on his part and had caused him serious trouble with Senator Russell. He later repeated this story to naive reporters for *Life, Time,* and *Newsweek,* and they wrote that he was a courageous innovator.

In a conglomerate version, Johnson said he told Russell he planned to order the Senate Democratic Steering Committee (in charge of making committee assignments) to carry out his decision regarding the freshmen. No longer were freshmen to be shunted onto the dreary and second-rate Post Office and Civil Service, Rules and Administration, and the District of Columbia Committees.

Russell was supposed to have told him, "But Lyndon, you're dealing with the most sensitive thing in the Senate—seniority." *Time* said that when "old hands objected" along with Russell, Johnson simply offered them a pointed story to show why he intended to carry out his plan. "There was this boy in the Hill Country whose daddy wouldn't let him ride to the nearby town," Johnson was said to have drawled. "And the boy complained that his brother had been 'twowheres and I ain't been nowheres.' So it makes no sense to stick seniority-high senators twowheres when the freshmen ain't been nowheres."

"I shoved in my whole stack," *Life* quoted Johnson. He put Stuart Symington on the Armed Services Committee, Mike Mansfield on Foreign Relations, John Kennedy on Labor, Henry (Scoop) Jackson and Price Daniel on Interior and Insular Affairs, and Albert Gore on Public Works. Yet these "somewheres" that Johnson created were minor compared with the assignments Majority Leader Scott Lucas had made in 1949. That year Lucas put four freshmen including Johnson on the Armed Services Committee and three other freshmen on the Labor Committee, and no older senators registered a complaint.

Besides convincing his six freshmen that he had given them a remarkable break, Johnson singled out one other senator for special attention. It was his decision to bend Hubert Humphrey to his will and make the fiery liberal his secret lieutenant inside the antagonistic Northern liberal bloc. It was also his intention to make Humphrey respectable to the Southern bloc. This would be quite an undertaking, for Southern senators had been fuming and sputtering at the mention of Humphrey's name ever since the Minnesotan had caused an uproar at the 1948 Democratic Convention with his strong civil rights plank. As Bill White took note of his friend's scheme, "Johnson fixed his restless, reckoning eyes on him."

Humphrey had gone on from his convention play to antagonize Southerners still further. In 1949 he had fought bitterly with Johnson on the Senate floor over Leland Olds. Then he had taken on the entire Southern bloc with his marathon ridicule of an appropriation for Senator Harry Byrd's Joint Committee on Reduction of Nonessential Federal Expenditures. The Byrd Committee was a fraud which permitted the apple-cheeked Virginia apple grower to gain some publicity with press releases showing the changes in the numbers of federal employees. But it was Byrd's fraud, and the Southern senators would not accept this denunciation without a sharper attack on Humphrey in return.

After this the gulf between Humphrey and the Southerners approximated an ocean. However, Johnson did not avoid Humphrey as the other senators did, and when he ran for minority leader, he saw no reason for not talking directly to Humphrey to gain his support.

The Johnson plan for Humphrey called for buying him off while praising him as a man who could not be bought. It also called for convincing Humphrey that he was no more liberal than Johnson, but that the difference between them was that Johnson "knew how to get there." Bill White called it an "operation," and it began when Humphrey made the caucus motion to elect Johnson by acclamation. A few hours later, said one of Humphrey's assistants, the new minority leader walked into the Minnesotan's first-floor office. "You name the man you want on the Policy Committee," Johnson told Humphrey. "I'll see he's appointed. Name the men you want on the major committees. I'll put them on."

Humphrey stared at him and wanted to know why Johnson was being so generous. "You're one of those fellows not playing both sides of the street like some of your liberal friends," Johnson replied. "I want to work with you. I want you to help me."

When flattered Humphrey said he would, Johnson told him he was putting him on the Foreign Relations Committee. Their special relationship was kept out of the press because the only reporter who understood it was Johnson's friend, Bill White. Although Humphrey continued to spout his extreme liberalism, when Johnson needed his help or vote, he made himself available. In return, said his aide, Johnson "rewarded Humphrey often with powerful help for special projects or liberal legislation causes."

One of Johnson's chief efforts on Humphrey's behalf was to make him acceptable to the Southern bloc. He pushed hard on Walter George, "in favor of his protégé-target," said White. Casually, he would approach the aging Georgian, who liked to hold court in the Democratic cloakroom, where he sat by the hour, chain smoking, smoothing his white hair, and acting as adviser to younger members. "Senator," he would remark as though the thought had just struck him, "Hubert isn't such a bad fellow, you know. On such and such a matter, he has shown a great deal of responsibility and ability." The first dozen or so times Johnson put in a plug for Humphrey, old George cocked a white eyebrow above his thick-lensed glasses in disbelief. But Johnson did not end his campaign, and one day Senator George told him, "Hubert is doing much better these days."

Johnson also worked on Senator Russell, who was even more skeptical about Humphrey than George had been at the outset. But Russell succumbed to Johnson's ploy that he wanted him to go over a piece of farm legislation that Humphrey planned to introduce, and Humphrey utilized this opportunity to show deference by his repeated "Sir" to Russell when they discussed the measure. By the end of the session Humphrey was to declare that the degree of unity among Democrats that Johnson brought about was "a near miracle." Other Northern Democrats who disliked seeing the two conferring so frequently charged that Humphrey was "selling out to Johnson."

Even though Johnson was already Russell's protégé, he put Russell in his permanent debt when he thoughtfully flew to Winder, Georgia, fifty miles northeast of Atlanta, to attend the funeral of the senator's mother, Ina Dillard Russell, who died at eighty-five on August 30, 1953. Once there, he gave Russell a sympathetic audience for the stories he wanted to tell about his beloved mother. Not only had she raised fifteen children, but she was the youngest of thirteen children in her original family. Bachelor Dick was her oldest son, and his memories of fifty-five years of living with her in the big white house surrounded by the pecan trees and mimosas poured out in profusion. Until he was well along in school he had believed that mothers did not sleep because he had never seen her in bed. When a horse bit him, she had nursed him without respite, and one spring she worked the foot pedal of the old Singer sewing machine seemingly without end in order to make about two hundred garments for her children. Russell related that at thirty-three, when he became governor in 1931, she and his father, then Chief Justice of the State Supreme Court at a salary of seven thousand dollars a year, lived with him in the governor's mansion in Atlanta. Because of her character and her successful way of life, said Russell, the town of Winder had declared a holiday in her honor in May 1950.

Besides earning Russell's eternal gratitude for coming to his mother's funeral, Johnson made use of his trip to Georgia in another way. He had kept his eyes wide open on his visit to the Winder area, and he shrewdly observed that Russell had collected far more than a reasonable share of American taxpayers' dollars for the benefit of his constituents. For miles and miles around his home town, he had plastered the countryside with a breathless array of pork-barrel projects and government contract activities that put to shame what Johnson had been doing recently for his people in Texas. For instance, not far from Winder was the town of Marietta, which the 1930 Census credited with eight thousand inhabitants. Here at Marietta Johnson saw a Lockheed plant working on government plane contracts and employing twenty-five thousand workers. Georgian friends of Dick Russell laughingly confided that he had done more for the peanut than George Washington Carver. According to Representative Jamie Whitten of Mississippi, who served on the House Appropriations Committee, year in and year out Russell invariably slipped another agriculture research station or two for Georgia into the Department of Agriculture's annual appropriation when the bill reached the Senate. Despite the opposition of the Department, Russell would not let the bill get through Congress unless the stations were retained.

When Johnson returned to Washington, he told his staff: "I want us to start at least one dam in Texas every year from now on." This order was carried out in his remaining years as a senator.

In addition to acquiring a faithful lieutenant in Northern liberal ranks in the person of Hubert Humphrey and solidifying his standing with Russell, Johnson made it his firm practice to maintain friendly relations with the Senate's Republican leadership. In fact, this was a policy he had started a few years earlier when Republican Senator Kenneth Wherry of Nebraska was the minority leader. He did his biggest job on Wherry, "the Merry Mortician," because he was the Republican who could be of most use to him at the time. Other Democrats had warned him that as a politician Wherry had his chief sport in helping to kill Democratic legislation. But Johnson made it a point to be diffident in Wherry's presence, and the Nebraskan senator was so pleased that Johnson became the exception to his rule of hatred for Democrats. This paid off brilliantly for Johnson during a Senate night session. The Democratic leadership intended to report the Calendar of Private Bills that evening. Private bills were not of a national character and required unanimous approval to get through Congress. When Johnson learned that Wherry planned to object to every private bill and thus kill the lot, he went directly to him, turned his voice into a plea to a superior, and whispered, "You know how I never do anything except Senate work. Well, tonight I made a rare commitment to go to one of Mrs. Maurice Cafritz's dinners. So couldn't you just let my one little bill go through to save west Texas long-staple cotton?"

Tongue-twisted Wherry replied, "I'd rather do business with you than anybody else on your side, London." Johnson's private bill passed without Wherry's objection.

When Wherry died in November 1951, and Styles Bridges succeeded him as minority leader, Johnson also played up to Bridges, who was as partisan as Wherry. However, Bridges felt a lack of sincerity on Johnson's part, and immediately after Johnson was elected minority leader, said Bill White, "Bridges called on him in his chambers, sat down across the table, look straight at him, and said without pause: 'Now, I know that you can get around dear old So and So [a fellow member of the Republican hierachy] and you can very often persuade dear old Such and Such [another member of the Republican hierarchy] before he really knows what's going on. But . . . you won't persuade me unless I want to be persuaded. And that is that.' "

According to White, Johnson rose, "shook Bridges' hand and said: 'Fair enough, Styles. We know where we stand.' " Afterward, the two had some harsh exchanges on the Senate floor in view of the press gallery, but they met privately over drinks to conclude amiable deals on legislation.

In 1953 Johnson was especially attentive to humorless Majority Leader Taft, even though the Ohioan did his best to humiliate him in return by ignoring his existence. Frequently, in order to draw Taft's attention, Johnson would lean across the center aisle, pretend that he had forgotten his glasses in his office, and ask Taft to read a fine-print paragraph in a bill or committee report to him. Taft squirmed but took on the chore.

At the time that Truman referred to Eisenhower as a "squirrel-head," Johnson told Taft he did not agree with this description. Whenever a Republican senator made a fool of himself in debate, Taft would snap his teeth together and suck in his breath. Johnson never let such an opportunity slip by without sympathizing with the majority leader. On one of numerous occasions when Republican Senator George "Molly" Malone of Nevada disgraced himself in a colloquy, Johnson let out a stage whisper across the aisle: "Bob, Bob! You must be very proud of your party today. How do you manage to find such great minds as that?" Taft smiled wanly and replied, "Now, now, Lyndon."

Although he courted Taft publicly, in private Johnson resented the publicity the Ohio senator received. Even though Taft had been a national figure for almost fifteen years, and was the son of a former President, a four-time aspirant for President himself, and was now the powerful "Mister Republican" and Senate majority leader, Johnson chided reporters for giving Taft far greater newspaper coverage than they gave him. A few newsmen who failed to praise Johnson in print after he spent hours with them in interviews learned that he had a special name for them. Senator Harley Kilgore, one of the Democratic liberal crew who called Johnson "Lying-Down Lyndon," said that in the cloakroom Johnson referred to nonrewarding newsmen as "piss-ant reporters." One time, irked by Bill White's frequent newspaper stories about Senator Taft, Johnson called White on the phone and told him: "This is Lyndon Johnson, the minority leader of the Senate, you may remember. I would take it very kindly if I could have an appointment with the Senate correspondent of *The New York Times*. Now, of course, I don't want to put you out—I would be glad to meet you in Senator Taft's office."

Besides the Congressional Republican leaders, Johnson had no intention of creating poor relations with the White House, though he almost succeeded in doing so shortly after becoming minority leader. That year he was also serving as president of the thousand-member Texas State Society, a social club for Texans in Washington. When the TSS held its big affair in April 1953 to celebrate San Jacinto Day, Johnson decided that President Eisenhower would have to attend because he was born in Texas. However, Eisenhower begged off because of his Presidential duties.

This only spurred Johnson on to make another request, and when Eisenhower again refused, he repeated his invitation. By now Eisenhower realized Johnson would give him no peace, so he accepted. But he had the last word, for when he was called upon to address the Texans, he referred to his own lack of ties to his native state in this fashion: "Just because a cat gives birth in a stove, that doesn't make the kittens biscuits."

Chapter 39

DURING THE TWO years that Lyndon Johnson served his apprenticeship in taking firm control of Senate Democratic machinery as minority leader, the Eisenhower Administration was settling into national authority by fits, jolts, bombast, and occasional wisdom. This was a period of completing action on some events that had been hanging fire since midpassage of the Truman Administration, paying off campaign promises, developing a new foreign policy vocabulary which included such frightening terms as "brinkmanship" and "massive retaliation" should the Soviet Union overstep the boundary of its European containment. It was also a time to begin a few Republican programs at home.

Sam Rayburn, now in his twenty-first House term and reduced to minority leader, had determined immediately after the 1952 election what the policy of the Democrats should be toward Eisenhower, and Johnson concurred with him. "Any jackass can kick a barn down," said Mister Sam, "but it takes a carpenter to build it." Democratic policy, at least from the Congressional end, would be friendly and cooperative, unlike the rough treatment Rayburn had joined Garner in giving President Hoover.

This did not mean that Rayburn considered Eisenhower a proper choice for President. "The Democratic Presidents took him as a major and made him a great general," said Sam on one occasion. Rayburn talked about his own forty years spent trying to learn the political ropes, and he concluded, "And I still didn't know all the answers on domestic and foreign problems." Here was Eisenhower, forty years in the Army and fresh in politics, at the very top. "He's no better qualified to do that job [as President] than I was to do his [as military leader in World War II]. But you know how folks feel about fellows who come back from war with medals and ribbons. . . . I was bothered by the thing that happened in 1952. The people were all stirred up, but they'll settle down." But regardless of Rayburn's small opinion of Eisenhower the politician, he refused to go after him "like a man with a meat ax in a dark room."

After the Senate Democratic caucus elected Johnson minority leader, he unwound his long legs and read five minutes of remarks he had prepared for this occasion. His central theme was a reiteration of Rayburn's stand that there should be no war with the Republican Administration. "I have never agreed with the statement that 'it is the business of the opposition to oppose,'" he said. "I do not believe the American people have sent us here merely to obstruct."

This was a stunning remark to the Northern liberal contingent, and it set the stage for eight years of trouble between them and Johnson. When he quoted Sam Rayburn's remark that "the difference between Republicans and Democrats is that we don't hate their Presidents," the liberals called him "Lying-Down Lyndon" and said he was preventing the party from presenting a positive program of its own.

Johnson's reply to this charge by Lehman, Douglas, and Kefauver was to deny that he was "petticoatin' around with Eisenhower. That's not true." And it was not true in 1953, in the sense that he was collaborating directly with the Republicans, for Eisenhower did not call him to the White House on a single occasion while Taft was majority leader to discuss legislation. Sam Rayburn did not fare much better in 1953. Not until June, when a reporter for the San Antonio *Light* wrote that Johnson and Rayburn had expressed their "curiosity about the new decorations in the White House," did Eisenhower invite Mister Sam to a private lunch at the Executive Mansion.

The Rayburn-Johnson strategy of never attacking Eisenhower directly applied to members of his official family who were from Texas. Thus was Presidential immunity extended on the old Alamo kinship to Secretary of the Navy Robert Anderson, who had been one of the owners of KTBC in Austin before Johnson acquired the radio station, and to Oveta Culp Hobby, the pretty World War II head of the Women's Army Corps and wife of one-time Governor William Hobby, publisher of the Houston *Post*. Mrs. Hobby became head of the new Health, Education and Welfare Department, and when a storm enveloped her in 1955 over the maldistribution of Dr. Jonas Salk's polio vaccine, she was forced out of office by an undiminishing Democratic attack, despite Johnson's efforts to end it.

Secretary of Defense Charles "Engine Charlie" Wilson, however, the former boss of General Motors, who was not from Texas, was a special target of Senate Democrats, including Johnson. When Wilson's name came before the Senate Armed Services Committee for confirmation, Russell already had his case built to show that Wilson was involved in a conflict of interest because he owned thirty-eight thousand shares of GM stock, and the giant firm held about four billion dollars in defense contracts. Russell also baited Wilson during the committee hearings on his nomination by demanding to know if he would "make a decision adverse to General Motors."

"For years I thought that what was good for the country was good for General Motors and vice versa," Wilson replied. This was all Russell needed to promote to the press that Wilson had said, "What is good for General Motors is good for the country."

The truth was that there was little need for the Democrats to attack the Administration when the Republicans were doing this job for them. One time when Eisenhower complained of this, Speaker Joe Martin told him, "Maybe that's the result of these last twenty years that we spent out in the wilderness."

Taft hit Eisenhower a sledge-hammer blow at a White House meeting in the Cabinet Room on April 30, 1953, on the issue of the Administration's first budget. Sherman Adams, the "Assistant to the President" and former governor of New Hampshire, reported that after Eisenhower said that his budget had a 5.5-billion-dollar deficit, "Taft exploded, losing control of himself, pounding his fist on the Cabinet table, and shouting at the stunned President, who was sitting opposite him, 'With a program like this, we'll never elect a Republican Congress in 1954. You're taking us down the same road Truman traveled. It's a repudiation of everything we promised in the campaign!' Taft went on to declare that he had no confidence in the Joint Chiefs of Staff and that Eisenhower was being badly taken in by these professional military people."

Representative Daniel Reed of New York, chairman of the House Ways and Means Committee, was another Republican who made it unnecessary for the Democrats to attack the Administration. Seventy-seven-year-old Reed, in Congress since 1919, believed that at last he held the power to slash income taxes 11 per cent and eliminate the wartime excess profits tax; and budget deficit or not he intended to do so. Eisenhower, who had little understanding of taxes, budgets, and economics but could repeat what professional economists in the Administration told him, called Reed to the White House to attempt an explanation of the folly of cutting taxes at a time of spiraling inflation. Egged on by House Democrats, Reed, who looked like a neat and smug Yankee general store operator, listened absently and remained determined to continue on his course despite the repeated pleas of Eisenhower. So adamant was he in his scheme to move on his own and thus force the Administration to accept his independent step that he became known as "the Syngman Rhee of Capitol Hill." However, Democratic members who had urged Reed to fight with Eisenhower joined Administration friends on the House Rules Committee in preventing Reed's bill from being reported out to the House floor and it died there. Then after Democrats convinced old Reed that he should retaliate against the Administration's bill to extend the excess profits tax by not calling a meeting of his committee, they double-crossed him again by working with Republicans on the Rules Committee to order the Eisenhower tax bill reported directly to the floor. Joe Martin said afterward that Reed could get support from Mister Sam's boys "when he didn't need it, but he could not get it when he did need it."

Taft also gave Eisenhower a hard time when it came to fulfilling the plank in the 1952 platform that stated: "The Government of the United

States, under Republican leadership, will repudiate all commitments contained in secret understandings such as those of Yalta which aid Communist enslavements." Taft wanted to push a resolution through the Senate that would nullify the Yalta Agreement reached between Roosevelt, Churchill, and Stalin, as well as the Potsdam Agreement entered into by Truman. However, Secretary of State John Foster Dulles considered such a resolution would end any hope of bipartisan support for Eisenhower's foreign policy. Besides, as he told Taft at a White House wrangle, those treaties were valid. The only resolution he would propose, he told the Senate majority leader, was one in which Congress assured those living behind the Iron Curtain that the Administration would utilize all "peaceful means" to help them win their freedom; and instead of mentioning the agreements by name, the resolution should also simply repudiate "any interpretation" of agreements that "have been perverted" to enslave people under communism.

Taft denounced this as a wishy-washy effort that did not meet the requirements of the party platform. But his long-running argument with Dulles and Eisenhower ended when Soviet dictator Stalin died on March 5, 1953, for he recognized that the President needed an opportunity to deal with the new Communist masters without a resolution that in effect condemned Roosevelt and Churchill and threatened war with the USSR.

A few weeks later Taft had another opportunity for slapping the Administration, when Eisenhower nominated Charles Bohlen, Roosevelt's interpreter at Yalta, as ambassador to the Soviet Union. This nomination enraged Republican members of the Foreign Relations Committee, and when a dozen Republican senators called it a "blunder," Eisenhower invited Taft to the White House for a meeting.

This time, despite his own opposition to Bohlen, Taft agreed to promote the confirmation. Leaders of the hate pack were McCarthy, Malone, Goldwater, Dirksen, and Mundt, and charges flew that Bohlen's FBI file would reveal him totally unacceptable because of its load of derogatory information. To check the truth of this, Taft and Senator John Sparkman were given Presidential permission to examine the file. After reporting back to the Senate that "there was no suggestion anywhere by anyone reflecting on the loyalty of Mr. Bohlen," Taft pushed through his confirmation by a vote of seventy-four to thirteen. Eleven of the adverse votes were Republican.

Following the Bohlen success, Eisenhower wrote in his diary: "Senator Taft and I are becoming good friends." However, Taft's health was already on the decline, and though he went downhill fast with spreading cancer, he continued to utter strong opinions on the issues. Finally on June 10, 1953, he resigned as majority leader, and on July 31 he was dead. Johnson told a reporter that on hearing of Taft's passing, he walked into the Senate Chamber, approached Senator Clinton Anderson, who held the floor at the time, and whispered while tears coursed down his cheeks, "Clint, Clint! Have you heard? Bob is dead."

As it turned out Johnson had good reason to weep at Taft's passing. For when Governor Frank Lausche of Ohio appointed Democrat Tom Burke to succeed Taft, the Democrats swept into a forty-eight to forty-seven lead over Senate Republicans. But since Wayne Morse, the gravel-voiced, self-proclaimed Independent Party of one, would not end his feud with Johnson, his continuing vote for the Republican organization of the Senate prevented Johnson from becoming majority leader.

When Taft departed from the scene, Eisenhower could have named his successor as majority leader because of the willingness of Senate Republicans to accept his choice. However, because he remembered his schoolbook glorification of the doctrine of "Separation of Powers," he declined to do so, with the result that Senate Republicans proceeded to choose Senator William Knowland of California as their leader. This was an unfortunate choice, said Sherman Adams, because "it would have been difficult to find anyone more disposed to do battle with much of the President's program in Congress." The bull-necked, bull-voiced Knowland was a McCarthy supporter, a competitor of Vice President Nixon, and a man obsessed with a desire to place American military might behind an invasion of the Chinese mainland by Chiang Kai-shek.

From this point on, until Knowland left the Senate in 1959, Adams said, President Eisenhower "struggled patiently, trying to win cooperation from Knowland." Frequently he invited the burly Californian to breakfast and he praised him publicly almost as warmly as he lauded Winston Churchill. "Then Knowland would knock over the apple cart, and Eisenhower had to try all over again," Adams noted. One time in anguish Eisenhower told an aide, "I will spend hours here in the office staring out these windows, sometimes a little hopelessly, with Senators Dirksen or Millikin or Knowland here, to tell me what industries I have to protect with higher tariffs—or how the folks back home don't like these big bills for Mutual Security."

Even though he missed out on the opportunity to become majority leader, the passing of Taft was a fortunate event in Lyndon Johnson's career. Taft had dominated the Senate in a one-man display of authority, but Knowland, lacking both his prestige and his parliamentary mastery, was no match for power-hungry Johnson fortified by advice from Senators Russell and George. Still another gain for Johnson was that for the first time President Eisenhower took note of his existence and came to depend on him more and more to aid passage of his legislative program. As Sherman Adams explained the oddity of a Republican President working with the leaders of the minority party, "Many of the President's aims and hopes actually received more sympathy from the Democratic leaders in

Congress, Lyndon Johnson and Sam Rayburn." Because of this Eisenhower took to inviting them along with Senators George and Fulbright to his second-floor oval White House office, where "over a drink and a canape, Eisenhower smoothed the road for many of his goals and legislative purposes."

However, this warm relationship between Eisenhower and the minority leaders served to bring on further suspicion of Johnson by Northern liberals, for Eisenhower had openly boasted of removing all traces of former President Truman from the White House with the exception of the balcony Truman had added to the Executive Mansion. The Truman piano was banished along with the large world globe that had been a feature of the President's office, and the downstairs bowling alley was closed. This Eisenhower animosity extended also to Adlai Stevenson, who gave the impression that the intellectuals, or "eggheads," backed him while only dollar-grubbing businessmen were for Eisenhower. In rebuttal, Eisenhower jeered at Stevenson by telling his bridge-playing cronies one evening, "An egghead is a guy who thinks he has to step out of the shower to take a leak."

As Eisenhower stepped up his castigation of Truman and Stevenson, his praise of Johnson and Mister Sam grew steadily more enthusiastic. It reached such heights, Johnson told a *Time* reporter, that on one occasion when he visited Eisenhower in his office, "the President pointed to the leather chair behind his desk. 'Some day,' he said, 'you'll sit in that chair.' " Johnson said that his reply was, "No, Mr. President, that's one chair I'll never sit in. I wouldn't trade desks with you for anything in the world." To this, he claimed, Eisenhower said "with a burst of laughter, 'Well, I'll trade with you any time.' "

This oddity of a Republican President who was more at ease with the Democratic leaders of Congress than his Republican leaders interested Washington reporters, and at one Presidential news conference a newsman wanted to know why he did not punish Republicans who voted against his legislative proposals. "I don't think it is a function of a President to punish anybody for voting what he believes," he said. Another time he explained further, "You don't 'lead' a man by yelling at him in public or forcing him to say publicly, 'Yes, it's true—I've been voting like a fool ever since I came to Congress.' If I forced him to do that, he would stay converted only long enough to get off his knees and curse me."

Chapter 40

D URING THE EISENHOWER years of Johnson's Senate minority leadership, several important actions occurred. Foremost among these was the Korean Armistice, which brought to a halt the two-and-a-half-year nightmarish war where meaningless hills were taken and retaken and American soldiers were brainwashed by the Communists at an alarming rate. It was also a time when the Shivercrats were rewarded with the tidelands for their desertion of the Democratic party; and when the McCarthy assault upon free thought was finally checked. In addition, it was a period that witnessed the decision of the Administration not to save the French in their eight-year attempt at the physical reconquest of their Indochinese colony.

Understandably, Johnson's most earnest effort came on the tidelands issue. On foreign affairs he had no voice, though he spoke out freely; and on McCarthyism he stayed silent, playing a waiting game until an overwhelming number of senators could no longer tolerate the Wisconsin firebrand.

When Senator Richard Russell went to Denver in alien country in his preconvention campaign swing on June 27, 1952, he condemned the Truman Administration for relying on "cheap security" in fighting the Korean War. He promised that if he were President, he would speed jet plane production and then devastate North Korea into bomb-crater surrender.

Early in the next Republican Congress, he promoted this view with the assistance of Johnson and Symington on the Armed Services Committee in an effort to force Eisenhower's hand. Secretary of State Dulles proved a ready ally on a hard-line foreign policy that was predicated on heavy military involvement; but President Eisenhower, who could vividly recall that when he entered the Falaise Gap Zone in Normandy in 1944, "it was literally possible to walk for hundreds of yards at a time, stepping on nothing but dead and decayed flesh," took a frowning view of a cocked foreign policy pistol.

When Stalin died on March 5, 1953, Eisenhower disheartened the hard-liners by making a speech that expressed his desire for peaceful co-existence with the Soviet Union. Stories in Congress had Eisenhower ready to hit North Korea and China with atomic bombs when word came from the new Soviet dictator Georgi Malenkov through Chinese Communist Foreign Minister Chou En-lai that a fair Korean truce was negotiable at last.

Eisenhower quickly accepted the basic truce conditions, which permitted only voluntary repatriation of prisoners of war, and reset the boundary at the Thirty-Eighth Parallel. This failed to please Syngman Rhee, who was counting on an expanded war to capture all of Korea, and the seventy-eight-year-old Rhee preferred igniting the world in World War III to an acceptance of the truce talk results. Rhee's position won support from Congressional extremists, who added to the confusion by demanding total war against Red China. Fortified by this news, Rhee revealed his contempt for the negotiations by deliberately releasing twenty-five thousand North Koreans from Allied prisoner-of-war camps and proclaiming his intention of freeing the northern part of Korea by force, dragging the Americans in behind him.

The weeks of dealing with Rhee gave Eisenhower a feeling of "helplessness." At a Cabinet meeting on the subject of Rhee he wailed, "There's one thing I've learned in the five years I served in the Army out there [in the Philippines]. We can never figure out the workings of the Oriental mind. . . . If anybody has any ideas, for God's sake, don't hold them back." He was met with silence.

But eventually Rhee backed down, and the truce was signed on July 26, 1953. The United States was once more at peace, though the hardliners found this an error. Johnson's view was that if any Communist satellite became involved in military action in the future, the United States should attack the Soviet Union. As he said in a speech made some months earlier but recirculated now: "We should announce that any act of aggression, anywhere, by any Communist forces, will be regarded as an act of aggression by the Soviet Union. We should keep strength ready, the strength we are now building. If anywhere in the world—by any means, open or concealed—Communism trespasses upon the soil of the free world, we should unleash all the power at our command upon the vitals of the Soviet Union."

Bill Kittrell, the lobbyist friend of Sam Rayburn, enjoyed retelling Mister Sam and Lyndon that it was through him that the train of events developed to make Eisenhower the tidelands hope of the Texas oil crowd.

Right after Pearl Harbor, said Bill, he and a friend were traveling to Washington with oilman Sid Richardson aboard the *Blue Bonnet,* the crack express train on the Missouri, Kansas-Texas Railroad. After a time, Richardson grew tired of "shooting the bull," and he grunted at Kittrell to wander through the train and corral someone who knew how to play bridge. Bill said he picked up a stranger, a grinning Army colonel named Dwight Eisenhower, and they passed hours together playing bridge and talking.

In February 1952, more than a decade later, Sid Richardson flew to London with George Allen—a Truman friend who was a business partner of Eisenhower in a downtown Washington restaurant. Richardson became one of the long list of people who begged Eisenhower to seek the Republican nomination and fight "Trumanism." By this he meant the Administration's stand on tidelands oil, and if Ike became the Republican nominee, he said, he could count on campaign help from him. This was a substantial promise, for Richardson's wealth was estimated at almost a billion dollars.

During the campaign the Texas oil men had led the charge away from the Democratic camp, and even Richardson's young attorney, John Connally, who was on his way to becoming a millionaire because of this association, joined the flight to Eisenhower. Afterward, newly elected President Eisenhower gave notice he would redeem his pledge to the tidelands oil-holding states.

Happily, with Taft in charge of the tidelands bill in the Senate, Johnson had no need to play an obtrusive role. During the April 1953 debate he spoke only twenty minutes for the bill. Afterward he told a reporter: "I proceed on the rule you don't have to explain what you don't say." The irony was that had he been majority leader instead of minority leader, he would have been forced to lead the floor battle for the measure. This would have cost him dearly with the already suspicious Northern liberals and endangered his future relations with them.

While he sat back, sure that Taft, who was not enthusiastic for the bill, would win in the end, he listened to Senator Millikin lead the Republican attack on the measure; read the testimony of Eisenhower's Attorney General Herbert Brownell, who told a Senate committee that the offshore wealth belonged to the nation and not merely to California, Texas, and Louisiana; heard oil-state Democrats blast Stevenson and defend Eisenhower and nonoil-state Democrats cry out about a "steal" and a "give-away."

One Southern oil-less Democrat attacking the bill was Lister Hill of Alabama, who read a forty-five-thousand-word statement. Another Southern Democrat, Johnson's new colleague Price Daniel, had much to say in the bill's favor, for he had argued the Texas offshore oil land case before the Supreme Court in 1950. Daniel's wife Jean was a great-great-great-granddaughter of Sam Houston, and this fact had been made known to Chief Justice Fred Vinson before the case was heard. The camel-faced Vinson, who had a historic thirst for anything pertaining to Houston, told friends afterward that he had almost been swayed by clever Daniel, who had carefully larded his argument with numerous references to the Texas hero. But when it came time to make his decision, said Vinson, he was swayed more by his good friend Harry Truman than his love of

Sam Houston, and his vote in that 1950 case made the Supreme Court's decision four to three against Texas.

The Senate debate grew overheated and reached its climax when anti-tidelander Senator Wayne Morse set a filibustering record on April 24 by talking twenty-two hours and twenty-six minutes without rest to publicize the issue in favor of federal ownership. During his marathon talk he dramatically had his aides taste his food and sip his beverages, for he believed the oil crowd, expecting great favors from the states with the passage of the bill, planned to drug him and end his filibuster. The Washington *Post*'s comment on his effort went: "If it is endurance that he wishes to demonstrate, it is a pity that he does not take up pole sitting or marathon dancing."

The five-week debate finally ended on May 5 when the Senate voted 56 to 35 to approve the award to Texas, California, and Louisiana. Then on May 22 Eisenhower signed it. Governor Shivers could now claim his desertion of the Democratic ticket in 1952 had been wise.

During the time that the ownership of the submerged tidelands underwent Congressional debate, Shivers was quietly trying to ruin Sam Rayburn. Early in 1953, when the Texas State Legislature considered a bill to redistrict Congressional seats to meet the 1950 Census changes since 1940, Shivers attempted to slip the Republican silk-stocking area of Dallas into Rayburn's Fourth District. For a time it looked as though he would succeed, but in the end a majority of state legislators refused to sanction his mean, spiteful move.

The years 1953–1954 encompassed far-reaching foreign policy matters, of which the Korean armistice was one of many events. Johnson was not a member of the Senate Foreign Relations Committee, but he had deliberately helped create an Adlai Stevenson vacuum in Democratic party policy in order to raise his own importance, and he injected himself into this gap despite his lack of background.

One tempestuous issue was the Bricker Amendment to curtail the President's Constitutional authority over foreign affairs. Even before Eisenhower was inaugurated on January 20, 1953, Senator John Bricker of Ohio, a handsome but dull-eyed former governor, railroad attorney, and Republican Vice-Presidential nominee in 1944, introduced his resolution calling for an Amendment to the Constitution. Bricker's purpose was to prevent future "Yaltas" as well as United States acceptance of such United Nations measures as the "Covenant on Human Rights," written under the guidance of Mrs. Franklin Roosevelt. Although it was a slap at Democratic Administrations, sixty-two senators including many Democrats joined him as cosponsors. A Democrat who announced himself in favor of the Bricker Amendment was Lyndon Johnson.

When Eisenhower first heard about the Bricker Amendment, he did not know what to make of it. But after State Department lawyers explained its ramifications, his conclusion was that "Bricker is trying to save the United States from Eleanor Roosevelt." Under the proposal, Congress would have "power to regulate all Executive and other agreements." This was one encroachment on Executive authority. Another provision, known as the Which Clause, stipulated that a treaty could not "become effective as internal law" inside the United States without special legislation by Congress.

What disturbed Eisenhower was that Bricker already had almost enough support for the two-thirds vote required for a Constitutional Amendment. In addition Bricker had resurrected a year-old speech by Dulles, in which the Secretary of State expressed concern that, because treaties were "the supreme law of the land," a ruthless President might make one with another country that contained provisions to curtail American civil rights or the powers of states. But Dulles backed away from this speech, and during the rest of 1953 the Administration fought a delaying action with Bricker by feigning the need for further discussions to arrive at a satisfactory compromise.

Bricker finally caught on to what was happening, and at the beginning of 1954 he pushed for immediate passage of his resolution. When the Senate Judiciary Committee reported it out favorably, Knowland plucked it from the Senate Calendar and brought it to the floor for action. Vociferous support came from the DAR, the Chicago *Tribune* and the Vigilant Women for the Bricker Amendment, and Texas papers said that Senator Johnson had given it his blessing.

"The vote on the 'Which Clause' came on February 17," said Senator Kilgore. "As a rule, Lyndon's boy, Bobby Baker, would call you so you knew what was on deck. But I received no call, and it was by accident that I walked on the floor just after a 43-to-43 tie vote. So I quickly voted against the 'Which Clause' that required a special bill to put treaties into operation domestically, and that was the death of it."

However, the Democratic leaders in the Senate came to the conclusion that the Bricker Amendment without the "Which Clause," or one that would hog-tie a President if he desired to make an Executive Agreement with the head of another country, should be enacted. This produced the George Amendment, sponsored by Senator George and promoted by Minority Leader Johnson. Before the vote on February 26, 1954, George reacted irascibly to news that Attorney General Herbert Brownell had sent a memo to Knowland questioning one of the amendments to the proposed Constitutional Amendment. "The United States has a very odd little Attorney General," George told the Senate, adding that in all probability "some kloik in the department was the real author."

The close tally on February 26 showed that of the 91 senators voting, 60 said *Aye*. With only a single additional vote in its favor, the George Amendment would have had the necessary two-thirds required. Afterward, Johnson, who had voted for it, confided to a doubting reporter that he had engineered this cliff-hanging vote. He said he had done so in order to make the Administration sweat.

In his determined sweep toward making himself the Democratic party's spokesman, Johnson also considered it to his advantage to push himself into the CIA's 1954 adventure to foment a revolution in Guatemala. Here the cruel military dictator, General Jorge Ubico, had finally been over-thrown in 1944, and in 1950 the Communist-oriented government of Jacobo Arbenz Guzmán gained control, seized the property of the United Fruit Company, and began large-scale imports of Czechoslovakian arms.

Secretary of State Dulles started the Administration's plan of action against the Arbenz Government by winning approval of his March 1954 resolution from the conference of the Organization of American States (OAS). This was a declaration of "solidarity for the preservation of polit-ical integrity of the American States against international communism," and it was followed by United States Navy stoppage of "suspicious for-eign-flag vessels on the high seas off Guatemala to examine" and seize cargo. Then in June came the CIA invasion of Guatemala from Honduras through the person of Colonel Carlos Castillo Armas, an exiled Guatemalan, and his United States-armed ground troops and tiny air corps.

In the midst of this operation, the United States origins and strategy of which were being kept secret, Johnson devised a plan to make it ap-pear that the Senate Democrats under his direction were forcing the Administration to do something about "Soviet interference" inside Guate-mala. This came in the form of his resolution, approved by a vote of 69 to 1, calling for United States intervention to end "the beachhead in the Americas now." The Johnson Doctrine proposed treating Communist and Communist-oriented regimes differently from other dictatorships. His resolution limited action solely to "Communist penetration of the Western Hemisphere"; and, as he explained his lack of concern with home-grown American dictatorships: "We are concerned only with external [Soviet] aggression," which eliminates any "question here of United States inter-ference in the domestic affairs of any American state."

A friend of Johnson once remarked, "Lyndon will go which way the wind blows." And another friend added, "Maybe, but if he does, he'll probably beat the wind there."

This was Johnson's approach in the McCarthy affair, which reached its climax while he was minority leader.

The McCarthy scourge had risen so dramatically that by 1952 the nation was whipped into hysteria over his charges that Communists had in-filtrated into the departments of the United States Government. McCar-thyism spread like lava into the private sector of the economy as well. Fearful of damage to their profit levels, many firms were engaged in cowardly wholesale firings and blacklistings of employees against whom charges of Communist affiliation and guilt by association had been leveled. That year's Presidential campaign showed the effect of McCarthyism when General Eisenhower deleted a favorable reference to General Marshall in his Wisconsin speech, to appease McCarthy, who was using Marshall as a punching bag. And in the Congressional elections political observers said that McCarthy had influenced eight Senate contests.

In the Senate that year McCarthy was arrogantly calling complaining senators by a variety of derogatory nicknames in his effort to ridicule anyone who challenged him. Senator William Benton, who found himself referred to as "Connecticut's little mental midget" in floor debate, finally brought charges against the Wisconsin senator, and a Senate Privileges and Elections Subcommittee undertook hearings. Benton's chief charge was that McCarthy had committed perjury in denying that he had made the statement at Wheeling that he held a list of 205 card-carrying members of the Communist party who were employed by the State Department. Other charges involved McCarthy's speculation in soy bean futures based on his inside information, his receipt of ten thousand dollars to write a pamphlet for a firm under investigation by a committee on which he served, and immense "loans" made to him by a bank in his home town of Appleton, Wisconsin.

Johnson was involved in discussions regarding the decision of the Senate Privileges and Elections Subcommittee, for the Democrats held a majority of seats. But after the 1952 election, when the Republicans gained control of the Senate and Benton lost his re-election contest, Johnson's opinion was that the subcommittee should quietly fold its tent without making any recommendations and let the Republicans handle their own problem when they took over in January. This was the course followed by Senators Tom Hennings of Missouri and "Silent Carl" Hayden, who were jeered at by the victorious McCarthy as "lackeys of the Truman Administration." With Benton no longer a member of the Senate, he had no recourse against the Johnson strategy.

As a member of the victorious party McCarthy had gained enormous official power in 1953 in his "crusade," because seniority elevated him to chairmanship of the Government Operations Committee and its Permanent Subcommittee on Investigations. This allowed him to hire investigators and hold hearings of his choice, and before long he was including the Eisenhower Administration as an object of his attacks along with the departed Truman Administration.

In his own party McCarthy's closest allies were Vice President Nixon and Senators Taft, Knowland, Dirksen, Mundt, Jenner, and Hickenlooper. Among the Democrats he had admiration for his rival Communist hunter, Pat McCarran, as well as for Jim Eastland and Ed Johnson. McCarthy's view of Lyndon Johnson was that he was on the right track with his call for total destruction of the Soviet Union the next time any Communist aggression occurred anywhere on the globe.

Although he was now numbered by Eisenhower aides as friendly to the Administration, Minority Leader Johnson was not above using McCarthy to upset the smug tone of righteousness at the White House. In May 1953, for example, urged on by Johnson's pal Stuart Symington, who sat on his committee, McCarthy wrote a letter to Eisenhower demanding a Presidential statement denouncing British trade with Red China. Since Britain was the principal American ally, such a statement would have jeopardized American foreign policy.

"It was Nixon who finally got us out of it," said Sherman Adams. McCarthy withdrew his letter after Nixon convinced him that "his Democratic fellow senators, Symington and McClellan, had gotten him to embarrass the Republican Administration."

Eisenhower's early decision was not to "get into the gutter" with McCarthy but to ignore his existence. Unfortunately, this decision was interpreted by Secretary of State Dulles as a policy of appeasement, when McCarthy's two young gumshoes, Roy Cohn and David Schine, made a whirlwind two-week European trip for his subcommittee to investigate Communist influence in the Department's Overseas Information Program. On their return, after insulting embassy employees in every capital and demanding special privileges, they reported "appalling infiltration." Instead of ignoring their written nonsense, Dulles ordered all personnel fired whom they had named, and he sent a directive to the Department's overseas libraries to destroy books "by any Communists, fellow-travelers, etc."

Despite demands by Senator Lehman that Johnson support him in a move to condemn McCarthy after the Cohn-Schine hi-jinks, Johnson stubbornly refused to do so, arguing that Lehman should leave McCarthy to the Republicans. By now Eisenhower was aroused, and when he went to Dartmouth to get an honorary degree in June 1953, he told his audience, "Don't join the book-burners. Don't be afraid to go in your library and read every book." A month later he revoked Dulles' directive. Then when J. B. Matthews, McCarthy's chief investigator, wrote in a summer issue of *American Mercury* that the "largest single group supporting the Communist apparatus in the United States today is composed of Protestant clergymen," Eisenhower let out a blast at Matthews. This disturbed even Senator McCarthy, and when the three Democrats on his subcommittee, Protestants all—McClellan, Symington, and Jackson—walked out in protest against his investigator, he fired Matthews.

McCarthy next jumped on the CIA as a Red haven, and when he failed to make headway, he turned on the Army. In January 1954 he began digging his own political grave by attacking the generals and other officers at Camp Kilmer, New Jersey, for permitting Major Irving Peress, an Army dentist, to resign with an honorable discharge after he refused to sign a loyalty certificate. "You're shielding Communist conspirators!" he screamed at Brigadier General Ralph Zwicker, Kilmer's commander, when he heard that Peress had been given a promotion before his discharge.

Senator Dirksen, one of McCarthy's friends and a member of his subcommittee, attempted to head off the growing battle between McCarthy and the military by inviting Secretary of the Army Robert Stevens to join the Republicans on the subcommittee in a secret fried-chicken lunch in his office. Stevens came to this clandestine session only to find a hundred reporters in front of Dirksen's door. Afterward, Stevens returned to his office and reported that McCarthy had promised not to harass Army officers in the future. But this was in conflict with the "Memorandum of Agreement" Senator Mundt read to the newsmen after the fried chicken was gone. According to Mundt, Stevens had agreed to supply "Joe" with the names of all officers who had had anything to do with Peress' promotion and honorable discharge.

It was freshman Senator Charles Potter, Republican member of McCarthy's subcommittee and a war hero who had lost both legs in the European fighting, who induced Stevens to make public a chronology of McCarthy's threats and demands. The Stevens paper told in detail the efforts by McCarthy and Cohn to gain special privileges for Schine, who had been drafted into the Army. One of these lobbying attempts had centered on forcing Stevens to accept Schine as his special assistant in ferreting out Army subversives. When McCarthy offered a rebuttal of forty-six countercharges, the controversy was suddenly too large to ignore.

At McCarthy's suggestion, Senator Mundt took over the chairman's seat temporarily for a showdown hearing with the Army. McCarthy's error was in agreeing to televise the hearing, for his dark beard, nasal monotone, and the detailed story of his underhanded activities could only result in his undoing before a nationwide audience.

For thirty-six days national productivity was sharply reduced as the Army-McCarthy spectacle went on, with McCarthy constantly calling out, "Point of order; point of order, Mr. Chairman." Testimony revealed he had engaged in wire-tapping, picture-cropping, and pressuring government employees to steal confidential files for him. Before the hearings McCarthy's chant had been "Twenty years of treason" (referring to the Roosevelt and Truman Administrations). But when Eisenhower expressed his opposition to the McCarthy tactics revealed in the hearing, McCarthy said, "The evidence of treason has been growing over the past twenty—[long pause]—twenty-one years!"

On June 17, 1954, the hearings ended with such damage to McCarthy that for the first time most Republican senators thought he should be punished. However, it was not until July 30 that Republican Senator Ralph Flanders, a crusty seventy-four-year-old Vermonter, introduced a resolution to censure McCarthy for bringing "the Senate into disrepute." Friends of

McCarthy immediately argued that no valid precedent existed for such action, but Johnson raced into the cloakroom and asked Senator George, who was talking to friends and smoking, if he knew of previous instances. George replied that old Jim Preston, the superintendent of the Senate press gallery, often spoke of the time in February 1902 when Senator John Mc-Laurin of South Carolina called "Pitchfork Ben" Tillman, the other South Carolina senator, a "willful, malicious, and deliberate liar," a charge that led old Ben to punch him in the face and bring on a slugging, wrestling fight in the Senate Chamber. The Senate had not only censured them but also suspended both men for six days. Then there was the Bingham censure in 1929, said George, while Johnson led him into the chamber.

Senator George spoke at length to his colleagues on the 1929 action, one in which he had personally participated. Senator Hiram Bingham of Connecticut had brought a tariff lobbyist into closed-door hearings of the Finance Committee deliberating the Hawley-Smoot Tariff Bill's individual rates. Bingham had brought the man in under the guise that he was his "secretary," and for this activity the Senate overwhelmingly approved the Senator George Norris resolution of censureship, calling Bingham's subterfuge "contrary to good morals and senatorial ethics, and tends to bring the Senate into dishonor and disrepute, and such conduct is hereby condemned."

After George's discourse the Senate on August 2 voted on a joint proposal by Johnson and Knowland to set up a special six-man committee, composed equally of Democrats and Republicans, to study charges of misconduct against McCarthy. The vote to appoint the committee was an overwhelming 75 to 12, but the shocker was that nine Democrats (Chavez, Douglas, Fulbright, Hennings, Hill, Humphrey, Lehman, Magnuson, and Monroney) considered the action too weak to bring about adequate punishment for McCarthy, and they voted against the six-man committee.

Johnson had promised Knowland he would get George and Russell to serve on the special select committee. But when neither would accept, Johnson dug deeper in the conservative barrel and came up with Senator John Stennis of Mississippi, Ed Johnson of Colorado, and Sam Ervin of North Carolina. Knowland in turn failed to talk Senator Millikin into serving, and his final list noted three uninfluential Republicans, Arthur Watkins of Utah (to be chairman), Francis Case of South Dakota, and Frank Carlson of Kansas. When Vice President Nixon made the formal appointments of these six, the committee began two weeks of hearings.

On September 27 the Watkins Committee issued its report, calling for McCarthy's censure on two counts: his contempt for the Senate, and his vicious treatment of General Zwicker. The Senate went into recess until the November elections ended (Johnson was one of the members re-elected), and it returned on November 8 for a month of deliberations in the Senate chamber on the McCarthy question.

McCarthy's defense was to attack, and he denounced the special session as a "lynch bee." As for Watkins, McCarthy told reporters the Utah senator was guilty of "the most unusual, most *cowardly* thing I've heard of." He also said, regarding Watkins, that he "didn't think he'd be *stupid* enough to make a public statement." Then after calling the committee "the unwitting handmaiden" of the Communist party, he retired to the hospital with a sore elbow that he claimed came from banging it on a table top while shaking hands.

The debate found tempers short and arguments long, and for a time friends of the ailing senator discussed running a filibuster until the session terminated. When Johnson's turn came to speak, he cautiously avoided any mention of the McCarthy activities that had precipitated the formation of the select committee. Instead, Johnson, who was noted for his profanity, concentrated on crying out at the language McCarthy had used in attacking Watkins and the committee. Portraying the role of a shocked gentleman, the minority leader's voice quavered as he declared, "The words that were used . . . would be more fittingly inscribed on the wall of a men's room." These obscene words, said Johnson, were the characterization of Watkins as "cowardly" and "stupid."

Dirksen, Mundt, and Bridges tried to save McCarthy by offering motions to let him off with a slight slap on the wrist. But their efforts were voted down by more than a 3-to-1 margin, and at last on December 2, 1954, time ran out for further delay or absolution. The question before the Senate was the McCarthy Condemnation Resolution: its wording almost a verbatim copy of the Norris resolution on Bingham's censure in 1929. Like Bingham, McCarthy was charged with conduct that "tends to bring the Senate into dishonor and disrepute . . . and such conduct is hereby condemned."

As the final vote approached, Senate Republican leaders felt sudden remorse that they had agreed to the appointment of the six-man committee. But they could not halt the tide against McCarthy, and the vote stood 67 to 22 in favor of the resolution. Eisenhower was reported to have revealed his low boiling point when he learned that Knowland, Dirksen, Bridges, and Millikin had all supported McCarthy.

On the Democratic side every senator present supported the resolution. Only Senator John Kennedy, who was then in a hospital, laid himself open to charges that he was pro-McCarthy when he refused to tell how he would have voted had he been present. His past record gave evidence that he might have voted against the resolution had he responded to the clerk's call. "Hell, half my voters in Massachusetts look on McCarthy as a hero," he had earlier justified his inactive position at the height of the McCarthy furore.

For this solid-front Democratic party vote Johnson took total credit, adding to the picture his friends in the press were trying to create—that he was the greatest legislative wizard ever to appear on the American scene. Johnson also told reporters that it was he who had talked McCarthy into permitting the tell-tale television cameras into the Army hearings and ruining his image.

So the nightmare of McCarthyism faded temporarily into McCarthy-wasm; and the Wisconsin senator shuffled brokenly about on the scene for another three years begging strangers to smile at him, before dying in 1957 at the age of forty-seven. Senator Watkins also claimed that he was ruined by his McCarthy role, for when he ran for re-election, McCarthy's friends in Utah, an unforgiving lot, helped defeat him.

Chapter 41

A DECADE LATER, when Johnson became President, he made one of his rare displays of humility when he told Eisenhower he knew little about foreign policy. Yet in Eisenhower's first term he expressed himself freely on a host of foreign issues, including one that would dwarf all other matters in his own Administration.

This was the problem of Indochina, a far-off area that Johnson once described as being "as big as Texas." Factual history of Indochina went back more than two thousand years, and because it was known as "the fat man of Asia" with its excess production of rice and rubber, surrounding powers successively invaded it. Then in the nineteenth century it fell under the heel of France, intent on extending its empire to the Far East. French rule over the five Indochinese protectorates and their capitals— Cochin-China (Saigon), Annam (Hué), Cambodia (Pnompenh), Laos (Vientiane), and Tongking (Hanoi)—was noted for the brutality of European governors in keeping the natives in subjugation.

In 1940 Japan entered upon the scene when it demanded and won military bases in northern Indochina after France fell to Nazi Germany. Then when Japanese forces moved south and occupied Camranh Bay, President Roosevelt grew concerned that this would lead to an early attack on Malaysia, Singapore, and the Netherlands East Indies. To signal his displeasure, he froze Japanese assets in the United States and closed the Panama Canal to Japanese ships. Afterward, in talking to Japanese Ambassador Admiral Nomura, Roosevelt proposed that Japan begin to ease the tension between both nations by agreeing to the neutralization of the five Indochinese provinces. But Japan refused, later rejecting an even more comprehensive demand that it reduce its forces in northern Indochina to twenty-five thousand men and promise to withdraw entirely in the future. Two weeks later came Pearl Harbor.

At the time Lyndon Johnson was acquiring his radio station in 1943, Roosevelt was meeting with British Foreign Minister Anthony Eden on Indochina, and he advocated a postwar international trusteeship in preparation for an independent nation there. "France has had the country—thirty million inhabitants—for nearly one hundred years, and the people are worse off than they were at the beginning. . . . France has milked it for one hundred years," Roosevelt told Secretary of State Cordell Hull.

Unfortunately, when Roosevelt died, Jimmy Byrnes, who became Truman's Secretary of State, accepted the view of State Department old-schoolers that France should regain her colony and grant at some future time "an increasing measure of self-government in Indochina." At Potsdam, in July 1945, the conferees agreed that Chiang Kai-shek's troops should accept the surrender of Japanese forces north of the Sixteenth Parallel in Indochina, while British soldiers would intern Japanese troops below that line.

Ho Chi Minh, a wispy, bearded Communist from Annam (Hué), and at one time sentenced to death in absentia by the French, had headed the underground resistance movement during the war against the Japanese. As a collaborator of the American Office of Strategic Services (the forerunner of the CIA), and supplied with American weapons, Ho and his army (the Vietminh) harassed the Japanese and their Vichy French collaborators throughout the conflict.

It was after the Japanese surrender on September 2, 1945, that Ho Chi Minh announced in Hanoi the independence of the Democratic Republic of Vietnam (Indochina). This created a problem for British Major-General Douglas Gracey, in charge of handling the Japanese surrender below the Sixteenth Parallel, for Gracey was aghast at the idea of Asian natives on the mainland ousting a European colonial power. So Gracey rearmed the surrendered Japanese troops, combined them with French troops who had been interned in Saigon, and then joined the two armies with his own forces to fight the Vietnamese until fifty thousand French reinforcements could be landed. When General Douglas MacArthur learned of this action as well as similar episodes in the Netherlands East Indies, he snapped fiercely, "If there is anything that makes my blood boil, it is to see our Allies in Indochina and Java deploying Japanese troops to reconquer the little people we promised to liberate. It is the most ignoble kind of betrayal."

Six months later the French seemingly came to terms with Ho by agreeing to recognize him as the premier of the Republic of Vietnam, a nonforeign affairs government centered at Hanoi. The French Government also induced Ho to permit the stationing of large numbers of French troops in northern Vietnam in exchange for the calling of a referendum in other parts of Indochina to determine whether the people wanted a single independent country with jurisdiction throughout Indochina, whose external affairs would be directed by France.

But on June 1, 1946, only three months afterward, the French set up a South Vietnam puppet government, refused to withdraw the troops dispatched to the north, and disavowed the proposed referendum. Eight years of war now broke out between the French and Ho's Communist forces and non-Communist Indochinese nationalists leagued with him. The point of no return came on November 23, 1946, when a French air and sea attack on the city of Haiphong killed 6,000 civilians.

Little international attention was paid the bitter fighting in Ho Chi Minh's Vietnam, and in the course of a few years his Vietminh guerrillas gained possession of the back country, while the French were masters only of the deltas and big cities. Then in 1950 this war erupted into news dispatches when the Soviet Union and Red China recognized the Ho Government in January and the United States and Britain recognized France's puppet government of Emperor Bao Dai a month later. Bao Dai was an early-day "Jet Set" type who passed his time as a playboy on the Riviera, but Secretary of State Dean Acheson believed he had no recourse but to champion him as the stalwart friend of democracy in Southeast Asia. After denouncing Ho Chi Minh as "an agent of world communism," Acheson declared that the United States would work through Bao Dai to "develop genuine nationalism" in Indochina. This was followed in August 1950 by the arrival of thirty-five American military advisers in Indochina and the promise of large-scale American aid.

Truman found several reasons for supporting the French, who were obviously the Bao Dai Government. For one thing, with the fall of China to Mao Tse-tung in 1949 and the Red invasion of South Korea in 1950, Truman and Acheson saw the French not as colonial despoilers but as brave fighters against the spread of communism in Southeast Asia. Just as compelling a reason was the French hesitancy to accept the American proposal to include France's old enemy, Germany, in the European Defense Community. Truman and Acheson were convinced that unless they appeased France in Indochina, France might not agree to a unified defense alliance for Western Europe that included goose-stepping Germans.

The crisis period in Indochina arrived at the beginning of 1954, at the start of Eisenhower's second year as President. At this juncture, after almost eight straight years of continuous warfare, the French had suffered one hundred and fifty thousand casualties and spent five billion dollars fighting Ho Chi Minh. On top of this the United States had shipped over a billion dollars worth of supplies to the French in Indochina. The French forces numbered two hundred thousand men and combined with an equal number of natives on their side; the anti-Vietminh army stood at four hundred thousand troops. Arrayed against these fighters were three hundred thousand guerrillas who supplied themselves locally except for five thousand tons of supplies that came monthly from Red China. The Chinese Communists across the border demanded full repayment even for these small shipments, and opium and raw materials moved north. Yet with inferior numbers and supplies, Ho Chi Minh's guerrillas controlled four-fifths of the north and half of the south, and an air of impending doom hung over the French.

The crisis arose because of a plan developed by General Navarre, French commander in Indochina in 1953. Under Navarre's plan, French troops would be increased to two hundred and fifty thousand and French native forces to three hundred thousand, creating an edge of one hundred thousand over the Vietminh. With this superiority Navarre hoped to lure the Communists into open-field fighting, instead of the costly guerrilla actions. Eisenhower thought so highly of Navarre's plan that he promised sufficient United States aid to underwrite its cost.

It was late in November 1953 that the French moved ten thousand crack troops to a spot ten miles from Laos and not far below the Chinese border. This was the isolated town of Dien Bien Phu, soon to become world famous. French strategy behind this action was to control a place that sat athwart the supply route from China to the Reds. Dien Bien Phu lay in a plain, and when the Vietminh discovered the French in position in a fortress on flat land they would be expected to fight a hand-to-hand European-style pitched battle in order to reopen the supply route.

Study of the topography made Eisenhower gulp. High hills overlooked the plain, and what if the Vietminh dragged heavy pieces of artillery to the heights and pointed them at the French below? The French assured him that China would not give artillery pieces to the Vietminh, and even if the Reds gained possession of large cannon the hills were too steep to drag the pieces to the top. Eisenhower remained unconvinced, and as the paymaster of the Navarre plan he was derelict in not demanding the removal of the French troops from the harebrained enticement.

In January 1954 the Ho Chi Minh forces accomplished the impossible: artillery pieces ringed Dien Bien Phu; and at a ratio of more than three to one, the Communists outnumbered the French below (who could be supplied solely by air). Eisenhower was aware that should the French fortress succumb, the loss would have little military significance in itself. But psychologically a French defeat here might cause the government of Premier Joseph Laniel to quit Indochina. This would be a blow to the Eisenhower Administration, which had been propagandizing the American people that unlike the Truman Administration it was stopping the spread of communism. In addition, should the French quit Indochina they would be less subject to pressure to permit Germany to become a member of the European Defense Community. Eisenhower now gave some thought to increasing American aid in order to keep the French in action against Ho Chi Minh.

An erratic six months lay ahead for him. On January 4, 1954, at a joint meeting of his Cabinet and Republican Congressional leaders for an advance reading of his State of the Union Message, he was bluntly asked if he planned to send American troops to Indochina. His abrupt reply was *No.* But a month later he was wavering, even though he had long held two beliefs: (1) The United States must avoid a land war in Asia; and (2) United States military action must never be unilateral. As he once said, "If you go it alone in one place, you have to go it alone everywhere."

To pave the way for possible direct American intervention, he found it necessary to give such action meaning other than the restoration of French colonial rule. He therefore requested the French Government to issue a statement promising to grant independence to the three associated states of Laos, Cambodia, and Vietnam "as soon as military victory should be obtained." This was necessary, he said, to depict the French soldiers as fighting not "to sustain their former domination over the area" but as "a clear case of freedom defending itself from Communist aggression."

However, the French refused to issue the statement on the ground that it would serve to promote an independence movement in French North Africa. Yet even this rebuff did not end Eisenhower's concern about what to do regarding Dien Bien Phu's worsening situation. On a cold wintry morning early in 1954 I met him at the padded-cell studio room in the White House where he was taping a television broadcast for that year's Red Cross drive. Afterward we walked to his oval office in the West Wing for an interview. He was tense and preoccupied, and his replies to questions were indecisive outpourings of words that were little related to the subject.

Included in Eisenhower's developing aid program was a large number of B-26's for the French in Indochina. When the Defense Department said that the French were incapable of maintaining the planes, Eisenhower made a fateful move by ordering two hundred Air Force technicians to accompany the planes to the war zone. But since the law barred sending Air Force men overseas on a permanent basis, he created the fakery that they would be away from the United States only until mid-June. Then, concerned that this subterfuge might arouse Congressional animosity, he invited Congressional leaders of both parties to come to the White House and hear his explanation.

Johnson was a member of this group. However, it was Russell who was the principal spokesman for the Democrats. On learning of the B-26 technicians dispatched to Indochina, Russell, always a big war man, did the unexpected. "If you send two hundred now, you'll send twenty thousand before it's over," he prophesied. Senator John Stennis not only supported Russell but went further and opposed any American participation in the French defense of its Indochinese colony.

"I told Eisenhower he was making a terrible mistake sending in those two hundred Air Force men," said Stennis. " 'They are soldiers and they represent our flag, and if they are attacked, we will have to put the force of the government behind them. Why not hire two hundred civilian mechanics and send them in instead?' I asked him. But he would not listen."

Afterward, Johnson told reporters that had they been present they would have seen him "pounding on President Eisenhower's desk" in opposition to the shipping of the two hundred Americans. Other participants denied he had done so. This meeting with Congressional leaders came up at Eisenhower's news conference on March 10. Asked about the reported Stennis warning that the shipment of the two hundred Air Force technicians was the beginning of an American war there, Eisenhower's reply was that he would never violate the exclusive right of Congress to declare war.

While Eisenhower was embroiled in this controversy, events in Europe also involved the war in Indochina. In January-February 1954, the Big Four Foreign Ministers met in Berlin to discuss the long overdue Austrian and German settlements. Nothing worthwhile resulted on these topics, for the Russians would not cooperate. But during the sessions French Foreign Minister Bidault, with the backing of Anthony Eden, proposed a conference at Geneva in late April to discuss a solution of the Indochinese war. Dulles opposed a Geneva Conference, until Bidault said that unless one were held "the moral obligation to carry on the war in Indochina would have to be shifted from French shoulders to American."

When the date for the convening of the Geneva Conference was set for April 26, CIA chief Allen Dulles, brother of John Foster Dulles, told Eisenhower that the Communists would now double their effort to capture Dien Bien Phu and as much of the hapless country as they could before the conference began, in order to dominate the proceedings. Dulles' prediction was borne out by the major attack that began against Dien Bien Phu on March 13. After this, French appeals for air strikes, dropping of atomic bombs, and direct American ground participation reached a crescendo.

Confusion overtook the White House and the Capitol, as full-scale arguments broke out within the Administration and in the Senate. Admiral Arthur Radford, head of the Joint Chiefs of Staff, first proposed air strikes from carriers in nearby seas around the besieged town. Army Chief of Staff Matthew Ridgway opposed this vociferously as of only temporary and indecisive value, yet of a nature that would drag the United States into a big war, as in Korea. "The same old delusive idea that we can do things the cheap, easy way," Ridgway derided the Radford proposal. First would come air attacks, and when these failed to change the situation, ground troops would be sent. In such ground fighting, he foresaw greater casualties than the one hundred and fifty thousand in Korea, because of the Indochinese jungles, climate, rainfall, tropical diseases, lack of transportation facilities, and the failure to convince the people there of the Communist menace.

On Saturday, April 3, Secretary Dulles held a secret conference in his office with eight members of the House and Senate Armed Services Committees. Johnson and Russell were among those present as Admiral Radford outlined a plan to drop atomic bombs on the supply route from China to the Vietminh. Dulles then went into a long ramble, repeating the Domino Theory of Truman and predicting that if Indochina fell, Burma, Thailand, Malaya, and Indonesia would be next, India would be "hemmed in," and Australia, New Zealand, the Philippines, and Japan would not be free states for long. After completing his horrifying picture, Dulles produced a joint resolution he asked the eight congressmen to promote in the House and Senate. This resolution would authorize the President to take whatever action he deemed necessary in the Indochinese theater.

Russell was the spokesman for the congressmen, and backed by Johnson, he offered his own three-point program—U.S. intervention in Indochina must be in coalition with the British Commonwealth and the neighboring countries to Indochina; the United States must not be made to appear to be fighting to save French colonialism; and the French must remain in the war and not pull out.

Russell and Johnson could not speak for the Senate, and here the sentiment was decidedly against American participation under existing conditions. Said Senator John Kennedy: "I am frankly of the belief that no amount of American military assistance can conquer . . . 'an enemy of the people,' which has the sympathy and covert support of the people. . . . To pour money, material, and men into the jungles of Indochina without at least a remote prospect of victory would be dangerously futile and self-destructive."

Stuart Symington told his colleagues that he had learned in Paris that there was no military or political solution in Indochina. Mike Mansfield, former professor of Far Eastern history and a recent observer in Indochina, accused the Administration of purposely bypassing the Senate Foreign Relations Committee to consult with the more warlike Armed Services Committee. Mansfield opposed committing American troops and denounced the proposed joint resolution to give the President a blank check for Indochinese action as an "abdication of responsibility by Congress."

Eisenhower was not a reader of the *Congressional Record,* but he was a listener to the hard-line approach of his Secretary of State. At his April 7 news conference he gave a part of his half hour to a long explanation of the Domino Theory, and in private he sent a request to ailing Prime Minister Winston Churchill that the British join a United States-French coalition "willing to fight if necessary." Churchill's reply revealed his caution, for he said he would not be able to discuss this subject before April 12.

Dulles flew first to Paris, where Premier Laniel issued a statement promising independence to Indochina in a "fraternal association" under a French Union. Pleased by this belated statement, Dulles rushed off to London, where he apparently won quick approval from Churchill to send a token British force if needed to fight alongside Americans in Indochina. But

Churchill backed down on second consideration and opposed joint intervention. "What we are being asked to do," he said, "is to assist in misleading the Congress into approving a military operation which would be in itself ineffective, and might well bring the world to the verge of a major war."

After this British turndown Vice President Nixon made a short campaign for unilateral American intervention. In an off-the-record speech on April 16 at a luncheon of the American Society of Newspaper Editors, he said, "If in order to avoid further Communist expansion in Asia and particularly in Indochina, we must take the risk now by putting American boys in, I believe the Executive Branch of the government has to take the politically unpopular position of facing up to it and doing it."

But if Nixon frightened many editors and newspaper readers with his war-hawkism, his opinion had no influence with the Administration. In a meeting with Republican Congressional leaders on April 26 Eisenhower reported his failure to win Churchill's agreement for a joint venture in Indochina. As a result, he said, "Without allies, we are not going to carry the rest of the world on our back. We are not going to send in American ground forces independently." Dulles, who felt momentarily like a martyr, remarked, "We are confronted by an unfortunate fact. Most of the countries of the world do not share our view that Communist control of any government anywhere is in itself a danger and a threat."

On the day Eisenhower met with his Congressional leaders, the Geneva Conference began, with Red China sitting at the table. At that very time the French defenders at Dien Bien Phu were in their death throes; and on May 7, while the conferees were in the midst of their debate, the French surrendered there.

The day before the French surrender, the Democrats held their one-hundred-dollar-a-plate Jefferson-Jackson Day dinner at the Mayflower Hotel in Washington. Long before the Eisenhower Administration began, the Republicans had continually belabored the Democrats as being "soft on communism" and appeasers. Earlier in 1954 Nixon had aroused the Democrats to fury by his rhetorical question to a nationwide television audience: "Isn't it wonderful that finally we have a Secretary of State who isn't taken in by the Communists, who stands up to them?"

Johnson chose the Mayflower Hotel's Democratic clambake to strike back at Nixon and the Republican accusers. Wild cheers bounced off the walls as he attacked the Administration, and Dulles in particular, for operating a weak foreign policy and not taking more decisive action in Indochina. "Ours is the tradition of Valley Forge and Iwo Jima," he bellowed. "Tomorrow Asia may be in flames. And the day after, the Western Alliance, which the Democrats painstakingly built up brick by brick, will lie in ruins."

Under Dulles, he charged, the United States had suffered a "startling reversal" and stood "in clear danger of being left naked and alone in a hostile world. . . . What is American policy on Indochina? All of us have listened to the dismal series of reversals and confusions and alarms and excursions which have emerged from Washington over the past few weeks. . . . We have been caught bluffing by our enemies. Our friends and allies are frightened and wondering, as we do, where we are headed." Then, as though he were concerned that he sounded too warlike, he added, "This picture of our country needlessly weakened in the world today is so painful that we should turn our eyes from abroad and look homeward."

Dulles stayed only a week at the Geneva Conference, and during his short face-to-face encounter with the Chinese Reds, he made it a point not to glance in the direction of Chou En-lai, the Communist premier. An important conference change occurred after his departure. Mendes-France, campaigning on a pledge to bring peace to Indochina by July 20, succeeded Joseph Laniel as French premier and immediately set to work to honor that pledge. Mendes-France fell a day short of his goal, for on July 21 the British and French on one side and the Communists on the other signed an agreement on Indochina.

Ho Chi Minh fared far worse from the Geneva Conference terms than the gloomy Eisenhower Administration expected at the outset, for after Dien Bien Phu he could easily have overrun the rest of the country. But he agreed to independence for Laos and Cambodia and a two-year split of Vietnam at the Seventeenth Parallel. During that time he would control the north, while Bao Dai and his premier, Ngo Dinh Diem, would be in charge of the south. Then in July 1956 a nationwide Vietnamese election under international supervision would reunite the two halves into a single Vietnam.

The Eisenhower Administration's explanation for these soft terms on the part of Ho was that his Chinese Red ally feared an American attack if the terms were harsher. Other explanations were that the Soviet Union wanted a Ho compromise in order to build French support to kill Eisenhower's hope for a European Defense Community, while the Chinese Communists wanted to present the world with a kinder image of themselves. From Ho Chi Minh's point of view, he saw no need to demand total French capitulation because he expected Laos and Cambodia to turn Communist, and he knew that he would easily win a Vietnamese election because he was the symbol of nationalism and independence.

Eisenhower would not sign the agreement, though he gave his word that the United States would "not use force to disturb the settlement. We also say," he threatened, "that any renewal of Communist aggression would be viewed by us as a matter of grave concern."

As the eight-year crisis was put temporarily to rest, General Ridgway wrote prematurely: "When the day comes for me to face my Maker and account for my actions, the thing I would be most humbly proud of was the fact that I fought against, and perhaps contributed to preventing, the carrying out of some harebrained tactical schemes which would have cost the lives of some thousands of men. To that list of tragic accidents that fortunately never happened I would add the Indochina intervention."

Afterward, Johnson saw a monolithic communism more determined than ever to destroy the West and capture the world. At a dinner for David Sarnoff he dwelt on this theme and proposed establishing a Cold War general staff to counteract the Soviet Union. He would have this staff "direct and coordinate the weapons for a cold war—diplomatic, economic, propaganda." He would give no peace or quarter to the Communists.

PART FIVE
Sam Rayburn's Boy

Chapter 42

~

AT THE 1952 Democratic National Convention Senator Mike Monroney
of Oklahoma had attempted to whip up support for Sam Rayburn as the
party's standard bearer. Mister Sam was pleased with Monroney's effort
because he knew that at seventy this would be his last opportunity to gain
such high office.

"When a few ballots have gone by, and it becomes obvious that none
of the candidates is going to get past first base," said Monroney, "the
delegates will be ready to switch to someone who can hit a home run."

But Rayburn and Monroney planned without taking Truman and Adlai
Stevenson into account, and when Stevenson won the nomination, Mister
Sam knew his historic reputation would be only the footnote that he had far
surpassed Henry Clay's record of serving as speaker of the House for
3,056½ days. This did not deter Rayburn from working hard in Stevenson's behalf, despite the hatred it engendered in the Shivers camp. In that
fall campaign he shouldered many burdensome organizational details, because Wright Morrow, the Texas Democratic committeeman, was working
for Eisenhower.

Following Stevenson's overwhelming defeat and Rayburn's relegation
from speaker to minority leader in the House with the Republican sweep
of Congress, Mister Sam's chief political pleasure lay in his protégé's
rise to minority leader in the Senate. It was at one of his get-togethers with
Lyndon Johnson that he agreed to transfer his now discarded ambition to
the young senator and use what power and strategic sense he possessed to
help him become President.

One considerable problem was that Adlai Stevenson had recovered from
the shock of his 1952 battering and was talking as though he headed the
Democratic party. If he were permitted to do so without challenge, this
would place him in line to win the Democratic Presidential nomination
again in 1956. Therefore, when reporters asked them for their opinions

379

about Stevenson's remarks, Rayburn and Johnson put on pained expressions and acted as though Stevenson were just another former Democratic officeholder without current credentials. In addition they refused to discuss party business and legislative policy with him or to pass along information sent them on foreign and defense matters by the State and Defense Departments. "We won't butt into his business, and he better not butt into ours," Johnson told newsmen. A sensitive man, Stevenson did not hold Rayburn responsible for these snubbings, but added them to the grievances he had already placed in his Johnson file.

Another problem Johnson and Rayburn discussed was the fact that Johnson suffered from the handicap of not being well known to the public, even though his Preparedness Subcommittee had drawn some news stories. Major attention had to be given to the task of whipping up more publicity and sustaining it over a period of time in order to make the Johnson name familiar in all parts of the country and give him a distinctive national image. This publicity had to be favorable, of course, if it were to help him.

It was, therefore, a sharp slap to Johnson when the *Saturday Evening Post* and *Collier's* refused to authorize new profiles of him because they had done him as recently as 1951. There were smaller magazines willing to publicize him, and one of these was the struggling new periodical, *The Reporter*. Douglass Cater, later one of Johnson's White House assistants, wrote an article that appeared in the January 20, 1953, issue, but instead of the friendly résumé Johnson had expected, the tone was highly critical. Cater reported that most of Johnson's colleagues said they could "admire" him but did not "like" him. Cater rated Johnson "stern and ruthless" and "hard as nails," and quoted a fellow senator who had known him since the 1930's as saying: "Lyndon used to talk a great deal about his father and the underdog. He doesn't talk that way any more. He doesn't seem to care for anything any more except power." There was also a quote from Johnson about his pet fret: "I'm damned tired of being called a Dixiecrat in Washington and a Communist in Texas."

A high point in Johnson's publicity hunt came on June 22, 1953, when *Time* magazine featured him with a cover story. He was described as the Democratic politician who had jumped "into the midst of the vacuum" created by Stevenson's defeat and was attempting to keep the party afloat by holding the divergent elements together. *Time* wrote him up as a "nervous boss with a hot temper" who "works three secretaries simultaneously," "has six phones in his office," orders his staff to turn out "as many as four thousand letters a day on electric typewriters," and dresses ostentatiously with "gold diamond studded cuff links shaped like the map of Texas." The cover story also quoted Senator Russell, his Senate Daddy, who paid him a left-handed compliment that went: "He doesn't have the best mind on the Democratic side of the Senate; he isn't the best orator; he isn't the best parliamentarian. But he is the best combination of all those qualities."

As a meat and potatoes politician, Johnson knew that upstaging Adlai Stevenson and gaining a distinctive national image were primary weapons in his drive toward the Presidency; but these would become immediately meaningless should he lose his Senate seat in 1954. As he told Douglass Cater, one qualm he had about becoming minority leader in 1953 was his observation of what had happened to Scott Lucas and Ernest McFarland, his predecessor Democratic leaders. He had accordingly ordered the Library of Congress to make a survey of the fate of floor leaders, he said, and felt better when he learned they were the only two who lost their re-election contests. Had the survey been more accurate, he would have found that John W. Kern, a freshman senator who had been Woodrow Wilson's first-term majority leader, had also suffered defeat when he ran for re-election in 1916.

Johnson took no chances, and he began his 1954 campaign in the fall of 1953, shortly after the first session of the Eighty-third Congress adjourned. He labeled his extensive tour of Texas "nonpolitical," claiming that it had no connection with his race the following year. But there was nothing nonpolitical about the more than two hundred speeches he delivered at county fairs, building dedications, barbecues, and hotel luncheon meetings, or about his lead position in a cowboy get-up astride a sleek horse in parades.

To reporters who asked him questions about his "nonpolitical" tour, Johnson smilingly quoted Sam Rayburn's advice when he was first elected to the House in 1937: "The best way to keep your job is to use your franking privilege in Washington and your heel leather when you're back home." He also quoted Mister Sam's three primary rules for successful politicians: "Do right; make yourself available; and tell about your product."

In his extensive swing around the mammoth state, Johnson put on a good show "pressing the flesh," as he called the important job of shaking hands with the little fellow, who would remember the physical contact the next time he cast a ballot. As Johnson explained the process he had learned from John Connally: "When you extend a handshake to a fellow, you can tell from his pulse and evaluate him by the way his hand feels. If it's warm and if it has a firm grasp, then you know he is affectionate and that he is direct. And if he looks you in the eye, you usually know that he is dependable."

Johnson also considered it basic to exchange a "Howdy" and a few other choice Texas expressions with the voters. "I want them to know Lyndon Johnson," he told a reporter, "so that when I ask them for their votes they won't be likely to say they elect me and then never hear of me again. I want them to ask me questions about their problems, and naturally I want to do everything a senator can do to help them."

Wherever he appeared, there was an uproar. Behind the scenes, and sometimes openly, he upbraided his aides because his hotel bed was too

short, the food tasteless, the scheduling stupid, the speeches too bombastic
—even for a Texan. From Horace Busby and other writers he demanded
speeches with remarks "that will make me sound goddam humble." Disappointed with an aide's performance, he would utter such scalding jibes
as: "You couldn't even pour piss out of your boot," and "You can't
even reach your ass with your right hand."

Besides "pressing the flesh," Johnson held small dinners in a score of
cities with local Democratic chieftains. Here he emphasized his importance
to Texas in his role as Senate minority leader, and he explained why he and
Rayburn had adopted the policy of treating President Eisenhower kindly.
To Democratic liberals, who urged him to attack Eisenhower, Johnson's
stock reply was: "If you're in an airplane flying somewhere, you don't run
up to the cockpit and attack the pilot. Mr. Eisenhower is the only President
we've got. We must help him when we can." If this failed to stop the
grumbling, he added, "It's up to us to save Eisenhower from the Republicans."

After Johnson's return to Washington from this grueling tour, the large
Marsh-Fentress newspaper chain, the influential Houston Harte's San Antonio *Express* and the rest of his extensive Texas chain, and Sam Fore's
paper in Floresville, in the county below San Antonio, took the editorial
position that no Democrat should be his rival candidate in the July 1954
primary. Political insiders recognized immediately a hopeful bit of Johnson
strategy pointing at only a single person—Governor Shivers. Johnson still
believed that despite his continuing appeasement of Shivers, the governor
planned to enter the Senate primary. However, Shivers remained silent on
his future political plans, as he relentlessly continued to teach a men's Sunday School class at the First Baptist Church in Austin after a week's work in
the governor's office at the capitol.

While he waited fearfully for Shivers' decision, Johnson continued to
campaign by long distance. It was customary, for instance, for members of
Congress to praise the leadership in the dusky days of each session. But
Johnson personally solicited overpraise in 1953 among his colleagues, so
that he could frank home to Texas an impressive flood of eulogies. Senator
Albert Gore, Tennessee liberal, was quoted on Johnson's "phenomenal
success . . . patriotism . . . ability and his standards of integrity." Eighty-six-
year-old Theodore Green of Rhode Island commented that "both old and
young have followed him gladly"; Mike Mansfield reported that for the first
time in his eleven years in Congress (ten of which were under Sam Rayburn), he felt like "a member of a unified party." The street of praise grew
so heavy with traffic at one point that Senators Symington, Clyde Hoey, and
Ed Johnson all shouted at the same time to Vice President Nixon for recognition so they could add their fulsome plaudits.

In addition to distributing this praise under his free-mailing privileges,
Johnson filled mailbags each week with his staff-written newsletter, which
went to the several hundred weekly newspapers in Texas, copies of his

speeches for general distribution, and tapes of his weekly recording for radio stations of his "Report to the People."

Johnson's worries about Shivers increased early in 1954 when the governor frequently praised him. But finally Shivers announced his decision to run for an unprecedented third term as governor, and at this good news Johnson's friends called to congratulate him. However, they found him almost as concerned as before, because a political unknown, thirty-year-old Dudley Dougherty, a Beeville millionaire rancher-oilman, had entered the Senate primary against him.

Young Dougherty, a long-sideburned candidate in dude cowboy attire, was a state representative whose only point of political reference was that he had made the largest single contribution in Texas to Adlai Stevenson's 1952 Presidential campaign. But once in the race with Johnson, Dougherty managed a ninety-degree turn from liberal to reactionary, because he believed this was the majority level of Texas thinking in 1954. Coke Stevenson, who became the young candidate's campaign manager in order to win revenge against Johnson for 1948, agreed with Dougherty's analysis, and the two planned the campaign to portray Johnson as a dangerous radical.

Dougherty launched his senatorial venture with a twenty-four-hour radio and television marathon that made a joke of the ten-thousand-dollar campaign limitation. Unfortunately for him, his endurance stint revealed stark naked so many personality shortcomings that his backers realized they had committed a major blunder by permitting this needless exposure. Viewers found him a fumbling, bumbling, tiresome bore, though there were few phoned-in complaints about what he said. One of his repeated points was that the United States must quit the UN. Monetarily, he demanded a return to the Hoover gold standard; and he managed to combine religion, McCarthyism, and anti-federalism into the single slogan: "Clean the Godless Commies out of the State Department."

After this failure, Dudley Dougherty attempted to bring a touch of Pappy O'Daniel–Farmer Jim "Pa" Ferguson color into his campaign by racing across the state in a shiny red fire truck and speaking from the rear of this clanging vehicle. His message remained the same, though he grew personal about his opponent. He charged Johnson with backing the international policies of Presidents Roosevelt and Truman, and he placed newspaper ads that featured a Dallas *News* editorial for September 22, 1952, attacking the Johnson wealth. Dougherty also liked to read the *News* story that said Johnson "went to Congress as a barefoot boy with absolutely no resources of his own. Although his entire pay as a public servant has not exceeded two hundred thousand dollars, his net financial worth today is certainly over one million dollars, perhaps several times that amount. . . . The public is entitled to know how the wealth was achieved."

On the basis of reports of Dougherty's failure on radio and television and the small crowds his fire truck was attracting, Johnson decided not to return home to campaign in person. Instead, he left much of the face-to-face work with local politicians in the hands of old friends, like Tom Miller and Jimmy Allred. Allred, because of his position as judge of the Federal District Court, a position Johnson had helped him get, could not operate openly for Johnson in 1954, but this did not prevent him from working behind the scenes under long-distance masterminding by Johnson.

Although Johnson asked, "What campaign?" when Texas reporters attempted to discuss the Beeville contender with him, he geared all his Senate activities to the Dudley Dougherty campaign. Since his radio and television catastrophe and his first campaign swing, Dougherty was under strict orders from Coke Stevenson and old Dan Moody, his special adviser, not to utter a single *ad lib*. Instead, he stood on the rear of his fire truck and continued to read the same hard-core charges against Johnson at every stop. He would point the finger of personal aggrandizement at Johnson, denounce him as soft on communism, hard on American labor, and a milksop of a Senate leader.

Johnson did not bother to comment on his radio and television wealth, but he showed great concern about Dougherty's "soft-on-communism" charge. When the televised Army-McCarthy hearings ended in mid-June 1954 with McCarthy severely damaged, Johnson was so influenced by Dougherty's campaign that he suggested caution and silence to Senators Fulbright, Lehman, and Kefauver, who wanted an aggressive Democratic line taken toward the Wisconsin senator. As for Dougherty's demand that the United States quit the UN, Johnson believed that any defense of the international organization would lose votes. So he made an oblique attack on both the UN and international communism in a Senate speech on July 2, by insisting that the United States quit the UN if Red China was ever admitted to membership. This led Senator Fulbright to chide him that a "permanent" exclusion did not take into consideration internal changes that could possibly occur in the future in China. In this same speech Johnson also attempted to bury the Dougherty camp's nonsense that he favored any action other than an aggressive military approach toward communism. In a sharp slap at Prime Minister Winston Churchill and the British Government over their unwillingness to go to war in Indochina and their recognition of Red China he said, "A top official of the government of our closest ally states a doctrine which smacks strongly of the appeasement at Munich."

The Coke Stevenson–Dan Moody line for inept Dougherty was to have him beat both sides of the labor drum simultaneously against Johnson. Branding Johnson a New Dealer, Dougherty then pointed out that Johnson had favored drafting striking railroad workers in 1946. With Texas labor anti-Johnson since the 1948 campaign, Dougherty hoped to swing the growing labor force vote in his own direction. However, by clever strategy Johnson outwitted him.

A reporter called his accomplishment, "Changing sides while standing still." When the Senate Labor Committee reported out a revised Taft-Hartley Bill, both AFL and CIO leaders bellowed that the revision was worse than the current act. Johnson saw his opportunity to gain personal advantage by killing the revision and maintaining the original Taft-Hartley Act. So, with the solid backing of Democratic liberals who opposed the revision and the Southern bloc who were pleased with the original Taft-Hartley measure, he was able to put up a united Democratic front, which, acting along with only a few Republicans, succeeded in sending the changed bill back to its death in the committee. In appreciation Texas labor leaders now made substantial contributions to the Johnson campaign chest.

He also had to dispose of the Dougherty charge against him of milksop Senate leadership. "Everybody's Friend; Nobody's Leader," was the title of a forthcoming article in the *New Republic* on Johnson, and Dougherty voiced similar slogans. Johnson's approach in attacking this charge was to issue releases showing the unanimous and near-unanimous votes by the Democratic side of the Senate, such as the unanimity he achieved on the Taft-Hartley revision. One unanimous Democratic vote joined a few Republican liberals to add an antimonopoly amendment to the Administration's Small Business Bill; another that had only two Democratic defectors successfully tied Alaskan statehood to the Administration's bill to grant statehood solely to Hawaii. Texas reporters were given these tales of Johnson's legislative "wizardry" to write up as news stories for home consumption, although a few charged that when he could not gain Democratic unity, he tried to prevent voting on bills.

Johnson's avoidance of any public campaign against his young rival was enhanced when he announced he was so busy concentrating on the affairs of the nation that he had voted by absentee ballot. Late on Saturday night, July 24, 1954, the Senate was in session on a bill to revise the Atomic Energy Act of 1946. Northern liberals were in filibuster heat, charging that the Administration's revision was a nuclear giveaway to big business; and for days and nights without respite they had been talking against the bill and snatching sleep on Marine cots set up in the lobbies.

This was also primary election night in Texas, and when Senator George Smathers wandered to the news teletype machine, he read that Johnson held a three-to-one margin over Dougherty. Elated, he rushed to Johnson and said he planned to read the report to senators on the floor. However, Johnson begged him not to on the ground that it would jinx him and result in Dougherty's victory. But Senator Barry Goldwater of Arizona thought such superstition was nonsense and he hurried into the Senate chamber to announce to his colleagues: "My neighboring state of Texas is showing intelligence in backing solid American thinking in these trying hours." Majority Leader Bill Knowland added in full basso that Johnson was "a great American, a great leader," and for ten minutes such praise rang through the Senate.

The figures put out by the Texas Election Bureau showed Johnson with 875,000 votes to 350,000 for Firetruck Dougherty. No longer could anyone call him "Landslide Lyndon," and to celebrate his overwhelming victory he joined with Knowland that very evening to break up the liberal Democratic filibuster against the Atomic Energy Act revision.

There was other good news for Johnson in the July 24, 1954, primary. The haunting specter of a Shivers powerful enough to continue to bedevil his career disappeared with Shivers' whisker win over Ralph Yarborough, Shivers' weak opponent two years earlier. Shivers collected only 668,913 votes to 645,994 for Yarborough, and because several other candidates were in the field, he was forced into a degrading run-off for lack of a majority of the votes cast.

Yarborough had approached the 1954 primary without an organization or campaign funds. About all he had going for him was support from labor and minority groups, his own energy, and the homework he had done on Shivers that enabled him to publicize scandals involving the governor and his administration. This time Mister Sam did not mind when Yarborough called himself a "Sam Rayburn Democrat," because he sensed that this might help the Austin lawyer pull the political upset of the year.

At every stop Yarborough hammered away at the numerous irregularities uncovered in the state's land office; at the one thousand dollars a month John Van Cronkhite, Shivers' 1950 campaign manager, was collecting from a discredited insurance firm; and at Shivers' success in gaining easy wealth. Handsome, young Lloyd Bentsen had not only become a county judge at twenty-five and a member of Congress two years later, but he was also the son of an immensely rich Texan who had a plan to bring quick wealth to Shivers. Bentsen, senior, was so philanthropically disposed toward Shivers, Yarborough disclosed, that he sold him thirteen thousand Rio Grande Valley acres in Hidalgo County for twenty-five thousand dollars, and then bought them back six months later for four hundred and fifty thousand dollars. This time lag in the repurchase enabled Shivers to pay only the 25 per cent capital gains tax on his profit instead of the graduated income tax rate. Yarborough estimated that Shivers used only a microscopic part of his gain in an attempt to buy an endorsement for Yarborough from "Friends" in the Communist New York *Daily Worker*.

Despite the unrelenting Yarborough charges, Shivers and Jake Pickle, his campaign manager, had expected little trouble from the Austin attorney in the primary. Therefore the results in the July 24 vote-count stunned them, and the shock deepened with the realization that the governor had to enter a run-off race with Yarborough.

But far from being elated with his showing, Yarborough believed he would have won the primary, had the election laws been honored. Among his charges was the assertion that Allan Shivers had not only violated the campaign expenditures law by spending a million dollars in the primary, but had conspired with Jack Porter, the Republican National Committeeman and general election opponent of Johnson in 1948, to have Republicans vote in "the Democratic primary and save Shivers."

Shivers' margin in the run-off a month later was 91,956 out of a total vote of 1,458,220. This time Yarborough accepted his defeat publicly; privately he said, "I was counted out by the border county dictators. But the Texas political code is to swallow defeat in a crooked election or be labeled a poor loser. This can be fatal for your future in politics."

Johnson's delight in Shivers' close call was tempered by his intense personal dislike for Yarborough, the political liberal. Yet he knew he would be forever indebted to him for making it unnecessary to appease the governor any longer.

Chapter 43

ONCE HE DISPOSED of Dudley Dougherty, Johnson viewed the coming general elections in November 1954 as an excellent opportunity to increase his national standing. If the Democrats could gain control of the Senate, this would make him the undisputed boss of the Upper Chamber—the majority leader, instead of the reacting minority leader, a post he had been only a single vote away from attaining during the past year. Furthermore, if he played an active role in bringing this about, he could further challenge Adlai Stevenson for leadership of the Democratic party.

Johnson's opening move toward becoming majority leader came on August 11, when his secret lieutenant, Hubert Humphrey, introduced a bill to outlaw the Communist party. Reports from Minnesota were that the Republicans intended to concentrate on the "soft-on-communism" line to beat Humphrey, and Johnson had worked out this legislative ploy with Humphrey to kill the Republican campaign before it began. Eighteen other Democrats, all up for re-election and fearing the same Republican attack, raised such a clamor that Johnson and Humphrey let them into the act by permitting them to be cosponsors of the measure.

Johnson's concern that Humphrey was in great political danger had no foundation. Three years earlier Humphrey had, with the help of President Truman, eliminated the one Republican who could have defeated him. This was popular Governor Luther Youngdahl, who accepted the proffered bait in September 1951 and resigned to become a federal judge. But in mid-1954 Humphrey was jittery and almost hysterical about his political future, and Johnson could not let him fail. The two had grown so close, despite the pleas of liberals to Humphrey that he show more independence, that Johnson wrote him pep letters and notes of thanks because he would not listen to his fellow liberals. One such note went: "Dear Hubert—They have tried on many occasions, but one thing I would never let them do was to come between us. I have too much sense. . . . Hubert, as I leave Washington, I want you to know how grateful I am for all the help that you gave me."

Johnson believed that merely introducing the bill to outlaw the Communist party would be a sufficient weapon for Humphrey and his co-sponsors. But Humphrey wanted the bill to pass the Senate because this would strengthen his case many times over. Johnson undertook to do so; and it proved a simple task because it gave each supporting senator the opportunity to gain a record for anticommunism of the McCarthy stripe. Despite the charge of the Justice Department that it would lead the Communist party to change its name and its members to go underground, and the condemnation of Senators John Sherman Cooper and Estes Kefauver that the measure was "of doubtful constitutionality," the Communist Control Bill of 1954 sailed through the Senate by a unanimous vote of eighty to nothing. Eisenhower signed it into law, and Humphrey later credited the legislation with saving his political career, though he also said, "It was not one of the things I'm proudest of."

Johnson further helped Humphrey by putting him on the Senate Agriculture Committee in May 1954, a necessity for a man from a farm state. In addition, to add to Humphrey's friends among the old Farmer-Labor populists, he named him to the select Small Business Committee. Both committee assignments, when coupled with Humphrey's seat of prestige on the Senate Foreign Relations Committee, made him appear to be a top voice in the Senate. Then there was the quotation Johnson got from old Senator George that the country needed Hubert during the trying next six years. And far from minor, Johnson furnished him with campaign funds through his aides, Senators Clements and Smathers, who had the job of managing the Senate Democratic Campaign Committee.

It was too much for Johnson to expect that Adlai Stevenson would abstain from the 1954 Congressional elections. Yet for a long time it looked as though he would. Following April surgery to remove a kidney stone, he had returned pale and weak to his home at Libertyville, Illinois, vowing to forget about politics. But when September came and the smell of politics was in the air, he went out to do a little talking—and soon he was on a tour of thirty-three states, with eighty major stops, alongside Congressional candidates, speechifying.

Richard Nixon took on the job for the Eisenhower Administration of retaining Republican control of the Senate and House, and despite the Communist-outlawing act, he worked hard to pin the Red tail on the Democratic donkey. In his nationwide name-calling sweep, he labeled Democratic candidates as politicians who favored "imposing the Truman Socialist left-wing policies on the country again." A typical campaign remark of the Vice President was one he made in Butte, Montana: "All over the United States in the key Senate and House races, the Communists are in the forefront calling for the defeat of Republican candidates and the election of an anti-Eisenhower Congress." Stevenson called the Nixon method of dirty in-fighting "McCarthyism in a white collar."

Eisenhower found the campaign an affront to his desire for quietude. Commenting to Jim Hagerty, his press secretary, on the slanderous noise emanating from the public platform, he said, "By golly, sometimes you sure get tired of all this clackety-clack." In the opinion of Sherman Adams, his top assistant, the President found it difficult "to work up much enthusiasm for many of the Republican candidates who were up for re-election." Nor did he care for most members of the Republican National Committee because he had found them "either lukewarm or openly hostile" to him.

Nevertheless, when Eisenhower was told that Nixon was not getting his message across, he went out on the speaking trail to save his Republican Congress. He was inept at making partisan remarks, and his generalities stood out in sharp contrast to the elegant language of Adlai Stevenson. Jealous of Stevenson's reputation as a Lincoln scholar, he ordered his speechwriters to sprinkle his talks with Lincoln stories. One that made him pause and smile every time he read it was the story of Lincoln's crooked fence, which he attempted to relate to the Democratic "prophets of gloom and doom." The Lincoln crooked fence tale involved "a farmer who built a fence that was so crooked that every time a pig bored a hole through it, he found himself on the same side from which he started."

While Stevenson (the phrasemaker), Nixon ("McCarthyism in a white collar") and the President (who wanted to be home) were rushing from coast to coast, Lyndon Johnson was also on the hustings. His was a tour of nine states, concentrating entirely on Senate races. This was his first campaign invasion of the North, and at first he was far from comfortable away from Dixieland. But as the days stretched into weeks, he grew more at ease.

One man he wanted to help was Joe O'Mahoney of Wyoming, a Senate leader in the defeat of Roosevelt's Court-packing plan seventeen years earlier. O'Mahoney had been chairman of the Appropriations Subcommittee on the Defense Department. There he had always been a firm advocate of increased defense spending, when he could spare time from yelling about Wall Street and the monopolies. "Joe's approach was to ask the generals and admirals, 'Are you sure you don't need more money?' " Senator Kilgore, a member of his subcommittee, complained. "If I threatened to cut off some of their fat, they'd get Joe to talk to me, and if that didn't work they'd get newspaper editors to run scare headlines about Communist submarines sighted off our coast."

O'Mahoney had lost his race for re-election to a fourth term in 1952, and now in 1954 he was running against Representative William Henry Harrison, the great-great-grandson of the ninth President. The old Democrat presented a tired appearance on the platform, and he had the misfortune of rambling on about subjects that were not directly involved in his campaign.

At his big tabernacle rally with Johnson as guest speaker, O'Mahoney worked along gustily for an hour, relating a government "loyalty" case in which he had represented the accused. His exhibition sickened Johnson, who finally interrupted him in a stage whisper that carried to the rear of the hall with the suggestion that he start a campaign speech about what he was going to do for his state when the voters returned him to Washington. After a lengthy interval, during which time he continued to tell about the loyalty case, O'Mahoney managed to utter a few campaign promises. Then Johnson jumped forward and delivered the campaign speech that O'Mahoney should have given.

Johnson also had hardship duty in Montana, where he spoke for seventy-eight-year-old Jim Murray, but when he went to Minnesota to help Humphrey the trouble was of another nature. Here both were compulsive speakers who had to raise their voices to be heard above the other until they were fairly screaming. Johnson had in addition considered going into Illinois to speak for Paul Douglas. However, Douglas needed no help, for he had found the perfect campaign formula in a state where Eisenhower's popularity ran high. Day after day Douglas infuriated Eisenhower by charging that Joseph Meek, his Republican opponent, "wants to scuttle everything President Eisenhower has proposed."

It was during the fall campaign that President Eisenhower violated his self-imposed rule to avoid a public dispute with the Democrats. Carried away by the drama in which he found himself, he listened to pleas of Republican leaders that he use some "scare tactics" to win Republican votes for Congressional campaigners. This bore fruit early in October, when he warned about "the cold war of partisan politics" that would break out between him and the Democrats if the latter gained control of Congress.

While several Democrats now called anew for a policy of open warfare against him because of his words, Mister Sam would not tolerate this even though he was hurt by Eisenhower's lack of gratitude for the aid

Democrats had given him during the Eighty-third Congress. In a telegram he and Lyndon Johnson sent Eisenhower at the Denver home of the President's mother-in-law, they told him, "It takes two to make a war. . . . There will be no cold war against you by the Democrats."

Eisenhower had been warned by advisers that he would lose the House, and when this came true on election day, he told his Cabinet that the loss had come because "there were just too many turkeys running on the Republican ticket." But his sadness was Sam Rayburn's joy, for the House Democrats were augmented by twenty-one freshmen members, returning Mister Sam to the dais once more as House speaker.

The Senate situation was another matter. Democrats O'Mahoney, Murray, and Douglas won, as did Alben Barkley, the former Vice President, who returned to the Senate from Kentucky. Humphrey won by a margin so large that he carried the entire Democratic-Farmer-Labor slate into office with him. Yet despite these victories, when Johnson went to bed on election night, it did not appear probable that he would match Rayburn and become the Senate's majority leader.

In the morning, however, the contest for control of the Senate had become a horse race, because of the fight in Oregon between Republican incumbent Guy Cordon and free-lance writer and state politician, Democrat Richard Neuberger. The night before Johnson had written off Oregon because Cordon had a ten-thousand-vote lead; but by daybreak it had vanished. It was the final and breathless count in Portland during the morning that gave Neuberger the victory by a measly margin of twenty-four hundred votes.

The scorecard made one name stand out among all senators. Even with Neuberger's success, the Senate contained the same total number of Democrats and Republicans as in the last session: forty-eight Democrats and forty-seven Republicans. So once again the organization of the Senate rested squarely with cantankerous Wayne Morse, the one-man Independent party, who, said his friend Paul Douglas, "reminds me of the German Ph. D. who could go down deeper, stay down longer, and come up muddier than anyone else."

This time Johnson had no intention of continuing his feud with Morse, for without the Oregonian's support he could not become majority leader. As for Morse, he had no intention of continuing to join the Republicans so they could control the leadership and committee chairmen, though he knew it was best to pretend he had to be coaxed into supporting the Democrats by being given top committee assignments and promises of pork barrel.

Morse could no longer sit on the Republican side of the aisle because Republican senators were treating him to a continuing barrage of scurrilous, personal attacks. Herman Welker of Idaho and Irving Ives of New York, for instance, constituted themselves a two-man whispering insult squad whenever Morse denounced President Eisenhower. While Morse spoke, a typical Ives whisper told him, "You silly jackass. Why don't you shut your silly mouth and go out and drop dead?"

Welker's specialty was to walk up and down the aisle while Morse spoke, and when he passed him, he spat out in a whisper, "You stupid ass. Everybody knows you're a dope."

Morse had campaigned vigorously for Neuberger, his former law student, in 1954, and after Neuberger's victory over Cordon, Johnson called Morse to congratulate him for his fine work. Morse was susceptible to flattery, as Johnson discovered, and in the gushing warmth of the moment, Johnson told him he could make a claim of any dimension to any reward that a *majority leader* had to offer. Morse said he wanted to think about this.

Johnson's campaign moved ahead on November 5 when he visited with Sam Rayburn on Mister Sam's small ranch, and he spoke to reporters. "Morse should never have been kicked off his committees," he said, adding that the Oregon senator could expect to get some important committee assignments from him during the next session. Then he returned to Washington for the Senate's climactic action on the McCarthy censure, and here he told newsmen, "I don't know what Senator Morse may want, but whatever he wants, he's going to get it—if I've got it to give."

Morse agreed he would vote to make Johnson the majority leader, and become a Democrat, in exchange for an assignment to the Senate Foreign Relations Committee. The Southern bloc had to be consulted because Russell and George had to make up their minds whether their animosity toward Morse exceeded their own desire to become committee chairmen again through the Democratic organization of the Senate. Reluctantly they agreed that Morse should be given the seat he wanted, and on that basis Johnson became at last the majority leader of the United States Senate.

Chapter 44

A<small>T HIS NEW</small> peak of power as majority leader, Lyndon Johnson should have been elated. But instead of an expected great surge of satisfaction and joy, he found he could not bellow out some good old Texas Yeeeaaaaaayhooos for a variety of reasons.

There was Adlai Stevenson still standing in the Presidential road, showing holes in his soles and mopping his bald head with a wrinkled handkerchief, while uttering elegant English sentences that continued to excite a substantial number of Democrats. The recurring Johnson wish that Stevenson would fade as a giant factor in the 1956 nomination was not coming true. After the 1954 elections Johnson had to call reporters to claim that he had saved a half dozen Democratic senators by campaigning for them. But Stevenson had not been forced to such action, for dozens of Democratic congressmen and governors told the press on their own that Stevenson's aid in their campaigns had spelled the difference between their close victories and what would have been close defeats.

One opportunity to downgrade Stevenson came immediately following the McCarthy censure on December 2, 1954, when the Democratic National Committee met in New Orleans to elect a new chairman. Stephen Mitchell, a Chicago lawyer and political amateur Stevenson had installed as chairman in 1952, after forcing Truman's man Frank McKinney to resign, was quitting, and a majority vote was to name his successor.

Johnson had intended to go to New Orleans to help install a non-Stevenson National Committee chairman, but sudden and sharp back pains kept him in Washington. Sam Rayburn went instead to protect his protégé's interests, and because of Mister Sam's prestige Johnson assumed that this would be done. Unfortunately, Rayburn would not go by plane, his train arrived late on December 4, and four names were already in nomination when he took off his black hat and walked into the meeting room. Paul Butler, a skinny, gray-haired, young South Bend lawyer, Democratic National Committeeman from Indiana and a fiery Eisenhower detractor, was Stevenson's choice; squat Mike Di Salle, former mayor of Toledo and head of the Office of Price Administration, was the anti-Stevenson choice of Harry Truman; Jim Finnegan, president of the Philadelphia City Council and the candidate of the city bosses, was the third nominee; and F. Joseph "Jiggs" Donohue, former District of Columbia commissioner, was the fourth. When Rayburn learned that Butler was an odds-on favorite, he delivered an impassioned plea for a two-month delay in the vote. But the one-hundred-and-five-member National Committee disagreed and ordered an immediate tally. When Butler drew seventy votes, Mister Sam saw 1956 as a rerun of 1952.

That evening at the Democratic party banquet he sat on his hands during much of Adlai Stevenson's speech. The only pleasant parts of Stevenson's euphonious talk, outside of his quips—Eisenhower should sign a nonaggression pact with Senator Knowland—came after his formal television performance ended. Besides pointing out that he had wiped out the eight-hundred-and-forty-thousand-dollar Democratic party debt by his series of fund-raising speaking engagements, Stevenson cheered his party opponents when he said, "Henceforth, I cannot participate in public life and party affairs as vigorously as I have in the past." He would

be going home to Libertyville, Illinois, for a semipolitical retirement, he
added. But with Paul Butler left behind as his legacy to the National
Committee, this promise had a hollow sound to Rayburn and Johnson.

Another factor diminishing Johnson's complete satisfaction in becoming
majority leader was the continuing unwillingness of the Senate liberals to
accept him unquestioningly as their spokesman. Since they numbered
twenty members—or almost half his total force—this was a situation
that infuriated him. On one occasion in 1953 when Senator Douglas had
taken an hour to protest against the public works appropriations bill,
Johnson had openly revealed his contempt by complaining, "What's he
want to waste all that time for? I told him they just haven't got the votes.
So why don't we get the show on the road?"

Besides his open lack of respect for liberals chasing lost causes, two
chief issues prevented a closer relationship between Johnson and this
group. He would not agree to changes in Rule XXII so that filibusters
over motions to take up civil rights bills could be thwarted. Second, he
would not drop his public courting of Eisenhower. In the safety of the
cloakroom he could ridicule Eisenhower by a hilarious imitation of the
President's syntaxless, rubbery replies to questions at his news conference
in the Indian Treaty Room at the Old State Department Building next
door to the White House. He might also say that Eisenhower was the only
President he had known who signed anything put on his desk; and he
could quote from a Republican who got it straight from Sherman Adams
that Eisenhower disliked being interrupted when he practiced golf shots
with his Number 8 iron on the White House south lawn in the late afternoon, unless Adams brought him "some good news." Then there were
comments passed on by other White House staffers that on days when
Eisenhower wore a light brown suit, he was bound to explode at an aide
or two before the day ended; and that he once asked his wife to join him
before photographers with the order, "Mamie, fall into formation."

But all such jesting was grist solely for the cloakroom. In the open
Johnson maintained a heavy show of respect for Eisenhower.

When it became generally known that Morse was going to vote for the
Democratic organization of the Senate and make Johnson the majority
leader in the process, several liberal members asked Johnson to issue a
statement of principles and a legislative program. Johnson saw through
this maneuver, for what they wanted was a program at odds with the
Administration and what would in effect be a sharp rap at Eisenhower.
"There will be no personal attacks upon the integrity of the President
or upon his intentions," Johnson issued a public broadside aimed at the
frustrated liberals. It would be better, he said, if both parties were to follow the simple virtues of democratic cooperation he had learned as a
youngster from his father, Samuel Ealy Johnson, Jr.

"My Daddy would get all of us kids around the table at home when there was a decision to be made," he told reporters an apocryphal story at a news conference in Washington after the 1954 elections. "Daddy would start off with words from Isaiah, 'Come now, and let us reason together.' My Daddy's advice to the five Johnson children will serve well Democrats and Republicans in the next Congress."

Eisenhower got the drift of Johnson's effort to avoid creating a separate Democratic legislative program, and he replied, "If there are any road-blocks thrown in the way of cooperation, I am not going to be responsible." This brought a further Johnson comment that it would be "a good idea if the Administration consulted Democratic chairmen in order to avoid 'crash-landings only' bipartisanship."

Eisenhower quickly replied that he had drafted a letter to department heads to follow this course, and he added, "I want you to know, Mister Rayburn and Lyndon, that I am available for consultation at any time."

Senate liberals who followed this exchange realized that Johnson was painting them into a corner, especially when he defined cooperation as being in the national interest. There was only increased frustration on their part, a short time later, when newspapers printed the story that Johnson and Rayburn had presented Eisenhower with an expensive Texas steer for his farm at Gettysburg, Pennsylvania. Said Senator Harley Kilgore, "Lyndon didn't want us to have a program because that would have brought out clearly the chasm between the liberal and Southern wings of the Democratic party. But in doing this, he gave us nothing on which to establish a record to run on in 1956."

Regardless of Johnson's unwillingness to write a detailed legislative program, the liberals decided to upset his debut as majority leader on January 5, 1955, by staging a fight to change Rule XXII. Two days before the convening of the Eighty-fourth Congress, Senator Herbert Lehman called a meeting of nineteen Democratic senators to discuss strategy. One who attended was Senator Humphrey, who realized the unfavorable Johnson publicity that a battle at the start of the new Congress would yield.

Far in advance of this meeting Humphrey had telegraphed what his position would be at the meeting when he told reporters, "It's no great service to the party to be stubborn and dogmatic in one's views. The old New Dealer's sole idea was to 'get it done,' and the Devil take the method. Today liberals are more concerned with protecting procedural rights and the use of proper constitutional methods." At the precaucus session of the liberals, Humphrey talked the proposed fight on Rule XXII to death. In a scolding tone, he told his fellow liberals to abandon the "Devil's theory of politics and recognize Southern Democrats as reasonable, constructive men, rather than as fiends from the pit." The meeting ended in a decision not to fight for a weakening of the Cloture Rule.

The third factor preventing Johnson from fully enjoying his new power was the poor state of his health. The December backaches had worsened, and an examination revealed he was suffering from a kidney stone. His physician proposed immediate surgery, but Johnson knew he had to suffer along somehow until he was officially elected majority leader. This event took place on January 5, 1955, and on the following day, when President Eisenhower came to the Capitol to read his State of the Union Message, Johnson gasped through the reading.

The next time the Senate met was on January 10. Johnson was not present, and Senator Earle Clements, the Democratic whip, explained that he would be serving as acting majority leader until Johnson returned from the Mayo Brothers Clinic in Rochester, Minnesota.

Johnson was absent from the Senate for two months, making his reappearance on the Senate floor on March 8, despite the warning of his Mayo Clinic internist, Dr. James C. Cain, that he might suffer a relapse without further rest. Johnson knew that Dr. Cain had his best interests at heart, for he was the son-in-law of Johnson's late Daddy, Alvin. Wirtz, having married Ida May Wirtz. But two important months had already disappeared from the Congressional session. There was little time remaining to establish a record as a majority leader of action. Furthermore, Earle Clements, who had acted in his stead during his absence, had proved highly successful in creating fairly harmonious relations between the liberals and the Southern bloc. Nor could the White House find any fault with the cooperation Clements had given the Administration. The first time Johnson trudged into the President's Oval Office to pay his respects, he talked about the operation to remove his kidney stone, waited for Eisenhower to tell him how sorely he had been missed, and when this did not happen, he said, "I'm still weak."

With a display of his famous grin, Eisenhower replied, "I hope we can depend on that."

Despite Dr. Cain's warning, and the reminding pain in his back, even though his torso was encased in a steel brace, Johnson moved swiftly to establish himself as the boss of the Senate. Clements was ordered out of the seat of power on the center aisle in the front row and from staff central headquarters in the majority leader's office in a corner of the Senate wing of the Capitol on the gallery floor level. Here in his special office under the tinkling glass of the immense chandelier, Johnson and his young protégé, Bobby Baker, whom he had ordered elected secretary for the majority, examined the thousand details that gave him control of the Senate.

Johnson was soon thriving on overwork, and the brace was discarded. On the wall over the fireplace in his office was a framed quotation: "You ain't learnin' nothin' when you're talkin'." But visiting politicians and reporters found they could not complete a sentence without being interrupted by a torrent of words pouring from Johnson, as he explained plans to push the Administration's small legislative program, told stories about his heroic work to win support for bills by inserting compromise amendments or by making pork-barrel promises, revealed statistics to prove he was the most effective majority leader in history—as well as the youngest at forty-six—and related a few funny stories from his stock of "bedroom and barnyard" tales. Almost all these office visits found Johnson sitting throughout with his mirror-bright shoes propped against his desk lid and his eyes below the level of his bent knees.

Johnson found he could make columnists like Stewart Alsop and Douglass Cater feel on the inside of events and on his side by telling them about the shortcomings of his Senate colleagues. He also discovered that most reporters would print anything he told them without checking the "facts." One story on his life reported that his father spent twenty-four years in the Texas House instead of the eleven he really spent; another had his mother dramatically forging his father's signature to a letter asking Dr. Evans at Southwest Texas State Teachers College to enroll her son, instead of calling Evans by phone; still another told of his modesty about his "bombing missions" in World War II. Asked about the Austin radio and television empire, he told how "Claudia Alta" Johnson had shown business genius by taking a business heavily in the red and single-handedly turning it into a profitable venture. "Now it's on a national TV network and doing very well," he quoted Lady Bird.

To reporters, he scoffed at reports that he was aiming for the Presidency. "Talk of being a potential candidate is a lot of foolishness," he said. "I have no interest, no ambitions in that direction. I'm conscious of my limitations. I think it's fair to say nobody but my Mama ever thought I'd get as far as I am."

Adlai Stevenson came to Washington in the spring of 1955 to pin Johnson down on this point. In their stiff conversation Stevenson asked about his intentions for 1956, and Johnson replied with a smile that he would probably be for Stevenson again.

To this, Stevenson asked, "What do you mean 'being for me' in 1956? You said that in 1952 and you didn't take part in the campaign. Will you campaign actively for me next year?"

"I can't commit myself," Johnson told him. "I might have an awkward situation in Texas."

Little had changed in the two months Johnson was away from the Senate. Before he left for Rochester, Minnesota, two major issues had replaced the McCarthy frenzy on the front pages; and when he returned they were still unsettled. One involved whether to go to war over the off-shore Chinese islands of Quemoy and Matsu; the other concerned the effort of the Administration to weaken the TVA through what became known as the Dixon-Yates affair.

As a major achievement of the New Deal, the Tennessee Valley Authority, with its regional rehabilitation of a multistate area, evoked an

emotional response from most Democrats. So there was anger when
President Eisenhower cited the TVA to his news conference as an ex-
ample of "creeping socialism." Then the anger turned to rage among
congressmen from TVA country when Eisenhower rejected the Authority's
proposal to construct a free one-hundred-million-dollar power plant for
the city of Memphis. Instead of this, Eisenhower asked Budget Bureau
Director Rowland Hughes and Atomic Energy Commission Chairman
Lewis Strauss to promote private power companies in the TVA area.
Shortly afterward Hughes and Strauss negotiated a contract with Edgar
Dixon's Middle South Utilities and E. A. Yates' Southern Company to
build a power plant at West Memphis to supply electricity for Memphis.

Johnson became involved in the battle by TVA congressmen against
the Dixon-Yates contract because they came to him for help. Back in
World War II days Johnson had several run-ins with Strauss, who worked
on Navy contracts, and he was happy to help damage him now from a
safe distance. His suggestion to the congressmen was that since Eisenhower was not a fighter, he would back down if Senator Clinton Anderson's
Joint Committee on Atomic Energy voted to recommend the cancellation
of the contract. When Anderson's committee did this in January 1955, and
Eisenhower refused to comply, Johnson's advice was that there was nothing
more to do.

But Senator Lister Hill of Alabama, the leading TVA champion,
would not surrender. Every week Senate liberals honored him by attending the Lister Hill Luncheon Club, and at one meeting Hill proposed that
they investigate every person involved in the contract.

Hill was the one who discovered that Adolph Wenzell of the First
Boston Corporation, which was financing the Dixon-Yates deal, had
been the Budget Bureau's consultant on the contract award. Finally in
November, after hearing the cry "scandal" for many months, Eisenhower
considered it best to cancel the contract. But he still would not permit the
TVA to build the steam plant for Memphis, and the city had to underwrite the cost of a plant that it built for itself. The final result was such
that both the admirers of public power and the Administration claimed
a victory—and Johnson could be called a friend by both sides.

Shortly after the 1954 elections Secretary of State Dulles had noticed
that eighty-seven-year-old Senator Theodore Green of Rhode Island was
slated to become the next chairman of the Senate Foreign Relations
Committee. As a New and Fair Dealer and an Eisenhower detractor,
Green could prove troublesome. However, any analysis of Green's political career would have revealed that he would cooperate if further in-
stallments were paid on his insatiable appetite to make his little state the
center of activities for the United States Navy. Green had already acquired
so many Naval Stations, yards, and installations by World War II that, when
he requested further Navy pork barrel, President Roosevelt chided him

gently, "Please, Theodore, Rhode Island is already below the Plimsoll Line."

Frightened by the prospect of dealing with the Republican-disliking Green and the need to shout at him because he was hard of hearing, Dulles proposed to Eisenhower that he call Senator George to the White House and ask him to accept the chairmanship of the Foreign Relations Committee. George was top Democrat in seniority on both the Foreign Relations and Finance Committees, and his colleagues knew that in the past he had chosen to head the Finance Committee because his chief Georgia sponsors, Coca-Cola and Georgia Power, wanted him in charge of the tax-making committee.

One of Eisenhower's favorite bridge partners, however, was Bill Thompson, the head of Coca-Cola, and behind the scenes the agreement for George to shift his chairman's seat to Foreign Relations had already been arranged before George came to the White House. Nevertheless, he argued that he should not make the move: There were many social demands made on the chairman of the Senate Foreign Relations Committee, and he and Mizz Lucy, his wife, disliked night-owl activities. However, he agreed to be "ree-ee-eesonable" and shift to the Foreign Relations' head chair when Eisenhower assured him he did not have to attend nighttime banquets. "If I am summoned to a White House function at night, I will come— once!" George said, shaking hands on the deal.

The immediate reason for wanting George to be chairman of the Senate Foreign Relations Committee was to make use of his immense influence with his colleagues in support of the Administration's policy in the Far East. In September 1954, the Chinese Reds had begun a bombardment of the island of Quemoy, which is as close to the mainland off Amoy as Staten Island is to Manhattan. Quemoy lay in the hands of Chiang Kai-shek's Nationalists, whose presence prevented the Communists on the mainland from making use of the port facilities at Amoy. The far-reaching effect of the bombing of Quemoy, and the Matsu Island group two hundred miles northward off the mainland port of Foochow, came with the crowing of the Chinese Reds that the bombings would be followed by an invasion of Formosa, the Nationalist stronghold, a hundred miles off the coast. Coming so soon after an economic recession at home, the Indochinese troubles, and the refusal of France to join the European Defense Plan, the Chinese Red bombings left Eisenhower with "spells of depression," said an aide.

As the shelling of Quemoy persisted, Eisenhower put into effect the same pattern of dealing with this crisis that he had used in Indochina. All top officers in his Administration were free to advocate openly whatever policy they favored, while Eisenhower remained silent. Even though the confusion might lead to public hysteria, the enemy would remain equally confused regarding the true course of the Administration. The longer the crisis was drawn out in this cloudy fashion, the more time the enemy would have for thinking about the possible consequences of carrying out its intentions. By neither withdrawing nor going on the offensive, the Administration's surface inertia could result, in time, in the enemy's change of heart.

The range of proposals completed a circle. Senator Knowland, leader of the China Firsters and known as "the Senator from Formosa," demanded that Eisenhower blockade China; the head of the Joint Chiefs of Staff, Admiral Radford, and Secretary Dulles advocated an immediate attack on Chinese airfields and factories, with Dulles pulling the Domino Theory out of his well again and wailing that if Quemoy and Matsu fell "we face disaster in the Far East." Adlai Stevenson wanted to know how the honor and prestige of the United States came to be "staked on some little islands within the shadow of the China Coast." Former British Prime Minister Clement Attlee thought the problem would end if the UN ran Formosa as a neutralized country. Anthony Eden wanted Quemoy and Matsu neutralized. Senators Kennedy, Morse, and Lehman wanted those islands abandoned, and Syngman Rhee and Chiang Kai-shek proposed that Eisenhower join them in a holy war against Mao Tse-tung.

In the past Johnson had been in the Knowland camp of China Firsters, but with Senator George now the key man in the Senate on foreign affairs, he favored whatever George thought necessary. In this instance George believed that the Administration should set its Far Eastern policy on the basis of the national interest, and not on the basis of pressure from Knowland.

In his State of the Union Message in February 1953, at the behest of Knowland, Eisenhower had revoked the Truman Korean War order stationing the Seventh Fleet between Formosa and the mainland to prevent attacks on either side by the other. Eisenhower's revocation was commonly called the "unleashing of Chiang Kai-shek," for it gave the impression that the United States would back him in an invasion of the mainland.

George called this a dangerous situation which might lead to Chiang's dragging the United States into war with Red China at any time he chose to land men ashore. While the Quemoy bombing was going on, Dulles was busy writing a mutual defense treaty with the Nationalist Government on Formosa, which Chiang had requested. George insisted this was a good time to "releash" Chiang by writing into the treaty his promise not to invade the Chinese mainland without American approval. Eisenhower agreed to do so.

On January 10, 1955, when Johnson had started for Rochester, Minnesota, the Chinese Reds airbombed the Tachen Islands off the coast and then successfully invaded Yikiang, a nearby island. Eisenhower possessed sufficient authority as Commander-in-Chief to put American soldiers into the defense of Nationalist Chinese holdings, had he chosen to do so, but this would have resulted in the war he wished to avoid. To continue the tension and yet not show weakness or pugnacity, he sent a special message to Congress on January 24 requesting approval to use American forces "for the specific purpose of securing and protecting Formosa and the Pescadores [forty miles west of Formosa] against armed attack." The resolution did not mention the offshore islands, though it purposely gave him the authority to protect vaguely delineated "closely related localities."

With strong attacks on the resolution from Senate liberals of both parties, only the support of Senator George could save it from being defeated. George soon saw that a major concern of his colleagues was the possibility that an admiral or general could decide on his own that Quemoy or Matsu or any other offshore island was a "closely related" locality to Formosa and the Pescadores that needed American protection, thus bringing on World War III. For this reason he called Eisenhower and obtained the clarification that under the resolution the President alone would have the right to make this decision.

George explained this in a forty-minute speech which determined the fate of the resolution. At one point in his explanation he noticed two senators whispering to each other, and he paused to stare coldly at them until they dropped their heads in embarrassment. If Eisenhower alone could decide on action, and because Eisenhower was "a prudent, patient man who knows the horrors of war," said George, the Senate had nothing to fear in the resolution. It passed by a vote of eighty-five to three, with the Senate according George a standing ovation.

While the mutual defense treaty and the resolution were important weapons for Eisenhower, their passage did not result in the immediate lessening of tension. Admiral Robert Carney threw the country into further panic in March when he leaked the story to reporters of an imminent Red Chinese invasion of Quemoy and Matsu which would be answered by an Eisenhower order to bomb Chinese industries. Johnson had returned to the Senate only a short time before the Carney "scare" and was sitting in his aisle seat when Knowland delivered a vigorous attack on the Eisenhower Administration for favoring "appeasement" rather than Carney's promise of a withering bombardment of China if the islands were attacked.

Senator George, who occupied the desk next to the majority leader, leaned over and told Johnson to answer "that wild boy who is trying to force Ike into a flat commitment to defend Quemoy." Johnson agreed with Knowland's basic position, but in deference to George he stood up and attacked Knowland for proposing an "irresponsible adventure."

If Eisenhower derived any pleasure from Johnson's assault on Knowland, it was lessened by Johnson's determination to reopen the Indochinese period squabble regarding the trustworthiness of American allies. At a White House luncheon for Senate leaders, he interrupted Dulles' explanation of the current situation in the Far East to yell out a demand that Dulles tell him whether Britain and France would join the United States if war started over Quemoy. Dulles' headshake led to the further question whether the two allies would join in a war over Formosa. Again Dulles shook his head. By then, Eisenhower sensed that Johnson might be building up material for a speech condemning the Western allies and thus upset their growing pressure on Red China to be less warlike. To head this off, Eisenhower cut in to insist that Britain and France could be counted on for military aid in a defense of Formosa. Eisenhower said this so fiercely that the discussion ended.

Late in May the period of hysteria over Quemoy, Matsu, and Formosa subsided when Chou En-lai, the Red Chinese Premier, announced that China would attempt "the liberation of Formosa by peaceful means." So the "wait-and-see" policy Eisenhower and Senator George had fashioned proved successful.

However, George did not believe that drift should be the total philosophy behind American foreign policy. Once a week he had breakfast with Secretary Dulles, and one February day in 1955, while drinking his quart of buttermilk and eating a melon, he suggested a conference between Eisenhower and the Soviet leaders to consider what parts of the Cold War might be thawed to ease East-West tensions. Dulles reacted strongly against such a conference by calling the Russian Communists totally treacherous.

When George brought this up to Eisenhower, the President said he would be interested only if the Communists offered proof they would negotiate constructively. Georgi Malenkov, the Soviet dictator, had been exiled to Siberia in February 1955, and his two successors, Nikita Khrushchev, head of the Communist party, and Nikolai Bulganin, the Soviet Premier, accepted the Eisenhower call for a worthwhile deed and agreed in May to sign the Austrian Peace Treaty. When Eisenhower still refrained from requesting a conference, Senator George went on TV to suggest "a meeting at the Summit" of the Big Four. A conference was arranged shortly afterward, and it was set to begin on July 18 at Geneva, Switzerland.

Johnson's initial reaction to a summit conference was that it should not be held. On May 15 he had spoken in New York at the banquet in honor of David Sarnoff, and his theme was that the United States must "prepare for a full-scale Cold War." But he fell in line behind George after the chairman of the Foreign Relations Committee spoke on TV in its favor. This position approving the summit conference gave him the opportunity to make a belated personal attack on Senator McCarthy, now fast on the downgrade.

McCarthy's reaction to the Geneva meeting was, of course, negative. Solely to gain headlines for himself after a long absence from the front pages, he introduced a resolution directing the Secretary of State to insist that the status of the Red satellite nations of Eastern Europe be made an agenda item at the conference. McCarthy had expected his resolution to die in the Foreign Relations Committee, but Johnson would not let this happen. He told George it would be in the best interest of the Administration to have the Senate debate the McCarthy resolution, and the old

Georgian induced the other seven Democrats on the committee to vote in favor of reporting it out to the floor. The anguished seven Republicans on the committee were short one vote to kill this move.

Once the resolution came up for debate, Johnson enjoyed a field day attacking the now-defanged McCarthy. He mimicked his nasal voice as he quoted his condemnation of "the striped pants boys from the State Department." Knowland and Capehart attempted to intercede and save the bewildered McCarthy from further embarrassment, but Johnson would not stop. McCarthy rose at one point to ask for unanimous consent to withdraw his resolution. Johnson prevented this, and his attack continued. The stench of acrimony filled the Senate chamber, and before long McCarthy was in a name-calling match with his strongest Republican defenders—Knowland, Capehart, and Hickenlooper. "The issue before the Senate is a very simple one," Johnson said before the vote. "It is whether the President of the United States shall be sent to the Big Four Conference in a straitjacket." The vote of seventy-seven to four killed the resolution and permitted McCarthy to slip back on his road to oblivion.

While the Far Eastern controversy raged, slow-walking, poor-sighted, seventy-seven-year-old Walter George showed Lyndon Johnson that his enormous influence extended to domestic as well as foreign affairs. George's personal authority was not dependent on his age, for there were older senators; nor was it dependent on his committee power, for there were more than a dozen other committee chairmen. It was an authority Johnson could study, yet never develop for himself, because it was intangible and was based on the peculiar willingness of other senators to accept George's position as being superior to their own. "Senator George does not merely rise in the Senate as other men do," wrote one observer. "He takes the floor. . . . He manages to look down over his colleagues. Or so it appears."

George put on a demonstration of this mysterious quality one May day in 1955, after Senators Albert Gore and Richard Neuberger offered an amendment to the federal roads bill that would have banned highway ads. George rose in opposition, and the two senators "wilted as he stood and glared about him," wrote a thrilled reporter. "The Senator from Georgia had won half his battle simply by standing up." When he said with annoyance that the proposal was an extension of federal control over the forty-eight states, Senator Bob Kerr, who was pushing the bill for the Senate Public Works Committee, defended the ad ban by claiming high motives for Gore and Neuberger. Kerr was in the midst of praising George as a statesman, as a disarming gesture, when George interrupted him with "I'm sorry the senator continues to pay me these fulsome compliments when I'm not asking for them." As soon as he sat down, Neuberger and Gore requested that their proposal be removed from the bill. It was.

Chapter 45

L YNDON JOHNSON'S FRIENDS were surprised by the speed of his recuperation from his kidney operation. After missing the first two months of the
Eighty-fourth Congress in 1955, he set a galloping pace during the next
three months as he managed the remaining business of that session. But
the debilitating effects from the relentless use of his power and the irritations caused by Democratic liberals who had to be scolded, courted, and
bought began to show on his lined face by May. That month Senate friends
saw him clutch at his chest while leading floor action against the McCarthy
resolution involving the summit meeting. Two months later came a total
collapse.

After his return from the Rochester clinic, Johnson refused to follow
Dr. Cain's order to sleep late. Instead, he started the day by being roused
from sleep at six-thirty by a clock-radio and then pressing a bedside buzzer
that notified Zephyr Wright to bring up his breakfast. During the night a
green Government Printing Office truck had delivered yesterday's *Congressional Record,* and while he swallowed his cups of coffee and smoked
a few cork-tip cigarettes, he skimmed the debates in both the House and
Senate. The ink on the *Congressional Record* was still wet, and it stained
his long fingers.

Lady Bird still laid out his clothes for the day, attire described by *Life*
as making him look like a "Mississippi River boat gambler," and she had
the proper items in the proper pockets. As majority leader, he had the
services of a long, black, sleek limousine and Norman Edwards, a chauffeur.
At seven-thirty, after he warned daughter Lynda for the last time (until
tomorrow) to quit eating candy bars and lose weight, roughhoused with
Little Beagle Johnson, and picked him up by his ears in farewell, Johnson
made a fast trip to the Capitol, giving driving instructions to Norman and
skimming *The New York Times* and the Washington *Post* en route.

Bobby Baker was on hand to go over the day's work and pass along
Senate gossip when he arrived, and the fourteen-to-sixteen-hour day began.
Even with recurring backaches from his operation, Johnson spent six
full days at the Capitol and part of Sunday. In the morning there were
committee meetings, committee chairmen to call about bills, individual
senators to see about their personal legislative problems. Then at noon,

when the Senate almost always convened, he was at his desk of power on the front-row center aisle. Senator George had insisted on occupying the seat next to him, and a daily ritual was Johnson's twenty-minute explanation to George of that day's business. George demanded this even though Johnson saw to it that each senator's desk held a printed calendar for the day's expected work. In addition, at the end of each week, Johnson told the Senate what the legislative program would be for the following week.

As a rule, Lady Bird called him about 6:30 P.M., after she thought he would be back from his daily visit to Mister Sam's Board of Education, and she would suggest that he think about coming home for dinner. If he would not leave, she would insist that he eat dinner in the Capitol area. "If I had let him alone," she said, "he wouldn't have eaten until midnight." Sometimes she stopped in to visit him during the day when she joined other Senate ladies in their patriotic task of rolling bandages for the Red Cross. He still complained about her clothes and ridiculed shoes she wore that did not have slim, high heels. One time he sent her to New York to learn about facial makeup from a Hollywood makeup man.

When he did go home of an evening, he generally brought several guests. "While everyone was drinking and talking," said a friend, "he sat under a floor lamp signing foot-high mail with a quick scrawl, rapidly read staff memos, raised his head from time to time for comment on his work or on the conversation."

At midnight a Capitol messenger showed up at the white painted brick house with a heavy box of mail, memos and staff and committee reports to replenish the supply he had already handled. Johnson would either read this material until he fell asleep or break his rest in the middle of the night to read the contents and sign the mail. If he thought he might forget something that had to be done the next work day, he would blithely telephone the assistant involved, at 2 or 3 A.M., and relate the assignment. Mary Rather, who was overworked as his secretary and as part-time babysitter for his daughters, on occasion got such calls. "Once in a while I'd look up from my typewriter during the day and ask myself," she said, "whether I would work this hard for anybody else, including myself. I decided I wouldn't."

A major Johnson failing was his continuing inability to relax. He took lessons from Sammy Snead, the famous golf pro, and he joined the exclusive Burning Tree Country Club. But he was a duffer who found the game a bore, and his only record at Burning Tree was his ownership of the biggest shoes (size fourteen) in the locker room. His closest Senate friend, George Smathers, recalled a frustrating attempt to relax him. "I took him on a fishing trip to Florida," said Smathers, "but he refused to go fishing once we got there. He would just get mad and sulk in the house when the rest of us went out on the boat. He wanted us to stay around and talk politics all the time."

In the confines of the cloakroom Johnson gained a reputation as the "suave compromiser." He was there to keep his one-man majority in line behind him by whatever means necessary. If a bill needed trimming, expanding, disfiguring, delaying, or swift passing, he would do what had to be done to gain the goal that would indebt his Democrats to him. There were also the petty details to care for—notifying a member in the Senate dining room when his amendment had reached the floor for action, praising individual senators to their home-state press, warning a liberal senator that he was courting danger if he continued to bait vicious-tongued Bob Kerr, who ran the show on Public Works bills, and whose rule of thumb was to give his own state of Oklahoma 10 per cent of the total pork barrel. At other times Johnson had to beg Kerr to stop teasing liberal senators on the floor about their wanting "just a teeny weeny dam."

Other majority leaders before Johnson had run small errands for their colleagues, but Johnson was so eager to be of service that more and more small chores were pushed on him, creating a huge backlog of favors owed him in return. Nor was he above doing small favors for Republican senators, because of the accruing power credit to his account. On one occasion, for example, Republican Senator Frank Carlson was promoting an Administration bill involving the Post Office, and when he learned that it was to come to a vote the next day he was chagrined because he had to keep a vital engagement back home in Kansas the following afternoon. Johnson not only sympathized with troubled Carlson but called the Senate into session early the next morning so the Republican senator could be present for the vote and still keep his date in Kansas. Carlson never forgot Johnson's action.

The most difficult aspect of Johnson's position was trying to satisfy every whim of the crusty Southern committee chairmen, and at the same time keep the liberals in a fairly weak condition to prevent them from rebelling.

Although Walter George had offered to go to Minnesota to campaign for Hubert Humphrey's re-election in 1954, he told Johnson he would not abide having another liberal on the Foreign Relations Committee in 1955. As matters stood, he pointed out, he was the sole Southern conservative on his committee, for the others were Theodore Green, William Fulbright, John Sparkman, Hubert Humphrey, Mike Mansfield, and Johnson's newest addition, Wayne Morse. All backed him unstintingly, he agreed, and especially Mike Mansfield, who was his protégé, but still it would be good to have another Southern conservative to fill the remaining vacancy. When Johnson pointed out that only hot liberals were asking for the seat, George agreed to accept old Alben Barkley, Franklin Roosevelt-era Senate majority leader and former Vice President, who was returning to the Senate as a freshman.

The new Finance Committee chairman, Harry Byrd, the brother of Antarctic explorer Admiral Richard Byrd, had a similar request regarding two committee vacancies. Johnson agreed with the concerned Virginia reactionary that Senator Paul Douglas held seniority priority for a committee shift to Finance, and he also agreed that Douglas would be a troublemaker because he favored tax reforms to eliminate special privileges, such as the oil depletion allowance. Johnson settled the problem by giving one of the Finance seats to Barkley and taking the other seat himself. Douglas had to be satisfied with the chairmanship of the innocuous Joint Economic Committee and a half promise of better future treatment when he quit attacking tax and appropriations bills.

There was also a sharp warning: The Senate leadership was tired of Douglas' exposure of pork-barrel bills, especially his ridiculing and self-righteous tone, as on one bill about which he said "a million-dollar dredging of a Georgia river was being done to save a single paper company $135,000 a year in freight costs; that $242,000 was being spent so that fifty-nine fishing vessels at a Florida port would not have to wait for the tide to come and go; $1,400,000 to construct a harbor for six hundred persons who lived at a spot on the south shore of Lake Superior in Michigan so they could attract summer vacationers; and millions for a bridge in Nebraska that had no river under it and no approaches." More talk like this, Douglas was told, and he would find "all public works projects for Illinois removed from appropriations bills."

To go on the Finance Committee, Johnson had to give up one of his committees, and he chose to relinquish his seat on the Commerce Committee rather than Armed Services. He already had a thriving radio and TV operation which no longer required the Commerce Committee's power over the FCC. What he lost by the shift was the continuation of his long denunciation, during committee hearings, of "powerful interests" who he claimed were blocking use of the Columbia Broadcasting System's color development so they could saturate the country "with millions upon millions of black and white sets." He had persisted in this charge even though CBS kept admitting that its system was not perfected for commercial use.

On the green wall of the gallery-floor majority leader's office, Johnson had a framed quotation from Edmund Burke that caused him to sigh in the presence of those who read it. The quotation read: "Those who would carry on great public schemes must be proof against the worst fatiguing delays, the most mortifying disappointments, the most shocking insults, and worst of all, the presumptuous judgment of the ignorant upon their designs." Johnson said that the quotation fitted him perfectly.

But Senate liberals knew that Lyndon Johnson had no great public schemes or political principles he was attempting to promote. Franklin Roosevelt, on being interviewed about his political philosophy, had said simply in reply, "I am a Christian and a Democrat." However, Roosevelt had his New Deal as proof of tangible goals.

Pressed by the liberals, Johnson finally issued a statement regarding his views. As he explained his political purposes, they were "to proceed as rapidly as possible to build up the nation's defenses, assure farmers a fairer share of the nation's income, break the bottleneck of foreign trade, broaden the credit basis, and put an end to the evil effects of the hard-money policy."

Many of the Senate liberals reacted to this by saying that if he had a policy it was to hold down their attacks on President Eisenhower. What bothered them especially was their observation that while he was quick to frown upon any of their attacks on Eisenhower, he always let out some anti-Eisenhower words at Democratic clambakes, as though to prove that the liberal wails were without foundation. For instance, in April 1955, when thirty-five hundred Democrats ate a cold meal at a fund-raising dinner in Washington, he drew cheers and laughter when he screamed into the microphone: "Back in 1952 a lot of our folks in Texas got excited about tidelands oil, so they voted Republican. Well, we got Ike and we got our tidelands and it hasn't rained since. Now we are caking our cows—feeding them expensive cottonseed meal cakes—because of drought-stricken range grass, quarreling with our wives, and praying to God for forgiveness and a Democratic Administration." Another time he spoke critically of the President's performance at a news conference and remarked: "After all, Ike spent last week in New England and may not fully understand what he is talking about."

Yet he showed sharp displeasure when liberals Matt Neely of West Virginia and Richard Neuberger baited the President on the Senate floor. Old Matt, five times elected to the House and four times to the Senate and now serving as chairman of the lowly District of Columbia Committee, was known to Republicans back home as "that three-fingered S.O.B." and to coal miners as "Billy Sunday of the Stump." Neely wore immaculate white suits much of the year and was the senator most frequently called up for a few choice words at a colleague's passing. When he said in hushed tones, "The dull swain treads on it lightly with his clouted shoon," other senators nodded thoughtfully, though thoroughly puzzled. Neely had memorized the sixty-six books of the Bible, all of Shakespeare, Longfellow, Tennyson, Coleridge, and others, but he did not use any of the melodious language from these works to describe Eisenhower. One of his mildest expletives was "hypocrite," a term he used in charging the President with posing as a religious man, yet failing to join a church until after his inauguration. Johnson knew that Neely could be contained temporarily if his insatiable appetite for petty patronage was satisfied. But sooner or later he would be on his feet again to denounce Eisenhower or some of his conservative colleagues with such assessments as "a dead loss without insurance," "the biggest hog in Washington," and "a fat squirt."

Neuberger's attacks on Eisenhower were of such a nature that they led to reprimanding editorials in Washington and New York papers, which labeled them as petty and mean. Typical was his taunting of the President in the spring of 1955 for ordering squirrels removed from the White House grounds so that his putting green would not be damaged. Johnson found that Neuberger, too, could be contained by offering to whip up support for some of his Oregon-important bills. Furthermore, by this course he could be turned into a hardworking helper and defender of the majority leader; and Johnson successfully used this technique on him.

By 1955 Sam Rayburn was having misgivings about the "Be Kind to Ike" policy he had fashioned with Lyndon Johnson for the Democrats in Congress. While the Republicans felt free to oppose the Administration on important issues, Mister Sam found that his Democrats were expected to save the President each time. When the Eisenhower proposal to continue the Reciprocal Trade Program came to the House in February, the bill lost by a vote of 207 to 178. Rayburn manipulated for a second vote and on the morning before he called it, he asked twenty Democratic freshmen members to breakfast and ordered them to vote for the bill. This time it passed by a single-vote margin, 193 to 192.

Then there was the Formosa Resolution. When it came to the House, the position of a substantial number of Democrats was expressed by one opposing member in this fashion: "This is just a method of sucking the Democrats in on whatever trouble he [Eisenhower] gets us into around Formosa."

Rayburn's reply was to tell his Democratic charges, "I don't want one word said against this resolution when it gets to the floor of the House." Out of respect for Mister Sam all Democrats obliged him on this dictum of silence, though one voted against the resolution.

Mister Sam grew concerned early in 1955 that a continuous defense of Eisenhower and the absence of Democratic legislation were preventing the Democrats from building a record for next year's election. With the disapproval of Johnson, he pushed a bill through the House to reduce taxes for each taxpayer by twenty dollars. Eisenhower's public condemnation of Rayburn's action as "irresponsible" hurt the Speaker; and his feelings suffered further injury when Eisenhower sat three chairs away from him at a White House correspondents dinner and would not talk to him.

The next day Mister Sam was in a furious mood when Sid Richardson telephoned him. Rayburn knew of Richardson's close relationship with Eisenhower and he complained to the second richest man in Texas: "What does Eisenhower mean by saying I am 'irresponsible'? When I put through the Reciprocal Trade Treaty they thought differently down at the White House. And when I passed that Formosa Resolution for him, it saved Ike's neck. But when I push a twenty-dollar tax reduction to give the little fellow a break, I am 'irresponsible.' "

Richardson's reply was: "The trouble with Ike is that he probably didn't even know you passed the Reciprocal Trade Treaty for him. The boys around him forgot to tell him. Don't forget, Ike *never* reads the newspapers."

Because of this show of independence, Mister Sam was cheered wildly at the April 16 National Guard Armory Democratic fund-raising dinner. In his honor, the crowd rose to applaud him before he spoke, and he cried like a baby when the band played "The Eyes of Texas."

The performances of Walter George and Sam Rayburn underwent close scrutiny by Johnson, but he realized he could never rival them. While George could sway the Senate by a short speech, Johnson's talks added no votes, and in fact, if he did not order staff aides to sit in the gallery and applaud resoundingly after he finished reading a speech, his talks would have gone unnoticed by the few colleagues who did not run for the cloak-room when he rose. Rayburn's total control of House members was simply a matter of personal loyalty and respect. But how could Johnson achieve this with his clumsy lot of suspicious liberals?

Humphrey, Neuberger, and Morse were behind him now, and Johnson made some attempts in the spring of 1955 to lessen the animosity of the other liberals toward him. Morse had been kept happy by giving him the seat on the Foreign Relations Committee, but that had been a political necessity, and there was no way of knowing when he would stop praising Johnson. Before he gained the seat, he had said, "If Johnson should ever have a liberal idea he would have a brain hemorrhage." Afterward he warbled another tune: "I consider Lyndon Johnson not only a great states-man but a good man."

The other liberals might temper their distrust of the majority leader if he could pass legislation they favored. He made a test case of John Spark-man's Public Housing Bill. Given the Administration's opposition to the measure and Johnson's general unwillingness to tangle with Eisenhower, the liberals considered the proposal to construct one hundred thousand housing units a year a lost cause. But Johnson quietly rounded up support by promising aid to Southern members on their special bills. To throw a roadblock into the path of the growing support for Sparkman's bill, Repub-lican strategists promoted the Capehart Amendment, which would permit the small number of thirty-five thousand housing units to be started each year.

The vote was to come on June 7, and a week before that date Johnson knew he had the Capehart Amendment defeated. However, he would lugubriously admit only that Capehart was no doubt correct in his boast that his amendment would pass by an eight-vote margin. On the morning of the vote Hubert Humphrey left Minneapolis by plane at seven-thirty with Washington arrival time scheduled for 2:30 P.M. Humphrey had worked hard for the Sparkman bill, and Johnson had promised he would hold off the vote on the Capehart Amendment until Humphrey arrived.

At two-thirty, when the time came for voting, Humphrey was still absent. Johnson maneuvered to waste time. He remembered that Senator Prescott Bush, Republican from Connecticut, had two innocuous amendments and he chose them to pass time. While they were under discussion, Capehart wandered to Johnson and said jeeringly, "Your stalling won't help you a bit. This time, Lyndon, I'm going to rub your nose in it."

At four, Johnson called the control tower at Washington's National Airport. He learned that Humphrey's plane had not landed because of fog. "Dammit!" he screamed. "I've got a senator up there somewhere on Northwest's Flight 30. He's two hours overdue and I want him down quick. He's got to vote. You better be awful sure he's not stacked up there."

A few minutes later Humphrey's plane landed and Capitol police raced him to the Capitol, where he ran up the stairs and burst into the Senate chamber just as the vote was getting under way. His vote was not needed, for the Capehart Amendment failed 38 to 44. But afterward Humphrey took the floor and his emotional praise of Johnson was applauded by the other liberals. Then Johnson brought the Sparkman bill to a vote and it passed easily, 60 to 25. Senator Paul Douglas, always the most skeptical liberal on the subject of Johnson, stood up and told his colleagues: "I am frank to say I did not think it would be possible to defeat the Capehart Amendment." For the moment he sang Johnson's praise, calling his performance "extraordinary political virtuosity."

The liberals also wanted the Reciprocal Trade Agreements Bill that Sam Rayburn had yanked through the House by the 193-to-192 vote. This was the continuing symbol of the Franklin Roosevelt effort to cut tariffs. Johnson's expressed conclusion was that the enormous trouble to pass the 1954 version portended the defeat of the 1955 bill. The preceding year he had saved Reciprocal Trade when Republican Dan Reed, then chairman of the House Ways and Means Committee, would not consider the Administration's one-year extension bill. At that time, Johnson had passed false word to Reed that he had more than enough votes to push Senator Gore's three-year extension bill through the Senate. Reed had grown frightened at this prospect and quickly rushed the one-year extension through the House.

Johnson knew how to get a favorable vote for the supposedly tariff-reducing bill. This was to turn it cynically into a highly protectionist measure. Six Southern senators, who had been in opposition, quickly agreed to vote in its favor when he added bans against heavy imports of Japanese textiles, and he won other Southern support plus flattering letters from large oil firms by his limitations on oil imports. When the bill came to the floor, heavily laden with such satisfying exceptions, the expected debate of several weeks failed to materialize, and on the third day it passed by a vote of 75 to 13. But instead of thanking him, the liberals charged him with showing reactionary stripes again.

One further Johnson effort to gain liberal support was his work on minimum wage legislation. A few years earlier he had favored the Ellender bill to cut the minimum hourly wage from seventy-five cents to sixty cents. Now he promoted an increase to a dollar an hour; and though the bill for which he won passage did not contain the broad extension of persons covered or the $1.25 rate, as requested by Senator Douglas, it was ten cents higher than the Administration's proposal. But here again, as with the Reciprocal Trade Agreements Bill, the liberals found displeasure in a bill that did not meet their standards.

Johnson found Senator Lehman as critical as Senator Douglas about accepting compromises on new legislation and working slowly to change existing legislation. One of Lehman's special hates was the illiberal McCarran Immigration and Naturalization Act of 1952, and he tried to induce Johnson to join him in a major effort at immigration reform. However, Johnson would not agree to this method, and he wrote Lehman: "As you know, it has seemed to me that the way to handle this issue is to begin nibbling at it. If we nibble long enough, we will break its back." Lehman replied that nibbling was not the correct approach.

By June 1955, Johnson gave reporters the impression he was operating like a smooth-riding jet. "I'm just trying to be like my Daddy," he said. "He talked less and passed more bills than anyone else." Magazine articles applauded the speed with which major bills cleared the Senate. One columnist quoted Johnson as saying he had used "no slipperies or trickeries" to win passage. "But you've got to know the rules," he added. Senate employees in the chamber said he sometimes held his forefinger up and twirled it, as a signal to whoever was presiding at the moment to speed up proceedings. At other times he turned an imaginary crank of a make-believe early tin lizzie to get the same result. And there were times when he wanted to stall and he did this by whispering to the clerk to slow down his reading of the roll call.

"Lyndon involved himself in every petty Senate matter as well as the important business," said Senator Smathers. While majority leaders before him generally asked committee chairmen to handle floor action on private bills (for the benefit of individuals or companies) and routine changes in executive agency activities or titles, Johnson undertook these himself. These were subjects handled by the unanimous consent method, which did not require a time-consuming vote, and in the course of an afternoon he could clear a hundred such bills. (The record was 136 bills cleared in four hours by Republican Majority Leader Charles Curtis on December 30, 1924.)

"I ask unanimous consent that the Senate proceed to the consideration of Calendar Number 615, House Bill 4221," Johnson began. When no objection was voiced, he proceeded to give a short explanation of the bill. This was followed by a statement from the presiding officer that the bill was open to amendment, and finding none, he would proceed with "The bill was ordered to a third reading, read the third time, and passed." Then Johnson moved on to the next minor bill.

Johnson's unwillingness to take time off to recuperate from his kidney operation; his swift and hard pace after he returned to the Senate on

March 8, 1955; his inability to consider the Senate liberals with anything except gritting irritation; and his planning for the Democratic Presidential nomination the next year all showed their effect on his health in June. When the Americans for Democratic Action blasted him early that month as a Republican in disguise, even though Hubert Humphrey defended him against the ADA charges in a Senate speech, Johnson was ill from the venom he felt against the liberals.

"On Saturday, June 18," said Senator Smathers, "Lyndon and I had lunch in the Senate dining room. He ate his usual double meal and gulped the food. Then Norman, his chauffeur, drove us to the Mayflower Hotel, where we stopped to cheer up Senator George, who was ailing.

"Later that afternoon we were supposed to drive out to Middleburg, Virginia, about forty miles from Washington, to visit with Lyndon's friend, George Brown, of Brown and Root, who had an estate there. Norman hardly drove us across the Memorial Bridge when Lyndon clutched his chest and gasped out, 'It's killing me. I've got indigestion.' He asked Norman to stop for a Coke, but even after he drank it, he didn't feel better.

"When we got to George Brown's place, Lyndon insisted on playing dominoes. The pain was still bad, and I said, 'Why don't you take soda?' A servant brought some, and Lyndon tried to burp and belch and play dominoes. Finally, he went to bed, and the next morning he said he was better.

"But he didn't look better, and I asked him to go to his doctor and get a checkup when we got back to town. He kept saying, 'No—No,' as though I was looking for trouble. He did go to see Dr. George Calver, the Capitol physician, when he went back to work on Monday, but this wasn't a real exam, and Dr. Calver told him he was okay.

"What he had suffered, as he later learned, was not indigestion but a heart attack."

Having received assurance from Dr. Calver that his health was good, Johnson plunged ahead as usual into his work load, determined to wind up the session before the end of July. On June 27 he told this to reporters, adding that he was well satisfied with his record in the Eighty-fourth Congress. The Senate had passed fifty major bills, he said, and in a rare jibe at Eisenhower he went on: "I think this should be contrasted with a statement made by a certain party leader last fall that a Democratic Congress would mean 'a cold war of partisan politics.' "

The following day, after being prompted by White House Press Secretary Jim Hagerty to repeat this statement in the form of a question at Eisenhower's weekly news conference, a reporter was the bridge to a reply. The President just happened to have a typed list of sixteen major bills the Senate had yet to act upon, measures such as a military reserve program and the highway construction authorizations, and he suggested that Johnson work hard and get these passed.

Johnson's reaction to the Eisenhower crack was one of lightning anger.

"We are not going to carry out instructions like a bunch of second lieutenants," he said. While Eisenhower was serving as a "hands-off Congress"
President, playing golf and bridge and taking numerous vacations, Johnson
explained to reporters, he and Sam Rayburn had run themselves ragged
to make the President's program a legislative success. Bill White agreed in
The New York Times a few days later: "He has served President Eisenhower as few Senate leaders have served a President, even when both were
of the same rather than differing parties." White pointed out that he
had not only pressured committee chairmen for action on legislation on
a continuing basis, but "he has even taken the unusual step of keeping in
close personal touch with the clerks and technicians of Senate committees
to keep them going full tilt."

Friday, July 1, 1955, was one of Johnson's busiest days. A steady stream
of senators wanted help with their bills before they were shelved in the
rush to adjourn. Republican Senator Francis Case of South Dakota came
to his office four times during the day to discuss legislation. Dick Neuberger
wanted to know Johnson's reaction to a copy of the article, "Making a
Scapegoat of Lyndon Johnson," which he had written for the July 4, 1955,
issue of the *New Republic*. Johnson told him that he and Lady Bird had
read this favorable article, and both were grateful. That evening Johnson
had dinner with Stuart Symington and Sam Rayburn, and Johnson took
time during the meal to telephone Wayne Morse to urge him to slow his
pace. Mister Sam told Lyndon he should take the same advice because he
looked worn out. Johnson said he would do a lot of deer and dove shooting
as soon as Congress adjourned.

"On Saturday morning Lyndon asked me to go with him again to George
Brown's place for the weekend," said George Smathers. "But I had a golf
date, so he asked Clint Anderson and two other senators instead."

After lunch Johnson held a news conference with the Senate wire-service
reporters from the AP, UP, and INS. He had expected to lay out next
week's schedule and put in a few plugs for himself, before abruptly ending
the meeting. However, as soon as it began, he found himself excessively ir-
ritated by the expressions on the faces before him. Then their questions
roused him to make sarcastic replies. One question by an AP man, doubting whether he would work this session with Senator Lehman to repeal the
McCarran Immigration Act because he had supported McCarran's original
bill in 1952, moved him to give a cursing personal reply. Other reporters
quickly defended their colleague, and when Johnson assailed them with
obscene ridicule, they stamped out of the meeting.

By now Johnson was feeling physically out of sorts to an extent that
matched his emotional disturbance. Yet he did not go home, but went instead to the Mayflower for another visit with Senator George, who was
still ailing with respiratory trouble. Then about 4:45 P.M., he climbed into
his official limousine and asked Norman to take him to "Huntlands,"
George Brown's estate.

Just across the Memorial Bridge Johnson broke into a beady sweat, and as on his ride two weeks earlier with George Smathers, he suffered excruciating pain in his midsection. Again he had Norman stop for a Coke to relieve his nausea, and when no change occurred, he stuck his forefinger down his throat in an effort to regurgitate. But he could not vomit, and the pain grew so fierce, he said, that "it was as though I had jacked up a truck and the jack slipped and the truck had crushed my chest in."

When he stumbled into George Brown's place, he declined an invitation to join other guests in the swimming pool. "Lyndon told me afterward that when he walked into one room he found Clint Anderson sitting on a couch," said Smathers. "Clint had had a major heart attack, recovered from it fine, and knew the symptoms. Lyndon walked up to him and asked, 'Clint, what is it when you hurt right across here?' He pointed to his chest.

" 'Does it hurt up and down your left arm?' Clint asked back.

" 'It hurts!' Lyndon told him.

" 'My God, man! You're having a heart attack!' Clint yelled.

" 'If that's the case,' Lyndon said he gasped, 'you get off the couch and let me lay down.' "

Anderson said he rushed to Brown and told him, "Call a doctor, or there's a good chance we'll read in the papers tomorrow that the Senate majority leader expired in the home of George Brown." Brown called every doctor in Middleburg, said Anderson, "but they were all at the horse show. Finally we got one.

"When the doctor came in and pulled a long needle from his satchel, Johnson said, 'I knew it wasn't indigestion.' "

Senator Anderson had also called Bethesda Naval Hospital, where Johnson preferred going, and an ambulance was soon speeding westward on the hour's drive to George Brown's. In addition Anderson, at Johnson's request, called Lady Bird, George Reedy, his press man, and Skeeter Johnston, the secretary of the Senate, and asked them to meet Johnson at the hospital.

When Johnson was brought inside the hospital, the receiving doctor warned him, "Senator, you're going into shock at any minute."

"Let me have a cigarette," Johnson demanded.

"You can have one, but it's the last one you'll ever smoke," said the doctor.

"Tell the wire men I've had a heart attack—a real belly buster—and that I won't be back this session," Johnson told Reedy. "Don't tell them I'm here for a rest or a checkup."

His message to Skeeter Johnston was, "Get ahold of Earle Clements. Tell him to quit campaigning at home and get back here fast and take over the Senate for me."

To his wife, he said, "Bird, my money clip is in my coat pocket. My will is in Jesse Kellam's desk. Call the Mayo Clinic and ask Dr. Cain to fly here and take care of me."

Then he told the doctor, "I'm ready for you."

He was taken to a sixteenth-floor room, put into bed under an oxygen tank, and soon fell into unconsciousness and deep shock.

Acting Majority Leader Clements stood up on July 5 and read a statement by Dr. Cain to his Senate colleagues. "Senator Lyndon B. Johnson has had a myocardial infarction of a moderately severe character. He was quite critically ill immediately following the attack, but his recovery has been satisfactory. . . . He should be able to return to the Senate in January."

Senator Lehman proposed a silent prayer for his noncooperating leader, and members of the Upper Chamber vied with one another in their oratorical praise of Johnson. Hubert Humphrey said, "I wish he could step up here and advise me, as he has done so often, in order to see that things went right along." Neuberger told the Senate he did not agree with the recent attack on Johnson by the ADA, even if Johnson had supported the tidelands giveaway to the oil states and now wanted to remove natural gas pipelines from federal control.

The New York Times ran Bill White's weeping tribute to his friend in the July 4, 1955, issue. "A sensitive and delicate man," White described Johnson before leveling blame for the heart attack at Democratic liberals. "He had been deeply hurt, compounded both of exasperation and sorrow, at the criticisms made so often of him by the advanced liberal Democrats, who have accused him of undue co-operation with the President. . . . He has found it increasingly hard to bear the sense of alienation from some in the extreme liberal wing. . . . This situation has borne very heavily, almost crushingly, upon him."

The object of this veneration returned to consciousness uncertain whether he would live or die. Lady Bird had taken the room adjoining his, and when he came to, she told him that Sam Scogna had called. On that last busy Saturday, Lyndon had gone down to Scogna's tailor shop at Connecticut and K Street to be fitted for two expensive suits. "Tell him to go ahead with the blue suit, Bird," he told her. "We can use that no matter what happens."

Rebekah Johnson made her first plane trip to be with her son, and reporters found Lyndon's mother a never-ending source of Lyndon stories. Letters, telegrams and postcards poured in; the final count totaled more than four thousand.

Cowboy singer and Western actor Gene Autry, who had done some campaigning for Johnson in his 1948 race against Coke Stevenson, wired him from Hollywood: "Get back in the saddle real soon."

Humphrey wrote him, "I miss having you get after me."

Adlai Stevenson had difficulty composing his note, and finally he addressed one to Lady Bird after Lyndon was well on the mend. "I understand that Lyndon is being a juvenile delinquent in the sick room," he wrote. "If he doesn't behave, let me know and I'll bring a posse of assorted Democrats to bring him into line."

Dr. Cain had ordered strict bed rest and no mental work, if the effects of the blood clot within the heart artery were to subside. But Johnson had no intention of remaining supine for long. First, he told the floor nurse he would recuperate much more quickly if he were permitted to have a radio so he could hear his favorite hillbilly music. Permission granted, he kept at the radio dial for a continual blaring of news reports and political commentaries.

He heard so little mention of himself that he told Lady Bird to call Earle Clements to prepare a major statement on Lyndon's accomplishments during his few months as majority leader. "Everybody loves Lyndon," he said sarcastically.

The report was actually whipped up by Johnson's staff and released with the hospital as its place of origin, as though he had written it himself in his hospital room. The heart of the report compared his record in office with that of Senator Taft in 1953, an unfair comparison because Taft's six months covered a time of changeover in Administrations and a period when the Eisenhower Administration was in the process of formulating legislative policy.

"More responsible and thorough work was done than in many, many years," the Johnson report boasted. "A comparison of this session with the first session of the Eighty-Third Congress [1953] illustrates the point. This session passed about 30 percent more bills in about 30 percent less time; it left fewer measures lost in committee files; it confirmed nearly 40,000 Presidential nominations, as compared to about 23,500 during the first session of the Eighty-Third Congress." Still angry with the liberals over their charge of his "petticoatin' Eisenhower," Johnson also had something to say on this score at the close of his statement. "The President's recommendations were considered thoroughly and examined from the standpoint of how they fitted into the needs of the country. In many cases they were improved; in some, they were passed practically without change; others were not acted upon at all."

Johnson also had a story to pass on to George Dixon, the political humorist-columnist, to typify his own hard work putting over the bills of lazy liberals. The anecdote, as printed, pointed out that Johnson was so busy in the last session he had never taken his wife to a social affair. One time he promised he would, but he could not leave the Senate floor and Lady Bird went alone as usual. That night she told him, "I don't see why you couldn't make it. Every other senator made it. Why even Senator Green was there, and he's getting on for ninety."

Said George Dixon, "At this her imperturbable husband perturbed, 'Senator Green! Was he there? That's why I had to stay up on the Hill—to push his blasted bill through!'"

Within a week after being carried into the hospital, Johnson was already fretting over his lack of work. Homer Thornberry came for an occasional game of dominoes, but the nurses hurried the game so he would leave. One day when several nurses were in his room, he bellowed at the head nurse, "I'm tired of female talk. I want my staff to be let in to see me."

The floor physician rejected his demand for several days, pointing out that Lady Bird had converted her next-door room into an office. Here, with the help of a typist, she was plowing into the sacks of mail between his calls to sit with him in his room. "Lyndon wanted me around twenty-four hours a day," she said. "He wanted me to laugh a lot and always to wear lipstick." Many of the letters contained food recipes for heart patients. "I'm either going to have to turn registered chemist or jump out of the window," she told a reporter—an unfortunate remark, considering that former Secretary of Defense Jim Forrestal had leaped to his death from the diet kitchen on the same floor.

By dogged persistence, Johnson wore down his doctors' resistance and his staff moved in like an army, preempted the office of the floor physician, and set up a humming, makeshift center for their boss. Some made scrapbooks of the newspaper clippings and letters sent him, others kept in close touch with committee chairmen and reported on business to him. One friend, on entering the hospital, was told he could visit Johnson because the senator was in a rest period. When he walked into Johnson's room, he found him watching a baseball game on TV, listening to the news on his transistor radio earphone, and bantering with the head nurse. During his second week in the hospital he ordered Clements to come four times for talks, and on one of these occasions, said an observer, Johnson "filled the air with angrily colorful phrases when a nurse asked Clements to depart."

But the nurses made no fuss on July 15 when President Eisenhower came for a fifteen-minute visit. Vice President Nixon had arranged this get-together through Bobby Baker. Eisenhower was to leave that day for the Geneva Summit Conference and he wanted to report that he did not expect anything positive to result from his meeting with Khrushchev and Bulganin. The nurses also made no objection when Nixon came for an hour on July 30.

On August 7 the weary doctors judged Johnson sufficiently recovered to complete his recuperation at home. Congress had adjourned five days earlier, and Dr. Cain believed the absence of Johnson's political buddies would prevent a relapse. Even Mister Sam had to leave for a series of promised speeches, a departure that made Johnson lonely.

Finally, after he had mumbled for days his father's words about wanting to go back to the Hill Country "where the people know when you are sick and care when you die," the doctors said he could fly home to his ranch. He made the flight on August 25, with brother Sam Houston Johnson, who had recently remarried, detailed to accompany him, Lady Bird, and a doctor to Fredericksburg, where their sister Josefa, also recently remarried, was to meet the plane.

As the plane approached Austin, Lyndon burst into the cockpit and ordered the pilot to make immediate radio connection with the airport control tower below. His instructions were for the control tower to dial 8-2793 by phone and keep the radio-telephone connection alive in order that he could talk to his mother in her Austin home. The cowed pilot did as he was told, and Johnson had his conversation with "Mama."

From the loud and energetic quality of her son's voice, Rebekah Johnson knew he would mend without damage.

Chapter 46

JOHNSON'S RETURN TO the L.B.J. Ranch in August 1955 heralded a period of planning that was to end with his pushing Governor Shivers off the top of the Texas political hill. But his scheming to take charge of the next Democratic National Convention ended in failure.

These episodes in his life began with the bouncing ride to the ranch from Fredericksburg. He was pale and his suit was baggy, for his weight had dropped from two hundred and twenty pounds to one hundred and seventy-nine. In his pocket was an unopened pack of cork-tip cigarettes, and after he rode across the Pedernales dam and walked into the ranch house, he set the cigarettes next to his bed as a grim reminder of the three packs a day that had helped bring on the heart attack. Instead of cigarettes, he now chewed gum and crunched low-calorie candy.

The ranch house and grounds were far different from what they had been in Aunt Frank's time. "When we bought the ranch in 1951," said Lady Bird, "the first thing we did we built the dam in the Pedernales [*Purd-in-alleys*]. Then the road and all the irrigation tanks followed in quick succession before we did anything to the house."

Max Brooks worked fast but carefully on the architectural plans for the reconstruction, and in 1952 the new ranch house was beginning to take shape. That was the year of the big flood that washed away chickens and outdoor furniture, and when it struck, Lady Bird was alone at the ranch with her two daughters. "Lady Bird was here and Lucy was just a baby," said Lyndon, "and she was carrying another baby, and she lost that baby as a result of the flood."

He came to the rescue by inducing a friend to offer his single-engine plane for a flight to the ranch. But on take-off the plane flipped over and tore off a wing. Johnson had to rescue his family by car, bringing them out along a back road. The flooding Pedernales brought him more trouble when he and Ray Gordon, a pilot, acted as Good Samaritans to rescue people stranded by the deep running water. At one place they picked up an old lady, but she refused to leave without her dog. Johnson went back for the animal, and it bit him.

With the acquisition of the ranch Johnson had begun a drive to buy surrounding land, and in time Lady Bird was able to say, "We've got four hundred and thirty-eight acres on the main spread. It's shaped like a shoe box, going back from the river. You look to the horizon and you see old mountains, old hills. We planted little bitty pecan trees by the road that runs along the river. . . . There's the Johnson family cemetery down the river road. The tombstones are pink granite. . . . Nearby is Harvey Jordan's house and the scrap of land—two acres—with the little house on it where Lyndon was born. We've planted trees around the irrigation tanks. We call a pond a tank in Texas. We've stocked the tanks with catfish and bass." She also noted the number of heifers ("a heifer is a new bride"), Hereford steers, black Angus bulls, Columbia sheep, and Poland China hogs they owned, and added, "Lyndon gets so mad when they wander in front of the house."

When Johnson came home to the ranch that August, he admitted he had not glanced at more than a half-dozen books since leaving college a quarter of a century before. Lady Bird sought to remedy this by buying him copies of Marquis James' biography of Sam Houston and John Gunther's *Inside Africa.* He sat outdoors near the kidney-shaped swimming pool then under construction and let the sun bake him while he read, dozed, listened to piped-in hi-fi—sterilized, homogenized music that came through the tree receivers outdoors and into loudspeakers in every room. An intercom alongside the pool permitted him to be in instant touch with anyone in the house. "Bird! Bird!" he called, whenever he wanted something brought to him. "When this is over," she confided to a friend, "I want to go off by myself and cry for about two hours."

Despite his weak condition he began making forays back into politics from the start of his ranch stay. The day after his return was his forty-seventh birthday, and he told a Houston *Post* reporter that he was formulating plans to lead a tax cut drive in the next session of Congress. Staff aides made their appearance within a week after he was at the ranch, and he had them take on Senate chores, while two secretaries tapped out page after page of dictated letters and reports on the porch. The old office routine was back when he started placing long-distance phone calls to various senators.

But this would never do if his doctors found out. So he told a reporter for publication: "I've thrown away the whip. That heart attack taught me to appreciate some things that a busy man sometimes almost forgets. I've found it's fun to play dominoes with my two girls. I've found out again that it's pleasant to make small talk with my wife and neighbors. I take a nap every afternoon, and I spend my evenings quietly with Lady Bird and the girls."

In September 1955 political visitors began trooping across the spillway of the river dam to the ranch to pay their respects to Johnson, and reporters who could be trusted to write favorable stories were also invited. But Johnson's hopes for enlarged national publicity were dashed on September 24. President Eisenhower had returned from his Geneva Summit meeting and had gone to Denver for a golfing vacation. Here at 1:30 A.M. he suffered a coronary thrombosis and was put under an oxygen tent. "The difference between Lyndon's heart attack and the one Ike had," said a Democratic senator, "was that the stock market suffered a serious drop when Ike's attack happened."

This Presidential coronary immediately produced speculation that Eisenhower would not run in 1956, even if he should survive. Vice President Nixon, hardly an Eisenhower favorite, was the logical Republican substitute, and a half dozen Democrats, including Johnson, believed they could defeat the brutal-tongued Nixon, who was now presiding at meetings of the Cabinet and the National Security Council.

Reporters tried to smoke out the intentions of Adlai Stevenson, but while the defeated 1952 candidate was noncommittal, he acted the role of top leader of the Democrats. He came to Austin on September 28 to talk on "America, the Economic Colossus," as one of the speakers in the Great Issues series at the University of Texas. Sam Rayburn showed up at Austin's Commodore Perry hotel an hour before the school address for a chat with Stevenson, and Mister Sam was impressed at the applause Stevenson drew from the outsize audience of fifty-five hundred persons.

After Stevenson finished, Rayburn and he drove to the LBJ Ranch to spend the night, and in the morning when Stevenson waked up at seven, he found Johnson conducting a tour of the immediate ranch grounds with a thick pack of reporters. Stevenson joined them in time to visit the family cemetery, where on the ground next to the graves of his grandparents, Big Sam Johnson and Eliza Bunton Johnson, Lyndon dramatically scratched an "X" with his foot. "Sixty days ago," he said, looking about sadly, "that's where I thought I was going to be."

After breakfast of Pecos cantaloupes, venison sausage, bacon, scrambled eggs, hominy grits, and popovers, Johnson told reporters that he and his two guests would submit to a news conference. They sat outdoors in canvas chairs with microphones set in front of them. No, said Johnson, the three politicians had not discussed politics. There was one thing he wanted understood, though, he added, "I like Ike." Mister Sam cut in quickly to agree—"We're not haters. We never hated Mister Eisenhower and we never will."

Stevenson opened his mouth, as though he wanted to talk, but Johnson shook a sheet of paper and said he had a copy of the telegram he had sent to Eisenhower, who, he had learned, was finally able to leave his oxygen tent. He read the telegram in a loud voice: "Dear Mister President, yesterday I went dove hunting and got my limit. I am now extending you an invitation to come to Texas and hunt with me."

Stevenson again made a motion to talk, and Johnson shouted into the microphones that he admired Stevenson, too, and had supported him in 1952. When a reporter asked, "Governor Stevenson, do you think Texas will switch back to the Democratic column in 1956?" Stevenson said, "It's my opinion . . ."

"I think Sam and I are in a better position to answer that question," Johnson took over. "Texas will definitely be in the Democratic column next year by a substantial margin."

Another reporter wanted to know from Stevenson whether the President's illness would change Democratic policy in dealing with the Administration. Johnson replied to this, too, with a quick, "I will continue to act on the basis of what is best for the country."

After several more minutes of Johnson domination, Stevenson finally spoke out above his host's voice. With a broad smile on his face he told the newsmen: "I'd like to come back to Texas and either talk or listen—whatever they'll permit me to do."

Other visitors came to the ranch. Estes Kefauver, known as "The Hand," because of his handshaking technique for picking up support in the 1952 Presidential primaries, was among those who dropped in to discuss the 1956 Presidential politicking. Johnson had long disliked the slow-moving, slow-talking Tennesseean, both for his political competition and his year-after-year arguing for the writing of a Democratic legislative program by a Senate Democratic caucus. After Kefauver's hard sixty-six-mile ride from Austin to the ranch, Johnson kept him from talking politics by showing him his latest electrocardiogram, medical reports, and weight chart, with dozens of explanatory oral footnotes, and when this prolonged recital grew too repetitious even for Johnson, he launched into a sermon against the Demon Cigarette that dangled between Kefauver's lips. He was glad when Kefauver finally stumbled away, just as he was pleased a few days later, on November 24, when Republican Senator Styles Bridges came for Thanksgiving dinner.

Johnson enjoyed steering guests around his property in a large, motorized golf cart. Besides frightening cows in his path and ritualistically scratching a sympathy-evoking "X" on the sod next to Grandpa and

Grandma Johnson's cemetery plots, he always paused before the little house where he was born. Here, he asserted, was where he spent all his years before leaving as an adult. His statement and the current rundown condition of the house embarrassed Rebekah Johnson when she went along; and invariably she chided him with "Why, Lyndon, you know you spent most of those years in the nice house where you live now and in our home in Johnson City." Also in defense of the Lyndon Johnson birthplace, Lady Bird admitted, Rebekah Johnson "used to say proudly that when she lived there it was always freshly painted, with flowers growing by the door."

Toward the close of November Johnson felt sufficiently recovered to make a one-hundred-and-fifty-mile trip northward past Waco to the town of Whitney. The town had a population of 1,379, but 1,510 Democrats were sitting in the Whitney High School gym when he loped in to deliver the big speech at the fund-raising dinner. Adlai Stevenson had announced his candidacy for the 1956 nomination on November 15, and to offset this, Johnson worked his mumbling way through his own offering of a thirteen-point legislative program for next year. He would promote legislation, he promised, to build more schools and highways, help farmers and the poor, broaden Social Security, build dams, and remove natural gas pipelines from federal price control. The ten-dollar-a-plate audience cheered his last proposal most of all. Afterward, when the newspapers across the country reported his "Program with a Heart," as he named it, the ADA labeled it a vague set of generalities that differed little from the vague set of generalities proposed by Eisenhower. When Hubert Humphrey was asked to comment on his friend's program, he called it "twelve hits and one strikeout." The strikeout, said Humphrey, was the natural gas idea.

What pleased Johnson the most about this trip to Whitney was that he did not feel weak upon returning to the L.B.J. Six physicians who examined him in December corroborated this. "Barring unforeseen complications, there is every reason for him to return to his duties and to resume major activity," their unanimous report agreed.

Johnson was on hand for the convening of the second session of the Eighty-fourth Congress on January 3, 1956, a day of congratulations from Democrats and Republicans on his recovery. The President was also back in Washington from Denver via a two-month recuperation in Gettysburg after his heart attack. When the two got together to compare heart attacks, Eisenhower was careful not to repeat the comment he had made to Republicans that "Geneva was not a Yalta." By now, in the Republican vocabulary, Yalta was synonymous with "a sellout to the Communists by Democrats." Eisenhower confessed he had not read a newspaper since his attack and expressed amusement over an editorial a friend sent him that said the Cabinet had functioned better without him.

Keeping his promise to Alvin Wirtz's son-in-law, Johnson started slowly on the job. He slept late, came to the Capitol at ten, stayed on the floor from twelve until one, enjoyed a two-hour nap after a light lunch, returned to the floor in mid-afternoon to check on activities, let Bobby Baker do most of the talking on Capitol intrigues at their meetings, went back to the floor to close the Senate between five and six, and then had Norman drive him home. That month he also took time off for a ten-day vacation in Florida; and the next month he flew back to the ranch for another ten-day absence from the Senate.

But promises were not meant to be kept. On February 6 he stayed in the Senate Chamber without a break between 10 A.M. and 8:30 P.M., in order to win passage for the Harris-Fulbright Bill, which removed federal control over natural gas prices. And by March Sam Rayburn said Johnson looked well enough to devote time and energy to the task of dislodging Shivers from political control of Texas. The appeasement had gone too far, said Rayburn, offering a home-area saying: "What goes around the Devil's back will some day come around under his belly!"

Only a year ago Mister Sam had believed in the necessity of pacifying the governor. In March 1955 he invited Shivers and Democratic National Committee Chairman Paul Butler to a secret summit meeting in the kitchen of his apartment at 1900 Q Street Northwest. Here Butler agreed he would not enforce a loyalty pledge on delegates at the 1956 convention and promised that a Shivers-bossed delegation would be welcomed without questioning. Butler also said he would accept any person named to fill the vacant Texas Democratic national committeeman seat who was jointly approved by Shivers and Rayburn-Johnson. Dwight Morrow, the last national committeeman, had been ousted for the same crime Shivers and Price Daniel had committed—supporting Eisenhower in 1952. Later Eisenhower named Morrow a member of the United States delegation to the UN. Johnson blocked confirmation, and Eisenhower then accepted a man proposed by Johnson, though he weakened Johnson's victory in this instance by labeling the new delegate "a Democrat for Eisenhower."

The continuing appeasement of Shivers made Rayburn pause and ponder for the first time in September 1955, when Adlai Stevenson came to the L.B.J. Ranch for their "powwow," and Shivers told reporters a few days later that he would not support Stevenson in 1956. Rayburn suddenly realized that if Shivers controlled the Texas delegation to the national convention, the general animosity toward him would weaken the Presidential candidacy of Lyndon.

Shortly after the Stevenson visit, Shivers came to the L.B.J. for talk with the convalescing Johnson and old Mister Sam. There was the question of the national committeeman to settle, and Rayburn agreed with Lyndon that this was not the moment to begin a fight with Shivers. So the two said they would accept Shivers' grayhaired Lieutenant Governor Ben Ramsey, who was the governor's watchdog to prevent passage of liberal legislation in the Texas Senate. Shivers pointed out that Ramsey was a good choice because Ol' Ben claimed he had voted for Stevenson in 1952, even if he had not opened his mouth for him during the campaign. Johnson said he would take Ramsey in trade for Shivers' support for Johnson for President, and when Shivers nodded, the pact was sealed.

Texas liberals feared that Rayburn was playing a double game because of his desire to promote Johnson for President. On the one hand Rayburn was maintaining friendly relations with Shivers; and on the other hand, he had been the man most responsible for organizing the Democratic Advisory Council of Texas liberals (DAC). Rayburn's uncomfortable tightrope walk was clearly visible on November 5, 1955, when he attended the big Waco meeting of the DAC. After Creekmore Fath, the fighting Texas liberal, proposed a resolution to bar the 1952 Eisenhower Democrats from the 1956 Democratic National Convention, Mister Sam reacted with such antagonism that the delegates defeated Fath's resolution. But Rayburn could not control Byron Skelton, the newly elected chairman of the DAC, who delivered a ringing attack on Shivers and the "corruption in Austin."

The DAC followed up their meeting by sending a delegation to talk to Johnson. On becoming the national committeeman, Ben Ramsey had vowed to support the national ticket in 1956. What the DAC wanted to know was whether Johnson would lead an anti-Stevenson drive before the convention and oppose him afterward if he won. Even though his eyes gave away his anger at being questioned, Johnson softly replied he was at least as regular a Democrat as Ramsey.

The truth was that Shivers was rapidly growing sorry he had named Ben Ramsey, because Johnson was piling on errands for Ramsey to run at the national committee headquarters and was treating him generally as an employee. One day Shivers ordered his lieutenant governor to come to his second floor office, and when Ramsey entered, he demanded an explanation.

"Well, Allan, it's this way," Ramsey said, embarrassed. "Lyndon got me by the lapels and put his face on top of mine and he talked and talked and talked. I figured it was either getting drowned or joining."

When Rayburn told Johnson in March 1956 they had no time to lose in pushing Shivers off his pedestal, Johnson showed so little taste for the public brawl which would have to result that Rayburn said he would start it himself. Time was indeed an important factor, because the precinct conventions would come on May 5, the county conventions only days afterward, and the state convention on May 22.

So one day early in March, at one of his "five minutes to noon" press conferences, Mister Sam told reporters that "Lyndon will be Texas' 'favorite son' for President at this year's convention and he will also serve as chairman of the Texas delegation to that convention." Rayburn also repeated this in a statement he asked his hometown Bonham *Daily Favorite* to print. "Under his [Johnson's] leadership, we can now begin to put our house in order," Mister Sam claimed. Borrowing from Franklin Roosevelt's famous characterization of Al Smith, Rayburn also called Johnson "a happy warrior."

The import of Rayburn's remarks hit Shivers like a thunderclap, for he was again making plans to lead the Texas procession to the national convention and cause an uproar against Stevenson. In addition, Shivers had grown so accustomed to Johnson-Rayburn appeasement that he had lulled himself into believing it would continue. On a "Meet the Press" radio and television interview program on March 25, the governor slapped lightly at Johnson, who had not publicly ended his appeasement, but tore into Mister Sam, who, he believed, was the real troublemaker. All Johnson had to do to get his support, said Shivers, was to go "on record so far as his views on certain vital issues are concerned"—such as federal aid to education, state interposition against carrying out the Supreme Court's decision on desegregation, and the restoration of the two-thirds rule for nomination at Democratic national conventions. But, Shivers went on, "If Johnson is sponsored by the Democratic Advisory Council [that Rayburn had helped organize], I could not support him."

Johnson's silence emboldened Shivers, and three days after his nationwide interview appearance he made a speech in Houston to dispose of Rayburn. The old speaker's proposal for his protégé was painted as a "cynical and calculated" idea. Rayburn was "a Democrat first and an American second"—a "brass collar" Democrat who followed his party blindly and was without principle. His current operation for his protégé revealed him as "an angry, confused and frustrated man." As for Johnson, said Shivers, "Lyndon, I'm for you, if you're for us."

Allen Duckworth, the excellent political reporter on the Dallas *Morning News,* noted that Shivers' attack failed to bring on a Rayburn retreat. All it did, said Duckworth, was to raise Mister Sam's ire so that on reading it he became "hotter than a ninety-eight-cent toaster." After recovering his general aplomb, Rayburn told newsmen, "Shivers appears to realize he is on a leaking boat which may go down at any time. If I was as alarmed and cruel as Shivers," he said, lighting a Camel cigarette, "I might say Shivers likes Shivers better than anything else, but I wouldn't say that about any man."

In the quiet of Rayburn's Board of Education room, he angrily told Johnson he had gone as far as he could unaided. Johnson now had to leap into the fray, or he (Rayburn) would become a laughingstock in Texas. Mister Sam also pointed out that Shivers might prove to be "a paper tiger because he is a lame duck governor. He might fall over if you blow on him."

Johnson started out cautiously to end his years of appeasing Shivers. Instead of name-calling or charge-making, he began by defending his record as a nonliberal. "No one knows better than Allan Shivers," Johnson said, "that I'm not and never have been the creature of the ADA, the DAC, the PAC [the CIO's Political Action Committee], the NAACP, the CIO, or any other group the governor may have in mind. Nor have I ever been an errand boy of reactionary big business or the Republican party."

On April 10, the competition between Shivers and Johnson became public record when both announced their availability to serve as chairman of the Texas delegation to the national convention. Johnson's statewide address that day was his first appearance on television and he seemed ill at ease. But he had an evangelical air as he asked Texans to unite behind him at the precinct conventions and quoted from Psalm 133: "Behold how good and how pleasant it is to dwell together in unity"; and from Isaiah, against internecine warfare: "Come now, let us reason together." Unless he were given control of the Texas delegation and made the "favorite son," Johnson implied, Texas would be left with a situation in which "Republicans and the radicals [Shivercrats] are trying to destroy the Democratic party in Texas and leave it to the hotheads [liberals]." Shivers' retort to all this was: "I might still back him if he will stop playing footsie with Sam Rayburn and the leftwingers of the DAC-PAC who are trying to take him into camp."

This was now a fight to the end, and though Joe Belden's polls showed Johnson far in front of Shivers for chairman of the Texas delegation and ahead of Eisenhower for President in Texas, Johnson decided to run "scared" in his springtime competition with Shivers. Before long the no-holds-barred politician in the Governor's Mansion was whining to precinct workers in the Houston area that Johnson and his crowd were using "some of the toughest and rawest political and economical pressure that has ever been used in this or any other state." Shivers was referring to the 176-man Johnson statewide committee, which was bringing pressure to bear on local politicians through their bankers, preachers, local editors, and business associates. Johnson was also out zigzagging over Texas in a tieless khaki shirt, brown ranch pants, and big-heel cowboy boots, waging a major campaign effort to browbeat those local politicians who had remained uncertain about promoting him at the precinct conventions, even after the threats to their livelihood by the Johnson statewide committee.

As for Allan Shivers' complaint about his tactics, Johnson scoffed innocently, "Shivers is a frightened, frustrated, and fearful man, and somewhere, somehow, he seems obsessed with a delusion that someone is closing in on him." It was the other way around, Johnson claimed. "All those who open their mouths against Shivers are tarred with the brush of that smear artist."

Besides his 176-man statewide committee and his own personal politicking with precinct politicians, Johnson campaigned with the voters. One technique was his mail gambit, a "Dear Friends" letter sent out to a half million Texans. This mailed enclosure included his April 10 TV talk plus favorable Johnson editorials and told readers to round up all their neighbors and make sure they voted at the precinct conventions. Johnson was also doing some speechmaking, using over and over again, from town to town, an attack on Shivers for deserting the party in 1952 and wanting to be in charge in 1956: "I suppose a woman has the right to leave her husband," he said, "but she doesn't have the right to come back four years later and beat him every morning before breakfast." He also defended his own brand of states' rights, declaring himself opposed to federal aid to education except for school construction in depressed areas. As for the Shivers variety, he said, it included so much state scandal that "we ought to be against state wrongs, just as we are for states' rights." Shivers had no business going to a Democratic convention, let alone serving as chairman of the Texas delegation, he argued. "Why, in 1952, Allan Shivers took a Republican delegation to the Democratic National Convention," he said, ignoring his own role in getting that delegation seated. "Now here in 1956 Allan has not found a single Democrat that he can even conscientiously support, unless Brownell thought one up for him when they were having that secret conclave in Woodville." (The attorney general had come to Texas in early April and was a guest at Shivers' home in Woodville.)

Shivers started to worry about his chances of success when the two leading contenders to succeed him as governor, Senator Price Daniel and Ralph Yarborough, endorsed Johnson as delegation chairman. On April 26 Shivers began a daily radio broadcast against Johnson, raced to several cities to build support for his cause in person, and enriched several TV stations by his special political broadcasts. This was a frenzied effort to paint Johnson as the darling of "the CIO, the UAW, and the Texas Federation of Labor," who, Shivers cried, were spending an unlimited bankroll to buy local support for Johnson. Shivers also remembered that it was Rayburn who had started the contest. Johnson had been honoring his speaker-daddy by characterizing Texas history as "from Sam Houston to Sam Rayburn." Shivers maintained that it would be more appropriate to say "from Santa Anna to Sam Rayburn." Rayburn denounced the governor's "rat alley politics."

There was cause for Johnson-Rayburn rejoicing on May 5 when the precinct conventions favored Johnson as chairman of the Texas delegation by a margin of 3 to 1. Then on May 7 there were boisterous Johnson "yeeeeaaaayhooos," with 185 of the 254 county conventions declaring in his favor. Only the May 22 state convention lay ahead, but this would be a Johnson picnic.

A theatrical production ushered Mister Sam and his boy back to Washington on May 9 for Congressional business and a respite before the state convention gathered. On April 12 Senator George had made a statement endorsing Johnson for the Presidential nomination, and two days later loyal friends Tom Miller and E. H. Perry of Austin had printed "Lyndon Johnson for President Committee" on a rented office door. This Presidential initiative coupled with his victory over Shivers in the precincts and counties brought out a crowd of more than a thousand Texans plus several Southern senators and newsmen to greet Johnson's plane at the Washington National Airport. A cowboy band struck up "The Eyes of Texas"; husky young men held up signs reading "Love That Lyndon" and "The USA Needs LBJ"; and a long red carpet was rolled out at the foot of the plane's ramp for the returning hero.

"I'm going to have first call on you to be my Secretary of State," Johnson greeted old George. "I can't be like Roosevelt. I can't be my own Secretary of State." Then to the crowd of Texans he shouted, "It was a victory of moderation over the rash extremists and hotheads of passion." Openly he bragged that his next victim back home after Shivers would be the liberals. "Next time we'll knock down the extreme left wing," he said. "We won't allow either the right or the left to carry our buggy off the road."

Johnson's warning should have alerted the liberals, yet they arrived in Dallas for the state convention under the mistaken notion that he had merely spoken idly for the press. Far in advance of the May 22nd state convention, Johnson had assigned John Connally the job of controlling the statewide meeting, and Johnson's conclusion was that while the liberals outnumbered other factions, they were fortunately far from united in their goals. He knew that if they could be kept this way, they represented no problem. If they became monolithic in their demands, his task would become hopeless. A Maury Maverick on the scene could have ruined Johnson's aspirations, but Maury was now two years dead.

Nothing mattered more than making certain Johnson was chosen by the state convention to be the chairman-dictator of the Texas delegation to the national convention and "favorite son" candidate for the Presidential nomination. Also important, but to a slightly lesser degree, Connally was to deprive the "Red-Hots," as Johnson called the liberals, from gaining control of the state's Democratic party organization.

Johnson's timetable called for attaining his goals first and then spanking the Red-Hots. But the liberals upset his plans with their preconvention commotion at the Adolphus Hotel gathering of twelve hundred delegates on May 21. Here the liberals cried "Shame" at Shivers for his appalling, reactionary leadership of the state. Despite the stereotyped picture of the cowboy-booted Texas millionaire oil and ranch man, the truth was that 30 per cent of the population was impoverished. Texas stood near the bottom in the nation in per capita spending on pupils (more than a half-million adults could not read or write) and in aid to the blind, old, and mentally ill. Small-loan interest rates were legally very high, and taxes were designed to soak the poor, applying to necessities such as bread and medicine. Industrial safety bills and a twenty-five-cent-an-hour minimum wage law could not clear the legislature, while appropriations for libraries and prison rehabilitation that did were met by the governor's vetoes.

At this meeting in the Adolphus, several liberal leaders also announced their determination to replace the State Democratic Executive Committee, which was a Shivers puppet, with a liberal membership. This would be the first step in modernizing Texas. But Johnson was horrified at this prospect, and he begged Sam Rayburn to talk his DAC friends out of this proposal. Mister Sam happened to be in tune with the liberals' demand that the Shivers organization be ousted, but his sense of loyalty to his protégé overrode such feeling, and he complied. "We Democrats are big enough to hold the door open for those who have strayed," he argued the cause for not pushing the Shivercrats off the committee. The silence that greeted his remarks stunned him, and he stalked from the Adolphus a short time later to go to the bedside of his sister, Mizz Lou, who was dying.

After Rayburn's flat talk Johnson used a different approach when he addressed the rally. Why go to all that trouble against the Governor Shivers-run executive committee? he asked. The committee's life would expire in only three more months when the September governor's convention would approve a new slate. So there was no point in causing a big war now.

Prolonged booing and cries of "Throw 'Lying-Down Lyndon' Out" and "Shivercrat stooge" greeted the close of his argument. But they served only to reinforce his determination to throttle the Red-Hots. Late that night John Connally and his helpers fanned out for further talks, threat-making, and promise-making among delegates. Federal jobholders were threatened with reprisals, while federal jobs were dangled before those who were known to covet them.

By the time the state convention convened the next day, Connally knew from a head count that despite the enormous unpopularity of Johnson's position, Shivers would be left in charge of the executive committee. After a liberal motion was made to replace the membership of the committee, Connally made an attacking speech and then smugly called for a vote to table the motion. Liberal leaders were shocked when Connally won by the wide margin of 1,306 to 525.

Just how impressive was the Connally feat became clear afterward, when Ralph Yarborough, the liberal candidate for governor, and Lyndon Johnson both spoke from the platform. When Yarborough finished his rousing speech, the applause was almost deafening. Johnson followed with a justification for maintaining the Shivers executive committee control— "Let us leave the politics of retribution to small-minded men," he preached, and if Connally had not whipped his small Johnson claque into a fervor of whistling cheers, the lack of response would have been embarrassing.

It was after Johnson became the "favorite son" and chairman of the Texas delegation that the liberal leaders decided to fight back. Promoted by Yarborough, the convention voted to establish a Democratic Campaign Committee to bypass the State Democratic Executive Committee, which would have given campaign help only to Johnson and Shivers candidates. In addition, the convention voted not to adjourn at the close of its business, but to recess instead in order that it could reassemble quickly to combat later moves by the Shivercrats.

A further liberal fight came over the naming of a national committeeman to succeed Ben Ramsey, and a national committeewoman. Rayburn and Johnson had made an agreement with Yarborough and other liberal leaders in which the liberals would select the committeeman, and Johnson the committeewoman. Johnson readily accepted Byron Skelton of the DAC to serve on the national committee and he proposed Beryl Ann Bentsen, wife of former Congressman Lloyd Bentsen, for committeewoman.

But Johnson's selection galled the liberals, who recognized Bentsen as a Shivercrat. Their immediate charges were that Bentsen's father had given Shivers a quickie-get-rich deal, and that young Bentsen had supported Eisenhower in 1952. Mrs. Frankie Randolph of Houston, wealthy leader of the liberal women, refused to honor the deal, and Johnson, unwilling to tangle in a public shouting match with her, had to stand by helplessly while the convention voted Mrs. Randolph onto the national committee instead of Beryl Ann Bentsen.

As one observer afterward described the Texas political situation: "The Democratic party of Texas today is a series of armed camps, acknowledging no one leader or group of leaders. Senator Johnson's 'moderates' are one of the smaller and more ineffectual of the camps."

Chapter 47

ALL OF JOHNSON'S enormous home-state efforts were, of course, pointed hopefully toward his domination of the coming Democratic National Convention, scheduled for Chicago in mid-August. This was why he could not accept the latest public opinion polls, which placed him in the miscellaneous category. According to Dr. George Gallup, Adlai Stevenson was the favorite of 39 per cent of the Democrats; Kefauver, of 33 per cent; New York's Governor Averell Harriman, 6 per cent; Senator Russell, 4 per cent; and Johnson, only 3 per cent. After all, as Johnson's friends passed off his low score, this same Gallup was just as wrong when he predicted a Dewey landslide victory over Truman in 1948.

Had logic taken precedent over dreams, Johnson should have been working just as hard in the Senate to create a Roosevelt-type national image as he had been toiling in Texas to control the state convention. However, by the time he went to Chicago in August for the every-four-years Democratic hatefest, he still bore the label of Eisenhower's chief collaborator, champion of the Texas oil and gas industry, anti-labor senator and Southern segregationist.

The label of defender of Texas oil and gas producers came early in 1956. Since 1949, when President Truman had vetoed the Kerr Bill, which would have ended federal price control over natural gas, Humble Oil, Phillips Petroleum, Kerr-McGee, Brown and Root, and other producers had continued their fight for freedom from strict federal authority. With the arrival of President Eisenhower and his amenability to Sid Richardson and other Texas friends, the situation suddenly improved. All that now remained was the creation of a favorable Congressional vote; and to this end the General Gas Committee, with John Connally on its steering committee, undertook a million and a half dollars worth of lobbying.

By exerting his leadership, Sam Rayburn managed to squeeze the industry's Harris Bill through the House on July 28, 1955, by a vote of 209 to 203. The Senate could not act on the legislation before adjournment time, and Johnson, recuperating from his heart attack at the LBJ, appeared to have been put on the spot between his home state industry and his own national ambitions. But Johnson revealed his intentions by making passage of the natural gas bill Point Seven in his thirteen-point "Program with a Heart" speech at Whitney on November 21. This had drawn as much applause as his charge that the Republicans "gave our air academy to Colorado."

The Harris-Fulbright Bill, as the Senate version was called, became Johnson's first order of business when the second session of the Eighty-Fourth Congress convened in January 1956. Bobby Baker's head count showed passage a certainty because of the coalition of Republicans and Southern Democrats; and with a winner's generosity, Johnson permitted the liberals under Senator Paul Douglas to talk themselves out at their leisure. When Douglas, whose appearance was that of a big, floppy sheepdog, threatened to read a one-hundred-and-fifty-page speech, Johnson told him, "Go right ahead." Then when Douglas stumbled in anger, reciting the cupidity of the industry for wanting the bill passed because they would milk another twelve billion dollars a year from consumers in higher prices, Johnson walked to Douglas' desk and whispered that he should cool off for the sake of "party unity."

Only on one occasion did Johnson try to speed up proceedings, and this came one day when he entered the chamber and found Senator William Langer of North Dakota alone in the chamber with presiding officer Senator

Strom Thurmond and the Senate clerks. Langer was silent, while an unhappy clerk was droning aloud reading from a thick manuscript. Johnson learned that Langer, claiming weak eyes, had asked for unanimous consent to have his ninety-three-page speech read by the clerk, and being the only senator on the floor at the time, he had granted himself the permission. Johnson ran to Langer's desk, where the Nonpartisan League-Republican senator sat chewing on a cigar still encased in a cellophane wrapper, and begged him to call off the reading and simply insert his speech in the record. But Langer refused, and the afternoon disappeared.

This kindness to the liberals turned out to be a strategic blunder. By the beginning of the last week in January they had run out of talking material, yet Johnson took no step to close the debate, for fear of antagonizing them needlessly. Then on February 3 his aplomb was shattered when Republican Senator Francis Case of South Dakota, a supporter of the Harris-Fulbright Bill, gained the floor and said: "Mister President, I rise to make a difficult speech." Case, who bore a resemblance to former President Truman, went on to explain he had received a telephone call from a friend that day, reporting that a stranger had given him twenty-five hundred-dollar bills as a "campaign contribution" for Case. The stranger, who was an out-of-state lawyer, had passed along the money from the Superior Oil Company because of Case's favorable stand on the natural gas bill.

An immediate public furor arose over lobbyists in Washington. Johnson tried to turn the situation around when Case said he could no longer support the bill because of the pressure from the industry. "In all my twenty-five years in Washington," Johnson charged, for the record, "I have never seen a campaign of intimidation equal to the campaign put on by the opponents of the bill. Those of us who support the bill are called 'gas robbers' in newspapers across the land." But to demands of liberals that he agree to a full-scale lobbying investigation by Senator Tom Hennings, chairman of the Subcommittee on Privileges and Elections, Johnson refused, appointing instead a select committee under Senator George to restrict itself to the "Case case." As Johnson explained his action to reporters, he saw need only for a "cowcatcher" (a wire net in front of a streetcar to scoop up a fallen pedestrian) and not a "general fishing expedition."

The Case incident may have dirtied Johnson but it did not materially affect Bobby Baker's head count; and on February 6, three days after the senator made his charge, Johnson pushed the bill through by a vote of 53 to 38. However, President Eisenhower confounded his Texas supporters by vetoing it on grounds of immoral lobbying in the Case affair, yet declaring that the bill "is needed." Johnson's irate comment afterward was: "I think we ought to investigate the morals of some people in South Dakota for bringing this up. . . . When a gas and oil bill comes in here, everybody says it's crooked, for the same reason they think a girl on the street after midnight is probably up to something. But for me, I don't accuse a girl until I see her doing more than walking."

As a Presidential candidate Johnson also damaged himself with Democratic insiders because of his anti-labor stand on the twenty-five-billion-dollar Gore Federal Aid Highway Bill of 1956. The Administration's highway construction bill proposed its financing through the sale of federal bonds; the Gore Bill, through tax revenues. A question arose regarding wage standards, and Senator Chavez proposed an amendment bringing highway workers within the Davis-Bacon Act of 1931, which stated that building and construction workers on federal projects should be paid prevailing wages. The Chavez amendment authorized the Secretary of Labor to set the prevailing wages for each county.

Johnson opposed the Chavez amendment, and immediately aroused the ire of organized labor. On May 29, when the Senate voted on the bill, great confusion reigned as the Upper Chamber passed both the Chavez amendment and one by Senator Knowland, which would give the states the power to determine the prevailing wages, and not the Secretary of Labor. The Senate fell into turmoil, with Senator Douglas and other liberals demanding to know what had been voted. Johnson could have straightened out the milling confusion, but after starting the day in the majority leader's seat, he had slipped out in order to avoid being forced to go on record with his anti-Davis-Bacon Act views. Later, after much haggling with the House, the Gore Bill, including the Chavez amendment, was signed into law by Eisenhower.

On still another score did Johnson weaken his national image, and this resulted from his continued stand as a sectional candidate who "smelled of magnolias." He had an opportunity to undo this reputation when a bloc of ninety-six congressmen signed a "Southern Manifesto" on March 11, 1956. This document, which declared sectional war on the Supreme Court's decision of May 1954 against continued segregation of school facilities, was drawn up by Senators Russell, Stennis, and Ervin, and its nineteen Senate signers were the members from Alabama, Arkansas, Florida, Georgia, Louisiana, Mississippi, North Carolina, South Carolina, Virginia, and Price Daniel of Texas.

Neither Johnson nor Rayburn signed it, and when Johnson's name did not show up on the document, Senator Neuberger, his liberal champion, hailed it as "one of the most courageous acts of political valor I have ever seen take place in my adult life." But Johnson could not hold his silence, and he disillusioned some who had praised him by pointing out that he had refrained solely because by signing he might have endangered his position as majority leader. "I am not a civil rights advocate," he told reporters; and in answer to a question about the white citizens councils in the South, which were using economic and physical intimidation of Negroes, he replied, "Wise leaders at the local level will work to resolve differences."

Disillusionment of militant civil rights liberals deepened in July 1956 when

Johnson killed the Administration's Civil Rights Bill of that year. The far-reaching Eisenhower proposal involved a four-point program: the establishment of a bipartisan Civil Rights Commission to look into charges that Negroes were being deprived of their right to vote and were subjected to economic pressures to keep them in line; a Civil Rights Division in the Justice Department with authority to bring legal action against civil rights violations; new legislation to permit federal prosecution of persons intimidating voters in federal elections; and amendments to existing laws to permit the federal government to bring civil as well as criminal action against "conspirators" attempting to repress the civil rights of others.

The bill had gone to the House in April after long arguments in the Cabinet, with Dulles leading the fight for the status quo. The Dulles position was that no matter how unfair a situation, "laws which depart from the established customs of the people are impractical." While the bill was in the House, it came under the denunciation of another "Southern Manifesto." But with almost total Republican support and half the Democrats for it, the bill cleared the House on July 23 by a vote of 279 to 126.

Through Senator Humphrey Johnson had been alerted to the plan of Senators Paul Douglas and Herbert Lehman to keep the bill from being assigned to its death in Senator James Eastland's Judiciary Committee. On the day the bill passed the House, Lehman was to remain on the Senate floor to guard against its quick referral to the Mississippi senator's graveyard, while Douglas was to walk the length of the Capitol to the House chamber and physically walk the bill back to the Senate. The rules required that each bill transmitted from the House to the Senate be read twice before being referred to committee. The usual procedure was to have the reading clerk read it first on the day of its arrival and then again the following day. This would give Douglas and Lehman sufficient time to employ a complex parliamentary maneuver to keep the bill on the Senate floor for action without going to committee.

Their plan proved a total failure. "As a rule, it usually takes an hour to go through the detailed fuss after a bill passes the House before it's delivered to the Senate," said Howard Shuman, Senator Douglas' administrative assistant. "Paul thought he had a lot of time when he started walking to the House chamber on being told the Civil Rights Bill had just won approval there. He would walk alongside the clerk transmitting the bill to the Senate and then he and Herbert Lehman would work to keep it from going to Eastland."

But Johnson had earlier been in touch with the clerk of the House. As soon as the bill was signed by Rayburn, it was spirited out a side door and brought on the run to the Senate. While Douglas walked purposefully toward the House, the bill passed him in the corridor. Then when it came to the Senate chamber, genial Senator Lehman was called off the floor by a ruse. "By the time Paul walked back into the Senate," said Shuman, "he learned that the bill had been referred to Eastland's committee. Johnson had made certain that Lister Hill, an opponent of the bill, was serving at the time as presiding officer. And Hill had had the bill read twice and referred it to the committee in the blink of an eye.

"Paul then tried to reclaim the situation by an attempt to have the bill discharged from the Senate Judiciary Committee. But again Johnson owned the situation. For thirteen straight days—perhaps in anticipation—he had not adjourned the Senate at the end of each day but had simply recessed the Senate late every afternoon, so that the original legislative day did not change. As a result, no new action was possible under the rules until the Senate was adjourned and a new day begun.

"Douglas made a motion to adjourn the Senate, but Johnson was intent on teaching him a lesson, and he humiliated Paul. The vote was 76 to 6 not to adjourn. Hennings was the only Democrat to vote with Douglas and Lehman, and the three Republicans were Ives of New York, Bender of Ohio, and Bill Langer of North Dakota. So the Civil Rights Bill was dead."

In the opinion of Joseph Rauh, national chairman of the ADA, Johnson had "brought the Democratic party to its lowest point in twenty-five years," and was "running the Democratic party for the benefit of the Southern conservative viewpoint."

"A Johnson Boom Starts in the South," read a front-page headline of a story written by Allen Drury in *The New York Times* on March 12, 1956. Besides public declarations of support by Senators George, Russell, and Thurmond, other Southern senators told Johnson privately that he could count on their aid at the national convention in August.

Johnson made no strategy plans for the sweaty gathering to take place in the Chicago International Amphitheatre. As majority leader he had watched obsequious Democratic leaders from every state as they begged him for favors, and he made the assumption that since they, as well as most Democratic senators, would be at the convention, his same position of authority would apply.

This lack of Johnson preparation became public knowledge shortly before the convention began, when he called Sam Shaffer of *Newsweek* and belligerently ordered him to come to his office. When Shaffer appeared, Johnson gave him a severe dressing down because he had quoted a Democratic politician in *Newsweek* on Johnson's plans at the convention.

"If you want to know what Lyndon Baines Johnson was going to do at the national convention," Johnson screamed, "why didn't you come to Lyndon Baines Johnson and ask him what Lyndon Baines Johnson was going to do?"

"All right," said Shaffer, hiding all signs of intimidation, "what is Lyndon Baines Johnson going to do at the convention?"

"I don't know," was the answer.

Although Sam Rayburn believed Adlai Stevenson was an odds-on favorite to win the Presidential nomination a second time, Johnson refused to accept this. There were nine favorite sons to be nominated, he argued, and they could cause a great deal of trouble for the former Illinois governor. Furthermore, Scott Lucas, the former Senate majority leader, now a Washington lawyer and lobbyist, had confided that he would keep part of the Illinois delegation out of the Stevenson column. Lucas' animosity stemmed from the fact that Stevenson had refused to support him against Senator Paul Douglas in the Democratic primary in 1954.

Johnson was wrong, despite the appearance in the spring of a weak Stevenson candidacy. In March Senator Kefauver claimed all twelve New Hampshire delegates after the primary. Then a week later Kefauver shocked the Stevenson admirers by trouncing him in the Minnesota primary. At the time of his town-to-town tour of handshaking Minnesotans, Kefauver complained that Humphrey had contrived with Johnson to call up the 90 per cent parity bill for a vote so that Minnesota farmers could be told Kefauver was more interested in his own political status than in the welfare of farmers. Having got wind of their scheme, said Kefauver, he made a desperate flight to Washington to vote and then flew back to his Minnesota campaigning.

After his Minnesota victory over Stevenson, Kefauver had an opportunity to wipe Stevenson out as a candidate by taking the California primary on June 5. But Stevenson also realized this, and he campaigned up and down the Pacific state as though he were in a general election. His smashing 2-to-1 victory over Kefauver deflated the Tennessean's national campaign, and in time he announced his own withdrawal from the race with a statement that he was supporting Stevenson.

All these primaries and home-state pronouncements by the variety of candidates and local bosses were of little concern to Johnson as he flew to Chicago as head of the large Texas delegation and the state's favorite son. He had reserved a big suite on the twenty-third floor of the Conrad Hilton Hotel for himself, Lady Bird, and his mother; extra phone lines were installed and his political friends were told he expected them to drop by for talks. Rebekah Johnson knew her son as the leader of the Senate, and now she had an opportunity to meet and be photographed with Harry Truman, Adlai Stevenson, Eleanor Roosevelt, and a host of other Democratic celebrities. Unfortunately, in the midst of her glory, Lady Bird noticed nodules on her mother-in-law's arms. Later examination revealed her to be suffering from cancer of the lymph glands.

Although Johnson had several offers to speak to delegations regarding his own candidacy, he preferred that the heads of the delegations and other candidates visit him privately. Young Senator John Kennedy was one who came. So did Stuart Symington. Symington confided that he was hoping for a deadlock to develop after a few ballots so that the delegates would turn to him with the nomination. This was exactly the idea Johnson had for himself, and so did Stevenson, who came to Johnson's suite and asked for the support of his fifty-six Texas votes. Johnson said he might do this on the second ballot if Stevenson agreed to three concessions. These were to let Johnson name the next chairman of the Democratic National Committee; to include Johnson in the top advisory group to determine the Vice Presidential nominee; and to accept a moderate Johnson civil rights plank in the platform. Stevenson rejected all three conditions.

Harry Truman brought Averell Harriman with him to seek Johnson's support for the New York governor. Truman had already declared his opposition to a Stevenson nomination on the ground that he could not defeat Eisenhower. But privately Truman seethed at Stevenson for not defending him in his 1952 campaign and for firing Frank McKinney, Truman's chairman of the Democratic National Committee. Mrs. Roosevelt had already chastised Truman for his intemperate remark on Stevenson's chances against Eisenhower by telling him it was time to let young Democrats run the party.

John Kennedy was almost hysterical with joy when a Stevenson aide telephoned him with word that Stevenson was giving him permission to make his nominating speech. Kennedy's interpretation of the call was that Stevenson had decided on him as his running mate, and his speech dripped with unctuous praise. John Connally made Johnson's nominating speech, and his convention oratory included such gushing oil as calling Johnson "that son of the Texas hills" and a man who "knows people and they love him, and from that love burns an unquenchable flame of trust." Senator Allen Frear of Delaware made the seconding speech for Johnson, and when he began: "Ladies and gentlemen, fellow delegates, President Truman, Lady Bird"—loud murmurs arose: "Who is Lady Bird?"

There was noise and confusion, parades with waving placards, more nominating speeches, and Mister Sam, as permanent chairman, standing on the platform under the burning spotlights and relentlessly pounding his two-tone yew gavel for order. Rayburn had need to plow through the chaos of only a single ballot. When the first states were polled, and the trend was for a large Stevenson lead, Jim Finnegan, Stevenson's floor manager, asked Johnson if he would switch the fifty-six Texas votes from himself to Stevenson. There were hints of political repayment for this, but Johnson refused, and Texas cast its votes for him as did Mississippi.

It was Michigan that began the stampede for Stevenson by changing its vote, and when the first ballot finally closed, Stevenson had the nomination with 905½ votes; Harriman, 210; Johnson, 80; Symington, 45½. At this point, Mister Sam put into effect his famous "Rayburn Rules of Order for National Conventions" to give Stevenson the nomination by acclamation. Like a locomotive at full throttle he called out, "Those in favor say *Aye*. There are no *Noes*. It is unanimous."

Asked afterward why he had not acted as a kingmaker for Stevenson, just as Tom Connally had done for Roosevelt in 1932, Johnson said he could not switch Texas because it would have been interpreted as proof of Governor Shivers' earlier charge that Johnson was "the stooge of Stevenson."

At this point Johnson was chagrined that his power as majority leader had not rubbed off on the Irish and Italian city bosses who had powerful voices within their state delegations. Nevertheless, he believed he could still land the Vice Presidential nomination, and he asked Sam Rayburn to tell Stevenson he would take it. However, before Rayburn had an opportunity to lobby for his protégé, Stevenson told the whistling, cheering delegates: "I have decided that the selection of the Vice Presidential nominee should be made through the free process of this convention." Johnson, who did not care to get into a general free-for-all, showed open disappointment at Stevenson's unusual move; but this was minor compared with its emotional effect on his friend Hubert Humphrey. The Minnesota senator believed that Stevenson had "tapped" him for his running mate when he had told him before the convention began that he considered him "best qualified" and asked him to "talk up" his candidacy. Stevenson's remark about an open contest for Vice President moved Humphrey to rage.

Kefauver and Kennedy had brought large staffs to Chicago, and they moved quickly to saturate the fifty-three delegations with appeals and promises. But poor Humphrey, operating on a thin shoestring, had only himself on whom to rely. Johnson assured him of support, but this was not the United States Senate where such assurances meant success. All that night, while his son and his staff fanned out among the delegations, Joe Kennedy, basking on the French Riviera, was glued to the phone, barking out promises to a long list of city bosses in Chicago on behalf of his boy.

The younger Kennedy's strategy was to concentrate on gaining public support from top political figures. One person he called on was popular Mrs. Roosevelt, but when he requested her aid, she told him coldly, "I'm concerned about your failure to have taken a position on McCarthy." He replied that political necessity in Massachusetts had not made this practical. To this, she chided him for being the author of a book titled *Profiles in Courage,* yet failing to act courageously himself. Kennedy also joined the long line of candidates who called on Johnson for aid. Said Kennedy about the pleasant doubletalk Johnson handed him: "Maybe Hubert thought Lyndon was for him, and maybe Symington thought the same thing, and maybe Gore thought that too—and maybe Lyndon wanted them all to think that. We never knew how that one would turn out."

By the morning after Stevenson's announcement, it was apparent to the pros that the fight was between Kennedy and Kefauver, with Senator Albert Gore owning an outside chance. The Midwest and Rocky Mountain states' delegations were dubious about Kennedy because of his vote against rigid farm price supports earlier that year, while anti-Catholicism was voiced among some Southern delegations. Yet these handicaps did not seem likely to defeat him, for Kefauver was undergoing general hazing by city bosses who distrusted him. Harry Truman, making the rounds, showed his opposition by pronouncing Kefauver's name as "Cow fever."

By the time Sam Rayburn was ready to pound his gavel and begin proceedings that day, the big amphitheatre was plastered with freshly made signs, and delegates were arm-weary from carrying leaflets and swinging banners for various candidates. Kefauver was available on the scene for last-minute handshaking, handsome Gore for flashing smiles at delegates, while Kennedy was next door, having commandeered the Stockyard Inn, where free liquor was available for thirsty delegates.

Several delegations argued through fiery caucuses before the balloting began, and Texas was no exception. To the packed gathering of delegates before him, including the first Negro delegate—Hobart Taylor, a Houston businessman—Johnson minced no words. He had intended to cast all fifty-six Texas votes for young Governor Frank Clement of Tennessee, and since Clement had withdrawn from the race, the Texas vote on the first ballot would go to Senator Gore. Then on the second ballot, Texas would vote for Hubert Humphrey.

Opposition to Humphrey was tremendous, but there was also little love for Gore, a strong liberal, as angry comments revealed. Former Senator Tom Connally raised his voice to a blast and what came out was: "You vote like you damn please, Lyndon, and I'll vote like I damn please. You're just a tinhorn."

On the first ballot Texas voted for Gore, who emerged third in the ratings behind Kefauver with 483½ and Kennedy with 314. Downcast Humphrey was a poor fifth behind fourth-runner Mayor Robert Wagner of New York City. Before the second ballot Johnson staged another caucus. "I went to see Lyndon," said Gore, "because I had picked up South Carolina, Kentucky, most of North Carolina, and other states, and if Texas had stayed with me on the second roll call, I would have won the nomination. But Lyndon wouldn't do it, so I threw my votes to Kefauver."

At this caucus, Johnson announced his switch from Gore to Kennedy. Tom Connally argued for Kefauver, but Johnson was insistently for Kennedy, despite his own small opinion of the thirty-nine-year-old Massachusetts senator. "You sent me here as your leader," he growled. "I've worked in the Senate with these men, and I want you to know I favor Kennedy."

Not long afterward, when Rayburn recognized the Texas delegation, Johnson told the convention: "Texas proudly casts its fifty-six votes for the fighting sailor who wears the scars of battle." By the end of the second ballot, it appeared likely that Johnson was backing a winner; for Kennedy led with 648 votes to 551½ for Kefauver. Kennedy, enjoying the show on television while lying on his bed at the Stock Yard Inn and wearing only his shorts, decided that the time had come to dress and walk into the amphitheatre in time to be told that his total had risen beyond the necessary 686½.

As he kept an eye on the television screen, several delegations were waving their state standards for recognition from Rayburn. Obviously, they intended to switch their votes to him and give him the nomination. But suddenly House Majority Leader John McCormack of Massachusetts, a fierce anti-Kennedy-family Democrat, was standing before the platform and he could be heard screaming, "Sam! Sam! Missouri!"

Mister Sam listened and gave the floor to Missouri in the midst of the tumult. A groan went up from the Kennedy supporters when Missouri announced a switch from Gore to Kefauver. Other states jumped on the Kefauver bandwagon and swiftly the nomination was his: 755½ to 589 for Kennedy. A Humphrey aide reported that "tears [were] streaming from his eyes as the surge to Kefauver crushed his candidacy." Old Tom Connally, who enjoyed Johnson's defeat when he attempted to become a kingmaker, loudly proclaimed, "Once again the Democratic party has saved the nation from Texas."

But Johnson did not suffer a total disaster at Chicago. He and Sam Rayburn were determined to emerge with a mild civil rights plank in the platform, despite Stevenson's insistence on a strong plank. In February, before a Negro audience in Los Angeles, Stevenson had been booed and called "a phony" when he said he opposed using federal troops to enforce desegregation. But by the time the convention began, his views on civil rights were more militant.

Johnson had allies in his fight for a mild plank. Lady Bird's girl friend Marietta Brooks landed on the platform committee through his efforts, and she kept him up-to-date on the civil rights fight. Also Hubert Humphrey was of help with his nationwide TV speech calling for patience on civil rights goals and a better understanding of the South by the North.

On August 16 Johnson's mild plank and a Northern all-out civil rights plank came before the convention for decision. Mister Sam, wise in the ways of convention affairs, passed along word to Johnson to pack the galleries with supporters of the moderate position. He permitted only thirty minutes of debate. Then when the time arrived for the voting, Rayburn again applied his "Rayburn Rules of Order for National Conventions."

"Clear the aisles!" he yelled. Then he announced quickly that a voice vote was coming on the mild plank. All the while, the chairman of the New York delegation called in vain for a roll call vote. "Those in favor say *Aye,*" Sam snapped. The galleries boomed out their approval, with little response coming from the delegates on the floor. "There are no *Noes,*" he called out. "It is unanimous." The champions of the strong plank almost collapsed in shock at what had happened.

Mister Sam went back to his big white house on Highway 82 at Bonham convinced that the convention had been a success despite the agonies of his protégé. "I feel the Democrats were in the best humor with each other," he told Frankie Randolph, the Texas national committeewoman. "There were no brawls, no fist fights, there was no pulling and hauling at state standards, and everyone looked to be at their best. It seemed that everyone wanted to get a winning ticket and go home and work to elect it."

Mister Sam was wrong on a few scores. Jack Kennedy's last memory of the convention was hearing the band play the "Tennessee Waltz" in honor of Estes Kefauver. Afterward, he fled to the Riviera in remorseful conjecture of what might have been, while his young wife remained at home and suffered a miscarriage.

Mister Sam was also wrong about Lyndon Johnson. The tall Texan went back to his ranch, his heated, kidney-shaped swimming pool, piped-in Muzak music and jungle of telephones to brood a short time and then leap into action to renew his springtime control of the Texas Democratic political machinery.

Trouble between the liberal and conservative factions had broken out anew over the gubernatorial election set for July 28. Six candidates had entered the field, all of them united on only a single issue—to clean up the Shivers state government if elected. Senator Price Daniel, Johnson's candidate and Eisenhower Democrat in 1952, was the front-runner, while Ralph Yarborough, already a two-time liberal loser for governor, was conceded to be a strong contender. The other four candidates were a resuscitated Pappy O'Daniel, traveling across Texas with a red fire truck and his hillbilly band; Evetts Haley, Texas historian and right-wing right-winger; Reuben Senterfitt, former Texas House speaker; and J. J. Holmes, a racial integrationist.

Johnson had sent orders to his friends to work hard for Price Daniel, and when the votes were tallied by the Texas Election Bureau on July 28, Daniel led the field with 628,914. But since he failed to gain a majority, he was forced into a chagrining runoff with "Raff" Yarborough, the next high man with only 463,410 votes.

This margin appeared sufficient at the outset to guarantee Daniel's runoff victory on August 25. However, a vengeful Pappy O'Daniel, hating both Daniel and Johnson, asked his 347,757 backers in the first primary to shift their votes to Yarborough. As a result, the Daniel-Yarborough contest turned into a brawl, with the odds shifting for a Yarborough victory.

Immediately, a variety of nuisance tactics were used against Yarborough. One such stunt involved radio studio engineers who turned off the lights while he was in the midst of reading a speech. "But the big job done on me came on the run-off vote on August 25," said Yarborough. "That night the Texas Election Bureau gave Daniel a slight lead, but they reported that thirty thousand votes were still to be counted, and almost all were in counties favoring me. At midnight I learned that Daniel's men were seen at the airport leaving with briefcases for all parts of Texas to fix the vote. Instead of the expected thirty thousand votes, only five thousand were sent in during the next two weeks, and the fictitious certified totals sent to Shivers' Democratic Executive Committee gave Daniel a thirty-five-hundred-vote margin. There was nothing I could do about this stolen election."

The State Governor's Convention was scheduled for Tuesday, September 11, at Fort Worth; and Johnson and Rayburn came as heads of their county delegations. An immediate head count of the eighteen hundred delegates after the August 4 county conventions had convinced Johnson that only strong-arm action would prevent the "Red-Hots" under Yarborough from gaining control of the next State Democratic Executive Committee and the party platform. Johnson had made his plans since that time, and the events that followed revealed his superiority over the disorganized liberal majority.

On convention eve the liberals held a rally at the Fort Worth Pioneer Palace on the convention grounds. Talks by Yarborough and Austin attorney Fagan Dickson called for an all-day effort the following day to prevent Executive Committee Chairman George Sandlin—"the mouthpiece of Shivers"—from "stealing the convention from us." Lyndon Johnson was not attacked, though private apprehension was expressed that he would be working for Price Daniel at the convention, as he had during the campaign against Yarborough.

Mrs. Kathleen Voight, the executive director of the liberal Democratic Advisory Council, laid bare the Johnson strategy in advance of the rally with her pamphlet titled, "The Big Steal of the Texas Democratic Party 1956 Style." Her warning was of a "Shivercrat-Republican conspiracy" to send contesting reactionary delegations to the state convention and have them seated instead of the elected liberal delegations.

Mrs. Voight was correct, yet neither she nor her liberal friends were a match for Johnson when eight counties sent contesting delegations of conservatives to Fort Worth, and he put into effect "the big steal." When the convention opened at 11 A.M. on Tuesday, Johnson had already placed Ray Buck, his 1941 and 1948 Senate race aide, on the Credentials Committee as vice chairman, along with his friend, Frank Wilson, the committee chairman. He had also borrowed Shivers' strategist, Jake Pickle, to lead the fight to prevent the seating of liberals, including Mrs. Voight, on the Executive Committee, even though her district caucus had elected her. In addition he had personally hired the Palo Pinto County sheriff's posse to drag Red-Hots out of meetings if they proved too argumentative. Furthermore, he had ordered Texas members of the United States House of Representatives to report to Fort Worth and work as his assistants. Said Larry King, an aide to freshman Congressman J. T. Rutherford, Johnson brusquely ordered them to "fan out" to the delegations from their districts and return with information about delegates "flirting with the Red-Hots." Such individuals, said King, would soon be confronted by their "banker, preacher, lawyer, congressman, brother, and threatened unless they got back into the fold."

Johnson's scorecard showed that he could not win if the Harris County (Houston) liberal delegation with its 270 votes was seated. What infuriated him most about this situation was that Frankie Randolph, the Democratic national committeewoman, was a member of this delegation, and the sight of her reminded him of his failure at the May state convention to seat Mrs. Bentsen. So along with his determination not to seat the liberals from Harris County he resolved to have Mrs. Randolph removed from the national committee. This latter task he took on with pleasure, grasping lapels of delegation chairmen to argue for summary action through convention resolution to oust her. There were scenes where Johnson asked delegates to tell him how they liked their federal jobs, and there were times that he talked mayhem. One liberal leader said he heard Johnson bark at a henchman: "You tell those Mexicans from Laredo I'll break their legs if they don't vote for us."

At one point spectators were treated to the sight of Johnson standing nose against nose with an old college friend from Houston and screaming, "If you don't he'p me get rid of her and put Mrs. Bentsen in, you ain't never gonna get to be a federal judge!" But Johnson was unable to win enough support for his proposal, because it was too raw even for the conservatives, and Mrs. Randolph remained on the national committee until 1960.

However, Johnson was more fortunate in barring her delegation from being seated at the convention. One of the Red-Hot delegations whose seating was in dispute was from El Paso County, in Representative Rutherford's Congressional District. County Judge Woodrow Wilson Bean, chairman of the liberal delegation, wanted to take part in the convention, and he went to Johnson, said Larry King, and offered to make a deal. "See that my El Paso liberals are seated," said Bean, "and I'll deliver their votes to you."

Johnson recognized the offer as an excellent opportunity to have some Red-Hots under his thumb. And when Bean also agreed to vote for the seating of the Harris County conservatives and not Frankie Randolph's liberals, Johnson quickly telephoned Ray Buck on the Credentials Committee, and Judge Bean's group was seated.

Unfortunately, after Bean told his delegation the good news to the accompaniment of cheers, his admission of the *quid pro quo* exacted by Johnson stirred talk of revolt. Spies in the group passed word along to Johnson that the majority of Bean's delegation were not going to serve as "Lyndon Johnson's rubber stamp," and in a ferocious tone he telephoned Bean to report to him for a talk. After upbraiding him, Johnson asked, "Well, can you deliver them or not?"

"I can try, Senator," Bean hedged.

"Trying don't count. You with me or against me?"

"Well, I tell you," Bean said finally, "it looks like we'll be forced to go the other way, Senator."

Johnson pounded Bean's chest with a finger. "Woodrow Bean, I'm gonna give you a three-minute lesson in integrity. And then I'm gonna ruin you."

For three minutes he yelled out a lecture on the importance of "being a true friend to Lyndon Johnson." Then he called Buck again and ordered Bean's delegation replaced by the conservative El Paso County delegation.

Through Buck's help and his own personal browbeating techniques, Johnson managed to seat the conservative Harris County delegation, rather than Frankie Randolph's Red-Hot delegation. Now the convention belonged to him, for this gave him a margin of 1,006 to 869 for the Red-Hots. He pushed through a Price Daniel platform with ease, brought into being a sixty-two-member State Democratic Executive under right-wing Chairman J. H. Blundell, which did not include Mrs. Voight, and ordered Texas National Committeeman Byron Skelton to announce, "Now that we have a loyal Democratic Executive Committee, there is no need for the Democratic Advisory Council." Johnson also had Lady Bird's friend Marietta Brooks named vice chairman of the Executive Committee. Afterward, when Price Daniel appeared on the platform and began his victory speech, there was so much booing he could not be heard.

Sam Rayburn resented the critical letters liberals sent him following the September convention. Comments about "the stealing of the Fort Worth Convention" gave him "a heaviness of heart," said friends. But Johnson suffered no regrets or pains from his work at the convention. As a reporter friend put it, he was proud that "in the spring he defeated the Texas Democratic conservatives and in the fall the liberals."

Texas liberals moved toward a final break with Johnson when they learned he and Rayburn had convinced Stevenson not to come to Texas to campaign before the November election. Not only that, Johnson made a one-hour campaign speech, reputedly in behalf of the Stevenson-Kefauver ticket, yet he did not mention the name of either man. In addition he used a large part of the treasury of the Texas State Democratic Campaign Committee to reprint and mail a column written by Holmes Alexander, a conservative reporter. The column flayed Stevenson but applauded Johnson, "the tall traveler [who] came to Congress as a follower of Franklin Roosevelt but a number of years later . . . was riding in the first-class coach of arch-Republicanism, the Taft-Hartley Act."

When Eisenhower defeated Stevenson in Texas by a larger margin than he had in 1952, reporters said Johnson was "not saddened" by the election. The coast was now clear to build on his record for the 1960 Presidential race and to strengthen the image that he and Sam Rayburn represented the Democratic party. As one political observer noted, "The only things holding the Democratic party together are its debts and its Texans."

Chapter 48

As soon as the 1956 election was over, Johnson went hunting in his "Zane Grey Country" with his Johnson City friend and new business partner, Blanco County Judge A. W. Moursund. With Moursund, Johnson could momentarily forget politics and concentrate on deer and doves. Before his heart attack Johnson's notion of a hunting expedition was racing up and down knolls to get a buck in his sights. Afterward, in order to conserve his energy, he built a forty-foot-high, heated glass enclosure complete with elevator, which served as a sumptuous hunting tower for him and "A.W." The tower stood just beyond some wooded acres that deer frequented during the day. It also stood at the edge of a field richly sown with oats to lure the animals into the open when it grew dark. Johnson and Moursund enjoyed coming to the tower with guests and several Negro servants for dinner, drinks, and a good shoot. Once the table was cleared and everyone held his telescopic rifle in readiness, Johnson would turn on baseball park night-lights on the field; the bucks would freeze as they ate and be felled by the marksmen. One time when Roy and Jack Howard of the Scripps-Howard papers were his hunting companions in the tower, they described their evening as one that "equalled hunting with the Maharajah of Mysore, who invited his guests to shoot tigers from a royally equipped and danger-proof structure in the jungles of India."

With Johnson as the Senate's majority leader and Moursund as the local judge, hunting laws could be conveniently disregarded. Texas regulations barred dove hunting after sundown, but Johnson and Moursund decided this was the best time to pepper the flocks as they rested en route to their Southern winter homes. One night Captain Sprott, in charge of law enforcement for the Texas Game and Fish Commission, heard after-dark shooting on Moursund's ranch. When he and Warden Grover Simpson investigated, they found Moursund, Johnson, and Ernie Stubbs, the Johnson City banker, on Moursund's range. Simpson demanded to see the game bags, and a long argument followed when Moursund refused to open them. Johnson had meanwhile gone to Moursund's car to escape interrogation, only to hear Simpson yell at Moursund, "Who is that big-eared s.o.b. in the front seat?" Johnson made no reply.

Despite the seriousness of the hunters' offense, it was Sprott and Simpson who suffered. Another local judge dismissed the case before the regular hearing time. Then at a later date, Johnson's persistence in demanding the removal of Sprott and Simpson from their jobs was not only successful but Judge Moursund was named a member of the Texas Game Commission!

Following his period of relaxation on the range, Johnson headed back to Washington for what he believed would be the most crucial four years of his life. With Eisenhower flattening Stevenson by an electoral count of 457 to 74, the chubby, bald, Illinois word-slinger should be finished politically. And with no one else of Johnson's stature on the horizon, he was certain that an astute four-year effort to portray himself as a Westerner and not a Southerner, as a statesman, and as "Mister Democrat" should yield him the Presidential nomination.

To become "Mister Democrat," it was necessary for Johnson to continue to give the Democratic National Committee the gripless end of the political stick. But Adlai Stevenson had no intention of letting this happen. Shortly after his defeat he told National Committee Chairman Paul Butler to establish a party spokesmen committee that would meet regularly to issue policy statements on current issues. Butler, who agreed that Johnson and Rayburn had failed to give the Democrats a legislative program, lost no time organizing a Democratic Advisory Council with a membership set at seventeen, Stevenson as its unofficial leader, and himself as chairman.

In December 1956 Stevenson came to Washington to arrange the membership of the DAC and to explore ways of getting cooperation from Johnson and Rayburn. A meeting with Senate liberals in the office of Senator Clinton Anderson led to the selection of DAC members, but failed to solve the Johnson-Rayburn problem except to name the two to membership. A fascinating aspect of the announced roster was that it contained the names of every Democrat who nurtured Presidential ambitions for 1960—Stevenson, Johnson, John Kennedy, Hubert Humphrey, Stuart Symington, Kefauver, Averell Harriman, and Michigan's Governor G. Mennen Williams.

Johnson saw the DAC as a dangerous competitor, and neither he nor Rayburn would recognize its existence. In a bristling press interview he stated flatly that he and Rayburn would set all Democratic legislative goals by themselves. Asked for his reason, he replied that he and Mister Sam were elected officials representing constituents, unlike Adlai Stevenson who held no office and Paul Butler who was an appointed officer. But Butler refused to dissolve the DAC, and a four-year battle began. Without Johnson and Rayburn the DAC was merely a vocal forum; yet the existence of the DAC prevented Johnson from portraying himself as the spokesman of the Democratic party. At one point in this intraparty struggle Mister Sam publicly decried his own action after the 1956 convention in convincing Stevenson to retain Butler as national committee chairman when Stevenson wanted to replace Butler with genial Jim Finnegan.

Despite the Eisenhower landslide over Stevenson, the composition of the

Senate—forty-nine Democrats and forty-seven Republicans—remained un-
changed, though it took some doing by Johnson to retain his majority
leadership.

In Texas his strategy was to have Price Daniel resign his Senate seat on
the same day he was sworn in as governor so that he would have authority
to name his successor, who would serve until the general election. However, Shivers would not agree to this, and he demanded that Daniel resign
and the governor name the temporary senator. Johnson quaked at this
latter possibility, because Shivers had supported Eisenhower in 1956, and
there were Austin stories that he planned to "fix" Lyndon by appointing
a Republican senator.

It was Shivers who bested Daniel in this war of the senator. But instead
of naming a Republican to succeed Daniel, he chose reactionary Dallas
Democrat William Blakley, chief stockholder in Braniff Airways and a self-
made ranch and real estate millionaire five hundred times over. Johnson let
out a whistle of relief when Shivers called him with the good news, and
to reporters he said gleefully, "Shivers is tough. He'll grab the flag and
take his folks somewhere. I like that in a leader."

However, Johnson was still not out of the political timber country. Five-
term Ohio Governor Frank Lausche, a wide-faced, slow-thinking and
talking, reactionary Democrat, had defeated Republican Senator George
Bender, and there was talk Lausche planned to join Knowland in helping
the Republicans take control of the Senate in the Eighty-fifth Congress.

This rumor gained credence on January 3, 1957, when Lausche failed
to attend the Democratic caucus in the big conference room in the forty-
eight-year-old Senate Office Building. After a long wait for him, Johnson
finally told his Democratic charges, "I don't know if I'll be the majority
or minority leader."

The test came in the Senate chamber, with Democrats and Republicans
introducing motions to elect Johnson and Knowland as majority leader. A
crackling air of electricity hung over the Senate when the roll call began
on the Knowland motion. On the call of Lausche's name, the Ohio senator
made no immediate reply, and loud murmurs arose on the floor and in the
galleries. Finally, Lausche shouted a slow "No," and Johnson retained his
authority as majority leader.

Johnson found the composition of the Senate changed in several respects
at the beginning of Eisenhower's second term. Alben Barkley, who considered him with amused contempt, was dead, and so was Harley Kilgore
of West Virginia, who had described Johnson as a "roughneck." Senator
George was also gone into forced retirement, and Theodore Green, in his
ninetieth year, had taken George's place as chairman of the Foreign Relations Committee.

The most respected member of the Senate, George had paid the price back home for concentrating on foreign relations at Eisenhower's request. His Coca-Cola and Georgia Power sponsors had second thoughts after suggesting he leave the chairmanship of the Finance Committee for Foreign Relations, and they had shifted their support to "Young Gene" Talmadge, governor of Georgia and son of former Governor "Ol' Gene" Talmadge, a redneck, race rabble-rouser.

George heard that word was spreading throughout Georgia that "Ol' George has gone high-hat"; he's become a Yankee"; and "he's forgotten Georgia." When George went back home to assess the situation, he saw that Talmadge had sewn up the Democratic primary. So he announced his retirement and accepted the Administration's offer to become United States Ambassador to NATO.

Earle Clements, Johnson's chief aide and majority whip, was also out of the Senate after losing to former Assistant Secretary of State Thruston Morton. "Earle knew he was in serious trouble, so he went back to Kentucky in February 1956 for an all-year-long campaigning," said Senator George Smathers. "And with Earle gone, Lyndon asked me to be his acting whip.

"It was a grueling year for me," Smathers recalled. "Lyndon came by my house on Garfield Street every morning at seven on the dot and I was with him until ten-thirty at night. As soon as we walked into the Capitol, he started his sixty-cylinder engine, and he didn't slow up during the entire work day. He wanted me at his side all the time, and the only real break we got came about six-thirty, when we went over to Sam Rayburn's to join the Texas delegation for drinks. While most of the others wanted to talk nonpolitics, Lyndon spent that respite talking politics without pause. If we stayed awhile, Sam would send out to Pierre's on Q Street for dinners, and he'd also order a special plate of raw onions for himself. We didn't go home afterward as a rule, because Lyndon believed in night sessions in the Senate for everything; so we didn't leave the Capitol until hours later. Then it seemed like only a few hours later Lyndon and his limousine were back at my front door to start a new day.

"That summer and fall, too, he and I put in long hours on Senate election campaigns, because I was in charge of the Senate Campaign Committee and we determined how much money and speech help Democratic candidates would get."

After Clements lost to Morton, Johnson called Smathers in Florida and ordered him to come to Washington immediately. "When we met," said Smathers, "Lyndon greeted me with, 'Can you get Magnuson to be for you?'

" 'Be for me for what?'

" 'For my whip.'

" 'I don't know whether I want to be the whip,' " Smathers said he told Johnson. "It was as though I had kicked him in the solar plexus. He couldn't understand how anyone could refuse the job.

" 'Why not?' he yelled at me.

"I told him that my wife wouldn't tolerate it. 'You tell that Lyndon you already have one wife,' I repeated her words."

Johnson was incredulous. "Well, if I don't get you, who will I get?"

Smathers suggested he get Mike Mansfield of Montana because he was a Westerner. "I'm a Southerner and you're a Southerner," said Smathers. "You'd have a hard time getting me elected."

Johnson would have preferred Humphrey rather than Mansfield. But he needed Humphrey as a seemingly free liberal, so he asked tall, thin, professorial Mansfield to take it. Now he was stunned again when Mike also turned him down, insisting he wanted to concentrate on his Foreign Relations Committee work. "Lyndon insisted I had to take it because I was the least objectionable to most of the Democratic senators," said Mansfield. "It was not a flattering argument, but after several meetings I finally lost my resolve against becoming whip."

With the pipe-smoking Montanan as his whip, Johnson began his third year as majority leader. Yet instead of feeling at ease about the Senate, he suffered from gnawing discomfort because of unfinished business back home. Looming over the horizon was a special election to choose a man to finish out the year and three quarters remaining of Price Daniel's term, and the vision of having Ralph Yarborough as his Texas colleague envenomed him.

Johnson made two efforts to prevent this. With the help of Governor Price Daniel, serving as his front man, Johnson tried to promote a bill through the Texas legislature to continue the appointed Blakley in office as a United States senator. But his hope was short-lived because on March 12, 1957, the state senate rejected this proposal.

Johnson's second scheme was to alter the existing law regarding special elections. The day set by Daniel for the election was April 2, and at first Johnson believed he need do nothing to prevent Yarborough's election when Martin Dies, the old Un-American Activities Committee blowhard, entered his third contest for United States senator. With the state Democratic organization behind Dies, as well as the border county dictators and conservatives of both parties, Johnson saw Yarborough as an obvious loser. His smile faded when Republican Thad Hutcheson of Houston paid his filing fee and announced he was running with President Eisenhower's endorsement. Hutcheson's entrance into the race meant only one thing to Johnson: He would split the conservative vote with Dies, and Yarborough would emerge as the next senator! This called for a desperate effort to prevent such a catastrophe.

"The first I heard of any scheming against me," said Yarborough, who was out campaigning against "the interests" and his eighteen fellow candidates, "was when friends told me that Lyndon and Sam Rayburn were telephoning people in the state legislature to vote for the Pool Bill. This legislation would require a run-off election in a special election if no candidate won a majority of the votes the first time. The existing law only required a plurality."

Sam Rayburn had supported Yarborough for governor the preceding year against Daniel; and he now wrote friends that unless the Pool Bill was passed, Yarborough and Dies would split the Democratic vote and Hutcheson would win. Yarborough, who liked Rayburn, concluded that Mister Sam had been taken in by Lyndon. "The Pool Bill was obviously aimed only at me," he said. "I had sixty-four friends in the Texas House pledged against it, but Johnson and Rayburn swung it with a one hundred-vote majority and the help of Waggoner Carr, the speaker.

"As in the house, the bill needed a two-thirds approval in the Texas Senate, and Johnson and Rayburn worked on members without let-up. 'If they can pass it,' one senator told me, 'they plan to file a mandamus suit in the Texas Supreme Court right afterward to force a run-off.' But when the vote came in the senate, they were able to get nineteen votes out of thirty-one, or only one vote fewer than they needed for their required two-thirds. So I was saved on this score."

Tuesday, April 2, was a bad weather day in Texas, and voting was not especially large, even for a special election. "The tricks were not over," said Yarborough. "At nine-thirty that night the Texas Election Bureau announced that Martin Dies was seventy-five thousand votes ahead of me. Despite the tornado, reporters came out to see me, and one of them named Duncan told me, 'You're seventy-five thousand behind. So why don't you concede?'

"Because I know I've won," I said to him. "I've had elections stolen from me before. But this is no Democratic primary. This is a general election and the federal law applies. I'll see that whoever is manipulating the votes will go to jail.

"At midnight the Texas Election Bureau declared me the winner by that same margin of seventy-five thousand votes."

After Yarborough's victory Sam Rayburn announced, "I am glad that I could finally win with him because I lost with him when I voted for him four times before this and he had my vote again this time."

Johnson's welcome to Yarborough when he came to the Senate was to shunt him off to the minor Post Office and Civil Service Committee, Government Operations, and Interstate and Foreign Commerce Committees. This was his way of telling him that a state of war was continuing.

Before he left the Senate, Walter George reminisced: "Mister Roosevelt had a real gift for separating his personal feelings from his political feelings. He never mixed them. That's a gift Lyndon Johnson doesn't have," the old man added.

From his vantage point as majority leader, Johnson hoped to throttle all would-be opponents for the Democratic Presidential nomination in 1960. With the exception of Stevenson, all the panters after this honor were members of the Senate whose careers and work he could alter at will. Adlai Stevenson would always be able to waft out an uplifting phrase, but as a two-time loser and as the little star of the Democratic Advisory Council, which Johnson believed he had ignored into oblivion, Stevenson did not appear to present a real threat for 1960. But Estes Kefauver, with his friendly handshake, tireless campaigning in primaries, crime committee reputation, and 1956 Vice Presidential nomination, had all the earmarks of becoming Johnson's chief competition for the Presidential nomination.

This was why Johnson acted quickly in January 1957 to prevent Kefauver from gaining further glory as a Democratic party foreign policy spokesman. When Walter George left the Senate, he also opened a seat on the Foreign Relations Committee. Kefauver claimed it on the basis of his Senate seniority, and although other members considered this to be a firm rule for filling committee openings, Johnson gave the post to freshman Senator John Kennedy, despite Kefauver's denunciation of this unfair maneuver.

At the time, Johnson considered the young Kennedy to be no threat to his bigger political aim, for the Massachusetts senator was among the Upper Chamber's leading absentees and infrequent debaters. He had a book that had won him a Pulitzer Prize, but common talk in the Senate cloakroom was that his rich father had paid a ghost-writing syndicate of college historians to write it for him. This had seemed to be borne out when the Senate put him on as chairman of a committee to select five outstanding senators in its history. One Kennedy suggestion was that perhaps Oliver Ellsworth merited inclusion among the holy five. Those familiar with early American history knew Ellsworth was a member of the first Senate and later Chief Justice of the Supreme Court, and a man whom colleagues called "Endless Ellsworth" because he talked almost continuously and in a foolish fashion. Ellsworth was also known as a hot opponent of the Bill of Rights during the undeclared War of 1798 with France.

While Kennedy was unsuccessful in promoting Ellsworth, he had no trouble winning acceptance for the late Senator Robert Taft as one of the immortal senators along with Daniel Webster, Henry Clay, John C. Calhoun, and the elder Bob La Follette. As a paid Kennedy campaign biographer later stated, Kennedy wanted Taft included because his own voting record "was becoming increasingly down-the-line liberal [and] he still wanted to keep some ties with the conservative camp." Kennedy believed "that many conservatives, if denied the substance of right-wing policies, will settle for symbolic recognition of the justice of their cause."

To Johnson the harmless status of the Kennedy candidacy for 1960 seemed to hover at a degree close to the bottom of the political thermometer; and at only a few degrees higher were the candidacies of his friends, Stuart Symington and Hubert Humphrey. Few political pros judged Symington to be more than a lightweight, while Humphrey lay anchored by his chains of "Endless Hubert" and his public image of a firebrand liberal. Oddly, Humphrey was to claim he had Presidential stature on the basis of an eight-hour-and-twenty-five-minute conversation he held in the Kremlin with Soviet dictator Khrushchev on December 1, 1958, a talk with only a midway break when Khrushchev told him, "Let's go to the toilet."

Humphrey continued to be Johnson's hard-working lieutenant, even though they were competitors for 1960. When Democrat Joseph Clark, former mayor of Philadelphia, defeated Republican Senator "Big Red" Duff and came to the Capitol in January 1957, Humphrey's advice to him was: "Keep your mouth shut and your eyes open. It's a friendly, courteous place. You will have no trouble getting along. Paul Douglas and I will help you. Lyndon Johnson runs the Senate and will treat you well." Johnson followed up by inviting Clark and five other freshmen senators to lunch in the office of Skeeter Johnston, then the Secretary of the Senate. Each senator found a copy of *Citadel*, by Johnson's friend Bill White, at his table place, and in a paternalistic manner Johnson "urged them to read it as a Bible." White's book extolled the Senate club of Southern committee chairmen.

While Joseph Kennedy began staging large audience luncheons for his son across the country and putting a copy of *Profiles in Courage* at each plate as a trademark for his boy, Johnson had to make use of his newspaper and magazine friends to portray him as a lofty statesman and the towering master of politics. Reprinting from the *Texas Quarterly*, the *Reader's Digest* lent him a hand by running a first-person article on Johnson's creed that said: "I am a free man, an American, a United States Senator and a Democrat, in that order. I am also a liberal, a conservative, a Texan, a taxpayer, a rancher, a businessman, a consumer."

Time, Life, and the *Saturday Evening Post* found him a worthy subject for eulogizing articles and their references to him followed the awestruck Stewart Alsop line that as majority leader "there was something magical about his performance." As Alsop had Johnson explain it: "When we get the football in our hands, we just don't sit back with it—when we don't hit the line, we throw a forward pass. But mostly the job of being majority leader is just doing what's right—that and hard work. . . . There's no mystery about being Senate Leader," Alsop quoted Johnson. "You've got to be interested in the other man's problems, you've got to treat him fair and you've got to know enough of what's going on to do your job right."

Johnson's friendly reporting crew printed his confession on why he was so superb a majority leader. "Sam Rayburn once told me that an effective leader must sense the mood of the Congress. He doesn't see it, smell it, hear it—he senses it. I usually know what's going to happen within the first fifteen or twenty minutes of the day."

The torrent of printer's ink devoted to Johnson encomiums became a Niagara of praise. A *Reader's Digest* article on him was titled: "Face of the Democratic Party"; a syndicated column, "Lyndon Johnson Moves

Mountains"; *Time* magazine, "One-Man Show." The *Time* piece found him the exciting ringmaster and all the acts in a three-ring circus. On one day, the magazine told readers:

He seemed everywhere at once: describing a new electric vibrator to Vice-President Richard Nixon, eating breakfast with Defense Secretary Neil McElroy and again with Army Secretary Wilbur Brucker, holding seven-hour committee sessions, making television films for a Texas network, striding down a corridor tossing off orders to two press secretaries who took notes as they scurried after him, slipping into a dinner jacket for a banquet, speaking to the Women's National Press Club and 1200 steelworkers in a snowstorm outside the Capitol.

"The second most powerful man in the United States," one article declared—and perhaps the most powerful because President Eisenhower could have only that legislation Johnson chose to give him. His control of the Senate was such, said a reporter, that when he walked into the Senate chamber he was like "a Bavarian landgrave stepping into his castle."

Another reporter declared that "he runs the Senate like a caged tiger"; still another said, "Sitting slumped in his aisle seat, he can sense everything that is going on behind him without turning around."

Many reporters wrote about the source of his power. Bill White tried to ascribe it more to his personality than to his formal position. Johnson was a great convincer, he claimed: "No single man ever left a *tête-à-tête* with Lyndon B. Johnson feeling he had won a single round of the discussion."

Some reporters quoted Johnson as saying he was merely carrying out the precepts he had learned at his daddy's knee. Sam Johnson, identified as "My Daddy," was the keen judge of life and men, said Lyndon Johnson, who "used to tell me": "that the time to kill a snake is when you've got the hoe in your hands"; "that it's better to win a convert than a fight"; "that if I didn't want to be shot at, I should stay off the firing lines"; "that you ain't learnin' nothin' when you're talkin'"; "that so-and-so's a damned smart man, but the fool's got no sense"; "that you shouldn't rock the boat just for the fun of it."

Never, never, Johnson was quoted as complaining, did his power depend on acting the role of a wheeler-dealer. "People don't understand one thing about me," ran one quotation, "and that is that the one thing I want to do is my job. Some are always writing that I'm a back-room operator. They say I'm sensitive. How would you like your little daughter to read that you are a 'back-room operator,' a 'wire-puller,' or a 'clever man'?"

By whatever name others chose to call Johnson's method of operation, wrote Mary McGrory in the Washington *Evening Star*, his personal approach was "a rather overwhelming experience. The full treatment is an incredibly potent mixture of persuasion, badgering, flattery, threats, reminders of past favors and future advantages."

Stewart Alsop, rivaling Bill White as Johnson's principal booster, saw more humaneness in Johnson's approach. "Like a great professional athlete, Lyndon Johnson of Texas makes no wasted motion," he purred. "A word here and there, a casual political arm around a recalcitrant shoulder, a brief, companionable colloquy with his opposite number, William Knowland of California, and the chances are that the bill under consideration will slide through the Senate almost without debate."

Alsop also offered his own personal experience in running into what he described as Johnson's "Treatment A" to paralyze reporters who had disagreed with him in the slightest. On this occasion Johnson asked him to come to his office and began the conversation by reminiscing about President Roosevelt as being the true source of Johnson's interest in national defense, not the current untidy state of world affairs, as Alsop had suggested.

By gradual stages the relaxed, friendly and reminiscent mood gave way to something rather like a human hurricane.

Johnson was up, striding about his office, talking without pause, occasionally leaning over, his nose almost touching the mesmerized reporter's, to shake the reporter's shoulder or grab his knee. Secretaries were rung for. Memoranda appeared and then more memoranda, as well as letters, newspaper articles and unidentifiable scraps of paper, which were proffered in quick succession and then snatched away. Appeals were made, to the Almighty, to the shades of the departed great, to the reporter's finer instincts and better nature, while the reporter, unable to get a word in edgewise, sat collapsed upon a leather sofa, eyes glazed, mouth half open. "Treatment A" ended a full two hours later, when the Majority Leader, a friendly arm around the shoulder of the dazed journalist, ushered him into the outer office. It was not until some days later that the reporter was able to recall that, excellent as Johnson's record on national defense undeniably is, the two sentences he had written had been demonstrably true.

Another reporter found a comparable "Treatment A" applied to senators when Johnson went after a vote. "It was a form of hypnosis by movement," said Russell Baker of *The New York Times*, "which seemed to leave the victim pliantly comatose. He might saunter up to his man and begin by seizing his lapels. Then the big hands would start, flashing around the fellow's ears and the Leader would lean into him, nose to nose, talking constantly, pounding fist into palm, kneading the victim's elbows, bobbing and weaving, withdrawing abruptly, then thrusting his face just as abruptly against the gentleman's own, forcing him to retreat in mental disarray."

On reading this description, Johnson once boasted that he could work senators over so roughly that "the skin comes off with the fur."

This did not quite jibe with Johnson's own description, on another occasion, of the need for handling his colleagues gently. "This Senate is like a dangerous animal that you're trying to make work for you," he said. "Push him a little bit, and he'll go. Push him a little bit harder, and he may go or he may balk and turn on you. You've got to sense just how much he'll take and what kind of mood he's in each day; and if you lose your feel for him, he's going to turn around and go wild."

So the hunting-tower rifleman viewed the Senate as a wild animal; its members as Whales and Minnows. He added a new member to his menagerie now when he referred to his chief lieutenants, like Hubert Humphrey, as his "lead horse" and "stud duck."

As the printed praise of Johnson expanded, several senators called it unrealistic in several respects. For instance, Mike Mansfield, his whip, commented, "Lyndon attempted to be the whole show. Instead of letting committee and subcommittee chairmen handle their bills on the floor when he called legislation off the Calendar, he demanded that they fill him in quickly on the subject and then he would serve as floor manager. He gave me no duties, and about the only thing I did as whip was to pull on his coattails when he was talking too long and beginning to lose votes because of this. Sometimes he sat down before it was too late."

Republican Senator John Williams of Delaware viewed him in a different fashion. "Lyndon was majority leader at a time when Eisenhower presented a small and moderate program that was not too unpopular. There were usually forty to forty-five Republicans for each bill, so all Lyndon had to do was to get a third of the Democrats behind it. In addition, with only a slim majority in the Senate, the Democratic senators felt a natural and psychological need for uniting. So he could brag that the expected successes came about solely because of him.

"This did not mean that Lyndon was satisfied to win easily. He liked to play tricks on you, and the game to many members was always one of trying to outfox Lyndon. If you had a vital interest in a bill, and he didn't like you, he would call the bill up from the Calendar when you walked out of the chamber."

Senator George Aiken of Vermont, another Republican, considered Johnson a "strong-fingered man without finesse." Said Aiken, "Lyndon would go around and try to change votes by pounding his forefinger into your chest and yelling at you, 'You better vote the other way.' If you got in bad with him, he punished you by never calling your bills off the Calendar."

A personal admirer of Johnson, yet a senator who saw him objectively, was Russell Long of Louisiana. "Johnson was a take charge man and a driver," Long described him. "But he never took a chance and wouldn't keep pushing a bill if he felt it might not get through. He also could not bear to have anyone operating outside his camp. When he saw this developing, he would either reconcile or isolate them. As for Senate loners, he could make their lives miserable."

So these varying views of Lyndon Johnson existed: one promoted by his tremendous publicity machine in the press; the other, kept to quiet behind-the-scenes talk by his colleagues. Only the first mattered, and John-

son basked under the floodlight of printed praise, in the belief it would
carry him into the White House in 1960.

Chapter 49

L YNDON JOHNSON'S COMPETITORS for the Democratic Presidential nomination could choose at their leisure the issues and stands they believed
would enhance their candidacy. Johnson was not as fortunate, because his
position forced him to become involved in all the controversial issues of
Eisenhower's second term. In some instances he wanted the association
because of the possible salutary effect on his national image; in other
cases, he played a reluctant role, fearful he might damage himself.

These issues encompassed a wide range of political matter—from the
Middle East controversy of 1956-1957, civil rights legislation, budget cutting, recession fighting, and labor racketeer controls to missile-gap filling.
Ironically, while his involvement helped him to write the history of the era,
it prevented him from taking the time to saturate the country with barnstorming speaking tours and state-by-state courtship of probable convention delegates.

The overriding crisis at the beginning of the second Eisenhower term
lay in the Middle East. British inroads inside Egypt, begun in 1882, and
blossoming into a protectorate in 1914, were on the wane following World
War II. Fat King Farouk symbolized the disintegrating colonialism when
he fled during the *coup* that brought in the government of General Mohammed Naguib in 1952. Then in 1954, when Lieutenant Colonel Gamal
Abdel Nasser, the power behind Naguib, took charge, a major push began
to oust remaining British colonialism. The British readily agreed to pull
out the eighty thousand English troops, and President Eisenhower promised
economic aid to Nasser. But a deep, remaining concern of the London
Government was the fate of the Suez Canal, completed in 1869 and
functioning as the lifeline to the East. In 1889 England and eight other
European nations had agreed by treaty to keep the Suez Canal open in
war and peace to military and civilian commerce. The Nasser Government
was not bound by this pact.

Besides the uncertainties regarding the Canal, the Middle East was held in tension by unending Arab belligerency toward the state of Israel, established in 1948 from a part of the British Mandate of Palestine. Following the heavy warfare in 1949 between Israel and her Arab neighbors, Jordan chose to lob shells into Israel and raid villages across the border in a monotonous but deathly repetition that witnessed severe retaliatory raids in return by Israel each time. To make certain that neither side would grow strong enough to overcome the other, the British, French, and American Governments signed an agreement in 1950 to maintain the status quo in the Middle East.

A further, menacing complication arose late in 1955 when the Soviet Union undertook a penetration in Egypt. Aware of the competition between that communist nation and the West, Nasser began a policy of blackmail to increase his military strength. Requests for aid to Washington and Moscow contained the threat that he might join the other camp unless he got what he wanted. When Eisenhower hesitated about supplying him with twenty-seven million dollars worth of arms, the Soviet Union agreed to send him two hundred million dollars worth.

Nasser's major dream was the construction of the Aswan High Dam on the Nile, a goal that he soon put up to the rival nations to fulfill. Dulles believed the United States had no alternative but to take care of this billion-dollar chore for Nasser, and he and the President called a meeting of Congressional leaders to discuss the financing of the dam in June 1956. Because of Johnson's expressed thought that "foreign policy is the responsibility of the President," Dulles expected the meeting to be routine. But hardly had he broached the subject of the dam when Johnson interrupted to declare his opposition to the project.

Dulles heatedly replied that construction would be under a grant-loan arrangement "with no side deals between Egypt and the Soviets," which would tie Egypt to the United States for at least ten years. Egypt was at that very moment dickering also with Russia, he added, so the United States had to build the dam. The President's contribution to the discussion was to remark that it was ironic the Soviet Union, with a weaker and less developed economy than the United States, could nevertheless compete. "This shows the advantage which a dictatorship possesses in being able to choose its own ground and then moving very fast," he said.

Mister Sam, who was also present, conjectured whether Nasser was not already a Soviet tool. Then to soften his rebuke to Dulles, he asked whether Nasser believed that American aid to Israel was much larger than aid to Egypt. Dulles wandered off into this extraneous subject and failed to return to the subject of the Aswan Dam.

By the time Johnson returned to the Capitol, he viewed the rejection of the dam as a popular vote-getter for the Democrats. Senator Russell was easy to convince that the dam meant severe competition with Southern cotton by its irrigation aid to Egypt's long staple variety, and the Senate

Appropriations Subcommittee, in its report on the Mutual Security (foreign aid) appropriations, stated that "none of the funds provided in this act shall be used for assistance in connection with the construction of the Aswan Dam . . . without prior approval of the Committee on Appropriations."

Eisenhower angrily charged that this statement "would render the Executive powerless in his conduct of foreign relations," though he asked Dulles to mention this Congressional problem in continuing his negotiations with Nasser. It was Nasser's gambit now to object to the Administration's demand that he enter into no side deals with the Soviet Union. To show his independence, he recognized Red China, armed Algerian Arabs to fight the French, fortified the Israeli border, and denounced the Baghdad mutual defense pact existing between Britain, the United States, and Turkey, Iran, Iraq, and Pakistan.

After completing his display of independence, Nasser then informed Dulles that he was accepting the American proposal to construct the dam. Dulles reacted with undiplomatic fury and called off the offer. Nasser now took the retaliatory action that precipitated the stormy Middle East crisis: on July 26, 1956, Egypt seized control of the Suez Canal.

An immediate Cabinet crisis developed in Britain, and Prime Minister Eden, fearful that other areas under British domination would take actions similar to Egypt's, demanded that Eisenhower join him in putting down the Nasser Government. However, Eisenhower put into effect his foreign policy of waiting calmly for a propitious moment to seek a compromise. His initial delaying action was to have Dulles arrange a conference in London for August 16 for twenty-four countries that used the Suez Canal. Cautioned that it might be wise not to ignore the existence of the Democratic party, Eisenhower, at Dulles' suggestion, decided to entangle Democratic leaders behind his policy.

Johnson was in his suite at the Chicago Conrad Hilton, planning how he would dispose of Stevenson's candidacy at the opening of the national convention the next day, when Eisenhower telephoned him and Sam Rayburn on August 12 to return to Washington for an important White House meeting on the Suez crisis. The Presidential plane, the *Columbine*, rolled into Chicago a few hours later and a party of loud-talking Democrats flew back to Washington discussing convention matters all the way. The conversation continued without letup into the Cabinet room before "a serious President and a grim Secretary of State" called the meeting to order, said Sherman Adams.

After Dulles painted a frightening picture of a situation in which Nasser could cut off two-thirds of the oil Western Europe needed for industry and home heat, the desire of the British and French to go to war over Suez, and the threat of a developing Soviet sphere of influence south of the Mediterranean, he spoke glowingly of the User-Nation Conference to be held in London four days later. Senator Russell called this ridiculous because Egypt had announced it would not attend. Then Sam Rayburn asked "how much kicking around" the British and French would take before using military force against Nasser. "They have only agreed to bide their time until the conference," said Dulles. "They call Nasser a wild man brandishing an ax."

Eisenhower assured the group of twelve senators and twelve House members that if the Users evolved a fair proposal and Nasser rejected it, the United States would probably consider "more forceful measures" to support the British and French. Afterward, Eisenhower tried to close the meeting by requesting Mike Mansfield to accompany Dulles to the London conference. Mansfield shocked him by saying he "had more urgent business elsewhere." Eisenhower then asked Johnson to go, but Johnson, with the convention on his mind, also declined. Eisenhower's final request was made to William Fulbright. The Arkansas senator put it the bluntest of all by rejecting the Administration's hoped-for facade of bipartisanship. "No Democrat is available," he told Dulles later.

The London Users Conference proved to be only a delaying action. An agreement to recognize Egypt's sovereign rights over the Canal, plus an economic right to fair compensation for its use, met with summary rejection by Nasser. When Eisenhower's earlier promise of "more forceful measures" failed to materialize, leaders of the two countries accused him of letting Presidential election precautions influence his foreign policy. This seemed to be borne out when Henry Cabot Lodge, the United States representative to the UN, voted for a British-French resolution for a UN study of Nasser's acts in "bringing to an end the system of international operation of the Suez Canal," and for an Egyptian resolution calling for UN measures "against some powers, particularly Britain and France, whose actions constitute danger to international peace and security."

After this, Prime Minister Anthony Eden and French Premier Guy Mollett withdrew from close association with the Eisenhower Administration. Eisenhower's concern about what action the two were secretly planning soon heightened. On September 23 Jordan shelled across the Israeli border, and Israel retaliated with a major raid. This was followed by a buildup of Israeli military forces and a fear by Eisenhower of imminent war between Israel and Jordan. No CIA consideration was given to the possibility of war between Israel and Egypt, even though Egyptian raids into Israel were a regular event.

Eisenhower's misjudgment became clear on October 29, when Israeli forces invaded the Sinai Peninsula inside Egypt and began a rapid advance toward the eastern bank of the Suez Canal. That this was part of a plan devised by Britain and France with Israeli collaboration was evidenced the next day by the invoking of the 1950 Tripartite Pact by Eden and Mollett. Ultimatums went out to Israel and Egypt to quit fighting and withdraw ten miles from either side of the Suez Canal. If this were not done, said Eden, British and French armies would enter that zone "in whatever strength may be necessary." Then before Eisenhower could protest that he did not agree with their interpretation of the Tripartite Pact, British air attacks on Egypt had already begun.

Eisenhower's worry now was that the Soviet Union would join with Egypt if a cease-fire and withdrawal of forces were not effected. When Britain and France vetoed a United States resolution before the UN Security Council calling for all members to end the use of force in the Middle East, Dulles asked for action by the UN General Assembly. Here on November 2 the vote of 64 to 5 ordered a cease-fire between Israel and Egypt and a withdrawal by Israel to the 1949 truce border. A UN peace-keeping force was also approved.

Three days later, when British paratroopers landed on the west bank of the Canal and French troops entered Egypt, Eisenhower's alarm grew when the Soviet Union proposed joint American-Soviet action to drive the invaders from Egypt. His pressure on Britain and France finally resulted in their agreement to halt further military activities on November 6. A sad Anthony Eden called Eisenhower and requested a Washington meeting on Suez, but when State Department officials vetoed this talk until British troops withdrew from Egypt, Eisenhower accepted their decision, he said, "with reluctance and impatience." Only a personal appeal to Israeli Prime Minister David Ben-Gurion by Eisenhower produced a cease-fire on the east bank of the Canal.

A major problem yet remained following the cease-fire, and this was to force the withdrawal of British, French, and Israeli troops from Egypt. Anthony Eden considered this meant the end of his government, and he would not agree. Not until December 3, after his health broke down, did his temporary substitute, Selwyn Lloyd, accept Eisenhower's demand for an unconditional withdrawal. But he did so only after the American Government secretly proposed to fill British oil needs. As British troops pulled out of Egypt, the Suez Canal was gutted by sunken vessels, all oil pipelines except one had been sabotaged by Arabs, and worst of all for England and France, they were no longer a factor in Middle East affairs.

When 1957 dawned, Eisenhower was faced with two major problems in the Middle East: If the United States did not fill the Western Power vacuum following the British-French withdrawal, the Soviet Union would attempt to do so; unless stubborn, little Israel moved out of her 1956 conquests, the United States would lose face among the Arab nations.

Eisenhower and Dulles attempted to move swiftly on the first issue by drawing up what they called the "Eisenhower Doctrine" for the Middle East. Upon the request of the government of any country in that area, the Doctrine called for the sending of American military forces to repel Red aggression. The Doctrine would also provide the President with two hundred million dollars to parcel out in economic and military aid to Arab nations.

Because of its top priority, Eisenhower called Johnson, Rayburn, and other Congressional leaders to the White House for a meeting on New Year's Day, 1957, to give the Eisenhower Doctrine an energetic send-off. Unfortunately, before they arrived, printed explanations were already in the newspapers following leaks by State Department officials. In addition, several of the congressmen were the worse for wear after attending New Year's Eve celebrations.

No one made a sound during Eisenhower's reading of his Doctrine and his long explanation. "The existing vacuum in the Middle East must be filled by the United States before it is filled by Russia," he said. Then he awakened those still suffering from their parties by adding, "Should there be a Soviet attack there, I can see no alternative to an immediate United States move to stop it."

Almost four hours of questioning followed, with Johnson and Rayburn so noticeably quiet that Eisenhower felt obliged to tell them at the close of the session: "You know you are as welcome in this house—in this office—as anyone." The preceding year he had neglected to call Rayburn in to discuss the foreign aid bill, and when the House slashed the appropriation, Mister Sam had scolded him for not working closely with the sympathetic Democratic leadership to save the bill. "Naturally, I work normally and properly with my own party leaders in the Congress," Eisenhower now attempted to explain his predicament. "But you have the right and you have the duty to call on me when you think something is necessary, just as I have the duty to call it to your attention when I think something is needed. . . . When I say Happy New Year to you I mean it from the bottom of my heart, even though we belong to different parties."

If Eisenhower thought this little speech would win him speedy passage of the Eisenhower Doctrine, he was mistaken. On January 5, 1957, he delivered a Special Message to Congress on this subject and sent up a bill in the form of a joint resolution. First the Democratic Advisory Council under Stevenson-Butler opposed its passage, and then former Secretary of State Dean Acheson, a notable lawyer but a man obsessed with the specter of Communists lurking everywhere, declared the bill "vague, inadequate, not very useful." Johnson thought it should be rewritten, and in deference to Mister Sam he asked his aides and outsiders for help in writing a Rayburn Doctrine. This thirty-four-word declaration read: "The United States regards as vital to her interest the preservation of the independence and integrity of the states of the Middle East and, if necessary, will use her armed force to that end."

Dulles was outraged at such tampering with his handiwork, and when the President asked if he could live with Rayburn's revision, he uttered a flat *No*. Dulles gave as his reasons the absence of any mention of economic aid, the call for a freeze of the Middle East boundaries by the United States, and the violation of the UN Charter in ordering United States military action even if a country voted peacefully to establish a communist government.

A chastised Rayburn remained the perennial good soldier. "I think we've got to give the President the authority he requested to use American military forces," he told House members. "I lean very strongly toward giving Mister Eisenhower the power to spend, as he sees fit, two hundred million dollars by next June 30 to bolster the economies of the Middle East." So compliant was he that when the bill came to the floor, he invoked a "gag rule" barring amendments, and though members charged he was working to protect the big oil interests, he pushed the bill through the House on January 30 by the overwhelming vote of 355 to 61.

But Johnson served notice that he was not Dulles' good soldier when he had the bill sent to a joint Armed Services-Foreign Relations Committee for protracted hearings. Here Senate hecklers told Dulles that Eisenhower was requesting power that Constitutionally belonged to Congress; that he was attempting to force Congress to share responsibility that was only his; that he was requesting authority to cover an indefinite future emergency; and that his economic proposals showed his favoritism toward Arabs over the Israelis.

Senator Russell decided that the two-hundred-million-dollar request was a blank check untied to specific needs—"We are being asked to buy a pig in a poke." Senator Fulbright infuriated Dulles by softly asking him to supply a complete review of the Department's policy in the Middle East since his 1952 trip to Egypt to present General Naguib with "a silver-plated pistol." Wayne Morse caused a weary Dulles to blunder badly when he asked why England and France were not included as partners under the Eisenhower Doctrine so that "American boys won't have to fight alone." Dulles' reply, which brought him reams of criticism across the nation, was the angry retort: "If I were an American boy, I'd rather not have a French and a British soldier beside me, one on my right and one on my left."

While these rasping hearings continued, Johnson made several changes in the Administration's bill. One alteration eliminated a separate Middle East fund and assigned such aid under the regular foreign aid appropriation; another deleted Congressional authorization for military aid and left this entirely to the President. Dulles agreed to these but not to an amendment by Russell that would "cut the heart out of the resolution," said Eisenhower, by deleting all references to military and economic aid to the Middle East. When the Democrats split on the Russell Amendment and the Republicans united with only five exceptions behind the President, it lost on March 2 by a vote of 58 to 28. Then three days later, when the Johnson version of the Eisenhower Doctrine came off the Calendar, it passed the Senate 72 to 19, and became law on March 9 when Eisenhower signed it.

During the next year, Eisenhower applied his Doctrine twice. After anti-Israeli and pro-communist riots were tearing Jordan's stability to shreds, King Hussein asked for American aid, and Eisenhower ordered the Sixth

Fleet into the Eastern Mediterranean. This action was followed by the end of the Jordanian rioting.

The other invocation came in Lebanon, where the government of President Camille Chamoun asked for American troops, ostensibly to put down a communist attempt to take over the country. Reports to the White House revealed that the principal cause for unrest in Lebanon came from Chamoun's intention to amend the Lebanese constitution because it barred a second term. When a *coup* took place in nearby Iraq by pro-Nasser forces, and Syrian invaders made raids into Lebanon, Eisenhower considered the Lebanese situation so serious that he called a meeting with Congressional leaders.

Sam Rayburn took one extreme view that if American troops were sent into Lebanon, they would be getting embroiled in "strictly a civil war." Senator Fulbright quoted a study by UN Secretary-General Hammarskjöld which stated that there existed no proof that the rebel support from Syria was communist. Uncle Carl Vinson piped up with the suggestion that the United States should make up its mind "to go the distance"—nuclear war with the Soviet Union. Johnson offered no opinion.

As a group the congressmen showed little enthusiasm for action in Lebanon. But Eisenhower had decided even before the meeting to send Marines in, and he did. The Marines stayed three months in Lebanon and Eisenhower claimed that the landings had quashed the rebel movement. Yet a year later, the rebel leader became the premier of Lebanon and came to the White House as a Presidential guest.

After the British-French withdrawal from Egypt at Eisenhower's insistence, the President expected little Israel to do the same quickly. However, Ben-Gurion refused to budge without winning assurances from the United States on two issues before retreating behind the 1949 armistice line with Egypt. The Egyptians had mounted a tiring number of raids into Israel from their Gaza Strip along the Mediterranean, and Ben-Gurion now demanded that a UN police force occupy that twenty-five-mile strip, which pointed like a finger inside Israel. Ben-Gurion's second condition for his withdrawal was the guarantee that Israeli and foreign vessels steaming up the Red Sea to Israel would pass freely through the Strait of Tiran and into the Gulf of Aqaba bound for the Israeli port of Elath. Since 1950 when Egypt mounted artillery at Sharm el Sheikh, Arab control over the narrow Tiran Strait opening into the Gulf of Aqaba barred ships heading for Israel. Yet the use of the Gulf of Aqaba was as important to Israel's economic stability and growth as the Gulf of Mexico was to the United States.

Dulles, with a free hand from Eisenhower, made the decision that Israel must relinquish her newly won military control of Sharm el Sheikh and the Gaza Strip without exacting any prior guarantees from Egypt. Only after this was done, Dulles told Ben-Gurion, would the United States commit herself to help Israel win approval of her demands from Nasser. To prove his good intentions, Dulles on February 11, 1957, handed Israeli Ambassador Abba Eban an Aide-Mémoire showing the extent of United States commitment to the stubborn nation. The two-page statement agreed that to head off future "armed infiltrations and reprisals" by Egypt, the United States pledged to seek the establishment of a UN Emergency Force to "move into this area and be on the boundary between Israel and the Gaza Strip." As for the Gulf of Aqaba, the Aide-Mémoire declared that the United States "believes that the Gulf comprehends international waters and that no nation has the right to prevent free and innocent passage in the Gulf and through the Straits. . . . The United States . . . is prepared to exercise the right of free and innocent passage and to join with others to secure general recognition of this right."

Distrustful of Dulles, even with the Aide-Mémoire commitments, Ben-Gurion continued to occupy the Gaza Strip and Sharm el Sheikh at the Strait of Tiran. His suspicions grew when King Saud of Saudi Arabia came to Washington as a Presidential guest, and they boiled over when Dulles threatened to propose a resolution to the UN calling for sanctions against Israel for failing to withdraw. The Dulles resolution would ban private as well as government aid to Israel, a severe restriction because Jews in various countries were contributing substantial sums to aid the Israeli economy.

With Adlai Stevenson supporting Israel's position, Johnson believed he had much to lose as a Presidential hopeful in 1960 unless he involved himself personally in the unsettled conflict. The so-called "Jewish vote" had supported Eisenhower in 1952 and 1956, but it normally was considered the property of the Democratic party. So Johnson added his support for Israel by writing a letter to Dulles on the same day Dulles handed the Aide-Mémoire to Ambassador Eban. The Johnson letter of February 11, 1957, insisted that the United States must oppose any UN resolutions for sanctions against Israel "with all its skill." Under no circumstances, said Johnson in a more sweeping afterthought, should the United States permit a vote to be taken on sanctions.

Without knowledge of the Johnson letter, Minority Leader Knowland also championed Israel by letting the Administration know he intended to resign as a member of the United States delegation to the UN General Assembly if that body imposed sanctions against Israel. Knowland also found it contemptible that UN reprisal action was contemplated for Israel while the Soviet Union's military brutality in putting down the Hungarian democratic rebellion the preceding fall was not to be punished by the UN.

Eisenhower was enjoying himself shooting quail in Georgia at the time, but Dulles' urgent request that he return to Washington for a face-to-face meeting with Johnson and Knowland made him put aside his gun. Early on the morning of February 20 he faced those two plus about fifteen other Congressional leaders in the White House Cabinet Room. Impatiently he explained why he favored UN sanctions against Israel unless she withdrew immediately. There could be no future peace with the Arabs unless Israel took this step, he said. Furthermore, there would be no large-scale oil shipments over the Suez Canal until she relinquished her war gains. Even worse, it would lead the Arabs to seek Soviet aid. "And then the whole thing might end up in a general war," he threatened.

Sherman Adams, who was present, observed the congressmen, to judge their reaction to Eisenhower's presentation. "Lyndon Johnson turned and looked at Senator Russell with a determined expression which seemed to say that he was not going to yield an inch," said Adams. "Knowland was wearing his classical toga of lofty defiance. Only Carl Hayden preserved his appearance of utter benignity, but then . . . Carl had no other appearance."

Eisenhower next tried to disarm the legislators by the "sincere" approach, telling them that he "could understand their attitude" against sanctions. But what else could he do? he asked. If he did not support the UN in setting sanctions on Israel for not withdrawing, "it would be a lethal blow to the UN. Nobody likes to impose sanctions," he said as though he were deeply pained by the necessity.

When he saw he was not convincing the congressmen, he asked Dulles to take over. But while Dulles' mouth was open to say his first word, Johnson interrupted to discuss the appearance of his private letter to Dulles in the New York *Herald Tribune* the preceding day. This was his letter ordering Dulles not to apply sanctions against Israel, and he insisted he had not leaked the letter to reporters. His implication was that Dulles had done the leaking, though the benefits were all in Johnson's favor in the reading area around New York City. Johnson also ran on with praise for Knowland for taking his own position without any discussion between the two on sanctions. This was one time when the Executive Branch had no monopoly on foreign policy, he said. "After all, there are times when Congress has to express its views."

"I certainly have no objection to that," Eisenhower said.

Adams noted that "Johnson looked at the President for a moment with a wry smile and said, 'Thank you.' "

Dulles then went on to divulge the details of the Aide-Mémoire, and commented that both he and Hammarskjöld had given Ambassador Eban assurances that Nasser could be brought around to the acceptance of a neutral administration over the Gaza Strip and would not dare oppose free passage through the Tiran Strait into the Gulf of Aqaba.

However, Johnson and Knowland still argued that Dulles was applying a double standard: "cracking down" on little Israel and doing nothing against the Soviet Union for its Hungarian massacre. UN Ambassador Lodge cut in to explain that this had to be so because "the UN will never vote sanctions against either Russia or the United States."

This brought Eisenhower back into the conversation again with a suggestion that the legislators agree to a statement for publication that they favored UN sanctions against Israel. "I am not sure all would agree unless it could be made certain that Israel would get justice after she withdraws," Senator Fulbright told him. House Majority Leader John McCormack called out that he would not be a party to any statement Eisenhower composed, while Senator Russell said that any statement would have to be the President's alone.

On this note the meeting broke up, and the congressmen filed out, with an Eisenhower aide telling the President that Johnson's and Knowland's discussion was "a can of worms." Reporters grouped around the congressmen in the corridor, and Johnson stepped in front to assume the role of spokesman for the group. "Our views have not been changed," he told them for national publication.

Two days later the UN General Assembly began debate on the resolution for military, economic, and financial sanctions against Israel. However, the vote never came because Israel's Foreign Minister, Mrs. Golda Meir, announced to the UN on March 1 that Israel had agreed to a "full and complete withdrawal."

Eisenhower's assurances to Israel that the Aide-Mémoire was a full commitment suffered a blow not long afterward. The promise that a UN Emergency Force would alone operate in the Gaza Strip was shown to be worthless when Nasser poured Egyptian administrators into this twenty-five-mile-long territory, and the Eisenhower Administration did not even protest. All that now remained was the American commitment to free passage of vessels in the Gulf of Aqaba.

Chapter 50

H AVING AIDED HIS Presidential candidacy by championing Israel over the Administration's determination to apply sanctions against her, Johnson also decided he needed a positive achievement in the civil rights field to gain Northern support. As he told Douglass Cater, Negroes had noticeably shifted their votes from the Democratic party in the 1956 elections. They would have to be brought back into the fold by a civil rights bill, and 1957 was a good year for getting this chore out of the way.

The Eisenhower Civil Rights Bill of 1956, the measure Johnson had killed in the Senate, returned to the House as top business in January 1957. Little trouble was expected in the Lower Chamber because it had passed there the previous year by the large vote of 279 to 126. However, more than four months passed before Minority Leader Joe Martin guided it through the House shoals. Martin encountered little opposition to Part I, which set up a Civil Rights Commission empowered only to conduct investigations; or with Part II, which established a Civil Rights Division under an Assistant Attorney General. But Judge Howard Smith, chairman of the House Rules Committee and mastermind of an army of one hundred Southern representatives plus dozens of Republicans, centered his fire on Parts III and IV.

There was good reason on the part of the Virginian Smith for this. Ever since Reconstruction days, United States criminal statutes authorized fines up to five thousand dollars and imprisonment up to ten years for anyone found guilty of depriving another person of his right to vote and other civil rights. However, the catch was that the injured party had to exhaust redress possibilities through the anti-Negro state courts before being permitted to file suit in federal court. Few could expend the time and money required. To place civil rights enjoyment above such nullifying levels, Parts III and IV permitted a plaintiff to come directly to federal court when someone threatened to violate or had violated his civil rights. Part IV was specifically tied to voting rights, while Part III was a general catch-all that included other matters, such as school desegregation.

It was Senator Sam Ervin, a former justice on the North Carolina Supreme Court, who provided Howard Smith with a gimmick for emasculating the Civil Rights Bill. The planned new procedure of initial federal court action provided that the injured party would notify the Justice Department, and the Attorney General would ask a federal judge for an injunction against a named defendant. If the judge granted the injunction, and the defendant continued on his old course, the judge would then find him guilty of contempt of court, punishable on the spot by imprisonment and a fine.

Even though Senator Ervin had four times in his own court ruled that the courts had the authority to try individuals for contempt without a jury trial, he gave Smith the war cry that Parts III and IV of the bill were a threat to the Constitutional right of a trial by jury. Most Northern liberals saw through this hoax, for they realized that white Southern juries would not convict a white defendant in a case where a Negro was the plaintiff. But enough people were taken in by "the principle above the facts" to make Joe Martin grow concerned. However, this only made him increase his effort, and though his old-fashioned, box-toe shoes did not reach the floor when he sat in his swivel chair, he was a big fighter. While buttonholing Republicans for support, he let the Southerners talk as long as they wished; and the longer they talked, the more bored and angry other members became. When it came, the vote against the Jury Trial Amendment was too close for Martin's comfort, but the Administration's total bill with some changes breezed through afterward, on June 18, by a vote of 286 to 126.

The task was now the Senate's as the bill came over from the House. Senator Eastland already had the original Administration bill pickled in brine in his Judiciary Committee, and on the basis of Johnson's action of last year, Eastland expected the House Civil Rights version to be shipped to him also. But Johnson made no move to strong-arm Paul Douglas and Bill Knowland, who were combining forces to promote the House bill. After the second reading of the bill, Johnson remained silent when Knowland asked that it be placed directly on the Calendar and kept out of committee, as permitted under Senate Rule XIV. Russell took up Eastland's cause by demanding that the bill be shipped to the Judiciary Committee, according to the almost invariably used Rule XXV.

Five hours of loud debate followed before a motion was made that Vice President Nixon decide which rule to follow. But Nixon passed the question back to the Senate for a vote, and three more hours of snarling talk followed. All the while Russell was operating at full steam in the cloakroom, rounding up votes for Rule XXV. A year earlier the Senate had killed the Hells Canyon Dam project—a half-billion-dollar public dam on the Snake River in Idaho—by a vote of 51 to 41. Idaho Power, a private company, had then won FPC approval to build three smaller dams in the mile-deep Hells Canyon. Russell now proposed a swap with senators favoring public power: If they would vote to send the Civil Rights Bill to committee, he would get an equal number of Southern senators who had voted last year *against* the Hells Canyon Federal Dam to vote *for* it this year. Five Northern liberal Democrats agreed to do this. Four were from the public power Northwest area—Morse, Magnuson, Mansfield, and Murray; the fifth was John Kennedy, whose interest in this swap was to gain Southern friends for his 1960 try for the Presidential nomination.

On June 20, by a vote of 45 to 39, the Senate approved Knowland's motion to use Rule XIV and put the civil rights bill directly on the Calendar, bypassing the Judiciary Committee. Johnson was numbered among those voting to give Eastland the bill. The next day Russell nevertheless honored his pledge when he and Eastland, Ervin, Long, and Smathers changed their vote of last year and supported the Hells Canyon Dam. The bill cleared the Senate 45 to 38, but this vote became meaningless a short time later when the House Interior Committee voted down the dam 16 to 14. President Eisenhower later said he discerned "a curious relationship between the voting on civil rights and one on public power."

Russell opened the debate on the civil rights bill while it still rested on the Senate Calendar. On July 2 he rose at his usual early hour, cooked his breakfast of scrambled eggs and grits in his Woodner apartment, donned the new dark blue suit he had purchased for the occasion, and headed for the Capitol to deliver a sweeping attack on the civil rights proposal. The bill would cause "unspeakable confusion, bitterness, and bloodshed," he predicted. There would not be enough jails to hold Southerners opposed to the "use of raw federal power forcibly to commingle white and Negro children in the state-supported schools and places of public entertainment." The real purpose of the bill, he claimed, was "to punish the South."

Senator Dirksen laughed off Russell's speech with a declaration that he had never seen "so many ghosts discovered under the same bed." But little did Dirksen know that Russell had planted some of these ghosts under the Presidential bed. The following day at his news conference Eisenhower dealt Knowland and Douglas a low blow when a reporter asked if he would favor a bill including only the protection of the right to vote (Part IV) and eliminating protection of other rights, such as to public school integration (Part III). His astounding reply was not a ringing defense of his bill but the following: "In reading over parts of the bill this morning, I found certain phrases I didn't completely understand. Before saying more on this subject, I want to talk with the Attorney General and see what they mean."

The civil rights measure moved forward on July 8, when Knowland offered a motion to take the House bill off the Calendar and make it the Senate's pending business. Ordinarily the procedure to bring a bill to the floor took only a few minutes, but Russell insisted on a full debate on Knowland's motion. During the next eight days, sixty-six speeches were heard. Russell's tactics were to select Senators Fulbright and Sparkman to lead off, because they were both known as liberals and moderates and would gain good press attention. Part of his tactics also called for him to visit the President personally on July 9 to weaken his stand further on his own bill. This was a fifty-minute conversation in which Russell reiterated that Part III was a monstrosity which would mean sending an enormous number of federal troops into the South to enforce integration. Before he left, the President told him that he had anxiety about the great problems the South faced, and perhaps the bill should be restricted to the Negro's right to vote. "With his right to vote assured," said Eisenhower, "the American Negro could use it to help secure his other rights."

These sweet words to Russell against including Part III were perfumed further by the editorial in the respected *New York Times*. Ever faithful to Eisenhower, the *Times* wrote: "It is the part of wisdom to take one step at a time and concentrate now, in this law, on the basic right of a free ballot." Buttressed by such support, Russell called a happy strategy caucus of his eighteen Southern senators in his Senate Office Building Suite Number 205. Senator Thurmond blustered out a brave call that all present should march in a body to 1600 Pennsylvania Avenue Northwest and order the President to back down and end his support of the bill. His South Carolina colleague, Senator "Olin the Solon" Johnston, solemnly declared to the gathering that he had a forty-hour speech ready for filibustering delivery. Russell told him to hold it in readiness, though he saw no need to consider a filibuster. Then on July 16, feeling certain that Eisenhower had weakened the opposition, he made little fuss when the Knowland motion to consider the House bill came to a vote and passed, 71 to 18.

Lyndon Johnson now took charge of the strategy Russell had begun. First, Part III would have to be eliminated under the guise of concentrating on a strong federal guarantee of the right to vote. Then when this was accomplished, the Part IV voting rights section would be so watered down as to become meaningless. After this the disemboweled bill would be passed, and Johnson would be able to claim he had led the fight to win passage of the first civil rights bill in eighty-two years.

Johnson's warning to his Southern colleagues, according to Douglass Cater, was that they would have to refrain from their usual "corn and pot liquor" arguments. This would have to be a quiet operation without the raucous cries that would antagonize Northern fence-sitters.

It was Nixon, hardly a civil rights advocate before, who now joined Knowland and Douglas to save Part III. The incongruity of the battle lines was revealed when the ADA worked closely with Nixon, while Dean Acheson and Clark Clifford from the Truman Administration days joined Johnson with advice on the need to drop from the bill Part III, with its grant of authority to the Attorney General to bring civil action against civil rights violators. Acheson called the elimination of Part III an "undiluted gain."

Rather than have a Southerner push for this, Johnson asked his friend Clinton Anderson to sponsor an amendment to drop Part III. Anderson willingly complied and found a cosponsor in Republican Senator George Aiken of Vermont, who believed that for the time being it would be sufficient to pass a civil rights bill centering solely on federal protection of the right to vote.

Knowland counted on his hard core of thirty-nine Republicans and ten Democrats to save Part III, but another Eisenhower blooper made him gasp. At his July 17 news conference Eisenhower was asked if the Attorney General should be allowed to bring suits on his own motion to enforce Southern school integration. Part III gave him this power because Southern school authorities would not be expected to ask for integration. But Eisenhower replied that he should not act without a "request from local authorities."

"The President has pulled the rug out from under us," Douglas wailed.

When the vote on the Anderson-Aiken Amendment came on July 24, Part III was crossed out of the bill by a vote of 52 to 38. Knowland's hardcore Republicans had dropped to twenty-five. Johnson had so many additional votes at the roll call that he advised some Northern Democrats to vote against dropping Part III, for their own political future.

There was still Part IV to consider, and Nixon, Knowland, and Douglas concentrated now on getting this section approved intact. However, John-

son had other ideas. After calling Nixon's following "his goon squad" and
deriding Knowland as "a man who can't stand a little power" and who was
able to operate only when "he is in a minority," Johnson asked Ben Cohen,
Dean Acheson, and Abe Fortas to lend their excellent legal minds to help
him make a joke of Part IV.

The point of their handiwork was to make certain that anyone who
deprived a Negro of his right to vote and continued to do so after an injunction was issued by a federal judge could not be tried for contempt solely
by that judge, but was entitled to a jury trial by his Southern neighbors.
This was the old scheme of Senator Ervin, yet to lure maximum support,
this trio wrote four versions of an amendment to Part IV.

The first edition found a willing sponsor in old antitrust fighter Senator
Joseph O'Mahoney of Wyoming. Then a longer second version became
known as the O'Mahoney-Kefauver Amendment. A third version, the
Church Amendment (after Senator Frank Church of Idaho), extended the
jury trial provisions on criminal contempt cases far afield of voting rights to
such extraneous subjects as antitrust actions and violations of the Federal
Power Act, the ICC Act, and the Securities Act of 1933. The fourth added
the feature of declaring anew the right of Negroes to serve on juries.

The result was a four-page, six-hundred-and-fifty-word statement requiring a jury trial for criminal contempt cases. But it was so sloppily
drafted that its meaning was not comprehensible. Eisenhower told his news
conference that the undecipherable amendment reminded him of the story
about the bright young Mississippi law school graduate who twice failed the
bar examination. His father went to the examining board to see the test
questions, and after a hurried glance he gasped out: "For goodness' sake,
you gave him the Negro examination!"

Voting day for the jury trial amendment was set for August 2, and
both Knowland and Johnson went to work on the Senate membership for
support. Johnson sought an ally in labor by conjuring up to union leaders
the specter of criminal contempt actions being applied in labor injunctions
by judges instead of by juries. George Meany, head of the AFL, immediately came out for the amendment, as did the Railroad Brotherhoods.
Johnson's old friend Welly Hopkins, now general counsel for the UMW,
got croaky-voiced John L. Lewis to send him a telegram in favor of the
jury trial amendment. Lewis "had never communicated with me, directly
or indirectly, until 2:48 P.M. today," Johnson told reporters of the
"surprise, unsolicited" telegram. But Walter Reuther, head of the CIO,
was furiously opposed to the amendment because he realized its purpose
was not to safeguard labor but to circumvent the right of Negroes to vote
in the South.

On August 2 Knowland spoke with Hubert Humphrey, who assured him
of victory on the ground that thirty-nine Republicans and ten Democrats
were the rock-bottom total the anti-amendment forces claimed. But Knowland was not aware of defections via the pork-barrel trail. Republican

Senators Schoeppel of Kansas and Butler of Maryland had been assured by Johnson he would see to it that they named the judges to fill the existing vacancies on the federal courts in their states. There were others.

In the final debate Johnson had a catch in his voice when he said, "By adopting this amendment we can strengthen and preserve the right to a trial by jury. The people will never accept a concept that a man can be publicly branded as a criminal without a jury trial." Then later that evening, after watching Johnson race about the cloakroom, Nixon said to him, "You've really got your bullwhip on your boys tonight."

The vote came at midnight, after a long fourteen-hour legislative day. As it proceeded, there were some doubts that Johnson's jury trial amendment would win, but in the end he collected 51 votes to 42 opposed to his dilution. Among those voting on Johnson's side was John Kennedy, who was not in a mood to affront Southern voters. Then on August 7 the Senate passed this disemboweled bill by 72 to 18. Afterward, Douglas called it a piece of legislation all of its enemies could live with happily; Nixon labeled it "a vote against the right to vote."

But Johnson had yet to do further work in order to make good his claim as producer of a civil rights measure. Immediately after the Senate vote his handiwork was greeted with enormous anger by House liberals, who demanded that it be killed. They gathered sufficient votes on August 13 to prevent the establishment of a conference committee of House and Senate members to find a compromise solution between the versions of both chambers, and almost in shock, Johnson watched helplessly as tired old Mister Sam let the House and Senate versions go to wrinkled Judge Smith, who smilingly locked the two bills in his Rules Committee desk drawer. Joe Martin put it on the line for his Republican charges who wanted no compromise with Johnson after he had knocked their bill to pieces: "We're not at all interested in pushing a Democratic bill through, particularly when it doesn't provide anything."

However, Johnson intended to force Martin to become interested, and he telephoned Eisenhower to bring pressure from the top. After bathing Eisenhower in compliments, Johnson won his concurrence for a White House effort to soften Martin and Knowland's stand against a compromise. Dean Acheson had a proposal that had bargaining possibilities, and one morning, while riding to work in his air-conditioned Cadillac, Johnson called Knowland on the car phone with a compromise offer on the jury trial amendment. Instead of forcing a federal judge to send all criminal contempt citations to the jury for trial, why not give the judge authority to set jail sentences up to thirty days and fines up to two hundred dollars?

Primed by Eisenhower that Johnson would bargain with him on the bill, Knowland made a counter-offer of ninety days and three hundred dollars. The two peppered each other with figures during the next few days, and finally Johnson called Eisenhower again to close the bargaining door. Eisenhower later reported the pressured threat behind Johnson's final offer: "I can get Ervin and the others to agree to a compromise of three hundred dollars and forty-five days." Eisenhower agreed, even though Johnson was so beset by necessity that he would have accepted any figures the President offered.

Martin grumbled and fell in line; Mister Sam used his own brand of narrow-eyed, thin-lipped threats to pry open Judge Smith's drawer; the House voted to send the bill to conference, and after two weeks agreed to the latest Johnson version, 279 to 97. Johnson was all smiles in the Senate chamber on the evening of August 28, with plans for hurried passage of the compromise bill, when Strom Thurmond took the floor at 8:54 and began the most garrulous speech in Senate history. He did not finish until 9:12 the following night, setting a new filibustering record of twenty-four hours and eighteen minutes. When he finished, Wayne Morse, the old champion, came over to congratulate him, and shortly afterward Thurmond collapsed. Johnson lost little time, following this pointless exhibition, pushing the bill through the Senate by a vote of 72 to 18.

Yet his concern still existed, because national pressures began to descend on the White House for a Presidential veto of the bill. Deputy Attorney General William Rogers, when asked for his advice, called the Johnson version of civil rights "the most irresponsible action I have seen in all of my experiences in Washington. The law is like handing a policeman a gun without bullets."

UN official Ralph Bunche wrote Eisenhower, "It would be better to have no bill."

A. Philip Randolph, Negro union leader, told the President, "It is worse than no bill at all."

However, Eisenhower realized that if he vetoed the bill, he would lay himself open to the spurious charge of having done so because he was anti-Negro. So on September 9, 1957, he signed a useless civil rights bill that had to be redone in 1964 and 1965. But in Dean Acheson's jubilant words, as expressed in the *Reporter*: "The bill as passed seems to me the legislative process operating at its best."

As a Presidential candidate, Johnson gained more than a reputation as the "father" of civil rights legislation in 1957. With the assistance of a bumbling Administration, he was also able to clothe himself in the hardly recognizable attire of the "government economizer."

At the New Year's Day 1957 Congressional leaders' gathering at the White House, Eisenhower had graciously told Johnson and Mister Sam that they were "as welcome in this house—in this office—as anyone." But as the months stretched on into the first session of the Eighty-fifth Congress there were many times when Eisenhower had cause to regret his friendliness.

The President's troubles erupted in mid-January when Secretary of the

Treasury George Humphrey told reporters the budget of seventy-three billion dollars that the President had submitted to Congress was so large that, if it were not cut "over a period of time, I will predict that you will have a depression that will curl your hair."

Shortly afterward Eisenhower added to the public's concern that his budget was inflated when he agreed to the release of a letter Humphrey said he had written to him. In this letter Humphrey said that the government agencies had made cuts in their spending programs for next year, but that "the overall net results are not sufficient. Only the most drastic action will suffice."

At his news conference Eisenhower, in a strange attempt to defend Humphrey, deepened the hole into which he was sinking by remarking on the letter: "I not only went over every word of it; I edited it; and it expresses my convictions very thoroughly. . . . If Congress can cut the budget, it is their duty to do it."

This was a White House-sent opportunity for Johnson—and he took it. "The Democrats are the party of economy," he told newsmen, who winked at each other when his words sank home. Economy on the President's budget by the Democrats in Congress would best describe the mood in this session of Congress, he said. "What we need," he added, "is not a Republican Congress but a Democratic President." In the Senate cloakroom he told willing Democratic members that this was the time for gaining a new party reputation if they would unite behind him and fight the budget.

Unfortunately for Johnson he could not levy an immediate attack on any agency's budget because the spending bills were on the other side of the Capitol in the House Appropriations Committee. But there was a way to keep himself in the limelight, and this was to remain vocal on the issues raised by Humphrey and the President. In one announcement he said he had sent out thirty-nine thousand questionnaires to Texans on the budget, and almost all were demanding severe cuts. Another time, on the Senate floor, he made a vibrating-voiced plea to the President to tell Congress how to reduce his inflated government spending.

By spring Eisenhower was talking about "an unexpected phenomenon. The Democrats [had] inexplicably become economy-minded." Then he began sputtering to associates that he was being deliberately misinterpreted by Johnson and his Senate crew. They were wrapping themselves in the toga of economy, when in truth they were big-time Treasury money spenders. The fraud of it all, said Eisenhower, was that Johnson was publicly crying for less spending and privately asking the House Appropriations Committee to add 1.8 million dollars to George Humphrey's budget to buy some Coast Guard cutters to protect Texas shrimp fishermen in the Gulf of Mexico. And here was benign-expressioned Carl Hayden, chairman of the Senate Appropriations Committee, voicing support for Johnson, yet pushing so many new pork-barrel projects that Sam Rayburn had to admit he "had smiled more billions through Congress than anybody else in history."

The Battle of the Budget turned into a brawl in May. A short, black-haired Oriental man in a double-breasted suit had come to the White House for an official visit and a demand for increased foreign aid at a time when the House was hacking away at the foreign aid program. The man was Ngo Dinh Diem, boss of the Republic of South Vietnam, whose message was that last year's four hundred and fifty million dollars in United States aid had not ended the "impatience" of the people of his country "to reduce their technical backwardness."

Eisenhower took time off from entertaining his guest to go on nation-wide TV on May 14 to urge pressure on Congress to save his budget. He said the answer to the question of how large the budget should be was similar to the answer given by Lincoln to the question of how long a man's legs should be. "They ought to be long enough to reach the ground," said Lincoln. "And so should the budget," said Eisenhower, launching into a defense of his money requests.

Johnson answered him the next day as the self-appointed spokesman of the Democratic party. "I never considered it a reflection on me when the President disagrees with me," he told the Senate. "I do not think it ought to be a reflection on the President when I disagree with him. I heard the President's talk last night. I have had to make some TV speeches, at times, to appeal to people to get them to go along with my program."

Johnson had left his seat on the Finance Committee for a place on the Appropriations Committee at the beginning of the session, and when the appropriations bills reached the committee, after being cut in the House, Hayden gave Johnson a free hand to trim the bills item by item as he saw fit. Johnson also chairmaned the subcommittee holding hearings on the appropriation for the United States Information Agency, a job he could hardly wait to begin.

Arthur Larson, the young head of the USIA, had written a book, *A Republican Looks at His Party,* in which he lauded the Eisenhower approach to government as "Modern Republicanism." In Larson's view the Dwight Eisenhower philosophy was akin to that of Abraham Lincoln, especially in the Lincoln quotation: "The legitimate object of government is to do for a community of people whatever they need to have done, but cannot do at all, or cannot so well do, for themselves—in their separate, and individual capacities."

Flattered by Larson's praise and finding the term "Modern Republicanism" a handy catch phrase, Eisenhower elevated Larson from a Labor Department job to the head of the USIA. But Larson was not content with concentrating on his new job. On April 16 he made a speech in Hawaii in which he lashed out at the Democratic party as an un-American body. One widely quoted sentence had him saying that "throughout the New and Fair Deals, this country was in the grip of a somewhat alien philosophy, imported from Europe."

Eisenhower had asked Congress for 144 million dollars for the USIA for fiscal 1958, beginning in July 1957, and the day following Larson's speech the House cut his agency to 105 million dollars. Johnson told reporters, before his hearings on the USIA began on May 2, that perhaps the cuts should have gone deeper.

For four days Larson experienced a nightmare. At the outset Johnson ushered in the inquisition with a sarcastically delivered introduction. "You appear before us under conditions which guarantee a considerable amount of distinction," he told Larson. "Of all the agency heads, you are asking for the most money to be restored to the funds cut by the House. We look to you as the distinguished *author* and *spokesman* for your party, to enlighten us."

Larson proved to be another Leland Olds, unable to cope with Johnson's insinuations and speech inflections as he fumbled through one reply after another. Laughs from other senators and clerks came frequently, before he stumbled out four days later. Johnson's subcommittee report cutting the USIA still further to 90.2 million dollars drew further laughs with its advice to the agency to "concentrate on improving its personnel." Then for four hours on another day Johnson held the Senate floor to continue his attack on the USIA, after telling his colleagues of his fairness in holding "one of the longest and largest records of any subcommittee in the history of the Senate—1,249 pages of testimony." A reporter said he went through a great deal of "fencing, flattering, cajoling" of other senators present and wound up with a vote of 61 to 19 favoring his appropriations cut. Even after he relented in the conference committee afterward and raised the figure to 96 million dollars, Eisenhower still labeled his action "irresponsible."

By the time the last appropriations bill went to the White House, Johnson could claim a major role in cutting the total budget by 5.5 billion dollars. This included a billion from Foreign Aid and 2.4 billion from Defense.

As the session faded, Johnson believed he had advanced his cause in his drive for the Presidential nomination by his stand on the Middle East crisis, his control of the civil rights bill, and his work to slash the budget. All in all his name had appeared far more frequently in the papers than any of his rivals. But as to his legislative achievements, Senator Joseph Clark took a bleak view. Said Clark: "As the session of the Eighty-fifth Congress rolled by it became obvious to me that there was no real Democratic Senate legislative program; and none in the House. It was not fashionable to refer to the national party platform. President Eisenhower had no particular Republican platform he wanted enacted."

Despite Clark's view, Johnson felt elated with his achievements, and Eisenhower believed he had been put through a wringer. When the session closed on August 30, 1957, Johnson called him and said, "Mr. President, I'll bet you're just as happy to see us go as we are to go."

Chapter 51

J OHNSON SEEMED TO have good reasons for believing he was far ahead of the Presidential pack when he flew back to Texas at the beginning of September in 1957. Adlai Stevenson was talking to the wind like a worn-out has-been, denouncing the Eisenhower foreign policy between work assignments for the Encyclopedia Britannica and his Chicago-based law firm. Stuart Symington and Hubert Humphrey were having trouble getting their names in the paper, while John Kennedy, after a Congressional session of sporadic attendance, had been able to garner his little cup of publicity chiefly by blasting the nomination of an ignorant Republican campaign contributor as ambassador to Ceylon, attacking France in a Senate speech for not granting independence to Algeria, and voting the Southern position on the Civil Rights Act of 1957. One ardent Northern civil rights advocate had gone so far as to label Kennedy's votes to send the bill to Eastland's committee and for the jury trial amendment "A Profile in Cowardice." Little wonder that Johnson called out to his wife when they reached the ranch, "Bird, I want to count our blessings."

But time did not stand still. Once back home, Johnson put on his Texas blinders, and unmindful of his need to meet local politicians in Northern states, began a fall tour of "Lyndon Johnson Appreciation Day" celebrations his friends had arranged for him throughout the Lone Star State. Taking a wise, opposite approach, Kennedy set off on a ten-thousand-mile, six-week speaking tour of the country as the handsome young senator who had won that year's Pulitzer Prize. At the same time a large staff helped him prepare a virtual flood of articles for dozens of magazines. There were in addition banquets and dinners paid for by the Kennedy family.

Adlai Stevenson also gained new prominence late in the year, when he traveled to Washington at Eisenhower's invitation to work closely with Dulles in the preparation of American policy positions for the forthcoming Paris meeting of NATO heads of state. Eisenhower then asked him to accompany him to Paris, but Stevenson declined because he believed the Administration predicated the chief communist threat to be "military aggression." Stevenson thought the real threat was "by propaganda, economic bribery, and political penetration."

Johnson's belief, that his Congressional work in the last session set him far ahead of the pack, proved short-lived. For one thing his assertion that the Civil Rights Act he had forced upon Congress and the Administration would fix the rules for improved race relations suffered a low blow on September 4, 1957, when Governor Orval Faubus of Arkansas called out the National Guard to prevent the integration of Little Rock's Central High School. The Civil Rights Act contained nothing to cope with this situation, and Eisenhower was forced to federalize the Arkansas Guard and send in paratroopers to maintain order. Johnson did not enter this controversy, but Senator Russell, who was not a Presidential candidate, publicly accused Eisenhower of "applying tactics that must have been copied from the manual issued to the officers of Hitler's storm troopers."

There was also Johnson's record as a budget cutter that rose like a ghost to haunt him briefly. This came about when the Soviet Union began a new chapter in world history by successfully sending *Sputnik I,* an earth satellite, into outer space orbit on October 4, 1957. National hysteria arose because of a fear that the Communists would press their advantage in some military fashion, and it could not be allayed by comments from within the Eisenhower Administration that the Soviet lead in outer space was not significant. Sherman Adams made light of the Soviet accomplishment by asserting that the United States was not interested in "an outer space basketball game"; and Rear Admiral Rawson, in charge of naval research, called *Sputnik* a "hunk of iron almost anybody could launch."

Johnson's work in cutting the defense budget by almost two and a half billion for the next fiscal year had also reached into the missile program; and his first reaction on learning of *Sputnik* was to remain quiet. But Stuart Symington blasted the Administration for an economy policy that had produced "an inexcusable delay," and he added that "if this now known Soviet superiority develops into supremacy, the position of the free world will be critical." When papers headlined candidate Symington's roundhouse swings at the Administration, plus those of the would-be favorite son of Washington State, Senator Henry "Scoop" Jackson, Johnson recognized that he would have to step in and wrest control of the issue from his two fellow Democrats.

Even though he had refrained from campaigning up North, Johnson had carefully cultivated "advisers" in several Yankee areas, and one of these was the influential legal and money field in New York City. A leader of the Wall Street advisers to Johnson was Edwin Weisl, a senior partner in Simpson, Thacher and Bartlett, an executive committee member at Paramount Pictures, and "the eighteenth partner of Lehman Brothers." Weisl, as counsel for the Hearst papers, had won Hearst endorsement for Johnson in his 1948 Senate race against Coke Stevenson. Johnson's strange approach to Weisl and the others in the New York set was to pretend that he was a weak, indecisive man who urgently needed their ideas and repetitious beseeching to adopt courses of action that he had already decided to take. So hard did he play at this game that several members of the New York group nicknamed him "Yellow-Dog" Johnson.

While Eisenhower was working himself into a dangerous fury, trying to decide whether to answer Symington and Jackson and expose Democratic budget economy in the last Congress, Johnson's political eye told him he would enhance his candidacy enormously by making his own name synonymous with the American space race. A call to Russell at home in Winder, Georgia, led to a discussion about bringing the seven members of the Preparedness Subcommittee back to Washington to investigate the missile lag. Hardly had the two agreed that this would be an excellent move when Weisl telephoned Johnson with this same suggestion. Johnson's feigned reluctance induced Weisl to call Russell and plead with him to work on Johnson. After more calls from the New York "advisers," Johnson said they had convinced him, and on October 8 Russell made the announcement that Johnson's Preparedness Subcommittee would begin hearings on Wednesday, November 25. This time Johnson decided that the New York advisers should work for a change. Since Weisl had done so much urging, Johnson now telephoned him and snapped, "You're always telling me about what I should do. Now you come down here and help me do it. I want you to be the Preparedness general counsel." Weisl tried to talk Johnson out of this, for his Wall Street practice earned him almost five thousand dollars a week. But "Yellow-Dog" Johnson was tough and unyielding, and Weisl had to agree, bringing with him his young junior partner, Cyrus Vance.

Before the investigation began, Johnson revived his long-time philosophy of the need to turn the United States into an armed camp. At the Rose Festival at Tyler, Texas, on October 17, he painted a frightening picture of the horror that would overtake the United States if it did not treat Soviet leadership in missilery as a war. Then at Waxahachie, in a prepared speech, he denounced the forty-hour week as a serious menace. The eight-hour, five-day week, he charged, "will not produce intercontinental ballistic missiles." The entire nation "must go on a full, wartime mobilization schedule."

This scare approach to the Soviet 22-inch-in-diameter orbiting satellite made no sense to Texas labor-union leaders, who watched unemployment figures rise to an eight-year high in the recession that had descended on the country. While they were castigating Johnson as fascist-minded, the Soviets, on November 2, orbited *Sputnik II,* a satellite ten times as heavy as the first *Sputnik,* and which carried a dog inside.

Johnson found further justification now for his armed camp demand and for taking on the role of champion of the American people against the Defense Department. The day after *Sputnik II* he went to the Pentagon for a seven-hour briefing on the American space effort. Later he told reporters he had given top defense officials unshirted hell because they had postponed a vital development-production decision from July to October. As he recounted the conversation, he had told the generals: "Gentlemen, you'll be seeing a lot more of my committee and my staff. You need a great deal of help."

With the worried national interest in the space program, Johnson's hearings, which opened on November 25, were a headline catcher. That same day, when President Eisenhower suffered a mild stroke at his White House desk, some of Johnson's friends passed word around that it had been brought on by the Preparedness Subcommittee's investigation. Eisenhower had tried indeed to undercut the hearings by naming James Killian, highly respected MIT president, as his science adviser and by promising the successful launching of a Vanguard satellite in early December. Eisenhower had also been expending a lot of "Damn it! Damn it!" to aides and friends about the Democratic attack on his space program. "The idea of them charging me with not being interested in defense," he screamed in one conversation. "Damn it, I've spent my whole life being concerned with defense of our country." He had figures to prove that Truman had spent a measly seven million dollars on long-range missiles development from 1947 to 1953, and he had last year's Johnson budget cut that would have permitted him a strong weapon for attacking the Democrats. But he did not publicize these charges because Johnson also held high cards. He could reveal former Defense Secretary Charlie Wilson's fight against research spending and the Defense Department's blunder in emphasizing military missiles instead of its space-missile program.

In the two-month subcommittee hearings, a parade of more than two hundred scientists and government officials passed before the seven senators and Weisl. The entire investigation could have gone up in smoke on December 6 when *Vanguard I* left the Cape Canaveral launching pad following the countdown. But once in the air it exploded and crashed back to earth. At his hearings, Johnson told the crowd the news and then declaimed: "How long, how long, oh God, how long will it take us to catch up with the Russians' two satellites?"

For the most part Johnson was content to lead witnesses into their own condemnation of the Administration's space program. When CIA boss Allen Dulles passed on his collected rumors of the Soviet advantage, Symington tried to get into the center stage by calling out: "A sad and shocking story!" Johnson watched him carefully after that to prevent Symington from gaining publicity mileage at his own expense. To Symington's complaint that Johnson was hindering his cross-examination of the new Defense Secretary, soap manufacturer Neil McElroy, Johnson snapped in return, "Certainly there is no disposition to interfere with your questioning or keep you from having a reasonable length of time. [But] we do have plans to conclude the hearings."

For saving McElroy, Johnson demanded in return that the Defense Secretary let announcements on the Administration's space program emanate from his subcommittee room and not from the Pentagon. One afternoon, for instance, Johnson had McElroy send Major General John B. Medaris to his subcommittee room so that Johnson could lead the general into the hall to announce before assembled TV cameras the changeover from liquid to solid fuel for powering missiles.

The extremes of the hearings were reserved for William Holaday, the Pentagon's guided-missiles boss, and Lieutenant General James Gavin. Johnson and Weisl belittled Holaday mercilessly when they found he had no space-science background, and they led him into repetitious squirming by forcing him to admit that the research and development work on the Army and Air Force intermediate-range ballistic missiles was only 10 per cent complete.

On the other hand Johnson showed every kindness toward Gavin, a World War II paratrooper hero and head of the Army's research and development work. With gentle assistance from Johnson, Gavin testified at a closed session that the Pentagon mess was forcing him to resign from the Army. He said he had learned he was not to get his fourth star and the promised command of the United States Continental Army because of Eisenhower's opposition to his proposed sharp increase in space spending and his plans for substantially increasing a highly mobile, nuclear-weaponed Army to fight "brush wars" abroad. When Gavin finished, Johnson hurriedly scribbled words on a sheet of paper, told Gavin to check its accuracy as a summary of his testimony, and then ordered him to read it to reporters waiting outside the room.

The next day, when an assistant showed Eisenhower the news story that Gavin had resigned, Eisenhower expressed surprise, for he had planned to give Gavin his fourth star within the year. Friends of Johnson said the senator had done a magnificent job, "conning" Gavin in order to lend excitement to the hearings.

At the close of the hearings Symington demanded a report that would rip the Administration. However, Johnson decided he had achieved his purpose and there was little to gain from this tack. Furthermore, *Explorer I* had been successfully launched on January 31, 1958. So he withstood the protests from Symington; and after a first decision not to issue any report, he finally produced one that offered no criticism of the President's space program. "The past is already for historians. Let us seek solutions," he said, angering fellow Democrats who saw the value of promoting the issue of a missile gap in the 1958 elections. Instead of an attack, Johnson's report listed seventeen technical recommendations for improving the existing program, and the Administration relaxed.

Having gone through these hearings and noted the excitement they had generated, Johnson saw continuing personal value in assuming the role of Democratic leader of the Space Age. In February 1958 he moved ahead into this position when he introduced a Senate resolution to establish a Senate Committee on Aeronautical and Space Sciences. The Senate approved this 78 to 1, and Johnson became chairman. The one vote in opposition came from Senator Ellender, whose reason was that he was opposed to the creation of any new committees. It was as chairman of the Space Committee that Johnson helped bring about both the separation of the space-missiles from the military-missiles program and the establishment of the civilian space-missiles agency, the National Aeronautics and Space Administration (NASA).

As 1958 dawned, Johnson took early opportunities to act the role of the Democratic Party's statesman. On January 7 Democratic senators filed into the caucus room and sat on the metal folding chairs in bored anticipation of another perfunctory annual get-together. Johnson faced the forty-nine senators, and chair shuffles of disapproval by the liberal contingent arose when he announced that he did not want to hear any anti-Administration speeches on the Senate floor before President Eisenhower delivered his State of the Union Message on January 9.

Then as he asked for close attention, his aides passed out mimeographed documents to each senator and to newsmen outside the door. This was a Johnson speech that he had still been revising in the middle of the night, and he announced to his fellow Democrats that this was his own "State of the Union Message."

In a drawled reading, he emphasized the need to strengthen the nation's defenses and catch up with the Russians in outer space. "Our national potential exceeds our national performance. Our science and technology has been, for some time, capable of many of the achievements displayed thus far by Soviet science. That the Soviet achievements are tangible and visible, while ours are not, is the result of policy decisions made within the governments of the respective nations. . . . At the root this Congress must— before it does much else—decide which approach is correct." Afterward he sought out Senator Saltonstall and attempted to get him to make the same pitch in the Republican caucus.

A few weeks later Johnson presented the Senate with his own list of "must" legislation, most of which covered economic programs. The economic recession had deepened—industrial production was down 14 per cent in nine months; profits, 25 per cent; and unemployment had risen to 7 per cent of the labor force. Johnson offered a ten-point antirecession program, including a 1.8 billion dollar housing bill and a .5 billion dollar public works bill. In a showy display to portray himself as the leader in the fight to right the faltering economy, he promoted a resolution declaring it "the sense of Congress" that public works projects pump-prime the economy without delay. Explaining why his solution was best, he said he had worked it out with "my Cabinet of committee chairmen." A short time before, Eisenhower had announced conditions under which Vice President Nixon could become Acting President; and when Johnson spoke about his "Cabinet of committee chairmen," columnist Doris Fleeson waggishly asked the Democratic statesman if he had made similar disability arrangements with Mike Mansfield, his second-in-command.

Within a single week Johnson pushed through his pump-priming measure; and when he bragged that it had been "one of the most productive and constructive weeks" of his Senate career, Minority Leader Knowland paid him homage by complaining to the Senate, "It is only in the dictatorships of the world that legislation whizzes through." However, Eisenhower undid Johnson's work on April 15 by vetoing the public works bill and calling it a "waste of public funds."

Johnson's antirecession program did not contain a tax reduction bill, which economists in both political parties, as well as responsible newspapers throughout the country, declared was a far better tool for fighting the recession than a clumsy, time-consuming public works program. Leaders within the Administration who were for a tax cut were Vice President Nixon and Labor Secretary James Mitchell; while the big gun against this technique was Mister Sam, operating through his secondary protégé, the new Secretary of the Treasury, Robert Anderson. Only a few years earlier Rayburn had fought for a twenty-dollar deduction for each taxpayer, but now he suddenly feared a large budget deficit with reduced taxes, and Johnson obeyed his command to head off tax-cut legislation in the Senate.

At a secret White House meeting to settle the Administration's policy toward a tax cut, Eisenhower followed his bent for inertia and sided with Anderson against Nixon and Mitchell. When Nixon quietly returned to the Capitol, Johnson greeted him with "Well, you and Mitchell got on that high horse, and here Ike and Bob Anderson rode off and left you."

Despite rumors that Eisenhower wanted an open Republican convention in 1960, Johnson believed Nixon would be the nominee, and he sought ways to weaken and embarrass him. On one occasion when the Senate took up a bill to raise interest rates on veterans' loans, Johnson kept a sufficient number of Democrats away so that the vote was 47 to 46 to increase the rate. Then when Nixon gloated that he was certainly happy not to be forced to state his position on a touchy subject like this, Johnson signaled to Senator Fulbright to enter the chamber and make the vote a tie. Nixon was now forced to vote, and he glumly cast his ballot in favor of higher interest rates. Another nod passed from Johnson, this time to Wayne Morse, who stood up and denounced Nixon.

In the spring of 1958 Nixon gained a great deal of publicity when he and his wife made a dangerous trip to South America. University students in Lima, Peru, booed and stoned him, and in Caracas, Venezuela, a mob smashed the car he sat in and spat in his face. The House of Representatives immediately passed a unanimous resolution praising the Vice President for his "courage" in meeting the communist youth rabble in South America. Senator Charles Potter, who had lost his legs in the World War II European fighting, showed Johnson the resolution he wanted to introduce in the

Senate—one congratulating the Nixons for their "dignity and courage." Johnson saw this as a possible Nixon weapon in the Presidential election, so he induced Potter not to submit it. In return for this Johnson led all the senators to the Washington National Airport on May 15, 1958, where they were inconspicuous in the throng of one hundred thousand persons who had turned out to welcome Nixon home.

In 1958 Mister Sam was treated to a steady verbal pounding by Texas national committeewoman Frankie Randolph for his "get-along, go along" policy with the Administration. Rayburn was tired at seventy-six, but he intended to throw his weight behind Lyndon's candidacy, and he made a few bids to promote pieces of legislation Democratic liberals favored. One such measure related to statehood for Alaska. The Eisenhower priority system was to bring Hawaii, with its supposedly large Republican organization, into statehood first. Judge Smith had the Alaskan statehood bill bottled up in his Rules Committee and adamantly insisted it would die there. However, when Johnson told Rayburn he could get a favorable vote for Alaska in the Senate, Mister Sam dug into his own "Speaker Rayburn's Invented House Rules" to thwart Smith. From his high-backed chair in the House, he announced he was using a rarely employed rule, under which a statehood bill possessed a privileged character and could be brought up for action by a simple majority vote. Angry charges met his announcement, but with his "Those in favor say *Aye*, the *Ayes* have it. . . . It is approved," statehood for Alaska passed.

The next year, when Hawaii joined the Union as the Fiftieth State, Mister Sam told Johnson he did not want to go to the White House for the signing of the Statehood Proclamation because Eisenhower had not invited John Burns, the Democratic delegate to Congress from Hawaii, who had worked tirelessly for statehood. "If they're counting Jack Burns out, they can count me out also," Rayburn growled. But Johnson and Burns told him he should attend the ceremony. Mister Sam did with reluctance, and when Eisenhower offered him the pen that had signed the proclamation, Mister Sam barked, "I don't believe I want that!" Later he changed his mind, and he walked back to the signing table and told a crimson-faced President, "I'll take that pen after all. I'd like to give it to Jack Burns."

Chapter 52

W HEN CONGRESS ADJOURNED on August 24, 1958, Johnson flew back
to Texas, where Rebekah Johnson lay dying of cancer. After her death on
September 12, he went through a short, sad period reminiscing about
Mama before the needs of the Presidential campaign brought him back
to the present.

John Kennedy was clearly stepping up his pace in the race for the
Presidency, giving more and more speeches in more and more states, after
having missed hundreds of Senate roll calls and committee meetings. An
aide said of his speaking tour: "We continually searched for new topics,
themes, and writers . . . and [gave] a $10,000 guarantee" to Lou Harris
to conduct polls for Kennedy. College students felt close rapport with him,
women liked his good looks, men respected his background of family
wealth.

The political issues and his Senate record were of little importance in his
Presidential bid, though he collected a Harvard-MIT "brain trust" to pass
along their deepest thoughts on public affairs. Assistants collected political
humor for him, and the funny story files went with him on his travels. One
story especially successful in his 1958 tour went as follows: Said Kennedy,
"Several nights ago I dreamed that the Good Lord had touched me on the
shoulder and said, 'Don't worry. You'll be the Democratic Presidential
nominee in 1960. What's more, you'll be elected.'

"I told Stu Symington about my dream. 'S'funny thing,' said Stu, 'I had
the same dream myself.'

"We both told our dreams to Lyndon Johnson, and Johnson said, 'That's
funny. For the life of me I can't remember tapping either of you two boys
for the job.' "

Simultaneously with his Presidential swings, Kennedy was faced with a
campaign for re-election to his Senate seat. Johnson had been of tangible
help to him in this effort, promoting his private bills and pork-barrel projects, as well as lending his prestige to win downtown agency approval of
contracts and other matters for influential Massachusetts constituents of
Kennedy. Johnson had also made the path simple for a Kennedy labor bill
in the last session. Kennedy had served on the Special Senate Investigating
Committee on Labor Rackets, and his bill on this subject was written for

him by seven outstanding attorneys under Harvard Professor Archibald Cox. Among other features the Kennedy-Ives Bill required unions to report on their trust funds, make financial reports, and operate secret-ballot elections. Johnson plucked the bill off the Senate Calendar out of sequence, and it passed in June 1958 by a vote of 88 to 1. However, the House took no action, and it died. But the Senate action gave Kennedy a talking point as an active legislator, though the effect of this was in no way measurable in his astounding re-election victory, by 874,608 votes.

With two chief exceptions, Johnson continued to wear his Texas blinders in 1958. Both the exceptions that carried him outside Texas were intended to build up his image in the foreign affairs field. One trip took him to Mexico as a four-day guest of President-Elect Adolfo Lopez Mateos. The other trip took him to New York in November as a member of the United States delegation to the United Nations. With Eisenhower's approval Johnson made his first speech to the United Nations—a call for peaceful exploration of outer space. His invitation to member nations to "join in this adventure in outer space together" was followed by his proposal that the UN establish a study committee to look into it.

While foreign correspondents sent home favorable stories about the senator's speech, American reporters gave it little attention because of the weak next step, calling for the study group instead of instant action. "These men writing for foreign papers seem to understand me better than the men writing at home," Johnson said in a snarling tone to American reporters.

In the few days Johnson stayed in New York, he managed to gain additional publicity. V. K. Krishna Menon, India's representative at the United Nations, was a sharp-tongued leftist with a lack of manners. Other UN delegates considered it wise not to tangle with him because of his ability at diatribe. When Johnson finished his outer space brotherhood talk to the UN Political Committee, he felt highly satisfied with his effort. But as he stepped down from the platform, Menon confronted him with a blast of loud sarcasm that carried about the room: "That was a very impressive presentation," said the British-educated Indian; "I wish that your country would give as much time to disarming as you give to preparation for arming."

Menon always insisted he was not a Communist, and Johnson turned him speechless with words delivered slowly and derisively, "Well now, Mister Ambassador, we're ready. We'll disarm tomorrow. Can you deliver the disarmament of the communist bloc?"

Johnson did not fare as well in a news conference he held with sixty foreign correspondents. "Texas 'Country Boy' Leaves Many at UN Bewildered," read the headline the next day on the reporting story in the St. Louis *Post-Dispatch*. Johnson's problem was one of language. From the moment he began, by saying, "I'm just a country boy from Texas come to howdy and shake," chaos descended. Few present knew what he meant by "country boy," and none fathomed "howdy and shake"; and as the bewildering interview continued, more Texas talk brought additional confusion. There were some who wondered what his daddy had to do with foreign affairs, for he quoted his daddy frequently. For instance, when he was unwilling to take a detailed stand on a highly controversial matter, he brushed aside questioners with "My daddy taught me a long time ago that the chicken that sticks his head up above the weeds is liable to get it knocked off with a rock."

Except for his few forays outside of Texas, Johnson spent the rest of his 1958 campaigning season either on the move through his state or as a host to politicians at the L.B.J. Ranch.

Sixty miles west of Austin, over the winding Hill Country roads, came the politicians from other parts of the country whom Johnson believed could be of help to him in 1960. Here to the land of the chalky earth, long-rising hills, peach trees, gnarled live oaks, chicken hawks, buzzards, doves, and deer they traveled for a novel visit. The entrance to the L.B.J. was noted by two big pillars on either side of the blacktop road; then came a fording of the Pedernales on Johnson's property by driving across the spillway of the dam, and onward to the white stone and wood, two-story rambling ranch house.

The host was usually either outside near the swimming pool, sipping a low-calorie soft drink as he listened to the piped-in music, or indoors talking long-distance. Guests entered through the white gate, crossed over the concrete walk, and walked into a hallway past a mounted head of a buck deer whose antlers served as a hat rack. At Christmastime Lady Bird covered the buck's nose with red velvet, so that everyone could make sport of "Rudolph the Red-Nosed Reindeer." The spacious living room, with its sofas, chairs, and fireplace, had one corner reserved as the domino center, with a table ready for players. When Homer Thornberry came, the two put in hours in that corner playing one fierce game after another. Johnson enjoyed reminding Homer that when he was recuperating from his heart attack at the Bethesda Naval Hospital in 1955, he had lived up to his boast— "I can beat you lying down, Mister Congressman." Johnson set packages of cigarettes about the house to test his own will power, and he lectured company on the dangers of smoking. If he saw Lady Bird smoking a cigarette, he would pull it out of her mouth and crush it.

Johnson rose early at the ranch, and guests tried to match him. One morning George Smathers appeared from his bedroom with purple lips, and said he had frozen all night. Johnson walked him back into the room and showed him he had been sleeping under an electric blanket, which he had not switched on. When asked why he rose so early on the ranch, Johnson explained, "My Star Route mail carrier leaves the mail across the river at six." He enjoyed telling guests about the day after a flood, when he asked one of the Negro servants to bring the mail. "Yassuh, we don't hab no mail. We don't eben hab no mailbox," was the reply.

In the fields surrounding the ranch, Lady Bird had put in acres of Texas bluebonnets, and once she put in a carpetlike, bright green lawn, after he ordered her to have it in place within three weeks because special guests were coming. Another time, when John Connally bragged about the Coastal Bermuda grass pastures he installed on his ranch, Johnson talked him into supervising a similar installation on the L.B.J. pastures.

Every guest had to be taken on a walking tour of the immediate area around the ranch house and on an auto tour of the ranch. Generally, half a dozen dogs yelped along on the walking tour, and on occasion Johnson's two iridescent peacocks came by to cackle "Ulp, Ulp." The walk to the swimming pool was over 12-inch-square cement blocks that contained the autographs of famous guests.

In his guided tour, Johnson usually plucked the heartstrings of company with a highly emotional but fictitious story or two about the ranch house. "My Daddy lost this house before I was born, and that's why I was born in a shack," he said on dozens of occasions. This bore no relationship to the facts, but he told it well. If this imaginative tale did not move his listeners, he made a further effort with "When I was thirteen the price of cotton dropped from forty to six cents a bale and wiped out my Daddy."

Sometimes Johnson extended the story of family poverty into the near-current period. The way one reporter wrote down his recital of the acquisition of the ranch, "Lady Bird was opposed to the idea but took a long look at what was in her husband's eyes and said yes." The true story of the trade with eighty-one-year-old Aunt Frank of her ranch house for the Johnson City house was also cast aside for the more exciting fiction that when he wanted to buy the ranch he lacked money for a down payment. Ignored was the fact that he was by that time a multimillionaire. He described a worrisome visit to the Blanco Bank to ask old Mr. Brigham about a loan. " 'Well, boy, I'll lend you the money,' " he said Brigham told him after he described the property. " 'But you better not expect to pay it back off cattle. However, if you're going to play cowboy and stomp in boots around the post office on Saturdays, I'm not going to interfere.' " Johnson said he "winced at this, but he took the money and earned enough to pay it back."

On occasion, after a walk to the picturesque family graveyard and to the house where Johnson was born, he might take guests to visit Cousin Oriole, whose mother, Kate Keele, born a Bunton, was buried in the Johnson cemetery. But he preferred leading guests to her little red house by flashlight along the lane near the river late at night. Her house had a tin roof and was cooled only slightly during the summer heat by surrounding live oak and hackberry trees.

As he approached her house Johnson would call out, "Cousin Oriole, we've brought some people to see you." If she did not come out, he rapped on her screen door, and she usually emerged in a robe and bare feet. Cousin Oriole was a widow and answered to others as Mrs. J. W. Bailey.

Visitors saw a tall, seventyish, pioneer-type, rough-hewn woman, with sharp and kind eyes. On her porch was a horsehair loveseat, and in her combination bedroom-sitting room was a white metal bed. Cousin Oriole was a Christadelphian in her religion and opposed to political action, so conversation fell on other subjects. Johnson usually nagged her until she read some of her poems, though she could easily be led into religious subjects. "I believe that when you die you are as dead as this chair, until Resurrection Day, when all shall rise and be judged," she offered this and other strong opinions. She had little time for bluff, and when Johnson came with an autographed picture for her, she scolded him for signing "Lyndon Johnson" instead of "Lyndon." Before they left, visitors heard several samples of her rich Texasese, such as: "Come see me now, hear"; "It frets me"; and "Don't be grieving."

When the ranch guests numbered half a dozen, Johnson and Lady Bird divided the group in two, and each climbed behind the wheel of a late-model Lincoln or Cadillac to show visitors around the ranch. With intercoms in the cars, Lyndon and his wife kept in continual touch with each other, and each could hear the other's guided tour comments on the squawk box. One time, when Lady Bird drove past a little house in the valley, her comment was, "I can just picture Marshal Dillon riding up to that place." Every Saturday evening, no matter what other event was taking place, she insisted on taking an hour off to watch the latest TV episode of "Gunsmoke." On one wedding anniversary, Johnson's present to her was a framed picture of James Arness, the actor who portrayed Marshal Dillon on "Gunsmoke."

Johnson had put in four artificial ponds for cattle water holes, and he stocked them with fat catfish and black bass. Visitors were sometimes told, as they bounced over plowed fields, that they were going to do some fishing in a pond. Negro servants who trailed behind in jeeps raced to set up folding chairs and thread worms on fish pole hooks so the fishermen could be comfortable while trying their luck. After a few bass were hauled in, Johnson was anxious to move on, and before the fishermen could protest, he ordered the catch thrown back. With promises that bigger fish awaited them at the next pond, he herded the guests into the cars for a repeat performance down the line.

In late fall visitors were also taken on deer-hunting trips. With the hunting tower reserved for himself, Moursund, and special VIP's, run-of-the-mill senators received the second-class hunting treatment. George Dixon described this as a safari on which the hunters were "driven to a deer hunt in a Cadillac and encouraged to shoot a buck without getting out of the car." At a select spot Johnson would stop the car, windows would be lowered so that rifles could nose out, and servants would force captured deer to run alongside the car. As a gracious host Johnson wanted everyone to have a good time; if he learned that a guest was a poor shot, he fired simultaneously at the same animal and congratulated his fellow hunter when the buck fell dead.

Guests had to see his herds of cattle, which he had carefully expanded from the initial few heads on Aunt Frank's place. With beaming face, he pointed out the Bar-J brand he had devised for his steers. His greatest pride was reserved for his Herefords, whose white faces, he said, were "a real part of the Old West." He enjoyed speeding across the fields to within "smelling distance" of a herd of cows; then he would blow his special horn that sounded like the mating bellow of a bull. If this did not bring them to their feet, he drove closer and bellowed at them himself to stand. Once, when Stewart Alsop was his guest, he took him on a cattle visit and singled out various steers for comparison with "a politician he knows." He also told Alsop how much money each animal had cost him and he bragged about the "staggering profit" he would make when he sold it.

On another day Johnson took a *New York Times* reporter in an open car to look at his cattle. As they rode along, Johnson boasted of his successful Senate strategy on various bills the week before, and he was giving the reporter the lowdown on how he had gone about creating a winning vote when a dove flew into view. Without dropping a syllable, said the reporter, Johnson stopped the car, aimed a rifle, and killed the bird. A servant in a trailing car leaped out to retrieve the bird, while Johnson rode off, continuing his story.

As a compulsive talker, Johnson turned his guided tours into long monologues. There was one exception. This occurred when Johnson took Allen Duckworth, the Dallas *News* political columnist, on a ride around the ranch. "Mr. Ed, the Talking Horse" Clark, mustached, up-from-poverty millionaire lobbyist, banker, lawyer, and lumberman, sat his big, hulking frame in the back seat of the car, and he was off talking as soon as Johnson turned on the motor. Over a few hills Johnson sped; then in mounting anger, he ordered Clark to quit talking. Six more times in quick succession, as they rode toward the next dirt hill, he screamed at The Talking Horse, "Clark, please shut up! I want to tell Duckworth something."

But Clark wouldn't and couldn't quit. Finally Johnson gripped Duckworth's thigh and told him, "If Clark won't stop talking, you quit listening to him."

Johnson permitted few persons to drive him around on the ranch. One who did was his secretary, Mary Margaret Wiley. But even with her, he sat hunched and tense, ready to explode as she barely missed the cattle guards protruding from the ground. "You get only a B-minus for missing that one so close," he muttered. "You get an A for that one . . . now you got an A-plus . . . "

From the pastures he alerted the kitchen help by car telephone to have the meal ready at a stated time for his guests. If fewer than twelve were present, they ate in the dining room. Representative Bob Poage, who came to the House a year before Johnson, said that Johnson liked his roast beef so rare "it could walk off his plate."

Johnson was especially partisan to barbecues for large crowds, and for herds of visitors he asked Walter Jetton, the Texas barbecue master, to bring his chuckwagon and take over. For a long time Johnson dreamed of a trademark food he could serve guests. Finally, when he decided that his prize would be a hamburger shaped like the perimeter of Texas, experimenters could not keep it in shape throughout the frying. But Harry Aiken, owner of the Nighthawk Cafes in Austin, succeeded, just as Johnson was ready to give up. As a reward, Johnson ordered the Senate Dining Room to put Aiken's cole slaw on the daily menu. However, Johnson remained dissatisfied with the geographical Lone Star hamburger because the jutting western Panhandle spoiled its symmetry, and he walked among guests with the request that they "eat the Panhandle first."

When Democrats were guests, Johnson frequently gave his hilarious imitation of Eisenhower at a news conference. One hand on hip, shoulders squared, chest up, his face screwed into a deep listening frown as he pretended to concentrate on a question being asked him, Johnson would then deliver a rambling meaningless paragraph or two. He had no further to go for an actual example of a Presidential reply to a reporter than Eisenhower's words to a question at the August 26, 1958, news conference: "I believe there is still, we have got great savings, I believe that we have got to offer things in a better packaged way, we've got to do better advertising and above all things let the public buy when they think they are getting a bargain and not worrying about what is going to be the possible future of some possible future action."

Sometimes Johnson drove visitors at a ninety-mile-an-hour pace over the highway for a look at Johnson City. Here he pointed out the house he had lived in (Aunt Frank was dead and he had reclaimed it, in addition to buying the entire block); the Opera House, where he had watched silent movies; and the First Christian Church, to which he belonged. The assassinated President James Garfield, he would add, had also belonged to the same sect, which was sometimes called Campbellites or Disciples of Christ. Under a mulberry tree beside the Casparis Restaurant, Otho Summy, who had gone to California with him as a boy, might be found playing dominoes. Or Ohlee Cox, a Johnson City car dealer and old Johnson friend, might shout out, "Howdy, Lyn," and repeat to those around him that Johnson had talked to him about the White House, vowing, "Some day I'll be up there."

Guests found that Johnson treated his ranch employees exactly as he handled employees in his Senate office. In the kitchen he quizzed the help on household details; and outdoors he wanted equally clear answers to questions on the L.B.J. pastures, cattle, crops, and irrigation. Dale Malechek, his young foreman who had graduated from Texas A & M College, expected any sort of question or order to be thrown at him. One time Johnson greeted him in front of others with "Everything working, Dale? Toilet pressure okay?" A guest noted that Lady Bird frowned and said "reprovingly, 'Lyndon.' " On a ride over the pastures, Johnson might converse with Malechek about breeding problems or grass types, or he might grow exasperated at anything his foreman did on his own initiative. On one occasion that Johnson conferred with him, he caught sight of a tall stack of lumber and told Malechek it was too close to an entrance.

Malechek guessed it could be moved in ten minutes, and Johnson barked at him, "You get those two other fellows and move it. And I'm going to time you."

A reporter said Johnson "drove off to a pasture and returned in fifteen minutes. 'How long did it take you?' " he asked.

"Ten minutes," his sweaty foreman replied with a wide grin.

Another time Cousin Oriole discovered that Malechek had deposited some farm machinery in her yard, and she ordered him to remove it from her property. Since Johnson had told him to put it there in the first place, he was in a quandary. "I just can't do that without Mr. Johnson's okay," he told her, walking out of earshot before her retort came.

When guests left the ranch after a stay, Lyndon and Lady Bird, in cowboy attire, waved them off with fond farewells. "Y'all come back real soon, hear now," she called after them. And if a Southern lady were among those who departed, Lady Bird might turn to remaining guests and summarize, "She's a sturdy oak with magnolia blossoms all year long."

Chapter 53

❴—❵

POLITICAL TROUBLES DESCENDED on Lyndon Johnson when the Eightysixth Congress descended on Washington in January 1959. The continuing recession, farmer unrest in the Midwest, and public reaction to businessmen promoting state "right to work" laws barring compulsory union membership had contributed to the smashing Democratic victory at the polls the preceding November 4. Johnson's Senate majority showed a gain of fourteen on the Democratic side of the aisle, and the total now stood at sixty-four Democrats and only thirty-four Republicans.

Mister Sam toted up his own scorecard, and when he arrived at the total of two hundred and eighty-two Democrats in the House and only one hundred and fifty-three Republicans, he shook his weary head and told a reporter, "It adds up to trouble."

He knew the importance of Lyndon's continued razzle-dazzle in the Upper Chamber to his Presidential candidacy, and he had chuckled in the past when reporters wrote up the unanimous and near-unanimous Democratic votes in the Senate as examples of Lyndon's genius. Rayburn was well aware that when a political party held only a cat's whisker of a majority in either house, members were like a family, closing ranks against outside attacks. But with a tremendous majority—such as the thirty-senator lead Lyndon now held and his own one hundred and twenty-nine in the House—unity went out the transom, and members became obnoxiously independent. Even worse, Rayburn knew from past experience that in times of top-heavy majorities, members who had been storing up animosities toward the leaders believed they had gained a license to attack them openly and at will.

Rayburn feared such attacks on Lyndon—and they were not long in coming. Senator Joseph Clark tipped off the coming troubles with a letter to Johnson on November 18, 1958, in which he first congratulated him unctuously for helping bring about the smashing Senate Democratic victory, and then bluntly told him that the increased contingency of Democratic liberals wanted stronger representation on the Steering and Policy Committees to help determine committee assignments and the legislative program.

Johnson boiled with rage at Clark's audacity, and his anger increased when Clark's letter appeared in the newspapers. Nor did his vehemence decline when the Stevenson, Truman, etc., Democratic Advisory Council demanded that a big package of liberal legislation go through Congress in the Eighty-sixth Congress so that the party would have legislative achievements to boast about in the 1960 campaign.

He handled the Clark question at the Democratic caucus on January 7, 1959, by ignoring it. After the re-election of officers, and his brief "State of the Union Message" declaring his independence of the White House on that session's legislative program, Johnson quickly turned over the meeting to Hubert Humphrey for his lengthy talk on the eight-hour conversation he had held in the Kremlin with Khrushchev. Then the caucus adjourned with a Johnson aside that the next one would be held the following January.

But the liberals did not give up so easily. Once Reverend Frederick Brown Harris, the chaplain of the Senate, finished his prayer, and new members were sworn in at noon that day, the liberals began a fight to amend the Cloture Rule, Rule XXII, so that a majority vote could end a filibuster.

Johnson was unmoved by their arguments that this change was needed to prevent Russell and his Southern allies from blocking progressive bills. He viewed the fight strictly as a challenge to his leadership, and he was soon at work holding on to lapels and steaming the glasses of the new crop of Democratic senators to win their support. When freshman Senator Edmund Muskie, former governor of Maine and an oddity as a senator from that rock-ribbed Republican fortress, first showed up in Washington, Johnson had delivered a sermon to him, telling him not to succumb to pressure from lobbyists on bills. "Wait until they get to the *M*'s in the roll call," was Johnson's advice.

Now he had 6-feet 3-inch Muskie before him, and he suggested that Muskie take his side. Muskie would be a major triumph for him because the Maine senator had become an instant leader of the liberal pack. Finally Johnson demanded to have a preview of the way he intended to vote. "Well, Senator," Muskie said with his twinkling-eyed smile, "I think I'll follow your advice and wait until they get to the *M*'s in the roll call." After this conversation, said a cloakroom hanger-on, "Bobby Baker passed word around that Johnson had written Muskie off as a 'chickenshit.' "

Muskie had detected that Johnson would settle for a compromise, and he made an effort to talk the liberals into receding from their simple majority stand. "If the liberals would have settled for a three-fifths vote approval to bring cloture, they could have had it," said Muskie. But they would not, and Johnson wore a beaming expression when the liberal motion for a simple majority vote to invoke cloture was defeated 60 to 36. Then three days later, on January 12, he paternalistically pushed through a motion to return Rule XXII to its pre-1949 status, so a filibuster could be ended by the vote of two-thirds of the senators present rather than the existing requirement of two-thirds of the entire Senate membership.

Afterward, when he passed out committee assignments to his freshmen, Johnson determined to punish Muskie. The Maine senator had asked for Foreign Relations, Commerce, and Judiciary before the cloture fight. "Instead of these," said Muskie, "he shunted me onto Banking and Currency, Government Operations, and Public Works—none of them considered as having top prestige." But this punishment turned into a blessing, because in time Muskie's service on the committees made him subcommittee chairman on such major problems as pollution, urban renewal, and federal-state relations.

One of the recently elected senators with whom Johnson believed he had a warm relationship was William Proxmire of Wisconsin, who had succeeded Senator McCarthy in August 1957. Typical of Proxmire's *Congressional Record* insertions was his November 12, 1958, statement in which he said, "I think Lyndon Johnson has made an excellent party leader. He has been fair to everybody."

But, belatedly, Proxmire looked back on his re-election contest in 1958 and found fault with the Democratic Senate Campaign Committee for its minute contributions to his campaign. Proxmire ascribed this action to his sharp attacks on the oil depletion allowances, and when the Eighty-sixth Congress began, he was certain Johnson was punishing him, because his request for a seat on the Finance Committee was rejected.

The issue that brought a break between Proxmire and Johnson was the majority leader's decision not to call further Democratic caucuses in 1959. On February 23 Proxmire began his attack on Johnson with a Senate speech in which he charged: "There has never been a time when power has been as sharply concentrated as it is today in the Senate. . . . In January 1958 senators assembled [in the Democratic caucus] and listened to the majority leader read a speech which he had previously released to the press in full. There was not a single matter of party business discussed. There wasn't even a mention of party program, not a whisper concerning any legislation. . . . The next meeting of the Senate Democratic caucus was a full year later. The only business of the entire caucus had taken less than two and one-half minutes. And senators had to surrender for another year their right and duty to determine the Democratic party's policies and programs."

Johnson was in Texas when Proxmire made this first attack, and when he returned to Washington, he told other senators he would have a private conversation with the Wisconsin senator to "calm him." But after they met, Proxmire gave his account of what had taken place: "It was a very interesting experience," he said. "It was a one-way conversation with Lyndon doing the talking. That was both the beginning and the end of the meeting."

After this Proxmire made a series of talks on the Senate floor and attacked Johnson not only for "one-man rule" but also for lacking any legislative policy. On March 8, for instance, he ripped into Johnson for devising Democratic policy in the Senate "on an ad-lib, off-the-cuff basis." Every time he spoke, Paul Douglas, Wayne Morse, and Joseph Clark stood by to say "Amen," and though this trio did not cause Johnson to lose sleep, he was concerned that any bad publicity would damage his Presidential candidacy.

This is why he made Proxmire the first Democratic senator he attacked openly in the Senate. On May 28 he spoke in gasps of anger, yelling that Proxmire needed "a fairy godmother" or a "wet nurse." Only weeks earlier he had boasted anew to reporters of his tight control over all the activities of the Senate. Now he called the charge of dictatorship utter nonsense. "This one-man rule stuff is a myth," he spat out at Proxmire in hardly a confessional tone. "I do not know how anyone can force a senator to do anything. I have never tried to do so. I have read in the newspapers that I have been unusually persuasive with senators. I have never thought these were accurate reports. Usually when a senator wants something done and does not get his way, he puts the blame on the leadership. It does not take much courage, I must say, to make the leadership a punching bag." Finally getting down to his excuse for failing to put more liberals on the policy committee or to call more caucuses, he chided Proxmire with "Our policy is what each individual senator's conviction tells him is good for America. . . . I have no illusion that there is any super policy committee or super caucus which could have the slightest influence on the senator from Wisconsin . . . or any other senators, to make them act contrary to their convictions."

Johnson failed to convince the liberal senators that he spoke from the heart, and though Proxmire continued with his charges for a time, he finally quit, admitting that he had failed to make "any real dent in the Johnson leadership program."

Most members, conservatives as well as liberals, enjoyed a burst of laughter involving Johnson's pious declaration to Proxmire that "there is not anything the leadership can or should do to require a member of the Senate to change his convictions on any bill, and I have never tried to do it." The laughter came on a tax amendment and involved small, bow-tied Allen Frear, senator from Delaware, who was known as a "200 per cent Johnson man." Johnson had wanted the amendment passed, but it had failed by a single vote, 41 to 40. Frear had voted against the amendment because it would have stripped his state's biggest firm, the Du Pont Corporation, of a special tax loophole. When Johnson heard the disappointing vote total, he remembered Frear's high-pitched *No!* when his name had been called.

"Change your vote, Allen!" Johnson screamed out to Frear in full hearing of more than eighty senators and the galleries. When Frear remained silent, Johnson screamed even louder, "Change your vote!" This time Frear did as he was ordered, and the amendment carried.

There were more than the liberal fleas who stung Johnson in 1959. President Eisenhower was belatedly acting as boss of the White House, and this proved a serious trial to Johnson. Eisenhower had lost his chief of staff, Sherman Adams, in September 1958 after House investigators found he had accepted gifts and favors from a New England textile manufacturer and had made phone calls to government officials on behalf of the businessman. During the investigation Eisenhower had attempted to save him by telling his news conference, "I need him." But he had to part with Adams because the morality of his Administration was at stake. Then the following May, Secretary of State Dulles died of cancer, after logging 559,988 miles around the globe to promote his policy of brinkmanship. As he lay dying, the President used the same expression he had used in the Adams imbroglio: "America needs him. And I think each of us needs him."

Left on his own for the first time, Eisenhower became obsessed with only a single political approach—to balance the budget. Galled by the twelve-billion-dollar deficit that was developing in the current fiscal year, he was determined to have receipts exceed expenditures in the next fiscal year. At the beginning of the year, House Republicans, blaming Joe Martin for their decline in numbers, had deposed him by voting Charlie Halleck of Indiana as minority leader. In the Senate, Bill Knowland was gone, having run and lost in a race for governor of California; and Senator Everett Dirksen was the new minority leader, after defeating John Sherman Cooper by a vote of 20 to 14.

To Halleck and Dirksen, Eisenhower now divulged his plan for preventing the enactment of legislation involving large expenditures. His solution was simple and required little physical effort. He would let Lyndon Johnson and Sam Rayburn go through the enormous expenditure of time, thought, and energy to pass such bills, and then he would merely veto them. "Every sort of foolish proposal will be advanced in the name of national security and the 'poor' fellow," he told Dirksen and Halleck at their first leadership meeting on January 13, 1959. "We've got to convince Americans that thrift is not a bad word."

It mattered not that air safety control had been dangerously neglected and needed immense and costly updating, that city slums, seed-bedding crime and disease, had expanded to a menacing level, and that a host of other social ills had too long been ignored. Vetoes came swiftly and frequently; there was talk that Eisenhower intended to set a record. Not until September 10 did Congress for the first time muster the necessary two-thirds in each house to override an Eisenhower veto. "In health, education and welfare," Eisenhower boasted afterward, "I insisted that spending more money did not necessarily hasten progress."

Housing legislation became a major battleground between the Administration and the Congressional Democrats. Mister Sam faced a high hurdle in the House merely to get a bill to the floor for a vote. At the beginning of the session Chet Holifield of California, spokesman for House liberals, had asked Rayburn's cooperation in a major effort to amend House rules in order to prevent Judge Smith's Rules Committee from holding up traffic on liberal legislation. Rayburn did not relish the fight this would entail, and he promised Holifield that if the liberals would not proceed with their plan, he would personally guarantee that Judge Smith would not hold up or kill liberal bills.

His test came early in February when the Rules Committee, by a vote of 6 to 6, refused permission for a multibillion-dollar urban renewal bill to go to the floor. Rayburn brooded over his inability to convince Smith to release the housing bill. But after a short vacation at home in Bonham, he found his solution. This was to make use of his Rayburn Rules of Parliamentary Procedure to meet any problem, and he informed Smith that he would simply bypass his committee. The threat of such action convinced two of the six in opposition to change their votes and permit the housing bill to reach the floor.

In the Senate, Senator Clark had attempted to meet the stated requirements of American mayors for an urban renewal program providing six hundred million dollars a year for ten years. Johnson told him it would be vetoed, and the bill was cut to four hundred and fifty million dollars a year for four years. An Eisenhower veto caused Johnson to slice an additional amount off the proposal, following the failure of Congress to override the veto. This new bill was also vetoed. Finally Johnson pushed through another housing bill that liberals denounced—one calling for three hundred million dollars a year for three years—and Eisenhower signed it.

As the Eisenhower vetoes grew in number, Johnson slashed the money amounts of a wide variety of bills in order to head off more. An airport aid bill shriveled. A temporary unemployment compensation bill, to extend payments to those who had received the maximum in the recession, was altered, forcing such individuals onto relief.

As the months of 1959 went by, the yowls and howls against Johnson for attempting to placate an implacable President grew to a roar. The Democratic Advisory Council, ignored by Johnson since its establishment late in 1956, gained front-page stories with attacks on him and Rayburn. In a June blast the DAC declared that the voters "expect and are entitled to have in this Congress more tangible results of the mandate they gave the Democratic majority last November than they have received to date." The DAC charged that the Congressional leaders were engrossed in "time-consuming efforts to water down proposed legislation to the limits the President might accept."

Paul Butler, the national committee's chairman, personally entered the growing controversy when he chidingly suggested on July 5 his hope "that we will be laying a bill upon the President's desk even though knowing in advance that he may veto it and letting it be known . . . we will take the issue to the American people."

This last comment incensed Johnson, and he asked Butler to come to the speaker's office in the Capitol for a talk. Reporters heard Johnson's loud voice coming through the closed door throughout the hour-long argument. Afterward, when Mister Sam opened the door, he told newsmen, "We had a very friendly meeting. There was no loud talk . . . no violent disagreements . . . no fighting and scratching."

Johnson piped up with satisfaction, "It was a pleasant and constructive meeting; it ought to do a lot of good." When the TV cameras and photographers were ready to roll films of the three, Butler remarked wanly, "Let's try to look happy together."

Stuart Symington found his issue in 1959, and it was a repetitious cry of "missile lag" and "missile gap." He was also trying to revive his charge of the year before, when he made a Senate speech about the "surrender studies" he claimed the Pentagon had conducted to evolve a plan for American surrender after a surprise nuclear attack by the Communists.

At that time Eisenhower had asked the Pentagon whether such studies existed, and when the reply was *No* his reaction to Symington was volcanic. "Well," he said in dwindling fury, "I'd better not get a stroke over a thing like that."

John Kennedy was also searching for an issue or a handle by which he could identify himself to the public. When opponents pointed out that in six years as a senator he had no record as a lawmaker, Kennedy decided that now was the time to correct this shortcoming as well as to put down the charge that he lacked political management experience. As one of his friends wrote that year, "If he took the initiative on any bill and made it his project, his success or lack of it would become a test of his Presidential quality. . . . If he did nothing he would be written off as a cipher."

Kennedy quickly saw that the most logical bill to promote was the labor antiracketeering bill, which had won Senate approval in 1958 only to die in the House. He should win an even easier Senate victory this year, and then his friends could work on House Democrats to give him the successful piece of legislation he needed.

So again he introduced his bill and went through subcommittee hearings. There was little opposition from labor leaders, for they had generally come around to the acceptance of his proposal to reform internal union operations in order to prevent racketeers from gaining or holding control of union membership, policies, and funds. The chief spark-maker at the hearings proved to be Labor Secretary Mitchell, who favored the addition of strong antilabor features. But Mitchell failed, and Kennedy's bill was reported out intact onto the Senate Calendar.

A ticklish point now arose: Kennedy wanted to be floor manager for his bill, and this was an area Johnson almost invariably reserved for himself. Few committee and subcommittee chairmen had complained in the past when Johnson took over the direction of their bills on the floor, because he insisted on this authority. Besides, he seemed to have a strange ability to learn the enormously complex details of hundreds of bills. An old friend explained this as a memory trick: "He told me once that when he had to know the contents of a bill or a report, he could scan it and fix it in his mind so well that if you gave him a sentence from it, he could paraphrase the whole page and everything that followed. But once they'd finished the piece of work, even if it was only a week later, he wouldn't remember the contents or even the name of the report."

Fully aware of Kennedy's lack of experience in floor-managing legislation and the importance the younger senator was attaching to the antirackets bill, Johnson eagerly agreed that Kennedy should boss the floor show. And for a short time Kennedy confounded him by adroit handling of minor opponents.

But one April afternoon Kennedy's floor-managing suffered a total collapse. This occurred when Senator John McClellan of Arkansas, who had been conducting long hearings on labor racketeering, rose and offered his "Bill of Rights" Amendment to the Kennedy bill. This amendment, which would permit a union member to go to federal court over any point of disagreement he had with union leaders on membership, union meeting procedures, and voting, conceivably could disrupt every labor organization in the country to the point of chaos.

Johnson offered no help to Kennedy when the lawyers in the Senate slammed down every argument Kennedy made against the "Bill of Rights" Amendment. The Kennedy management exhibition was so lame that even his friends were embarrassed. One offered the excuse that he "was bone-tired, he was disconcerted by the quick turn of events, and most of his recent homework on labor reform had been sandwiched between exhausting campaign trips and legislative duties."

Nor did Johnson and Bobby Baker aid him in the necessary behind-the-scenes rounding up of friendly votes. Kennedy's own assistants, naive and inexperienced, undertook this job; and when the nightmarish vote on McClellan's Amendment came on April 22, it carried 47 to 46. Kennedy managed to gain a reconsideration of the vote, and this time the result was a 46-to-46 tie, with Vice President Nixon casting the deciding vote afterward in favor of the amendment. The next day's *New York Times* summed up the wild Senate evening by calling the passing of the amendment a "grave defeat" for the Presidential candidate.

Following the Kennedy disaster, Johnson moved back to his front-row, center-aisle seat and helped Kennedy win approval for a milder bill of rights to replace the McClellan version. But Kennedy was still not out of the pit. The House was considering three labor bills: an innocuous measure supported by the AFL-CIO; a Kennedy-type antiracketeering bill; and the Administration-backed Landrum-Griffin Bill, a harsh measure containing provisions curtailing picketing and boycotts which even the Taft-Hartley promoters had considered too extreme a decade earlier.

Mister Sam favored the Kennedy approach, dealing solely with internal union reforms, and he told the Texas House delegation to support this measure (the Elliott Bill). But Johnson came almost running to Rayburn when he heard this and "cautioned Mister Sam that for Texans to vote for anything less than the toughest possible labor bill would mean their political death back home." Johnson telephone calls went to each member of the Texas delegation, and the Landrum-Griffin Bill passed, with Texas House members voting 17 to 4 in its favor.

As a result, when Kennedy led the seven-senator delegation to meet with seven House members in the conference committee, the two bills whose differences were to be ironed out were basically dissimilar. Joyous reports came to Johnson that in the two and a half weeks the conference committee sat, Kennedy was no match for the House members who refused to budge from Landrum-Griffin provisions. Nor could he match the insults thrown at him by House Education and Labor Committee Chair-

man Graham Barden. Kennedy had asked Harvard Professor Archibald
Cox to sit behind his chair as his adviser, and Barden kept up a steady
stream of ridicule of Kennedy's "crutch." After listening to Cox's excited whispers interjected steadily throughout one conference committee
session, Barden yelled at Kennedy, "I'm sick and tired of these intellectual outsiders nit-picking and scratching for little holes." Kennedy's retort
was, "And I'm sick and tired of sitting here and having to defend my aide
time and time again from your attacks."

But Kennedy's accomplishment proved to be little more than a defense
of Cox, for when the final version of the labor bill was sent to both houses
for a vote, it was essentially the Landrum-Griffin Bill. Kennedy requested
that his name be removed from the measure, and this was done before it
successfully cleared the House and Senate. So the chief achievement of
the first session of the Eighty-sixth "liberal" Congress was an extremely
stringent antilabor law. Kennedy had not gained a record as a lawmaker,
but as he was to find out, he needed none.

If Johnson pleased neither the liberals nor the Administration with the
tepid spending bills he fashioned, and John Kennedy failed to reveal
managerial qualities in the legislative arena, Wayne Morse, the senator
most devoid of humor, provided the only laughter in the session.

This came about when Eisenhower nominated Mrs. Clare Boothe Luce,
wife of the influential magazine publisher, as ambassador to Brazil in
February 1959. Mrs. Luce, a tart-tongued former playwright, congresswoman, and ambassador to Italy, had been a subject of Democratic dislike since the 1944 Presidential campaign when she called President
Roosevelt "the only President who ever lied us into war."

Morse was chairman of the Foreign Relations Subcommittee on American Republic Affairs, and when her nomination reached him, he first
quizzed her sharply, then observed her expressions and mannerisms almost clinically for another two hours. Mrs. Luce claimed she had been
forced to resign her Rome post because the ceiling paint in her bedroom
contained arsenic and particles had fallen into her breakfast coffee. Morse
now called her New York doctor to determine whether she was mentally
ill, because the story from Rome was that the ceiling had not been painted
in half a century.

Despite Morse's plea to the Senate to reject her, she was confirmed by
an overwhelming vote of 79 to 11. But seething at the senator's attack,
she could not hold her tongue. She struck back at him at a news conference, remarking, "My difficulties, of course, go back some years when
Senator Wayne Morse was kicked in the head by a horse."

Morse happened to be reading the AP news wire teletype printer in the
cloakroom when her words appeared. Rushing onto the floor, he called
out, "Mr. President, I rise to a point of personal privilege," and he
read her comment to his colleagues. "Shocking!" yelled several smiling

senators, as Morse went on: "This is an old, old pattern of emotional instability on the part of this slanderer; the same pattern which caused her to put on a scene in the Roman Parliament after her candidate for President of Italy was defeated."

Democratic senators jumped up to defend Morse with noble oratory, and this exhibition continued until Minority Leader Dirksen, in an effort to end the speechifying, innocently brought down the house with his histrionic wail—"Why thrash old hay or beat an old bag of political bones?"

While this talk was going on, the Democratic Presidential hopefuls were suddenly stricken by the crushing thought that Henry Luce, the husband of Mrs. Luce and publisher of *Time* and *Life,* would give them poor publicity or none at all because of Morse. A State Department official said that Kennedy called him "in a voice of some urgency" and pleaded, "Get her to withdraw her statement." Johnson was more direct with a telephone call to the White House oval office. Eisenhower said that Johnson asked him to "induce Mrs. Luce to temper her 'kicked in the head' remark."

"Well, I have not felt exactly complimented by some things that Wayne Morse said about me," Eisenhower replied.

"I've sometimes found myself in the same boat," Johnson agreed.

Mrs. Luce ended the war by resigning her post three days later. She gave as her reason "the climate of good will was poisoned by thousands of words of extraordinarily ugly charges against my person" by a senator whose "natural course" would be "a continuing harassment of my mission."

There was one Eisenhower appointment fight that year in which Johnson played an important role. In October 1958 Eisenhower had nominated Admiral Lewis Strauss as Secretary of Commerce, yet the Senate Commerce Committee did not start hearings on the nomination until mid-March 1959, or four months after Strauss joined the Cabinet. This delay would not have had an ominous tone were it not for the incessant demand of Johnson's pal, Senator Clinton Anderson, that Strauss be rejected.

Anderson, as chairman of the Joint Committee on Atomic Energy, had carried on long warfare with Strauss, who had been head of the Atomic Energy Commission. Anderson had criticized him for his role in the Dixon-Yates affair, labeled him generally untrustworthy, and accused him of withholding necessary information from his committee. Strauss, who had not gone to college, had taken delight in telling Anderson that he had not sent him more detailed information because Anderson had "a limited understanding." It became apparent to Eisenhower that if he appointed him to a second term at the AEC, Strauss would not win confirmation because of Anderson; hence the appointment to the Commerce Department. At the same time, Anderson, who had been a regular member at Eisenhower's evening bridge games, received no more invitations to play cards at the White House.

Anderson was not a member of "Maggie" Magnuson's Commerce Committee, which heard testimony on Strauss' nomination, but Magnuson permitted him to attend committee sessions. In addition, young Senator Gale McGee of Wyoming, who agreed with Anderson on the Strauss issue, served as the committee's focus of attack on the admiral. However, Magnuson expected no fireworks because a poll of committee members before Strauss appeared as a witness revealed a count of 14 to 3 in Strauss' favor.

Unfortunately, Strauss turned out to be his own worst witness, displaying such rudeness and arrogance in answer to questions that the final committee vote was only 9 to 8 for confirmation.

Only after the Strauss nomination reached the Senate floor did Johnson suddenly decide to fight his confirmation as repayment for the many humiliations Eisenhower had heaped upon him that year. However, he would not work openly, nor would he announce that he intended to vote against Strauss.

Throughout American history, since the Civil War Reconstruction period, Presidents assumed that their Cabinet appointments would win automatic Senate confirmation. The only rejection in the twentieth century had come in 1925, during the Coolidge years, when his nominee for Attorney General, Charles Warren, failed of confirmation.

Old Walter George used to sit in the Marble Room off the Senate floor and pat his white hair in place as he recounted the Warren story. "I had a live pair with an absent Republican," said George. This meant that even though George was present, he would follow the practice of courtesy and not vote, in order to balance a vote on the other side by a senator who was away. "But when the voting came, I saw it was going to be 40 to 39 for confirmation. So I violated my live pair and rushed onto the floor to vote against Warren. This gave Vice President Charlie Dawes the opportunity to cast the tie-breaking vote, but he was taking a nap in his hotel room a few miles away. The Republicans woke him up when the voting began; he ran half-dressed into Pennsylvania Avenue to flag a taxicab; and broke the twenty-miles-an-hour speed law by fifty miles getting here. Some of the younger Republican senators met him when he came running into the Capitol, and they carried him up the stairs and into the chamber. But we had moved on to other business by then and he was not given the privilege of voting."

On June 18, 1959, when he noted that five Republican senators were out of town and all sixty-four Democrats were present, Johnson suddenly called for the vote on Strauss. Dirksen immediately launched a hoarse-voiced filibuster while Eisenhower dispatched Air Force jets to deliver the absentees to Washington.

The voting finally began after midnight, following Senator Harry Byrd's continuing praise of Strauss, his fellow Virginian. Republican Whip Thomas

Kuchel's count placed Kennedy, Symington, Fulbright, and Neuberger among the twenty Democrats expected to join a united Republican army for Strauss—far more than the number needed for confirmation.

But Johnson, who had remained quiet for publication, now came out openly in opposition, and the paper majority for Strauss began to show erasures. Kennedy and Symington suddenly decided that a vote for the very conservative nominee would be hard to explain to liberal audiences. Neuberger's reasoning was far more simple: He would back his majority leader as a party principle. Fulbright, who was torn between holding to his promise and loyalty to Johnson, solved his dilemma by wandering off the floor and going uncounted.

Only fourteen solid Democratic votes remained for Strauss, and Dirksen was faced with a need to have the entire Republican membership support Strauss or suffer defeat. In the middle of the roll call the break came, when Senator "Wild Bill" Langer, a Nonpartisan League politician from North Dakota and only a nominal Republican, voted against Strauss. Dirksen was still hoping that a Democrat who was supposed to be against the nominee would vote for him and offset Langer. But his hope vanished when Republican Senator Margaret Smith of Maine was called on for her vote. Mrs. Smith had spent the day reading the committee hearings, and her conclusion was that Anderson and McGee were correct in charging Strauss with "deception—falsehoods—evasions." When she voted *No*, Senator Goldwater slammed his fist on his desk in fury and yelled out, "Goddam!"

Had Langer and Mrs. Smith voted for him, Strauss would have been confirmed, for the vote that rejected him was 49 opposed to 46 in his favor.

Besides their sullen rage at his watering down of their legislation for fear of an Eisenhower veto, Senate liberals found another reason for attacking their majority leader. Johnson was publicly labeling himself as a ruthless opponent of government spending, yet his personal extravagance was large. Since becoming majority leader, Johnson had chafed at the indignity of being held to a small office on the echo-laden gallery floor of the Capitol, one flight above the Senate chamber level.

Then one day he told the seven-man Senate District of Columbia Committee that he was ousting them from their spacious quarters across the lobby from the Senate chamber. Interior decorators and a large working crew appeared, and the rumors were that Johnson spent between one hundred and two hundred thousand dollars of taxpayers' money to create a Hollywood setting for himself in the old D.C. rooms. The glittering office was decorated in royal green and gold with plush furniture, and if visitors were not immediately awed on entering his new headquarters, they generally felt insignificant on entering his inner office, where a lighted, full-length portrait of the majority leader hung on the wall. In addition, as a reporter noted, two overhead lamps focused "an impressive nimbus of golden light as he sits at his desk." Johnson's new office became a virulent subject to most of his colleagues, and they jeered at it as the "Taj Mahal" and the "Emperor's Room."

Sam Rayburn, too, was on a personal spending spree. Despite the angry opposition of the American Institute of Architects, he called on Johnson to help him bludgeon a twenty-one-million-dollar bill through Congress to extend the East Front of the Capitol in front of the dome by thirty-two feet. The extension became known as "Rayburn's Madness," but Mister Sam felt it was worthwhile when President Eisenhower came on July 4, 1959, to lift the first bit of dirt with the same silver trowel George Washington had used to lay the Capitol's cornerstone on September 18, 1793.

Held to Washington by his legislative duties and his unwillingness to let Mike Mansfield, his whip, do any work, Johnson was forced into a long-distance favor-granting outburst to win the friendship of politicians around the country. Sometimes this produced strange results, because Johnson lacked time to learn the details of the requests. For instance, an FBI agent in the Midwest said: "I caught a gang of young bank robbers who had been rifling safety deposit boxes of farmers, and they hired the Democratic national committeeman of the state as their attorney. One day when I was interrogating them privately, one of them bragged to me, 'Our lawyer knows the guy who runs the Capitol, and he lives across the street from J. Edgar Hoover. He's going to get rid of you and have you taken off our case.'" The agent scoffed, but a few days later he was notified he had been transferred to another city.

Johnson's relationship with FBI boss Hoover had grown closer over the years, and he thought of Hoover when some problems arose. Lady Bird told a reporter that her husband was on the telephone one evening when their older daughter, Lynda, went out on her first date. When he hung up, he was outraged, she said, because he had not talked to the youth who had called for Lynda.

As the evening wore on, between other phone calls, Lady Bird said, he paced the floor and kept screaming, "Why did you allow Lynda to get into a car with a boy?"

At 11 P.M., he announced that his daughter had only two minutes to come home before he would cross the street and ask Hoover to put out an area-wide alarm for her.

Punctually at two minutes after eleven, he started up the stairs to telephone Hoover that he was coming when Lynda walked into the living room. Down the stairs he pounded like a heavy bear and bellowed at his daughter: "Where did you go? Where were you? Why weren't you home by eleven?"

Lynda waited until he paused for breath, then explained that she and the boy and another young couple had decided not to go out. Instead, they had spent the evening dancing in the basement, while her father had done his yelling overhead.

As the summer of 1959 wore on, Johnson grew anxious to end the fruitless session of Congress and go home to campaign for the Presidency. This desire was spurred by the news that Eisenhower had invited Soviet dictator Nikita Khrushchev to visit Washington on September 15.

Johnson had no intention of permitting this "Red Menace" to address a joint session of Congress, a courtesy customarily granted visiting heads of state. So he and Mister Sam set the adjournment date for September 12 and planned a last week of feverish effort to complete outstanding business and send Congress home by then.

With time so short Johnson ordered the Senate to stay in session over the Labor Day weekend. But this interfered with Wayne Morse's plan to attend the Oregon State Fair, and he determined to become a legislative spoiler. Johnson was counting on unanimous consent agreements to permit committees to operate while the Senate was in session and to cut the talk on the floor in order to finish the voting on more than one hundred bills. He was soon to find that every motion for unanimous consent was met with a gravel-voiced objection. Even when Johnson asked for unanimous consent to dispense with the reading of the previous day's Senate *Journal,* Morse caused his face to redden by objecting; and the glum clerk had to read all fourteen thousand words.

On Labor Day, when Morse appeared with a rose bud in his lapel, his signal for a long speech that day, Johnson rose from his seat and begged Vice President Nixon "for protection of my rights." When Morse spoke up, Nixon told him to shut up.

Finally when Morse concluded that he had taught Johnson a lesson and also computed that his tactics would keep Congress in session until after Khrushchev arrived, he ended his war. But Johnson outwitted him. In three days he passed one hundred and sixty-six bills, keeping the Senate up all night for a 6:22 A.M. adjournment on September 15, six hours before Khrushchev's expected arrival.

He also placed Morse in debt to him. When Senator Fulbright, now chairman of the Foreign Relations Committee, suggested to Johnson that it might be useful for the committee to meet with Khrushchev, Johnson had no objection. In fact, he considered it an excellent Presidential campaign tool for himself to hold a confrontation with the Red dictator, just as Humphrey and Nixon were promoting themselves as Khrushchev confronters. When Morse made a similar suggestion to Johnson for the committee meeting, Johnson called Fulbright and told him to pretend that Morse had originated the idea. In this way, Morse believed he was not only responsible for the meeting but that kind Lyndon had helped arrange it.

A few days later Johnson flew back to Texas with a story designed to raise his stature with the dozens of audiences he addressed. "When I met with Khrushchev in Washington," he said slowly but firmly, "Khrushchev told me, 'I have read your speeches. And I don't like any of them!' "

Chapter 54

For a man who desperately wanted the Presidency, Johnson made a mockery of the judgment of friendly reporters who hailed him as the most astute politician in the nation. In 1957, 1958, and 1959, John Kennedy had created a profession of running for President, to the detriment of his Senate duties. But while his Senate colleagues considered him with a shrug as a legislative force, he had made deep inroads in local Democratic organizations throughout the nation. When a poll of delegates to the 1956 Democratic National Convention revealed in 1959 that they would give 409 votes to Kennedy, 259½ to Symington, 244 to Stevenson, 195½ to Johnson, and 120½ to Humphrey, Johnson's friends clamored for him to get to work on the national campaign trail and firm up convention commitments. However, he refused, and when Congress adjourned in September 1959, he headed back to familiar Texas—and disaster.

At most he would continue his last year's approach, which was the baffling act of campaigning throughout Texas for the Presidency of the United States. Hundreds joined him in this effort. A few months earlier Governor Price Daniel had won a change in the Texas Election Code which shifted the state's primaries from traditional July and August to May and June. The sole purpose of this change was to enable Johnson to get his renomination for the Senate out of the way in the spring of 1960 before the Democratic National Convention met in the summer.

Mister Sam was also at work for his protégé, even though he tired easily and his eyesight had receded to the point where print was a blur. Failing to convince Johnson of the need to campaign in the North, Rayburn had been buttonholing members of the House to work in Johnson's behalf when they returned home. Mister Sam also opened a twelve-room "Johnson-for-President" headquarters in Austin on October 17, 1959, and a small staff was hired to pass out handbills declaring "All the Way with LBJ." One of the fourteen employees was Elliott Roosevelt, Jr.

When Kennedy learned of this, he sent his younger brother Bobby to the L.B.J. Ranch to determine how seriously Johnson planned to campaign. Johnson had come straight to the ranch after Congress adjourned, changed into cowboy clothes, fired at some deer, doves, and varmints, and mapped out a strenuous airplane, helicopter, and auto tour of the state as a Presidential candidate. He put up the thirty-four-year-old youngster, whom he had known as chief counsel for the McClellan Rackets Committee, and in the morning he told Bobby to tell his big brother he had no intention of running for President. Bobby thanked him for his frankness.

The Johnson Presidential tour through Texas was hectic. This was his country, and he treated it as though he were its feudal lord. He had ordered Texas congressmen to pitch in their labors as his assistants, and he requisitioned their office assistants to handle the more menial tasks. One congressman's assistant remembered the fury with which Johnson screamed orders and his running complaints about the inadequacies of the staff's work in arranging the dozens of meetings, luncheons, press conferences, receptions, publicity, and hotel accommodations. His wide-ranging temperament made it impossible for others to gauge his reaction to any event.

At one hotel reception Johnson was the shy, small-town boy personified, as he told the assemblage "how good it is for me and Lady Bird to get out of the steel and stone of the cities and come back here to feel the soil of home under our feet, and draw close to all the things we hold dear while we gaze at the Texas moon." He begged the crowd to visit his little, plain Washington office at any time. "The coffee pot is always on," he promised, "and sometimes Lady Bird bakes a bunch of little cookies in the shape of the state of Texas to go with the coffee."

But afterward, when he and Lady Bird and his travel aide got into the hotel elevator, he poured out a torrent of obscene oaths at the assistant for arranging the talk at that reception.

Nights later, after a successful dinner in his honor, Johnson's reaction was to scream at his assistants: "Who was that redheaded son-of-a-bitch set two chairs down from me? Whoever he was, I don't want the goofy s.o.b. setting in the same room with me again. Ruined mah whole night."

On another occasion, he got into an argument with his aides because they claimed he had agreed to a press conference in a hotel ballroom and he said he had not. His voice rose to such full pitch that the entire lobby soon filled with people who had come running to learn the cause of the noise. Then when he finally held the press conference, and an unfriendly reporter asked a question, Johnson first ignored him, and when the question was repeated, Johnson shouted, "That's it! Thank you, boys."

Jake Pickle traveled with Johnson for several days, and one night they were stuck in a small town whose hotel boasted only two beds in a single room. Pickle argued for pushing on to a city on the ground that Johnson was the king of the snorers. But Johnson was the boss, and they took the room. An hour later Johnson's snoring was so loud that Pickle leaped from his bed and stood upright in total disgust. A moment later Johnson sat up and laughed almost hysterically at the joke he had played on Jake.

In sharp contrast to this setting was the fund-raising rally for Johnson at oil multimillionaire Pat Rutherford's ranch near Austin. A thousand wealthy guests came from every section of Texas, and they arrived either in private planes on the ranch's runway or in chauffeured limousines. Said Rutherford, "I have a rich friend in Fort Worth. He flew down in a single-engine, came down low over the runway, and saw sixty-two twin-engine planes. Hell, he went over to Austin and came back by cab."

There was also an unusual rally at Bastrop, in Johnson's old House district, where thousands of REA members staged a facsimile political convention in his honor. A gigantic parade into the hall, snake dances, and waving banners urging Johnson for President were everywhere in sight. Some of those present expected Johnson to commit himself for 1960 on the spot, but he would go no further than to thank them for the fish fry and comment on the Presidency: "We have to take this one step at a time. There's a lot of work to do in the Senate; so we'll go just one step at a time."

Johnson was himself the host at a rally, though it was camouflaged as "foreign relations." This was his L.B.J. Ranch spectacular in October 1959 that brought Mexico's President Mateos to the Pedernales. A Dallas paper called it "one of the most dramatic outdoor shows since they produced Aida with live elephants." When Mateos' helicopter settled down on Johnson's runway, a red carpet was rolled out to the whirlibird, and Mateos walked across it to the native music of a Mexican band. Former President Truman and Sam Rayburn arrived shortly afterward in a helicopter, and Mister Sam pointed to the dozens of signs that read: "Lyndon Johnson sera Presidente." While the eight hundred present feasted on barbecued steaks and listened to Mateos' speech of friendship for the United States and Johnson's proposal for a "Liberty Bank" to make low-interest loans to underdeveloped nations in the Western Hemisphere, Truman and Rayburn drank their bourbon and branch water and discussed Presidential politics.

Truman admitted he was nominally for Symington, his fellow Missourian, but his heart was with Johnson. The possibility that young Kennedy might emerge the nominee was enough to make them gulp their drinks. Mister Sam then told him of his concern about Johnson's failure to talk in Northern states, but tempered this with the thought that Kennedy would probably burn himself out long before the convention. Early in the year, he said, he expected to get a Washington headquarters for Lyndon in operation, with John Connally running it. Lady Bird was also helping out, said Rayburn, and when Lady Bird came by, she confirmed this.

To overcome her shyness, she had taken a course in public speaking earlier that year at the Capitol Speakers' Club in Washington from Hester Provensen. When she started, her nervousness produced fast-running, high-pitched talk. Mrs. Provensen had not only made much progress in relaxing her, but also taught her how to speak, organize material, and how to sit and stand on the speaker's platform. And Lady Bird was ready now to do some speaking in Lyndon's behalf. In fact, she was already making plans for a women's organization to work for him. Neiman-Marcus in Dallas was ready to turn out a red, white, and blue "Ladies for Lyndon" uniform for only twenty-seven dollars and eighty cents. Included at this price was a white sailor hat with "Lyndon B. Johnson" stitched on the hatband.

Just before the second session of the Eighty-sixth Congress convened, Rayburn had another talk with Johnson in the Speaker's Office to beg him to announce his candidacy and enter some of the Democratic primaries in the spring.

"Lyndon would have had no trouble winning the Indiana primary in May," said Senator Vance Hartke of that state, whose strength was such that he had originally won his nomination to the Senate at the Indiana Democratic convention despite the opposition of two chairmen of the Democratic National Committee, Frank McKinney and Paul Butler. "I told Lyndon this, but he wouldn't enter," Hartke added. West Virginia Democrats also wanted Johnson to enter their state's primary. But again he refused.

Kennedy later offered the opinion that "if he'd made a fight out of it," Johnson might have won the West Virginia primary. According to a Kennedy aide, "The majority leader's decision to stick to his Senate duties and enter no primaries at all was a fatal flaw in the Johnson campaign."

As Kennedy put it: "Johnson had to prove that a Southerner could win in the North, just as I had to prove a Catholic could win in heavily Protestant states. Could you imagine me, having entered no primaries, trying to tell the leaders that being a Catholic was no handicap? . . . When Lyndon said he could win in the North, but could offer no concrete evidence, his claims couldn't be taken seriously."

Only two explanations for Johnson's behavior appeared plausible: He was rigidly committed to his long-time belief that his prestige as majority leader would give him the nomination, and he had never been comfortable outside the South. As he once told a reporter, in the North "you think we all have tobacco juice on our shirts."

When John Kennedy formally announced for the Presidency on January 2, 1960, he told reporters how hard he had already campaigned for that office: "In the past forty months I have toured every state in the Union." He also jibed at his rivals—and at Johnson in particular—in adding, "Any Democratic aspirant should be willing to submit to the voters his views, record, and competence in a series of primary contests." Johnson held his silence; Stevenson, hopeful for a draft at the convention, issued a statement declaring he was not a candidate; Symington also said he was not running but "certainly would like to be President." Only Hubert Humphrey accepted Kennedy's challenge and put himself into the Wisconsin and West Virginia primaries.

Although Johnson expressed a few worried thoughts about his course to George Smathers, he fell back on his belief he was taking the right road. He was more certain when a poll taken of Democratic senators found him the "favorite son" of the Upper Chamber. In addition, a poll of Washington correspondents gave him an overwhelming vote for the title of "the most able Democrat in the Senate." Furthermore, almost all committee chairmen in both the House and Senate were for him.

So while Johnson continued in his dream world, convinced that these friends in Congress would convert their state delegations into Johnson supporters, if they were not already for him, Kennedy was following a practical course based on a vital discovery. A Senate committee chairman might be a powerful figure in his own arena of legislation, but back home he might be lucky to be selected as a member of his state's delegation to the national convention. In Illinois, for instance, neither Senator Douglas nor National Committeeman Jake Arvey was influential at the convention delegates level. This honor belonged to Chicago's Mayor Richard Daley, the Cook County boss.

With this discovery Kennedy had gone to work relentlessly on the key controllers of delegates. To buttress this activity, his staff also built a file of seventy thousand local party leaders, and these persons received autographed copies of *Profiles in Courage,* Christmas cards, telephone calls, and what appeared to be casual drop-in visits. Mrs. Roosevelt, who was promoting Stevenson, bitterly assailed the lavish Kennedy venture and told a TV audience that his father, Joseph Kennedy, was spending a fortune to buy the nomination for him. Kennedy immediately demanded a retraction, but she refused. Mister Sam, whose hopes for Lyndon never waned, nevertheless was beginning to view the Kennedy operation throughout the country as a steamroller. "Everywhere he goes, he leaves behind an organization," Rayburn said of the masterful politicking of the young man from Massachusetts. "There are some good young fellows working for him, too."

Johnson, on the other hand, was ready, when Congress reconvened, to show the nation the wonders of how a Senate statesman controlled the pulsebeat of the Upper House and the legislative aspirations of the country. But even before the session began, the Senate liberals, who fell into his category of "nitpickers . . . weak men . . . little men," resumed their assault on his bossism.

At the Senate Democratic caucus on January 6, 1960, Senator Clark proposed that the caucus, or conference, meet at least every two weeks at the request of fifteen senators. In any other year Johnson would have ignored the Pennsylvania liberal. But this was 1960, and he let his Democratic senators debate it. Finally, Johnson announced a course far beyond the wildest dream of the liberals: He would convene a caucus any time any senator requested one.

The favorable newspaper publicity that followed seemed at first to be worth the concessions he was making. But the liberals knew no moderation. Senator Gore struck at him openly, with a speech on the Senate floor in full hearing of the Republicans and the press, attacking him as a dictator. The Senate Democratic Policy Committee, said Gore, "should represent all the Democrats in the Senate, not merely *one*." Senator Smathers, defending his Texas friend Johnson, came back with a shout at Gore that Democratic dirty linen should not be put on display in public; but Gore rejoined that this was better than to suffer a Johnson steamroller behind closed doors.

Johnson stepped in by calling a Democratic caucus on January 13 to air his Policy Committee selections. Senator Clark described the two-hour liberal attack as a "spirited discussion." But when the vote came, the count was 51 to 12 to let Johnson continue as total boss of the Policy Committee. Mister Sam was described as "peeved and angry. . . . He sulked! He fumed!" because Senator Yarborough was numbered among the unfriendly dozen.

At the swift request of Senator Muskie for another caucus, Johnson obliged by calling the Democratic conference to another session on January 15. Muskie expected a host of liberal-sponsored bills to be aired, but instead Johnson monopolized the meeting with a reading of his "State of the Union Message" for 1960. This was a ten-point program of generalities and included proposals "to bring water to our arid, nonproductive wastelands"; to accept "the challenge of the exploration of space"; "to mount a massive battle against disease"; "redevelop our great cities"; and carry out "our obligation to our elderly citizens."

On January 18, after the liberals badgered him further, Johnson held another caucus to discuss specific tax legislation for the session. When the meeting ended, excited liberals emerged with plans for several other party conferences. But Johnson had suffered enough indignities for the year, and he refused to call another caucus meeting during the rest of the session, even though this might cost him the delegation support at the national convention of the senators involved.

The caucus embroilment was not his sole trouble with Senate liberals in 1960. There was also a rage of antagonism that developed over civil rights. With the 1957 Civil Rights Act proving a farce, Johnson had introduced another civil rights bill in January 1959. His new bill, born of a need to portray himself anew in a softer light to Northern politicians, would extend the life of the Civil Rights Commission, establish a federal Community Relations Service, authorize federal prosecution of bombings, and provide federal courts with the right to subpoena witnesses and records in voting-rights cases.

Johnson's many veto problems with Eisenhower had kept this bill on ice in the 1959 session, but when 1960 came, he issued a statement vowing Senate action on civil rights by February 15. Senator Russell complicated matters by insisting there would be no additional civil rights measures; Senator Douglas, by calling for the passage of Part III, omitted from the 1957 Act; and Attorney General William Rogers, by sending Congress a bill to have federal judges appoint federal referees to determine whether individuals had not been permitted to register to vote because of racial discrimination.

Late in January Johnson used his civil rights bill as the reason for a three-day foray into Illinois and New York, into the land he called the centers of "Northern bigotry." If Kennedy was at first concerned that this short trip heralded the beginning of a long campaigning effort by Johnson for Northern delegates, he was soon relieved, for his majority leader raced through a series of luncheon and dinner speeches on civil rights in his continuing strategy to pose as a statesman-legislator who had to get back to Washington to do his job. Even in this limited arena, reports did not rate Johnson's performance highly: He appeared uncomfortable, and his speeches lacked the content and polish that the dozens of Kennedy professors and speechwriters put into the Bostonian's speeches. A novelty to the Northern audiences he addressed was his frequent use of sayings "My Daddy told me." He also used Sam Johnson to show he was not a Johnny-Come-Lately to civil rights. "My Daddy, looking down upon us from heaven, fought the Ku Klux Klan in Texas," he intoned like a preacher, "and in nineteen and twenty-eight my Daddy was for Al Smith's election."

On February 15—his deadline for starting Senate action on civil rights—Johnson hunched upright and asked for unanimous consent to proceed with the Stella School Bill. This was a minute measure to authorize the leasing of an unused army barracks at Fort Crowder, Missouri, to nearby Stella, whose schoolhouse had burned. When there were no objections, he immediately announced that the civil rights amendments could be offered to the Stella Bill. While almost all Senate civil rights advocates applauded Johnson's strategy, Morse proved the exception by denouncing this as trickery—"I am opposed to legislation by rider," he rasped, joining Russell of the Southern diehards, who condemned Johnson for "lynching orderly procedure."

So the civil rights battle began over an army barracks, and it lasted fifty-three days. Russell had only a force of eighteen Southerners, but they knew how to dance "The Filibuster." Once the various civil rights amendments to the Stella bill were introduced, Russell divided his men in pairs, with each team told to hold the floor for four hours. One man drawled for two hours, and as his replacement entered the chamber, the speaker suggested the absence of a quorum, or a simple majority of the total Senate membership. It generally required at least an hour to round up fifty-one senators to answer when their names were called; and fifty had to be non-

Southerners, because Russell did not want the quorum to be reached without the greatest difficulty. Northerners had to respond to the quorum call because all Senate business was suspended until a quorum was produced.

There was only one way to defeat the Russell strategy, and this was to invoke cloture, or get two-thirds of the senators present to vote for an end to talk and the taking of the "Ayes and Noes" on the amendments in question. After a few weeks this became the goal of the Paul Douglas liberals who had introduced their own strong measure, which would make the full power of the federal government available to enforce school integration and all other civil rights. But when Douglas asked Johnson and Minority Leader Dirksen for aid to bring cloture and take up his civil rights additions to the Stella School Bill, both leaders revealed their unwillingness to insure passage of the Douglas measure by opposing cloture. However, Douglas went ahead on his own and to defeat, for his cloture failed even to get a majority, let alone the two-thirds he needed, because of this leadership combination with Russell's filibusterers.

On February 29 Johnson undertook his own plan for breaking the filibuster, and this was to put the Senate in continuous, around-the-clock session. Cots were installed in the cloakrooms and in offices in order that senators could answer quorum calls in the middle of the night. This total Senate day approach lasted through March 8, and throughout its existence, it proved a nightmare for those favoring civil rights legislation. For every two hours when the suggestion came from a Russell man that there was no quorum, the agonized opponents of the filibuster had to drag themselves onto the Senate floor.

Mike Mansfield blamed this Johnson strategy for the eventual defeat of the liberal proposals. "We debated civil rights shaven and unshaven. We debated it without ties, with hair awry, and even in bedroom slippers. In the end we wound up with compromise legislation. And it was not the fresh and well-rested opponents of the civil rights measures who were compelled to the compromise. It was, rather, the exhausted, sleep-starved, quorum-confounded proponents who were only too happy to take it."

What Russell would permit to pass was an innocuous bill establishing the federal referee device to enlarge Negro registration in the South—but only for federal elections. Other provisions extended the life of the Civil Rights Commission and made it a federal crime for anyone to make bomb threats by mail, telephone, or telegraph. The Douglas proposals would have to wait until 1964 and 1965. Yet despite the sorry legislation, when Eisenhower signed it into law on May 6, most newspapers in the North editorialized in its favor and praised Johnson as its father.

To round out the statesman's approach for his Presidential quest, Johnson wanted desperately to gain some public recognition that year as an influential figure in foreign relations. Bill White tried to portray him as a man able to cut through the sham and rituals of world affairs. "When a genuinely sticky world problem was on the agenda" of the Foreign Relations Committee, White claimed, his friend Lyndon would modestly slip into the end seat of the committee table and listen attentively to the talk back and forth between the Secretary of State and committee members. When he saw that the discussion was leading nowhere, said White, he would throw aside "his spurious meekness, loudly clear his throat, and say, 'Now, Mr. Chairman, if I may just butt in here a moment!' He would fix the witness with a cold eye and demand: 'Now, Mr. Secretary, to cut this down to some size [meaning to cut the cackle], what you are really saying is this, is it not?' The witness, who had not meant to be nearly so blunt, and would certainly not have been required to be in Johnson's absence, would look both pained and reluctantly approving of his interrogator's instinct for reaching the kernel of the business. Then he would say, 'Well, yes, Senator.' "

But Bill White's press agentry was not sufficient; for what he needed was a hot, current issue with which the public could identify him.

He believed he had this in May 1960 when Eisenhower and Khrushchev had an unpleasant encounter. The background was this: For six years the Eisenhower foreign policy had been the Dulles foreign policy. The Secretary of State had sought to satisfy his mania for paper alliances and treaties to contain the Communist bloc. After Dulles' death in 1959, Eisenhower tried his own approach to foreign affairs, and this was the use of personal diplomacy to further peace.

In December 1959 he made a twenty-two-thousand-mile trip in *Air Force One* on a goodwill mission through Italy, Turkey, Pakistan, Afghanistan, India, Iran, Greece, Morocco, Spain, and France. He talked privately to the leaders and made public speeches to crowds as large as a half million (in New Delhi), promoting the theme of "Peace and Friendship in Freedom." Then in February 1960 he continued his goodwill touring with a fifteen-thousand-mile trip through Argentina, Brazil, Chile, and Uruguay.

There were to be two major events that year, a Summit Meeting set for Paris on May 15 and an Eisenhower visit to the Soviet Union that summer. However, on May 1 Eisenhower's peace offensive fell apart when an American turbojet plane was shot down over Sverdlovsk in the Urals, twelve hundred miles inside Soviet borders. The plane was a U-2, a speedy craft flying at eighty thousand feet and capable of taking immensely clear day and night photographs. At first, the State Department claimed that the spy plane was a weather plane that had wandered off its course. Next, when the wreckage and the captured pilot were photographed for the world's press and the location of capture noted, the White House lamely said the flight had not been authorized. Finally, when several Democrats charged that Eisenhower did not know what his own Administration was doing, he admitted he had authorized the spy flight as "a distasteful but vital necessity."

Rumors spread that Khrushchev would call off the Summit Meeting, but he traveled to Paris as though he meant to go through with the conference despite the U-2 incident. Here, while Khrushchev rained insults on Eisenhower, Johnson conceived a plan to involve himself in the situation. Adlai Stevenson was testifying before the Senate Commerce Committee on his proposal that the FCC waive its rules so that the three networks would donate free time for debates between the Presidential nominees in the coming campaign. Johnson asked him to come along to a Capitol meeting with Sam Rayburn and Senator Fulbright to save the Paris conference. Newsmen noted that front-runner Kennedy was not invited.

The four, led by Johnson, proceeded to write a cablegram to Khrushchev, sternly requesting him not to "torpedo the conference." Then, instead of sending it to the Soviet leader, Johnson dispatched the cable to Eisenhower with instructions to deliver it to Khrushchev. By that time Khrushchev had broken up the conference and canceled the Eisenhower trip to the Soviet Union, labeling the President "a thief caught red-handed in his theft."

Added to Eisenhower's chagrin was the cablegram, and his reaction was one of compressed-lips anger as he charged the four Democrats with attempting "to interfere in the day-to-day conduct of foreign relations." Secretary of State Christian Herter caught the brunt of the Presidential indignation by being ordered to call Johnson "to ask whether the authors desired to withdraw the cable." Even though the conference was over before it began, Johnson nevertheless told Herter that he still wanted the cablegram delivered. Unaware that Johnson intended to use the cable to prove his own role in world affairs, Eisenhower expressed amazement at the seeming pointlessness of the Johnson demand. But he had the sheet of paper sent to the Soviet Embassy in Paris, and Johnson could now tell of his effort to save the Summit Meeting.

But when Eisenhower returned home with the full sympathy of the press, and one hundred and forty congressmen lined the airport apron to express their loyalty, Johnson chose the opposite tack. This gave him the opportunity also to strike at Kennedy, who had expressed regret "that the flight [the U-2] did take place," and that Eisenhower should not have permitted its flight so near to the time of the Paris Summit. Strongly hinting that Kennedy favored appeasing the Communists, Johnson bellowed out during several speeches at that time, "I am not prepared to apologize to Khrushchev—are you?" Then at a political dinner, where Kennedy bemoaned the loss of the Summit Meeting because of the U-2 incident, Johnson attempted to flatten him with "I'm not much of a summit man."

PART SIX

A Profitable Vice Presidency

Chapter 55

WHILE THE PRESIDENTIAL race heated up, Johnson continued to hold unswervingly to his strategy that he was "minding the store" as his patriotic duty. "This country can't stand, the party can't stand, the Senate can't stand having three active Presidential candidates in the Senate—of whom one is the majority leader," he cast aspersions on his rivals who were racing about the country. "I simply cannot be a real candidate: I can't get away from here to do all the speech-making and delegation-hunting that would be necessary. I have simply got to stay here and mind the store."

The storekeeper candidate read in the papers in March that Kennedy had won the New Hampshire primary. Then on April 5 Kennedy proceeded to sweep two-thirds of Wisconsin's delegates into his convention bucket in a surprise victory over Hubert Humphrey. Hubert had said he would withdraw from the Presidential contest if he lost in Wisconsin, but after charging that the Kennedy clan had bought that primary, he entered the May 10 primary in West Virginia, a state that was 97 per cent Protestant.

Kennedy's gains were also coming from other directions. In Ohio, for instance, Governor Mike DiSalle committed his state's sixty-four convention votes to the young candidate; in Arizona, Representative Stewart Udall "stole" the state convention from benign Carl Hayden's friends in April and transferred the expected seventeen Johnson votes into the Kennedy column. Mister Sam was angry enough with these actions, but what infuriated him was the partisanship of the supposedly impartial National Committee chairman, Paul Butler, who publicly declared that a Kennedy victory in Wisconsin portended his nomination in July—perhaps on the first ballot.

Mister Sam's regret was that he was not younger than his seventy-eight years at a time when his protégé needed him most. At the coming Democratic National Convention in the Los Angeles Sports Arena he would be unable to help Johnson, for he was no longer permanent chairman. No more would he be the towering figure of control on the convention's rostrum. In an effort to salvage what he could from the situation, he had promoted Lyndon's friend Congressman Hale Boggs of Louisiana as his successor, but the post had gone instead to Governor LeRoy Collins of Florida.

Although Rayburn was by now concerned with the Kennedy trend, he was still unable to convince Johnson of the urgent need to declare his candidacy and forget about the Senate. During the April Easter recess Johnson was back on his ranch studying the political polls and the delegate tabulations that crammed his pockets. So far as he could tell, Mister Sam was overanxious. One poll said he would easily defeat Nixon, and all the delegate tabulations he had compiled himself gave him between five hundred and five hundred and fifty delegates, even if he did no campaigning. His friends in the South were good for three hundred and nineteen votes; border state delegates should total one hundred and ten; and the Midwest and West should give him a scattering sum of at least a hundred. While the total was still a few hundred under the seven hundred and sixty-one votes necessary to carry the convention, it should serve as an excellent base on later ballots, when the favorite son candidates did their switching.

Nevertheless, despite his tabulated totals, Johnson sought to please Rayburn by spending the weekend of April 23 on a swing through Colorado, Wyoming, Utah, and Nevada for talks with politicians. And when he returned to his Taj Mahal in the Capitol, he told visitors he would accept "Sonny Boy," as he and his Senate friends called Kennedy, as his running mate. "I can see it all now," said one of Johnson's aides, caught up in the sweep of the senator's optimism. "Johnson will be standing in the hotel room after he wins the nomination, and he'll say, 'We want Sonny Boy for Vice President. Go fetch him for me.' "

But by the first week in May Johnson's spirits were dampened. The Kennedys were spending so much money in West Virginia that a Kennedy upset seemed in the making. There was talk that even Boston's Cardinal Cushing was contributing money to Protestant churches in the Mountain State in order to lessen anti-Catholic feeling. At this point Johnson considered it politic to add an anti-Kennedy tone to the primary to help poor, beleaguered Humphrey, and he went on a two-day speaking tour that carried him to East Liverpool, Ohio; Pittsburgh, Pennsylvania; and Clarksburg, West Virginia. He was so well received in West Virginia that it was apparent he would have held an edge over Kennedy had he entered the primary instead of Humphrey. But he hadn't, and when Kennedy was an easy victor over the Minnesotan, Kennedy was suddenly the front runner, far out in the lead.

Faced with a twenty-thousand-dollar campaign debt and his withdrawal from the Presidential contest, Humphrey said bitterly, "Bobby Kennedy said if they had to spend a half million to win here they would do it. Anyone who gets in the way of papa's pet is going to be destroyed."

Mister Sam hoped that Lyndon would announce after he won his own renomination to the Senate in the May 7 Texas primary. But the storekeeper candidate would not; nor would he after the State Democratic Convention at Austin in June, where he won all sixty-one delegates to the national convention, a pledge that Presidential electors would vote for the ticket, the denial of a seat in the convention delegation to Senator Yarborough, and the ouster of his enemy, Mrs. Frankie Randolph, from her post as national committeewoman.

As Kennedy continued to win primaries, Mister Sam, now sinkingly worried that it was almost too late, went ahead on his own and asked John Connally to establish a national headquarters in Washington for Lyndon. Connally organized the Citizens-for-Johnson Committee, with Truman's former Secretary of the Interior, Oscar Chapman, and the former head of the National Committee's Women's Division, Mrs. India Edwards, as official heads. So while Johnson remained an unofficial candidate, Connally from the Ambassador Hotel headquarters began what he believed was the only way to stop the Kennedy drive. This was to use some good old time-tested Texas campaign tactics on the young Massachusetts senator. He was an "absentee senator," too young, sick, inexperienced, a sure loser against Nixon. Sure, he looked healthy, Connally told the press, but Jack had a fatal disease.

Truman joined the questioning of Kennedy's candidacy in a nationally televised news conference in which he endorsed Symington and praised Johnson. Kennedy was not ready for the country, and the country was not ready for Kennedy, Truman charged. "We need a man with the greatest possible maturity and experience. May I urge you to be patient?"

Kennedy reacted to Truman by assembling data about young men in history who had held power. As for the Connally outpouring, Kennedy told friends that Johnson was the "riverboat gambler . . . in ruffles and a long black coat . . . and aces up his sleeve."

In June Johnson made his last small effort at campaigning by embarking on a five-day flight by private plane through the West and then back into New York and New Jersey. Everywhere he stopped, he pleaded one point: Delegates who were not legally bound to vote for Kennedy should shift their votes to Johnson at the convention. He also tried to counterattack the successful Kennedy line that opposition to the Massachusetts senator necessarily meant religious prejudice. As Johnson argued in Newark, "I told a friend of Jack's last week, we Protestants have proved we'll vote for a Catholic. Now we want you Catholics to prove you can vote for a Protestant."

When Johnson was back in his Capitol Taj Mahal, Kennedy insiders passed word to friendly reporters that Johnson was engaged in blackmailing Kennedy supporters. They charged that he had held a two-hour talk with Representative Lee Metcalf of Montana, who was running for the seat vacated by Senator Jim Murray, and had warned Metcalf that unless he switched his support from Kennedy to him, he would receive no money from the Senate Democratic Campaign Committee. They charged further that Johnson had called Iowa's Governor Herschel Loveless, who was also a Senatorial candidate, and told him he could expect the worst possible Senate committee assignments if he dropped his favorite son role at the convention and threw his state's twenty-six votes to Kennedy.

Not until July 5—five days before the national convention was to meet in Los Angeles—did Johnson finally declare himself an official candidate. He and Rayburn had recessed Congress from July 3 until August 8 for the Senate and August 15 for the House; and by the timing of his announcement after the recess began, he pointedly showed how steadfastly he had held to his Senate duties. But in case anyone had forgotten why he had run so shadowy and inept a campaign, he had this to offer reporters: "Those who have engaged in active campaigns since January have missed hundreds of votes. This I could not do—for my country or my party. Someone has to tend the store."

At the end of the first week in July 1960 Mister Sam climbed into his 1955 Plymouth and rode to the train station near his home in Bonham for the trip to the Los Angeles slander and libel contest in convention hall. "Jack could win it on the first ballot," he told an interviewer sadly before leaving. Truman had held another nationally televised news conference in which he said there was no point in holding the convention because it would be a "prearranged mockery controlled by one candidate."

Mister Sam's heavy heart was occasioned by the fact that his protégé had failed to work out a deal with Adlai Stevenson to derail the Kennedy express. Johnson had met privately in Washington for conversations with the former Illinois governor on this very question, but Stevenson would not agree to Johnson's tactics, even though he considered Kennedy a "parvenu . . . calculating and cocksure," and said so openly even to Kennedy's friends. Stevenson later spoke about these "stop Kennedy" talks with Johnson "with some amusement" and referred to them as "a series of profane discussions" by the Texan, who wanted "to form a political alliance." What Johnson proposed was that Stevenson tell his supporters to back Johnson at first and if Johnson saw he could not win the nomination himself, he would then throw his own delegate strength to Stevenson. Certainly the two could easily "take" that blankety-blank Kennedy, said Johnson, and he wailed to Stevenson, "I can't stand to be pushed around by that forty-two-year-old kid." Stevenson, however, while commiserating with him, remained aloof, and the reason became clear on July 8, when he said he would accept a draft by the convention for his third nomination.

There was another reason why Stevenson had refused to form a Johnson alliance. It could have been arranged only over the strong opposition of Stevenson's chief supporter, Mrs. Roosevelt, who would be against his close association with Johnson, even to stop Kennedy, whom she disliked as much. In 1935 she had been pleased by Johnson's appointment to head the Texas NYA, but by mid-1960 she had a strong distaste for him. On a nationwide TV show earlier that year she had hit at him as a politician operating without a program or ideals by describing him as "one of the ablest people at maneuvering that we have in the party."

Once when Mary Lasker, widow of the advertising tycoon, argued that Johnson was really "a secret liberal," her blunt reply was, "You're crazy!" Another time, when her son Jimmy invited Johnson to be the speaker at the Hyde Park rose garden memorial exercises for her late husband, Mrs. Roosevelt told Jimmy he had made an unfortunate choice.

Rayburn had advised Johnson to rush to Los Angeles as soon as he made his announcement so that he would have at least a few days to combat the Kennedy army before the convention began. But again Johnson wasted precious time before catching the plane from Baltimore's Friendship Airport. And by the time Mister Sam arrived in Los Angeles, it was common knowledge that Kennedy aides were already operating within each state delegation to increase his votes. In addition, the elder Kennedy was in control of the convention's machinery from his hideaway in the rented Marion Davies mansion. When reporters spied Rayburn, they asked if he had seen Joe Kennedy, and his reply was, "I haven't seen him, but he's in the bushes around here."

The Johnson suite on the seventh floor of the Biltmore lay two flights below Jack Kennedy's and a floor below the large suite at 8315 where Bobby Kennedy directed his brother's dealings with delegations and leaders. From his suite Johnson had ordered a half-ton of taffy flown in from Austin to be passed out by his "red, white, and blue girls" in the Biltmore lobby. In addition his friends paid fifty thousand dollars for a full-page newspaper ad in his behalf. But it was already evident to him that only a slim chance remained that Kennedy might not win the nomination on the first ballot.

Too little, too late, he began a mad scramble, dashing from delegation to delegation to disclose Kennedy's poor Senate record both as a legislation innovator and as an absentee. He also hit at Kennedy's wealth, even though his own holdings rivaled the ten million dollars the elder Kennedy had given his son. "I haven't had anything given to me"—he told delegations to consider the superiority of the self-made man over the born-rich man. "Whatever I have and whatever I hope to get will be because of whatever energy and talents I have." In addition, he brought up Joe Kennedy as a sinister pro-Hitlerite who strongly influenced his son. "I don't want any Chamberlain umbrella man!" he yelled at the Washington state caucus, referring to Kennedy's role as ambassador to Great Britain when Neville Chamberlain was Prime Minister. Other Johnson aides were quick to join the innuendo campaign against Kennedy on all these scores, but it was John

Connally and India Edwards who again threw up a medical scaresheet by asserting that Kennedy suffered from Addison's disease and was kept alive only through injections of cortisone.

However, with his computed majority of delegates, Kennedy never lost his aplomb or ridiculing wit. "I asked Jack to talk to the Florida delegation," said Senator George Smathers, who was his state's favorite son candidate. "Jack knew I favored Lyndon for the nomination because I thought Lyndon was better qualified. Jack came, and after I introduced him, he told the delegation, 'I was feeling pretty good until lately. George has been a friend of mine a long time: We were elected to the House together; and he was the best man at my wedding. [Smathers was an usher at Kennedy's wedding.] The only thing about him is that he's never given me the right advice.

" 'In 1952, he said, "Don't run for the Senate. You can't beat Lodge." In 1956, he wanted to nominate me for Vice President. He said I would win. In the Wisconsin primary, he said, "Don't do it. Humphrey will beat you." In West Virginia, he said, "Humphrey will kill you down there." So I ran. I felt good until now when he told me that I'd get the Presidential nomination.' "

A desperate Johnson pushed Kennedy into a debate before the joint Texas-Massachusetts delegations. On the Senate floor Johnson had always held the upper hand with Kennedy, and he believed he would show him up as an innocuous young politician now. But he found himself in error, for Kennedy did not operate under Senate strictures.

When he attacked Kennedy for following the reactionary farm policies of Eisenhower's Secretary of Agriculture, Ezra Taft Benson, Kennedy made him sound like a nitpicker. "I don't think I will argue," he said softly, "because I don't think Senator Johnson and I disagree on the great issues that face us."

As for Johnson's charge that he had missed every quorum call during the 1960 filibuster on civil rights, while Johnson had answered all fifty, he passed this off flippantly with the comment that Johnson was apparently "talking of some other candidate, not me." He also said in a paternalistic tone with a beaming grin, "I want to commend him for a wonderful record answering those quorum calls." Since few present knew what a quorum call was, Johnson seemed to be a small-minded debater. Then in answer to Johnson's chief theme, that he was far better qualified to be President because of his long service as majority leader, Kennedy produced a wave of laughter by retorting, "I came here today full of admiration for Senator Johnson, full of affection for him, strongly in support of him—for majority leader."

Hubert Humphrey was the most dejected figure at the convention. Having come as a primary candidate twice beaten by Kennedy, he was being further tortured by Kennedy aides urging him to support the Massachusetts senator. The climax to this pressuring came on Tuesday, July 12, said Humphrey, when Bobby Kennedy rushed up to him, jabbed a stiff index finger hard against his ribs, and warned, "Hubert, we want your announcement and the pledge of the Minnesota delegation today—or else!" Humphrey said he "jabbed a finger back at Bobby's chest and retorted, 'Bobby, go to hell!' "

If he could not get the nomination himself, Humphrey wanted it to go to Johnson, and so did Humphrey's fellow Minnesotan, Senator Eugene McCarthy. But at the instigation of Johnson, who believed that Stevenson would be a better rallying force than he on the first ballot, Humphrey announced for Stevenson, while McCarthy agreed to make the nominating speech for the former Illinois governor.

The time for nominations came at last. This would be Mister Sam's and Eleanor Roosevelt's last Democratic convention, and the two old pros drew tremendous applause from delegates and galleries. On Tuesday Mrs. Roosevelt made an impassioned speech for Stevenson and asked the delegates to pause and think about the nation's future before voting lightly. On Wednesday Rayburn put Johnson in nomination, calling him "a tall, sun-crowned man who stands ready now to lead America." By this time McCarthy was worked up in his belief that the former governor was by far the best candidate, and his speech for Stevenson was judged the finest nominating oration in decades.

But at eleven that same evening it was all finished. Kennedy emerged the victor on the first ballot with 806 votes. Johnson was second with 409; then came Symington with 86; and Stevenson trailed with 79½.

When the significance of the vote hit Mister Sam, his face screwed up into deepest disappointment, and tears coursed down his cheeks. Later, after regaining a semblance of control over his emotions, he told reporters, "Of course I'll support Mr. Kennedy. That's the Democratic way—and I'm a Democrat."

Governor Price Daniel, his fists clenched tightly, could not speak because of the outrage he felt. Wright Patman was flabbergasted. "We didn't realize how many votes Kennedy had in his pocket," he said. On the seventh floor of the Biltmore, where Lady Bird and Lyndon watched the balloting, their unhappiness permeated the room.

On the day before the convention opened, George Smathers had approached Johnson to ask if he would accept the Vice Presidential nomination should he lose the Presidential contest. "I wouldn't want to trade a vote for a gavel," Johnson had replied.

The possibility that he might make himself subservient to Kennedy seemed preposterous to many of Johnson's friends. In the Senate they had watched him treat Kennedy for years as a junior protégé, and for the past year and a half, as the Kennedy machine developed, he had spoken with increasing acerbity about the audacity of the younger senator to run for President. Then at the convention the Johnson bitterness, which developed during their confrontation at the Massachusetts-Texas delegations meeting, had appeared to burgeon into full warfare that same evening, when the two spoke to the South Carolina delegation. Afterward Johnson was wild with rage, because Kennedy had unmercifully ridiculed him, and an observer said he had grabbed Kennedy by the shoulder and set his nose against his as he screamed, "Jack, if you don't stop acting the way you are, we're liable to have to support that little fellow we nominated in fifty-two and fifty-six." Kennedy had torn himself loose, smiled weakly, and left the room without answering.

After Kennedy was nominated on Wednesday night, July 13, Mister Sam, having recovered his dignity, telephoned Johnson because he had a premonition. "They are going to try to get you to go on the ticket," he said gruffly. "You mustn't do it. It would be a terrible thing to do. Turn it down."

"Nothing will happen," Johnson assured him. He told Rayburn he had not been asked, did not expect to be asked, and if he were he would not make any decision without Mister Sam's approval.

But Johnson had already given thought to the Vice Presidency as a way out of a coming crisis. "Had Lyndon returned to the Senate as majority leader in 1961," Senator Vance Hartke later remarked, "he knew he would have been stripped of his power. The growing revolt against his leadership was approaching success."

Said Senator Russell Long, in an off-the-record aside to a reporter, "Lyndon was living on borrowed time as a strong majority leader. Those guys would have pinned his hide to the wall. His methods were suited only to a small majority that has to stick together for mutual protection."

Two days before his nomination Kennedy had received two visitors at his North Rossmore apartment hideaway who came to ask that he take Johnson as his running mate. This pair of busybody prince-makers were Philip Graham, the bright, high-strung son-in-law of the late Eugene Meyer, who had purchased the Washington *Post,* and Joe Alsop, the Roosevelt cousin and romanticist of wars in his syndicated column. Graham, who spoke for the two, said that Kennedy had agreed to accept Johnson "so immediately, as to leave me doubting the easy triumph." Alsop later said his impression was that Kennedy was not that enthusiastic—perhaps "about 80 per cent" convinced. Nor did Johnson sound convinced that Kennedy wanted him, when the conversation was passed on to him.

After his nomination when Kennedy returned to his hideaway he found a warm, congratulatory telegram from Johnson. He made his move the next morning at eight-thirty, on his return to the ninth-floor Biltmore suite, by calling Johnson. Lady Bird answered. "At first I had a mind to say, whoever it was, that he was sleeping, and I didn't want to awaken him, but when he said it was Mr. Kennedy, I felt that I certainly must, and so I said 'Just a minute' and put Lyndon on," Lady Bird afterward recalled that Thursday morning.

Kennedy said he wanted to come down to Johnson's suite for a talk. Johnson said he would go to Kennedy's suite. Finally, Kennedy asserted his new authority and said he would come down at nine-thirty. When Johnson hung up, Lady Bird told him, "I know he's going to offer the Vice Presidency, and I hope you won't take it."

As soon as he leaped from bed and began dressing, Johnson remembered his pledge to Rayburn, and he called him. "Turn it down," Mister Sam repeated, when Lyndon told him Kennedy was coming to discuss the Vice Presidency. Johnson also called Homer Thornberry. Homer answered with his face lathered for his morning shave, and when his boyhood friend explained the situation, Homer advised: "I wouldn't touch it with a ten-foot pole. Tell Jack anything you want, but don't take it." But a few minutes later, while Homer stood shaving, he told his image in the mirror, "I don't have any right to tell Lyndon he shouldn't become Vice President." He called Johnson back and told him his new view, and Johnson said glumly, "But Homer, what'll I tell Mister Sam?"

Kennedy came at 10 A.M., and he and Johnson sat down on a sofa for their talk. It was a ludicrous scene, with Kennedy, who had been "Sonny Boy" the day before, now talking down paternalistically to Johnson, and Johnson playing the role of subservience. "Jack started by telling me he had said many times that he thought I was the best qualified man for the Presidency by experience," said Johnson long afterward. "But he went on to say that as a Southerner I couldn't be nominated. He said he felt that I should be the one who would succeed if anything happened to him."

Kennedy's memory was that when Johnson talked enthusiastically about the Vice Presidency as a worthwhile office, he had been "astonished." As he explained the scene to a friend, "I didn't offer the Vice Presidency to him . . . he grabbed at it."

But Kennedy should not have been astonished, for even his lack of straightforwardness could not obscure the reason for his visit. He knew and Johnson knew that he had no other purpose in paying this early call than to discuss the Vice Presidency. Nor should he have blinked his eyes in surprise when Johnson first said he wanted the Vice Presidential nomination and then fell back into the political routine of saying he would have to think it over for a few hours. He asked Kennedy for the names of others he might choose if he turned him down, and Kennedy blurted that his next choice was Governor Orville Freeman of Minnesota, while other alternatives were Symington and "Scoop" Jackson.

By now Kennedy was on the defensive, and he wanted to know who opposed Johnson's acceptance of the Vice Presidential nomination. When Johnson replied, "Lady Bird and Mister Sam," Kennedy asked if Rayburn had personal animosity toward him. Rumors had spread through the Sports Arena that Rayburn had remarked that "a Catholic couldn't and shouldn't become President." Johnson's reply was that Mister Sam's opposition was not to Kennedy but to Johnson's relinquishing the important post of majority leader. Kennedy finally left, promising, "I'll call you back in two or three hours."

When Kennedy walked back into his own suite, he startled his aides and family members when he closed the door behind him and exclaimed, "You just won't believe it. . . . He wants it!"

Word flew to Southern governors and senators of the Kennedy proposal, and Johnson's suite was soon a madhouse, with his friends arguing that he must not accept. Price Daniel said it would be fatal because "we in the South just can't carry this boy [Kennedy]." The party platform that Chester Bowles, a Kennedy man, had put over on the convention was just too much of a burden, Daniel added. Among the planks were declarations to close such "tax loopholes as depletion allowances," to enforce racial integration, and to end "unfair" restrictions on labor. Besides listening to the frenetic pleas in his room, Johnson also made several phone calls for advice. One to Cactus Jack Garner down in Uvalde brought this estimation: "I'll tell you, Lyndon, the Vice Presidency isn't worth a pitcher of warm spit."

Someone told Wright Patman that Price Daniel was looking for him. "When I saw him," said Patman, "he told me what was going on, and the way he put it, 'Sam Rayburn is stopping Lyndon from taking the Vice Presidential nomination.'"

As one of the old lookouts for the welfare of Sam Johnson's boy, Patman stormed into Rayburn's suite. "Sam was in the bathroom in his shorts, and he was shaving," Patman recounted. "He was blistering mad about Lyndon's even considering the Vice Presidency, and he shouted at me, 'It will ruin him for the future.'"

"That isn't so, Sam," Patman replied. "It's the second biggest office in the United States next to the President. No man can turn it down."

"Others were after Rayburn, too," said Patman later, "and he changed his mind before the morning ended."

Once word reached Kennedy that the speaker was resigned to Johnson's taking second place, he arranged to call on him. The old man saw that the young nominee "looked a little flustered," and he led him to a corner of the room, looking unblinkingly into Kennedy's eyes while listening to his arguments for including Lyndon on the ticket. Kennedy said he wanted a united party behind him, and he promised to give the Vice President important domestic duties and send him on trips abroad.

"Well," said Mister Sam when he finished, "up until thirty minutes ago I was against it, and I have withheld a final decision until I could really find out what was in your heart. You know, Jack, I am a very old man . . . in the twilight of my life, walking down into the valley. My career is behind me, but Lyndon is only approaching the summit of his. I am afraid I was trying to keep him in the legislative end where he could help me. Now the way you explain it, I can see that you need him more. . . . Lyndon is a good soldier and he will hear the call of duty. I yield on one condition . . . that you go on the radio or television and tell the people you came to us and asked for this thing." Kennedy agreed.

When Kennedy left, Mister Sam telephoned Johnson. "Lyndon, you've got to go on the ticket," he said resignedly.

"But last night you told me that whatever happened, I shouldn't. What's made you change your mind?" Johnson teased him.

"I'm a wiser man this morning than I was last night," Rayburn said. "Besides, that other feller Nixon called me a traitor, and I don't want a man who calls me a traitor to be President. We've got to beat him, and you've got to do everything you can to help."

Following his visit to Rayburn, Kennedy was plagued by second thoughts about having Johnson on the ticket, despite his outright promise to Mister Sam. On the positive side, he had counted fewer than a dozen Southern delegates who had voted for his nomination out of the 319 votes in the Southern bloc, and Johnson on the ticket could certainly attract vitally needed electoral votes in the cotton and molasses country. But on the negative side the ADA and labor unions had been shrieking against Johnson for so many years that his inclusion on the ticket would be interpreted by them as a cynical deal. Before the Presidential nomination, United Auto Workers boss Walter Reuther had begged Mrs. Roosevelt to get Stevenson to support Kennedy and "keep Johnson from slipping in." Furthermore, Johnson had always treated Kennedy as an inferior—and why should he change merely because Kennedy held the upper half of the ticket? He could become an immense troublemaker.

To add to Kennedy's indecisiveness, he saw that the Johnson matter had thrown almost all his assistants into a condition of shock. They had joined in the ridicule of Johnson so long during the campaign pull that they could not believe Kennedy might be serious. Nor could labor leaders and liberals believe it when the news reached them.

As a prime delegation, Walter Reuther, his lawyer Arthur Goldberg, and Alex Rose, the Hatters Union boss and leader of the New York Liberal Party, called on Kennedy and "violently and vehemently objected to Johnson" because he would drive the Negro vote away from the Democrats. Furthermore, they predicted a mutiny on the convention floor if Johnson's candidacy were pushed by Kennedy, and their suggestion was that at this late hour he should word his offer to Johnson in such an insulting way that Johnson would have to turn it down. When Kennedy asked Goldberg how George Meany, head of the AFL-CIO, felt about Johnson, Goldberg frowned and said that Meany was in a rage over him, charging Johnson with having tried "to use his control over labor legislation" as majority leader to force Meany "into neutrality." But Goldberg admitted that no matter who shared the ticket with Kennedy, labor would have no choice except to support the Democratic party.

While the liberal-labor tempest boiled over, three hours passed, and instead of calling Johnson as he had promised, Kennedy sent his brother

Bobby to discuss the revolt with Johnson. Rayburn was there, and he talked to Bobby, but he told the young man that Lyndon would speak only to his big brother.

There were further revolts in Northern state delegations, hysteria in the corridors and over telephones, exchanges of rumors in the dining halls. Phil Graham had Kennedy's private phone number and he reached him by telephone. Bluntly Graham wanted to know why he hadn't phoned Johnson, who was expecting his promised call. Kennedy was hesitant and apologetically replied that he "was in a general mess because some of the liberals were against Johnson." Graham called him later and this time Kennedy asked his advice about Johnson. "It's too late to be mind-changing," Graham claimed he replied, "and remember, you ain't no Adlai."

Resigned at this point to the necessity of ending the convention chaos, Kennedy then called Johnson, who sat on his bed and listened while Kennedy read a draft statement announcing his selection as the Vice Presidential nominee. Kennedy told him he planned to make it public at 4 P.M. When he finished, Johnson asked point-blank whether Kennedy *really* wanted him on the ticket, and with a reply that this was so, Johnson said he would be his running mate.

But the gruesome day was not yet over. Before the last Graham call, Kennedy had sent Bobby to tell Johnson that if he were hesitant to become the nominee, he should withdraw because of the liberal opposition. Bobby did not arrive until after the phone pact was settled between his brother and Johnson, and without knowledge of that, Bobby painted a picture of an "ugly floor fight" to Johnson and suggested that he withdraw for the sake of the party and its fall campaign. When Bobby offered to guarantee appointment of Johnson to the chairmanship of the Democratic National Committee if he withdrew, Mister Sam yelled out, "Shit!" "I want to be Vice President," Johnson told Bobby.

After Bobby left and Johnson was immediately enveloped by fears that the Kennedys were making a fool of him, his young assistant Billie Moyers, who knew Phil Graham had Kennedy's private phone number, found Graham and brought him to Johnson's room. When Graham came, Johnson wailed out his tale of confusion and when he finished, Rayburn ordered Graham to call Kennedy. Several delegates from Hawaii were in Johnson's bedroom, and Lyndon had to ask them to leave so that Graham could call.

Graham's memory of the scene was that "L.B.J. seemed about to jump out of his skin." "Jack," he said when the call went through, "Bobby is down here and is telling the speaker and Lyndon that there is opposition and that Lyndon should withdraw."

"Oh," said Kennedy, "that's all right. Bobby's been out of touch and doesn't know what's been happening."

"Well, what do you want Lyndon to do?" Graham asked.

"I want him to make a statement right away. I've just finished making mine."

Graham told him to speak again to Johnson, and when he handed the receiver to him, Johnson lay sprawled over the bed. "Yes . . . yes . . . yes," he said into the phone at intervals. Kennedy was telling him he had already told reporters that Johnson would be the Vice Presidential nominee.

While Graham had been putting through the call, Bobby Baker was sent to find Bobby Kennedy and bring him into Johnson's bedroom. When they returned, Bobby Kennedy spoke to his brother. "Well, it's too late now," he said, before half slamming down the phone.

With the subject now settled beyond recall, Lyndon and Lady Bird walked into the hall, stood on chairs before the sweaty crush of reporters and cameras, and he read his statement accepting the Vice Presidential nomination. Then he signified the complete change in his relations with Kennedy since the week began by going to Kennedy's suite, where he pledged "total commitment" to his new leader. Afterward, Johnson confessed, he fell into a deep depression.

There was still the task of winning the approval of the convention. The Kennedy-Johnson announcements were taken with poor grace by several Northern delegations and a name-calling floor fight loomed. But probable floor disorders were avoided because of a scheme hatched by House Majority Leader John McCormack and Governor Collins, who was presiding. McCormack called out for a "voice vote" to nominate Johnson by acclamation. There were yells for a state-by-state roll call, but Collins announced from the platform he would ask for the "Ayes" and "Noes" on McCormack's motion. Passage required a two-thirds vote, and though both sides were equally loud, Collins blithely declared: "The motion is adopted and Senator Lyndon B. Johnson of Texas has been nominated for the Vice Presidency of the United States by acclamation."

Afterward Johnson received a note from his old friend Senator Barry Goldwater expressing contempt at his accepting second place to Kennedy. "I'm nauseated," Goldwater wrote.

Chapter 56

MISTER SAM STAYED in Los Angeles long enough to see Lyndon gain the place that neither he nor his protégé really wanted. Johnson's staff and relatives had cried unabashedly, and as Lady Bird's niece put it: "We felt as if he were stepping out of the driver's seat he occupied as majority leader, to take off his coat and pick up the broom." Before he left, Rayburn was also embarrassed by Lyndon's public temper tantrum when Lynda Bird could not be found to take part in the happy family scene on the convention's platform. She had gone to Disneyland, and when she finally turned up long afterward, Lyndon was still so angry that he scolded her sharply.

Once he was back in Bonham, Rayburn had little opportunity for rest because anti-Johnson mail came by the mailsack. Angry Texans wanted an explanation for Johnson's "double cross" in going on a ticket with Kennedy; others questioned the propriety of supporting a Catholic for President. As a Democrat first and last, Rayburn began to develop a public rationalization for Lyndon's lowly position on the ticket and a defense of young Kennedy that carried him over his personal misery.

He had advised Lyndon to give himself no time to brood about the convention, and Johnson took his counsel. On July 17 he and Lady Bird and the Homer Thornberrys flew to Acapulco for a vacation in a house owned by President Mateos of Mexico. Then on his return to the ranch he took thirty-seven Texas editors and reporters on a chartered flight to Hyannis Port, Massachusetts, to the Kennedy family compound at this summer resort.

This was Johnson's first meeting with Kennedy since the convention, and some observers said that he compensated for his reduced status by enlarging his speaking volume and dominating the two-day session with his compulsive talking. His voice was so loud while discussing privately the coming Senate session of August 8 and the post-Labor Day Presidential campaign that reporters wandering in the yard outside heard him distinctly.

At one point during his visit Johnson held a confidential talk with Kennedy's cigar-smoking press secretary, roly-poly Pierre Salinger, to discuss ways to improve his image. Talking through Salinger's advice, Johnson proposed that he be built up as a real-life counterpart of Lady Bird's hero on the TV "Gunsmoke" show. "You know," he told Salinger, whom he called "Peer," "like Marshal Matt Dillon . . . big, six-feet-three, good-looking—a tall, tough Texan coming down the street."

On Saturday, July 30, Kennedy held a joint press conference for the dozens of newsmen on hand. Reporters threw questions at both on the Democratic team but Johnson answered most of their queries as though he were in charge. Finally, when he left for the ranch, some of Kennedy's aides laughed almost hysterically at Johnson's exhibition.

Back home again, Johnson still had not given his friends an explanation of his action at the convention. This came at Blanco on August 3 at a barbecue in his honor. With the temperature dancing above one hundred degrees, he drove up in his cream-colored Thunderbird with Lady Bird and Governor Price Daniel, and ten tanned cowboys astride ponies escorted him inside Blanco State Park. Here the barbecue, turning to a crisp, sizzled in open pits. Red beans in black iron kettles bubbled over fires, and barrels containing pickles and a half ton of onion rings were rapidly being emptied by the five thousand guests.

Mayor Wayne Smith introduced Johnson, while the Vice Presidential nominee gulped down the last tasty morsels handed him at the pavilion. Smith revealed his partiality by throwing a dig at Kennedy. "This is a kangaroo ticket," he told the crowd. "All of its strength is in its back legs."

Johnson made no effort to correct this slur, though he conceded, "I ran for the Presidential nomination and I lost in a fair fight." However, catching sight of the sea of doubting faces before him, he cried out, "When Kennedy asked me to run with him, what was I to do? Say 'No' and return to pout in Texas? I could have taken my baseball bat and gone home. It's not easy to try for first place and get second." But there were some advantages in being on the ticket, even in second place, he argued. This was an excellent place for guarding the 27½ per cent oil depletion allowance and preventing racial desegregation. Then spying a few reporters from national magazines, Johnson changed his course of talk abruptly. "I want it clearly understood that it's a privilege to run with John Kennedy," he said with a smile. "I can tell a man by looking in his eyes. I looked in John Kennedy's eyes and liked what I saw. . . . I didn't run for Vice President, but I have never run from anything."

After the Blanco barbecue Johnson showed up at an Iowa farm meeting where the large Midwestern crowd called repeatedly to him to pour it on with every thrust he made at the Republican party and its candidates, Richard Nixon and Henry Cabot Lodge. He also appeared in Nashville, where an eight-state Democratic rally was in progress. And on August 5 one of the three planes he owned landed at Jones Field in Bonham. Johnson had bought these planes originally (in Lady Bird's name) so that his radio and TV advertising time salesmen could fly around the country.

Mister Sam climbed aboard the plane and flew to Oklahoma City, along with Lyndon, Lady Bird, Texas Secretary of State Zollie Steakley, Johnson's 1941 Senate rival Gerald Mann, and Grover Sellers. Here Senator Bob Kerr, reconciled now that his friend had taken the stupid Vice Presidential nomination, was throwing a shindig for "a thousand of my closest and dearest friends," so they could congratulate him on his new ghostwritten book, *Land, Wood and Water*.

While the barbecue and the rainbarrels of lemonade were disappearing, Kerr regaled the crowd with such stories as the one about the time he called President Eisenhower a man "without brains," and Johnson had made him modify his language for the printed *Congressional Record*. In this friendly Oklahoma setting, Johnson wandered about and "pressed the flesh" and got in hundreds of "howdy's," while Mister Sam reminisced on his early political days. Then he suddenly turned bitter and denounced the recent Republican nastiness in calling the "Democratic party" the "Democrat party." Rayburn said he was of a mind to label that little old opposition party the "Publicans."

A protocol problem arose on August 8 when the Senate convened. Johnson was the top senator, but Kennedy was the top Democrat. It would have been a friendly gesture for Johnson to lend Kennedy his Taj Mahal across from the Senate chamber. However, he refused, and finally Joe Duke, the Senate's sergeant-at-arms, surrendered his smaller ell-shaped office to the Presidential nominee. Kennedy had delegated the management of the special session's business to himself, and since it would not have looked proper for him to go to the majority leader's spacious quarters for conferences on bills and strategy, the Senate's hierarchy had to squash into Duke's rooms for meetings.

In this three-week session Kennedy wanted four bills passed in order to amass a legislative record to campaign on during the two hard months that were to follow. The four were Medicare for the aged, a boost in the minimum wage, and housing and education bills. Kennedy tried to take on floor leadership, but he knew too little about behind-the-scenes maneuvering. The Republican liberals would not cross sides because it was a campaign year, and Johnson was not in favor of the bills.

In his restrained form of jesting, Republican Senator Hugh Scott of Pennsylvania watched the two Democrats in their dance of agony and labeled Kennedy "the Majority Leader's Leader." Some of Kennedy's friends were convinced that Johnson and Rayburn had arranged this embarrassing special session so that if he lost at the convention he could make the winner look inept afterward. A Washington columnist reported that Johnson stomped into Minority Leader Dirksen's office during the special session and after fortifying himself with Dirksen's scotch complained to the many Republicans present that if he weren't on hand like a Daddy to help Kennedy, "Jack would fall flat on his face."

During this short session about forty thousand tourists clogged the Senate galleries and halls to catch a glimpse of Kennedy and Nixon. It was a time of total frustration for Kennedy because not a single one of his "must" bills became law. Finally, on September 1 when Congress adjourned, he returned to what he could do best—campaigning.

During the campaign Johnson went into forty-three states, but like other Vice Presidential candidates in the past, he garnered insignificant newspaper coverage. All eyes were on the standard-bearers—Kennedy and Nixon—whom *Time and Tide* of London described as "two junior featherweights," some American publications as "young men in too big of a hurry," and local ADA chapters as a choice between an impossible Republican and a lesser-of-two-evils Democrat. TV commentator Eric Sevareid called the Presidential candidates "tidy, buttoned-down" junior executives, "sharp, ambitious, opportunistic, devoid of strong convictions and deep passions, with no commitments except to personal advancement."

The Kennedy hope as the campaign got under way was that Johnson would boost the party's electoral count in the South far above the Adlai Stevenson total against Eisenhower in 1956. Stevenson had won 6 of the 11 Confederate states from Eisenhower, and had amassed 60 electoral votes compared with 67 for the General. Above the old Stevenson vote, Kennedy wanted most of all the 24 electoral votes from Texas that Stevenson had never won; and he was counting on Johnson, whom he erroneously believed to be the political boss of the Lone Star State, to supply them on November 8.

Even though Kennedy and his lieutenants held this mistaken notion about Johnson, Kennedy nevertheless considered it essential that he serve as his own spokesman on the major political issue he faced in the South that year. This was the Bible Belt's anti-Catholicism, the concern that he would be the Vatican's puppet in the White House. If this question went unanswered, Kennedy knew that it would rise to overwhelm him not only in the South but in Northern pockets of religious prejudice.

His assault on suspicious Protestants came early in the campaign. On September 12 he crossed into Texas, and Johnson joined him in plane stops at El Paso, Lubbock, San Antonio, and Houston. The trip started poorly because Johnson's plane arrived first at El Paso and Kennedy, flying in from California, ordered him via plane radio to stay aboard until his own plane landed an hour later. Larry King, assisting Johnson, reported that "in poolroom language he fumed because Kennedy was late," and when the top nominee finally arrived and spoke, "Johnson sat glumly on the platform." Later, "Johnson was in Sam Rayburn's face, crying out some terrible woe and emphatically poking the speaker's chest with that stabbing forefinger. The speaker looked tired and faintly agonized."

At each stop Kennedy warmed up on the religious issue, and at the sacred Alamo he singled out the names of McCafferty, Bailey, and Carey as men who gave their lives here. "But no one knows whether they were Catholic or not," he threw in for emphasis.

All these short speeches pointed to the major stop of the trip, which came that evening at Houston, where he addressed the Greater Houston Ministerial Association's three hundred members in the ballroom of the Rice Hotel. The speech was carried throughout Texas over live TV and made part of nationwide TV news programs the following day. "I believe in an America where the separation of church and state is absolute," Kennedy began a talk that did much to ease the concern of borderline anti-Catholics; "where no Catholic prelate would tell the President (should he be a Catholic) how to act, and no Protestant minister would tell his parishioners for whom to vote—where no church or church school is granted any public funds or political preference."

On the following day, Mister Sam joined Kennedy and Johnson in a barnstorming tour of Texas towns. So pleased was he with Kennedy's talk to the ministers that in reply to a questioner who had not seen or heard it, he remarked, "as we say in my part of Texas, he ate 'em blood raw!"

In his turns about Texas with his running mate, Kennedy's opinion that Johnson was the state's political boss was reinforced by the way local Democrats jumped at Johnson's orders and did not reply to his frequent obscene words of exasperation at the way they handled crowds or tried to provide comforts for the candidates. Because of inept staffwork, he was totally unaware that beneath the surface Johnson had an unusually large number of political enemies in Texas that year. Unbridled animosity had developed over the special favoritism granted him by the new state laws that shifted primary day from July to May just to permit Johnson to run simultaneously for two federal offices. A lawsuit had been filed in Federal District Court to force him to give up his Senate contest, but the court ruled early in August that his double race was legal. Yet talk rumbled on that he had so little faith in the ability of the Democratic ticket to win over Nixon that he was making certain he remained on the federal payroll.

The Johnson opposition revealed itself again on Tuesday, September 20, a few days after Kennedy left Texas, when the Governor's State Convention met at the Dallas State Fair Music Hall. Every mention of Johnson's name provided a signal for loud booing and little cheering. This time the booing came from both the liberal and conservative forces, who on other issues saw fit to engage in fist fights and floor-rolling wrestling melees when words proved insufficient.

As in the past the chief issues were the seating of contesting delegations and loyalty to the national party. At one point Lady Bird's friend Marietta Brooks, the vice chairman of the Executive Committee, attempted to intimidate the conservatives from Harris County (Houston) when she saw they wore Confederate flags in their lapels. "How about letting us have the names of all the people wearing Confederate flags?" she demanded, only to be met by a mammoth outcry of "Dictator" and "Totalitarian." Seldom flustered, she shouted back, "This is a Democratic convention, not a Confederate reunion!"

Governor Daniel, who controlled the convention's machinery, had little control over individual delegates on the floor. After he told the convention that this would be a "harmony" meeting of Texas Democrats, he added that he would see to this even if he had "to fight for it." When two Presidential electors popped up to say they had no intention of casting their votes for Kennedy and Johnson if the Democrats carried Texas, Daniel suggested they resign. One did, but the other man proved unwilling to take his suggestion, so Daniel had the convention oust him. Harmony was disrupted still further by a Houston woman with a loud voice who called out, "I take full responsibility for trying to expose Lyndon Johnson. If we want to get this country back, it will be by the people, not by yellow-dog Democrats."

Days before the convention met, reporters had predicted a bloodletting fight over the state Democratic platform. The liberals came determined to insist on the total approval of the national platform, while the conservatives called for its repudiation. Daniel rammed through what he called his "harmony" platform—not a stated repudiation of the Los Angeles product, but close to that. Then before either set of opponents could get to the microphones he gaveled the convention to adjournment. A surly mob of hundreds yelled out foul names at Daniel and his entourage as he sneaked away.

So what Daniel did for his friend Johnson was to give him a states'-rights platform to campaign on for senator as opposed to a "New Frontier" platform of broadened federal activities as his campaigning stand for Vice President. The Daniel platform denounced "the growing and menacing power in central government," opposed racial sit-in demonstrations, insisted on the "retention of the present oil and gas depletion allowances," demanded continued racial segregation, opposed Medicare and "the entry of the federal government in the general field of public education." The Kennedy platform was the opposite on all these points.

Johnson had paid a courtesy call on Harry Truman at Independence, Missouri, before going to the Hyannis Port conference with Kennedy, and although the sharp-tongued ex-President was not yet reconciled to Kennedy as the Democratic nominee, as a loyal Democrat he wanted the party to win. He had many suggestions for Johnson's campaigning, for he had handled a similar chore in 1944. Chief among these was that Johnson make a thorough back-platform, whistle-stop tour of the South of the sort he had made in his successful 1948 campaign against Tom Dewey.

Early in October Johnson's eleven-car train, the *LBJ Victory Special,* dubbed the "Cornpone Special," set off on a thirty-five-hundred-mile trip through the South. Johnson's chief assistant was Bobby Baker, who arranged the stops and hauled thrilled local Democratic politicians a stop or two so they could "ride a ways and talk a bit."

Into town after town slid the Cornpone Special, blaring over stepped-up amplifiers its theme song, "The Yellow Rose of Texas." "God bless yuh, Rocky Bottom. Ah wish ah could stay an' do a little sippin' an' whittlin' with yuh. . . . God bless yuh, Gaffney," Johnson screamed over the microphone at whistle-stop towns; and then in a bellowing aside that was just as audible, he was heard yelling, "Bobby, turn off that damn Yellow Rose!"

A typical stop came at Culpeper, Virginia, about seventy miles west of Washington. When the music was turned off, and he introduced Lady Bird, Johnson told the crowd, "Ah jes' wanta tell yuh how happy ah am that yuh-all would come here and howdy and shake hands with us this mo'nin'. Ah'd appreciate so much if yuh-all would come jes' a lil bit closer. Yuh make us feel so wonnerful to come out here and look us in the eye and give us a chance to press the flesh with yuh. Give us yur he'p now."

Johnson had told Bobby Baker the stop would last only a few minutes, and at this point Baker signaled the engineer to start out of town. Johnson still had things to say as the train began moving, and he screamed out, "They tell me we can't carry Virginia. Ah don't believe it, do you?"

The disappearing crowd, containing dozens of Johnson shills disguised in old, ill-fitting clothes, yelled back, "No!" and Johnson's faint voice could be heard calling, "When they tell yuh that, yuh jes' ask 'em, 'What did Richard Nixon ever do for Culpeper?' "

After his nomination Kennedy took some speech lessons to correct his nervous mannerisms and too-rapid pace; and when he conferred with Johnson one time during the special session, he suggested that Lyndon do something about his slovenly speech. Often between stops and at night Johnson practiced talking slowly and accenting important words in the short speeches Horace Busby wrote for him. He also practiced speaking in a softer tone because his customary screaming into the lip of the microphone muffled his words. But during the day, on that trip south on the Cornpone Special, the excitement of the crowds made him forget what he had practiced. Nor did it matter in the South, where ears were attuned to hear unpronounced consonants and syllables. Everyone could laugh and applaud his drawling description of the way Nixon had permitted the makeup man to turn his face into a pale death mask for his first debate with a suntanned Jack Kennedy.

"Cold hotcakes and early sunrises," Lady Bird recalled that trip. At one stop in Alabama twenty-five of her cousins were at the station. One of her relatives said this was only a tiny part of her kin: "Afta aw-awl, Lady Bird's daddy's Mama had thirteen chillen in the fo' times she was married."

Lady Bird found that she enjoyed talking, and her Southern accent, so much thicker than Lyndon's, made crowds respond enthusiastically when she spoke. She had a gracious thing or two to say about each locality where the train stopped, and when townspeople gave her a present, she knew how to say breathlessly, "Ah can tell you ah'm powerful proud." By the time the trip ended at New Orleans, with the Democrats staging an out-of-season Mardi Gras, she was an old-timer at campaigning.

Johnson ruined the final scene of the Cornpone Special in New Orleans by a change of mind. He had intended moving on to other campaign places, but once in New Orleans, he decided he and his staff would stay overnight. With two giant conventions then going on, no hotel rooms were available. Johnson, however, staged such a massive temper tantrum that a hotel manager ousted most of the guests on one floor to provide the demanded space. Then, when all the turmoil between the hotel and the ousted guests was beginning to ebb, Johnson announced he had changed his mind again and was mushing on to the next campaign post.

There were other trips in a chartered Convair Lady Bird nicknamed the "Lucy B," with the pilot who was named "Big Deal" chauffeuring her and the Kennedy sisters plus Bobby Kennedy's wife, Ethel. At a Corpus Christi rally she worked up a paragraph formula that she used throughout Texas: "Lyndon wants you to write a card to all your kinfolks; have a coffee or tea party for your friends; phone ten people and ask each of them to phone ten more; write a letter to the editor of your paper; and drive a full car to the polls on November 8." When people wanted to know which lady was Lady Bird, the answer was "the one in the red dress," because she always campaigned in red. Lady Bird had no need for the crowd shills that her husband did. Ladies in the South loved a gracious, drawling lady campaigner. But after Culpeper Lyndon found that some crowds did no applauding; so he continued to carry along a group of about forty aides to Texas congressmen, who were told to yell themselves hoarse at every stop.

Lady Bird learned to stand in receiving lines for hours, shrug off near accidents, such as the occasion when her plane skidded in a pea-soup fog beyond the landing strip, and substitute for Lyndon at a moment's notice. One time Washington attorney Leonard Marks, who was in charge of Johnson's TV and radio campaign and handled Washington legal problems for the Johnson broadcasting empire, had to put her on the early-morning *Today* show, because Johnson claimed he had a sore throat. When she traveled with Lyndon on the chartered jet-prop Electra, nicknamed "Swoose II," he expected her to take care of his personal details as well as to campaign. One time he rode a palomino horse in Albuquerque, and when he climbed down he found the knee of his trousers had split. Almost exploding in tension because he was scheduled to appear on TV afterward, he wrung his hands and bellowed, while Lady Bird bent down and sewed his pants.

"If it hadn't been for Lady Bird," said one of Johnson's friends, "Lyndon would have gone off the deep end many times."

It was during the campaign that Lady Bird's father, raucous Cap'n Taylor, "Dealer in Everything," failed physically. He was eighty-five and suffering from advanced hardening of the arteries. Throughout her cam-

paigning Lady Bird worried she would not be with him at the end. She
was out on a campaign swing with Mary Rather in mid-October, when
she got word he lay dying in the hospital at Marshall. Dropping everything, she flew there and sat at his side for two days. Finally he died during the afternoon of October 22.

Back in Washington, Johnson's friend George Smathers was handling
the Senate Campaign Committee's funds, and this gave Johnson a great
deal of leverage in rewarding Southern politicians who promised to support the ticket. To combat this and the Johnson campaign tours of the
South, Nixon sent Senator Barry Goldwater to build up Southern states'-
rights support for the Republican ticket. In his wanderings Goldwater was
not averse to hitting at Johnson, his Senate buddy, for his mysterious TV
and radio fortune and his unexplained TV monopoly in Austin. "When I
left Dallas," Goldwater said in his sarcastic speaking tone, "I asked a
man how to find Austin. The man said, 'You just fly down in this direction
and when you come to a town with just one television tower, that's it.' "
In his Texas tour Goldwater also hammered hard at Johnson for running
for two offices at the same time.

Nixon, too, came to Texas, and instead of restricting his attacks to
Kennedy, he put Johnson into the act in his effort to prove that the Democratic ticket was born in cynicism. Johnson and Kennedy, he said, "flatly
disagreed 264 times on roll call votes in the Congress. . . . They have dis-
agreed on farm policy, disagreed on taxes, disagreed on civil rights, dis-
agreed on foreign aid, disagreed on foreign policy, disagreed on defense.
They have disagreed on labor issues, disagreed on public works, disagreed
on housing, disagreed on Tidelands oil. Name it, and they have disagreed on it—from antitrust, atomic energy, banking and controls, to the
national economy, education, clean elections, natural gas. They have disagreed on highways, mail rates, and loyalty oaths. They have even disagreed
on fireworks."

While liberal Texas Democrats would not work for Johnson, many conservative Democrats worked for the Republican ticket. Former Governor
Allan Shivers headed "Democrats for Nixon," whose campaign propaganda labeled the national Democratic platform as "Socialism" and Johnson as a "turncoat" and "opportunist." Democrats who were even more
right-wing than Shivers spread stories that "Joe Kennedy had a half million dollars flown to Los Angeles as a bribe to Johnson to take second
place on the ticket." Another rightwing-rightwing story was that Texas
oil men gave Johnson a million dollars to spend in Los Angeles to win the
Presidential nomination, but he pocketed the money and refused to return it.

Foolish Texas Republicans did more than talk about Johnson. A large
Republican crowd had assembled at Love Field, at Dallas, to cheer Nixon
on the morning of November 4. Afterward some fight-seekers in the as-

semblage of thousands harangued the Nixon-cheerers to go downtown and jeer at Johnson, who was scheduled to address a Democratic luncheon at the Adolphus Hotel.

Lyndon and Lady Bird drove from Fort Worth to Dallas in a motorcade that morning, and as they approached the corner of Commerce and Akard Streets he spied a street-choking crowd of about two thousand persons. Like any normal campaigner, he waved, thinking they were on hand to greet him. But as he came closer he saw the Nixon-Lodge banners, plus dozens of others that carried such messages as "Texas Traitor"; "Texas Tombstones for Lyndon"; and "Yankee." He also caught sight of tall Texas Republican Congressman Bruce Alger, working a big sign up and down like a piston. The Alger placard showed a picture of Johnson holding a carpetbag and the caption read: "He Sold Out to the Yankees." Another demonstrator on the scene was little John Tower, Johnson's Republican opponent for the Senate.

The ugly mob would not let the car pull up at the Adolphus, so Lyndon and Lady Bird were forced to get out at the Baker Hotel across the street. Later Lady Bird said that they had intended to get out at the Baker anyhow in order to change their clothes before proceeding to the Adolphus. But in the Baker a yelling mob also filled the lobby, and even to enter proved an effort. Then once safely past the lobby, past the crowd that was now cheering itself for thwarting Johnson, Lyndon decided he had no alternative other than to cross the street back to the Adolphus. He gripped Lady Bird's arm, and they began a grim walk, reversing their field. Said Lady Bird, "I just had to keep on walking and suppress all emotions and be just like Marie Antoinette in the tumbrel."

They made it out of the Baker, through a constant stream of insults, and into the street where the mob enveloped them. Ordinarily Johnson employed a burly brute who crashed through crowds, elbowing, pushing, and punching friendly Democrats to make a path for him. But his rough aide was not present now when he needed him most.

Some of the screaming Republicans spat in their faces, and one hit Lady Bird over the head with a sign; but the Johnsons inched ahead with frozen, frightened faces until they reached the Adolphus. Here the situation was just as bad as outdoors, and it required almost a half-hour of inching along in order to cross the 75-foot lobby to the ballroom. The national image of Dallas as a strange city of odd oil millionaires now gained a new addendum as a dangerous place for pro-Kennedy Democrats.

Johnson went on to finish the campaign after the Adolphus incident. Hauled out repetitiously were the sayings "My old Daddy once told me . . . ," stories from the Tom Connally collection on Southern politicians, and frightening pictures of a Nixon Presidency. Reporters said that behind the scenes he reassured Southern political leaders that the national platform's civil rights promises were not to be taken seriously; and *The*

New York Times accused him of handing out advance texts of speeches and then "departing from his prepared text," so that entirely contradictory statements were made public. In her remaining electioneering, Lady Bird never entered political controversy, but showed herself as a girl of the old cotton-day South at outdoor meetings and at "How to cook a Republican goose" coffee klatches.

And so the campaign came down to the wire. The two Democrats met at the exciting closing rally at the Coliseum in New York on November 5, where they compared their experiences. To Johnson and others in his entourage, Kennedy spoke about the new breed of political parade watchers, the teen-agers, whom he described as "jumpers," "double-jumpers," "touchers," "grabbers," and "roadrunners"; and at the Coliseum that night Kennedy jibed to the receptive crowd about Nixon, but deep down he was concerned about the effectiveness of the late campaigning by President Eisenhower for Nixon.

On November 8, after Lyndon and Lady Bird voted in Johnson City, they returned to Austin to wait for the election results. Lady Bird wrote two statements: one to be released to the press if the Democrats lost; the other if they won. Only the latter was needed.

The first Gallup Poll of the campaign had put Nixon safely ahead; the last gave Kennedy 49 per cent and Nixon 48 per cent. As the vote totals became known, Kennedy's vote was 34,221,463, or 49.7 per cent of the total; Nixon's was 34,108,582, or 49.6 per cent. The Kennedy margin of victory was only 112,881 out of a total of 68,832,818 votes cast, yet the distribution of the votes was such that his electoral count was 303 as against Nixon's 219.

When the race was over, Nixon's advisers assessed his minute defeat as resulting from his excessively pale makeup at the first of the four TV debates he held with Kennedy; his strange insistence on squandering precious time campaigning in Alaska; his failure to lambast Reverend Norman Vincent Peale and his Protestant clergymen's association for anti-Catholic comments; his unwillingness to follow Kennedy's lead and telephone sympathy to Mrs. Martin Luther King, Jr., whose young husband, the nation's leading civil rights figure, had been arrested in Atlanta for leading a restaurant sit-in; his inability to undo the Ivory Soap nature of the 99.44 per cent pure Catholic vote for Kennedy; his blunder in not requesting Eisenhower to campaign for him before the final week; and the slipshod Republican poll-watching to prevent crooked elections in several states—especially in Texas and Illinois.

On the Democratic side, the Kennedy statisticians had time to study the significance of having Johnson on the ticket. In his own re-election race for the Senate in Texas, Johnson's total was 1,210,386, but this was surprisingly low, for Republican John Tower, a small college professor and a political unknown, collected 42 per cent of the total ballots cast, or 936,000 votes. And throughout the old Confederate States, where Stevenson had amassed 60 electoral votes four years earlier, Johnson could not keep Florida, Tennessee, and Virginia from supporting Nixon (even Culpeper, Virginia). Nor could he prevent the eight Mississippi electoral votes that had gone to Stevenson in 1956 being wasted in 1960 on Senator Harry Byrd, along with six others from Alabama.

The Kennedy gain over Stevenson in the old Confederacy was a measly twenty-one electoral votes, and even this would not have been possible without the twenty-four Texas electoral votes that moved from the Republican to the Democratic column. Yet this Kennedy victory by 46,233 votes in Texas out of 2,311,845 votes had a tainted odor, as did the Kennedy victory by less than 9,000 in Illinois. Had an honest count been taken in these two states, Nixon would have been President, not Kennedy.

But the Republicans did not howl until it was too late. In Texas Thad Hutcheson, the Texas Republican chairman, uncovered a situation in which an estimated 100,000 Republican voters were disqualified from having their votes counted. Under state law voters did not check the name of the candidate they favored but crossed out the names of *all* other candidates. In county after county those precincts known to favor Nixon had as many as 40 per cent of all ballots disqualified by election judges, because they had not crossed out unwanted names of minor party candidates; only Kennedy's. In adjacent precincts, where Kennedy was well-liked, few ballots were thrown out, on the ground that the election code also permitted polling officials to count ballots with more than one name unscratched if they could determine "the intent" of the voter. In one precinct in Angelina County, a total of 68 applied for ballots; yet the recorded vote was 147 for Kennedy and 24 for Nixon. In the south Texas counties populated by Mexicans and bossed by Anglo dictators, investigation revealed that poll-tax certificates in blocks of 300 to 3,000 were purchased at $1.75 each, and the Mexican "purchasers" were recorded as Democratic voters. In several cities where voting machines were used, Republican keys could not be moved into place.

The Republican charges went to a state board dominated by Price Daniel and his secretary of state, who made a determination that they could not do anything about them. Afterward, a federal court in Houston rejected the Republican complaint and the matter died.

Kennedy had only seventy-three days to prepare his administrative machinery and program before his inauguration on January 20, 1961. Having declared his election victory "a miracle," he busied himself with exhausting rounds of conversations to set the stage for his takeover of the government's reins.

Vice President-Elect Johnson was among those who flew to Florida to confer with the President-Elect at Palm Beach. At his insistence, Kennedy flew to Austin on November 16, just eight days after the election, to be a guest at the L.B.J. Ranch about which Lyndon had raved.

From Austin the two took a small plane to the ranch, where the mayor of Stonewall stood in front of a crowd of reporters and Johnson's neighbors to give the welcoming speech he had memorized and present the President-Elect with a big cowboy hat. Kennedy would not put the hat on his head despite the entreaties of news photographers. Then the host and his guest climbed into a limousine and drove about one hundred feet to the ranch house. Inside the house as well as outdoors, Kennedy felt constantly rattled by the never-ending Muzak music piped into every room and onto the grounds, and by the chatter of orders and replies on the squawk boxes.

At 6 A.M. the next day Johnson roused Kennedy to set off on a deer hunt. Kennedy, who later told his wife how much he "loathed the prospect of shooting" a deer, apparently believed himself obliged to honor his host's urging. They drove off in a white Cadillac and ranch employees forced some bucks to cross their path. *The New York Times* reported the next day that each hunter had killed two deer. The Johnson story was that each had killed one; and bowing to his inferior political position, Johnson hailed the President-Elect as a magnificent marksman who brought down his buck from a distance of four hundred yards. Long-time deer hunters questioned the four-hundred-yard tale, while Johnson friends were willing to wager that he had been up to his old trick of firing simultaneously at the same deer as Kennedy.

Afterward, when Johnson presented Kennedy with the dead deer's head on a wall plaque, Kennedy told his wife: "The three most overrated things in the world are the State of Texas, the F.B.I., and mounted deer heads."

Chapter 57

W HEN TRUMAN HAD been President, he came to the Capitol one day for lunch in Les Biffle's office. There he regaled Johnson and other senators with a story about a President facing innumerable crisis problems involving the economy, labor strikes, and impending war. In the midst of his agony, the Truman story went, the President had glanced out a White House window in time to spy the Vice President walking by on Pennsylvania Avenue, twirling his cane, and whistling a tune. "There goes the

Vice President," said the President, "with nothing on his mind except the health of the President."

Johnson fully understood the natural impotence of the Vice Presidency, but he had some plans of his own to circumvent it. He might be resigned to calling "Sonny Boy" "Mister President"; and to being called "Lyndon" in return. He might also be resigned to walking a pace behind young Kennedy in public and sitting on the speaker's platform and pretending to be thrilled by the monotonous, machine-gun delivery of a Kennedy speech and the nervous index finger puncturing the air downward as though it were in search of a typewriter key. But behind this protocol facade he had no intention of vegetating.

One area in which he planned to expand the Vice President's figurehead role was in the Senate, where he had come to believe he was indispensable. Therefore, it hurt Johnson to listen to Kennedy, in meetings with Senate Majority Whip Mike Mansfield, plead with the Montanan to put his name before the coming caucus for majority leader "because you're the best catalyst, Mike, among the factions up there—and I need you." Mansfield required a great deal of begging before he finally agreed to do it.

Once Johnson got over his pain at hearing Kennedy's praise for Mansfield, it had been a simple job to gain their agreement to elevate his ally, Hubert Humphrey, into Mansfield's old whip slot, even though there would be a more difficult task ahead convincing Dick Russell that the two Northern liberals would be fair to the South. And amenable Mansfield had put up no argument either, when Johnson suggested he retain Bobby Baker as the secretary for the majority. Senators expected Bobby to carry out Lyndon's orders in the next Congress, just as he had in the past.

Besides having Humphrey tell him what Mansfield was planning and having Baker lobby among senators for votes on bills according to Johnson's dictates, Johnson had still another scheme. "Lyndon was still a senator and majority leader when we held our first caucus on January 3, 1961," said Mansfield. "He had come to me earlier and asked if I would propose that he be permitted to attend future caucuses as Vice President and also to preside. In my view this would only constitute an honorary position, and I had no objection."

But Johnson considered this as giving him control of the caucus procedures and activities, as did the other senators, and when Mansfield offered his resolution, a storm of protests followed. Looking directly at Johnson, Senator Gore, the leader of the opposition, snapped angrily, "We might as well ask Jack Kennedy to come back up to the Senate and take his turn at presiding. I don't know of any right for a Vice President to preside or even be here with senators. This caucus is not open to former senators."

Mike Monroney, long a Johnson friend, almost floored him when he said, "We are creating a precedent of concrete and steel. The Senate will lose its powers by having a representative of the Executive Branch watching our private caucuses."

The vote was 46 to 17 to approve the Mansfield resolution. "But even though we lost, we won," said Gore, "because the size of the vote didn't reflect the true sentiment. You could feel the heavy animosity in the room, even from many who voted for Lyndon—and Lyndon does possess a long antenna."

"Johnson presided at one caucus meeting after that," Monroney recalled, "and he received a great deal of press attention for his new power. But we greeted him with so much coldness that he handed his gavel over to Mansfield and left—never to return."

So the Johnson grab for authority in the Senate fizzled, and he lost face among his old colleagues. Still another damaging blow came within the week when it became known that Kennedy had called Gore on the Johnson-caucus incident. "He congratulated me," said Gore, "for leading the fight against Lyndon."

An additional slap came not long afterward when newspapers reported Mike Mansfield's comments on what sort of majority leadership he envisioned for himself. His words emerged as a negative portrayal and were commonly accepted as referring to Johnson. "I am neither a circus ringmaster, the master of ceremonies of a Senate nightclub, a tamer of Senate lions, or a wheeler-dealer," he said between puffs on his favorite pipe.

On January 3, 1961, after his chagrining experience in the caucus, Johnson walked into the Senate chamber and went through the ceremony of being sworn in for another term as senator. After this he put on a show of resigning from the Senate so that his and Price Daniel's choice to succeed him, William Blakley, could be sworn in as an appointed senator. Johnson's aides had come to the galleries to listen to weepy speeches about "our comrade who is leaving the Senate after twelve glorious years"; but his departure went unnoticed, even though Mike Mansfield had slipped into his front-row-center seat and taken charge.

Only in one small way did Johnson gain revenge. The Vice President had use of an ornate office with a large chandelier next to the Marble Room off the Senate floor, plus a spacious workshop in the new Senate Office Building, a block northeast of the Capitol. When Mansfield became majority leader, he asked Johnson to move out of his Taj Mahal. But Johnson, who had argued that this movie-set headquarters was so necessary to the dignity of a majority leader, now stubbornly refused to leave. Unwilling to engage in a stupid scene that might rock the capital and damage the incoming Administration, Mansfield quietly moved into the smaller quarters Kennedy had used during the summer session and bequeathed the Taj Mahal to Johnson by default.

Washington bulged with Democrats in the seventeen days that remained between the convening of Congress and the Inauguration. Some had come for the fun; some for jobs; others for contracts. "The bland leading the bland" was the description young and untried New Frontiersmen gave the outgoing Eisenhower Administration.

Little wonder that Eisenhower's remarkable Farewell Address to the nation on January 17 went almost unnoticed. "An immense military establishment and large arms industry [are] new in the American experience. The total influence—economic, political, even spiritual—is felt in every city, every statehouse, every office of the federal government," he said. "We recognize the imperative need for this development. Yet we must not fail to comprehend its grave implications. Our toil, resources and livelihood are all involved; so is the very structure of our society. In the councils of government, we must guard against the acquisition of unwarranted influence by the military-industrial complex. The potential for the disastrous rise of misplaced power exists and will persist. We must never let the weight of this combination endanger our liberties or democratic processes."

Cold, snowy Inauguration Day dawned, and at noon the swearing-in ceremony for both the new President and Vice President took place on the temporary platform in front of the new Rayburn East Front of the Capitol, which was built, of course, of Texas pinkish granite. The wind and the sun's glare forced poet Robert Frost to recite his poetry from memory, while Cardinal Cushing went on with his interminable prayer as firemen put out the smoldering blaze in the lectern. As for Rayburn, when he swore Lyndon in, he gave him so many words to repeat at a time that his protégé stumbled about, making up his own oath as he placed his left hand on his mother's Bible and held his right hand high.

After the forty-three-year-old new President cried out in his inaugural address that "the torch has been passed to a new generation of Americans," top Democrats attended the Kennedy inaugural luncheon in the old Supreme Court chamber in the Capitol. Harry Truman was conversing with Johnson and Rayburn when he suddenly rose and slipped out to the cloakroom. A reporter asked him why he was leaving the lunch so early, and Truman looked at the dozens of Secret Service men hovering about and then looked toward the feasting Democrats before replying, "That coat of mine is twenty-five years old, and I don't want anybody to steal it."

Mister Sam was another who did not derive maximum pleasure from the luncheon celebration, even though he had made his peace with Kennedy. "That boy grows on you," he told others about the new President.

Mister Sam's concern was that he had placed his entire prestige on the line in an argument with Johnson and with Kennedy congressmen over the problem of what to do with the legislation-killing House Rules Committee. This committee decided what legislation would reach the floor, how long debates would be, and if amendments could be considered. "Well, Sam," old Chairman Howard Smith told him at the beginning of the Congressional session, "I'm going to be generous and let about five New Frontier bills clear my committee."

"But there will probably be forty or more," Rayburn replied.

Smith, who believed his chief function in Congress was to stem the tide of liberal legislation, merely repeated what he had earlier told reporters: "My people didn't send me to Congress to be a traffic cop. I don't intend to let the Kennedy Administration spend the country broke."

The Democrats held a nominal 8-to-4 lead on the Rules Committee. But with Judge Smith and Bill Colmer of Mississippi voting with the Republicans, the resulting 6-to-6 tie meant the defeat of Kennedy's legislation, for only a positive vote could bring floor action. Johnson's solution was to purge Colmer, who had deserted Kennedy in the last election. But Rayburn argued in return that if he did so, Colmer's martyrdom would result in a unification of the one-hundred-member Southern bloc, and its combination with Republicans would doom any Kennedy bills. House liberal leaders supported the Johnson position with zeal at Democratic caucuses, yet Mister Sam refused to yield. Instead he offered his own solution: Expand the Rules Committee to fifteen members by adding two liberal Democrats and one Republican. This would change the committee to an eight-to-seven majority vote for Kennedy legislation without antagonizing the hundred Southern members.

The fight over the Rayburn proposal became an issue that would have ruined the speaker had he lost. A nose count on January 25, when the House vote was to take place, showed that this catastrophe would occur; so Mister Sam postponed the vote until January 31. Lobbyists for conservative and liberal groups flooded the Capitol and the House Office Buildings in a belligerent effort to influence individual votes. Johnson talked to many Southern members whom he knew well, and even Uncle Carl Vinson, whose heart was with Judge Smith, joined Johnson and House liberals to save Mister Sam. Joe Martin, the deposed Republican leader, was another who came to Rayburn's aid with a tireless effort to win support for him from Northeastern Republican congressmen.

Rayburn worked personally on the other twenty Democrats from Texas, and he also prepared a short speech for the day of the voting. When he gave it, he made the important point that Smith had been put on the committee in 1933, and Colmer in 1939, solely to "pack" the committee, just as he now planned to do again. The roll call took twenty-five minutes, and Johnson aides in the galleries noisily kept count throughout the tense balloting. When the announced results gave Rayburn the narrow victory of only 217 to 212, Judge Smith spoke with his long cigar still in his mouth and said, "Well, we done our damnedest." Even though Mister Sam won, he decided that the six Texas members who had voted against him had to be punished, and he eliminated them from special committee assignments and junket trips abroad.

Two days after Kennedy's inauguration he was talking with his brother Teddy and an old friend, Paul Fay, whom he had named Undersecretary of the Navy, when Fay glanced about the President's Oval Office and remarked, "I feel any minute somebody's going to walk in and say, 'All right, you three guys, out of here.'"

It was during this early period of newness and gawkiness regarding his position that Kennedy picked up some typewritten sheets of paper that his secretary had laid on his desk. The sheets proved to be an Executive Order Johnson had written and sent to Kennedy for his signature, in order to make it legal. On reading the document, Kennedy's expression revealed his surprise at the Vice President's audacity. What Johnson was proposing was that he turn over "general supervision" of a host of Executive duties to Johnson, plus ordering Cabinet members and agency heads to send the Vice President copies of all written items sent to the President.

Kennedy passed this proposed Executive Order to his aides, who immediately spread the story through Washington that "Lyndon wants to pull a William Seward." This referred to Lincoln's Secretary of State who had sent Lincoln a memo ordering him to turn over his Presidential duties to him and spend his time on patronage matters. Eventually the Seward comparison story reached Johnson, and in rage he hurried to the White House to denounce to Kennedy the implication of his assistants. Kennedy said he would have the Seward talk stopped, but he would not sign the proposed Order. And though he did talk to his staff, the anti-Johnson joke-making continued and swelled throughout New Frontier circles.

Even though Kennedy did not sign the Presidential-sharing Executive Order, he soon realized that a busy Johnson presented far less of a problem for himself than a frustrated, idle man. Yet there was no room at the top of the New Frontier for Lyndon Johnson. Friend and foe alike agreed that Johnson had been put on the ticket solely to attract Southern votes. If this were not so, why had Kennedy avoided joining him on a single Northern campaign platform until the wrap-up meeting in New York? they asked.

As an outsider and second-string man who had so recently been an insider and captain of the team, Johnson presented a particularly difficult problem for Kennedy. "After all," Kennedy once explained to one of his Harvard assistants, "I spent years of my life when I could not get consideration for a bill until I went around and begged Lyndon Johnson to let it go ahead."

A Johnson aide also pointed out what a wrenching had to occur between the two men to place their new relationship into practice. Kennedy had walked into the Democratic Policy Committee "two years before the nominating convention . . . hugely agitated about the prospects for getting a certain resolution passed out of the Senate before the weekend. The resolution," the aide said, "was to commemorate, in Boston, an Arthur Fiedler–Boston Pops Day."

Johnson listened to him impatiently, then "shook his head negatively. 'I haven't got time,' he finally said, 'to worry about your damn fife and drum and bugle corps up there.'"

To give Johnson the feeling he was part of the Executive Branch team, Kennedy presented him with a six-room second-floor office in the eyesore of a building next to the White House, a structure built in President Grant's era as the State, War, and Navy Building and now called the Executive Office Building. He also invited him to attend the Tuesday leadership meetings with Rayburn, House Majority Leader John McCormack, Mike Mansfield, and Hubert Humphrey; Cabinet meetings; Presidential news conference briefings; and asked for his opinion on speeches and other matters. By law the Vice President attended National Security Council sessions.

At the Tuesday legislative meetings Johnson was generally morbidly silent, brooding because he no longer possessed power on the Hill. Cabinet meetings also found him quiet and out of character, as he sat at the coffin-like Cabinet table with excited administrators. Kennedy considered the institution created in Washington's time a waste of effort and took to holding them infrequently. In the Eisenhower Administration the National Security Council, established by Truman in 1947 to advise him on defense and foreign affairs, had turned into a burdensome welter of committees and reports. Kennedy soon stripped away the committees, decided that he could not bear to listen to the endless, drawling opinions of Frank Ellis, a member because of his position as director of the Office of Civil and Defense Mobilization, and seldom convened the NSC, with the chief exception being the almost continuous sessions during the Cuban missile crisis in October 1962.

On the morning of the President's news conference Johnson joined Press Secretary Pierre Salinger, special counsel Ted Sorensen, Secretary of State Dean Rusk, Undersecretary of State George Ball, Chairman of the Council of Economic Advisers Walter Heller, and White House special assistant for foreign affairs McGeorge Bundy for an eight-forty-five breakfast with Kennedy. Here Salinger and Sorensen threw questions at Kennedy which they believed might be asked later by reporters, and Kennedy made replies. While other eaters cut in occasionally, Johnson made no sound. Nor did he when Kennedy, in embarrassment, asked him to attend an occasional staff meeting. "Everybody would have ideas and want to talk about them," said a Kennedy aide. "But not Johnson. You'd have to put a direct question to him."

Nor did Johnson evidence his internal roiling when young whippersnapper Kennedy aides, who only months before had worked as Senate clerks when he was majority leader, acted the role of the nouveau powerful and addressed him as "Lyndon." There were other mortifications from the White House crowd that Johnson would not forget, even though he had started the warfare with Kennedy's loyal crew by his attack on Kennedy and his father at the convention. There were Kennedy messages to him that went undelivered, and his calls to Kennedy that did not get through. Jokes made the round: "Lyndon? Lyndon who?"; and "Whatever happened to Lyndon Johnson?"

At the posh parties given by Kennedy friends, Johnson found himself snubbed by the others attending. For weeks White House circles rocked with laughter because Johnson showed up in white tie, tails, stiff collar, and piqué weskit for the unveiling of the Mona Lisa at the French Embassy, while all other male guests came in the simple black tie garb. All that evening he either stood with bent knees behind Lady Bird or held a covering hand over his conspicuous white tie. Others present almost choked with laughter because the only male present attired like Johnson was the butler.

At the same time the Kennedy crowd was laughing at Lyndon, the President was seeking to appease him in the field of patronage and high-level appointments. After the election Johnson had submitted several suggestions to Kennedy for Cabinet posts: Chief among these were Senator William Fulbright for Secretary of State and Representative William Dawson, Negro boss of Chicago's second ward and chairman of the House Government Operations Committee, for Postmaster General. Kennedy had quickly rejected both—Fulbright because of his strong, independent personality and prosegregation voting record for his Arkansas constituents; Dawson, because he was seventy-five, a Negro, and inexperienced in the necessary business techniques.

However, Kennedy agreed to appoint a dozen Johnson men to lesser posts, and among these were John Connally as Secretary of the Navy, Ken BeLieu of the Senate Preparedness Subcommittee as Assistant Secretary of the Navy for Installations and Logistics, Cyrus Vance, Ed Weisl's junior partner, as general counsel of the Defense Department, Solis Horwitz as troubleshooter for Defense Secretary Robert McNamara, and O. D. "Bill" Lloyd, as public relations director of NASA.

Connally, the son of an impoverished tenant farmer and farm-to-farm cattle butcher, had risen to millionaire status in recent years while executor of the late Sid Richardson's estate. Now he wore three-hundred-dollar suits, handmade shirts and shoes, and when invited to a ranch, he would drawl, "Sure, if you got an airstrip long enough to handle a DC-3." In his *Congressional Directory* biography, he carefully avoided any references to himself as a many-time assistant to Johnson, but described his job background instead as an involvement in "oil field services, radio-TV, carbon black, ranches and corporation director of several corporations." That Kennedy would agree to give him any post came as a surprise to those who knew it was Connally who had authored the desperate convention week pitch in Los Angeles that Kennedy was dying of Addison's disease.

But Kennedy was willing to do this and more to appease Johnson. One startling Johnson demand on the President was that he be awarded all federal patronage control beyond postmasters' appointments in the state of Texas. This job disposal, by century-old custom, gave senators of the same party as the President the right to name all federal appointees in their state whose jobs extended beyond the borders of the Congressional district of any member of the House.

In the case of Texas such authority meant that Senator Yarborough, whom Johnson considered the enemy and who was the heir to Maury Maverick's position as leader of the Texas liberals, would be the beneficiary; and Johnson refused to tolerate this situation. To Kennedy he insisted that since "my people back home still consider me their senior senator, I deserve the right to fill all those jobs."

Another President would have laughed out loud at this preposterous demand, but Kennedy's response was to appease his loud-talking Vice President. When Yarborough learned of the unwarranted Johnson *coup*, as a loyal Kennedy man he paid a call on the President. If he were deprived of job-giving to his supporters, he pointed out, he would be in a weakened position when he came up for re-election in 1964. "Besides," he added, "it's a matter of pride not to be raped of my patronage."

To his disgust, Yarborough found Kennedy not only stubborn in Johnson's behalf but willing to go even further. Yarborough believed that what Kennedy had given Johnson was authority to fill the hundreds of federal jobs in Texas that did not require Senate confirmation. Now he learned that the young President had also awarded Johnson the right to fill the sixteen federal vacancies that needed confirmation—four federal court judges, four marshals, four United States attorneys, and four Customs collectors.

However, Yarborough possessed a weapon to prevent this. "I went to Jim Eastland, whose Judiciary Committee held hearings on the legal nominations," he said, "and I told him I intended to declare all persons named by Johnson to those positions as 'personally obnoxious' to me." Since the Senate held strictly to the rule that no federal official below the Cabinet level could be confirmed if a senator from his state found him "personally obnoxious," Eastland assured him he would honor his declaration.

Nevertheless, Johnson was not finished, and he stormed to such an extent to Kennedy that the President in weariness turned the matter over to his younger brother, Bobby, now the Attorney General and the Administration's boss over patronage. Bobby's Solomon-like court-of-last-resort final solution was to dole out the sixteen appointments equally between Johnson and Yarborough, with each agreeing not to name anyone the other might find "personally obnoxious." A Johnson aide at that time spoke of the Vice President's fury because he had been forced to deal "with such a young squirt like Bobby."

The operation Johnson next launched on Yarborough in order to retain the right to name all the judges was merely an extension of the manner in which he had operated in the Senate.

"I had to concern myself with my work as a senator," said Yarborough, "while Lyndon could stay up nights figuring out ways to name all four federal judges instead of only two."

Tiny Sarah Hughes was one of the Texans Johnson had promised to promote for a seat on the Federal District Court in Dallas. Miss Hughes, long a Johnson supporter, had been the first woman state district judge in Texas, and in 1946 she had tried unsuccessfully to become the first Texas woman to win election to the House of Representatives.

Even though Johnson wanted her appointed, he did not want to waste one of his two judge seats on the "dynamo from Dallas," as she billed herself in political campaigns. So knowing that Mister Sam liked her, he asked Rayburn to talk to Yarborough and request that the senator approve her as one of his two choices as a special favor to the speaker. Yarborough, who had no objection to Sarah Hughes, might have grown suspicious that the Rayburn move was Johnson-inspired; but Johnson immediately set up a billowing smokescreen by passing word to Yarborough's office that he was considering holding out against her appointment. Yarborough fell into his trap by declaring himself more than ever for her nomination.

Yet despite the success of his trickery, Johnson did not quit. A Texas politician said, "Lyndon sent Cliff Carter, one of his assistants, back to Texas to spread the false story that Yarborough was working against Sarah Hughes' confirmation."

Johnson had expected the Senate to give her quick approval, but Bobby Kennedy now appeared on the scene. When the Yarborough recommendation reached his desk in the Justice Department, he decided not to send her name to the Senate because the American Bar Association called her too old at sixty-four to handle the job. Since Johnson had assured her privately that she would soon be wearing the federal black robe through his work, he held a rough but unsuccessful meeting with Bobby in an effort to save her. At this dark moment Bobby had to go to the Capitol on departmental business, and Mister Sam arranged to meet with him. Without preliminary greetings Rayburn warned the Attorney General that a bill he was particularly interested in would not win House approval before Sarah Hughes was confirmed by the Senate. Bobby remonstrated about her age until Rayburn slapped him with "Sonny, everybody seems old to you." Shortly afterward Bobby's brother submitted her name to the Senate, and she was confirmed.

Johnson later duplicated the Hughes machinations in tricking Yarborough to use his other Federal District Court choice to name a man

Johnson wanted; and again he had Cliff Carter report in Texas that Yarborough was blackballing his own selection. So in the end, Johnson wound up with all four judgeships and managed to blacken Yarborough in the process.

This vengeance against Yarborough continued throughout Johnson's Vice Presidential years. When Johnson left the Senate, he opened a vacancy on the vital Appropriations Committee, and when Yarborough requested the Democratic Steering Committee to give it to him, Johnson hurriedly asked Hubert Humphrey, who had more seniority than the Texas senator, to request the committee seat. Senator Russell had a talk with Humphrey and pointed out that an unwritten Senate rule barred a member from serving on both the Foreign Relations Committee and Appropriations. However, when Humphrey replied that the rule be damned because he had seniority to make the request, Russell, who believed unswervingly that length of Senate service was the prime consideration, withdrew his complaint and Humphrey went on the Appropriations Committee.

When another vacancy arose in the Appropriations Committee in February 1963, Yarborough guessed who was behind the move that put Democratic Senator Bob Bartlett on the committee even though Bartlett had come to the Senate almost two years after Yarborough. No doubts remained when Senator Kefauver, who was a member of the committee, died on August 10, 1963.

In his attempt to bring fairness to the Senate, Mike Mansfield had democratized the seventeen-man Steering Committee so that it selected new members for all Senate standing committees by majority vote and by secret ballot, instead of the Johnson system of deciding committee membership on his own. Unfortunately, under the new idealistic system Bobby Baker collected the votes, tallied them, and announced the results. He also left with the ballots, so no one checked on him.

One senator said: "Ralph Yarborough had announced for Kefauver's committee seat, and it was expected he would get it this time. But Bill Proxmire, Lyndon's in-again, out-again friend and detractor, ran against him, even though Yarborough had more seniority. Bobby Baker counted the ballots and he announced a tie. Then there was a second vote, and this time Bobby announced, 'I've got all the proxies for those who aren't here, and they're all against Yarborough. So Proxmire wins.'

"Just then Senator Olin Johnston, who was a member, walked into the Steering Committee room and he called out, 'You haven't got my proxy, Bobby. I'm for Yarborough.' Bobby was flustered only a moment before he yelled back, 'It doesn't make any difference. It's overwhelming for Proxmire.' Then he scooped up the ballots and lit out of there. Proxmire, who was also there, went out into the hall and met Lyndon Johnson, and they exchanged congratulations."

A few days later Senator Russell, who still believed that length of Senate service was the prime consideration, came over to Yarborough and asked, "Tell me, who's senior? You or Proxmire?"

"I am," Yarborough replied.

"Why, that Bobby Baker!" Russell exclaimed angrily. "I was told a lie!"

After Yarborough's defeat by Proxmire, he opened his smoldering controversy with Johnson to public view. In a statement carried by Texas newspapers, he disclosed that "the lackeys and henchmen of a powerful Texas politician [had] lobbied with other Senators against me. . . . It is more than strange," he charged "that Texas politicians should work to advance that Senator [Proxmire] who is the bitter foe of Texas petroleum interests and the hardest working advocate of cutting the 27½ per cent depletion allowance."

Not until January 8, 1965, when Johnson's boy, Bobby Baker, was no longer employed by the United States Senate, did Yarborough finally get on the Appropriations Committee.

Besides depriving Yarborough of his rightful patronage and scheming to keep him off the Appropriations Committee, Johnson tried during his Vice Presidency to destroy Yarborough back home in Texas by repeated attacks on his personality, beliefs, and work as a senator.

False accusations rained on him. Stories cropped up and spread that Yarborough was paranoiac, a madman who suffered from delusions that he was being persecuted by Johnson. Other stories portrayed him as a crook who took bribes from unsavory characters. In some tales he was subjected to ridicule, and in others he was labeled a radical.

Kennedy was warned to watch out "for that nut who does nothing but complain." The White House crowd, already laughing at Johnson, recoiled in distaste from Yarborough and added the hapless senator to the list of those to be jeered.

Chapter 58

W HEN KENNEDY GAVE his old Senate boss a fancy six-room suite in the Executive Office Building, he realized that in addition to permitting Johnson to attend advisory meetings, he should give him some Executive functions that did not infringe on the authorized activities of the established government agencies.

While pondering the vast array of federal functions in search of jobs for Johnson, Kennedy staked out two areas. One of these was in the space program; the other involved ending discrimination against Negroes by federal contractors. At both tasks, Johnson began by pouring his unusual energy into the jobs and ended by pretending they did not exist.

Space seemed a natural program in which to make use of Johnson's background of Senate interests. This was an area in which he had specialized, following the successful flight of the Soviet Sputnik into outer space in October 1957. With the help of Ed Weisl, Johnson in 1958 had authored the National Aeronautics and Space Act, which placed all space activities, except those the President labeled as military, into a civilian agency, the National Aeronautics and Space Administration (NASA). The Act also established a Space Council, whose members were the President, the Secretaries of State and Defense, the heads of NASA and the Atomic Energy Commission, plus four appointed members. The Space Council was empowered to advise the President on space matters and serve as the connecting link between the civilian space exploration program and the military missiles undertaking, adjudicating controversies between the two.

In practice Eisenhower had activated NASA by using as its nucleus the old National Advisory Committee for Aeronautics and by naming Dr. Keith Glennan, president of the Case Institute of Technology in Cleveland, to boss NASA. As for the Space Council, Eisenhower did not call its members to a single meeting, and in fact, asked Congress on one occasion to abolish it.

In Johnson's "pulling a Seward" Executive Order to Kennedy, he had given himself control over several agencies, including NASA. Much of Kennedy's campaign pitch in 1960 had centered on the theme that the Republicans had produced a space and missile gap, and because of his own need now to prove he would eradicate such gaps, he was affronted by Johnson's request to stake out NASA for himself. However, he had no objection to Johnson's taking charge of the advisory Space Council, and following a talk with his eager Vice President, he won approval from Congress to replace the President with the Vice President as chairman of the Council.

In Keith Glennan's two years with NASA he had sent up some satellites, begun Project Mercury to put an astronaut into orbit, and managed to work up annual expenditures of more than nine hundred million dollars. Even before his inauguration Kennedy had asked Dr. Jerome Wiesner, his special science aide, to find a Democratic head for NASA and formulate a New Frontier space program. Wiesner had restricted his search for a new NASA boss to fellow scientists, and all whom he approached rejected the offer on the ground that operating control would either be swallowed up by the Pentagon missiles crowd or by Johnson's Space Council. As for a space program, Wiesner misread Kennedy's romanticism, called the sending of astronauts into outer space mere "stunts," and said that emphasis should be placed on sending scientific equipment into space instead.

Because of Wiesner's failure to find a man to replace Glennan, Kennedy brought Johnson into the search. The first Johnson recommendation was retired General James Gavin, former head of the Army's research and development projects, but Kennedy wanted no military man for the job and appointed Gavin as Ambassador to France.

Johnson's second suggestion won quick Kennedy approval. In a conversation with his old pal Senator Bob Kerr Johnson agreed to push James Webb, a director of Kerr's oil company, Kerr-McGee. Kennedy was aware that this appointment would be of value in further dealing with Kerr, who was now chairman of the Senate Space Committee. In addition, despite his reputation for garrulity, Webb knew the governmental ropes as a Truman Director of the Bureau of the Budget and Undersecretary of State. So one day, with Johnson sitting at his side, Kennedy asked Webb to come to his office for a chat.

Webb knew what was coming, and was not surprised in the least when Kennedy made the offer. But Johnson was surprised when Webb declared volubly that he would not accept NASA if he were to be window dressing for Johnson. Sitting in cold silence, Johnson heard Kennedy assure Webb that this would not happen. And in April 1961, a short time later, Johnson suffered further when Congress appropriated almost two billion dollars to Webb's NASA, while slashing Johnson's request of one million dollars for the Space Council to a half million.

However, Johnson's status in the space program momentarily gained a boost on April 12, when Soviet cosmonaut Yuri Gagarin orbited the earth and landed safely. After congratulating Khrushchev, Kennedy sent Johnson a five-paragraph memo featuring a single question: "Can we beat the Russians to the moon?" Johnson's reply was in the affirmative, and Kennedy asked him to work up data showing the cost, manpower, and facilities necessary to achieve this goal. Unfortunately, the Space Council lacked a technical staff, and Kennedy had to turn to NASA and the Defense Department for the answers. When Kennedy went to Congress in May to ask in person for a crash program of at least twenty billion dollars to put an astronaut on the moon and bring him back "before this decade is out," Johnson's Space Council had been shown up as a paper organization.

Nevertheless, Johnson made innumerable efforts to portray himself in the public's eye as a top figure in the space program. He dashed from one space installation to the next in the late summer and fall of 1961, with local reporters on hand to write newspaper stories on his visits. Earlier that year, when astronaut Commander Alan Shepard missiled into space like a cannonball that dropped back to earth, Johnson upstaged Jack and

Jackie Kennedy, who were having their picture taken during the tense countdown before blast-off. Johnson held center stage in the newspaper photo that showed the Presidential couple merely watching the TV scene at Cape Canaveral, for he was pictured holding a telephone as though he were directing the Shepard flight.

Then the following February 20, when Colonel John Glenn became the first American to orbit the earth, Johnson told Kennedy he was flying to the Bahamas to be on hand to greet Glenn after his reentry. Kennedy yelled out his refusal, though Johnson wore down his resistance when it came to joining the hero Glenn and his wife Annie in their triumphant parades in Washington and New York. It was Johnson who warned the eloquent astronaut that when he addressed the joint session of Congress, the legislators would be bored with a long speech, and Glenn shortened it to a banal little talk. In New York Johnson stepped ahead of Glenn to sign the city's guest book on March 1, and he was later portrayed by the New York *Herald Tribune* as a camera hog because he intruded into almost all shots of the Glenns.

After the Glenn parades Johnson stopped his touring of space installations and settled into infrequent calling of Space Council meetings. So far as he was concerned his lack of direct association with NASA was all to the good, for Webb was soon involved in trying to put an end to featherbedding practices and settling massive labor strikes at the installations, answering charges that billions of dollars were being squandered in pork barrel space projects, and suffering through Congressional hearings, where he was criticized for spending money that could better be used to fight poverty, slums, disease, and ignorance.

There were two matters, other than the "man on the moon" project, in which Johnson involved himself as chairman of the Space Council. Kennedy asked him to look into the feasibility of the United States' producing a supersonic transport plane, the SST, to compete with the joint British-French venture to produce a commercial plane that would fly at twice the speed of sound. The Space Council's recommendation was that the government go ahead with plans for an SST to fly at four times the speed of sound and to be produced by private industry with a heavy federal subsidy.

The other matter was the establishment of a communications satellite system; and the view of Senator Kerr, as accepted by Johnson and finally by Kennedy, would establish a Communications Satellite Corporation jointly financed by the federal government and private industry, but run entirely as a commercial enterprise. Senate liberals conducted a fifteen-day filibuster against what they termed "a giveaway to American Telephone and Telegraph," but after cloture was voted, the bill passed. James Wechsler, editor of the New York *Post,* charged that the bill was Johnson's handiwork—"It is a matter of fact," Wechsler added, "that Tom Corcoran's law firm, with which Johnson has continuous and intimate relations, displayed an active interest in AT&T's cause."

Besides the space program, Kennedy tried to keep Johnson busy as chairman of the President's Committee on Equal Employment Opportunity. This was not a new organization, for in 1953 President Eisenhower had put Nixon in charge of a similar committee to end racial discrimination by government contractors. Nixon had signified his sincerity at this enterprise by joining the National Association for the Advancement of Colored People (NAACP); and his chief success, with the help of committee colleagues George Meany and John Roosevelt, was to convince the Capitol Transit Company of the District of Columbia that Negroes should be hired to drive buses. Eisenhower's contribution to solving the "colored problem" at the national level was to hire a Negro as a White House administrative officer, another as a White House secretary, and a third as an Assistant Secretary of Labor.

When Johnson became chairman of the old Nixon committee, there were ample reasons for skepticism among liberals. At the outset of the Presidential campaign, newspapers had reported his speech at the Blanco barbecue in August 1960, in which he promised the crowd: "I will support the Democratic platform on civil rights during the campaign but oppose parts of it when it gets to Congress—not in the November election, but I'll put the opposition in the proper place." In addition, behind closed doors he used the word *Nigger* instead of his public *Nigra*.

Total federal appropriations for fiscal 1962, beginning on July 1, 1961, came to 86.6 billion dollars, with at least half this sum going to government contractors who employed twenty million workers in all sections of the country; so the task of the Johnson committee could be enormous if it so chose. Under Nixon the committee's endeavors had been insignificant because it had authority to act only when individuals brought in complaints of discriminatory hiring and employment practices. To show his new sincerity, Johnson asked Abe Fortas to draft a tough Executive Order for Kennedy's signature that would force all private contractors on government projects to sign statements that they did not practice discrimination. The committee would then possess authority to cancel contracts of violators. Kennedy viewed Fortas' handiwork as an excellent approach because it provided for government initiative, and he signed the Order.

Armed as he was now with aggressive power, Johnson had an excellent opportunity to gain a reputation as a civil rights advocate and as an executive. But the job soon turned into a nightmare. He knew his old Senate comrades from the South would never approve an appropriation for his committee. So he illegally bypassed Congress and picked up more than a million dollars by making calls for money on several government agencies. This brought him into immediate controversy with members of his committee, who wanted their activities based on a legal foundation. In addition his secretive action subjected the committee to continuing attacks from Senator Russell, who fruitlessly demanded to know where the committee was acquiring its operating funds.

A more fundamental antagonism quickly developed between committee members and Johnson over his seriousness about ending job discrimination. Two leaders on this score were the Very Reverend Francis Sayre, dean of the Washington Cathedral and grandson of Woodrow Wilson, and United Auto Workers President, Walter Reuther. Johnson's clash with Sayre came soon after the committee was formed, when he staged a one-day meeting in St. Louis with contractors and union officials. Sayre later reported to the full committee in a Washington meeting that Johnson had occupied the first morning hours at the St. Louis session jawing on Missouri politics and giving a long talk praising the St. Louis mayoralty candidate he wanted to win in the next election. Then when the meeting finally got under way, he leaped up and announced he had to run for his plane to take him to another city where he was to make a luncheon address. The session was half-heartedly progressing when he suddenly reappeared in midafternoon, talked local politics again, and then adjourned the meeting. Johnson was present when Sayre gave his report, and when the churchman concluded, Johnson turned on him with a nonstop hour-and-a-half name-calling outburst.

As for Reuther, his complaint was that Johnson was wasting the time of committee members by not preparing an advance agenda of topics to be discussed at their meetings. Johnson reluctantly agreed that members could appoint an agenda subcommittee, but when Dean Sayre became its head, he ignored its work.

Below the committee level, Johnson also faced serious staff problems. The two top men had been named by Kennedy, and at the same time that they fought with each other, Johnson despised both. One was Robert Troutman, an Atlanta businessman and Harvard roommate of Kennedy's older brother Joe, whose plane had disappeared beyond the English coast during World War II. Johnson remembered Troutman well because of his energetic work among the Southern delegations against him at the 1960 convention. The other staff director was John Feild, formerly with the Michigan Fair Employment Practices Commission, whom Kennedy had named on the recommendation of the two anti-Johnson senators from Michigan.

With divided authority between Troutman, a go-slow civil-righter, and Feild, an aggressive opponent of discriminatory practices, trouble was bound to erupt. Troutman's contribution to the committee's work was his invention of a "Plans for Progress" program, under which the heads of industrial firms with government contracts and union leaders trooped to the White House to sign documents pledging not to discriminate against jobseekers and jobholders. However, Feild considered the Troutman approach meaningless because the signers were taken at their word and compliance investigations did not follow. What Feild advocated instead was a hard-hitting on-the-scene check of government contractors, with contract cancellations for violators, as spelled out in the "Fortas" Executive Order.

Open arguments developed between the Troutman and Feild staffs. Johnson tried at first to ignore them, but when *The New York Times* exposed the fight in June 1962, some action on his part became necessary. Arthur Goldberg, Secretary of Labor and a member of Johnson's committee, played down the controversy's meaning to reporters when he said, "I like a little healthy diversity. There is bound to be disagreement in a group as varied as this one." After the story was in print, Johnson interpreted it as an attack on himself, and he wrote a letter to the editor of the *Times,* disclaiming any committee troubles. "In my opinion none exists." Then, concerned that the Troutman approach might be damaging to his image in New York, he added, "The committee operates a compliance program, and, as I have said frequently, we mean business."

He meant business now so far as Troutman and Feild were concerned. Rather than adjudicate the differences between them, he had a reorganization plan drawn up that eliminated their jobs. Kennedy agreed to his proposal to dump Troutman despite his personal family tie after jealous White House staff aides reported that Troutman was a phony with none of the important Southern political connections he was constantly claiming. Then Johnson personally fired Feild, whose views he found obnoxious, and appointed a new top staff director, Hobart Taylor, Jr., a mild, go-slow civil-righter and son of the Houston Negro millionaire who had been a Johnson-appointed Texas delegate to the 1956 Democratic National Convention.

Only a few months after Johnson and young Taylor busily concluded more "Plans for Progress," committee statistics showed that more than fifty had been signed by firms holding billions of dollars worth of defense contracts. However, sitting in his office in the Justice Building on Pennsylvania Avenue, with his big shaggy dog barking outside his door, Bobby Kennedy grew suspicious of these pious signing ceremonies. In those firms involved, statistics of Negro employment revealed only microscopic gains; while among the hundreds of thousands of contracts negotiated with companies in the South, not a single one had been canceled for discriminatory practices.

The Johnson–Bobby Kennedy encounter came shortly afterward on a morning when Johnson was presiding at a committee meeting. Bobby slipped into the room and listened for a while to the talk. Then he suddenly turned on Jim Webb, NASA's talking-machine administrator, and asked how many employees he had. Webb replied, "Forty thousand."

Then Bobby Kennedy pointed out that NASA had been authorized by Congress to spend 3.8 billion dollars in the current fiscal year, and he snapped at Johnson: "How many of your people are working on the discrimination program in NASA contracts?"

"One full time and one part time," Johnson told him.

Bobby snorted that this was ridiculous, and he proceeded to scold Johnson in front of the two dozen committee members. When Hobart Taylor started to break in, Kennedy cut him short with an angry glance. After his stern lecture that his brother expected some results, Bobby hurried out, and an observer reported that Johnson sat in silence "slumped in his seat." Not for months afterward did he call another committee meeting, and when he did, it was with little enthusiasm.

Chapter 59

IF JOHNSON'S EXECUTIVE Branch assignments proved disagreeable to him, his numerous trips abroad during his thousand days as Vice President were the opposite. In that interval he traveled 120,000 miles and raced on foot and by car through cities, towns, and villages of thirty-three countries.

At the national convention Kennedy had used the goodwill ambassador travel bit on Rayburn in order to gain his consent to Johnson's taking the Vice Presidency. As Kennedy put it to the old Texan, he planned to broaden the duties of that office, and he promised among other things "to use Johnson's finesse in handling people on an international level." Kennedy had seen enough of Johnson to know he lacked finesse in handling people, but Mister Sam was reaching out for a kind word about his protégé, and Kennedy was willing to give him one.

When Kennedy came to the L.B.J. Ranch for the deer shoot, he proposed that his Vice President-Elect go on the foreign road the way Nixon had for Eisenhower, and Johnson revealed his pleasure. Only once before —not counting his wartime trip to Australia and his four-day visit with Mexico's President Mateos—had he gone on a junket, and he liked the sweep of foreign lands. Kennedy was pleased, too, that Johnson showed enthusiasm, for it meant that his Vice President would not be relentlessly on the Washington scene.

Only a few weeks after his visit to the ranch the President-Elect suffered doubts about his proposal when he heard of Johnson's late November 1960 trip to the NATO Parliamentary meeting in Paris. Reporter friends of Kennedy relayed word that Johnson had abruptly left a special dinner in his honor by the Macmillan Government in London to spend half the night in a nightclub, that he had shouted at American embassy staff personnel, failed to keep a schedule or observe protocol rules, and insulted reporters.

Nevertheless, when France gave Senegal on the coast in West Africa her freedom, Kennedy asked Johnson to represent the United States at the independence celebration in April 1961. Cases of Cutty Sark scotch and a seven-foot-long bed went ahead to Dakar before Johnson and Lady Bird arrived by Presidential jet. "Africa is a many-splendored continent of bright colors and contrast," Lady Bird's story of the six-day trip began afterward in the Washington *Post*. It ended, she said, when "we were back [in Washington] on Friday night in time to spin the wheel at the Cherry Blossom Festival."

In that short span of time, Johnson put the State Department's embassy staff into a state of collapse, running errands for him and altering his schedule (which he ignored). He also had Lady Bird fill in for him and talk about poetry, women's rights, and Senegalese illiteracy with President Senghor, while he ran down streets passing out L.B.J.-inscribed ballpoint pens, told local officials he had come "to press the flesh and look them in the eye," shook hands with fingerless lepers, and made speeches to native groups who knew no English.

Lady Bird went with him one morning at four-thirty to the fishing village of Kayar, where he told the chief and the villagers that their low standard of living need not be permanent. "The rural per capita income of Texas was only $180 in 1930 and it's $1,800 today," he said to one interpreter, who translated his Texasese into French to a second interpreter, who translated the French into Wolof for the chief and his people. Gurtil N'Doye, the chief, asked him why he had chosen to come to Kayar of all places, and Johnson told him, "I came to Kayar because I was a farm boy, too, in Texas. It's a long ways from Texas to Kayar, but we both produce peanuts." Then he told how "My Daddy went busted waiting for cotton to go up to twenty-one cents a pound, and the market fell apart when it hit twenty."

After a few days in Senegal, Johnson flew on to Geneva, since Kennedy said he ought to listen to talk at the Nuclear Test Ban Conference, where the Soviet delegates were fighting for a *troika,* or three-power inspection system. But once he and Lady Bird reached Switzerland, Lady Bird wanted to see Spain, so they hurried there after getting permission from the new Secretary of Defense, Robert McNamara, to do some "inspecting." McNamara's helpfulness confirmed Johnson's early impression of him, for Johnson had liked McNamara at first meeting, exclaiming at the time, "That young fellow with all that Stacomb in his hair is a smart one." Kennedy had also characterized McNamara. His assessment ran: "half genius—half S.O.B."

Hardly was Johnson back in Washington when Kennedy sent him on another diplomatic escapade, this time on a twenty-thousand-mile trip through Southeast Asia to talk to government leaders in Formosa, South Vietnam, Thailand, India, Pakistan, Hong Kong, and the Philippines. Johnson set off on May 9, 1961, in an Air Force silver-colored Boeing 707, while about twenty-five correspondents traveled by Pan-Am jet to record his trip for posterity. Besides Johnson and Lady Bird, among his party of twenty were Johnson's speechwriter, Horace Busby; the President's sister Jean and her husband, Stephen Smith; Deputy Assistant Secretary of State for Public Affairs, Carl Rowan; Far Eastern expert and aide to Mike Mansfield, Frank Valeo; and an assortment of personnel from the Executive Branch.

Trouble erupted over mid-Pacific, said one of the passengers, when Johnson suddenly exploded in a screaming fit of rage directed toward Busby, who gave him no provocation. "You're fired!" Johnson bellowed at one point. "Get the hell out of this plane!"

"But we're over the ocean," Busby reminded him.

"I don't give a f------ damn!" Johnson swore. "You're fired. Get off this plane."

An hour later Johnson apologized to Busby for his outburst, after Lady Bird told him he was being perhaps too rough on his long-time ghostwriter.

The classic pattern of foreign visits by a high dignitary had been planned for Johnson: He would be greeted by the chief of government or state in each country and treated to an honor guard and a local band playing "The Star Spangled Banner" ("Lyndon looked four inches taller and ever so stern as they played," said his loyal wife); there would be a formal exchange of dinners by both sides; symbolic visits to hospitals, handicraft centers, and institutions for the mentally retarded by the ladies; a so-called private talk between Johnson and his host (with a half-dozen aides from each side present); an occasional prepared speech; and a joint, vague, but statesmanlike, communiqué at the close of each visit, written by the staffs of both men and cleared with Washington.

Johnson went through all these—and more. It was his additions, played by ear, that gave protocol officers chest pains. At no time, Johnson was lectured, should he violate Oriental custom by shaking hands or patting heads. Handed a speech to read in Formosa, he glanced at it, declared it dull, and flung it back, yelling, "Don't give me that pap. Give me something that will bring them off their seats, ready to grab buckets of water to put out the fires of hell—and do it!" It was also in Formosa that his poor briefing revealed itself when he grew wild with excitement listening to old Generalissimo Chiang Kai-shek confide his rote recitation of the imminent collapse of the Mao Tse-tung Red regime and the need for American backing for an immediate invasion of the mainland. Johnson was on the verge of promising such support when an embassy official reminded him that his instructions did not give him authority to commit the United States on the spot.

In South Vietnam, where the Diem Government controlled less than a third of the countryside and the French had managed to hang on to the banking, public utility, and commercial interests, Johnson handed the short, black-haired president a letter from Kennedy promising money to support twenty thousand more native soldiers, to teach guerrilla warfare to the one-hundred-and-fifty-thousand-man force, and to send additional United States military advisers and technicians. Johnson met with Diem and American Ambassador Fred Nolting on the second floor of Diem's magnificent Independence Palace, and again he was carried away by the practiced spiel of his host. After the three-hour session, Johnson issued a statement in which he flatly declared that "Diem was the Churchill of Asia" . . . who would "fight communism in the streets and alleys, and when his hands are torn, he will fight it with his feet!" While Diem preeningly took this remark to mean total American support for his regime, and was therefore pleased with Johnson, he and his sister-in-law, Madame Nhu, who also wielded great power in the country, viewed with contempt Johnson's excursions into the streets to shake hands with everyone he encountered.

On to Thailand went Johnson, where he plowed through the formal rigmarole and quickly reverted to the Texas rancher and political campaigner. He met with Premier Sarit Thanarat, the military dictator, on a teakwood sofa flanked with elephant tusks. After presenting him with a letter from Kennedy that stated a United States assurance to send troops to Thailand if the Geneva Conference on Laos failed, Johnson pulled him close, looked him in the eye, and added: "Now is the time to separate the men from the boys." Thanarat, who was filling his Swiss bank account with American-aid millions, agreed.

Johnson had again been warned to avoid handshaking in Thailand because it was considered offensive there. But he raced through the streets of Bangkok pressing the flesh of surprised pedestrians, leaped on a bus, and pushed his way through the aisle grasping hands, and invaded a large Chinese-owned store, where he gave an impassioned speech on democracy and the need to consider China an enemy to the crowd of customers who were Chinese and did not understand English.

On to India the Johnson entourage moved. Here he considered Prime Minister Jawaharlal Nehru with suspicion because of his academic manner, and his neutralist stand against communism. But he tried to be pleasant during their talk and controlled the conversation by giving the Brahmin-caste leader a detailed description of the way he had set up the Pedernales Electric Co-operative when he was in the House. It was after the session, when he asked his press aide in Nehru's presence if he had arranged a news conference and received the reply, "No," that he forgot where he was and snapped, "The only way to deal with you is to handcuff you to my belt so you'll be there when I need you!" Then he blistered Carl Rowan, who argued for the elimination of one sentence in the Johnson-Nehru communiqué.

Johnson's swift forays down the streets of Delhi and through several villages to mingle with the natives won him many friends in the Indian press. In the poorest slums he altered his giveaways to pencils instead of pens, and these pencils read: "Compliments of your Senator, Lyndon B. Johnson—the greatest good for the greatest number."

Daily he gave his protocol guides recurring concern by teasing them with "Dammit, I haven't patted anyone on the head yet." Then suddenly the threat became reality when he deliberately began patting heads. The most unpleasant embarrassment to his Indian hosts came at the real Taj Mahal at Agra, where he committed the sacrilegious act of kissing Lady Bird. Even worse was the fifteen-second-long Texas cowboy "Yeeeaaaayhoooo" he screamed out at the top of the marble landing. "Ah'm jes' testin' the echo," he explained matter-of-factly to the choleric Indians afterward. Then to Jean Kennedy Smith, whose father's large and self-made fortune rankled him, he said in a biting aside, "Maybe someday you'll build a place like this for your husband Steve."

Ayub Khan, the military dictator of Pakistan, was more to his liking than the intellectual Nehru, and he invited him to his ranch with the promise to put a Stetson on his head and treat him to a Walter Jetton barbecue, complete with a Mexican mariachi band and Ernie Tubbs, the cowboy singer and electric "gee-tar" string plucker.

The major event of Johnson's Asian trip occurred along the five-mile motorcade from the airport into Karachi. During the ride, Johnson astounded his protocol aides by jumping from the car, racing alongside the natives lining the road, and yelling, "Howdy and shake!" At one corner he spied a barefoot man dressed in white cotton work clothes who was waiting for the motorcade to pass so he could lead his camel-driven cart and its load of sacked straw across the blocked traffic lane. The Pakistanian was Bashir Ahmad, and pausing a moment before him, Johnson glibly invited him, as he had dozens of other natives in the countries he visited, to come to the L.B.J. Ranch.

In this instance, a cameraman and a politically important local reporter caught the meeting and invitation, and from the resulting press publicity around the world, a test of Johnson's sincerity was at hand. Later, after returning to the United States and checking on the high cost of bringing Bashir to America, Johnson induced the Conference of Mayors to bear the expense. Then arrangements were made, and Johnson put up the lowly Pakistanian camel driver in the same bedroom at the ranch that Ayub Khan had used. Johnson also gave him a pickup truck that the Ford Motor Company donated on request, and he asked Lady Bird to show the charming visitor the sights of Washington before sending him home via Mecca. The enormous goodwill Johnson earned from this venture was priceless.

When the madcap tour of Southeast Asia neared its end, and the last Navy plane had been dispatched to Hong Kong for more Cutty Sark scotch, Kenneth Young, American Ambassador to Thailand, with the assistance of Carl Rowan, wrote a report for Johnson of his "Mission to Southeast Asia, India and Pakistan" for delivery to President Kennedy.

Bill White, Johnson's press buddy, hailed the report as revealing Johnson's "perceptive awareness of what was happening and what might happen in Southeast Asia." The pages that Johnson handed Kennedy on May 24, after a Marine helicopter brought him and Lady Bird to the White House lawn from Andrews Air Force Base, announced, "Our mission arrested the decline of confidence in the United States. It did not—in my judgment—restore any confidence already lost. . . . We didn't buy time— we were given it. If these men I saw at your request were bankers, I would know—without bothering to ask—that there would be no further extension on my note."

Portending what would be Johnson's policy as President, the "Young" report declared, "There is no alternative to United States leadership in Southeast Asia," and "Asian Communism is compromised and contained by the maintenance of free nations on the subcontinent." But in an opposite vein, the report also said that Asian leaders "do not want American troops involved in Southeast Asia other than on training missions" and "American combat troop involvement is not only not required, it is not desirable" because "recently colonial peoples would not look with favor upon governments which invited or accepted the return this soon of Western troops." However, Young covered Johnson's tracks by adding that "this does not minimize or disregard the probability that open attack would bring calls for U. S. combat troops."

In August 1961, after the Communist East Germans began building a concrete "Berlin Wall" to prevent East Germans from escaping to the West, and made oral boasts that they intended to take over West Berlin, Kennedy asked Johnson to fly to the beleaguered city and assure the hysterical citizens that the United States would not abandon them. Johnson stunned Kennedy by refusing to go on the ground that it was dangerous, and finally brother Bobby was sent to tell Johnson that it was an order.

As the trip turned out, it proved of inestimable publicity value for Johnson. White House aide Walt Rostow wrote a speech for him that he delivered to three hundred thousand West Berliners on August 19 and won for himself hero stature. "I have come to Berlin by direction of President Kennedy," he began. "To the survival and to the creative future of this city we Americans have pledged, in effect, what our ancestors pledged in forming the United States: Our lives, our fortunes, and our sacred honor."

Everywhere he went, crowds followed and cheered him. Only once did he drop the saintly expression, and this came when he met Willy Brandt, the mayor of West Berlin. Brandt was running against Chancellor Konrad Adenauer for political control of the Federal Republic of West Germany, and he mentioned casually to Johnson that in view of his current fame in Germany the fact that he had recently entertained Adenauer on his Texas ranch would now help the old chancellor. A bystander reported that Johnson turned on Brandt with burning rage, "bawled hell" out of him, and finished the scolding with a curdling "Didn't I have you the hell out to my ranch back in 1954?"

Several other trips followed during the next few years; visits with kings, queens, shahs, premiers, presidents, and the Pope. Linden Hjalmar, owner of Lenz-Linden tailors in San Antonio, complained that he was given too short a time to stitch Johnson's new suits after Johnson tore into his shop like a cyclone, insulted his fitters, and dashed out the door.

The protocol shambles seldom diminished. In Helsinki he sang an off-key "Happy Birthday" to a woman selling vegetables on learning she was seventy that day. In Rome, where he had gone to attend the funeral services for Pope John XXIII, he ordered the CIA to locate a tie shop proprietor in the middle of the night so that he would be waiting outside Johnson's rooms with his wares before breakfast the next morning. In Copenhagen he kept the hotel management in a condition of wringing hands and sweaty foreheads by his many-hour upbraiding of a Danish artist over the asking prices for his paintings. In Stockholm he had a temper tantrum because he had failed to see the fashion show put on for Lady Bird and Lynda Bird, and the fashion show manager had to bring the models and clothes to his suite so he could enjoy a private viewing. It was here in Sweden that he barely avoided injury, when the helicopter carrying him and King Gustav Adolf VI hooked its landing gear on a fence and almost flipped. At Paris, when General de Gaulle haughtily asked him, "Now, Mister Johnson, what have you come here to learn from us?" he spat back with biting sarcasm, "Why, General, simply everything you can possibly teach me."

In the wake of a seventeen-day sweep in August 1962 through Lebanon, Iran, Turkey, Cyprus, Greece, and Italy, he shook thousands of hands, passed out L.B.J. pens and gilt-edged cards admitting visitors to the Vice President's gallery over the Senate floor, and joined girls in street dances. At every stop he produced Lady Bird and Lynda Bird, and in the style of Harry Truman's famous whistle-stop campaign, introduced them to crowds and asked them to "say something to the people." The two had been carefully coached in memorizing a sentence or two of the native language, and their recital won warm applause. At Beirut, Lebanon, he climbed onto a bulldozer and told about hard times in his youth when he, too, worked on a road gang. He also wanted to see Baalbek, a village two hours away, where Cain was supposed to have fled after he slew his brother Abel. While he bounded in and out of countries, Lady Bird wrote travelogue notes in her daily diary, never entering any mention of his robust nature. She found German-born Greek Queen Frederika, who had been involved in the Hitler youth movement, "a mixture of Grace Kelly and Eleanor Roosevelt." And her view of Italians was that "their burgeoning industrial muscles are busy marketing age-old artistry."

Chapter 60

WHILE KENNEDY WORRIED about keeping Johnson busy and out of his hair, Johnson was equally worried that Kennedy would give him so many busywork jobs of no importance that he would have little time to spend on his private business activities and Washington entertainment.

The house on Thirtieth Place was all right for a congressman, but to Johnson it lacked dignity as a residence for the nation's second citizen. So he sold it to one of his old Senate Policy Committee assistants, after signing a lease on an eight-room, four-bedroom, five-bathroom suite at the Sheraton Park Hotel, formerly the Wardman-Park, on Connecticut Avenue above Rock Creek Park. But when Lady Bird said she did not like hotel living, and could not hold large parties, Johnson moved again, this time buying "Les Ormes," or "The Elms," on Fifty-Second Street Northwest in the exclusive Spring Valley area. This was a hilltop French chateau owned by Perle Mesta, whom Truman had appointed as minister to Luxembourg following her frenetic social entertainment of the Trumans in their short Vice Presidential period. Perle was so loyal a Johnson friend that when Kennedy won the Democratic nomination over Johnson, she announced her support of Nixon.

Many of the walls and floors of her house had come from centuries-old French chateaux and the furniture in several rooms was copied from French originals. Lady Bird, who still sat in theater balconies when she went alone and informally to plays, and was highly pleased when Lyndon gave her a tool kit one Christmas so that she could make her own minor household repairs, talked Mrs. Mesta into throwing in the furniture in the sales price of her house. Afterward Johnson told friends that he had spent an extra three hundred thousand dollars remodeling the chateau, including piping Muzak into each room and installing a heated swimming pool. This outlay, he claimed, was in addition to spending an average of one hundred thousand dollars a year above his Vice Presidential salary, which came to thirty-five thousand dollars plus ten thousand dollars for expenses.

But making ends meet was not Johnson's problem. What did concern him was that he was still far from the wealth level of the big boys in Dallas, Fort Worth, and Houston; and he worked earnestly as Vice President to close this gap.

His KTBC radio and TV net profits had risen to more than five hundred thousand dollars a year, and to replace the small, rented quarters that housed the LBJ Co. there was now an eight-story windowless building erected in Austin at a cost of eight hundred thousand dollars, with a luxurious private apartment for himself.

Despite his new position as the nation's Vice President, he constantly exhorted his salesmen to bring in more time advertisers. Since advertising rates depended on the number of potential listeners, on one occasion he took on the job of expanding the KTBC market. In 1962 the FCC was enforcing a freeze that barred existing stations from relocating their transmitters, but Johnson was Vice President, and the FCC made an exception to the freeze by permitting the LBJ Co. to move its Austin transmitter and pick up an additional sixty-five thousand potential listeners. When questioned about this, FCC officials insisted that KTBC's lease on its old transmitter site was about to expire and the owners would not renew it. However, a check revealed that the lease had several years yet before possible termination.

Down in Alabama Johnson and Lady Bird employed agents to add to the 3,800 acres of land she had inherited from her Aunt Effie and Uncle Claude. Alabamans talked about the farms in Autauga and Chilton Counties that moved into her possession and were seeded with pine trees. In addition Johnson was putting in hour after hour in his four official Washington offices and in Texas to expand his ranch holdings at home.

From 1961 onward through his Vice Presidency, he and his agents bought more than 12,000 acres in Blanco, Gillespie, Llano, and Burnet Counties, close to his 438-acre Blanco County L.B.J. Ranch, for about a million and a half dollars. In this acreage were three excellent ranches: the Scharnhorst place, the Lewis ranch, and the Haywood place.

The Scharnhorst place—ten miles away—cost Johnson $54,000. He put air conditioning into its red-frame ranch house and hung on the walls the stuffed heads of deer Lady Bird and Lynda Bird killed. Of its eighteen hundred acres, a mile and a half of the ranch property fronted on the Pedernales. This became Johnson's favorite deer-hunting ground and the chief source of the venison sausages he enjoyed for breakfast.

The Lewis ranch, costing sixty-five dollars an acre, covered eight hundred acres and had a fieldstone house that Lady Bird remodeled and decorated.

Six times as large as the Lewis ranch was the Haywood place, twenty-five miles from the L.B.J. Ranch and Johnson's prize possession. After his return from Southeast Asia, he and his hunting pal, Judge Moursund, acquired it in June 1961 from Texas Christian University, which had gained it initially from the will of Lula Haywood. The university wanted $550,000, but Johnson and Moursund got it for $500,000 with $200,000 down and a ten-year note due in 1971 for the other $300,000 plus 5 per cent interest.

After the purchase the two partners then sold 242.7 of the 4,718 Haywood acres for $326,660 to the Comanche Cattle Corporation, which Moursund managed for himself and Johnson. These 242 acres were on the shores of the artificial, government-built, twenty-two-mile-long Granite Shoals Lake, later renamed Lake Lyndon B. Johnson at Johnson's request. This lake and several others west of Austin were the backwash of the dams built by Alvin Wirtz. The water of Lake L.B.J. came specifically from the nearby Llano and Colorado rivers.

Moursund and Johnson's original group of lakeside lots numbered about one hundred, and they peddled them as "Comanche Rancherias" and "Comanche Ranchettes" at advertised prices running from six to seven thousand dollars each. They sold one group at a "discount" to Arthur Krim, a Johnson friend who was head of United Artists and a Democratic fundraiser. Krim was given a bargain price of $28,047 for eight lake-front lots. To help the sale of the other lots (and boost lot prices), Johnson got after the Texas Highway Department to put up a $725,000 bridge across the Llano River so the rancherettes would have shopping facilities at the town of Kingsland, across the river.

On some of his excursions back to Texas, Johnson was drawn to the excellent ranch house on the Haywood place. Tall, thick hedges surrounded the house and kept the cattle from coming close. Behind the house was Packsaddle Mountain, and in front ran a hill to the water below. Suddenly taken with water sport, Johnson built a boathouse on Lake L.B.J. to moor his new swift motorboat and his new nineteen-foot, sixty-m.p.h. cabin cruiser. Secret Service agents attached to the Vice President were then forced to buy a jet boat and house it on the lake. After Johnson put a radio-telephone relay system on his cruiser, he could roar his jeers from the cabin at the Secret Service agents because they could not attain his speed in their effort to maintain a close watch on him. From his boat he could also call the L.B.J. Ranch and have servants deliver meals to him twenty-five miles away.

In addition to his ranch holdings, which also included the 2,785-acre Nicholson ranch that he purchased for "$10 and other valuable considerations," Johnson purchased twenty-five acres of land in Johnson City along with several buildings, and increased his Austin land holdings to include some property worth up to thirty thousand dollars an acre. The Austin Muzak franchise also became his, and four Austin banks considered his shareholding to be substantial.

Johnson's control of the dummy Brazos-Tenth Street Corporation, an Austin real estate holding company, did not become known until a plane crashed west of Austin in February 1961. Friends of a Houston oil millionaire and long-time Johnson supporter said that this man had lent Johnson his white Convair CV in 1960 in order to give him as much campaigning class as John Kennedy, who was traveling across the country in his family's Convair, the *Caroline*. In order to protect Johnson from Republican charges that he was an oil stooge, the man's friends reported, he had written a phony lease giving Johnson the option to buy the half-million-dollar plane for two hundred thousand dollars. The oral agreement was that Johnson would return the plane after the campaign. However, when the last speech ended and the final votes were counted, upon the owner's request for his plane, said his friends, Johnson told him he was exercising the option to buy.

This produced an immediate problem for Johnson, for the jet could not land on the 3,000-foot, thin asphalt runway at the L.B.J. Ranch. But it was solved by the laying of a thick asphalt runway 6,300 feet long, though mystery developed regarding who paid the seventy-five-thousand-dollar cost. There was no mystery, however, about the thirty thousand dollars spent for navigational lights and radio instrumentation, because this was paid by the Federal Aviation Agency upon its declaration that the ranch landing field was the "Johnson City Airport."

On the night of February 17, 1961, while at his ranch, Johnson called his pilot, Harold Teague, at the Austin Airport and ordered him to fly the Convair to the L.B.J. Teague had been told by the tower that the fog was too soupy for safe take-offs and flights, but when he passed this on to Johnson, according to witnesses, he was treated to a tongue-lashing and a penetrating question: "What do you think I'm paying you for?"

Ordered to take off, Teague finally did, and in the fog he and Charles Williams, his copilot, lost their lives when the plane crashed into a hill. Afterward, a friend of Johnson reported that the Vice President had sobbed when word of the crash reached him.

Johnson disclaimed ownership of the plane, and when newsmen checked on the Convair's title they found that the Brazos-Tenth Street Corporation was listed as the owner. But a further check revealed that Brazos-Tenth, with extensive ranchland and city real estate and the possessor of more than a million dollars worth of bank stock, had no telephone and was housed in the same building as the LBJ Company.

"A lot of people think I'm just a front for Lyndon Johnson," Donald Thomas told a *Wall Street Journal* reporter. "I'm not. There are no facts to suggest the company [Brazos-Tenth] is owned by anyone but me."

But Thomas, who was a law partner of Mr. Ed "The Talking Horse" Clark, was also a director and executive secretary of Johnson's broadcasting empire, a trustee of the LBJ Profit-Sharing and Incentive Plan and of the Johnson Foundation. If Brazos-Tenth Street Corporation was not a front for Vice President Johnson, then its business operations made no sense.

Wall Street Journal investigators found, for instance, that on February 1, 1962, the LBJ Company, with Thomas signing the sales papers as executive secretary, sold parcels of Austin real estate to Brazos-Tenth with Thomas signing as purchaser. Then before sunset that day Brazos-Tenth sold the same property to Vice President Johnson. So the property in reality went from Johnson to Johnson to Johnson. Another such deal involved forty lots in two counties, with the real estate moving from the LBJ Company through the dummy company to Lyndon Johnson.

There were so many more of these strange deals by the Vice President that there was wonder by those who knew about them that he had time for the duties Kennedy assigned him. And what was the point of these real estate transfers? The *Wall Street Journal* could find no explanation except a probability that he wanted to make use of the capital gains provisions of the tax laws—to get an immediate profit on the property and still retain it for future profits by a reversal of sales. Had the LBJ Company sold the real estate directly to him without an intermediate sale, said the *Wall Street Journal,* the Internal Revenue Service would not have allowed it. But this was only an extra precaution, for Bob Phinney, his former employee, was now the Internal Revenue Service director for the southern Texas district.

These wheeler-dealer real estate transactions—the ranch and city lots purchases and the three-step tax dance—were only one part of Vice President Johnson's cyclonic business activities. There was also his insatiable interest in gaining control of banks.

The American National Bank in Austin had assets of 117 million dollars. Johnson moved in with the help of LBJ Company money and became a large stockholder. His hunting pal and business partner, A. W. Moursund, became a member of the bank's board. At Austin's Capital National Bank, with 122 million dollars in resources, Ed Clark was chairman of the board of directors and Brazos-Tenth Street Corporation became a stockholder. Clark was wearing one of his loud checked suits and a bright colored shirt when a reporter asked him for details of Johnson's interest in the bank. Mr. Ed laughed and said nothing except, "Spell my name right. I need the business." The *Wall Street Journal* noted the peculiarity that wherever a Johnson interest was involved in a business deal, Clark, Moursund, and Thomas were also participants.

Besides Clark's bank, Brazos-Tenth Street Corporation had investments in three other Austin banks plus stock in financial institutions elsewhere. The hometown boy who made good in Washington also made good in Johnson City. Here the Citizens State Bank with three million dollars in resources had been functioning profitably for years when Brazos-Tenth showed up one day as owner of four-fifths of its stock and installed Moursund, Thomas, and Jesse Kellam, now president of the Johnson broadcasting interests, as the controlling members of its board of directors.

Johnson and Moursund enjoyed a major banking *coup* in the spring of 1963, at a time when Kennedy was trying to keep the New Frontier alive in the face of harsh Congressional resistance. "Look at him. He's a man," Johnson said proudly of Moursund's ability to strike a hard bargain. "He can survey a line, brand a cow, break a horse, skin a deer, go to Houston and lick ten big-city attorneys in the courtroom, and he can whip Heavyweight Champion Sonny Liston right now, tonight."

The Vice President and Moursund drove to Llano one morning that spring and entered the Moore State Bank for a private conversation with Tom Moore, the president. The bank was a sound institution and had paid dividends twice a year for thirty years. Moore enjoyed running the bank as boss, yet when his two visitors stood up to leave they had his agreement to turn controlling interest over to Brazos-Tenth, which would put five men on the bank's board, including Moursund, Thomas, and Moursund's law partner, Tom Ferguson, the former Texas Insurance Commissioner. In addition, Moursund would draw a thousand dollars a month as counsel to the bank. The conclusion of the *Wall Street Journal* was that the Johnson bunch wanted to finance "other ventures by borrowing from this bank."

As Vice President, Johnson also busied himself with the LBJ Company's Profit-Sharing Plan and the Johnson Foundation. The Profit-Sharing Plan was reputedly established as a trust for rewarding employees. But in 1963, thirty-eight employees went to court to request an accounting of its funds. Rather than parcelling out profits, there were indications that its chief function was to buy bank stock and invest in oil, gas and mining properties, and to lend money at interest to outsiders.

The Johnson Foundation, established in 1956 with Moursund, Thomas and Kellam as trustees, was proclaimed as a charitable organization to dole out some Johnson monies to needy and worthy groups. Yet in 1963, its assets increased eleven times more than the money it paid out and it was busy increasing its investments on a tax-free basis in Austin banks and private commercial enterprises. One such investment by the Johnson Foundation was its major stock purchase in the Austex Chili Company, a food canning firm in Austin, which merged with the Frito-Lay corn and potato chips company in Dallas.

In addition to his own frenzied business activities in the raw pursuit of great wealth, Vice President Johnson did not forget his principal political backers—especially Brown and Root. On a single night during Johnson's 1948 race for the Senate, Herman Brown had raised fifty thousand dollars for him by telephoning a few contractor friends; and who could forget the fun weekends at George Brown's Virginia place? Fresh from a billion-dollar construction on Guam and a two-billion-dollar air bases contract in sunny Spain, Brown and Root were ever on the lookout for more federal contracts.

In 1961, when the National Science Foundation decided to ask Congress to authorize Project Mohole, Brown and Root indicated to Johnson its desire to land the contract. Project Mohole involved boring a hole three miles below the bottom of the Pacific Ocean to study "the mantle of the Earth." While the scientific benefits were of little consequence to the company, new, acquired skills in such deep drilling might be applicable for future oil ventures at these depths. In 1962, when the contract panel of the National Science Foundation reviewed the five construction bidders, it rated Brown and Root as the least qualified of the lot by far. Ten other firms were highly endorsed, yet a strange thing happened on the way to the contract signing, for after Vice President Johnson expressed an interest in science, Brown and Root landed the Mohole contract at a bid for its fee as project constructor of almost twice the low bid. Then when work started, the estimated cost of twenty million dollars was revised upward to 127 million dollars.

Brown and Root also gained a foothold in the military construction program in South Vietnam, which was to expand from 21 million dollars in 1962 to a 1.2-billion-dollar program a few years later. In addition Johnson joined George Brown and his Rice Institute classmate, Representative Albert Thomas, in successfully moving the NASA Space Center to Houston, far from the Cape Canaveral launching pads. Thomas played the major role, for he happened to be Appropriations Subcommittee chairman on NASA's budget.

In 1962 a serious behind-the-scenes struggle took place at the Pentagon over the awarding of a contract to produce the TFX fighter and bomber planes for the Navy. Secretary McNamara's top military advisers and technical experts favored Boeing over General Dynamics, and said that Boeing's plane plans were superior and cheaper. However, Senator Henry "Scoop" Jackson noted that great pressure was coming from Texas in favor of General Dynamics, and Republican congressmen began calling the TFX the "L.B.J." In the end McNamara awarded the contract to General Dynamics despite the charge that he was wasting an unnecessary four hundred million dollars and would give Navy fliers an inferior carrier plane. An estimated seven to ten billion dollars was involved in the TFX contract.

H. P. "Pat" Zachary, wealthy San Antonio builder, was another who benefited year after year from federal contracts through Johnson's interest. To Johnson, Zachary's rise was the Horatio Alger story of Texas, and one time when he was discussing with Zachary possible solutions for the filthy Mexican slums in San Antonio, he blurted: "I wish you would tell the

Mexicans to get out and work with the grass, prune the trees, work with the flowers. Tell them that's how you got started, Pat—and now you're a millionaire."

This was the homespun advice of the Vice President for those on the lowest rungs of American society.

Chapter 61

OBSERVERS WHO WATCHED the President and Vice President in their offices and at meetings noted few similarities between the two men. One likeness was that both were highly nervous: Johnson had pocket cases of salve to rub on his skin rashes and inhalers to inject into his nostrils, while Kennedy was forever adjusting his belt, pushing his hair off his forehead, running a hand down his tie, and hitting his teeth with a finger nail to show impatience with a speaker. Representative Hale Boggs, the House Democratic whip, remembered that the handsome young President was "always pulling up his gray socks and pulling on a middle finger." One dissimilarity was that Johnson kept his desk and office neat, while Kennedy's desk and closet were in great disorder.

But the dissimilarities extended beyond such trivia into the thinking of both men on foreign and domestic policy. Johnson's favorite foreign leaders were Chiang Kai-shek, President Ayub of Pakistan, President Diem of South Vietnam, and Moise Tshombe—leader of Katanga Province in the Congo and bedfellow of the European mining cartels—none of whom stood high on the Administration's list of worthwhile allies.

Nor did Johnson agree with the Kennedy approach toward a more peaceful and just international society. He viewed foreign aid as he did his private business transactions: You don't give something for nothing; there must be a *quid pro quo,* such as a promise of alliance. He saw the Administration's desire for the beginning of a détente with the Soviet Union, even to the extent of selling American surplus wheat to her, as a colossal blunder. When Kennedy finally authorized the wheat sale, Johnson was quick to judge this action as "the worst political mistake we have made in foreign policy in this Administration."

So far as Johnson was concerned, the most exasperating aspect of the Vice Presidency was that he was not free to express his strong opinions on foreign policy to Kennedy as a normal routine. An attendant at National Security Council sessions remembered Johnson's agonizing periods of silence while Kennedy restricted his questioning to his special advisers; Johnson sat with "his fingers locked and working together until sometimes the knuckles were white." And frequently, Johnson believed he was being sent on busywork errands so that he could not attend critical meetings. Secretary of State Dean Rusk, who found early that Johnson's views were similar to his own, was one of the few Kennedy officials who briefed Johnson on his department's activities.

Afterward some Kennedy men expressed their regret that Johnson had been treated to the neglect that was the historical lot of Vice Presidents. Yet the blunt truth is that on those occasions when Kennedy did bring Johnson into the discussion, he was quickly apprised that Johnson's views were discordant notes. And had he accepted those views, his own foreign policy would never have developed.

As it was, the Kennedy foreign policy faced serious troubles from the outset. In December 1956 Fidel Castro had walked ashore with eighty-one men on the southern coast of Cuba and started a revolution that witnessed the fleeing of the leaders of the sadistic and corrupt Batista regime and the establishment of the Castro Government two years later. In April 1959 Castro had come to New York and Washington, but Eisenhower would not see him, and not long afterward the bearded Cuban announced that the small nation of six and a half million persons was part of the Communist international.

Early in 1960 Eisenhower empowered the CIA to train and arm Cuban exiles in Guatemala for a return to their homeland, though he did not sanction such action during the remaining time he held office. It was after Kennedy became President that CIA Director Allen Dulles, Chairman of the Joint Chiefs of Staff General Lyman Lemnitzer, and Chief of Naval Operations Admiral Arleigh Burke convinced the green new Commander-in-Chief that he should sanction their harebrained scheme to manage an invasion of Cuba by fourteen hundred exiles. Their assurance that all of Cuba would rise to throw off the Communist yoke when the fourteen hundred arrived, plus a concurrence by Secretary of State Dean Rusk and Defense Secretary Robert McNamara that this would happen, led Kennedy into the worst blunder of his Administration.

What was to be a dramatic curtain raiser on his Administration, the tragic Bay of Pigs incident, was a traumatic experience for the new President and a blow to American prestige abroad. On April 15, 1961, eight United States B-26 bombers, manned by Cuban exiles, left Nicaragua and attacked three Castro airfields, inflicting little damage. Then on April 17, after Cuban refugees in the United States spread word to dozens of newspapers that an invasion was imminent, the fourteen hundred came ashore through the Bay of Pigs to be greeted by a large Castro force.

Kennedy had told Johnson nothing of this venture, and in fact, had asked him to entertain West German Chancellor Adenauer the weekend of the invasion on his Texas ranch. While Johnson was showing the old man what a real Texas barbecue was like and taking him to Fredericksburg so the German Texans could listen to a speech in their mother tongue, Kennedy was wrestling with the decision whether or not to use United States fliers as a cover for the Cuban invaders and if necessary to undertake an American invasion. At the same time that Johnson was kept in the dark, Kennedy passed word to Adlai Stevenson, now the United States representative at the UN, that "no United States personnel participated" in the planning of the invasion and "no United States Government airplanes of any kind participated." Stevenson, who was duped, argued these points vehemently in answer to a charge by Cuba of United States aggression.

Despite the advice of Adolf Berle, Jr., an old Johnson friend in F.D.R.'s State Department, and Thomas Mann, a Texan friend of Johnson, former Assistant Secretary of State for Eisenhower, and now Kennedy's Assistant Secretary of State for Inter-American Affairs, that the President commit the United States military might behind the unlucky fourteen hundred, Kennedy's decision on April 18 was to avoid war. When Castro then crushed the invasion forces in three days, Kennedy publicly accepted personal responsibility for the stupid and humiliating business.

Both Stevenson and Johnson had arguments with Kennedy afterward. On returning to Washington, Johnson blistered the CIA in a harsh interview with Kennedy and demanded that the intelligence agency be stripped of its bungling officials and undergo rebuilding. "Lyndon, you've got to remember," Kennedy interrupted him, "we're all in this, and that when I accepted responsibility for this operation, I took the entire responsibility on myself, and I think we should have no sort of passing the buck or backbiting, however justified." In this manner Kennedy was telling him not to involve himself in Presidential business. Some time later, in public, Kennedy tried to praise Johnson's role in the international field but succeeded only in offending him when he said, "Lyndon's been in on every major decision except, that is, for the Bay of Pigs." Johnson's response was an immediate protest: "That's one of the few I was really involved in."

Stevenson's reaction on learning that he had been speaking untruths at the UN was his decision to resign his post; and this was reinforced when he found that Kennedy was referring to him as "my official liar." But he came to the White House, and Kennedy, who generally had difficulty talking to him, convinced him on this occasion that he was truly sorry for misusing him. As a reward for staying on the UN job, where member countries considered him the most prestige-laden individual, Kennedy asked him to go on a goodwill tour of South America and offset the bad taste of the Bay of Pigs.

While Kennedy aides, through specious rhetoric, found countless plus points for him in his Bay of Pigs experience, Kennedy saw the need to recoup American stock abroad for moral world leadership and as a force for peace, not war. He had read a translation of Soviet dictator Khrushchev's speech of January 6, 1961, vowing not to engage in nuclear war; then received a warm note from him on his inauguration; and was told that two American fliers shot down over the Arctic in July 1960 would be released. Although he did not believe that the Cold War could be ended by a face-to-face meeting with Khrushchev, he saw no harm in discussing mutual problems with the Soviet leader; so he arranged a summit meeting in Vienna with him in June, to go over an agenda including ending internal warring in Laos, and working toward disarmament and a settlement of German problems.

This time Johnson knew of Kennedy's plan for summitry, and he argued with him privately against this course. The Johnson view was that the Cold War was permanent, that the Russians understood only sword rattling and massive military buildups. Johnson's position was also argued by his 1960 supporter, former Secretary of State Dean Acheson, whose browbeatings and public denunciations by Republicans for failing to include South Korea in the American first-line defense perimeter had so traumatically affected him that he believed that extreme military aggressiveness was the only way to deal with the Soviet Government around the world. But Kennedy's answer to Johnson, Acheson, and others who took this extreme position was that it was better to talk than to fight.

A bad omen for the forthcoming trip to Vienna was Kennedy's visit to Canada shortly before going to Europe. While shoveling ten spadefuls of dirt in a tree-planting ceremony in Ottawa, he suffered excruciating back pains which would not disappear and forced him to use crutches after his Vienna meeting. In addition Canadian Prime Minister John Diefenbaker was not only furious because Kennedy had met with his opponent, Liberal leader Lester Pearson, but also claimed that a Kennedy staff paper left behind on the conference table contained a marginal scrawl by Kennedy on the Prime Minister that read: "What do we do with the S.O.B. on this point?"

The Vienna Summit in June 1961 proved a debacle for the still-green President. Khrushchev's rudeness and roughness caught Kennedy unawares, and in retaliation for all the browbeating and bullying that he suffered, Kennedy attempted to retaliate by warning Khrushchev about a Communist "miscalculation" of Western resolve. And to Khrushchev's warning that he planned to sign a treaty with East Germany by the end of the year, thus making it necessary for the West to negotiate with his satellite over Berlin, Kennedy's reply was, "It is going to be a cold winter."

Afterward, Johnson strutted triumphantly about, for he recalled his advice that the West should not negotiate with the Communists. "It was a shock to the President," he was quoted as saying, "though he was well-briefed, to see it at firsthand. A man knows his daughter will leave him when she marries, but he does not feel it really until after the wedding. In the end the Vienna meeting was good for us by alerting us, as the Communists so often have helped us!"

Following the Vienna Summit, when Kennedy returned in a mild state of shock to Washington, he held a series of meetings and asked advisers to write memos outlining proposals for handling the expected Berlin crisis. The paper prepared by Dean Acheson, after talks with Johnson and other promilitarists, became the basic memo, serving as the focal point for agreement or disagreement by others. Acheson proposed a military showdown with the Communists by sending a division of troops down the Autobahn into Berlin; and if the Reds fought these men, then nuclear war would be the answer.

Johnson was not asked to prepare a work paper, and he did not openly enter the Berlin problem until called upon for his opinion at the July 13 meeting of the National Security Council. Secretary of State Dean Rusk supported the Acheson approach to avoid diplomatic negotiations with the Soviet Government and to concentrate on a military showdown; and when Johnson spoke he agreed with this approach and more. He would have Kennedy declare a national emergency, expand the Army, call up reserves, sharply increase the Defense budget by at least five billion dollars, raise taxes 2 per cent to cover the immediate cost of the military buildup, and order standby wage and price controls.

Kennedy's decision favored the Johnson approach, though it was not as drastic. Nevertheless, by asking Congress for a 3.25-billion-dollar increase in the Defense budget, calling up 160,000 National Guard and Reserve units, and painting a picture of impending nuclear war over nationwide TV, he set off national hysteria and a frenzied building of backyard underground air-raid shelters. It was Adlai Stevenson, returning from a trip to Europe, who looked about and then reported that Western Europe was shaking far less over fear of war than the United States.

When the Communists began erecting their Berlin Wall on August 13 around West Berlin, American hysteria reached its feverish height. It was then that Kennedy had ordered "Showdown Johnson" to go to Berlin and reassure West Berliners that the United States would not let them down; and it was then that Johnson balked about proceeding to a zone of possible personal danger. But he went, staying up all night in the plane crossing the Atlantic. Kennedy had ordered fifteen hundred troops to march through the Autobahn in East Germany to West Berlin in a test of Red intent. Concerned that he might now become a sitting duck, Johnson on arrival ordered Charles "Chip" Bohlen, former United States Ambassador to the Soviet Union and now special assistant to Dean Rusk, to roam through East Berlin and note the military preparedness there. Bohlen added to his concern by reporting a great deal of military activity, but the marching Americans entered West Berlin without incident, and the Johnson speech in West Berlin was the high point of his visit, both for himself and for the immense listening throng.

After his return Johnson gave reporters a mimeographed news story that he wanted them to push on their editors for publication. "When the Communists put up the wall in Berlin," the Johnson analysis read, "the immediate reaction was panic on the part of the German people. There was so little will to resist that the Communists could have virtually walked into West Berlin and taken it over.

"The Vice President went to Berlin, bringing the people the direct pledge of the President of the United States that this country would support West Berlin to the hilt. The visit reversed the depression and today Berlin remains free."

In de Gaulle's opinion Khrushchev had only been bluffing about signing a treaty with East Germany, and Kennedy's military buildup—flying fifty thousand soldiers to Germany—had been unnecessary. Whichever was true, when 1962 came, no treaty was signed, and the Berlin crisis evaporated. One casualty of this happy result was that Johnson's ally, Dean Acheson, was dropped by Kennedy as an adviser on foreign affairs.

The third of the four major international crises involving the Kennedy Administration—that of Laos—saw Johnson participating almost entirely as a seat warmer. After the 1954 Geneva Accords on Indochina, which provided for a neutral government for Laos, a kingdom with a population of three million persons, Secretary of State Dulles, citing the Domino Theory, committed the United States to expenditures of almost a half-billion dollars to install a military, right-wing government in power. At the same time the Soviet Union and China supported the Pathet Lao Communist armies in their effort to seize control.

At the hour Kennedy became President, the Pathet Lao was gaining the upper hand, and shortly afterward by his references to this tiny land at his news conferences, he gave the impression the United States would soon become involved in a major war there. This was not an entirely incorrect conclusion, for as he told an aide long afterward, "If it hadn't been for the Bay of Pigs, we'd be fighting in Laos by now—and that would be a hundred times worse."

For advice, as the Laos crisis deepened, Kennedy went to New York to talk to General MacArthur, and the old Asia hand told him: "Don't commit American foot soldiers on the Asian mainland." This advice was later objected to by the most hard-line of Kennedy's civilian advisers, Professor Walt Rostow of MIT and now Kennedy's assistant at the National Security Council, who argued the need for sending a substantial contingent of American troops to Laos. Added to Rostow's proposal that the American troops be placed in the path of the Pathet Lao to "deter" them from aggressive action was the advice of Richard Nixon, who came to the

White House and clamored in person to Kennedy for "a commitment of American air power" to Laos.

As for the Joint Chiefs of Staff and the three civilian service Secretaries, Johnson participated in the meeting where they expressed their views. From an earlier request for committing sixty thousand troops to Laos, their proposals now included one to send one hundred and forty thousand men and nuclear weapons. It was Johnson who suggested to Kennedy that, with all seven military and civilian service Secretaries contributing a garble of different proposals, they be asked to put their thoughts on paper. What Kennedy then received were seven different plans.

From all these divergent proposals Kennedy's decision was first to get the Soviet Union to ask the Pathet Lao to agree to a cease-fire, then to establish a neutral government once more. After the contending forces in Laos agreed to a cease-fire in May, a Geneva Conference undertook the task of establishing a neutral regime. Typical Communist stalling tactics in negotiations while continuing military action in the field led to Kennedy's decision to send five thousand Marines to the Thailand border of Laos and dispatch an American fleet to the trouble zone. Finally in June 1962 a neutral government was reestablished.

However, this settlement brought forth charges of a Kennedy defeat from hard-liners, who pointed out that Communists had been taken into the government and the contingent of United States military advisers had to leave Laos.

In the fourth major foreign crisis of the Kennedy Administration— the Cuban missiles crisis—Kennedy permitted Johnson to participate in the key discussions, though he considered Johnson's views too extreme to follow. This crisis began on October 16, 1962, when Kennedy learned from U-2 photos that Soviet medium-range ballistic missiles capable of hitting the lower half of the United States with nuclear warheads were at Cuban launching sites. Immediately he organized an Executive Committee of the National Security Council to determine what should be done. Johnson was a member of the Executive Committee, and an observer later remembered his nervous tension from the way he "tightened his mouth, pushed his lips up and backwards at the same time, and stiffly rubbed them with three midfingers of his right hand."

Over the next four days the group discussed six possibilities in great detail, and five task forces probed deeply into the legal, diplomatic, military, intelligence, and public informational aspects. The six alternatives ranged from doing nothing, holding diplomatic talks with the Soviets, and getting Castro to drop his Communist adherence, to blockading Cuba, attacking Cuba from the air and destroying the missile bases, and launching an invasion of the island.

Johnson was not present at all sessions, for he was away one day from the capital to campaign for Democrats in the 1962 Congressional elections. But when he was present, he agreed with Walt Rostow that the answer should be an all-out military liberation of Cuba. This also gave him an opportunity to belittle Attorney General Robert Kennedy's belief that even a much milder air strike would be "a Pearl Harbor in reverse" and "would blacken the name of the United States in the pages of history." According to one write-up that Johnson later called reliable, the Vice President called Bobby Kennedy "confused in his thinking," and "the only real way to remove that threat—to cut out the cancer soon enough—is to overthrow the Communist regime—and the only way to do that is by invasion and occupation."

In the end Kennedy accepted the proposal of Defense Secretary Mc-Namara to establish a sea and air blockade, or quarantine, against shipments of military matériel to Cuba and declare that any missile launched from Cuba against the United States would be considered as coming from the Soviet Union. With the threat that an invasion of Cuba was also in the works, on October 28 Khrushchev ended his Cuban venture by promising to dismantle his missiles there and take them back to the Soviet Union. For a few days the threat of nuclear war had terrorized the world, but it ended as suddenly as it had begun.

Joseph Kennedy and Senator George Aiken of Vermont served together on President Truman's Hoover Commission on the Organization of the Executive Branch in the late 1940's, and on one occasion, said Aiken, Kennedy confided that his son Jack hoped to make a political career beyond the House of Representatives. Aiken, with a wry smile, asked what advice the reactionary isolationist had given his thirty-year-old son.

"Simple but smart," said Kennedy. "I told him, 'Just stand for everything your old man's against and you might even become President.' "

John F. Kennedy's New Frontier, a modern counterpart of Franklin Roosevelt's New Deal and Harry Truman's Fair Deal, was diametrically in opposition to his father's narrow and archaic political philosophy. The term *New Frontier* had first appeared in his acceptance speech at the Democratic National Convention; and as Kennedy defined it that night, it referred to the "uncharted areas of science and space, unsolved problems of peace and war, unconquered pockets of ignorance and prejudice, unanswered questions of poverty and surplus."

As it unfolded in its three legislative years, the New Frontier included a potpourri of liberal proposals. Domestically, Kennedy wanted large-scale federal aid to education, a strong civil rights program, tax reform, federal aid to poverty areas, medical aid for the old, and manpower retraining for the computer age. In the foreign field, his New Frontier wanted a peace corps of idealistic Americans to work in underdeveloped nations, an "Alliance for Progress" for Latin America, or a stepped-up Roosevelt "Good Neighbor Policy," and a major trade expansion program empowering the President to cut tariffs by 50 per cent.

In the foreign New Frontier, Kennedy's success was significant more in intent than accomplishment. In the domestic end, he floundered as badly as had Truman with his Fair Deal.

At the outset of his Administration Kennedy's former associates in the Senate did not expect much from a man who had missed 331 Senate roll calls out of 1,183 in seven and a half years. Only a year earlier, when he was absent on his campaign tour for the West Virginia primary, Senator Joseph Clark had been quoted as saying, "I think the Senate will pass a minimum wage increase if we can just get Sonny Boy back from the cricks and hollows long enough to report it out of his committee."

But Kennedy had purpose now and a desire to win historic rank with Washington, Lincoln, and Franklin Roosevelt. Fulfillment of this desire depended to a large extent on his control of Congress, and it was here that he encountered a stone wall. Each year the Administration handed statistics of legislative achievements to the press: In 1961, total major recommendations by Kennedy—53, enacted into law—33; in 1962, recommendations—54, enacted—40; in 1963, recommendations—129, enacted—62. These figures boasted of legislative success, yet they were highly misleading, because the major New Frontier bills could not gain Congressional approval. As time passed, the same Senator Clark, once a Kennedy jeerer but now a New Frontiersman, denounced Congress as "the sapless branch" and called for a reform that would force both houses to hold votes on all Presidential bills.

Much of the trouble that Kennedy encountered with Congress over his New Frontier was simply a matter of timing. New legislation required long and repeated committee hearings and a public dialogue over a time period generally of three years' duration. Given another year as President with his Democratic Congress, he would probably have changed his record of legislative failure to legislative success.

However, some of Kennedy's poor rating as a legislative President resulted from other causes. For one thing, about three hundred members of Congress had run ahead of him in 1960 and did not believe they were indebted to him. This sense of independence made these congressmen difficult to deal with, and they rebuffed him at will, thus helping to nullify the two-thirds majority the Democrats held in the Senate and the 60 per cent held in the House.

For another thing, a great deal of resentment developed on the Hill over the approach of the White House liaison staff. "Those boys expected Congress to heel like a dog," said one who had many dealings with them. "Their approach was to use crude power, bare-knuckled, shanty Irish Boston politics; and what they built up instead was resentment and indignation. When Kennedy started in 1961, he could count on a dozen moderate Republican senators to provide the margin of victory on liberal bills. Before the session ended, half deserted him."

Just as Kennedy had incorrectly counted on Johnson to sweep the South for him in 1960, so the new President hoped vainly for some lapel-grabbing, glasses-steaming aid on legislation from his Vice President. One of the first Kennedy efforts in Congress on the domestic side was his promotion of a bill to raise the minimum wage from $1.00 an hour to $1.25, a level Johnson had opposed as majority leader. When the bill went to the House, Kennedy asked him to help bring Southern members into line behind the proposal. However, Johnson did nothing, because Representative Carl Albert of Oklahoma, the Democratic whip, took charge of this task. But when the Albert bill as amended came to the floor for a vote and lost by 186 to 185, Johnson told Texas reporters Rayburn had arranged this defeat as a special favor to him to teach Kennedy a lesson for holding back on some Texas patronage that Johnson wanted.

Although Rayburn denied the story and said that Albert's bill had lost because some lazy, liberal Democrats did not show up since they thought the bill would pass without them, the fact that Johnson owned all non-confirmation patronage in Texas lent credence to his story. Later, when the Albert bill passed by a substantial majority, Washington insiders agreed that through his control over Rayburn, Johnson was actually the boss of Kennedy.

But whatever use Johnson actually hoped to make of his special relationship with Rayburn ended that same first year of the Kennedy Administration. In the spring of 1961, Mister Sam had to discontinue his daily walk around the Capitol grounds because he found them too strenuous. Then in the summer he experienced such dizziness while sitting on the House dais that he had to grasp his desk's edge to keep from falling.

When pains developed in his back, he told reporters "that old lumbago is fretting me again." Kennedy aides who tried to talk to him about legislation were almost blown out of his office by his grouchiness. In September he deserted the House and went back to Bonham for tests. On October 2 he entered the Baylor Medical Hospital in Dallas, where doctors confirmed he was suffering from a metastatic cancer. Johnson came and sat at his bedside, and Kennedy and Truman flew to visit him. In great pain he was taken back to Bonham at his request, and he rapidly wasted away. "This is the damnedest thing that has ever happened to me," he gasped. Finally, on November 16, 1961, Mister Sam died, and another Johnson "Daddy" was gone.

After 1961 Johnson was never observed promoting a Kennedy bill on Capitol Hill, and in private he had complaints about several pieces of legislation and legislative tactics. In his single major action affecting the Kennedy program as presiding officer of the Senate, he served to reinforce opinion that he was not only out of step with the New Frontier but anxious to use what little authority he had as Vice President to do it harm.

Johnson's friend Senator Clinton Anderson was the man who brought on his problem in January 1963. Anderson expected a Kennedy Civil Rights Bill to come to the Senate that year, and he knew its chances were better if the Senate's Cloture Rule to cut off a filibuster required the affirmative vote of only three-fifths of the senators on the floor instead of two-thirds. But to change a Senate rule in a liberal direction was impossible so long as Russell's bloc could talk it to death. So Anderson began a floor argument in January 1963 that the Senate was not a "continuing" body. Each numbered Congress was a "new" Congress, he insisted, and therefore could adopt new rules by majority vote. One of these new rules, he went on, should be the lowered cloture requirement.

With his interests in jeopardy, Russell was soon on his feet, decrying this view and launching into a defense of the Senate as a "continuing" body. But even as he restricted his talk to such legalities, it was apparent to everyone present he was actually defending the filibustering powers of the South.

The Anderson-Russell argument was not an original debate. In the Wilson Administration senators had argued this issue at the top of their lungs; and in the Eisenhower Administration, Vice President Nixon, first in 1959 and again in 1961, had ruled from his presiding seat that each Senate was "new" and rules could be adopted by majority vote. But on neither occasion would the Senate majority leader (Johnson and then Mansfield) permit action to adopt any new rules.

In 1963, however, the Senate liberals had sufficient voting strength to enact the Anderson cloture change by a majority vote, and by maneuvering, forced the issue upon Vice President Johnson. If Johnson ruled that each Senate was "new," he would get cheers from the liberals; if he ruled it was "continuous," his Southern brethren would applaud.

Johnson's moment of truth finally came. But instead of a yes or no decision, he declared that he lacked authority to make any ruling on this issue, and that the Senate would have to decide the matter itself. Since his answer was a victory for Russell because a two-thirds Senate vote would now be necessary to declare each Senate "new," anger quickly developed among some Senate liberals.

Johnson watched this happen, and to head off criticism he announced that he had done the right thing, that no one was going to force him to take on "the authority of a military *junta*." Then he took the aggressive road in order to head off exploding criticism from the liberals. "Anxious as the Vice President may be at times to choke off debate," he snapped out, "this Vice President is not going to choke it off except in accordance with the rules!"

"We are not trying to make a dictator out of the Vice President," Senator Clark called up to him. "All we are trying to do is ask the Vice President to exercise his undoubted authority."

Senator Jacob Javits, New York Republican, gave him the unkindest cut of all. "There comes a time," he said, "when the Chair must recognize he is Vice President of the United States."

Chapter 62

B Y THE FALL of 1963 talk was common in Washington that Johnson would be dropped from the 1964 ticket because he had turned into a negative factor. A Midwestern senator, who traveled to Connecticut with the Vice President for a fund-raising affair for the Vice President's pal Senator Tom Dodd, reported to his Senate colleagues afterward that Johnson had lugubriously remarked during their New England visit, "I'm going to be out of it for a second term. Jack has another man in mind for Vice President." So concerned was Johnson over what he believed would be his political doom that he developed severe stomach pains. But in this instance, the doctor's diagnosis found it a coincidence of timing, that he was suffering from an oversupply of calcium and should eliminate milk from his diet.

Johnson had good reasons for being concerned about his future. Kennedy had discovered that his Texas political base was actually set in quicksand, and Johnson was no longer a political necessity to entice Southern votes. In addition, in every political scandal that erupted in 1963, Johnson's name was somehow entangled with that of the culprits.

In 1960, Kennedy had made the broad and unwarranted assumption that Texas Democrats were a noisy but monolithic group entirely under Johnson's control. Even when the Democratic ticket barely carried the state by 46,000 votes and the Republicans cried fraud to the tune of more than 100,000 uncounted Republican votes, Kennedy accepted their charges with stoic disdain. So had he ignored the loss of face suffered by Johnson when Republican John Tower, the little professor from Wichita Falls' Midwestern University, picked up 936,000 votes in the 1960 race with Johnson for the Senate.

But the Johnson reputation as the political boss of Texas suffered a White House decline shortly after the inauguration. The Administration was counting on a Democrat to win the special election set for April 4, 1961, for the six-year Johnson term, and Johnson spoke assuredly of appointed interim Senator William Blakley, the half-billionaire from Dallas, winning easily.

A total of seventy-one candidates entered that race, though only two counted: Blakley and Tower. Sam Rayburn, not yet seriously ill, knew how important the race was for Johnson's reputation, and he made appeal after appeal to Texas Democratic liberals to support Blakley. Unfortunately, the liberals had no use for Blakley because he had voted against Kennedy's depressed areas bill and the emergency feed grain program. In addition, Mister Sam, who was a personal friend of Blakley, could not talk him into a positive campaign stance with liberal appeal. "He is the hardest fellow to help I ever saw," said Rayburn. "He never does say what he is for—only what he's against."

Tower, with the help of Senator Barry Goldwater, who again campaigned for him by throwing digs at the Johnson radio-TV monopoly in Austin, emerged victor over Blakley in the primary by 135,000 votes. Yet since he lacked a majority, a run-off came on May 27. But the liberal Democrats could not be enticed to the polls, and Tower won again, to become the first Republican senator from Texas since Reconstruction days, when Jim Flanagan and Morgan Hamilton served.

Tower's swearing-in as a senator in the spring of 1961 was a blow to Johnson's political prestige at the White House. Yet he managed to ride out that storm and actually gained increased standing with Kennedy by plunging personally into the Bexar County campaign between State Senator Henry Gonzales and Republican John Goode, Jr. This race was for the House seat of Johnson's friend, Representative Paul Kilday, whom Kennedy had appointed to the Military Appeals Court in late 1961.

Gonzales, of Mexican ancestry, had been a fighting liberal in the state senate, opposing burdensome taxes on the poor and all forms of segregation. Goode was a proclaimed "Goldwater-oriented Republican," and when former President Eisenhower lent his prestige to him by campaigning for him in San Antonio, Johnson moved in as the champion of Gonzales, to the puzzlement of liberal Democrats.

Soon Washington and New York papers were describing the unusual efforts of the Vice President in behalf of Gonzales. Not only did he round up campaign funds for Gonzales, he also brought Mexican film star Cantinflas to the Twentieth Congressional District to entertain and electioneer for the Latino. In addition, Johnson came on the scene as a hard-working campaigner, and for an entire day and far into the evening, he stood on the back of a pickup truck and delivered speeches at a long run of street corners.

Gonzales beat Goode by 10,000 votes out of 95,000 on November 4,

1961, and for the time being Johnson could claim a showy success as a Texas political leader who sponsored the liberal cause. Liberal Texas Democrats, who tried to find the reason for his out-of-character behavior, had only to examine his shaky pre-Gonzales status in Washington.

But there was no home-state political rest for the Vice President, despite the Gonzales effort and his astute doling out of federal patronage. Only the next year Johnson was again put to the test when John Connally quit as Secretary of the Navy to run for governor of Texas. Johnson cared little when the right-wing extremist General Edwin Walker announced his candidacy and the little-known Attorney General Will Wilson also filed. However, he and Connally did a great deal of swearing when Governor Price Daniel broke his word against running for a fourth and unprecedented term and joined the contest. Rounding out the candidates was the choice of the liberal Democrats, thirty-six-year-old Don Yarborough, a Houston lawyer and a World War II and Korean War veteran, who believed Kennedy could do no wrong. Don Yarborough was not related to Senator Ralph Yarborough.

The campaign took unexpected turns. Johnson had hoped to do some work for Connally, but Connally had hardly begun his twenty-five-thousand-mile tour of the state when he noted that any mention of Johnson brought resounding "boos." "Don't you come back and campaign for me, Lyndon," he warned his "Daddy"; and to Texas crowds he bellowed with Johnson mannerisms: "When John Connally sits in that governor's chair, you're going to know who's governor of Texas. No man will occupy that chair with me or stand behind me."

Almost all the 125 daily newspapers and the 555 weeklies in Texas were behind Connally, and his campaign chest bulged with so many large contributions from the wealthy that he frequently made use of costly TV shows. In addition hundreds of billboards throughout the state showed the handsome, prematurely gray Connally with a look of stubborn integrity in his eyes. But as the primary progressed, it soon became evident to Connally and Johnson that Don Yarborough, who lacked newspaper backing and campaign funds, was making serious gains with his sincerely stated support of the entire New Frontier. A saving grace was that Price Daniel, who would normally have split the conservative Democratic vote, was now being clobbered by the charge that he had "used his office to accumulate two million dollars worth of land."

Johnson could take a deep breath when the May 4, 1962, primary totals were announced, for Connally had 422,000 of the 1,400,000 votes. Even though he held only one-third of the total and would be forced into a run-off with Don Yarborough, who had come in second with 312,000, Connally should win easily because the Daniel and other conservative votes would now be his.

But the month-long run-off campaign revealed the serious intent of the liberals to defeat Connally and destroy Johnson nationally. In every city and town the liberals searched out votes for Don Yarborough, and the young candidate, whose only previous political campaigning had been an unsuccessful run for lieutenant governor in 1960, made impassioned speeches backing Kennedy. Tens of thousands of bumper stickers appeared on cars, reading: "Scratch Lyndon's Boy, John."

Connally was now concerned, and with a newly filled campaign chest he set off by train across Texas to destroy his opponent by character assassination. His banners and billboards cried: "Connally Go Ahead versus C.I.O. Red"; and at every stop, to the roaring boos of his shills in the crowd, he charged Yarborough with being the candidate of the Americans for Democratic Action. Yarborough's reply was that Connally was "a confessed lobbyist for Eastern oil and gas monopolies and a man weaned on the big lie technique, such as saying John F. Kennedy was suffering from a 'death-dealing disease.' "

Reporters noted the strange situation where the Vice President was supporting a man who campaigned against much of the Kennedy program and opposing a Kennedy admirer. Yet the situation was even more bizarre. At one point Don Yarborough requested White House aid in the form of a Kennedy statement, but Kennedy rejected his plea. In fact, said James Wechsler, a Kennedy confidant and editor of the New York *Post,* "It is even reported that the President tried to persuade some Texas labor chieftains to desert Yarborough and endorse Connally."

Despite his immense war chest and Presidential backing, Connally won the run-off by a mere 27,000 votes out of 1,100,000. Even so, he could not claim an untainted victory, because liberal Democrats insisted they had evidence his campaign aides had purchased far more than his winning margin in the George Parr country close to the border and in the poverty-stricken Mexican section of San Antonio. Afterward, liberals charged Kennedy with being either naive or double-dealing; and to show their anger and continuing hatred of Johnson, they deserted their party to vote for Republican Jack Cox in the November election.

The insecurity Johnson suffered in his Texas political base was not the sole excuse he believed Kennedy might use for replacing him on the 1964 ticket. Several scandals broke in 1962 and 1963, and because of Johnson's association with the individuals involved, many Democratic politicians were already wincing at probable Republican charges of a scandal-ridden Administration in the following Presidential campaign.

After John Connally quit his Navy post, Johnson had won Kennedy's approval to appoint Fred Korth, president of the Fort Worth Continental National Bank and a former Truman Assistant Secretary of the Army, as his successor. Korth's bank was the principal money source for the General Dynamics Corporation, and when this firm won the TFX fighter-bomber plane contract, reporters uncovered the connection. A political furor developed, a Senate investigation got under way, and Kennedy, sorely vexed by questioning at a news conference in October 1963, told a reporter, "I have no evidence that Mister Korth acted in any way improperly in the TFX matter." But Korth resigned and returned quickly to Fort Worth, while reporters began to conjecture about the role Johnson had played in the affair.

There was also Billie Sol Estes, a short, plump, bespectacled young man from Pecos who could have written volumes on wheeling and dealing and financial fakery. Billie Sol, who opposed dancing and swore he "never took a drink, smoked, or cursed," had been chosen one of the "Jaycee Outstanding Young Men of 1953." Behind this facade Estes, a rare financial genius, was involved in such a tangle of fraud that when his empire toppled, hundreds of investigators, including seventy FBI agents, could not entirely comprehend what he had been doing. For one thing, he stored government grain in his grain warehouses for fat fees, yet how much of this grain was quickly moved out was only a guess. Another scheme involved giving mortgages to farmers on fertilizer tanks that did not exist and selling those mortgages to banking institutions and private firms at a discount that netted him millions of dollars.

Estes was a Democrat, and he contributed frequently to the campaigns of various party members. Among contributions known were his $15,000 to the Democratic National Committee in 1960; $7,900 over seven and a half years to Ralph Yarborough campaigns; and $1,500 in 1962 to Texas Congressman R. T. Rutherford. His home boasted autographed pictures of Kennedy, Truman, and Adlai Stevenson, and when he came to Washington, he was entertained by the Johnsons at The Elms.

Neither Johnson nor Ralph Yarborough knew of Estes' manipulations, and because of his reputation as the saintly pillar of Pecos, Johnson decided to win him away from Yarborough for 1964. "Early in 1962," said Senator Yarborough, "Rutherford called and asked if I would attend a meeting with him and Estes at the Department of Agriculture, where Estes wanted to get approval for a cotton acreage allotment in Alabama, which he then wanted to transfer to Texas. This was evidently one of the few legitimate matters Estes was in, though I refused to make any recommendation to Charlie Murphy, the Undersecretary of Agriculture, who ran that meeting. This was the only time I ever attended a meeting with Estes, and when Murphy rejected his request, I returned to the Senate."

From the Department of Agriculture, Estes went directly to Johnson's office, where Cliff Carter spoke knowingly about the meeting before Estes could talk. "What are you going to Yarborough for?" he asked. "He's not important at all. Why, Billie Sol, you're a great man! When you walk, Wall Street shakes!"

An Estes acquaintance later reported that Carter took him in to see

Johnson. "Lyndon, I'm in trouble," Estes wailed, and Johnson said assuringly, "I'm going to see if I can help you, Billie Sol. We'll just go down to the White House and see about that."

When they returned, Estes told Carter, "I couldn't get to see the President." But shortly after that, he won his cotton acreage allotment and transfer privileges.

As the Estes acquaintance viewed this petty story, Johnson, on learning that Yarborough was going to Agriculture with Billie Sol, had called Murphy, who had worked in the 1960 Johnson campaign effort, and told him to reject Estes' request. Then when Johnson later could get him what he wanted, Billie Sol would be indebted to the Vice President.

But nobody wanted to know Estes when his scandals were exposed. Rather than admit any relationship with Billie Sol, Johnson tried to clear himself by shoving all onus in Senator Yarborough's direction. Murphy, denying that he was a Johnson friend, said that Yarborough had lobbied with him for Estes, and pro-Johnson papers in Texas printed the lie: "Do you know that Estes gave Yarborough fifty thousand dollars?" Secretary of Agriculture Orville Freeman, who had named Estes a member of the honorary Cotton Advisory Commission in July 1961, said he had done so on Yarborough's letter of recommendation, even though Yarborough's letter was dated the previous February. However, when a staff aide of the McClellan Senate Investigating Subcommittee "leaked" word that Johnson and Murphy had aided Estes, the damage to Johnson was apparent from the reams of newsprint that continued to link his name with the Pecos wheeler-dealer.

The Estes river had other eddies. In 1960 Jerry Holleman, the president of the Texas AFL-CIO, had been a leading opponent of the drive to make Johnson the "favorite son" candidate at the national convention, until Johnson held a private talk with him and changed him into a rooter. Later Kennedy appointed Holleman Assistant Secretary of Labor and a member of Johnson's Committee on Equal Employment Opportunity. Here Holleman's demands for action produced friction between him and Johnson, leading to Johnson's public warning one time: "You get too upset about the Nigras, Jerry." When Holleman was discovered to have accepted a thousand dollars from Estes, and Kennedy ordered him to resign, Johnson was delighted because the Estes spotlight was momentarily shifted from his own face.

The Estes river also flowed over three high officials at the Department of Agriculture in Washington who were fired because of their warm relationship with him. Yet Agriculture Secretary Orville Freeman undid such high-minded action by demoting a fourth official who had charged the Department with abetting Billie Sol's schemes. And when the latter's secretary, a mild Southern lady named Miss Mary Jones, who was about to retire from the federal service, protested her boss' fate, she was dragged from the office to a mental hospital, stripped of her clothes, and declared mentally ill. Only through the efforts of Johnson's old Senate opponent, Senator John Williams of Delaware, was Miss Jones finally liberated from her nightmare.

Then down in Texas Dr. John Dunn, who owned the Pecos *Independent*, the newspaper that originally exposed Estes and connected him to Johnson, was barred from practice in the local hospital by the City Council after fraudulent charges of malpractice. Dr. Dunn was also hounded and threatened so relentlessly, and called "Nigger lover" to his face, that he finally had to move. While Dunn was ruined, his editor, Oscar Griffin, who wrote up his Estes findings, won the Pulitzer Prize.

The most significant blow dealt Johnson during his Vice Presidency resulted from the revelations involving his protégé, Bobby Baker. Young Bobby, the fourteen-year-old Senate page from Pickens, South Carolina, in 1942, had moved up to the point where he was often referred to as the "one hundred and first senator." In the early days, said one Senate observer of Johnson's protégé, "Bobby was an unabashed lackey— a bootlicker—and he'd think of any excuse to come to the office and see Johnson." Another Baker-Johnson watcher said, "Bobby even tried to be Johnson. He copied Lyndon's clothes and mannerisms. When he came into the Senate chamber, he'd take the Johnson stance, smooth his sideburns, brace his shoulders, and scowl up at the balcony—the whole bit. The only thing wrong with his act was that he was six inches too short."

Senator George Smathers gave his version of why Baker was the closest person in Washington to Johnson: "Bobby Baker was an energetic little fellow—the only one around who could keep up with Lyndon." In turn, Johnson had this to say about Bobby: "He is my strong right arm, the last man I see at night, the first one I see in the morning."

Opinions of Baker varied among the Senate membership, for like Johnson, Baker divided senators into "Whales" and "Minnows," and he treated each group accordingly. One Senate Minnow admitted, "I never liked him very much, but if you wanted to know what was going on, Bobby was the guy you called. He had the head count. He knew who was drunk, who was out of town, who was sleeping with whom. He knew who was against the bill and why, and he knew how to approach him to get him to swing around." American University thought so much of Baker's political work that it awarded him an honorary degree in 1961.

Baker's political existence had grown so entwined with Johnson's that there was some question whether he would continue to function full-steam after Johnson left the Senate. But he continued to do so because he had the support of Senator Bob Kerr, the arrogant Oklahoman, who possessed a thirst for political power and money as unslaked as

Johnson's. Baker frequently told the story, with a proud air, of that wild morning in Los Angeles when he was advising Lyndon to take second place on the ticket, and Senator Kerr, who had walked into the room, "in his anger swung and slapped me as hard as I've ever been hit." But Bobby continued talking, and after five minutes, he said, Kerr came around to his point of view and conceded, "You're right. You're smarter about this than I was, Bobby."

Baker remained full of tricks and power in the Kennedy era because of Kerr and the hesitancy of Majority Leader Mike Mansfield to fire him and replace him with his own choice for secretary for the majority. Senator Yarborough attributed his lack of success in getting on the Appropriations Committee to the intrigue of Baker in combination with Vice President Johnson. Senator Quentin Burdick of North Dakota told Baker in 1961 he wanted to land a seat on the Judiciary Committee, but Baker told Senator Joe Clark of the Democratic Steering Committee, which voted on committee memberships, that Burdick did not want it and Senator Edward Long of Missouri got it instead. Then there was the occasion when Kennedy called Baker to the White House at the outset of his Administration to discuss a possible enlargement of the Senate Finance Committee to add some liberal Democrats who favored tax reforms. But when Baker told Kennedy he did not believe he could collect the necessary votes to expand the committee, Kennedy accepted his verdict and dropped the idea. When Baker returned to the Capitol and reported this to Kerr, who was second man on the committee and a devout antireformer of the oil depletion allowance, Kerr might have danced a jig, said an observer, had he not been hindered by a hanging midsection.

It was only natural that Baker should decide to imitate Johnson and Kerr in the money-making department while holding public office. How well he succeeded can be gauged from a study of his ballooning net worth. In 1954 he reported it as $11,025; in 1960, as $262,102; and on February 1, 1963, as $2,166,866.

One of his relationships was with Don B. Reynolds, a former Air Force and Foreign Service officer, who was in the insurance business in Maryland. In 1957 Johnson took out two $50,000 life insurance policies through him, and in 1961 Johnson added another $100,000. Premiums were to be paid by the family's LBJ Co., which would also be the beneficiary. Asked afterward why Johnson had wanted the $200,000 worth of life insurance, a Johnson lawyer replied that this amount would be used to pay his inheritance taxes when he died.

But there were some unusual activities connected with these policies. After the initial ones, said Reynolds in testimony before a Senate committee on the day Johnson became President, Johnson's aide, Walter Jenkins, had badgered him into using part of his commissions to buy advertising time on Johnson's KTBC-TV station in Austin. Since Reynolds operated only in Maryland, such an expenditure was ridiculous, yet he bought $1,208 worth of time and then resold it at a cut-rate price to a pot and pan manufacturer. In addition, in 1959, Baker told Reynolds to send Johnson a stereo set, and Reynolds did in July, a set costing him $542. The invoice Johnson received with the set revealed Reynolds as the purchaser. When the set proved larger than she had anticipated, Lady Bird voiced a complaint, said Reynolds. Later when this Reynolds testimony was released by the Senate committee, Johnson was then President, and he told reporters that the stereo set had come from Baker—"a gift that an employee of mine made to me and Mrs. Johnson."

Reynolds also told the committee that Bobby Baker and other Democrats had involved him as a "bag man" to deliver political kickbacks. This was the case with the D. C. Stadium. Matt McCloskey, a builder and chairman of the Finance Committee of the Democratic National Committee, and later Kennedy's ambassador to Ireland, was successful in winning the low-bid construction contract for the Stadium, and then was successful in getting the government to add three million dollars to his bid after construction started. Baker told McCloskey to take out his performance bond through Reynolds, a charge of $73,631. But "in error," the McCloskey check was for $109,205, said Reynolds. Of this sum, Reynolds said he gave $4,000 to Bobby Baker, $2,500 to the clerk of the House District Committee, and an additional $25,000 went to the Democratic party as a 1960 campaign contribution.

From the great expansion of Baker's side activities, said Senator Russell Long on the Senate floor afterward, "Bobby Baker's boss must have known what he was doing. . . . His boss could have called a halt to those activities." Johnson voiced no objection in 1959 when Baker combined his Senate work with a restaurant project in partnership with Governor Luther Hodges of North Carolina, who later became Kennedy's Secretary of Commerce. Nor did Johnson object when Baker went into partnership with two builders to construct the Carousel, a million-dollar motel at Ocean City, Maryland. In fact, on opening day, Vice President and Mrs. Johnson were the guests of honor among the dozens of Senate freeloaders at the "high-style hideaway for the advise and consent set," as Baker described his motel. To help with the grand opening, Baker had the chef of the Senate Restaurant and several employees on hand as well as food from the restaurant, table linen, cooking utensils, and warming pots; a group of lobbyists supplied the liquor; and the Washington, D. C., Transit bus company carried the guests to and from the Carousel at no charge.

While Baker was riding high, he collected money from a California bank that won a charter as a national bank, received a payment of a half-cent a pound on all beef imported into the United States from Haiti, helped a company get a favorable tax ruling and acquired an enormously profitable stock option, dabbled in Florida real estate in a deal with Senator Smathers, operated a travel agency, and was involved in a pipeline company and the vending machine business. On frequent occasions individuals entered into "Texas deals" with him—they put up all the money in a venture and he received half the profit.

Many times Baker was in need of sudden cash, and he told a jury of one experience in July 1962 when he needed $300,000. He said he told Johnson of this, and the Vice President called Kerr, who arranged a loan for $250,000. The rest of the money, Baker claimed after Kerr's death, came from Kerr as the result of a pay-off to the senator as campaign contributions from savings and loan bank executives. Baker said that in 1962 the Kennedy Administration wanted to impose high taxes on the savings and loan business, and Kerr had written a Senate Finance Committee report calling for the tax increase. Baker said he then brought an official from the industry into the Vice President's ceremonial office off the Senate floor for a talk with Kerr, and afterward Kerr not only killed the tax increase but saw to it that a bill the savings and loan people favored passed Congress. For this, said Baker, he picked up $99,600 from the individuals in the industry to be given to Kerr, and out of this, he claimed, Kerr gave him the rest of the loan he needed.

The Baker balloon was pricked in September 1963 as a result of his vending machine operations. He had been receiving $650 a month from a food vending machine company for his help in landing a contract with the Melpar Corporation, a Defense Department contractor, to put its vending machines in Melpar's Falls Church, Virginia, plant. Baker demanded $1,000 a month, and when the company refused to pay this, Baker got the Melpar president to revoke the contract and issue a new one to Serv-U, a vending machine company that Baker and a few friends had organized.

With the Senate secretary for the majority connected with Serv-U, and his friend the Vice President chairman of the Space Council, little wonder that Serv-U could trade on such prestige. In only eighteen months of existence business boomed to an annual rate of $3,500,000, and *The New York Times* quoted *Vend* magazine's observation that "Serv-U's success in aerospace plants contracts was the talk of the vending machine industry."

But in September 1963 when the Capital Vending Company sued Baker for $300,000 for the loss of the Melpar contract, and the Washington *Post* mentioned the suit, Senators Mike Mansfield and John Williams asked Baker for an explanation. However, Baker quickly acquired Johnson's lawyer and adviser, Abe Fortas, as his attorney, and on legal advice, he refused to keep his scheduled appointment with the senators. On October 8 the Washington *Post*'s front-page headline read: BAKER RESIGNS SENATE POST.

The biggest scandal of the Kennedy Administration had begun. Reporters delved into the *Congressional Record* for Johnson comments on Baker and came up with "He is a man who truly serves his country, and I consider him one of my most trusted, most loyal and most competent friends. . . . He gives of himself unsparingly, and without regard to what he will get in return." Newsmen also found that Baker lived not far from Johnson in a Spring Valley $124,500 home, and that his two youngest children were named Lynda and Lyndon Baines.

As the clamor arose for a Congressional investigation of Baker and his activities (most of them still unknown), Johnson experienced the sinking feeling that Kennedy would drop him. "There are some funny things going on in Washington," said Republican Senator Thruston Morton in a public talk. "The Secretary of the Navy—Fred Korth—has left town rather hurriedly. Lyndon Johnson's boy Bobby Baker resigned. I wonder if Lyndon is expecting a purge." Kennedy was asked about Morton's remarks at his news conference on October 31, and he replied in a tone that seemed to have too much conviction that he wanted Johnson on the ticket and expected him to be his running mate again.

Before the Bobby Baker resignation Kennedy had already made plans for a trip to Texas. The Washington *Post* reported on October 5 that Governor John Connally had visited the President the day before to "arrange a trip for Kennedy to Texas November 21-22." Connally bragged after leaving the White House that the Joe Belden Poll showed Kennedy leading Goldwater in the Lone Star State by an 8 per cent margin.

Why was Kennedy going to Texas? "The common story," said Senator Yarborough, "was that JFK planned this trip to Texas in order to settle political differences between John Connally and me and 'save' the Democratic party in the state. But this was nonsense—a romantic myth for those who wanted to assess blame for the Dallas tragedy that followed.

"If JFK wanted to settle our differences, he could have called me to the White House when Connally was there arranging the trip. Kennedy was a shrewd and able politician, and he wouldn't have taken two whole days off as President, with all the duties his office required, just to have the two of us talk it out with him fifteen hundred miles away in Texas.

"The truth was that the trip was for the President's benefit. First, he wanted to raise money for the Democratic party for the next year's campaign. At a recent fund-raising affair in Boston, he raised more than $600,000; and he thought that a Boston-Austin tie-up would be good luck. So he was going to Texas to raise more money. Second, the polls showed he had slipped badly in the South, and he believed a personal appearance tour there would boost his popularity and give him the state's twenty-five electoral votes in 1964."

When news spread that Kennedy was going to Texas, foreboding appeared in many Democratic quarters. A month earlier, when Adlai Stevenson visited Dallas to speak on United Nations Day, a large congregation of local nutcake right-wing extremists booed and threatened him, and one woman hit him over the head with a sign while a man spat in his face. Stevenson voiced his concern over Kennedy's safety to a White House aide. Byron Skelton, the liberal Democratic national committeeman from Texas, wrote Bobby Kennedy of his worry over the sanity of Dallas. Two of Yarborough's brothers, both Dallas lawyers, wrote the senator of their fear of an attempted assassination. Senator Fulbright went further, and spoke to Kennedy directly, imploring him to omit Dallas from his itinerary. But Kennedy was obdurate about the Dallas stop on Friday, November 22, as a point of honor to prove that he was not frightened.

If Johnson was on the defensive in November 1963 because of Estes, Korth, and now Bobby Baker, so did Kennedy find little to cheer him in his Presidential efforts. The appropriations bills that were supposed to have become effective the last July for the fiscal year had yet to clear Congress; and his four major pieces of legislation—the Civil Rights Bill, the tax cut, aid to education, and Medicare—were doomed in the current session. In Latin America the Alliance for Progress had not produced expected results either in raising living standards or in buttressing constitutional governments. In four countries, Guatemala, El Salvador, the Dominican Republic, and Honduras, military *coups* had upset civilian-run governments. In other areas the Agency for International Development (AID) was on the defensive following General Accounting Office investigations showing widespread waste and inept administration of foreign aid. One cheering note came on October 7 when Kennedy signed the limited Nuclear Test Ban Treaty. But this was more than offset by growing turmoil in South Vietnam and the assassination of President Diem earlier in November.

Yet despite a weak record of political achievement after almost three years in office, Kennedy had caught the imagination of a major share of the American people. The current decline in his Gallup Poll rating was of little import, for his grace and youth seemed in themselves sound reasons for the mounting adoration of him both at home and abroad. In addition, his steady maturing in office was indicative of an evolving major President for the period ahead.

Johnson spent the first week of November racing through the little Benelux countries of Northern Europe, reading dull speeches and pressing the flesh untiringly. He also gave speeches that month in West

Virginia, California, and Dallas, and he returned to the L.B.J. Ranch to inspect preparations that were being made for the night of November 22, when Jack and Jackie Kennedy would be overnight guests.

There was bad news from Washington. Senator John Williams of Delaware, who had rocked the Truman Administration by uncovering the widespread scandals in the Internal Revenue Bureau, and who had persisted in looking into the details of the Estes operations, was working on Don Reynolds to confess his relations with Baker, McCloskey, and Johnson. As yet these had not been brought to light. One day Williams invited Reynolds and his wife to his office, and after Mrs. Reynolds wept and told her husband she would leave him unless he talked, he agreed to do so. Reynolds was scheduled to testify in executive session before the Senate Rules Committee on November 22, and there would be only additional trouble for Johnson in holding on to the Vice Presidency when his damning testimony was eventually released. And here the Kennedy speech for the big Austin fund-raising rally that night, which Johnson had seen in advance, referred to the Vice President as "my strong right arm."

Despite the immense and friendly crowds, backstage bickering featured the Kennedy visit to the major cities of Texas. One White House aide, Arthur Schlesinger, who was naive about Texas politics, believed that during the short tour Johnson would "use his personal influence with Connally and his ideological affinity with Yarborough to end the wracking fight in the Texas democracy." But Yarborough considered the two—Johnson and Connally—as operating the same tandem bicycle. Johnson was openly seeking a conservative Democrat to run against Yarborough in the coming 1964 primary, while Connally was using the Kennedy trip to humiliate the senator. At the climactic affair in Austin scheduled for the evening of November 22, Connally had arranged to seat Yarborough at the non-VIP table, and had excluded him and his wife from the long guest list at the governor's reception.

When *Air Force One* set down in San Antonio, Yarborough realized he would be damaged in the eyes of his liberal followers if he followed motorcade orders and rode in the Johnson limousine. So he "hitched" a ride with popular Congressman Henry Gonzales and left Johnson fuming at him. Then in Houston Yarborough repeated the act, this time riding with Congressman Albert Thomas, the pork-barrel king of the Texas delegation.

That night in Houston's Rice Hotel, Johnson and Kennedy exchanged loud words in what proved to be their last meeting. Hotel servants later said that the name of Senator Yarborough was prominently mentioned. The next day Yarborough agreed reluctantly to ride into Dallas with Johnson, and he did, though Johnson would not look at him as they rode from Love Field toward the Trade Mart.

A young man in his early twenties had gone from New Orleans to Mexico that fall to get a visa to travel to Castro's Cuba. When he was unsuccessful, Lee Harvey Oswald headed back to his wife and child in Dallas. On the way he stopped in Alice, in Jim Wells County, where Precinct Box 13 had put Johnson into the Senate in 1948. Here in Alice, Oswald tried to find work, but failing, he went on to Dallas and to employment as a laborer in the Texas School Book Depository, along the route of the Kennedy parade into town.

Don Reynolds was testifying in closed session before a Senate committee in the early afternoon of Friday, November 22. He was in the midst of detailing his connection with Bobby Baker and Lyndon Johnson when word was brought in that Kennedy had been shot.

PART SEVEN
Taking Command

Chapter 63

All around him after the assassination, everyone was in various states of shock, nearing collapse. But the new President sat there like a large gray stone mountain, untouched by fear or frenzy, from whom everyone began to draw strength.

He began to give orders in clear, audible tones, yet the voice was soft, the words unhurried. And suddenly, as though the darkness of the cave confided its fears to the trail of light growing larger as it banished the night, the nation's breath, held tightly in its breast, began to ease and across the land the people began to move again.

—From the hilarious speech "I Sleep Each Night a Little Better, a Little More Confidently, Because Lyndon Johnson Is My President" by Jack Valenti.

My God! There's a difference between testifying against a President of the United States and a Vice President. If I had known he was President, I might not have gone through with it.

—From remarks by Don Reynolds to Senator John Williams after Reynolds' testimony to the Senate Rules Committee on the day of Kennedy's assassination.

O N THE LAWN of Parkland Memorial Hospital in Dallas that Friday, November 22, 1963, Senator Ralph Yarborough stood sobbing. A friend said that his chief reason for crying was his affection for the slain President, whose stilled body lay inside the hospital. But another reason was his realization that his fellow Texan was now President.

Only minutes before, Yarborough and Johnson had been nontalking passengers in the same vehicle, two cars behind the Kennedys and the Connallys. "There were three rifle shots," said Yarborough, who had seen combat in Europe during World War II. "They came from the right rear, and how many people fired them I don't know."

When they reached the hospital, Johnson jumped out of the car and held his left bicep with his right hand while he rushed indoors with five Secret Service agents, leaving Lady Bird with Yarborough. Rumors spread that he had been shot, that he had suffered a heart attack. Once inside the hospital, Johnson and the agents were ushered to the rear of the Minor Medicine area, where between deep sniffs from his nasal inhalator, he said repeatedly, "The International Communists did it!"

After viewing the Kennedy body before it went to Major Medicine, Lady Bird followed her husband into Minor Medicine Booth 13. Here, as she later said, "Lyndon and I didn't speak. We just looked at each other exchanging messages with our eyes. We knew what it might be."

In the chaotic period that followed, she wandered into the Major Medicine area to attempt a few comforting words to Jackie Kennedy and Nellie Connally, whose husband had been seriously wounded by a rifle shot. Afterward, John Connally was to insist that the shot that injured him was independent of the two that tore through the President's body.

Kennedy had been hit fatally at 12:30 P.M. Dallas time, though surgeons went through the medical motions until one o'clock, when they declared him dead. This information was passed on to Johnson at 1:13 by a Secret Service agent, who said Johnson appeared to be in shock, though he managed to say, "Make a note of the time."

Kennedy's press secretary, Pierre Salinger, had not made the trip to Texas because he had accompanied six Cabinet members to Honolulu and Japan. Nor had Salinger's chief assistant, Andrew Hatcher, gone to Texas, because Kennedy had been considerate of the anti-Negro bias in that Southern state. This was the reason Malcolm Kilduff, another assistant press secretary, was present at the hospital and became the first person to call Johnson "Mr. President." Kilduff had come to Booth 13 to ask his permission to make a statement that Kennedy was dead, but Johnson barked at him, "No, wait. We don't know whether it's a Communist conspiracy or not. I'd better get out of here and back to the plane. Are they prepared to get me out of here?"

Johnson turned to Homer Thornberry, whom Kennedy had recently elevated to the federal bench, and he whispered, "This is a time for prayer if there ever was one, Homer."

At 1:26 Johnson left Parkland for Love Field. Dallas Chief of Police Jesse Curry had been ordered to supply two unmarked cars for the fleeing trip to the airport, with Lady Bird in one and her husband in the other. Congressman Jack Brooks remembered that the cars took off "like a striped-assed ape." Johnson sat on the floor of his car, and as they raced ahead with the agents fearful of an attack, one radioed ahead to Johnson's valet, Paul Glynn, to move his belongings from the Vice President's plane to *Air Force One,* the Presidential plane. On arrival, all occupants of the two cars ran full speed into the plane; and once aboard, after ordering all plane shades closed, Johnson watched Kilduff's announcement and the initial pictures and stories of the assassination on TV.

After a few minutes of CBS news, Johnson was ready for work, even though the plane was so hot without the air conditioning turned on that it smelled like a men's gymnasium. In the hospital, while they had been waiting for final word that he was President, Johnson had turned to his wife and ordered, "Bird, why don't you take some notes on all this?" Ordinarily, Lady Bird spent part of each day filling her diary, and now, as she sat sweating on the plane, she scribbled furiously, while he barked orders to aides, Secret Service agents, and Texas congressmen.

Johnson quickly made two decisions. Kennedy's remains would travel to Washington with him so that he would not appear to be in unseemly haste to take charge. There was only one trouble with this, and it was the adamant insistence of the Dallas County Medical Examiner that the body would have to be subjected to an autopsy because a homicide had been committed. The use of brute force by loyal Kennedy aides was necessary before his remains could be shoved and wrestled out of Parkland Memorial Hospital.

Johnson's second decision was that he would be sworn in on the plane before taking off for Washington. Using Kennedy's bedroom phone on the plane, he telephoned Bobby Kennedy at his Virginia home. Although the President's brother was in a state of shock, he took the call. After telling Bobby that his brother's murder "might be part of a world-wide plot," Johnson asked whether he should take the oath in Dallas, and if so what was the form of the oath? Bobby ignored the first question and said he would call him back on the second.

While he waited, Johnson also called Walter Jenkins and told him to go to the White House. Then he talked briefly to McGeorge Bundy, Kennedy's schoolmarmish special assistant on foreign affairs, to J. W. "Waddy" Bullion, a Dallas lawyer and business crony, and to Abe Fortas, whom he ordered to meet his plane when it landed at Andrews Air Force Base, a half-hour southeast of Washington. To these and others he said that Bobby Kennedy had told him to take the oath of office in Dallas. As for the person to administer the oath to him, Johnson decided on tiny Sarah Hughes, the federal judge whom Sam Rayburn had forced on the Kennedys, because she had her court in Dallas.

Johnson had boarded *Air Force One* at 1:33 P.M., an hour and three minutes after the shots had been fired at Kennedy, and he had almost forty-five minutes for phone calls before the half-ton casket was carried into the tail compartment by superhuman effort on the part of the late President's aides. Mrs. Kennedy, in her blood-soaked, rose-colored suit, stepped into the plane's bedroom and stopped, stunned to find Johnson lying on the bed and dictating to a secretary.

The Kennedy and Johnson aides immediately exchanged harsh words, and there was continuing trouble all the way to Washington. It began with an order from a Kennedy man for a direct takeoff and a countermanding order by Johnson, and it was fired by the anger of the Kennedy group that Johnson had usurped *Air Force One* instead of taking the other plane. "I thought, oh Lord, they've already taken over," said

Evelyn Lincoln, the late President's secretary. Eighteen years earlier, the Roosevelt staff, returning by train to Washington from the Hyde Park funeral, had become so aroused by the sight of the Missouri twang-talk aides of President Truman that they drank themselves into savage animals long before the train pulled into Union Station.

Johnson's Texas congressmen friends infuriated the Kennedy help by their nonstop, complacent political talk. One who was not present was Senator Yarborough, who had tried to get on the plane, but was kept out on orders from Johnson. On the other hand, Judge Sarah Hughes, for whom he was waiting, almost did not get on board, for when she arrived at the field, the guard would not let her through. Finally, after a bystander identified her, she was permitted to scamper toward the plane.

Meanwhile Johnson had prettied himself for the pictures of the swearing-in and had ordered clean clothes set out for "Honey," as he called Mrs. Kennedy. Johnson believed it was utterly essential that she appear in the pictures with him and Lady Bird, and he did not want her to wear her blood-clotted suit. But she would not change her garments. When the crowd of twenty-eight persons had crammed into the state-room, meant for eight, two-thirds back from the front of the plane, Johnson tightened his lips in growing anger when she did not appear. Finally, just after he snapped, "I'm going to get her," she entered the stateroom. "This is the saddest moment of my life," Johnson told her, relieved, as he set her into position on his left.

Sarah Hughes, shaking and sweating, was ready to begin, when a voice asked, "What about a Bible?" "Someone thrust a small Bible with soft leather backs in my hands," she said. "I thought someone said it was a Catholic Bible." This was a momentary concern to her, but she felt she had no alternative except to use it. (Actually, it was not a Bible, but a missal, for the Mass.)

Following the twenty-eight-second oath, as taken from Article II, Section 1 of the Constitution, said Judge Hughes, "He gently kissed Mrs. Kennedy and leaned over and kissed his wife on the cheek. . . . As I left the plane, I heard him give the order to take off."

The swearing-in had taken place at 2:38 P.M. in the stifling, gold-upholstered cabin. Only two hours and twenty minutes ago the man who was now President of the United States had been convinced he would not be retained on the Democratic ticket as Vice President at the next nominating go-around. In Washington the Treasury Department noted a change in Administration by increasing Johnson's salary from $35,000 to $100,000 a year starting at 2:00 P.M. that day, or 1:00 P.M. Dallas time.

After he took the oath, Johnson felt hungry, and he ordered some soup, while Mrs. Kennedy fled to the tail compartment to sit with her husband's loyal aides and his remains. Between frequent summoning of various Kennedy assistants who refused to go forward, and detailing a moment-by-moment account of his day for posterity and a future Lyndon B. Johnson Library, the brand new President edited a short statement for the Andrews arrival, held conferences with Texas congressmen, watched the endless TV rehashing of the assassination, and made more telephone calls. One call went to Rose Kennedy, JFK's mother, but he was able to blurt only a single sentence to her before his mind went blank, and he handed the phone to Lady Bird. Another call went to Nellie Connally, who reported that her husband would recover. Johnson also ordered a call to go to the Cabinet to meet him at Andrews, and for the first time he learned that six Secretaries were in a plane over the Pacific. The plane had already turned back toward Washington at the request of White House aides.

After a flight of two hours and twenty-one minutes, *Air Force One* landed at 5:05 P.M. on a dark night at Andrews Base. A crowd of three thousand persons was at hand to witness the aftermath of the Texas trip. Johnson had expected to leave the plane in company of Mrs. Kennedy, the casket, and her husband's staff, but a member of the latter group said that "they felt Johnson wanted to use Kennedy's body for his own purposes." Johnson reacted with fury when the Kennedy entourage jumped off the plane before him, removed the casket, and left immediately for the autopsy at Bethesda Naval Hospital.

The next day Johnson spoke of his "real problems with the family" to a Cabinet member, as he detailed what had happened at Andrews: "He said when the plane came in . . . they took the body off . . . put it in the car, took Mrs. Kennedy along, and departed, and only then did he leave the plane, without any attention directed or any courtesy toward him, then the President of the United States." He admitted he did not care to battle with the Kennedys because "the aura of Kennedy is important to all of us."

Not until an hour later, at 6:14, after "pressing the flesh" of some of the dignitaries who had come to Andrews, did Johnson, wearing his saddest face, read his fifty-seven-word statement for the TV cameras. As he spoke, the loud roar of nearby jets mingled with his words, and Lady Bird, standing beside him, looked grim, until she suddenly smiled broadly and waved to a friend in the crowd.

On the helicopter ride to the White House Johnson was accompanied by Lady Bird, staff aides, Secret Service agents, Defense Secretary Robert McNamara, Undersecretary of State George Ball, and McGeorge Bundy. Before the helicopter touched down on the South Lawn at 6:25, he asked the three Kennedy men to stay on as his helpers by pouring fulsome praise on them.

Lady Bird did not tarry at the White House, but went home to The Elms at 4040 Fifty-Second Street NW. Kennedy's body was to lie in state in the White House, and "Honey," his widow, would be permitted to continue living in the Executive Mansion until she chose to leave. Once she reached The Elms, Lady Bird ordered several chickens fried for Lyndon and the staff aides he would probably bring home with him.

As for Johnson, he paused to study the President's Oval Office in the West Wing of the White House, a room to which he had come as a supplicant, sitting at the side of the desk to talk to Franklin Roosevelt, Harry Truman, Dwight Eisenhower, and Jack Kennedy. This unpretentious room, this seat of top world power, was now his.

Yet he did not try out the chair behind the desk, but went through the Cabinet Room and continued through the building and across the narrow street to the Executive Office Building and the gaudy six-room Vice Presidential suite at number 274. Here he resumed his compulsive phone-calling, talking to Truman and Eisenhower, and because he could not bring himself to talk to Herbert Hoover, a politician before his time, he asked one of the dozen staff aides scurrying from room to room to find a Hoover friend who could convey a message from him. Finally Johnson decided to call the eighty-nine-year-old ex-President at the Waldorf Towers, where he lived, but when the call went through at 7 P.M., one of Hoover's retinue said that "the Chief" had gone to bed and could not be disturbed.

There were other calls. These went to Senator Ted Kennedy, Dick Russell, Speaker McCormack, Justice Arthur Goldberg, J. Edgar Hoover, and Sargent Shriver, the Peace Corps director and a Kennedy brother-in-law. Reports of FBI ineptness at Dallas were not yet in the news, and Johnson asked his former neighbor to flood Dallas with FBI agents to work up a memo on the assassination. With Shriver, who was still angry because someone had stolen his expensive topcoat earlier in the day from a White House closet, he discussed funeral arrangements.

Johnson also had his first visitors: Senator Fulbright and Ambassador Averell Harriman. He was in the midst of scribbling two short notes to the Kennedy children—Caroline and John—when an aide walked in at 7:40 and reported that the bipartisan mob of Congressional leaders whom he had asked to come had arrived. For men who had ostracized him since he became Vice President, the Democrats from the Senate now showed unusual friendship. To bind the entire Congressional contingent for what he hoped would be far into the future, he told them that the Kremlin was watching him carefully, hoping for American political party strife so "international communism" would have a free hand to do its dirty work abroad. The effect was immediate, for each man pledged . himself against any partisan behavior during the transition period ahead. As an added precaution he played up to Senator Everett Dirksen, the minority leader, just as he had observed other Presidents cater to Senate leaders of the opposing party.

After forty-five minutes the pledges were repetitious, and the session broke up, with Hubert Humphrey, his old liberal agent in the Senate, hanging back for private words, as had been the custom in their Senate days. Humphrey later wrote that Johnson "put his arm around me and said that he needed me desperately." Finally, at 9:42, Johnson piled into a limousine with Jack Valenti, Billie Don Moyers, Horace Busby, and Cliff Carter, and sped out to Lady Bird in Spring Valley.

There was fried chicken, Cutty Sark scotch, endless talk, the TV marathon on the assassination, and more phone calls. On landing at Andrews, Johnson had missed greeting Abe Fortas, and he called him now. The immigrant's son from Memphis, who owned a Rolls-Royce and was married to a brainy little lady lawyer who smoked cigars, had maintained his special relationship with Johnson since his magnificent performance in the "Landslide Lyndon" affair of 1948. As Vice President, Johnson had made Fortas chief adviser on his Washington existence, a status that irked many Johnson employees, who viewed the private attorney as a meddler. "On any problem we had," a staff member of the Committee on Equal Employment Opportunities recalled, "we were told to 'check it with Abe.' "

Fortas was a man brimming with ideas for his friend, the new President. He thought Johnson should install a rocking chair in the Oval Office as a symbol of continuity with the Kennedy Administration. He also had ideas on what should go into Johnson's first Address to Congress, and he agreed to serve as its editor. Another Fortas thought was that there should be a bipartisan probe of the assassination, led by outstanding public figures.

Fortas was also Bobby Baker's lawyer, and Johnson wanted to know what had happened that day at the Senate Rules Committee's closed meeting with Don Reynolds. Reynolds had talked, bringing up the Mc-Closkey D. C. Stadium deal, the stereo hi-fi set, and the arm-twisting by Walter Jenkins to get him to kick back part of his insurance premium by buying commercial time on KTBC. On the stereo, Reynolds said he had passed along a Magnavox catalog to Lady Bird so she could make her selection. Reynolds also swore that Bobby Baker had opened a satchel filled with paper money and claimed it added up to a one-hun-dred-thousand-dollar payoff to Johnson for the seven-billion-dollar TFX plane contract by a subcontractor of General Dynamics.

Another Reynolds story was that as Vice President, Johnson had stopped at Hong Kong on his Southeast Asia trip in 1961 and drew one hundred thousand dollars in Hong Kong counterpart dollars. Counterpart dollars are money earned by the federal government in foreign countries which can be spent only there. Visiting congressmen are accorded the privilege of drawing local expense money from these counterpart funds. Reynolds' story was that Johnson had spent one hundred thousand dollars of this public money "in a period of twelve to fourteen hours in buying gifts for people who were loaded."

Senator B. Everett Jordan from North Carolina was chairman of the Senate Rules Committee, and some of his friends said he had been peeved at Johnson when he came to the Senate in 1958 from his home town of Saxapahaw. Johnson had a reputation for doing right by freshmen Democrats, so Jordan had been told, but outside of an assignment to the middling Agriculture Committee, Johnson had scratched the bottom of the barrel, putting him on the Rules Committee and the Post Office and Civil Service Committee.

However, Jordan was almost convinced now that the Reynolds charges were chiefly a Republican attempt to smear the Democrats. On this basis—and with a six-to-three margin of Democrats on the committee—he could easily be talked into keeping the Reynolds testimony secret and not releasing even a doctored version for months. Everything depended on whether the Republicans leaked Reynolds' charges to reporters. With good luck, if this did not occur, Johnson would have time to gain some seniority as President, so that when the Rules Committee eventually released the Reynolds charges, they would appear as a ridiculous attack on the nation's First Citizen.

Johnson's further view was that Reynolds and the man who had induced him to talk—Senator John Williams of Delaware—should be punished. Perhaps Williams could be wrapped up by an income tax charge, and if not, the Democrats would pour money into Delaware to defeat the chicken farmer when he ran for re-election the next year. Johnson also thought that Fortas should drop "that little sonofabitch Bobby Baker" as a client, because it would look bad for Johnson if his adviser were associated with Bobby.

The four Johnson aides who rode to The Elms with him that Friday night were exhilarated by their proximity to decisive national power. Horace Busby would take time off from his weekly reactionary newsletter for businessmen to write speeches for Johnson as he had done so frequently in the past. Cliff Carter would be his Washington political-insider, just as he had been his Texas hatchetman during the Vice Presidency; Jack Valenti, his jack-of-all-trades, would be at his side all day long as a sort of political valet; and Billie Don Moyers, still in his twenties, would be second among all staff assistants, a step or two down the ladder from Walter Jenkins.

Valenti, a small, dark young man, had met Johnson at a "get-acquainted" *kaffeeklatsch* for the then senator in 1957. Valenti was in advertising in Houston at the time and also wrote a weekly column in a Hemingway imitation for the Houston *Post*. After meeting the senator, Valenti wrote the wildest line of the year in describing the Johnson personality: "There is a gentleness in his manner." Valenti later met and courted Mary Margaret Wiley, Johnson's secretary, and though Johnson seemingly made an effort to break up the match, he gave the bride away in June 1962.

Valenti's advertising company had handled the Kennedy-Johnson publicity in Texas in the 1960 campaign, and on Kennedy's last trip to Texas, Valenti had organized the testimonial dinner to Representative Albert Thomas at Houston on November 21, the night before the assassination. Throughout the meal he had squatted below table level at Kennedy's side, telling friends afterward that Kennedy's hands had shivered convulsively from nervousness as he read his speech. At Parkland Hospital, Johnson ordered Cliff Carter to find Valenti and have him come along on the flight to Washington. Valenti had momentary doubts when he heard of this invitation, because his baby daughter, Courtenay Lynda, was only three weeks old, and he was worried about leaving his wife behind in Texas; but he did.

Billie Don Moyers had made his Johnson connection by writing him a letter and asking for a job in 1954 during the "Firetruck Dougherty" campaign. Afterward he went to work for Johnson's KTBC radio and TV stations and graduated from the University of Texas. Then he attended the University of Edinburgh for a year and Southwestern Baptist Theological Seminary in Fort Worth for two years, emerging as an ordained preacher. But when Johnson offered him ten thousand dollars to help him in his 1960 Presidential campaign farce, Moyers returned to politics. At first a Vice Presidential aide, Moyers deserted Johnson during the Kennedy Administration to become deputy director of the Peace Corps. This action caused one of the few troubled times between Abe Fortas and Johnson, for it was Fortas who helped Moyers land the job as deputy to Sargent Shriver.

The pale, bespectacled young former preacher was in Austin when he heard of the assassination. With a rush, he caught a plane for Love Field in time to board *Air Force One*. Once aboard, he sent a note to Johnson's cabin—"I am here if you need me." Johnson said he did.

Busby had brought his wife to The Elms that night, and another person who had come along was Dr. Willis Hurst, a heart specialist, who had accompanied Johnson back to the L.B.J. Ranch after his heart attack in 1955. Until midnight, Johnson and his guests watched the Kennedy assassination news on TV, a sickening rehashing of the day's events plus other available movie shots on Kennedy's early life and career. Then, at twelve, when Johnson said he was going to bed, Hurst and the Busbys left. As for the other three, Johnson insisted that they sleep in his house that night.

It was about one o'clock when each of the three got a call from Johnson as they were preparing for bed. "I can't sleep," Johnson said. "I want to talk some more. Come to my room."

When they walked in, he was sitting up in his bed with CIA reports and other Presidential papers strewn on the top of the bedspread. "We've got a lot of work ahead," he greeted them excitedly. "I want to think out my agenda."

He kept them at his bed until 3:30 A.M., rambling on almost nonstop to the exhausted young men. "Good night, boys," he finally told them. "Get a lot of sleep fast. It's going to be a long day tomorrow."

Before his first day as President ended, Johnson said he walked to a sitting room at the back of the house, where he knew a framed photograph of Sam Rayburn was featured. Johnson said he filled a glass with a drink and then remarked: "Well, Mister Sam, I wish you were here tonight."

Chapter 64

THE JOHNSON OBJECTIVE in the immediate period following the assassination was to give the impression he had taken such complete charge of the federal government that there would be no skip in the national heartbeat.

This meant retaining the Kennedy crew intact for a time beyond their period of mourning in order to create an aura of continuity. It also meant posing for pictures with nationally known political leaders; holding briefings, meetings, and a long series of private conferences with Cabinet members and congressmen to elicit their emotional support; and overawing newsmen by granting them long, private interviews in which he successfully portrayed himself as crushed by Kennedy's death, yet strong and wise enough to bear all national burdens.

Johnson had much going for him when he climbed out of his long bed at The Elms that Saturday morning, November 23, 1963, after three hours of good sleep. Ignored and distrusted as Vice President, he held the nation's best wishes and solid backing as he began his first full day as President. He was the man who would carry the torch for the fallen leader, gone before he could complete his glorious purposes, said a sobbing nation, part of which had been bitterly partisan to John Kennedy only yesterday.

Notified over the Pacific of the assassination, the six Cabinet members and Press Secretary Pierre Salinger had returned to Andrews Base at

12:31 A.M., on Saturday. At 4:25 the black hearse bringing Kennedy's body crept into the White House grounds, and Mrs. Kennedy and her brother-in-law Bobby Kennedy led the sad procession into the East Room, where the casket would be on display that day before going to the Capitol for public viewing on Sunday.

Because of the hour, Jackie invited the Kennedy aides to sleep in the White House, and they went to bed on the third floor at 7 A.M. An hour later, said Salinger, the phone rang, and when he answered it groggily, a voice drawled, "Peer, this is Lyndon Johnson." The new President was ready to begin his work.

Johnson had decided to use the facade of humility to hold the Kennedy people to their jobs until he could safely discard them. Doris Fleeson, the astute Washington columnist who had studied Johnson over the Senate years, noted that he "keeps books on his helpers and hinderers rather too openly and at first hand." Johnson's book of grievances, which he carried in his head, had a large section for certain Kennedy aides, but at the moment his expressions of regard for their abilities and the abject confession of his own lack of credentials to be a successful President without their experience and guidance was a performance worthy of a dramatic award. "Peer, I need you more than *he* needed you," proved so winning a bleat with Salinger that Johnson used it repetitiously and to good effect long afterward.

When Evelyn Lincoln, Kennedy's secretary, came to work at 8:30 A.M. in her office next door to the Oval Office, Johnson was suddenly at her side and he asked her to step into the President's office, which had been luxuriously refurnished during Kennedy's Texas trip. "I need you more than you need me," Johnson told her. But as he said it and looked into her face, he abruptly changed his mind. "Can I have my girls in your office by 9:30?" he asked her in a commanding manner.

"I was shocked," she recalled later. "He was giving me an hour to get out." When she reported this, sobbing, to grief-stricken Bobby Kennedy, he said, "Oh, no," and assured her he would talk to Johnson.

It was the new President who caught sight of Bobby first, and he invited him to a conversation. "I need you more than your brother did." He trotted out once more his line to the person in the last Administration whom he detested most. He then probed into the delicate subject of taking over the White House physically and said "my advisers are pressuring me to move into this office." When the Attorney General frowned and remarked that it would take time to clear out his brother's belongings, Johnson backtracked and said he would remain in his Vice Presidential trappings across the street for the time being.

When Bobby returned to Evelyn Lincoln's office, he told her she need not move out by 9:30. "He says you can stay until eleven." Shortly afterward an enormous framed portrait of Johnson arrived in her office to be hung on the wall.

That Saturday was a whirlwind of a day for Johnson, considering the many talks he had set for himself. There were other members of Kennedy's staff to be treated to a display of entreaty and humility. One whom Johnson did not see that day was Arthur Schlesinger, who submitted a letter of resignation. "Tell him to take it back," Johnson snapped at McGeorge Bundy. "I don't want any such letters. And tell everyone I mean that."

But Johnson had special contempt for Schlesinger and was planning unique humiliation for him. Walking through the line at Andrews the previous evening, Johnson had heard what he considered the most presumptuous greeting of all coming from Schlesinger: "I'll do all I can to help." When he finally saw Schlesinger, a few days had passed, and he flattered him with the old line, "I need you far more than John Kennedy ever needed you. He had the knowledge, the skills, the understanding himself. I need you to provide those things for me."

Flattered by Johnson's histrionics, Schlesinger agreed to stay, and when he returned to his White House East Wing office, he made the notation that Johnson had "said all this with simplicity, dignity, and apparent conviction." But the new President never followed up by calling him to discuss duties, and after four months of the blank existence Johnson had planned for him, Schlesinger finally quit. Later, when he expressed differences with Johnson on foreign affairs, Johnson's columnist mouthpiece, Bill White, attempted to ridicule Schlesinger by claiming Kennedy had told him personally that he had isolated Schlesinger in the East Wing to get him out of his hair and was tired of the long memos Schlesinger kept sending him that he threw away unread.

That Saturday, also, Johnson and Lady Bird observed the expected rituals by walking past the coffin in the East Room after the Kennedy family Mass and then crossing Lafayette Park in front of the White House to attend the memorial service at St. John's Church. In his Vice President's office he issued his first Executive Order as President, closing the Executive Branch on Monday, November 25, for the funeral.

And his telephone circuits were busy. He called labor leaders George Meany, Walter Reuther, David Dubinsky, Alex Rose, and David McDonald to tell each, "I need you more than he did." This line forestalled any necessity for thinking out special pleas and was just as effective as with the Kennedy aides. He also repeated this by phone to A.T.&T. President Frederick Kappel, who doubled as chairman of the President's Business Council. He had additional phone conversations with Governors George Romney of Michigan and John Reynolds of Wisconsin, Speaker McCormack, Senators Dirksen, Yarborough, Smathers, and Humphrey, and House Majority Leader Carl Albert. One special call went to Bob Anderson, Eisenhower's Secretary of the Navy and Treasury Secretary, and early owner of Johnson's KTBC radio station. Johnson ordered Anderson to come to Washington the next day for a long conversation. Still more calls went to Negro leaders: Martin Luther King, Roy Wilkins, and Whitney Young.

There were also several visitors, including former Presidents Eisenhower and Truman, Senator Eugene McCarthy, and Justice Arthur Goldberg. Eisenhower came in the rain from his Gettysburg farm, to pay his respects in the East Room to Kennedy, then went to Johnson's suite in the Executive Office Building at 12:35 P.M. for a twenty-minute appointment. Johnson buttered up the aging general, saying he was concerned about his own lack of experience in foreign affairs and the poor staff at hand that was supposed to advise him. Eisenhower's name would be an important source of support behind any of Johnson's actions, and Johnson, showing even more humility than he had revealed that day to Kennedy aides, begged Eisenhower "to write down the things you think I ought to know." He got rid of Eisenhower by giving him a pencil and a legal-sized lined pad of yellow paper and asking him to spend as much time as he wanted at the conference table in another room. Later the general dictated his notes—on what he thought Johnson should know—to a stenographer in the office. Eisenhower also supplied him with a list of "good people who know foreign affairs," none of whom Johnson hired, though he thanked the former President several times for coming to his rescue.

At 2:30 P.M. that Saturday Johnson called his first Cabinet meeting. These were the same men who had, with few exceptions, ignored him when he was Vice President. When he entered the Cabinet Room to take the honored seat at the mahogany table, Secretary of State Dean Rusk jumped up, and the others followed suit as Rusk called out pompously, "Gentlemen, the President of the United States!" It was generally known that Kennedy had intended to retire Rusk after the 1964 election and replace him with Robert McNamara, for among Rusk's poorer qualities was his eagerness to apply military solutions to international problems instead of taking a diplomatic course. In addition, Rusk took a black view of the wisdom of worikng toward a détente with the Soviet Union.

Johnson began the meeting with a silent prayer for his predecessor and ended it in scarcely concealed anger with the late President's brother, the Attorney General. Following the prayer he had launched into still another recital of his humility pitch: "I need you a lot more than Kennedy did." Then Rusk officiously reminded him that long-standing custom required Cabinet members to hand in undated resignations to a new President. Johnson might have nodded and said nothing. Instead, he argued so strenuously against such letter writing that one man who was present later viewed it as Johnson's technique to make certain all would submit the undated resignations.

McGeorge Bundy had written a memo of suggested subjects for the Cabinet meeting, and Johnson was in the midst of reading the memo aloud when there was a great stir as Bobby Kennedy entered the Cabinet Room. Kennedy said afterward he had not known of the meeting but had come to the West Wing to see if his brother's possessions had been collected from the Oval Office. Bundy had spied him, he said, and insisted he walk into the meeting. An emotional outpouring occurred as the other Cabinet members saw him, and they interrupted Johnson's reading to shake his hand and press his arm.

Following this, Johnson finished his stumbling reading, and Adlai Stevenson added to the dismal twenty-five-minute session by delivering his own wretched reading of a panegyric to Johnson that bore none of his own low regard for the new Chief Executive. "Your unique qualities of character, wisdom, and experience are a blessing to our country in this critical hour, and our confidence in your leadership is total," Stevenson said with little conviction.

After telling the Cabinet to let him have their recommendations for legislation on Monday, the day of the funeral, Johnson stalked out with a cold glance at the Attorney General. Defense Secretary McNamara, a highly sensitive man, was aware of this, though he turned the situation around by telling Jean Kennedy Smith: "Bobby should take a rest and go away and forget everything for a while. I'm afraid he'll get into a fight with Johnson."

As for Johnson, when he later met with Treasury Secretary Douglas Dillon in the Vice President's office, he burst into a tirade against Bobby. The little soandso had deliberately spoiled his talk to the Cabinet by coming late, said Johnson, adding that he had it from good authority that Bobby had told "an aide" he did not plan to "go in until Johnson has already sat down."

Before Johnson went back to The Elms at 9:30 P.M. that Saturday, he busily sought a consensus on a variety of decisions he had already reached. One of these was to deliver an Address to a Joint Session of Congress, for this would have the full dignity and authority of the Office of the President on display for the American people. When he learned that Cabinet members and others favored an evening TV speech without the facade of a crowded House Chamber with the mustered Supreme Court, Cabinet, Congress, and diplomatic corps applauding him repeatedly, he buttonholed all in this group, and by asking leading questions, thanked them before the conversation ended for proposing the Joint Session Address. Johnson also used the consensus approach to gain backing for a Tuesday Address. However, he failed to convince one listener, and this was Bobby Kennedy, who thought it crude that he would want to make a major speech on the day following his brother's burial. Once again, anger rose in Johnson, but he agreed to delay his Address until 12:30 P.M. on Wednesday, November 27.

As for the Address itself, Johnson utilized another of his old techniques when he begged several persons in private, and individually, to save him at the outset of his Presidency by composing the speech for him. Kenneth

Galbraith, the six-and-a-half-foot-tall Harvard economist and Kennedy Ambassador to India, who had been Johnson's tour guide there in 1961, was one who believed he was working alone on the speech. Among others who were also asked to be the speechwriter were Adlai Stevenson, Ted Sorensen, Horace Busby, and Charlie Murphy, the former counsel to President Truman and Johnson go-between in the Estes business at Agriculture.

That Saturday evening Johnson took home the same young assistants he had the night before, and he expressed pleasure (between sharp complaints) about the various networks' running pictures of him on their dinnertime TV news programs, showing the steady flow of his office visitors that day. By now utter weariness had gained the upper hand over his exhilaration at being President, and after his valet massaged him, as he lay on his bed, Johnson asked pudgy Horace Busby to stay behind and talk to him.

Busby later told Stewart Alsop that he sat in a chair by Johnson's bed in the dark, and when he concluded from the snoring sounds that Johnson was asleep, he tiptoed toward the door. But just as he had his hand on the knob, Johnson called out, "Buz . . . Buz . . . are you still there?" Resignedly, Busby said he was, and walked back to the chair.

Again, after a long period, Busby headed for the door, and again came the "Buz . . . Buz." After this, Busby waited until he was certain Johnson appeared to be in a coma-type sleep, but once more he was trapped at the door by the call "Buz . . . Buz . . ." Not until 2 A.M. Sunday morning was he able to sneak out and go home.

There were still two days to live through before the physical remains of Kennedy were underground and two more days after that before his speech at the Joint Session of Congress would serve as Johnson's true inauguration as President.

That Sunday morning, November 24, Johnson felt he had to follow the tradition of Presidential churchgoing, and he went to Lady Bird's church, St. Mark's Episcopal on Capitol Hill, with her, daughter Lucy, and Homer Thornberry.

After church Johnson went gingerly to the White House, where the large Kennedy clan and friends were collecting for the funeral ceremonies. It was while he and Lady Bird were in the Blue Room to meet Jackie Kennedy that Secretary of State Rusk called him with news that Lee Harvey Oswald, the suspected Kennedy slayer, had been "shot on TV" by Jack Ruby inside the Dallas city jail. "You've got to do something," Johnson yelled at Bobby Kennedy as a greeting. "It's giving this country a bad name around the world." Kennedy made no reply to him.

Ten minutes after one, Johnson and Lady Bird joined Mrs. Kennedy, her children, and Bobby Kennedy in the lead car behind the horse-drawn caisson for the trip to the Capitol. The twenty-block ride up Pennsylvania

Avenue witnessed a crowd of at least one hundred thousand grief-stricken spectators. Then the heavy casket was borne up the steep stairs to the Rotunda for all-afternoon and night viewing by the public, following eulogies by Chief Justice Earl Warren, Speaker John McCormack, and Senate Majority Leader Mike Mansfield. Mansfield, in his loud, crisp voice with the Irish lilt, delivered a magnificent eulogy. Johnson's task was to set a wreath at the casket, and because the red and white carnations, set in a sea of green, was so enormously Texas size, he needed the help of an Army sergeant, who was sobbing his heart out for the dead Kennedy, to drag it into position.

After this gloomy business, Johnson went back to his Vice Presidential office in the Executive Office Building to do some Presidential work. The job of saving Oswald's life had been botched by the doctors in the same Parkland Hospital where Kennedy had been carried, and when Johnson learned Oswald had died at five minutes after two, he pressed the button on his twenty-button telephone box that brought tall, bald Deputy Attorney General Nicholas Katzenbach to the phone in the Justice Department. In a rasping tone, Johnson ordered him to submit a report on Oswald to him.

Johnson's principal visitor on Sunday was Robert Anderson, who came to the office because of the urgent invitation of the day before. Anderson, the dull-eyed Texas protégé of Mister Sam, had also been the protégé of the late Sid Richardson, and the combination of "Daddies" had been sufficient to put him into the Eisenhower Cabinet and to win Eisenhower's remark toward the close of his first term that Anderson would make an admirable Vice Presidential nominee in 1956. As a member of the Eisenhower Administration Anderson had overseen the multi-billion-dollar annual import-quota program of special favor to the largest oil importers. He had also held the tax line against any lowering of the 27½ per cent depletion allowance for oil. One of Richardson's top oil men told the story of Anderson's being raised to the millionaire class by a phony deal concocted by Richardson which permitted him to "buy" oil stock for $1.00 and then sell it for $970,000. At the moment Anderson was being groomed by General Eisenhower as his number one candidate for the Republican nomination in 1964.

Anderson sat with Johnson for hours on Sunday afternoon, spouting his conservative economic line and advising his fellow Texan to drop the Kennedy proposal for an 11.5-billion-dollar tax cut. Johnson expressed concern on this point, for although he had personally told Kennedy of his opposition to the tax cut, if he failed to promote it now, he would immediately lose the good will of the Kennedy admirers. But Johnson told Anderson he would seriously consider his advice, and in return he asked Anderson to serve as his special troubleshooter on foreign affairs because of his lack of faith in the State Department. Anderson agreed to take on such assignments.

Besides the Anderson talk, Johnson's Sunday witnessed his plunge into two of the most vexing current problems. Ambassador to South Vietnam Henry Cabot Lodge and CIA boss John McCone briefed him on the military situation there, and publicly Johnson announced he would retain the Kennedy program to bring home a thousand American soldiers from Vietnam by the end of the year and the fourteen thousand other American troops by the close of 1965. There was no reason to doubt him, even though Bill White, his mouthpiece columnist, wrote early the next week that in foreign affairs Johnson was a militarist and could be expected to step up the war in South Vietnam.

Johnson also held a meeting on the next fiscal year's federal budget, which had to be pinned down within a month if it were to go to Congress on schedule on January 17, 1964. At this Sunday 5:15 P.M. session were Treasury Secretary Douglas Dillon, Budget Bureau Director Kermit Gordon, and Chairman of the Council of Economic Advisers Walter Heller, all government officials who had ignored Johnson when he was Vice President.

The original budget estimates submitted by the various government agencies to the Budget Bureau that fall had totaled about 120 billion dollars. Kennedy had pared this down to 103 billion dollars by mid-November; then shortly before leaving on the Texas trip he had cut it to 101.5 billion dollars and ordered Treasury Secretary Dillon to trim it below 100 billion dollars because crusty Senator Byrd, chairman of the Senate Finance Committee and a Kennedy enemy, would not take up the tax cut if the budget stood above that figure. Johnson now decided to publicize the 103-billion-dollar figure as the Kennedy rock-bottom budget, so he could gain public recognition as an economizer who magically cut the budget below 100 billion dollars.

Not long after the attendants at the budget meeting filed out, an aide found Johnson at his desk angrily cursing the "chickenshit" Kennedy crowd. Walt Heller had lagged behind to disclose like a pupil trying to win favors from the teacher that Galbraith had called a meeting in Secretary of Agriculture Orville Freeman's office at which Secretary of Labor Willard Wirtz, Secretary of the Interior Stewart Udall and Heller had been present. Galbraith had asked the others to listen to his "very good draft" of the speech he had written for Johnson to read at the Wednesday Joint Session.

Johnson exploded when he listened to Heller's recital. No one in his Administration was going to hold meetings without gaining his advance approval. He wasn't going to tolerate White House staff people and Cabinet members meeting "secretly" like conniving crooks—especially those damned liberals. And one other thing, he bellowed out, the weak Kennedy action in letting working officials issue press releases under their own name about census changes, Gross National Product estimates, and cost-of-living index figures and every other government statistic was ended. From now on, the White House would release these numbers and percentages, and the press releases would all begin: "President Johnson reported today that . . ."

Monday, November 25, was the final Kennedy day, for the late President's remains were to be taken from the Capitol, brought back to the White House, and then, with the widow in the lead, two hundred world chiefs of state and government were to walk behind her up Connecticut Avenue to old St. Matthew's Church on Rhode Island Avenue. Following the Roman Catholic Mass would be the burial on a hillside below the Lee Mansion in Arlington National Cemetery, across the bridge from the Lincoln Memorial.

Johnson did not go to the Capitol with the Kennedys, as the family assumed he would, to participate in the return of the casket to the White House. Instead he took this opportunity to move into the West Wing Oval Office. Because Mrs. Kennedy had ordered her husband's desk removed, Johnson brought in his large Taj Mahal desk as a replacement.

When the military procession back to the White House was under way, the Secret Service made its last argument with Johnson not to walk to St. Matthew's. "You damned piss-ant bastards are trying to take over," he spat out. "I'm going to walk those eight blocks." And he and Lady Bird did, walking behind the Kennedy family and in front of a car bringing little Caroline and John, who in turn were followed by de Gaulle, Haile Selassie, and the other two hundred foreign dignitaries, in rows of twelves.

At the graveside ceremonies Johnson expected to be in the front row with the Kennedys. But in the rush for places at the final rites he found himself pushed into the Supreme Court delegation. "What the hell am I doing here?" he screamed at a Secret Service agent. But there was nothing the hapless agent could do to bring him into a better position for the TV cameras.

There were yet other Kennedy ceremonies late that afternoon. Mrs. Kennedy held a reception at the White House at four o'clock for the foreign mourners, and Johnson held one for the same crowd at five at the State Department. The individuals who went to the White House to cry rode afterward to the State Department to study the new President with whom they would now have to deal.

State Department officials had drawn up short resumes on cards for each person in the line, and while Rusk detained each guest in front of him, an aide quickly whispered into Johnson's elephantine ear the information on the appropriate card. In an hour the entire group of two hundred and twenty had the opportunity to undergo Johnson's pressing of the flesh and to have photographs taken with the new President.

Then while the guests went to the John Quincy Adams Room for the buffet, Johnson slipped into the Thomas Jefferson Room, where arrangements had been made for him to speak with sixteen guests, allotting four minutes to each. Unfortunately, Johnson enjoyed the show so much that his schedule collapsed, and as a time saver he met with the three members of the royal families of Sweden, Norway, and Denmark and their premiers. But this conference was hardly under way when Charles de Gaulle suddenly stood in the doorway. Dean Rusk came dashing over to de Gaulle and took him and Johnson to his own seventh-floor office, leaving the Scandinavians behind.

De Gaulle had been proving obstreperous about accepting American domination of the Western allies and British partnership in the European community. Knowing little about the complications of these problems, Johnson was silent at their conference while the French leader and Rusk engaged in general conversation, with Rusk rudely giving combat to the general when he spoke of an existing close working relationship between his country and the United States.

Johnson left this session with de Gaulle to meet with thirty-five governors in the Vice President's quarters in the Executive Office Building. He came bursting into the reception room and apologized for being late because "my conversation with General de Gaulle lasted much longer than I expected. Even then," he confided, "we did not finish, so we have another meeting set up for early in the year when he comes back to this country."

When French Ambassador Hervé Alphand later asked Paris for a confirmation, back came a denial that any such promise had been made. However, said de Gaulle, he would certainly be pleased if Johnson traveled to Paris to see him—as etiquette demanded of a junior partner.

One major hurdle remained for Johnson, and this was his Address to the Joint Session of Congress at 12:30 P.M. on Wednesday, November 27. For this important address, besides the numerous writers of speech drafts, Johnson also acquired the services of Hubert Humphrey and Abe Fortas as editors.

Humphrey came into the editing of the speech in an oblique fashion. On Sunday night, while crowds stretched thirty blocks from the Capitol to pay last respects to Kennedy by passing his bier in the Rotunda, Johnson called Humphrey at his home in Maryland to discuss a bill that Larry O'Brien, Kennedy's Congressional aide, said was on the Senate program for the coming week. As Vice President, Johnson had opposed the Kennedy bill to sell wheat to the Soviet Union; but now as President he more firmly believed, after the badgering Bob Anderson had given him earlier against the tax cut bill, he would be off to a poor start if he did not support all Kennedy "must" legislation. The call to Humphrey was occasioned by an amendment to the wheat bill by butterball Senator Karl Mundt of South Dakota. This amendment would in effect bar the wheat sales by prohibiting interim government credits to finance the shipments, and since the Soviet Union had no credit rating with commercial banks in the United States, shipments could not be made.

The man Johnson should have called was Majority Leader Mike Mansfield, but Mike had never been his agent and always made him feel uncomfortable. Throughout the four years Mansfield had served as majority whip under Johnson's majority leadership, stories floated around the Senate that Johnson was attempting to get him to quit by ignoring him. Nevertheless, in 1960 Mansfield had supported him at the national convention, even though the ascetic Montanan afterward developed a doting-uncle relationship with young President Kennedy.

"When Lyndon became Vice President," said Mansfield, "he told me, 'Mike, they are going to try to split you and me. They are going to put stories into the papers of things I'm supposed to have said about you. But don't believe any of them.'" Mansfield puffed on his pipe, eyed Johnson warily, and replied, "Lyndon, as far as I'm concerned, it won't happen."

But it happened. Stories spread that Johnson considered Mike a weakling because he had failed to push him out of the Taj Mahal. Nor could he respect a Mansfield who had meekly agreed to ask the other Democrats at the first caucus to let the Vice President boss the conferences. There was a story that Johnson considered Mike the only Minnow who served as majority leader and yet remained a Minnow. Then there was Bobby Baker, Lyndon's boy, who was openly calling Mansfield "the nothing majority leader," and bragging that he was really the majority leader who met with Kennedy on committee and legislative problems.

Mansfield had brought democracy to the Senate by calling for Steering Committee secret ballots to elect Democrats to standing committees. He had also eliminated the use of the Senate Calendar as a prime weapon of the majority leader by ordering all bills on the Calendar brought in turn to the floor for action. Yet most senators knew that Baker had made use of the Steering Committee's democratization to electioneer Johnson choices into the best committee vacancies. It was also true that behind Mansfield's back Baker would meet with Johnson on pork-barrel and government contracts. It was these two, for example, who arranged the construction of a plant by North American Aviation Company in House Majority Leader Carl Albert's Third Congressional District in Oklahoma, when Albert was worried that lack of such activity would defeat him in the next election.

Because senators who were mistreated by Baker did not complain to Mansfield, Mike remained unaware of the enormity of the plotting and secret dealings of his young secretary for the majority. Only after Baker was exposed, six weeks before Kennedy's assassination, did Mansfield's eyes suddenly open wide, and he became a strong majority leader passionately concerned with instilling in the rest of the Senate the integrity he possessed.

Baker's quick resignation before he could be fired, however, now left the new Chief Executive without what would have been his chief ally in the Senate. Therefore, it was Senator Humphrey, the Senate's majority whip, whom Johnson called that Sunday night instead of Mansfield. "Hubert," he asked after exchanging pleasantries with his old agent, "don't you think this Tuesday is a poor time to bring up the Mundt Amendment?"

Humphrey replied that nothing could be done about it because a unanimous consent agreement two weeks earlier had set November 26 for the vote.

"Can you beat it?" Johnson bellowed. "How many votes do you have?"

"Well, I'm not sure," Humphrey stammered.

"That's the trouble with that place up there." Johnson jeered at Mansfield, who had ordered an end to the practice of prying from senators how they intended to vote on various bills. "You fellows just don't have the votes counted."

Humphrey and Larry O'Brien made a vote count on the day Kennedy was interred, and the actual vote the following evening bore out their figures that the Mundt Amendment would be easily defeated. That Tuesday night Humphrey called Johnson at The Elms at 9:15. "I just wanted to report your first victory as President," Humphrey said smugly. "We've defeated the Mundt Amendment 57 to 35."

"Keep it up, Hubert," Johnson told him. "Come on over and have something to eat. I want to talk to you."

Around the table when Humphrey walked in were Johnson, his inseparable young aides, and Abe Fortas. Johnson had the Galbraith, Busby, Stevenson, and Sorensen drafts of his speech for tomorrow, and he read aloud parts from each. After Humphrey finished eating, Johnson tossed all the drafts to him and said, "Hubert, you and Abe go ahead and redraft these speeches and get me one that will be suitable for tomorrow."

Fortas had become Johnson's chief adviser and listening post in these first days. It was he, for instance, who suggested that to head off a Senate Judiciary Committee investigation of the assassination, Johnson should organize a special commission composed of old and well-known Americans. Fortas also gave him the names of the individuals he should appoint, and Johnson's task became that of browbeating these persons to serve. The Fortas names were Chief Justice Earl Warren; Senator Richard Russell; former CIA boss Allen Dulles; banker, former Assistant Secretary of War for Roosevelt, and disarmament troubleshooter for Kennedy, John McCloy; Senator John Sherman Cooper of Kentucky; plus two fifty-year-olds as a concession to youth—Republican Representative Gerald Ford of Michigan and House Democratic Whip Hale Boggs of Louisiana.

Johnson had to do a great deal of arguing before he could issue his Executive Order of November 29 naming these seven. Earl Warren had come to the White House to tell Johnson he would not accept. Warren said: "The President told me how serious the situation was. He said there had been wild rumors, and that there was the international situation to think of." Johnson built up a spurious picture of worldwide disaster if Warren did not head the commission. "He said he had just talked to Dean Rusk," Warren recalled the Johnson histrionics, "and he also mentioned the head of the Atomic Energy Commission, who had told him how many millions of people would be killed in an atomic war. The only way to dispel these rumors, he said, was to have an independent and responsible commission, and that there was no one to head it except the highest judicial officer in the country. I told him how I felt. He said that if the public became aroused against Castro and Khrushchev, there might be war."

"You've been in uniform before," Johnson told the seventy-two-year-old Chief Justice in a roll beat of patriotic drums. "And if I asked you, you would put on the uniform again for your country."

The old first lieutenant of infantry in World War I said, "Of course."

"This is more important than that," Johnson pushed forward.

"If you're putting it like that," Warren said helplessly, "I can't say no."

Johnson tried a different approach on Senator Russell, whom Kennedy alive had considered as a form of Senate gangrene. "Lyndon, I'm too busy," Russell told him over the phone. "There's the civil rights bill and all those other bills coming up. And besides, I'm having trouble with my breathing."

"Well, Dick, this is going to be mighty embarrassing for me," Johnson elbowed his arguments aside. "We've already given the press an advance statement naming the members of the commission, and you're on it. I hope you won't let me down." Russell grumbled that he would not.

Having landed these two big names, Johnson had little trouble winning the consent of the other five. His chief problem came with Boggs, whose home phone gave back a busy signal for more than an hour. Johnson scolded him for having such a talkative family.

Another service Abe Fortas provided Johnson in those first days was to advise him to put the Johnson businesses and investments into a trust. Johnson had checked into the wealth of other Presidents, and he was excited and proud that he was the richest Chief Executive in history, millions higher than the ten million dollars Joe Kennedy had given his son Jack.

Fortas told him he must not give the impression he was still involved in money-making, but should sign an irrevocable trust putting his holdings into the hands of trustees, as Eisenhower had done at the outset of the Presidency. In the Eisenhower trust, no information regarding sales or investments was given him by the trustees—only the amount of taxable income the trust earned each year.

Johnson was amenable to Fortas' suggestion, provided he named the trustees. And he did name the two. One was his old hunting pal and business partner A. W. Moursund, and the other was his Dallas business friend and lawyer J. W. Bullion. So the trust that was dated November 29, 1963, served the purpose of answering any public charge that the new President was involving himself with profitable sidelines; and at the same time, by appointing two business associates as his trustees, Johnson could continue actively in business.

As a show of good intent, the LBJ Company broadcasting empire was changed back to its more impersonal name, the Texas Broadcasting Company. But this was the only facade. For forty-six-year-old Moursund, who studied inquiring, nosy reporters from behind rimless glasses and would only shrug and reply, "I'm just a country boy," soon possessed a telephone that connected by private line to the President's White House phone. And Texas bankers and businessmen reported that instead of dealing directly with the Vice President, as they had before the assassination, they now dealt directly with the President of the United States. Others said they knew when they discussed deals with Johnson trustees and associates that Johnson was pulling the strings. As the *Wall Street Journal* assessed the business scene north and south of Austin six months later: "Some of the area's businessmen feel a certain uneasiness about the growing financial strength of the Johnson circle." Johnson's repetitious denial that he had been involved in the slightest way with the LBJ Company from its inception evoked a tart rejoinder from the Washington *Evening Star* that "several Texans who dealt with the Johnsons prior to last November say that they always dealt with Mr. Johnson, never with his wife."

Fortas and Humphrey went to work on the Johnson Address to the Joint Session at 10:15 P.M. that Tuesday, and they used as their base the Sorensen draft. "I added some corn pone," Fortas later explained his role. Fortas also told Johnson to practice his pronunciation of certain words —especially "Americans," instead of his usual "Amurrakins."

The two editors liked the first sentence because it would give Johnson the image of humility that they thought he should portray so soon after Kennedy's burial. Dropping three words and adding one, they altered the first sentence slightly so that it now read: "All I have I would have given gladly not to be standing here today." They also liked the next sentence, because it too projected humility. "The greatest leader of our time has been struck down by the foulest deed of our time."

Not until 2 A.M. did they finish their editing, and at noon, when Johnson rode to Capitol Hill with Pierre Salinger and Ted Sorensen, Salinger remarked, after reading the draft, "That's a helluva speech, Mr. President." Johnson gave Sorensen the credit, but when Sorensen said that only 50 per cent of what he wrote had been retained, Johnson nodded and said, "The best 50 per cent."

The high emotional climax of this first Johnson talk to Congress was his utterance of "Let us continue," as a follow-up of Kennedy's inaugural remark, "Let us begin." He told Congress, "This nation will keep its commitments from South Vietnam to West Berlin"; and he asked that Kennedy's civil rights bill and tax reduction proposal be enacted. "I firmly believe in the independence and integrity of the Legislative Branch," he assured those sitting before him, "and I promise you that I shall always respect this. It is deep in the marrow of my bones." There was hardly a dry eye in the House Chamber when he closed by reciting the familiar ending that Sorensen had in his draft:

> "Amurrika! Amurrika!
> God shed his grace on thee.
> And crown thy good with brotherhood
> From sea to shining sea!"

Lady Bird recorded in her every-evening one-hour diary tape that night that Lyndon had been applauded thirty-two times by her own count. As for Johnson, he knew he had glided over his first hurdle, and he was eager to boss the nation and the world.

Chapter 65

From the moment Johnson acknowledged the welcome praise from the assembled congressmen at his first Address to Congress, he was already at work on the 1964 election. There was much to do before then. The party machinery had to be taken over—all the Kennedy men on the National Committee who did not cry out fealty and grovel before their new master had to be ousted; the local organizations, led by the tough city bosses, of whose existence Johnson had not been aware in 1960, had to be turned into a tireless Johnson army by pork barrel and patronage; the do-gooder elements throughout the nation, labor leaders and minority group leaders had to be transformed into rousing Johnson champions.

Johnson also needed a legislative program, plus national exposure of the old blarney that he was "a legislative genius" who cracked a whip and made 535 senators and representatives do his bidding. In addition, he needed a legislative reputation as "a great humanitarian" if he was to retain the Kennedy following; and he required a mantle reading "the great economizer" to gather in the dissident elements of the business community. This was the crowd Kennedy had antagonized in 1962 when he reacted to U. S. Steel's inflationary six-dollar-a-ton price increase with the remark: "My father always told me that all businessmen were s.o.b.'s, but I never believed it until now."

Above all, Johnson had to create a solid public acceptance of himself as "President Johnson," whose umbilical cord was not attached to his predecessor. Said one of his assistants at the time: "He feels that he has to make the public aware of the man who's in the office now and show them a man who looks like he can do the job. Beyond that, he feels that his own Administration can't afford to be anything less than energetic and productive."

How well he believed he had succeeded at this task was revealed the following April, when he told a reporter, "They [the people] have a babylike faith in me. It's just like the faith that you have in the pilot that's flying your airplane."

On Saturday, December 7, 1963, while the rest of the country noted the twenty-second anniversary of the Pearl Harbor attack, Jackie Kennedy finally moved from the White House to the Averell Harriman brick place on N Street in Georgetown. In the two weeks and one day that had passed since his oath-taking on *Air Force One,* Johnson had been growing increasingly uneasy that Mrs. Kennedy might remain at the Executive Mansion far beyond her promised departure date of two weeks after the funeral. He had covered his concern by careful inquiries about her packing schedule and by generous comments, such as: "Honey, you stay as long as you want. I have a nice, comfortable home, and I'm in no hurry. You have a tragedy and many problems." Nevertheless, he chafed with each passing day, because the White House was not only his due, but it was important as the awesome symbol of *the* President.

Now she was gone, and Lady Bird brought to the White House her porcelain bird collection and the Porfirio Salinas paintings of the Texas Hill Country. Zephyr Wright came to cook, and Helen Williams to serve as housekeeper of the 163-year-old Executive Mansion. The thirteen rooms at The Elms chateau had seemed a major undertaking, but the White House had 132 rooms, and as Lady Bird found, when she asked chief usher J. Bernard West to take her on an attic to basement tour, it was tiring. West also introduced her to the seventy-seven White House employees, and she was pleased to learn that besides appropriating money to pay their salaries, Congress gave the First Family $670,000 a year to meet living expenses in the Executive Mansion. Asked by lady reporters how she liked her new life, Lady Bird replied happily, "I'm busier than a man with one hoe and two rattlesnakes."

But there was one unhappy note that night. When it was time to retire, Johnson decided to use the Abraham Lincoln bedroom and Lady Bird the adjoining room. The Lincoln room, with its large canopied bed, had served as bedroom for several Presidents, and its white marble mantel was carved with the following inscription: "In this room Abraham Lincoln slept during his occupancy of the White House as President of the United States. March 4, 1861-April 13, 1865."

Staring at the mantel, Johnson became aware that Mrs. Kennedy had left a reminder that he was a usurper. Beneath the Lincoln inscription, a new inscription had been carved, reading: "In this room lived John Fitzgerald Kennedy with his wife Jacqueline—during the two years, ten months and two days he was President of the United States. January 20, 1961-November 22, 1963."

Although Johnson was careful to keep the Kennedy crew on hand because of the positive benefit to him in public esteem, even before he and Lady Bird moved into the second-floor living quarters at the White House, his own advisers and staff had begun to take shape. Abe Fortas was collecting Johnson's speeches and planned to take them to the Atheneum Publishers in New York to be turned out as a book. Fortas was also going over current speeches and policies and talking three or four times a day by phone to his friend. It was Fortas' idea to keep Walter Jenkins from testifying before the Senate Rules Committee, after Don Reynolds told the committee of the KTBC-TV "kickback time" Jenkins had ordered him to buy following his sale of life insurance to Johnson. As a witness Jenkins might prove too emotional and unreliable, even though he was totally dedicated to Johnson. So some properly placed phone calls brought the decision of Rules Committee Chairman Jordan that Jenkins need not come if he signed an affidavit after talking to committee investigators in his office. In his signed statement Jenkins insisted he "had no knowledge of the TV advertising arrangement," and though this meant that either he or Reynolds had committed perjury, Jordan said, "There's no conflict. There's nothing to get excited about."

The frenzied friendship between Johnson and Senator Humphrey also continued on its old level. "I've had ten calls from that man in the White House," Humphrey complained with pride, shortly after Johnson became President. "He has a new idea every thirty minutes, and he calls me up about it. I can't do anything he wants done because I don't have time to get going between calls."

Other individuals besides Fortas and Humphrey became frequent visitors to the White House. Dean Acheson, whose warlike advice Kennedy would not take at first and then would not even listen to, was a welcome guest. So were Tommy the Cork Corcoran, now sixty-two and a leading Washington wheeler-dealer and moneymaker; James Rowe, lobbyist for Haitian sugar interests, Corcoran's partner, and also a former F.D.R. aide; Clark Clifford, a Truman speech writer, lawyer for General Electric, Phillips Petroleum, and the El Paso Natural Gas Company, and self-proclaimed authority on the Presidency; and Bill White, whose column in the Washington *Evening Star* would soon be transferred to the Washington *Post,* a larger circulation newspaper.

Chief assistant and coordinator on the Johnson White House staff in the emerging Presidency was Walter Jenkins, Old Reliable, who had been with

Johnson since 1939. Only once had Jenkins made an attempt at independence, and this had come in 1951, when he ran unsuccessfully for a House seat. After losing in the Democratic primary (with the excuse that his failure stemmed from his professed Roman Catholicism), he returned to Johnson's service as his chief administrative officer and treasurer of the Johnson broadcasting empire.

The closeness of Johnson and Walter Jenkins was revealed in many ways. On the night of the new President's move into the White House, he and Lady Bird went for dinner to the Jenkins home on Huntington Street in Washington. Then on December 22, Lady Bird's fifty-first birthday, the Johnsons celebrated by going again to the Jenkins for a family get-together. For this occasion Johnson gave Lady Bird an autographed picture of himself that read: "For Bird, still a girl of principles, ideals and refinement—from her admirer, Lyndon." Yet another evidence of the Jenkins tie to Johnson was that one of the six Jenkins children was named Lyndon.

For a man who was the closest assistant to the new President, florid-faced, bespectacled, forty-five-year-old Walter Jenkins possessed a strange characteristic: he was a mystery man who fled from interviews and photographs and resisted all newspaper and magazine attempts to publicize him. In Jenkins' mind there was good reason for this, for he feared recognition by certain individuals. In January 1959 he had been arrested in the downtown YMCA, a notorious homosexual hangout, and was booked on a morals charge. The notation in police records referred to him as "disorderly (pervert)," but no action had resulted, because he had posted collateral and then elected to forfeit it rather than stand trial. Like Johnson, Jenkins was a close friend of J. Edgar Hoover, whose organization failed to inform the White House of Jenkins' past. From his new position in the Presidential entourage, Jenkins was an acknowledged fighter to keep the federal service clean, and on one occasion he wrote a memo that warned agency heads: "It would be unfortunate if undesirable individuals were put on the Federal payroll simply because sufficient precautions were not taken prior to their appointment."

When swarthy Jack Valenti left his wife and three-week-old daughter Courtenay Lynda to travel to Washington on order from Johnson, he little knew what the future portended, though his expectancy ran high. Initially he had no stated duties, but Johnson's affinity for him was revealed by his residing first at The Elms and then in the White House on the express invitation of the new President. However, this had its shortcomings, for newsmen at the outset believed he was Johnson's valet. When Johnson glanced about for the bottle of soda to pour into his Cutty Sark, Valenti leaped to oblige. On one occasion, early in 1964, when Johnson, some reporters, and Valenti rode over the low hills on the L.B.J. Ranch, Johnson braked the car to a halt, pointed to a bottle on the road, and remarked that it could cause a blowout. Valenti was out of the car before he finished

and threw the potential danger out of range. "Now there's a valuable hunk
of humanity. He can do anything for you and do it fast," Johnson told
the reporters in a loud stage whisper.

Newsmen began to observe the gradual, growing importance of the little
Houston advertising man. At first, without an assigned office, Valenti
wandered about from room to room for temporary desk space. Then he
acquired a closet-size office and finally moved into the spacious appointments secretary office adjacent to the President's oval office. Reporters
found he was clearing appointments for Johnson, telephoning top government officials on major government problems, and editing Johnson
speeches. Valenti's specialty on Presidential speeches was to turn long
paragraphs into short ones, long sentences into short sentences, and fancy
words into short, clear words. On one speech that Johnson tossed to him,
the order was: "Sex it up a little, Jack." On Johnson's speech to the UN
on December 17, 1963, Johnson told Valenti: "Put some peace in it, Jack."

In addition to these duties, Valenti was Johnson's untiring promoter
with the press, and for this activity he was aptly described as "an aging
cheerleader." His knack for finding good in all Johnson actions prompted
one observer to remark, "If Johnson dropped the H-Bomb, Valenti would
call it an urban renewal project." That Johnson liked this whirlwind of a
publicity agent was publicly acknowledged one time when he said: "The
first man I appointed to my staff when I became President was Jack
Valenti, whose grandfather came from Italy, and who, incidentally, is
about the best fellow with me. He gets up with me every morning. He
stays up with me until I go to bed at night, around midnight, and he is the
only one who can really take it. The rest of these fellows are sissies."

But if Valenti derived enormous pleasure from operating so close to the
top of the nation's business, he was to find Johnson's personality an offset-
ting factor. Long before, a Johnson friend had observed, "Lyndon has a
clock inside him with an alarm that tells him at least once an hour to chew
somebody out. . . . He is given to great pettiness." One time Johnson's
voice carried down the corridors of the small West Wing of the White
House as he bellowed, "I thought I told you, Jack, to fix this f---ing doorknob!" Another time, when Valenti stepped out of his office to get a quick
cup of coffee, Johnson buzzed him to come into his office. Valenti walked
in three minutes later, and with visitors alongside him, Johnson cursed
gutturally, "Where the goddam hell ya bin? How many times have I got to
tell you not to leave your office without telling me where you're going?"
One of the visitors later said, "Imagine what would happen if an assistant
walked into the President's office and told him he was going to get a cup
of coffee?" The day after this incident, Johnson burst into Valenti's office
and shouted at the drawling aide, who was on the phone, "For Chrissake,
do you spend all your time on the phone?"

Billie Don Moyers, who would one day replace Jenkins as Johnson's top aide, after Jenkins was publicly exposed on another morals charge, was swiftly emerging as Johnson's chief ideas man on legislation, expert on press relations, and devil's advocate for liberal domestic causes. Moyers' main drawbacks were that he continued to maintain friendly relations with Bobby Kennedy and Sargent Shriver and that he once tried to gain some personal publicity by appearing as a contestant on a TV show, *To Tell the Truth,* where the announcer had said, "Will the real assistant to Vice President Lyndon Johnson please stand up?"

Moyers was one of the few Johnson aides to escape the Presidential bullyragging. Some said he did so because Johnson knew the young man considered him with amusement, an attitude he found baffling. However, Moyers toiled long hours and possessed mature judgment, even though he was only twenty-nine years old. "That boy has a bleeding ulcer," Johnson spoke of Moyers with pride to a visitor. "He works for me like a dog, and is just as faithful. He never asks for anything—but for more work. He won't go home with that bleeding ulcer until nine or ten o'clock. I don't know what I'd do without him."

George Reedy, a large, rumpled man of forty-six with white hair, thick horn-rimmed glasses, and a tired philosopher's air, proved to be an even more useful punching bag than Jack Valenti. Reedy had become a Johnson employee in 1951, after working as a UP reporter on Capitol Hill, and he was being groomed to replace Pierre Salinger as the President's press secretary as soon as Johnson could insult Salinger to the point of forcing his resignation. In front of others Johnson once addressed Reedy as "you stupid sonofabitch," and his aide, who happened to be right about the subject under discussion, merely shrugged helplessly. On another occasion a visitor listened annoyed while Johnson abused Reedy with a string of four-letter words over the telephone. After Johnson hung up, he told his guest, "Well, let's give George his Christmas present now." When the man's mouth fell open, Johnson offered this explanation: "You never want to give a man a present when he's up—you want to do it when he's down."

Other Presidential employees who had not worked for Johnson in the past found they were not only expected to give their lives to him but to chance insults at any meeting. Budget Bureau Director Kermit Gordon took his first evening off after weeks of slave labor to go to a concert. Of course, that was the evening Johnson telephoned him. The following morning when he came to a White House meeting, Johnson sprinkled him with sarcasm. "Well, playboy," he snarled, "did you have a good time?" McGeorge Bundy, nicknamed the "human computer" and the "efficiency expert" because of his cold, stilted personality and high I. Q., had Kennedy's permission to walk into his office at any time on urgent foreign policy matters. Johnson was going over plans to escalate the fighting in Vietnam with Ambassador Henry Cabot Lodge when thin-faced Bundy strode into the Oval Office. "Goddammit, Bundy!" Johnson snapped, annoyed, in his direction. "I've told you that when I want you, I'll call you." Bundy stumbled out like a rejected suitor.

Even White House employees who did not enter the Oval Office felt Johnson's wrath. One guest said sadly, "Why, he's mean to the lowest servants." Walking about his new domain, Johnson could find much that displeased him. Once he confronted the girls at the White House telephone switchboard and scolded them so savagely for alleged poor service that one girl began sobbing uncontrollably. Another time he appeared in the press office, and, after studying the messy desk of Assistant Press Secretary Malcolm Kilduff, he said, rolling his eyes, "Kilduff, I hope your mind isn't as cluttered as your desk." Kilduff quickly cleared his desk, but the following day Johnson was back, this time scoffing at the change, "Kilduff, I hope your brain isn't as vacant as your desk." Johnson also went after Secret Service agents whom he spotted wearing the PT-109 tie clips that Kennedy had given them. "Don't you know that you've got a new President!" he railed; and the tie clips disappeared.

Najeeb Halaby, administrator of the Federal Aviation Agency, once remarked that he required more than a year on the job before any policy he announced was put into effect. "It took that long before the people who worked there quit carrying out the policies of my predecessor," he said.

As President, with twelve Departments, dozens upon dozens of independent agencies, and two and a half million civil servants scattered around the world, Johnson could not expect to influence the daily operations of the federal establishment before an even longer period than a year elapsed— if at all, in many cases. But he believed it vital that he give the impression he was wiggling a finger in every government pie, and almost all his Cabinet members were willing to play this game. Most compliant was Secretary of State Dean Rusk, who had gained an extension at his post by the death of Kennedy. Years before, Senator Walter George had introduced Rusk, who was also from Georgia, to his Senate colleagues as "the Georgia Fat Boy," a derisive name that did not increase Rusk's already low opinion of senators. Rusk had carefully supplied Johnson, as Vice President, with State Department briefings, and for a grateful Johnson he was now willing to tell reporters that Johnson was his own Secretary of State.

Secretary of Agriculture Orville Freeman was another who declared that Johnson's finger was on his Department's pulse. "President Johnson doesn't give suggestions," Freeman told reporters. "He gives orders." But there was one Cabinet member who would not march in the ranks, and he was Attorney General Bobby Kennedy. It was Johnson's fond hope that Bobby would quit after the Arlington National Cemetery ceremony. However, Bobby stayed on, some said to challenge Johnson for the Presidential nomination in 1964; according to others, to force Johnson to put him on the ticket as the Vice Presidential nominee.

Johnson was already referring to him as "a little chickenshit" when he asked Bobby to stop in the Oval Office for a talk during his second week as President. "People around you are saying things about me." Johnson took an aggressive stance. "I wouldn't let people around me say anything about your people," he added, his voice growing into a loud warning, "and don't let any of your people say anything about me." Kennedy tried to talk, but Johnson spoke through him and then asked him to leave after a five-minute session.

That the name of John Kennedy galled Johnson as much as that of Bobby Kennedy became evident on the afternoon of December 5, 1963, when Johnson met with top government officials in his office. The occasion was to remind Johnson of the December 7 Medal of Freedom Award ceremony at which he was to preside and make the presentations. The discussion was cozy until Johnson heard that Kennedy had planned a forty-five-minute ceremony to award the medals to the thirty-one distinguished recipients the late President had selected the previous summer.

Immediately the atmosphere blackened, as Johnson clenched his fists and declared, "I'm sick and tired of all you telling me to do this, that, and the other thing because that's the way Kennedy planned it. If I had to do all the things people like you claim were the most important things in the world to Kennedy, it would take me fifteen years to do them all. After all," he added, in an unpleasant tone, "I'm President now. And I don't think I'll give more than ten minutes to the whole damn ceremony. Besides, who the soandso scheduled it for the exact same time as the Jack Benny show?"

George Ball, the dignified Undersecretary of State, who was present, looked as though he had been slapped across the face and had no hands to strike back. Ted Sorensen, another participant, took the easy route out, by rushing from the room.

Johnson held the ceremony as scheduled, adding two recipients of his own—John Kennedy and Pope John XXIII. He also traveled to New York to attend the funeral of former Senator Herbert Lehman, who dropped dead while preparing to fly to Washington to pick up his Medal of Freedom.

This opposition to participating in activities laid out by the late President also extended to appointments Kennedy had made unofficially in ambassadorial ranks and other government posts. One such appointee, Professor Samuel Beer of Harvard, was turned down as ambassador to Uruguay by Johnson with the excuse that he was a friend of Arthur Schlesinger. Another expectant ambassador to Panama guessed that his nomination was never sent to the Senate because he had told Johnson to his face two years earlier that he was in error regarding a foreign aid matter.

During Johnson's first weeks in office, American newspapers worked overtime to help him establish the image he wanted, of a man who more than filled Kennedy's shoes—or more precisely, a man who was an incomparable President possessing uncanny genius for the job, know-how about all government activities large and small, good intentions, and high moral character. James Reston of *The New York Times* described the immense pro-Johnson publicity as "almost a Texas 'tall story'—Johnson conquering George Meany and Henry Ford, Martin Luther King and Harry Byrd, the savers and the spenders, Wall Street and Main Street."

Just as he had in the past attempted to overawe Capitol Hill reporters by giving them carrots of inside news and feigning utter frankness, so did he now continue this approach with carefully selected Washington newsmen. He invited a wary Walter Lippmann to the White House and won him over by begging him for advice on a number of national and international issues. That he never intended to follow Lippmann's advice was a decision he made in advance. Yet by permitting Lippmann to expound to the President at length, he gained immediate favorable publicity in the columns of the highly regarded Washington observer.

Other carefully selected reporters and publishers were similarly cultivated, given food and liquid refreshments, urged to give their opinions, and slipped inside stories. Much of this paid off early. In a flight of fancy, the Washington *Post* hailed his first Address to Congress as "among the best of the State Papers in American history"; and the Boston *Herald* called Johnson a man who "demonstrated a sense of grandeur of language." Some reporters were so impressed with being invited to swim naked in the White House swimming pool with Johnson that their stories afterward were almost shrieks of praise.

Even a word of caution by *Editor and Publisher* in its November 30, 1963, issue failed to slow down the initial pro-Johnson gushing. In a warning of what might be the true state of affairs once the honeymoon ended, *Editor and Publisher* said: "Mr. Johnson has shown himself to be exceedingly sensitive to news stories, calling up individual newsmen and berating them at some length." With advice to reporters who had not covered Johnson before, *Editor and Publisher* quoted a reporter on the Hill as recalling "a session at the Capitol with newsmen when, thinking photographers had finished taking his picture, Lyndon then put on his glasses. Just at that moment a flash bulb went off. Lyndon was furious, angrily told the photographer not to use the picture."

Having read this *Editor and Publisher* story, Johnson took an opposite tack in the early weeks. Cecil Holland of the Washington *Evening Star* had been openly comparing Johnson to Kennedy as a midget to a giant. But when Holland had some kind words for the new President in a news story, Johnson phoned him directly and praised him nonstop for a half hour.

There were additional ways in which Johnson attempted to influence and manage the news. Twice a day the press secretary held news conferences in his office with White House correspondents, and to be apprised of what was going on and which reporters needed special treatment, Johnson ordered his press secretary to keep his desk squawk-box telephone circuit open, so he could listen to the talk in his Oval Office.

Johnson also kept close watch over the wire services teletype machines, for the stories that came clickity-click onto the butcher-paper rolls of the machines were bound to appear across the country in newspapers that belonged to the AP and UPI services. Frequently, Johnson took a personal hand in stories as they were being manufactured. When a wire-service reporter telephoned in a story to his office from the White House, his story appeared on the teletype machines only a few paragraphs behind his actual dictation. One time Pierre Salinger interrupted a wire-service man on the telephone and surprised him with "The President says to tell you you've got the wrong emphasis in your article." Nor was Johnson above phoning the wire-service reporters directly to correct their copy. He called one to say, "That's not Adenauer who's coming to see me. It's Erhard." Ten minutes after a story came from Johnson City noting that Johnson's boyhood home would become a national shrine, Johnson called the UPI bureau from the White House with an angry complaint that the "r" in "free" had been dropped from the phrase "free tours," changing the meaning completely.

Johnson employed still another technique when dealing with the press. The President's News Conference, begun in March 1913 by Woodrow Wilson, had reached institutional status in Franklin Roosevelt's era with regularly held weekly meetings for question-and-answer sessions with reporters. The three succeeding Presidents—Truman, Eisenhower, and Kennedy—had maintained and added to the institution; for it not only gave them the front page in the next issue of newspapers, but as Eisenhower once put it, "It gives me a chance to find out what's on the mind of the American people, and it lets them know what's on my mind."

Johnson was opposed to being put regularly in the dock by the better quality Washington correspondents, yet he wanted the front page. His answer was one that brought on a slow disenchantment of the reporters with him. He would hold no set-time sessions each week, only occasional spur-of-the-moment get-togethers. By suddenly calling the press into his office for a news conference, he knew that the more skilled Washington reporters would not be able to come, because they would be on Capitol Hill or at Executive agencies. In this way the only participants would be the lower quality White House correspondents (with a few exceptions) who habituated the White House press room on an assigned basis and were forbidden to enter any West Wing office without special authorization. Except for the AP and UPI wire-service reporters, others assigned to the White House were generally fledgling newsmen.

Johnson's initial news conference portended the body blow the institution of the press conference was to be dealt in his administration. At noon on Saturday, December 7, 1963, Pierre Salinger casually told the weekend contingent of White House reporters, "The President would like to have you come in and have coffee with him." There was no time for anyone to call the top Washington reporters for the New York, Chicago, and other big-city papers, for Salinger walked briskly for a stout man, and the reporters in his office followed him hurriedly into the Oval Office. Johnson "pressed the flesh and said howdy" to each reporter, then he sat in his "Kennedy rocker," and when no questions were asked him, he ended the painful silence by calling out, "If there is anything you would like to ask me, I'd be glad to answer."

The first question was not about vexing national and international problems but was instead a feeble query about the way he felt knowing this would be his first night to sleep in the White House. "I feel like I have already been here a year," he replied, and then launched into a twenty-minute monologue. Before the meeting ended he fielded a few more banal questions tossed to him, such as, "What is your biggest problem?" "Being President," he said, after a moment of reflection.

Although Johnson enjoyed a boundless press honeymoon during his first weeks as Chief Executive, he became an unhappy man whenever he considered his newspaper coverage. He believed he was not getting as much of the front page and the front section of newspapers as should have been accorded him. It was good to read that a top Budget Bureau spokesman told reporters that the President's immediate comprehension of the complex budgetary problems "seemed incredible." And Bill White's columns in the editorial section were always a delight, as were those of Joe Alsop and Max Freedman. In one column White called the new President a "combat naval officer," described him as a sweet, gentle man, and said only "one form of criticism and one alone can move him to swear—that's the criticism of malice based on motives that are small and ugly." But there were not enough Budget Bureau spokesmen to quote, nor enough Bill Whites.

The climax came on December 23, 1963, just after the month of mourning for John Kennedy ended. That afternoon Pierre Salinger asked the top public relations staff men from the government Departments to come to the White House for a conference with Johnson. When they arrived, Salinger led them into the Fish Room, across the narrow corridor from the President's Oval Office.

He began by warming up the group with a pep talk focused on Johnson's interest in seeing to it that the government's exciting and important activities were well publicized throughout the nation. Finally he ran out of words, and subsided into a silent wait for Johnson.

It was a long time before Johnson swept into the Fish Room, with the expression on his face of a displeased teacher. "Peer says you're a hard-working bunch of men," he greeted them, "but in my opinion you're hardly doing anything at all.

"I don't see my name in the paper as often as I'd like to," he scolded them. "The only front-page story I got today was lighting that big White House Christmas tree on the Ellipse. Well, we did get a good play on that," he admitted, grudgingly. "You used to get Kennedy on the front page a helluva lot more than you're getting me there. And I'm warning you you've got to get more publicity for me. Now, I'm going down to the ranch over Christmas," he went on, "and I don't want you to put out a single big announcement about your Department's business with a Washington dateline. Send them all down to the ranch, and we'll announce them from there."

Chapter 66

JOHNSON'S NEED DURING his initial period as President to establish himself in the public mind as a legislative superman with mastery over Congress meant the enactment of laws Kennedy had not been able to obtain. Having told Congress and the nation in his first address on November 27 that he planned to work hardest for the Kennedy Civil Rights Bill and the 11.5-billion-dollar tax-cut proposal, Johnson was on a shaky-legged seat when Mike Mansfield and Speaker McCormack told him both measures were dead in the current Congress.

Nevertheless, Johnson felt it was important to keep both bills and himself in the news in order to show that he was working relentlessly toward their passage. This he accomplished by staging a flurry of interviews at the White House with civil rights leaders, tax cut advocates, and congressmen. In addition he took well-publicized trips to the Capitol for lunches and drinks with legislators.

He had Roy Wilkins, the dean of the Negro organization leaders and NAACP executive director, to a White House meeting on November 29; Urban League head Whitney Young on December 2; Martin Luther King, December 3; and James Farmer of CORE on December 4. Newsmen reported these meetings as important indications of Johnson's hard work to get the Kennedy bill passed, even though the place for such action was the Capitol. White House aides later said Johnson held these meetings to reassure the civil rights leaders of his position in favor of legislation and to gain their agreement for a moratorium on protest demonstrations throughout the nation. After his forty-five-minute meeting with Johnson, Roy Wilkins denied that a moratorium had been discussed; yet he gave himself away by telling reporters, "If Congress continues to postpone action as though a man had not been murdered in Jackson, Mississippi, and as though four girls had not been killed in a church in Birmingham . . . there is nothing for Negroes to do but demonstrate."

Johnson also kept himself and civil rights in the papers by other techniques. For the country's Negro newspapers he had copies of a 1960 interview on his personal emotional attachment to their cause. "I think I have had to go through the same kind of struggles as the colored people," the interview quoted him. In an inaccurate set of remarks on his own background, Johnson pleaded a dubious kinship in this fashion: "My family was poor and I was poor. When time came for us kids to go to college the money wasn't there. We couldn't go to the university. Because of all that, I had to suffer." For reporters from white-owned newspapers, he quoted Cactus Jack Garner as saying that "there comes a time in every poker game when a man has to shove in his whole stack." "Well, I'm shoving in all my stack on this civil rights bill," said Johnson. One further Johnson action that produced a front-page story came the morning he sent a limousine to pick up House Minority Leader Charlie Halleck and bring him to breakfast. Halleck confirmed the report that he had told Kennedy shortly before the assassination he was for a civil rights bill, but he informed Johnson what he already knew—that he would have to wait until next year for any action. Afterward, Johnson told reporters he had worked hard on Halleck for action on civil rights and had fed the heavy-jowled Republican "thick bacon, just the kind I know a fellow from Indiana would like."

While Johnson was creating the impression he was laboring furiously day after day to push a civil rights bill through Congress that December, he was also attempting to create a similar impression regarding the temporarily defunct tax-cut bill. Early in December he made a show of inviting Everett Dirksen to a poached-egg breakfast, and he told reporters he had asked the Senate minority leader to limit debate on the tax bill in the Finance Committee to ten minutes for each member. Dirksen almost exploded later when he learned of Johnson's words, because he had no authority to do this, nor did he want to for "Ol' Lyndon."

Johnson next had Senator Harry Byrd, the chairman of the Finance Committee, for a potato soup and salad luncheon at the White House on December 5. Afterward he led him on a tour of parts of the White House and to the basement swimming pool for which Franklin Roosevelt's friends had paid. Then he took Byrd's arm and directed him to the White House lobby, where he loudly proclaimed that he and Byrd were in "general agreement" on the need for a tax cut. Byrd's apple cheeks grew even redder in astonishment at Johnson's remark, but he said nothing to contradict him. Later, back in the Capitol, Byrd issued the statement that "Lyndon and I don't agree on a damned thing."

Johnson's talkfests on the Kennedy Civil Rights Bill and tax-reduction proposal helped create the picture he desired, that he was a perpetual motion machine on public business and a wizard over Congress. But he knew this portrayal could be maintained only by some tangible legislative success.

Fortunately, other Kennedy legislation already in the works was passed that December, and Johnson made a production of signing each new law and taking credit for it. The first bill of his administration was Public Law 88-204, a five-year, 1.2-billion-dollar program of loans and grants to construct college facilities. Johnson had played no part in its passage, but he called sixty congressmen to crowd about him at the White House ceremony while he signed the bill. One accepted the Presidential pen that made part of the top loop in the "L" of "Lyndon," and the others reached for pens proffered by Johnson as though they were made of gold. And to the reporters and news cameras, he not only claimed authorship, but offered the highly inaccurate comment that this was "the most significant education bill passed by Congress in the history of the Republic."

Three days later he gave another vigorous picture of the successful master of Congress and congressmen, when he signed a Kennedy bill that provided for a three-year 435-million-dollar manpower retraining program for unemployed persons in vocational schools or on the job. Again the large Congressional flock stood behind him, and he appeared to be humming during the twenty minutes he required to sign "Lyndon B. Johnson." He made a big show of awarding one of the pens to Senator Joe Clark, his old Senate enemy, and when he passed it to him, he said with a paternalistic smile, "You're the 'y' in Lyndon." Clark beamed in appreciation.

Of the many bills still before Congress in December 1963, and among those Johnson wanted to submit on his own, two stood out above the rest. The first was the Kennedy foreign aid appropriation bill, caught as usual in a House wrangle; the second, a Johnson proposal to change the line of Presidential succession. According to the 1947 law, because he had no Vice President, if he should die Johnson knew he would be succeeded by Speaker John McCormack, already slow-moving as he approached his seventy-second birthday. And next in line after McCormack was eighty-six-year-old Senate President *Pro Tem* "Silent Carl" Hayden. However, after furtive talks with House Democratic leaders, Johnson learned that the affront accorded McCormack by this proposal would severely damage the Presidential record in Congress in the next session. Moreover, there was small likelihood that a new succession bill would pass, for as Johnson put it, "Too many of those little Democratic chickenshits in the House won't go take a piss without consulting the speaker first." So he dropped the idea.

Reporters wrote up the House battle over the foreign aid bill as a Johnson "showdown." As Vice President, he had taken the position that only countries that proved they were American allies should receive foreign aid. But here again he changed his public stand because a key Kennedy bill was involved. Kennedy had tied foreign aid expenditures in his arguments not so much to humanitarian endeavors abroad as to their inexpensiveness in preventing "a successful Communist breakthrough in these areas." Yet this argument had failed to impress Representative Otto Passman of Louisiana, a leading Congressional junketeer, nominal Democrat who opposed Kennedy in 1960, and intransigent opponent of foreign aid as chairman of the House Appropriations Subcommittee on Foreign Operations. After one meeting with Passman, Kennedy told his aides, "Never bring that man here again."

Kennedy had sent Congress a request for 4.5 billion dollars for foreign aid in the next fiscal year, and by dint of a sharp pencil Passman cut the figure back to 2.7 billion dollars and added the Mundt Amendment to prevent the sale of wheat to the Soviet Union. When the Senate passed a 3.3-billion-dollar foreign aid bill, the Passman and Senate bills went to a joint conference committee, which reported back to both chambers a 3.0-billion-dollar bill without the Mundt Amendment. Passman quickly won House rejection of the conference bill and had it sent back to the conference committee. But the obstinate conference committee produced a new bill appropriating 3.6 billion dollars and again omitted the Mundt Amendment.

Johnson expected his friend Senator Fulbright, who was losing his appetite for shepherding foreign aid bills through the Senate, to be a good soldier and direct passage of the conference committee bill through the Upper Chamber. The problem lay in the House, where Speaker McCormack put it bluntly at his Board of Education glass-lifting ritual when he told Johnson to forget about foreign aid until the next session.

But the controversy had been seized upon by newspapers as a prime story, and Johnson realized that his inaction at this point would send his press-built reputation as a "can-do" legislative President down the drain. Highly agitated, he made calls to other House leaders, and he calmed down only when House Majority Leader Carl Albert and Majority Whip Hale Boggs assured him there was no reason for his hand-wringing. The job was to haul the hundred Democrats who had gone home for Christmas back to Washington and then to exert the influence of his office on them.

The order went out from McCormack to all absentee congressmen on Sunday, December 22, to return to Washington for a December 24 vote on the conference committee's report. Then to make certain that Democrats got back in time, Johnson ordered military jets dispatched to transport them. Next, on the night of December 23, he invited all House members to a White House party, to drink and eat and listen to his pep talk on the foreign aid bill.

Despite a snowstorm, two hundred came for spiked eggnog and fruitcake and a friendly scene in the State Dining Room, where Johnson stood on a velvet-covered gold chair and praised the legislators as men and women who "have labored through the vineyards and plowed through the snow." At the gathering, Johnson spied Charlie Halleck, whose face showed his angry mood, for he had learned from reporters that Johnson had been calling him a variety of unpleasant names.

"Charlie," Johnson told him, slapping him on the back, "I'm sorry if anybody here said anything ugly about you. We can disagree without being disagreeable." Halleck had worked closely with Passman to reject the first conference report, and afterward he had told House Republicans, "I guess this shows it takes more than a piece of thick bacon to buy me." But now, with Johnson's hand on his back, Halleck blurted in embarrassment, "I guess the House will pass the bill tomorrow."

When the guests were walking out of the White House, Johnson had a sudden idea for increasing his press coverage. Aides were sent scurrying after four female reporters who had left, to lure them back by promising they would have their pictures taken with him and Lady Bird. "Hey, ya want to see my swimming pool?" Johnson asked the ladies, following the snapshots. He led them to the pool, to his "think room" near his office, paused to stroke a bust of Franklin Roosevelt and remark, "Look at that chin. That's what I loved about him." Then he took them into his office and showed them a photograph of himself in which only the top of his head was seen above the high-backed Presidential chair. "There sits the loneliest man in the world," he said in his best imitation of a wail, and the ladies commiserated with him and later wrote appreciative stories of their tour.

The meeting of the House the next day, December 24, was set for the miserable hour of 7 A.M., and when members tottered in, each was handed a Johnson memo that warned: "The countries of the Communist world are watching anxiously to determine whether the new President is so strong they will have to come to terms with him or so weak that they can start hacking away at the free world with impunity."

Halleck's enormously unified crew did not buy the Johnson message, for only two of the 135 Republicans present supported the conference bill. But Carl Albert and Hale Boggs had made their count of Democratic sentiment before the morning, and knew they had more than enough votes to offset the Halleck unity. The final vote was 189 to 158 for passage, with twenty-five Democratic defectors joining the Republicans.

An analysis of the House vote on foreign aid revealed that Johnson's White House party, his memo and last-minute phone calls to Democrats had not changed a single vote. Those twenty-five Democrats who had opposed the first conference report that omitted the Mundt Amendment voted against the second conference report bill. What made the difference— and final success—was that other Democrats, who favored the bill but had been out of Washington when the first conference report was voted upon, were on hand for voting on December 24, thanks to Johnson's "air-lift."

Nevertheless, Johnson aides talked up the foreign aid success as a victory made possible only by Johnson's wizardry in persuading legislators to change their votes. One AP correspondent in Washington wrote that Johnson "had demonstrated—as his predecessor had not been able to do—that he could move Congress off its dead center to give him legislation he wanted."

At the end of Johnson's first month in office, Billie Moyers wrote out for newspaper use a statistical summary of his boss's activities. From his repetitive employment of the words "talked to," it was apparent that Johnson's interpretation of the Presidency was that it was a job for a monologist. Johnson "talked to the top policy officials of the State Department," said Moyers. "He talked to the top policy leaders of the Defense Department. . . . He talked to the ambassadors of the OAS countries. . . . He talked to all the ambassadors stationed in Washington. . . . He talked to farm leaders. . . . He talked to eighty of the nation's leading businessmen. . . . He talked to the Executive Council of the AFL-CIO. He talked to the United Nations. . . . "

This "talking to" extended to literally hundreds upon hundreds of individuals in person and an even larger number over the telephone. George Meany, the aging, rough, ungrammatical AFL-CIO president, had opposed Johnson's candidacy in 1960 both for the Democratic Presidential nomination and for the Vice Presidential slot. But Johnson overwhelmed him now by hard courting. He telephoned him, invited him to breakfast, and even had him join a morning meeting with the legislative leadership of Capitol Hill. He talked to him about Roosevelt, about labor's hard battles, and about raising the employment total by five million to seventy-five million persons drawing wages. Camaraderie between "George" and "Mister President" ran high, and Meany made no mention of Johnson's antilabor record as a House and Senate member and his successful fight to keep the AFL-CIO or any other kind of union from organizing his own workers at KTBC in Austin.

But to Pakistan's young Foreign Minister Z. A. Bhutto, Johnson talked in a different fashion. Bhutto was one of Johnson's first callers after the Kennedy funeral. The 3-by-5 card of pertinent data worked up by the State Department on Bhutto pictured him as leading his country into a closer relationship with Red China, and Johnson had absorbed this information before their meeting.

The young caller expressed his sorrow at Kennedy's passing, and just before he stood up to leave he expressed an unfavorable general comment about the course of American foreign policy in the Far East. "Sit down!" Johnson yelled at him, and with a pointing finger and straight-line mouth, he bellowed at Bhutto that if Pakistan continued to be friendly to Red China, his country might wake up one morning without any foreign aid from the United States. Unable to stop after he delivered his message, Johnson ran on while Bhutto sat speechless.

After Congress gave him the Kennedy foreign aid legislation, Johnson flew to the L.B.J. Ranch for Christmas. This was his first return since the Dallas murder a month and a few days earlier, and he made only one detour as Christmas Eve approached. This was a stop in Philadelphia to attend the funeral of Representative William Green, the Catholic Democratic boss of Philadelphia, who had supported him against Kennedy in the 1960 contest. Green's death had been hastened by a trial for misuse of his public office.

When Johnson awakened the next morning, twenty-seven relatives were on the scene to eat turkey. "My brother, my sisters, my uncles, cousins, aunts, and my family," he explained to reporters, whom he had asked to come before the meal to write newspaper stories of the President's Christmas Day. Humility and folksiness were the themes that day. Johnson mentioned a few of his past hardships and Lady Bird told how "I used an oil lamp until I was nine years old, and I can remember what a big day it was when we finally got indoor plumbing."

The relatives stood in a straggling line behind the seated First Family for the picture-taking on the lawn, after Johnson reminded the photographers not to photograph the right side of his face. Back in Washington this had led to the in-story of the news-photographer crowd that "Lyndon's right side is going to become as big a mystery as the dark side of the moon."

Once the posing was over, Johnson introduced some of his relatives to the newsmen. Aunt Ava Bright, with whom he had lived in Houston while he taught debating at Sam Houston High, had died in 1955. So to add color to the news stories that might come out of this Christmas Day, he assigned Aunt Ava's role to Aunt Jesse Hatcher, Sam Johnson's youngest sister. "This is Aunt Jesse," he told reporters. "She's Mrs. Silas Hatcher, who did all my cooking, washing, and sewing for me when I was in school in Houston. And I was in her dining room when I announced I was going to run in 1937."

Johnson also introduced a tall, blond youth to whom his daughter Lynda was engaged: "This is Ensign Bernie Rosenbach."

"He's a jay gee now," Lynda corrected him.

"I reckon he is," said Johnson, moving on to a description of the scene when he was Vice President and had taken Lynda along to meet Pope John XXIII at the Vatican. He had told the Pope that Lynda was "pinned to a Catholic boy, and she'll probably marry him." The Pope had blessed the proposed union and given Lynda matching rosaries for herself and the young man, who had recently graduated from the Naval Academy.

Then, after an aside that he expected his daughter to get a Ph.D. before

she married, he moved on to introduce seventy-nine-year-old Uncle Huffman Baines, and he teased his mother's younger brother when Uncle Huff
couldn't remember his age. By now Johnson was feeling like a warm host,
and he blurted to reporters, "Come in and see our house. It'll take but a
minute."

Lady Bird made a desperate move to prevent this tour from taking place.
"Honey, I promise I'll give all these folks a wonderful tour when they come
for the barbecue on Friday," she said in an uneven voice.

"Whatever you say, Honey," he told her, just before he opened the door
and led sixty reporters inside the house.

He had a story about every object. "Now this here framed letter," he
said at one point, "is from my great-granddaddy to Sam Houston. Great-
Granddaddy Baines was a Baptist preacher, and he was writing to renew
a note at 8 per cent interest and also to complain that his congregation was
behind on pledges." At a framed picture of Stuart Symington, Johnson
winked broadly and said, "He's Lady Bird's boyfriend."

Lady Bird came along once to complain that "the turkey dressing isn't
getting any better," but he glanced down only momentarily at his orange
cowboy boots before continuing the tour. As he finished and signaled he
would come to the table, he handed the reporters ashtrays with his signature. "They cost me only a few pennies, so they don't come under Paul
Douglas' two-and-a-half-dollar rule that separates a gift from a bribe."

That day, as he tucked his napkin into his shirt front and heaped his
plate with turkey and the usual side dishes, the first of an outpouring of
Presidential statements and reports on the economy and the body politic
was released to reporters under dateline of the "L.B.J. Ranch." His angry
talk to government press agents only two days earlier to let him release
their Department's announcements had produced swift results.

In addition to this grinding-out of ranch-released government junk mail,
Johnson also ordered his top public officials to fly to the ranch in a steady
stream. Each man who came, whether on business or not, had his picture
taken with a serious-faced President, and from the number of photographs
appearing in the newspapers, Johnson was easily doing far more work on
vacation than his predecessor had done in the White House.

The Joint Chiefs of Staff came resplendent in their uniforms. There was
also "Mister Stacomb," as Johnson sometimes called his Secretary of Defense; and chain-smoking Secretary of State Dean Rusk, an easy and prolonged talker; academic Walter Heller, the chairman of the Council of
Economic Advisers, whom Johnson confronted with some of his local
cattle rancher friends in order to show him up as an unrealistic professor;
other Cabinet members and agency heads; and an assortment of Johnson's
private business associates who avoided the photographers and reporters.

While there was a great deal of drinking and horseplay, there was also
work. Loose strings on the next federal budget had yet to be tied, and the

month-long struggle to write his first annual State of the Union Message, as required by the Constitution and tradition, still continued. Johnson had asked Horace Busby to write his Thanksgiving Day Address, and it was such a resounding flop that when he needed a speech for his UN appearance on December 17, he asked Ol' Adlai to work one up for him.

Now, on the State of the Union Message, because it would lay out his program in an election year, he needed an experienced hand. So he turned to Ted Sorensen and had him come to the ranch to do the job. In charge of coordinating the material for the Message was Bill Moyers (as his young aide wanted to be called, instead of Billie Don Moyers). Johnson was impressed with Moyers' attention to details as well as with his creative abilities. At the televised Thanksgiving Day Address, he had watched Moyers bark at the stage setters in a manner imitating his own, "That lectern won't do! Get one sixty-two inches high."

For the Sorensen draft of the Message, Moyers pulled together statistical material from two dozen agencies, ordered separate reports from individual Cabinet members, and asked Abe Fortas and others to read some of the submitted material. Johnson later claimed there were about sixteen drafts of the Message, including the Sorensen production, and that he submitted the "final" draft to 123 persons for criticism and suggestions. The Sorensen draft, which was essentially the annual State of the Union Message Congress and the nation heard on January 8, 1964, was one of the shortest in history. Even in his slowest speaking voice to captive audiences on the ranch, where he practiced reading it aloud in his living room, Johnson could not stretch it beyond forty minutes, allowing about fifty pauses for expected applause.

Johnson's first foreign visitor, balloon-jowled Chancellor Ludwig Erhard of West Germany, also flew to the ranch during the Christmas holidays. Kennedy had made the Erhard date before his Texas trip, and Johnson had insisted that it be kept despite the great American tragedy. To build excitement, Johnson told Rusk and McGeorge Bundy that he was terribly concerned because Lady Bird wanted a White House setting for the Erhard visit, while he wanted the ranch. By the time the two worked up sufficient nerve to tell him he should do "whatever came naturally," he had long completed arrangements for the ranch visit.

Before Erhard arrived, Rusk gave Johnson a quick briefing on the latest status of the Berlin controversy with the Reds, the Common Market tariff reduction activities of the six member nations—West Germany, Belgium, Holland, Luxembourg, France, and Italy—and the West Germany-Soviet Union coldness. Then came the German for an overwhelming Johnson welcome and ranch hospitality.

Johnson took him on auto trips to spot deer, sat with him on overstuffed living room chairs while they exchanged jokes and bantered with the clustered Johnson relatives and German neighbors, and went into Fredericksburg so Erhard could sample a German town in the midst of Texas. There was also a gala barbecue in Erhard's honor in the Stonewall High School gym, with six hundred invited guests. A chorus regaled Erhard with "Tief in dem Hertzen von Texas" (Deep in the Heart of Texas), "Cactus" Prior told jokes, a folk-singing group twanged out wailing songs, and Van Cliburn performed at the piano with a Chopin concert. Johnson gave the cigar-smoking German a cowboy's ten-gallon hat, to the merriment of the crowd, and the party was declared a success by most on hand.

Reporters felt sorry for Pierre Salinger that day. Before the trip to the ranch it had appeared that Salinger would successfully make the transition from Kennedy to Johnson as press secretary. One Saturday night the Johnsons had gone to the Salinger home in Falls Church, Virginia, for dinner. "You know, that's the first coffee cup I ever had that didn't burn my lips," Johnson praised the then Mrs. Salinger for her homemade ceramic cups. When she gave one to him, he acted as though he would be eternally grateful.

But on the ranch Johnson insisted that Salinger wear cowboy clothes, even though the pudgy press secretary looked ridiculous in his western getup. Johnson also ordered him to climb onto a small horse to be photographed. Then he began treating him like a despised servant, ordering him to carry out little errands and scolding him in front of others. At the Erhard barbecue he made Salinger a laughingstock by forcing him to don ten-gallon hats that were too wide at the brim for him. But the crowning embarrassment came when Van Cliburn concluded his brilliant playing, and Johnson yelled, "Would Mr. Salinger please go to the piano." "Me follow Van Cliburn?" Salinger, who had claimed to be a child prodigy, asked incredulously. Johnson nodded and ordered him to play.

Ludwig Erhard gave Johnson the impression he would have an easy time dealing with other foreign leaders on international affairs. Erhard had only recently succeeded Konrad "Der Alte" Adenauer, who had grudgingly retired in his late eighties, and by training, Erhard was an economist and not a politician. No, he would not push the Adenauer-de Gaulle scheme for a German-French togetherness against the world, he assured his Texas host. Yes, he would increase his military budget and buy war matériel from the United States. Yes, he would name West German representatives to a working party on Soviet relations that would include American, British, and French officials of ambassadorial rank. The group would concoct a "peace package" which the Soviet Union would be bound to reject, thus making the Communists look bad to the neutral nations. Erhard was so amenable that Johnson called him "my best friend" as the German left for home.

On the ranch, Johnson also quietly attended to state political business. The Kennedy assassination had done strange things to Texas politics. In the period of remorse and guilt that the murder had taken place in Texas, politicians there whose names were associated either with Kennedy or Johnson were suddenly immune from political defeat, whether they were hidebound reactionaries or strong liberals.

When Kennedy put Homer Thornberry on the federal bench as a favor to Johnson, Johnson picked Jake Pickle to occupy the seat he and Homer had held. But in the November 9, 1963, primary fight for the Tenth Congressional District seat, Johnson's influence was nil, and an almost equal three-way split developed. Jake collected 14,306 votes, Republican Jim Dobbs got 13,702, and Jack Slattery, a liberal Democrat, hung close to Dobbs' shirttail. But Slattery was third, even if by a few votes, and the December 17 runoff involved Jake Pickle and Jim Dobbs.

Johnson sadly considered his old pal Jake a loser for an obvious reason. Both Jake and Dobbs were right-wing extremists, campaigning in opposition to civil rights legislation, foreign aid appropriations, federal aid to schools, Medicare, and the Kennedy tax-cut proposal. But since Pickle had already received the computed reactionary Democratic vote in the first primary, Johnson realized he could not expect to do better in the runoff, because those Red-Hot liberals for Slattery were bound to stay home. In fact, their opposition was directed more against Pickle than Dobbs, for Pickle had bolted to Eisenhower in 1952 and had produced the 1954 film "The Port Arthur Story," an absurd piece of propaganda to place blame for labor troubles there on Ralph Yarborough, then Shivers' opponent for governor.

But the Kennedy assassination produced a closing of the Democratic ranks, and Pickle swamped Dobbs by a vote of 27,227 to 16,946.

Kennedy's death also insured Yarborough's re-election to the Senate in 1964, because he had been closely associated with the late President's legislative program. This was a turn of fate that angered Johnson, because he had been working for months to develop conservative Democratic candidates to run against Yarborough the following year. Now all such effort would prove a waste of time.

Following the assassination Yarborough had called Johnson at the White House to assure him of his support. But Johnson had accepted his promise gruffly and told him not to expect any Texas patronage as a result. For the first time in history, a President would direct all patronage appointments in his home state. And now on the ranch, when a telephone call came, and Johnson was asked about the $350,000 that had been collected for the $100-a-plate November 22 Austin banquet that had not taken place, he said not a penny was to go to the campaign of Red-Hot Yarborough.

John Connally's re-election as governor of Texas was also assured by the assassination. "Connally couldn't lose," said Yarborough. "He knew all he had to do was to appear on TV and hold up the arm that had been shot and rub it as though it still hurt." From the ranch that Christmas, Johnson was several times in touch with his long-time assistant, though he did not visit him in person. It was not until early January that Connally

was sufficiently recovered so he could return home to his 4,500-acre ranch
—the "Four C"—near Floresville, the scene of his boyhood poverty. The
Four C was named for the four Connally children, one of whom was already four years in her grave. This was sixteen-year-old daughter Kathleen,
John Connally's delight, who had eloped early in 1959. Later that year,
when her young husband came home one night, he claimed she held a
shotgun and threatened to take her life. He said he had fought with her
for the gun, but it had gone off, killing her.

Besides the press handouts, the steady stream of visitors, the Erhard
conference, work on the budget and the State of the Union Message, and
talk on state politics, Johnson also went hunting for deer and used part
of his vacation time on his private business affairs.

He went over to Moursund's spread the day after Christmas, and he
returned to the ranch with word that he had bagged a big buck. While he
was away with his estate trustee, Johnson also had an opportunity to discuss their mutual businesses, current problems, and future gains. There
was a minor problem in their control of the Moore State Bank at Llano,
which they had taken over early that year. The problem was that Moursund had decided to end the twice-a-year dividends the stockholders had
been drawing since Tom Moore had started the bank thirty years earlier,
and stockholders were complaining. Johnson proposed a solution to shut
them up, and this was to tell them that if they were dissatisfied they could
sell out to the new controllers at the book value of their stock. This should
start them on a new and pointless argument that would draw their attention away from the dividend matter, because the book value was about
half the six-hundred-dollar market value for each share. Moursund later
told a *Wall Street Journal* reporter, when he carried out Johnson's suggestion, "If any stockholder is unhappy, I don't know about it."

Johnson and Moursund also discussed the possibility of Moursund's acting as Johnson's property and assets trustee to branch into Louisiana and
pick up KLFY-TV in Lafayette for the usual hard-bargain low price. These
negotiations lasted throughout 1964 before Johnson's Texas Broadcasting
Company acquired KLFY.

At the same time that Chancellor Erhard was his ranch guest, Johnson
asked two executives of Midwest Video Company of Little Rock, Arkansas,
to be his guests, too. Newsmen were not informed of the visit of these
guests, nor were they told that Johnson was conducting foreign policy
negotiations with Erhard and private business negotiations with his other
guests.

The background of his business conference was as follows: Midwest
Video was an industrial firm engaged in receiving out-of-town TV programs on its mountain-top antennas and relaying them through strung
cables to TV receiver owners for a monthly charge. Midwest Video wanted
to operate in Austin, but this required a franchise from the city council.

Former Mayor Tom Miller and Johnson set up a dummy company called Capital Cable. Then Johnson, who was Vice President at the time, appeared on the scene with a proposition for Midwest Video: It should operate Capital Cable, which had no assets or business, as its wholly-owned subsidiary in Austin in the TV program relay business. The catch was that Johnson would have to be given a three-year option at no cost to acquire half ownership in Capital Cable. The three-year option would begin after the Austin city council approved the operating franchise. Midwest Video agreed because of a lack of alternatives if it rejected his proposition. It would bear all operating costs (except for Johnson's permission to run its cable from the KTBC-TV tower 1,280 feet high on top of Mount Larson); and when Johnson decided to take up the option, Midwest Video would lose control of its Capital Cable subsidiary.

The city council's approval came in January 1963, but a new problem soon arose. A rival Austin firm, TV Cable, came into existence, and it erected an antenna on top of a mountain thirty miles south of the city. TV Cable was able to pick up the four San Antonio TV channels, and by using an inexpensive microwave system that did not require high-cost strung cables, it was soon transmitting the San Antonio programs to Austin set owners for $4.95 a month.

There was no question that TV Cable, with its cheaper system, would not only ruin Capital Cable but would eliminate KTBC-TV's network monopoly in Austin unless a solution were soon found. With Vice President Johnson's connections, there was little surprise in Washington when the FCC undertook to determine whether TV Cable required a license and what its operating conditions should be. On the day of Kennedy's assassination, the FCC was supposed to make its ruling; and as Johnson made the touring circuit with Kennedy that Friday, he had this on his mind as well as the Bobby Baker revelations.

Despite its years of lavishing favors on him, the FCC ruled that morning against Vice President Johnson by its decision to permit TV Cable and other microwave users to operate outside FCC regulations. After word of the assassination came, however, said a senator, the FCC decided to reconsider its decision. When the FCC made its new ruling on December 13, Johnson had already served three weeks as President. According to the FCC, TV Cable would not be permitted to run any network programs for thirty days after they originally appeared, in order to give Johnson's KTBC-TV the right to rebroadcast those programs in the interim. The FCC also ruled that microwave transmission systems, such as those of TV Cable, were under FCC control, but strung-cable systems, such as Capital Cable's, were not covered.

This decision favoring Capital Cable made it obvious that within a few years this subsidiary of Midwest Video would be worth between five and ten million dollars. Disheartened by the back-to-the-wall deal Johnson had forced on them by promising to acquire a city franchise for them, Midwest Video officers hoped that Johnson would agree to forget his option to take control of Capital Video because he was now President of the United States and presumably totally engrossed with statesmanship.

But at the ranch that Christmas, they found Johnson's mood was far from charitable. According to John Barron of the Washington *Evening Star,* who later spoke to Midwest Video executives, Johnson was not only insisting that the option deal remain in effect, but threatening not to take up option control over Capital Cable until the end of the option period in 1966. This meant, of course, that he was telling them that they must continue to work and incur expenses until then in order to hand him the gift of a multi-million-dollar property. In addition, he said pointedly, he expected them to buy out Capital Cable's rival, the microwave transmitting company, TV Cable, and make it part of Capital Cable. He thought they should be able to swing this for less than two million dollars.

One of the Midwest Video participants told Barron that Johnson laced them as he spoke with such choice language that Lady Bird, who was present, cut in at one point with "Lyndon, don't you think you're being rather rough with these gentlemen?"

Johnson's reply was, "I'm speaking so frankly because I want all matters clearly understood."

As an aftermath of this Christmas session, when a reporter asked Johnson at a Presidential news conference early the next year about any possible connection he might have with Capital Cable, he emphatically denied any knowledge of the option his company held.

On New Year's Eve, with his first Presidential vacation almost over, Johnson paid a surprise visit to the drinking party Washington reporters away from home were holding at the Driskill Hotel in Austin. He had done handsomely for certain reporters during the vacation, and they were excited to see him now.

Earlier in the week he had invited Phil Potter of the Baltimore *Sun,* a long-time Johnson booster, Douglas Kiker of the New York *Herald Tribune,* and Tom Wicker of *The New York Times* to come to the ranch from the hotel for a fish fry. With his knack for instant friendship, he had made the latter two feel for the moment a rare kinship and bond with a President of the United States. In Wicker's case, this was somewhat watered down the next day when Johnson sat at the wheel of his Presidential Lincoln with the *Times* reporter alongside him and raced across the countryside at hair-raising speeds.

Johnson knew that Hugh Sidey, the young White House correspondent for *Time,* had been a Kennedy worshipper. So in order to effect a transfer of affections, he had Sidey come to the ranch for a chicken dinner and then for a ride in the nineteen-foot, sixty-m.p.h. Johnson motor launch on twenty-two-mile Lake Lyndon B. Johnson. Johnson was also especially attentive to Marianne Means, the blonde Hearst reporter at the White

House. Not only did he request that she sit next to him at a ranch dinner, but when he used three helicopters to transport guests on one flight, he asked her to join him in his helicopter. James Reston of *The New York Times* was in Phoenix, Arizona, with his wife during that vacation when he learned of the Johnson fraternization with some of the reporters, and he called the ranch to ask for an invitation. Johnson obliged by sending his own airplane to Dallas to pick up the Restons.

To assuage the less influential reporters holed up at the Driskill, Johnson invited the entire contingent to a ranch news conference one day. This was on Friday, December 27, the day before Erhard arrived for his two-day conference. The setting for the press meeting was unusual, as *The New York Times* pointed out: "The President of the United States held a news conference with a haystack as a rostrum. In the background smoke drifted up from barbecue pits. . . . After the conference the President rode off on a horse." His choice bits of news that day were that he had cut one hundred persons from the 2.5 million employees on the federal payroll during the last month, and that he and his old friend, Mexican President Mateos, would be picking up honorary degrees at UCLA the following February.

At the Driskill party Johnson tried instant friendship with the lot, sliding into easy barnyard language, slapping backs, pressing the flesh, and downing a half dozen drinks. Then on the trip back to Washington aboard *Air Force One*, he continued his effort to put the working press into the Presidential propaganda machine. "I'm gonna make big men outa all of you," he enticed the reporters. "We're gonna get along just peachy. And if you play ball with me, I'll play ball with you."

A few leaned forward to hear further details about the ball playing. "If I have one too many scotches under my belt, and you see it," Johnson explained, "I don't expect to read about it in the papers."

Chapter 67

B<small>Y THE TIME</small> the second session of the Eighty-eighth Congress convened in January 1964, the national trauma resulting from the Kennedy assassination was subsiding, though a numbing sorrow lingered among the late President's admirers.

Still another change was apparent: Johnson was no longer being accepted as the dimly outlined, Constitutionally required successor to the martyred President, but as the boss of the White House, the Executive Branch, and the Democratic party in his own right. He had brought this about, not by wearing the public humility and occasional cockiness of a Harry Truman, but by propagandizing an image of a tall, tough Texan who needed only an hour or two of sleep in each twenty-four as he rode roughshod over the enemies of the people.

Newspapers reported he was phoning senators, Presidential aides, and lawyers in the middle of the night in his continuous effort to bring good government. As a typical Johnsonism, newspapers epitomized him as a leader who received a morning call in his bedroom late in 1963 from Larry O'Brien, the carry-over Kennedy legislative aide. O'Brien was supposedly almost in tears because he had failed to prevent "a disastrous foreign aid vote."

"When did they vote?" the tale had Johnson asking sternly.

"At four-fifteen in the morning."

"Why didn't you call me?" Johnson snapped. "Next time wake me up. I want to bleed with you."

The implications of this story were twofold: Unlike Kennedy, Johnson was willing to work at any hour of the day; and had O'Brien called him before the disaster occurred, somehow he would have saved the situation.

Politics and history were never static, as Johnson well knew, and with a new year on hand, the tall, tough Texan would have to add to this image of dogged omnipotence because he faced a Presidential campaign in the fall. Although his three top idea men, Abe Fortas, Clark Clifford, and Jim Rowe, were already proposing a number of suggestions for ballooning this image, Johnson realized that the key to success would be the one that opened the door of Congress. Defeat this year on the Kennedy program would ruin him.

Johnson's legislative year began on January 8, 1964, when he donned his surest man-in-charge expression and stepped to the Presidential level on the House dais to deliver his State of the Union Message to Congress. With TV cameras photographing the stern yet occasionally kindly left side of his face, he deliberately gave the impression he was speaking from the heart and not from a printed speech by utilizing mirrors in front of his lectern on which the running words of the message appeared at his eye level. On each line, words were underlined to remind him to emphasize them; and other reminders were written into the margin: "Look right"; "Pause"; and "Look left."

When he finished, he told one enthusiastic senator who congratulated him, "Yeah, I know. I was interrupted eighty times by applause." A later check of the applause bursts revealed there were exactly that number.

The first order of business in the new Congress was to win approval of the Kennedy tax-cut proposal. But the chief stumbling block in January 1964 was the same Senator Harry Byrd, chairman of the Finance Committee, who had adamantly opposed the cut in December 1963. The way to meet a federal deficit, the Virginia apple grower said with the simplicity of a man in business, was to cut all loafers off the payroll and get rid of all nonessential programs, such as those dealing with social welfare.

As in December, the obstinacy of Byrd against the proposed tax cut could not be talked away by a President who could neither explain the New Economics nor show real belief in it himself. Six years earlier, during the 1958 recession, Senator Paul Douglas had failed completely to explain to Majority Leader Johnson why a tax cut would snap the economy out of its downward spiral. Johnson could understand pump-priming public works to create employment and a slash in government spending to balance the budget. But economist Walter Heller in 1963 and 1964 found Johnson a poor student in comprehending the proposition that when the economy was operating below capacity, the best way to offset a large federal budgetary deficit was to reduce taxes and thus stimulate industrial expansion and larger tax revenues. "Lyndon has never been able to understand monetary or fiscal policy," said Wright Patman.

It was Mike Mansfield who quietly rescued the tax-cut bill when it seemed dead in the Senate Finance Committee. In a talk with Byrd, the Senate majority leader pointed out that the House had passed the tax cut and Byrd was thwarting democracy in the Senate by bottling up H.R. 8363 in his committee and preventing ninety-nine other senators from voting on it. When Byrd agreed to drop the role of dictator, the bill was assured of success. "It's hard to be contrary with a man like Mike, who's always nice and fair to you," said Byrd.

But after the conference committee report for a unified House-Senate tax-reduction measure overwhelmingly cleared the Senate on February 26 by a vote of 74 to 19, newspapers hailed Johnson rather than Mansfield as a legislative genius. Johnson signed the bill that day using sixty-four pens, and then gained additional publicity when he rode to Mrs. Kennedy's home in Georgetown to deliver three of the pens to her and her two children.

In his first talk to Congress on November 27, 1963, and again in his January 8, 1964, State of the Union Message, Johnson had called on the Legislative Branch to pass the Kennedy Civil Rights Bill. Here again it was Mike Mansfield, who without any publicity, pushed it through the Senate.

The bills Johnson and Russell had permitted the Senate to pass in 1957 and 1960 had not contributed in any tangible degree to the realization by American Negroes of first-class citizenship status. Especially resented by Negroes were continuing restrictions preventing them from using public facilities, such as restaurants, hotels, and bathrooms, available only to whites; continuing bars to voting, lack of equal employment opportunities, and desegregated schools.

In his campaign for the Presidency, Kennedy had said in 1960 that "with a stroke of the pen" he would sign an Executive Order if elected, banning discrimination in federally financed housing. But it was not until 1962, and after the White House had been fairly flooded with pens sent by dismayed civil rights proponents, that Kennedy finally signed this Executive Order.

Trouble broke out in Mississippi that fall when the state government tried to bar a Negro from enrolling at the lily-white University of Mississippi. This was a foretaste of the growing Negro revolt that burst into the open in Alabama in 1963. At the beginning of that year's Congressional session, civil rights advocates had asked Vice President Johnson for a ruling that they claimed would make it easier for them to get a strong civil rights bill through the Senate. But Johnson had ruled against them by refusing to make any decision. Yet on May 30, 1963, he appeared at Gettysburg, where he delivered a strong pro-civil rights speech written by Horace Busby, hardly a civil rights champion. In this centennial celebration of Lincoln's Emancipation Proclamation, Johnson read: "Until justice is blind to color, until education is unaware of race, until opportunity is unconcerned with the color of men's skins, emancipation will be a proclamation but not a fact."

It took the Negroes themselves, acting in the dangerous environment of Birmingham, Alabama, in April 1963, to push Kennedy to federal action. Rev. Martin Luther King, young president of the Southern Christian Leadership Council, inaugurated a massive "Freedom Now" nonviolent protest, and the local police reacted with brutality. More than three thousand Negroes, including King, suffered drenchings, beatings, and draggings as they were carted off to jail for sitting at segregated lunch counters and picketing stores that practiced segregation in employment and service.

Finally, the sight of the mad events in Birmingham on TV moved Kennedy to ask Congress on June 19, 1963, for a civil rights law. "Frustration and discord are burning in every city, North and South, where legal remedies are not at hand," wrote Ted Sorensen for Kennedy's delivery.

But instead of taking quick action during that hot summer of Negro discontent, the House began what turned into eight months of deliberation. The Kennedy bill contained two chief features: a ban enforced by the federal government on discriminatory practices in places of public accommodation; and the granting of authority to the Attorney General to assume the initiative to end segregated schooling. Then, when the measure underwent hearings in Representative Emanuel Celler's House Judiciary Committee, disgruntled Republican liberals declared it inadequate. This led to strengthening additions installed by the Republicans, including the establishment of a Fair Employment Practices Committee and the 1956–1957 Senator Paul Douglas Part III broad authorization to federal courts to protect all civil rights.

The Kennedy bill had gone to Congress over the protest of Lyndon Johnson, whose opinion it was that Kennedy should have waited until Congress passed the appropriations bills for the next fiscal year before opening the civil rights keg. But Kennedy had ignored him because of great pressures from the black community. However, Kennedy had been busy behind the scenes in a futile effort to prevent the full House Judiciary Committee from sending to the floor the much stronger Republican bill of Representative William McCulloch of Ohio. Kennedy believed that the Republicans were loading the bill so the House wouldn't accept it.

Not until February 10, 1964, a month after Johnson's State of the Union Message, did the House finally vote, and the strong Republican bill breezed through by 290 to 130. "A lot of Republicans voted for the bill," said a disgruntled Southern member, "because they were sure it would go to Jim Eastland's Judiciary Committee in the Senate, and Eastland would bury it there. Lyndon Johnson's claim that he did a lot of arm-twisting had nothing to do with the House vote."

"Mike Mansfield took total charge of the civil rights bill when it came to the Senate from the House," said Charles Ferris, the counsel for the Senate Democratic Policy Committee. "He had no intention of letting the bill go to the Judiciary Committee, so he met it at the Senate door. And by utilizing a seldom-used procedure, he had the bill placed directly on the Senate Calendar."

Of course this was an understatement, for Senator Russell fought like an English bulldog. He made a point of order against permitting Mansfield to use Rule XIV, the obscure rule in question, and when the chair ruled against him, he appealed the ruling to the Senate, only to find a now angered Mansfield mustering his forces to table Russell's appeal by a vote of 54 to 37.

"On March 9," said Ferris, "Mansfield made a motion to take the civil rights bill onto the floor and make it the Senate's pending business. But it took two and a half weeks for him to get past the filibusterers before he could get a vote on the motion. The vote on March 26 was 67 to 17 to proceed to the consideration of the bill.

"Then the month of April disappeared. First the Senate leadership for the bill devoted a week to explaining it. Then the filibusterers took over. At the end of April Mansfield told the Senate, 'The bill has been thoroughly explained, and the opponents have had time to digest it and attack it. So let's have the debate.' But this had no effect on the filibusterers.

"Mansfield had made himself the background chief on the bill as well as its political strategist, and he saw in April that the key to passage of the civil rights legislation was Senator Dirksen, the minority leader. Dirksen was barking against the FEPC provision of the bill and also the public accommodations section, and Mike realized that without Dirksen's approval no civil rights bill would pass, even if the filibuster ended. So he told Dirksen one day, 'We should sit down and work out a substitute acceptable to you and me and solve the serious problem we have in this country.' "

Dirksen was willing, and so were Tom Kuchel, the minority whip, Jacob Javits and Kenneth Keating from New York, and Clifford Case from New Jersey. As another Republican senator put it, "We knew Mike Mansfield well enough to know that his integrity was complete, and he would work out a fair bill and a strong bill. With Mike, we Republicans didn't need to monitor the Senate floor at all times the way we had to with his predecessor Lyndon Johnson, who would do something sly if we were not there."

For seven weeks of mornings, Dirksen's staff, Mansfield's staff, lawyers from the Justice Department, and Charlie Ferris met to hammer out the new civil rights bill. Then in the afternoons the senators directly involved met, to see what progress the morning staffs had made and to render decisions. "Mansfield kept the structure from breaking down," said Ferris. "He insisted, for one thing, that all the meetings must be held in Dirksen's office, because it was Dirksen who needed special attention and the limelight. Mansfield's even temperament also helped spread the bipartisan spirit that the negotiations required."

All the time the daily meetings were proceeding, Russell's forces held the Senate floor. Leading Northern Democratic advocates of civil rights angrily demanded that Mansfield hold around-the-clock sessions to break the filibuster. But Mansfield refused. "I remembered too well that when Lyndon did this in 1960, we wore out first from having to answer all the roll calls and caved in to the filibusterers," Mansfield said. So he now adjourned the Senate every evening about six or seven o'clock and ignored complaints.

By the beginning of June the base of the Civil Rights Bill had been broadened and clarified to gain acceptance by Dirksen, while the filibusterers were growing hoarse, and their talk was embarrassing even to themselves. On purpose Mansfield paused to speak to fence-straddling senators, sadly muttering, "It looks like the Senate can't do its job," and thus created animosity toward the Russell crew. Mansfield now moved in to line up the necessary votes for cloture.

The vote to shut off the filibuster came on June 10. Johnson called Mansfield and insisted that Mansfield give him the names of five undecided senators who needed special attention. Mansfield obliged, and of the five only one supported cloture. But this one vote was not needed, for the vote for cloture was 71 to 29, four more than the required two-thirds.

Nine days of cogent debate still lay ahead, and Mansfield turned over his front-row, center-aisle seat to Senator Hubert Humphrey, the chief Senate sponsor of the bill, to handle floor debate according to the basic strategy laid out for him by Mansfield. There were eleven sections in the new bill, including public accommodations and FEPC coverage, but with Dirksen now satisfied that all the Mrs. Murphys whose boarding houses of five rooms or fewer were exempted from the public accommodations section of the bill, the Southern cause was hopeless. The one-sided vote of 73 to 27 on June 19, when this landmark bill cleared the Senate, proved this.

With Mansfield's silence regarding the behind-the-scenes Senate slavery to "free" Negroes, all credit for passage of the Civil Rights Act accrued to Johnson. While Southern newspapers denounced him as a traitor and a Congressional manipulator, the Negro and liberal votes in the nation were now solidified behind him.

Even with the success of the tax cut and civil rights measures, Johnson chafed under the image of the horse that had pulled the master's cart up the steep mountain and into the master's castle. What he wanted was his own program of Johnson bills—not Kennedy bills—for Congress to pass. But trapped by a lack of originality among his advisers, he had to settle for another Kennedy program that he now called his own.

It was on November 23, 1963, the day following the assassination, that he had a talk with Walter Heller and first heard about a Kennedy proposal to coordinate a program for the economically underprivileged in America. The true genesis of welfare programs for "the forgotten man" on the economic totem pole was the New Deal of Franklin Roosevelt. "I see one third of a nation ill-housed, ill-clad, and ill-nourished," Roosevelt had said.

Following his visits to the hills and hollows of West Virginia, and seeing firsthand the abject, hopeless misery of other Americans, Kennedy, in his 1960 campaign, promised a "war against poverty and degradation." Once in office, his fight against poverty had included Senator Douglas' Area Redevelopment Bill which Eisenhower had earlier vetoed, an eleven-state Appalachian program, a Manpower Training and Redevelopment Bill, and vocational education appropriations. Late in 1963, before Kennedy went to Texas, he had given much thought to creating a unified 1964 war against poverty, Heller told Johnson.

But Kennedy had not actually prepared a package of antipoverty legislation as he had on the tax cut, civil rights, and Medicare. So Johnson pushed the war on poverty as his own program. On January 8, 1964, it showed up as a major section in his State of the Union message, in which he declared "an unconditional war on poverty in America." Then on March 14, he sent a special message to Congress requesting an appropriation of about one billion dollars to establish an Office of Economic Opportunity. The OEO, he said, would "direct and coordinate youth programs, community action programs, antipoverty programs in rural areas, small business incentive loans, and work experience programs, in an effort to alleviate poverty." About 380,000 poor youths who were school dropouts were to have a thousand dollars of federal money spent on each of them during the next year through a job training program. Three hundred and fifteen million dollars were to be earmarked to "stimulate" towns and cities to operate local wars on poverty under their own direction. There would also be small loans to low-income rural families, aid to migratory farm workers and needy children, and adult education programs. In short, it would be a variety of individual Kennedy programs brought together under one roof to be directed by Sargent Shriver, the late President's brother-in-law.

Mike Mansfield brought action in the Senate on the poverty war before the House took up the proposal, for he knew he had the necessary votes for passage. Trouble arose chiefly over a single Republican amendment, which would grant state governors the authority to veto local community action programs. On the first vote the amendment carried 45 to 44, and Mike asked his whip, Hubert Humphrey, to dig up some absent Democrats. Humphrey found only one, and the next roll-call vote was 45 to 45. Mike asked him again to find more Democrats. The third time around, the amendment was finally defeated, 46 to 45. Following a ringing denunciation of the entire bill by Senator Goldwater, saying that it was a "Madison Avenue stunt" by Lyndon Johnson, the Antipoverty Bill easily cleared the Senate by a vote of 61 to 34, with twelve Democrats and twenty-two Republicans in opposition.

However, it sailed a rougher course in the House. Speaker McCormack gazed over the sea of Southern Democratic faces and decided that to insure passage a Southern Democrat must be the sponsor. The man he chose was Phil Landrum of Georgia, a high-seniority member of the House Education and Labor Committee. Johnson considered this choice excellent, for Landrum had been the cosponsor of the antilabor Landrum-Griffin Act of 1959, and his Southern colleagues could not charge him with being a Red-Hot. So he could be expected to drag some Southerners in his wake to support the bill. But Landrum was not easy to convince, until McCormack talked about finding a seat for him on the powerful Ways and Means Committee, a transfer Landrum desired.

Even with Landrum as sponsor, Southerners tried to kill the bill. Judge Howard Smith, Mister Sam's old friend and nemesis, now eighty-one and at his shrewdest, sat at the head of the Rules Committee table, chewed on his long cigar, cleared his throat and his head at the same time, and told his fourteen committee members that they must keep this "dangerous" legislation from going to the House floor. But McCormack called the Democratic members in for talks, and on July 28, while Johnson sat helplessly in the White House waiting for word, eight loyal Democrats defeated Smith and Bill Colmer of Mississippi and the five Republican members of the Rules Committee.

So the bill came to life on the House floor, and a massive lobbying effort began to win passage of the measure. McCormack sent notices to Democrats to pay him a call in Rayburn's old quarters, and they were asked what pork-barrel projects were dearest to them. Johnson was also on the telephones from the White House, and Presidential legislative aides, led by Larry O'Brien, roamed through the House office buildings. Landrum, who was being attacked by some of his Southern colleagues and treated suspiciously by some Northerners, had this to say during the midst of the lobbying circus, "If I live through this without getting two ulcers, I'll be lucky."

Landrum believed he faced an insurmountable mountain because of the existence of a short, dark, rude special assistant to Defense Secretary Robert McNamara, named Adam Yarmolinsky. This young man had helped draw up the Antipoverty Bill and had been told by Sargent Shriver that he would become deputy director of the program. But right-wing members of the South and North Carolina delegations passed word along to Landrum and Johnson that they might support the legislation if Yarmolinsky were not involved in its administration. Their charge was that Yarmolinsky was a dangerous New York radical who came from even more radical parents.

Despite the nonsense of their charge, Landrum attempted to placate them by announcing on the House floor, "This gentleman will have absolutely nothing to do with the program." But white-haired Mendel Rivers of South Carolina, who would succeed retiring Uncle Carl Vinson as chairman of the powerful House Armed Services Committee, wanted assurances from a higher level. He and Harold Cooley of North Carolina, the chairman of the House Agriculture Committee, baited Shriver to call Johnson and get the Presidential word on Yarmolinsky, and after stalling the two for a time, Shriver finally put in the call. Johnson, who had previously told Yarmolinsky he could be Shriver's deputy, had been mulling over the situation for several days before the Shriver call, and he had reached a decision. "We're not going to have the whole thing wrecked just because of one little chickenshit," he had confided to an aide that morning. When Shriver hung up he told Rivers and Cooley, "The President has not objected to my saying that if I were appointed, I would not recommend Yarmolinsky."

On August 8, 1964, by a vote of 226 to 184, the House passed the Senate version of the Antipoverty Bill. A check of the vote showed that Yarmolinsky had been needlessly sacrificed. When Johnson was asked about the Yarmolinsky offering to Rivers and Cooley at a White House Rose Garden news conference on August 15, he replied unpleasantly: "Mr. Yarmolinsky is employed by the Defense Department. . . . The first information that I had that Mr. Yarmolinsky was, in effect, appointed to one of these places that did not exist was the columnist rumor. . . . We [don't] plan to make any assignment because some columnists think we ought to."

So Johnson had what he hailed as his very own first legislative program. However, it began a state of affairs that reporters in time would call the "Johnson credibility gap," because they knew Johnson's remarks on Yarmolinsky were false.

Johnson might have placed the Kennedy programs to raise the economic level of the eleven-state Appalachian Region within the antipoverty legislation. Here was an area covering 165,000 square miles and inhabited by fifteen million persons, of whom millions were reduced to the barest subsistence level. But a separate Appalachia bill meant two bills to his credit instead of one, and since this was an election year, the more numerous the items on the record, the safer would be the campaign. Unfortunately, after the hauling and pulling by those really interested in eliminating the wretched poverty pockets in the worst 355 counties in Appalachia, the Johnson request for a billion dollars to help these poor people asked that 840 million dollars, or more than four-fifths of the money, be spent on highway construction and not on direct, human welfare.

Despite their poverty, the mountain people of West Virginia and Kentucky, with their old-time religion, moonshine, feuds, and Daniel Boone customs, formed a romantic image for most Americans; and in April 1964 Johnson decided it would be politically advantageous to be televised, photographed, and recorded as their on-the-scene champion and savior. So he set out with Lady Bird and an army of reporters on a running glance at the depressed areas of Indiana, Pennsylvania, West Virginia, and Kentucky.

The depressed areas had to wait until he put in an apearance at a $100-a-plate banquet in Chicago on April 23, where the crowd of six thousand, including overweight Cook County Democratic precinct bosses and their heavy-jowled leader, Mayor Richard Daley of Chicago, cheered themselves hoarse. In this attack on poverty, Johnson told the gathering through the thick cigar haze, "Lady Bird is my Secretary of War." The crowds that Daley, his sewer commissioner, and other officials had collected on the streets to cheer Johnson on the rides to and from the airport pleased Johnson immensely. The old foreign-travels pressing-the-flesh syndrome suddenly returned, to the shock of his Secret Service agents, not yet recovered from their Dallas nightmare, as he leaped from his limousine to rush into the crowds to shake hands. At one point, his right hand was bleeding.

Then the next day he came closer to the depressed areas with a motorcade through Pittsburgh and a speech there. Along the spectators' route, he seized a bullhorn from a policeman and called out for several blocks a drawling imitation of the Kennedy remark: "Ask not what we can do for you, but what you can do for your country." Before setting out on this trip, he had been in touch with his business trustees to discuss their latest deals. But as a bullhorn preacher in the streets of Pittsburgh he espoused a simpler philosophy for his cheerers. "The one good thing about America," his voice rang out, "is that our ambitions are not too large. They boil down to food, shelter, and clothing."

In his speech he drew his loudest applause with his attack on former Vice President Nixon, who he believed might edge Goldwater out for the Republican nomination. Nixon had gone on a three-week tour of the Far East, ostensibly for his client, Pepsi-Cola. Always a big war promoter, Nixon had recently returned and advocated a step-up in the fighting in South Vietnam plus an invasion of North Vietnam. The public opinion polls had shown the mood of Americans was not for war, and Johnson gained yells of "Hooray" when he said, "One of my friends that drinks Pepsi-Cola—a former Vice President—went out to Vietnam and said we ought to have a little more war. Well, we won't."

The heart of his trip now came with a swing through the backwash of subsisting Americans. Johnson had sent notices to top Democrats in the depressed-area states to prepare a massive welcome for him by closing the schools, painting signs to be set along his route, and ordering union leaders to get their coal miners on the road with the school children.

At one stop he attempted to establish instant kinship with the poor people he met by calling his own father "a tenant farmer," a description Sam Johnson would have declared false. At a shack, he called on departure to the sickly, unemployed father of a malnourished family, "Take care of yourself now, yuh hear!"

Tom Fletcher, thirty-eight, with a wife and eight children crowded into a small, three-room shack near Inez, Kentucky, had been carefully selected for a staged conversation between "a President who cares" and one of life's unfortunates. Fletcher poured out his woeful tale of sickness and poverty to Johnson, who sat alongside him and his brood on the porch with the left side of his face in camera view. Finally, when the schedule called for the conversation to end, Johnson rose and told Fletcher, "Don't forget, now. I want you to keep those kids in school."

"Bye, chillen," Lady Bird yelled cheerily to them.

Then to reporters she spoke her rehearsed piece about the trip and her husband. "This is the sort of day that makes Lyndon feel like going back and working harder to live up to the faith that he has found people have in him today."

Chapter 68

I N A TRUE sense, Johnson's 1964 campaign for the Presidency began when he stood against the wall in Cubicle 13 at Parkland Hospital in Dallas and contemplated his new position. By the spring of 1964, no Kennedy Democrat could be heard in opposition to his nomination, and there was a significant force within the business community as well as the solid front of labor, liberal, and minority-group organizations behind his candidacy.

Big business support was a new experience for a Democratic President. A.T. & T. board chairman and head of the President's Business Council Frederick Kappel told the President, "I want to assure you in behalf of the Council that we have undiminished confidence in the economic and moral strength of our country under your leadership." Ben Heineman, chairman of the board of the Chicago and North Western Railway, was willing to take on special assignments for Johnson, and dozens of other business leaders, like Henry Ford II and Crawford Greenewalt of Du Pont, were similarly inclined. When he spoke to the U. S. Chamber of Commerce's convention in early spring of 1964, Johnson enjoyed the pleasure of being interrupted by applause exactly sixty times. He promised business a thirty-billion-dollar profit that year and added, "But I must apologize to you this morning. We haven't done anything for business this week. . . . But please remember, this is only just Monday morning."

Much of the business goodwill that came to Johnson was the result of the settlement of a dispute between railroad management and labor that had appeared to be heading toward a major national strike.

In 1959, when the time came for new contracts with the five Railroad Brotherhoods, railroad management insisted that new work rules be installed and featherbedding eliminated. Work restrictions written into previous contracts included the paying of a day's wage and a change in crew every one hundred miles, an iron curtain separation of yard and road work, and the employment of unneeded locomotive firemen and maintenance workers. The railroads claimed that these featherbedding practices cost them 500 million dollars a year. But the Brotherhoods had serious gripes against callous treatment of workers—no vacation pay, no away-from-home arrangements for food and lodging, no job security. Little public sympathy was directed toward either side, though animosity was probably stronger toward a "Let the public be damned" arrogant management, which discouraged passenger traffic by providing dirty, slow trains and continually dwindling schedules.

Each year that railroad management declared it would impose new work rules, the Brotherhoods threatened to strike. Both Eisenhower and Kennedy established study boards to examine the featherbedding problems, and each time the boards upheld the position of the railroads. Furthermore, on three occasions federal courts upheld the boards, and in March 1963 the Supreme Court authorized railroads to install new rules, while declaring that the Brotherhoods had an equal right to strike. Finally, on the eve of a nationwide strike call in late August, Kennedy wrested the first compulsory arbitration law in American history from Congress. A new arbitration panel would study and decide what should be done, while the unions would be barred from calling a strike for six months.

Johnson had never been involved in a labor-management dispute except at KTBC, and he now had his first test when a wildcat strike took place on Illinois Central commuter trains out of Chicago early in April 1964. The Illinois Central had retaliated by ordering nonfeatherbedding work rules put into operation on April 10, and this in turn had led to the call for a national strike by the Brotherhoods should this be done on that day.

As that deadline neared, Secretary of Labor Willard Wirtz dug up a report Walter Heller had written for Kennedy in 1963 regarding the effect of a strike, and he showed it to Johnson. Such a strike by 200,000 union members, said Heller, would immediately force a half-million other railroad employees off the job, and by the end of a month six million nonrailroad workers would be unemployed, and New York and possibly other large cities would be suffering from serious food shortages.

Johnson's order to Wirtz was to settle the dispute before the April 10 deadline, but even though Wirtz talked until 3 A.M. on April 9 to the representatives from both sides, he found their positions rigid. His advice to Johnson when he reported his lack of success was to let the strike occur. However, Johnson believed he could be more convincing, and he asked the five management representatives and the five Brotherhood heads to a 6 P.M. meeting in the Cabinet Room.

When they came, he asked for a twenty-day delay while a settlement was worked out. "I am your President," he told them. "All I want is for you to give me a chance. I want you to tell me you'll do this for me." Both sides withdrew for consultation, and when they returned, the management group agreed, but the union leaders would not. One railroad president called Johnson's efforts to win a change from the Brotherhood men a sickening sight. "He was practically on his knees with them," he said. "I thought the President really demeaned himself with his begging and pleading."

Even this failed, and as a last resort Johnson led the union leaders into his office. "Charlie," he begged Charles Luna, the heavy-faced chief of the Railway Trainmen, "you're from Texas like me. It ain't one of those damn Yankees asking you to do it." Charlie finally agreed to a fifteen-day delay, and the others mumbled their willingness. Johnson then told the ten-man labor-management crew that he was providing space for them in the Executive Office Building across the street. In addition, on the advice of Willard Wirtz, he was naming two professional labor mediators, Professor George Taylor of the University of Pennsylvania and Ted Kheel, a New York attorney, to work with them for a solution. Again there was objection from the union men, this time on bringing in the mediators; and Johnson took Charlie Luna into a corner to plead again with him as a loyal fellow Texan. Finally, at 10:30 P.M., Johnson walked into the Fish Room to inform the nation that he had prevented a strike and won a fifteen-day delay.

During the days of negotiations, he frequently walked into the meeting room to ask how things were proceeding. One day he brought octogenarians Carl Sandburg and his photographer brother-in-law Edward Steichen to meet the disputants, and he told the two in his loudest stage whisper, "I wanted you to see some of the toughest people operating today. These men can throw seven hundred thousand people out of work." On another occasion he asked the group to drop into his office for a howdy, and when they came, he went into a patriotic spiel. "Johnson has a flag in the corner of his office," said one of the union negotiators. "He picked it up and ran around the room waving it."

The Brotherhoods were expecting railroad management to insist on the elimination of all featherbedding practices. But the management negotiators came prepared to accept only one antifeatherbedding work change —the elimination of firemen on freight diesel locomotives. However, they argued as though they would accept nothing less than a total overhaul of the antiquated work rules. So it was a relief to the Brotherhoods when the mediators, after an all-night session on April 21, drew up a settlement that not only ignored all other featherbedding practices but proposed that 90 per cent of freight firemen be eliminated by attrition—upon their retirement or death. In addition the settlement proposed a seven-day vacation with pay each year, and lodging and a $1.50 meal when workers were away from home.

When the union leaders accepted the proposals, it was now the turn of the management negotiators to show stubbornness. Pretending that the agreement was unsatisfactory, Joseph "Doc" Wolfe, a Chicago railroad man and chief management negotiator, told Johnson that the railroads would not take the settlement unless two unrelated concessions were made part of the arrangements. The first was legislation permitting railroads to adjust many freight rates without going through the endless Interstate Commerce Committee hearings. The second was a reversal of an Internal Revenue decision barring them from any depreciation allowance on their four-billion-dollar investment in mountain tunnels and grading. For the sake of a settlement, said Johnson, he would agree to both conditions.

Late on the afternoon of April 22 Johnson met with Wolfe and nine railroad presidents in his upstairs family room at the White House for a final discussion of the settlement. "I'm proud of you fellows," he told them when they accepted the mediated proposals. "Now you can go home and brag to your wives a little."

He asked them to come to his office in a half hour to join him in a statement to the press. At that time he met them, the union negotiators, and the mediators in the appointments secretary's office and led them into his Oval Office, where they were surprised to find Walter Lippmann sitting. "These men have just saved collective bargaining," Johnson told Lippmann. "They did a wonderful job for their country."

It was 6:20 P.M. and Johnson had an idea how they could get maximum publicity for the settlement and he could gain maximum praise for saving the country from a strike. Dashing outdoors, he jumped into a Presidential limousine with Doc Wolfe and Roy Davidson of the Brotherhood of Locomotive Engineers and sped in a fifty-mile-an-hour race to the CBS-TV studio miles away. And at 6:45, prime news time on TV, he broke the news of the railroad peace by reading a letter from "Little Cathy," a seven-year-old girl who lived in Park Forest, Illinois. Little Cathy, he said, had written him that she hoped he would prevent a strike so that her grandmother could come from New York to attend Cathy's first communion. "Cathy's grandmother can now go to see her," he assured all America.

Cathy's grandmother had already made the trip and was back home in New York at the time he read the letter. But the effect was homey and warm, and this was what Johnson wanted. As for the two conditions on which Wolfe had won Johnson's promise in order to agree to the settlement, the promise was never kept.

Not long afterward, when some history professors visited Johnson, he related how he had settled the railroad strike: "If both sides knew what I would do," he told them, spinning an imaginary tale, "they would have outmaneuvered me. So for three days I kept them guessing, and they caved in." The professors remarked later on his brilliance.

In a tally of Johnson pluses and minuses that could influence the 1964 election, the assets as heralded by the press were formidable indeed. He was the magician of labor-management harmony, wizard of Congress, master of government administration, tireless worker for public good, and the leader for international peace. Hubert Humphrey summed up what he called the positive qualities of Johnson by telling reporters he expected all Johnson "must" bills to pass Congress, because "he has a Mystery Kit of Legislative Remedies."

But there were minuses that cropped up and gave indication that they •

could explode into serious trouble for Johnson. The largest incendiary bomb was the Baker Case.

No matter what the efforts of Abe Fortas, the Senate Rules Committee could not hide forever the Don Reynolds testimony, especially since three Republicans served on the committee of eight, and Senator John Williams of Delaware, who had forced the investigation, continually demanded a report. Reynolds' censored testimony was leaked to reporters on January 17, 1964, and when Johnson learned that front-page stories were being written, he tried to head off those destined for what he called the influential newspapers. In one instance, said a writer, "the reporter's editor received a telephone call from a well-known aide to President Johnson. . . . He suggested, according to the editor, that the paper might want to kill the article outright."

On January 20 the committee issued its own heavily trimmed testimony, which revealed a feeble investigation—"Thanks to the behind-the-scenes string-pulling by Johnson and Abe Fortas," said one senator. Jenkins had not been called to refute in person the Reynolds charge of a forced kickback to buy KTBC-TV time; nor had Matt McCloskey been asked to take the witness chair and speak on Reynolds' accusation that he had made a bagman for Democratic political contributions and payoffs out of the insurance agent for the D. C. Stadium that McCloskey was constructing. Nor had Johnson been asked about the stereo hi-fi gift from Reynolds; and equally interesting, in the months that the committee held hearings, it had never called Bobby Baker.

If Johnson were now Vice President, he would have been in trouble. But with Johnson now serving as President, there was widespread press reticence to make direct accusations against him. *Time* magazine set the pace when it wrote: "On the basis of the record so far, neither Johnson nor Baker was guilty of using his public office for private gain." *Newsweek* excused Johnson, though one of its columnists called it a flaw in "our government and social order . . . that permits members of Congress and their employees to serve their own private interests while pretending to serve the public interests only."

Some of Johnson's advisers suggested that he ignore the released committee testimony, but when Fortas proposed that he take aggressive action, he did. At a hastily announced news conference a few days after the release, he told reporters, "The Baker family gave us a stereo set. . . . He was an employee of the public and had no business pending before me and was asking for nothing, and so far as I knew, expected nothing in return, any more than I did when I had presented him with gifts." No reporter brought up the fact that the invoice attached to the delivered set read: "Charge to Don Reynolds, 8484 Fenton Street, Silver Spring; shipped to Lyndon Johnson, 4931 30th Street NW, Washington, D.C., one stereo."

Nor did reporters ask about the alleged forced buying of time on KTBC-TV, after Johnson brought up the insurance policies he had bought from

Reynolds. Johnson said that "the company in which Mrs. Johnson and my daughters have a majority interest, along with some other stockholders, were somewhat concerned when I had a heart attack in 1955, and in 1957 they purchased insurance on my life made payable to the company." His further statement was that the company was paying the premiums. Again, no reporter asked why he dealt with Don Reynolds in Maryland, when there were a great many insurance agents in Texas, including his first cousin, Huff Baines.

At later news conferences Clark Mollenhoff, Pulitzer Prize-winning reporter from the Des Moines *Register and Tribune,* attempted to probe deeper, but Johnson would not permit this. One Mollenhoff question went: "How do you feel about the general ethical question that's been raised, relative to high government officials . . . who have an interest in government-regulated industries, such as television?"

Johnson's lips pressed together like a vise before he replied that he owned no stock in the Texas Broadcasting Company, and that his wife's stock was under the tight control of trustees. "I see no conflict in any way," he spat at Mollenhoff.

In this election year Johnson used a maneuver of distraction to take the minds of Americans off the Baker business. The very day that the Reynolds testimony broke, January 20, Johnson ordered twenty-five Budget Bureau officials to the White House, and he gave them a preview of what would soon become known as the "Lightbulb Lyndon" affair. "Somebody told me that the light bill in the White House ran several thousand dollars a month," he barked at them. "I challenged Mr. John Valenti over there and my maid this morning when I left to turn out all those lights in those chandeliers when there is no one in the house. Mrs. Johnson had gone to New York and I was the only one there, and I didn't require that much light. I don't know how much we saved today.

"And see that that kind of economy goes down to every government building. A stitch in time saves nine. You don't accumulate anything unless you save in small amounts." He offered a philosophy alien to his own.

His purpose was served, for according to the heated letters to the editor that poured into newspapers, more public indignation arose over the sudden lights-out at the White House than over the Baker affair. The White House belonged to the nation, went the arguments, and Johnson had no right to dim its beauty. For a time he was Lightbulb Johnson, encouraging an aroused public on this issue, and to show he was really sincere on the personal economy issue he added the feature of ordering the Pentagon to reduce the number of limousines supplied its top officials to ten cars. A reporter bothered to check and found that before the Presidential order the number of limousines supplied at the Pentagon totaled exactly ten.

"Get a dollar's value for every dollar spent," he also admonished Defense Secretary McNamara, "and see that military contractors reduce their costs." At that time over in South Vietnam, Johnson's friends Brown and Root, in their construction combine, were, according to the GAO, in process of squandering hundreds of millions of dollars of a 1.2-billion-dollar contract.

Having successfully passed the hurdle of the released Reynolds testimony, Johnson determined to get revenge against both Reynolds and Senator Williams. Jack Anderson, the partner of Drew Pearson, had become a director of the Riddle Airlines, which Senator Williams exposed as being involved in a Bobby Baker caper. In addition, Drew Pearson's stepson, Tyler Abell, was Johnson's Assistant Postmaster General, and Tyler's wife, Bess, the daughter of Johnson's Senate pal Earle Clements, was Mrs. Johnson's social secretary.

Several Pearson columns that now appeared were devoted to a character assassination of Reynolds. Secret intelligence reports on Reynolds in the State Department and the Air Force, said Pearson, had data on Reynolds' "German mistress . . . black market operations . . . that one of the senators with whom Reynolds worked was Joe McCarthy . . . that a security review board in the U.S. Air Force . . . concluded in 1953 that Reynolds' past led to a reasonable belief that he was a security risk." Reynolds was not to be believed now, Pearson claimed, because he was a man "who had brought reckless charges in the past."

In examining the Pearson columns, *The New York Times* concluded that this smear of Reynolds came from 1600 Pennsylvania Avenue. "Persons within and close to the Johnson Administration have attempted to use secret government documents to impugn the testimony of a witness in the Robert G. Baker case," said the *Times*.

The bad odor of the Baker affair was soon removed entirely from Johnson's area, with Pearson and Anderson engaging in a name-calling contest with the *Times* on the subject of leaks from classified files. "It's only natural that the *Times* seethes with professional jealousy when it sees another newsman apparently getting an inside track," Anderson jeered in a column. Here was the earnest President, he said, who "went out of his way to have dinner with the moguls of the *Times* . . . but it didn't do any good. . . . Twenty-four hours later they kicked him in the teeth with a front-page story accusing him of leaking the Don Reynolds documents."

Johnson's effort to punish Reynolds did not stop with character assassination. Friends warned Reynolds that it would be safer if he hid, and he did so, later leaving the country. His friends and business associates were soon subjected to investigations by the Internal Revenue Service under direction of its chief, a young law associate of Abe Fortas named Sheldon Cohen. So widespread was this activity that a Washington physician who had purchased insurance through Reynolds had his financial records examined microscopically with the implication that he could expect trouble because he had dealt with Reynolds.

It was Senator Williams whom Johnson wanted ruined most of all. The method selected was to paint this highly moral man as a crook, for if he had not stubbornly demanded Senate action after Bobby Baker was exposed, the Rules Committee would have ignored the subject instead of going through an investigation. When its carefully staged, tepid investigation concluded with the insinuation that Reynolds and Williams were the guilty parties and not certain Democrats, Williams taunted Johnson with the comment, "Whitewash put over dirt won't stick. We country boys know that."

To charges by some Democrats that he was just a hater of Democratic Presidents, as shown by his earlier relentless attacks on the Truman Administration, Williams replied, "From my investigations, President Truman was a completely honest man. It was the people around him who were not."

Johnson had several allies in attacking Williams' character. Drew Pearson asked in a column why Williams was so affronted by Johnson and Baker when he kept quiet about the numerous, expensive gifts Eisenhower had accepted while serving as President. The Washington *Post* was another Johnson ally. Philip Graham, the publisher of this influential, liberal newspaper, noted for its integrity, had committed suicide in August 1963 after a period of psychiatric treatment for manic depression. Following his death, the newspaper lost its news objectivity. When the Baker case broke, the *Post* ran the unchecked, false story that Senator Williams employed hidden microphones in his own office to record what others said about Baker.

Only days after the Reynolds testimony was released, Williams noticed that his office mail service had developed strange behavior. In February 1964 a former Democratic member of Congress from Delaware, who had taken a job in the Johnson Administration, called Williams and arranged to meet him privately. "I couldn't risk going to your office," he blurted when they met, "but I can't stomach what they are doing to you. Your mail is being intercepted. Every letter you write to any federal official asking about the Baker case is immediately routed to a special handler. He sends the Senate Rules Committee copies of any information sent you. Sometimes he even checks with the committee before deciding whether your inquiry is to be answered at all. You'd better be careful about what you put in writing."

With this information, Williams felt concern for several Texans with whom he had been corresponding about Johnson's business activities. The typical reply he received was a typed letter telling him to go to hell. However, an accompanying unsigned letter on cheap paper told him the answers to the questions he had asked. His concern now was that the White House probably had copies of this correspondence.

When Williams announced he had new evidence that warranted the re-opening of the Senate Rules Committee investigation in mid-1964, committee Democrats called him a crackpot. Bobby Baker had appeared before the committee in February with a new lawyer, and in two and a half hours Baker took the Fifth Amendment 125 times. On that note the committee believed its work was finished. But Williams' daily persistence was so jarring that the committee agreed to renew the investigation. However, a White House strategy meeting decided that the probe could not be reinstated until after the 1964 election, and in the meantime a massive effort would be undertaken to defeat Williams, who was up for re-election to his fourth Senate term that November.

The variety of moves to destroy Williams was broad. Bobby Baker's secretary, Carole Tyler, a young girl who was involved in his businesses, took on the unusual chore of delivering a speech to the Tennessee Press Association. Here she made the charge that Williams was implicated in a sex scandal, that she had seen this so-called family man with a pretty girl at 6:30 A.M. on a specified morning. Williams did not sue, nor did he answer the young Miss Tyler, who lived in an expensive house that Baker owned. Reporters who checked learned that the girl with Williams was his granddaughter.

Another move came from the Internal Revenue, which went to work to find a way to imprison him. His income tax returns for several years underwent close scrutiny, and a two-year-old return was selected as the test case. This was a year Williams had paid $34,000 in taxes. Notified by Internal Revenue that he was under investigation, he had to drop his Senate work and drive back to Delaware to be questioned by Internal Revenue agents. His accountants had to be called to answer questions about his records, and days of examination of the figures followed. Finally the agents said they had found their case of dishonesty. "I had taken off $150 as a business expense to have some timber acres appraised for sale," said Williams. "The agents insisted that I should have paid a $90 tax on the $150 that year and then deducted it from capital assets the following year. Their entire argument was nonsense, but I wrote out a check for them for that amount. Not long afterward Internal Revenue wrote me they had found an error in my favor in that return for $30.16 above the amount I had paid, and they sent me a check for that sum."

When Williams had run for election in the past, it was unusual for outside Democrats to appear in Delaware to speak against him. In 1964 wave after wave of Democrats deluged the state to denounce him. Reporters who traveled with Johnson in the campaign were popeyed when he wasted the important Saturday before the November 3 election to speak at Dover, Delaware, which had a population of only seven thousand persons. "Give me men I can work with!" he cried. Johnson got almost twice the vote in Delaware that Goldwater collected, yet Williams was returned to the Senate.

Besides the Bobby Baker business, there were other Johnson minuses in 1964. One of these was the reporting of his behavior back on the ranch. Editorials of prudish dismay appeared in the national press, following a story published on page 23 in the April 10, 1964, issue of *Time,* on Johnson at Easter on the L.B.J. Ranch.

A cream-colored Lincoln Continental driven by the President of the U. S. flashed up a long Texas road, swung into the left lane to pass two cars poking along under 85 m.p.h., and thundered on over the crest of the hill—squarely into the path of an oncoming car. The President charged on, his paper cup of Pearl beer within easy sipping distance. The other motorist veered off the paved surface to safety on the road's shoulder. Groaned a passenger in the President's car when the ride was over: "That's the closest John McCormack has come to the White House yet."

One afternoon, the President gazed dreamily around . . . sighed contentedly to reporters assembled: "The cows are fat. The grass is green. The river's full and the fish are flopping." To prove it, he hopped into his Continental to play tour guide, invited in four reporters, including Hearst's pretty blonde Marianne Means and two other newswomen. . . . At one point, Johnson pulled up near a small gathering of cattle, pushed a button under the dashboard—and a cow horn bawled from beneath the glistening hood. Heifers galloped toward the car while photographers clicked away and the President looked pleased. As he drove, Johnson talked about his cattle, once plunged into what one startled newswoman called a "very graphic description of the sex life of a bull."

During the tour, Reporter Means, her baby-blue eyes fastened on Johnson, cooed: "Mr. President, you're fun."

Through all the fun, the President sipped beer from his paper cup. Eventually, he ran dry, refilled once from Marianne's supply, emptied his cup again, and took off at speeds up to 90 m.p.h. to get more. In the President's car, someone gasped at how fast Johnson was driving. Quickly, Lyndon took one hand from the wheel, removed his five-gallon hat and flopped it on the dashboard to cover the speedometer.

Reporters added to the *Time* story with a description of their harrowing ride to church at Fredericksburg on Easter Sunday as they tried to follow Johnson, who was driving at a speed of ninety miles an hour. With an immediate public reaction of distaste for these tales of Presidential speed and beer-drinking, Johnson added to his growing credibility gap by denying he ever exceeded seventy on the highway. He also caused raised eyebrows when he sent a letter to highway officials across the country demanding they declare war on speeders—"We cannot tolerate this terrible . . . loss of life," he wrote.

But Johnson, who screamed with anger at *Time* for printing the story of the speeding President, soon fell back on his usual technique of laughter and ridicule to neutralize the incident. Former Venezuelan President Romulo Betancourt was planning an auto trip across the United States, and Johnson told him for publication, "Now, you be careful, because we've got a lot of crazy drivers in this country." And to Dorothy McCardle of the Washington *Post,* who had been one of the three women reporters accompanying him and columnist Marquis Childs on the wild ride, he called at a White House gathering, "How about coming for another ride with us?"

Still another Johnson minus came late in April, when he led a thirteen-man task force promoting foreign investments in the United States on a stroll to the White House flower garden. Here romped the Johnson beagles, Him and Her, and he pushed sugar-coated vitamin pills into their mouths.

Then while the group watched, embarrassed, he picked Him up by his ears. Him howled, and when none of the men spoke up, a woman reporter asked, "Why did you do that?"

"To make him bark," said Johnson. "It's good for him."

Then he yanked on Her's ears, and she also yelped.

Public indignation at such cruelty to animals sounded like a million hounds barking simultaneously. Johnson said nothing as dog-lovers condemned him. A typical reaction was that of a West Virginia Humane Society officer who growled, "If Johnson were here, I'd run him in."

At the height of the public outcry, Jacob Potofsky, the bearded president of the Amalgamated Clothing Workers of America, telephoned Johnson with the request that he drop his scheduled appearance at the union's convention. Johnson gave his interpretation of his conversation with Potofsky to reporters in an effort to ridicule the union leader. "I asked him why he didn't want me to come," said Johnson, "and Potofsky told me, 'Well, Mr. President, those people are pretty mad because you pulled the ears of a bagel.' "

So there were sufficient Johnson minuses to gladden the hearts of Republicans. But there was no joy, and a reading of the springtime polls revealed the reason. A Lou Harris poll in April 1964 clearly indicated the indifference of Americans to the moral implications of the Bobby Baker investigation. Throughout the nation, reported Harris, 73 per cent of Americans admitted that their opinion of Johnson had not been affected by the Baker revelations; only 14 per cent said they thought less of him; and 3 per cent declared that the investigation had increased their regard for the President!

Chapter 69

"I CAN'T REMEMBER a time when a President had prosperity and poverty going for him at the same time," said discouraged Leonard Hall, former Republican National Chairman, in May 1964.

The early polls gave Johnson 60 per cent or more of the votes in a race against any of the leading Republican candidates—Goldwater, Nixon, Rockefeller, Romney, and Lodge. There were still many months ahead for the Republicans to close the gap through hard and intelligent campaigning. Yet these early polls tended to discourage optimism in the G.O.P., and a sinking spirit hit Republicans every time Johnson was described pulling copies of popularity polls from his stuffed pockets and showing them to reporters. As Bill Moyers said afterward, "We were delighted to use the popularity polls to create a bandwagon psychology in 1964."

In planning the 1964 convention and campaign, Johnson wanted to make certain he would be in complete charge of all phases and that all his aides were totally devoted to him. He had learned with some surprise that on November 12, 1963, Kennedy had held a three-hour strategy meeting with his staff and John Bailey, his Democratic National Chairman, to map out the 1964 campaign. Kennedy had not notified him of the meeting, nor had he discussed its details with him afterward. This had caused Johnson to brood when he heard about the meeting, and he hastened the departure of most of Kennedy's "Irish Mafia." But he retained highly useful Larry O'Brien, who had proved himself as loyal a Johnson servant as a Kennedy employee, and John Bailey, who knew the political network stretching from the National Committee into each state. However, he did not trust Bailey, and he assigned Cliff Carter and Walter Jenkins to manage Bailey and the National Committee for him.

In their continuing role as chief Johnson advisers, Abe Fortas, Clark Clifford, and Jim Rowe moved into the political campaign area as well, although they were rank amateurs at this activity. However, this made no difference, for Johnson would have no fight to get the Democratic nomination, and his campaign would be against the weakest candidate the Republicans could have nominated—the warmongering, right-wing Barry Goldwater, who conveyed the impression that nuclear wars were not to be dreaded, and who voted against the Civil Rights Bill, costing the Republicans their reputation since Lincoln's Emancipation Proclamation as champions of Negro rights. Goldwater had also cost the Republicans the votes of the aged citizens by favoring a voluntary social security system, and he caused tremors among those interested in the government's fiscal and monetary stability by advocating the abolition of the graduated income tax. As one unhappy liberal Republican senator put it, "Every time Barry opened his mouth, he was campaigning for Lyndon."

One of Fortas' suggestions was that Johnson take on the role of "Mr. Average Everyday American" until after the Democratic National Convention. It was on the morning of April 11 that he first tried out this act of a man without pretenses, when he walked to the Southeast Gate of the White House with Moyers. About a hundred persons, mostly students, were on the other side at the time he appeared, and he called out, "Would you like to take a walk with me before lunch?"

A gasp arose and then a chorus of yesses, and over the objections of the Secret Service, he ordered the gate opened and the crowd admitted onto the White House grounds. "All right," he yelled at his guests, "all you ugly men go up there and all you pretty girls stay here with me." He asked one startled student from India, "Is Mr. Nehru getting better?" (Johnson already knew that Nehru was not expected to recover.) To a girl from the Philippines he said, "We've got our Secretary of State out in the Philippines right now." (Rusk had been sent there on a fruitless mission to badger the six other SEATO members to join the United States in escalating the war in Vietnam.)

After this initiation Johnson made frequent excursions to the gates to shake hands through the bars with tourists, banter with them, and on occasion invite them inside to join him and reporters in a walk around the White House grounds. As his aides had predicted, this exposure won him great newspaper publicity as a warm and unusually friendly man. Only Harry Truman joined the Secret Service in objecting to his "taking too many chances mixing with crowds." One time Johnson and Lady Bird took a stroll around Lafayette Park across Pennsylvania Avenue, and on several occasions she joined him in the hand-shaking at the gate of the White House and the laps around the walking track with hundreds of tourists. Him and Her were also included in the walks, with Lady Bird holding the leashes, and Johnson occasionally stopping to pick them up by their paws and make joking references to their strong ears.

Newspapers reported many strange questions and answers made on these walks. One man, weighted down with camera equipment, asked Johnson, "Do you cut this grass yourself?" "No, sir, I don't. But I'd probably feel better if I did," Johnson told him with a straight face.

When the opportunity arose, Johnson made use of his encyclopedic knowledge of the byways of Texas. One family of tourists proudly announced to him that they hailed from Falfurrias, Texas, a small town not far from the George Parr duchy of Duval County. Johnson had been there often as a guest on George Brown's nearby ranch. "Do you know Percy Hunter?" he shot back at them without pause. Then he added, "The best creamery butter in the world comes from Falfurrias," and Lady Bird nodded agreement.

During his temporary portrayal of John Doe, American, the simple small-town man who was your good neighbor, Johnson also engaged in other middle-class American pastimes. He played some rounds of golf at Burning Tree, with photographers on hand to snap pictures of him in golf slacks. But as for his playing ability, said George Smathers, the best golfer in Congress, "He hits the ball as though he were clubbing a snake." Johnson also held White House dances, and newspapers reported that he danced long past midnight and with every lady present. Helen Thomas, a UPI reporter who was invited to one party, wrote, "I danced with the President." The more indiscreet of his floor partners said that he could dance only the simple two-step, and he was at his best when the band played "Alexander's Ragtime Band."

Johnson was working so hard to add this new image to his numerous other images that James Reston wrote with awe at the close of April in *The New York Times*:

In the last seven days, President Johnson has held two formal and two informal press conferences, made seven impromptu statements after White House meetings, delivered a major foreign policy address to the Associated Press, helped settle the national railroad dispute, opened the New York World's Fair and talked at a political rally in Chicago. The White House is now more open than any residence in Washington. "Welcome to *your* house," he tells his visitors, and that's the way it is. No majestic aloofness for him. He regards himself as the temporary occupant of a public building and simply does what comes naturally.

During this period his friends thought his public performance was superb. However, they had some qualms about his private activities, and fear that they might be publicized. One such activity was his heavy drinking, but the newspapers made no mention of this, and it came out only after the election was over, in the book *The Making of the President 1964* by Theodore White and in *Life*. Another activity that might have proved damaging then was his frequent showing at White House social occasions of his home-made movie of deer mating, along with his own vivid soundtrack description. But it was not until December 1965 that this was given publicity by *Life*, with the notation that whenever he had shown the pictures, "the effect had been electrifying."

At the beginning of 1964 Johnson decided that Hubert Humphrey would be his running mate in the coming election. However, he wanted to create an aura of suspense for what would otherwise be a cut-and-dried convention, so he did not divulge his selection to Humphrey.

But there were penalties attached to this secrecy, and the heaviest was that Bobby Kennedy wanted the Vice Presidency. The thought that Kennedy might maneuver himself into a position that could force his hand sickened Johnson. After the assassination he had hoped that Kennedy would quit as Attorney General, and as the weeks passed without his resignation, Johnson grew increasingly troubled by his presence in the Cabinet. Early in 1964, after avoiding private meetings with him (except for one in which Johnson contradicted Mrs. Kennedy's observation and insisted he had taken off for Washington as soon as the Kennedy casket was aboard *Air Force One*), Johnson telephoned Kennedy at the Justice Department. The purpose of his call was to suggest that Kennedy go on a fact-finding mission to Southeast Asia and hold talks with political leaders in Japan, the Philippines, Malaysia, and Indonesia.

This was comparable to the trips Johnson had taken abroad for President Kennedy, and the results were as inconsequential. Upon his return Bobby Kennedy went to the White House on invitation to report to Johnson. But Johnson was not alone—he had several congressmen with him—and he embarrassed Kennedy by ordering him to speak his piece to the legislators. Later, when Kennedy tried to arrange a new and private appointment with Johnson, he failed to make connection. Nor did Secretary of State Rusk, who only a few months before had deferred to him as his brother's chief adviser, invite him to relate his talks with Indonesia's Sukarno and other Asian leaders.

In the spring Kennedy waited for Johnson to give him a sign he would be his Vice President. When word did not come, Kennedy made an attempt to force the issue by staging a six-hour interview with Ben Bradlee of *Newsweek,* a personal friend and a reporter highly regarded by his brother. In this marathon talk Kennedy said he wanted to be Vice President but would accept the Cabinet posts of Secretary of Defense or Secretary of State as second choices. He offered as his reason for meriting the Vice Presidency his opinion that he was his brother's link for "striving for excellency" in the Johnson Administration and the fact that "most of the major leaders in the North want me—all of them really."

With the release of this interview Johnson met in a council of war with Fortas, Clifford, and Rowe on the "Bobby Kennedy problem." The Fortas solution was so direct that Johnson dismissed it at first, only to accept it as the easiest answer. It called for a face-to-face confrontation with Kennedy to show him that the President was not intimidated; and it called for the leaking to the press of the Johnson version of that meeting so that Kennedy would appear in a poor light. There would also be a final phase: Without mentioning Kennedy by name, Johnson would publicly declare an entire category of government officials, of whom Kennedy was one, as ineligible to be his running mate.

On Monday, July 27, Johnson telephoned Kennedy and invited him to his office on Wednesday for a private meeting. "I could tell Bobby's voice was kind of funny," Johnson later told a trio of reporters over a four-hour lobster, watermelon, and liquid refreshments lunch in his upstairs dining room. These were the newsmen who were expected to leak what he gossiped on the Kennedy confrontation. "I knew about his voice," Johnson went on, "because I was once in that same position.

"And when he came on Wednesday, I told him I didn't have any objection to his desire to run the U. S. some day, but I'd given the matter a great deal of thought, and I decided I wasn't going to ask him to run on the ticket with me this time. I was looking at Bobby closely, and he said nothing—only gulped. [Johnson gulped to show the newsmen Kennedy's reaction.] But Bobby took it okay, and he said he would not only support me but would give me any help I asked for. So I jumped right in then and asked him to be my campaign manager—like he'd been for his brother. So he tried to back out by saying he'd have to resign as Attorney General to do this. But I just cut in and urged him to quit. He said then that he would if I agreed to name Katzenbach to succeed him."

As expected, the Johnson story was soon all over Washington, and when Kennedy learned of it, he went to the White House to protest directly to Johnson the publicizing of a private meeting. Johnson acted stricken and swore he had not told a soul. Kennedy then blurted that Johnson was lying, and to this Johnson replied, "Well, I'll have to check my ol' calendar and see if I had a talk with someone I can't remember just now."

Afterward Kennedy gave his version of their meeting. Johnson had not been able to look him in the eye, but "had stared at the wall and then at the floor before he finally said he had been thinking about the Vice Presidency and who'd be the biggest help to the country, the Democratic Party, and to himself personally. He said that person was not his Attorney General."

Kennedy said his own conversation had been strained because he noticed that Johnson's tape recorder was running. He said he had replied immediately that the President's decision suited him fine, and he had offered to help in the campaign. Johnson had then offered to name him ambassador to Britain, France, or Italy or to another Cabinet post, if any opening should appear in the future. When Kennedy had said he liked being Attorney General, Johnson then had praised the staff at the Justice Department and complained about the low caliber of his own White House staff.

After this, Johnson shifted the talk to the coming campaign, said Kennedy, and the Attorney General mentioned Bobby Baker. Johnson's reaction was to call his former protégé a string of names and to declare incorrectly that Baker had become embroiled in his troubles only after Johnson left the Senate in 1961. Johnson also expressed the opinion that "the Republicans won't dare open the Baker case up," and he listed several Republicans whose activities would embarrass them if Johnson cared to expose them. As Kennedy left, after forty-five minutes, he said he told Johnson, "I could have helped you, Mr. President."

Kennedy's friends later claimed that Johnson had offered to accept any Vice President selected by Kennedy. But this was not true, nor was the claim that Kennedy had suggested the means the President used to eliminate him as a candidate. It was the Johnson inner circle who prepared, in advance of the Kennedy meeting, the statement that Johnson read over TV on Thursday, July 30. "I have reached the conclusion that it would be inadvisable for me to recommend to the convention," said Johnson, "any member of my Cabinet or any of those who meet regularly with the Cabinet."

"I'm sorry I took so many nice fellows over the side with me," said Kennedy when he heard the news. Adlai Stevenson, who had also hoped for the Vice Presidency, took action when he saw that he was included in Johnson's sweeping statement. He immediately phoned Senator Humphrey and said, "It's you, Hubert."

With Johnson suspensefully maintaining public silence about possible favorites, reporters added daily to the names they believed were in contention. Those most frequently mentioned were Senate Majority Leader Mike Mansfield, Senators Eugene McCarthy of Minnesota, Tom Dodd of Connecticut, and Ed Muskie of Maine, New York Mayor Robert Wagner, Governor Edmund Brown of California—and Hubert Humphrey. As the list continued to grow, Johnson added to the mystery by praising the various Democrats, and in some cases teasing them personally that they were under consideration. But some were not taken in by his talk.

"I knew it would be Hubert," said Mike Mansfield, "and I would have preferred staying in the Senate even if I was being considered. So I went to Lyndon and told him that under no circumstances would I be interested."

Muskie expressed a similar opinion. "The President was going to take Humphrey from the beginning. I never gave any thought to the talk about me."

Humphrey knew on the night after the Cabinet and Stevenson had been eliminated that his own chances were excellent, for Jim Rowe came to his Senate office with some advice from Johnson. If Humphrey would agree to be a totally subservient and loyal Vice President, he was to call Johnson and tell him so. Humphrey placed the call without delay.

Then a week later Johnson had Rowe grill Humphrey regarding his background. Was he for hire by any Minnesota backer? Why hadn't he served in World War II? Did he have a past love life that could be uncovered by Republicans? Humphrey's answers were satisfactory.

While Johnson was stirring up interest in the Vice Presidency, the Republican National Convention had taken place in San Francisco in mid-July. Here former President Eisenhower, who had failed under McCarthy pressure in 1952 to speak out for his McCarthy-maligned sponsor, General George Marshall, again failed, this time under right-wing extremist pressure. After encouraging Pennsylvania's governor, the personable moderate William Scranton, to enter the contest against Barry Goldwater, Eisenhower backed out at the convention and left Scranton stranded. Right-wing radicals, in control of the convention, booed Rockefeller and ridiculed Scranton, while Goldwater blandly referred to the Eisenhower Administration as a "dime-store New Deal."

Johnson enjoyed watching the Republican Convention on the three TV sets lined up in a row in his White House bedroom, and when the time came for the big nominating scene, he made an attempt to steal the show. TV networks were alerted, and cameramen followed Lyndon and Lady Bird on a walk around Lafayette Square, stops at the Andrew Jackson and Baron von Steuben statues in the park, and then a hugging and kissing scene between the Johnsons at the Portico entrance to the White House.

If the Goldwater crowd believed it had achieved total mastery of a convention, there was much to learn from the Johnson hold over the coming Democratic barbecue at Atlantic City, scheduled to start on August 24. Johnson's grip was so unyielding that an advance tape recording of the keynote address had to be sent him, the contents of the convention's souvenir book required his approval, and the cover picture of himself would be one he selected. In addition, an enormous portrait of "your President" would be staring at the delegates in the convention hall, and a White House aide would be backstage to control the duration of the applause whenever the Johnson name was mentioned. As for the program, the President and Vice President were to be nominated the same evening—Wednesday, August 26; movie clips shown at the convention were to be cropped of all shots of Bobby Kennedy; a special movie on President Kennedy was not to be shown until after the nomination, and a rousing fifty-sixth birthday party was to be held on the convention floor for Johnson on August 27, and only those paying one thousand dollars each would be invited for a slice of cake.

Furthermore, the entire platform had to meet with his approval, and the Platform Committee could make no decisions on planks without a nod from him. Among the planks he rejected were those endorsing "peaceful demonstrations," legislative reapportionment, and disarmament.

But despite this Johnson straitjacket, one event threatened the total subservience. A Negro-led Freedom Democratic Party of Mississippi held its own conference and sent a delegation to Atlantic City to demand that it be seated instead of the Jim Crow "Regulars." This was a vocal group, and its counsel was Joe Rauh, Johnson's long-time pest; and when Johnson heard about it, he detailed Abe Fortas to shut them up by arranging a compromise. Johnson knew that the Mississippi Regulars planned to return home after the convention and campaign for Goldwater, but he would endanger his entire Southern vote if he ousted them in a body. And as little regard as he had for the Regulars, he had even less for the Freedom Democrats, because he believed they were trying to get TV coverage as unwanted Democrats. A reporter later wrote that a top officer of a national TV network was pushed into swift action after his secretary told him that the President of the United States was calling from Washington. "Get your goddam

cameras off the niggers out front and back on the speaker's stand inside,
goddam it!" was the Presidential message. The cameras moved to the convention floor scene.

The Fortas compromise worked out with Senator Humphrey and Credentials Committee Chairman Governor Dave Lawrence of Pennsylvania called
for the seating of the Regulars and naming two Freedom Party members
as delegates-at-large. When Rauh rejected this as a ridiculous compromise,
Johnson then ordered Walter Reuther, whose union Rauh served as counsel,
to fly to Atlantic City and demand that he accept it. As the situation developed, the Regulars walked off the floor when a few Freedom Party delegates
sat in the Mississippi seats. But by then the convention was engrossed in
other matters, and the Negroes were considered tedious troublemakers.

Once the convention began on August 24, Senator McCarthy's conviction grew stronger that Johnson was using him as a dupe to enliven a dull
convention. On the following day he sent Johnson a telegram withdrawing
himself from the Vice Presidential competition and suggesting that Humphrey be chosen. As soon as he dispatched the wire, McCarthy gave copies
to reporters. This was fortunate, for only minutes afterward, Johnson had
an aide call McCarthy to demand that he stay in contention. But McCarthy
said with satisfaction that it was too late.

That same afternoon, Tuesday, August 25, Humphrey learned finally
that he was Johnson's choice. Johnson had phoned Jim Rowe in Walter
Jenkins' suite at the Deauville Hotel with the request that he have Humphrey read the President's statement in Tuesday's Washington *Evening Star*
about his qualifications for a Vice President. Humphrey did this, and when
he found that the chief point was the expected subservience that he had
already promised Johnson, he knew he had been selected.

Wednesday evening had been set aside for nominating both the President
and Vice President, and Johnson wanted to squeeze into the day as much
tension and mystery as he could. He told reporters he had invited Senators
Dodd and Humphrey to fly from Atlantic City for a White House meeting
that afternoon, and as the day progressed, excitement grew that the great
decision would finally be made. TV cameras were on hand to film the two
senators as they landed and rushed to the White House, but Johnson ordered a blackout because Lady Bird's arrival by helicopter in Atlantic City
was then on TV screens.

While the two senators were on their flight to Washington, Johnson
heightened the suspense by leading reporters on a fifteen-lap walk and interview around the South Lawn in 85° heat, a 4.35-mile trudge in which
he passed out the blarney that he had not yet decided which man would
be his Vice President.

Then came the two senators, and Johnson spoke first to Dodd, who soon
saw he had merely come along for the ride. After this useless conversation
ended at six, Johnson put his arm around Humphrey's shoulder and led

him into his office. First he asked him if he would be his Vice President, and Humphrey replied, "Yes, sir, I would love it, Mr. President."

As they talked, Johnson warned him anew he would demand total co-operation. "I've done a lot of research on Vice Presidents," Johnson told him, "and not a single President ever got along with his Vice President."

Instead of impolitely querying Johnson on his relationship with Kennedy, Humphrey said, "Yes, sir, I know that, Mr. President."

"But we will be different," said Johnson, "because no two men ever got along better than we do."

"Yes, sir, Mr. President," Humphrey agreed. "You can count on me to be completely loyal, sir."

After further clarification of the Vice Presidency, Johnson took him to the Cabinet Room, where Rusk and McNamara were seated at the table. Johnson told Humphrey that the two were among his biggest boosters— "Why, I've been asking everyone here in the White House and right down to the cleaning women they're for you."

Then Johnson said, "Let's call Muriel," and in a moment he had Mrs. Humphrey on the line 140 miles north in Atlantic City. "How would you like to have your boy be my Vice President?" he asked her, winking at Rusk and McNamara. She thought that would be fine.

All that remained was a swift flight by the two to the convention. John Connally had made the nominating speech and Johnson had been nominated before the two reached the hall. Once there, Johnson seized the gavel from John McCormack, pounded for order, and nominated Humphrey for Vice President.

This was an easy campaign for the Democrats, one with scarcely a doubt by Johnson and his aides on the outcome. Any time Johnson had a momentary qualm he had only to pull the June Gallup Poll from his pocket and read the joy of assurance that 81 per cent of Americans favored him over Goldwater at that time. The Republicans were bound to make some gains as the campaign proceeded, but unless a terrible tragedy occurred, Democratic political statisticians could not foresee an upset.

The handsome, gray-haired Arizona Republican in the distinctive black horn-rimmed glasses was doomed by the preconvention attacks against him by moderate Republicans and by his own words. Rockefeller and Scranton had effectively nailed him to a war scene as "trigger happy," and Johnson had only to pose as the untiring man of peace to arouse a national cheer against his opponent. Goldwater's championing of extremists and his actual use of the term in his acceptance speech had also added to the revulsion against him by the great majority of voters, who did not consider themselves in that category. What remained for Goldwater was a bitter struggle to prove that he was a responsible citizen, as his personal life portrayed him. But his fight was hopeless, and in the end the Republicans were left only with their slogan: "In your heart you know he's right."

The oddity of the campaign was that Johnson agreed with much of Goldwater's aggressive, big-stick military stance. But he sensed the national mood in this year of his biggest election, and he campaigned as a tireless champion for peace. "Barry laid out the blueprint, Johnson followed afterward," said a bitter Republican.

"All the Way with LBJ," "LBJ and the U.S.A.," "Prosperity and Peace" were the Democratic slogans—and there was one more. Roosevelt had his "New Deal," Truman his "Fair Deal," Eisenhower his "Great Crusade," and Kennedy his "New Frontier." Johnson had earnestly sought a catchphrase for his own Administration, and the slogan he wanted was supplied him early in 1964 by Richard Goodwin, a young Kennedy aide. This was the "Great Society," once the title of a pre-World War I book by the social psychologist Graham Wallas, the mentor of Walter Lippmann. Johnson tried the term at the May graduation exercises at the University of Michigan, and when it went over well he made it his own. "The Great Society rests on abundance and liberty for all," Goodwin gave Johnson the philosophic underpinnings to explain what the Johnson Administration was all about.

While the Goldwater campaign ran into money troubles, the Johnson campaign was opulent. A masterstroke was Johnson's establishment of a personal "President's Club." Thousands were to join, and membership was based on contributions of at least a thousand dollars to the Democratic National Committee. In order to avoid the pitfalls of the Federal Corrupt Practices Act's restrictions on contributions, Johnson had his "President's Club" organize state chapters. There were additional benefits to members besides the tax write-off. Surface gains were opportunities to "press the flesh" with Johnson and be photographed with him, plus finding in the mail pens he used signing bills and a copy of the "First Family Photo Album." More important gains were invitations to swim naked with the President and to attend White House affairs and the friendly receptions accorded members by agency officials at negotiated contract meetings.

This campaign was also unusual because the Democrats had the press behind them. Few newspapers had supported Roosevelt and Truman, but in 1964 only three large newspapers—the Los Angeles *Times,* Chicago *Times,* and Cincinnati *Enquirer*—came out for Goldwater. Even such crusty Republican magazines as *Life* and the *Saturday Evening Post* joined the Johnson bandwagon.

Then there were the crowds, large and enthusiastic for Johnson, smaller and sometimes antagonistic toward Goldwater. The Secret Service, conditioned by the Kennedy assassination, looked initially with horror upon Johnson's tried and effective campaign technique of enveloping himself physically in a mob. But a new conclusion developed: He was safer there than he would be if he stood alone on an outdoor speaking platform, where he made an excellent target for a mad rifleman. Nevertheless, a lingering doubt remained that with the riots in the streets that summer of 1964 a great deal of Negro anger existed toward governmental authority and the officials in charge.

Democrats traditionally opened their campaigns with a Labor Day visit to Detroit, and Johnson was no exception. After this, White House aides told newsmen that Johnson was considering a White House campaign, comparable to the minor effort made by Roosevelt in 1944 against Tom Dewey. And for most of September he did act as a storekeeper type of candidate, with a flurry of Presidential announcements and nonpolitical trips on Presidential business. He wore the face of a statesman as he joined the President of Mexico in dedicating a new international bridge, and he was the alert Commander-in-Chief as he inspected the Strategic Air Command at Offutt Air Force Base in Omaha with his guest, Manlio Brosio, the Secretary-General of NATO. On the plane Signor Brosio had been witness to a strange scene. The President had invited the reporters who had gone along to join him and the Italian for some conversation. No sooner had they sat down, than Johnson stood up and told the gathering, "I'll be right back. I'm going to take a piss."

Toward the end of September he made a few forays into familiar haunts in Texas and Oklahoma, and the crowds were not as large or as noisy as he had hoped they would be. He rode a horse to the speaker's platform at the opening of the Oklahoma State Fair, screamed out his cowboy "Yeeee-aaaayhoooo," waved his big Stetson, and dug his spurs into what he called an important speech. Goldwater had been crisscrossing the country, decrying "crime in the streets" and blaming the Administration for this and for turning Americans into long numbers on computer machines. "Ah come ta talk 'bout happy people," Johnson told the Fair crowd. "Ah dint come here ta talk 'bout what's wrong. . . . Ah'm proud of Amurrika an' Ah'm proud of Oklahoma. . . . Seventy-five years ago, on an April morning, startin' guns signaled the opening of this land. No one called it a give-away. . . . What came out of it? It gave us Oklahoma, and no one thought it would dull initiative."

Reporters on the Johnson campaign noticed an immediate change in both the size and enthusiasm of his crowds following the weekend of September 26. The explanation was that the Warren Commission report of 880 pages was carefully released at that time to draw maximum newspaper and Sunday TV coverage. There were the names of Chief Justice Warren, Allen Dulles, and Senator Russell to give integrity to the judgment that Lee Harvey Oswald was the sole slayer of President Kennedy and that a single bullet had passed through the bodies of Kennedy and John Connally. Not until much later would the Warren Commission come under fire as a tired group of old men, busy at other tasks, who let fledgling lawyers handle the actual investigation and make the commission's conclusions. But at the time of the release that September weekend, the nation accepted the judgments as authoritative, and credit accrued to Johnson for putting the national mind at rest.

The heightened enthusiasm for Johnson was revealed on September 28, when he came to New England for his first campaign sweep through the old Kennedy country. He grabbed thousands of outstretched hands, teased the enormous crowds with his bullhorn calls—"I want to ask you just one question: Are you gonna vote Democratic in November?" "YES," came the roar. "I didn't hear you. Did you say *yes*?" "YES!" And there was the sad message: "About ten months ago there was this terrible tragedy, and we lost our beloved President John F. Kennedy. Give me your help, your hand, your prayers, and I'll do the best job I can as your President."

In this swing he grabbed a Democratic senator by the arm and ordered him to tell the reporters that the crowds were much larger than those Kennedy had attracted in New England in 1960. The senator refused. Johnson also pushed a White House AP reporter to a fence behind which were hundreds of semihysterical people reaching out to touch Johnson. "Write that in your story," Johnson told him. "Tell the whole country you have proof that the people like me!"

After New England the crowds belonged to Johnson, and he was master, brother, friend, teacher, storyteller, man of the cloth, prosecutor, and your 'umble servant as the mood and occasion demanded. He told some audiences to "just go back to the Good Book and practice some of the teachings of the Lord." He gave others his belief that the American workingman doesn't ask for much. "He would like to have a little sick leave, a little medical attention, a rug on the floor, and a picture on the wall and a little music in the house, and a place to take Molly and the babies when he retires. . . . His boys go to war, and they fight to preserve this system, and he likes his boss and respects him."

He felt it necessary in Albuquerque to explain his 1948 Senate election and his old nickname "Landslide Lyndon." In this 1964 version he claimed that the election had been entirely honest, and he gave credit for his victory to his womenfolk and not Abe Fortas. He said, "I won the nickname of Landslide Lyndon because I won by the magnificent total out of a million and a half by eighty-seven votes, and the Republicans have been talking about it ever since. I have been thinking about it ever since, because if it hadn't been for that extra work that Lady Bird and my mother and my sisters and my cousins put in that day [telephoning everyone in the Austin phone book], Texas would have lost a good senator."

Other crowds felt the tug of sympathy while he told them of the awful responsibility and the long hours he was putting in as President in their behalf. "Not many of you get waked up in the night about Cyprus or Zanzibar or Vietnam," he said, working his arms up and down like pistons. "But I never send a reconnaissance mission out about eleven o'clock with our planes and our boys guiding them to take a look at what is developing and realize they have to be back at three-thirty in the morning, but what promptly at three twenty-five, I wake up without an alarm clock, because I want to be sure my boys get back. . . . And sometimes they don't get back. . . . "

In the early part of the campaign, Barry Goldwater came in for some Johnson ridicule as a perspiring candidate to whom there was no road to the White House. "There was this fellow down in Blanco County." Johnson frequently related this story. "He wanted to find the courthouse, and he asked the town drunk, who hunched up and tried to give him directions. 'You go down to the creek, take the first right past the bridge, then go left—No—You can't go to the courthouse that way.'

"So he tried again. 'Let's see, you go on up to the top of the hill, turn left at the live cedar grove and cross the bridge. No—You can't get to the courthouse that way neither.'

"After a couple more stabs at it, the drunk gave up, looked at the other fellow, and said, 'You just can't get to the courthouse from here.' "

It was LBJ all the way, except for two sour notes. The Very Reverend Francis Sayre, Dean of Washington Cathedral, who had suffered through a ninety-minute tirade delivered against him by Johnson when the two served on the Equal Employment Opportunity Committee, found this a good time to strike back at Johnson. Newspapers publicized the hard-hitting Sayre remarks, which included the following: "The electorate of this mighty nation is left homeless by such a pair of nominees. It knows not where to turn . . . frustration and a federation of hostilities in the one party [Republican]; and in the other, behind a goodly facade, only cynical manipulation of power." Sayre characterized Goldwater as "a man of dangerous ignorance," and Johnson as "a man whose public house is splendid in its every appearance, but whose private lack of ethic must inevitably introduce termites at the very foundation."

Johnson ignored the Sayre attack, and it was soon forgotten. But another form of trouble leaped onto the front pages early in October, and it seemed to be the one spark Goldwater needed to ignite his campaign.

Abe Fortas had almost abandoned his lucrative law practice to help his friend win the election. It was Fortas who helped kill off a threatened Goldwater campaign issue that Johnson had used his public office to amass 12 to 20 million dollars. Fortas did this by hiring the reputable accounting firm of Haskins and Sells to prepare a study of the Johnson family holdings based on their original cost and not on their current value. As a result the low figure of $3,484,098 was released and not a truer one several times as large. Goldwater dropped this issue following the disclosure.

Fortas had also advised on the convention's operations, settled the trouble with the Mississippi Negroes in Atlantic City, written speeches for Johnson, worked closely with Clark Clifford, Bill Moyers, and Douglass Cater in their strategy meetings on the campaign, and served as squadron leader to combat Republican attacks on Johnson. He was now confronted with the job of covering up or shrugging off the Walter Jenkins scandal.

On October 7 chief White House aide Jenkins went to a dinnertime cocktail party at the Washington office of *Newsweek,* then wandered a block away to the basement bathroom at the YMCA, where District Police arrested him as they had in 1959 on a morals charge. He and his companion, a Soldiers Home resident, were taken to a police station and booked. As in the old case of arrest as a pervert, Jenkins paid the collateral and was released.

Jenkins' luck in avoiding publicity, however, was not present in 1964. An employee of the FBI passed the story on to the Republican National Committee and to several reporters. Without naming Jenkins, Republican National Chairman Dean Burch issued a statement charging: "The White House is desperately trying to suppress a major news story affecting the national security." But to Burch's accusation White House aides did not even bother to issue a denial.

It was on October 14, a week after Jenkins' arrest, that a Washington *Star* reporter went to District of Columbia police headquarters to examine the arrest book. Case No. 2208 for October 7, 1964, and No. 174 for January 15, 1959, left no doubt that "Jenkins, Walter Wilson, 3704 Huntington St., NW, Born 3-23-18, Jolly, Tex., Occupation: Clerk, married. Read and Write, yes. Male. Collateral: $25. Mother Enna Morgan, father John B., charge disorderly conduct (pervert)" was Johnson's aide.

The reporter called Liz Carpenter, Mrs. Johnson's press secretary, and asked if the President knew of the two arrests. Her retort was that the charge was ridiculous, and she called the reporter back a short time later to say she had mentioned this to Jenkins, who said he would call the *Star* and make a denial. However, Jenkins did not call the reporter. Instead he phoned Fortas and told him he was in serious trouble. Fortas suggested he come to his law office, but Jenkins said he wanted to talk privately with him at Fortas' Georgetown home. When Jenkins arrived, said Fortas, he was in a state of "emotional collapse." After he finished his story of the October 7 arrest, Fortas had two suggestions: Jenkins should go to a hospital for a rest and be out of reach of reporters; and Fortas would make an appeal to the *Star* not to print the story.

Editors of the *Star* later recalled his masterful performance, as he and Clark Clifford appeared for the defense. In a low voice, Fortas begged for compassion on the part of the newspaper. He said that Jenkins had been working day and night for Johnson, and his wife had to bring his meals to his desk. Fortas claimed that the night of the arrest, Jenkins had swallowed a few drinks at the cocktail party and could not remember having gone to the YMCA afterward. This was an isolated incident, the lawyer said, brought on by great overwork and exhaustion. "Think of Jenkins' wife and six children," he added. But Fortas was startled when the editors told him about the 1959 arrest. Nevertheless, he continued his appeal until the editors promised to withhold the story upon learning that Jenkins was going to the hospital and would soon resign his White House post.

Visits by Fortas and Clifford to the editors of the other two Washington papers were equally successful. But that evening at eight o'clock the UPI broke the story over its wires.

Johnson was in New York that day when George Reedy told him the news. He was scheduled to pay a call on Mrs. Kennedy at her apartment that evening and then speak at a memorial dinner for Al Smith. A reporter said that when a Secret Service agent told him it was time to go to Mrs. Kennedy's place, he asked absently, "Where?" And those at the dinner who sat near him said he read his speech as though it were a series of chemical formulas.

The advice of Fortas was that Johnson should announce he had asked for and received Jenkins' resignation, and that he had asked FBI Director J. Edgar Hoover to make "an immediate and comprehensive inquiry on the case and report promptly to me and the American people." At the same time an effort would have to be made to take the sting out of an expected Republican attack by creating sympathy for Jenkins. In addition Johnson's pollster, Oliver Quayle, must get to work on a quick survey to determine public reaction to the Jenkins revelations.

Director Hoover jeopardized the program at the outset when he sent Jenkins a bouquet of fall flowers and a note reading, "J. Edgar Hoover and Associates." This removed the FBI aura of cold authority when he then announced Jenkins had had "limited association with some individuals who are alleged to be, or who admittedly are, sex deviates," but "there was no information that Jenkins had ever engaged in improper acts with them."

The sympathy campaign included a statement by Jenkins' doctor, who said his patient was suffering from "extreme fatigue," and one from Lady Bird, who commented, "Mah hah't is achin' today fo' someone who has reached the point of exhaustion in dedicated service to his country. . . . Ah know that the love of his wife and six fine chillen and his profound religious faith will sustain him through this period of anguish." Johnson's statement was almost a copy of Lady Bird's, except that his heart didn't *ache* but *went out* "with the deepest compassion for him and for his wife and six children."

Johnson also took the offensive by charging that Eisenhower had suffered from "the same type of problem" with one of his White House aides. Eisenhower denied this, but his denial got far smaller news coverage than the charge. In addition, a White House leak revealed that Jenkins was a lieutenant colonel in a Reserve Air Force Squadron commanded by Senator Goldwater.

Finally, Johnson ended all concern over the Jenkins business when Oliver Quayle's quick telephone poll reached his hands. People were deeply moved by Governor Rockefeller's divorce, but they were not influenced either by the Bobby Baker shenanigans or by the Jenkins police record.

In the last two weeks of the campaign, with the news of Khrushchev's fall from power replacing the Jenkins fall in front-page coverage, Johnson returned to his earlier type of raucous electioneering. "Come down an' hear the speakin'!" he urged crowds through his bullhorn. "Bring your children and the family to hear the speakin'!" He flew to all parts of the country, stumping city and town, certain of victory. As for his opponent's attack on Johnson's lack of public and private scruples, it had foundered on the shoals of poorly written speeches and Goldwater's unwillingness to call Johnson names. So the Arizonian was left chiefly with his demand for the escalation of fighting in southeast Asia.

Johnson had quick answers as he battered Goldwater as a man of war and hailed himself as the peace candidate. "We are not going to send American boys nine or ten thousand miles away from home," he yelled on October 21, "to do what Asian boys ought to be doing for themselves." And at Los Angeles on October 28, he said, "Just because we are powerful, we can't mash a button and tell an independent country to go to hell, because they don't want to go to hell, and we don't get very far rattling our rockets or lobbing them into men's rooms. . . . The only real issue in this campaign, the only one that you ought to get concerned about, is who can best keep the peace. In the nuclear age, the President doesn't get a second chance to make a second guess. If he mashes that button—that is that. . . . I tell you, as your Commander-in-Chief of the mightiest nation in all the world, we can keep the peace, in the words of the Prophet Isaiah, by reasoning together, by responsibility, by negotiation."

Had Alvin Wirtz been alive, he would have been highly amused at Johnson's description of their relationship to one audience before the 1964 campaign ended. "One time when I got into a fight with the head of a power company that wouldn't let me build a little REA line in my country district of Texas," Johnson related, "I said, 'As far as I'm concerned, you can take a running jump and go straight to hell!' and everybody applauded me, and the board of directors thought I was brave and great. One old man, though, the general counsel, who had been a lawyer a long time, and mighty wise and had been in a lot of fights, didn't applaud. He looked serious. He was an ex-senator.

"I said, 'Senator, what did you think of my speech?' He said, 'Come by my office, and I'll tell you.' I went by his office, and I said, 'Senator, what do you think of my speech?'

"He said, 'Young man, you are just in public life. You are just starting. I hope you are in it a long time. I hope you go a long way. I'm going to try to help you, but the first thing you have to learn is this: Telling a man to go to hell and then making him go there is two different propositions.' He said, 'First of all, it is hot down there and the average fellow doesn't want to go. And when you tell him he has to go, he just bristles up and he is a lot less likely to go than if you hadn't told him anything. What you better do is get out the Good Book that your mama used to read to you, and go back to the Prophet Isaiah and read what he said. He said, "Come now, let us reason together." ' "

After a last-ditch effort to defeat Senator Williams in Delaware, Johnson went back to Texas to hear the election results. He had endorsed Ralph Yarborough shortly after the Atlantic City convention and assured him he would campaign hard for him, but he managed to squeeze all the campaigning into a single day, November 2, the day before the election. "And he came to Texas at 4 P.M. on the second," said Yarborough, who had not expected even this.

Johnson was happy on November 3 as he sat sipping a Cutty Sark in the Jim Hogg Suite at the Driskill Hotel and watching the returns on TV. Poor Barry was going to lose by fifteen million votes, he laughed. He watched the percentage split carefully, because he hoped to set a record, beating the F.D.R. total of 60.8 per cent of the vote in 1936 against Landon. When it became clear that he would get 61.2 per cent, he rode to the Austin Civic Center, where the roar of the joyous crowd could tell him how great a victory was his.

PART EIGHT

On His Own in the Oval Office

Chapter 70

I~N~ 1952, ~WHEN~ General Eisenhower grinned his way to the Presidency, he believed he had a "mandate for change" from the turbulent Truman era he was succeeding. In his simple interpretation of national existence, the federal government must be honest, stingy, and quiet, and foreign relations must simmer down within the confines of an expression of American moral leadership for the outside world plus a handout of foreign aid to small nations to keep them from the Communist camp. Discounting the oral brinkmanship bravado of his Secretary of State, the Eisenhower times were in reality the "Digestive Era" and he was the "Caretaker President."

Then in 1960 came a new national approach, when John Kennedy gained power and pledged: "It is time to get this country moving again." This was to be an intellectual and technical approach by experts with new ideas, programs, and excitement. But he was gone after only a brief 1,036 days in office, and his material accomplishments were nil.

Johnson's victory over his archaic Republican opponent in November 1964 was open chiefly to two explanations. The first, and minor, view was that the electorate considered him the lesser of two evils. But this could not have accounted for the massiveness of his success over Goldwater. For the Arizona senator collected only the electoral votes of his own state plus five Deep South states, and the 15,952,000-vote plurality Johnson held over him was the largest in history.

The second explanation was far more plausible. Johnson's enormous victory was translatable as "a mandate for progress long overdue." The nuclear-space-computer age had come to America. So had decayed cities, decayed race relations; an inadequate educational system, and an inadequate economy; polluted air, and polluted water. To solve these and other problems required a herculean effort, and great expectations were centered on Johnson to lead the way to his promised Great Society.

But this did not happen; and the vote of the nation proved in vain. For once Johnson no longer needed to operate in the shadow of Kennedy, his inner person and philosophy now boldly asserted themselves. He soon lost sight of the beckoning beacon light that had led him to victory, and what the nation witnessed was how the product of a lifetime of unceasing battle for personal wealth and political power would operate a government—using the same rough methods.

Johnson's long-time militarism gained top priority early in his Administration, and his lack of perspective and deep interest in domestic issues soon disheartened millions of his followers. The result was that the difficult job of establishing the Great Society for two hundred million Americans became a bothersome bore to him compared with the task of bringing two hundred thousand Viet Cong guerrillas and fifty thousand North Vietnamese Communist troops to their knees some eighty-five hundred miles from the United States.

So Johnson's opportunity for greatness vanished in the steaming jungles of far-off Asia. Cities continued to decay, race relations worsened, and pollution spread. And the Johnson legacy to his country and the world would be the era of brutality, confusion, and frustration that followed in the wake of his toxic role as Commander-in-Chief.

In the sweet afterglow of his November 3, 1964, swamping of his friend Barry Goldwater, Johnson asked his new Vice President, Hubert Humphrey, to come to the ranch for a victory celebration. Together they pored joyously over the election returns to find reasons for their enormous success. One columnist had claimed that the public support of the Democratic ticket by Dr. Benjamin Spock, the eminent baby care book writer, was a decisive factor. "The exact moment when all hope oozed away from the Republican candidate," wrote Inez Robb, was when Spock took his stand, because "millions of American mothers and grandmothers in the United States would as soon question Dr. Spock as they would Holy Writ." Spock later said that Johnson had phoned him the day after the election to thank him for his support.

Johnson had several amusing campaign experiences to relate to Humphrey, but the wrinkled telegram from Goldwater that Johnson pulled from his pocket and showed Hubert was not funny. Instead of a simple wire of concession, Goldwater had sent the following belligerent acknowledgment: "Congratulations on your victory. There is much to be done with Viet Nam, Cuba, the problem of law and order in this country, and a productive economy. Communism remains our No. 1 obstacle to peace, and I know that all Americans will join you in honest solutions to these problems."

After Humphrey swore renewed oaths of fealty and promised to be a totally subservient Vice President, Johnson made a Hill Country man of him. Reporters howled to see the Vice President-elect stumble about with his size eight feet in size eleven cowboy boots, and his big head popping out of a small-size cowboy Stetson. It was equally amusing watching Humphrey astride a horse, bumping up and down in his race to keep abreast of Johnson as the two horsemen galloped over hills. When they returned, Humphrey slid off and muttered, "I'll do anything for my President—but no more horses." Later, Humphrey left Johnson open-mouthed when the President admired his jacket and asked where he got it. Humphrey pretended he was examining the label, and he said with a straight face: "It says here . . . 'Neiman-Marcus, courtesy of Billie Sol Estes.' "

Other Administration officials and politicians flew to the ranch in profusion, and there was hard work on the budget and the State of the Union Message and the Inaugural Address, plus briefings and tours and humorous stories. Johnson led reporters to two picnic tables, and while his peacocks watched from riverbank trees, he let the newsmen in on a secret. "The federal budget was written there around those tables," he declared, "and that's where you lost billions of dollars this week." He insisted that he had been unable to push the budget under the one-hundred-billion-dollar mark. But from the look of too great despair on his face, newsmen were certain he was misleading them again. They knew he would send Congress a budget bill below that figure and then tell how much he had agonized to get it down. (The bill he eventually submitted was one requesting Congress to appropriate 99.7 billion dollars.)

Secretary of State Dean Rusk flew down to brief Johnson on Vietnam, and the two went over plans to bomb North Vietnam after a "proper" incident occurred. When a reporter asked Johnson how serious things were out there, the reply was a jocular "The mess in Vietnam is no worse than the mess inside the Republican party."

There was loud laughter on the ranch as joyous Democrats told their best stories. One was the apocryphal tale about a senator whose mother broke her collarbone. "When Dirksen heard about it, he took hold of the poor senator's elbow, and his voice quavered with his promise to ask the Lord to heal her. Lyndon Johnson pressed the senator's flesh, clouded his glasses by breathing his regrets that the senator would not be present for a major vote, and then pulled out the enormous wad of paper money he always carried and peeled off several hundred to meet her hospital expenses. Hubert Humphrey leaned his head into the senator's neck and sobbed like a baby."

President Johnson's State of the Union Message preceded his inauguration, and he drove his aides mercilessly to spell it out in understandable language that would not cost him any of his carefully gathered consensus support. "Remember, I'm President of all the people," he enjoined them, "so let's not make a lot of people mad. Besides, I don't want to come up to this Congress and scare it half to death." He had a vision of what constituted a perfect speech, and he repeated it to each new person who worked on drafts of all his speeches and messages. "I want four-letter words, and I want four words to the sentence, and I want four sentences to the paragraph," was his line. "Now that's what I want, and I know you want to give it to me." One Washington correspondent, Robert Sherrill, revealed an inside episode involving Johnson and his assistant, Douglass Cater, who had handed Johnson sheets of a draft. "Johnson scanned it rapidly and judged it to be 'pretty good, Doug. You've got the idea. But you've got to get more PAY-thohs into it, hear? We gotta have more people livin' in wretched hovels and things like that. Doug, you've gotta get your hand up under the dress!'—accompanied by a descriptive gesture."

The Eighty-ninth Congress was to Johnson's liking. Both the Senate and House showed a wide comfortable Democratic margin, with the Senate sporting a 68-to-32 and the House a 295-to-140 division. Furthermore, the House caucus had adopted a new rule at his suggestion, one that would grant power to the speaker to order any bill to the floor after the Rules Committee had held it twenty-one days.

So it was with a feeling of exuberance that he came with his entourage on January 4 to tell a joint session of Congress and the nation what the Great Society meant. "The Great Society asks not how much, but how good; not only how to create wealth but how to use it," he explained in this State of the Union Message of 1965. He asked Congress for a Medicare Bill, aid to education, a cut in excise taxes on luggage, jewelry, and other items, a step-up in the poverty program, a new immigration law which would give priority to skilled foreigners, the establishment of an Urban Affairs Department, a program to purify air and change sea water to fresh water cheaply, aid for the arts, and a fast train between Washington and New York and Boston.

Praise for the State of the Union Message was widespread among Republican as well as Democratic newspapers. Kennedy had intended to send the nomination of Harvard Professor Samuel Beer to the Senate for confirmation as American ambassador to Uruguay. But Johnson recognized Beer as a former chairman of the ADA who had joined the attack on his candidacy in 1960, and on becoming President he killed the intended appointment. Apparently Beer was working now to rehabilitate himself in Johnson's eyes, for he praised the Message lavishly. Kennedy had been concerned with a redistribution of wealth, said Beer, but "Johnson is less concerned with redistribution of material things than he is with raising the general level."

Once the State of the Union Message was out of the way, Johnson concentrated on his inauguration. Having heard from his President how spectacular it would be, Humphrey put in a call to Sam Scogna, a Washington tailor, for the formal garb Kennedy had ordered his entourage to wear in 1960. Humphrey thought he was renting a suit of tails for the customary $12.50, but Scogna told reporters he was cutting garments to his measurements for $125. While Humphrey was in the midst of a fiery hassle with Scogna, Johnson added to his misery by sending him word that he was expected to wear an "oxford gray suit, black shoes, and a fedora."

These were happy times leading to Johnson's day of days, and yet there were irritations. Part of the happiness stemmed from the increase in value of the four thousand acres of land he had quietly purchased during his first year as President, from the acquisition of another six thousand acres on a lease-possible sale basis to graze his growing herd, and from the completion of the deal to gain control of KLFY-TV in Lafayette, Louisiana.

There was also happiness in having twenty-two relatives and acquaintances from his distant past stay at the White House prior to the inauguration to see how powerful Sam Johnson's boy had become. Hatred of the railroads was still strong in his part of the country, and he enjoyed telling the way he had settled the strike in 1964 when the Brotherhoods and the railroad tycoons were fighting. "One of the biggest and richest of those railroad presidents," he said, "was against the settlement, and he told me, 'I'm just a country boy.' So I just hauled off and told him, 'When I hear someone say "I'm just a little ol' country boy," I just clamp my hand around my wallet.' So he just caved in and said he was for my settlement."

Kate Deadrich, now Mrs. Chester Loney, Johnson's first teacher, was in her seventies, but she could recall every antic of her most famous pupil with undimmed memory. Probably what might have deterred Lyndon from becoming a serious disciplinary problem, she hinted, was that at nineteen, as the mistress of the Junction School, she stood almost six feet tall and weighed about 170 pounds. "He had to sit on my lap to recite," she said as though by rote, "and he would put a little finger under each word." Johnson added the story about riding a donkey to the school at Albert later and the way the older children teased him so unmercifully that he wept rainbarrels of tears every day. "It helped a little when my mother told me that 'Jesus rode into Jerusalem on an ass,'" he said. But what ended the ridicule was the horse his father finally gave him for the ride to and from school.

Old friends from Southwest Texas State Teachers College talked about his whirlwind days at the small college that squatted on top of Chatauqua Hill in San Marcos. The mention of Dr. Evans' name conjured up several stories. Willard Deason, whom Johnson had promised to appoint to the Interstate Commerce Commission, recalled Lyndon's ability to sell Real Silk hosiery. "Dr. Evans wound up with more socks than anyone else in the United States," he declared. Jesse Kellam remembered that Dr. Evans permitted Lyndon and his roommate occupying the room in the garage to paint the garage in lieu of rent whenever they were short of cash—"That little building had more coats of paint on it than any building in the United States."

Someone else recalled that for a time Lyndon was known as "Bull" Johnson at school, but the moot point was whether this related to his bullheaded manner of driving ahead to win what he was after or to doubts about the veracity of his remarks. Then there was the description of Lyndon's debating technique by Professor Howard Mell Greene that the old schoolmates remembered: "When Lyndon had the last word in the debate, he just threw the string around the necks of opponents so slick." They also brought up his fabled boardinghouse reach and the amount of food he shoveled in at mealtime. They would have laughed uproariously at the woeful tale of his food miseries back in college that he was describing to reporters—"My dinner used to consist of a fried egg between two pieces of cold bread, and I was glad to get it, too," he had allowed reporters to quote him.

Johnson had his own stories to air to his White House inauguration guests. He told about his year at Sam Houston High, where he handled his big debate program, campaigned for Kleberg, and also taught the first Dale Carnegie course for businessmen in Houston, even though he was only twenty-two at the time. "I used to stand along the side wall and heckle these successful businessmen to death while they gave their talks, so they'd gain some confidence," he said. When he talked about the two years he bossed the Texas NYA, Deason recalled Johnson's big staff meeting, when he stood in front of his office crew and told the gang, "I carry aspirin in this pocket [he rattled them in the box] and Ex-Lax in this pocket [rattle-rattle-rattle]. And I tell you we're gonna get the job done one way or the other."

His irritations in this preinauguration period came from his insistence on handling many of the details. This would be an opulent inauguration— a 1.5-million-dollar affair—with invitations going out to two hundred thousand persons. Lady Bird could tell he was laboring under mental pressure because of the "rash on his hands." He wanted to know about the parties, the food, the minute-by-minute schedule for inauguration day, and he demanded that changes be made. Nor would he accept assurances from the top three arrangers of the President's finest hour that everything could be expected to move smoothly without his close attention. These three were Dale Miller, the Johnson family friend and lobbyist for Texas Gulf Sulphur, as his father had been before him, who was officially in charge of the inauguration; Jim Rowe, the foreign agent for the Haitian American Sugar Company of Port-au-Prince in the land of voodoo dictator Francois "Papa" Duvalier, who was in charge of the Inaugural Citizens for Johnson-Humphrey Committee; and Abe Fortas, lobbyist for the Commonwealth of Puerto Rico, and sponsor of the special preinaugural party for Johnson.

Fortas' supper-dance party in the Benjamin Franklin Room in the State Department on January 19 produced Johnson's first public outburst. Arthur Krim, the movie magnate, national chairman of the President's Clubs and lot owner at Lake Lyndon B. Johnson, was present, and Johnson had hardly begun to twirl Mrs. Krim around the dance floor when the photographers moved in for pictures. Johnson immediately stopped dancing, clutched one photographer, and half-wrestled him toward the door, where Secret Service agents took over and ejected him. Then he blasphemed other photographers not to take his picture.

This hardly augured a pleasant beginning for the inaugural events, though the next morning, when he had breakfast with Lady Bird at 6:40, the incident seemed forgotten. As was traditional, a President attended church on inauguration day, and Johnson and Lady Bird went early to the Washington National City Christian Church for services. But the sight of photographers at the church triggered a rekindled fury, and he took time to berate the group as "little piss-ants, and I hope you know how much I hate photographers at church." Inside, Billy Graham was present to emote in his loudest and most emphatic manner the nation's love for Johnson, and he told the congregation: "There is a spiritual dimension to leadership, which this Administration has already recognized."

There was another reason for Johnson's general irascibility, and this was his realization that his writers had failed to draft a better Inaugural Address than the one delivered four years earlier by Kennedy. Richard Goodwin, originator of "the Great Society" catchphrase, had been put in charge of the Johnson inaugural speech; but despite additional work by Douglass Cater, Horace Busby, Adlai Stevenson, Willard Wirtz, Bill Moyers, and Jack Valenti, the Goodwin speech lacked depth and excitement. What had emerged was a dull and quaint twenty-minute sermon, at Johnson's speaking rate of only sixty-nine words a minute, that only the sycophantic part of the press would hail as "notable and memorable."

To give off an aura of Presidential health, Johnson wore no coat despite the cold weather, though he was protected somewhat by his thermal long-handle underwear. Then to show proper humility for this august occasion, he walked slowly, with short steps and bowed head, to the lectern. Finally, to depict how important his wife was to him, he gave Lady Bird an inaugural "first" by asking her to hold the Bible on which he rested his left hand for the oath-taking ceremony. "How incredible it is," he preached to the sea of faces before him on the Capitol's broad parking lot, "that in this fragile existence we should hate and destroy one another. There is world enough for all to seek their happiness in their own way."

Following his speech and the inaugural lunch, Johnson and Humphrey, their families, and special guests watched the traditional parade and floats moving past the reviewing stand in front of the White House. Johnson was in good spirits at last, but it proved short-lived when word came to him about the activities of Bobby Kennedy. Bobby had resigned from the Cabinet in the summer of 1964 and was now the elected United States senator from New York. Both before and after Johnson's oath-taking, Bobby had visited his brother's grave, and a crowd of news photographers had snapped hundreds of pictures for tomorrow's papers in competition with news of the inauguration.

That this Bobby Kennedy action helped induce Johnson's illness was doubtful. It was the following evening, January 21, that Johnson developed severe chest pains and a tearing cough, bringing on fears he was suffering another heart attack. At 2:55 A.M. the next morning, doctors rushed him to Bethesda Naval Hospital, and Vice President Humphrey was alerted by the Secret Service that the President's health had become a matter of their prime concern. But once Johnson was ushered into the VIP seventeenth-floor suite and examined, the diagnosis was that he was suffering only from a cold and needed about five days of hospital rest and care.

During Johnson's stay at Bethesda Naval Hospital the press tried to develop a feud between him and Humphrey. One story making the rounds in Washington was that when Johnson woke up in the hospital the first thing he screamed was, "You tell Hubert to get out of my chair!"

What led to such newspaper stories was the death of England's great statesman, Winston Churchill. Johnson had been nudged awake at 3:30 A.M. on Sunday, January 24, and told that the ninety-year-old World War II leader had passed away. An immediate order of business was to select his special representatives to attend the London funeral, and since he could not go, a logical choice was Humphrey.

But Johnson ignored his Vice President and selected instead Secretary of State Rusk, Chief Justice Warren, and United States Ambassador to the Court of St. James, David Bruce. While Humphrey was mortified, and his friends were angry, newspapers dubbed Johnson the "Great Emasculator," who had acted solely to deprive his Vice President of publicity.

Following a stay of several days in the hospital, Johnson returned, coughing, to the White House after berating the hospital staff for keeping his rooms too warm, for the slowness of the elevator, and for the permeating food odors that seeped into his suite from the kitchen. Reporters hounded him to tell if he had any special reason for omitting Humphrey from the funeral entourage, and his angry reply was a hacking "No!"

However, in the days that followed his recovery, he revealed a suspicion and jealousy of Humphrey's frequent speechmaking and press talks. "When I was Vice President," Johnson pointedly told newsmen, "I never held a press conference, and I don't think that the Vice President should." Johnson also had some unkind comments to make about a Vice President who needed a personal staff of forty-five persons. In addition, when Humphrey spoke to a labor convention and said that Johnson would shortly ask Congress for an increase in the minimum wage, Johnson bitingly remarked to newsmen, "I see by the papers that I have a minimum wage program."

Johnson had gone a year as President without a Vice President, and it took time to accept the existence of a waiting-in-the-wings figure, even if it was his long-time friend and the man he had personally selected. His order was that Humphrey should act as the totally quiet chairman of the Space Council, the Peace Corps Council, the Cabinet task force on youth, honorary chairman of the advisory council to the Office of Economic Opportunity, and silent member of the National Security Council.

After his short spree, Humphrey bowed to Johnson's commands and became subservient once more. "I am Vice President because he made me Vice President," he confessed to reporters. "There are no Humphrey policies; there are no Humphrey programs." On one occasion in February, Johnson and Humphrey visited NASA headquarters for a briefing on the Mariner IV Rocket destined for an eight-month flight to Mars. Humphrey's speech to the gathering made many wince, though it pleased Johnson. As Humphrey zoomed through his oratorical flight, his chief point was that space flight was made possible only because of Johnson. "He has put his heart into it," Humhprey cried out. "He has put his spirit into it, his hands and his mind into it."

So the Johnson Administration moved into its era.

Chapter 71

WHEN THE FIRST session of the Eighty-ninth Congress got under way on January 4, 1965, Johnson was determined to surpass the Franklin Roosevelt record of fifteen major bills pushed through Congress in those frightening Hundred Days in 1933.

This did not appear to be too difficult a contest, because the shelves were heavy with New Frontier bills which had already gone through Congressional hearing after Congressional hearing, and opponents were admittedly exhausted. In addition, Johnson had months earlier appointed fourteen task forces consisting of leaders in industry, labor, and the academic communities, and he had ordered them to hand him "bold new steps" for his Great Society before Congress convened.

White House aides had already digested the task force reports and recommendations, and these were now available as legislative proposals for presentation to Congress. So Johnson had a heavy bag of bills to drop on the Capitol, even though the task forces had in reality produced a mouse. Their proposals contained nothing newer than the New Frontier except for a rent subsidy proposal, textbook aid to parochial schools in public welfare areas, and a "Demonstration Cities" program for urban renewal.

"Now take Bill Moyers," Johnson said proudly, with reference to the young man who had succeeded Walter Jenkins as his top aide and had worked his way through most of the task force reports. "I think he'll be dead at forty. . . . And Horace Busby—he can take a lot of legal language and make something out of it. And Jack Valenti, he's a genius, comes along and he takes a paragraph of Busby and makes a sentence out of it. It gets Busby mad, but it's even better. And Dick Goodwin, he's wonderful, that boy. He can cry a little. He cries a little with me whenever I need to cry over something. And Hubert, he's another who can cry pretty good over something. They get a lot of emotion into their work."

On a top floor of the Federal Aviation Agency building, across the wide street from the Smithsonian Institution, Najeeb Halaby, FAA's capable administrator, was holding a meeting with the Supersonic Transport (SST) report-writing task force. "You've written too complex a report," Halaby complained. "You've got to remember that you're writing it for Bill Moyers. So you have to make it ABC simple so Moyers can understand it, because Johnson won't read the report and will only hear what Moyers tells him orally." With this, Halaby doomed his own continuation in the Great Society, for every agency now had White House informers.

"Mah preachuh," Johnson called his young ordained minister, who was different from his other aides because he dared talk back on occasion to his master and utter jibes at the holy-crusade atmosphere Johnson tried to affix on his Great Society to make detractors look like atheists. On one occasion Moyers was pronouncing grace at lunch with his boss, and Johnson yelled to him, "Speak up, Bill! I can't hear a damn thing." Moyers looked up and said, "I wasn't addressing you, Mr. President." Another time, when a White House worker passed around the order that all Johnson scribbled notes, chits, and side margin comments on papers were to be saved for posterity, Moyers continued to throw such material into his wastebasket. Finally, after undergoing a scolding for his sacrilegious activity, he handed the Johnson memorabilia collector an envelope. When it was opened, the contents turned out to be chicken bones. "That's what the President had for lunch," Moyers intoned loftily.

With Moyers, Cater, Busby, Goodwin, and the others having done their jobs for the unveiling of the Johnson Administration's legislative program, Johnson ordered Larry O'Brien's contingent of legislative lobbyists to meet with him at the White House just before leaping out of the trenches to attack Congress. To lend excitement to his determination to outperform Roosevelt in the Hundred Days competition, Johnson tried to fire up the O'Brien crew with his own erroneous historical presentation of the way popular Presidents could be undone by Congress. He was depending on them, he said, to see to it he did not suffer the same fate. He pictured Warren Harding wracked and tortured by the Senate investigation of the Teapot Dome scandal involving naval oil holdings. (This investigation did not occur until Harding lay in his grave and Calvin Coolidge was President.) He also pitied Herbert Hoover, battered and bleeding, from 1931 to 1933, from attacks by a mean Democratic majority in the Senate. (Jim Watson, the Old Guard Republican, was in control of the Senate during that Congress. It was the Democrats in the House under Speaker Garner who had mangled Hoover.) And he portrayed poor Franklin Roosevelt sitting "there in his wheelchair in the White House," a prisoner to paralysis who "just couldn't get around to all the Congressional offices" in 1937, and was cut to pieces by Congress as a result. (The Roosevelt network to Congress by phone, legislative aides, and congressmen helpers was excellent.)

O'Brien's boys had to work fast, he pleaded, because even the one-sided victory he had enjoyed the preceding November was bound to dissipate itself in time. "Just by the natural way people think, and because Barry Goldwater probably scared hell out of them, I figure I've already lost about two of my fifteen-million lead, and am probably getting down to thirteen million," he said in the tone of self-pity necessary to get his message across. "If I get in any fight with Congress, I'll lose another couple of million." He let his voice falter: "I may be down to only eight million by the end of the summer."

The push to emulate Roosevelt's New Deal Banking Act, AAA, TVA, NRA, HOLC, CCC, FDIC, PWA, and the rest of that breathless show in the terrible spring of 1933 bogged down quickly in the winter of 1965. By May 1 seventeen bills had come across Johnson's desk for signature, and only two—Aid to Appalachia and the Elementary and Secondary Education Act—were of top significance. Among the others he signed were laws establishing a professional photography week (May 2-9, 1965), Goddard Day (March 16, 1965) for the father of modern rocketry, the Nez Perce National Park in Idaho, and a clarification of civil service retirement provisions. But Johnson briskly passed over the minor nature of most of the bills and told reporters that his one hundred days formed "a record of major accomplishment without equal or close parallel in the present era."

Johnson's failure to come close to the Roosevelt one hundred days record did not detract from his total record later that year. One hundred and fifteen Presidential legislative recommendations—not counting appropriations bills—were to make the mile-long trip from the White House to the Capitol. And of these, ninety made the round trip and were signed into law by Johnson before Congress fled Washington 293 days later on October 23. "You passed so damn much legislation," Johnson told Senator Pat McNamara of Michigan, chairman of the Public Works Committee and ranking Democrat on the Labor and Public Welfare Committee, at a bill-signing ceremony, "I'm gonna give you an extra pen to take home with you."

Within this avalanche of legislation were a voting rights law; Medicare;

a Highway Beautification and Scenic Development Act; establishment of a Department of Housing and Urban Development (HUD); a new immigration law; a cut of four billion dollars in excise taxes on furs, playing cards, jewelry, luggage, etc.; a two-billion-dollar pork-barrel measure for rivers and harbors improvements in forty-one states; and a whopping 5.2-billion-dollar NASA outer space appropriation—the modern-day pork barrel.

Unfortunately, Johnson did not emerge from the hectic year as a popular President with Congress. "There were a lot of us who broke our backs on some of these bills, but Lyndon claimed he did it all himself. And you don't make friends that way," said one senator. "All you ever read in the papers and magazines was that he carried the whole load by himself."

Newsweek declared him "Lyndon the Powerful. . . . He summons the dukes and barons of Congress to his chambers and they dutifully carry out his royal decrees." *Newsweek* quoted him as saying: "For thirty-five years I have watched people read and write and talk about things that should be done; and in the limited time that I have, I'm going to do them." The frothy Kiplinger Letter said his friends "call him a 'human dynamo.' Enemies are bitter . . . say he's trying to run a one-man show, be both ringmaster and performer." The opinion of a *New York Times* writer was that "Lyndon Johnson seems 20 feet tall—when he really measures no more than 10. . . . He dominates any room by walking into it and any conference by taking his seat. . . . Mr. Johnson is generally regarded as a 'wizard' who exerts some magic on a 'rubberstamp' Congress and therefore rules that proud body as imperiously as he does his own staff."

The facts were frequently at odds with these views, especially on important legislation. Two cases in point were voting rights and Medicare.

In his State of the Union Message Johnson had pledged himself to "eliminate every remaining obstacle to the right and opportunity to vote." Despite his hoopla remarks in 1957 and 1960, neither of those so-called civil rights bills had proved the least effective in insuring Southern Negroes of their Constitutionally guaranteed voting rights. The 1964 Civil Rights Act, with its concentration on public accommodations and public education and job desegregation, had not covered this vital point for full citizenship. The time was at hand to pass the strong voting rights provisions of the 1957 and 1960 acts that Johnson had eliminated before their passage.

Even with Johnson's declaration in January 1965, Dr. Martin Luther King remained unconvinced that any action would take place in Washington before a grass roots fire was started in Confederate territory. The place he selected as the nonviolent battleground for his voting rights drive was Selma, Alabama, a town of 15,100 Negroes and 14,440 whites, with a voter-registration roll book that revealed 99 per cent of the local eligible voters were white. Selma's other distinction was that following the Supreme Court's 1954 decision against segregated schools, it had organized the South's first White Citizens Council.

The King drive in Selma was a complex matter of inducing frightened Negroes to march with him to the Selma courthouse to register to vote. Local Sheriff Jim Clark and his bullyboys planted their feet athwart the courthouse walk to prevent this, sometimes by beating the Negroes with clubs, sometimes by hauling them off to prison. Without Clark's presence, King later admitted, his drive might have faded; but each time it gave indication of flagging, Clark's savagery revived his movement.

In the first seven weeks King was in Selma and chanted, "We shall overcome," Clark arrested two thousand Negroes. Then, on February 18, came a heightening of brutality, when Clark's men plus Governor George Wallace's state troopers clubbed unarmed demonstrators and killed a young Negro woodcutter. Following this incident, King called a march of fifty miles on Sunday, March 7, from Selma to the state capital at Montgomery in protest. This time, after Alabama troopers demanded that the 650 protesters turn back and were met by a brave rejection of their order, they used their billy clubs and tear gas on the Negroes, and the national press expressed outrage.

Now the symbol became another march on Montgomery, with clergymen and white civil righters from the North hurrying to Selma to participate. Johnson told reporters he "deplored the brutality" and said that both sides should "cool down." Governor Wallace came to Washington at his own request to confer with Johnson on the deteriorating situation. At the confrontation Wallace promised that the Alabama National Guard would protect those participating in the new march on Montgomery. But when he returned home, he denied he had made this agreement, which led Johnson to nationalize the Alabama guard and send federal troops to prevent interference with the marchers.

However, this still did not solve the question of voting rights for Negroes in the South. "From the beginning of the session," said Charles Ferris, counsel for the Senate Democratic Policy Committee, "the Administration kept saying it was working on a voting rights bill. But nothing ever came to the Hill. Then the morning after the big Selma incident, Mike Mansfield called me and bluntly ordered me to have a one-page bill ready in a half-hour. I dropped everything and worked on the legislation, and came up with a three-page bill after three hours.

"Senator Mansfield took my bill, but he was angry with the Administration for its lack of action. So he phoned Nick Katzenbach, the Attorney General, and he told him he was going to introduce the bill, and he wanted to know where the Administration's bill was. No such bill existed, for none had ever been written. But after Mike gave him what for, Katzenbach's staff at Justice worked up a forty-eight-page bill, and he brought it to Mansfield."

By now Johnson appeared on the scene as the man in charge. On March 15, he came to the House at prime evening TV time to deliver a message on civil rights. "I want to be the President who helped the poor to find their own way and who protected the right of every citizen to vote in every election. I want to be the President who helped to end hatred among his fellow men and who promoted love among the people of all races and all religions and all parties. I want to be the President who helped to end war among the brothers of this earth," he told the nation.

"Just as in 1964, it was Mike's job again to make sure that a civil rights bill passed the Senate," said Ferris. "Once more it was Senator Dirksen who expressed doubts about many of the details of the two bills. So Mansfield had me meet with Dirksen's staff and lawyers from the Justice Department in Dirksen's office to develop a bill Dirksen would approve. Then, as in 1964, Mansfield and other interested Democrats and Republicans met in Dirksen's office in the afternoons to go over what the staffs had done in the mornings."

Senator Paul Douglas, the Senate's acknowledged civil rights champion, was peeved that the meetings took place in Dirksen's office, and he complained bitterly to Mansfield that when the afternoon's session was over, Dirksen glided into the hall outside his office and talked to the TV cameras waiting there.

"Why not let Dirksen get the temporary glory?" Mansfield chided him. "He likes the limelight, and it helps us get his cooperation. In the long run, what will be remembered is that a Democratic Administration and a Democratic Congress passed voting rights for Negroes in the South."

Douglas grudgingly acquiesced, and the work was completed without further hitch in the bill-writing committee. The final bill, as passed by Congress and signed by Johnson on August 6, suspended all literacy and "device" tests as voter qualifications in any county where less than 50 per cent of voting-age residents were registered on November 1, 1965. The act also abolished the requirement of any poll tax payment to vote in a federal election.

Kennedy had promoted a Medicare bill without success in the three years he served as President. The bill to provide medical care in hospitals for old people under Social Security failed in the Senate one year by a vote of 51 to 44 and in 1962 by 52 to 48. One of the opponents was Senator Smathers, Kennedy's close friend, and a remark came from the White House that "George hasn't stood up for me since my wedding." But Smathers was a minor opponent compared with Chairman Harry Byrd of the Senate Finance Committee and Chairman Wilbur Mills of the House Ways and Means Committee.

Johnson had opposed President Truman's Fair Deal proposal for health insurance, but in 1964 he came out for Medicare, and he wanted desperately to have the bill pass that year so that he could brag about this accomplishment during the campaign against Goldwater. He had believed that even though the old Virginian had told him flatly he would never let the bill out of his Finance Committee, Byrd could be softened up if Congressman Mills would permit a House vote.

"Wilbur," he told him over the telephone in late September 1964, "I've just been looking through the polls here, and I've got only a few weaknesses, and the worst of them is that I'm not doing anything for the old folks. I need some help from you, Wilbur. How about letting Medicare get to the House floor?"

"No!" Mills told him.

"But what am I gonna tell the old folks?"

"You've got the Kerr-Mills Act," said Mills.

"But that's got that mean means test," Johnson begged helplessly.

When the Eighty-ninth Congress began its work in 1965, Mills decided he would no longer block Medicare, and he permitted the Ways and Means Committee to hold four weeks of hearings on the measure. The Administration's bill was a mild one, providing only a short hospital stay with payment coming from the Social Security system. Chief objection to it was that it was inadequate, yet because of this it experienced little difficulty clearing the committee for floor action by a vote of 17 to 8.

It was here that its nature changed. The Republicans came up with their own bill, one providing far broader coverage and more extensive services but limited to those who met a means test. Before the Republicans knew what was happening, Mills swept in, adopted their bill as his own, and dropped only one provision—the means test. When he pushed this through the House by the lopsided vote of 313 to 115, old Speaker McCormack, his normally ashen face now red with pleasure, cried out to him, "Congratulations, my dear friend. Magnificent!"

"This was a tremendous bill that came from the House," Charles Ferris recalled. "But it accentuated the Senate problem, which was Senator Byrd's opposition." Byrd had gone to the White House, where he agreed on TV to permit Senate committee hearings, but once safely back in the Capitol he said he would not. However, Mike Mansfield had another talk with Byrd about his high sense of fairness, and once more the senator said, "I'm not going to block it in committee, but only as a favor to you, Mike." So Byrd agreed to step aside and permit Senator Russell Long of Louisiana, the ranking Democrat on his committee, to handle the bill.

Months earlier Russell Long had won the caucus election for the post of majority whip, as the replacement for Hubert Humphrey. To pick up support among his fellow Democrats, he had made several promises, and in one case he traded Senate Chamber desks. His father before him, the late Huey "Kingfish" Long, had once occupied Russell Long's desk, and in a loud "Father, forgive me" prayer, he gave the desk to Senator "Olin the Solon" Johnston of South Carolina, who coveted it because John C. Calhoun had used it in the first half of the nineteenth century. For this piece of furniture, Johnston cast his ballot for Long as the next whip.

The oddity of Long's taking over committee and floor leadership on Medicare was that he had been a vehement opponent of the bill before Mansfield gave him the assignment. In fact, besides voting against Medicare in the past, he had opposed most of the New Frontier, including the Peace Corps, the Nuclear Test Ban Treaty, aid to education, foreign aid, and the Kennedy Civil Rights Bill. However, he worked hard for Medicare and promoted it through the Senate on July 9 by the vote of 68 to 21. Three weeks later Johnson signed Medicare into law.

Because Congress lacked a publicity machine, the vital efforts of Mansfield gained no public attention as he worked quietly behind the scene to clear the Senate Calendar of pending legislation. Nor did Mills, Long, Lister Hill, and other Congressional promoters of legislation gain notice for their work. Instead, with Johnson talking about "my Medicare Bill" and "my Voting Rights Bill," when these and other measures passed, all credit accrued to him, and unsophisticated newsmen called Congress "an able legislative body" and Johnson the "one-man show" who made "Congress seem another pygmy at his feet."

In fairness to Johnson, there were a minority of bills whose passage he assisted by patronage and pork-barrel grants, threats, bribes, persecution, and a barrage of barnyard Johnsonese. On one occasion he boasted to reporters that he had insured passage of the cotton acreage allotments in Title 4 of the Food and Agriculture Act by personally changing "twenty-one or twenty-two votes in the House."

Two bills in particular revealed a Johnson who would use any of his powers to bring about their passage. The first was the rent subsidy, and the second was the 325.5-million-dollar Highway Beautification Bill.

Jeered at by Kennedy liberals for his lack of new legislative ideas, Johnson brought rough action into play to promote a section providing a thirty-million-dollar rent subsidy for low-income families in the Administration's four-year 7.8-billion-dollar Housing Bill. Representative Otis Pike from Long Island, a Kennedy Democrat who opposed the rent subsidy, received the typical Johnson treatment on this bill. First came "a warning call from the White House," he said, "followed by a barrage of others from Administration men." Then when he continued in opposition, a White House assistant delivered word that "a vote against rent subsidies might cost his district an important research project." Democratic Representative Edith Green of Oregon expressed her view of what was happening in this fashion: "We have in the House a determined effort to silence those in opposition."

Representative Tom "Tip" O'Neill from Cambridge, Massachusetts, in the Kennedy heartland, was generally a Johnson stalwart, but on the rent subsidy he was a renegade. When he told John McCormack he planned to oppose it in the Rules Committee and then on the floor—if it got out of committee—McCormack passed this intelligence on to Johnson with his judgment that O'Neill owned the swing vote on Judge Smith's Rules Committee, and his vote on the floor could spell life or death for rent subsidies.

"That night, after I told McCormack," O'Neill later recalled, "the President called. He thanked me all over the place for the fine things I had said about him in a speech I had made in my home district and for all the help I'd given him in the past. Then he got to the point. He said it would be damned embarrassing for him to lose this one, and didn't I know what problems he had without this thing falling flat. Well, hell, what do you say to the President of the United States?

"I told him I'd sleep on it. Then the next morning I said to myself, I've always been a party man, and if he really needs me, of course I'll go along, even if the bill wasn't set up exactly the way I wanted it. Probably I took a half-dozen guys with me. We won in the crunch by six votes—208 to 202. Now, I wouldn't have voted for it except for his call. He made me feel a little guilty and cheap for letting him down."

Over in the Senate, Democratic Senator Ed Bartlett of Alaska intended to vote against the rent subsidy, until a White House lobbyist passed word to him that he could have his ten-million-dollar Eskimo housing project if he changed his mind. When the Senate passed the rent-subsidy proposal by a vote of 46 to 45, Bartlett said glumly of his decisive vote, "I'm not proud of myself."

Yet after all his arm-twisting and intimidation to win approval for his post-Kennedy idea, Johnson suffered defeat, even though he signed the Housing Bill into law on August 10, 1965. Angry House Republicans examined the rent supplement section closely and discovered that it was so poorly written it was not in reality restricted to elderly and handicapped low-income families. Instead, an elderly couple with net assets of twenty-five thousand dollars could become eligible to have the federal government pay 75 per cent of their rent. Following this disclosure, House Democrats joined Republicans to cancel any rent subsidy appropriation.

The Highway Beautification Bill was Johnson's present to Lady Bird, and he was wild with rage toward all who opposed its passage. When he first succeeded Kennedy, Johnson attempted to create an Eleanor Roosevelt image for Lady Bird. She was his eyes and ears on the nation's social problems, he told reporters, but he could not win acceptance for her on this score because of her previous lack of interest in welfare matters. In addition, with so many problems centering in the South's treatment of its Negro population, her Southern accent was immediately suspect.

However, Lady Bird worked hard on this "great lady concerned with the masses" image at the outset, and when Johnson declared war on poverty, she took her first trip as First Lady in a sad-faced, sympathetic, head-shaking tour of the Appalachian area in March 1964. But the Eleanor Roosevelt image collapsed in May, when two Republican congressmen disclosed that four Negro families were living in miserable squalor on property she owned in Autauga County, Alabama. The carefully devised White House reply, written by Elizabeth Carpenter, made the bold assertion that these poverty-stricken families were there only because of Mrs. Johnson's overwhelming sense of kindness, that the acreage they occupied could more profitably be used to raise pine trees. When the press turned on the two Republicans for the crime of attacking the First Lady, they retreated into silence. But Lady Bird could no longer be billed as an Eleanor Roosevelt.

Another build-up for Lady Bird was the attempt to picture her as an astute businesswoman and as a woman who could set an example for other women born with handicaps. The successful businesswoman creation told about the fine lady who was so devoted to her politician-husband and children, yet had drawn a salary of fifty thousand dollars a year as the head of a large broadcasting company. Johnson was described as a man who had nothing to do with private business. "Bird is the brains and money of this family," he told a lady reporter.

As for the effort to describe her as a woman who successfully overcame handicaps, a story that had once appeared in the *Daily Oklahoman* was put to work as the prototype: "She is a gal with gumption. Although frightened of the public forum, she took a public-speaking course to steel herself to face audiences. Timid with firearms, she nevertheless learned to shoot several years ago and now handles a .28 shotgun in the Texas dove season and a rifle for the November-December deer season."

When this build-up failed to attract public enthusiasm, White House aides and the President looked further. Lady Bird could always be a limited sort of success by acting her own nostalgic self. She could make Southern audiences sigh with pleasure when she recalled, as she did in the spring of 1964, "Until I was about twenty, summertime always meant Alabama to me. With Aunt Effie, we would board the train at Marshall and ride to the part of the world that meant watermelon cuttings, picnics at the creek, and a lot of company every Sunday. . . . My uncle John Patillo would take me walking through the pine trees when I was a little girl."

The search to find a cause for Lady Bird ended with the need to beautify the nation. To help Lady Bird's campaign as a landscape beautifier, Mary Lasker, who had defended Lyndon to Mrs. Roosevelt, contributed twenty-five thousand dollars worth of azaleas to plant along Pennsylvania Avenue. Unfortunately, the District Government failed to water the plants, and they died. But the idea of a champion for planting trees and flowers and bushes was met with friendliness by the press, and so Lady Bird found her role in her husband's Administration.

Lady Bird acquired a committee of advisers on beautification, and she met in the White House with Mrs. Lasker, Laurance Rockefeller, and other millionaires to decide what to plant and where to plant it. Johnson's contribution was the Highway Beautification Bill to pay outdoor advertisers to remove highway signs, and junkyard owners to move at least one thousand feet from the pavement.

When the bill entered the crucial Senate floor debate stage, Johnson had his aides supply him with an up-to-the-minute tally of support and opposition. Democratic senators who opposed the Lady Bird bill were deluged with phone calls from the Oval Office and given material reasons for changing their position. One stubborn senator admitted: "I was awakened at 2:30 A.M. one morning, and it was Lyndon telling me to come right over to the White House for a meeting in the upstairs family quarters. I didn't ask, but I guessed that he wanted my advice on one of the major crises that had come up suddenly. But when I got there, he was in his bathrobe, and he immediately listed every bill I wanted passed and he screamed at the end, 'You aren't going to get a damned one of them passed unless you vote for the Beautification Bill!' "

Johnson dissipated even more energy in the House to promote this legislation. He had scheduled a party for the Legislative Branch on the evening of Thursday, October 7—"Lyndon Johnson's Salute to the Eighty-Ninth Congress"—and he wanted the Beautification Bill to clear the House before then, so he could announce its passage to the assembled guests. Maryland Representative George Fallon, chairman of the House Public Works Committee, had scheduled the vote for October 8, but Johnson was adamant. It must come before his party.

When the House convened on October 7, the leadership was so optimistic about quick action on the Lady Bird bill that Democratic members planned to leave early, and their wives visited the beauty parlors to make themselves ready for the evening party. But things did not turn out as expected. At 2 P.M. Johnson was on the phone to McCormack, and he was steaming angry. "You keep that House in session as long as it's necessary, just so the bill passes," he told the speaker. "I've got to have this tribute to Lady Bird to announce at my party."

The spoilers were the Republicans, for, when news of Johnson's order leaked out, an aroused GOP minority was determined to show House independence from the White House. While McCormack sat uneasily in his presiding chair, Republican members offered a steady stream of amendments to the bill, and the afternoon and evening vanished as more amendments were debated and House members filed down the aisle for twelve teller vote counts.

Johnson's salute to Congress began that evening with movie actors and opera singers giving their free performances. But there were no House members present and only a few wives of representatives had come. Most of the ladies were at the Capitol waiting for the nonsense to end. At 9 P.M. some members asked McCormack to put the bill over until the next day. His doleful answer was that he could not, and jibes and more amendments greeted his announcement. One amendment which failed proposed giving Lady Bird authority to enforce the law instead of the Secretary of Commerce. Iowa's H. R. Gross, the House's one-man Treasury watchdog, made the suggestion that when the bill passed, Johnson should hold the signing ceremony "on Route 290 outside of Austin, in the shade of a billboard advertising the Johnson TV and radio station."

It was not until 12:51 A.M., after Jim Wright of Texas beat off a motion to recommit the bill to the Public Works Committee, that the House finally passed the Beautification Bill by a vote of 245 to 138. Following its passage, one member yelled out, "You wouldn't find me dead near the White House!" and an angry group of congressmen and their wives stamped out of the Capitol while Majority Leader Carl Albert called after them, "The party's still on."

The sequel of this episode was that, after Johnson signed the bill on October 22, it proved a monstrous mess in operation. The generous compensation to outdoor advertisers and junkyard owners to remove their unsightly properties was computed to run into the billions of dollars, even though the program was restricted solely to the interstate and primary highway systems.

Hardly a day went by throughout the entire year without Johnson's domination of newspaper space with stories relating to the absolutism with which he ruled Congress, the Executive Branch, the press, industry, labor, and the long line of foreign leaders who came hat in hand to Washington for handouts. Most of the stories were poppycock, but a sufficient number were true to lend credence to the lot. In many ways Lyndon Johnson was a type of President the country had never experienced before—a man who was more interested in being portrayed for the use of his Office's power than in the programs and policies he was promoting.

It became common for him to use the herd technique, a device that robbed others of their dignity. He would announce the appointment of several officials at one time, hold mass swearing-in ceremonies, call droves of congressmen to the East Room for briefings by several officials and pinch off questions by dismissing everyone. Reporters were kept on edge, always uncertain when he would spring a news conference, whether questions would have to be thrown on the run in laps around the White House South Lawn, whether they might be reprimanded before fellow newsmen. One news photographer, whose picture of Johnson's right profile appeared in the papers, found a Presidential index finger pointed in his direction at a news conference and heard a Presidential blast, "You sonofabitch!" According to Michael Davie, a British correspondent, when a newsman asked Johnson a silly question, Johnson replied, "Why do you come and ask me, the leader of the Western world, a chickenshit question like that?"

When he disliked what he heard or read in the news about himself, he sometimes reacted in unusual ways. After *The New York Times* expressed opposition to his foreign policy in Southeast Asia in 1965, he told Hubert Humphrey and General Maxwell Taylor to fly to New York and convince

John Oakes, the editorial-page editor, to change his slant. After their return, when the *Times* continued its opposition, he sent others to talk to Oakes. Still the *Times* would not shift. Finally he asked Secretary of State Rusk to reason with the *Times* people, and Rusk helped him end his mission by asking, "What in hell do you care what the *Times* says, Mr. President?"

Johnson had tried reasoning with *The New York Times* because he had always been in awe of this publication. With other critics, his approach was far more severe. On one occasion, an 11 P.M. TV news commentator made a mildly critical comment about the President. "I was expecting a tax refund from Internal Revenue at the time," he said, "but a few days later I was notified that court action would soon be instituted against me for failure to pay my taxes. I was certain the I.R.S. had made a mistake, but my lawyer told me I was in for real trouble: Johnson had heard me make the offending remark. So I took the only course available to me. I called Sheldon Cohen, the director of I.R.S., and told him I wanted to run a special half-hour show directly with him and also work up a series of a half-dozen shows on the wonders of the Internal Revenue Service. The tax action was dropped."

Sometimes Johnson employed censorship techniques to prevent publication of material dealing with him. Ralph Schoenstein wrote a book for Doubleday in 1965 about Johnson and his three beagles, Blanco, Him, and Her. Ken McCormick, chief editor at Doubleday, claimed he paid Schoenstein ten thousand dollars for the sixty-five-page manuscript. "It was understood by Liz Carpenter and by Doubleday, and we thought by Ralph Schoenstein, that his manuscript would be checked out by the White House for accuracy and taste," said McCormick. "But the White House was outraged . . . and a really heavy blue-penciling took place." This was an understatement, for Mrs. Carpenter told Doubleday that if it printed the book it would "sacrifice the cooperation of the White House with its future writers." Specifically, Doubleday hoped for Johnson's memoirs after he left office, and dropped the dog book. "The whole thing was a mess, and it cast no virtue on the writer, the publisher, or the White House," said McCormick. Doubleday also attempted to censor a book by Clark Mollenhoff by eliminating criticism of Secretary of Defense Robert McNamara. Each time that Mollenhoff restored his text, the blue-pencil lines were redrawn in his manuscript by his Doubleday editor.

Nor were private individuals immune from the pressures of Presidential power applied against them by a displeased Mr. Johnson. In May 1965, for instance, Mrs. L. Cummings, a campaign worker for the Democrats in 1964, tried to sell a short note Mrs. Kennedy had sent Lady Bird inviting her to watch the first Nixon-Kennedy debate. Obviously, Mrs. Cummings had no right to sell the letter because it did not belong to her. Nevertheless, Johnson's response was again the harsh act of punishing her through the taxing device. George Dixon reported in his column that before she tried to sell the letter Mrs. Cummings was told she would get a tax refund. A few days later, after Secret Service agents descended on her and attempted to terrorize her, the inevitable letter came from Sheldon Cohen's office at Internal Revenue that she was in tax trouble.

The Administration's approach to force an end to Senator John Williams' provocative opposition on a host of issues went beyond tax accusations, the direct Johnson effort to defeat him in his 1964 re-election fight, and the continuing smear on his character for instigating the Bobby Baker investigation. Early in 1965 Williams infuriated Johnson when he made public that the USIA had spent eighty thousand dollars on the film *The Texas Story*. Then toward the end of that summer he lashed at Johnson again for naming David Bress, a Washington lawyer and the attorney for Bobby Baker's Serv-U vending machine company, as United States Attorney for the District of Columbia, where a grand jury was to probe the Baker activities.

The novel scheme now used in an attempt to destroy Williams was to send him unsigned reports about alleged Johnson Administration scandals. The reports were false, and if Williams publicized them, he would immediately be shown up as a vicious slanderer. But he did not swallow the bait "because I could tell from experience it was fishy," said Williams. So this scheme to destroy "Whispering Willie," as the deriders of the soft-spoken senator called him, failed.

The *Journal du Dimanche* of France summed up what it described as the animal-like approach of the American President in dealing with others: "There is something of the hunting dog in the way of sniffing the air around him, of the bear in the way he greets his guests, of the fox in his manner of watching someone present a problem, of the bird of prey in the way he jumps on an adversary during a debate."

Johnson's personal need for publicity resulted in some bizarre activities in 1965. "Lightbulb Johnson" struck again and gained newspaper attention when he turned off the lights in the ladies room in the West Wing press quarters. But far more newspaper space came his way because of the unusual places he found to sign legislation into law.

On April 11 he traveled to the one-room tin-roofed Junction School a mile from his birthplace to sign the 1.344-billion-dollar Elementary and Secondary Education Act. "Miss Kate," his first teacher, was present, and a wag who knew their story wondered why he didn't sit on her lap while he read his statement on the bill. Scott Klett, who had been the Johnson City school superintendent and Lyndon's history teacher, was sought out by reporters, and he told how Lyndon had to be thrashed one time for jumping on a board and splashing mud on the girls.

On July 30 he signed the Medicare Act in the presence of former President Truman in Independence, Missouri; and on August 6 he sat at a desk in the President's Room off the Senate Chamber and used fifty pens to sign the Voting Rights Act. This was the room where Lincoln had signed the Emancipation Proclamation on New Year's Day of 1863. A week after Johnson signed this bill a devastating riot took place in the Negro community of Watts, in Los Angeles, revealing that the race problem in the United States was far from reconciled. Still another trip to sign a bill came on October 3, when Johnson traveled to New York to affix his signature on the Immigration Act in the shade of the Statue of Liberty.

There was also a special trip to Hye, five miles from the L.B.J. Ranch, in November, to swear in Larry O'Brien, the last remaining Kennedy aide, as his Postmaster General. The ceremony took place on the porch of the town's gingerbread-topped post office, and when Johnson spoke to Hye's 134 residents and the crowd of newsmen and visiting dignitaries, he recalled that "I was four years old when I came to Hye to mail a letter to my grandmother. And she never got it. But Larry O'Brien told me that he is going to find that letter and deliver it."

Then Johnson went on November 8 to his Alma Mater, Southwest Texas State Teachers College at San Marcos, for the signing of the Higher Education Act, which provided a three-year 2.3-billion-dollar program of federal scholarships to needy students and a college building construction grant.

Johnson's secrecy in trying to manage his operations and in naming appointees to federal positions provided him with additional newspaper publicity. If reporters learned the name of the person Johnson planned to appoint, and this was divulged in the press before the White House could make the announcement, a peeved Johnson would cancel the appointment. James Farmer, the national director of the Congress of Racial Equality (CORE), was told he would head a massive literacy drive in the Office of Economic Opportunity, but when word leaked out, Johnson was in a fury and cancelled both the program and Farmer's appointment. In another of many examples, Johnson informed Lloyd Cutler, a Washington attorney, he would be named as Undersecretary of Commerce. However, when the Washington *Post* mentioned this, Johnson told Cutler that the job was no longer his.

This penchant for secrecy extended also into the operations of the federal government, with public officials ordered not to discuss their agencies' problems with the press. Above all, they were not to bring into the open any troubles they were having with one another, because this would spoil the Johnson image of running a consensus government. To seven men who had lived through weeks of fear that reporters would discover that Johnson had proposed their appointments, Johnson delivered a warning lecture when he ordered them to fly to his ranch for final presentation to reporters. His stern command was that he expected them to do their "giving and taking" in dealing with each other "in privacy, not on the television screens or the front pages. . . . Time after time when I was Senate majority leader," he said, "I tried to talk it out with one of the folks opposing me or opposing what I knew a majority of the Senate wanted to do. The next thing I knew, everything I said was on the front page of, first, that fellow's hometown paper and sure enough on the front page of the Washington papers the next day."

The absolute manner in which Johnson ran the White House also gained him press attention. His demands for complete subservience grew during 1965, and unctuous professions of loyalty uttered publicly by Jack Valenti and others became even more shrill. "A sensitive man, a cultivated man, a warmhearted man," Valenti called him; and Moyers declared he had special antennae "to divine the pulse of the American people." When a Herblock cartoon showed Johnson with a whip striding past the scraping figures of Valenti and other slaves at the White House "plantation," Johnson was so enraged he canceled the July 12, 1965, Medal of Freedom awards ceremony.

Rapidly spreading jokes depicted Johnson and Lady Bird as believing the Valenti deification of their persons. One story had the Johnsons strolling along the Pedernales, and Johnson said, "Bird, are there any reporters or Secret Service men around?"

"No, honey."

"Then let's try that walking on top the water once more."

Another story had German Ludwig Erhard visiting at the ranch, and in a conversation he said to Johnson, "I understand you were born in a log cabin, Mr. President."

"No, Mr. Chancellor, I was born in a manger," was the reply.

Early in 1965 Johnson brought Marvin Watson to the White House as his appointments secretary and hatchet man in dealing with the White House staff and the Democratic National Committee. Forty-year-old Watson had been the chairman of the Texas State Democratic Committee under John Connally and worked as the assistant to the president of the Dallas Lone Star Steel Company, a firm with a record of aggressive antiunion activities. "Marvin is as wise as my daddy, gentle as my mama, and loyal to my side as Lady Bird," Johnson introduced his new aide to reporters. Lady Bird added, "I'd give Marvin one hundred thousand dollars a year to run my business."

Reporters soon found out that Watson was running a White House gestapo on orders from his boss. All employees were required to keep a log of their telephone calls, noting who called and the point of the discussion, and give an accounting of their work day. A check was also made on users of White House cars.

Although the picture of a President who wanted to be the complete master of all he surveyed did not dovetail with the image of a President who sought a consensus as his mode of operation, in Johnson's case the two were similar. As one observer described the Johnson consensus approach, it was simply a modern-day version of the ancient Isaiah's remark. The Johnson version went like this, "Come let us reason together, you little chickenshit."

Essentially the Presidential call for consensus was no different from that of Majority Leader Johnson, which Senator William Fulbright had once described: "Johnson is an extraordinary man, and he goes to extraordinary lengths to convert people, and if not, to neutralize them. It is all personal, because he has never shown any interest in issues or substantive matters."

By putting George Meany's phone directly onto the Presidential line, inviting him frequently to the White House, and promising him full White House aid to repeal Section 14(B) of the Taft-Hartley Law, which permitted state "right to work" laws, Johnson was able to win his grudging approval of the Council of Economic Advisers' low wage-price increase guideline of only 3.2 per cent for labor contracts in 1965. This was the wage increase percentage the United Steelworkers had been forced to accept after Johnson put their president, I. W. Abel, into Room 275½ in the Executive Office Building with R. Conrad Cooper, the steel management negotiator, to end the strike threat.

By inviting industrialists to lunch and on rides in *Air Force One,* he found he could gain support from business. Support was surer when they joined one of the President's Club chapters and contributed their thousand dollars or more to the Democrats, for this had its own rewards for loyalty. Not long after the executives of Anheuser-Busch gave the President's Club ten thousand dollars, the Department of Justice canceled its antitrust suit against the St. Louis brewery. Anheuser-Busch celebrated by flying Vice President Humphrey and the head of the Antitrust Division to a baseball game in St. Louis aboard a company plane. In another instance, when the Washington director of a company contributed three thousand dollars to the President's Club, his firm won a 1.3-million-dollar antipoverty contract, even though four far more experienced firms were in competition.

To gain popular backing from the intellectual community, Johnson hired a historian-in-residence for the White House, though he totally ignored the man. Johnson also passed word to reporters that he was a disciple of Barbara Ward, the highly regarded British economist and wife of Sir Robert Jackson, the commissioner of development in dictatorial Ghana. Miss Ward had written a short book, *The Rich Nations and the Poor Nations,* in 1962, and Johnson ordered his staff aides to read it. One of Miss Ward's chief points was that it was the duty of rich nations to assist poor countries, and Johnson told reporters he had assured her, "I read it like I do the Bible."

Johnson also tried his consensus technique with august William McChesney Martin, chairman of the board of governors of the Federal Reserve System. When Woodrow Wilson established the Federal Reserve and gave it control over the nation's monetary policy, he made it independent of the

President. The Federal Reserve would control the amount of money and credit in circulation, while the Treasury Department would be restricted to raising revenue to meet the government's expenses.

When Martin made a speech comparing 1965 and 1929, the Treasury Department was concerned that he planned to tighten credit by raising the interest rate charged banks that borrowed money from Federal Reserve Banks. At the insistence of Treasury Secretary Henry Fowler, Johnson asked Martin to come to a meeting in his office one morning at 11:30. On Martin's arrival, Fowler and Johnson argued that he must not take any action, and when Martin refused to agree, Johnson kept him there without lunch until 4 P.M. Even though he grew hungrier with each passing hour, Martin argued in return that the government should raise taxes to curtail the inflation. When he finally staggered out it was with a Presidential admonition not to dare take independent action.

It was early in the morning, December 5, that Martin announced an increase in the interest rate from 4 to 4.5 per cent. When a reporter asked Martin's aide if Johnson had been informed in advance, the man smiled and replied, "Mr. Martin would have, only it was two hours earlier at the ranch and he didn't want to awaken the President. But he had to act without delay to stop the hemorrhaging of the U.S. gold supply."

Johnson's chief press attention in 1965 did not come from his legislative accomplishments but from a personal experience instead. The day following Labor Day he had suffered severe abdominal pain. Doctors told him he must have his gallbladder removed, but he refused to do so before the principal bills cleared Congress. In addition he wanted to wait until after Pope Paul VI's visit to New York during the first week in October.

The press was not informed that anything was amiss, and Johnson actually stepped up his working schedule to throw them off the scent. In the meantime Lady Bird had twenty classrooms cleared and remodeled on the third floor at Bethesda Naval Hospital for his one-dollar-a-day stay there. This low charge was his by virtue of being Commander-in-Chief, and therefore a military man. When the Pope arrived, Johnson flew to Manhattan for a forty-six-minute conversation with him on the thirty-fifth floor of the Waldorf Towers and gave him an autographed picture of himself. Then on his return to Washington, he held out until Lady Bird's Beautification Bill passed the House shortly after midnight on October 8.

Three Secret Service agents in surgical gowns and masks stood in the operating room a few hours later along with ten doctors. Surgeons quickly removed the gallbladder and in addition removed a kidney stone. One of Johnson's conversation pieces had been the kidney stone from the 1955 operation that he carried in a small box and showed visitors. Now he had an additional quarter-inch stone for the box.

When Johnson regained consciousness, he asked for Moyers. "Bill, how are you?" he greeted him wanly.

Moyers bent over him excitedly and replied, "I've got good news. The stock market opened strong today, Mr. President."

Johnson had arranged with Moyers to portray him to the press as a physical superman to whom a major operation was like a scratched finger. Moyers' success was swiftly in evidence when an AP bulletin in the next day's paper read: "President Johnson was up before dawn today and signed into law thirteen bills." One Johnson wisecrack that was printed was his apocryphal order to the surgeons to use one hundred and fifty scalpels and pass them out to congressmen afterward.

But one true story was Lady Bird's devotion to her husband and her own image. She came to the hospital with a fifteen-foot willow oak and planted it under his window in thanks for his successful operation.

Johnson spent twelve weeks convalescing at the end of 1965. Before he left the hospital for the ranch, he contributed to Presidential photography by exposing his twelve-inch abdominal scar for news photographers. This recovery was not spent in idleness, since there was a budget to prepare, a State of the Union Message to write, and a stream of advisers and visitors to consult on a variety of matters. William McChesney Martin was one who flew the 1,384 miles from Washington to the ranch to receive a mild reprimand from Johnson for increasing the interest rate. In return he told Johnson this would not have been necessary if the President had asked Congress for a tax increase.

Other visitors brought word that Mayor Daley of Chicago and other Democratic local bosses were incensed over a provision of the War on Poverty law that weakened their power. This was the section with revolutionary overtones that declared that local programs had to be "developed, conducted and administered with the maximum feasible participation of the groups served." Who thought up the wild idea that the poor should run their own programs? they wanted to know.

But if this was an unhappy note, there was a moment of amusement for Johnson in reading the *Life* excerpts of the book on Kennedy by Arthur Schlesinger, who divulged Kennedy's unmanliness after the Bay of Pigs disaster. According to Schlesinger, Kennedy had "put his head into his hands and almost sobbed."

Among the many visitors was Johnson's favorite foreigner, Ludwig Erhard, and it was an unhappy occasion for the German Chancellor when he heard the bad news that Johnson had cancelled the MLF, the Multilateral Force of a mixed-manned NATO fleet of vessels equipped with nuclear weapons. Another visitor was British Prime Minister Harold Wilson, who attempted to show Johnson his knowledge of the President's background by mentioning his 1948 Senate fight "in which you won an eighty-six-vote victory." Johnson stared into his eyes, shook his head, and growled finally, "You haven't been here six hours, and you've already taken one vote away from me." Wilson, whose Labor party held only a two-vote margin in Commons, replied, "Mr. President, you can afford to lose one vote. I can't."

While Johnson recuperated, Bill Moyers was his man in charge of "Project 66," the legislative program to be dumped on Congress during the coming year. Goodwin again wrote the first draft of the State of the Union Message, and Moyers and Valenti refined it. This was a speech the press labeled a "stock-taking and promise-making message," because it lacked the fire of Johnson's two previous messages.

With the polls showing Johnson's popularity declining, the Republican leaders in Congress gave their own State of the Union Message, a program reporters dubbed the "Ev and Gerry Show," after its two participants, Senator Dirksen and House Minority Leader Ford. Johnson ruined their attack by making public his confusing notes to each. He told newsmen he had written Everett Dirksen a message of thanks, telling him he was "grateful" for his support on foreign policy; and his note to Ford told of his delight to find the House Republican leader supporting "programs which the President has been promoting."

However, the Johnson "victory" over Dirksen and Ford was dimmed by newspaper stories playing up Bobby Baker's indictment by the local grand jury. And Senator Williams was in the news again with his charge that the 178-page Democratic book of praise for the Eighty-ninth Congress, *Toward an Age of Greatness,* carried a million dollars worth of ads by defense contractors.

A thousand times worse than any scandal in 1966 was the pall that settled over the nation because of Johnson's continual escalation of a war in Southeast Asia that appeared to be without solution, yet required more and more American boys, and was costing the United States the goodwill of old allies.

In 1966 the legislative output revealed a total of 1,001 bills passed and 66,289 nominations confirmed. Yet few of these measures pertained to the Great Society, even though in his State of the Union Message Johnson had called the United States strong enough "to pursue our goals in the rest of the world while building a Great Society at home."

The minimum wage was increased to $1.40 an hour and eight million additional workers were covered. Among those now included under the minimum wage law were agricultural workers, and when Southern farmers mechanized rather than pay Negroes such wages, a great movement northward by blacks began. Another Great Society measure was the Demonstration Cities Act of 1966. Federal funds were to be used to help cities rebuild and restore large areas of "slums and blight" to decent living sections. High on the list of cities requesting aid was Laredo, Texas, with the sorry record of possessing the lowest per-capita income of all American cities.

In 1967 the Great Society gained only lip service as a Johnson rallying point as the budget for the War on Poverty was slashed. Riots in the Negro ghettos of Newark, Detroit, and other cities in the summer of that year were frightening spectacles. But they also pointed to the despair of a large minority group whose welfare was no longer considered of key concern by the Administration. Disillusionment grew widespread among liberal Democrats and Republicans because the domestic needs of the country were not being met.

Floyd McKissick of CORE called the Administration insincere, even about the Great Society legislation already approved. McKissick said that he and Dr. Martin Luther King had organized an enormous staff to assist federal registrars register a million Southern Negroes under the Voting Rights Act of 1965, but their effort failed, he added bitterly, because "Johnson failed to send those registrars into the South except in token force."

When Johnson came to the House to deliver his State of the Union Message on January 17, 1968, he offered a listless talk to an audience that did not include thirty-four of the one hundred senators, a record of absentees. The Great Society had lost its flag to the war in Vietnam.

Some Democrats recalled a Humphrey speech in the spring of 1966, in which he said even then, "The struggle in Vietnam has overshadowed the record of domestic programs." Said a House liberal about the Great Society: "It sounds like the title of a book that hasn't been written."

Chapter 72

D ESCRIBING THE REACTION of various members of Congress to international crises, President Eisenhower once compared the peacelike approach of Sam Rayburn to the warlike Johnson approach to these problems. "Sam Rayburn, for example," he wrote, "was always anxious to make certain that the United States would do everything possible to negotiate. Senator Lyndon Johnson, on the other hand, appeared to be anxious to be able to take some action, visible to the world, to indicate we had—or the Senate had—strengthened our Armed Forces."

Johnson had to be told repeatedly that the United States was strong enough to blow up the rest of the world. For example, on March 6, 1959, when Eisenhower consulted with both men on the perennial Berlin crisis, he said he "assured Speaker Rayburn that we would not go to war because of rigidity in attitude and emphasized the recent exchange of notes in which we kept the chances for negotiation open. To Lyndon Johnson, I reiterated my confidence in the nation's military power. In fact, I said, 'If we were to release our nuclear stockpile on the Soviet Union, the main danger would arise not from retaliation but from fallout in the earth's atmosphere.' "

Shortly after Johnson became President in November 1963, a former Senate associate added to this assessment of what could be expected from him as the man with the finger ready to "mash the button" of American foreign policy. "Lyndon's ideas were set in thick concrete by World War II," the senator said. "Every big action he takes will be determined primarily on the basis of whether he thinks any other action will look like a Munich appeasement. The reasons he will give publicly for his actions will not be those he really believes, because in the Senate he said what he thought you wanted to hear. And he will not change course even when he knows he is wrong, because he has a preposterous idea he is bound to lose face if he does. The only advisers he will listen to are those who will tell him what he wants to hear, for he is not a man who tolerates listening to both sides of a problem.

"In addition, Lyndon sees the Cold War as permanent, the enemy unchangeable, and every anti-United States activity anywhere on the face of the earth as a deliberate act controlled by an international monolithic Communist network operating from the Kremlin in Moscow. He will pay lip-service to an East-West détente, but he doesn't believe in it. Furthermore, since his entire training has been that of a politician trying to overpower other politicians, he will rely on personal diplomacy to buy off, threaten and coerce other nations."

Johnson's first test in foreign affairs came on January 9, 1964, when serious rioting broke out in the Panama Canal Zone. Panama, which had been taken over by Spain in 1538, gained its freedom in 1821 and then became a part of Colombia. A French firm had begun construction of a canal across the isthmus of Colombia's State of Panama in 1882, but after spending 250 million dollars, had gone bankrupt. When the French interests had offered to sell the United States its rights for forty million dollars and Colombia refused to sanction the sale, President Theodore Roosevelt instigated a jungle revolution which resulted in the breaking away of Panama from Colombia. Once the shooting began, Roosevelt immediately recognized the independence of the Republic of Panama and in 1903 imposed a treaty on that tiny nation which gave the United States a ten-mile-wide canal zone "in perpetuity" for ten million dollars, plus an annual rental of $250,000.

Angry demands by Colombia for reimbursement for her territorial loss led to a United States payment of twenty-five million dollars in 1921. Minor treaty concessions were also made with Panama, but this was not the end of the trouble, for nationalistic demands grew in Panama for political control over the Canal Zone, a matter of concern to the thousands of Americans living a comfortable existence there.

In 1960 President Eisenhower yielded slightly to Panamanian nationalism by permitting Panama's flag to be raised along with the United States flag at the U. S. Panama Canal Building. Then two years later Kennedy agreed to establish fifty dual flag sites, including eighteen schools. The concern of the American Zoners was that the flag concession would be the initial breakthrough that would eventually end their colonial existence, and they initiated a program to eliminate all flags at the designated places, rather than fly the Panamanian colors anywhere.

At the beginning of January 1964, while Johnson was concentrating on his first State of the Union Message, Canal Zone authorities ruled that no flags would fly in front of Balboa High School, at the Pacific Ocean end of the Canal. However, on January 7, American pupils there defied the order and raised the United States flag on the school pole. When the United States governor of the Canal Zone spied it in place, he ordered it hauled down, but the pupils sent the Stars and Stripes up again.

Two days later came a "protest" invasion of the Canal Zone by Panamanian youngsters, who raised the flag of Panama. As the youngsters were leaving, a group of workers in a labor dispute joined them for a second protest. This turned into a riot. United States troops were called out; they fired into the mob, and snipers from rooftops fired back at them; the Panama flag, which had been raised by the "invaders" at the school, was pulled down and torn; extensive damage was done to neighborhood structures; and tragically, when the rioting ended, twenty persons lay dead, including three Americans, and three hundred others were wounded. The reaction of President Roberto Chiari of Panama was to break off diplomatic relations with the United States and demand that the United States agree to end the 1903 treaty.

It was Secretary of State Rusk who designated the episode a Communist plot when detailing the riot to Johnson. "There were a lot of Molotov cocktails appearing pretty fast," he emphasized, adding, "and there were a good many snipers who appeared who perhaps had to have had arms in known localities available to them."

Johnson immediately visualized another Castro–Cuba type Communist foothold in the making, and he decided to try personal diplomacy on the head of tiny Panama that day to order him to keep his Panamanians in line if he did not want real trouble with the United States. "Hey, get me the President of Panama—what's his name, anyway?" he barked at a White House assistant. "I want to talk to him."

"Mr. President," the aide said hesitantly, "that isn't protocol. You just can't do things that way."

"Who the hell said I can't?" Johnson bellowed. "Now you just get him on the phone fast."

"This is President Johnson," he yelled into the phone when Chiari came on the line. "Now, I know you have your own troubles because you've got an election in May. But I want this violence to stop right now." When he asked about the loud noise in the background and learned that demonstrators were just outside Chiari's quarters, Johnson was furious.

Chiari countered with the request that Johnson agree to negotiate a new treaty and tear up the 1903 pact. This would be the best way to end the agitation, he said.

In a rough reply, Johnson said he would have none of this. The rioting would have to stop first, and peace be restored, before there could be any talk about treaties.

There was no meeting of minds in this phone conversation of January 9, and only hours after Johnson hung up, Panamanian rioters attacked the United States Embassy.

Johnson, the tall, tough Texan, could not see how a large country could be conciliatory toward a tiny country without appearing weak. "We are not going to make any precommitments before we sit down on what we are going to do in the way of rewriting new treaties with a nation we do not have diplomatic relations with," he told reporters on February 29, 1964, as the problem remained unresolved. "And just because Panama happens to be a small nation no larger than the city of St. Louis is no reason why we shouldn't . . . be equally insistent on no preconditions."

To others, Johnson explained his position: "They were killing people, and some thought we should write a new treaty right away. But you just can't say, 'I'll give you a blank check,' when there's a pistol pointing at your head."

While Johnson held to his rigid position, the Organization of American States (OAS) established a five-member team to find a peaceful path out of the woods. By March the team was putting its thoughts on paper, and Johnson insisted upon seeing each sentence and changing words in their tentative proposal. Finally on March 12 a compromise joint Panama-United States declaration appeared ready for issuance by the OAS. This was a statement calling for future "discussions and negotiations," with Panama issuing a follow-up memorandum stressing "negotiations" and the United States issuing one stressing "discussions."

Undersecretary of State Thomas Mann was ready to issue the United States interpretation that night to reporters, when Johnson abruptly called off the agreement. At this late hour, Chiari had asked that the word *review* be substituted for *discussions,* and as a White House aide described Johnson's reaction, "He went through the ceiling. 'Who do they think they are?' he screamed."

By now OAS leaders believed that their organization was in danger of collapsing, and in self-defense they issued the joint declaration on March

15 without the interpretive statements from the two countries involved. Mann jeeringly called the statement "wishful thinking."

That night Johnson ordered Rusk, Humphrey, and Mann to the White House along with Senators Fulbright, Mansfield, Morse, Dirksen, and Russell to discuss the situation. Called upon for his opinion, Dirksen counseled him to be firm. "Hell, Mr. President," he gasped in his rumbling voice, "if we give an inch we'll be saying to every little country in the world that the way to get something out of us is to break off relations, attack our embassy, and make demands on us."

"That's right," Senator Russell, his fellow emphysema sufferer, supported his view.

The view of the other four senators was that Johnson should drop his concern over the words *discuss, review,* and *negotiate,* and magnanimously resume relations with Panama according to the OAS declaration. After all, they pointed out, even if he agreed to negotiate a new treaty, this did not bind him to whatever was produced. Said Fulbright, it was ridiculous for the United States to treat its troubles with tiny Panama "as a test of our courage and resolve."

Johnson's reaction was to turn with anger on the senators who wanted him to accept the OAS declaration. The last thing he would do, he declared, was make a new treaty just because mobs down in Panama were pressuring him. As he rumbled on, said one of those present, Johnson's derision of the conciliatory senators "was rough."

The following day the OAS was staging its third anniversary celebration of Kennedy's Alliance for Progress, with Johnson scheduled as the featured speaker. This was expected to be a bland affair at the Pan American Union. But Johnson shocked his audience when he digressed from his printed text of praise for the "Alianza" to disavow the OAS declaration on the Panama-United States squabble. Using a conciliatory tone to coat his words, he gave the impression that while he was patiently willing to do anything to bring agreement with Panama, the little country was holding out against a peaceful settlement. He said he would meet with Panama "any time, anywhere, to discuss anything, to work together, to cooperate with each other, to reason with one another, to review and to consider all of our desires and all our concerns, but we don't ask Panama to make any precommitments before we meet, and we intend to make none." Then he added in a weary manner, "As of this moment I do not believe there has been a genuine meeting of the minds between the two Presidents of the two countries involved."

This was not all. Listeners seethed when he implied that the OAS had tried to trick the United States. "Press reports indicate that the Government of Panama feels that the language which has been under consideration for many days commits the United States to a rewriting and a revision of the 1903 Treaty," Johnson said contemptuously. "We have made no such commitment, and we would not think of doing so before diplomatic relations are resumed and unless a fair and satisfactory adjustment is agreed upon."

In reply to this undiplomatic outburst by Johnson, the OAS struck back by giving its five-man mediation team an overwhelming vote of support. This led Johnson's foreign policy aides to wring their hands in concern that he was destroying goodwill for the United States throughout the Americas.

During the following week Johnson himself came belatedly to this view. On March 21 he opened the door on Press Secretary Reedy's news conference and told surprised reporters, "We are prepared to *review* every issue which now divides us, and every problem which the Panamanian Government wishes to raise. I don't say *discuss*," he went on, "because that is a sticky word. Some of them do not quite understand what it means. But I say *review*. We are glad to do that."

After this, Johnson gave the order to the State Department to sign an agreement on this score with Panama, and diplomatic relations were soon resumed. In addition he named Robert Anderson as his troubleshooting ambassador to do the reviewing of the sixty-one-year-old treaty and to find a new spot to build a sea-level canal to replace the Panama Canal. By September 1965, Johnson was so amenable that he promised President Robles of Panama a new treaty which would "recognize Panama's sovereignty" over the Canal Zone.

But in the eyes of Latin American diplomats, President Johnson's public display of irascibility and his unwillingness to accept a consensus of his "Good Neighbors" did not augur pleasant future relations.

Other countries saw different aspects of the new President's foreign policy methods that first year. The danger-fraught Cyprus crisis revealed a Johnson who did not want to commit the United States beyond the point of warning both Turkey and Greece that their continued antagonism over this Mediterranean island would benefit only the Communists. For the most part, as he put it, he preferred, on this squabble, to "hunker down like a jackrabbit in a hailstorm."

In 1960 the island of Cyprus had gained its independence from the British Empire with a written agreement by Britain at Zurich, Switzerland, to guarantee its freedom. Because of the rampant home-country nationalism of the two Cypriote groups, the 400,000 Greeks and the 100,000 Turks, a strange constitution of compromises had gone into effect. There would be a Greek President, a Turkish Vice President, and each community would have legal authority to veto government action involving it.

It was only a matter of time before this tenuous government produced bloodshed. A climax came when robed, bearded Archbishop Makarios, the President, decreed that no longer could the Turks retain their veto on the government. Fighting and killings resulted immediately, and with their home countries, Greece and Turkey, involving themselves in Cyprus' affairs, the British Ambassador to Washington told Undersecretary of State George Ball in January 1964 that his government could no longer guarantee peace on Cyprus. The British suggestion was that a NATO force take over this task.

Johnson, who was involved with Panama and with the need to gain a domestic legislative record for the forthcoming Presidential campaign, dumped the problem in Ball's lap, and the competent undersecretary hurried overseas to talk with the Greek and Turkish government leaders and with Makarios. A menacing note as he flew to the scene was the tough warning .from the Soviet Union that the establishment of another NATO stronghold would be "the source of international complications fraught with grave consequences."

Ball's stumbling block in his attempted settlement turned out to be the archbishop, who opposed the NATO peace-maintenance force at that time and preferred a UN Security Council endorsement of his government. "For God's sake, your Beatitude," Ball scolded him, "this killing must stop."

When Ball returned to Washington, after further visits to Ankara and Athens to restrain those governments from invading Cyprus, Johnson told him to have a memo covering his activities on the President's desk by nine o'clock the next morning, "and be damn sure it doesn't appear in *The New York Times* first."

The murders on Cyprus increased all that spring, and in June, preparatory to an invasion, the Turks bombed Greek installations on the island. On June 5 Rusk wrote a blunt letter for Johnson's signature to Turkish Premier General Ismet Inonu. The letter warned the Turks they must not use arms supplied them as a member of NATO against a NATO ally. The letter also told Inonu not to take any action without consulting the United States in advance, because a Turkish invasion of Cyprus would lead to war with Greece and "to the slaughter of tens of thousands of Turkish Cypriotes." In addition, Johnson wrote, if Turkey became involved in war with the Soviet Union, the other NATO nations would not come to her aid.

When the Turkish Government reacted by inviting Soviet trade experts and cultural personnel to Ankara to discuss friendship, Johnson took Ball's advice and invited Inonu and Greek Premier George Papandreou to the United States. Inonu visited the White House on June 22 and the Greek leader came on June 24, following a White House effort to get Greek-Americans to write to Greek officials in Athens on the need for a calm solution on Cyprus. Papandreou left the White House to denounce the Johnson-Inonu communiqué, calling for the "binding effects of existing treaties," a quotation that referred to the original treaty of independence, which bound England as guarantor of freedom. As for Johnson's suggestion that he negotiate directly with Inonu, Papandreou rejected this entirely, declaring that he wanted *enosis*, the union of Cyprus with Greece.

It was U Thant, the Secretary-General of the UN, who finally arranged talks on Cyprus in Geneva later in the summer, with the UN, Greece, Turkey, Britain, and the United States as participants. Johnson chose as his representative Dean Acheson, who had played a major role both in the Truman Doctrine for aid to Greece and Turkey against communism in 1947 and in the establishment of NATO. Here Acheson produced a plan for Cyprus' union with Greece, enclaves on the island for the Turkish population protected by a Turkish military base, and the cession of a Greek island in the Dodecanese to Turkey. Just when it appeared that his plan might be accepted, renewed fighting broke out on Cyprus, with Greek Cypriotes destroying Turkish villages, and Turkish military planes dumping their loads on Greek towns.

A truce came on August 9 only because the Soviet Union did not oppose a UN Security Council resolution calling for a cease fire and a UN police force on Cyprus. With peace restored momentarily, Acheson returned home to denounce Makarios as "a political priest with considerable gifts of demagogy and ruthlessness" who "threw monkey wrenches into the machinery."

In the case of Cyprus, the Johnson performance puzzled those familiar with his temper tantrums on Panama. One explanation for his aloof approach and his delegation of responsibility to Ball and Acheson was that the United States was not directly involved in the dispute. Another explanation was that as it dragged out, it would have cut into the time he needed to devote to the 1964 campaign.

If Johnson played the pious, public role of a man who earnestly wanted peace in Cyprus, in other areas he played the unpublicized role of a war maker.

One such place was Laos. Here in July 1962 President Kennedy, through Averell Harriman, had effected at another Geneva Conference a loose neutralization under Prince Souvanna Phouma, with the left-wing Pathet Lao leader Prince Souphanouvong and right-wing General Phoumi Nosavan as his Vice Premiers.

By 1964 the Pathet Lao officials had withdrawn from the capital at Vientiane, near the Thailand border, and began a military campaign to take over all of Laos. Johnson's reaction to this was to give a secret order to the United States Air Force to bomb Pathet Lao installations and strafe Pathet Lao troops. Only in June 1964, after months of such secretive activity, was the American war in Laos publicized, and then by the Chinese Communist press.

Johnson denied such activity when asked about it, and even when two American planes were shot down within Laos, he claimed they had been there on a peaceful mission, to search for violations of the 1962 neutralization agreement. After this, when the CIA pinpointed the location of the Pathet Lao headquarters and an American plane bombed it, Johnson blandly insisted this had been done by mistake. The Washington *Post,* so friendly to Johnson, considered the attacks and the denials puzzling activities, and complained in an editorial that "the country has come to a sad pass when it must turn to Communist China's New China News Agency for reports on covert military operations being conducted by the United States."

But this was not all. In Africa's Congo, Moise Tshombe, round-faced, bright-eyed Katanga Province leader, had gained control of the central government, and Johnson gave him secret air support in attacking rebel groups.

Following eighty years of ownership of the Congo and brutal suppression of her population, Belgium had agreed in 1960 to Congolese independence. Because the people had been kept uneducated, chaos enveloped the Congo and native power seekers fought each other with murder and imprisonment and exile. That same year the government of President Kasavubu, fearing a Communist takeover, asked the UN to step in with troops and economic aid, plus advisers to help write a new constitution.

When Kennedy became President, Moise Tshombe was the major problem in the Congo. Tshombe's Katanga Province had seceded from the government and multiplied the Congo's troubles because three-fifths of the nation's revenue came from Katanga's rich cobalt and copper mines. Furthermore, Tshombe was in league with the white mining interests, and had become a symbol of hatred to the rest of nationalist Africa, especially after he hired an army of white mercenaries and employed white lawyers to promote his cause before both the UN in New York and the American government in Washington.

One of his leading champions in Washington was Senator Thomas Dodd, a Johnson friend, who took up the cry for the "Katanga Freedom Fighters." At one point, Dodd, ostensibly as a member of the Senate Foreign Relations Committee, went to Katanga, where he was Tshombe's guest. Edmund Gullion, American Ambassador to the Congo, phoned Kennedy that Dodd was telling Tshombe that the State Department was influenced by international communism.

Despite Tshombe's pressure, Kennedy supported the UN effort to prevent a separation of Katanga from the rest of the Congo, because this would deprive the Congolese Government of 85 million dollars in annual copper-cobalt royalties. Another factor in Kennedy's decision was his unwillingness to associate the United States with Tshombe because of the latter's image in Africa. In December 1962 Tshombe's mercenaries boldly attacked the UN force, but when U Thant, the new UN Secretary-General, unhappily gave the order to return the fire, Tshombe's army collapsed in days, he fled to Europe, and Katanga was reunited with the Congo.

But Tshombe had a charmed life, and in June 1963 he was back in the Congolese capital of Leopoldville as Prime Minister of the entire country. However, his hold was shaky, and when the UN army quit the Congo in

June 1964 for lack of funds, various tribes began a fight with his government to win their local independence.

It was at this point that Johnson, after talks with Dodd, came to Tshombe's aid by permitting United States pilots to join Tshombe's air force in attacking the rebels. Then, when the secessionists held hostages in Stanleyville, Johnson ordered an airlift rescue operation to save them. Here again it was the Washington *Post* that carried the news of Johnson's aid to the hated Tshombe. "In the Congo," said the *Post,* "the Peiping news agency accused the United States of air strikes against rebels in Kivu Province. The State Department first issued a denial and yesterday, embarrassed by news reports, confessed that Americans under contract to the Congo had flown the planes. What in heaven's name does the United States think it is doing by trying to keep these air strikes secret?"

But secret or open air strikes, Moise Tshombe could not be maintained in power. General Joseph Mobutu took over, Tshombe went into hurried exile with a price on his head, and chaos returned to the Congo, despite a misleading billboard at the Leopoldville airport, which announced: "Welcome, amiable tourists to the land of hospitality. Visit the interior and see picturesque falls, pygmies and volcanoes in eruption"—plus the Congolese in eruption, the sign might have added.

Shortly after he took office, heads of foreign governments realized that Johnson was evaluating them entirely in terms of their country's power and the degree to which they supported his policy in Southeast Asia.

An early use of the Johnson scale of values involved Pakistan's President Ayub Khan and India's Prime Minister Lal Bahadur Shastri. Ayub had been a guest on the L.B.J. Ranch when Johnson was Vice President, and he looked forward to his invitation to visit the White House in April 1965. Shastri was to come in June.

However, early in April, Johnson suddenly announced he had cancelled both visits because he could not spare the time to see them. Ayub and Shastri immediately had unpleasant comments to make about their rude party-spoiler, especially when they noted that Johnson had not called off the visit of South Korea's President, an American puppet. One White House aide offered the explanation that Johnson did not want to give Ayub, who was friendly to Red China, the opportunity to blow communism in his face; nor did he want to listen to Shastri's plea to stop the escalation of the Vietnam war. Johnson privately claimed he had committed his diplomatic sin because the two were unpopular with Congress, and the foreign aid bill was coming up for consideration. "Suppose your mother-in-law dropped in on you just five minutes before you were supposed to go to a baseball game?" he asked in a defensive tone. "Well, that's the way it was with me."

Johnson's animosity toward Shastri was later transferred to Indira Gandhi, Nehru's daughter, who succeeded to Shastri's post as Prime Minister early in 1966, on the death of the little leader. Mrs. Gandhi visited Johnson in March, when the question of foreign aid to the half-billion people of India was discussed. American aid to India was then running at an annual rate of sixty-five cents per capita compared with $20.69 for Libya.

After agreeing to a two-million-ton food shipment for famine-hit India, Johnson suddenly ordered shipment held up in November 1966. The official reasons given the press were the Administration's desire that India reform its agricultural products distribution system and also liberalize its laws pertaining to foreign investors. However, the real reason was Mrs. Gandhi's opposition to a continuation of U. S. bombing of North Vietnam. "I'm damned tired of people taking our aid and then slapping the hand that feeds them," Johnson told a reporter, expressing ire toward Mrs. Gandhi for holding a meeting in New Delhi with Yugoslavia's Communist President Tito and Egypt's President Nasser and stealing headlines from his own Manila Conference on Vietnam.

But following Johnson's order to stop food shipment, one month later Canada gave India a gift of 250,000 tons of wheat; the Soviet Union 200,-000 tons; and Australia 150,000 tons. Solely because of the Soviet gift, Johnson decided he had to offset the Communists and he grudgingly ended his freeze on December 22, 1966.

Any foreign leader who made a remark against a Johnson policy while on American soil could expect a personal show of Presidential ire. Canada's Prime Minister Lester "Mike" Pearson stopped in Philadelphia on April 2, 1965, on his way to a meeting with Johnson at Camp David, Maryland, and he spoke out for an end to American bombing in North Vietnam. Word of this reached Johnson, of course, and when Pearson arrived, Johnson's lips were set in tight, parallel lines. Almost their entire meeting vanished with Johnson on the phone making calls. Then afterward, Johnson warned the Canadian Ambassador to the United States: "Don't let your man come down here again to make speeches."

To gain American aid, British Prime Minister Harold Wilson was willing to support Johnson's foreign policy. Johnson liked this, but he despised the Wilson penchant for making trips to Washington to be photographed with him in order to help his sagging political image back home. At one time the London *Daily Mail* commented on these frequent cross-Atlantic flights that "the nation is becoming accustomed to waving farewell to Mr. Wilson just as things get uncomfortable." On one occasion, when Wilson begged Johnson to let him come to Washington, Johnson screamed over trans-Atlantic phone, "I won't have you electioneering on my doorstep. Every time you get in trouble with Parliament you run over here with your shirt-tail hanging out. I'm not going to allow it this time."

Another visitor who felt the lash of Johnson's long tongue was Fernando Maria Castiella, the Spanish Foreign Minister, who visited Johnson early in 1965. Castiella was in the midst of flattering Johnson by bragging about his own Texas relatives on his mother's side when Johnson interrupted with a snarling demand that he explain why Franco Spain was doing business with Castro Cuba. Castiella was giving his reasons when Johnson spat at him, "Ol' Pat McCarran would turn in his grave if he knew what you were doing." (McCarran had been the Senate's chief apologist for the Spanish dictatorship, as well as its principal lobbyist for American aid.) Castiella left the oval room bristling in anger.

When a visitor represented a country that had neither power nor meaningful prestige to lend the United States in backing Johnson's foreign policy, Johnson had little time to spare. The Prime Minister of Trinidad came for a Presidential appointment, was kept waiting an hour and a half, and then was dismissed by Johnson after a quick handshake and a loud "Howdy." When Prince Bernhard of the Netherlands came for his appointment on April 13, 1965, Johnson would not confer with him in private but called out instead to a dozen persons who were watching the official greeting, "Come on, have your picture taken with a *real* prince!" Prime Minister Bjarni Benediktsson of Iceland came for a conference, and Johnson had him join a fifteen-minute walk around the South Lawn with reporters. "That's the Washington Monument," Johnson told his visitor, pointing to the Jefferson Memorial. Johnson also introduced him to one of his beagles and confided, "Him is a little bit stubborn. He's the one that got me in all that trouble." Then they walked back to his office with a lady reporter who was invited inside to talk about her home-state politics. After she and Johnson talked through the next fifteen minutes, Johnson stood up and dismissed the astonished Icelander, who had been unable to squeeze in a single word about the subject of their meeting. "It's been very good to see you, Mr. Prime Minister"—Johnson waved him out—"and I'll look forward to seeing you again."

Such ignominious treatment was not accorded Ferdinand Marcos, the President of the Philippines, when he came on a visit with his beautiful wife Imelda. Johnson held a party for them, and he danced with her. Then Imelda entertained the gathering by singing a song to Johnson that was titled, "Because of You."

Later, when the couple left the United States, a White House aide commented on Marcos' success in getting the economic and military aid for which he had asked. "He's taking back everything but the crown jewels," was the analysis of the Marcos visit.

An imprudent remark could be costly to a foreign visitor no matter how dire his problem. Israeli Foreign Minister Abba Eban discovered this at the end of May 1967 when he flew to the United States to see Johnson about the climactic crisis with Egypt over Nasser's closing of the Gulf of Aqaba to Israeli vessels and the massing of the Arab armies to push Israeli citizens "into the sea."

Before he called the White House to arrange an appointment, Eban unwisely told reporters he would meet with Johnson. When Johnson read this on the news teletype machine, despite the crisis he ordered Marvin Watson to keep Eban away for an entire day as punishment. Eban was told he could not see the President until late the following evening because Johnson was too busy. And while Eban suffered great anxiety because of the worsening situation at home, Johnson spent a long day conferring at leisure with the newly arrived ambassador from Iran, bidding farewell to the Italian ambassador, discussing local problems at home with the ambassadors of El Salvador, Venezuela, and Peru, and accepting a season pass to the soccer games of the Washington Whips.

When Eban finally saw him, Johnson was vague about an American commitment. Eban had a copy of the Dulles Aide-Mémoire of 1957, which declared that "the Gulf of Aqaba comprehends international waters and that no nation has the right to prevent free and innocent passage through the Straits." If Johnson would agree to send an American ship into the Gulf, the Egyptians were bound to backtrack rather than take on the United States. But although Johnson said he agreed with the Dulles statement, he warned Eban against Israel's going to war with Egypt to end the blockade.

If Eban considered that Johnson had been rough with him, he should have sat in on some of Johnson's staff meetings with foreign affairs employees and advisers. At one such meeting, Johnson belittled Dean Acheson, who sincerely admired him, by replying to an Acheson comment: "You're the man who got us into the war in Korea, and we had to get Eisenhower to get us out of it."

Acheson made no reply. However, after Johnson bullyragged Undersecretary of State Ball and Secretary of Defense McNamara as incompetent "experts" and purveyors of false information, Acheson could stand it no longer and he barged in with "Mr. President, you don't pay these men enough to talk to them that way—even with the federal pay raise."

Chapter 73

JOHNSON'S INTERVENTION IN the Dominican Republic's fratricidal spat in the spring of 1965 was a classic example of the way he reacted to a crisis in the Western Hemisphere. The key to his response was the identification of the rebel forces in any uprising. In his view, there was nothing to admire about a military *coup* against a democratic regime. However, if this was a homegrown business that was not directed from the outside, it was not to be condemned. In contrast, a leftist rebellion against any regime was *ipso facto* a Communist conspiracy from abroad intent on establishing a second Castro Cuba in the Americas. As such, it must be opposed with all the strength the United States could muster. In Johnson's black-white appraisal of the Dominican Republic's troubles, the rebellion in 1965 was of this variety.

On May 30, 1961, following thirty-one years of operating the Dominican Republic as a prison-state, sadistic dictator General Rafael Trujillo was killed. Kennedy rushed economic, political, and social-welfare aid, and in December 1962 the three million people who had lived through a long nightmare participated in a free election, choosing writer-philosopher Juan Bosch as their President. As his representative to Bosch's inauguration in February 1963, Kennedy sent Johnson; and following Johnson's bear hugs of the white-haired new leader, in the name of the Alliance for Progress, Bosch gave Lady Bird copies of his short stories and his biography of David.

But the weak and inept Bosch could not cope with the enormous problems he inherited, and the people remained as poor as before, with few reforms undertaken to improve their lot. Bosch made no effort to dismiss or separate the right-wing military men, who remained virtually as intact as they had been under Trujillo. As a result, only seven months after the Bosch Government began, it succumbed to a military *coup,* and Bosch fled to Puerto Rico to add further time to the twenty years he had already spent in exile.

A three-man military *junta* succeeded Bosch on September 26, 1963, and eventually power went to Donald Reid Cabral, of one of the island's "better" families. Reid was serious about improving his country and he undertook an economic austerity program. To his credit, he also made an effort to fire some of the corrupt and power-greedy generals, but his sincerity on both scores aroused the animosity of the hungry peasants, burdened by an unprofitable sugar economy, and the arrogant generals. By 1965 he was doomed, despite some accomplishments.

United States Ambassador W. Tapley Bennett had gone back to Washington to ask for a commitment of twenty-five million dollars in aid for Reid when the rebellion broke out back on the island on Saturday, April 24, 1965. That day Reid had received word that some young Bosch army officers were planning a *coup* against his government, and he sent his army chief of staff to their camp to arrest them. However, they outnumbered the arresting group and seized the general.

Word of their action spread swiftly into the capital of Santo Domingo, where Bosch supporters seized the government-owned Radio Santo Domingo that afternoon and yelled into its microphones that the revolution had begun and the fight was now on to restore Bosch to the Presidency. The radio station was retaken by Reid, who could have squashed the opposition by swift follow-through action. However, General Wessin y Wessin, one of the top military men, was more interested in forcing Reid out and taking charge, and this excellent opportunity to demolish the would-be revolters was lost while Wessin became boss.

That same evening the Bosch forces—now called the *Rebels*—undertook to arm civilians to fight the right-wing generals led by Wessin and his followers—now called the *Loyalists*. About ten thousand weapons, including machine guns and bazookas, were passed out, and the Rebel section of the capital became an armed fortress. The city fell siege to rioting, fires, and killings, and the death toll quickly mounted.

Now that he had pushed Reid out of power, Wessin attempted to destroy the Rebels quickly. In an effort to bring his Loyalist troops from their suburban fortress at San Isidro into the city, he ordered them to cross over the Duarte Bridge. But the Rebels met his force along the way, and after a prolonged exchange of firing occurred, the frightened Loyalists retreated. While this was going on, Loyalist airplanes bombed Rebel strongholds inside the city. By midnight the city had no electricity or water, the streets were filled with corpses, and the police force was eight hundred men short because of a Rebel ruse of putting in calls for emergencies and then killing the arriving policemen.

Just twenty-four hours after the attempt to arrest the young officers at the camp, hundreds of Americans and foreign nationals collected at the Embajador Hotel for the trip to the port of Haina, where the American Navy would evacuate them to Puerto Rico. While they were there, Rebels attempted to drag off a Loyalist; the Loyalists fired at the Rebels; and bullets flew about the hotel for four hours. No foreigner was hit, and none was in danger after this incident.

On Monday, April 26, Ambassador Bennett was told to return to Santo Domingo. Johnson personally gave him orders that under no condition did he want "another Cuba in this hemisphere." Above all, said Johnson, he did not want the return of Bosch to power. "Giving the Dominican Republic back to Juan Bosch," he remarked, "would be like turning it over to Arthur Schlesinger, Jr."

Certainly there were Communists among the Rebels, and they were disciplined to play a role far greater than their numbers would indicate. But in that early period of the rebellion they did not hold key positions among the Rebels, whose acting President was non-Communist José Rafael Molina Ureña, a high official in the Bosch Dominican Revolutionary Party (PRD). Nevertheless, Bennett made the assumption that all the Rebels were Communists, and because Johnson's order was not to permit Bosch back into power, he must work on the side of the Loyalists.

The chaos might have ended on Tuesday had Bennett not taken this view.

He showed his bias that afternoon when two of the Rebel leaders, Colonel Francisco Caamaño Deñó and Colonel Miguel Angel Hernando Ramirez, and six of their aides came to the U.S. Embassy to ask him to initiate talks with the Loyalists to arrange a cease-fire. Bennett saw this as an effort by the Rebels to gain a breathing spell and stave off an imminent Loyalist invasion of their stronghold inside the city. So he coldly rejected their plea and lectured them on the sin of permitting Reds to "take advantage of their legitimate movement." Shortly afterward, when acting Rebel President Molina took refuge in the Colombian Embassy, Bennett believed the rebellion was on the verge of collapsing.

But he was wrong. Certainly Wessin had another advantage besides Bennett's support, for he possessed tanks; and late on Tuesday, when one of his tank units crossed into town over the Duarte Bridge, the Rebels panicked. Had he continued forward, the Rebels would have surrendered, as they later admitted. However, he feared Molotov cocktails in the alley-like streets, and in fear he pulled back his tanks. At sight of this, the Rebel forces gained courage, and on Wednesday, April 28, they were ready for further fighting.

This was the decisive day for Johnson. Bennett sent three cables that day to the State Department, all of which were later published. The first message, coming shortly after noon, read:

While I regret reliance on a military solution for a political crisis engendered by a confused, democratic left, all valid elements of which are either in hiding as much from the extremists (in their own camp) as from the military forces, the plain fact is that while leftist propaganda may fuzz the issue, the issue here now is a fight between Castro-type elements and those who oppose. I do not wish to be overdramatic but we should be clear as to the situation. If we deny communication equipment and the anti-Rebel forces lose for lack of heart, we may well be asked in the near future for landings of Marines to protect United States citizens and possibly for other purposes.

At 3 P.M. Bennett sent a second cable, disclosing that Colonel Pedro Bartolomé Benoit, a Loyalist right-wing leader, had asked for twelve hundred U. S. Marines to aid him. Bennett said, "He was given no encouragement. I do not believe the situation justifies it."

Then at 5:15 P.M. came Bennett's third cable. He described Wessin's Loyalists as "tired and discouraged" and said that when one of his men visited the Loyalist base at San Isidro, a top officer was in a "hysterical mood, urging retreat . . . a number of officers [were] weeping." Bennett concluded that with the situation "deteriorating rapidly . . . I recommend immediate landings" of Marines. Bennett suggested that the excuse could be "the purpose of protecting the evacuation of American citizens."

The U. S. Aircraft Carrier *Boxer* with eighteen hundred Marines aboard had been lying off the Dominican coast since Sunday. At 6:30 P.M. Johnson ordered the Marines to land.

To head off possible Congressional opposition to his move as a form of "gunboat diplomacy," Johnson asked legislative leaders to a White House meeting an hour after giving the landing order. When they came, he said bluntly that the requirement for speed had made it necessary for him to ignore Congress until after he had acted. As for the reason for his decision, he said that the sole purpose was to protect American lives. Then he read the group a statement he intended to deliver over TV shortly afterward, and the only suggestion came from Mike Mansfield, who wondered why he did not mention the Organization of American States, since the OAS held primacy on inter-American affairs. "Good idea, Mike," he said, telling Rusk to scribble in a few kind words for the OAS. No one bothered to ask if he had notified José Mora, the Secretary-General of OAS, of the landing.

"The United States Government has been informed by military authorities in the Dominican Republic that American lives are in danger. . . . Four hundred Marines have already been landed," he told his TV audience at 8:50 P.M. José Mora happened to have his set turned on at the time, and he learned about the American unilateral action in the Caribbean.

Once the action was under way, Johnson insisted that the historic record must justify his decision. One aspect of this meant that Ambassador Bennett had to climb into a helicopter and fly almost twenty miles to visit Colonel Benoit, who had asked for Marines in the 3 P.M. cable. In a predated dictated statement, which he signed the day after the landing began, Benoit said: "American lives are in danger and conditions of public disorder make it impossible to provide adequate protection. I therefore ask you for temporary intervention and assistance in restoring order in this country."

Johnson also wanted the record to show that the National Security Council had deliberated the intervention question, and he held an NSC meeting after the fact. This was an instance he likened to his intervention in Vietnam, describing it as being "just like the Alamo. . . . It would be hard for me to live in this Hemisphere if I sent in the Marines, and I couldn't live in this country if I didn't," he yelled, with a sweeping-arm gesture. "Hell, it's just like you were down at that gate, and you were surrounded, and you damn well needed somebody. . . . Well, by God, I'm gonna go."

Yet for all his bravado, he experienced real terror shortly after the first Marines were to have come ashore. About fifteen feet away from his Oval Office desk, Johnson kept two teletype ticker machines, and one report that clattered on the UPI machine stated that twelve thousand Rebels were on hand to kill the U. S. Marines as they landed. Johnson ripped the paper from the machine and in great agitation called Defense Secretary McNamara to determine the accuracy of the news item.

McNamara immediately phoned General Earle Wheeler, chairman of the Joint Chiefs of Staff, who called one of his colonels, who called General

Bruce Palmer, the American commander in the field. But by then, Johnson had already talked to Palmer, who assured him that the landings were without mishap, and his regular breathing resumed.

On the following day, when the Loyalist forces, with the moral backing of the Marines, failed to enter the Rebel fortress area in downtown Santo Domingo, Johnson was in a quandary. The initial Marine intervention had secured the area around the Embajador Hotel for the airlift evacuation of Americans and foreign nationals. But if the Marines now left, the Rebels would probably win. So at 11 P.M. on Thursday, April 29, Johnson ordered two thousand troops of the Eighty-Second Airborne Division to land in the Dominican Republic.

That day, too, he decided that the OAS should meet to approve, as a multi-nation organization, what he had done on his own. His blunt instructions to Ellsworth Bunker, the United States Ambassador to OAS, were to bring about such collective agreement, though he did not believe the OAS was capable of arriving at any decision without being forced into it or of following through on any course of action once it made a decision. As he put it, "The OAS couldn't pour piss out of a boot if the instructions were written on the heel."

When the OAS met all day Thursday until 2 A.M. on Friday, April 30, Johnson was furious that it had not made its decision to support U. S. action, and his anger increased when Bunker told him that it had adjourned until Saturday. "The only thing they're interested in is the cocktail hour," he barked.

That night he appeared again on TV, this time to scold the OAS. "The eyes of the hemisphere are now on the OAS," he said unpleasantly. "Loss of time may mean that it's too late to preserve the freedom which alone can lead to the establishment of true democracy." On Saturday, despite many misgivings, the OAS gave him the hemispheric support that he ordered.

However, by now Johnson was under blistering attack from Walter Lippmann, the ADA, *The New York Times,* the Washington *Post,* and a long string of college professors, who charged him with supporting military dictators in the Western Hemisphere. An editorial in *The New York Times* charged him with showing "little awareness . . . that the Dominican people—not just a handful of Communists—were fighting and dying for social justice and constitutionalism."

As the attacks built up against him, Johnson did not hold his peace but lashed out at his critics in an intemperate display of ridicule and self-justification. If he had done nothing, he insisted, things would have been worse. "When you duck, dodge, hesitate, and shimmy, every man and his dog gives you a kick." He made personal phone calls to editors for hours on end to denounce their charges; and he told newsmen in dizzying walks around the South Lawn that their patriotic duty was not to criticize him. And the more he railed, the wider grew the credibility gap.

There was the concocted story he told at a news conference to show that the intervention was based on human kindness. "It has been necessary for a few Marines," he said in justification, "to go out and take an old lady and her little belongings—and with a crippled hip—and carry her down through the streets where the firing is taking place."

Then there was his fanciful tale to base his action on supposed attacks on the American Embassy, which he claimed lay in the midst of a battleground. "There has been almost constant firing on our American Embassy," he excitedly told reporters. "As we talked to Ambassador Bennett, he said to apparently one of the girls who brought him a cable, he said, please get away from the window, that glass is going to cut your head, because the glass had been shattered, and we heard the bullets coming through the office where he was sitting while talking to us."

Added to this tale was another imaginary scene, which he described to a later news conference: "Some fifteen hundred innocent people were murdered and shot, and their heads cut off, and . . . as we talked to our ambassador to confirm the horror and tragedy and the unbelievable fact that they were firing on Americans and the American Embassy, he was talking to us from under a desk, while bullets were going through his windows, and he had a thousand American men, women, and children assembled in the hotel who were pleading with their President to help preserve their lives."

Ambassador Bennett was stunned when he heard of Johnson's description and called this entire story a fabrication when hailed before the Senate Foreign Relations Committee. He had never had to hide under his desk, the Embassy had not been splattered with a continual barrage of bullets, and no one had been beheaded.

When the attacks on Johnson continued, he dropped his stated reason for the intervention—to save American lives on the island—and found a new justification that made his detractors appear un-American. His new argument was the one that had motivated him from the outset—his concern that Communists might establish a second beachhead in the Western Hemisphere unless he intervened.

On Friday night, April 30, he unveiled this new approach on TV when he said, "There are signs that people trained outside the Dominican Republic are seeking to gain control." Then two days later, on Sunday, May 2, having made this start, he added to this picture with another TV speech, telling the nation that "what began as a popular democratic revolution, committed to democracy and social justice, very shortly moved and was taken over and really seized and placed into the hands of a band of Communist conspirators."

Johnson's weariness in that Sunday speech revealed itself when he repeated two entire paragraphs. Nor was his argument aided when he said in the speech that he had been in touch with the former President of Venezuela, the liberal anti-Communist Romulo Betancourt, for "counsel and advice." Reporters learned that he had not talked to Betancourt, and that the Venezuelan's analysis of the Dominican situation was that the Communists had not gained control of the rebellion. One newsman wanted to know why Johnson had not gone to the aid of the Rebels when they first rebelled, if he thought they were "popular" and "democratic."

At the outset Johnson had asked the new CIA boss, Admiral William Raborn, for information regarding Red penetration of the Rebels, and the answer was that perhaps two Red agents held positions of power in the Rebel force. When Johnson's man-on-the-scene, the magazine writer and former ambassador to the Dominican Republic John Bartlow Martin, telephoned him on Saturday, May 1, that he was "now convinced after having talked to many people on the Rebel side that this is Communist-dominated," Johnson pressed Raborn's phone button and ordered a new Red count.

"After I tell you this," he snapped, "I don't want to hear anything but the click of your phone. I want seventy-five of your people in the countryside down there today. And if you need a submarine to get 'em in, we'll get you one."

A frenzied effort to prove Johnson's point began, and Raborn soon phoned Johnson with fifty-four names, a more than sufficient number to substantiate Johnson's new justification. However, here again, a press check revealed that some of those named as Reds were dead and others were not in the Dominican Republic.

With the continuing attacks on his motives, Johnson made a further effort to justify intervention on Monday, May 3, by racing in his limousine to the Washington Hilton Hotel for an impromptu talk to the AFL-CIO Building Trades Council. "Now I am the most denounced man in the world," he wailed to the union crowd, asking for its support. "All the Communist nations have a regular program on me that runs twenty-four hours a day. Some of the non-Communist nations just kind of practice on me." Some who were present called his exhibition "very embarrassing to listen to and watch."

"What is important is that we know, and that they know, and that everybody knows, that we don't propose to sit here in our rocking chair with our hands folded and let the Communists set up any government in the Western Hemisphere!" Johnson screamed. "If they are going to put American lives in danger, where American citizens go, that flag [he turned and indicated with a long finger the American flag behind him] goes with them to protect them!"

Yes, to justify his intervention in the Dominican Republic, he told the labor leaders, he was reminded of the time Senator Huey Long of Louisiana went into Arkansas to campaign for tiny, quiet Mrs. Hattie Caraway for the United States Senate in 1932. Senator Joe Robinson, also of Arkansas, had denounced Long on the Senate floor for his "invasion," said Johnson, and Long walked over to Robinson to explain to the Democratic leader,

"I wasn't in Arkansas to dictate to any human being. All I went to Arkansas for was to pull those big, pot-bellied politicians off this poor little woman's neck." (The facts of Huey Long's invasion of Arkansas were otherwise. He and Robinson were enemies and were not on speaking terms. In addition, it was Robinson who supported Mrs. Caraway's opponent.)

Throughout all the charges and countercharges, activity was proceeding on the Dominican front. In time 31,000 Marines were present, and they quietly joined with the Loyalists to make it impossible for the Rebels to gain military control. Once, when Johnson heard reports that Commanding General Palmer was openly sanctioning Marine combat against the Rebels instead of remaining a covert ally of the Loyalists, he ordered Cy Vance, the Deputy Defense Secretary, to check this.

"Tell Palmer," he warned, "I'm going to bust him down to private, just another buck private, if he doesn't have the right answers."

After the fighting fronts gained a semblance of stability, a four-OAS-nation peace force landed in May. Then Ambassador Ellsworth Bunker and other OAS diplomats went through four months of labor before both sides would agree to a cease-fire in September 1965 and the establishment of a provisional government under Garcia Godoy until an election could be held. By then 35 Marines were killed and 192 were wounded, and two reporters were killed by Marines. It was a year later, in June 1966, that the election was held, with Bosch a surprising loser to right-wing Joaquin Balaguer, and the Dominican crisis ended for the time being.

From this episode Johnson emerged with a tarnished image. His credibility gap was widened, the American liberals were lost to him, and his reputation was now that of a fast-shooting Commander-in-Chief who manufactured reasons to suit his actions. This would harm him in the major undertaking of his Administration—the waging of war in Vietnam.

PART NINE
Vietnam Escalator

Chapter 74

It all seems to have been in vain. Memories are short and appetites for power and glory are insatiable. Old tyrants depart. New ones take their place. Old allies become the foe. The recent enemy becomes the friend. It's all very baffling and trying.

— *From the remarks by Harry Truman to Lyndon Johnson on the Cold War, in January 1966, when President Johnson presented him and Mrs. Truman with applications Nos. 1 and 2 for Medicare.*

I'd like to have a Scotch and water right now. But I can't. I've got planes out tonight.

— *Lyndon Johnson to a visitor on the burdens of the war in Vietnam, quoted in* The New York Times, *May 23, 1965.*

ALTHOUGH VIETNAM REMAINED a center of turmoil and intrigue following World War II and the Geneva Conference on Indochina in 1954 (see Chapter 41), it did not gain and hold front-page attention in the United States until late in 1963.

In reality the Geneva agreements had been a surprising military settlement. For after France's disastrous defeat at Dien Bien Phu, following eight years of war against the Vietminh, the loss of tens of thousands of men, and the expenditure of billions of dollars, the Communist Ho Chi Minh, with control over three-fourths of the southern sector of Vietnam, could easily have overrun the rest of the South.

Instead, Ho had agreed at Geneva to withdraw his military forces north of the Seventeenth Parallel and leave the South to Emperor Bao Dai, the fun-seeking chief of state living a high life on the French Riviera. Furthermore, although the French, after almost a century of brutal political control, were now deprived of their colony, their businessmen were permitted to continue as before in the South.

President Eisenhower's explanation for Ho's generosity at Geneva had been a self-praising claim by the President that the Chinese Reds feared an American nuclear attack if Ho insisted on all of Vietnam. Some observers, on the other hand, believed that the Soviet Union had forced Ho into this decision so that the appreciative French would then reject the Eisenhower proposal that France join a European Defense Community.

Yet there existed another important factor. As the man who had fought the longest against French tyranny in Indochina, and as the best known man in Vietnam, Ho Chi Minh expected to win handily in the July 1956 national election, called for by the Geneva agreements to unify North and South into a single Vietnam. So far as he judged matters, the split at the Seventeenth Parallel would be of only a temporary two-year duration.

Prior to Geneva, the policy of the United States had been to back the French in their attempt to regain colonial mastery after the Japanese occupation in World War II. And following Geneva, the Eisenhower policy was set on preventing Ho from taking over the entire Vietnamese people by denying him the promised election.

Under the agreements, Ho was to pull his Vietminh armies out of the South, and most of his forces withdrew above the Seventeenth Parallel. However, he was not a naïve sort, and as a precautionary measure, he left strategic guerrilla groups behind with ample supplies of arms.

When the dissolute Bao Dai elected to remain in Europe, he appointed a Vietnamese nationalist, Ngo Dinh Diem (*Dzee-em*), a short, broad-faced man in a business suit, as his premier. Diem stemmed from a highly respected mandarin family in Hue that had served Annamite emperors as administrators since the 1500's. The Ngos were strong Catholics, having been converted by missionaries before the United States was founded. What Diem and Ho Chi Minh had in common was a hatred of Caucasians and a dislike and distrust of Chinese.

The situation that Diem stepped into was disheartening from every approach. The people were exhausted from years of ceaseless war; malnutrition and disease were rampant; Diem's army commander, General Nguyen Van Hinh, would not take orders from him; and Bao Dai, with frequent pangs of jealousy, was dispatching demands to Diem to resign. Added to these problems, the agreements had called for freedom of movement in both temporary sections of Vietnam, and a million persons had run southward across the Seventeenth Parallel to escape the Communist reign of brutality directed from Ho's capital at Hanoi. About 90 per cent of these refugees were Catholics who hurried into the Buddhist South because the northern Communists were in process of killing almost 100,000 known anti-Communists and landlords.

But these were not all of Diem's difficulties. The French had not trained a native civil service, and he had to organize a government. Then there was the gangster sect, the Binh Xuyen, which under French rule had run the national police and operated the gambling and prostitution concessions in Saigon and other cities. In addition, a large part of South Vietnam was the fiefdom of two religious sects, the Hoa Hao and the Cao Dai, which possessed their own armies and controlled over three million people in the area north and west of Saigon.

"I can lift my telephone, issue one command, and have Diem deposed in a few moments' time," Army General Hinh openly boasted. And he could have, at the outset. When, a short time later, Diem ordered him to go to France "for indefinite study," Hinh induced the gangster Binh Xuyen leader to join him in cabling Bao Dai to fire Diem. But Diem outmaneuvered General Hinh by intriguing with his junior officers at the Saigon army posts. Finally Hinh, in fear of his life, quit Vietnam, and Diem appointed a personal friend, General Le Van Ty, to succeed him.

Diem moved now against his other opponents. When he closed the gambling and prostitution dens in Saigon, the Binh Xuyen announced a declaration of war. But Diem's army routed the gangsters and ended their police rule. He also weakened the autonomous religious sects that were in opposition to him by impressing their armies into his own.

In October 1955 Diem held a referendum to let the people of South Vietnam choose between himself and Bao Dai. His popularity was such that he drew crowds of thousands of cone-shape-hatted peasants in the cities he visited. "Ten thousand years for our Premier Diem!" was a common call to him from admirers. Even had he done no campaigning, it was apparent he would have overwhelmingly defeated the absent Bao Dai. But Diem had already begun to develop a dictator complex, and with the help of one of his brothers he rigged the totals so that he emerged with 98 per cent of the votes. Now he called himself President and Chief of State, the one-man boss of South Vietnam.

With the backing of President Eisenhower and Secretary of State Dulles, Diem refused in 1956 to permit the India-Canada-Poland International Control Commission, established under the Geneva agreements, to hold the promised national election and unify Vietnam. Diem's excuse was the lame argument that South Vietnam had not signed the Geneva agreements, but it was obvious to observers that Ho would have been an easy victor over Diem even in an honest election in both sectors. "I will not permit the eleven million people of our area to be surrendered into the clutches of the Vietminh," Diem announced, adding the extra excuse that Ho Chi Minh would not allow a free election among North Vietnam's thirteen million citizens. Diem might also have stated that he would have nothing to do with the wispy-bearded Red leader who had years earlier ordered Diem's brother, Ngo Dinh Khoi, buried alive.

So the two Vietnams went their separate ways, with the Eisenhower Administration taking nominal tutelage over the South. An Eisenhower letter to Diem, dated October 23, 1954, which offered Diem American economic aid on the condition that he reform his government, was later seized upon by Lyndon Johnson as the basis for his own war there. But Eisenhower made no promise of military intervention to maintain South Vietnam's continued existence.

The Eisenhower letter, which was so misused later, read:

> I am, accordingly, instructing the American Ambassador . . . to examine with you in your capacity as Chief of Government, how an intelligent program of American aid given directly to your government can serve to assist Vietnam in its present hour of trial, provided that your Government is pre-

pared to give assurances as to the standards of performance it would be able to maintain in the event such aid is supplied.

The purpose of this offer is to assist the Government of Vietnam in developing and maintaining a strong, viable state, capable of resisting attempted subversion or aggression through military means. The Government of the United States expects that this aid will be met by performance on the part of the Government of Vietnam in undertaking needed reforms. It hopes that such aid, combined with your own continuing efforts, will contribute effectively toward an independent Vietnam, endowed with a strong Government. Such a Government would, I hope, be so responsive to the nationalistic aspirations of its people, so enlightened in purpose and effective performance, that it will be respected both at home and abroad and discourage any who might wish to impose a foreign ideology on your free people.

Backed by American aid, Diem proved an excellent government administrator during his first few years in office. About six hundred American military advisers, known as the American Military Assistance Advisory Group, were helping to train his new army of 150,000 men, and American military equipment was sent for their use. The United States also sent trucks and ships to resettle refugees under Diem's land-reform program, and Diem made use of American technical assistance to improve education, public health, and agriculture. New methods doubled the rice crop, and rubber and pig production rose markedly. "I am determined to show the whole world," said Diem, "a contrast between our free land, where the people have liberty and are governed by duly elected representatives, and the slave regime of the Communists in the North."

But by 1957 the character of the Diem regime changed, as he took on authoritarian control over South Vietnam. He instituted censorship over the press, barred anti-Diem remarks in parliament, and added to the prison population of Communists those non-Communists who expressed opposition to him. He also extended one-man rule into the thousands of villages of South Vietnam, where villagers had elected village chiefs probably before the time of Chinese control over Vietnam, which dated from 111 B.C. to A.D. 907. Diem now moved in, ousted the elected headmen, and arbitrarily installed his own men from Saigon to run the villages. In addition, his regime took on an anti-Buddhist tone as he chose members of his family to serve as his chief advisers. These included his brother, Roman Catholic Archbishop Ngo Dinh Thuc; another brother, Ngo Dinh Can, who ran the central section of South Vietnam with unbridled one-man savagery; and a third brother, the overbearing Ngo Dinh Nhu, plus his wife, the outrageously dictatorial Madame Nhu, who was given authority by her brother-in-law to decree the morals of Saigon.

In February 1957 came the first attempt by non-Communist opponents of Diem to assassinate him; and when it failed, he retaliated by a renewed reign of terror and murders. Many who escaped death wound up in his concentration camps. The Eisenhower Administration was apprised of these goings-on, and at any point Eisenhower might have fallen back on his letter of October 23, 1954, to demand democratic reforms as a *quid pro quo* for continued aid. But Eisenhower remained silent.

By 1960, with Diem living in splendid isolation from his cruelly treated countrymen, eighteen of his friends bravely signed their names to an open letter requesting him to install administrative, economic, and military reforms, so that he would return to his initial purposes. Diem did not kill them, nor did he listen to them. Then on November 11 of that year, while the small American colony in Saigon was celebrating Veterans Day, elite paratroop battalions attempted a *coup* against him. Although this attempt also proved a failure, it revealed how widespread was the non-Communist opposition to Diem.

It was a month later, in December 1960, that a large group of South Vietnamese dissidents, most of whom were Communists, held a conference and formed the National Liberation Front of South Vietnam (the NLF). Their intention was to wage guerrilla civil war against the Saigon Government with the support of arms, strategy, and some troops from the Ho regime in Hanoi. Two thousand of their guerrilla troops had been among the ninety thousand Communists who had gone north in 1954, and after guerrilla training had returned to their villages in the South.

There was some confusion as to the ultimate objective of the NLF, for of the forty NLF leaders who had spent their lives in South Vietnam, not many wanted to unite with North Vietnam if they succeeded in overthrowing the Diem government. Donald Zagoria, analyst with the Rand Corporation, viewed the formation of the NLF as Hanoi-inspired, but resulting apparently from the disappointment of its members with the United States for not creating a neutralized South Vietnam modeled after Laos.

In January 1961, as Eisenhower prepared to retire to Gettysburg, he held a meeting with Kennedy to run down the checklist of serious international problems, but, said Kennedy with some bitterness only weeks afterward, "Ike never briefed me about Vietnam."

Nine days after Kennedy's inauguration, Radio Hanoi announced that Ho Chi Minh's Government had recognized the NLF and was promising aid to the NLF guerrilla fighters, the Viet Cong "peasants in soldiers' clothing," as they called themselves. Kennedy's first detailed intelligence report on South Vietnam told of a Viet Cong force that had grown to fifteen thousand men, only one-twentieth of Diem's army, yet capable of killing a half-dozen Diem-appointed village chiefs a day, burning villages, and controlling more than half the countryside of South Vietnam. The report also told of a Diem filling prisons, dismissing and exiling young military officers, and providing little effective opposition to the Viet Cong. Elbridge Durbrow, the American Ambassador to Saigon, was asking to be relieved: Diem had not spoken to him in months and believed Durbrow had been involved in the paratrooper *coup* attempt.

The inexperienced young President, whose chief forte had been as a Presidential campaigner, was suddenly beset by a host of international problems, and his first concentration in Southeast Asia was Laos, a small nation of two million adjoining Vietnam. This was a land that Dulles had tried to sculpture into a right-wing principality, despite the Geneva agreements that had called for Laotian independence as a neutral country. When Kennedy became President, the Pathet Lao Communist forces were slowly wresting control from the Dulles puppets, and Kennedy frightened the United States at his first news conference by talking about involving the United States in a major war there. War was avoided, though Kennedy committed diplomatic blunders before arranging with the Soviet Union in 1962 for Laotian neutrality.

Two reliable sources offered a disquieting explanation for Kennedy's motive early in 1962 in suddenly altering United States policy in Vietnam, the land adjoining Laos, from the Eisenhower approach of not committing American armies in Asia, to an opposite approach. James Reston of *The New York Times* wrote: "A few minutes after this meeting [the Vienna conference with Khrushchev in June 1961] President Kennedy told me that apparently Khrushchev had decided that 'anybody stupid enough to get involved in that situation [the Bay of Pigs] was immature, and anybody who didn't see it through was timid and, therefore, could be bullied.'" Reston said that Kennedy then sent twelve thousand American troops to Vietnam to show Khrushchev that his estimate of him was wrong, "although he was aptly warned that he was creating an unlimited commitment and was violating all his pronouncements about not getting into an Asian land war."

Newsweek reporters Edward Weintal and Charles Bartlett, the latter a Kennedy family friend, charged that "had he not suffered reverses in the Bay of Pigs and Laos, it may well be that President Kennedy would have thought twice before expanding the Vietnam commitment early in 1962 from seven hundred to eleven thousand advisers. Had he followed a long-range policy plan rather than an understandable concern for his image, as a result of the Bay of Pigs fiasco, he might have reduced rather than increased the Vietnam commitment."

This shocking picture was later fortified by Robert Manning, the Assistant Secretary of State for Public Affairs in the Kennedy Administration. Manning recalled that "one day late in 1961 President Kennedy discussed with his counselors a decision to increase the American 'presence' in South Vietnam from a few hundred 'military advisers' to a military force of fifteen thousand men.

"Undersecretary of State George Ball opposed this, arguing that it would seriously alter the character of the war and might eventually suck more than three hundred thousand American men into action there. Secretary of State Dean Rusk and Secretary of Defense Robert McNamara agreed that Ball's reservations were fair ones, but they were willing to risk the consequences. Kennedy decided that he was, too.

"Hindsight marks that decision as a critical step in this country's creeping escalation toward international tragedy and a domestic crisis of politics and morality. Yet in the news reports of the day it was characterized only as a 'modest' increase in American advisory help to the beleaguered South Vietnamese Government."

Before Kennedy held his disastrous meeting in Vienna with Khrushchev and made the fateful Vietnam decision based on his determination to change Khrushchev's opinion of him, he had given Vice President Johnson direct exposure to Southeast Asia in May 1961. Kennedy aides spread the story that Johnson was so fearful he would be killed in that Asiatic powder keg that he argued with Kennedy for two weeks against the trip. "Mr. President, I don't want to embarrass you by getting my head blown off in Saigon," they reported Johnson had told Kennedy.

The Kennedy reply was supposed to have been, "That's all right, Lyndon. If anything happens to you out there, Sam Rayburn and I will give you the biggest funeral in the history of Austin, Texas."

The aides said that Johnson finally agreed to go only if Kennedy's sister, Mrs. Stephen Smith, went along as proof that the trip was not dangerous.

In his two-day stay in Saigon, Johnson was carefully sheltered from anyone who could tell him of Diem's sadistic activities, while Lady Bird and Kennedy's sister Jean were turned over to baleful Madame Nhu for tea in the presidential palace and for tours of selected hospitals, museums, and a language school.

It was after talks with Diem that Johnson likened him to Winston Churchill and issued a joint statement signed by himself and Diem that read: "The United States recognizes that the President of Vietnam, Ngo Dinh Diem, who was recently re-elected to office by an overwhelming majority of his countrymen, despite bitter Communist opposition, is in the vanguard of those leaders who stand for freedom on the periphery of the Communist empire in Asia."

On Johnson's return to Washington, he proposed a "major American commitment" to South Vietnam, a position that was combatted by Chester Bowles, then an Undersecretary of State. Bowles' proposal was that a major conflagration be avoided by establishing a neutralized Southeast Asia consisting of South Vietnam, Laos, Cambodia, Burma, Thailand, and Malaya, with neutralization guaranteed by the United States, the Soviet Union, India, China, and Japan.

It was following his slap in the face by Khrushchev that Kennedy adopted the Johnson approach, which was to back Diem's Government with American military support. In order to establish a justification for such

activity, Kennedy found it necessary to ignore the essential nature of the
struggle inside South Vietnam. Facts had to be turned inside out so that
what was basically a civil war was now called a war on South Vietnam by
Communist North Vietnam. As Secretary of State Rusk so piously and
tirelessly stated his position, if the Government in Hanoi willed it, the
fighting in the South "could end literally in twenty-four hours."

The Kennedy strategy for South Vietnam consisted of political and economic programs as well as military aid. This was contrary to Dean Rusk's
position, for he believed that Vietnam was not a political problem but was
solely a military concern. Following Kennedy's death, he said that instead
of a mere fifteen thousand American soldiers sent to Vietnam, Kennedy
should have put up more "blue chips" at the outset, made the struggle an
American war against North Vietnam, and won a complete victory.

Shortly after Johnson's visit to his "Winston Churchill of Southeast
Asia," Kennedy sent Professor Eugene Staley, a Stanford economist, to
Saigon to study means to make American aid more meaningful. The Staley
study proposed a substantial increase in the size of Diem's army, the Civil
Guard, and village militiamen, plus an accompanying large flow of war
matériel. Staley also sold Kennedy on the Strategic Hamlet concept,
whereby villagers would be moved into fortresslike compounds, comparable
to early-time American fortresses, which protected colonists from savage
Indians.

Theoretically, the Staley programs were excellent, but in practice they
failed. Much of the war matériel shipped to South Vietnam wound up in
the hands of Viet Cong guerrillas. As for the Strategic Hamlets, great
animosities developed when Vietnamese people were uprooted from the
land that had been in their families for centuries and were pushed into
prisonlike compounds. So the Staley programs resulted chiefly in a further
breakdown of Diem's political authority.

To devise a military program, Kennedy sent General Maxwell Taylor
and Walt Rostow, a garrulous White House aide and war enthusiast, to
Saigon in October 1961. As publicly stated, the Taylor-Rostow mission
was requested to determine "whether Vietnamese nationalism had turned
irrevocably against us or still might serve as a basis for the fight against
communism." Secretary Rusk had declined to name a State Department
official to participate in the mission, again holding to his position that the
only solution to the Viet Cong problem was through bullets and bombs.
This stand was hotly contested by Averell Harriman, his soon-to-be-
appointed Assistant Secretary of State for the Far East, who argued that the
Vietnamese problem was political and could be met with a more progressive
governmental approach by Diem in meeting the needs of his people. Should
this be done, the NLF arguments would lose their popular appeal, he insisted.

Taylor and Rostow and their staffs made their examination of the strange situation in which the heavily armed and well-trained Diem army of a quarter of a million soldiers was unable to cope with fifteen thousand peasant-guerrillas whose weaponry and supplies were simple. The report Taylor submitted to Kennedy contained three groups of recommendations. The first group consisted of suggested political, governmental, and economic reforms. The second group proposed that Americans take on air reconnaissance and air bombing duties, plus air-lifting Vietnamese troops to fighting areas. The third group recommended sending an initial force of ten thousand regular American troops and six full divisions, eventually, to operate in northern South Vietnam to bar infiltration and permit Diem's troops to wipe out the Viet Cong trapped in the middle. Rostow would go further than Taylor, as his special proposal revealed. He recommended that the United States bomb North Vietnam to "seek out and engage the ultimate source of aggression."

Kennedy's basic acceptance of General Taylor's report led to his exchange of letters with Diem on December 15, 1961, in which he promised a major step-up in American aid, though he stressed the point that Americans would only help him and not take over his fight for him. Diem, in return, let him know that while he would accept increased numbers of American troops and military equipment and economic aid with pleasure, he did not intend to carry out the proposed social and political reforms. Then to show that he meant this, his controlled press in Saigon accused the United States of attempting to interfere in the internal affairs of a sovereign state.

With the landing of four thousand American troops in South Vietnam in the spring of 1962 and the avoidance by Diem of reforms, the Kennedy solutions to the Viet Cong problem dwindled to military means. The new ambassador to Saigon, Frederick Nolting, mouthed the helpless line in dealing with the intransigent and ruthless South Vietnamese ruler when he publicly praised Diem for his "dedicated and courageous leadership." *The New York Times* claimed that the White House had ordered the American mission to Saigon "to get along with President Ngo Dinh Diem's regime come hell or high water and forget about political reforms." Homer Bigart, of that paper, called it "Sink or Swim with Ngo Dinh Diem."

Additional American military "advisers" arrived in South Vietnam until General Paul Harkins, Commander of the Military Assistance Command, had about fifteen thousand men in his charge. Military supplies poured into South Vietnam and Diem's troops received modern training and weapons. Yet small Viet Cong forces easily defeated and routed much larger government forces. In a typical action, one in the Mekong Delta in January 1963, two hundred Viet Cong guerrillas chased two thousand South Vietnam regulars and shot down five American helicopters, killing American pilots.

Nevertheless, the Kennedy Administration's propaganda line was that Diem was a remarkable leader, and the war was being won. Undersecretary of State George Ball, ordinarily a man of mature judgment, had this to say about the Viet Cong guerrillas who were moving from military victory to victory and were killing and kidnapping thousands of South Vietnamese civilians who favored the government of Diem: "The guerrillas whom the Vietnamese Army are fighting are under distinct handicaps. In many cases they are poorly trained and equipped and not motivated by deep conviction. Rather, they are merely unsophisticated villagers or peasants who have been conscripted by terror or treachery."

Others offered false notes of optimism. Said Defense Secretary McNamara in February 1962, "By every quantitative measure we are winning the war in Vietnam." A year later Rusk announced that Diem's troops "clearly have the initiative in most areas of the country."

All such comments, plus those praising Diem, failed to find corroboration from American reporters in South Vietnam. There were stories of defeats, blunders, corruption, and growing dislike for Diem, his brother Nhu, and his sharp-tongued sister-in-law, who was managing much of the legislation passed by the National Assembly.

By the summer of 1963 the Buddhists of South Vietnam broke with Diem. When Diem decreed that Buddhists could not fly Buddhist flags during religious festivals, a protest was held in Hue. Diem had the crowd dispersed by ordering his troops to shoot into the lines of protesters, twelve of whom were killed. Demonstrations by Buddhists then occurred in Saigon, and a rage of suicides by self-immolation took place. On August 21 Buddhist pagodas in the capital and several other cities were raided by Diem's hated Special Forces, and Buddhists were dragged off to jail. When students demonstrated in protest, Diem ordered the universities in Saigon and Hue shut down, as well as the secondary schools in Saigon, and four thousand students were imprisoned. High government officials and top military officers were later found roaming through the jails in search of their children.

The madness of the Diem repression of the Buddhists was apparent from the fact that of South Vietnam's estimated fourteen million citizens, only 1.5 million were Catholics like Diem, three million were members of the special sects, such as the Hoa Hao and the Cao Dai, and the rest were Buddhists. True, some Buddhist leaders had political ambitions, and their continued troubles with Catholic Diem and his brother Nhu would serve to enhance their status among fellow Buddhists. However, the troubles did not stem from their own instigation but from the Government's policy toward the Buddhists. Making use of his own loose definition of his enemies, Diem's view was that the Buddhists were Communists, and his sister-in-law, Madame Nhu, who agreed with him, dismissed the increased number of cases of self-immolation as a delightful "barbecueing of monks" that caused her to "gaily clap her hands."

Kennedy had made a strong effort to have American correspondents in South Vietnam serve his own purpose by writing up Diem as an inspiring man and the only leader who could rally the people of South Vietnam against the NLF and the Viet Cong guerrillas. However, several American newsmen took the approach that Diem had to be replaced. When David Halberstam of *The New York Times* persisted in this anti-Diem line, Kennedy exploded with "I'll be damned if I intend to let my foreign policy be run by a twenty-seven-year-old reporter," and he asked the *Times'* publisher to pull him out of Vietnam.

Only a few reporters defended Diem. One was Joe Alsop, who accused his fellow-American reporters in South Vietnam of "conducting a crusade against the government." When Admiral Harry Felt, Commander-in-Chief in the Pacific, met Neil Sheehan of UPI, an opponent of Diem, he told him, "So you're Sheehan. Why don't you get on the team?"

Diem was also treating American newsmen like enemies, ordering some ousted from the country, and on one occasion setting Government plainclothesmen to administer beatings to a group of American reporters at a Buddhist pagoda religious ceremony in Saigon.

It was in this summer of the anti-Buddhist madness that Kennedy replaced Ambassador Nolting, Diem's friend and admirer, with Henry Cabot Lodge, whom he had trounced in the Senate race in 1952. Kennedy saw Lodge as adding bipartisan blessing to the war in Vietnam, for the former Republican senator had also served as the Eisenhower Administration's representative to the UN. In addition, Kennedy realized that if he changed his policy toward Diem, it would be simpler to put it into effect without having Nolting in Saigon.

Before Lodge arrived in Saigon, a White House statement declared that Diem's assault on the pagodas was "a direct violation by the Vietnamese Government of assurances that it was pursuing a policy of reconciliation with the Buddhists." Shortly after this, Lodge sent word back to Washington that several South Vietnamese generals had spoken to him about their desire to effect a *coup* against Diem, who, they claimed, was plotting to kill them. Lodge requested advice on what to tell the generals.

On Saturday, August 24, 1963, a group of anti-Diem American officials held a meeting in Washington to draft a cable to Lodge. Around the table were Averell Harriman, George Ball, Assistant Secretary of State for the Far East Roger Hilsman, and Michael Forrestal, who was McGeorge Bundy's assistant on Far Eastern matters. The cable they wrote told Lodge to give Diem an opportunity to end his repression of the Buddhists and to remove his nefarious brother Nhu from his position as chief administrator and adviser to Diem. If Diem would not comply, said the cable, the United States would support "an interim anti-Communist military regime."

It was preposterous that this signal for ending the Diem rule should have been sent, because Rusk, McNamara, and CIA chief John McCone favored the continuation of the Diem Government. However, McNamara and McCone were on vacation, and Rusk was in New York, and their next-in-line men accepted it in the confusion of belief that it came from

the President. Kennedy, in turn, was vacationing at Cape Cod and agreed
to the draft because he believed his top advisers had approved it.

On the twenty-sixth, when Kennedy returned to Washington, he had serious misgivings about the cable. All that week he met with Cabinet members and the National Security Council to determine whether it would be
foolish to hold to the cabled policy. In the August 28 National Security
Council meeting, a bitter argument broke out between Frederick Nolting,
who defended Diem, and George Ball, whose position was that the continuation of the Diem-Nhu Government along its current policy line would
make certain that the war against the Viet Cong would not be victorious.

On August 31, when Kennedy was away from Washington on a weekend
vacation, Secretary Rusk ran the National Security Council meeting on
Vietnamese policy. Rusk took the position that disaffection with Diem was
only in the cities, and that the war was going well. This incredible position
was attacked by Harriman, Ball, Hilsman, and Forrestal; and in turn the
opinion of these four that the war had been affected by the repression and
lack of reforms by Diem was rebutted by McNamara and General Taylor.
These two argued that the war was not only going well but that Vietnam
required a dictator in order to defeat the Viet Cong.

Throughout the discussion Vice President Johnson had been silent, and
Rusk asked for his views. Johnson said he agreed with McNamara and
Nolting. "I don't believe in this cloak and dagger stuff," he emphasized.
"I think we should try to live with what we've got. I've never been happy
that Otto Passman has complete control of our foreign-aid appropriations.
But since Passman has this control, we try to get along with him as best
we can. We don't try to overthrow him. I think we ought to keep trying
to do the best we can with Diem."

When Diem was told of rumors that the Americans would work for his
overthrow unless he changed, he reacted by making personal threats to a
few of his generals. And when General Ton That Dinh (not to be confused
with departed General Nguyen Van Hinh), in charge of the Saigon area,
told his fellow generals he would not join in their contemplated *coup,* they
lost heart and canceled their plans. Diem and Nhu celebrated by stepping
up the rate of civilian arrests.

Although the question of continued American support for Diem seemed
settled at this point, Kennedy reopened the entire issue again in a TV interview on September 2. "I don't think that unless a greater effort is made
to win popular support that the war can be won out there," said Kennedy.
"We can give them equipment, we can send our men out there as advisers,
but they have to win it, the people of Vietnam, against the Communists."
Diem's Government, he went on, "has gotten out of touch with the people"
and could reestablish popular support only by "changes in policy and perhaps with personnel."

This interview made it clear to Diem that the road was now open again to his ouster unless he mended his ways. But to Defense Secretary McNamara it brought anguish, because as he told Kennedy in the National Security Council meeting on September 6, the facts would show that even with the Diem Government's activities, the war against the Viet Cong was being won.

To check this once more, Kennedy sent a Marine general and a Foreign Service officer to "get the facts." But they returned with such opposing conclusions that Kennedy, in pain, asked them, "Have you men been to the same place?"

This led McNamara to say he would go himself to "get the facts," and he left on September 24 for Saigon. Afterward, a Vietnamese general explained the basis for the ebullient spirit in which McNamara returned to Washington. "Your Secretary of Defense loves statistics," he said. "We Vietnamese can give him all he wants. If you want them to go up, they will go up. If you want them to go down, they will go down."

McNamara had taken General Taylor with him and on October 2, 1963, the released White House summary of their report read: "Secretary McNamara and General Taylor reported their judgment that the major part of the U.S. military task can be completed by the end of 1965, although there may be a continuing requirement for a limited number of U.S. training personnel. They reported that by the end of this year, the U.S. program for training Vietnamese should have progressed to the point where 1,000 U.S. military personnel assigned to South Vietnam can be withdrawn."

The appalling lack of touch with reality by these two did not buy time for Diem. While his atrocities were continuing, General Dinh was persuaded away from his caution, and he took a "blood oath" with his fellow generals to prepare for the *coup* against their President. Another roadblock was pushed aside when Ambassador Lodge sent CIA chief McCone a cable asking him to recall John Richardson, the CIA station chief in Saigon. Lodge did not explain his reason, and McCone, who was a strong Diem supporter, opposed this at first, then grudgingly ordered Richardson home on October 5. Richardson had been especially close to Diem's brother Nhu.

In a frenzied last-ditch effort, Madame Nhu went on a worldwide tour to build support for her brother-in-law. But when she came to the United States her bitter tongue did Diem harm. In Rome she had ridiculed American soldiers, and her remark had preceded her across the United States— "The junior officers of the United States military mission are acting like little soldiers of fortune." And she slapped at the Kennedy Administration by calling it "much closer to communism than we are." A public opinion poll showed that 90 per cent of Americans disliked her.

On November 1, 1963, General Paul Harkins, in charge of the Military Assistance Command in Saigon, was quoted as saying, "Victory . . . is just months away, and the reduction of American advisers can begin any time now." That day also the Vietnamese generals told Lodge they were springing their *coup* at 1:30 P.M., and Lodge cabled Kennedy with the news.

A third event that day was a visit Lodge and American Admiral Harry Felt, Commander in Chief in the Pacific, made to the Independence Palace to see Diem. The generals were concerned about this call because Diem was noted for his six- and eight-hour-long monologues, and their timetable would be upset if this should occur today. But it did not, though Diem held Lodge back momentarily when the ambassador started to leave, and in a humble tone he asked, "Tell me what you want me to do, and I will do it. If you don't know what you want me to do, cable Washington for instructions, and then tell me."

Lodge escaped from his pathetic clutching, and the generals telephoned Diem and Nhu to surrender. That afternoon the palace was taken, though the Ngo brothers escaped through a tunnel, only to be captured the next day in a little Catholic Church. On their way back to the Joint General Staff Headquarters as prisoners, they were murdered.

President Kennedy's assassination, coming three weeks after the slaying of Diem, produced a profound change in American policy toward Vietnam. The young President, who had reacted so immaturely to Khrushchev's ridicule by attempting to show his manliness with an escalation of the American presence in South Vietnam from six hundred to fifteen thousand American troops, had come to realize, said one of his aides, "that Vietnam was his great failure in foreign policy." Pouring in these men plus military and economic aid had not improved the situation because the emphasis had been on treating the struggle as a military rather than a political problem.

Only two months before the *coup* had Kennedy come to realize this. There is ample evidence—such as his ultimatum to Diem—that he agreed with the policy expounded by his young Assistant Secretary of State Roger Hilsman, that "the only way the Viet Cong could be defeated in a permanent, political sense was through a political and social program to which military measures were subordinated. The only sure success in guerrilla warfare was to win over the peasants, so they could be armed to defend themselves."

Hilsman went on to say that "President Kennedy made it abundantly clear to me on more than one occasion that what he most wanted to avoid was turning Vietnam into an American war. He was skeptical of a policy of escalation and of the effectiveness of an air attack on North Vietnam."

Two days after Kennedy's assassination, on Sunday, November 24, Johnson placed a wreath on his predecessor's casket in the Capitol Rotunda, and then with a motorcycle escort he sped off to his Vice Presidential suite in the Executive Office Building for his first foreign policy meeting on Vietnam.

Present were General Taylor, Rusk, McNamara, Ball, Harriman, McCone, and McGeorge Bundy, and all sitting around the conference table knew Johnson's view regarding that small dot on the earth's surface. Their only doubt was whether his holding the sobering powers of the Presidency might produce a change in his outlook. There was also an uneasiness around the table, for with the exception of Rusk the others had ignored him during his Vice Presidency.

Johnson was in charge of the meeting, with a stern expression fixed on his face as he drawled out his views. He would never have brought off the Diem *coup* (he called it "coop"), he said, because he agreed with Rusk and McNamara that the only way to subdue the Viet Cong was to kill them and not to bring the New Frontier to South Vietnam.

Johnson was envious of the great rhetorical skill that Rusk unleashed at this meeting, for he had seldom expressed his views under Kennedy. The senior South Vietnamese general involved in the *coup,* General Duong Van Minh—"Big Minh," as he was called—had succeeded Diem, and there was little doubt, Rusk pointed out, that Big Minh was probably only an interim boss. (Big Minh was not to be confused with exiled General Hinh or General Dinh, who took part in the *coup.*) But whoever became the general in the Independence Palace was the man the United States should support unquestioningly.

Rusk's view of the war was that it had nothing to do with nationalist aspirations or so-called yearning for social justice. Nor was it a civil war, he said. It was simply an aggression on South Vietnam by North Vietnam, aided by Red China. All trouble in South Vietnam would end, Rusk insisted, if China and Ho Chi Minh would "leave their neighbors alone."

Johnson's primitive view was that Ho was another Adolf Hitler carrying on agression, and if he were not stopped, it would be Munich appeasement repeating itself. At the close of the meeting Johnson made his decision: "Increase the pressure and press on."

In the months that followed, Johnson received much advice. President Charles de Gaulle repeated his offer of August 29, 1963, to Kennedy, to help create "an independent but neutral South Vietnam." UN Secretary-General U Thant came to Washington to say that he had Ho Chi Minh's approval for private, unofficial talks between American and North Vietnamese officials in a neutral country to start peace negotiations. General Curtis LeMay, bombastic Chief of Staff of the Air Force, who staged drag races on government airfields, called for carrying the war to North Vietnam. "We are swatting flies," he said through teeth clamped on a cigar, "when we should be going after the manure pile." Strategic Air Command boss, General "Tough Tommy" Power, asked for authority to "pulverize North Vietnam" and plaster the Viet Cong in South Vietnam with his B-52's. Power believed that such bombings, plus later warnings to the Communists to quit, would do the trick. "Every time we have told our enemies to get their greasy hands off something, they have gotten their greasy hands off," he said toughly. "They know all about you and what you can and will do to them if they ever get real foolish. But those hoodlums want the world." Walt Rostow also had a program for the new Chief Executive—

an escalation of the fighting in the South, bombing in the North, and reconnaissance over Laos and bombing the Pathet Lao bases there.

Additional suggestions came from Republicans Barry Goldwater and Richard Nixon. They would not only bomb North Vietnam but they would deliberately entice Red China into the war so that her budding nuclear plants could be destroyed. The Eisenhower and MacArthur tenet against American land wars in Asia should be ignored, their proposals cried.

Johnson's initial decision was to concentrate on exterminating Viet Cong guerrillas and his first public announcement of "an open-end military commitment" to South Vietnam came on New Year's Day 1964, when he sent a message to Big Minh. "Our aims are, I know, identical with yours: to enable your government to protect its people from the acts of terror perpetrated by Communist insurgents from the north," said his letter. "The United States Government shares the view of your government that 'neutralization' of South Vietnam is unacceptable. As long as the Communist regime in North Vietnam persists in its aggressive policy, neutralization of South Vietnam would only be another name for a Communist takeover. Peace will return to your country just as soon as the authorities in Hanoi cease and desist from their terrorist aggression. . . . We shall maintain in Vietnam American personnel and material as needed to assist you in achieving victory."

Big Minh was not in power much longer than it took him to read Johnson's message. On January 30, 1964, after the CIA had decided on him as the new ruler, General Nguyen Khanh, a tiny, round-faced man in high, laced boots and a beret, arrested Big Minh and took over the government.

Johnson was quick to praise Khanh, just as he had extolled Big Minh. But one problem that now arose in using Khanh as a rallying figure for the South Vietnamese was that he was entirely unknown and lacked the stature of the late Diem or the devilish Ho Chi Minh. So Johnson called in Defense Secretary McNamara, gave him a rousing briefing of his own campaign techniques in Texas, offered him pointers on the "electioneering" style he had used in the various trips he had made abroad for Kennedy, and ordered him to Saigon to serve as Khanh's teacher.

The crux of Johnson's explanation was that little people like to meet important people who are friendly, and the strategy he laid out for McNamara and Khanh was to dash into several villages and mingle with the inhabitants. So McNamara made his fourth trip to South Vietnam, this time to race about the countryside with the new local military boss. At this endeavor, Khanh managed to generate a few cheers, but McNamara was considered dubiously, for he committed the sins of shaking hands, patting heads, and plowing through crowds.

Afterward, McNamara hailed South Vietnam's new chief as "an able and energetic leader" who had already "demonstrated his grasp of the basic elements—political, economic, and psychological, as well as military

—required to defeat the Viet Cong." But American newsmen in Saigon remained unconvinced that Khanh would lead South Vietnam out of a morass in which his armies could not defeat Viet Cong guerrillas, the National Liberation Front was collecting taxes in forty-one of the forty-four provinces of South Vietnam, and only 20 per cent of the 8,600 Strategic Hamlets were operating with any degree of effectiveness.

Khanh was not to be given an extensive or a quiet opportunity to develop his image, for other generals were jealous and hoped to succeed him. In a single year nine changes in leadership were to occur, and Khanh was ousted and regained power three times before his luck ran out in February 1965, and he agreed to disappear from the scene as an "Ambassador-at-large to the UN."

A modicum of stability was not to come until June 1965, when ten military men, none of whom had gone past high school, formed the National Leadership Committee to run the government, with General Nguyen Van Thieu as Chief of State and Vice Air Marshal Nguyen Cao Ky as Premier. Nine of the ten were from North Vietnam, and the same number had fought on the side of the French against Indochinese independence.

Thirty-four-year-old Ky, who had been born near Hanoi, had attended a French air school during the independence fight, and later he went to Algeria, where he was a French fighter pilot against the Algerian nationalist forces. Before he became Premier, "the cowboy," as Ky was called because he strapped a pearl-handled, chrome-plated revolver to his side, flew regularly into North Vietnam with the Forty-Third Air Transport Group to drop South Vietnamese guerrillas and saboteurs by parachute into Ho Chi Minh's domain.

In early February 1964 Johnson chafed under his proclaimed restriction to hold the war within the confines of South Vietnam, and he went to California in the middle of the month to release a trial balloon on expanding the war into North Vietnam and possibly China. Those two Communist countries, he charged, were playing "a deeply dangerous game" against South Vietnam, and he implied they might have to be stopped. Eagerly, he read editorials during the next few days to see if he had support. But when newspapers with few exceptions stated with loud objections that he sounded as though he intended to bring on another Korean-type war, he ordered Rusk to hold a news conference and say that the war would be kept within South Vietnam.

While Rusk was offering this assurance, Johnson also ordered a step-up in the program to drop South Vietnamese guerrillas into the North and to use American naval vessels to escort South Vietnamese boats in raids on northern installations and cities along the coast. In addition, Johnson requested that large numbers of South Vietnamese pilots be sent to the United States for training on bombing planes and bombing missions. Furthermore, Johnson had on his desk in March a three-part plan for future use. It called first for the creation of "sonic booms" over northern cities; then the employment of electronic ships sent north to snarl radio communication with the Viet Cong; and third, air bombardment, naval blockade, and invasion.

By this time the first rumblings of a growing national concern were heard about his true policy on Vietnam. Senator Mansfield told the Senate on February 19, 1964, of his dread that the Administration might turn the struggle in Vietnam into an American war, and that in doing so it could focus the entire foreign policy of the nation on events in that tiny place. "There does not exist today a basis in our national interests which would justify the assumption of primary American responsibility which might involve the sacrifice of a vast number of American lives," said Mansfield.

Senator William Fulbright, one of Johnson's oldest Senate friends and a proponent of swift American military action to destroy the Soviet missile sites in Castro Cuba, considered it necessary to preach to Johnson in a ninety-minute speech of caution in March. In talking about "old myths and new realities," Fulbright told his friend that the Kennedy Administration had successfully begun a policy of firmness but flexibility in dealing with the Soviet Union, and that this policy should not lightly be tossed aside. This could happen in Vietnam, depending on Johnson's policy there. "The character of the Cold War has, for the present at least, been profoundly altered: by the drawing back of the Soviet Union from extremely aggressive policies," he said, "by the implicit repudiation by both sides of a policy of 'total victory,' and by the establishment of an American strategic superiority, which the Soviet Union appears to have tacitly accepted because it has been accompanied by assurances that it will be exercised by the United States with responsibility and restraint."

But Johnson scoffed at those who were afraid to live dangerously. In a reply to Fulbright, Johnson said at an Associated Press lunch in New York that the Cold War was permanent policy of the Communists. "Communists, using force and intrigue," he said, "seek to bring about a Communist-dominated world. Our convictions, our interests, and our life as a nation demand that we resolutely oppose with all of our might that effort to dominate the world."

In the early summer of 1964, Johnson decided that the time had come to exclude Congress from playing any role in the Vietnam decisions. McGeorge Bundy drew up a draft resolution to this effect to be sent to Congress for approval, and, said Tom Wicker of *The New York Times,* "He [Johnson] had been carrying it around in his pocket for weeks waiting for the moment." Asked about the draft, Bundy said later, "We had always anticipated . . . the possibility that things might take a more drastic turn at any time."

The right moment came in August. On July 30, the U. S. Destroyer

Maddox escorted South Vietnamese vessels raiding naval and radar installations on a North Vietnamese island in the Gulf of Tonkin. On August 2, when the *Maddox* was, by the admission of Secretary of State Rusk, "six to eleven miles" off the coast of North Vietnam (which claimed twelve miles of territorial waters), three North Vietnamese patrol torpedo boats approached the American ship. The skipper of the *Maddox* later said he fired the first shot—a warning shot across the bow—then he sank two of the P T boats.

After this incident *The New York Times* asked the Defense Department if U. S. destroyers and other Navy vessels were escorting South Vietnamese raiders. The answer, as quoted in the August 3 *Times,* was: "Destroyers on patrol have sometimes collaborated with South Vietnamese hit-and-run raids on North Vietnam cities."

When Hanoi admitted that the August 2 incident had occurred, it generated little outcry within the United States for avenging this "attack on the national honor." However, late on the night of August 4, Johnson went on TV with a story told in patriotic fervor that the *Maddox* and the *C. Turner Joy* had been subjected to another unprovoked attack by North Vietnamese P T boats sixty-five miles from the enemy's coastline. Resolutely he told the nation, "These acts of violence against the armed forces of the United States must be met not only by alert defense, but with positive reply. . . . That reply is being given as I speak to you. Air action is now in execution against gunboats and certain supporting facilities of North Vietnam which have been used in these hostile operations."

As a result of this attack of August 4, Johnson added, he was sending Congress a resolution to make "clear that our government is united in its determination to take all necessary measures in support of freedom, and in defense of peace, in Southeast Asia."

Congress gave him his resolution on August 7, the Senate giving him his blank check by a vote of 88 to 2, and the House by 416 to 0. Under the resolution, he was authorized to "take all necessary measures to repel any armed attack against the forces of the United States and to prevent further aggression." In signing the resolution in his Oval Office, with congressmen and high military officers lined up like sheep behind him, he added to United States activity in the Far East by saying, "To any in Southeast Asia who ask our help in defending their freedom, we shall give it." He could now do as he wished in Vietnam and elsewhere by his possession of this piece of paper.

Grave doubts later arose in the Senate whether the August 4 incident had actually occurred, but it was too late by then to rescind the resolution without appearing to be un-American. "I thought Johnson's story was on the level," said Senator Fulbright, "but the story of the attack didn't hold up. It was an arranged incident to get a resolution creating unity behind any action he wanted to take."

A *Maddox* officer was quoted as saying that the enemy P T boats "were nothing more than a flock of geese on radar screens." Commander Herbert Ogier, the *Maddox*'s skipper, admitted to reporters, "Evaluating everything that was going on, I was becoming less and less convinced that somebody was there." And Lt. Raymond Connell of his ship added, "I had nothing to shoot at. I recall we were hopping around up there, trying to figure out what they [on the *Turner Joy*] were shooting at because we didn't have any targets."

Johnson himself gave several versions afterward. Questioned on one occasion whether the "attack" had actually taken place, he replied, "Hell, I think we might have fired at a whale." Another time he painted an opposite picture for reporters of a deliberate Communist plan to expand the war by firing on American Seventh Fleet destroyers in mid-ocean "with lots of torpedoes"; and he said that what had disturbed him was that few of the P T boats had been destroyed—"Those Navy boys need more target practice." He also told a tale of acting the role of a prosecuting attorney when his aides first brought him word of the second incident, because this "proved" that the first attack was not an isolated incident. "Are you sure we were attacked? How come they were such bum shots?" he said he went after his aides, before he gave the order to retaliate and bomb North Vietnamese torpedo boats and bases.

As for this retaliatory action, Secretary Rusk was in the forefront of advisers advocating bombing right up to the Chinese territorial limits. But in his version of that decision meeting, Johnson pictured Rusk as a man of diplomacy, a man of caution. "When we were going in to take out those P T boats that hit our ships in Tonkin," said Johnson, "it was Dean Rusk who said: 'Now, just a minute—one of those bases is oh-so-close to the Chinese, and if one of our planes gets over there, and they don't understand what we're trying to do, then what?'

"Oh, he wanted to get them all right, because they hit our ships. But then he asked how many boats they had in all, and Bob McNamara says forty-seven, and he asked how many at that target up there, and Bob says thirteen, and Dean Rusk finally says, 'I'm for getting about thirty-four just as hard as we can, and forgetting about those thirteen.' And that's what we did."

Following this single strike in North Vietnam, Johnson could not broaden the bomb drops at this time, for he was faced with the 1964 Presidential election, and his slogan was "Peace and Prosperity." For a short time Henry Cabot Lodge, the Ambassador to South Vietnam, gave the impression he might gain the Republican nomination after winning the New Hampshire primary, but he faded in the Goldwater blooming. At one point General Eisenhower considered backing Lodge, his own chief booster for President in 1952, and he told Lodge he might if the ambassador would assure him that he had not taken any role in the assassination of "the king and his brother" (Diem and Nhu). Lodge blandly replied that he had been oblivious of the entire business, and in fact, when the *coup d'état* was under way, he added, he had actually offered asylum in the American Embassy to the two men.

Goldwater proved a perfect foil for the "peace" candidate. "Ten years ago we should have bombed North Vietnam, destroying the only access they had to South Vietnam with no risk to our lives," he told audiences, and added matter-of-factly that low-yield atomic bombs should be dropped to "defoliate the trees."

Although Johnson's military planners were already drawing up North Vietnamese bombing targets, the screaming outcry from editors and citizens against the Goldwater proposals made it necessary for Johnson to insert antiescalation remarks into his own campaign speeches. A rundown of these remarks reveals what he believed would add to his vote total in November:

August 16, 1964: Some others are eager to enlarge the conflict. They call upon us to supply American boys to do the job that Asian boys should do. They ask us to take reckless actions, which might risk the lives of millions and engulf much of Asia.

August 29: I have had advice to load our planes with bombs and to drop them on certain areas that I think would enlarge the war and result in committing a good many American boys to fighting a war that I think ought to be fought by the boys of Asia to help protect their own land. And for that reason, I haven't chosen to enlarge the war.

September 25: There are those that say you ought to go north and drop bombs, to try to wipe out the supply lines, and they think that would escalate the war. We don't want our American boys to do the fighting for Asian boys. We don't want to get involved in a nation with seven hundred million people and get tied down in a land war in Asia.

September 28: We are not going north and we are not going south; we are going to continue to try to get them to save their own freedom with their own men, with our leadership and our officer direction, and such equipment as we can furnish them.

October 21: We are not going to send American boys nine or ten thousand miles away from home to do what Asian boys ought to be doing for themselves.

It was in October 1964, as Johnson later confided to Charles Roberts of *Newsweek,* that he had reached a firm decision, despite what he was saying in the Presidential campaign, to escalate the war by bombing North Vietnam. That this constituted a direct violation of the Geneva agreements of 1954 was of shoulder-shrugging consequence, for he agreed with Dean Acheson that ethics and morality held only baggage space in international relations: "The overriding guide must be achievement of a major goal of policy," as Acheson put it.

The major goal of policy in Vietnam was to exterminate the Viet Cong, and reports showed that the VC problem had increased during 1964. An estimated seven thousand North Vietnamese had infiltrated into the South during the past year to join the thirty thousand South Vietnamese Viet Cong regulars, and in their hit-and-run and terrorist actions they were more than a match for the half million Army of the Republic of Vietnam (ARVN) troops, the succession of Saigon governments, and the twenty thousand American "advisers" on the scene.

If only Hanoi could be delivered a painful message to quit sending supplies and military strategists into South Vietnam, Johnson reasoned, the Viet Cong in the South could be chased and killed and the Communist menace ended in the country. And the solution was not to enter into peace negotiations, as U Thant was suggesting, because the enemy would be bargaining from its momentary strength. Furthermore, what was there to bargain? Neutralizing South Vietnam like neighboring Laos? Never. Bringing the NLF into a coalition government? The NLF was to be eradicated.

Stubbornly, Johnson refused in the fall of 1964 to consider a political solution to the vexatious problems within South Vietnam. He wanted a swift conclusion and not the do-gooder approach of weaning Vietnamese peasants away from the Communist Viet Cong guerrillas by installing social, economic, and political reforms so they would have a reason for taking up the fight against the VC's. The swift conclusion, he believed, was attainable by dropping bombs on North Vietnam. "It was Hanoi who was 'hurting' us," he explained to Roberts after he had escalated the war. Supplies traveling south over the Ho Chi Minh trail, he said, were forcing the United States to fight "at a crippling disadvantage." (Actually, as Defense Secretary McNamara told the Senate Preparedness Subcommittee on August 25, 1967, the one hundred tons a day shipped southward was "a quantity that could be transported by only a few trucks.") But as Johnson viewed the situation, this infiltration of supplies and men was the crux of the Vietnam problem: North Vietnam was the real enemy, and bombs dropped above the Seventeenth Parallel would be hitting back "at the people who were hurting us the most." In addition, Johnson said, "These air operations would raise the morale of the South Vietnamese people."

At the very time that he was continuing his campaign as a man of peace who would not send American boys to fight battles South Vietnamese boys should be fighting, Johnson put McNamara on the alert to supply him with an incident to justify an escalation of the war. An attempted assassination of the American ambassador, such as the grenade-throwing at Ambassador Nolting in 1961, would have met the specifications, as would an attack similar to the Viet Cong assault against the American Special Forces camp at Plei Mrong in 1962.

A suitable incident became available in October 1964 when Viet Cong guerrillas made a surprise attack on an American air base at Bien Hoa, fifteen miles from Saigon. Here the Viet Cong killed four Americans, wounded seventy-six, and destroyed six multi-million-dollar B-57 bombers.

Aroused to a feverish pitch by the mortar attack, General Maxwell Taylor, who had succeeded Lodge as ambassador in June, demanded that the Defense Department immediately launch a reprisal attack on North Vietnam. After all, he emphasized, the B-57's had been sent to Bien Hoa after the Tonkin Bay incidents specifically to warn Hanoi what was in store for the North if further incidents took place. But Johnson refused to sanction the reprisal bombings, and Taylor expressed his contempt for Washington pulsillanimity until Johnson told him he was waiting for a more appropriate time.

Johnson had an excellent reason for not using Bien Hoa for mounting his acceleration. The election was only three days away, and he did not want to destroy his image as the man of peace. The enormous national concern that Goldwater would involve the United States in a war with China by bombing North Vietnam was too large a pro-Democratic factor to throw away at this point. "We know there are two hundred million in the Chinese army," Johnson said as a man of proper caution, in contrast to "trigger-happy Goldwater." "And if only one little general in shirt sleeves can take Saigon, like what's his name [Nguyen Khanh], think about two hundred million Chinese coming down those trails. No, sir! I don't want to fight them."

A second trigger incident occurred on Christmas Eve in the heart of Saigon, when pajama-clad Viet Cong soldiers made a daytime attack on an American officers' quarters and killed two Americans and wounded sixty-three. But again Johnson delayed action, for he wanted to get through the splendor of his January 20 inauguration before he went after North Vietnam.

Sunday, February 7, 1965, became the day that Johnson escalated the war. At 3 P.M. the preceding day he had been sitting in the Cabinet Room with Cy Vance, Bill Moyers, George Ball, and General Earle Wheeler, the new Chairman of the Joint Chiefs of Staff, when he was handed a message that had just come from General William Westmoreland, who had replaced General Harkins as American Commander in South Vietnam. Westmoreland's message was that the Viet Cong had attacked three military installations, with the worst damage coming at the American base at Pleiku, 240 miles north of Saigon, where seven soldiers were dead and 109 were wounded.

This was what Johnson had been impatiently waiting for since his inauguration. That evening at 7:45 P.M., he held a meeting of the National Security Council. "I've had enough of this," he snapped, waving the Pleiku report. A week earlier the State Department had guessed that Pleiku would be the Viet Cong target, but Johnson did not ask at this meeting why the base had not been protected. For four months now Johnson had been receiving the superb photographs of North Vietnam taken by U-2 planes, and he was more familiar with the terrain, installations, farms, factories, villages, cities, roads, and rivers than most of the air reconnaissance experts at the Pentagon. He knew the targets he wanted to hit in North Vietnam; and McNamara and Wheeler, whom he called upon for suggestions, chose the two they had heard him mention at an earlier time.

The Dong Hoi guerrilla training and staging area, just north of the Seventeenth Parallel, and Van Linh, a communications center, were circled for retaliatory action. Word was sent to Ambassador Adlai Stevenson at the UN to pass on sugared excuses to U Thant that the raids were merely "defense actions" in reply to "intensified Communist aggression in South Vietnam." Then Johnson gave the order for American planes to flatten the targets. "There is something about an emergency that puts an extra hunk of steel in his spine," said little Jack Valenti, proud of his master.

The bombs dropped on Dong Hoi; then three days later the Viet Cong guerrillas raided another American billet, this time at Qui Nhon. Johnson now ordered further bombing of North Vietnam, and on a regular basis, escalating from minor targets, such as bridges and rural roads, to major installations. "They woke us up in the middle of the night, and we woke them up in the middle of the night," he explained and justified his increased bombing of the North. "Then they did it again, and we did it again."

At the end of February 1965 the State Department issued a *White Paper* on the war, in an effort to establish a justification for Johnson's escalation. This was a seventy-one-page document that accused North Vietnam of causing all the trouble in the South and stated anew the repetitive Rusk remark that the war would end if North Vietnam would "let its neighbors alone." The presence of the United States in the encounter, said the *White Paper,* stemmed from South Vietnam's request to her for aid through the "collective-self-defense" doctrine expounded in Article 51 of the UN Charter. Much later North Vietnam issued its *Black Book* on the war, placing the blame on the United States for violating the Geneva agreements of 1954.

The escalation of the war was like a spreading cancer. At the beginning of 1965, an estimated twenty thousand American "advisers" were stationed in South Vietnam to man bases and train South Vietnamese troops, of whom an estimated ninety thousand were deserting annually. When an additional 3,500 Marines landed in March, Johnson had McNamara tell reporters they were sent merely to relieve South Vietnamese soldiers who had been assigned to protect American bases and not to "tangle with the Viet Cong." At the end of March Viet Cong guerrillas bombed the American Embassy in Saigon, and Johnson in retaliation dispatched another forty thousand American soldiers to South Vietnam. Instead of being called advisers, these June arrivals were referred to as combat-support troops, and their stated function was to fight the Viet Cong only in emergencies when South Vietnamese troops were busy elsewhere.

The emergencies started coming in increasing numbers, and American casualties began to grow. By the end of the year they totaled 1,350 Americans killed and 5,300 wounded. There were now 190,000 American troops in South Vietnam, and despite the assurances by Defense Secretary Mc-Namara that all was going well, stories made the rounds in Washington that Johnson and the Joint Chiefs of Staff were discussing putting perhaps a half million or even a million soldiers into Vietnam before long. This was now the American War that Johnson had campaigned against in 1964.

As 1965 progressed, the war began to drown out all other Presidential activities. It was preposterous that so tiny an opponent would want to continue fighting with the United States. Yet it was happening, and Johnson started to sound like a beleaguered Winston Churchill in that statesman's fateful "Battle of Britain" summer of 1940 against the Nazi war might. Johnson was speaking about "my Security Council" and "my State Department" and "my troops," and he visualized himself on the battlefields and in field headquarters. "I've got to go to Da Nang," he said as he excused himself from partying White House guests with a heavy sigh, signifying that duty called him back to work. "I could have bombed again last night, but I didn't," he told a visitor.

Of the early Viet Cong raids on American billets and bases, Johnson explained, "They actually thought that pressure on an American President would get so great that he'd pull out of Vietnam. They don't know the President of the United States. He's not pulling out!" Asked about the U.S. position toward Red China, he replied, "I don't want China to spit in my eye, and I don't want to spit in China's eye." When he visited a small federal project and was told that the agency head back in Washington had been generous enough to provide it with a one-million-dollar budget, Johnson's shoulders tightened and he insisted, "He gave you one million dollars of *my* money!"

He was putting in long days, chiefly on Vietnamese strategy, and he told a friend he was waking up at 3:30 A.M. without an alarm to read the first reports of bombing raids. He had his first complaints about living in the White House. "It's not a home," he declared. "I wake up at five some mornings and hear the planes coming in at National Airport, and I think they are bombing me. Then at 8 A.M., when I'm trying to read a report from a general, all the tourists are going by right under your bed. . . . And some days I suddenly realize at five o'clock that I haven't had lunch."

Cabinet members confided that if he were consulting one of them on Vietnam, and he had to go to the bathroom, he would ask his visitor to accompany him inside so they could continue their conversation without a pause. He was cutting down now on his evening's normal quota of six scotch-and-sodas, and he was finding more relaxation from showing his

World War II movies of his Australian trip than from his photos and sound track of deers mating. And to head off any criticism of the widening involvement of the United States' economy and military strength in the small, backward dot of a place in Southeast Asia, he had his stock answer: "Hell, Vietnam is just like the Alamo."

In the spring of 1965 Johnson had sent a photograph of himself to Senator William Fulbright, and under it he wrote: "To Bill Fulbright—who listens—maybe—perhaps."

Fulbright, his old Senate ally and friend, had emerged as his chief critic on foreign policy, and the criticism hurt because Fulbright was chairman of the Senate Foreign Relations Committee. First had come his unwillingness to floor-manage the foreign aid bill in 1964 because it combined military and economic aid in a single package. Johnson had been forced to ask Senator Sparkman of Alabama to take on this chore for him.

There was also Fulbright's unwelcome advice that he should be more generous in dealing with little Panama on the revision of the 1903 treaty and not act like a bully. Then there was Fulbright's chastisement of Johnson in a speech of March 25, 1964, for holding to "certain drums [that] have to be beaten regularly to ward off evil spirits" and "certain pledges [that] must be repeated every day, lest the whole free world go to rack and ruin—for example, we will never go back on a commitment no matter how unwise." Yet despite this widening chasm, Fulbright had campaigned hard in 1964 for Johnson in Arkansas, and political observers agreed that it was chiefly through Fulbright's effort that Johnson had carried the state that November.

The break between Johnson and Fulbright had come not over Vietnam but over Johnson's Dominican Republic action in April 1965. Fulbright, from the prestige of his committee pulpit, had labeled Johnson's intervention a "grievous mistake" and said that his voodoo belief in an international monolithic communism bent on taking over the world would "make us the enemy of all revolutions and therefore the ally of all the unpopular and corrupt oligarchies of the hemisphere." Fulbright had also attacked the Johnson action as being "based on fragmentary and inadequate evidence. . . . His story about 1,500 people having their heads cut off and the American ambassador hiding under his desk and the bullets whizzing in just wasn't so."

Before the Dominican intervention Johnson had made much use of Fulbright's prestige to cut down those who gave the impression they had come to his office to argue with him. "Bill Fulbright was sitting in that chair right over there two days ago," he would announce loudly, without proceeding to disclose what Bill Fulbright might have discussed while he sat there. But Fulbright told a reporter, "Whenever I went to the White House to talk to Johnson, I didn't get to say a word. He did all the talking."

Fulbright's relations with Johnson over Vietnam had begun in a friendly manner. As a man who liked to sit alone in his office in the late afternoon and read and think about world affairs while munching an apple, Fulbright had acknowledged in the spring of 1964 that Johnson had two chief choices in Vietnam. "The hard fact of the matter is that our bargaining position is at present a weak one," he said in his slow manner. "And until the equation of advantage between the two sides has been substantially altered in our favor, there can be little prospect of a negotiated settlement.

"It seems clear," he went on, "that only two realistic options are open to us in Vietnam in the immediate future: the expansion of the conflict in one way or another, or a renewed effort to bolster the capacity of the South Vietnamese to prosecute the war successfully on its present scale."

It was Fulbright's early opinion that Johnson was following the latter course. When the Tonkin Bay Resolution came before the Senate in August 1964, Fulbright took the lead to fight off an amendment by Senator Gaylord Nelson of Wisconsin. The Nelson Amendment would have eliminated the blank check given the President and restricted American action to "aid, training assistance, and military advice" but not "direct military involvement." Fulbright also offered no immediate objection when Johnson ordered a "retaliatory" raid on North Vietnam after the Pleiku incident of February 1965.

"But after other bombings came, and we began to send in more troops," said Fulbright, "I voiced objections verbally and by memo to Johnson that we were turning the conflict into an American war by our escalation and our false reliance on a military solution. Then after the Dominican intervention, this crystallized the feeling that we were becoming just another imperial power butting in whenever we felt like it, and my opinions started to rile Johnson.

"In his years as a senator, Johnson had never been interested in substantive matters—only in power; and his growing animosity toward me was not based as much on what I was saying but on the fact that I was offering any objections to what he was doing because he was President. I was reminded of an argument we had in 1957 over the Dulles foreign policy after the Suez action. When I told Johnson at that time I planned to oppose the Administration's proposed action, he said, 'Ike's our President and has responsibility for foreign policy, and it's my duty to support him,' although, of course, there were many instances when he didn't support the President on foreign affairs. In addition, although Eisenhower also proclaimed this doctrine that no one should attack a President on foreign policy, he had bitterly assailed Truman on Korea during the 1952 campaign."

For a time after Fulbright began his criticism of Johnson's Vietnam policy, Johnson continued to invite him to the White House for briefings on the fighting and other activities in Vietnam. "You found yourself in the Cabinet Room with Johnson, members of his Cabinet, high-level brass, the House speaker and majority leader, Senate leaders and several committee chairmen," Fulbright recalled. "The idea evidently was to make everyone present from Congress feel cowed by the time the very doctrinaire anti-Communist Dean Rusk and other briefers finished their recitations. Afterward, Johnson would ask, 'Are there any questions?'

"Each listener would chirp up in turn, 'Mr. President, we have great confidence in you, and we are behind you.' Then he came to you, and Mike Mansfield and I were the only two who said we didn't agree. And when we did, all the others looked down on us like a horse's ass."

By the fall of 1965, following Fulbright's sharp attack on the Administration for its Dominican intervention, Johnson no longer included Fulbright in the Congressional group called to the White House for briefings on Vietnam. Two members of Fulbright's committee, Democratic Senators Russell Long and Tom Dodd, were prodded by Johnson to attack Fulbright on the Senate floor for his anti-Administration stand on foreign policy.

Fulbright reacted to this hazing by trying flattery at first. "Lyndon Johnson has a great capacity," he said. "He could make a great President if he could get back on the track in foreign relations." When this failed to elicit the response he wanted, he sent Johnson a program for neutralizing all of Southeast Asia. The response was a cold letter from the White House that more or less told the chairman of the Senate Foreign Relations Committee to stay out of foreign affairs. "I feel so isolated and discouraged," Fulbright told a reporter. "The war fever is increasing. We Americans are so powerful, so self-righteous."

Fulbright was not alone in the Senate. Wayne Morse made the loudest noise against the war in Vietnam, but his gift for antagonizing those who agreed with him was actually a Johnson asset.

Then there was Senator Ernest Gruening of Alaska, a former physician, editor of the *Nation* magazine, and high official in the Interior Department during the Roosevelt era. Gruening presented a threat in 1965 with his amendment to an appropriations bill, which would have restrained Johnson from sending draftees to South Vietnam. Only Gruening and Morse had voted against the Tonkin Bay blank check resolution in the Senate, and White House aides now considered his proposal on the draft a difficult problem for the President. But Johnson called him to the White House, gave him his solemn oath that "the boys will begin to come home by 1966," and begged him to hold off until then.

Gruening later told a reporter, "I had made a speech praising the Johnson domestic policy, an unremarkable speech that found its place amongst a barrel of the same kind of pap that goes into the *Record* every day. But the next morning Johnson called me at home and praised me fulsomely. I should have suspected then that something was wrong." Johnson told him he wanted to hold a discussion with him on Vietnam, and he invited Gruening to a White House briefing by General Taylor, McNamara, and Bundy.

Then he called Gruening to come for another discussion on Vietnam. This time, said Gruening, "I asked the President not to interrupt me for ten minutes. I didn't want him punching my chest or slapping my knee or doing those things he likes to do to keep you rattled and off balance." Johnson then let him talk a few minutes on his proposed amendment to keep the President from sending draftees to Vietnam before cutting in with "Oh, no, don't do that. If we don't have the boys out of there by January, you can do it."

After that White House meeting Gruening did not push his amendment, and by 1966, when a growing influx of American troops appeared in South Vietnam, the reintroduction of his amendment would have been academic.

A greater problem for Johnson was Senate Majority Leader Mike Mansfield, a former professor of Far Eastern history, one of a few Americans to serve in the Marines, Navy, and Army, and a man who had made many trips to Asia, including a World War II mission to China for Franklin Roosevelt. Johnson's animosity toward Mike, which had resulted from the role he and Senator Williams had played to start the Bobby Baker investigation, grew larger with Mansfield's opposition to the open-end escalation of the war in Vietnam and his frequent calls for an end to American bombings of the North and a negotiated settlement. In private, Johnson referred to him as "that cross between Jeannette Rankin [she had voted as a congresswoman against American entrance into both World Wars I and II] and Burt Wheeler [a leading pre-World War II isolationist senator]."

When the United States involvement in Vietnam started on its escalating course, Johnson liked to pull a piece of paper from his pocket and read to visitors certain provisions of the Southeast Asia Treaty Organization pact (SEATO) of September 1954 as the justification for American presence in Vietnam. "This is the grounds for our action and policies in Vietnam," he would introduce his reading. "I carry this paper around with me most of the time. It's my constitutional authority for the fight against aggression over there."

But Mike Mansfield shook his head and objected, and this infuriated Johnson. "I was a member of the three-man American delegation to Manila, along with Secretary of State Dulles and Senator Alexander Smith of New Jersey, in the writing of the SEATO agreement," said Mansfield. "We agreed on an alliance of anti-Communist countries there, but the American-type action in Vietnam was not included in that pact."

Nor did Mansfield buy the Johnson justification that he was merely carrying out the policy "forced" on him by the Eisenhower letter to Diem in 1954. "Our basic commitment to Vietnam was made in a statement ten years ago by *our* President, Dwight D. Eisenhower," Johnson was telling newsmen in an effort to blame Republicans for his predicament. Eisenhower himself found this reprehensible in 1965, and he told a group of

House Republicans that Johnson's military action could not be based on his own 1954 offer of economic aid to Diem.

Nor did Mansfield accept Johnson's frequent rendition of the Domino Theory, his hand-wringing claim that "if we quit in Vietnam, tomorrow we'll be fighting in Hawaii and next week we'll have to fight in San Francisco." Senator George McGovern of South Dakota, a member of Mansfield's Democratic crew, offered this conjecture about the inanity of the Domino Theory: "We are left to wonder how a flotilla of Chinese junks is going to get by the Seventh Fleet en route to San Francisco." As a matter of fact, even Secretary of State Rusk scoffed at the concept of the Domino Theory, and so did McNamara, though both agreed it was a handy tool for gaining the support of the American people.

Despite Mansfield's opposition to Johnson's policy of escalation for a military victory, the gentlemanly senator from Montana refrained from attacking him openly because he believed his position as majority leader precluded this. So he was not the roadblock to Johnson that he might have been had he chosen to do more than write secret reports on the war to Johnson, deliver speeches on his own position on Vietnam, and play the role of "angel's advocate" in behind-the-scenes, face-to-face confrontations with Johnson.

Mansfield first grew concerned that Johnson might be planning a big war when the Pleiku attack in February 1965 inaugurated the bombing of North Vietnam. Then a month later, when Johnson sent in the thirty-five hundred Marines as his first new batch of ground soldiers, Mansfield's already wrinkled brow wrinkled further, though he hoped that Johnson did not intend major American ground action in South Vietnam.

However, this hope was shattered on March 30, when Viet Cong guerrillas bombed the American Embassy in Saigon, killing two Americans and nineteen Vietnamese and wounding 156. Johnson was offering a toast that evening at a White House affair when word of this attack reached him. After reading the note, he passed it to Rusk and nodded toward the door as a signal for Rusk to get back to his office. Then in a great show of fury, he told his party guests, "Our Embassy in Saigon was just destroyed by the enemy, and a lot of fine American girls working there as secretaries have been killed, and I'm not going to tolerate this any longer." He also said he was sick and tired of the demands of certain senators and others that he stop the bombing of North Vietnam. In fact, he went on, right now he was going to send forty thousand more American troops to Vietnam, and he was going to pay for raising, equipping, and training an additional one hundred and fifty thousand South Vietnamese soldiers.

To the public outcry that he was escalating the war by sending "combat-support troops," Johnson blandly insisted that no escalation was occurring. Troops already there, he said matter-of-factly, had served as more than "advisers"; so this was no more of an American war than it had been previously.

But Mansfield was not satisfied with this explanation, and he took the lead in needling Johnson to offer some hope that the United States was willing to negotiate a settlement of the Vietnam conflict. This pressure led Johnson to make a conciliatory-sounding speech at Johns Hopkins University in Baltimore on April 7, 1965. Much of this Baltimore talk was devoted to a promise that the United States would make "a billion-dollar investment" in the economic development of Southeast Asia *after* the fighting ended. As for the war, Johnson proclaimed his willingness to engage in "unconditional discussions" to find a way to peace. However, Mansfield's belief in the sincerity of this pledge foundered almost immediately afterward when word spread through the Capitol that Johnson aides were explaining, "Sure we have to say we're for negotiations, but under the circumstances we would have to go in with pretty tough terms." The tough terms amounted to the surrender of the enemy.

Within days after the Baltimore speech, the Hanoi Government replied by offering its own four-point "tough terms." These four points resulted in a severe propaganda loss for Hanoi, for though Johnson was actually a man of war, he was not so stupid as to put his stand down on paper. These hard-line points by Hanoi called for the withdrawal of American troops from the South, a promise by both North and South not to form military alliances with foreign countries, recognition of the National Liberation Front as the government of South Vietnam, and the reunification of Vietnam "without any foreign interference."

With a temporary lead in the propaganda war because of Ho Chi Minh's heavy-handed conditions for negotiating a settlement, Johnson saw an excellent opportunity to persuade European friends to get behind him in Vietnam. In addition, he spied a chance to divide and confuse and rout the American academic community that was now in process of uniting against further escalation of the war.

A large crowd of university pipe-smokers was scheduled to descend on Washington in mid-May to stage a "teach-in" protest against the war, and Johnson recognized both a danger and an opportunity. He took one direct step against the teach-in by ordering former professors on his staff to join the gathering and argue vigorously in his behalf.

In addition, to take the starch out of the teach-in, just before it began, Johnson suddenly announced that a bombing pause over North Vietnam would start on May 12. And behind the scenes, he acted on the urging of Defense Secretary McNamara to send a message that same day to Hanoi through the offices of the Soviet Union. Ho Chi Minh was told that Johnson would be "watchful" for indications from him that he wanted to negotiate peace. If no sign was given, the note said, the United States would end the bombing pause.

A quick reply came from Mai Van Bo, head of the North Vietnamese Diplomatic Mission in Paris. Hanoi would negotiate on condition that Johnson recognize in principle the four-point program. If he did, then

Ho Chi Minh would not press for its application as the basis for making a peaceful settlement.

But now Secretary of State Rusk stepped forward and dispatched ultimatum-like terms to Hanoi: South Vietnam must be recognized as a separate and independent nation; North Vietnam must withdraw all its troops and aid from the South. The bombing pause ended on May 18.

The news from Saigon continued bleak. The dozenth upheaval in the unstable South Vietnamese Government had put "the cowboy" Nguyen Cao Ky in as Premier on June 19. The effort of the Johnson Administration to establish an image of the ten-man military *junta* in charge as a democratic force suffered a blow almost immediately when an interview with Ky was made public. "People ask me who my heroes are," said Ky. "I have only one—Hitler."

Johnson did not see how Ky and the other tiny mites in the *junta* could manage a war against the terrorist Viet Cong forces. So he put his staff to work to determine how many American soldiers were needed to finish the search-and-destroy job against the Viet Cong in the South while the North was pounded from the air. The figure Johnson thought sufficient at the moment was 125,000 additional Americans, to be raised through the draft, but if he made an announcement to this effect, he was certain the outcry would be so great that he would feel obliged to lower it.

The surest method to get what he wanted and emerge as a moderate was to frighten the nation. In June 1965, he was responsible for releasing a trial-balloon figure of four hundred thousand Americans who would be called up. Then Secretary McNamara was featured in news stories, declaring that perhaps the President would be forced to declare a state of emergency and call up the National Guard and reserves. By the time a month elapsed in this horrendous uncertainty, Johnson knew that when he got around to announcing the 125,000 figure and no call-up of the Guard, there would be a national sigh of relief.

In July, while the public was told only that an important decision would soon be reached on the number of troops to be sent to Vietnam, and that the Cabinet was meeting daily on this matter with the President to push him into a large-scale mobilization, Johnson did not share his secret figure with Vice President Humphrey. Instead, he ordered Humphrey to get to work on his Senate liberal friends and argue the need for turning the Vietnam conflict into an American war, with a massive build-up that would reach into almost every American family. Humphrey did as he was told, and for the first time he found himself considered a renegade and a Presidential lackey.

If Hubert Humphrey, the Second Citizen, was kept from decision-making, Abe Fortas, a private-practice lawyer earning a quarter of a million dollars a year, was not. During this period, when Johnson wrestled with the problem of how to devise an American war in Vietnam that was palatable to the American people, Fortas came daily to the White House to discuss with his friend the strategy of (I) bringing Ho Chi Minh to his knees, begging for an end to bombing, and (2) wiping out Viet Cong soldiers in the South and hustling those who surrendered into prison stockades. Like Dean Acheson, Walt Rostow, McGeorge Bundy, and Clark Clifford, Fortas belonged to that school of amateur war strategists defined at one time by Herbert Hoover as men to whom a military objective was worth whatever human cost was involved. At a battle at the Somme River in northern France, where Hoover had been an observer in 1916, a quarter of a million men had perished in a fight involving some acres of ground. Said Hoover, the Germans with him had been elated because British losses were twice those of their own nationals.

Johnson was anxious to have Fortas available to him several times a day, and he found the way that July. Adlai Stevenson, that sensitive, intellectual politician and ambassador to the UN, whom Kennedy had degraded by making him an unwitting liar in the UN discussion of the American role in the Bay of Pigs disaster and then by telling reporters Stewart Alsop and Charles Bartlett he had been the lone dissenter in the Cuban missile confrontation, was away in Europe during the vital policy talks on Vietnam. When Stevenson died on a London street on July 14, 1965, amidst charges that he opposed the Administration's policy in Vietnam and countercharges that he championed it, Johnson saw his opportunity to move Fortas into his official family.

This was a complicated operation that first required inducing Supreme Court Associate Justice Arthur Goldberg to resign from the "Jewish seat" on the Court and succeed Stevenson at the UN. Goldberg was pursued to the hospital room of his dying mother-in-law, where, flattered by this exciting attention and the apparent opportunity to have an active part in current affairs again, he finally agreed. Now Johnson quickly named Fortas, whom *The New York Times* described as the "crony of Lyndon Johnson," to Goldberg's seat on the Court, and with the lax schedule of the top judiciary body, he was almost as available for White House consultation as some of Johnson's West Wing aides.

After the public hysteria over the extremes Johnson might decide to carry out in Vietnam reached a roar, Johnson scheduled a TV appearance on July 28, 1965, to inform the nation of his "moderate" plan. The evening before his appearance, he had ordered Congressional leaders of both parties herded into the Cabinet Room for a preview, and after attacking the absent Humphrey for taking an extreme warlike stance, he told of his decision to turn the conflict into a mild American war.

As Johnson finished and perfunctorily asked for questions, expecting none, Mike Mansfield extricated a three-page typewritten statement from his pocket, and while mouths fell open, he read a sharp and loud criticism of American involvement in Vietnam. Lodge, who had recently been re-appointed ambassador to South Vietnam, was seated a few chairs away from Mansfield at the Cabinet table, and he stared vacantly ahead as Mansfield charged that there had not been a legal government in Saigon since Diem's murder. Mansfield also charged that the bombings in North Vietnam would not bring peace. "This is not an American war," he said, "and the United States must not make it one."

Johnson broke the stifling silence when Mansfield finished. "Well, Mike, what would you do?"

Mansfield made no reply, but stared into his face.

When Johnson went on TV the following night, he offered two excuses for the American war in Vietnam. The first was the Domino Theory, that the loss of South Vietnam to Ho Chi Minh "would imperil the security of the United States itself." Besides this hoary argument, he also called himself helpless to do otherwise because "three Presidents—President Eisenhower, President Kennedy, and your present President—over eleven years have committed themselves and have promised to help defend this small and valiant nation."

Bombing raids in the North were increased to five thousand sorties a month, and General Westmoreland sent his new large ground force into Viet Cong–infested areas, for Johnson had ordered a swift victory.

But no victory came, despite the figures delivered nightly at 3:30 A.M. to Johnson as he lay in the four-postered Lincoln bed under the canopy. The statistics showed a steep step-up in the number of enemy killed and captured and in the flattening of northern and southern targets. Yet baffling estimates revealed that 1964 figures of 32,000 VC regulars, 60,000 VC irregulars, and 7,400 VC infiltrators from the North showed an actual increase, despite the American nature of the new war, to 75,000 VC regulars, 100,000 VC irregulars, 40,000 political cadre, and 19,000 infiltrators, including ten North Vietnamese regiments. In the Mekong Delta southwest of Saigon, a triangle measuring about 180 miles to each side, and where 60 per cent of the South Vietnamese lived and amassed 60 per cent of the country's wealth, the NLF continued in political control. The effect of the American escalation in late 1965 was that it produced a corresponding escalation on the enemy side. But it also brought on a stalemate in the South and prevented a Viet Cong victory, one that appeared possible early that year.

Yet the Johnson victory over the bearded little Ho Chi Minh in the North and the National Liberation Front in the South seemed as far away as before the escalation began.

In November 1965 Mansfield infuriated Johnson again when he asked for the use of the Presidential plane to talk to the heads of sixteen governments on what could be done to end the war in Vietnam. "He had a nerve making his request," said a Johnson friend, "because he intended to take four other anti-war peace doves with him, and he was going to talk to a lot of government heads who were opposed to us in Vietnam."

But Johnson wanted no trouble with Mansfield, and he approved the trip. "Just convey my views that I want to find a way to the negotiating table, Mike," he said.

"Did you mean what you said about not remaining in Vietnam and acquiring special privileges after the war?" Mansfield asked.

"That's right," Johnson told him. "All I want is to negotiate an honorable settlement that will allow the people of Indochina to choose their own government."

Republican Senator George Aiken, who participated in that thirty-seven-day trip around the world, said, "Everyone we talked to spoke frankly because they knew Mike would talk to LBJ on our return. In Japan, anti-war groups called off their picketing for three days while we were there so there wouldn't be any disturbances during the talks. Mike's thirty-page secret report to Johnson on our return was an independent view —not the junk Johnson's advisers and diplomats were writing him, which was what he wanted to hear."

The point of the Mansfield report was that Johnson's objective—to give the puppet military regime of Premier Ky control over all of South Vietnam—was not attainable, regardless of the degree to which the United States escalated the war. Mansfield suggested that Johnson revise his objective downward, establish a holding operation, and work to institute political and land reforms to win widening support from the Vietnamese peasants for an anti-Communist government of their own choosing.

Even though Johnson viewed with contempt any advice not calling for total victory in South Vietnam, he acted on another Mansfield proposal. This was to call a bombing pause as an inducement to the enemy to negotiate.

The original suggestion for this second pause had come from Defense Secretary McNamara, for he was slowly changing his mind about the power of the bombings to end North Vietnamese shipments southward and the ability of a military solution in the South to end the Viet Cong problem there. But McNamara was almost alone in supporting the pause as an opportunity to bring the enemy to the talk table. Among outside advisers, Clark Clifford and Abe Fortas were in vehement opposition, declaring that this would give the enemy a free opportunity to prepare future offenses. Dean Acheson went further, and said that Johnson should make no effort to negotiate but should work steadfastly for military victory. Within the Administration, soft-spoken Rusk and brittle-speaking Bundy had argued the most strenuously to keep up the bombing without pause. "Rusk and Bundy are always a little bit readier to hit than McNamara," Johnson explained with amusement to visitors.

Johnson added to the drama of the bombing pause that began on

December 24, 1965, by sending Averell Harriman, Arthur Goldberg, and McGeorge Bundy on jet flights around the world to ask the support of leaders in various national capitals to bring the Communists of North Vietnam to the negotiating table. This was a pointless gesture, because the American ambassadors on the scene could have delivered the messages, yet it was of political value to Johnson at home, for it presented him as a man who was sincerely trying to establish peace. But his effort to acquire support abroad was doomed, since his negotiating position was clear: He would deal only with North Vietnam and not with the NLF, thus making Ho Chi Minh admit he was an aggressor and an invader of South Vietnam. On this basis, the minimum Johnson terms would be Ho's withdrawal of aid and interest in the affairs of South Vietnam.

There were some Johnson associates who insisted that the President had called the bombing pause and dispatched his emissaries abroad merely to offset the bad publicity he had received from a *Look* magazine article on Adlai Stevenson in November 1965. In the article Stevenson had been quoted as having been highly critical of Johnson for not cooperating in the peace efforts of UN Secretary-General U Thant.

For a year now Johnson had seethed at the mention of Thant's name because the UN official would not buy his view that the war was totally an invasion of South Vietnam as part of an international Communist plot and was not a civil war. As Thant put it: "It is nationalism, and not communism, that animates the resistance movement in Vietnam against all foreigners, and now particularly against Americans." Thant had also made the remark that "Vietnam is not vital to Western interests," and Rusk had swiftly rushed in to censure him with "Four [U.S.] Presidents have not taken that view." Over a period of time, said a reporter at the UN, "uncomplimentary remarks about Thant attributed to Rusk have filtered through the bureaucracy here." But it was Johnson who made the slurs on Thant, and Rusk merely passed them along.

Johnson's animosity toward Thant went back to August 1964, when the former Burmese schoolteacher asked the former Cotulla schoolteacher for a meeting on making peace in Vietnam. Thant came to Washington at that time, spoke to Johnson and Rusk, and returned to New York with the belief that the President had agreed to his suggestion for private, unofficial talks between American and North Vietnamese representatives.

Elated by his Washington conversation, Thant got in touch with the Hanoi Government through the Soviet Government in September 1964, and shortly afterward he reported to Adlai Stevenson, the American ambassador to the UN, that Ho Chi Minh was willing to appoint someone to speak privately with an American on preliminary peace negotiations. Stevenson reported this excitedly to Rusk, but a Washington blackout occurred and he was unable to get any response. One plausible explanation to Stevenson for this silence was that Johnson did not want to begin negotiations at a time when the war was going badly for the unstable succession of Saigon Governments. Another explanation was that talk of negotiations during the Presidential campaign would give Goldwater an issue that Johnson was "soft on Communism."

In January 1965, while Johnson was searching for a "good" incident that would make palatable to the American public the escalation of the war through bombing of North Vietnam, Thant asked Stevenson to inquire whether the President was still interested in peace negotiations. This time Stevenson was told by Rusk that the United States had conducted its own appraisal of the possibility of preliminary talks with the Hanoi Government, and that a negative response had been received. Thant considered this peculiar, and on investigation he learned that the State Department had asked a Canadian official in Hanoi to check, and this official had spoken not to Ho Chi Minh but to middle-level North Vietnamese government employees. "All our indications were that there was no serious intent on the other side," said Rusk, recalling this slipshod check ten months later, in November 1965.

After learning of the Canadian official's statement, Adlai Stevenson did not permit the issue to die but asked Thant to suggest who should conduct secret preliminary negotiations and where they should meet. Thant believed this should be done by the American and North Vietnamese envoys in Burma, and on January 18, 1965, he told Stevenson that his Government had agreed to meetings at Rangoon.

Stevenson now passed on this news to the State Department. Ten days of silence followed. Then came a strong *No*, with the explanation that "any rumors of such a meeting might topple the Saigon Government." This was ridiculous, Thant told a dispirited Stevenson, for Saigon Governments were toppling with regularity. "What Saigon Government are they talking about?" he demanded. "Minh, Khanh, Suu, Tri—or what?"

Twenty-four hours after Thant told Hanoi that the Johnson Administration was not interested in negotiations, American air bombing strikes took place over North Vietnam in retaliation for the Viet Cong attack on Pleiku near the Fourteenth Parallel on February 7. In sadness, Thant said, "The great American people, if they only knew the true facts and the background to the developments in South Vietnam, will agree with me that further bloodshed is unnecessary."

Johnson recognized that he would look like a warmonger after the recital of Thant's efforts for negotiations. So he tried the swinging-ax approach and ordered Press Secretary George Reedy to tell reporters: "The United States has received no proposal from U Thant." As another credibility gap was now in the making, Rusk shifted the blame to Adlai Stevenson after Stevenson's death in July 1965. Rusk said that Stevenson had not been told to reject the meeting in Rangoon but had merely been informed that Rusk was "skeptical" about positive results from the meeting. Johnson brushed even this explanation aside when he later told a news conference: "Candor compels me to tell you that there has not been the slightest indication that the other side is interested in negotiation."

In an article in the Washington *Post* on December 5, 1965, Murrey Marder was the first to use the term "credibility gap," and he had this to say about the Administration's denial of U Thant's peace efforts: "It represents a perceptibly growing disquiet, misgiving or skepticism about the candor or validity of official declarations." Nor did Thant help Johnson when he offered the undiplomatic comment that "in times of war and hostilities, the first casualty is truth." Johnson tried to counter this with a White House statement that "there are no *meaningful* proposals for negotiations that are before our Government." But he emerged from his word battle with U Thant under great suspicion as to his truthfulness, and knowing of Johnson's animosity toward him, U Thant stopped traveling to Washington to discuss peace efforts.

Johnson originally had planned to continue the bombing halt for forty days because of the biblical quality of that number. But pressure from the Joint Chiefs of Staff brought his approval to end it after thirty-seven days.

By the time Johnson ordered an end to the bombing pause on January 31, 1966, he had acquired several new opponents in Congress. Senator Hartke, previously considered a Johnson man, formed a group of fifteen senators willing to sign their names to a request to Johnson not to resume bombing of North Vietnam. Johnson wrote Hartke a short, mean letter in reply and referred to him in the White House as "Chickenshit Hartke." Orders went to the White House social secretary to bar Hartke from future functions. Then Johnson curtailed Hartke's patronage and passed word to the State Department to instruct American embassies to hinder Hartke on his trips abroad. Not long afterward, when Hartke went to Greece and England, he found the embassy people unfriendly to him and obstreperous about arranging appointments for him with government officials.

This animosity toward Hartke burgeoned because the Indiana senator, who was on the Finance Committee, began making inquiries about the cost of the Vietnam conflict. Hartke found that the figures were hidden in defense appropriations, except for supplemental small amounts specifically requested for South Vietnam from time to time. When asked by Hartke about the cost of the war, Secretary of the Treasury Henry Fowler and Bureau of the Budget Director Charles Schultze shrugged off the question as of little importance, though they made no numerical reply. As for Johnson, his stock reply to reporters was that the costs of Vietnam were minor, the Great Society would grow, and the nation would not have to make a choice between guns and butter. But Hartke foresaw the eventual growth of the cost of the conflict to a level of thirty billion dollars a year, which meant the strangulation of the Great Society at a time when domestic needs required enormous attention. He also noticed that while Johnson's budget message to Congress in Janurary 1965 mentioned the Great Society four times on the first page, the 1966 message mentioned it only once in the entire document.

So angry was Johnson with Hartke that he passed along to reporters a fictitious conversation with the Indiana senator. "I told him, 'Now you look here,'" Johnson said. "'I remember you when you were just a two-bit mayor of a two-bit town in Indiana, and I made you a United States senator.'"

Hartke told newsmen after this story was printed that it had never taken place. "Johnson was one of eighteen senators who came through Indiana when I ran in 1958, and he spoke at a single rally—in Indianapolis," said Hartke.

Other senators opposed to Johnson's Vietnam policy were also subjected to imaginary conversations that friends of Johnson "leaked" to the press. One story claimed that after Senator Frank Church of Idaho criticized Johnson policy in Vietnam, the President scolded him, and Church was supposed to have replied, "I didn't go any further than Walter Lippmann."

The fictitious tale had Johnson flattening him with "Well, Frank, the next time you need money to build a dam in your state, you better go to Mr. Lippmann."

A true sequel to this story came after it appeared in print. Church was at the White House, and Johnson asked with delight, "Well, Frank, how are all the dams in Idaho?"

"Just fine, Mr. President, and the next one we build, I think we'll name the Walter Lippmann Dam."

When one senator complained directly to Johnson that he had heard that some of the President's aides and the President were criticizing him, Johnson denied it, saying he had in reality been praising him to others. "You remind me of the story about this here good judge in the Hill Country," he said, "who was told by one of his friends that a legislative committee had voted to abolish his court."

"'Who testified against me?' the judge hankered to know."

"'Well, for one, there was your pal Banker Jones.'"

"'He's usurious. Why, he cheats lil ol' ladies and widders out of their life's savings. Who else?'"

Several other names were mentioned, said Johnson, and the judge fiercely denounced each as a scoundrel from way back.

After pouring it on about all the people who had testified against the judge, the friend admitted he had been joking from the start. None of them had; and furthermore, his court had not been abolished.

To this, the judge drew himself up and bellowed, "Now why did you go and make me say all those things about the finest group of men I know?"

"And that's the way you ought to feel," Johnson told the senator.

Johnson's troubles with Fulbright reached a high point at the beginning of February 1966, when Fulbright's Senate Foreign Relations Committee held hearings on the war in Vietnam that were televised for home viewing across the nation. One eloquent witness against the Johnson escalation was retired General James Gavin, whom Johnson had convinced back in 1957 to resign as Army research chief in protest against the inadequate Eisenhower missile program. Gavin proposed that General Westmoreland, who had been his chief of staff in the Normandy invasion, dig into strong areas, or enclaves, that could be easily defended against the Viet Cong, and maintain control there until the Communists decided to negotiate. Former Army Chief of Staff Matthew Ridgway submitted a statement backing Gavin, and former Ambassador to the Soviet Union and Yugoslavia George Kennan, formulator of the Truman containment policy against Soviet expansion in Europe, chose as his focal point: "There is more respect to be won in the opinion of the world by a resolute and courageous liquidation of unsound positions than in the most stubborn pursuit of extravagant or unpromising objectives." Yet Kennan supported the Gavin enclave approach because "we should not turn tail and flee the scene" before negotiations for a settlement were made with the enemy. What Kennan found strange in the American involvement was that "here is an obligation on our part not only to defend the frontiers of a certain political entity against outside attack, but to insure the internal security of its Government in circumstances where that Government is unable to assure that security by its own means."

In order to pull the publicity rug out from under the Fulbright hearings Johnson flew to Honolulu on February 5, 1966, for a spur-of-the-moment two-day war-and-peace council meeting with Ky and Thieu, the American-backed puppet leaders of South Vietnam. At the close, Johnson and Ky proclaimed themselves "brothers in arms," and the two, in what appeared to be an afterthought, agreed that besides American armies and bombing crews, also of importance in winning the war were social and economic reforms and the establishment of a future democratic government in South Vietnam. Secretary of Agriculture Orville Freeman was dispatched from the conference to South Vietnam to be photographed upturning a spadeful of dirt, as a symbolic gesture of future agricultural reforms combined with American farming techniques. Vice President Humphrey was also sent on to Saigon to continue the effort to downgrade the Fulbright hearings. Joe Alsop, who was there, after denouncing Fulbright and Mansfield as "timid and/or inexperienced," said that Humphrey should take home from Vietnam the message that "this war . . . with serious effort, may even be won rather soon."

Johnson was not in a good mood when he returned home. He had failed to drown out the Fulbright hearings; Ky was having trouble with the political Buddhists in Saigon, Da Nang, and Hue, and the Viet Cong refused to disappear; De Gaulle was ordering NATO to move its headquarters out of France; anti-war demonstrations were going on regularly from Atlantic coastal states to the Pacific; in addition to the academic community, church leaders were overwhelmingly against the war; irresponsible Republican leaders had joined with right-wing crackpots to yell that

Johnson had not escalated the war sufficiently. Perennial campaigner Richard Nixon was quoted anew about the risk of the Chinese coming into the war if Johnson should follow the Nixon plan of massive escalation. Nixon replied, "We must recognize that they might. My answer is that this is the time to take that risk. . . . Now we can win."

Evangelist Billy Graham came to Washington on February 17 to join Johnson and several hundred others at an 8 A.M. grilled-lamb-chops, hash-fried-potatoes, and fried-apple prayer breakfast at the Shoreham Hotel. The Reverend Mr. Graham recalled words of Jesus to support the war in Vietnam. "There are those who have tried to reduce Christ to the level of a genial and innocuous appeaser!" Graham boomed in his best voice. "But Jesus said, 'You are wrong—I have come as a fire-setter and a sword-wielder. . . . I am come to send fire on the earth' (Luke 12:49). . . . 'Think not that I am come to send peace on earth: I came not to send peace, but a sword. For I am come to set a man at variance against his family. And a man's foes shall be they of his own household' (Matthew 10:34)."

When Johnson spoke, he thanked Billy Graham for his many kind words and said he wanted to read a letter from a "dear little lady" whose son had been killed in Vietnam. "My countrymen," Johnson said—after finishing the dear little lady's letter to him invoking "God to bless you and your little family"—"in those words from that dear mother are to be found the greatness of this nation and also the strength of its President."

By mid-February 1966, Johnson was aware that upward of thirty of the sixty-seven Democratic senators were opposed to his military policy in Vietnam. But among this growing list of Democratic opponents of his policy of escalation and unconditional surrender, Johnson reserved his greatest hatred for Fulbright and Senator Robert Kennedy.

The young senator from New York was not by nature a dissenter, and he stood apart from the Fulbright-Mansfield-Morse-Hartke-Young-McCarthy-McGovern-Gore-Gruening-Clark-Aiken-Church-Burdick-Moss-Bartlett "doves" who met secretly from time to time to discuss how they might influence a President who was deaf to their proposals. Johnson could grow angry at reports he read of these closed-door meetings, but they did not give him the chest pains a single speech by Bobby Kennedy gave him. At one "dove" meeting, Senator Eugene McCarthy of Minnesota was reported to have said, "We've got a wild man in the White House, and we are going to have to treat him as such"; and Senator Albert Gore of Tennessee called Johnson "a desperate man who was likely to get us into war with China, and we have got to prevent it."

Yet because Bobby Kennedy was the living embodiment of his late brother's mystique, Johnson became more overwrought at Kennedy's news conference statement on the war on February 19, 1966, than he did with these statements by McCarthy and Gore. On this occasion, Kennedy prefaced his attack with the comment that an American withdrawal was "impossible for this country." Then he went on to propose a solution that involved telling Ho Chi Minh that the United States did not want him to surrender but rather to negotiate. Kennedy also proposed establishing a coalition government in South Vietnam that would include the NLF.

Johnson sat in his rocking chair in the Oval Office, too depressed to move for hours. Then he ordered McGeorge Bundy, George Ball, and Vice President Humphrey to pound Kennedy as naïve and as an unpatriotic American. Later Bundy wrote Kennedy a long letter of apology for his assault on him, although neither Bundy's nor Ball's attacks gained much public attention. However, Humphrey's did, for he used the striking word picture comparing Kennedy's proposal for a coalition government to "putting a fox in the chicken coop or an arsonist in a fire department."

Now that Johnson believed from the newspaper stories that Humphrey had discredited Kennedy, he went after Fulbright. On March 2, 1966, the Morse Resolution to repeal the Tonkin Bay Resolution of August 1964 came to the Senate floor for a vote. Fulbright had attempted to keep this from a tally because White House propaganda had twisted the issue so that most Senate "doves" feared that a vote for Morse would be interpreted back home as an antagonistic act toward the boys fighting in Vietnam. But Morse had shown characteristic adamancy, and it failed by 92 to 5, with Fulbright glumly casting one of the losing votes.

On the very next day Johnson retaliated by announcing a further escalation in the war by ordering an additional thirty thousand soldiers sent to Vietnam. He also spoke at a Democratic dinner in the Washington Armory at which Fulbright was present, and he gleefully told the crowd, "You can say one thing about those Foreign Relations Committee hearings, although I don't think this is the place to say it."

What infuriated Johnson most about Fulbright was the senator's standing as an intellectual, for this to a large extent had turned the professors, who as a group had supported Wilson, Roosevelt, and Kennedy, into Johnson opponents. Johnson said flatly that Munich and Vietnam were identical, but the professors applauded Fulbright when he said, "The treatment of slight and superficial resemblances as if they were full-blooded analogies— as instances of history 'repeating itself'—is a substitute for thinking and a misuse of history." Then to throw Winston Churchill, the staunchest symbol of the anti-Munich spirit, into Johnson's face, Fulbright quoted the British statesman: " 'Appeasement from strength is magnanimous and noble and might be the surest and perhaps the only path to world peace.' "

As the father of the Great Society, Johnson especially resented Fulbright's charge in April 1966 that he was also its pallbearer. "The inspiration and commitment of the Great Society have disappeared," said Fulbright. "In concrete terms, the President simply cannot think about implementing the Great Society at home while he is supervising bombing missions over North Vietnam. There is a kind of madness in the facile assumption that we can raise the many billions of dollars necessary to rebuild our schools and cities and public transport and eliminate the pollution of air and water while also spending tens of billions to finance an 'open-ended' war in Asia."

Then there was Fulbright's lecture on "The Arrogance of Power," delivered at Johns Hopkins University, in which he accused the Administration of being "a seeker after unlimited power and empire" with a "self-appointed mission to police the world, to defeat all tyrannies, to make their fellow men rich and happy and free."

On the evening of May 4, Johnson was waiting for Fulbright to come down the receiving line at the Diplomatic Reception in the Blue Room. When Fulbright approached, Johnson reached into his pocket, pulled out a penciled note from his cook, Zephyr Wright, and held Fulbright there. "A man can hardly have an arrogance of power," Johnson threw at him, "when he gets a note from his cook talking up to him like this."

With a worried expression on her face, Lady Bird was yanking at his arm and repeating that they were supposed to go to the East Room to dance. "Bird, I'll be ready in a minute," he told her as he angrily began reading Zephyr's note to Fulbright: " 'Mr. President, you have been my boss for a number of years and you always tell me you want to loose [*sic*] weight, and yet you never do very much to help yourself. Now I'm going to be your boss for a change. Eat what I put in front of you and don't ask for any more and don't complain.' "

Fulbright gave him a quizzical smile at the conclusion and moved on.

Even with the increase in ground-troop strength and the step-up in napalm and explosive bombings, the expected military victory in South Vietnam did not come into view in the spring of 1966. In fact, a civil war within a civil war was occurring there, with Buddhist leaders refusing to cooperate with the Ky Government. But with American backing, Ky's troops moved into Hue, Da Nang, and other places, and after months of skirmishes extinguished the Buddhist threat. One puzzling matter to Johnson was the growing animosity of South Vietnamese to Americans. On May Day, for instance, ten thousand persons marched in a Saigon parade and shouted slogans such as "End the War" and "Yankee Go Home." The marchers were finally dispersed after a clubbing by ARVN troops and the police.

There was further military escalation that spring. On April 17, Johnson permitted a one-time testing raid by South Vietnam–stationed fighter-bombers on two Soviet-built surface-to-air missile sites fifteen miles from Hanoi, and two days later there was a similar raid on the Uongbi power plant fifteen miles from Haiphong. In addition, that same month giant B-52 bombers stationed on Guam were thrown into the war on Johnson's orders to make daily flights to drop their payloads over Vietnam.

By June, the Washington rumor factories were alive with stories that Johnson was working on another major escalation. There was talk that he was considering an Inchon-type invasion of North Vietnam, mining the port of Haiphong, bombing the centers of Hanoi and Haiphong, and egging the Chinese Communists into a showdown.

While Johnson let the situation simmer along before announcing another escalation, he held briefings with congressmen to insure support for the course he planned to follow. One whom he wanted to convert or neutralize was Senator Stephen Young of Ohio, whose outbursts against the war had gone on far too long to suit Johnson.

Young, a veteran of World Wars I and II, had come to the Senate in 1959, and at the specific request of former President Truman, Johnson had assigned him to top committees. The principal reason for Truman's interest was that Young had defeated Senator John Bricker, who had grossly insulted Missouri's Harry at a Gridiron Club banquet during his Administration. In return for Johnson's kindness, Young had not participated in the revolt of the Senate liberals against Majority Leader Johnson that year.

It was after Johnson had been President a year that Young began his persistent attack on the Administration over the war in Vietnam. Young recalled his first visit: "I took a trip there with Senators Tom Dodd and Howard Cannon. Tom spent two days holed up in an air-conditioned suite in Saigon while Howard and I went to every American air and field base in South Vietnam; six of the eight bases we had in Thailand; and we flew over North Vietnam in a helicopter. I asked General Westmoreland if the Viet Cong soldiers were Communists from the North because I wanted to know the nature of the conflict. And he frankly told me, 'The bulk of the VC's fighting us in South Vietnam were born and raised in South Vietnam.'

"So when I returned to the United States I began making speeches in which I said, 'President Johnson has made the most serious mistake that any President of the United States has ever made by involving our armed might in a civil war more than eight thousand miles from Washington.' " Young also challenged the Administration's claim that the fighting in Vietnam had the same justification as the Korean War. "That was an invasion of South Korea by North Korea," Young insisted. "Besides, we had a definite commitment there from the World War II postwar settlement; and in addition, Truman had immediately turned the war into a United Nations effort."

Before long, Young focused his antagonism on Dean Rusk, and the two had serious flare-ups on occasion. One such scene took place in the White House theater after Rusk denounced the Viet Cong for their "sneak attack" on Pleiku in February 1965. "Would you call George Washington's crossing the Delaware on Christmas Eve in 1776 to capture the Hessians at Trenton a 'sneak attack'?" Young asked. Rusk's face grew livid, but he made no reply.

Johnson stepped into this antagonism in February 1966, when Young mounted an attack on Rusk as a peace-poser who loved war. Mimicking the famous speech of Jack Valenti on Johnson, Young said in a speech he could sleep better at night if Rusk were not Secretary of State. The next day Johnson told a group of congressmen at the White House, "I'm sorry I'm a little late, but I stopped at the drugstore and bought some sleeping tablets for Senator Steve Young because Steve ought to get his sleep, because Dean Rusk is going to be Secretary of State a long, long time."

As the time drew near for Johnson to make his announcement of the next escalation, said Young, "Johnson asked the twenty-eight members of Congress who had been to Vietnam to come to his second-floor office in the White House for a briefing on June 22. We sat in two rows of chairs around a large table: Johnson was seated in a large leather chair; McNamara sat at his right; Rusk was two places away at his left; and Hubert Humphrey was close to him in the midst of several impressively dressed generals, plus White House advisers.

"After the briefing Johnson called for our opinions; and almost everyone there with the exception of Mike Mansfield, George Aiken, and me was very warlike and said we should bomb all of North Vietnam, mine the harbor at Haiphong, and get tough with our non-helping allies—even breaking diplomatic relations with them. One House member from my state pleased Johnson by denouncing 'American legislators who were quoted by *Pravda* as being against the war—and I don't exclude some U. S. senators from my remarks, because they are giving aid and comfort to the enemy.'

"Mansfield and Aiken spoke out loud and clear against what we were doing, and they opposed further escalation. When my turn came, I agreed with them and added, 'It's a miserable civil war. And it does not involve in any strategic importance the defense of the United States or any real commitment. We don't have a mandate from Almighty God to police the entire world. This talk about there being an international Communist conspiracy that we must repel wherever it rears its ugly head is a myth. Southeast Asia, Mr. President, very definitely is not within our sphere of influence. South America? Yes.' Johnson seemed impatient to move on to a war-lover, but I took the time to look at the bemedaled Chiefs of Staff and tell them, 'Your required reading should include the *Battle of Dien Bien Phu,* by the French officer Jules Roy.' "

Johnson decided to "raise the price of aggression" that Ho Chi Minh would have to pay for continuing the war. The opening move came on June 29, 1966, with bombing attacks on the oil installations at Haiphong and Hanoi.

To one reporter Johnson explained, "I had to do something to help the morale of the Joint Chiefs. We weren't winning and they were frustrated." To another, he said he was moving because of a talk Ho Chi Minh had held with a Canadian diplomat in Hanoi. Johnson said he had learned that Ho had expressed his willingness to fight a long war against the United

States, but Ho had added that he did not think this was necessary because "we won't have to wait too long—only until November, when American voters defeat those who favor the war."

Once the first attacks were made, there was some concern that this would bring China into the war. Johnson told guests at the annual White House Judicial Reception a year later that he had felt apprehensive about this. The Washington *Post* reported that while "standing in a corner of the State Dining Room, consuming a huge meal," Johnson recalled the night of June 29, 1966: "My daughter Luci complained that I looked tired, and I told her to sit down and learn some history. 'You may not wake up tomorrow,' I told her. 'Your Daddy may go down in history as having started World War III.' " Johnson said "he went on to tell of the restless night he had waiting to hear if the American planes returned, and said that the prayers and hopes of Luci and himself had gone with the men on their mission."

In another version of June 29, Johnson told a reporter he had expressed his worries to Luci, and she said, "Come with me to the monastery and my little monks will pray for you." Johnson went on, "So I went with Luci to her monastery and I prayed with her little monks. Then I went back to the White House and slept like a baby." The next day, he said, he told Luci he felt better because the raid had not produced World War III, and she replied that she had not worried "because I knew my little monks would come through."

On the day following the first air strikes on the oil depots, Johnson flew to Omaha, where he excitedly announced in a speech at the stockyards, "We have begun to turn the tide!" His chief planner, Walt Rostow, who had been urging him into an open-end escalation, added that the Viet Cong have been "tactically defeated." Rostow had other deep thoughts. "We're closer to an era of real global peace than at any time since 1914" was one. As for Ho Chi Minh, Rostow said that the Communist leader should be thankful for American intervention in Vietnam, since it was a protective shield against Red China's intervention. "The men in Hanoi cherish their independence," Rostow remarked, claiming that they would lose it to China "if we left the Asian mainland."

Back on his ranch after another speech at Des Moines, Johnson held an outdoor news conference before TV cameras to tell the American people of the coming end of the war. "Our diplomatic reports indicate that the opposing forces no longer expect a military victory in South Vietnam," he said. However, at another point he quickly threw in the thought that additional men and equipment would have to be sent to Vietnam.

In the first boom of the bombing escalation and Johnson's optimism that the end was now in sight, his popularity showed a ten-point surge in the polls, so that an estimated 55 per cent of Americans approved of him as President. This was apparent to reporters who accompanied him in late

July on a nine-speech day into four states. He was drawing cheers when he compared himself to the late President Kennedy and bellowed through his bullhorn: "Some are more interested in style. I'm interested in accomplishments." There were even louder cheers when he said in effect that congressmen and columnists who criticized the war were un-American. "Stop, look, and listen as you hear the voices talking about what's wrong with your country," he screamed. "It may be old-fashioned, but I still believe that my country does most things right." In all his talks he referred to the soldiers and guerrillas fighting Americans and Premier Ky's forces as "North Vietnamese." One time he called "speakers and columnists and many commentators" propagandists for the enemy and said jeeringly, "I doubt if they will lecture you about bombings by the North Vietnamese of hospitals for American servicemen in South Vietnam."

In August, Johnson celebrated his improved standing by campaigning in five states in three days for congressmen up for re-election in November. "Johnson made a field trip into Indiana," said Senator Hartke, "and in the flush of his new popularity over his latest escalation he criticized Senate critics of the war while I was sitting on the platform. The crowds were large and enthusiastic because they believed that the war would soon be over, and he said he planned to campaign in all fifty states.

"But when the war went on and American casualties kept rising, his popularity poll dropped, and he knew that only the war hawks like Paul Douglas wanted him to campaign for them. Everyone else clamored for Bobby Kennedy to come to their states and speak for them. So Johnson said, 'We may get licked in this election, and I'm going to be blamed, and I need an escape hatch.' He found it by deciding to be out of the country on a hurriedly arranged conference in Manila."

After the July 1966 raids on the oil depots, intelligence reports reaching Johnson revealed that Ho Chi Minh was escalating his side of the war in answer to the American escalation. "Hanoi, Haiphong, and other cities and enterprises may be destroyed," Ho told his countrymen, "but the Vietnamese people will not be intimidated." More than six hundred thousand of Hanoi's eight hundred thousand residents were sent out of the capital; North Vietnam's trained reserves were called to duty; fifty thousand Chinese road and railroad laborers came across the border to repair bombing damage; and immense Soviet military assistance plus some Soviet missile crews went to North Vietnam.

By September, with the polls showing his popularity falling rapidly following his failure to end the war, Johnson put into effect the second half of the "Johnson Vietnam Syndrome" while he considered his next move. This syndrome, a swinging pendulum on no regular beat between "the man of escalating warfare" and "the man of negotiating peace," was a magnificent instrument to render his critics helpless and to confuse the public.

Ambassador Arthur Goldberg led off for him with a hoarse-voiced speech at the UN, declaring that the United States wanted only peace in Vietnam and would halt the bombing of North Vietnam when "a corresponding and appropriate de-escalation on the other side" went into effect. This was the old pitch of Dean Rusk, requiring Ho to remove his troops and influence over the Viet Cong fighters as a precondition to the end of the bombings. Goldberg, however, added a new element to the cauldron when he expressed for the first time the promise that representation of the Viet Cong at the negotiating table would not be "an insurmountable obstacle." But Rusk quickly scotched any loose interpretation of Goldberg's promise by saying that Ho Chi Minh was capable of representing them.

After the Goldberg speech Johnson made an attempt to shift the blame for the lack of negotiations on the Communists. On a quick trip to New York on October 7, he made a speech to the influential National Conference of Editorial Writers, replacing Rusk, who had been the scheduled speaker. The Johnson thrust in the small luncheon room was to call for "peaceful engagement" between the United States and the Soviet Union despite their severe differences over Vietnam. That same day Johnson's conciliatory words spilled over in a spur-of-the-moment talk he held with U Thant on the thirty-eighth floor of the UN Building. Johnson asked him to get Ho Chi Minh's agreement to negotiate, and he also insisted that Thant accept United States promotion for a second term as UN Secretary-General, even though Thant argued that he was weary and wanted to retire.

The visit to U Thant was marred by chanting groups of youth who, despite threats by New York policemen, called out to Johnson: "Hey, hey, LBJ! How many kids did you kill today?" But this was quickly forgotten when Johnson rushed afterward to Newark, where a Democratic crowd applauded his forty-five-minute attack on Richard Nixon. Yet even here there was an unhappy note, for the loudest cheering came whenever he mentioned the name of John Kennedy.

On the following Monday, October 10, Johnson shifted the onus for the continuing conflict in Vietnam to the Soviet Union when he met with Andrei Gromyko, the Soviet Foreign Minister. Gromyko had asked to enter and leave the White House through a back-door route so that the meeting would not be publicized, but Johnson lost no time calling Drew Pearson and giving him his version of the conversation. "During this historic visit," Pearson wrote in his column five days later, "the President treated Gromyko like a misguided congressman who needed to be shown the light. He argued the American case in Vietnam with powerful logic, speaking one moment in the name of humanity, the next as one politician to another. . . . Gromyko repeated the Soviet complaint that a settlement is impossible as long as American planes are bombing North Vietnam."

To this, said Johnson, "he reminded Gromyko that he had halted the bombing from December 24, 1965, to January 31, 1966, in response to a private plea from Soviet Ambassador Anatoly Dobrynin that this might lead to a truce," but that "during the 'Dobrynin pause' you kicked me in the groin" by sending in large amounts of Soviet weapons. "Actually, he used a more earthy term than groin," Pearson acknowledged, reporting that Johnson had asked the Russian diplomat, "Would you kick me again?"

At one point, Johnson told Pearson, he had emphasized to Gromyko how easy it would be for the Soviet Union to cut red tape by pulling "a knife out of his pocket and [making] slashes in the air. . . . As Gromyko prepared to leave, LBJ wrapped a friendly arm around his shoulder and stabbed him in the chest with an emphatic forefinger. 'Now remember what I said,' he admonished."

With a continuing drop in the popularity barometer, Johnson decided to take a quick trip abroad to stem the downward trend, just as he had flown to Honolulu in February to draw attention away from the Fulbright hearings.

This time, with the fanfare of a potentate, he flew from Washington on October 17 on a seventeen-day, thirty-one-thousand-mile tour of Southeast Asia, climaxed by a two-day Manila Conference on October 24 and 25. Before he left, he arranged with Bill Moyers to call him daily to report on the amount of coverage he was getting on radio and TV. There was little need for this, because from the number of reporters and TV camera crews accompanying him, he would receive almost total news saturation back home.

His first stop was New Zealand, where his plane was greeted with signs reading "Bobby Kennedy for President." But the crowds were friendly, outside of some shouting anti-war demonstrators, and enjoyed his frequent leaps from his limousine to rush among them for his unique style of "howdy and shake." Then it was on to Australia, where breezy "Mr. Ed, the Talking Horse" Clark was now the American ambassador to the "down-under" land of twelve million persons. Although Johnson repeatedly asserted that "Australians are the kind of people I can go to the well with," in Sydney his driver sped his car at fifty miles an hour past anti-war demonstrators to avoid the experience of the day before at Melbourne, where the Presidential limousine was splattered with bags of green and red oil paint.

The next stop was Manila, for the summit meeting with South Korea, South Vietnam, Thailand, the Philippine Islands, Australia, and New Zealand. President Marcos, host to the seven-country conference, favored an end to the bombing of North Vietnam, but he offered no objection when asked to sign the hard-line joint communiqué Johnson's staff had prepared for the occasion. This was a document pledging the South Vietnam Government's allies to remove their troops from that country within a six-month period after North Vietnam removed its "military and subversive forces" from the South. Rusk and Clark Clifford had argued in vain with Johnson not to propose the withdrawal promise.

The "Spirit of Manila" was actually a hardening of Johnson's terms for negotiations, because no mention was made of stopping the bombing of the

North. In addition, Premier Ky defined the "subversive forces" who would have to go north as including the Viet Cong guerrillas, who were native to the South. There was also a Johnson declaration at Manila committing the United States to enforce peace throughout Southeast Asia. Walter Lippmann called this the "messianic megalomania which is the Manila madness." But Vice President Humphrey took an opposite view: The "Spirit of Manila" was an immense addition to the "Spirit of Honolulu," which was of as "much significance to the future of Asia as the Atlantic Charter had been for the future of Europe."

There was still time for Johnson to return home and campaign for Democratic congressmen, but he went instead to Thailand, Malaysia, and South Korea, in addition to paying a surprise call on American troops in South Vietnam on October 26. Johnson's arrival in Thailand, a country under a military dictatorship and where an estimated fifty thousand American troops were stationed to prepare the daily bombing raids over Laos and North Vietnam, was dampened somewhat by news that Red China had just exploded a missile with a nuclear warhead. Nevertheless, Johnson assured his audience at a state dinner that the war in Vietnam was almost over, though there were "rivers still to cross and mountains to climb." Johnson's speechwriter was Walt Rostow, whom friends called "an anti-Communist with machine guns"; newsmen recognized his style from the frequent insertion of the terms "Munich" and "appeasement" in describing why the United States was in Vietnam. They also recognized the Rostow pen in Johnson's definition of his objective in South Vietnam as the bringing about of "the principle of self-determination on a one-man, one-vote basis by secret ballot."

Before Johnson proceeded to Seoul, South Korea, his aides had gone there earlier to handle the welcome, and he was pleased with the huge signs reading "The Tall Texan." Marquis Childs, who was along, reported that when Johnson said in South Korea that his great-grandfather had died in the battle of the Alamo, "this came as quite a revelation to the Texas newsmen at hand." Johnson's visit to Camranh Bay on the coast of South Vietnam at the Twelfth Parallel featured an exhortation to Westmoreland's generals at the Officers' Club to kill as many Viet Cong as they could search out and destroy. "Come home with the coonskin on the wall," he told them.

It was on the evening of November 2 that the Presidential plane landed at Dulles Airport in a downpour after a 3,500-mile flight from Anchorage, Alaska. Federal employees had been ordered to be at the airport to greet him, and thousands were on hand when he stepped from the plane and walked over the 150 feet of red carpeting to the microphones. Signs read, "Well Done, Mr. President," and the applause was loud as he finished shaking hands and stood under the umbrella held over him by Hubert Humphrey. But instead of acknowledging the peaceful aspects of the Manila trip, Johnson's message was a declaration of further escalation:

"The war effort will be increased from the 336,000 American servicemen now in Vietnam. We shall never let them down." Then in a warning to Fulbright, who had come to the airport, Johnson said that criticism of what he was doing in Vietnam must end—"When there is deep division in a land, there is danger."

Johnson returned from the Spirit of Manila puffy-eyed, tired, and ill, and although doctors told him he needed two operations, he was determined to join in the last-minute campaign effort for pro-war candidates. All that fall Bobby Kennedy had garnered enormous publicity flying across the nation on speaking trips to help Congressional members in their campaigns. The polls had revealed a surge for Bobby for President in 1968 and a growing percentage of Democrats who thought Johnson should retire.

But Johnson had second thoughts about campaigning even for the small number of Democrats who wanted him when he experienced pain on the right side of his abdomen the day following his return home, despite the girdle he had been wearing over his hernia since April. He therefore notified pro-war Democratic candidates Senator Paul Douglas in Illinois, Governor Edmund "Pat" Brown of California, Representative Robert Duncan (running for the Senate in Oregon), and former Governor Endicott Peabody (a Senate candidate in Massachusetts) that they would have to get along without him. All four expressed sharp disappointment. As compensation, however, Johnson publicly ridiculed Nixon, who was dashing about the country on a speaking tour, as a "chronic campaigner," and he ordered Defense Secretary McNamara to declare a cutback in the draft call (to be raised after the election) and White House aides to issue economic statistics showing a continuing prosperity.

Yet when the votes were counted, the four who had depended on his personal help failed miserably. As for the Ninetieth Congress, it would come to Washington in January showing an increase of forty-seven Republicans in the House and three in the Senate. "This Congress isn't going to do a damn thing," predicted Representative Richard Bolling of Missouri, a Democratic leader in the House.

Johnson waited until November 16 to have his operations—one to eliminate an abdominal hernia and the other to remove a 5-mm. benign polyp from his throat. Three hours after these operations Alvin Wirtz's son-in-law, Dr. James Cain, announced that his condition "couldn't be better." Lady Bird was in his hospital room when he returned wide-awake from surgery, and he scribbled a note for her to turn on all three TV sets at the foot of his bed plus two radios. She said afterward, "This is the first time in my life I've ever seen him speechless, and we're going to make the most of it." At 11:30 A.M., five hours after his operation, he asked that reporters be brought to his bedside. The conversation turned out to be a sore-throated denial that he was fat. "I weigh two hundred and twelve pounds and that's not fat for six feet three inches," he insisted with thrashing gestures. He rolled up a pajama leg and said, "See, this isn't a fat leg." Then he rolled up a sleeve. "And that's not a fat arm." One reporter was tempted to ask him about the condition of his head.

Despite his quick alertness so soon after the operation, Johnson's recovery at the ranch was slow, and he could not return to the White House for several weeks. At the First Christian Church in Johnson City he looked wan as he sat clipping his nails and listening to the preacher pray for "the rapid recovery of Thy servant, our President"; and he was out of sorts as he commuted between the ranch and Austin to work in his "Texas Taj Mahal," as local residents dubbed the glittering ten-room Presidential suite in the new Federal Office Building. Nor was he happy when Democratic governors at the Governors Conference suggested he retire from office. He asked them to come to the ranch for a barbecue in December and successfully browbeat them into submission during a two-and-a-half-hour gripe session.

Johnson's dismal mood in 1966 also revealed itself when the White House Historical Association commissioned Peter Hurd, one of Johnson's favorite artists, to paint his portrait. Johnson promised to pose and Hurd went to the ranch, where he was given a twenty-minute session to study Johnson's expressions and skin coloring. Johnson would not sit still, however, and spent the time conversing with Arthur Goldberg in a series of lopes around the room and quick leaps off his chair while he incessantly rubbed his forehead, nose, and chin. Afterward, Johnson gave Hurd another appointment and promised he would model this time in a quiet, thirty-minute session. But Hurd had hardly set up his equipment when Johnson dropped his head on his chest and began snoring. Hurd roused him gingerly after ten minutes and offered to return another day. "No!" Johnson bellowed. "I promised Bird I'd give you a half hour and I'm going to give you a half hour." With that, his head fell and he slept again.

Following this, Hurd returned in disgust to his own ranch in New Mexico and completed the portrait of Johnson in three-quarter left profile from photographs. When the egg tempera portrait, with the U. S. Capitol Building as a backdrop, was completed, Hurd and his wife Henriette brought it to the L.B.J. Ranch for the unveiling.

"That's the ugliest thing I ever saw!" Johnson told him, scowling. He jerked open a desk drawer and pulled out a reproduction of a portrait of himself that Norman Rockwell had produced. "That's what I call a real good likeness," he spat at Hurd.

"I wish I could copy a photograph like that," Hurd replied heatedly.

"That's not a photograph," Johnson bellowed. "Rockwell made that while I posed twenty minutes for him."

"Nonsense!" Hurd yelled. "He couldn't have painted that from life in twenty minutes if he had nineteen more hands."

Johnson was now in a fury after having been called a liar to his face, and he began jingling coins in his pocket with a heavy clunk. "Let's get out of here, Henriette," Hurd told his wife, and they left, slamming the door.

Johnson sent the portrait back to him—C.O.D. Not long afterward, Lady Bird called Hurd and apologized for the scene Lyndon had put on. "The only thing that didn't go wrong that day," she said, "was that the Government in Vietnam didn't fall."

She wanted him to try again, and she sent him a photograph to use as his model. But after he tentatively agreed, he said he found this photograph in every post office and "framed on every bureaucrat's desk," so he quit.

"What we ask for we are going to get, we are going to keep, we are going to hold!" was the way Johnson had described his intentions in Vietnam during his trip to the Manila Conference. He was determined to win a military victory in South Vietnam, and he had promised General Westmoreland three thousand new troops each week for the war furnace. The North was hurting far more than it admitted, read the optimistic intelligence reports that crossed Johnson's desk.

Continued escalation had raised the total number of American troops in Vietnam from 15,000 at the beginning of 1965 to 190,000 in January 1966; then to 380,000 a year later; and at the rate promised Westmoreland, the total would reach 465,000 by 1968. These were in addition to the 50,000 men in the U. S. Seventh Fleet off Southeast Asia and a similar number of American troops stationed in Thailand. All these, plus 750,000 South Vietnamese ARVN troops, 45,000 from South Korea, and an extra 10,000 from Australia, New Zealand, Thailand, and the Philippines, were engaged in "search and destroy" warfare against 225,000 Viet Cong guerrillas and an estimated 50,000 DRV (Democratic Republic of Vietnam—North Vietnam) soldiers.

As 1966 began to fade, an enormous worldwide effort to bring the war to a halt before it escalated to the point where it involved other major powers and nuclear weapons became evident. Necessity now forced Johnson to work both parts of his Vietnam Syndrome simultaneously—to escalate the war further and express his desire for an end to the conflict.

Johnson critics at home and abroad were soon confused by his apparent sincerity in asking the enemy to give him only the slightest signal that it would join him in talks and he would travel anywhere to bring peace to Vietnam. But while he spoke softly and as a man who yearned for peaceful negotiations, he refused to meet the two minimum requirements that all insiders recognized as necessary before the Communists could enter into talks. The first essential was the halting of the bombing of the North without a *quid pro quo;* the second was the recognition of the NLF as an independent political entity in the South. Because of his adamant stand on these two issues, Johnson knew he could prevent negotiations from taking place while, at the same time, gaining great political mileage as a man who wanted peace.

Never since Johnson had become President were so many attempts to end the war taking place at the same time. President De Gaulle was reiterating his belief that the United States should withdraw from South Vietnam and respect "the principle that every people should settle its affairs itself, in its own fashion and by its own means." U Thant was calling into the wilderness for the United States to end the bombings as proof that it wanted negotiations. Then there was British Foreign Secretary George Brown, who went to Moscow on November 23 to gain Soviet approval of his peace plan, which would have the United States halt its bombings of the North while a conference negotiated a cease-fire and political settlement.

But when Soviet Premier Aleksei Kosygin told Brown that an unconditional end of the bombing must come first, American "spokesmen" said that this proved the insincerity of the Communists, and Johnson escalated the fighting by ordering heavy air strikes over Hanoi on December 2, 3, and 4. This was the first time North Vietnam's capital had been bombed since the preceding June 29.

There was also a Polish effort to establish peace talks between North Vietnam and the United States, and North Vietnam was reported to have agreed to discussions at Warsaw without a prior end of the bombing. But North Vietnam withdrew its offer when Hanoi again underwent heavy bombing on December 13 and 14. British Prime Minister Harold Wilson, who had been kept apprised of the Polish attempt, refused to blame the United States for deliberately ruining the project and called its failure a "two-way misunderstanding."

When U Thant criticized American bombing of Hanoi during these preliminary negotiations, Johnson ordered Ambassador Goldberg to counteract this by making the Secretary-General appear less a peacemaker than the United States. This was cleverly accomplished on December 19, when Goldberg asked Thant to "take whatever steps you consider necessary to bring about the necessary discussions which could lead to . . . a cease-fire." One UN observer called this "a message to Thant to produce the Communists [on the United States' terms] or stop criticizing." Since Johnson had no intention of weakening on the two basic requirements, the Administration knew that U Thant would be effectively stymied.

In addition, Goldberg had an opportunity to read off a high-sounding fourteen-point peace proposal when he "pleaded" with Thant to find a way to bring about a cease-fire. These fourteen points did not include the three-point program of Thant: (1) an unconditional end to the bombing, (2) a mutual scaling down of the fighting, and (3) the inclusion of the Viet Cong in the negotiations. So the American bombing of Hanoi was offset in the propaganda war by the Goldberg request to Thant, and Goldberg's insistence that "our objective remains the end of all fighting, of all hostilities, and of all violence in Vietnam—and an honorable and lasting settlement there."

When the three-day Christmas truce began on December 24, Mike Mansfield asked Johnson to extend it until February 12 and propose to North Vietnam a mutual freeze in military strength so that a cease-fire could be arranged. But Johnson ordered the air attacks resumed, and he told reporters at the ranch, "You just can't have a one-sided peace conference or a one-sided cessation of hostilities." Ambassador Lodge went further and said that no peace negotiations would probably be necessary because he expected the enemy to "fade away." In any case, he added a double-talk judgment: The Viet Cong must end their military activities "to earn a cease-fire."

British Foreign Secretary George Brown was still looking for an answer to the Vietnam dilemma. On December 30, he came up with the idea of holding an international peace conference—a proposal advanced by Mike Mansfield the preceding April. But Hanoi quickly torpedoed Brown's plan because he would not invite the NLF.

On January 10, 1967, having recovered from the Johnson-Goldberg gambit, U Thant declared that the United States would have to accept three propositions if peace were to come. The first one, said Thant, was that the Viet Cong forces were not "a stooge" of North Vietnam, even though the NLF "received substantial help from the North." In addition, he went on, the Domino Theory was not valid, nor was South Vietnam "strategically vital to Western interests."

The results of his stated views were predictable. Secretary Rusk pounced on all three propositions as wildly incorrect. And Johnson ordered new air strikes on Hanoi on January 15 and 16. These attacks were followed by White House assurances that the civilian population had not been bombed, and these assurances were followed by admissions that some civilians might have perished "by accident" in the attacks on military targets.

Although the North Vietnamese peace terms continued to be the hard four points of the April 1965 declaration, the first softening came in January 1967 with the announcement by Mai Van Bo, head of the North Vietnam diplomatic office in Paris, that if the United States ended its bombings without demanding conditions, "this fact will be examined and studied by the Hanoi Government." Near the end of the month North Vietnam's Foreign Minister, Nguyen Duy Trinh, said that after the bombings and "other acts of war" terminated, "there could be talks between the two countries."

Johnson's reply on February 2 was that the bombings would have to continue until a matching "de-escalation" was made by North Vietnam. Putting the entire blame for the continuing conflict on the enemy, Johnson told his news conference in a tone of self-righteous patience, "I cannot report that there are any serious indications that the other side is ready to stop the war." Dean Rusk added to this picture of the impossibility of negotiations until the other side surrendered when he promised that the

NLF could become a "full negotiating party"—if the Viet Cong troops "were to lay down their arms."

At this point, even though he was continuing to escalate the real war, Johnson was winning the propaganda war inside the United States as to his being a man who wanted peace. In all the purposely confusing pleas for peace that he issued ("a matching move [to a bombing stoppage] by the Hanoi Government would be just almost any step"), he showed the experts that he wanted the war to continue by refusing to budge on the two minimum requirements of the enemy: an unconditional bombing halt and recognition of the NLF as an independent force in the South. As one observer noted, "This country seems to have, not so much a policy for starting talks, as a stance to head them off."

But now came trouble with news stories from Paris, linking Senator Robert Kennedy with a peace proposal by the Government of North Vietnam. Immediately there were headlines in newspapers across the United States and a hope that Kennedy would be able to bring about the peace that seemed to be eluding Lyndon Johnson.

A phone call to Rusk brought details of what had gone on in Paris. Kennedy had discussed the war with Etienne Manac'h, the director of the Far Eastern section of the French Foreign Ministry, who passed on to him a three-stage program by Mai Van Bo for settling the war after the bombing stopped. Kennedy had not considered this a vital advance in the published Hanoi formula, but an employee of the American embassy who had accompanied him considered it of enormous importance and cabled the State Department a detailed report. When it was leaked to the press in Washington, the garbled story was that Kennedy was returning from Paris with a peace proposal from North Vietnam.

On learning the true story, Johnson saw an excellent opportunity to rip away the persistent Kennedy political menace. This had been on his mind since the autumn campaigns, when Kennedy had generated excitement wherever he appeared. On December 2, David Broder in the Washington *Post* had called attention to Johnson's situation by describing him as being "in the gravest sort of political danger." Broder attributed Johnson's decline to his "abuse of public confidence, abuse of Administration talent, and abuse of political allies."

But Johnson saw his own standing as in inverse correlation with that of Bobby Kennedy's, and he sought ways to cut him down. In December one opportunity had come when he urged his friend, FBI Director J. Edgar Hoover, to make public a letter charging Kennedy with having expanded wiretapping by the Justice Department during the time he served as Attorney General. Kennedy immediately branded Hoover a liar, and Hoover replied with a similar statement; the publicity that poured out did Kennedy harm. After this came the heavily publicized controversy between Mrs. John Kennedy and the publishers of William Manchester's book *The Death of a President* over the inclusion of certain derogatory remarks Mrs. Kennedy and others had made about Johnson. The net result of this controversy had been to blemish Bobby Kennedy's reputation further.

And now, with the false newspaper stories about a peace offer Kennedy was said to be bringing home with him from Paris, Johnson saw an immense opportunity to demolish him. So when Kennedy returned to Washington, Johnson asked him to come to the White House on February 6, 1967, to brief him on his European tour.

Kennedy went to the White House with Undersecretary of State Nicholas Katzenbach, and the forty-five minutes they spent with Johnson were wild ones. Johnson demanded to know the details of the leaked so-called peace proposal, and Kennedy said he had told no one. A United States embassy employee had accompanied him to the French Foreign Office, he said, and "perhaps the leak came from your State Department."

Johnson turned on him wrathfully. "It's your State Department, not mine!" he screamed. And so far as Kennedy's making soft suggestions on the war, he went on, "If you keep talking like this, you won't have a political future in this country within six months. . . . In six months all of you doves will be destroyed! . . . The blood of American boys will be on your hands!" He continued, charging that those who opposed what he was doing were giving the enemy courage to continue fighting. "I never want to hear your views on Vietnam again!" he bellowed. "I never want to see you again!"

At one point Kennedy was reported to have called Johnson an S.O.B.; and at another point he was said to have interrupted Johnson with "I don't have to sit here and take that shit."

Throughout this stormy session Johnson threw what he thought were telling blows against the "stop the bombing" arguers, and every time he made a point, he would yell at Katzenbach, "Isn't that right?" and Katzenbach would nod like a puppet.

Before the meeting broke up, Johnson ordered Kennedy to hold a news conference and declare that the United States "has never received a genuine peace offer from Hanoi." When Kennedy said he could not until he checked all the records, Johnson again raised his voice. "I'm telling you that you can!" But Kennedy refused.

This was a private meeting, yet as soon as it ended, Johnson poured out the details to Walt Rostow. Within a few hours a blow-by-blow account spread throughout Washington, and the Washington *Post* reported: "One of the sources of information was known to be the British Ambassador to the United States, Sir Patrick Dean. Presumably he was informed of the session by Rostow."

Vice President Humphrey, who had much to gain personally from a Johnson-Kennedy political war, told a friend afterward that the February 6 confrontation between the President and the senator was merely a typical meeting between the two. "When Lyndon and Bobby get together," said

Humphrey, "all sense flies out the window, and they become two animals tearing at each other's throats."

Less than a month after the celebrated session, Kennedy added to the widening chasm between him and Johnson by delivering a speech on Vietnam to the Senate on March 2, 1967. In this highly publicized address Kennedy's broad implication was that Johnson did not sincerely want a negotiated settlement in Vietnam, since he was asking the enemy for "unconditional surrender" as a precondition. Kennedy offered a three-part program of his own: First, suspend the American bombings unilaterally and acknowledge a readiness to negotiate; second, each side was not to build up its forces during negotiations; and third, gradually withdraw American and North Vietnamese troops from South Vietnam.

"Lyndon embarrassed his friends in the volcanic way he reacted to this speech by Bob," said Mike Mansfield. "When he heard about it, he went on a rampage of activities to squeeze it—he hoped—off the front pages. That same day, he released a month-old letter from Soviet Premier Kosygin, agreeing to discuss a curb on nuclear missiles; he sent Scoop Jackson a letter to be read in answer to Bob on the Senate floor—that he would end the bombing 'when the other side is willing to take equivalent action'; he held two press conferences; went unannounced to Howard University's one hundredth anniversary to make an impromptu talk; and he showed up on TV at the ceremony noting the centennial of the U. S. Office of Education."

In addition to this flabbergasting performance, which only served to highlight the Kennedy speech, Johnson ordered a further escalation of the war by signaling the American Command in Thailand to bomb Hanoi from Thai bases. He also told Rusk to demolish Kennedy's argument that the Administration opposed a peace in Vietnam. "We have had bombing pauses of five days in May 1965," Rusk began, "thirty-seven days in December 1965–January 1966, and six days just two weeks ago. And we encountered only hostile action in response."

Ambassador Goldberg, then in Southeast Asia on a vacation and for talks, was also brought into the attack. In Saigon, after meeting with General Westmoreland, who put in a plug for an increase in his force of four hundred thousand American troops, Goldberg said, "We reaffirm our commitment of support to the Vietnamese people to be left alone and determine their own political destiny under conditions of freedom without external interference."

Next Johnson took a turn at attacking Kennedy's picture of him as a war-lover. In a talk to governors, Johnson insisted he had made thirty-three offers to Hanoi in four months. "If I propositioned a gal thirty-three times," he told the state heads, "and I didn't get one proposition in return, I just wouldn't have anything more to do with her."

Senator George Smathers, Johnson's friend and supporter, described Johnson's reaction to Bobby Kennedy as "pathetic." Said Smathers in early 1967: "Sometimes Lyndon calls me up and asks me to come over for a visit to the White House, and when I walk in I find him sitting there in his chair with his face all screwed up sadly and a fist against his cheek, and he greets me with a sort of cry: 'Tell me what I ought to do about Bobby, that little blankety-blank.'

"He can't remember that he is President of the United States and Bobby is just a little senator. What he does is react to Bobby for all the mistreatment he got during the three years he was Vice President. When he held the Vice Presidency and the boys around Jack Kennedy kicked him around, Johnson used to tell me all his grievances—real and imaginary—while we rode back to the Hill from the leadership meetings at the White House. And I relayed them back to President Kennedy. Johnson would never tell him directly because he believed Bobby was directing the mistreatment of him.

"As President, Lyndon reacts stupidly to Bobby, the way he runs around to get public attention every time Bobby makes a speech. All he has to do is stay calm and tell the press, 'I will pass Senator Kennedy's suggestion along to the State Department.' "

Two other peace offensives got under way and ended during that busy season. But each was doomed from the outset by Johnson's two-point formula calling for Communist reciprocity as a trade for a bombing halt and for the exclusion of the NLF as a direct bargaining power.

The two offensives were intertwined: One involved a Johnson letter exchange with Ho Chi Minh; the other, a Harold Wilson–Aleksei Kosygin–Lyndon Johnson–Ho Chi Minh backstage maneuvering. In January 1967, Johnson sent four letters to Ho through the relaying offices in Moscow, telling him to withdraw from South Vietnam in order to get negotiations started. On February 2, he sent his fifth letter, informing Ho he would stop the bombing and freeze the American troop total in South Vietnam after all infiltration of troops and supplies from the North ended. His letter read in part:

Dear Mr. President:
I am writing to you in the hope that the conflict in Vietnam can be brought to an end. That conflict has already taken a heavy toll—in lives lost, in wounds inflicted, in property destroyed and in simple human misery. If we fail to find a just and peaceful solution, history will judge us harshly.

We have tried over the past several years, in a variety of ways and through a number of channels, to convey to you and your colleagues our desire to achieve a peaceful settlement. For whatever reasons, these efforts have not achieved any results.

In the past two weeks, I have noted public statements by representatives of your Government suggesting that you would be prepared to enter into direct bilateral talks with representatives of the U. S. Government, provided that we cease "unconditionally" and permanently our bombing oper-

ations against your country and all military actions against it. In the last
day, serious and responsible parties have assured us indirectly that this is
in fact your proposal.

Let me frankly state that I see two great difficulties with this proposal.
In view of your public position, such action on our part would inevitably
produce worldwide speculation that discussions were under way and would
impair the privacy and secrecy of these discussions. Secondly, there would
inevitably be grave concern on our part whether your Government
would make use of such action by us to improve its military position.

With these problems in mind, I am prepared to move even further
toward an ending of hostilities than your Government has proposed in
either public statements or through private diplomatic channels. I am prepared to order a cessation of bombing against your country and the stopping of further augmentation of United States forces in South Vietnam as
soon as I am assured that infiltration into South Vietnam by land and by
sea has been stopped.

I make this proposal to you now with a specific sense of urgency arising
from the imminent new year holidays in Vietnam. If you are able to accept
this proposal I see no reason why it could not take effect at the end of the
new year, or Tet, holidays.

While this hard-line request was on its way to Hanoi, Aleksei Kosygin
was on his way to London for a visit that would last from February 6 to
February 13. On his arrival Kosygin told Prime Minister Wilson he believed that the recent proposal of North Vietnam's Foreign Minister Trinh,
made in an interview with Australian writer Wilfred Burchett in Hanoi,
should serve as the basis for negotiations. In this interview Trinh had said
"there could be talks" with the United States after an unconditional halting
of the bombings of North Vietnam. Kosygin also told Wilson that he believed he had some influence with Ho Chi Minh and could almost guarantee
negotiations in three or four weeks if a fair compromise were found between the American and North Vietnamese positions.

Wilson immediately telephoned Johnson with the details of this conversation, and numerous transatlantic calls followed between the two as Johnson offered further elaborations on the last letter he had sent to Ho. Besides
ending the bombing, said Johnson, he would also delay the arrival of
seventy-five thousand new troops destined for South Vietnam. But for this
he would expect the withdrawal of North Vietnam's troops from the South
and no further infiltration of weapons, ammunition, and troops—especially
the three North Vietnamese divisions reported near the border's demilitarized zone (DMZ). Wilson passed these increasingly harsher terms on to
Kosygin, who sent them to Hanoi.

In the meantime, the Tet (lunar new year) four-day truce holiday had
begun on February 8 with a plea by Pope Paul VI that it be continued
until arrangements for peace were made. On February 13 Kosygin returned
to Moscow without hearing from Ho, and on the following day Johnson
ordered the bombing pause ended and new strikes begun. A disturbed

Wilson took to TV that day, after the bombings were resumed, and as Johnson's champion, he put the blame for the continuing war on Ho Chi Minh. "Last weekend, I believe," he said erroneously, "peace was almost within our grasp. One single act of trust could have achieved it . . . one gesture by North Vietnam—which would have cost them nothing in terms of security or even face."

On February 15 came Ho Chi Minh's reply to the Johnson letter of February 2. This was a message proclaiming his unwillingness to accept the status as the aggressor in the conflict and turn over South Vietnam to the United States, as the Johnson terms demanded of him. His letter read in part:

Your Excellency:

On 10 February 1967, I received your message. This is my reply.

Vietnam is thousands of miles away from the United States. The Vietnamese people have never done any harm to the United States. But contrary to the pledges made by its representatives at the 1954 Geneva conference, the U. S. Government has ceaselessly intervened in Vietnam; it has unleashed and intensified the war of aggression in South Vietnam with a view to prolonging the partition of Vietnam and turning South Vietnam into a neocolony and a military base of the United States. For over two years now, the U. S. Government has with its air and naval forces carried the war to the Democratic Republic of Vietnam, an independent and sovereign country.

The U. S. Government has committed war crimes, crimes against peace and against mankind. In South Vietnam, half a million U. S. and satellite troops have resorted to the most inhuman weapons and the most barbarous methods of warfare, such as napalm, toxic chemicals and gases, to massacre our compatriots, destroy crops and raze villages to the ground.

In North Vietnam, thousands of U. S. aircraft have dropped hundreds of thousands of tons of bombs, destroying towns, villages, factories, roads, bridges, dikes, dams and even churches, pagodas, hospitals, schools. In your message, you apparently deplored the sufferings and destructions in Vietnam. May I ask you: Who has perpetrated these monstrous crimes? It is the U. S. and satellite troops.

The U. S. Government has unleashed the war of aggression in Vietnam. It must cease this aggression. That is the only way to the restoration of peace. The U. S. Government must stop definitely and unconditionally its bombing raids and all other acts of war against the Democratic Republic of Vietnam, withdraw from South Vietnam all U. S. and satellite troops, and let the Vietnamese people settle themselves their own affairs.

In your message, you suggested direct talks between the Democratic Republic of Vietnam and the United States. If the U. S. Government really wants these talks, it must first of all stop unconditionally its bombing raids and all other acts of war against the D.R.V.

The Vietnamese people will never submit to force, they will never accept talks under the threat of bombs.

Our cause is absolutely just. It is to be hoped that the U. S. Government will act in accordance with reason.

Once he received Ho's letter and went through the abysmal day following Bobby Kennedy's speech of March 2 calling for an unconditional end
to the bombings in the North, Johnson once again escalated American action. This time his orders to the Navy were to drop mines from planes into
North Vietnam's rivers. The Seventh Fleet was also ordered to travel up
Tonkin Gulf alongside the coastline of North Vietnam and shell fortifica-
tions and roads. In addition, American troops just south of the DMZ
were told to lob artillery shells into North Vietnam. Johnson, professing a
desire for peace, explained away the escalated violence to reporters by
saying, "I don't see any alternative."

As a counterbalance, the enemy also escalated by stepping up the killing and kidnapping of civilians above the 1966 figures of three thousand
killed and ten thousand kidnapped, increasing terrorist activities on air
bases and in cities, and making use of Soviet rockets for the first time.
Caught in the crossfire were tens of thousands of innocent civilians, who
were napalmed and bombed and strafed by mistake by American planes;
and taxed, drafted, and frequently terrorized by the Viet Cong.

By March 1967, Johnson was wearing the full armor of the man of
escalating war again. To dramatize this he planned to fly to Guam for a
two-day conference of "Johnson and his generals" on March 20–21 and
learn what was needed "to stop the aggressor in the South, increase his
costs in the North, and bring him ultimately to the bargaining table."

En route, he stopped off at Nashville to beat the war drums in a commemorative address before the Tennessee legislature on the occasion of the
bicentennial of the birth of Andrew Jackson. He wore the stern face of
the Commander-in-Chief who would not flinch before the mighty foe of the
tiny country of Vietnam but would persevere to the end because his side
was right. "Two years ago," he offered in justification for his stand, "we
were forced to choose between major commitments in defense of South
Vietnam or retreat in the face of subversion and external assault."

The 8,600-mile flight to Guam aboard *Air Force One* took eighteen
hours for Johnson, his advisers, and his limousine. Not far behind were
two jets carrying reporters and cameramen to cover this event, which Johnson had modestly called "a routine review of the war." Senator Fulbright,
aware of the Johnson Vietnam Syndrome and realizing that any talk about
peace and any Johnson conference abroad were usually followed by new
escalations, joined Mike Mansfield in expressing misgivings to newsmen
that an expansion of the war would follow Guam.

It had been Johnson's intention to hold an all-American conference,
and, in fact, embassy officials in Saigon had suggested that Ky not be invited because "it would seem like a kiss of approval" for him by the United
States Government. But Premier Ky could not be kept away, and Johnson
had been obliged to send him a "come if you can spare the time" note.

And when the dapper premier came, his superior and rival, Chief of State Thieu, went along to keep close watch on him.

Arrangements had been made to hold the conference in the U.S. Navy Station headquarters atop Nimitz Hill, looking out over the Philippine Sea and at two Soviet electronic spy ships bobbing about just outside American territorial waters. The Communist vessels were there to keep records and send signals when the B-52's left for raids on Vietnam and to maintain a watch on the Polaris submarines assigned to Guam.

Before his trip Johnson had made changes in the American civilian command in Saigon. Elderly Ellsworth Bunker, rated an excellent diplomat for trouble-shooting assignments, was to replace Ambassador Lodge; Eugene Locke, one of Johnson's "up-from-poverty-to-millions" Texas friends and whose nickname was Lyndon Junior, was to shift from his post as ambassador to Pakistan to serve as Bunker's deputy; and Robert Komer, a former CIA agent and Presidential aide, was to handle what was called the other war in Vietnam. The "other war" was the pacification program, and it amused some of Komer's associates, who called him Blowtorch because of his extremely quarrelsome nature.

It had been Johnson's intention to spring these appointments at a news conference on Guam as a high point of the meeting. But he had been compelled to make the announcements in Washington before the trip because reporters had learned of them. From his fury at being forced to reveal his new commands prematurely, some newsmen conjectured that the point of his trip had been flattened. Nor did the skimpy agenda tell a story of a broad-ranging conference; a senior officer on the scene was quoted by *Newsweek* as deriding the conference as a "political ploy to crowd Bobby Kennedy off the front page."

Ky was the hit of the conference. Dressed in somber civilian clothes instead of his gaudy uniform and without his oversize dark glasses and pistol, Ky symbolized the civilian statesman as he handed Johnson a copy of the constitution that an elected constitutional assembly had been writing since the previous September. "I looked at it just as proudly as I looked at Lynda, my first baby," Johnson later told reporters, pointing out that South Vietnam would hold a Presidential election the following September.

Much of the discussion was given over to what General Westmoreland considered an essential escalation in troop numbers above the 475,000 scheduled to be on hand toward the end of that year. There was talk that perhaps an additional 200,000 American boys might be necessary to finish the task to "search and destroy" the VC's. American battle deaths were averaging 750 a month, but this seemed to the generals a worthwhile price to pay. Johnson wanted to know how many American casualties had occurred last week, and the answer was 2,092. But he was assured that the Viet Cong losses had been "terrific. . . . They're down to using thirteen-year-old soldiers." When talk turned to increasing the war cost to North Vietnam, McNamara pointed out that air sorties were already averaging about thirteen thousand a month "over the infiltration routes and base areas." McNamara favored circumscribing the northern bombing to military targets south of the Twentieth Parallel, or below the Hanoi-Haiphong line. This proposal, plus his earlier suggestions for bombing pauses and now his proposal to erect a barrier just south of the DMZ and then eliminate the bombings as unnecessary, were no longer the handiwork of a man reckoned to be a human computer.

In Manila, only a few miles from some of the world's most squalid slums, Johnson had extravagantly promised five months earlier to lead the way "to conquer hunger, illiteracy, and disease" in Asia and to help other nations there "to be free from aggression." Now he wanted to know how the pacification and economic aid programs were progressing.

The pacification program, called Revolutionary Development, or R.D., had begun in 1966 as a way to insure the safety and progress of the strategic hamlets. The R.D. team for each hamlet consisted of fifty-nine persons trained in specialties such as police work, farming, and military techniques. The function of each native team was to move into a hamlet to manage its affairs and develop it into a support area for the Saigon Government. However, with the war rapidly moving to an *hourly* cost of four million dollars for the American Government, an *annual* expenditure of forty million dollars on pacification could not provide for many fifty-nine-man teams. And even if more money were available, the emphasis of R.D. on police vigilance, with each hamlet resident privately interrogated on the political opinions of his neighbors, was hardly conducive to a growing love for the Saigon Government.

Komer had written the Komer Report on pacification in 1966 for Johnson. This was a highly optimistic report, but White House aides assessed him as "another Walt Rostow—a man ready to tell Johnson what he thinks Johnson wants to hear." General Nguyen Duc Thang, in charge of R.D. for the Ky Government, called the Komer optimism unrealistic. However, Thang was not present on Guam, and American embassy reports on the pacification program called it a rising success. The odd reasoning behind this cheerful conclusion was that the Viet Cong had markedly stepped up their attacks on the R.D. teams in recent months because they were "desperate" to halt the program that would ruin them.

The situation of a million refugees in the South was glossed over. Senator Edward "Teddy" Kennedy of Massachusetts, Bobby Kennedy's younger brother, had adopted the refugees in South Vietnam as his special project, and any significant change in the program of ignoring them would serve chiefly to give him publicity. In the spring of 1967 these million persons were crowded in makeshift coastal-area camps and towns with almost no provisions made for health, food, education, job training, and rehabilitation. A witness before the U. S. Senate Judiciary Committee confirmed that the refugees fled their home villages to avoid American and the South Vietnam

Government's bombing and shelling and came to these American and South Vietnamese-held places because "the Viet Cong have no airpower."

Nor was mention made of the gross corruption that infested the Ky Government and the thousands of provincial leaders, or of the waste and extravagance that were commonplace in the AID and U. S. military construction programs. The ubiquitous Brown and Root, as part of the construction combine known as RMK-BRJ in South Vietnam, was charged by the General Accounting Office in a report in May 1967 with running a 1.2-billion-dollar contract in which "normal management controls were virtually abandoned." Among a host of detailed findings, the GAO found the combine guilty of losing accounting control of 120 million dollars; of "goldplating," or needless buying of super-quality supplies; shipping items such as business envelopes by airfreight from the United States; and failing to build warehouses or fence off the mile-long Cam Ranh Bay Depot, so that local sampans beached nightly and stole millions of dollars worth of diesel engines, electric cable, roofing, etc.

David Lilienthal, an old Johnson friend of the New Deal and Fair Deal era, was an invited participant in the Guam conference. Lilienthal's private economic-planning firm was operating under a lucrative contract to help plan the postwar developments in South Vietnam, and from the way the chief participants spoke, this might be needed soon.

Johnson exuded optimism throughout the day and a half of meetings in the headquarters of Rear Admiral Horace V. Byrd. "We are at a favorable turning point," he told reporters; and Ky, who stood on top two empty Coca-Cola crates to reach the microphone, assured newsmen that the Viet Cong were "on the run" and that the transportation and supply system of North Vietnam was "in near paralysis." Said the Washington *Post* in a front-page headline: "UNRELENTING WARFARE TO BREAK REDS' WILL EMPHASIZED AT GUAM."

But if the enemy's will was to be broken, it would have to be done solely by the American forces. For with the exception of a few hardened South Vietnamese ARVN units, South Vietnam's soldiers were still running away in battle and were deserting at a rate close to one hundred thousand a year. In addition, as American military men admitted to reporters, they treated their own civilian population on the ground as harshly as American pilots did from the air. One reporter noted: "American officers in the field with Vietnam troops make critical remarks about their behavior toward their own people—stealing, raping, burning down villages, generally kicking people around."

Now the Commander-in-Chief made ready to fly home, and as a last-minute gesture toward his "boys in Vietnam," he paid a call at the U. S. Naval Hospital on Guam, where wounded GI's had been brought from South Vietnam. There was pain on many young faces above mangled bodies, but he wanted them to know how proud he was of the job they had done for "freedom." One unpleasant note came when he walked toward the bed of a young serviceman who had lost both arms and his right leg. The soldier's wife was next to his bed, and when Johnson appeared, she pointed to her husband and said chokingly, "Aren't you proud of him?" Johnson did not reply to her question but walked quickly past her.

It was on his return flight from the war-escalating meeting that Johnson made important propaganda gains as a man of peace. To counteract the Guam conference, Ho Chi Minh had released Johnson's letter to him of February 2 and his reply to Johnson of February 15. The Johnson letter had offered to stop the bombing of North Vietnam and quit reinforcing American troops in South Vietnam after the enemy's "infiltration into South Vietnam by land and sea has stopped." Ho's reply had stated his refusal to purchase the bombing suspension by what amounted to a surrender by the NLF and his own total withdrawal from the conflict.

Patriotic fervor rocked American publications with the release of the letters by Ho. Typically, Kenneth Crawford of *Newsweek* found Johnson's letter "conciliatory" and Ho's reply "bellicose." Ignoring the contents of the exchange and what Johnson was requesting, Crawford took the position that since "it was the President who was making the peace overtures and he, Ho, who was turning them down," Johnson was therefore a man of peace. Other columnists and publications went even further and took the view that critics of the war were "un-Americans who should be shut up by law." Since few newspapers printed either the letters or a fair summary of their contents, the confused general public could only accept the patriotic judgments it read.

And again, as after Manila, Johnson returned home a short-term newspaper hero. Arriving at Andrews Air Force Base and flanked by Rusk and McNamara, Johnson wore his kindest expression when he told the crowd that Ho Chi Minh's rejection of his generous February 2 peace offer was "a regrettable rebuff to a genuine effort to move toward peace." Then he added in his best tone of undimming patience, "Nevertheless, we shall persevere in our efforts to find an honorable peace."

An hour later the man of escalating war was back with a blunt comment on his trip to White House aides. "There will be more planes and more helicopters," he told them. "And there will be more men."

The release of the letters by Ho was not Johnson's only bonus as a man of peaceful intent during this period. At the beginning of the year U Thant had proposed a three-point plan for peace, with the first point being a stop to the bombing of the North by the United States. But because of Johnson's opposition, Thant's plan died.

On March 28, 1967, Thant held a news conference and offered a new three-point proposal that did not include a halt to the bombing but proposed instead a continuation of military activity until "a general standstill truce" was reached. Thant suggested that preliminary talks between the United States and North Vietnam be held after the truce, followed by the reconvening of the Geneva Conference, with the NLF and the South Vietnam Government as participants.

When Radio Hanoi was quick to denounce Thant's proposal because it did not call for an end to the bombing, Dean Rusk was just as swift in recognizing a propaganda gain for the United States as a peace-lover, and he announced that President Johnson favored the Thant plan. Premier Ky was also told to announce his agreement with the dead plan, and he did, though he grumbled publicly afterward that because the plan excluded his Government from the preliminary talks he was "being treated like a puppet." But newspapers considered that a minor complaint, and once again the press hailed Johnson as a man of peace and the North Vietnamese Communist leader as a man of war.

After this propaganda victory by the United States, Thant angered Johnson by declaring that before negotiations began for the truce the United States would first have to stop bombing the North. At this clarification by Thant, Johnson told several visitors his low opinion of the UN Secretary-General, and word filtered back to Thant of some of these Texas-cowboy remarks.

"It was in May 1967 that I went to New York for a conference with U Thant," said Senator Vance Hartke. "This was shortly after he had held a press conference and spoke of World War III as likely to result from the continuing escalation of the Vietnam conflict.

"I tried to talk him into going to Washington once more for another talk with Johnson, but he refused. Thant told me, 'I've just spoken to Mohammed Hashim Maiwandwal, the Prime Minister of Afghanistan, who used to be his country's ambassador to Washington. The Prime Minister was in Washington last week for meetings with the President, and he made Johnson angry by calling for a cessation of U. S. bombing against North Vietnam, and Johnson read about this in the papers.

" 'The day after he said this the Prime Minister had to go to the White House for a conference with your President, and he wrote out reminders on a small slip of paper for five topics he wanted to discuss with Mr. Johnson. But he never had a chance to pull the sheet of paper out of his pocket.

" 'Johnson started out immediately by jabbing the Prime Minister's forearm steadily with a finger like a pecking bird while he kept repeating, "We've been awfully easy on North Vietnam so far."

" 'Then after a time he stopped this, and thrust his big fist like a piston that stopped only an inch from the Prime Minister's eyes, and he yelled: "We could really pound them if we wanted to!"

" 'And that is what would happen to me, Senator, if I went to Washington to see President Johnson,' said U Thant wearily."

After Guam and the Ho release of the letters, Johnson's increased price for negotiations was apparent even before he climbed into *Air Force One* in April 1967 for his flight to the Latin American Chiefs of State three-day conference at Punta del Este in Uruguay. His orders had been transmitted through the Joint Chiefs of Staff to Westmoreland to pound North Vietnam even harder, shoot more shells across the DMZ into the North, increase the search-and-destroy missions against the VC, bomb Mig airfields in North Vietnam, bomb downtown Hanoi, and level the power plants in Haiphong for good. In addition, spy-plane flights over China were to be increased, and "hot pursuit" of the enemy into Cambodia and Laos were to be made commonplace. Military victory must come.

Before leaving for Uruguay, Johnson had asked the Senate for advance support for the Latin American Summit Conference. However, after having gone through the experience of the blank-check Tonkin Gulf Resolution of 1964, Fulbright infuriated Johnson by substituting his own resolution putting Congress on record to give only "appropriate consideration" for any agreements reached at Punta del Este. Johnson angrily demanded that the Senate take no action, and no resolution passed.

Johnson told the delegates at the conference he had come to Uruguay to hasten the industrialization and economic growth of the continent. But a painful hour arose when President Otto Arosemena Gomez of Ecuador denounced the United States for spending billions in Vietnam and little in Latin America. "It is not that we seek charity," he said. "It is unfortunate that our brothers of the North should be so concerned with democracy in a noble but distant country such as Vietnam, whereas at their very door nations are trembling with guerrillas and misery corrodes not only the body but the very soul and minds of the people."

Johnson made no direct reply to Arosemena, but offered to join the others in forming a common market for mutual low-tariff trade by 1970. This dismayed several delegates who wanted preferential tariff treatment with the United States in order to compete with more industrialized nations.

Peruvian President Fernando Belaunde Terry, regarded as the outstanding democratic leader in Latin America, drew applause when he followed the Johnson theme that the individual countries must in the end depend on their own efforts. However, he too jibed at the United States and said it "must do more." Later he met privately with Johnson, and reports raced through Latin capitals that the two had engaged in a brawl. Johnson was said to have insisted that Vietnam was more important than Latin America, and he detailed the vast amounts of money he had to spend there. Belaunde, on his part, was reported to have raised his voice in an effort to point out that "whatever the United States spends in the Americas is insurance against another Castro Cuba."

The spring of 1967 was also a good time to render helpless the dissenters to the conflict in Vietnam. In public, Johnson referred to his Congressional critics as "Nervous Nellies" and "cussers and doubters," non-patriots who were endangering the lives of American soldiers in Vietnam and giving the enemy false hopes; and in private, he denounced them as "chickenshits and piss-ants." He also derided Senate opponents by affixing the title "general" to their names when mentioning them. In May, when he awarded the Medal of Honor posthumously to a Marine who died in South Vietnam, he said that if it hadn't been for the dissenters at home, the sergeant would probably still be alive.

Bill White helped out by lending his column to relentless attacks on Fulbright, Mansfield, Bobby Kennedy, and others as "lefties" and cowards who "have no real policy for Vietnam except the policy of cut and run." One morning in the New Senate Office Building, Senator Hartke came upon White and told him, "I read your latest attack on us that the White House dictated for you."

Johnson took great pleasure in conducting a major personal war on columnist Walter Lippmann, now moving away from Washington after a steady regime of columns written on Johnson's credibility gap and his lack of objectives in Vietnam except the country's physical destruction through escalating warfare. After a long period of four-letter-word barrages against Lippmann to private visitors, Johnson attacked him openly at a White House dinner for the President of Turkey as "a commentator who is still with us" who opposed Greek-Turkish aid in 1947. Lippmann retaliated by reprinting his 1947 column in favor of the Truman Doctrine. Then Johnson had a White House assistant write an attack on Lippmann in a letter to the editor in the Washington *Post,* just as CIA chief Richard Helms had written a letter-to-the-editor attack on Senator Fulbright in a St. Louis newspaper. Next came a speech by another White House aide, whose attack on Lippmann read: "God is not dead; he is alive and appears in the Washington *Post* three times a week." Then came another Johnson attack. This time he walked into a press dinner without notice, broke into the entertainment, and delivered a speech in which he derided Lippmann as "a political commentator of yesteryear."

As for the public demonstrators and private letter-writers, Johnson used other techniques. After a big anti-war rally in New York, he told reporters at the ranch that he was carefully reading an FBI report on "anti-war activity." In addition, after the prominent role played at this rally by Dr. Martin Luther King, Jr., the Nobel Peace Prize winner and civil rights leader, the FBI circulated to reporters a purported hotel-room recording to "prove" King was guilty of "moral turpitude." Those Americans who wrote Johnson of their sympathy for the demonstrations received letters in reply from the Internal Security Division of the Justice Department.

In an unprecedented action, Johnson ordered General Westmoreland to quit the battle area and join him in the attack on home-front critics. The general spoke in New York before the Associated Press on Monday, April 24, 1967, and said he was "dismayed" by "recent unpatriotic acts here at home." He also said he opposed all "cease-fire proposals." There was a great deal of criticism in both the House and the Senate before he spoke at a Joint Session of Congress on April 28, with the charge being aired that it was not "appropriate to have a general on active duty under military orders address Congress." "Backed at home by resolve, confidence, patience, determination, and continued support," Westmoreland told the legislators, "we will prevail in Vietnam over the Communist aggressor."

Said Fulbright in answer to the implied threat, "This criticism of dissent will lead to a charge of disloyalty, and from that . . . probably to treason." As for Westmoreland's pronouncements on the Far East, Fulbright commented, "General Westmoreland has neither the competence nor the right to discuss U. S. foreign policy on Southeast Asia."

In May 1967, the United States escalated the war further by sending ten thousand Marines to invade the neutralized DMZ area below the Benhai River on the border between North and South Vietnam. Bitter battles were soon in progress for Hills 861 and 881, north of Khesanh, with heavy casualties on both sides. And on May 20, Johnson ordered that Ho Chi Minh be given a present on his seventy-seventh birthday: the bombing of the heart of Hanoi. The Soviet Government gave Ho a different sort of present by vastly increasing his supply of missiles and missile sites.

At the end of the month and during most of June, the Vietnam war disappeared from front-page prominence as the war between Israel and her Arab neighbors gained top attention. There was general agreement among the military experts that if Johnson had followed the Dulles aide-mémoire of February 11, 1957, and sent an American vessel into the Gulf of Aqaba, Nasser would have ended his blockade. But Johnson had too much at stake in Vietnam in seeking military victory there to honor the U. S. commitment to Israel, and he would not do so.

This was not necessary, however, because of the swift and decisive blows by Israel against Egypt, Jordan, and Syria, once the Middle East war started in full force on June 5. Soviet Premier Aleksei Kosygin, whose Government had bestowed two billion dollars worth of military goods on Egypt's President Nasser in order to gain a Communist grip on the Middle East, was suddenly fearful that war might erupt between the United States and the Soviet Union if Johnson should live up to his commitment to Israel. So Kosygin made use of his "hot line" from the Kremlin to the White House and sent Johnson a message that his country would not get into the conflict if the United States would also abstain. Johnson quickly sent an acceptance of the Kosygin offer.

Only nine months earlier Johnson had castigated the leaders of Jewish organizations in the United States and told them that because so many American Jews opposed the war in Vietnam, he might not be kind to Israel in the future. But this was forgotten now as the Israeli armies swept forward to victory, and Johnson was for some unexplained reason hailed by these same Jewish leaders as having helped bring this about. However,

Israeli Premier Levi Eshkol called this nonsense. "We were first asked to wait two days before acting against Arab mobilization. Then we sent Eban to the United States and were asked to wait a further fortnight. President Johnson promised us great things. They told us that forty to fifty maritime powers would sign a guarantee for free passage through the Tiran Strait [the entrance to the Gulf of Aqaba that Egypt had blockaded].

"We examined the situation and found that it really came down to a dozen, and finally to only two countries . . . and perhaps only one—Israel.

"I once told President Johnson that it is likely that if we are attacked you will be very busy with other matters and that the nature of the American guarantee is unclear," he added sarcastically.

To save what he could for the Arab world after its devastating defeat by Israel and also to entrench Soviet influence anew and deeper in the Mediterranean region, Kosygin came to New York to demand that the UN "vigorously condemn Israel's aggressive activities" and order her to withdraw immediately from conquered territory. When Kosygin showed up for the Saturday, June 17, emergency special session of the UN General Assembly on the Middle East, speculation arose regarding the possibility of a Johnson-Kosygin summit meeting.

First came a fencing between the two over a meeting place. Johnson suggested Washington; Kosygin, New York. Finally Kosygin suggested a halfway point, somewhere in New Jersey. The White House staff found this midway spot at Glassboro, 135 miles from Washington and about 110 miles from New York. So the two met for five hours and twenty minutes on June 23 in the home of the president of little Glassboro State College, and they met again for a further discussion two days later.

In these talks, each man expressed his views on the Middle East and Vietnam and turned a deaf ear to what the other said. Johnson said he favored an Israeli withdrawal from conquered territory after other nations guaranteed freedom of the seas in the Gulf of Aqaba; Kosygin wanted a rollback first. On Vietnam, Johnson reiterated his desire for peace and said that he would stop the bombing in the North if the other side would reciprocate by, in effect, running up the white flag. Kosygin quoted a North Vietnamese spokesman who had complained: "Every time we have agreed to talk to the Americans, Washington has escalated the war." The bombing halt must come first, said Kosygin. He also pointed out that he had arrived in Hanoi on February 6, 1965, to talk to Ho Chi Minh about making peace and only a day later Johnson had ordered the bombing of the North. In addition, he mentioned his trip to England to work with Wilson to find a way to the truce table, and how he had promised he would get Ho to negotiate three or four weeks after bombing stopped. However, Johnson had refused to end the bombing and instead escalated it, hitting Hanoi directly. Kosygin now repeated that if Johnson stopped the bombing, negotiations could begin inside of a month. But Johnson refused.

Yet despite the stone-wall summit conference Johnson, in an optimistic tone that covered up a lack of any progress, told the crowd outside the meeting house that "this meeting today was a very good and very useful meeting."

Kosygin was scheduled to hold a TV interview in New York at 8 P.M., shortly after the second session ended, and Johnson was suddenly concerned that he would lose a propaganda battle to the Soviet Premier. So after lending Kosygin a slow White House helicopter for his return trip to New York, Johnson sped by jet to Washington, and instead of landing at Andrews Air Force Base, *Air Force One* set down at National Airport close to the White House. When the plane landed, he was at the back door ready to rush out and board his helicopter. However, the ramp was rolled to the front door, and he ran like a deer to that exit and bounded down the stairs. Five minutes later, at 7:42 P.M., he stepped from the helicopter onto the South Lawn of the White House and moved before TV cameras to give his assessment of the Glassboro summit fifteen minutes before the Kosygin show. Vice President Humphrey hailed this innocuous meeting as the "Spirit of Glassboro," just as he had hailed the "Spirit of Honolulu," the "Spirit of Manila," and the "Spirit of Guam."

By July 1967 General Westmoreland was chafing because he wanted more soldiers sent him from the United States. As back-up support for Westmoreland, Premier Ky sent word to the White House that he wanted 600,000 Americans fighting in South Vietnam, or 137,000 more than the number there at that time. So Defense Secretary McNamara made his ninth trip to Southeast Asia to discuss the war with Westmoreland.

Reports told of a serious disagreement between the two men, as well as trouble between the top two South Vietnamese political and military figures. General Thieu, the Chief of State, had entered the September Presidential contest as an opponent of Premier Ky; and with Cowboy Ky's greater publicity and American favoritism he was bound to humiliate Thieu. But Thieu handled this problem to his own satisfaction by calling a meeting of the *junta* of generals and establishing a new political ticket. Thieu would run for President and Ky for Vice President.

Westmoreland's insatiable appetite for more GI's for his war offensive irked McNamara, who saw no improvement in the fighting situation from two years earlier, when Westmoreland had first demanded a major troop increase. At that time, before the bombing of North Vietnam, no regular North Vietnamese troops were in the South; now ten regiments had crossed the Seventeenth Parallel. Two hundred thousand Viet Cong were said to have been slain, but great doubts existed in the Pentagon regarding the credibility of Westmoreland's "body count" of the enemy, for the same number of VC troops and guerrillas were in the field as had been present in 1965. In addition, McNamara's statisticians had figures to show that "Westy" was not making efficient use of the men he had. Only 37 per cent of his American troops were assigned to combat duty. And what about his own afternoon tennis games? Furthermore, in his April 28 speech before Congress, Westmoreland had incorrectly given the impression that South Vietnam's ARVN forces were carrying a large share of the fighting burden when he told the legislators, "Vietnamese troops have scored repeated successes against some of the best Viet Cong and North Vietnamese army units." Nor was there as much success in the pacification program as had been anticipated when Johnson transferred that function from the civilian hands of Ambassador Bunker to General Westmoreland. It was progressing "very slowly," McNamara complained.

McNamara also had strong doubts about the declared value of bombing the North. The number of American plane losses was approaching the one thousand mark, yet the expected breaking of the will in the North was not occurring even though the tonnage dropped on the Communists exceeded that dumped on Germany during the whole of World War II. As for the effectiveness of bombing the supply routes to the South, the amount of matériel customarily shipped was so small (one hundred tons) that no significant decrease had taken place. As for the persistent military demand to bomb and mine the harbor at Haiphong and take the risk of having Red China and the Soviet Union join the conflict directly, McNamara pointed out again that though 4,700 tons of North Vietnam's daily supply imports of 5,800 tons came through Haiphong, North Vietnam's seacoast ran four hundred miles and contained many locations suitable for "over-the-beach" nighttime unloading operations.

McNamara returned to the United States on July 11 from his five-day trip to Saigon, and when the rumors grew too strong regarding his hard talk and criticism of Westmoreland, Johnson stepped into the breach. He ordered McNamara to prepare a statement for reporters, declaring that political progress in South Vietnam since last year has been "noteworthy"; economic change, "remarkable"; and the Viet Cong military offensive, "blunted."

Westmoreland had also returned to the United States for his mother's funeral in Columbia, South Carolina, and Johnson had him come to the White House to join in a news conference with General Earle Wheeler, the head of the Joint Chiefs of Staff, McNamara, and himself. The meeting was held in the west sitting room of the family living quarters on the second floor of the White House, and newsmen witnessed a scene of a schoolteacher ordering pupils to recite memorized lines at a school assembly. A large bowl of yellow flowers sat on the coffee table, and the three guests were seated on the green damask sofa behind the table with Johnson, their prompter, leaning forward in a chair to their left.

Johnson gave the cues and each responded automatically with a fixed smile on his face to match that of the President. The war was progressing according to plans, said Johnson, and each man was called upon to repeat this. "The troops that General Westmoreland needs and requests, as we feel it necessary, will be supplied," Johnson said, then asked, "Is that not true, General Westmoreland?"

"I agree, Mr. President."

"General Wheeler?"

"That is correct, Mr. President."

"Secretary McNamara?"

"Yes, sir," came a helpless reply.

Johnson's technique of going down the line and asking for verification reminded reporters of a similar rote exhibition involving officials of the space program. In that instance, the punch line had been, "Are you satisfied with the return on that investment?"

"Delighted."

"Elated?" Johnson had growled.

"Elated."

In this exhibition with his war trio, Johnson continued to have them jump through the hoops. To the discomfort of McNamara, he repeated his optimism on the way things were going in Vietnam: "We are generally pleased with the progress we have made militarily, and we are very sure that we are on the right track." The three responded well. Then he addressed Westmoreland: "Touch on this 'stalemate' creature."

"Complete fiction," the general who was doing such a poor job in Vietnam said righteously. "The enemy has failed in achieving his objectives [while] we have succeeded in attaining our objectives."

Afterward, Johnson chose to ignore the McNamara charges of "waste and inefficiency" in Westmoreland's command, and on August 3 he authorized a 45,000-man troop increase to a total of 525,000. Mike Mansfield answered the progress report at a news conference with the comment: "Reports of progress are strewn, like burned-out tanks, all along the road which has led this nation ever more deeply into Vietnam."

"I got everything I asked for, all the flexibility," Westmoreland told his staff in Saigon on his return. He was also helped by the Senate Preparedness Subcommittee, which attacked McNamara for not stepping up the air bombing of North Vietnam to the total-destruction level.

While Mansfield, Fulbright, McCarthy, Hartke, and U Thant were calling into the dead air for the end to the bombing of North Vietnam and the start of negotiations, Johnson was wrapped in a dozen major efforts involving his thirst for more land and banks. Said one insider, "In 1967 Johnson and his coterie forced the owners of a thriving savings and loan bank in Austin to turn over their business to him. Then when he had the bank, he rushed back to Washington and, because of the tight mortgage-money squeeze, sent a message to Congress asking for a grant of money to the FHA to buy additional hundreds of millions of dollars of mortgages from savings and loan banks."

Said another insider, "Then there was the Citizens National Bank in Austin, in which Lyndon had stock. The man who devoted his life to building up this little bank was pushed aside so Lyndon's kid son-in-law, Pat Nugent, could be made a director in May 1967 on Lyndon's orders. Now the bank is called the Nugent Bank, and it's thriving because Frank Erwin, chairman of the board of regents of the University of Texas and Democratic National Committeeman, is depositing a chunk of the university's four-hundred-million-dollar endowment there."

Johnson was also busy with the Lyndon B. Johnson Presidential Library, which was being erected at breakneck speed on the campus of the University of Texas. A Johnson associate who had graduated from and taught at the university confided, "Frank Erwin, head of the regents, owed Lyndon a big favor. When Lyndon was majority leader and Frank was the lawyer for the gigantic Elgin-Butler Brick Company, Lyndon put through a nutty amendment to the tax laws so that the depletion-allowance break was extended to clay products.

"So Erwin let him move in now to turn the University of Texas into an LBJ University, even though Lyndon hadn't even gone there. To put up his library and create a special and bigger mall for it, the university has been forced to tear down essential buildings in its path. The LBJ Library has ruined the careful planning of the campus around the beautiful mall that was there. The former chairman of the board of regents, Bill [William H.] Heath, who was also helpful on the library, was rewarded by being named ambassador to Sweden."

By August 1967 the war dissenters in Congress were resigned to the fact that no argument had dented the Johnson obstinacy to hold out for military victory in Vietnam. Leaders of anti-war demonstrations and groups outside of Congress were also convinced that nothing they did would exert the slightest influence on the President.

However, if Johnson emerged now with a thoroughly discouraged opposition, he was still a loser in the popularity market. The polls of the period showed 52 per cent of the public disapproved of the way he was handling the war; 41 per cent believed American troops should never have been dispatched to Vietnam; and 56 per cent said that the war was either being lost by the United States or was in a stalemated position.

Nevertheless, the reading of such polls did not move Johnson to alter his policy. On the contrary, he became more convinced than ever that he was right and his opponents were in error. "This Administration hasn't lost its ass yet," he told his staff aides. He was another Harry Truman, he began telling visitors. Truman had been severely criticized as President, Johnson said, yet he was remembered for his wise and courageous decisions. Johnson found a new justification for continuing on for military victory in Vietnam: "Why, I remember back in 1948 when Truman was running for President. There were twenty-three members of the Texas delegation, and only two of us would get on the train and ride with him."

It was during 1967 that Johnson lost control over the federal bureaucracy and the budget. He saw only a few officials, and he was out of touch and had little interest in what the others were doing. Charges of inefficiency and lack of responsiveness were commonplace. Existing programs were not working well, and the General Accounting Office was shorthanded in uncovering waste, extravagance, and fraud. Nor were such findings restricted to Great Society programs. The Defense Department had lent eleven billion dollars worth of government tools and equipment to Defense contractors for use in 5,500 factories, and accounting control had been lost over billions of dollars in valuable tools. In addition, the Defense Department was signing war production contracts at the rate of 150 million dollars a day. Only 15 per cent of the contracts were based on competitive bidding; the rest were negotiated behind closed doors. In case after case, the GAO found that false costs had been submitted and become the basis for negotiated prices.

It was also during 1967 that Johnson lost control of Congress. No longer did the sound of his voice over the phone sway members, and he had to depend on the leadership on the Hill to salvage what they could of his programs. Chairman Wilbur Mills of the House Ways and Means Committee shook his head, and Johnson's proposal for a 10 per cent income tax surcharge was dead.

The Consular Treaty with the Soviet Union symbolized the decline of his power over Congress. Said Charles Ferris of the Senate Democratic Policy Committee, "The Consular Treaty was signed in 1964, and when it came up for a vote early in 1967, President Johnson told Senator Mansfield that the White House count showed it would fail to get the necessary two-thirds vote by at least twelve votes.

"But even though the White House had given up, Mike decided it had to pass because it was to the advantage of the United States. Among its favorable points, it would serve to protect Americans traveling in Russia, help us learn about Russian installations, and open a modicum of goodwill on our part to show that we didn't think that the Cold War had to be permanent. So while Johnson did nothing, Mike beat down proposed amendments, stayed on the Senate floor without respite, and fought it through against the anti-Red demagoguery and the spewed venom of some opponents. Of vital importance was that he brought Dirksen around to his view, and when the vote came, Mike had three more than he needed."

Johnson's concentration on the bleeding war in Vietnam had, of course, a harsh effect on the progress of his Great Society. In his State of the Union message in January 1966, he had called the United States strong enough "to pursue our goals in the rest of the world while still building a Great Society here at home." That fall, while campaigning in Newark, he had shouted through his bullhorn, "Measured by laws that mean something to the people, this Congress did more than all the other eighty-eight put together!"

By 1967, when he delivered his State of the Union Message to the first session of the Ninetieth Congress, his mention of the Great Society made it sound like a hoary, boring catch phrase. No longer adding butter to the diet of guns, he said he would "do all that we can with what we have, knowing that it is far, far more than we have ever done before, and far, far less than our problems will ultimately require."

That this approach was not enough was revealed within months. By midsummer 1967, the United States was engulfed by violent Negro ghetto riots across the nation. This was the fourth summer of such riots, but the 1967 variety was the costliest so far in human lives and property destruction. Several slum areas took on the appearance of bombed-out cities.

The first major riot occurred in Newark over the weekend of July 15, and by the time the burning ruins began cooling, twenty-six persons were dead. That the American society was beginning to look sick became apparent when the riots spread across the country and gave the appearance of a civil insurrection, with guns blazing and Molotov cocktails thrown at police and soldiers. But what characterized these riots was that they were not revolutionary marches against city hall but destructive moves solely within the slums.

The hardest hit city was Detroit, with twenty-seven dead, eight hundred wounded, 2,455 arrested, and property damage of more than two hundred million dollars. Governor George Romney of Michigan, whom Johnson considered his probable rival in 1968, was unable to reach Johnson by phone to ask for Army troops in the Detroit riots. After a day of Romney requests to Attorney General Ramsey Clark and Defense Undersecretary Cyrus Vance, Johnson finally went on TV to announce he was sending 4,700 Army paratroopers, and seven times he said that Romney had begged for aid because he "had been unable to bring the situation under control." Newspapers afterward condemned Johnson for playing politics while the lives of 1.5 million persons in Detroit were in danger.

When the riots struck, Johnson quickly took the offensive and blamed Congress for not acting on his small rent-subsidy bill and modest Model Cities budget for urban renewal. But the situation was too complex for such simplification. There was, for instance, evidence of a Johnson order to his Cabinet to slash non-defense spending 15 per cent, an amount that would have nullified most social-welfare programs. There was also evidence that federal agencies running those programs were too poorly staffed to handle them properly, and that the language of the authorizing legislation and the agency-made rules produced a legal maze of red tape and inaction.

As the depth of the slum problems was revealed by the actions of despair of the ghetto people, second thoughts began to be uttered about the Johnson concentration on the war in Vietnam. Mayor Jerome Cavanagh of Detroit was one who accused him of "sacrificing the poverty war to the hot war in Vietnam." Others said, "We must stop penning Negroes in poverty into cages in the centers of our cities." And one eastern paper, ardently for Johnson, posed the editorial question "whether the society really is healthy enough to wage an open-end struggle against a 'war of liberation' in Southeast Asia while something frighteningly like a 'war of liberation' is engulfing our cities, poisoning our politics, and raising the ugly image of a world policeman incapable of policing itself."

But the rioting finally ran its summer course, with threats of worse rioting promised for 1968, and Johnson returned to his plans and programs for the Vietnam conflict.

Every Tuesday at 1 P.M. when Johnson was in town, he had lunch with his war staff in the second-floor dining room in the White House to plan his next moves and decisions for Vietnam. He liked to sit in a high-backed chair at the south end of the table with Rusk at his right, McNamara at his left, Press Secretary George Christian near McNamara, and Walt Rostow opposite him at the north end. The wallpaper had one scene that seemed symbolic of the current struggle, but instead of Ho Chi Minh it portrayed General Cornwallis surrendering his sword at Yorktown.

At these Tuesday lunch meetings, the fare was simple: broiled liver, cooked vegetables, and gelatin, and as he ate and talked Johnson was another cool Franklin Roosevelt contemplating the world as he sat with his boys. Trusted Rusk would defend further escalation until the Commies gave up; McNamara would reveal some doubts on occasion; and voluble Rostow would speculate on the rainbow over the horizon after more offensive actions and bomb drops on the enemy occurred.

"It's going to break fast one of these days," was Rusk's principal thought about the war in 1967. He had many remarks about Vietnam that Johnson, as his superior, felt free to borrow. "They [Hanoi] keep hanging up the phone," Rusk would say, explaining the enemy's unwillingness to negotiate (on Johnson's terms). "You can't stop this war simply by stopping one half of it," he would offer in explanation of why it still continued. But at other times he would declare solely for surrender of the enemy in the South and the withdrawal of North Vietnamese troops above the Seventeenth Parallel. "There is one thing you had better understand—" and he would imitate Johnson by grabbing the jacket lapels of a reporter—"we are never going to let North Vietnam take this piece of real estate. That is the beginning of the story—and the end of the story."

Walt Rostow controlled the agenda at the Tuesday lunch, and during the rest of the week he was in touch with Rusk and McNamara to learn what topics they wanted discussed. On the basis of the agenda he would pour memos pertinent to the session over Johnson's desk, and he would shade key words and phrases with a yellow crayon pen. It was also Rostow's duty to turn every Johnson action into a "grand design" resulting from summit thinking and detailed research. Said one observer, "If Johnson belched, Rostow would declare it the culmination clarion call to a great transition in world affairs."

This small group had gradually taken on the functions of the National Security Council, though Johnson convened that body to record and legalize the lunchtime decisions. On occasion, when Johnson wanted to get further support for the unified view of his war staff, Vice President Humphrey, General Wheeler, and Helms of the CIA came for liver.

Humphrey had many personal experiences to relate at the Tuesday lunch meeting. He had traveled to Europe to talk to various government heads for Johnson. None would support the United States in Vietnam, nor did they control the anti-war demonstrators who made life miserable for Humphrey in the cities he visited. Humphrey had gone in early summer to the Far East and had proved just as controversial a figure there. In Seoul, where an election scandal had assisted President Chung Hee Park in winning a second term, the South Korean Government's newspaper had quoted Humphrey as suggesting "that arrest was appropriate for opposition party members who heckled at the inauguration of President Park."

In the riot-filled summer of 1967, Johnson still firmly believed he would get his military victory in Vietnam. Of the 427 targets on the target list in North Vietnam, he agreed with the Joint Chiefs of Staff in their recommendation that 359 targets were poundable. Of the others, he agreed with McNamara that they would "be considered for 'authorization' at a later date." Some were in the Chinese buffer zone at the top of North Vietnam, and the Tuesday lunch group would have to weigh further, as McNamara told the Senate Preparedness Subcommittee, "the risk of direct confrontation with the Communist Chinese or the Soviet Union."

While this pounding of North Vietnam was moving toward what Johnson hoped would be the eventual breaking of Ho Chi Minh's will, he had optimistic reports regarding the land fighting in the South. North of Khesanh below the DMZ the Marines had taken Hills 881 North and 881 South and Hill 861; and though the cost in lives was high and the hills had been evacuated upon capture, he believed they would serve as a reminder to the enemy that the American boys were better fighters than they. Heavy action had also taken place near the Cambodian and Laotian borders at Locninh, Dakto, and Conthien, where the Americans had also shown their bravery. "Slowly but steadily" the war was being won, was the good word from Westmoreland.

Westmoreland's optimism was also reflected in the statistical reports he sent to Washington. His figures showed the pacification program starting to come into its own, the number of Viet Cong defectors on the rise, and the search-and-destroy tactics resulting in skyrocketing body-count totals.

In the late summer of 1967 there was much talk at the Tuesday lunches about the Presidential election scheduled at the beginning of September in South Vietnam. General Duong Van Minh, or "Big Minh," had been exiled to Thailand, and concern had arisen in Saigon that because of his popularity he could defeat the ticket of Thieu and Ky in a halfway fair election. But with American pressure, Big Minh was disqualified as a contestant by the simple procedure of having the military *junta* label him "a security risk." Johnson was kept abreast of the strategy and moves of his ticket—Thieu and Ky—and it was his pleasure that they won, as everyone assumed they would, though they held only a third of the total vote.

The Tuesday lunch was not the only time in the week that the war staff met with Johnson. They got together on other days when summoned by Johnson, and as individuals they were on call for personal talks. In addition, Johnson sought advice from three other war hawks: Abe Fortas, Clark Clifford, and General Taylor, all of whom called for pressing the attack until victory came.

Then there was aging General Eisenhower, so careful in his own era to maintain his country at peace and oppose a land war in Asia. But Ike had changed after Johnson's relentless campaign to court him. There were frequent phone calls, visits, invitations to the White House, pleadings to represent Johnson abroad, and lavish briefings by Johnson aides, until now the flattered old man was not only Johnson's strong supporter but also his chief releaser of trial balloons. Among these were public calls for invading North Vietnam, engaging in hot pursuit of the enemy even into China, and using nuclear weapons.

General Taylor was in agreement with the view of the world that Johnson described as his own, a world in which the United States stood alone among rapacious neighbors. As Johnson put it in a talk to American soldiers in Korea on November 1, 1966: "There are three billion people in the world and we [the United States] have only two hundred million of them. We are outnumbered fifteen to one. If might did make right, they would sweep over the United States and take what we have. We have what they want."

Like Rostow, Taylor tried to give Johnson a "grand design" for aggressive action on the world scene. He divided other nations into three groups: (1) Troublemakers, who were to be contained or checked by the United States; (2) Victims, who were to be aided by the United States to withstand the Troublemakers; and (3) Bystanders, or the neutrals, who were to be turned into allies. Taylor believed that a priority system should be set up for the Victims, so that those closest to the Communist giants would be assisted first.

Taylor bluntly insisted that the United States should concentrate on a military victory in Vietnam and not waste strength on a political solution. Since the war in his opinion was simply an aggression by North Vietnam, he argued that it was winnable simply by getting her to quit the struggle in the South. Yet in a book that was published in 1967, Taylor wrote that even if the North were destroyed, "we would still have over two hundred thousand armed guerrillas in South Vietnam. . . . If they were determined to carry on the war, if their morale did not collapse at this disaster in the North, they could conceivably remain in action for the next ten years, or the next twenty years, and we might still be tied down by this vast guerrilla force."

On Johnson's fifty-ninth birthday on August 27, 1967, he saw his military tactics gaining the victory he wanted in Vietnam. Marquis Childs wrote a column about his new propaganda approach, which consisted of "calling in, either individually or in small groups, those on his approved list of opinion makers. The ritual is much the same in each instance," reported Childs. "The President's guests are shepherded into the small study off his oval office. It is a windowless room. . . . The exhortation follows a familiar pattern. The President reads from reports from his generals in Vietnam. It is an upbeat recital. The war is not stalemated. The enemy is hurting. The Vietnam critics will be confounded before too long. . . . Other Presidents have had even worse troubles and they have come through and triumphed in the end.

"All this is impressive, earnest, sometimes solemn. The big man, hunched forward in his chair, talking, talking, talking, with hardly an interruption in the dimly lighted little study, is the arch persuader. It all comes out in news stories, the columns, the news weeklies. And while no source is given, even the casual reader can hardly escape the conclusion that the inspirer was a man named Johnson."

Despite his preoccupation with military victory, Johnson's Vietnam Syndrome remained in full operation during the fall of 1967. The man of war ordered bombings almost to the Chinese border in a new escalation, in addition to a bomb drenching of the heart of Haiphong and a saturation attack on Campha, another major port in North Vietnam. To criticism by "Nervous Nellies" that the raids so close to Red China might bring her hordes into the war, Johnson assured reporters that his action posed no threat to her. But those bombings were, he added, another reason why "it is possible Hanoi may be unable to hold out through next summer." "It would be most ill-advised for Communist China to come into this war," Dean Rusk threatened, pointing out to newsmen that he knew some North Vietnamese fighter planes were based across the Chinese border between air missions.

The man of negotiating peace was also operative. "Maybe someday, somehow, sometime, somewhere, someone will want to sit at a table and talk instead of kill, discuss instead of fight, reason instead of murder; and when they do, I will be the first to come to that table, wherever it is." Johnson had first said this on his return from the funeral of Konrad Adenauer in April 1967, and he repeated it now to show his good intentions. He still had a penchant for remaining in secret touch with the little man in Hanoi who would not give up. In August 1967 he wrote Ho he was calling a halt to all bombing in the Hanoi area to give him the safety to think about Johnson's conditions for negotiations. A few months later, after Ho Chi Minh did not accede, Johnson ordered Hanoi pounded on four successive days.

Johnson knew that he alone was preventing negotiations, even though his repeated pleas for peace beclouded this truth. Vietnam experts agreed that negotiations would start within a month after he called off the bombings of North Vietnam. But he would not.

On September 21 Ambassador Goldberg, reading a murky speech on the negotiations issue to the UN General Assembly that Rusk had approved, gave Johnson additional propaganda gains with the American people. Not long before, North Vietnam's Premier Pham Van Dong had reiterated his stand against negotiations until an unconditional end of the bombings went into effect. "There will be no reciprocity . . . no bargaining . . . no blackmail," said Dong. Goldberg seemed to be softening the hardline Johnson stand when he said he merely wanted to ask North Vietnam what it would do if American bombing stopped. This gained the headlines, although further down in his speech he said that the United States would demand reciprocity in the form of a "mutual military restraint" or a "scaling down of the conflict." Goldberg also said that if there were negotiations the United States intended to keep Hanoi from all "external interference" in the affairs in the South.

The Goldberg speech led to the expected outburst by Hanoi. In addition, the NLF now made itself heard. One NLF official told an American TV correspondent, "If America stops bombing the North, Washington will be able to talk to Hanoi, but that will have no effect on the war in the South. If you want peace in the South, then you must talk with the Front there, for it is the Front that is fighting in the South, and you can't end a war except by dealing with the men fighting it."

Congressional Republicans, generally even more warhawkish than Johnson, revealed a serious split in their ranks when influential Senator Thruston Morton of Kentucky made a speech on September 27 declaring Johnson's policy in Vietnam "bankrupt." Johnson was "mistakenly committed to a military solution in Vietnam for the past five years," said Morton, who called for an immediate end to all bombings of North Vietnam and to all search-and-destroy missions in the South.

Because of Morton's prestige, Johnson sought to counteract it by another cloudy speech of his own. He had gone to Texas to inspect flood damage, and on September 29 newsmen were alerted to expect a major foreign policy address by the President that day in San Antonio.

The San Antonio Declaration, made before the National Legislative Conference, seemed to signify a tempering of the Johnson obstinacy against ending the bombing and getting negotiations under way. But the tune was the same, though the words were changed slightly. As he put it, the United States was "willing to stop all aerial and naval bombardment of North

Vietnam when this will lead promptly to productive discussions. We, of course, assume that while discussions proceed North Vietnam would not take advantage of the bombing cessation or limitation."

Although many newspapers, unaware of the Presidential battle of words against negotiations, applauded Johnson's San Antonio Declaration as a meaningful gesture toward peace, a bitter Senate debate broke out early in October on the war. Supported by Mansfield and Fulbright, Republican Senator John Sherman Cooper of Kentucky, formerly Eisenhower's ambassador to India, ridiculed Johnson's contention at San Antonio that the key to all he had done in Vietnam was his desire to protect American security. Blame for the lack of "negotiations and perhaps peace in South Vietnam lies with the Administration," he argued. Republican Charles Percy of Illinois added that every American escalation was matched by the enemy and yielded only more casualties and a massive increase in Soviet and Chinese military support. What was abominable, said Percy, was that Johnson had failed to understand that "widespread dissent indicates something may be wrong with Administration policies rather than with his critics."

As the fall progressed, Johnson took action to forestall competition from Bobby Kennedy at the next Democratic National Convention. Even though Kennedy continued to swamp him in the popularity polls, Johnson brought local Democratic organizations into line by offering promises and exacting pledges in return, until Kennedy realized he faced an uphill fight to win the nomination. Johnson strategists who believed Kennedy had no stomach for an underdog's role nodded knowingly when the young New York senator weakly muttered he would support Johnson even though he disagreed with him on both foreign and domestic policies.

Governor Romney, the Republican frontrunner and a constant winner against Johnson in popularity poll "trial heats" in early 1967, was nagged by pro-Johnson reporters until he blundered through a painful explanation of an incoherent position on the war that he hoped would not cost him the support of Republican warhawks. Romney's further utterance, that he had been "brainwashed" by Johnson men on a trip to South Vietnam, damaged him further, as had the Johnson TV speech declaring him incapable of handling the Detroit ghetto riot in 1967. Ruined though he was, it was not until February 29, 1968, that Romney removed himself from the race.

Johnson expressed his view to California Democrats on why he believed he would win in 1968 if the war were still on: "I don't seem to remember many Presidents that the American people turned their backs on in time of crisis or in a time of war. No President has ever been turned upon when he was trying to protect his country against a foreign foe."

By confusing and routing his principal Vietnam opponents of the moment in both parties, Johnson now believed he once more had a free hand in seeking his military victory. And the news was good. All reports coming to the White House from Saigon agreed with the Joe Alsop column heading one day in October: WESTMORELAND FORCES HAVE VIET CONG ALL BUT OVER A BARREL. The Westmoreland report to the SEATO military advisers meeting at Bangkok declared that the rate of enemy defectors was increasing; pacification was coming along on a firm foundation; the "population under Viet Cong control in Zone Two [of South Vietnam's four military zones] has fallen from 50 per cent to 11 per cent, and 90 per cent of the important highways are now open"; "approximately 50 per cent of North Vietnam's war-supporting industry, including its only iron and steel plant and its only cement plant, have been destroyed," and over a "half-million men have been diverted to road maintenance, repair, dispersal, and reconstruction tasks."

It was after such optimistic reports from Saigon that Johnson announced through Dean Rusk a change in the war's objective to cover all of Southeast Asia. In the past there had been statements that the United States had involved herself in Vietnam to show the Communists that "wars of national liberation did not pay"; to teach Hanoi to "let her neighbors alone"; to establish the principle of the "one-man, one-vote secret ballot"; "to make certain that the United States would not one day have to fight invading Asian Communists in San Francisco"; and "to honor our commitment and treaty obligations."

At his news conference on October 12, after being ordered to do so by Johnson, Rusk attacked the intellectual and scientific community, whose dissent with the war was almost total. "The fact that a man knows everything there is to know about enzymes," said the "Georgia Fat Boy" with heavy sarcasm, "doesn't mean that he knows very much about Vietnam. . . . As friends used to say of Einstein—that he was a genius in mathematical physics, an amateur in music, and a baby in politics." Then, moving on to the new objective for the conflict, Rusk caused gasps when he declared it was being fought to hold off the Yellow Peril—"a billion Chinese armed with nuclear weapons. . . . We are not picking out Peking as some sort of special enemy. Peking has nominated itself by proclaiming a militant doctrine of world revolution." For this reason, he insisted, the United States was in Vietnam.

Johnson's new objective as expressed by Rusk did not go without rebuttal. Said General David Shoup, retired Marine Corps Commandant and the winner of a Congressional Medal of Honor: "They just keep trying to keep the people worried about the Communists crawling up the banks of Pearl Harbor, or crawling up the Palisades, or crawling up the beaches of Los Angeles, which is of course a bunch of pure unadulterated poppycock." In much milder language, Professor Edwin Reischauer of Harvard, an acknowledged expert on the Far East and until recently the American ambassador to Japan, said that the United States was "overemphasizing" the menace of China. Reischauer said a better description was that the Mao Government was "politically militant, not militarily expansionist," that is, talkers and threateners rather than doers. He also pointed out that in his opinion "quite possibly a unified Vietnam under Ho, spared the ravages of war, would have gone at least as far toward the evolution of a stable and reasonably just society as the divided, war-torn land we know today. . . . In Asia, nationalism is the basic driving force and communism the technique sometimes adopted to fulfill it." In Asia, he said, because communism runs counter to nationalism and human nature, a Communist government was neither permanent nor a permanent enemy of the United States. Reischauer would end the Vietnam conflict "by prudent de-escalation of the conflict's purely military aspects—for instance, the bombing of the North."

If Johnson could not win friends among former Marine Commandants who owned Congressional Medals of Honor or in the intellectual and scientific communities, he still had powerful friends in the political community. One important group that he hoped to dominate was the Governors Conference, and in October, when the governors took off on a nine-day Caribbean cruise and conference aboard the S.S. *Independence*, Johnson sent Price Daniel, the former Texas senator and governor and now his Office of Emergency Planning chief, as liaison with the governors to win their vote of approval for his conduct of the Vietnam war. It was Governor Ronald Reagan of California who spoiled Johnson's scheme by coming into possession of a cable from the White House to Daniel telling the Texas politician to put special pressure on two Republican governors. When Reagan distributed copies of the cable, the hoped-for resolution on Vietnam was dead. At the island of St. Thomas a crew of FBI agents hustled aboard the ship in a vain effort to find the cable thief.

At the beginning of November the Gallup Poll revealed that Johnson's popularity was down to 38 per cent, and if the Presidential election were held then he would lose to any of five Republicans. But he did not feel like a loser, and he counted on Richard Nixon to be his opponent. The "perennial candidate" could easily be dubbed the "perennial loser"; and besides, with Nixon's harder line on Vietnam than his own, the war dissidents would have nowhere to go the following November. The decline of Romney and the disinclination of Governor Nelson Rockefeller to announce as a Republican candidate made Nixon appear Johnson's most likely opponent.

By the middle of the month there were other reasons to feel optimistic. Bunker, Komer, and Westmoreland flew to Washington for meetings, and they brought their "we are winning" spirit with them. Bunker told reporters that the United States was making "steady progress" in Vietnam; Komer thought the pacification program was succeeding, and he had computer compilations to prove this; and Westmoreland, impressive with the six rows of ribbon on his chest, said, "I have never been more encouraged in my four years in Vietnam." To congressmen, he predicted that a phase-out of

American troops could begin in less than two years. At the Tuesday lunch war council, Westy occupied McNamara's seat at Johnson's left and announced triumphantly that "the end begins to come into view." Within a few months, he boasted, he planned to turn over DMZ defenses to the ARVN forces of South Vietnam and remove the Marines.

A Johnson of a type newsmen had never seen before at a news conference displayed himself following the recital of the "happy tune" trio. (One observer of his new personality remarked that this was the first time on TV that he did not look "like he's fresh from a taxidermist's shop.") Johnson bounded about the stage in the East Room, clapping his hands, wringing them, and pointing his finger as he said "every American heart should swell with pride" knowing of the superb American leadership in Vietnam. He had harsh things to say about his war critics, but they were not as vehement as his private charge to Republican congressmen that the previous month's anti-war demonstration at the Pentagon was an international Communist plot directed by Hanoi.

Following his TV news conference, the polls showed the first improvement in his popularity rating since the Spirit of Glassboro. He now had a quip for almost every occasion. But none of his stories produced as loud a laugh as the article his daughter Lynda wrote for *McCall's* on the way she broke the news to her parents of her engagement to a young Marine officer on White House duty. She said that at 3 A.M. one day last August she had crawled on her hands and knees into her parents' dark bedroom and "inch by inch" made her way to the bed and touched her mother's hand. She said Lady Bird sat straight up and asked, startled, "Who is it?" That waked her father, she added, and the two pulled her into bed to hear her news.

It was in November, too, that Johnson dumped McNamara from his Cabinet and announced he would become the head of the World Bank. There was immediate concern among those seeking a de-escalation of the war that the only voice of moderation around the President would be lost. At a party, McNamara told other guests that he had been up until 4 A.M. one day last spring trying to decide whether to quit his job. In the summer and fall of 1967, when the news from Saigon was so cheering, Johnson told a senator that "McNamara has gone dovish on me," and he sarcastically referred to him as "that military genius" for proposing bombing pauses. When a friend asked McNamara how he felt personally about the growing number of American youths being sacrificed in Vietnam, "there was a long silence, a sideward glance, a look at the floor. 'Some day,' he finally replied, 'I'll tell you how I feel about the war. But not now.' "

In July 1967 Johnson had sent Clark Clifford and General Maxwell Taylor to talk to the government heads of the six American allies in Southeast Asia about arranging another summit conference on the war. To Johnson's disappointment, little interest was shown by most, who expressed their concern that he would badger them to send more than token forces to South Vietnam.

But Johnson got his meeting anyway when Australia's Prime Minister Harold Holt disappeared while swimming off Portsea on December 17. Before he left two days later for Holt's funeral rites, Johnson taped a TV show with three network White House newsmen. Many of the question-and-answer scenes were done repeatedly until Johnson was pleased with the final take. The most newsworthy item in the TV show was his suggestion, stated three times, that President Thieu of South Vietnam should hold informal talks with NLF leaders. Off in Saigon, American puppet Thieu immediately let out a howl of protest, declared he would talk only to Viet Cong defectors, and pointed to Secretary Rusk's statement of October 12 on the Yellow Peril, in which Rusk had said that "the NLF is directed from Hanoi on a daily basis. . . . I think the United States is affected by the fact that as far as peace is concerned, our problem is with Hanoi. We did not put our combat troops into South Vietnam because of dissident elements in South Vietnam. We put our combat forces into South Vietnam because North Vietnamese forces moved into South Vietnam."

Two months earlier the NLF had approached U Thant with the request that it be permitted to send representatives to the UN to discuss the war with delegates to the General Assembly. Thant had passed the request on to the United States State Department, which ruled against granting visas to the NLF's representatives for the purpose of lobbying with the General Assembly, which was a debating society. Rusk said, however, that the NLF could send men to any UN Security Council meetings on Vietnam, but only if the Council invited them. But since both the Soviet Union and France had blocked earlier attempts to permit the Vietnam conflict to be discussed in the Security Council on the grounds that the Council lacked jurisdiction over nonmembers, Rusk's decision effectively halted the NLF desire to express its views at the UN.

The possibility that the United States might soften its position toward the NLF put Thieu into agony. At the time of the NLF request to be heard by the UN General Assembly, the South Vietnamese Government had protested publicly and to Rusk against any recognition of the existence of NLF. Rusk had assured Thieu he need not worry. And on December 1, when a high-ranking NLF official came to Saigon on invitation for routine talks with CIA officers, South Vietnam's national police director seized him.

Reporters who accompanied Johnson and his bulletproof limousine to Holt's funeral in December 1967 and then followed him on a four-and-a-half-day circle of the globe called it the most exhausting trip of their lives. Two fellow-travelers suffered heart attacks along the way.

Johnson's first stop was in California, where he visited GI's wounded in Vietnam and passed out pens with the request that they send him letters. From here he flew on to Honolulu, where he was greeted in a downpour by chanting anti-war demonstrators. The next stop was Pago Pago in American Samoa, where natives had stayed up hours past their bedtime to dance for him after midnight.

Once he reached Canberra, he met with his allies and tried without success to exact more troops from them. The new Australian leadership revealed none of Holt's enthusiasm for the Johnson war. Thieu had also come for the funeral, and after a Johnson lecture about the importance of propaganda, he told reporters he did not mind meeting NLF representatives, even though he did not "regard the Front as an independent organization."

The funeral took place in Melbourne, and despite the fact that Holt had been relatively unknown in the United States, Johnson declared that all Americans mourned him. Afterward, Johnson flew on to Korat, Thailand, for a short visit at the United States base there, and with only four hours of sleep, he pushed on to Cam Ranh Bay to visit troops and talk to Bunker and Westmoreland. "We're not going to yield and we're not going to shimmy," he told the soldiers, and to Westmoreland he confided, "I wish I had things in as good shape in the United States as you have here."

Next it was an hour's stop at Karachi to visit with Ayub Khan, and then the weary travelers boarded their planes for Rome and the Vatican on December 23. Pope Paul VI had tried to keep Johnson away, but Johnson was determined to see the Pope and order him to stop his requests that the United States halt the bombing of North Vietnam.

Those who were there called the meeting a cool affair. Johnson tried instant friendship by declaring his joy in having his daughter Luci become a convert to Catholicism. The Pope heard him out and then grimly asked why he continued the bombing. Johnson's voice rose as he explained it was necessary in order to protect his troops in the South. "Why?" the Pope repeated.

An angered Johnson then told him of his own displeasure in knowing that Vatican diplomats were sticking their noses into the peace negotiations he had been conducting. The Pope merely shrugged, and when the meeting ended, noted an onlooker, "Everyone left unhappy. The encounter ended as a frigid meeting between two diplomats."

An old Southeast Asia hand once observed that the United States had moved into the French bed in Indochina but was dreaming different dreams. The folly of the dreamer became clear in January 1968.

The month started with a flurry of excitement that negotiations with Hanoi were fast approaching. North Vietnam's Foreign Minister Trinh, who had said talks "could" start if the United States halted the bombings unconditionally, now said "would" instead. Dozens of American newspapers and magazines urged Johnson to end the bombings and enter the discussion stage, and there was "a smell of peace in the air" despite Rusk's declaration that American troops in Vietnam would engage in hot pursuit of the Viet Cong into Cambodia and Laos. Pope Paul's behind-the-scenes effort was revealed on January 8, when the South Vietnamese Council of Roman Catholic Bishops called for a halt to the bombing and a start to peace negotiations. Then the marble rolled to the other side of the box when Israeli Premier Levi Eshkol, visiting Johnson at the ranch on January 7 and 8, was given permission to buy American Phantom fighter-bombers and Skyhawks only if he would praise Johnson's war in Vietnam and pledge "resistance to aggression wherever it occurs."

When Johnson remained silent on negotiations, politicians believed he was saving the news to tell the nation in his fifth State of the Union Message on January 17, 1968. He came to Congress that evening knowing of the general weariness and unrest of members regarding the war; so certain was he of a poor reception that he had ordered Appointments Secretary Marvin Watson to deliver more than forty White House employees to sit on the House floor among the legislators to form an applause bellwether group. Another employee was stationed in the gallery to keep notes on those who were applauding the loudest and most frequently.

"The enemy has been defeated in battle after battle," the Commander-in-Chief assured his listeners. But, added the man of peace, "Our goal is peace, and peace at the earliest possible moment." As for negotiations, listeners learned he still opposed the ending of the bombing of the North without a serious de-escalation by the enemy in the South.

After Johnson's talk, Republican Senator Aiken said that the President's objective in Vietnam "amounts to unconditional surrender" of the enemy. Mike Mansfield's reaction was: "No matter how much we have tried to avoid it, the Vietnam conflict has brought about a diversion of initiative, energy, and public attention, not to speak of funds, from the pressing problems of American cities. The logical consequence of greater American involvement in the war is still greater American involvement."

The first indication that Johnson's euphoria on the war was unjustified came six days after the State of the Union Message, when North Korean patrol boats captured the eighty-three crew members and the U.S.S. *Pueblo,* an electronic spy ship, off the North Korean coast near Wonsan. The *Pueblo* had roamed those waters for a month to locate the position and determine the strength of North Korean radar installations. President Park of South Korea, whose life had been endangered by a band of North Korean assassins a few weeks earlier, demanded that Johnson join him in a holy war against the North. Johnson, however, could not be distracted from the conflict in Vietnam.

Johnson was settling down now, as he said in his State of the Union Message, to the approach used by General Grant in the Virginia campaign —to gather "slowly but inexorably every kind of material resource" to force the enemy in Vietnam to give up. This dream exploded violently seven days later on January 30, 1968, during the Tet holiday in South Viet-

nam, when the Viet Cong mounted major offensives in three-fourths of
the forty-four provincial capitals.

In the midst of the stalemate the preceding summer (despite Westmoreland's recital of success), General Vo Nguyen Giap, the North Vietnam
Defense Minister and the conqueror of Dien Bien Phu, had taken charge
of Viet Cong operations and begun the planning of the current offensives.
The preliminary phase had been the coordinated attacks in the summer and
fall at Conthien, Dakto, and Locninh; terrorism against the pacification
R.D. teams and villages; and guerrilla attacks on military headquarters,
bridges, airfields, and towns. At the end of the year the specter of another
Dien Bien Phu arose at Khesanh, where Giap's soldiers surrounded thousands of American troops who could be supplied only by air.

Now came the erupting savage assaults on the cities at the end of
January, and for a short time part of the American embassy in Saigon
was occupied by the Viet Cong. To dislodge them from Hue, Mytho, Ben-
thre, Banmethuot, and other cities required a large sacrifice of American
ground forces and, in the process, the destruction of those cities by American air might.

By March 1968 the pacification (R.D.) program had collapsed in the
South; General Thang, the R.D. chief, had resigned, rightfully blasting the
immensity of the corruption that pervaded the Government and the army;
and President Thieu, operating under martial law, had arrested more than
fifty of his non-Communist political opponents. The rosy statistics on the
amount of land-reform acres distributed to peasants to "win their hearts"
were written off as false, as were the impressive figures on the number of
Viet Cong defectors during the last two years.

But as spring approached, the Commander-in-Chief back in Washington
and on his ranch saw no reason to find fault with his Vietnam policy or
commanders. He could not halt now or negotiate, said his friends, because
this would be an admission that the twenty thousand Americans killed in
the war had died for no purpose. McNamara became a scapegoat for
asking for the 37-day bombing pause in December 1965 and for his public
statement that the United States could not win in Vietnam by military
power. Newsmen who expressed doubts about the continuation of the
escalations in private talks with Johnson were summarily upbraided, and
he was enraged at the fun poked at him for using Abraham Lincoln's
words to justify what he was doing in Vietnam. But he was pleased to
learn of the way Rusk had disposed of a questioner who had asked about
the failure of the intelligence staff in Vietnam. "I'd like to ask you a
question!" Rusk had roared. "Which side are you on?"

Johnson was also comforted by the balance sheet Walt Rostow had prepared for him. The new euphoria read in part: "We're in the middle of
a battle that is unresolved but from their own [Communist] documents they
failed to achieve their objectives and may have left the South Vietnamese

Army and government institutions stronger than before the attacks."
Rostow also assured him that as a result of the attacks South Vietnam's
citizens "have come closer to a sense of nationhood than ever before."

By late March, Johnson slumped in the midst of his greatest political
crisis since the campaign for his House seat thirty-one years earlier. The
March 12 Presidential primary in New Hampshire had pitted him against
what Democratic professionals considered the ludicrous candidacy of Senator Eugene McCarthy. But McCarthy, with only a mild campaign manner,
little financial aid, and an aroused flood of college-student helpers, successfully revealed by his high vote the strong opposition, within a supposedly
hawkish state, to the war in Vietnam.

And then the most hated enemy of all—Bobby Kennedy—hitherto mumbling his support for Johnson in 1968, had leaped into the fray against
Johnson, ripping to shreds the false surface unity of the Democratic Party
across the nation.

If there was solace for Johnson in New Hampshire, it was that with the
withdrawal of George Romney, Richard Nixon had swept the state. For
Nixon was even more of a war hawk than Johnson, and Johnson knew that
historically a sitting President had a built-in advantage over an opponent
whose views were similar to his own.

In the face of widespread antagonism to continued warfare in Vietnam,
Johnson's reactions to McCarthy and Kennedy were to denounce them as
Hanoi helpers and to escalate the war further by sending more American
troops to the war furnace and by stepping up bombing raids on North
Vietnam from Okinawa and Thailand. He also phoned local Democratic
leaders around the country to hold them in line for the August Democratic
National Convention with promises and threats.

There were other political troubles. Growing inflation, deficit spending,
and an unfavorable balance of trade stemming from the war spending and
other causes produced a crisis on the gold market. Congress quickly removed the 25 per cent gold cover for United States dollars in circulation,
and the central bankers of the international Gold Pool, meeting in Washington, established a tenuous double standard for gold transactions abroad.

Still another crisis came when the National Advisory Commission on
Civil Disorders presented its report after eight months of work. Johnson's
open lack of enthusiasm toward the Commission's recommendations for a
massive effort to bring domestic peace and end the two-race society in the
United States brought forth sharp criticism from across the North. Even
newspapers favoring him on the war in Vietnam were apprehensive that he
was concentrating on also using military means at home in the expected
long hot summer of 1968.

Yet despite what appeared to be a serious decline in the political fortunes of Lyndon Johnson, not all of his foes were willing to consider his

career at an end. "Never underestimate Lyndon," said Senator John Williams. "And never count him out, for when he is in his worst trouble, that is the time he is most dangerous."

Nevertheless, at the end of March, when Johnson was apprised that he faced a drubbing by McCarthy in the April 2 Wisconsin primary and a pasting by Kennedy in the June California primary, he suddenly decided to quit the Presidential contest and retire in January 1969. He made this announcement on March 31 to a startled nation. As one opponent hailed it, "This is the principal constructive act of Lyndon's years in the White House."

What labors remained for Johnson in his final ten months of office were the direction of the Vietnam war and the tedious domestic crises involving racial troubles and treasury deficits. Again he announced a bombing pause over North Vietnam, this time a partial stoppage that did not include the Communist troop build-up centers just north of the demilitarized zone. Again he called on Congress to curtail domestic programs and increase taxes to help him out of the federal money quagmire resulting from his years as a budget buster in escalating the Vietnam war. As one paper understated the turbulent Johnson presidency, it would "influence world affairs for generations." Belatedly he began an effort to bring about a cease-fire with the Communist foe, and by this means his friends hoped to insure a draft for his renomination.

There was no question in April 1968 that Lyndon Johnson had failed in the necessary Presidential act of leading the American people and communicating with them. In fact, in the more than four years since he had succeeded John Kennedy as President, Johnson rivaled Herbert Hoover as the twentieth-century President most unable to establish a warm relationship with the citizens of the nation. He was a man apart, without the most important Presidential ingredients: the ability to inspire others and gain the affection and trust of the people.

He was only Sam Johnson's boy, who had grown up poor and earthy and ambitious in the Hill Country, and spent his lifetime fighting for personal power and wealth. In his unquenchable thirst for both, he failed to acquire any other purpose to guide his decisions, though he developed a remarkable talent for judging those who stood in his path. He learned how to seize authority from the lazy or slow, threaten and storm at the weak, flatter the vain, promise the greedy, buy off the stubborn, and isolate the strong.

In nearly twenty-four years in Congress, except for his recurring call that the nation become an armed camp, political issues intruded in his life only as a sideshow. So when he came to the White House, he brought no lofty ideals or causes to guide him, only a ceaseless determination to be recognized by all others as the man in charge. Because of this focus, he was unable to do what almost all of his predecessors had done—to grow in office. He explained his abysmal dilemma by saying on one occasion, "No President ever had a problem of doing what is right; the big problem is knowing what is right." Another time he discussed his perplexity with Bill Moyers: "If we know what the people of the United States wanted us to do, how could you be sure that we should do it?"

Because he lacked a grand Presidential sweep, Johnson was forced to find personal causes. To help win the election of 1964, he championed the New Frontier. Then he showed he could outdo Kennedy by promoting the Great Society in 1965. And after this palled that same year in the wake of his Vietnam excitement, he scuttled this pose to take on the role of a wartime Franklin Roosevelt.

Sitting in his Kennedy-type rocker in the Oval Office and surveying the troublesome world, he was the President from Texas. His was the land of the Alamo, where outnumbered men chose to die to show their bravery. He saw himself as a tall Texas Ranger riding into town to take charge and brooking no interference.

Unable to grow beyond his limited heritage and outlook, Sam Johnson's boy could not become more than the President from Texas. In the wake of these shortcomings, he failed to emerge as a President of the United States.

ACKNOWLEDGMENTS AND BIBLIOGRAPHY

The chief source of material for this book came from direct talks I had with hundreds of persons—Texans and non-Texans, politicians and non-politicians—whose lives at one time or another were intertwined with that of Lyndon Johnson. Many were kind enough to permit me to examine letters, reports, and other personal material as well. In a meaningful respect, this book began twenty years ago when I started covering Capitol Hill for several publications, one of which asked me to write a magazine article about Johnson shortly after he became majority whip in the United States Senate.

Of those who contributed their share of experiences relating to events in the life of Lyndon Johnson, I should especially like to thank Wright Patman, Mike Mansfield, Vance Hartke, George Smathers, Ralph Yarborough, Jennings Randolph, John Williams, John Stennis, Stuart Symington, George Aiken, Warren Magnuson, Harry Truman, Edmund Muskie, Albert Gore, William Fulbright, Lee Metcalf, Stephen Young, Russell Long, Mike Monroney, Joseph Clark, Eliot Janeway, Eleanor Lenhart, Frank Valeo, Charles Ferris, William C. Lewis, Howard Shuman, William McChesney Martin, Najeeb Halaby, and Elmer Staats. Most of all, I owe an unrepayable debt to my wife Florence for her untiring toil in helping with the interviewing, the organization of the material, and the editing.

Among those now gone who were of much help were Tom Connally, Sam Rayburn, Harley Kilgore, Joseph McCarthy, Leslie Biffle, Charles Watkins, Alben Barkley, Scott Lucas, Matthew Neely, Walter George, Estes Kefauver, Jim Preston, Robert Taft, Robert Kerr, Herbert Lehman, Joseph O'Mahoney, William Langer, Theodore Green, Pat McCarran, Joseph Martin, and Clarence Cannon.

In addition to talks, there was a grab bag of secondary sources. Some of these were:

BOOKS:

Adams, Sherman, *First-Hand Report,* New York, 1961
Adler, Bill, *The Johnson Humor,* New York, 1965
Amrine, Michael, *This Awesome Challenge,* New York, 1964
———, *This Is Humphrey,* New York, 1964
Baker, DeWitt Clinton, *A Texas Scrapbook,* New York, 1875
Baker, Leonard, *The Johnson Eclipse,* New York, 1966
Bell, Jack, *The Johnson Treatment,* New York, 1965

Bendiner, Robert, *Obstacle Course on Capitol Hill,* New York, 1964
———, *White House Fever,* New York, 1960
Bishop, Jim, *A Day in the Life of President Johnson,* New York, 1967
Bowers, Claude, *My Life,* New York, 1962
Boykin, Edward, *The Wit and Wisdom of Congress,* New York, 1961
Brown, Stuart, *Adlai E. Stevenson,* New York, 1965
Burns, James M., *John Kennedy,* New York, 1959
Chalmers, David, *Hooded Americans,* New York, 1965
Chase, Harold, and Lerman, Allen, *Kennedy and the Press,* New York, 1965
Clark, Joseph, *Congress: The Sapless Branch,* New York, 1964
Clemens, Cyril, *Mark Twain and Lyndon B. Johnson,* Kirkwood, Missouri, 1967
Coffin, Tris, *Senator Fulbright, Portrait of a Public Philosopher,* New York, 1966
Connally, Tom, and Steinberg, Alfred, *My Name Is Tom Connally,* New York, 1954
Davie, Michael, *LBJ: A Foreign Observer's Viewpoint,* New York, 1966
Dixon, George, *Leaning on a Column,* Philadelphia, 1961
Donovan, Robert, *Eisenhower: The Inside Story,* New York, 1956
Dorough, C. Dwight, *Mr. Sam,* New York, 1962
Draper, Theodore, *Abuse of Power,* New York, 1967
Eden, Anthony, *The Reckoning,* Boston, 1965
———, *Toward Peace in Indochina,* Oxford, 1966
Eisenhower, Dwight, *Mandate for Change,* New York, 1963
———, *Waging Peace,* New York, 1965
Evans, Rowland, and Novak, Robert, *Lyndon B. Johnson: The Exercise of Power,* New York, 1966
Fall, Bernard, *Last Reflections on a War,* New York, 1967
———, *The Two Vietnams,* New York, 1967
Farley, James, *Jim Farley's Story,* New York, 1948
Forrestal, James, and Millis, Walter, *Forrestal Diaries,* New York, 1951
Gantt, Fred, *The Chief Executive in Texas,* Austin, 1964
Geyelin, Philip, *Lyndon B. Johnson and the World,* New York, 1966
Graham, Frank, *Margaret Chase Smith,* New York, 1964
Griffith, Winthrop, *Humphrey,* New York, 1965
Gunther, John, *Inside USA,* New York, 1951
Haley, J. Evetts, *A Texan Looks at Lyndon,* Canyon, Texas, 1964
Harris, Joseph, *Advice and Consent of the Senate,* Berkeley, 1953
Haynes, George, *The Senate of the United States,* 2 vols., Boston, 1938
Hilsman, Roger, *To Move a Nation,* New York, 1967
Hoover, Herbert, *Memoirs,* 3 vols., New York, 1951–1952
Hughes, Emmet, *The Ordeal of Power,* New York, 1963
Hull, Cordell, *Memoirs,* 2 vols., New York, 1948
Ickes, Harold, *Secret Diary,* 3 vols., New York, 1953–1954
Johnson, Rebekah, *A Family Album,* New York, 1965
Kennedy, Robert, *To Seek a Newer World,* New York, 1967
Keogh, James, *This Is Nixon,* New York, 1955
Kraft, Joseph, *Profiles in Power,* New York, 1966
Lattimore, Owen, *Ordeal by Slander,* New York, 1950
Leighton, Frances, *They Call Her Lady Bird,* New York, 1964
Leslie, Warren, *Dallas City Limits,* New York, 1964
Lilienthal, David, *The Atomic Energy Years, 1945–50,* New York, 1964
Lincoln, Evelyn, *My Twelve Years with John F. Kennedy,* New York, 1965
Lyons, Eugene, *David Sarnoff,* New York, 1965

MacDowell, Charles, *Campaign Fever,* New York, 1965

Maguire, Jack, *A President's Country,* Austin, 1964

Manchester, William, *Death of a President,* New York, 1967

Martin, John Bartlow, *Overtaken by Events,* New York, 1965

Maverick, Maury, *A Maverick American,* New York, 1937

Mazo, Earl, *Richard Nixon,* New York, 1959

McKay, Seth, *Texas and the Fair Deal,* San Antonio, 1954

———, *Texas Politics, 1906–1944,* Lubbock, 1952

———, *W. Lee O'Daniel and Texas Politics, 1938–42,* Lubbock, 1944

Mollenhoff, Clark, *The Pentagon,* New York, 1967

Montgomery, Robert, *The Brimstone Game,* New York, 1940

Montgomery, Ruth, *Mrs. L.B.J.,* New York, 1964

Mooney, Booth, *The Lyndon Johnson Story,* New York, 1964

Nalle, Ouida Ferguson, *The Fergusons of Texas,* San Antonio, 1946

Nevins, Allan, *Herbert H. Lehman,* New York, 1963

Newlon, Clarke, *LBJ, The Man from Johnson City,* New York, 1964

Pearson, Drew, and Allen, Robert, *Washington Merry-Go-Round,* New York, 1931

Perry, George Sessions, *Texas, A World in Itself,* New York, 1942

Pike, Douglas, *The Organization and Techniques of the National Liberation Party of South Vietnam,* Cambridge, Mass., 1966

Pool, William, *Lyndon Baines Johnson: The Formative Years,* San Marcos, Texas, 1965

Porterfield, Bill, *The Hill Country,* New York, 1965

Provence, Harry, *Lyndon B. Johnson,* New York, 1964

Randel, W. P., *KKK,* Philadelphia, 1949

Reischauer, Edwin, *Beyond Vietnam,* New York, 1967

Report of the President's Committee on the Assassination of President John F. Kennedy, Washington, 1964

Roberts, Charles, *LBJ's Inner Circle,* New York, 1965

Rogow, Arnold, *James Forrestal,* New York, 1963

Roosevelt, Elliott, ed., *FDR: His Personal Letters,* 4 vols., New York, 1947–1950

Rowen, Hobart, *The Free Enterprisers: Kennedy, Johnson and the Business Establishment,* New York, 1964

Roy, Jules, *Battle of Dien Bien Phu,* New York, 1965

Salinger, Pierre, *With Kennedy,* New York, 1966

Schlesinger, Arthur, Jr., *A Thousand Days,* Boston, 1965

———, *The Bitter Heritage,* Boston, 1967

Sherrill, Robert, *The Accidental President,* New York, 1967

Sherwood, Robert, *Roosevelt and Hopkins,* New York, 1948

Singer, Jane and Kurt, *Lyndon Baines Johnson,* Minneapolis, 1964

Smith, A. Robert, *The Tiger in the Senate,* New York, 1962

Smith, Marie, *The President's Lady,* New York, 1964

Sorensen, Theodore, *Kennedy,* New York, 1965

Speer, John W., *A History of Blanco County,* Austin, 1965

Steinberg, Alfred, *Douglas MacArthur,* New York, 1961

———, *Dwight D. Eisenhower,* New York, 1968

———, *Herbert Hoover,* New York, 1967

———, *Man From Missouri,* New York, 1962

———, *Mrs. R.,* New York, 1958

———, with Senator Tom Connally, *My Name Is Tom Connally,* New York, 1954

———, *Woodrow Wilson,* New York, 1963
Strauss, Lewis, *Men and Decisions,* New York, 1962
Taylor, Maxwell, *Responsibility and Response,* New York, 1967
Texas State Historical Association, *The Handbook of Texas,* 2 vols., Chicago, 1952
Timmons, Bascom, *Garner of Texas,* New York, 1948
Trager, Frank, *Why Vietnam,* New York, 1966
Truman, Harry, *Years of Decision,* New York, 1955
———, *Years of Trial and Hope,* New York, 1956
University of Texas, *Cactus Year Book 1933,* Austin, 1933
Webb, Walter, *The Great Frontiers,* Boston, 1952
Weeks, O. D., *One Party Government in 1956,* Austin, 1957
———, *Texas in the 1960 Presidential Election,* Austin, 1961
———, *Texas Presidential Politics in 1952,* Austin, 1953
Weintal, Edward, and Bartlett, Charles, *Facing the Brink,* New York, 1967
Whalen, Richard, *The Founding Father,* New York, 1964
White, Owen D., *Texas, An Informal Biography,* New York, 1945
White, Theodore, *The Making of a President 1960,* New York, 1961
———, *The Making of a President 1964,* New York, 1965
White, William S., *Citadel,* New York, 1956
———, *The Professional: Lyndon B. Johnson,* Boston, 1964
Whitman, Alden, *Portrait: Adlai E. Stevenson,* New York, 1965
Writers Program, WPA, *Texas, A Guide to the Lone Star State,* New York, 1940
Zagoria, Donald, *Vietnam Triangle,* New York, 1967
Zeiger, Henry, *Lyndon B. Johnson, Man and President,* New York, 1965

ARTICLES:

Below are listed some of the articles that were of interest. They are part of the total files of the following magazines that I examined: *American Mercury, Atlantic Monthly, Business Week, Collier's, Fortune, Harper's, Life, Look, Nation, Nation's Business, New Republic, Newsweek, New York Times Magazine, Parade, Reader's Digest, Reporter, Saturday Evening Post, Time.*

Alsop, Stewart, "Lyndon Johnson, How He Does It," *Saturday Evening Post,* January 24, 1959
Barron, John, "Case of Bobby Baker and the Courageous Senator," *Reader's Digest,* September 1965
———, Article on Johnson's broadcasting business, Washington *Star,* June 9, 1964
Carpenter, Leslie, "Whip from Texas," *Collier's,* February 17, 1951
Cater, Douglass, "Lyndon Johnson, Rising Democratic Star," *Reporter,* January 20, 1953
———, "Trouble in Lyndon Johnson's Back Yard," *Reporter,* December 1, 1955
———, "How the Senate Passed the Civil Rights Bill," *Reporter,* September 5, 1957
———, "Coming to Terms with Lyndon," *Reporter,* July 2, 1960
Davidson, Bill, "Texas Political Powerhouse," *Look,* August 4, 1959
Dugger, Ronnie, "Texas Liberals Revolt," *Nation,* June 2, 1956
Guinn, Jack, "Screwball Election in Texas," *American Mercury,* September 1941
Harrison, Selig, "Lyndon Johnson's World," *New Republic,* June 13, 1960

Healy, Paul, "Frantic Gentleman from Texas," *Saturday Evening Post*, May 19, 1951

Johnson, Lyndon, "What I Believe and Why," *Reader's Digest*, April 1959

King, Larry, "My Hero: LBJ," *Harper's*, October 1966

Kohlmeier, Louis, Article on Johnson's broadcasting business, *Wall Street Journal*, March 23, 1964

———, Article on the business activities of the Johnson coterie, *Wall Street Journal*, August 11, 1964

Neuberger, Richard, "Making a Scapegoat of Lyndon Johnson," *New Republic*, July 4, 1955

Phillips, Cabell, "Way Lyndon Johnson Does It," *New York Times Magazine*, July 26, 1959

Pringle, Henry, "Velvet Gloves on Capitol Hill," *Nation's Business*, December 1950

Schendel, Gordon, "Something Is Rotten in the State of Texas," *Collier's*, June 9, 1951

Shelton, Willard, "New Truman Committee," *Nation*, October 21, 1950

Sidey, Hugh, "Measure of a Man," *Life*, December 3, 1965

Stavisky, Sam, "New Senate Leader," *Nation's Business*, December 1954

Steinberg, Alfred, "McCarran, Lone Wolf of the Senate," *Harper's*, November 1950

———, "How Harry Truman Does His Job," *Saturday Evening Post*, March 3–10, 1951

———, "Is This the Man to Beat McCarthy?" *Collier's*, November 24, 1951

———, "Shepherds of Capitol Hill," *Nation's Business*, January 1952

———, "Eisenhower: Toughest Job in the World," *Reader's Digest*, May 1954

———, "GAO: The Taxpayer's Best Friend," *Reader's Digest*, November 1967

Time, "Down on the Ranch, Hospitality to Washington Press Corps," January 17, 1964

———, "Mr. President, You're Fun," April 10, 1964

Tollman, Frank, "Everybody's Friend, Nobody's Leader," *New Republic*, August 9, 1964

White, William S., "Who Really Runs the Senate?" *Harper's*, January 1957

———, "Who Is Lyndon Johnson?" *Harper's*, March 1958

Wicker, Tom, "Lyndon Johnson Is Ten Feet Tall," *New York Times Magazine*, May 23, 1965

Young, Roland, "Lone Star Razzle Dazzle," *Nation*, June 21, 1941

OTHER PUBLICATIONS:

Congressional Record, Congressional Directories, Hearings of various Congressional committees, and *Reports* by the Comptroller General of the United States, in charge of the General Accounting Office.

NEWSPAPERS:

The New York Times, New York *Herald Tribune*, New York *Post, Wall Street Journal*, Washington *Post*, Washington *Evening Star*, Dallas *News*, Blanco County *Record*, Fredericksburg *Standard*, Johnson City *Record-Courier*, San Marcos *Record*, San Marcos *College Star*, Austin *American*, Austin *Statesman*, Corpus Christi *Caller*, Fort Worth *Star-Telegram*, Houston *Chronicle*, Houston *Post*, San Antonio *Express*.

Index